AF512881

To

my wife

Meenakshi,

and my grandparents

(Late) Mr. R. N. Sharma

and

(Late) Mrs. Girish Kumari Singh

COUNTER THE COUNTERFEIT & BUILD A STRONG FOUNDATION FOR SUCCESS

Books are our best friends, is the adage we have grown up with. However, the pirates of piracy are continuously forging 'our best friends'. Our books and their supplementary online resources are copyrighted, and we don't lend any right-to-copy. Piracy is synonymous to stealing books.

Knowledge comes real, let's not encourage its counterfeit. Therefore, we appeal all our readers to discourage pirated books and **choose authentic ones**.

HOW TO IDENTIFY THE PIRATED BOOKS?

1 TRANSPARENCY CODE ON THE BOOK

Congratulations! The book you have purchased is protected by Transparency. Transparency by Amazon is a unit-level product serialization service that verifies a unit's authenticity and enables you to view rich information about the product you purchased. Please look for the Transparency logo and code on the book back cover (Transparency barcode is a square code that can be found next to the "T" symbol). You can scan the barcode with the Transparency app to verify the book's authenticity. Simply download the Transparency app from the App Store or Google Play. Scan the barcode with the app. The app will display a green checkmark when the book has been verified as authentic.

2 COVER AND SPINE

- Look and feel (new or used book)
- Blurred images on the cover
- Hologram pasted on front
- Defective spine (wrinkles) or air pocket at its bottom
- Unclear ISBN/bar codes
- Missing/non-operational Unique Coupon Code for exclusive access to McGraw Hill Edge

3 TEXT/PRINTING/BINDING

- Uneven inking of pages
- Poor quality or blurred photographs/images/charts
- Substandard paper quality and opacity
- Misaligned pages
- Missing pages
- Inferior binding quality

You can further watch this video on How to identify a pirated book

For more information about identifying piracy, visit **https://www.mheducation.co.in/piracy**

To report a pirated book, send 'Hi' on WhatsApp code given on the back cover or write to us at **support.india@mheducation.com**.

Reported pirated books are examined to combat their piracy.

Let's fight the Pirates of Piracy and resolve to go for original!

8th Edition

How to Prepare for

DATA INTERPRETATION

FOR

CAT

Common Admission Test
& Other Management
Examinations

Arun Sharma

McGraw Hill Education (India) Private Limited

Published by McGraw Hill Education (India) Private Limited
Registered Office: Anjana Complex No: 5/90 A, Butt Road, St. Thomas Mount, Chennai – 600016, Tamil Nadu, India

How to Prepare for Data Interpretation for CAT, 8e

Copyright © 2023 by McGraw Hill Education (India) Private Limited

Third reprint 2024

No Part of this publication may be reproduced or distributed in any form or by any means, electronic, mechanical, photocopying, recording, or otherwise or stored in a database or retrieval system without the prior written permission of the publishers. The program listings (if any) may be entered, stored and executed in a computer system, but they may not be reproduced for publication.

This edition can be exported from India only by the publishers.
McGraw Hill Education (India) Private Limited

Print Edition:
ISBN-13: 978-93-5532-432-0
ISBN-10: 93-5532-432-4

E-Book Edition:
ISBN-13: 978-93-5532-433-7
ISBN-10: 93-5532-433-2

04 05 06 07 08 RAJ 28 27 26 25 24

Information contained in this work has been obtained by McGraw Hill Education (India), from sources believed to be reliable. However, neither McGraw Hill Education (India) nor its authors guarantee the accuracy or completeness of any information published herein, and neither McGraw Hill Education (India) nor its authors shall be responsible for any errors, omissions, or damages arising out of use of this information. This work is published with the understanding that McGraw Hill Education (India) and its authors are supplying information but are not attempting to render engineering or other professional services. If such services are required, the assistance of an appropriate professional should be sought.

Typeset at CoKrator Content Solutions Private Limited, Delhi - 110092, and Printed and bound in India at
Rajkamal Electric Press, Plot No. 2, Phase – IV, Kundli, Haryana.

Cover Design: Gyanendra Swamy

Visit us at: www.mheducation.co.in

Write to us at: support.india@mheducation.com

CIN: U80302TN2010PTC111532
Toll free Number: 1800 103 5875

Preface to the Eighth Edition

The importance of **Data Interpretation (DI)** to clear CAT and other MBA examinations can never be undermined. Right through the last decade of CAT, in spite of several changes to the examination pattern as the test evolved from its paper pen format to the online format, the importance of DI has, if anything, increased rather than decreased.

In the last few years, this importance has become even more stark, since there has been a perceptible increase in the difficulty level of the questions being asked in the DI-LR Section. Hence, as you set off on your journey to preparing yourself for Data Interpretation, you need to understand a few ground realities about DI preparation.

1. THE ALL OR NOTHING SECTION

All questions in the DI-LR section of the CAT come in sets – i.e. one situation/data set/puzzle is defined followed by anywhere between 3 to 6 questions asked based on that situation/data set/puzzle. Note here that CAT 21 had sets having 4 and 6 questions respectively, while the CAT 2022 exam had question sets containing 5 questions each. This is true for any other aptitude examination that tests you with either DI or LR questions also – be it, XAT, IIFT, SNAP, NMAT,MAHCET, Bank PO, etc. Hence, when you are solving a DI set inside an examination, there is an all or nothing situation that you face. The matter is accentuated in examinations where the quality of the questions becomes tougher – like CAT/XAT and IIFT. This is due to the fact, that a lot of times, aspirants taking these examinations get 'stuck' midway through the solving of a set – and cannot take their solving to fructification. This proves disastrous for aspirants, since leaving a DI (or indeed LR) set in between costs you anything between 5 to 8 minutes. It is very difficult to recover from such an experience whether it is a 40-minute section or a 60-minute section. If you are preparing seriously for the CAT and want to be amongst the toppers, you need to make sure that this does not happen to you. For doing that, one of the imperatives of preparation becomes getting to a point in your preparation, where you have supreme belief about being able to 'get through' those tough situations in the examination. We have tried to give you both the pedagogy and the practise content in this book in order to help you reach that stage of the supreme belief in DI where that internal voice inside you keeps repeating at the back of your head and keeps telling you: 'I can solve anything in Data Interpretation'.

2. THE QUESTION OF THE PATTERN

Between 2017 to 2019 , CAT had settled down into a 3 section 3 hour examination. The DI-LR section consisted of 8 sets of 4 questions each.

These 32 questions were typically divided between DI (16 questions divided into 4 sets of 4 questions each) and Logical Reasoning (16 questions divided into 4 sets of) questions.

In these papers (2017 onwards) you would need to solve only 14-16 questions in order to achieve around 98 percentile (in other words around 3.5 to 4 sets solved). If you could solve an additional set and get to 4.5-5 sets, it would take your percentile to 99.5+ and the 100 percentile would occur at around 24-26 attempts (of course with most correct). However, 2020 onwards the CAT became a 2 hour exam – and consequently, each section including the DI LR section of the exam was reduced to a 40 minute section. Naturally this changed the dynamics of what was required to score high in the exam. Also, it is important to note that even within the 2 hour CAT Paper, the pattern has varied quite a bit. In CAT 2020, for instance, there were 24 questions spread across 5 sets (4,4,4,6,6) while in 2021 it became 20 questions spread across 4 sets (4,4,6,6). It was easy to locate that the 6 question sets would have more logic involved and would hence be more difficult to solve. However, CAT 2022, retained the 4 sets and 20 questions structure, but made a crucial change of all sets carrying 5 questions each. The typical pattern of these papers has been 1 set exclusively based on DI, 1 set exclusively based on LR, while 2 sets are between DI and LR. Aspirants solving between 13-15 questions reported scores of 100 percentile or close to it. This converted to someone solving 3 sets in 40 minutes. Naturally, at around 10-

12 questions solved (2 sets and a bit) aspirants scored 99 percentile or thereabouts in the CAT. Going forward, we do not know whether CAT will remain a 2 hour examination or switch back to a 3 hour examination and also if the switch back happens, then when would it happen is another point on which an aspirant doesn't have any control of. Hence, the best thing to do is to prepare for both the patterns (as also any surprises) going forward.

If you compare the two patterns and the percentiles at various number of attempts, you would notice a few things with respect to each percentile range:

(a) The 100 percentiler on an average gets through one set in 10 minutes in the examination;
(b) The 99 percentiler gets through one set in around 12 to 14 minutes on average;
(c) As your per set time goes beyond 15 to 20 minutes, you are sliding down the percentile scale.

In the context of what I communicated in the previous point (the all or nothing section), your preparation flowchart has to look as shown here:

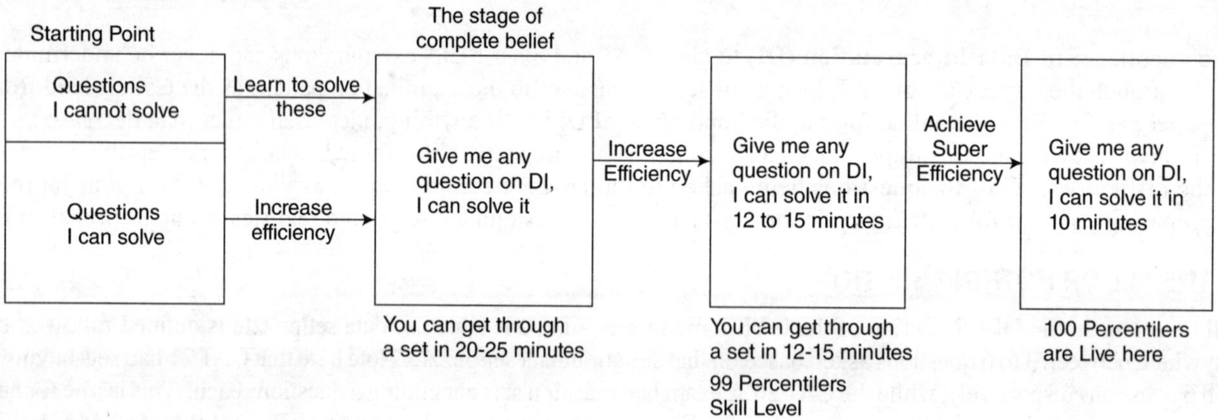

3. DO NOT UNDERDO YOUR DI

I have often seen that students prepare for hundreds of hours for their Quantitative Aptitude and Verbal Ability and Reading Comprehension section. Yet, when it comes to Data Interpretation and Logical Reasoning, they barely allocate a fraction of the time for which they do QA and VA/RC. Remember, inside the examination, you would be spending 1/3rd of the total time solving only DI and LR questions.

Hence, my advise again would be to make sure that you treat both these subjects DI and LR with intensity and do everything in your power to maximise your skill levels for them. Allocate at least 25-30% of your total preparation time for this section (DI and LR combined).

This then leads us to the question about how should you prepare your Data Interpretation, keeping in mind the increasing difficulty level of the examination? Let me try to answer that for you.

Unlike theory-oriented subjects, where you can feasibly define a portion and start studying the theory to understand the subject, Data Interpretation as a subject is an 'experientially learnt subject'—a subject learnt through experience. Your approach while studying DI should always be to identify Data situations and the typical specific solving skills that a particular DI question requires. Once identified, the DI situation and the specific thought process involved in that situation should then become part of your 'must have skills'.

Data Interpretation traditionally has been a section that has been dominated by your ability to understand graphs, charts, tables and caselets presenting information about various variables in the form of numerical values of certain variables. Variables would be either given or derived from the variables that were given (for instance, if you were given Revenues and Costs for a company over 5 years, then you could derive the profit or loss for the company over the five years as a derived variable). Traditionally, the questions would ask you questions about the variables (either given or derived variables) and would essentially involve a little logic and mostly calculations and observations. However, if you were to look at the DI sets asked in the CAT over the past 5-6 years you would realise that the traditional kinds of Data Interpretation questions have reduced drastically. These have been replaced by question sets that have been heavy on logic, analysis and reasoning – with calculations and the skills required to solve the traditional Data Interpretation questions being minimally tested. These questions require a completely different approach and completely different skills from what has been traditionally tested in DI. In my training sessions with my students, I have realised that the resources required and the approach required to prepare for the section has to change. The old approaches to DI preparation would leave you completely unprepared under the changed scenario – since Traditional DI and Logical DI are almost like two different subjects.

Naturally, given this change, I have observed that aspirants and students across the country have been finding it difficult to find appropriate resources for this section. Over the years, the first few editions of this book have been used by lacs of aspirants to successfully prepare for CAT and MBA and even for aptitude examinations like Banking etc. However, given the changes that I have described above, I realised that the pedagogy and the structure of this book have to undergo a major change.

It is in this context, that I have divided the book – into three major sections:

Section I: Traditional Data Interpretation
Section II: Logical Data Interpretation
Section III: Data Interpretation from the Archives (past 2 years CAT papers)

As you can see, this is perhaps the first book that gives you the opportunity to prepare separately for Traditional DI and for Logical DI. So let us have a look at the structure of this book and how and why this book is the one valuable resource you must have with you during your CAT and other examination preparation journey.

While doing this, I have retained the original strength this book had. This book has always been structured and written in such a way that you get an experience of all the possible situations, interpretation and calculation tasks that DI questions throw up. The endeavour in the book is to make sure that when you are solving the DI questions in any test, you have already 'experienced and done' what the question asks you to do – be it for CAT, XAT, IIFT, CMAT, Bank PO or any other examination having a DI component. In other words you are prepared for any eventuality that a DI question might throw up for you.

SECTION I: TRADITIONAL DATA INTERPRETATION

This section provides you with a comprehensive view and the study resources and the questions required in order to prepare for the traditional data interpretation questions. While CAT has been moving away from traditional DI, other examinations like XAT, NMAT, SNAP, MAT, CMAT as well as Banking and other competitive examinations still are rooted in traditional DI. Also, you cannot hope to master logical DI unless you are good at Traditional DI. Hence, this section retains its' importance for your DI preparation journey.

So how does this section help you master your Traditional Data Interpretation? The section is divided into 3 parts:

1. Basic Modes of Data Representaiton: The first thing we do in the book is to take you through an initiation into the various types of data representations. Chapters covered here include Pie Charts, Bar Charts, Tables, X-Y/Line Charts, Caselets, Mixed and Miscellaneous Graphs (covering triangular graphs, spider graphs etc). While this has to be naturally placed inside the traditional DI section of this book, we have divided the exercises of each of these chapters into Level of Difficulty 1, Level of Difficulty 2 and Level of Difficulty 3. Naturally, some of the Level of Difficulty 2 and 3 questions, would also delve into Logical Data Interpretation. We have done so in order to give you a heads up about the ultimate level of problem solving you would be required to be able to do, in order to crack CAT. Make sure that you try each set in each chapter on your own (at all levels of difficulty). However do not get too disheartened if you are not able to solve the Level 2 or 3 question sets, since they would be solvable only by someone who has strong DI skills. If you experience an inability to solve difficult question sets at the start of your preparation the approach you have to take is 'I will get stronger on my skills and come back to this at a later time'.
2. This is followed by Part 2: 'How to think In Traditional Data Interpretation' an invaluable DI study resource. This part provides you with two distinct resources → Under Chapter 1: Intro to Traditional DI and Mathematical Constructs in Traditional DI, help you go through the necessary mathematical understanding required for Traditional DI. Chapter 2 is a hands on, one-on-one training section, where the reader is taken through the step- by-step thinking and solving process that is gone through in a DI set. Original CAT and XAT questions that can be classified under Traditional DI, and provide us with huge learning opportunity have been handpicked and discussed from the thought process point of view in this section. I would expect the reader to make the most out of this resource in order to completely understand what it takes to solve a DI question set, before he/ she heads towards the next parts that are focused on practice.
3. Part 3 Mock Test Papers (On the latest CAT Pattern): Contains mock test papers – perhaps the most valuable practice resource in this part of the book. Each of the mock test papers have exactly 20 questions divided into Level of Difficulty 1 (Mock Test Papers 1 to 7) and Level of Difficulty 2 (Mock Test Papers 8 to 26). Do the Level 1 tests in a strict time limit of 30 minutes, while for the Level 2 tests, you can take 40 minutes for each test. There are a total of 540 questions, spread across 130-140 sets in this section and solving this section under strict time limit will not only help you close the loop of your Traditional Data Interpretation preparation process, but also give you varied exposure to various data interpretation situations that you are likely to face in your exams.

Students who can score 99.5+ percentile would be able to score 40+ in these tests and hence your endeavor should be to increase your speed and accuracy while solving these tests. Any questions you are not able to solve during the time limit for the test, you should solve after you finish the test. You have to know each data structure, relationship between variables, calculation structures and challenges. Make sure that you learn from every experience and every challenge you face while solving these questions.

SECTION II: LOGICAL DATA INTERPRETATION

This section provides you with a comprehensive view and the study resources and the questions required in order to prepare for the crucial Logical Data Interpretation questions, which are a feature of the current CAT papers. Hence, this resource is the most critical study resource of this book – and indeed of any study material or book you might be able to lay your hands on. The section takes you through 3 major Parts that would give you a comprehensive learning experience for Logical DI.

Part 1 of this section provides you with an invaluable write up on 'How to think in Logical Data Interpretation' which takes you through a hand held training experience of how to organise your thoughts while solving a Logical DI set. This section guides you through a series of Logical DI experiences, helping you to understand exactly how the toppers think in Logical DI situations. It will also give you a strong starting point in order to understand what logical DI is all about. You would be expected to go through each of the sets provided in this section – taking each set as a learning experience, first by trying to solve the set yourself without reading the explanations to the same and then try to look through the thought process and try to learn at what points your thinking was inferior to the toppers thinking in the same situation.

Part 2 of this section is 'Twelve Minute Tests' that consists of 30 Twelve Minute Tests which provide you with a challenge to test yourself against a logical DI situation under time pressure of 12 minutes for a set of 4 to 5 questions. The logic of why these are twelve minute tests, is because in the CAT examination these days toppers are solving between 3 to 4 sets in 40 minutes to score between 99.5 to 100 percentile in the DI and LR section. Hence, in my opinion the key test of how good you are at DI, is to check whether you are able to resolve a Logic based DI set in under 12 minutes. In this part, I would expect you to first solve each of the 30 tests in a 12-minute framework. The first thing you would aim for would be to get through the set in 12 minutes. You would only count your score for questions you were able to solve under 12 minutes. However, once you are through the 12 minutes, if you are not able to resolve the question, you should try to take yourself through a learning experience with every question set. After the 12 minutes are over, the focus shifts to learning how to take yourself through tough logical DI sets. These would go a long way in developing your belief in solving logical DI.

Part 3 of the Logical Data Interpretation section, provides you with 28 full length Mock Tests Papers, which are split between Level of Difficulty 2 (Mock Test Papers 1 to 8) and Level of Difficulty 3 tests (Mock Test Papers 9 to 28)). consisting of 20 questions per test – split between 4,5 and 6 question sets according to the latest pattern of the CAT exam. These tests have to be first solved under a strict 40-minutes time frame to check how much you are able to score in DI in 40 minutes. Of course, like you did in the previous part, once you are through the test in the time allotted, you should take each set and go through the invaluable learning experience derived out of taking yourself through to the answers of these intricate questions.

Logical DI, much like traditional DI, would be repetitive in nature i.e. logic and analysis and the reasoning in the sets would start repeating themselves across various sets and solving situations. Your task as a student is to make sure that you have seen enough Logical DI, so that when you actually go into the CAT, whatever they throw at you – you should be ready to handle, simply because, you've seen it and experienced it earlier. That is the best way to prepare for Logical DI and I am sure this section will create a highly engaging and invigorating learning experience for you that would take you a long way in cracking the CAT.

SECTION III: DATA INTERPRETATION FROM THE ARCHIVES

This section contains the indepth analysis and solutions of the CAT papers of the last 2 years viz: CAT 2021 and CAT 2022– and you are advised to first try to solve each set on your own before looking to learn through the provided solutions. Additionally, you can also have access to the DI section of previous years' CAT papers (2020-2022) on McGraw Hill Edge. To sum up, it would not be inappropriate to state that this book gives you an overall perspective to prepare for the all-important DI part of the DI and LR section of the CAT, while also providing you with an invaluable learning resource for all MBA entrance examinations as well as for other examinations based on aptitude and Data Interpretation. In its latest avatar of the eighth edition, I am confident that this book has become one of the most important resources for cracking Data Interpretation.

Wish you a great learning experience. May Data Interpretation provide you a flight, straight into the IIMs!

Arun Sharma

Acknowledgements

No book of mine can ever fail to recognise the extraordinary contribution that my students have made to my life and my learnings—something that is reflected in all my books you read. It is for this reason alone that any acknowledgements that are due have to first and foremost go to my wonderful students and as I write this, thousands of names flash through my mind, so mentioning any one of them would be a gross injustice to others.

Acknowledgements are also due to some exceptional people I have met over the past few years.

Special mention for the book you now hold in your hand must go to Pallav Jalan and Shaurya Sharma, without whom the redesign of this highly successful book would not have been possible.

Besides, I would like to extend thanks to all my colleagues at AMS Learning Systems and Mindworkzz— Mr Arun Chaturvedi, Koushik Rai, Bhavuk Pujara, Rajeshwar Tiwari, Saeed Khan, Sanjeeta Girotra, Ritika Sharma, Renu Rai, Kavita Jindal. Special mention has to be made about Palaan Haldar, Arjun Mehta and Santosh—to whom I owe immense gratitude for working with me and keeping the faith.

Any book I now write is more team work than it appears. This work would not have been possible but for the support and encouragement from McGraw-Hill, India. My sincere thanks and words of appreciation to them. I would like to make specific mention of Tanmoy Roychowdhury, Tanweer Ahmad and the entire team at McGraw-Hill. A special word of thanks to Aparna Kumar, Atul Gupta, Aarooshi Garg, and Anjali Nair whose untiring work was a strong support in helping me bring out a higher quality product in the Eighth edition.

Finally, I would like to acknowledge my family members—my parents, Mr. M. K. Sharma and Mrs. Renu Sharma; my wife, Meenakshi; my brother and his wife, Ravi and Aditi; and Shri. G. S. Upadhyay, Sachindra Upadhyay, Jayshree Sarma, Dr. Raju Sarma and Sandhya Upadhyay—who were a source of my inspiration and encouragement throughout the making of this book. Lastly, I would like to complete the list with the mention of the brigade of nephews that I have including Hurshey, Arjit, Rishi, Rakshit, and Shrey who always add joy and thrill to my life.

Arun Sharma

Developing Your Calculations

ADDITIONS AND SUBTRACTIONS (AS AN EXTENSION OF ADDITIONS)

IDEAS FOR ADDING AND SUBTRACTING WELL

Developing your calculations is perhaps the most critical step in doing well at traditional DI.

Addition is perhaps the most critical skill when it comes to developing your calculations. As you would see through the discussions in the other chapters of this part of the book, if you have the ability to add well you would be able to handle all the other kinds of calculations with consummate ease.

Skill 1 for addition: The ability to react with the addition of two numbers when you see them.

The first and foremost skill in the development of your addition abilities is the ability to react to 2 two-digit numbers when you come across them. You simply have to develop the ability to react with their totals whenever you come across 2 two-digit numbers.

For instance, suppose I were to give you two numbers at random – 5, 7 and ask you to **STOP!! STOP YOUR MIND BEFORE IT GIVES YOU THE SUM OF THESE TWO NUMBERS!!** What happened? Were you able to stop your mind from saying 12? No! of course not, you would say.

TRY AGAIN: 12 + 7 STOP YOUR MIND!! You could not do it again!!

TRY AGAIN: 15 + 12 STOP!! Could not?

TRY AGAIN: 88 + 73 = ?? STOP!! If you belong to the normal category of what I call 'addition disabled aspirants' you did not even start, did you?

TRY AGAIN: 57 + 95 = ??

TRY AGAIN: 78 + 88 = ??

What went wrong? You are not used to such big numbers, you would say. Well, if you are serious about your ability to crack aptitude exams, you better make this start to happen in your mind. You would know what I mean if you just try to look at a 5-year-old child who has just learnt to add, struggle with a calculation like 12 + 7 on his fingers or his abacus.

His struggle with something like 12 + 7 or even 15 + 12 would be akin to the average aspirant's ability to react to 88 + 78. However, just as you know 15 + 12 is not a special skill so also 88 + 78 is not a special skill. It is just a function of how much you practice your calculations especially in the domain of 2-digit additions.

So what am I trying to tell you here?

All I am trying to communicate to you is to tell you to work on developing your ability to react to 2 two-digit numbers with their addition as soon as these numbers hit your mind. What I am trying to tell you that the moment you make your mind adept at saying something like 74 + 87 = 161 just the way you would do 9 + 6 = 15 you would have made a significant movement in your mind's ability to crack aptitude exams.

Why do I say that—you might be justified in asking me at this point of time? In order to answer your question I would like to present the following argument to you:

In numerical questions, a normal student/aspirant would be roughly calculating for approximately 50% of the time that he/she takes to solve a question. This means that half the total time that you would spend in solving questions of Quantitative Aptitude or Data Interpretation would essentially go into calculations.

So the contention is this: If you can improve your calculation speed to $5x$, the time you would require to do the same calculations would come down to 1/5th of your original time. In other words 18 minutes would come down to 3.6 minutes – a saving of 14.4 minutes; 24 minutes would come down to 4.8 minutes – a saving of 19.2 minutes just by improving your calculation speed!!

In an exam like the CAT where you would always run out of time (rather than running out of solvable questions) 24 extra minutes could easily mean anywhere between 15 and 20 marks (even if you are able to solve an additional 6–7 questions in this time).

15–20 extra marks would be the difference between a 90 and 95 percentile, just as it would be the difference between 95 and 98 percentile in the CAT. Similar stories would play out in other exams like XAT, IIFT, NMAT, etc.

Addition being the mother of all calculations has the potential of giving you the extra edge you require to dominate this all important examination.

In the other chapters in this part of the book, all I am going to show you is how knowing additions well would have an impact on each and every calculation type that you might encounter for this exam and indeed for all aptitude tests. However, before we go that far you need to develop your ability to add well.

$$\begin{array}{r} {}^{1} \\ 7\ 8 \\ +\ 8\ 6 \\ \hline 1\ 6\ 4 \end{array}$$

Let us look at the simple calculation of 78 + 88. For eternity you have been constrained to doing this as follows using the carry over method:

The problem with this thought is that no matter how many times you practice this process you would still be required to write it down. The other option of doing this same addition is to think on the number line as this:

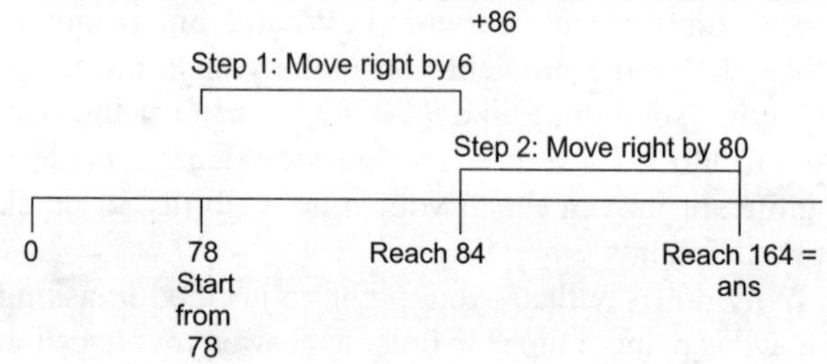

78 + 86 - How to think of this addition problem

As you can see, the above thinking in an addition situation requires no carry over and after some practice would require no writing at all. It is just an extension of how you are able to naturally react to 5 + 11 so also you can train your mind to react to 58 + 63 and react with a two-step thought (as 61 → 121—with practice this can be done inside a fraction of a second. It is just a matter of how much you are willing to push your mind for this). Once you can do that your next target is to be able to add multiple 2-digit numbers written randomly on a single page:

Try this: Add the following

48

27 73

18 68

43 56

In order to do this addition your thinking should go like this:

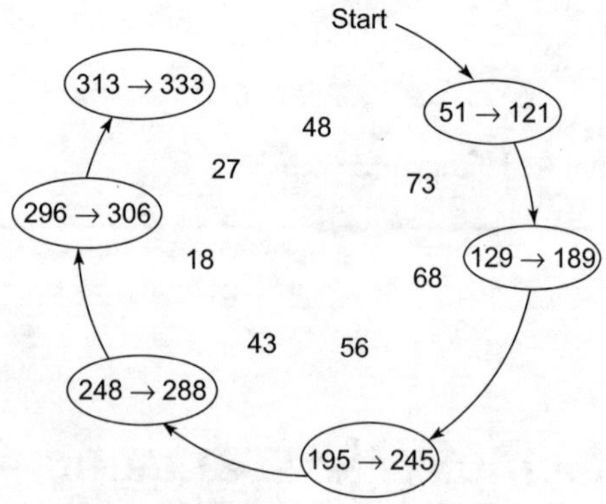

Alternately you may also do this the other way. The result would be quite the same.

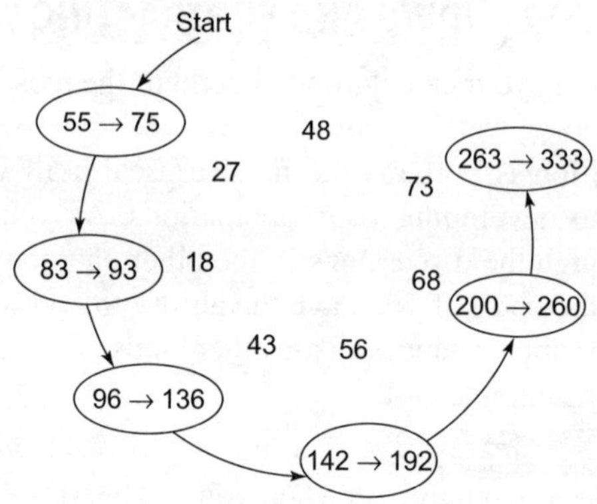

While you are trying to work on this addition you would realise the following about your abilities to add (if you belong to the normal category of aspirants)

1. Something like 121 + 68 would be easier than 189 + 56 because the latter requires you to shift hundreds- something that the former does not require you to do.
2. Something like 48 + 27 would be easier for you to do initially than 136 + 56; and 136 + 56 would be easier than 543 + 48 because your mind would be more comfortable with smaller numbers than you would be with larger numbers.

However, as you start practicing your additions these additions would become automatic for your mind – as they would then fall into the range where your mind can react with the answers. That is the point to which we would want you to target your skill levels for additions.

To put it in other terms, you would need to work on your additions in such a way that 10 numbers written around a circle (as shown above) should be done in around 10–12 seconds in your mind.

Till the time your addition skill levels reach that point we would want you to work aggressively on your addition ability.

The following 10 × 10 table done at least once daily might be a good way to work on your additions:

Inside the table you would broadly do two things:

(a) For each cell you would add the values in the corresponding row and the corresponding column in order to get the value inside the cell. Thus, the second row and 4th column intersection would give you 54 + 96 = 150, the sixth row and the sixth column would add to 73 + 32 = 105 as shown in the table.

(b) Add the total of the 10 numbers seen in each row after you finish doing the values inside the cells in the total. This would give you the final total of the row. Repeat the same process for the addition of the 10 numbers in the columns.

By this time, I guess you would have realised that we are targeting two broad addition skills:

(i) Your ability to react with the total when you see two 2-digit numbers (like 57 + 78 = 135)

(ii) Your ability to add multiple 2-digit numbers if they are given to you consecutively (like 57 + 78 + 43 + 65 + 91 + 38 + 44 + 18 + 64 + 72 = 570 in 8–10 seconds)

You might require around 1–2 months of regular practice to get proficient at this. However, once you acquire this skill, every conceivable calculation that any aptitude exam can throw at you (or indeed has thrown at you over the past 20 years) would be very much within your zone.

How do you do larger additions?

Once you have the skills to handle two-digit additions as specified above handling bigger additions should be a cakewalk.

Suppose you were adding:

57436 + 64123 + 44586 + 78304 + 84653 + 5836.

In order to do this, first add the thousands. 57 + 64 (= 121) + 44 (= 165) + 78 (= 243) + 84 (= 327) + 5 (= 332). Thus, you have an interim answer of 332 thousands. At this stage you know that your answer would be 332000 + a maximum of 6000 (as there are 6 numbers whose last 3 digits you have neglected). If a range of 332000–338000 suffices for you in the addition based on the closeness of the options, you would be through with your calculation at this point. In the event that you need to get to a closer answer than this, the next step would involve taking the 100s digit into account.

Thus for the above calculation: 57**4**36 + 64**1**23 + 44**5**86 + 78**3**04 + 84**6**53 + 5**8**36 when you add the hundreds, you get 4 + 1 + 5 + 3 + 6 + 8 = 27 hundreds. Your answer gets refined to 334700 and at this point you also know that the upper limit of the addition has to be a maximum of 600 more than 334700, i.e., the answer lies between 334700 and 335300. In case this accuracy level is still not sufficient you may then look at the last 2 digits of the numbers. Our experience tells us that normally that would not be required.

However, in case you still need to add these digits-it would amount to 2-digit additions again. So you would need to add 574**36** + 641**23** + 445**86** + 783**04** + 846**53** + 58**36** → **36 + 23 (= 59) + 86 (= 145) + 4 (= 149) + 53 (= 202) + 36 (= 238).**

	59	68	77	96	84	32	17	69	81	38	TOTALS
48											
54				= 96 + 54 = 150							
67											
89											
56											
73						105					
88											
24											
47											
96											
TOTAL											

Thus, the correct total would be 334700 + 238 = 334938 and while doing this entire calculation we have not gone above 2-digit additions anywhere.

Apart from that, the biggest advantage of the process explained above is that in this process, you could stop the moment you had an answer that was sufficient in the context of the provided options.

SUBTRACTIONS—JUST AN EXTENSION OF ADDITIONS

The better your additions are, the better you would be able to implement the process explained for subtractions. So, a piece of advice from me – make sure that you have worked on your additions seriously for at least 15 days before you attempt to internalise the process for subtractions that is explained in this chapter.

Throughout school you have always used the conventional carry over method of subtracting. But, we are here to show you that you have an option – something that would be much faster and much more superior to the current process you are using. What is it you would ask me? Well what would you do in case you are trying to subtract 38 from 72?

The conventional process tells us to do this as:

Carry over 1		
	7	2
–	3	8
	3	4

Well, the alternative and much faster way of thinking about subtractions is shown on the number line:

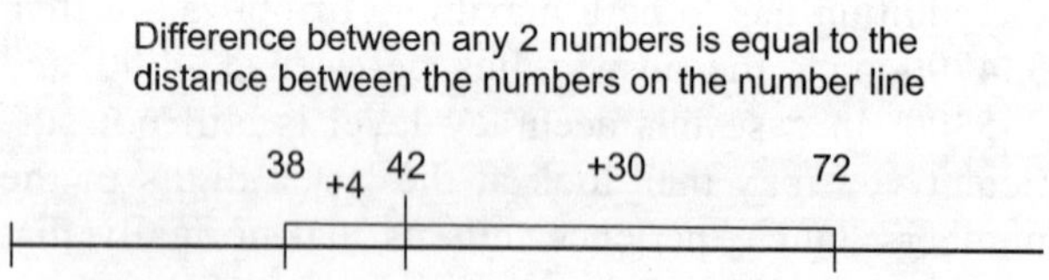

The principal used for doing subtractions this way is that the difference between any two numbers can be seen as the distance between them on the number line.

Thus, imagine you are standing on the number 38 on the number line and you are looking towards 72. To make your calculation easy, your first target has to be to reach a number ending with 2. When you start to move to the right from 38, the first number you see that ends in 2 is the number 42. To move from 38 to 42 you need to cover a distance of +4 (as shown in the figure). Once you are at 42, your next target is to move from 42 to 72. The distance between 42 and 72 is 30.

Thus, the subtraction's value for the numbers 72–38 would be 34.

Consider the following examples:

Illustration 1 95 – 39

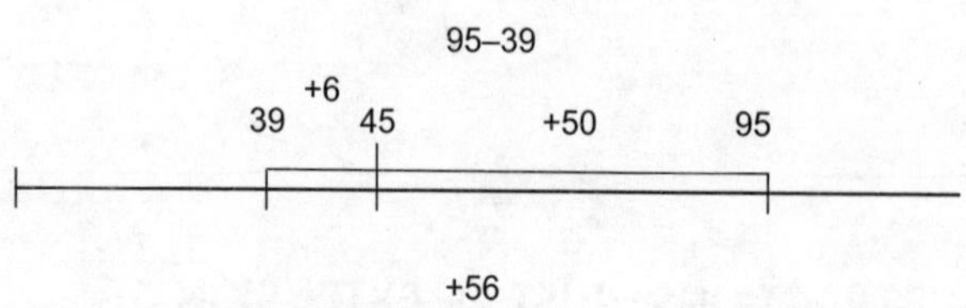

Illustration 2 177 – 83

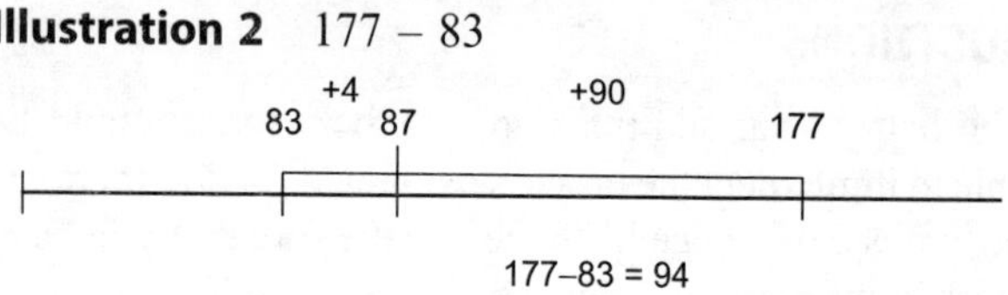

Alternately:

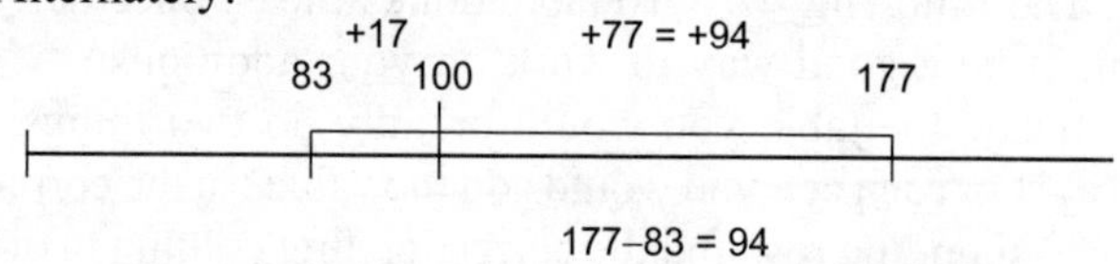

Illustration 3 738 – 211

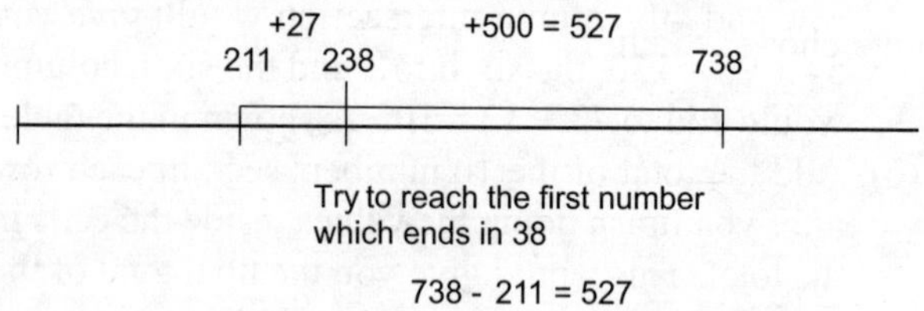

In this case the first objective is to reach the first number ending in 38 as you start moving to the right of 211. The first such number to the right of 211 being 238, first reach 238 (by adding 27 to 211) and then move from 238 to 738 (adding 500 to 238 to reach 738)

In case you need an intermediate number before reaching 238 you can also think of doing the following:

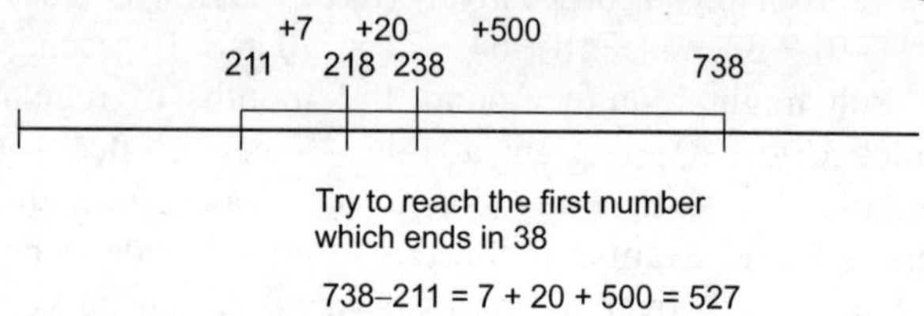

Illustration 4 813 – 478

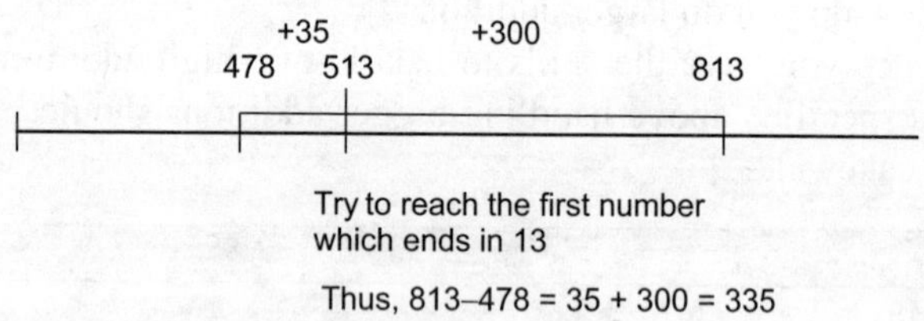

Alternately, this thought can also be done as:

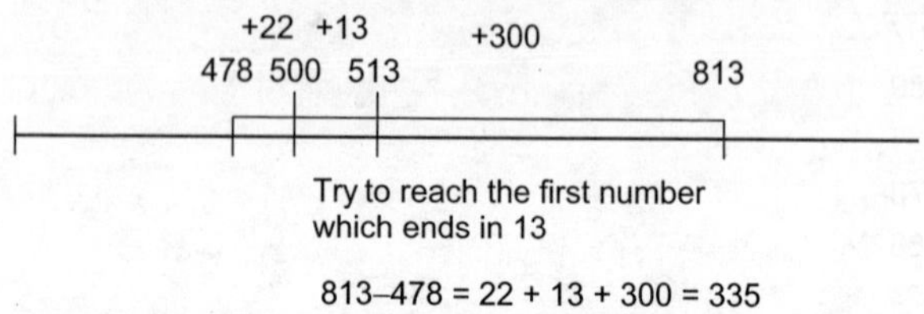

Also, you could have done it as follows:

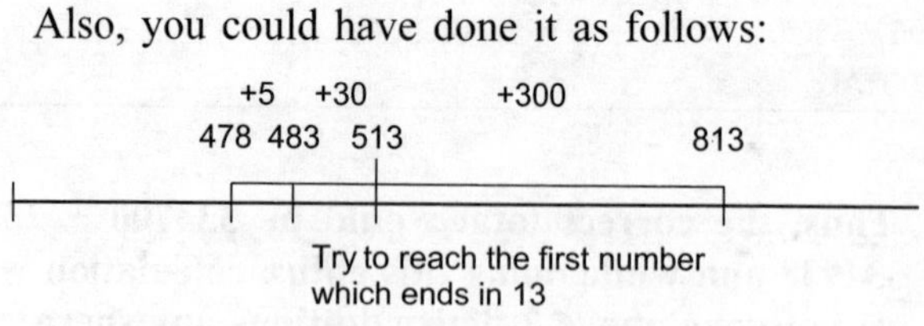

Even if we were to get 4 digit numbers, you would still be able to use this process quite easily.

DIVISIONS, PERCENTAGE CALCULATIONS AND RATIO COMPARISONS

CALCULATING DECIMAL VALUES FOR DIVISION QUESTIONS USING PERCENTAGE CALCULATIONS

I have chosen to club these two together because they are actually parallel to each other – in the sense that for any ratio we can calculate two values – the percentage value and the decimal value. The digits in the decimal value and the percentage value of any ratio would always be the same. Hence, calculating the percentage value of a ratio and the decimal value of the ratio would be the same thing.

How do you calculate the percentage value of a ratio?

PERCENTAGE RULE FOR CALCULATING PERCENTAGE VALUES THROUGH ADDITIONS

Illustrated below is a powerful method of calculating percentages. In my opinion, the ability to calculate percentage through this method depends on your ability to handle 2-digit additions. Unless you develop the skill to add 2-digit additions in your mind, you are always likely to face problems in calculating percentage through the method illustrated below. In fact, trying this method without being strong at 2-digit additions/subtractions (including 2 digits after decimal point) would prove to be a disadvantage in your attempt at calculating percentages fast.

This process, essentially being a commonsense process, is best illustrated through a few examples.

EXAMPLE 1

What is the percentage value of the ratio 53/81?

Solution The process involves removing all the 100%, 50%, 10%, 1%, 0.1% and so forth of the denominator from the numerator.

Thus, 53/81 can be rewritten as: (40.5 + 12.5)/81 = 40.5/81 + 12.5/81 = 50% + 12.5/81

= 50% + (8.1 + 4.4)/81 = 50% + 10% + 4.4/81

= 60% + 4.4/81

At this stage you know that the answer to the question lies between 60 and 70% (Since 4.4 is less than 10% of 81.)

At this stage, you know that the answer to the calculation will be in the form: 6*a.bcde* ....

All you need to do is find out the value of the missing digits.

In order to do this, calculate the percentage value of 4.4/81 through the normal process of multiplying the numerator by 100.

Thus the % value of $\frac{4.4}{81} = \frac{4.4 \times 100}{81} = \frac{440}{81}$

Note: Use the multiplication by 100, once you have the 10% range. This step reduces the decimal calculations.

Thus $\frac{440}{81}$ = 5% with a remainder of 35.

Our answer is now refined to 65.*bcde* (1% Range).

Next, in order to find the next digit (first one after the decimal) add a zero to the remainder;

Hence, the value of '*b*' will be the quotient of

$b \rightarrow$ 350/81 = 4 Remainder 26

Answer: 65.4*cde* (0.1% Range)

$c \rightarrow$ 260/81 = 3 Remainder 17

Answer: 65.43 (0.01% Range)

and so forth.

The advantages of this process are twofold:

(1) You only calculate as long as you need to in order to eliminate the options. Thus, in case there was only a single option between 60% and 70% in the above question, you could have stopped your calculations right there.
(2) This process allows you to go through with the calculations as long as you need to.

However, remember what I had advised you right at the start: strong addition skills are a primary requirement for using this method properly.

To illustrate another example:

What is the percentage value of the ratio $\frac{223}{72}$?

223/72 → 300 – 310% Remainder 7.
700/72 → 9. Hence, 309 – 310%, Remainder 52.
520/72 → 7. Hence, 309.7, Remainder 16.
160/72 → 2. Hence, 309.72, Remainder 16.

Hence, 309.7222 (2 recurs since we enter an infinite loop of 160/72 calculations).

In my view, percentage rule (as *I* call it) is one of the best ways to calculate percentages since it gives you the flexibility to calculate the percentage value up to as many digits after decimals as you are required to and at the same time allows you to stop the moment you attain the required accuracy range.

Of course I hope you realise that when you get 53/81 = 65.43% the decimal value of the same would be 0.6543 and for 223/72, the decimal value would be 3.097222.

The kind of exam that the CAT is, I do not think you would not need to calculate ratios beyond 2 digits divided by 2 digits. In other words, if you are trying to calculate 5372/8164 you can take an approximation of this ratio as 53/81 and calculate the percentage value as shown in the process above. The accuracy in the calculation of 53/81 instead of 5372/8164 would be quite sufficient to answer questions on ratio values that the CAT may throw up in Quantitative Aptitude or Data Interpretation questions.

RATIO COMPARISONS

Calculation Methods Related To Ratios

(A) Calculation methods for ratio comparisons:

There could be four broad cases when you might be required to do ratio comparisons:

The table below clearly illustrates these:

	Numerator	Denominator	Ratio	Calculations
Case 1	Increases	Decreases	Increase	Not required
Case 2	Increases	Increases	May Increase or Decrease	Required
Case 3	Decreases	Increases	Decreases	Not required
Case 4	Decreases	Decreases	May Increase or Decrease	Required

In cases 2 and 4 in the table, calculations will be necessitated. In such a situation, the following processes can be used for ratio comparisons.

1. Cross Multiplication Method

Two ratios can be compared using the cross multiplication method as follows. Suppose you have to compare

12/17 with 15/19

Then, to test which ratio is higher cross multiply and compare 12×19 and 15×17.

If 12×19 is bigger, the ratio 12/17 will be bigger. If 15×17 is higher, the ratio 15/19 will be higher.

In this case, 15×17 being higher, the ratio 15/19 is higher.

Note: In real time usage (esp. in DI) this method is highly impractical and calculating the product might be more cumbersome than calculating the percentage values.

Thus, this method will not be able to tell you the answer if you have to compare $\frac{3743}{5624}$ with $\frac{3821}{5783}$.

2. Percentage Value Comparison Method

Suppose you have to compare $\frac{173}{212}$ with $\frac{181}{241}$.

In such a case just by estimating the 10% ranges for each ratio you can clearly see that–

the first ratio is greater than 80% while the second ratio is less than 80%

Hence, the first ratio is obviously greater.

This method is extremely convenient if the two ratios have their values in different 10% ranges.

However, this problem will become slightly more difficult, if the two ratios fall in the same 10% range. Thus, if you had to compare 173/212 with 181/225, both the values would give values between 80% and 90%. The next step would be to calculate the 1% range.

The first ratio here is 81–82% while the second ratio lies between 80% and 81%

Hence the first ratio is the larger of the two.

Note: For this method to be effective for you, you'll first need to master the percentage rule method for calculating the percentage value of a ratio. Hence if you cannot see that 169.6 is 80% of 212 or for that matter that 81% of 212 is 171.72 and 82% is 173.84, you will not be able to use this method effectively. (This is also true for the next method.) However, once you can calculate percentage values of 3 digit ratios to 1% range, there is not much that can stop you in comparing ratios. The CAT and all other management exams normally do not challenge you to calculate further than the 1% range when you are looking at ratio comparisons.

3. Numerator Denominator Percentage Change Method

There is another way in which you can compare close ratios like 173/212 and 181/225. For this method, you need to calculate the percentage changes in the numerator and the denominator.

Thus:

$173 \rightarrow 181$ is a % increase of 4–5%

While $212 \rightarrow 225$ is a % increase of 6–7%.

In this case, since the denominator is increasing more than the numerator, the second ratio is smaller.

This method is a more powerful method for comparing close ratios – provided you are good with your percentage rule calculations. Another method has been explained in the next part of this book on page 1.3.11.

(B) Method for calculating the value of a percentage change in the ratio:

PCG (Percentage Change Graphic) gives us a convenient method to calculate the value of the percentage change in a ratio.

Suppose, you have to calculate the percentage change between 2 ratios. This has to be done in two stages as:

$$\text{Original Ratio} \xrightarrow[\text{numerator}]{\text{Effect of}} \text{Intermediate Ratio}$$

$$\xrightarrow[\text{Denominator}]{\text{Effect of}} \text{Final Ratio}$$

Thus if 20/40 becomes 22/50

Effect of numerator = $20 \rightarrow 22$ (10% increase)

Effect of denominator = $50 \rightarrow 40$ (20% decrease) (reverse fashion)

Overall effect on the ratio:

$$100 \xrightarrow[\text{Numerator Effect}]{10\%\uparrow} 110 \xrightarrow[\text{Denominator Effect}]{20\%\downarrow} 88$$

Hence, overall effect = 12% decrease.

Contents

PART 2: HOW TO THINK IN TRADITIONAL DATA INTERPRETATION

PART 5: MOCK TEST PAPERS (BASED ON THE LATEST CAT PATTERN)

Section II Logical Data Interpretation

PART 1: HOW TO THINK IN LOGICAL DATA INTERPRETATION

PART 2: TWELVE MINUTE TESTS

SECTION I

TRADITIONAL DATA INTERPRETATION

PART 1

BASIC MODES OF DATA REPRESENTATION

IN THIS PART YOU WILL LEARN:

- What is Data Interpretation?
- Various Types of Data Representations
  - Tables
  - Bar Charts
  - Line Graphs and X-Y Charts
  - Pie Charts
  - Caselets (Representing Data)
  - Multiple and Miscellaneous Charts

THIS PART CONTAINS:

- Individual chapters on each type of Data Representation
- Exercises and Practice Questions covering various question types asked in exams (like CAT, banking and other management and aptitude exams) on each type of Data Representation

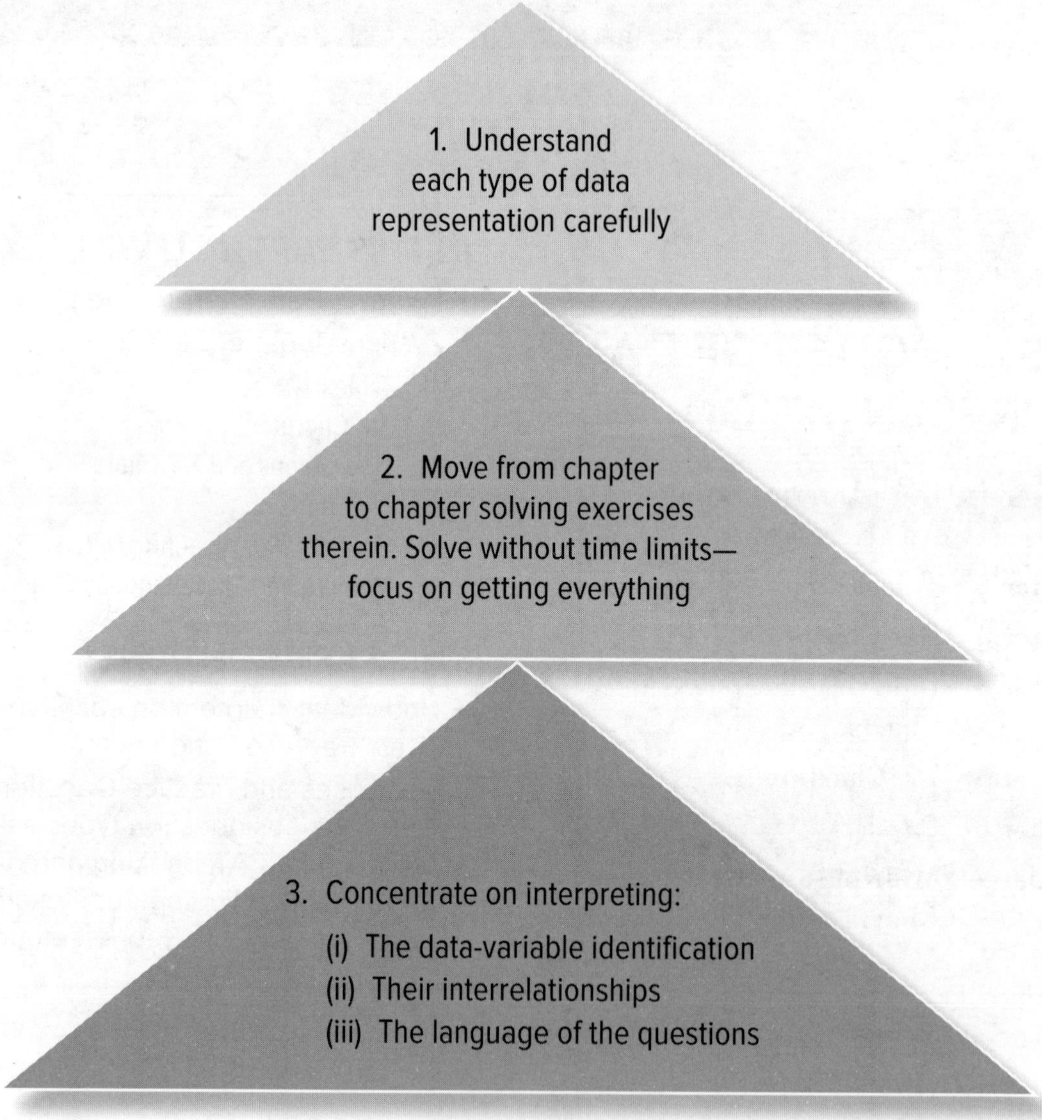
1. Understand each type of data representation carefully
2. Move from chapter to chapter solving exercises therein. Solve without time limits— focus on getting everything
3. Concentrate on interpreting:
(i) The data-variable identification
(ii) Their interrelationships
(iii) The language of the questions

CHAPTER 1

Data Interpretation—An Overview

Outline

Learning Objectives

- Get an overview of the various options for data representation.
- Answer the Question, 'What data interpretation is all about'?
- Understand how to study Data Interpretation.
- Understand the difference between Traditional and Logical Data Interpretation

Chapter Highlights

- What is data?
- What are variables (discrete and continuous)?
- Organisation and presentation of data (tabular, bar charts, X-Y charts, pie charts, reasoning caselets and numerical data-based cases).
- General hints for data interpretation.

Reading and understanding data is at the heart of all decision-making in today's world. So if you are deciding on a personal decision with regard to your budgets, a marketing manager making a decision about a marketing campaign, a finance CFO making an investment decision for his company or it is a decision that a head of government is contemplating about the budgets for the military establishment – all decisions whether complex or simple require the ability to read and understand data.

With the advent of the digital age and with the advent of technology and its ability to capture every piece of information generated from our day-to-day activities – the ability to read data, find patterns in it and draw inferences from it has become a critical part of almost all careers – but it marketing, finance, banking, sales, administration, sports, medicine and anything else one can think of.

Given the large part of your future professional life that you will spend with data and analysing and drawing conclusions from the same, it is no surprise hence that the CAT and all other management entrance exams have made Data Interpretation an integral part of their exams. In fact, DI as it is referred to (in short) is an integral part of all aptitude exams.

HOW SHOULD ONE STUDY DATA INTERPRETATION?

In order to formulate a plan of action to study data interpretation, you should first understand what it is.

When you are presented with any data, you can draw inferences and make conclusions from the data. Consider the following: 'The correct time of my train at the New Delhi Railway Station was 8 PM on 17th January. My train reached the New Delhi Railway station at 8:10 PM on that day.'

From this small piece of information, I have provided you with, you can easily draw the conclusion that my train was delayed by 10 minutes.

The art and science of making inferences and drawing conclusions about data is called as Data Interpretation. In other words, Data when Interpreted gives you information.

A typical Data Interpretation question presents you with data in the form of graphs/charts/tables/caselets followed by a set of questions.

A typical question in a DI set, asks you to draw out information from the given data. This you have to do by extracting the correct number/s from the given data and completing the required calculations to answer the question asked.

In order to be able to solve a DI set and the questions asked in the set, you should have a few basic skills. These include:

1. The Ability to read charts and graphs;
2. The ability to recognize variables – given variables and derived variables – presented in the data; (Note: Every Data set consists of given variables and derived variables. For instance, suppose you are presented with a set of data where you are given sales revenue and costs of a company across 5 years. From these two 'given' variables, the variable 'profit/loss' can be calculated for each of the five years.)

3. The ability to visualize and understand the equations connecting the variables in the problem;
4. The ability to understand the language of the questions asked (including the twists and turns of the same);
5. The ability to understand the information the question is seeking from you and what numbers from the data you would need to extract in order to answer the question asked;
6. The ability to do the requisite calculations that the question seeks from you.

DATA INTERPRETATION IN THE CAT

Needless to say Data Interpretation has always been an integral part in the CAT. However, the DI that you see in the CAT in the recent years has had a drastic transformation from what it used to be in the 1990s and the early 2000s. If we were to take a close look at this transformation, by taking a look at the sets that have been asked in the CAT over the last 2 decades, you will notice that the theme of the questions being asked in DI have moved from Data extraction to Data Analysis.

In other words, traditionally DI questions presented the test taker with data in the form of charts/graphs/tables. The questions asked on the DI sets, would seek information that was emerging from the data given in the charts. In order to get to the correct answer, the typical tasks required to be done are:

(a) Recognition of the equation to be used to find the information.
(b) Extraction of the relevant numbers from the given data to be placed inside the equation.
(c) Completion of the calculations required to get the value of the answer.

As you can imagine, the emphasis in such questions was on data extraction and calculations.

As against this, the changed emphasis in new age data interpretation questions is on the analysis of data. Problems on these can be set up based on various themes which you will encounter in the Logical DI part of the book. Some of these themes can be named as: Missing Data, Masked Data, Cross-Referenced data, data based on truth tables, and data based on multiple possibility situations. As you go through the contents provided in this book you will come across these themes and more and get a better understanding of them.

It is for this reason that, we have split the major parts of this book into two clear Sections:

Section I: Traditional Data Interpretation,
Section II: Logical Data Interpretation.

To help you get a better understanding of the difference between the two let me explain it to you through an example.

Consider the following bar chart:

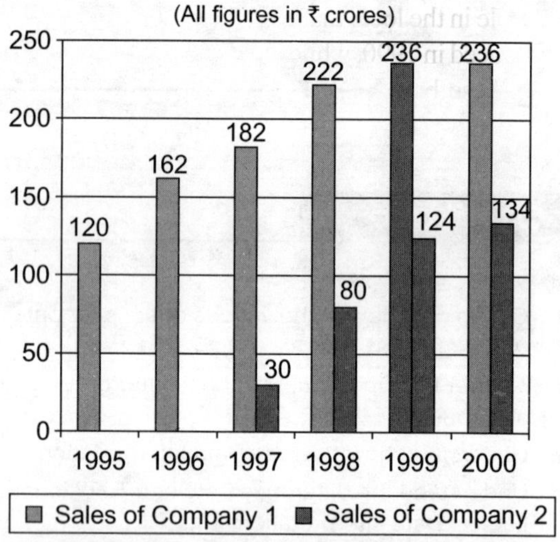

What kinds of information are extractable from this data? Remember, a DI question can only ask for information that can be extracted from the given data. Take a look at the following questions:

1. What is the percentage growth of sales For Company 2 in the year 1998, as compared to 1997? Answer: 166.66%. Sales for Company 2 have grown from 30 to 80 crores from 1997 to 1998, which represents a growth of 166.66 percent.
2. In which year did Company 1 show the highest percentage growth in its sales? Answer 1996 – as the percentage increase in sales from 1995-1996 for company 1 is 35%, (as it has grown from 120 in 1995 to 162 in 1996) and the percentage growth in any subsequent year is less than that.

Likewise, there could be questions about information regards, the total sales across years, the ratio of sales of a company from one year to the next, the ratio of the sales between the two companies for any given year etc.

As you can well see, these questions are all dependent on identifying the correct equation to be used to answer the information sought – extracting the correct numbers from the charts, inserting them into the appropriate places in the equations and executing the calculations required. This is the kind of question, that can be classified as a traditional Data Interpretation question.

To illustrate how sets based on data analysis change the nature of the tasks to be executed for solving a DI set, let's consider the following set, using the same bar charts as above:

EXAMPLE

Answer the questions on the basis of the information given below:

Purana and Naya are two brands of kitchen mixer-grinders available in the local market. Purana is an old brand that was introduced in 1990, while Naya was introduced in 1997. For both these brands, 20 per cent of the mixer-grinders bought in a particular year are disposed off as junk exactly two years later. It is known that 10 Purana mixer-grinders were disposed off in 1997. The following figures show the number of Purana and Naya mixer-grinders in operation from 1995–2000 at the end of the year.

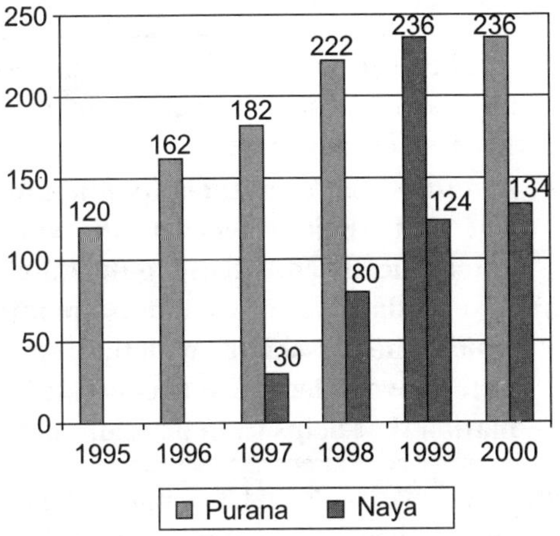

1. How many Naya mixer-grinders were disposed off by the end of 2000?
   (a) 10
   (b) 16
   (c) 22
   (d) Cannot be determined from the data
2. How many Naya mixer-grinders were purchased in 1999?
   (a) 44 (b) 50
   (c) 55 (d) 64
3. How many Purana mixer-grinders were disposed off in 2000?
   (a) 0
   (b) 5
   (c) 6
   (d) Cannot be determined from the data
4. How many Purana mixer-grinders were purchased in 1999?
   (a) 20
   (b) 23
   (c) 50
   (d) Cannot be determined from the data

Solution In the above question, the key variable shown by the charts is the number of mixer grinders in operation (and not the numbers sold). Thus, the 120 we see for 1995, is not the sales for that year, but how many Purana Mixer grinders were in operation for that year. What one needs to recognize from the given data, is that the increase of Purana grinders from 120 to 162 (in 1996), is happening because of two reasons. i) The addition of the Purana grinders that were sold in 1996; ii) The subtraction of 20% of the Purana grinders sold in 1994, which would be scrapped in 1996. (Note: This is to be done as the question mentions that 20% of the mixer grinders sold in a particular year are sold off as scrap exactly 2 years later).

Thus, the equation to be considered between 120 and 162 is:

120 + Purana Grinders sold in 1996 – Purana scrapped in 1994 (which will equal 20% of Purana grinders sold in 1994) = 162.

Again from the data we can observe that we do not have information about the number of Purana grinders sold in 1994. Thus, we cannot find the number of Purana sold in 1996.

Likewise, when you consider the year 1997, you have:

162 + Purana Grinders sold in 1997 – Purana scrapped in 1997 = 182.

In the textual information for the data, it is given to us that 10 Purana mixer grinders were disposed off in 1997. Hence, we can insert 10, for Purana scrapped in 1997 and find out the Purana grinders sold in 1997 as 162 + n -10 = 182 → n = 30.

Based on this logic we can answer the questions asked as:

	PURANA		NAYA	
	Purchases	Disposals	Purchases	Disposals
1995	50 (5 times disposal 1997)	Unknown	–	–
1996	Unknown	Unknown	–	–
1997	182 – (162-10) = 30	10 (given)	30	0
1998	Unknown	Unknown	50	0
1999	236 – (222 – 6) = 20	6 (20% of purchases 1997)	124 – (80 – 6) = 50	6
2000	Unknown	Unknown	134 – (124 – 10) = 20	10

1. 20% of 1997 will be disposed off in 1999 and 20% of 1998 will be disposed off in 2000.
   Hence, 6 + 10 = 16
2. 50 (As in 124 – 80 + 6)
3. Cannot be determined since this is asking the value for an even year.
4. 20 (from the logic 222 – 6 + purchases 1999 = 236).

As you could see, in a logical data interpretation set, while you still need to understand how to read data and also be able to identify the variables involved inside a question, the focus of solving such questions moves to the analysis of data, rather than the extraction of data.

In this section of the book, we will move you onto the various modes of Data Representation. Before you go into the individual charts and graphs that are commonly seen in DI questions, a brief word about Data.

WHAT IS DATA?

Data is the term used to refer to the raw numbers (facts and figures) which emerge from the occurrence of any event—physical, social, economic, corporate, geographical, individual, and all miscellaneous kinds of events that have the potential to throw out numbers and figures. These numbers and figures, however, make no sense by themselves unless they are qualified by a series of qualifiers explained as follows.

Nature of Data

A numerical value by itself represents nothing and describes absolutely nothing. Thus, if we imagine a number, say 37, it means absolutely nothing by itself. The number starts to gain some significance when it is qualified by saying that it is the temperature or weight, etc. However, just by saying that the number represents temperature does not complete the description of the number. It has to be further qualified by specific descriptions, that it is the temperature on 7 June 2023 in New Delhi at 2 p.m.

Thus, three facts get attached to the number to describe it more completely:

(a) It is a number representing temperature.
(b) It refers to a place called New Delhi.
(c) It refers to the date of 7 June 2023 and time of 2 p.m.

However, even with these qualifiers, the magnitude of the value is not imaginable. The natural question that will arise in the mind of the interpreter of this data is: 'What does a number 37, described as the temperature at 2 p.m. on 7 June 2023 in New Delhi, represent in terms of its magnitude'?

The unit provides meaning to the data. Data without a unit is meaningless.

The information provided does not give us an idea about the magnitude of the temperature. We need to further qualify the number by attributing to it a unit.

Thus, if the number is further qualified by the unit 'degree celsius' or '°C' then it suddenly makes sense to us. The introduction of the unit in fact automatically qualifies it as the temperature.

A unit also makes a number comparable to other values and we can thus make conclusions like 35°C < 37°C and that the temperature in New Delhi on 7 June 2023 is higher than the temperature in Lucknow at the same time on the same date. Further, that if Lucknow had a temperature of 35ºC we can say that Delhi had a temperature that was 2°C more than that of Lucknow or even that Delhi had a temperature that was (200/35)% higher than that of Lucknow, and so on.

These qualifiers can be seen as kinds of 'pointers' to the number and we conclude that for any number to make sense, it should have:

(a) A unit which quantifies its magnitude. The unit when attached to the number automatically adds sense to the number.
(b) A secondary set of qualifiers (pointers) which when associated with the data help us to convert the data into concrete information that helps us in decision making.

Hence, we have seen that the number 37 makes complete sense when it is qualified as: 37°C was the temperature of New Delhi on 7 June 2023 at 2 p.m. It could equally have been qualified as: ₹ 37 crore was the sales turnover of a company X in the year 2025.

You are encouraged at this point to think of alternative units and associated pointers which would make sense when attached to the number 37 (or for that matter any other number). While doing so, pay attention to how you are required to use a unit along with a few associated pointers to make any sense of a number.

Some Standard Common Pointers

Time

The time dimension is an overriding fact of our life and most data is measured in the reference frame of a particular time. Thus, we qualified the temperature of New Delhi by adding a date and a specific time to it.

Even figures related to companies/industries/corporations/organisations/departments have their respective time dimensions specified.

Other situations include movement of a car/train in a specified time duration, production in a factory in a particular time duration, etc. Units used for time are decades, years, quarters, months, weeks, days, hours, seconds, minutes, days, etc.

Place or Geographical Pointers

This is the second most common standard pointer which is used for making sense out of a number. Thus when we talk about economic data we talk about the country, state, area or region.

Other common pointers include: monetary value, temperature and number of units consumed/sold/produced, etc.

DATA REPRESENTS VARIABLES

This is another way to look at data and numerical values. A variable is a quantity or an attribute whose value is not fixed/is changeable and can change with a change of some of the underlying factors. Most data (numerical values/series of numbers) represent variables that can change their values.

As an example, we can think of the temperature of a place as a variable. This variable changes with time since the value of the temperature changes with time.

All series of numerical values will represent some variables that will underlie the set of values.

Types of Variables

Based on the way the value of the variable changes, it can be a discrete variable or a continuous variable.

Discrete Variables

Variables which have only discrete value change and have 'no in-between' values, e.g., continent, country, company, state, city, year, quarter, month, day and region. Change in these variables always occurs in discrete steps. Thus, the year may be either 2009 or 2013. There is nothing like 2009.05 or for that matter 2013.98 when we talk about the year as a variable.

Similarly, the country being mentioned could be either India or Pakistan or US or UK or Germany or any other.

Continuous Variables

These are variables which change continuously, e.g., sales revenues, unit sales, GDP, population, temperature, speed, etc.

In this context, it can be easily seen that while continuous variables can be easily represented by an unbroken line on the X-Y plane, discrete variables cannot be shown in such a fashion.

Further, if a continuous variable is taken on one of the axis in the X-Y plane, then each point on that axis will have a certain value. However, if an axis is used to represent a discrete variable, then not every point of the axis will necessarily represent an instance of the discrete variable. Hence, such an axis will have points which lie in between two values of the discrete variable and which will have no meaning or no value in terms of that discrete variable.

Thus, in Figure 1.1, the X-axis represents a discrete variable and the Y-axis represents a continuous variable.

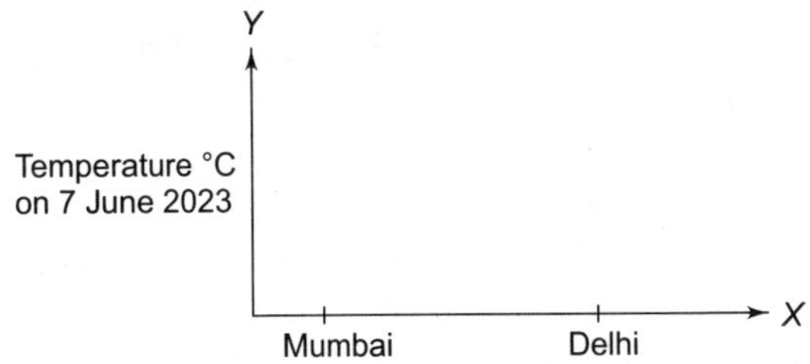

FIGURE 1.1 *Discrete and Continuous Variables*

Usually, continuous variables are represented by a series of numbers while discrete variables are normally represented by names. One possible case of exception could be the case of the year (time dimension). Here the discrete variable is represented by a number.

DEFINITION OF DATA INTERPRETATION

The interpretation of data is the process through which inferences are drawn about the data available for analysis. In other words, the process of drawing inferences and conclusions through the interpretation of data is what DI is all about.

ORGANISATION AND PRESENTATION OF DATA

Normally, data is generated in such volumes and in such great proportions that it becomes impossible to make any useful judgements through the volume of data. Unless organised in a condensed form that will highlight the main characteristics, facilitate comparisons and render it suitable for further processing and interpretation, raw data will have little meaning. Top management people rarely find time to go through the entire details of any report, be it daily production or the sales forecast. An effective presentation of data enables them to draw upon the information with the least effort and time.

One chart table or graph gives at least 10 times more information than one page of words.

There is thus a need to organise the data into meaningful presentations. Data is organised and presented through one of the several forms of presentations available. The most commonly used amongst these are tables, pie charts, bar graphs, the line charts, and so on.

Data can be represented by using any one or more than one of these. Normally data is represented through a graphical representation or a set of graphical representations linked to each other.

Effective presentation of data is broadly classified into the following categories:

1. Tabular presentation
2. Bar charts
3. X-Y charts
4. Pie charts
5. Caselets
6. Miscellaneous charts

We will now go on and analyse each of the types of charts briefly.

Tabular Presentation

Tabular presentation is the process of presenting data systematically in horizontal rows and vertical columns. This presentation of data makes it easily understandable and usable for further statistical analysis. The heading of each row and column helps the reader understand the data and the units used for the same. The units to be attached to the values within the row/column either may be mentioned in every row or column or might be mentioned commonly at the top/bottom of the table. In such a case there would be a reference to the units, e.g., 'All figures in ₹ crore'.

Either the columns or the rows will represent different values of a discrete variable, while the other represents a set of different continuous variables, which may or may not be related to each other.

Normally the rows represent the different values of the discrete variable, while the columns represent the multitude of continuous variables.

EXAMPLE 1

In Table 1.1 the discrete variable is the year and there are four values of it, viz., 2010, 2011, 2012 and 2013. Each of the columns represent different continuous variables with their own units.

The intersection of a row and a column denotes the value of the continuous variable for that instance of the discrete variable. For example, *x* denotes the value of the revenue (in ₹ crore) for the year 2010.

TABLE 1.1

Year	Revenue (₹ crore)	Costs (₹ crore)	Profit (₹ crore)	Sales (units) ('000s)	No. of Employees
2010	x				
2011					
2012					
2013					

EXAMPLE 2

The marks in Physics and Biology of 20 students are as follows:

Physics: 20, 21, 20, 21, 21, 24, 22, 22, 23, 20, 23, 22, 21, 22, 20, 24, 24, 22, 23, 20.

Biology: 30, 31, 32, 31, 33, 33, 32, 31, 34, 33, 34, 33, 32, 33, 32, 32, 34, 30, 34, 33.

This information can be presented as follows (Table 1.2):

TABLE 1.2 The Marks Obtained by Students in Physics and Biology

Marks in Physics → / Marks in Biology ↓	20	21	22	23	24
30	1		1		
31		2	1		
32	2	1	1		1
33	2	1	2		1
34				3	1

Bar Charts

Bar charts are one of the easiest, graphically attractive and hence the most commonly used methods of presenting all types of data. They are especially useful for representing various data series (normally 1–4). The data series comprises the continuous variables while the values of the specific instances at which the value of the data series is measured represents the values of the discrete variables.

Presentation of data as bar charts makes the comparative study of the data very easy. A bar chart consists of a group of bars which are equidistant from each other. The values on the bar charts are read by the measurement of the length or the height of the bars. The width of the bars is largely inessential and is used only for the clarity of the presentation. Example 3 will make the concept of bar charts clear.

EXAMPLE 3

The data related to the foreign exchange reserves of India for different years is as follows:

TABLE 1.3 Foreign Exchange Reserves of India

Years	₹ (Crore)
2008–09	5,334
2009–10	5,544
2010–11	4,123
2011–12	4,567
2012–13	6,127
2013–14	7,324
2014–15	7,909
2015–16	8,146

This data is represented on the following bar diagram (Figure 1.2).

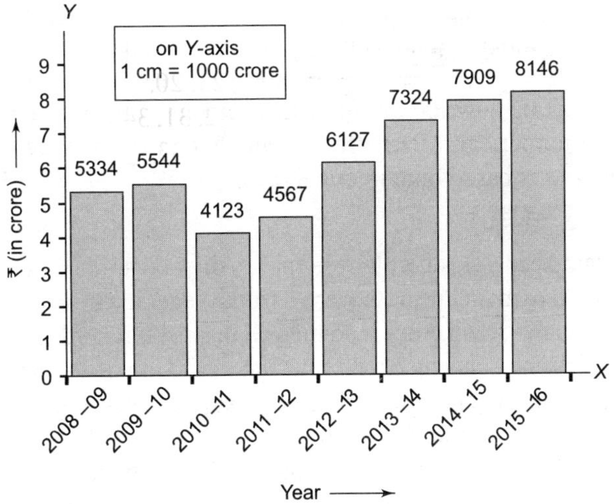

FIGURE 1.2 *Foreign Exchange Reserves of India*

X-Y Charts

As the name suggests, X-Y charts are graphs that are represented on the X-Y plane. In this case we normally have one axis representing one or more continuous variable(s) while the other axis is used to represent a discrete variable. In certain cases (like speed–time graph) both the axes could be used to represent continuous variables. X-Y charts, also known as line or point diagrams, are two-dimensional diagrams in which any point in the entire plane can be represented by the corresponding values read on the X and Y axes. Normally continuous variables are plotted on either of the two axes, while the other axis is used to represent the discrete variable.

An X-Y chart is a convenient and compact way of representing data series. It is also quite easy to understand. It is often used to denote single or multiple, related or unrelated, continuous variables against a specific set of values of a discrete variable. Such graphs are useful for exhibiting trends and rate of change.

EXAMPLE 4

The following data (Table 1.4) shows the number of questions solved by 330 students at Mindworkzz in a test on DI.

TABLE 1.4 Number of Questions Solved by Students at Mindworkzz

Number of Questions Solved	Number of Students
0	43
1	22
2	49
3	57
4	83
5	24
6	11
7	18
8	9
9	5
10	5
11	4

The data is represented by the following line diagram (Figure 1.3):

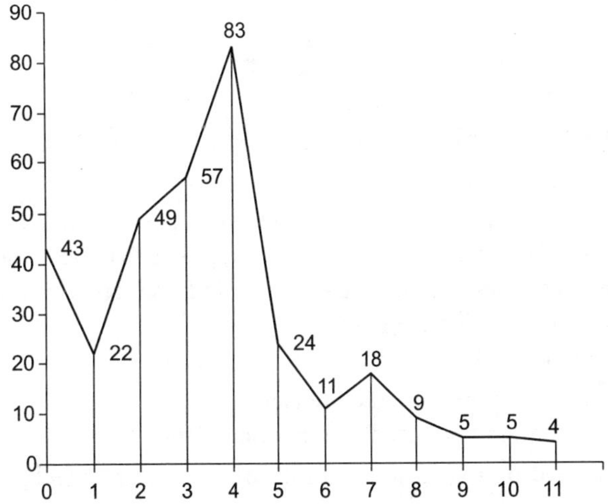

FIGURE 1.3 *Number of Questions Solved by Students at Mindworkzz*

Pie Charts

As the name suggests, pie charts are a circular representation of data. The data in question represents the break-up of a whole into its parts. The share of each part in the pie diagram is proportionate to its share of the whole data. The given data is distributed over a total angle of 360°. A pie diagram can also be described as a circular figure which is divided into different sectors or segments, each sector or segment representing in area and angle, the percentage contribution of a certain component to the total.

The following formula is used for the calculation of the angle of a sector of the pie chart:

$$\text{Angle of a sector} = \frac{\text{Value of Sector}}{\text{Total Value}} \times 360^\circ$$

EXAMPLE 5

Construct a pie chart based on the following data (Table 1.5).

TABLE 1.5 Number of Students Specialising in Select Subjects

Specialisation	Number of Students
Marketing	430
Human Resources	210
Finance	140
Systems	90
Production	65

Solution We need to compute the angle of each sector based on the formula given. This will result in the following diagram (Figure 1.4).

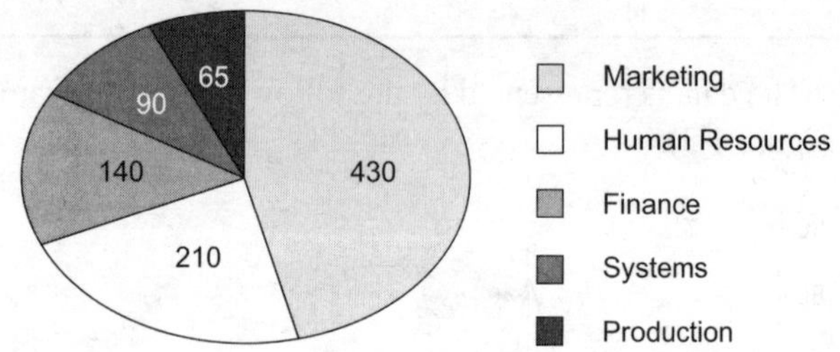

FIGURE 1.4 *Number of Students Specialising in Select Subjects*

Caselet Form

In this form of data presentation, the data is given in the form of a paragraph. The student is required to understand the data presented in a paragraph and convert it into a table for solving the questions.

Broadly there are two kinds of caselets:

1. Paragraph based on reasoning.
2. Paragraph based on numerical data.

The following is an example of a caselet based on reasoning.

General Hints for Data Interpretation

Data interpretation questions are based on information given in tables, graphs or diagrams. These questions test the ability of the solver to interpret the information presented and to select the appropriate data for answering a question.

1. Read the data very carefully. Even the minutest word must not be overlooked since many a times even a single word/group of words could become critical.
2. If there are more than one graphs/charts/tables, understand the relationship between them clearly before you proceed to solve the questions asked.
3. Answer only the questions asked. Do not answer/ calculate things which have not been asked for.
4. Be careful to use proper units and beware of charts and tables with non-uniform units.
5. Every DI question will present you with Variables – some given explicitly, others implicitly (or in a hidden fashion). The primary objective in a DI question is to identify the variables given in the data and work out the relationship between the variables. Questions on DI sets would involve either the given or the hidden variables.

Let us now look at the use of caselets for representing numerical information. Example 6 is an instance of a caselet based on numerical data.

EXAMPLE 6

Nath Seeds, an agriculture company divided its operations into five main business areas – fruits, vegetables, medicinal plants, cash crops, and miscellaneous. It recorded the following sales in 2011, 2012, and 2013. In 2011, sales in fruits, vegetables, medicinal plants and miscellaneous were ₹6,250,000, ₹2,200,000, ₹18,80,000 and ₹940,000 respectively. Cash crops accounted for 30 per cent of the total sales during the year.

In 2012, the total sales showed a 10 per cent increase over the previous year. While fruit and vegetables registered 8 per cent and 10 per cent increase over their corresponding figures in 2011, medicinal plants dropped by ₹130,000, while cash crops stood at ₹5,360,000.

In 2013, though the total sales remained the same as in 2012, fruits fell by ₹220,000, vegetables by ₹320,000, medicinal plants by ₹100,000 and miscellaneous by ₹120,000.

In order to make sense of the data presented in the form of a paragraph as above, it is normally advisable to convert it into a table. Something of the following nature will emerge and then the questions based on the caselet can be solved by just reading the values from the table (Table 1.6).

TABLE 1.6 Sales Figures for Nath Seed Company

	2011	2012	2013
Fruits	6,25,0000	6,75,0000	6,53,0000
Vegetables	2,200,000	2,420,000	2,100,000
Medicinal plants	1,880,000	1,750,000	1,650,000
Cash crops	4,830,000	5,360,000	6,120,000
Miscellaneous	9,40,000	1,430,000	1,310,000
Total	16,100,000	17,710,000	17,710,000

As we now move to look at each of these types of data presentations individually, it must be mentioned here that data generation and presentation is so vast a field that it is almost impossible to divide the individual types of tables/ graphs/charts into their subtypes. However, an effort has been made here to do so—the objective being to initiate the students into each of the types of data presentations. The student is expected to not just limit himself/herself to the tables and graphs that are part of this book but is expected to go much beyond and constantly be on the lookout for more and more data presentations in magazines, books, journals or even in statistical compilations.

CHAPTER 2

Tables

Outline

Learning Objectives

- Get a first-hand view of how data is presented through its organisation in the form of tables.
- Get an understanding of typical data which can be represented through tables.
- Get a first-hand feel of the typical question types that are asked on tables.
- Experience High Quality and difficulty level DI sets, to get a feel of High level DI - even if you cannot solve it at this stage.

Chapter Highlights

- Introduction to tables.
- Practice exercise on tables containing simulated examination level questions.
- LOD 2 and LOD 3 Exercises, to help you experience high quality DI question sets.

INTRODUCTION

The dictionary meaning of a table is – 'a chart of facts and figures shown in horizontal rows and vertical columns.' Tables are one of the most versatile methods of systematic presentation of quantitative data. In the context of the qualification of variables as either continuous or discrete variables, tables give the opportunity to present the maximum number of continuous variables with respect to a set of values for one discrete variable. Indeed, the amount of data that can be presented on a table is much higher than that which can be presented on any type of graph or chart. In fact, the data that can be represented on any type of chart (pie/bar/x-y) can also be represented on a table.

The reason for the versatility of a table over the standard charts is because if we want to present any additional information on a table, it is just a matter of adding one more column/row and describing the continuous variable to be shown in the heading of the column/row.

Normally, the discrete variable/s used in a table are:

(a) Geographical or location based (city, state, country, etc.).
(b) Time period in terms of months, quarters or years.
(c) Individual or company name based.
(d) Miscellaneous classifications.

The first three are the most commonly used.

A NOTE ON HOW LOGICAL DATA INTERPRETATION QUESTIONS CAN BE SET ON TABLES

While you might have come across various tables and how to read them – you need to understand that the Data Interpretation section of the CAT has undergone a massive shift from the days when questions were simply built on extraction of data and calculations.

Common themes of DI questions based on tables these days are:

(i) Missing Data questions;
(ii) Cross Referenced data and
(iii) Truth Tables

Let's take a brief while to understand each of these through an example of them:

Tables based on Missing Data

It is a very common questioning theme these days, where some data is removed from a tabular structure and clues are provided to trace back the numbers. A very simple starting level of example is explained here for your understanding.

EXAMPLE 1

Professor Tahiliyani, the HOD of the Electronics department at a college had marked his students based on their grades as Excellent, Good or Average. He had created a table for the same but due to a computer error, some of the data has gone missing from the table. However, he remembered a few crucial points regarding the table. Could you help him complete the table based on what he remembers?

	Excellent	Good	Average	Total
Girls		100		
Boys				
Total				

(a) 40% of the students in his class were girls.
(b) The ratio of number of excellent, good and average students was 2:3:4. The difference, between the number of excellent and average students was 200.
(c) The average students were equally split between girls and boys.

Q1. What is the ratio of excellent girls to average girls?
Q2. What is the difference between the number of excellent boys and good boys.

Solution: Based on the given information and the clues we can make the deductions that would lead us to the following table:

	Excellent	Good	Average	Total
Girls	60 (3)	100	200 (3)	360 (2)
Boys	140 (3)	200 (3)	200	540 (2)
Total	200 (1)	300 (1)	400 (1)	900

The bracketed numbers in the table represent the deduction numbers as explained below.

1. From clue b, we can work out that the number of students in excellent, good and average category are 200,300 and 400 respectively. From this we also get that there were a total of 900 students in the class.
2. Since 40% of the students are girls, we get that there must have been 360 girls and 540 boys in the class.
3. From clue c, we get that the 400 average students are to be split equally between boys and girls. Hence, 200 boys and girls. The remaining table can be filled using the row and the column totals and the left over values. For example, the excellent girls = total girls – good girls – average girls = 360 – 100 – 200 = 60 and so on.

The questions can be answered based on the completed table and the answers are: 3:10 and 60 for the two questions.

More complex questions on the same are provided in the LOD 2 and LOD 3 assignments of this chapter. Besides, you will also find a lot of them inside the 12 minute tests and the mock tests in the Logical DI part of the book. I would request you to go through these and improve your exposure and experience of how to think in such situations. Let's now take a look at cross referenced data – the second major theme on tables.

Cross Referenced Data

Let me explain what I mean by cross-referenced data: Imagine a situation, where there are 1000 students in a school. These are divided among boys and girls. When you categorise them as such, you have two kinds of students (boys and girls). Now suppose, the same 1000 students are again divided among senior, middle and junior school students. How many types of students (category-wise) do we now have? You should be able to perceive that there are now 6 types of students, based on cross-referencing them on the basis of their gender and school seniority. These are Senior Boys, Middle Boys, Junior Boys; Senior Girls, Middle Girls and Junior Girls. If I further introduce a new division of the same thousand people as: Scholars or Sportsmen, we will end up getting 12 different kinds of students in the school (Senior Boy Scholars, Senior Boy Sportsmen etc).

Such data structures are often used in Data Interpretation. It has been observed that students often lose control of the question, because they are not able to recognize how many variables they are dealing with. Just the bare recognition of the variables in such cases will go a long way in helping you to regain control of the set and solve it. Consider the following question, to help you understand how questions can be created based on cross referenced data:

EXAMPLE 2

The proportion of male students and the proportion of vegetarian students in a school are given below. The school has a total of 800 students, 80% of whom are in the Secondary Section and rest equally divided between Class 11 and 12.

	Male (M)	Vegetarian (V)
Class 12	0.60	
Class 11	0.55	0.50
Secondary Section		0.55
Total	0.475	0.53

Look into the table given. The situation divides the total 800 students based on two parameters – Male-Female and Vegetarian-Non Vegetarian. In order to solve questions on a set like this, you should first make the table with all divisions:

	Male (M)	Female	Vegetarian (V)	Non-Vegetarian
Class 12 (80)	0.60 → 80 × 0.6 = 48	80-48=32	424 – 352 – 40 = 32	80 – 32 = 48
Class 11 (80)	0.55 → 80 × 0.55 = 44	80-44=36	0.50 → 80 × 0.5 = 40	80 – 40 = 40
Secondary Section (640)	380 – 44 – 48 = 288	640 – 288 = 352	0.55 → 640 × 0.55 = 352	640 – 352 = 288
Total (800)	0.475 = 800 × 0.475 = 380	800 – 380 = 420 OR 32 + 36 + 352 = 420	0.53 → 800 × 0.53 = 424	800 – 424 = 376 OR 288 + 40 + 48 = 376

Solution: I will now explain some of the calculations done in the table:

The proportion of Male Class 12 students is given as 0.6. Hence, 0.6×80 = 48 Male class 12 students. We can similarly calculate the male class 11 students as 44 and the total Male students as 380. Once, we have these numbers we can work out the missing value in the Males column (i.e. Secondary Section Male students) as 380 – 48 – 44 = 288. The values in the other columns can be similarly calculated.

Once you have done these calculations, you are ready to solve the questions asked in the set:

1. What is the percentage of male students in the secondary section?
   Solution: 288 out 640 = 45%.
2. In Class 12, twenty-five per cent of the vegetarians are male. What is the difference between the number of female vegetarians and male non-vegetarians?

This question requires a further breakdown of the cross-referenced data. In order to solve this question, you need to realise that: There are 4 kinds of students in every class. Hence, Class 12 has Male Vegetarians (say a), Male Non-Vegetarian (b), Female Vegetarian (c) and Female Non-Vegetarian students (d).

Amongst these, we should realise the following five relationships:

Total Students: a + b + c + d = 80 ....(i);

Total male students a + b = 48 ....(ii); Total female students c + d = 32... (iii); Total Vegetarian students 32 = a + c ... (iv) Total Non-Veg Students 48 = b + d ... (v).

In such a case, if any one of these four values is provided to us, we can find the rest. The chain of thought from the information in the question goes as:

Since, it is given that 25% of the vegetarians are male, we get that since class 12 has 32 vegetarians (from our constructed table), male vegetarians = 0.25 × 32 = 8 (Value of a). Then, the value of b= 48 – 8 = 40 (From ii); c = 32 – 8 = 24 (from iv); d = 32 – 24 = 8 (from iii).

The question has asked us the difference between c and b. The required difference is the difference between 40 and 24, i.e. 16.

3. In Class 12, 50% of the students are non-vegetarian males. Which of the following statements is correct?
   (a) Except vegetarian males, all other groups have same number of students.
   (b) Except non-vegetarian males, all other groups have same number of students,
   (c) Except vegetarian females, all other groups have same number of students.
   (d) The number of non-veg females and the number of veg males is equal.

If 50% students are non-vegetarian males, it means that there are 40 non-veg males, 8 non veg females, 8 veg males and 24 non-veg females. Option (d) can be seen as correct.

As you go through the exercises in this chapter as well as the mock tests in the logical DI section of this book, you will come across a lot of practice sets based on cross-referenced data. I would advise you to make a clear mental note of the visualization of the various variables involved while tackling cross-referenced data sets. It's a very common theme in the CAT these days and hence very important for you to do so.

Let us now help you understand the logical Truth Table (To be differentiated from mathematical truth tables) and how to think while solving one:

LOGICAL TRUTH TABLES

A logical truth table is best explained through an actual example:

EXAMPLE 3

Consider the following:

In a history quiz, five students were asked to name the award winner from 2010 to 2014. As the anchor gave them a hint that the winners for the five years were Arjun, Bhim, Chitrasena, Duryodhan and Ekalavya not necessarily in that order. After getting the hint the contestants gave their respective orders as follows:

Students	2010	2011	2012	2013	2014
Pulkit	Chitrasena	Duryodhan	Arjun	Eklavya	Bhim
Qasim	Bhim	Chitrasena	Arjun	Duryodhan	Eklavya
Rahim	Chitrasena	Duryodhan	Arjun	Bhim	Eklavya
Sahir	Eklavya	Arjun	Chitrasena	Bhim	Duryodhan
Taufiq	Bhim	Chitrasena	Arjun	Eklavya	Duryodhan

Everyone got a different number of guesses correct.

Solution The key to the interpretation of the table is that of the 5 students, each one got a different number of bets correct. This means that the number of correct bets are 5, 3, 2, 1 and 0. (Note: Nobody can get exactly 4 guesses correct, since if for any person if 4 guesses are correct, the fifth would automatically be correct.) Thus, in the entire table there are a total of $5 + 3 + 2 + 1 + 0 = 11$ 'truths'. Also, since the total number of guesses is $5 \times 5 = 25$, it means that there are 14 'lies' in the table.

After this, it is just a matter of checking who can have all 5 guesses correct and matching the guesses with those of the others to see if the condition of 11 truths distributed as 5, 3, 2, 1, 0 is coming out to be correct. This is typically done through trial and error.

So, Assume that Pulkit is the one with all guesses correct. In that case, the winners for the 5 years are: Chitrasena, Duryodhan, Arjun, Eklavya and Bhim for 2010 through 2014 respectively.

Checking for the others, we get Qasim 1 truth (this we get by looking at Qasim's guesses and comparing them to Pulkit's); Rahim 3 truths, Sahir 0 truths and Taufiq has 2 truths. This fits the requirements of the truths in the table perfectly.

If you assumed Qasim's row as having 5 truths, Pulkit would have 1, Rahim 2, Sahir 0 and Taufiq 3. So Qasim's row is also a possible correct set of all 5 guesses.

If Rahim had all 5 correct guesses, then Pulkit would have 3 truths, Qasim 2, Sahir 0 and Taufiq would also have 3 truths. Thus, we can rule out Rahim getting all 5 guesses correct.

Likewise, if Sahir got 5 guesses correct, Pulkit would have 0 and Qasim also 0, which isn't possible. Hence, we can reject Sahir's row as the correct set of guesses in this situation.

For Taufiq having 5 correct guesses, Pulkit would have 2, Qasim 3, Rahim 1 and Sahir 1. This is again not possible – as it does not give us anyone with 0 correct guesses, while giving us two people with 1 correct guess each.

Hence, we conclude that either Pulkit or Qasim have all 5 correct guesses. From this analysis we can conclude that Arjun definitely won the award in 2012. Other award winners would be 2010: Bhim or Chitrasena and so on.

I would now advise you to move into the exercises at various levels of difficulty – and learn from each problem-solving experience you go through.

IMPORTANT NOTE: A Brief word about the LOD 2 & LOD 3 Questions in this chapter – and indeed in all chapters of this section of the book:

In the LOD 2 and LOD 3 questions in these chapters, you would find questions at a significantly higher level of difficulty than the LOD 1 questions. These have been provided here to give you a feel of what level of problem-solving ability you would need to develop in order to crack exam-level questions, that are being asked these days in the Data Interpretation section of the CAT. A lot of these questions might seem very difficult for you to do at this stage of your preparation, especially if you are at a starter or an intermediate skill level. You should not get daunted by this experience, even if you are able to solve a very small fraction of the questions that you come across at Level of Difficulty 2 and Level of Difficulty 3.

This is natural and to be expected because a lot of these problems require self-problem-solving experience of a minimum of 300 sets (split equally between about 150 sets of Traditional Data Interpretation and 150 sets of Logical Data Interpretation sets – before they can be solved by a student. My advice to you is that you should try to solve each of these sets on your own with a time limit of around 20–25 minutes for a set. In case you are not able to complete a set, mark it out and continue moving forward in the exercise. You should even move forward to the next chapter, leaving behind unsolved sets with the resolve that "I will keep practising my skills and raising them as I keep moving forward with my learning through the book. And I will come back stronger and solve these sets once I have a problem-solving experience of 300 + sets."

Remember that just as an athlete would not win every match they play, you would not be able to solve every question you come across at a starter or an intermediate level skill. Remember, in a skill development journey like the one you are going through for Data Interpretation (just like an athlete) - the losses are as important for your learning/skills as are the wins and are equally important when it comes to developing your skills. You should apply this principle while trying to learn from every experience. Remember, even the fact that you tried to solve the set will have raised your level of skill and this is an important component of your skill development process for Data Interpretation.

The following exercise will help you to clearly understand tables and the kinds of questions that might be created on tables.

EXERCISE

Level of Difficulty 1

Directions for Questions 1 to 4: *IIM Bangalore categorizes its students based on their academic performance for all its batches. The auditors of this report discovered something unique in the data set. The institute divided its students among three categories, namely Amazing, Good & Average. The total number of Amazing, Good and Average students are 200, 300 & 400 not necessarily in that order. The number of female students were found to be 25% more than the number of male students. The number of average female students was 1/6th of the total number of students. The ratio of the number of amazing male students to that of their female counterparts was 2:1. Half of the female students were good in academics.*

1. What is the total number of students who were average in their studies?
 (a) 400 (b) 300
 (c) 200 (d) Cannot be Determined
2. What is the total number of male students who were Amazing and female students who were Average in studies?
 (a) 350 (b) 200
 (c) 250 (d) 150
3. What was the total number of students who were amazing in their studies?
 (a) 200 (b) 300
 (c) 400 (d) Data Insufficient
4. Which of these values is the third lowest, if cross-references between male-female and Amazing-Good-Average are considered together?
 (a) Female Amazing Students
 (b) Male Good Students
 (c) Female Average Students
 (d) Both (b) and (c)

Directions for Questions 5 to 7: *Table 2.1 shows the courier charges (in ₹) for sending a 1 kg parcel from one city to another. Study the table carefully and answer the questions that follow:*

TABLE 2.1 Courier Charges for Sending Parcels

Cities	Allahabad	Mumbai	Kolkata	Delhi	Lucknow
Allahabad	—	10	5	15	10
Mumbai	10	—	7	25	20
Kolkata	5	7	—	20	15
Delhi	15	25	20	—	10
Lucknow	10	20	15	10	—

5. Amongst the following, the charges will be the least for sending a parcel from
 (a) Allahabad to Lucknow
 (b) Mumbai to Delhi
 (c) Lucknow to Delhi
 (d) Kolkata to Mumbai
6. For sending parcel from Kolkata, the least charges will be for:
 (a) Allahabad (b) Mumbai
 (c) Delhi (d) Lucknow
7. Which of the following routes of sending a 1 kg parcel, will have no extra cost even if the parcel had been sent directly from the origin, Allahabad, city to the destination city?
 (a) Mumbai-Allahabad-Delhi
 (b) Mumbai-Allahabad-Lucknow
 (c) Kolkata-Allahabad-Lucknow
 (d) All of these

Directions for Questions 8 to 12: *Study Table 2.2 and answer the given questions.*

TABLE 2.2 Employees Working in Various Departments of Hoola Boola Moola, Inc.

Years	Departments (Number of Employees)				
	Production	Marketing	Corporate	Accounts	Research
2007	150	25	50	45	75
2008	225	40	45	62	70
2009	450	65	30	90	70
2010	470	73	32	105	70
2011	500	80	35	132	74
2012	505	75	36	130	75

8. In which year did the total number of employees reach (approximately) twice the total number of employees that the factory had in the year 2007?
 (a) 2008 (b) 2009
 (c) 2010 (d) 2011
9. In which department did the number of employees (approximately) remain the same during the years 2007 and 2012?
 (a) Production (b) Corporate
 (c) Research (d) None of these
10. In how many years was the number of employees working in the production department more than 50% of the total employees?
 (a) 2 (b) 3
 (c) 4 (d) 5

11. In which year did each department have a larger number of employees than it had in the immediately preceding year?
    (a) 2010
    (b) 2012
    (c) 2009
    (d) 2011
12. Which department had less than 10% of the employees through all the years shown in the table?
    (a) Marketing
    (b) Corporate
    (c) Accounts
    (d) None of these

Directions for Questions 13 to 17: *Study Table 2.3 and answer the following questions.*

13. In 2011–12, the ratio of the difference between the maximum and the minimum production of polyethylene, to the difference between the maximum and the minimum production of polypropylene, is nearly
    (a) 14 (b) 15
    (c) 16 (d) 18
14. The ratio of the maximum production of polyethylene in 2012–13 to the minimum production of polyethylene in 2011–12 is:
    (a) 4.8 (b) 5 (c) 5.4 (d) 4.2
15. The maximum number of times the production in 2011–12 equals the production in 2012–13 (for the same month) is for which products?
    (a) Polypropylene
    (b) Polyethylene
    (c) Nylon Filament Yarn
    (d) None of these
16. For polypropylene, the production in 2011–12 is greater than the production in 2012–13, (for the corresponding month) for how many months:
    (a) 1 (b) 2 (c) 3 (d) 4
17. The difference between the minimum production of polypropylene in 2012–13 and the minimum production of polypropylene in 2011–12 is how many times the difference in July's production of polyethylene (of the two years)?
    (a) 3 times (b) 2 times
    (c) equal (d) 0.4 times

TABLE 2.3 Production of Three Types of Plastic Materials in the Island of Hoola Boola Moola

Months	Production of Plastic Materials					
	Polypropylene Production (in thousand tonnes)		Polyethylene Production (in thousand tonnes)		Nylon Filament Yarn Production (in thousand tonnes)	
	2011–12	2012–13	2011–12	2012–13	2011–12	2012–13
March	17.6	21.0	104	40	3150	2900
April	16.4	20.6	100	88	3050	2850
May	16.0	21.4	80	96	3000	2900
June	15.4	19.2	88	80	2520	2800
July	16.0	19.2	90	84	2600	2700
August	16.6	21.4	94	80	2650	2750
September	16.4	20.8	98	84	2500	2650
October	17.8	23.0	100	80	2200	3000
November	16.4	22.6	104	92	2000	2950
December	17.6	21.8	108	88	2250	3000
January	20.0	20.0	96	100	2750	2350
February	19.8	17.8	20	96	2600	2250
March	21.0	22	40	96	2900	–

Directions for Questions 18 to 19: *Study Table 2.4 and answer the questions given below.*

TABLE 2.4 Age-wise Brand Ownership of Television Sets

Brand	<1 Year Old	1–2 Years Old	2–5 Years Old	More Than 5 Years Old
LG	15%	45%	40%	
Samsung	5%	15%	25%	55%
BPL	10%	10%	10%	70%
Videocon	25%	55%	20%	
Sony	15%	50%	20%	15%

18. If 1,00,000 TVs were sold last year, how many LG sets were sold?
    (a) 10,000 (b) 12,500
    (c) 15,000 (d) Cannot be determined
19. If the total BPL sets sold to date are 500,000, how many are more than one year old?
    (a) 500,000
    (b) 450,000
    (c) 50,000
    (d) Cannot be determined

Directions for Questions 20 to 23: *Consider the following data of break-up of exports of services. Study Table 2.5 and answer the questions given below.*

TABLE 2.5 Export of Services across 4 Sectors (all values in million $)

	Food	Clothes	Labour	Vehicles
July	0.9	1.1	0.6	2.0
August	1.4	0.9	0.9	1.2
September	2.2	1.1	1.4	2.4
October	2.5	1.1	2.1	2.8
November	2.0	1.6	1.8	2.6

20. Over the period July to November, which of the four service sectors – food, clothes, labour and vehicles, has shown the least percentage growth in their exports?
(a) Food (b) Clothes
(c) Labour (d) Vehicles
21. What is the growth rate of total exports of the four sectors considered together in the time period August to October?
(a) 83.33% (b) 87.5%
(c) 88.88% (d) 93.18%
22. Over the entire five months, July to November, by what percentage is the total export of labour services lesser than the total export of food services?
(a) 16.66% (b) 18.88%
(c) 20% (d) 24.44%
23. Over the period July to November, which of the four service sector shows continuous percentage drop in their exports?
(a) Food (b) Clothes
(c) Labour (d) None

Directions for Questions 24 to 26: *Growth rate of Sales of facebook and that of whatsapp over the years 1995-1999. Study Table 2.6 and answer the questions given below.*

TABLE 2.6 Growth Rate in Sales of Facebook and that of Whatsapp

Year	Growth Rate in Sales (%)				
	1995	1996	1997	1998	1999
For Facebook	10	15	–10	5	–8
For Whatsapp	–5	12	–10	10	5

24. If the ratio of sales of Facebook to that of Whatsapp in the year 1997 was 2 : 1, find the approximate ratio of their sales in the year 1999.
(a) 3:2 (b) 5:3
(c) 9:5 (d) Cannot be determined
25. If the ratio of sales of facebook to that of whatsapp in the year 1997 was 2 : 1, find the approximate ratio of their sales in the year 1995.
(a) 4:1 (b) 3:2
(c) 2:1 (d) Cannot be determined
26. If the sales of whatsapp in the year 1997 was ₹150 crores, find the approximate difference in the sales values (in crores) between the year 1995 and the year 1999.
(a) 24.25 (b) 20.2
(c) 16.6 (d) 26.5

Directions for Questions 27 to 31: *The following table relates to five fictional countries, A, B, C, D and E and the arable land in the countries. Two types of data are given for each country for the years 2017, 2022 and 2027. One data is the percentage of total land of the country that is arable. And the second data is the arable land divided by the population of the country (hectare per person). Read the data carefully and answer the questions that follow.*

(Population density is defined as the ratio of population to the total area of the country.

Assume the total area of land in each of the countries to be constant across the years.)

27. What was the percentage increase in the total arable land in country A from 2017 to 2027?
(a) 6% (b) 6.5%
(c) 7.5% (d) Cannot be determined
28. What was the population density (persons/hectare) of country A in the year 2022?
(a) 0.3 (b) 0.33
(c) 0.37 (d) Cannot be determined
29. In which of the years was the population density of county C the least?
(a) 2017 (b) 2022
(c) 2027 (d) Cannot be determined

TABLE 2.7 The Percentage of Total Arable Land and the Hectare Per Person of Five Countries (A, B, C, D and E)

Countries	Arable Land					
	2017		2022		2027	
	Percentage of Total Arable Land	Hectare Per Person	Percentage of Total Arable Land	Hectare Per Person	Percentage of Total Arable Land	Hectare Per Person
A	12.30	0.37	11.30	0.3	13.10	0.3
B	19	0.35	23.10	0.36	24.40	0.32
C	17.60	0.27	19.50	0.26	20.00	0.27
D	38.90	0.52	30.80	0.43	28.40	0.4
E	13.70	0.35	17.00	0.37	19.00	0.35

30. In the year 2027, which country had the highest population density?
(a) B (b) C
(c) D (d) A
31. The population of country E increased by how much per cent from 1997 to 2007?
(a) 27.5% (b) 32.5%
(c) 38.5% (d) Cannot be determined

Level of Difficulty 2

Directions for Questions 1 to 5: *Study Table 2.8 and answer the questions that follow:*

1. Amongst the following countries, the highest average annual growth over the entire period (1999–2005) has been experienced by:
(a) Cambodia (b) India
(c) Myanmar (d) Vietnam
2. Which of the following statement is ***not true***?
(a) During 1999–2000, Myanmar registered the highest annual export growth.
(b) India witnessed the second highest annual export growth rate during 2003–04.
(c) Cambodia registered the third highest annual export growth rate during 2001–02.
(d) Thailand's highest growth rate was seen in 2000-01
3. Which of the following statement is not ***false***?
(a) South Korea registered the third lowest export growth rate during the year 2000–01.
(b) The sum of the export growth rates of India and Vietnam during 2001–02 is lower than the export growth rate of China during that particular year.
(c) Myanmar witnessed maximum number of years of positive export growth rate during the entire period.
(d) The difference between the export growth rate of China and Japan during 2004–05 was lower than the export growth rate of Vietnam during that particular year.
4. If we calculate the difference between the highest and the lowest annual growth rate experienced by the countries between 1999–2000 and 2004–05 ________would get the second rank amongst all countries.
(a) South Korea (b) India
(c) China (d) Japan
5. If we calculate the difference between the highest and the lowest average annual export growth rate experienced by the countries year-wise, the difference would be minimum during________.
(a) 1999–2000
(b) 2001–02
(c) 2004–05
(d) 2003–04

Directions for Questions 6 to 10: *Study Table 2.9 and answer the questions given below.*

6. Which of the following statements is false?
(a) Average annual level of SO_2 emission for Pondicherry over 1998–2003 is approximately 51.40 μg/m³.
(b) Average annual level of SO_2 emission for Anpara over 1997–2003 is approximately 48.24 μg/m³.
(c) Average annual level of SO_2 emission for Madras over 1999–2003 is approximately 25.02 μg/m³.
(d) Average annual level of SO_2 emission for Yamuna Nagar during 1997–2003 is approximately 23.74 μg/m³.
7. If the highest level of SO_2 emission amongst the given cities is noted year-wise, then their difference would be maximum for the following pair for years:
(a) 1998 and 2003 (b) 1997 and 2001
(c) 1997 and 2003 (d) 1998 and 2002

TABLE 2.8 Word Merchandise Exports by Select Countries *(Million Dollars)*

Countries	1999	2000	2001	2002	2003	2004	2005
Cambodia	1129	1389	1500	1923	2218	2798	3100
China	194931	249203	266098	325596	438228	593326	761954
India	35667	42379	43361	49250	57085	75562	95096
Japan	417610	479249	403496	416726	471817	565675	594905
South Korea	143686	172267	150439	162471	193817	253845	284419
Myanmar	1136	1646	2381	3046	2483	2380	2925
Singapore	114680	137804	121751	125177	159902	198637	229649
Thailand	58440	69057	64968	68108	80324	96248	110110
Vietnam	11540	14449	15029	16530	20176	25625	31625

TABLE 2.9 Industrial Emission Level of SO_2 in Select City Points (1997–2003)

City	1997	1998	1999	2000	2001	2002	2003
Anpara	54.1	57.9	59.3	64.6	53	30.1	18.7
Bangalore	28.1	37.2	37.9	19.1	19.3	12.1	7.6
Bombay	36	21.7	22.3	11.8	12	9.7	7.4
Calcutta	33.2	40.8	66.9	25.3	21.9	13.3	18.1
Cochin	7.4	4.9	10.5	41.6	24.6	31.5	23.4
Faridabad	37.8	35.7	31.3	37.3	23.1	13.1	9.5
Gajraula	25.8	19.7	25.7	26.6	35.5	41.1	39.3
Madras	26.3	14.2	11.7	20.1	26.1	40.9	26.3
Mysore	32.4	32.1	31	30.7	24.1	20.6	11.2
Nagda	81.8	55.2	26.9	52.6	46.5	36.5	36.5
Pondicherry	112.3	114.9	93.3	37.6	17.5	19.8	25.3
Solapur	19.4	17.2	18	18.9	19.4	20.1	19.9
Yamuna Nagar	27.8	32.2	9.8	18.9	22.1	28.6	28.2

Annul Mean Concentration Range (µg/m³)

8. Which of the following statement is true?
   (a) Bangalore in 2003 registered the lowest level of SO_2 emission in relation to the given dataset.
   (b) The difference between the average annual level of SO_2 emission during 1997–2003 for Pondicherry and Gajraula is lower than the corresponding average annual level for Mysore.
   (c) The average annual level of SO_2 emission during 1997–2000 for Faridabad is higher than the average annual level for the city for the entire period (1997–2003).
   (d) The sum of the average annual level of SO_2 emission during 1997–2003 for Bombay and Calcutta is lower than the corresponding average annual level for Anpara.
9. If the SO_2 emission level change for the given cities is noted year-wise, the difference would be maximum for which of the following option?
   (a) Cochin and Pondicherry during 1999–2000.
   (b) Calcutta and Nagda during 1998–99.
   (c) Madras and Anpara during 2001–02.
   (d) Nagda and Pondichery during 1997–98.
10. Which of the following statements is true?
   (a) While for Anpara, the SO_2 annual emission level declined consistently during 2000–01 and 2002–03, the same increased consistently for Yamuna Nagar between 1998–99 and 2001–02.
   (b) During 2002–03, the SO_2 annual emission level declined for maximum number of cities.
   (c) The absolute decline in annual SO_2 emission level for Bombay during 1997–98 was lower than the corresponding figure for Faridabad during 2000–01.
   (d) The number of cities which experienced a decline in their annual SO_2 emission level during 1999–2000 was more than the corresponding figure during 1998–99.

Directions for Questions 11 to 15: *Study Table 2.10 and answer the questions given below.*

TABLE 2.10 Estimate of Some Important Characteristics of Select Industries

Characteristics	Industry Groups and Year									
	2003–04					2004–05				
	A	B	C	D	E	A	B	C	D	E
Number of Factories	1085	916	652	239	403	5252	567	12656	3513	1152
Working Capital (₹ Lakh)	281895	149780	29662	28921	17729	401385	101370	600909	1884332	480972
Invested Capital (₹ Lakh)	464446	217230	421005	156983	121030	1862522	557576	4055974	9832961	2438776
Number of Workers	43977	34972	24259	13394	16169	139918	41274	381337	294973	57463
Wages to Workers (₹ Lakh)	42082	24245	13858	9691	8192	55829	20584	140109	293126	56924
Total Input (₹ Lakh)	1060692	474480	682340	197711	161375	2862201	425601	3209790	14046464	3729397
Depreciation (₹ Lakh)	23095	14544	27412	12619	12476	145745	43264	277640	636351	140743
Net Value Added (₹ Lakh)	303706	145547	53441	65180	42672	382864	128489	1062762	3944815	820172
Net Fixed Capital Formation (₹ Lakh)	4789	604	–12531	–250	464	168539	52500	100152	374612	220840
Profit (₹ Lakh)	131337	55952	–41774	35223	11756	142098	67338	563800	2735760	615832

11. Which of the following statement is ***not false***?
    (a) Between 2003–04 and 2004–05, the average no. of workers per factory increased for industry B and C, but decreased for A.
    (b) The percentage change in no. of workers between 2003–04 and 2004–05 is higher in industry A than industry E.
    (c) The average no. of workers per factory between industries D and E jointly increased by more than corresponding figure for B.
    (d) The average no. of workers per factory for factory C decreased between 2003–04 and 2004–05 by 6.
12. Which of the following statements is **True**?
    (a) The increase in invested capital per worker for industries B and D over the period is jointly higher than the same for E.
    (b) The invested capital per worker has remained the second highest for industry D both between 2003–04 and 2004–05.
    (c) The working capital per worker has been the highest for industry B during 2003–04 but not the lowest during 2004–05.
    (d) The working capital to worker ratio has declined by more than 50 per cent in case of industry A over the period, but by less than 50 per cent for industry B.
13. Which of the following statement is ***false***?
    (a) Working capital to invested capital ratio has been the second highest for industry E during 2004–05.
    (b) Industry C is the only industry for which the net value added to total input ratio has increased between 2003–04 and 2004–05.
    (c) If the average wage rate is defined by total wage bill divided by number of workers, then for a total number of three industries, the average wage rate declined between 2003–04 and 2004–05.
    (d) Net value added to total input ratio has been the highest for industry B during 2004–05.
14. If gross fixed capital formation is defined as net fixed capital formation plus depreciation, then which of the following statements is **true**?
    (a) Gross fixed capital formation has been the third highest for industry C during 2004–05.
    (b) Gross fixed capital formation is the lowest for industry E during 2003–04.
    (c) The increase in gross fixed capital formation between 2003–04 and 2004–05 for industry D is higher than the sum total of the same for industries C and E.
    (d) The increase in average depreciation per factory 2003–04 and 2004–05 has been the highest for industry D.
15. Which of the following statements is **false**?
    (a) Average profit per factory is the second highest for industry A during 2003–04 but the lowest during 2004–05.
    (b) Average profit earned per unit of input cost incurred is the second highest for industry A and C between 2003–04 and 2004–05.
    (c) The average profit to the number of workers ratio is the second highest for industry D both between 2003–04 and 2004–05.
    (d) The increase in average expenditure on input per factory between 2003–04 and 2004–05 has been the highest for industry D.

Directions for Questions 16 to 22: *Read the table below and answer the questions.*

16. During 2003–04, which pair of developed and developing countries registered the highest growth rate in their number of FDI projects outflow?
    (a) France, India
    (b) France, Singapore
    (c) Japan, Singapore
    (d) UK, India
17. An analysis of the annual FDI projects inflow growth rate reveals that the second largest decline has occurred for ________ during ________.
    (a) India, 2004–05
    (b) Russian Federation, 2003–04
    (c) China, 2004–05
    (d) Germany, 2004–05
18. The absolute difference between Singapore's highest growth rate in number of FDI projects inflow in a single year during 2002–05 and UK's highest growth rate in FDI projects outflow in a single year during the same period is:
    (a) 19.28 per cent
    (b) 15.28 per cent
    (c) 21.26 per cent
    (d) None of the above
19. Which of the following statements is ***true***?
    (a) The growth rate of FDI projects inflow in UK was lower than the same in Japan during 2002–03.
    (b) The average FDI projects inflow growth rate in Germany between 2002–03 and 2004–05 has been higher than its average FDI projects outflow growth rate over the same period.

TABLE 2.11 FDI Projects by Investor/Destination Region *(in Numbers)*

Country	World as Destination				World as Source			
	2002	2003	2004	2005	2002	2003	2004	2005
	By Source				By Destination			
Total World	5685	9348	9927	9488	5685	9348	9927	9488
Developed Countries	4903	7735	8443	8057	2746	3867	4144	3981
France	322	475	525	502	140	159	229	385
Germany	473	833	862	919	131	272	251	221
UK	438	709	746	752	326	414	490	541
US	1604	2397	2507	2479	417	589	584	527
Japan	472	878	1025	744	106	133	155	118
Developing Countries	707	1440	1294	1243	2362	4467	4806	4296
China	35	107	96	128	586	1303	1547	1196
South Korea	117	179	169	173	60	110	104	115
India	89	175	199	182	249	452	688	564
Singapore	57	90	103	79	108	154	174	154
Russian Federation	51	119	108	126	199	429	380	479

Note: FDI projects 'by source' is defined as 'outflow' while the same 'by destination' is defined as 'inflow'.

(c) The growth rate of FDI projects outflow from the US during 2002–03 has been higher than the corresponding figure for France.

(d) The growth rate in FDI projects inflow from the UK during 2003–04 has been lower than the corresponding figure for Japan.

20. Which of the following statements is ***false***?

(a) The growth rate of FDI projects outflow from the developed countries during 2004–05 has been lower than the same for the world as a whole.

(b) The growth rate of FDI projects inflow to Singapore during 2003–04 has been higher than the same for South Korea during 2004–05.

(c) The average growth rate of FDI projects inflow from developing countries between 2002–03 and 2004–05 has been higher than their corresponding figure for FDI projects outflow.

(d) The growth rate of FDI projects inflow to Singapore during 2004–05 has been more negative as compared to the corresponding figure for Russian Federation during 2003–04.

21. Which of the following statements is ***true***?

(a) The average growth rate of FDI projects outflow from India between 2002–03 and 2004–05 has been higher than it's corresponding figure for FDI project inflow.

(b) The average growth rate of FDI projects outflow from Germany between 2002–03 and 2004–05 has been lower than the average growth rate of FDI project inflow to South Korea over the same period.

(c) The average absolute FDI projects outflow from the UK during 2002–05 has been higher than the average absolute FDI projects inflow to India over the same period.

(d) Germany is the only country which did not experience a decline in FDI project outflow during 2002–05.

22. Which of the following statements is ***false***?

(a) The average FDI project inflow from South Korea expressed as a percentage of the total FDI project inflow from the developing countries during 2002–05 was higher than the average FDI project inflow to the UK expressed as a percentage of the FDI projects inflow to the developed countries during the same period.

(b) The FDI project outflow from the US expressed as a percentage of the total FDI project outflow from the developed countries in 2002 was higher than the FDI project inflow to China expressed as a percentage of the FDI project inflow to the developing countries in 2004.

(c) The average FDI project outflow from Germany expressed as a percentage of the total FDI project outflow from the developed countries during 2002–05 is higher than the average FDI project inflow to Russian Federation expressed as a percentage of the FDI project inflow to the developing countries during the same period.

(d) The FDI project outflow from India expressed as a percentage of the total FDI project outflow from the developed countries in 2004 is lower than the FDI project inflow to the US expressed as a percentage of the FDI project inflow to the developed countries in 2003.

Level of Difficulty 3

Directions for Questions 1 to 5: *The New Delhi Municipal Corporation(NDMC) is responsible for picking up garbage from Three different localities near Connaught place. The localities include Connaught Place, Laxmi Nagar and Roop Nagar. The NDMC also categorizes its garbage into three categories namely Wet, Dry and E-Waste. According to a report published by NDMC,11 families residing in the Connaught Place area produced on average 1500 kgs of waste every month, 25 families in the Laxmi Nagar area produced on average 140 Kgs and 15 families in the Roop Nagar area produced a total of 5000 Kgs. The Recycling wing of NDMC started to segregate the different kinds of waste and found that the E-Waste accounted for 8% of the total lot and Wet products were 59.782% of the ones that were left.*

The Recycling Wing further divided the waste into groups based on whether they are recyclable. The table below gives the data for different types of non recyclable waste .

(in Kgs)	Connaught Place	Laxmi Nagar	Roop Nagar	Total
Wet	3850	500	650	5000
Dry	2950	350	3250	6550
E-Waste	1200	150	100	1450
Total	8000	1000	4000	13000

NDMC also released the following information-

(a) Families from Roop Nagar produced only 2% E-Waste in that locality. However, of the total waste obtained from Roop Nagar, 25% was Wet.

(b) The Recyclable E-Waste from Connaught Place was 10 times the Recyclable E-waste from Laxmi Nagar.

(c) The ratio of Wet and Dry Recyclable E-Waste from Connaught Place was 3:5.

1. What percentage(approx.) of waste obtained from Laxmi Nagar was Dry?

(a) 61.24% (b) 65.42%
(c) 61.42% (c) 64.24%

2. Approximately, what percentage of waste generated in Connaught place was recyclable E-Waste?

(a) 2% (b) 3%
(c) 4% (d) 1%

3. If later it was found that, the person segregating the waste made a mistake and labeled half the non-recyclable waste as recyclable waste obtained from Laxmi Nagar, then what was the approximate percentage decrease in the total quantity of Recyclable waste from Laxmi Nagar if the mistake was taken care of?

(a) 40% (b) 0%
(c) 32% (d) 50%

4. If later it was found that, the person segregating the waste made a mistake and labeled half the non recyclable waste as recyclable waste obtained from Laxmi Nagar, then what was the approximate percentage decrease in the total quantity of Recyclable waste from Roop Nagar if the mistake was taken care off?

(a) 40% (b) 50%
(c) 0% (d) 32%

5. If all the area-wise and waste category-wise numbers for recyclable waste are arranged in decreasing order, which of the following would be the third lowest number amongst recyclable waste thus classified?

(a) Wet waste from Laxmi Nagar
(b) Wet waste from Roop Nagar
(c) E-Waste from Laxmi Nagar
(d) Dry waste from Roop Nagar

Directions for Questions 6 to 9: *In an examination there are five questions – Q1, Q2, Q3, Q4 and Q5 – each with five choices (a), (b), (c), (d) and (e). Five students – A, B, C, D and E – wrote the exam. The choices opted by the students for the questions Q1, Q2, Q3, Q4 and Q5 are shown in the table below. One mark is awarded for a right answer and no mark is awarded for a wrong answer. No two students got the same total marks in these five questions. Study Table 2.12 and answer the questions given below.*

TABLE 2.12

Name	Choice Opted For				
	Q1	Q2	Q3	Q4	Q5
A	b	c	a	d	e
B	c	d	a	e	b
C	c	d	a	b	e
D	e	a	c	b	d
E	b	c	a	e	d

It is observed that no two questions have the same choice as the right answer.

6. Who scored the least total marks?
   (a) B (b) A
   (c) C (d) D
7. What is correct answer choice for Q3?
   (a) a (b) b
   (c) c (d) Cannot be determined
8. If A's score is more than E's score, then what is the score of C?
9. If C's score is less than B's score, then what is the score of A?

Directions for Questions 10 to 13: *There are 3 levels of employees in an organisation – Level 1, Level 2 and Level 3. No employee can change his level during the job. The employees retire at 60 and get recruited at 25. Assume that apart from retirements at age 60 or recruitments at age 25, there are no more additions/ deletions from the companies' manpower. The table shown below depicts the average age of employees on the 31st of December for each of the given years from 2020 to 2024. The initial number of employees (in 2020) in Level 1 and Level 3 are 4 each and in level 2 there are 3 employees initially. Study Table 2.13 and answer the questions given below.*

TABLE 2.13 Average Age of Employees on the 31st of December from 2020 to 2024

Year	Level 1	Level 2	Level 3
2020	41	39	38
2021	36	30	39
2022	34	29	37
2023	26	28	38
2024	26.67	29	39

10. How many employees joined Level 1 in the given period?
11. How many employees retired from the company in the given period?
12. How many employees joined the organisation in 2024?
13. How many employees retired from the organisation in 2023?

Directions for Questions 14 to 17: *Table 2.14 shows the cost prices (in per kg) and selling prices (in per kg) of five food grains in five different states – Madhya Pradesh (MP). Uttar Pradesh (UP), Bihar (B), Chhattisgarh (C) and Goa (G).*

It is known that all the costs that may contribute in the cost price (like transportation cost, storage cost, etc.) of a food grain are included in the cost prices given in the table below. Study Table 2.14 and answer the questions given below.

14. A businessman buys 5 kg of wheat from Chhattisgarh and 10 kg of Bajra from Uttar Pradesh and then sells the entire stock in MP. What is his percentage profit?
    (a) 48.43% (b) 52.31%
    (c) 68.43% (d) 61.76%
15. A businessman buys 1 kg of each of the five food grains and then sells the entire stock. If he performs all the transactions in any one of the five states, then in which of the following states his percentage profit will be minimum?
    (a) Uttar Pradesh
    (b) Bihar
    (c) Madhya Pradesh
    (d) None of these
16. Prawin Tiwari a truck operator from Noida, buys 1 kg of each of the five food grains by spending the least amount of money and then sells the entire stock by earning the maximum amount of money. He performs all his transactions in one or more of the five states mentioned in the table, by picking the best possible cases. What is his percentage profit? (enter the nearest integer as your answer)
17. Rahul Jha, a shrewd businessman from Bihar, buys 1 kg of any one of the five food grains from each of the five states and then sells 1 kg of the stock in each of the five states. If he randomly decides on any one grain atleast how much profit (in ₹) he can expect to earn in that way?

TABLE 2.14 Cost Prices (in per kg) and Selling Prices (in per kg) of Five Food Grains in Five Different States

	Cost Prices					Selling Prices				
	MP	UP	B	C	G	MP	UP	B	C	G
Wheat	20	21	19	22	25	25	28	26	28	30
Rice	32	25	30	35	40	40	30	36	40	50
Jawar	45	40	35	40	30	50	50	50	50	40
Bajra	65	40	55	70	60	70	50	60	80	65
Makka	50	60	40	30	70	60	70	50	40	80

Directions for Questions 18 to 21: *The city of Hariyali conducted elections for electing four posts - Mayor, Councilman, Administrator and Commissioner. Each of five persons – Arun, Bishen, Chirag, Gemini and Markanday – contested for all the four posts. There are nine wards – Ward 1 through Ward 9 – in Hariyali. Further, each citizen casts exactly one vote, favouring any one of the five persons. After all the citizens voted, the four officials are elected based on the following criteria.*

1. *The candidate who received the highest number of votes across the nine wards combined is elected the Mayor.*
2. *For a candidate to be elected as the Councilman, he should have received at least 15% of the votes polled in a ward for each ward. Amongst the candidates who satisfy this condition, the candidate with the highest number of votes is elected the Councilman.*
3. *For a candidate to be elected as the Administrator, he should have received at least 15% of the votes polled in that ward for at least 6 wards. Amongst the candidates who satisfy this condition, the candidate who topped the maximum number of wards is elected the Administrator.*
4. *For a candidate to be elected as the Commissioner, he must have topped the maximum number of wards.*

The same person can be elected to two or more posts.

**A candidate is said to have topped a ward if he received a maximum number of votes across the five candidates in that ward. The following table provides the votes received by the five candidates in each ward of the city. Study Table 2.15 and answer the questions given below.*

TABLE 2.15 The Votes Received by the Five Candidates in Each Ward of the City

Ward	Arun	Bishen	Chirag	Gemini	Markanday
Ward 1	216	324	450	450	360
Ward 2	638	352	506	352	352
Ward 3	396	192	240	240	132
Ward 4	240	480	480	480	240
Ward 5	1000	300	300	300	100
Ward 6	400	400	384	160	256
Ward 7	50	250	250	100	350
Ward 8	180	240	240	180	360
Ward 9	140	280	210	490	280

18. What is the difference between the number of votes received by the Mayor in ward 8 and the number of votes received by the Administrator in ward 4?
19. Who will be elected for more than one post?
    (a) Bishen (b) Arun
    (c) Gemini (d) None of them
20. What is the difference between the total number of votes received by the Commissioner and the total number of votes received by the Councilman?
21. If the total number of votes received by the Mayor, Councilman, Administrator and the Commissioner as a percentage of the total number of votes polled is a%, b%, c% and d%, which of the following is true?
    (a) a > d > c > b (b) a > c = d > b
    (c) a > b = c > d (d) a = d > c > b

Directions for Questions 22 to 25: *Four persons went to a supermarket and each of the four persons purchase a certain number of tomato, apple, banana, cherries and pepper. The price of each item of a particular type is the same. Further, for each person, the number of items of each type that he purchased, when arranged in ascending order, form five consecutive integers.*

The following table provides the total amount spent (in ₹) in purchasing each type of item by each person. Study Table 2.16 and answer the questions given below.

TABLE 2.16 The Total Amount Spent in Purchasing Each Item by Each Person

Person	Tomato	Apple	Banana	Cherries	Pepper
Aradhana	320	396	840	680	288
Bisakha	240	300	648	520	224
Chandni	60	96	168	80	40
Devika	80	84	240	180	48

22. How many tomatoes did Chandni purchase?
23. What is the total number of items of the five types purchased by Bisakha?
24. What is the total number of tomatoes the four persons purchased?
25. For how many persons can it be said that the type of item on which they spent the highest amount and the type of item for which the number of items purchased by them is the highest are the same?
    (a) 0 (b) 1
    (c) 2 (d) More than 2

Directions for Questions 26 to 29: *A project at Dataman Infosys comprises four stages – Conceptualisation, Design, Execution and Testing. Four persons – Amitabh, Bharadwaj, Chetan and Daljit – are employed to work on the project. The following table gives the Information regarding the number of days taken by each of the four to complete the various stages of the project.*

TABLE 2.17 Number of Days Taken by Each to Complete the Project

Person \ Stage	Conceptualisation	Design	Execution	Testing
Amitabh	10	7	8	13
Bharadwaj	8	16	14	28
Chetan	12	24	5	11
Daljit	22	6	9	6

The project manager divides the projects in two assignments – A1 and A2. A1 comprises Conceptualisation and Testing and A2 comprises Design and Execution. The work of A1 is assigned to Amitabh and Chetan and that of A2 to Bharadwaj and Daljit. Amitabh and Daljit started working on their respective assignments on 2nd January, 2026, and Bharadwaj and Chetan started working on their respective assignments on 5th January, 2026. Amitabh and Bharadwaj work for two days and take an off on the every third day, while Chetan and Daljit work on one day and take an off the next day (i.e. an off every alternate day) Each person works only on one project in a day. Stages can be completed only in the order of Conceptualisation – Design – Execution – Testing. More than one person can work on a stage of the project at a time. Also, during the month of January, Amitabh was not keeping well and only worked on projects at 75% of his efficiency. New phases of a project can only be launched on fresh days – and if a phase is finished in a fraction of the running day, no work is done in the remaining part of the day. Study Table 2.17 and answer the questions given below.

26. Conceptualisation can at the earliest be completed by
    (a) 13th January, 2026
    (b) 14th January, 2026
    (c) 15th January, 2026
    (d) 16th January, 2026
27. The Design phase can at the earliest be completed by
    (a) 15th January, 2026
    (b) 17th January, 2026
    (c) 18th January, 2026
    (d) 20th January, 2026
28. The Execution phase can at the earliest be completed by
    (a) 10th January, 2026
    (b) 31st January, 2026
    (c) 3rd February, 2026
    (d) 1st February, 2026
29. The project can at the earliest be completed by
    (a) 15 February, 2026
    (b) 16 February, 2026
    (c) 12 February, 2026
    (d) None of these

Directions for Questions 30 to 33: *A, B, C, D, E and F are the six students in an academy. In training, they consumed four types of energy drinks, named Gatorade, Monster, Tzinga and RedBull, which have 40, 20, 20 and 40 Energy Points (EP), respectively. The numbers of different energy drinks consumed by them on a particular day were as shown in Table 2.18.*

TABLE 2.18 The Numbers of Different Energy Drinks Consumed

Student	Gatorade	Monster	Tzinga	RedBull
A	0	0	4	2
B	4	0	2	0
C	0	4	2	0
D	2	4	0	0
E	0	2	0	4
F	2	0	0	4

After consuming the energy drinks, they divided themselves into two groups having three students each and played 'Tug of war', in which the group having higher sum of the Energy Points of the participants won. Study Table 2.19 and answer the questions given below.

30. What is the probability that the winning team includes F?
    (a) 0.4 (b) 0.5
    (c) 0.6 (d) 0.8
31. What is the probability that the winning team includes both D and E?
    (a) 0.1 (b) 0.2
    (c) 0.3 (d) 0.4
32. If D is a member of the winning team, in how many ways can the other two members of the winning team be selected?
    (a) 2 (b) 4
    (c) 3 (d) 5
33. If A and C are the members of the winning team, in how many ways can the third member of the winning team be selected?

ANSWER KEY

Level of Difficulty 1

1. (c)	2. (a)	3. (b)	4. (d)	5. (d)	6. (a)	7. (d)
8. (b)	9. (c)	10. (d)	11. (d)	12. (a)	13. (c)	14. (b)
15. (a)	16. (a)	17. (d)	18. (d)	19. (b)	20. (d)	21. (d)

22. (d) 23. (d) 24. (b) 25. (c) 26. (a) 27. (b) 28. (c)
29. (a) 30. (a) 31. (c)

Level of Difficulty 2

1. (a) 2. (c) 3. (d) 4. (a) 5. (c) 6. (d) 7. (a)
8. (c) 9. (a) 10. (b) 11. (d) 12. (b) 13. (a) 14. (c)
15. (d) 16. (c) 17. (c) 18. (a) 19. (c) 20. (c) 21. (a)
22. (a)

Level of Difficulty 3

1. (c) 2. (b) 3. (a) 4. (c) 5. (d) 6. (d) 7. (a)
8. 2 9. 1 10. 4 11. 3 12. 1 13. 1 14. (d)
15. (c) 16. 101 17. 30 18. 300 19. (b) 20. 200 21. (d)
22. 6 23. 130 24. 70 25. (b) 26. (a) 27. (d) 28. (d)
29. (c) 30. (d) 31. (b) 32. (b) 33. 0

SOLUTIONS

Level of Difficulty 1

Solutions for Questions 1 to 4:

In order to solve this set, we would need to create a table as follows. Numbers in brackets show the deduction number that gives us the value in the table:

	Amazing	Good	Average	Total
Female	100 (4)	250 (3)	150 (2)	500 (1)
Male	200 (4)	150 (4)	50 (4)	400 (1)
Total	300 (4)	400 (4)	200 (4)	900

The following logic is followed for making this table:

Deduction 1. From the information about the number of Amazing, Good and Average students, we get that there must be a total of 900 students and since the number of female students is 25% more than the number of male students, we can work out that: Female Students = 500 and Male Students = 400.

Deduction 2. The number of average female students is given as 1/6th the total number of students. Hence, we get this number as 1/6th of 900 = 150.

Deduction 3. 'Half the female students were good in academics.' Hence, we get good female students as 250.

Deduction 4. We can now work out the numbers indicated by (4) in the table, starting with the number of female amazing students = Total Female students – Average female students – Good female students = 500 -150-250 = 100. Hence, Male Amazing Students = 200 (the given ratio is 2:1). This means that there are 300 Amazing students. Also, since we already have 250 good female students, the total number of good students cannot be below 250. Hence, the number of good students has to be 400 and the number of average students would be 200. The answers can be read off the table formed:

1. 200. Option (c) is correct.
2. 200+150=350. Option (a) is correct.
3. 300. Option (b) is correct.
4. The lowest number is 50 and the second lowest is 100. The third lowest number is 150 and occurs for both options (b) and (c). Hence, option (d) is correct.
5. Kolkata to Mumbai costs ₹7 only while the other three cost ₹10, ₹25 and ₹10 respectively.
6. Kolkata to Allahabad will involve the least cost.
7. It can be seen that there is no variance of cost in either of these three cases.
8. Total of 2007 is 345. In 2009, the total is 705 which is closest to 690 from amongst the options.
9. The number of employees in research is 75 for the years 2007 and 2012.
10. The value of the number of employees in production is greater than half the total number of employees in the company for every year after 2008. Hence, option (d) is correct.
11. Visual inspection gives 2011 as the correct answer.
12. If we look at the first years' numbers, we will get that the total number of employees in 2007 are 345. 10% of this being 34.5, marketing is the only department that can satisfy the below 10% for all years' condition. Checking the percentages for number of employees in marketing as a percentage of the total number of employees from 2008 to 2012, we get that the percent-

age of marketing employees is below 10% for each of these years. Hence, option (a) is correct.

13. Maximum production of polyethylene in 2012 is 108 while the minimum is 20. The difference between maximum and minimum is thus 108 – 20 = 88. Similarly, for polypropylene, the difference is 21 – 15.4 = 5.6. The required ratio would thus be 88/5.6 ≈ 16 (which is the closest value).
14. Maximum in 2012–13 for polyethylene = 100, minimum for polyethylene in 2011–12 is 20. Required ratio = 100/20 = 5.
15. Looking across the two years for each product in each month, you can see that this equality is achieved only for polypropylene in January.
16. This is again to be visually checked. 2011–12 is greater than 2012–13 for polypropylene only in 1 month viz. February.
17. Minimum polypropylene in 2012–13 = 17.8. Minimum polypropylene in 2011–12 = 15.4. Difference is 2.4. Difference in July production for polyethylene is 90 – 84 = 6. Required ratio = 2.4/6 = 0.4
18. The table provides for brand-wise figures with respect to the age of the TVs for each brand. Thus, of all the LG TVs in operation, 15% TVs are 1 year old, 45% are between 1 and 2 years old and 40% are between 2 and 5 years old. Thus, we do not have the information about the market shares of the 100000 TVs sold last year and we cannot determine how many LG sets were sold last year, just by knowing how many TVs were sold last year.
19. Following the logic of the above solution we can see that 10% of the total sets of BPL are 1 year old. Thus, the remaining 90% (= 450000) would be more than 1 year old.
20. Percentage Growth of exports of food = 1.1/0.9 = 122.22%

    Percentage Growth of exports of clothes = 0.5/1.1 = 45.45%

    Percentage Growth of exports of labour = 1.2/0.6 = 200%

    Percentage Growth of exports of vehicles = 0.6/2 = 3/10 = 30%

    Thus, least percentage growth has been shown by the sector of vehicles.

    However, you could have solved this much faster just by looking at the ratios that are visible between the first row and the last row's values for each column. Looking down the columns, it can be seen that food (0.9 to 2) and labour (0.6 to 1.8) have more than doubled during this phase, while for clothes and vehicles the growth is less than 100 per cent (as their numbers are less than doubling).

    Thus, we would have to do just two calculations that for clothes and vehicles.

    Even this could have been avoided by noticing that growth in clothes is 0.5 and that in vehicles is 0.6. But clothes grew from a very small base, 1.1 (and 0.5/1.1 is over 40%), whereas vehicles had a much larger base, 2.0 (and 0.6/2 is just 30%). Thus, percentage growth would obviously be less for vehicles. Hence, option (d) is correct.

Solutions for Questions 21 and 22: For such questions involving total across sectors or across time period, you just need to think, if you have to add across the columns or across the rows.

In Question 21, we would need to add all values in the row of August and that in the row of October. Thus, total exports of all 4 sectors in August = 1.4 + 0.9 + 0.9 + 1.2 = 4.4

And total exports of all 4 sectors in October = 2.5 + 1.1 + 2.1 + 2.8 = 8.5

The required growth rate = 4.1/4.4. Approximating it to 4/4.4 i.e. 10/11 = 90.90%, we know the correct answer has to be greater than 90.90%. Thus correct choice is (d)

In question 22, we would need to add all values in the column of labour services and that in the column of food services.

Total exports of labour services for entire period July to November = 0.6 + 0.9 + 1.4 + 2.1 + 1.8 = 6.8

Total exports of food services for entire period July to November = 0.9 + 1.4 + 2.2 + 2.5 + 2 = 9

Thus, percentage by which labour services is less than food services = 2.2/9 = 24.44%. Hence, option (d) is correct.

23. Clearly, from the table we can observe that none of the sectors shows a continuous per cent drop in export. Hence, option (d) is correct.

Solutions for Questions 24 to 26: Understanding the data:

In this question, the variables we are provided with are growth rate of sales for the two companies. What we need to understand here is that we do not know the actual value of the sales of Facebook. All that we know is the growth rate.

Using these growth rates, we can 'compare' the sales across the years. By 'compare' we mean:

(i) find the total growth rate over any period within the given range
(ii) find the ratio of sales for any two years for any one company.

Further, we can always understand that if actual sales value for any one year is known, we can find the sales value for all the years.

24. Assume Facebook Sales to be 200 in 1997 and Whatsapp Sales to be 100 (as per the 2:1 ratio). Facebook has grown by 5% in 1998 and reduced by 8% in 1999, while Whatsapp has grown by 10% and by 5% respectively in the two years. The required ratio will be given by:
$\frac{200 \times 1.05 \times 0.92}{100 \times 1.1 \times 1.05} = \frac{193.2}{115.5}$. The closest ratio to this from amongst the options is 5:3.

Note: In this case, 'the cannot be determined' option is rejected, as we are given the ratio of the sales of the two companies, thus connecting absolute values of the two, helping us find the ratios between subsequent absolute values.

25 Assume that the sales of Facebook in 1995 is 'f' and the sales of Whatsapp is 'w'. The equation for this would be got using:
$\frac{f \times 1.15 \times 0.9}{w \times 1.12 \times 0.9} = \frac{2}{1} \rightarrow \frac{f}{b} = \frac{2.24}{1.15}$. The closest answer is 2:1. Option (c) is correct.

26. If the sales of Whatsapp in 1995, were x, then $x \times 1.12 \times 0.9 = 150$ i.e. $x = 150/(1.12 \times 0.9)$
And the sales in year 1999 will be $150 \times 1.1 \times 1.05$.
The correct answer would be got by: $150 \times 1.1 \times 1.05 - 150/(1.12 \times 0.9)$. However, instead of doing this tedious calculation, you can think smartly in this question as follows:
Finding sales in 1995: From 1995 to 1997, sales increased by 12% and then decreased by 10%. A 12% increase and 10% decrease – using the PCG we can see that there is an effective increase of 0.8%. Thus after an 0.8% increase, the sales became ₹150 cr. Thus sales before the increase, in 1995 would have been marginally less than 150 cr. (approximately 0.7% lower). So you can approximate, the sales in 1995 to be around 149. For sales in 1999, use the PCG as follows:
150 → 165 (after a 10% increase) → 173.25 (after a 5% increase on 165).

Note: You can calculate 5% of 165 as half of 10% of 165 = half of 16.5 = 8.25.

Thus, the required difference is closest to 24.25. Hence, option (a) is correct.

Solutions for Questions 27 to 31:

27. Since the total area of a country remains constant, the percentage increase in the arable land will be the same as the percentage increase in 'arable land as a percentage of the total land'.
Thus, the required growth rate is the percentage increase from 12.3 to 13.10, i.e., 0.8/12.3. This can be seen to be closest to 6.5%. Hence, option (b) is correct.

28. The key in this question, is to understand the formula required to extract the population density. For any country population density is given as: $\frac{\text{Total Population}}{\text{Total Land}}$. In the given data, we have two pieces of information → Arable land as a percentage of total land. As an equation, this percentage can be taken as the percentage value of the ratio: $\frac{\text{Arable Land}}{\text{Total Land}}$. The other information given to us is: Arable land in Hectares per person. This would be given by: $\frac{\text{Arable Land}}{\text{Population}}$.
If you were to take the ratio of these two ratios you would get:
$\frac{\text{Arable Land}}{\text{Total Land}} \div \frac{\text{Arable Land}}{\text{Population}} \rightarrow \frac{\text{Population}}{\text{Total Land}}$. Thus, the required calculation for 2022 for country A is: Required population density = 0.113/0.3 = 0.37. Hence, option (c) is correct.

Note: We need to use the ratio value of 11.3% here, since we should not multiply the ratio by 100. Hence, we have taken the value as 0.113 (decimal value of the ratio of $\frac{\text{Arable Land}}{\text{Total Land}}$ for Country A in 2022.

29. Based on the thinking in the previous question, we can simply see that for this question, we need to compare the population density of the Country C over the three years 2017, 2022 and 2027. These values would be the ratios: 0.176/0.27, 0.195/0.26 and 0.20/0.27. It is clear that the least population density is in the ratio for 2017, i.e., 0.176/0/27. Hence, option (a) is the correct answer.

30. Population density of A, B, C, D and E in the year 2027 is 13.1/0.3, 24.4/0.32 and so on (since we have to compare them, the per cent sign of numerator is dropped). And we want to find the highest of these. Very rough calculations result in the ratios being 43, 80, almost midway of 66.66 and 80, 71, between 63 and 47. Thus, the largest of them can easily be found as for country B, thus option (a) is correct.

31. Since the total area of a country remains constant, the percentage increase in the population of a country is same as the percentage increase in the population density of a country. And the population density of E in 2017 = 0.137/0.35.

In 2027 = 0.19/0.35.
Increase = 38.6%.
Thus, Option (c) is correct.

Level of Difficulty 2

Solutions for Questions 1 to 5:

1. The average annual growth rate would be the highest for the country which has the highest ratio between the 2005 value and the 1999 value. Cambodia has a ratio of 3100/1129; India has a ratio of 95096/35667, Myanmar has a ratio of 2925/1136 and Vietnam has a ratio of 31625/11540.
   Myanmar is definitely lower than Cambodia because the numerator for Myanmar is lower while the denominator is higher.
   Further India's ratio is between 2.6 and 2.7 while the ratios of Cambodia and Vietnam are between 2.7 and 2.8.
   The comparison needs to be thus between Cambodia and Vietnam which means we are comparing 3100/1129 with 31625/11540 which can be seen as 31/11.29 against 31.62/11.54. The numerator grows from 31 to 31.62 which means a 2% increase in the numerator while the denominator grows from 11.29 to 11.54 – a growth of slightly more than 2%. Thus, 3100/1129 > 31625/11540.
   Hence, Cambodia shows the highest average annual growth rate.
   Option (a) is correct.
2. For this question we have to see which statement is not true. Statement (a) can be seen to be true as the growth in 1999–2000 is the highest for Myanmar
   Statement (b) is true because India's growth rate in 2003–04 was the second highest.
   Statement (c) is not true as Cambodia's growth rate in 2001–02 is not the third highest growth rate. Option (c) is correct.
3. The statements in options (a), (b) and (c) can be seen to be false based on the following observations:
   Option (a) is false because: South Korea's growth in 2000–01 was not the third lowest.
   Option (b) is false because the sum of India and Vietnam's growth rates in 2001–02 (13.5+ 9.9) is actually greater than the growth of China in that year.
   Option (c) is also false because the maximum number of years of positive growth was seen for Cambodia and not for Myanmar.
   Option (d) is not false as the difference between the growth rates of China and Japan 28.4 – 5.1 = 23.3 is lower than Vietnam.
   Option (d) is thus correct.
4. The highest difference is for Myanmar (around 63%) while the second highest is for South Korea (around 43%). Option (a) is correct.
5. The least difference is for 2004–05. Option (c) is correct.

Solutions for Questions 6 to 10:

6. Option (d) is false because the average for Yamuna Nagar is 167.6/7 = 23.9 which is not equal to 23.74.
7. The difference between 1998 and 2003 (which is 114.9 – 39.3 = 75.6) is the highest difference.
8. Statement (a) is not true as the least level is not for Bangalore in 2003 but for Bombay in 2003.
   Statement (b) is also not true as the difference between Pondicherry's average 418.7/7 and Gajraula's average 213.7/7 is actually higher than the average (and not lower than the average) of Mysore 182.1/7.
   Statement (c) is obviously true as the numbers for Faridabad are higher during the phase 1997 to 2000 and lower after that. Hence, the average of Faridabad for the period 1997 to 2003 would be lower than 1997 to 2000.
   Thus, option (c) is correct.
9. For the first option, the change in emission level for Cochin is +31.1 while for Pondicherry it is –55.7. The difference is 86.8.
   For the second option, Calcutta's level changes by +26.1 in 1998–99, while Nagda changes by –28.3. The difference is 54.4.
   For the third option, Madras's level changes by +14.8 in 2001–02 while Anpara changes by –22.9. The difference is 37.7.
   For the fourth option, Nagda changes by –26.6 in 1997–98 while Pondicherry changes by +2.6. The difference is 29.2.
   The highest value of this change is for the first option. Hence, option (a) is correct.
10. Option (a) can be seen to be incorrect as it can be seen that Yamuna Nagar does not increase consistently between the years 1998–99 and 2001–02.
    Option (b) can be seen to be correct as in the year 2002–03, ten of the 13 cities have shown a decrease in their SO_2 emission levels.
    Option (b) is correct.

Solutions for Questions 11 to 15:

11. For this question we are looking for the statement which is not false— which means we are looking for what is true. The statement in option (a) is false as it can be seen clearly that the

number of workers per factory decreased for C (as the ratio 24259/652 is greater than the ratio 381337/12656).
Similarly option (b) is also incorrect as the percentage increase in the number of workers for A is given by the ratio 139918/43977, while for E it is 57463/16169. The second ratio being higher, we can conclude that E has shown a higher percentage change than A. Thus, option (b) is also rejected.
The average number of workers for D and E changes from 29563/642 to 352436/4665, while for B it changes from 34972/916 to 41274/567. The value for D & E jointly increases by less than the corresponding value for B.
Thus, option (d) must be correct. The change in option (d) is from 24259/652 to 381337/12656 – a change of around 6 to 7.

12. Option (a) is incorrect because the increase in invested capital per worker has been lower for industry E than B & D combined together. Thus, option (a) is rejected.
The invested capital per worker is the second highest for D in both years shown in the table. Hence, option (b) is correct.
Option (b) is the correct answer.
13. When you check the statement in option (a) we can see that the ratio of working capital to invested capital is the highest for industry A in 2004–05. Hence, this statement is false.
But in this question we are solving for the false statement.
Since we have identified that option (a) is false we can mark this as the correct answer at this stage without checking the other options.
Option (a) is the correct answer.
14. Option (a) is incorrect as the gross fixed capital formation for industry C during 2004–05 is the second highest and not the third highest as desired by the option.
Option (b) is also rejected because the gross fixed capital formation is the lowest for industry D in 2003–04 and not for inductry E in 2003–04.
Option (c) is true as the difference between the gross fixed capital formation for industry D between its values in 2004–05 and 2003–04 is higher than the same for the totals of industries C and E.
Option (c) is thus the correct answer.
15. Option (d) can be seen as false as the increase for D in average expenditure on input per factory is not the highest for D.
Option (d) is hence the correct answer.

Solutions for Questions 16 to 22:

16. Japan shows the highest percentage growth amongst developed countries and hence only option (c) could be the correct answer.
17. The highest drop is for Japan between 2004–05 (it is between 23% and 24%) while for China in the same year the drop is the second highest drop (between 22% and 23%). Option (c) is correct.
18. Singapore's highest growth rate in inflows is for 2002–03 where it grows from 108 to 154 – a growth rate of 42.59%. At the same time, the highest growth rate for UK (in outflows) is for 2002–03 where it grows from 438 to 709 – a growth rate of 61.87%. The difference between the two is 19.28%. Option (a) is correct.
19. The statement in option (a) is false, as the growth rate for FDI projects inflow in 2002–03 for Japan is lower than that for UK.
The statement in option (b) is also false as the FDI projects inflow growth rate for Germany in 2004–05 is lower than the corresponding figure for FDI projects outflow for the same year.
The statement in option (c) can be verified to be true, as the growth rate for US (FDI project outflows during 2002–03) is from 1604 to 2397 which is close to 50%. At the same time the corresponding growth rate for France for the same year is represented by the percentage change from 322 to 475 – a growth of 153 on 322 which is definitely lower than the growth rate for US.
Thus, option (c) is correct.
20. The statement in option (a) is true – as the negative growth from 8443 to 8057 represents a growth rate of 4.6% which is a lower growth rate than the growth rate from 9927 to 9488 which is around 4.4%. Since we are looking for what is false we reject this statement as it is true.
The statement in option (b) is also correct – as the growth rate for Singapore for the given year from 154 to 174 is around 13% which is higher than the growth rate for South Korea for the given year – as it grows from 104 to 115 – a growth between 10% and 11%. Thus, we reject option (b) too as it is not false.
The statement in option (c) is false as the growth rate of FDI projects inflows between 2002 and 2003 has been lower than the corresponding figure for FDI projects outflows for the same year.
Hence, since option (c) is false it is the correct answer.

21. Option (a) can be seen to be true as the growth rate of India in 2002–03 for outflows (represented by the percentage growth from 89 to 175) is greater than the corresponding figure for growth rate of FDI inflows in 2002–03 (represented by the percentage growth from 249 to 452).
Similarly for 2004–05, the growth rate of India in 2004–05 for outflows (represented by the percentage growth from 199 to 182 – a growth rate of around –8.5%) is greater than the corresponding figure for growth rate of FDI inflows in 2004–05 (represented by the percentage growth from 688 to 564 – which is clearly lower than –10%).
Option (a) is correct.
22. Option (a) is clearly false as the required value of South Korea is around 2%, while for UK it is around 9%. The other options can be checked to be true. Hence, option (a) is the correct answer.

Level of Difficulty 3

Solutions for Questions 1 to 5:

From the starting text, we can make out that the total waste produced is:

Total waste Area wise	Total waste Area wise	Total waste Type wise	Total waste Type wise
Connaught Place Area	16500 kgs (11 × 1500)	Wet	9250
Laxmi Nagar Area	3500 kgs (25 × 140)	Dry	13750 (0.59782 x 23000)
Roop Nagar Area	5000 kgs (given)	E-Waste	2000 (8% of total)
Total Waste Produced	25000 kgs		25000

What you need to perceive in this question, is that this 25000 kg waste is split between Recyclable and Non-recyclable waste. The table provided to us in the question, is giving us the data for non-recyclable waste. Based on the numbers provided in the table, we can make the following table for (recyclable waste) the different kinds of waste produced in each of the localities. Note: In this explanation all numbers are in Kgs. We will also denote recyclable as (R) and Non Recyclable as (NR) for the rest of the solution.

Table for Recyclable waste:

(in Kgs)	Connaught Place (CP)	Laxmi Nagar (LN)	Roop Nagar (RN)	Total
Wet	3000 (6)	650 (7)	600	4250 (3)
Dry	5000 (6)	1800 (7)	400	7200 (3)
E-Waste	500 (5)	50 (5)	0 (4)	550 (3)
Total	8500 (2)	2500 (2)	1000 (2)	12000 (1)

Explanations for the numbers in the table:

1. Since the total waste is 25000, and 13000 of it is (NR), we get 12000 as the total here.
2. The total waste from CP, is 16500 and 8000 of it is NR (given in the table in the question). Hence, the R waste is 16500-8000=8500. Similar logic works for the LN and RN columns. R waste for LN = 3500 – 1000 = 2500 and R waste for RN = 5000 – 4000 = 1000.
3. Similar logic, gives us the numbers for total R waste that is wet, dry or E-waste. The calculations that fill these cells are: 9250-5000; 13750-6550 = 7200; 2000-1450 = 550. (Note: The numbers 5000, 6550 and 4000 are coming from the table given for NR waste in the question)
4. Interpretation of Clue A in the problem: Total E-Waste from RN locality is 2% of 5000=100, of which NR waste is 100 (given in table), hence we get RN E-waste (R) = 0.
Also, since 25% of total RN waste is Wet, it means that 25% of 5000 =1250 is total Wet waste and 5000-100-1250 = 3650 is Dry. These numbers when corelated to the NR table for RN give us the numbers indicated by (4) in the table we are constructing: 3650-3250 = 400 for RN Dry waste and 1250-650=600 for RN Wet Waste.
5. The numbers indicated by (5) in the table are an interpretation of the statement B. Since, the total Recyclable E-waste of 550 has to be divided between Connaught Place and Laxmi Nagar, and the ratio has to be 10:1, we will get 500 and 50 as the respective values.
6. The total Recyclable waste of Connaught Place left to be allocated between Wet and Dry is 8000 and when divided in the ratio 3:5, the division would be 3000 and 5000 as indicated by (6) in the table.
7. LN Wet waste in the table would be 4250 – 3000-600 = 650. Dry = 7200-5000-400 = 1800.

The answers can be read off the two tables.

1. Total dry waste from LN = 350+1800. Total waste from LN = 3500. Hence, the required answer = 2150/3500 = 61.42%. Option (c) is correct.
2. 500/16500 = 3% (approx). Option (b) is correct.
3. If half the non-recyclable waste from LN was actually labeled incorrectly, it means that the actual amount of non-recyclable waste from LN was 2000 and the recyclable waste from LN was 1500 – dropping from 2500. The drop is a 40% drop. Option (a) is correct.
4. The error would not have any effect in the Roop Nagar Recyclable waste. Hence, the decrease would be 0%. Option (c) is correct.

5. The dry waste from Roop Nagar is the third lowest value at 400 (above 0 and 50). Hence, option (d) is correct.

Solutions for Questions 6 to 9:

Since all the boys answered different number of correct questions, and since there are a total of 5 questions, the number of correct answers for the five boys would be amongst 0, 1, 2, 3, 4 and 5. However, if we look at the data and the conditions in the question, we realise that since each question had a different answer and the answers for the five questions for each boy are different, it means that if a boy got 4 questions correct, he would get all five questions correct. (Think of this as if: the answers of the five questions are b, c, a, d, e and the answers of a boy on four of the questions – say the first four – are correct and he has marked b, c, a, d in the first four answers, then his fifth answer would be e and the correct answer of the fifth question would also be e.) This implies the scores of the boys are 5, 3, 2, 1 and 0 in any order.

From this point, the process of solving this question is to check for which of the five boys can have all questions answered correctly.

If A's answers are right, then A's score is 5 and the correct answers to the five questions are b, c, a, d, e respectively. With this answer key, if we check the answers of the others, we see that:

B's score is 1; C's score is 2; D's score is 0 and E's score is 3. This is a possibility since all the conditions are satisfied in this situation. But we cannot conclude that this is the only case. We will need to check for whether there exist/s more than one possibility of someone getting all questions correct.

If B's answers are right, then B's score is 5 and the correct answers to the five questions are c, d, a, e, b respectively. With this answer key, if we check the answers of the others, we see that:

A's score is 1; C's score is 3; D's score is 0 and E's score is 2. This is also a possibility since all the conditions are satisfied in this situation

If C's answers are right, then C's score is 5 and the correct answers to the five questions are c, d, a, b, e respectively. With this answer key, if we check the answers of the others, we see that:

A's score is 2; B's score is 3; D's score is 1 and E's score is 1. This is not a possibility since all the conditions are not satisfied in this situation

Likewise, if we check for D's answer as all correct – we immediately see that A and B both have 0 correct answers and we reject this possibility. E also cannot be all correct as it leads to a contradiction with C and D both ending up with one correct answer.

This way we can deduce that the following are the two possibilities:

Score	Case 1	Case 2
5	B	A
3	C	E
2	E	C
1	A	B
0	D	D

6. It is clear that in both cases it is D who has scored the least total marks.
7. In both the cases, the correct answer for Question 3 is a. Hence, option (a) is correct.
8. This condition is referring to the scores in case 2 in the solution table above. In this case, we can see that C has scored 2 marks.
9. This condition is referring to the scores in case 1 in the solution table above. In this case, we can see that A has scored 1 mark.

Solutions for Questions 10 to 13:

Basic understanding of the data:

We can see that the numbers in the table give us the average age of the employees in each level of the company. Also given that the number of employees in each department are given at the start of the period, it implies that we can also calculate the total age of a department in the year 2020.

Looking through the columns in the table, you should also be able to deduce that if the group of employees remains the same from one year to the next, the average age of the group would go up by 1 – from one year to the next. This is seen to be occurring a few times in the table – for instance if we look at Level 3, from the year 2020 to 2021 the average age goes up by 1. This means that the number of Level 3 employees does not change in that year. The same deduction can be made about level 3 employees from 2022 to 2023 and from 2023 to 2024. In Level 2 employees this is seen only once between the years 2023 and 2024.

The next deduction you should have is that any disruption to this +1 in average age structure can happen either due to retirement of a 60 year old (number of employees would go down and the average age would go down) or a recruitment of a 25 year old (number of employees would go up and the average age would go down) or a simultaneous retirement and a recruitment in the same year (number of employees would remain constant if there is similar number of retirements and recruitments – the average age of the group would definitely drop).

The following set of numerical deductions can then be deduced based on the numbers given in the table and the logic mentioned above,

The average age in 2020 of L1 was 41.

Total age of L1 = 41 × 4 = 164

Total age of L1 next year = 164 + 4 = 168

If one employee leaves total age of L1 = 168 – 60 = 108. Average age 108/3 = 36 which matches with the value in the table. For 2022, then the total age would go up by +3 to 111. If there is a recruitment of 1 person in between, the total age for 4 people would become 136 and their average would be 136/4 = 34. This again matches the numbers in the table.

For 2023, what makes sense from this value, is 2 recruitments and 1 retirement. This would correspond to 5 people with a total age of 136 + 4 + 25 + 25 – 60 = 130 → average age = 130/5 = 26.

Likewise, there has to be a recruitment of a 25 year old, to make sense of the average age of 26.67 on 1st Jan 2024.

You would need to do a similar working out for Level 2 and Level 3.

In this way we construct a table as shown.

	Recruitment			Retirement		
	Level 1	Level 2	Level 3	Level 1	Level 2	Level 3
2021	0	0	0	1	1	0
2022	1	1	1	0	0	0
2023	2	2	0	1	0	0
2024	1	0	0	0	0	0

10. There are a total of 4 employees who joined Level 1 in the given period.
11. A total of 3 employees retired from the company in the given period.
12. In 2024, 1 employee joined the organisation (in Level 1).
13. In 2023, 1 employee retired.

Solutions for Questions 14 to 17:

14. Cost price of the stock (5 kg of wheat from Chhattisgarh and 10 kg of bajra from Uttar Pradesh)
    = 22 × 5 + 40 × 10 = 110 + 400 = 510.
    Selling price of the stock (5 kg of wheat and 10 kg of bajra to be sold in MP) =
    25 × 5 + 70 × 10 = 825.
    Percentage Profit =
    (315/510) × 100 = 61.76%,
    Hence, the answer is option (d).
15. In this question, we have to check the total cost and the total sales by adding the column values for each state. For example, for MP, his total cost would be 20 + 32 + 45 + 65 + 50 = 212. The total revenue would be 25 + 40 + 50 + 70 + 60 = 245. Percentage profit is 15.6% approx.
    In the same way if we check for all the states, we can see that the minimum profit percentage would occur in MP only, since the percentage profits for UP (22.6), Bihar (24), Chhattisgarh (20+%) and Goa (17.8%) are higher than the one for MP. So, the answer is MP. Option (c) is correct.
16. He will buy wheat in Bihar and sell it in Goa – Cost 19, SP 30, Profit 11. Similarly:
    For Rice – Buys in UP (Cost 25) and sells in Goa (SP 50)
    For Jawar – Buys from Goa (30) and sells in MP/UP/Bihar/Chhattisgarh (50)
    For Bajra – Buys from UP (40) and sells in Chhattisgarh (80)
    For Makka – Buys from Chhattisgarh (30) and sells in Goa (80)
    Total cost price = 19 + 25 + 30 + 40 + 30 = 144.
    Total selling price = 30 + 50 + 50 + 80 + 80 = 290.
    Percentage profit = (290 – 144)/144] × 100 = 101% approx.
17. In this question, he is buying 1 kg from each state and selling that kg in the same state. So, for each grain, we will have to look at the maximum profit (not the profit percentage) that can be generated by buying and selling 1 kg.
    For wheat: Profit (in ₹) = 137 – 107 = 30.
    For rice: Profit (in ₹) = 196 – 162 = 34.
    For jawar: Profit (in ₹) = 240 – 190 = 50.
    For bajra: Profit (in ₹) = 325 – 290 = 35.
    For makka: Profit (in ₹) = 300 – 250 = 50.
    The minimum profit he will get is in the buying and selling of wheat. The profit is ₹30. Hence, the answer is 30.

Solutions for Questions 18 to 21:

Candidate	Votes
Arun	3260
Bishen	2818
Chirag	3060
Gemini	3232
Markanday	2430

Ward	Votes	15% of Votes
Ward 1	1800	270
Ward 2	2200	330
Ward 3	1200	180
Ward 4	1920	360
Ward 5	2000	300
Ward 6	1600	240
Ward 7	1000	150
Ward 8	1200	180
Ward 9	1400	210

Selection of Mayor:
Arun would have been elected as the mayor, since he received the highest number of votes. ***Note:*** That is the only condition for appointment as mayor.

Selection for Councilman:
Arun received less than 15% votes in Ward 1, Ward 4, Ward 7 and Ward 9. Bishen and Chirag received at least 15% votes in all the wards. Gemini received less than 15% votes in Ward 6 and Ward 7. Markanday received less than 15% votes in Ward 3, Ward 4 and Ward 5.

Only Bishen and Chirag are eligible to be Councilmen. Amongst the two, Chirag received the higher number of votes and will be elected the Councilman.

Selection of Administrator:
Except for Arun, all the others are eligible for Administrator. Amongst them, Bishen received the maximum number of votes in two wards.

Chirag received the maximum number of votes in two wards. Gemini received the maximum number of votes in three wards while Markanday received the maximum number of votes in two wards.

Hence, Gemini will be elected as the Administrator.

Selection of Commissioner:
Arun received the maximum number of votes in four wards. Hence, Arun will be elected as the Commissioner as well.

18. The Mayor Arun, in ward 8 received 180 votes. The Administrator, Gemini, received 480 votes in ward 9.
    Hence, the difference = 300.
19. Arun will be elected for more than one post. Hence, option (b) is correct.
20. Required difference = Arun's votes – Chirag's votes = 3260 – 3060 = 200.
21. Since the mayor and commissioner are the same, a = d.
    From the options, only option (d) satisfies this requirement.

Solutions for Questions 22 to 25:

Understanding the Data:
The table provides us the total amount spent, which will be a product of the number of items and the price per kg of the items. Since the number of items and their price are all in integers, we need to look inside the factor pairs for each amount spent.

With this understanding, we can think of the possible values of prices of each of the commodities. Tomatoes, for example, can have a price, that is a common factor of 320, 240, 60 and 80. Since, the HCF of these numbers is 20, the price of tomatoes can be 20, 10, 5, 4, 2 or 1 (any common factor of these numbers can be the price). Likewise, the price of apples would need to be a common factor of 84, 96, 300 and 396. Hence, apples would be priced at any of 12/6/4/3/2 or 1. Likewise, bananas could be priced at 1/2/3/4/6/8/12/24, cherries at 1/2/4/5/10/20 and pepper at 1/2/4/8.

The next thing you need to use is that the number of kgs bought for each item for an individual person is a set of 5 consecutive integers. Through a trial and error, we can reach the following table, depicting the individual purchases of the items.

Number of items bought:

Person	Tomato (10)	Apple (12)	Banana (24)	Cherries (20)	Pepper (8)
Aradhana	32	33	35	34	36
Bisakha	24	25	27	26	28
Chandni	6	8	7	4	5
Devika	8	7	10	9	6

Numbers in brackets in the above table represent the prices of the items.

22. 6
23. 130
24. 70
25. This is only true for Devika. Hence, option (b) is correct.

Solutions for Questions 26 to 29:

Assignment	A1	A2
Stage	Conceptualisation, Testing	Design, Execution
Person	Amitabh, Chetan	Bharadwaj, Daljit

26. Conceptualisation can be done by either Amitabh and Chetan. Also in this question Amitabh, works at 75% of his efficiency, which means that he does 7.5% work per day (as against his normal work of 10% per day).

Day	Person		Percentage of Conceptualisation Completed
	Amitabh	Chetan	
Jan 2	7.5%		7.5
Jan 3	7.5%		15
Jan 4	Off		15
Jan 5	7.5%	8.33%	30.83
Jan 6	7.5%	Off	38.33
Jan 7	Off	8.33%	46.66
Jan 8	7.5%	Off	54.16
Jan 9	7.5%	8.33%	70
Jan 10	Off	Off	70
Jan 11	7.5%	8.33%	85.8333
Jan 12	7.5%	Off	93.333
Jan 13	Off	8.33%	100+

Hence, option (a) is correct.

27. The design phase can only be started on 14th January. Both Bharadwaj and Daljit can start working simultaneously. You can avoid making the complete table by doing a rough back of the hand calculation of how many days will be required. B's work rate on design is 6.66%, Daljit's work rate is 16.66.
Jan 14th, both work (23.33% work done), Jan 15th, only Bhardwaj (6.66, 30% work done); Jan 16th, Only Daljit (16.66% work done, 46.66 completed); Jan 17th only Bharadwaj (16.66% work done, 63.33% completed). Jan 18th both work (23.33, 86.66); Jan 19 (both off – no work done); Jan 20 both work and the work will be completed. Hence, the correct answer is Jan 20th. Option (d) is correct.

Note: You can also do 21 and 22 by using the LCM method of time and work. (Refer to the time and work chapter in my book QA for CAT for theoretical understanding of the same.) The process is illustrated in the next two questions and can be seen to significantly reduce calculations.

28. Execution would start on 21st January and can be worked upon by Bharadwaj and Daljit only. Assume execution has a total of 126 units of work. Bharadwaj would do 136/14 = 9 units of work, while Daljit would do 126/9 = 14 units of work. Their work days will be in continuation to the days when they were doing design. ***Note:*** Bharadwaj will take a leave on Jan 22, since he worked on design on Jan 20 (in the previous question).

Day	Person (Units of Work Done)		Units of Work Completed
	Bharadwaj	Daljit	
Jan 21	9	Off	9
Jan 22	Off	14	23
Jan 23	9	Off	32
Jan 24	9	14	55
Jan 25	Off	Off	55
Jan 26	9	14	78
Jan 27	9	Off	87
Jan 28	Off	14	101
Jan 29	9	Off	110
Jan 30	9	14	124
Jan 31	Off	Off	
Feb 1	9	14	Total work crosses 126 and is completed.

Option (d) is correct.

29. To complete the project, Amitabh and Chetan will start working on 2nd February. According to the question, Amitabh was not keeping well in January. In February, hence, he would be back to full efficiency. Assume total 143 units of work in testing. Amitabh does 11 units per day, while Chetan does 13 units per day.

Day	Person		Units of Work Completed
	Amitabh	Chetan	
Feb 2	11	13	24
Feb 3	11	Off	35
Feb 4	Off	13	48
Feb 5	11	Off	59
Feb 6	11	13	83
Feb 7	Off	Off	83
Feb 8	11	13	107
Feb 9	11	Off	118
Feb 10	Off	13	131
Feb 11	11	Off	142
Feb 12	11	13	Work Crosses 143 and is completed

Option (c) is correct.

Solutions for Questions 30 to 33:

30. Using the information given in the table, the following is the number of Energy Points consumed by the students:

Student	Gatorade	Monster	Tzinga	RedBull	Total
A	0	0	80	80	160
B	160	0	40	0	200
C	0	80	40	0	120
D	80	80	0	0	160
E	0	40	0	160	200
F	80	0	0	160	240

Total number of Energy Points consumed by the six students = 160 + 200 + 120 + 160 + 200 + 240 = 1080. Therefore, the team with more than 540 Energy Points wins the 'Tug of war'.
The teams having more than 540 Energy Points can be formed in the following ten ways:
ABE, ABF, ADF, AEF, BCF, BDE, BDF, BEF, CEF, DEF.

It can be seen that out of the ten ways of forming a winning team, F is present in 8 i.e. AEF, ADF, ABF, BEF, BDF, DEF, CEF and BCF. Therefore, the required probability is 0.8.
The correct option is (d)

31. Refer the above list,
It can be seen that out of the ten ways of forming a winning team D and E are present in only 2. Hence the required probability is 2/10 = 0.2.

32. Scanning the possible winning team lists, we see that D is a part of 4 teams. Hence, the two partners for D can be selected in 4 ways. Option (b) is correct.

33. None of the possible winning teams consists of both A and C. Hence, the answer to this is 0.

CHAPTER 3

Bar Graphs

Outline

Learning Objectives

- Get a first-hand view of how data is presented through its organisation in the form of bar charts.
- Get an understanding of typical data which can be represented through bar charts. Also understand the concept of time series.
- Get a first-hand feel of the typical question types that are asked on the basis of bar charts.
- Different Bar Charts covered include Simple Bar Charts, Composite Bar Charts, Deviation Bar Charts, Stacked Bar Charts, Percentage Representation on a stacked bar chart, etc.

Chapter Highlights

- Introduction to bar charts.
- Practice exercise on bar charts containing simulated examination questions.

In the chapter on tables, we discussed them as a convenient and versatile tool for presenting data. We saw their flexibility and versatility for presenting data. Besides, we also got an exposure to the kind of questions that can be created on a table.

However, it must be pointed out here that the visual impact created by tables is considerably lower than that which is created by graphs and charts. Charts and graphs give a bird's eye-view of the numerical data to be presented. Hence, they become easy to understand and facilitate comparisons. They have been used extensively since time immemorial, as due to their visual impact they save a lot of time and effort.

In the current chapter we will concentrate on bar charts as a device of presenting data.

Bar diagrams (or bar charts) are one of the oldest and the most commonly used diagrams for presenting data. A bar chart consists of bars, each of which is a thick box. The value of the reading of the bar is determined by the height of the bar.

Let us now take a look at a traditional DI question based on bar charts. Notice, that in this question, you would simply need to understand the charts, identify the variables involved, understand the language of the questions asked, identify the equation/formula to be used, extract data from the charts and calculate the answers. Typical of what a traditional DI question asks you to do.

EXAMPLE 1

The Horizontal Bars in the diagram represent 2022 aggregate profit of different companies. The top four belong to the Adani Group, Bottom four belong to the Reliance Group, and the rest belong to Nestle. For each of the product subcategories, there is a vertical line indicating the aggregate profit of the corresponding subcategory in 2023.

1. What is the approximate percentage difference in the profit of Nestle's products from 2022 to 2023?
   (a) 28.35% (b) 23.22%
   (c) 19.76% (d) 32.84%
2. Which company has increased their overall profit from 2022-23?
   (a) Nestle (b) Adani
   (c) Reliance (d) None of these
3. Rank the following companies in ascending order of their percentage decrease in profits?
   (a) Adani-Reliance-Nestle
   (b) Adani-Nestle-Reliance
   (c) Nestle-Reliance-Adani
   (d) Reliance-Nestle-Adani
4. Which of the following subcompanies of the parent companies have shown an increase in percentage growth of more than 20% in their profit?
   (a) Nespresso-Starbucks-Maggi
   (b) Adani Gas-Adani Enterprises-Adani Wilmar
   (c) Reliance Footprints-JIO-Reliance Industries
   (d) None of these

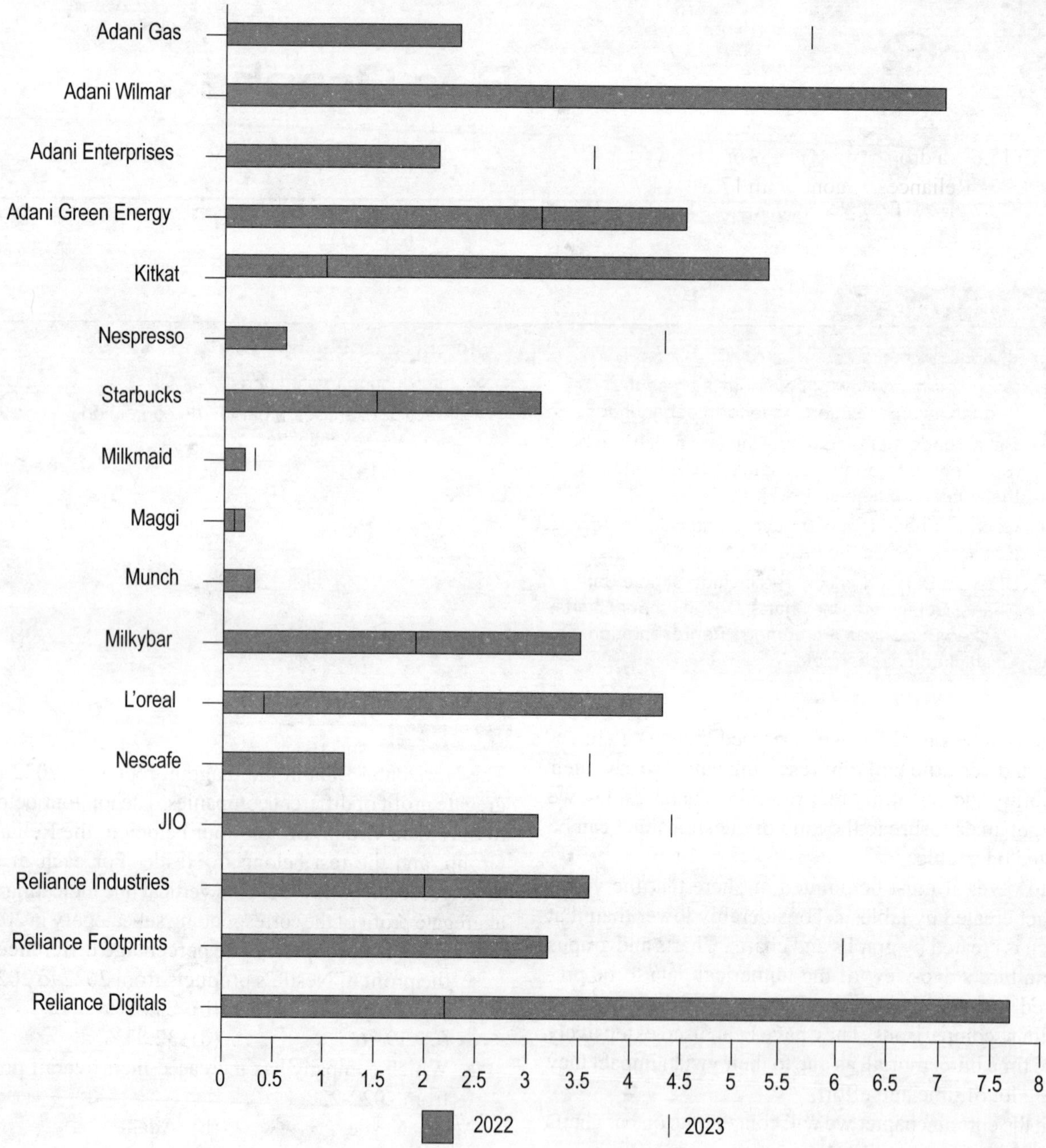

Solution: The exact values are shown in the table below:

	2022	2023
Adani Gas	2.3	5.7
Adani Wilmar	7	3.2
Adani Enterprises	2.1	3.6
Adani Green Energy	4.5	3.1
Kitkat	5.3	1
Nespresso	0.6	4.3
Starbucks	3.1	1.5
Milkmaid	0.2	0.3

	2022	2023
Maggi	0.2	0.1
Munch	0.3	0.3
Milkybar	3.5	1.9
L'oreal	4.3	0.4
Nescafe	1.2	3.6
JIO	3.1	4.4
Reliance Industries	3.6	2
Reliance Footprints	3.2	6.1
Reliance Digital	7.7	2.2

1. The total of Nestle has gone from 18.7 to 13.4 a drop of 28.35%. Option (a) is correct.
2. The profits of each of the companies is lower in 2023, than it was in 2022. Hence, option (d) is correct.
3. The Profits of Adani has gone from a net of 15.9 to 15.6 – a drop of around 2% or a growth of –2%, that of Reliance has gone from 17.6 to 14.7 – a drop of 16–17% roughly (or a growth of –16%), while Nestle can be seen to have an drop of close to 30%. The question has asked us to place the companies in ascending order of percentage increase. In this case, all the companies have a percentage decrease. The company with the maximum percentage decrease will be inferred to have the lowest percentage increase and will be placed first in the ascending order. In this case that is Nestle, followed by Reliance followed by Adani. Hence, option (c) is correct.
4. In this question, in order to select an option, all the companies given in a particular option should have exhibited an increase of 20%+. We can see that for option (a) Starbucks is not a greater than 20% increase, hence we reject this option, without even checking for Maggi. Likewise, option (b) is rejected because of Adani Wilmar and option (c) is rejected because of Reliance Industries. Hence, option (d) is correct.

As you just experienced, the above question set can be classified as an out and out Traditional DI question. Before you start solving the chapter exercises, it is important for you to feel how Bar chart questions can be made tougher analysis wise. It is important for you to appreciate what degree of complexity do logical DI analysis-based questions get to. It is important for you to understand this at this point of time, in order to get a clear idea of the level of solving skills and ability you have to get to in order to be able to score marks in the exam. Once you go through the solved examples based on bar charts explained here, you should go through the LOD 1, 2 and 3 exercises provided in the chapter trying your best to solve each of the sets of questions. However, I would like to remind you about the note I had explained to you- in the previous chapter – i.e. At this stage, if you are a starter in Data Interpretation, you would be able to solve only a fraction of the sets at the higher level of difficulties. My advice is that, you should not get disappointed by this, as this is to be expected. As you raise your DI Skills by proceeding on with the various chapters and practice tests provided in this book, you will doubtless raise your solving ability – and would be expected to come back to these sets and try them again. Remember the adage: it makes you grow only if it challenges you!

Try to read the following set and before reading the solution to the same, try your best to work out what's happening in this question.

The first thing you do in a set of Data Interpretation, is to identify the variables involved in the question. Any set of DI, will open the numbers and variables it is talking about as you go through it.

EXAMPLE 2

The IPL Mini Auction 2022 was held at Grand Hyatt Hotel in Kochi on 23rd December 2022. 10 Players namely Sam Curran 1, Liam Livingstone 2, Joe Root 3, Andre Russel 4, Shivam Mavi 5, Nicolas Pooran 6, Harry Brooke 7, Kane Williamson 8, Jos Butler 9 and Steve Smith 10 went under the hammer with base prices ranging from 50L to 3 CR with intervals of 50L. Base price of 50L or 1 CR is for bowlers, 1.5 Cr or 2 Cr is for Batters, and 2.5 Cr or 3 Cr is for All Rounders.

Following details are also known about the auction-

(a) Sam Curran, Joe Root, Shivam Mavi, Harry Brooke, Jos Butler are not bowlers; Liam, Andre, Nicolas, Kane & Steve are not batters; Joe, Nicolas, Jos are not all rounders.
(b) Andre Russel, Shivam Mavi, Nicolas Pooran, Harry Brooke, Kane Williamson, Jos Butler all have different base prices, with Harry having the highest base price and Kane the lowest.
(c) The bar chart shows the number of players with different base prices. Study the chart and answer the questions that follow:

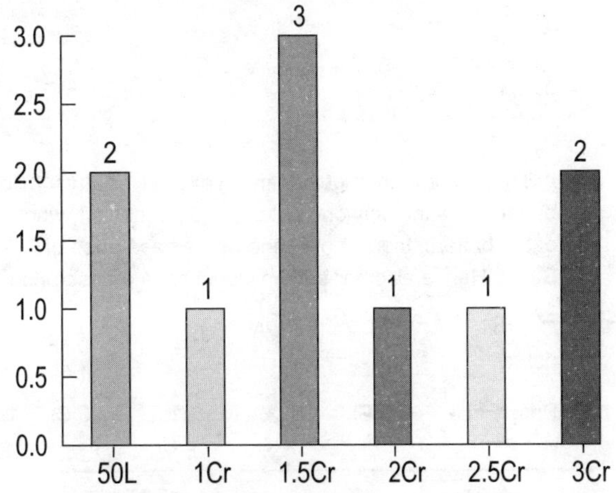

1. Which of the following is NOT necessarily true?
   (a) Sam Curran is a Batter
   (b) Shivam Mavi has a base price of not more than ₹ 2 Crores
   (c) Harry Brooke is an All Rounder
   (d) Steve Smith has a base price of not more than ₹ 2 Crores

2. What is the total base price of Sam Curran, Joe Root, Shivam Mavi, Harry Brooke, and Jos Butler?
3. If during the auction the Batters bagged a 50% hike in their base price and All Rounders bagged a 30% hike, then what is the difference between the salaries of Andre Russel and Sam Curran?
4. For how many players can we definitely determine their base prices?

Let us now take a look at the solution to this question:

We will first need to create a table to make sense of the information provided to us. In the table, I am using L to denote bowler, B for Batter and A for All rounder.

Solution:

TABLE 1

Row	Name	Sam Curran	Liam Livingston	Joe Root	Andre Russel	Shivam Mavi	Nicolas Pooran	Harry Brooke	Kane W	Jos Butler	Steve Smith	
1	Clue A	Not L		Not L		Not L		Not L		Not L		
2	Clue B		Not B		Not B		Not B		Not B		Not B	
3	Clue C			Not A			Not A			Not A		
4	Hence	B/A	L/A	B	L/A	B/A	L	B/A	L/A	B	L/A	
5	Clue D Base Price				x	y	z	3 cr. Hence, A	50 Lac. Hence L	M		
6	Consolidated	B/A	L/A	B	L/A	B/A	L	A	L	B	L/A	We know 2 B,2L and 1 A
7	Shift your focus now to the frequencies given in the Bar chars. You can make the following deductions here. i) Since Nicolas Pooran is a Bowler and his base price is different from Kane W, it means that his base price can only be 1 Cr. So the last remaining bowler would have a base price of 50 Lacs. ii) Between x, y and M one value of the base price has to be 1.5 crore, another 2 crore and the last one 2.5 Crore. However, Andre Russel is not a batter, hence his base price can only be 2.5 crore. Hence he is an all-rounder. iii) Shivam Mavi would then have a base price of either 1.5 or 2 crore and hence he can only be a batter.											
8					2.5 Cr	1.5/2 Cr	1 Cr	3 Cr	50 Lac	2/1.5 Cr		
	Consolidated	B/A	L/A	B	A	B	L	A	L	B	L/A	We know 3B,2L and 2 A
	i) Since we are short of identifying exactly 1 batter, 1 Bowler and 1 All-rounder, we can deduce that Sam Curran must be a batter (he is the only one out of the 3 people left, whose option of being a batter is still available). ii) Amongst the base prices of the batters, there is only one with a base price of 2 crore as per the bar chart. We have identified him as Shivam Mavi or Jos Butler. Hence all other batters would have a base price of 1.5 crore.											
10	Consolidated	B	L/A	B	A	B	L	A	L	B	L/A	
11	Base Price	1.5 Cr		1.5 Cr	2.5 Cr	1.5/2 Cr	1 Cr	3 Cr	50 Lac	2/1.5 Cr		

Notes to the table: It is given to us that the base price for Blowers is either 50 Lacs or 1 Cr. For Batters 1.5 or 2 Cr and for All rounders 2.5 or 3 Cr. From the frequency bar chart, we can make out that there are 3 bowlers, 4 Batters and 3 All-rounders in the list of people. In Table 1, after the use of clues A, B and C we were able to identify 2 batters and one bowler. After the use of Clue D, the fifth row of the table can be made. The clue tells us that the base prices of the six mentioned players are all different. This can only mean that their base prices are 50L, 1 Cr, 1.5 Cr, 2 Cr, 2.5 Cr and 3 Cr in some order. Since, Harry has the highest and Kane the lowest base price amongst the 6, we can allocate3 Cr and 50 Lacs to them. That makes, Harry Brooke an All Rounder and Kane a Bowler. We can modify Row 5 to Row 6. At this stage we still need to identify 1 L, 2 B and 2 A.

The answers to the questions can be read off from the Table.

1. We do not know whether Steve Smith is a bowler or an all-rounder. If he is an all-rounder, his base price would be 2.5 crore (since there is only 1 person with a base price of 2 crore and we have already identified him. Hence, we cannot conclude definitely about his base price being below 2 crores. Hence, option (d) is correct.
2. 1.5 + 1.5 + 1.5/2 + 3 + 2/1.5 = 9.5 crore
3. Salary of Andre Russel after the hike would be 3.25 crore (increase of 30% on 2.5 crore) and that of Sam Curran would be 2.75 crore (after 50% hike). The required difference is 50 Lacs.
4. We can determine the exact base price of 6 people out of 10.

Points Noteworthy with Respect to Bar Charts

- Bar diagrams are visual aids for presenting statistical data. Very often in bar charts, different colours, shades, dots, dashes, etc. are used in the bars to distinguish between different continuous variables being represented. There will always be an explanatory index indicating the meanings of the different colours, shades and markings.
- Each bar diagram has a title (which is displayed either at the top or at the bottom of the diagram) indicating the subject matter depicted in the diagram. Besides, at times, there may be footnotes at the bottom of the diagram to explain facts that are not covered in the title. The student is advised to be very careful about reading these footnotes and not to overlook these facts while interpreting bar diagrams.
- One axis (normally the X-axis) of every bar diagram will represent a discrete variable while the other axis represents the scale for one or more continuous variables.

We now move onto the different kinds of bar charts and the kinds of data that can be represented on a bar chart:

SIMPLE BAR CHART

The simple bar chart is the 'simplest' bar chart which has one continuous variable charted along with one discrete variable. Figure 3.1 shows an example.

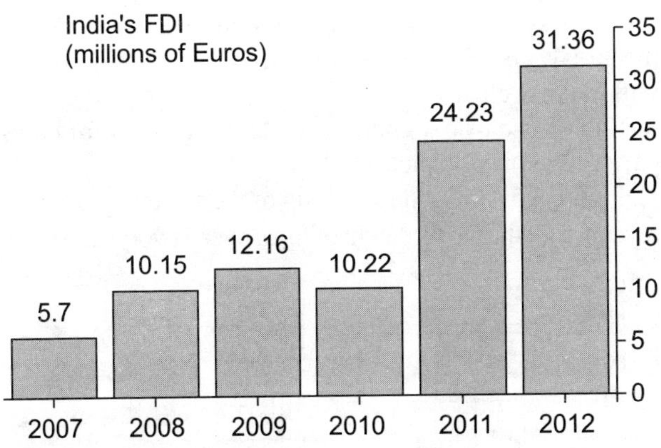

FIGURE 3.1 *Simple Bar Chart*

The following kinds of data can be represented on a simple bar chart:

Discrete Variable	Continuous Variable
Years	Sales (in ₹) trend of a single company
Years	Sales (in units) trend of a single company
Years	Profit trend of a single company
Years	Profit per unit trend of a single company
Years	No. of employees trend of a single company
Years	Population trend of a single country
Company names	Sales of each company for a particular year

Task for Student

Doubtlessly there will be varied types of data that can be represented on a simple bar chart. You are required to add to the list given and try to visualise simple bar charts for your own set of combinations of one discrete and one continuous variable.

STACKED BAR CHART

The length of a bar, on a bar chart, normally represents the magnitude of a single continuous variable. However, in certain cases it might be feasible and in fact required to break up the magnitude of the main continuous variable into its component parts. When this sort of representation is used, the chart formed is called a stacked bar chart.

Different shades, colours, etc. are used to distinguish the various components and an index is given along with the chart to explain these differences. Figure 3.2 gives an example.

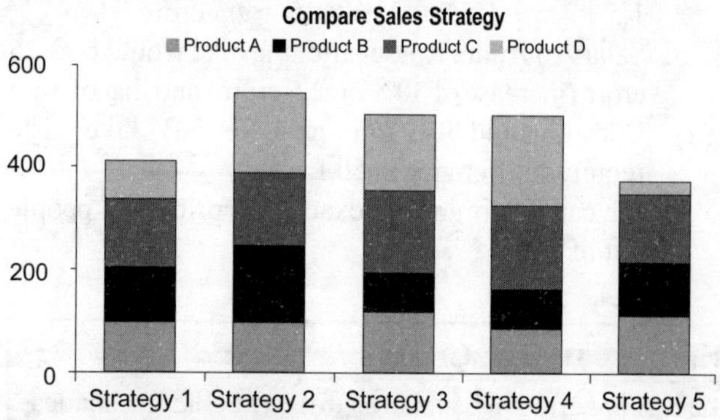

FIGURE 3.2 *Stacked Bar Chart*

COMPOSITE BAR CHART

One of the primary limitations of the simple bar chart is that it can only be used to display a single continuous variable. Similarly, although a stacked/component bar chart can display multiple continuous variables, it can only do so if all the continuous variables add up to a single continuous variable. In other words, it can only display one continuous variable and its constituent parts.

However, if two or more sets of continuous variables are to be shown on the same bar chart, we use what is called a composite bar chart. Figure 3.3 will make it clear.

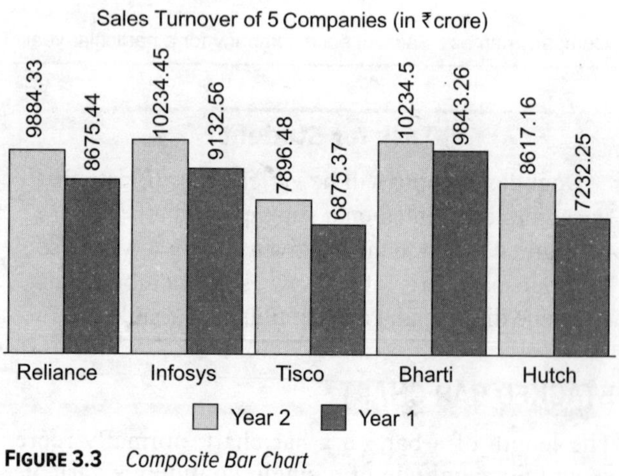

FIGURE 3.3 *Composite Bar Chart*

THE USE OF BAR CHARTS TO SHOW DEVIATIONS

Deviation bars are useful for graphic presentation of continuous variables which can have both positive and negative values, i.e., surplus or deficit, net profit or loss, net of imports and exports. In general, continuous variables which have both positive and negative values are the best represented on bar charts.

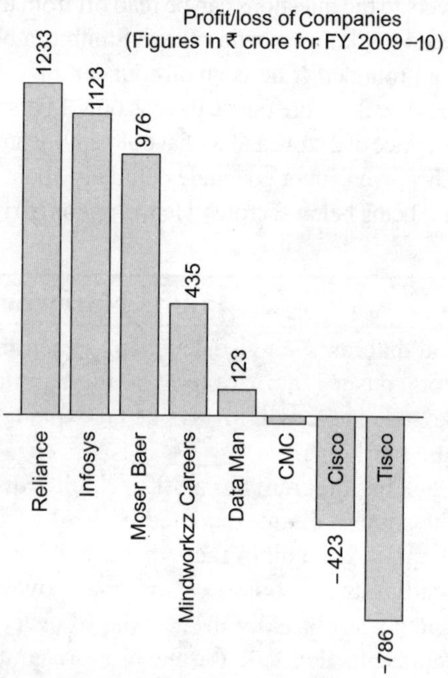

FIGURE 3.4 *Representing Deviation through Bar Charts*

A base line is created and positive values (such as profit, surplus), etc., are represented by bars above the base line while negative deviations (loss or deficit) are represented by bars below the base line. Figure 3.4 will make it clear.

REPRESENTATION OF PERCENTAGE ON A STACKED BAR CHART

Sometimes stacked bars can also be used to represent the break-up of some continuous variable. Figure 3.5 will make it clear.

Such a use of bar charts is quite convenient for comparing two or more sets of data.

Figure 3.5 shows the break-up of the various sources of revenues for the Government of India over a two-year period.

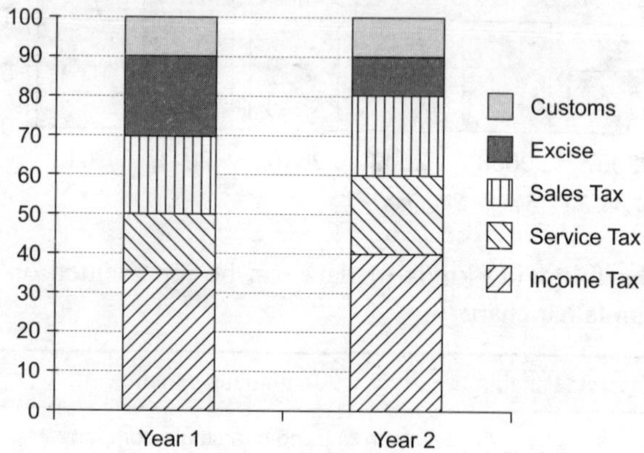

FIGURE 3.5 *Representing Percentage on a Stacked Bar Chart*

We now move on to give you a feel of the kinds of questions that can be created on bar graphs.

EXERCISE

Level of Difficulty 1

Directions for Questions 1 to 4: *The following chart (Figure 3.6) represents the number of students of Mindworkzz at its Lucknow centre who passed the CAT exam or the XAT exam or the CMAT exam or none of these exams. (Assume that there are no students who passed more than one exam.)*

1. What was the percentage of students who cleared CAT in 2010?
   (a) 19.56%
   (b) 12.65%
   (c) 14.28%
   (d) 11.76%
2. What was the percentage of students who succeeded in at least one of the three exams in 2010?
   (a) 82.4% (b) 82.8%
   (c) 82.35% (d) 83.3%

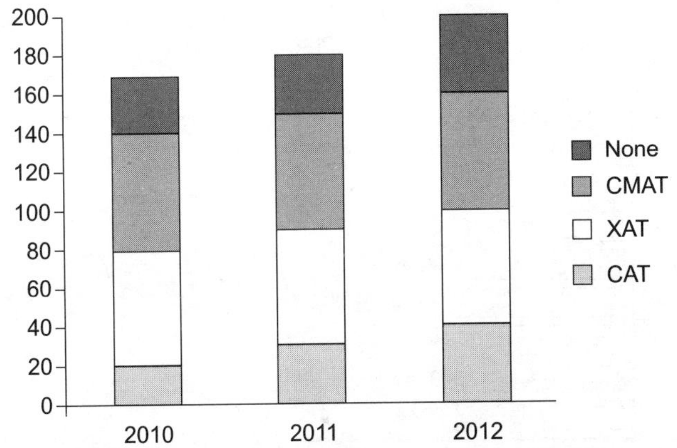

FIGURE 3.6 *Number of Students who Qualified CAT/XAT/CMAT Exams*

3. Which year showed the best result in MBA entrance exams for the institute (in terms of percentage of students who cleared)?
   (a) 2010
   (b) 2011
   (c) 2012
   (d) Cannot be determined
4. What is the percentage increase in the number of students in 2012 over 2010?
   (a) 30% (b) 17.64%
   (c) 117.6% (d) 85%

Directions for Questions 5 to 9: *Study the following bar chart (Figure 3.7) carefully and answer the questions given.*

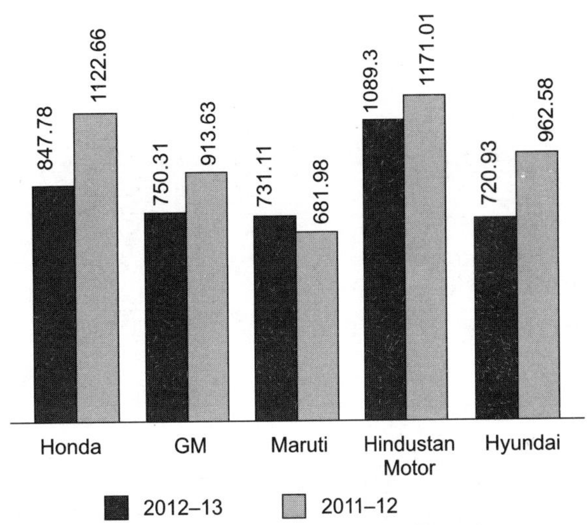

FIGURE 3.7 *Sales Turnover of 5 Companies (in ₹ crore)*

5. What is the approximate difference between the average sales turnover of all the companies put together between the years 2011–12 and 2012–13?
   (a) 133.45 (b) 142.48
   (c) 117.6 (d) None of these
6. What should have been the sales turnover of GM in 2012–13 to have shown an excess of the same quantum over 2011–12 as shown by the sales turnover of Maruti?
   (a) 953.76 (b) 963.76
   (c) 952.76 (d) 962.76
7. Which of the companies shows the maximum percentage difference in sales turnover between the two years?
   (a) Honda (b) GM
   (c) Hyundai (d) Maruti
8. What is the percentage change in the overall sales turnover of the five companies together between 2011–12 and 2012–13?
   (a) 17.21% (b) 14.68%
   (c) 12.67% (d) 21.24%
9. What is the absolute change in the overall sales turnover of the five companies together between 2011–12 and 2012–13?
   (a) 712.43 (b) 142.48
   (c) 683.53 (d) None of these

Directions for Questions 10 to 14: *The total of the first three deficit countries (in ₹ crore) = 3594.3. The total of the next five deficit countries (in ₹ crore) = 2588.5. The total of the last five deficit countries (in ₹ crore) = 334.2. The total of the four surplus countries (in ₹ crore) = 1860.4. Study Figure 3.9 and answer the questions given below.*

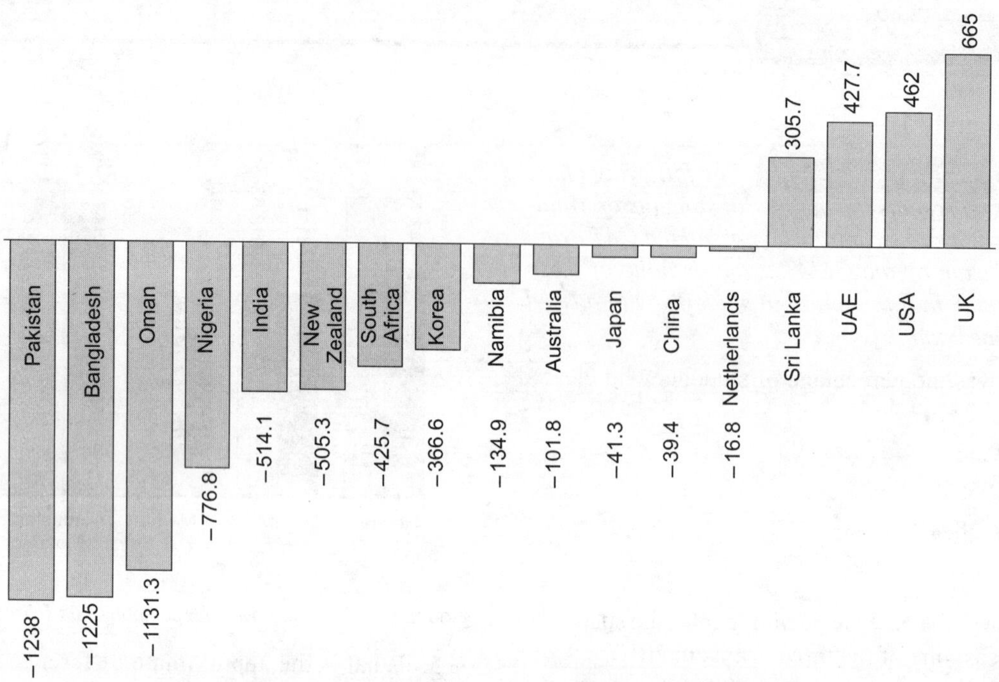

FIGURE 3.9 *Cumulative Trade Deficit/Surplus of Countries for the Year 2022–23 (All figures in ₹ crore)*

10. The country whose surplus is nearly equal to the average of the four surplus countries is
   (a) Sri Lanka (b) UAE
   (c) USA (d) UK
11. The ratio of the deficit of the first five deficit countries to the overall deficit of all the deficit countries is nearly equal to:
   (a) 0.72 (b) 0.75
   (c) 0.80 (d) 0.85
12. The average of the total deficit of the middle five deficit countries is the closest to the deficit of which country?
   (a) Korea (b) South Africa
   (c) UAE (d) None of these
13. The net total deficit/surplus is equal to:
   (a) 4656.6 surplus (b) 4656.6 deficit
   (c) 3836.5 deficit (d) None of these
14. The ratio of the difference between the highest and the lowest of the surplus countries to the difference between Bangladesh and Oman is:
   (a) 3.44 (b) 2.96
   (c) 4.5 (d) 3.83

Directions for Questions 15 to 19: *Study the following bar charts [Figures 3.10(A) and 3.10(B)] before answering the questions.*

15. How many countries exhibited a trade surplus?
   (a) 5 (b) 4
   (c) 3 (d) 6

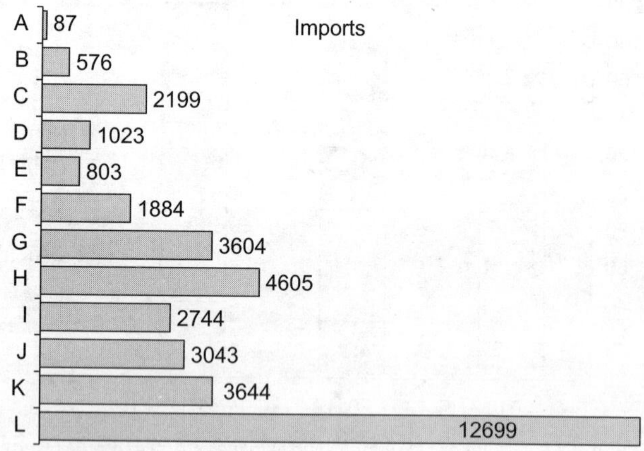

FIGURE 3.10(A) *Foreign Trade (Imports) by Countries for the Year 2008–09*

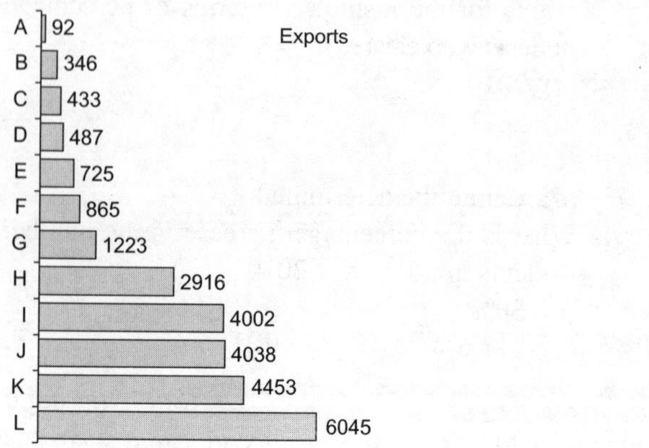

FIGURE 3.10(B) *Foreign Trade (Exports) by Countries for the Year 2008–09*

16. The highest trade deficit was shown by which country?
    (a) C (b) G
    (c) H (d) L
17. The ratio of exports to imports was the highest for which country?
    (a) A (b) I
    (c) J (d) K
18. The total trade deficit/surplus for all the countries put together was:
    (a) 11286 surplus (b) 11286 deficit
    (c) 10286 deficit (d) None of these
19. The ratio of the maximum exports to the minimum imports was the closest to:
    (a) 64 (b) 69
    (c) 74 (d) 79

Directions for Questions 20 to 24: *The following bar chart (Figure 3.11) shows the composition of the GDP of two countries (India and Pakistan).*

20. What fraction of India's GDP is accounted for by services?
    (a) 6/33 (b) 1/5th
    (c) 2/3rd (d) None of the above
21. If the total GDP of Pakistan is ₹10,000 crore, then the GDP accounted for by manufacturing is:
    (a) ₹200 crore (b) ₹600 crore
    (c) ₹2,000 crore (d) ₹6,000 crore
22. If the total GDP of India is ₹30,000 crores, then the GDP accounted for by agriculture, services and miscellaneous is:
    (a) ₹18,500 crore (b) ₹18,000 crore
    (c) ₹21,000 crore (d) ₹15,000 crore
23. Which country accounts for higher earning out of services and miscellaneous together?
    (a) India
    (b) Pakistan
    (c) Both spend equal amounts
    (d) Cannot be determined

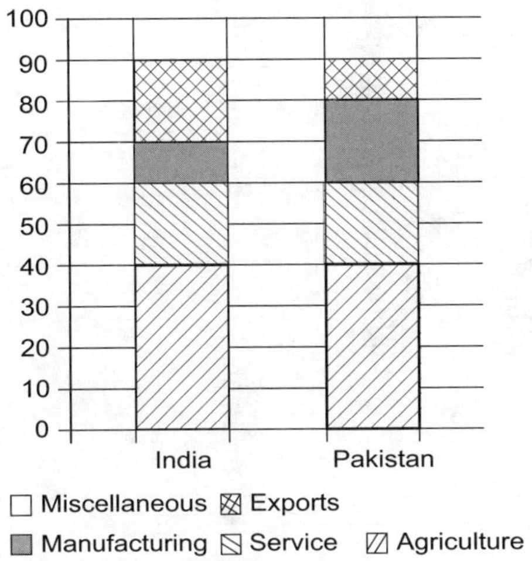

FIGURE 3.11 *Composition of GDP of Two Countries*

24. If the total GDP is the same for both the countries, then what percentage is Pakistan's income through agriculture over India's income through services?
    (a) 100% (b) 200%
    (c) 133.33% (d) None of these

Directions for Questions 25 to 28: *The bar graph given below shows the production of company A and B in the given four different years.*

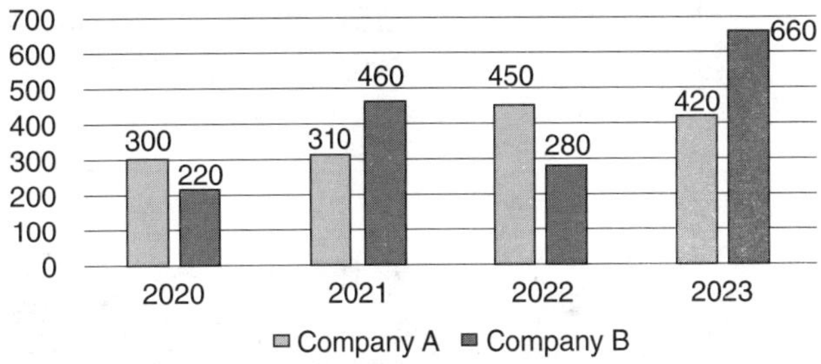

Note: In a year, total production = Total number of products sold + Total number of products unsold.

25. Half of the production of company A in the year 2022 is what per cent more or less than three-fifth of production of same company in the year 2020?
    (a) 25% (b) 80%
    (c) 125% (d) 75%
26. Find the average number of the production of company B in the year 2020, 2021 and 2022.
    (a) 320 (b) 240
    (c) 280 (d) 354
27. In the year 2024, the total sold products are 10% more than the production of company B in the year 2021 and total unsold products are 100 more than the production of company A in the year 2022. Find the total production in the year 2024.
    (a) 1000 (b) 1024
    (c) 1048 (d) 1056
28. Production of company A and company B in the year 2024 over the previous year has increased by 20% and 25% respectively. What is the total production of both the companies together in the years 2023 and 2024?
    (a) 1796 (b) 2256
    (c) 1850 (d) 2409

Level of Difficulty 2

Directions for Questions 1 to 5: *The line and bar graph below depicts the total area and the population density for 8 different countries. It is given that the area of the eight countries is the same for the two years 2002 and 2008. The population density is found by dividing the total population of the country by the area and depicted by the line graphs and is read off the left hand Y-axis. The two-line graphs refer to the population density in the years 2002 and 2008.*

1. How many countries had a higher population in 2008 as compared to 2002?
   (a) 8 (b) 7
   (c) 6 (d) Cannot be determined.
2. Find the increase in the population of Myanmar from 2002 to 2008.
   (a) 5.44 mn (b) 5.44 lacs
   (c) 5,440 lacs (d) Cannot be determined
3. Find the percentage increase in the population of Burkina Faso from 2002 to 2008.
   (a) 17.5% (b) 17.8%
   (c) 18.1% (d) Cannot be determined
4. The country with the largest population in 2008 amongst the given countries is:
   (a) Afghanistan (b) Ukraine
   (c) Myanmar (d) Cannot be determined
5. The area per person (area divided by population) is the highest for which country, amongst those given, in the year 2002?
   (a) Afghanistan
   (b) Burkina Faso
   (c) Nicaragua
   (d) Cannot be determined

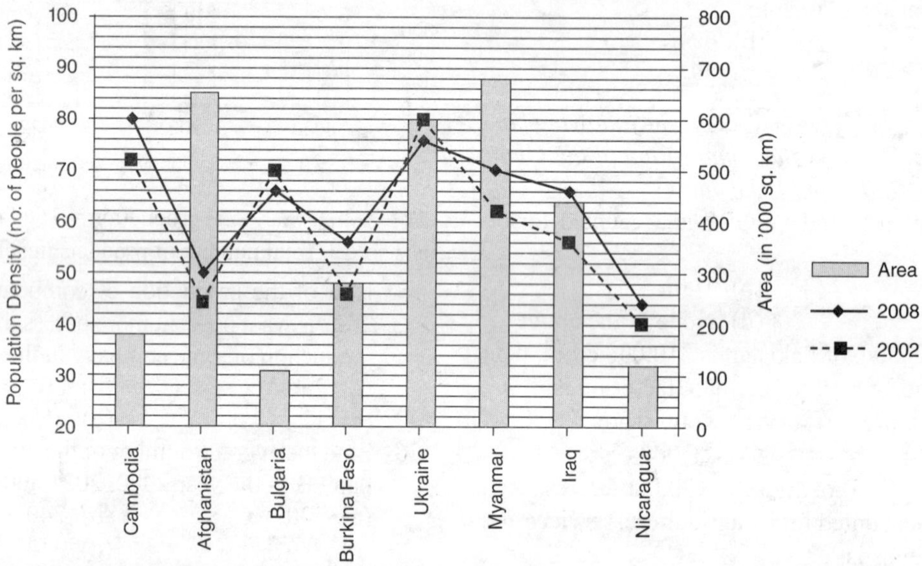

Directions for Questions 6 to 9: *Cash surplus is the excess of cash revenue over cash expenditure (deficit if this is negative). Rather than the absolute value of this surplus/deficit, it as a percentage of GDP is a more important measure. The following graph gives the cash surplus/deficit as a percentage of GDP for 6 countries for each year from 2003 to 2008. Deficits are shown above the X-axis and surplus below the X-axis.*

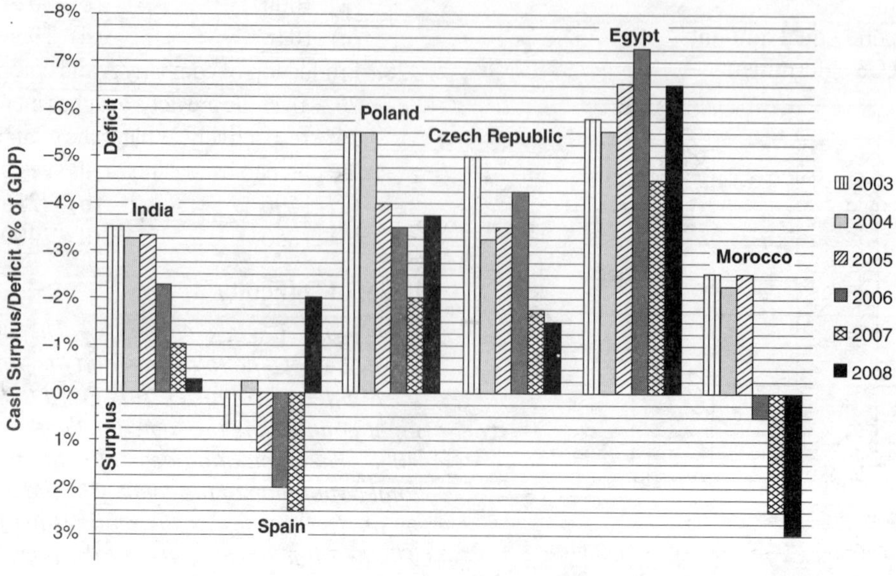

The following graph gives the growth rate of the GDP's of the same countries for the same time interval.

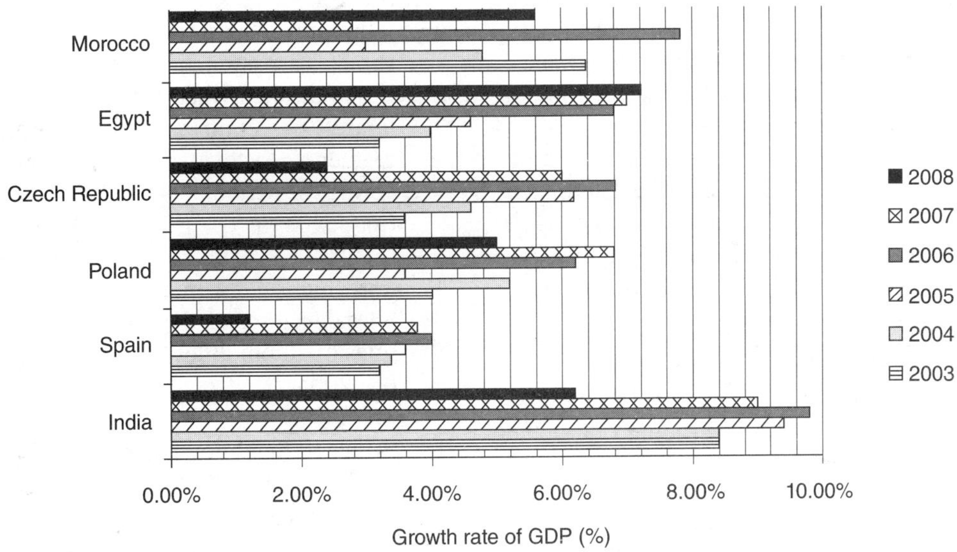

Each of the question below pertains to only the 6 countries for which data has been given in the above graphs.

6. Which country had the highest cash deficit in the year 2004?
   (a) Spain (b) Egypt
   (c) Poland (d) Cannot be determined
7. Which country's cash deficit increased by the greatest rate from the year 2004 to 2005?
   (a) India
   (b) Czech Republic
   (c) Egypt
   (d) Cannot be determined
8. Find the ratio of the cash deficit of Poland and Czech Republic in the year 2005.
   (a) 3 : 4 (b) 2 : 3
   (c) 1 : 2 (d) Cannot be determined
9. What was the percentage increase in Egypt's cash deficit from the year 2007 to 2008?
   (a) 44% (b) 50%
   (c) 55% (d) Cannot be determined

Direction for Questions 10 to 13: *A study conducted across four cities – P, Q, R and S collected information about the entire adult population (age >=18 years) in these cities across three parameters, marital status, employment status and gender. For each of the three parameters, the entire adult population of each city is divided into exactly two categories – as given in the respective bar-charts below. The three charts plot the number of adults in each city belonging to each of the two categories under each parameter. However, the respective scales along the Y-axis have not been mentioned in any of the charts.*

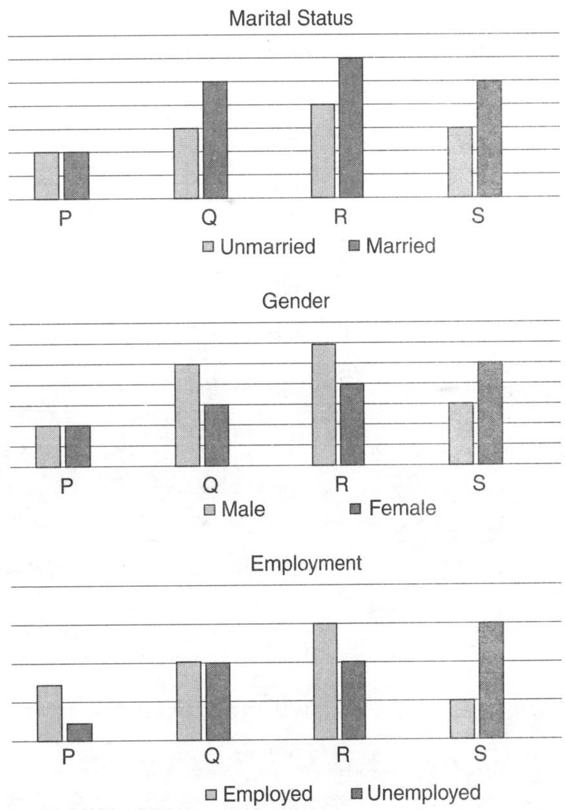

10. What is the total adult population (in million) of city S if the total number of adult unmarried across all the cities is 480 million?
    (a) 220 (b) 240
    (c) 320 (d) 360
11. Considering the adult population of city Q, the number of people employed is approximately what percentage of the number of unmarried?

(a) 66.67% (b) 100%
(c) 133.33% (d) Cannot be determined

12. If the unemployed adult population in each city comprises an equal number of males and females, which of the following cities has the maximum number of adult males who are employed?
(a) R (b) P
(c) Q (d) Cannot be determined

13. Which city can have the maximum number of adult females who are unmarried and also employed?
(a) P (b) Q (c) R (d) S

Directions for Questions 14 to 19: *Answer these questions on the basis of the following graphs.*

14. Which of the following years exhibited the highest percentage decrease over the preceding year in the automobile production?
(a) 2005 (b) 2006
(c) 2007 (d) 2008

15. Assuming whatever is not sold domestically was exported, then which year has registered the highest growth in exports of automobiles?
(a) 2005 (b) 2006
(c) 2007 (d) 2008

16. If the ratio of the domestic sale price of a commercial vehicle, a passenger vehicle and a three-wheeler is 5:3:2; then what per cent of earnings (approximately) is contributed by commercial vehicle segment to the overall earnings from domestic sales during the period 2004–08?
(a) 45% (b) 43%
(c) 11% (d) 27%

17. For which year were the domestic sales of automobiles the closest to the average (2004–08) domestic sales of automobiles?
(a) 2005 (b) 2006
(c) 2007 (d) 2008

18. Which of the following years exhibited the highest percentage increase over the preceding year in the automobile sales?
(a) 2005 (b) 2006
(c) 2007 (d) 2008

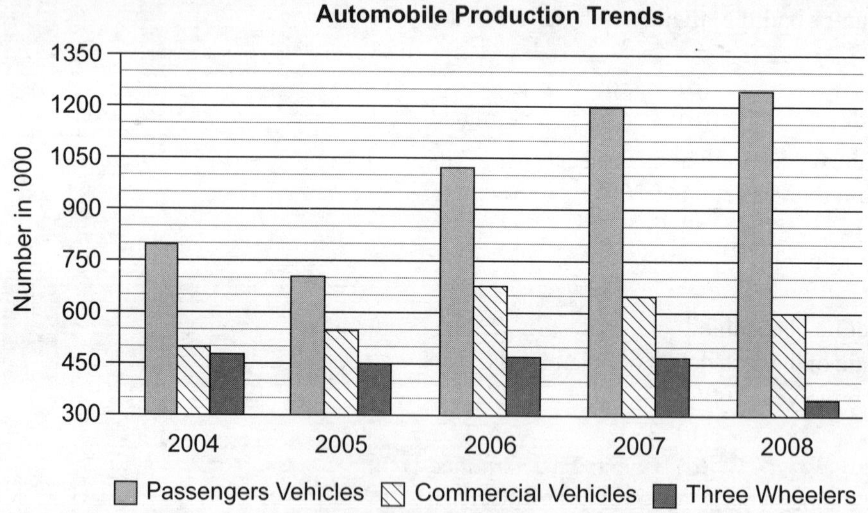

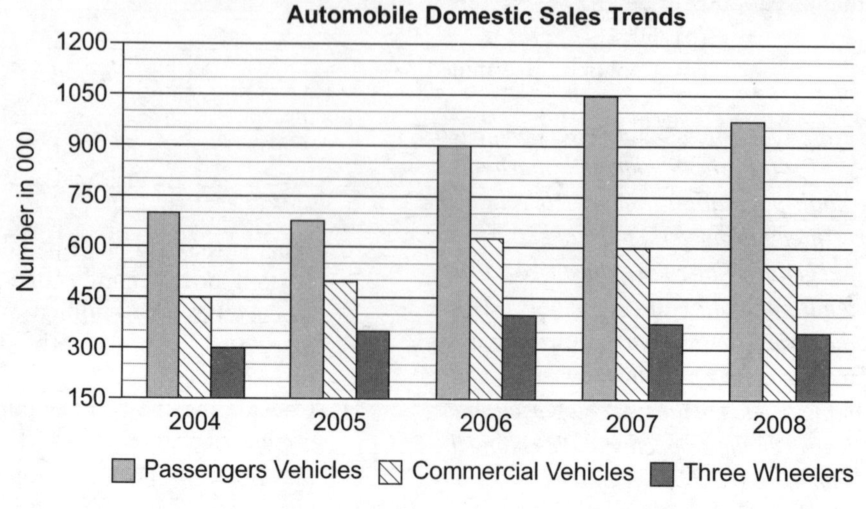

19. The ratio between absolute increase in domestic sales over preceding year and absolute increase in production over the preceding year is the highest during which year?
(a) 2005 (b) 2006
(c) 2007 (d) 2008

Directions for Questions 20 to 23: *Study the following graph and answer the questions that follow.*

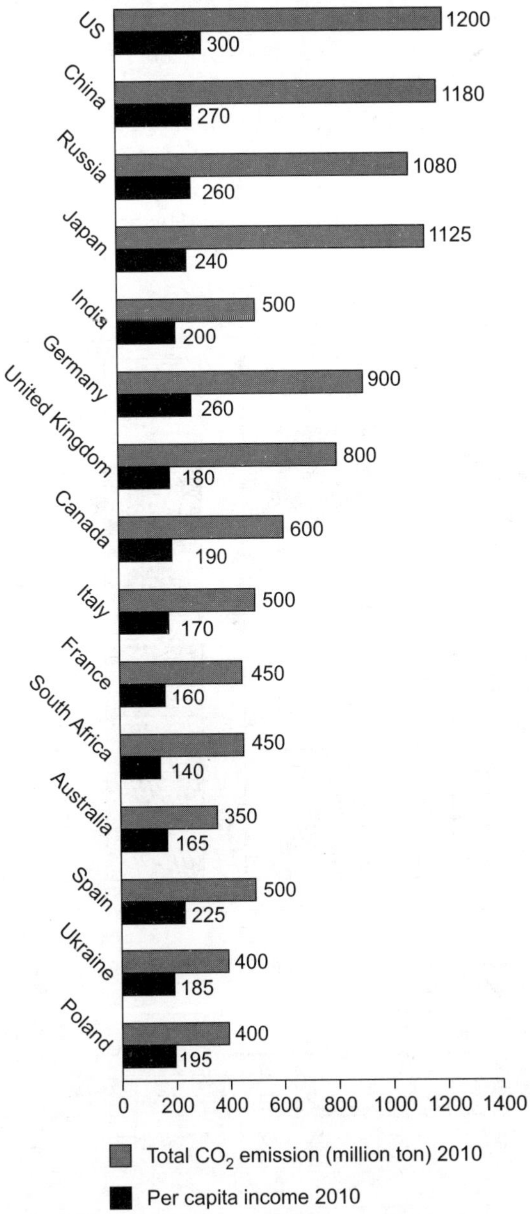

20. If the world energy council formulates a norm for high emission countries to reduce their emission each year by 12.5% for the next two years then what would be the ratio of CO_2 emission to per capita income of US, China and Japan after two years? (The per capita income of China, Japan and US is expected to increase every year by 4%, 3% and 2% respectively.)
(a) 3.5, 3.8, 4.1 (b) 3.4, 3.5, 3.4
(c) 2.9, 3.1, 3.4 (d) None

21. If US and China decide to buy carbon credits, from Spain and Ukraine to make up for their high emissions, then in how many years US and China would be able to bring down their ratio of CO_2 *emission* (million ton) to per capita income to the world standard benchmark of 0.75 (per capita income of the given countries remain same, 0.5 CO_2 emissions [million ton] is compensated by purchase of 1.25 units of carbon credit, and a country can buy carbon credit units in three lots of 15, 20 and 30 units in a single year).
(a) 3.8 years (b) 38 years
(c) 30 years (d) None

22. France, South Africa, Australia, Ukraine and Poland form an energy consortium which declares CO_2 emission of 350 million ton per annum as standard benchmark. The energy consortium decides to sell their carbon emission savings against the standard benchmark to high carbon emission countries. It is expected that the per capita income of each country of the energy consortium increases by 2%, 2.5% and 3.5% p.a. for the next three years respectively. The ratio of CO_2 emission to per capita income of each energy consortium country reduces by 50% and remains constant for the next three years. If by selling 0.5 CO_2 emissions (million ton) the energy consortium earns 1.25 carbon credits, then determine the total carbon credits earned by the energy consortium in three years.
(a) 3560 (b) 4506
(c) 5060 (d) None

23. Select the wrong statement in reference to the position of India vis-à-vis other countries in the graph in terms of the ratio of CO_2 emission to per capita income (increasing order).
(a) India stands at 5th position at the given CO_2 emission level and per capita income of each country.
(b) India stands at 5th position if 200 million ton CO_2 emission is deducted from the given CO_2 emission figures of each country.
(c) India stands at 5th position if 50 is added to the given per capita income figures of each country.
(d) India stands at 5th position if 200 million ton CO_2 emission is deducted from the given CO_2 emission figures of each country and 50 is added to the given per capita income of each country.

Level of Difficulty 3

Directions for Questions 1 to 4: *Baburao, Rahul, Raju, Shyam, Rohan and Rohit are six bright students at Bombay Public School. Recently they appeared for the final exam. The exam tested students on six subjects, namely, English, Marathi, Mathematics, History, Economics and Physics. The question paper on each subject was out of 100 marks and it is known that the marks scored by the students in each of the subjects can be only one integer out of the following: 40, 50, 60, 70, 80 and 90.*

All the percentages shown in the following graph are rounded off to the nearest two decimal points. (Interpretation of the graph – Baburao's score in English, Marathi, Mathematics, History, Economics, and Physics are 11.11%, 17.78%, 20%, 17.78%, 20%, and 13.33% respectively of the sum of his scores in the six subjects taken together.)

1. Who scored the second highest total marks in the six subjects combined?
   (a) Rohan (b) Raju
   (c) Shyam (d) Cannot be determined
2. In how many subjects out of 6, did at least two students out of the given six students score exactly 70 marks?
   (a) 0 (b) 1
   (c) 2 (d) More than 2
3. Which of the following was not the total score of any of the six friends?
   (a) 400 (b) 360
   (c) 440 (d) 450
4. In which subject was the sum of the marks scored by the six students taken together the third highest?
   (a) Mathematics (b) History
   (c) English (d) Marathi

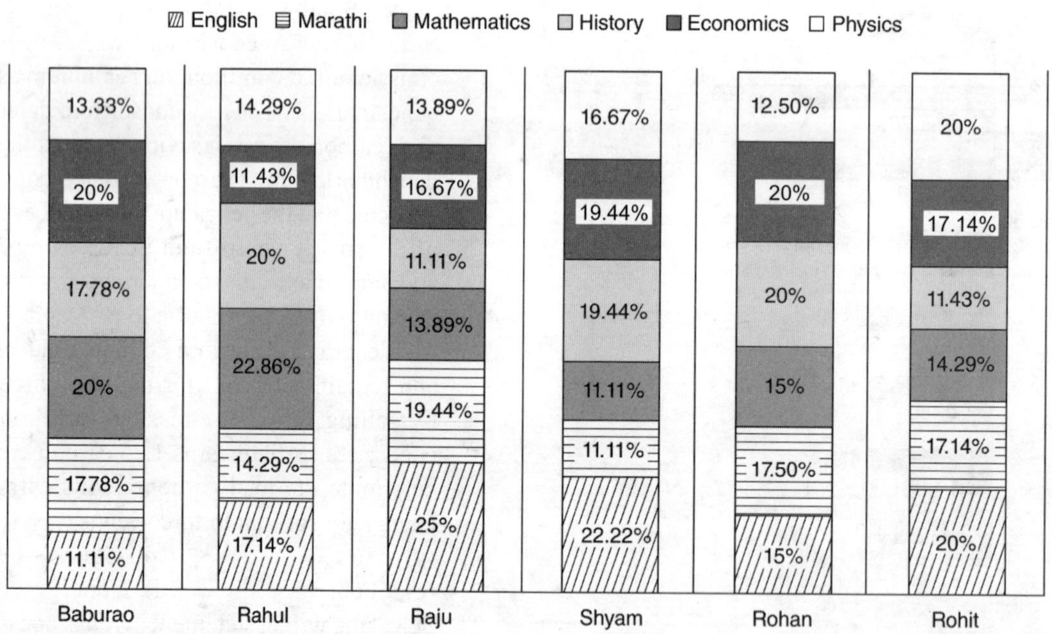

Directions for Questions 5 to 8: *Seven colleges, named A, B, C, D, E, F and G participated in a science competition. In the competition, a number of quizzes were arranged, and, in each quiz, the first three ranked colleges were awarded 5, 3 and 1 points respectively. The following bar graphs shows the college wise distribution of the quizzes in which the colleges received 5 points, 3 points or 1 point.*

3 Points

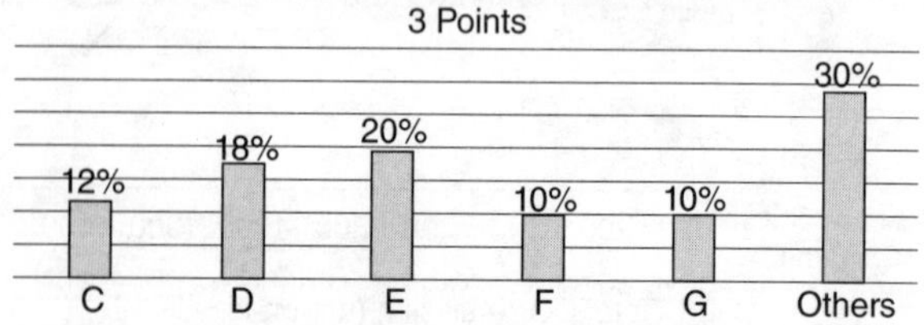

5 Points

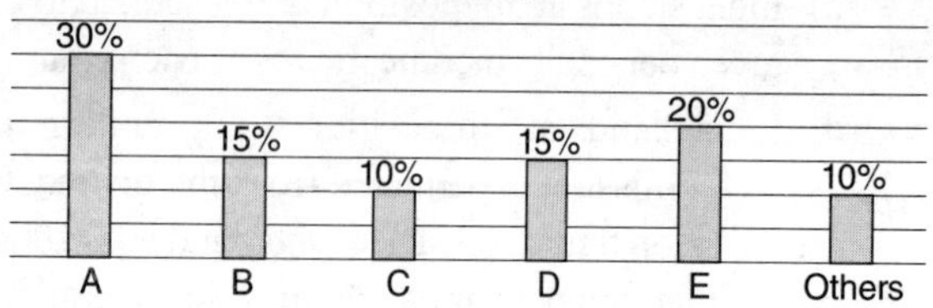

1 Point

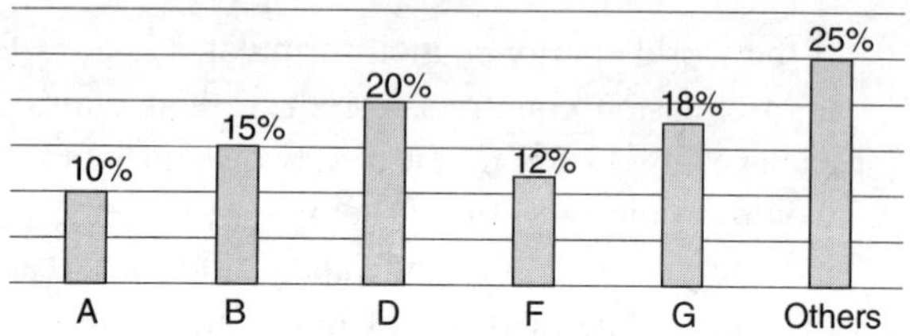

5. Which of the following could be the sum of the number of quizzes in which college F was awarded 3 points and 1 point?
   (a) 229 (b) 363
   (c) 374 (d) 588
6. Total points received by college D was at least what percentage of total points received by college B?
   (a) 93.25% (b) 77.25%
   (c) 82.77% (d) None of these
7. In all 500 quizzes were offered in the competition. Given that in each graph, the 'others' category belonged to exactly one college. What could be the maximum possible difference between points scored by colleges A and F?
8. In all 500 quizzes were offered in the competition. Which of the following cannot be the points received by college E?
   (a) 800 (b) 960
   (c) 925 (d) 924

Directions for Questions 9 to 12: *Urban Health Index of a city is computed on the basis of three parameters: Weight (W), Height (H) and Volume (V) of Bone. Parameters are ranked on a scale of 0–8. A family is then categorized based on the total score obtained by summing the scores of all the three parameters, as shown in the following table:*

Total Scores	0 to 4	5 to 8	9 to 13	14 to 19	20 to 24
Category	Bad	Very Bad	Average	Good	Very Good

The following diagram depicts the frequency distribution of the scores in W, H and V of 10 families – Smith, Jones, Williams, Miller, Clarks, Scott, Collins, Campbell, Bell and Murphy:

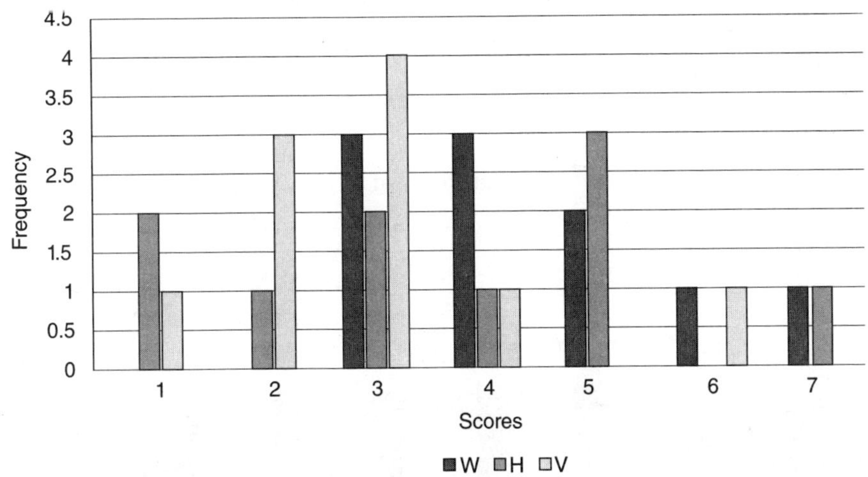

Further, the following are known:

(i) Smith and Jones jointly have the lowest total score, 7, with identical scores in all the three parameters.
(ii) Murphy has a total score of 17.
(iii) All the 3 families, which are categorized as Good, have the highest score in exactly one parameter.

9. What is Smith's score in H?
10. What is Murphy's score in W?
11. Williams and Miller, two families are categorized as good, are tied with the same total score. What is the best score they can achieve?
12. If Williams scores 16 and Miller scores 15, then what is the maximum number of families with a score of 13?

Directions for Questions 13 to 16: *Two rivers X and Y flowing in the same direction met at a point C and a new river Z is created. Z is flowing in the same direction. In river X, the distance between point A and C is 24 kms and in river Y, the distance in-between B and C is 18 kms. D is a point in river Z. The speed of the stream in all three rivers is equal.*

Swimming speed of 5 people is given in still water.

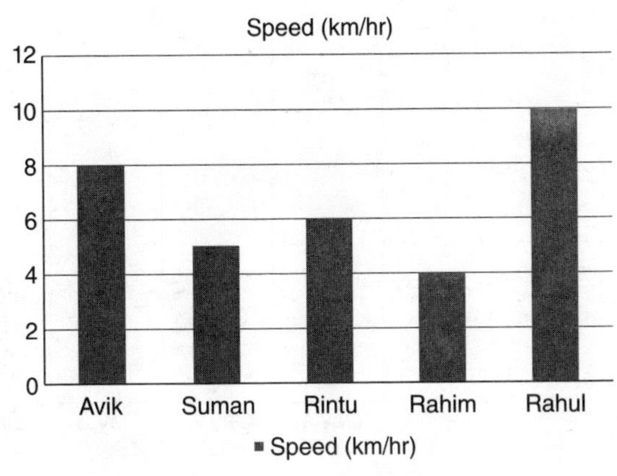

13. The speed of the stream is 4 km/hr. Suman is swimming from point A and Rahul is swimming from point B. How much earlier will Rahul reach point C than Suman?
(a) 1 hour
(b) 1.24 hours
(c) 1.12 hours
(d) 1.38 hours
14. Rintu is swimming from point C to A and Rahul is swimming from B point to C. They started journey at the same time. If Rintu finished his journey after 22 hours 48 minutes of the journey finished by Rahul, find the speed of stream.
(a) 6 km/hr
(b) 5 km/hr
(c) 2 km/hr
(d) None of these
15. Avik starts his journey from point B and goes to point A via point C. If the speed of the stream is 2 km/hr, find the time required to finish the total journey.
(a) 5.8 hours
(b) 6.2 hours
(c) 8 hours
(d) None of these
16. Rahul is swimming from point D to A. He finishes his journey in 10 hrs. What is the distance from C to D if the speed of the stream is 3 km/hr?
(a) 46 km (b) 41 km
(c) 40 km (d) 56 km

Directions for Questions 17 to 20: *The following bar-graph provides information about the number of shorts and t-shirts sold by a garment company on an online platform Fashion First in eight days – day 1 to day 8 of the sale period in October 2020. However, on each day some garments sold by the company were returned by the customers. The following bar-chart provides information about the aggregate number of shorts and t-shirts sold by the company and the number of shorts returned by the customers on each of the given eight days.*

All the shorts and t-shirts not returned by the customers are said to be accepted by the customers.

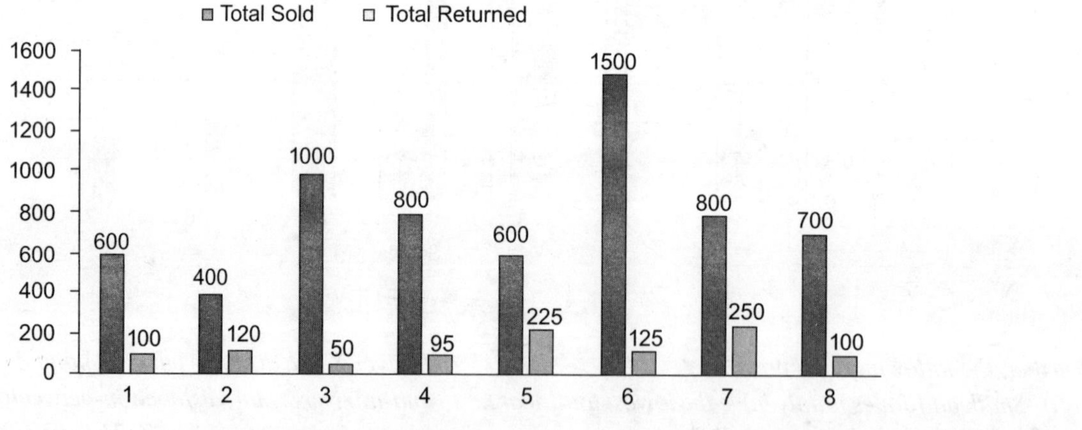

The bar chart given below provides information about the fraction of the number of t-shirts returned to the number of t-shirts accepted by the customers.

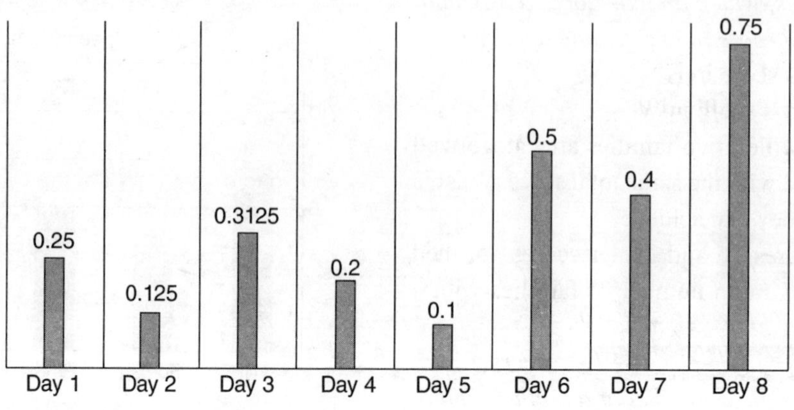

17. If the number of t-shirts accepted by the customers on each of the given eight days is same, then at least how many shorts were accepted by the customers on day 2?
18. On how many of the given eight days, the number of shorts accepted by the customer can be 0?
19. Which of the following can be the ratio of number of shorts and t-shirts accepted by the customers on day 1?
(a) 3:1 (b) 4:1
(c) 5:1 (d) 6:1
20. If the number of t-shirts accepted by the customers on each of the given eight days is the same and is equal to X, then how many distinct values of X are possible?

Directions for Questions 21 to 24: *Jacob rated 50 teams in a dance competition, each on the scale of 1 to 5, on four parameters, theme, creativity, coordination and choreography. The following bar graph provides the number of teams that were given each rating in each parameter.*

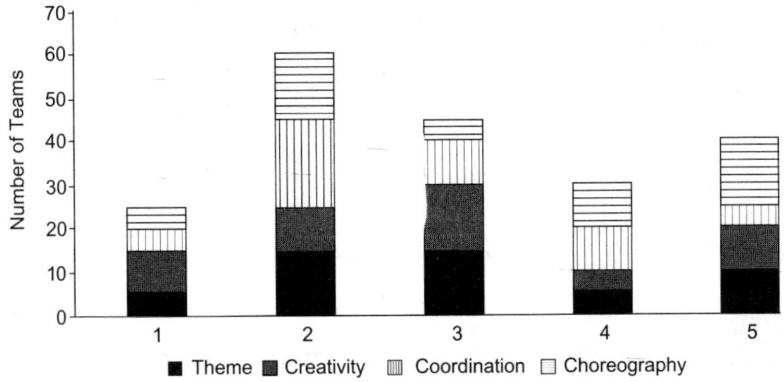

Note: Each of the values in the bar chart is a multiple of 5.

It is known that:
(i) The rating of any team in creativity was not greater than its rating in choreography.
(ii) The rating of any team in coordination was not greater than its rating in theme.

21. What is the maximum number of teams which have the same rating in both coordination and theme?
22. What is the maximum number of teams which are rated 2 in creativity, 2 in choreography, 3 in theme, and 2 in coordination?
(a) 4
(b) 5
(c) 7
(d) 0
23. What is the maximum number of teams which have the same rating in all the four parameters?
24. What is the maximum number of teams which have distinct ratings in all the four parameters?

Directions for Questions 25 to 28: *Ten students, A through J, appeared in a test which contained 20 questions in it. Each correct answer resulted into (+3) marks and each wrong answer attracted a penalty of 1 mark. A question left unattempted did not result in any marks. Following graph shows the scores obtained by each one of these ten students.*

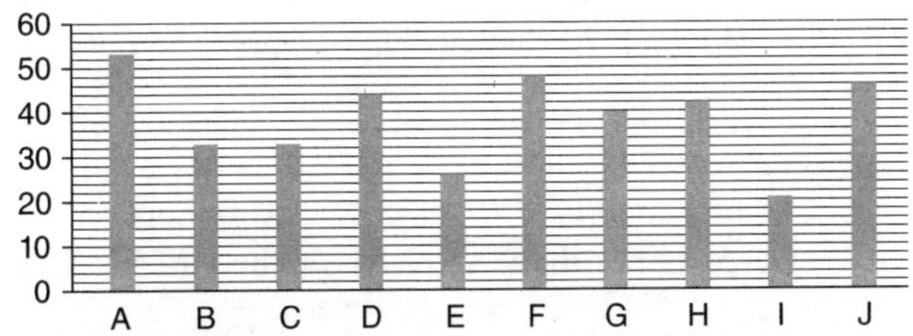

It is also known that:
(i) Out of these ten students, exactly five were boys and sum of their scores was 198.
(i) The difference between the lowest and the highest scores obtained by boys was equal to the difference between the lowest and the highest scores obtained by girls.
(iii) No two boys as well as no two girls scored the same number of marks.

25. What is the difference between the maximum and the minimum number of correct answers for boys?
26. At most, how many girls could have attempted all the 20 questions?
27. If one of the girls attempted exactly 14 questions then who amongst the following is definitely a boy?
(a) B (b) C
(c) F (d) G
28. For how many of these ten students is it not possible to determine the exact value of the number of questions answered correctly by them?
(a) 9 (b) 8
(c) 7 (d) 6

ANSWER KEY

Level of Difficulty 1

1. (d)	2. (c)	3. (b)	4. (b)	5. (b)	6. (d)	7. (c)
8. (b)	9. (a)	10. (c)	11. (b)	12. (a)	13. (b)	14. (d)
15. (b)	16. (d)	17. (b)	18. (b)	19. (b)	20. (b)	21. (c)
22. (c)	23. (d)	24. (a)	25. (a)	26. (a)	27. (d)	28. (d)

Level of Difficulty 2

1. (c)	2. (a)	3. (b)	4. (c)	5. (c)	6. (d)	7. (c)
8. (d)	9. (c)	10. (c)	11. (c)	12. (a)	13. (c)	14. (d)
15. (b)	16. (a)	17. (d)	18. (b)	19. (b)	20. (c)	21. (b)
22. (c)	23. (d)					

Level of Difficulty 3

1. (a)	2. (c)	3. (c)	4. (b)	5. (c)	6. (c)	7. 1040
8. (b)	9. 1	10. 6	11. 15	12. 1	13. (d)	14. (b)
15. (a)	16. (a)	17. 10	18. 1	19. (c)	20. 3	21. 40
22. (b)	23. 30	24. 10	25. 6	26. 2	27. (d)	28. (b)

SOLUTIONS

Level of Difficulty 1

1. The total students in 2010 can be seen to be 170 out of which 20 students have cleared the CAT. It converts to a percentage of $\frac{20}{170}\times 100 = 11.76\%$.
2. Out of a total of 170 students, 140 students have cleared either the CAT, XAT or the CMAT. The required percentage would be $\frac{140}{170}\times 100 = 82.35\%$.
3. Compare the respective pass percentages for the three years. $\frac{140}{170} < \frac{150}{180}$ and $\frac{150}{180} > \frac{160}{200}$
4. $\frac{30\times 100}{170}$ = 17.64 (approximately).
5. On the surface this looks like a very calculation intensive question. You would need to find the totals of the two years and then find the difference between the two and then divide it by 5 to get the difference in the average sales. Instead of this, a shorter process would be to look at the absolute differences between the sales values for each brand (using + sign for an increase in sales, and a – sign for a decrease in sales). This would give us (ignoring the decimals in the calculations):
   $-275 - 163 + 50 - 82 - 242 = -712$. Hence the difference in the averages would be $-712/5 = -142.4$.
   Note: Here since the question asks about the difference, you can drop the negative sign while checking the options. **Difference between two numbers is always a positive value.** The closest answer is option (b).

   Note: In this case since there is a none of these as one of the four options, you might need to finally account for the differences in the decimals too to see whether you would get the actual answer – this check would make you absolutely sure about the answer. When you do so, you can see that the decimals account for: $+0.12 - .32 - .87 + 0.29 + 0.35 = -0.43$. The average comes out as $-0.43/5 = -0.08$.

   Hence, the adjusted answer would be $-142.4 - 0.08 = -142.48$, which means the difference is 142.48.

   However, even if you do not do this last calculation exactly, you would need to be very very unlucky to get an incorrect answer in this case – even with the presence of the 'none of these' option in the set of options.
6. GM should have increased its sales turnover by ₹49.13 crore. Hence, the answer is: 913.63 + 49.13 = 962.76
7. Hyundai with a difference of 242 on 962 (ignoring the decimal values) is exhibiting a percentage change of slightly more than 25% (1/4th). The only company that comes close is Honda ,which has a difference of 275 on 1122, which is slightly less than 1/4th or 25%. Hence, Hyundai is the correct answer here.

8. Before solving this question, you might want to check out the degree of accuracy you would want to use in this case. Since, the percentages given in the options are at distances of 2–3% from each other, you can realize that you would not need quite exact calculations in this question. Since you have already calculated the difference between the sums of the two years in Question 5 (came out to be 712, remember), you can just work out the total for 2011–12 to calculate the percentage change. The total of 2011–12 (ignoring the decimals and the last digit) is 960 + 1170 + 680 + 910 + 1120 = 4840. ***Note:*** Do this addition as: 900 + 1100 + 600 + 900 + 1100 + 60 + 70 + 80 + 10 + 20 = 4840. The required percentage change we get is 712/4840 = 14.6%. Option (b) is the closest and the only feasible option.
9. We have already calculated this to be 712.43. Option (a) is correct.
10. Solvc this using the assumed average approach explained in the section 'How to think in Traditional Data Interpretation', in Part 2 of Section 1 of this book. If you assume 462 (USA's value) to be the average, you would get a deviation of – 157 – 35 + 203 → giving you a net deviation of only +11. Thus, the value of USA is the closest to the average. **Note:** If you were to assume 427 (UAE's value as the average), the deviation would increase as it would be given by: –122 + 35 + 238 = +151 which is clearly much larger than the deviation we get by assuming the USA's value as the average. Hence, USA's value is the closest to the average surplus of the four countries.

   Of course, you could also solve this using the actual calculation of the average. Thus, the average surplus is given by $\frac{1860.4}{4} = 465.1$.
11. The deficit of the first 5 deficit countries is 3594.3 + 776.8 + 514.1 = 3500 + 700 + 500 + 94 + 76 + 14 + 0.3 + 0.8 + 0.1 = 4885.2. The deficit of all the 13 countries is 3594.3 + 2588.5 + 334.2 = 3500 + 2500 + 300 + 94 + 88 + 34 + 0.3 + 0.5 + 0.2 = 6517.

   The ratio of 4885.2/6517 can be seen to be close to 3/4. In order to see whether this value is below 3/4 or more, we can look for a number thrice of whose value would give us 4885.1. Approximately, this number is 1628 (three times 1628 = 4884). If we add 1628 or thereabouts to 4885, we get a value of 6513 to 6514. Since the actual denominator is greater than 6514, we can clearly deduce that 4885.1/6517 is a ratio just smaller than 3/4. The next step would be to decide whether this value below ¾ is going to be so far below that we would need to change our answer to 0.72 from 0.75. If you consider the difference from 6514 to 6517, you can clearly see that there is a very minute difference (in terms of percentage this difference is about 0.05%). However, if you look at the difference between 0.75 and 0.72 in terms of percentage, you clearly see that this difference in terms of percentage is quite large comparatively (0.03/0.75 = 3/75 = 4%).

   Hence, we reject 0.72 as the correct answer and stick to 0.75.
12. The middle five deficit countries are India, New Zealand, South Africa, Korea and Namibia. Their average deficit is 1946.6/5 = 389.32. Korea's deficit is the closest to this value.
13. The total deficit of the 13 countries we already know as 6517 (from our calculations of Question 11. The total surplus of the 4 countries is 1860.4 (from our calculations of Question 10). The required answer would bc 6517 – 1860.4 = 4656.6 deficit. Option (b) is correct.
14. The required answer will be equal to 360/94 = 3.83 (approximately).
15. Out of a total of 12 countries, 8 showed a deficit while 4 showed a surplus.
16. Visually it is clear that L has the highest trade deficit.
17. I has a ratio of 4002/2744 = 1.45, which is the highest.
18. Sum of exports–sum of imports = deficit (11286).
19. 6045/87 = 69 (approximately).
20. Services accounts for 20%, i.e., 1/5th of the GDP of India.
21. 20% of 10000 = 2000.
22. (40 + 20 + 10)% of 30,000 = ₹21,000 crore.
23. Although the percentage on services and miscellaneous put together is equal for both the countries, we cannot comment on this since we have no data about the respective GDPs.
24. Since the GDP is same, the answer will be got by (40 – 20)/20 = 100%.
25. Production in 2022 = 450.

   Half the production = 225.

   Production in 2020 = 300.

   Three-fifth of production of company A in year 2020 = (3/5) × 300 = 180.

   According to question

   The required percentage by which 225 is greater than 180 = $\frac{(225 - 180)}{180} \times 100 = 25\%$.
26. Required average = (220 + 460 + 280)/3

   = 960 ÷ 3

   = 320.

27. In year 2024, total sold products = 1.10 × 460 = 506
 Total unsold products 100 + 450 = 550.
 Total production in year 2014 = 506 + 550
 = 1056.
28. Required sum
 = (420 + 660) + (420 × 1.2 + 660 × 1.25)
 = 420 × 2.2 + 660 × 2.25
 = 924 + 1485 = 2409.

Level of Difficulty 2

Solutions for Questions 1 to 5:

In any DI set, you need to first identify the set of variables that are given to you and based on that, you then identify the set of variables that can be derived. You need to understand that, for any set of DI questions, the questions asked will always seek to extract information from you about the given variables or the derived variables.

Once you have identified the variables (given and derived) you also need a clear understanding of the formulae connecting the variables that are part of the question set.

The key understanding in this question is that the given variables, we have here are: Population density in 2002 and 2008 and the area of the country (which is the same for both the years). You should be able to recognise the following formulae and relationships that exist here:

Population in 2002 (for any country)
 = Population density in 2002 × Area (in sq km);
Population in 2008 (for any country)
 = Population density in 2008 × Area (in sq km).

1. Since for all countries, the area remains same over the two years, 2002 and 2008, then if population density has increased from 2002 to 2008, population has increased and if population density has decreased, then population has decreased. The number of countries having their population density in 2008 more than that in 2002 is 6 (except Bulgaria and Ukraine).
2. Population of Myanmar in 2008 = 70 × 680000. Population of Myanmar in 2002 = 62 × 680000. The increase in population of Myanmar = (70 – 62) × 680,000, i.e., 8 × 680,000 = 5,440,000, i.e., 5.44 mn.
3. The population of Burkina Faso in 2002 = 46 × 280000. The population in 2008 = 56 × 280000. (Using the formula: Population density × area = Population.)
 However, we do not need to calculate the entire multiplied values in this case. Since, the area has remained the same in 2002 and 2008, the percentage increase in the population is same as the percentage increase in the population density. Thus, the required percentage growth is percentage growth from 46 to 56, i.e. 10/56, i.e., 17.8%.
4. The country with the largest population is going to be one that has a higher population density as well as a higher area. Looking for this combination in the graph, the choices are narrowed down to Ukraine and Myanmar. (Each of the rest of the countries has both the area and the population density lower than one of these two countries.)
 Population of Ukraine in 2008 = 76 × 600 = 45600 thousand.
 Population of Myanmar in 2008 = 70 × 680 = 47600 thousand.
 Thus, in 2008, the highest population is of Myanmar.
5. The Area per person is the reciprocal of population density.
 So it will be the highest for the country which has the lowest population density. In the year 2002, the country is Nicaragua.

Solutions for Questions 6 to 9:

Step 1: Understanding the Variables involved. In the first chart, the chart shows us the trade deficit or surplus of the country (as a percentage of GDP). So, the variables (given and hidden) that are underlying this data are:

Deficit/Surplus as a percentage of GDP (given in the first chart) × Actual value of the GDP = Actual value of the trade deficit/surplus.

Note: While reading this data, you should realise that until and unless you get the actual value of the GDP, you cannot make any calculations of the actual value of the deficit/surplus.

The second chart gives us the value of GDP growth rates for the given 6 countries for the years 2003–08. The formula used to calculate GDP growth rate in year

$$1 = \frac{\text{GDP in year 1} - \text{GDP in year 0}}{\text{GDP in year 0}} \times 100$$

6. Since we do not know the actual GDP values for any of the countries, we cannot have any idea of the value of the cash deficits for the countries. Hence, the answer to this question is option (d).
7. To solve this question, we have to understand the equation construct through which the variables

used in this question are connected. The value of cash deficit for a country for a particular year is: Value of cash deficit in a particular year = Absolute value of GDP × % cash deficit. The percentage growth rate of this value can be calculated using the percentage changes on each component and using them under a PCG structure for product change. (This thought structure is given in the part on Calculations development in this book and also explained in the percentage chapter of my book How to Prepare for QA for CAT.) Alternately, this can also be calculated using the formula $[a + b + ab/100]$, where 'a' is the percentage change in the first part of the product, 'b' is the percentage change in the second part of the product.

Looking at the options …

India: The growth rate in deficit will be a little more than 9.4% (since there is very little percentage growth in deficit).

Czech Republic: Growth rate of GDP in 2005 is 6.2% and the growth rate in deficit as a percentage of GDP (from 3.25 to 3.5) is 0.25/3.25, i.e., 1/13, i.e., 7.7%. Thus, the growth rate in deficit will be $6.2 + 7.7 + (6.2 \times 7.7)/100 \approx 13.9 + 0.4 \approx 14.3\%$.

Egypt: Growth rate of GDP in 2005 is 4.6% and the growth rate in 'deficit as a percentage of GDP' (from 5.5 to 6.5) is 1/5.5, i.e., approximately 18%. Thus, the growth rate in deficit will be $4.6 + 18 + 0.8 = 23.4\%$.

Thus, the largest growth rate in deficit will be for Egypt.

8. Since the ratio of GDP's of Poland and Czech are not known for any of the years, this ratio cannot be determined.
9. Using the same process as used in the question on percentage growth of cash deficits (2 questions ago).

   In 2008, Egypt's GDP grew by 7.2%. and the percentage growth in 'deficit as a percentage of GDP' from 2007 to 2008 (from 4.5 to 6.5) is 2/4.5, i.e., 4/9, i.e., 44.44%.

   Thus, the growth rate in the deficit = $44.44 + 7.2 + (44.44 \times 7.2)/100$, i.e., 51.64 + approx 3, i.e., 54.64% (approx).

Solutions for Questions 10 to 13:

Step 1: Understanding the Variables involved.

In this question, it is crucial to understand that the bar charts do not show the scale on which the measurements are done. Of course, since all the bars refer to populations of the four cities you should make the following connections between the three charts:

1. If you take the scale on the Y-axis of the first graph to be 'x', then the population of city P will be $2x + 2x = 4x$. Population of city Q = unmarried + married = $3x + 5x = 8x$; population of city R = $4x + 6x = 10x$; and population of city S = $3x + 5x = 8x$.
2. It can be noticed that the scale of the gender chart (second chart in the question) is also the same, since the sum for male and female adds up to the same heights. Thus, on the Y-axis on the gender chart, we can use the same 'x' as the height of an individual marking on this axis.
3. On the third chart, if we look at the sum of employed and unemployed, for city Q, we see that the sum of heights there is 4. On the first two charts the sum for Q was 8 each. Thus, we can understand that the scale of the Y-axis in the employment chart is double that of the other two charts. That is, a height of 1 on the third chart is equal to a height of 2 on the first two charts. Hence, if we take the scale as 1 unit as 'y' units on the Y-axis we can see that for city Q (for instance) employed + unemployed = $2y + 2y = 4y$. But the total population for city Q according to the scale used in the first two graphs is $8x$. Thus, the population of $4y = 8x \rightarrow y = 2x$.

10. The total represented by the bars for each city is the same. Let each gridline in marital status chart be x.

    Total number of unmarried 480 million.

    Therefore, $2x + 3x + 4x + 3x = 480$ million $\rightarrow x = 40$ million

    Total population of city S = $3x + 5x = 8x = 320$ million.

    The correct answer is 320.
11. The total represented by the bars for each city is the same. Let each gridline in marital status chart be x and each gridline from employment chart be y.

    For city Q. $3x + 5x = 2y + 2y$.

    Therefore, $y = 2x$.

    Number of people employed in city Q = $2y = 4x$.

    Number of unmarried in city Q = $3x$.

    Required percentage = $4x/3x$ = 133.33%.

    The correct option is (c).
12. In city P, unemployed population = $y/2 = x$.

    Number of unemployed males = unemployed females = $x/2$.

    Number of males = $2x$.

    Number of employed males = $2x - x/2 = 3x/2$.

    Similarly in city Q, employed males = $5x - 2x = 3x$.

In city R, employed males $6x - 2x = 4x$.
In city S, employed males $= 3x - 3x = 0$.
Hence, city R has the maximum number of employed males.
The correct option is (a).

13. In city P, females $= 2x$ and unmarried $= 2x$ and employed $= 3x$. Therefore, there can be a maximum of $2x$ female unmarried employees. (Minimum of $2x$, $2x$, and $3x$.)
In city Q, females $= 3x$ and unmarried $= 3x$ and employed $= 4x$. Therefore there can be a maximum of $3x$ female unmarried employees.
In city R, females $= 4x$ and unmarried $= 4x$ and employed $= 6x$. Therefore there can be a maximum of $4x$ female unmarried employees.
In city S, females $= 5x$ and unmarried $= 3x$ and employed $= 2x$. Therefore there can be a maximum of $2x$ female unmarried employees.
Hence, city R can have the maximum number of female unmarried employees.

14. This question can be visually solved as it can be seen that the automobile production has gone down twice during the period which is for the years 2005 and 2008. Of these the year 2008 shows a higher percentage decrease.
Option (d) is correct.

15. The production for the five years is seen as: 1775, 1700, 2175, 2325, 2200.
In the same years, the domestic sales were: 1450, 1525, 1925, 2025, 1875.
Based on exports = production – domestic sales we see that the exports for the 5 years were:
325, 175, 250, 300 and 325.
From these numbers it can be seen that the highest growth in exports has been registered for 2006 when it has gone from 175 to 250. Option (b) is correct.

16. The total revenues can be calculated by assuming passenger vehicles to cost 3 each, commercial vehicles to cost 5 each and three wheelers cost 2 each.
In such a case, the revenues from each of these can be tabulated as under:

Year	Passenger Vehicles	Commercial Vehicles	3 Wheelers
2004	2100	2250	600
2005	2025	2500	700
2006	2700	3125	800
2007	3150	3000	750
2008	2925	2750	700
Total Revenues	12900	13625	3550

Commercial vehicles contribute 13625 out of 30075, or 136 out of 300 which is close to 45%.
Option (a) is correct.

17. In the years 2004–08, the domestic sales were: 1450, 1525, 1925, 2025, 1875. This is a total of 8800 over 5 years which gives an average of 1760. 2008 is the year closest to this value of the average.
Option (d) is correct.

18. From the numbers for domestic sales, viz.,1450, 1525, 1925, 2025, 1875 we can clearly see that the highest percentage increase in sales was for the year 2006 when the value went from 1525 to 1925 a growth of close to 30% which is much higher than the other growth percentages in this series of numbers. Option (b) is correct.

19. The production for the five years is seen as: 1775, 1700, 2175, 2325, 2200.
In the same years, the domestic sales were: 1450,1525, 1925, 2025, 1875.
The required ratios are:
2005: need not be considered because production increase is a negative value in this year.
2006: 400/475 = 0.8+.
2007: 100/150 = 0.66+.
2008: need not be considered because production increase is a negative value in this year.
2006 is the year when the ratio is maximum.
Option (b) is correct.

20. For the US, the CO_2 emissions would drop to $1200 \times 7/8 \times 7/8 = 1200 \times 49/64$ = a drop of 1/8th of its value twice $\rightarrow$ 1200 would become 1050 and then approx 918.
Its per capita income in the same time would move from 300 to 306 and then to 312.12.
The required ratio of CO_2 emissions to per capita GDP would be given by 918/312 = 2.9 approx.
For China a similar analysis would give us 903/ 292 = 3.1 approx.
For Japan the same ratio would be 861/255 = 3.4 approx. Option (c) is correct.

21. The target reduction for the two countries can be seen to be:
For US: drop from 1200 to 225 – a drop of 975 units.
For China: drop from 1180 to 202 – a drop of around 978 units.
It can also be estimated that since the number of carbon credits that can be purchased per year is 65 (at the max.), the emission can only be compensated by around 65/2.5 = 26 units per year.
It would take close to 38 years to get the CO_2 emissions for these countries to the desired level.

22. Let us first do a sample calculation for France. France's current CO_2 emission is 450, which would drop by 50% as the ratio of Carbon emission to per capita income is becoming half as per the problem. This value would become 225 and give it a carbon saving of 125 tonnes against the benchmark standard of 350.
For all the five countries the benchmark standard would be 1750, against which the total carbon emission after the 50% drop would be 1025, a carbon saving of 725 units.
In the next year when per capita income rises by 2%, since the ratio of CO_2 emissions to per capita income remains constant, the CO_2 emission would also rise by 2%. Thus, the CO_2 emissions for all the 5 countries in the first year would be 1045, a saving of 705 tonnes. The next year this value of 1045 would rise by 2.5% to 1071, a saving of 679 tonnes and in the third year the savings would be dependent on an increase of 3.5% in carbon emissions from 1071. The carbon emission would become 1108, a saving of 1750 – 1108 = 642 tonnes.
The total saving in the three year period is: 2026 tonnes. Since the ratio of conversion of a CO_2 emission saved to a carbon credit earned is 0.5 : 1.25. i.e., 1 : 2.5, 2026 tonnes of carbon saving would mean 5065 carbon credits. Option (c).
23. Option (d) can be seen to be false, as if you make the reduction of 200 to CO_2 emissions and add 50 to GDP for all countries the ratio for the countries would be as shown in the table.

US	China	Russia	Japan
1000/350	980/320	880/310	925/290
Italy	**France**	**S. Africa**	**Australia**
300/220	250/210	250/190	150/215
India	**Germany**	**UK**	**Canada**
300/250	700/310	600/230	400/240
Spain	**Ukraine**	**Poland**	
300/275	200/235	200/245	

It can be seen that Poland, Ukraine, Australia having a ratio less than 1 would rank above India. Since India's ratio is 1.2, France and Spain would also be ranked above India. Hence, India would not be fifth in this situation in terms of the ranking with respect to the CO_2 to per capita income ratio.

Level of Difficulty 3

Set 1: Basic Understanding of the Data: As explained in the question, the basic understanding of the data is that each bar represents the total score of an individual student (i.e., the 100% of each bar shows the sum of all the scores of the particular student in all subjects). Thus, if we look at Rohan's bar chart, the lowest part of the bar (i.e., 15%, tells us that of the total score Rohan scored in all 6 subjects, he scored 15% of that in English). Other deductions follow as we look at Rohan's bar: He has 15% in Mathematics and 20% each in History and Economics – which means that his score in English and Mathematics would be equal (say x) and his scores in History and Economics would also be equal (say y). Further the value of 'x' would be 3/4th the value of 'y'. This we can correlate to the other information contained in the question: 'it is known that the marks scored by the students in each of the subjects can be only one integer out of the following: 40, 50, 60, 70, 80 and 90'. This helps us conclude that $x = 60$ and $y = 80$, since those are the only numbers possible such that $x = 3/4$th of y.

1. In order to solve this question, we would need to find out the total scores for each of the six individuals. The following deductions would lead us to the answer:
Deduction 1: Consider percentages given for Shyam. Shyam scored 11.11% in Marathi and Mathematics and 22.22% in English. So he must have scored 80, 40 and 40 marks in English, Marathi and Mathematics. As he scored maximum in English, he must have scored less than 80 in the remaining subjects. Since 11.11 = 40,we can make out that 16.67 = 60 and 19.44 = 70. Thus, we can conclude that his scores in History, Economics and Physics must be 70, 70 and 60 respectively.
Deduction 2: Consider percentages given for Rahul. Rahul scored 11.43% of his total marks in Economics and 22.86% in Mathematics. So his score in Economics and Mathematics must be 40 and 80 respectively (since his Mathematics score is double his Economics score – and the only two numbers that have a relationship of doubling are 40 and 80). As his maximum score is 80 (i.e., 22.86%), (20%, 17.14%, 14.29%) corresponds to (70, 60 and 50).
Deduction 3: Consider percentages given for Raju. That is 25%, 19.44%, 16.67%, 13.89% and 11.11% – i.e., he has 5 different scores out of the possible 6 (40, 50, 60, 70, 80 and 90). Hence his lowest score of 11.11% corresponds to either 40 or 50. If it corresponds to 50, then 22.22% would be 100 and there would be no value for 25%. So, 11.11% must be 40 marks. So, 25%, 19.44%, 16.67%, 13.89% correspond to 90, 70, 60 and 50 marks respectively.
Deduction 4: Consider percentages given for Baburao, i.e., 20%, 17.78%, 13.33% and 11.11%. 11.11% must be equivalent to 40 or 50 marks, i.e., 100% must be equivalent to 360 or 450 marks. This then means that 20% = 72 or 90 marks. As 20%

cannot be 72, 20%, 17.78% and 13.33% correspond to 90, 80 and 70 respectively.

Deduction 5: Consider percentages given for Rohan, i.e., 20%, 17.5%, 15% and 12.5%. The only possibility is 20% corresponds to 80 and hence 17.5%, 15% and 12.5% correspond to 70, 60 and 50 respectively.

Deduction 6: Consider Rohit. Since he has four different percentages, his 20% of English and Physics has to be either 70, 80 or 90. It cannot be equal to either 80 or 90, since in both these cases we do not get a feasible value for the other percentages (from amongst 40, 50, 60 and 70). Only if we take the 20% = 70, do we get the other numbers matching the situation. Therefore, 20% = 70, and 17.14%, 14.29% and 11.43% correspond to 60, 50 and 40 marks respectively.

Therefore, we have the following table to encapsulate the information:

	English	Marathi	Mathematics	History	Economics	Physics	Total
Baburao	50	80	90	80	90	60	450
Rahul	60	50	80	70	40	50	350
Raju	90	70	50	40	60	50	360
Shyam	80	40	40	70	70	60	360
Rohan	60	70	60	80	80	50	400
Rohit	70	60	50	40	60	70	350
Total	410	370	370	380	400	340	

From the above derived table we can say that Rohan scored the second highest total marks in the six subjects combined.

The correct option is (a).

2. Correct Answer: (c)
   This is happening in the subjects of Marathi and History. Hence, option (c) is correct.
3. Correct Answer: (c)
   Nobody has scored 440 marks and is evident from the table.
4. Correct Answer: (b)
   Again this is evident from the table.

Solutions for Questions 5 to 8:

Basic Understanding of the Data: From the first bar chart, we can read that in 30% of the total quizzes, college A scored 5 points. In 15% of the total quizzes, college B scored 5 points and so on. Likewise, the reading of the second bar chart of the question tells us that college C scored 3 points in 12 per cent of the total quizzes, while college D scored 3 points in 18% of the total quizzes and so on. The third bar chart tells us that A scored 1 point in 10% of the total quizzes, while B scored 1 point in 15% of the total quizzes and so on.

Another thing to notice for all the three bar charts is the others bar. In the first chart, we are given individual information about A, B, C, D and E. For colleges F and G, the individual information is not available. However, the other 10% shows that F and G together scored 5 points in 10% of the total number of quizzes. In the second chart, the 30% in the others bar is the combined value of the percentage of quizzes in which A and B scored 3 points. In the third bar chart this value is 25% and corresponds to the percentage of quizzes in which colleges C and E scored 1 point. Armed with this understanding, we can move into the questions for the set.

5. Let there be a total of X quizzes. In each of these X quizzes one or the other of the colleges were awarded 5 points, 3 points or 1 point.
   Number of quizzes in which college F was awarded 3 points and 1 point put together 10% of X + 12% of X = 22% of X.
   22% of X = 11X/50 must be an integer. Possible values of this expression could be 11, 22, 33, 44, 55 or any other multiple of 11.
   Looking at the options, we can see that the values in the options (a) and (d) are not multiples of 11. (229 and 588 are not multiples of 11).
   The key to distinguish between the other two options, is to find the value of X for each of the options and check whether all the percentage values across the three bar charts are integers or not.
   For option (b) 11X/50 = 363, X = 1650, but 15% of 1650 is not an integer (which will mean that if X is 1650, B scored 5 points in 15% of the quizzes → B scored 5 points in 247.5 quizzes, which is not possible). Hence, we reject option (b).
   For Option (d) 11X/50 = 374, X = 1700.
   It can be checked that all other values are integers.
   Hence, the correct option is (c).

6. In order to solve this question, you need to look at how many points college D got, and at the maximum, how many points college B got. Let there be a total of X quizzes. In each of these X quizzes one or the other of the colleges were awarded 5 points, 3 points or 1 point.
Points received by college D = 0.15X × 5 + 0.18X × 3 + 0.2X × 1 = 0.75X + 0.54X + 0.2X = 1.49X.
If college B accounts for entire 30% in Others Category of quizzes in the 3 points category, then the points received by college B (maximum possible) = 0.15X × 5 + 0.30X × 3 + 0.15X × 1 = 0.75X + 0.9X + 0.15X = 1.8X.
Required percentage = (1.49/1.8) × 100 = 82.77%
The correct option is (c).
7. It is given that 500 quizzes were offered.
College A received 5 points in 30% quizzes (150 quizzes) and 1 point in 10% quizzes (50 quizzes).
Amongst the colleges receiving 3 points, college A is a part of 'others' category.
The maximum possible points scored by A (i.e., if A accounts for this entire 30% in 'others') would be 150 × 5 + 150 × 3 + 50 × 1 = 1250.
The minimum possible points scored by A (i.e., if B accounts for this entire 30% in 'others').
150 × 5 + 150 × 0 + 50 × 1 = 800.
College F might be a part of 10% colleges counted in 'others' amongst those colleges who received 5 points. Also, college F received 3 points in 10% quizzes and 1 point in 12% quizzes.
The maximum possible points scored by F (i.e., if F accounts for this entire 10% in 'others').
= 50 × 5 + 50 × 3 + 60 × 1 = 460.
The minimum possible points scored by F (i.e., if G accounts for this entire 10% in 'others').
= 0 × 5 + 50 × 3 + 60 × 1 = 210.
0.48X = 210.
Therefore, the required maximum possible difference = 1250 – 210 = 1040.
The correct answer is 1040.
8. It is given that 500 quizzes were offered.
College E might be a part of 25% colleges counted in 'others' amongst those who received 1 point. Also, college E received 5 points in 20% quizzes (100 quizzes out of 500) and 3 points in 20% quizzes (100 quizzes out of 500).
Thus, E scored: Maximum: 100 × 5 + 100 × 3 + 125 × 1 = 925.
Minimum: 100 × 5 + 100 × 3 + 0 × 1 = 800.
Points received by college E has to be between 800 and 925 (both inclusive).
The correct option is (b).

Solutions for Questions 9 to 12:

Basic understanding of the data: Let us first draw a frequency table from the frequency bar chart: The table would look as follows:

Scores	W	H	V
1		2	1
2		1	3
3	3	2	4
4	3	1	1
5	2	3	
6	1		1
7	1	1	
Total	10	10	10

From the bar chart or this table, we can deduce that two families have a score of 1 in parameter H, while 1 family has a score of 1 in parameter V. Likewise 1 family has a score of 2 in H and 3 families have a score of 2 in V and so on.

Also, from the clues that follow, the bar chart in the question: 'Smith and Jones jointly have the lowest total score, 7, with identical scores in all the three parameters'.

Deduction 1: We can deduce that: Smith and Jones could total 7 only in two ways: 4, 2, 1 or 3, 3, 1. In either situation, since a score of 1 is only evidenced twice in the converted table above, we can conclude that both the families must have scored '1' in H.

Next from the statements (ii) and (iii) we get:

Deduction 2: The highest score in each parameter is 7(W), 7(H) and 6(V). These scores have to be given to the three different families that belong to the good category and have scored between 14 and 19 points. Also, using the numbers available, 17 for Murphy can be constructed as: 7 + 7 + 3; 7 + 6 + 4; 7 + 5 + 5 or 6 + 6 + 5. In this situation, if we correlate with the extracted table above, and clue (iii) we should be able to see that 17 is possible under the following cases:
Case 1: 7(H) + 6(W) + 4(V) (***Note:*** 7(W) + 6(V) + 4(H) is not possible since in this, Murphy family has the highest score in two parameters, which is not allowed. 7 + 7 + 3 is also not possible for the same reason.)
Case 2: 6(W) + 6(V) + 5(H).

Note: There is no other case possible for Murphy family to score 17 points – 7 + 5 + 5 is also not possible, since 5's are only available under W and H, and if we use them, we do not have a 7 in parameter V.

With these deductions you can answer Questions 9 and 10.

9. We can answer this question only on the basis of deduction 1 above. Smith must have a '1' score in parameter H.
10. The answer to this question can be read off from deduction 2 above. Murphy scores 6 points in parameter W in both its possible cases.

Solving Questions 11 and 12 requires further analysis from this point.

Case 1: If Murphy scores: 7(H) + 6(W) + 4(V), the available scores left in the various parameters (with their frequency would be):

Scores	W	H	V
1		2	1
2		1	3
3	3	2	4
4	3	1	0
5	2	3	
6	0		1
7	1	0	
Total	10	10	10

In this case, Williams and Miller would share the 7 of W and the 6 of V between them. One of them can reach a maximum of 7(W) + 5(H) + 3(V). The other can reach a maximum of 6(V) + 5(H) + 5(W). If they had the same total score, both of them would be able to score a maximum of 15 points.

In case 2, if Murphy scores 6(W) + 6(V) + 5(H) the available scores left in the various parameters (with their frequency would be):

Scores	W	H	V
1		2	1
2		1	3
3	3	2	4
4	3	1	1
5	2	2	
6	0		0
7	1	1	
Total	10	10	10

If we try to maximise both of them at a total score of 16, it is not possible, since 16 can only be constructed using 7 + 5 + 4, where the 4 would necessarily be in V. But V can contribute 4 only once, and hence 16 can be reached by only 1 family.

11. Thus, both the families can score a maximum of 15 points each, if they are scoring the same number of points. The correct answer is 15.
12. Since, the 7's and 6's are completely used in both case 1 and 2, in constructing the scores for Williams, Miller and Murphy, it follows that a score of 13 can only be achieved by 5 + 5 + 3 or 5 + 4 + 4.

In either of the cases, 5 + 4 + 4 cannot be used to get to 13 (since V's 4 would be used in constructing one of the three 'good' families scores). It is also seen that the 5's of W and H are used once and twice in case 1 (refer to the table for case 1 and the explanation about it). This would leave only one 5 each for W and H. Hence, in case 1, 5 + 5 + 3 structure can be made for only one family. A similar analysis in case 2 yields the same outcome. Hence, the correct answer is 1.

Solutions for Questions 13 to 16:

13. Suman has to cover 24 kms and Rahul has to cover 18 km to the point C. Rahul's speed would be 10 + 4, while Suman's speed would be 5 + 4. Suman would take 24/9 hours, while Rahul would take 18/14 hours. The time difference (required answer) = 24/9 – 18/14 = (336 – 162)/126 = 174/126 hours = 1.38 hours.
14. Rintu needs to cover 24 km, while Rahul 18 kms. Also, Rintu is moving upstream, while Rahul is downstream.

    This forms an equation as:

    $$\frac{24}{6-x} - \frac{18}{10+x} = 22.8$$

    On solving we get $x = 5$.

    So the answer is 5 km/hr.
15. (a). Avik will travel from B to C (18 km downstream) and C to A (24 km upstream). Avik's total time taken would be given by:

    $$\frac{18}{8+2} + \frac{24}{8-2} = 5.8 \text{ hours or 5 hours 48 minutes.}$$
16. The river is flowing from A to C to D. Rahul is swimming from D to C to A. Hence, Rahul is swimming upstream.

    Let the distance D to C be '*d*'. We know that C to A is 24. Also Rahul's swimming speed in still water is 10 km/hr. Hence, the speed upstream with a river speed of 3 km/hr (given) would be 10 – 3 = 7 km/hr.

    Thus, the total distance he covers in 10 hours is 10 × 7 = 70 kms. This is equal to 24 + d. Hence, d = 70 – 24 = 46 kms.

Solutions for Questions 17 to 20:

Understanding the data:

In order to control your solution to this set, you need to be able to spot the variables inside this set. There are 4 basic variables in this set: Number of t-shirts sold on each day (S_T); Number of shorts sold on each day (S_S); Number of t-shirts returned on each day (R_T); Number of shorts returned on each day (R_S). From these four basic variables, the following additional variables emerge:

Variables derived from the four basic variables:

1. Total units sold on each day ($S_T + S_S$). (This number is given to us for each of the days in the first bar chart.)
2. Total units accepted on each day for t-shirts ($S_T - R_T$). (Needs to be worked out – not given directly, since we know neither S_T nor R_T).
3. Total units accepted on each day for shorts ($S_S - R_S$). Again this one needs to be worked out, since we do not know S_S individually.
4. Total units returned each day ($R_T + R_S$). Again not known.

On the first bar chart, we are given two variables – one of which is the derived variable 1 – total units sold on the day; The other variable provided to us in the first bar chart is the value of the number of shorts returned by the customers on the day (R_S).

In the second bar chart, we have a ratio given to us. Understanding the ratio is important for us in order to solve this question. The ratio is the ratio of:

$\frac{\text{T-shirts returned}}{\text{T-shirts accepted}} = \frac{R_T}{S_T - R_T}$. Thus for instance on day 1, we can see that this ratio is given to us as 0.25. This means that if 4 t-shirts were accepted, 1 was returned. This also means that for every 1 t-shirt returned, 5 were sold. Similar deductions can be made for all other days, and we can proceed to do those for all days.

Day 1: Assume the number of t-shirts returned as 'a'. Then, the number of t-shirts accepted would be $4a$. Consequently, the number of t-shirts sold $= a + 4a = 5a$.

On similar lines, if b, c, d etc. are the number of t-shirts returned on days 2, 3, 4 etc. we can fill the table as follows:

Day	No. of Shorts Sold	No. of Shorts Returned	No. of Shorts Accepted	No. of T-Shirts Sold	No. of T-Shirts Returned	No. of T-Shirts Accepted
1	600-5a	100	500-5a	5a	a	4a
2	400-9b	120	280-9b	9b	b	8b
3	1000-21c	50	950-21c	21c	5c	16c
4	800-6d	95	705-6d	6d	d	5d
5	600-11e	225	375-11e	11e	e	10e
6	1500-3f	125	1375-3f	3f	f	2f
7	800-7g	250	550-7g	7g	2g	5g
8	700-7h	100	600-7h	7h	3h	4h

17. Given that the number of t-shirts accepted by the customer on each of the eight days is same, and let it be X.
$4a = 8b = 16c = 5d = 10e = 2f = 5g = 4h = X$.
LCM of 4, 8, 16, 5, 10 and 2 = 80.
Therefore, X = 80 or its multiple.
$a = 20k$, $b = 10k$, $c = 5k$, $d = 16k$, $e = 8k$, $f = 40k$, $g = 16k$ and $h = 20k$, where k is a natural number.
When $k = 1, 2$ and 3, the number of shorts accepted on days 1 to 8 > 0.
When $k = 4$, the number of shorts accepted on day $2 = 280 - 9b < 0$, which is not possible.
Thus, the maximum value of $k = 3$.
When $k = 3$, $b = 240/8 = 30$. The number of shorts accepted on day $2 = 280 - 9b = 280 - 270 = 10$.
Hence, the correct answer is 10.
18. 1. From the table; if we equate the values in the column 'Number of shorts accepted' to 0, we can see that only on day 1, we get $a = 100$, an integer value. For all other days, we do not get integer values for the values of b to h.
Hence, the correct answer is 1.
19. For day 1, the value of 'a' is a multiple of 20. (Since, $4a = 80k \rightarrow$ 'a' is a multiple of 20.) Thus, 'a' can be 20, 40, 60, 80, 100 and so on. The ratio of number of shorts accepted to the number of t-shirts accepted $= (500 - 5a)/4a \rightarrow$ This works out to 5:1 and hence, the correct answer is option (c).
20. Given that the number of t-shirts accepted by the customer on each of the eight days is same, and let it be X.
$4a = 8b = 16c = 5d = 10e = 2f = 5g = 4h = X$.
LCM of 4, 8, 16, 5, 10 and 2 = 80.
Therefore, X = $80k$ (a multiple of 80).
We can see that, for k = 1, 2, 3 the value of all the numbers in the table are positive and hence possible.
For $k = 4$, we get $8b = 320 \rightarrow$ 'b' becomes equal to 40. In such a case $280 - 9b$ will become negative.
Hence, there are 3 possible values of X (80,160 and 240 for k = 1, 2 and 3 respectively).

Solutions for Questions 21 to 24:

Basic understanding of the data: Since there are a total of 50 teams rated, we can see that the sum of rating scale 1 +

rating 2 + rating 3 + rating 4 + rating 5 = 50 (for each of theme, creativity, coordination and choreography).

Thus, from the bar chart we can create the following table:

Number of teams rated according to parameter.

Rating	1	2	3	4	5
Theme	5	15	15	5	10
Creativity	10	10	15	5	10
Coordination	5	20	10	10	5
Choreography	5	15	5	10	15

21. It is given to us that for all the teams, the rating in coordination ≤ rating in theme
All the 5 teams with a rating of 5 in coordination, would have a rating of 5 in theme too. These 5 teams would have the same rating of 5 in coordination and theme.
Next, if we look at the 10 teams with rating of 4 in coordination, out of these 10 teams, 5 would have a rating of 5 in theme, while the remaining 5 would have the same rating of 4 in theme too.
Similarly, thinking of rating 3 – there are 10 teams with a rating 3 on coordination, and each of these 10 would have rating 3, (since they cannot take a lower rating than 3 in theme).
The number of teams with rating 2 in coordination and theme, both would be 15; For rating 1, it would be 5.
The correct answer = 5 + 5 + 10 + 15 + 5 = 40.
22. In order to solve this, we would first need to see how many teams are ranked 2 in both creativity and choreography.
It is given to us that for all the teams, the rating in creativity ≤ rating in choreography.
Teams rated 5 in creativity (10) have to get a rating of 5 in choreography. Teams rated 4 in creativity (5 teams) can be rated either 4 or 5 in choreography. Teams rated 3 in creativity (15) have to all be rated 3, 4 or 5 in choreography. At this point – 30 teams rated 3, 4 or 5 in creativity would have corresponding ratings of 3, 4 or 5 in choreography. This means that the 10 teams rated 2 in creativity, would have rating 2 in choreography (compulsorily). In the previous question, we have seen that teams with rating 2 in coordination and 3 in theme, are 5.
Since there is no information on the link between these two pairs of ranks, we can take the maximum number of teams which satisfy all the four ranks to be 5. The correct option is (b).
23. From our deductions for the previous two questions, we have seen that:
The number of teams with rank 5 in both creativity and choreography is 10; while the number of teams with rank 5 in both theme and coordination is 5. Thus, the maximum number of teams with rank 5 in all parameters would happen if all the 5 teams with rank 5 in theme and coordination, also have a rank 5 in creativity and choreography. This works out to a maximum possible 5 such teams.
For 4, in all parameters: Maximum 5;
The maximum number of teams with rank 3 in all parameters = 5.
The maximum number of teams with rank 2 in all parameters = 10.
The maximum number of teams with rank 1 in all parameters = 5.
The maximum number of teams with same rank in all parameters = 5 + 5 + 5 + 10 + 5 = 30.
The correct answer is 30.
24. The number of teams with rank 5 in creativity and any other rank in choreography = 0.
The maximum number of teams with rank 4 in creativity and any other rank in choreography = 5 (these 5 teams can have rank 5 in choreography).
The number of teams with rank 3 in creativity and any other rank in choreography = 10 (these 10 teams can have rank 4 in choreography).
The number of teams with rank 2 in creativity and any other rank in choreography = 0.
The number of teams with rank 1 in creativity and any other rank in choreography = 5 (these 5 teams will have rank 2 in choreography).
Hence, for these two parameters, there are 5 teams with rank 4 in creativity and rank 5 in choreography; 10 teams with rank 3 in creativity and rank 4 in choreography; 5 teams with rank 1 in creativity and rank 2 in choreography.
The number of teams with rank 5 in coordination and any other rank in theme = 0.
The number of teams with rank 4 in coordination and any other rank in theme = 5 (these 5 teams will have rank 5 in theme).
The number of teams with rank 3 in coordination and any other rank in theme = 0.
The number of teams with rank 2 in coordination and any other rank in theme = 5 (these 5 teams will have rank 3 in theme).
The number of teams with rank 1 in coordination and any other rank in theme = 0.
Hence, for these two parameters, there are five teams with rank 4 in coordination and rank 5 in theme; five teams with rank 2 in coordination and rank 3 in theme.

Hence, there can be five teams with rank 4 in coordination, rank 5 in theme, rank 1 in creativity and rank 2 in choreography and another five teams with rank 2 in coordination, rank 3 in theme, rank 4 in creativity and rank 5 in choreography.

There can be maximum of 10 teams with four distinct ranks.

The correct answer is 10.

Solutions for Questions 25 to 28:

25. The scores are: 53, 48, 46, 44, 42, 40, 33, 33, 26 and 21.

We have to divide these 10 scores into two groups (one of the boys and the other of the girls) such that each groups has 5 scores.

Let's call these groups as Group 1 and Group 2. From second clue we can determine that 53 and 21 cannot belong to the same group.

Suppose the highest score in Group 1 is 53 and that in Group 2 is 'a'. Also assume that the lowest score in Group 1 is 'b' and that in Group 2 is 21. Then, $53 - b = a - 21$ or $(a + b) = 74$. The only values (other than 53 and 21) satisfying this condition are 48 and 26.

So. Group 1 has 53 and 26 as the highest and the lowest scores respectively, and Group 2 has 48 and 21 as the highest and the lowest scores respectively.

From third clue we can determine that one of the values in Group 1 as well as in Group 2 is 33.

Assume that the other two values in Group 1 are 'p' and 'q', and the other two values in Group 2 are 's' and 't'.

From first clue we can say that either $53 + 33 + 26 + p + q = 198$ or $48 + 33 + 21 + s + t = 198$. Further, we can conclude that either $p + q = 86$ or $s + t = 96$. But of the remaining four values (46, 44, 42 and 40) no two values can add up to 96 and that is sufficient to rule out the second case. So, $p + q$ has to be 86. But, that can happen in two ways in the given situation:

Case 1: p, q are 46, 40 → Group of boys: (53, 46, 40, 33 and 26) and Group of Girls: (48, 44, 42, 33 and 21).

Case 2: p, q are 44, 42 → Group of boys: (53, 44, 42, 33 and 26) and Group of Girls: (48, 46, 40, 33 and 21).

Now see the following table which shows all the possible combinations of number of right and wrong answers for each of the ten students.

Name	Score	(Right, Wrong)	Remark
A (Boy)	53	(18, 1)	
F (Girl)	48	(16, 0), (17, 3)	
J (Boy or Girl)	46	(16, 2)	
D (Boy or Girl)	44	(15, 1), (16, 4)	If J and G are boys then D and H are girls and vice versa.
H (Boy or Girl)	42	(14, 0), (15, 3)	
G (Boy or Girl)	40	(14, 2), (15, 5)	
B (Boy or Girl)	33	(11, 0), (12, 3), (13, 6)	If B is a boy then C is a girl and vice versa.
C (Boy or Girl)	33	(11, 0), (12, 3), (13, 6)	
E (Boy)	26	(9, 1), (10, 4), (11, 7)	
I (Girl)	21	(7, 0), (8, 3), (9, 6), (10, 9)	

The minimum number of correct answers by the boys (when D, H are boys) $= 18 + 15 + 14 + 11 + 9 = 67$.

The maximum number of right answers by boys (when J, G are boys) $= 18 + 16 + 15 + 13 + 11 = 73$.

Required difference is $73 - 67 = 6$.

26. Only three students, F, D and G could have attempted all the 20 questions but only two of them can be girls at a time – either F and D or F and G. So, the answer is 2.

27. Only H could have attempted exactly 14 questions and if H is a girl then D is also a girl and in that case G is definitely a boy. Hence, correct answer is option (d).

28. Only for A and J we can determine the exact number of right answers. We cannot determine that for the other 8 students. Hence, correct answer is option (b).

CHAPTER 4

Line Graphs and X-Y Charts

Outline

Learning Objectives

- Get a first-hand view of how data is presented through its organisation in the form of X-Y charts.
- Get an understanding of the typical data which can be represented through X-Y charts. Also understand the concept of time series as it applies to X-Y charts.
- Get a first-hand feel of what are the typical question types that are asked on the basis of X-Y charts.
- Experience higher level questions on line and X-Y charts

Chapter Highlights

- Introduction to X-Y charts.
- Practice exercise on X-Y charts containing simulated examination questions.
- Link between X-Y charts and time-series data.
- LOD 2 and LOD 3 questions to give you a feel of high quality DI questions on line charts.

In Chapter 3, we studied bar charts or bar diagrams as a mode of data presentation. In this chapter, we shall concentrate on *X-Y* graphs as a mode of data presentation. While bar charts are useful for visual presentation of categorical and geographical data, data related to time-series and frequency distribution is best represented through *X-Y* or line graphs. This representation is widely used by newspapers, television, government reports, magazines and research papers.

Besides, *X-Y* graphs are also very useful for determining trends, rate of change and for illustrating comparisons with respect to some time series.

THE TYPICAL DATA SHOWN ON AN X-Y CHART INVOLVES A TIME SERIES

A time series is an arrangement of data on the basis of time, i.e., in chronological order. The time period may be a year, quarter, month, week, days, hours, etc. Time series are extremely essential for the measurement of economic and business performance. Hence, most data relating to economics and business are in the form of time series. In time-series data, time (the independent variable) is seen as a discrete variable while the continuous variable being measured defines the other dependent variable.

Thus, we have continuous variables like the population of a country, GDP of a country, data on exports and imports in an economy, data of production, sales, profit, etc., of a company and so forth, which are measured against time.

Normally time is taken along the *X*-axis and the dependent continuous variable is taken along the *Y*-axis.

As you go through the exercise below you will see examples of various presentations of data, possible through *X-Y* charts. These are listed below for your quick reference. As you go through the exercise, familiarise yourself with the following representations.

Let's start directly with a logical DI set on the same.

EXAMPLE 1

Ted, on Barney's advice, decided to categorize all his dogs on the Cute-Crazy Scale. Till now Ted has purchased 15 dogs and has had some problems with each of his dogs due to which he had to leave them at a shelter. He plotted all the points but forgot to put the names of the dogs and handed over the list to his best friend Barney (That's right Marshall, I am his best friend.). Barney remembers a few things about the Dogs that Ted had in the past which are as follows-

(a) Vicky and Tommy were the only two dogs on the Cute-Crazy Diagonal. However, Barney remembered Ted telling him that Tommy always refused to take baths.

(b) Sheru, Rocky, Holly, Max, Stacy, Robin and Cooper were above the VM Diagonal while Ginger, Cathy, Jack, Tucker, Zoey, Lily were below it.

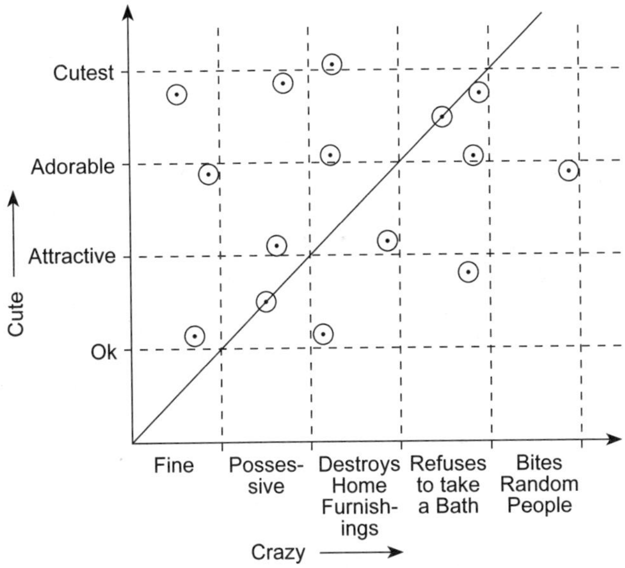

1. If Stacy, Cooper and Sheru were fine and Max, Rocky and Holly more than Adorable, then who could have been the Attractive Possessive Dog of Ted?
   (a) Vicky (b) Stacy
   (c) Cathy (d) Robin
2. If Ginger was the least attractive among all the dogs and Tucker was more Adorable than Lily, who used to bite random people, then who is the Cutest dog who refuses to take baths?
   (a) Max (b) Tucker
   (c) Zoey (d) Cannot be determined
3. In the previous question if it is known that Cathy and Jack were not as attractive as Tommy, then who could have been the Cutest Dog who refuses to take baths?
   (a) Tucker (b) Zoey
   (c) Jack (d) Both (a) or (b)
4. It is known that Robin, Stacy, Max, Sheru, Rocky, Tucker and Lily were more than attractive but less than Cutest. Moreover, Robin and Rocky were possessive, Max, Cathy, Holly and Ginger used to destroy the home furnishings. Also, Tucker, Jack, and Zoey refused to take baths. Then how many dogs lie between Holly and Vicky?
   (a) 9 (b) 10
   (c) 2 (d) Cannot be determined

Solution The first thing you should do is to make

The fifteen dog names are: On the diagonal (2 dogs): Vicky (V), Tommy (T),

Above the diagonal (7 dogs): Sheru (S), Rocky (R), Holly (H), Max (M), Stacy (Stacy), Robin (Robin) and Cooper (C)

Below the diagonal (6 dogs): Ginger (G) , Cathy (Cathy), Jack (J), Tucker (Tucker), Zoey (Z), Lily (L).

1. We can identify from clue A, that T is represented by the second point on the diagonal. This means that V is Possessive. In this question, we are told that Stacy, S and C were represented by the three points above the diagonal and in the fine category of dogs. Also, M,R, and H are above the adorable line. This leaves only one point above the diagonal – and that has to be the remaining dog of the 7 above the diagonal: Robin. Option (d) is correct
2. We do not have enough information to identify the cutest dog who refuses to take a bath. We are only able to identify G as the dog below the diagonal who destroys home furnishings, And Lily as the dog below the diagonal, who bites random people. This means, Tucker has to be above Lily – which gives us two possible points for Tucker (if you see the figure, there are 2 points in the refuses to take a bath column, that are above the point representing the dog that bites random people. The highest point in this column, representing the cutest dog who refuses to take a bath can go to any one of Tucker, Jack, Cathy or Zoey. Hence, we cannot determine the answer to this question. Option (d) is correct.
3. Adding to the deductions of the previous question, we can see that Cathy and Jack would be below Tommy. Hence, now only Tucker and Zoey could be the most adorable dog who refuses to take a bath.
4. From the given information we can make out that Robin and Rocky are the two possessive dogs, Max and Holly are the two dogs above the diagonal and in the destroy home furnishings column; while Cathy and Ginger are below the diagonal in the same column. When you are trying to find the number of dogs between Holly and Vicky, you need to find the number of points that are between them when you go from left to right and also lie between them when you go from bottom to top on the vertical. From the basic information, we know that Vicky is the dog who is represented by the lower leftmost point on the diagonal. However, from the description in this question, we are not able to identify the exact point representing Holly. We only know that she is one of the two dogs above the diagonal in the destroys home furnishings column in the figure. Hence, how many dogs there are between Vicky and Holly is something we cannot find. Hence, the correct answer is (d).

EXAMPLE 2

A survey of 13 classrooms in Bennett University was taken to understand the relation between the number of students and their pocket money spending. The X-Axis shows the number of students in the classrooms, while the Y-axis represents the average monthly pocket-money-spending by the students of the class. Additionally, the average marks of the students in the classes were also taken to check whether it had an influence on the expenditure.

The results can be seen in the chart below.

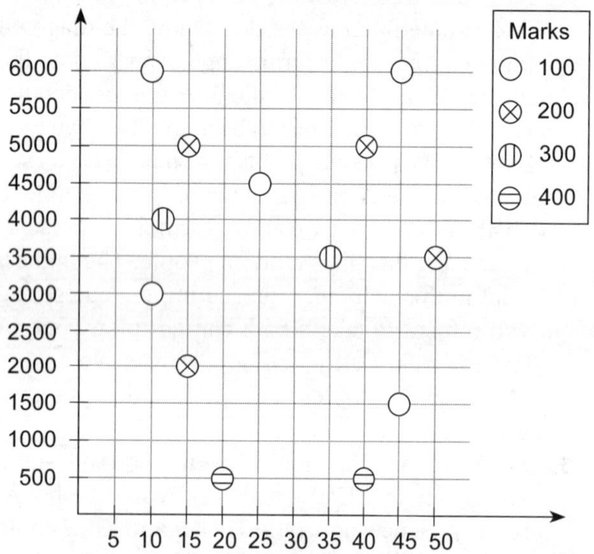

1. What are the average marks per student for the classrooms which have more than ₹ 3000 of expenditure (approximate integer value)?
2. What is the approximate average expenditure per student for classrooms with more than 30 students?
   (a) 3356 (b) 3353
   (c) 2876 (d) 3244
3. What is the difference in total expenditure between classrooms with exactly 40 students and classrooms with exactly 10 students.
   (a) 1,30,000 (b) -1,30,000
   (c) 3500 (d) 1,20,000
4. If the students of the classrooms with an expenditure of 6000 go to the classroom which has an average marks of 100 and an average expenditure of 4500, what will be the average expenditure per student of the new classroom?
   (a) 5470.25 (b) 4781.25
   (c) 5489.75 (d) 5531.25

Solution

1. There are a total of 8 classrooms where the average expenditure is above 3000. The total marks obtained by the students of these classrooms are:
   $10 \times 100 + 15 \times 200 + 25 \times 100 + 35 \times 300 + 40 \times 200 + 45 \times 100 + 50 \times 200 = 39500$.
   The total number of students are 220. Hence, the required average marks for these classes are: $39500/220 = 179.54$. The closest integer value is 180.
2. The total expenditure of all the classrooms (with more than 30 students) can be calculated as the sum of the product of the number of students per classroom and the average expenditure of the students of the classroom. The total expenditure is:
   $35 \times 3500 + 50 \times 3500 + 40 \times 5000 + 45 \times 6000 + 40 \times 500 + 45 \times 1500 = 855000$.
   The total number of students is: $35 + 50 + 40 + 45 + 40 + 45 = 255$.
   The required average is $855000/255 \approx 3353$. Option (b) is correct.
3. The classroom with exactly 10 students has an expenditure of $3000 \times 10 = 30000$ and $6000 \times 10 = 60000$ the total would be 90,000.
   The classroom with exactly 40 students has a total of 5000×40 and $500 \times 40 = 2,20,000$.
   So the difference is 1,30,000. Option (a) is correct.
4. The total expenditure of both classrooms are $(6000 \times 10 + 6000 \times 45) = 3,30,000$
   The total expenditure of the classroom with an average expenditure of 4500 and an average marks of 100 is $4500 \times 25 = 1,12,500$. Now the total Expenditure of the 3 classrooms combined would be 4,42,500 and the total number of students would be $25 + 10 + 45 = 80$
   Hence the average expenditure per student will be $\rightarrow 442500/80 = 5531.25$. Option (d) is correct.

EXAMPLES OF VARIOUS TYPES OF DATA PRESENTATION POSSIBLE THROUGH X-Y CHARTS

1. **Single Dependent (Continuous) Variable Graph:** These graphs show changes in a single variable over a certain period of time.
2. **More than One Dependent (Continuous) Variable Graph:** In this type of graph, two or more lines are drawn to represent tw o or more dependent variables.
3. **Graphs with Two Scales:** When two continuous variables having different units of measurement have to be shown on the same graph, we use two scales on the graph.

4. **Range Graph:** For some specific types of data (such as temperatures, run rates, etc.), it is essential to depict the range of the variation of the variable over a period of time. This is depicted using a range graph, which shows the deviation between different values of the variable under consideration.
5. **Band Graph:** Like a stacked bar chart, the band graph is a line graph used to display the total value of a continuous variable broken up into its different components for each period.
6. **Speed Time Graph:** This is a special case of an X-Y chart where the respective axes show the speed of a moving body against time.

EXERCISE

Level of Difficulty 1

Directions for Questions 1 to 4: Consider the following graph (Figure 4.1) and answer the questions based on it. The graph shows the trend of consumption of metals and plastics in the production of cars between 2007 and 2012.

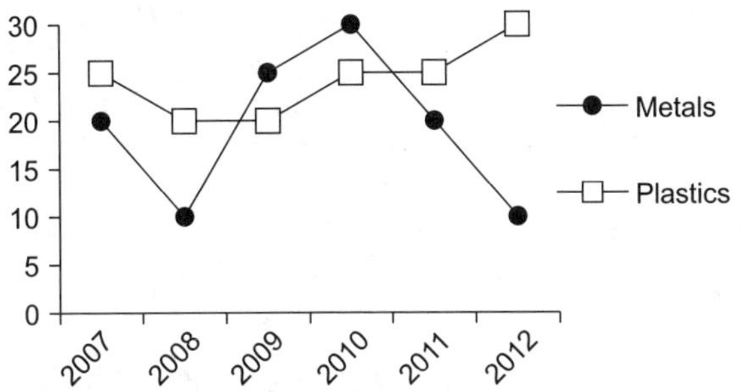

FIGURE 4.1 *Consumption of Metals versus Plastics in the given Years for Car Manufacturing (in thousand tonnes)*

1. The total consumption of plastic (for car manufacturing) divided by the total consumption of metals (for car manufacturing) over the period will give a ratio the closest to:
   (a) 4:3
   (b) 5:4
   (c) 6:5
   (d) 7:4
2. The ratio of the highest total consumption in any single year to the lowest total consumption of the two items taken together in any year was equal to:
   (a) 5:3
   (b) 7:4
   (c) 11:6
   (d) 11:7
3. Which year showed the highest percentage increase in the total consumption of the two metals?
   (a) 2008
   (b) 2009
   (c) 2010
   (d) 2011
4. Which year showed the highest percentage decrease in the total consumption of the 2 items taken together over the previous year?
   (a) 2008
   (b) 2009
   (c) 2011
   (d) 2012

Directions for Questions 5 to 10: Consider the following graph (Figure 4.2) and answer the questions based on it.

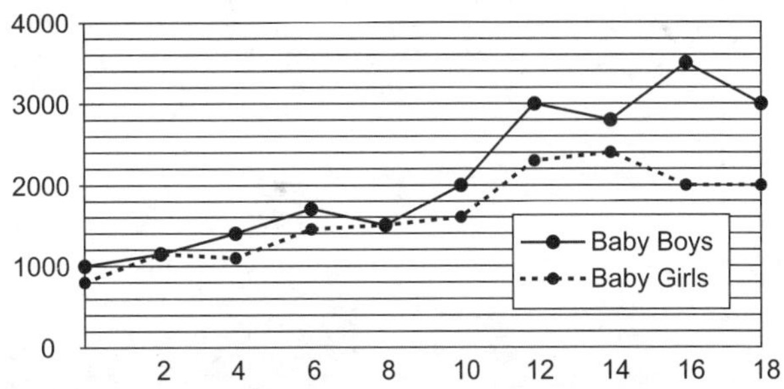

FIGURE 4.2 *Calories Required Per Day by Baby Boys and Baby Girls in the First Eighteen Months of their Lives*

5. At what ages are the requirements of calories for baby boys and baby girls equal?
   (a) 2 months
   (b) 4 months
   (c) 8 months
   (d) 2 months and 8 months
6. The difference between the calorie requirement for baby boys and baby girls at the age of 6 months is approximately equal to:
   (a) 300 calories
   (b) 250 calories
   (c) 400 calories
   (d) 200 calories
7. If in a family there are four baby boys aged 4, 6, 8 and 12 months respectively, and three baby girls aged 2, 8 and 16 months respectively, then what is the total calorie requirement per day for the babies in the family?

(a) 12,100 (b) 12,250
(c) 12,400 (d) None of these

8. For the previous question, if the baby girl aged 16 months goes away, what is the percentage change in the calorie requirement per month for the family?
(a) 16.3% (b) 17.4%
(c) 14.3% (d) 12.2%

9. For the previous questions, if the great doctor Raju informs Ravi that the graphs have got mixed up and what is shown for the baby boys is for the baby girls and vice versa, then the answer for question 10 would have been:
(a) 12,100 (b) 12,250
(c) 12,400 (d) None of these

10. It can be inferred from the graph that in general, calorie requirements for baby boys and baby girls:
(a) are quite different at all ages.
(b) are similar till the age of 17 months.
(c) reaches a peak value at the same age.
(d) increase at nearly the same rate till the age of 13.

Directions for Questions 11 to 13: *Consider the following graph (Figure 4.3) and answer the questions based on it.*

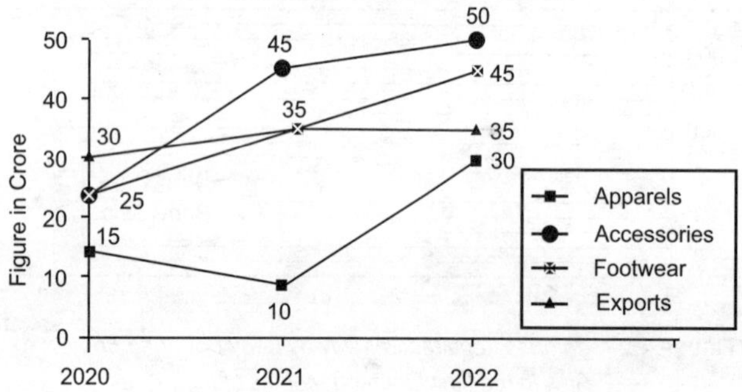

FIGURE 4.3 *Production of Select Leather Industries for the Period 2020-22 (Assume all production is consumed locally.)*

11. The percentage increase in the sales of footwear between 2020 and 2021 was
(a) 20% (b) 30%
(c) 40% (d) 50%

12. In 2011, if 20% of the footwear sold within the country had been additionally exported at the local price, the percentage increase in export income in the period 2020-21 would have been
(a) 20% (b) 30%
(c) 40% (d) 50%

13. If the sales of footwear had touched ₹80 crore in 2012, the average annual percentage growth of footwear for the two year period 2020-22 would have been (approximately):
(a) 50% (b) 75%
(c) 80% (d) 90%

Directions for Questions 14 to 16: *The following graph (Figure 4.4) gives us information about the number of washing machines produced by HLL. Answer questions 14 to 16 based on the graph.*

Note: Figures for 2011 are estimated figures. Also, assume that everything produced is sold in the same year.

14. What was the value of each machine in 2007?
(a) ₹20,000 (b) ₹8,333.33
(c) ₹2,000 (d) ₹833.33

15. What was the percentage drop in the production of the number of machines from 2008 to 2009?
(a) 20% (b) 25%
(c) 27% (d) 32%

16. What was the difference in the value per machine between the years 2007 and 2010?
(a) ₹2,000 (b) ₹5,000
(c) ₹4,000 (d) None of these

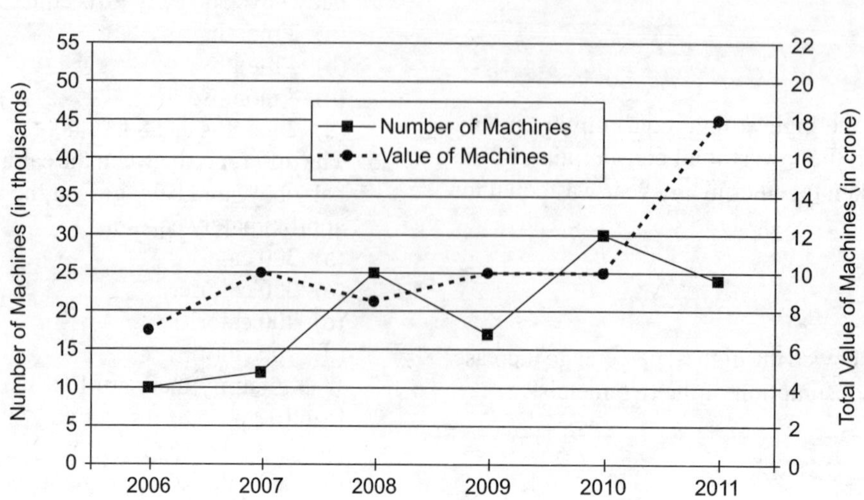

FIGURE 4.4 *Washing Machines Manufactured by HLL*

Directions for Questions 17 to 19: *Use the following graph (Figure 4.5) showing railway finances for the years 1997–98 to 2004–05, to answer the questions given.*

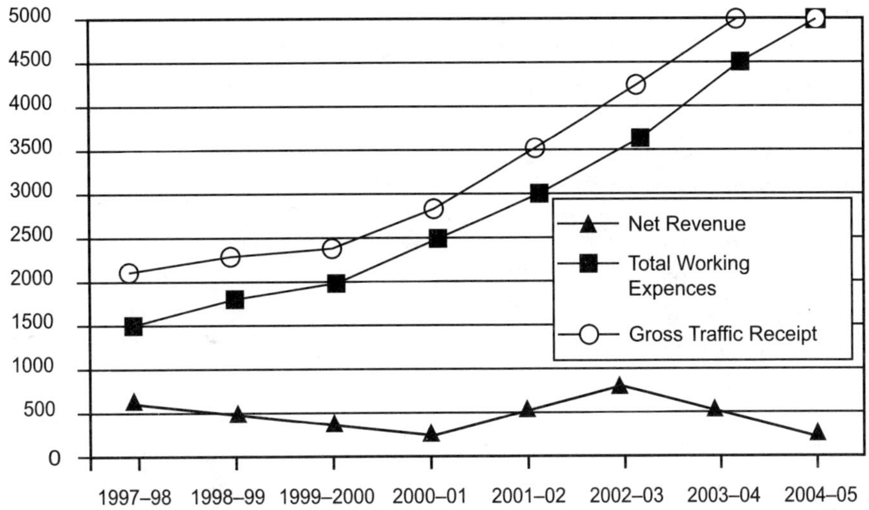

FIGURE 4.5 *Railway Finance: 1997—98 to 2004—05*

17. The difference between the gross traffic receipt and the total working expenses was the highest during which of the following years?
    (a) 1997–98 (b) 2001–02
    (c) 2002–03 (d) 2004–05
18. By what per cent did gross traffic receipts increase between 1997–98 and 2004–05?
    (a) 38% (b) 124%
    (c) 133% (d) 138%
19. Between the years 1997–98 and 1999–2000, the ratio of the increase in gross traffic receipts and total working expenses was:
    (a) 5:3 (b) 3:5
    (c) 2:3 (d) None of these

Directions for Questions 20 to 21: *Observe the given graph (Figure 4.6) carefully and answer the following questions.*

20. The minimum difference between day and night temperatures is:
    (a) 9.5 degrees
    (b) 11.5 degrees
    (c) 9.7 degrees
    (d) None of these
21. The highest ratio of the night to day temperature is for:
    (a) 1st May (b) 3rd May
    (c) 4th May (d) None of these

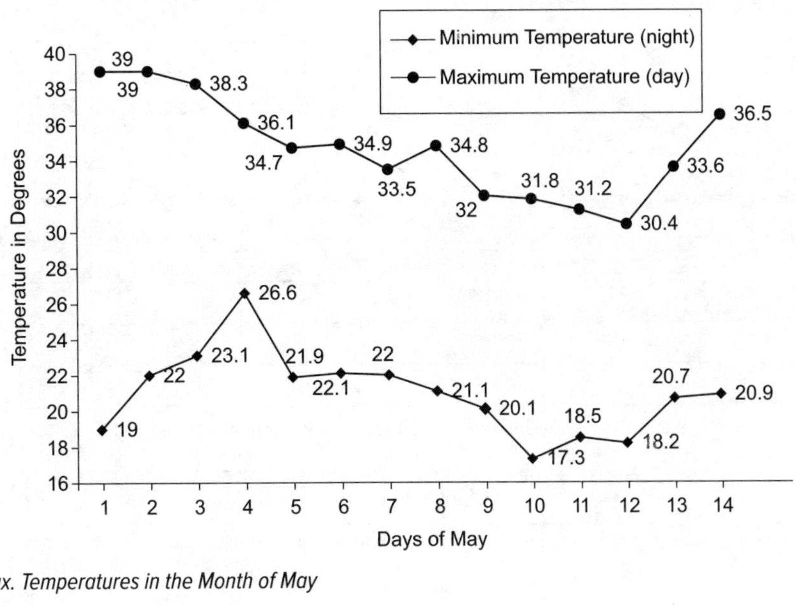

FIGURE 4.6 *Min. and Max. Temperatures in the Month of May*

Directions for Questions 22 to 23: *Study the following graph (Figure 4.7) carefully and answer the given questions. Assume that the curve between any two years marked on the graph is a straight line and the difference between any two years can be got by interpolation. Beyond 2003 the values go up to 2005 and are the projected values for 2004 and 2005.*

22. In 1963, the percentage of HBS students who were engineers was about
    (a) 18% (b) 25%
    (c) 30% (d) 35%
23. Which was the first year when more than 200 students were studying in a batch at HBS?
    (a) 1973 (b) 1978
    (c) 1983 (d) 1985

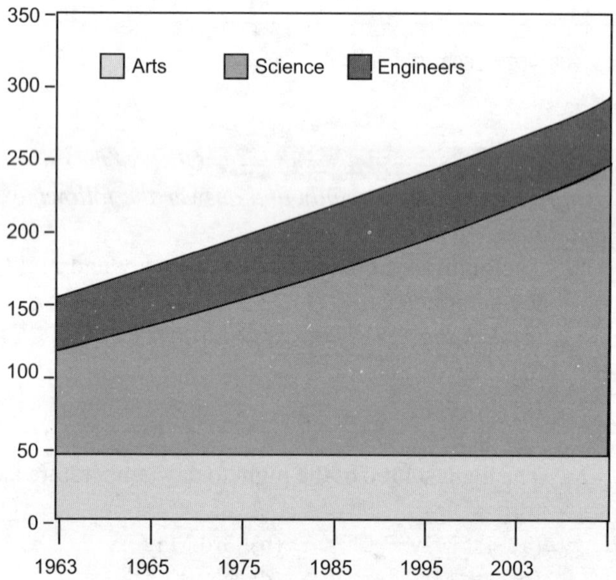

FIGURE 4.7 *Academic Background of Students Joining Harvard Business School (HBS)*

Directions for Question 24: *The following graph (Figure 4.8) gives the movement of a car with respect to time. (Assume that the speed dimension on the Y-axis is marked at every 10 kmph and there is uniform acceleration between hours.)*

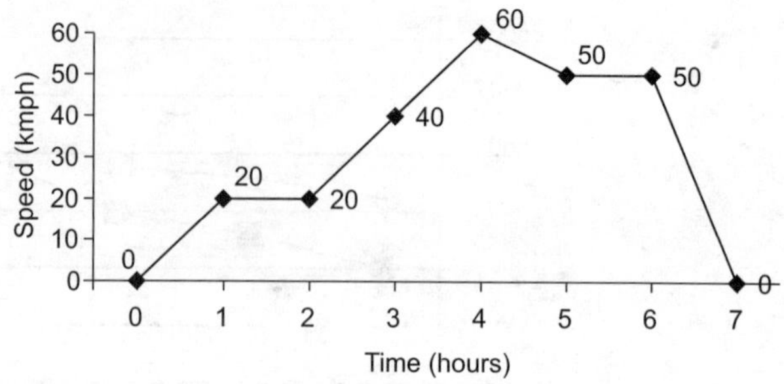

FIGURE 4.8 *Movement of a Car with Respect to Time*

24. Find the average speed of the car (in kmph).
    (a) 36.28
    (b) 34.28
    (c) 33.57
    (d) None of these

Directions for Questions 25 to 28: *These questions are based on the situation given below:*

The figure below presents sales and net profit, in ₹crore, of IVP Ltd. for the five years from 1994–95 to 1998–99. During this period, the sales increased from ₹100 crore to ₹680 crore. Correspondingly, the net profit increased from ₹2.2 crores to ₹12 crore. Net profit is defined as the excess of sales over total costs.

Note: Figure 4.9 has two Y-axis – one on the left representing the sales and the one on the right representing profit. The Y-axis on the right has a scale of 1 unit representing ₹2 crore.

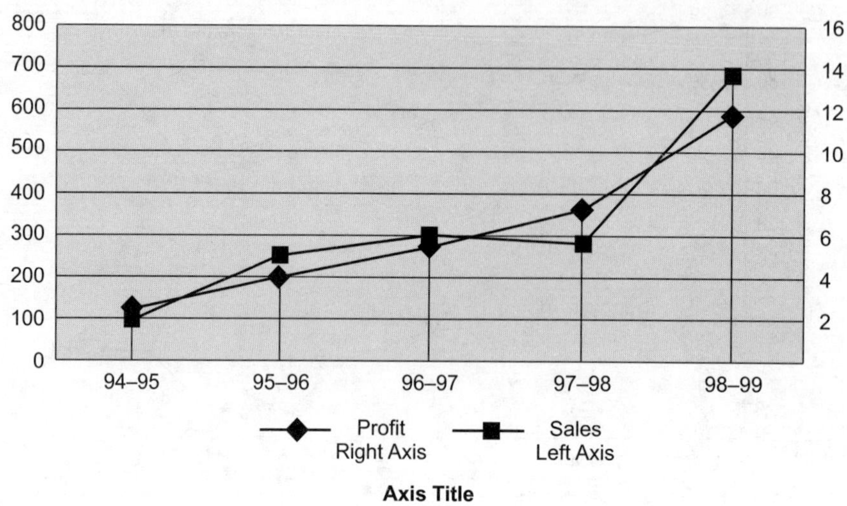

FIGURE 4.9

25. The highest percentage of growth in sales, relative to the previous year, occurred in:
    (a) 1995–96 (b) 1996–97
    (c) 1997–98 (d) Can't be determined
26. The highest percentage growth in net profit, relative to the previous year, was achieved in:
    (a) 1998–99 (b) 1997–98
    (c) 1996–97 (d) 1995–96
27. Defining profitability as the ratio of net profit to sales, IVP Ltd. recorded the highest profitability in
    (a) 1998–99 (b) 1997–98
    (c) 1994–95 (d) 1996–97
28. With profitability as defined in Question 27, it can be concluded that:
    (a) Profitability is non-decreasing during the five years from 1994–95 to 1998–99.
    (b) Profitability is non-increasing during the five years from 1994–95 to 1998–99.
    (c) Profitability remained constant during the five years from 1994–95 to 1998–99.
    (d) None of the above

Directions for Questions 29 to 32: *These questions are based on the price fluctuations of four commodities – arhar, pepper, sugar and gold – during February–July 1999 as described in Figure 4.10.*

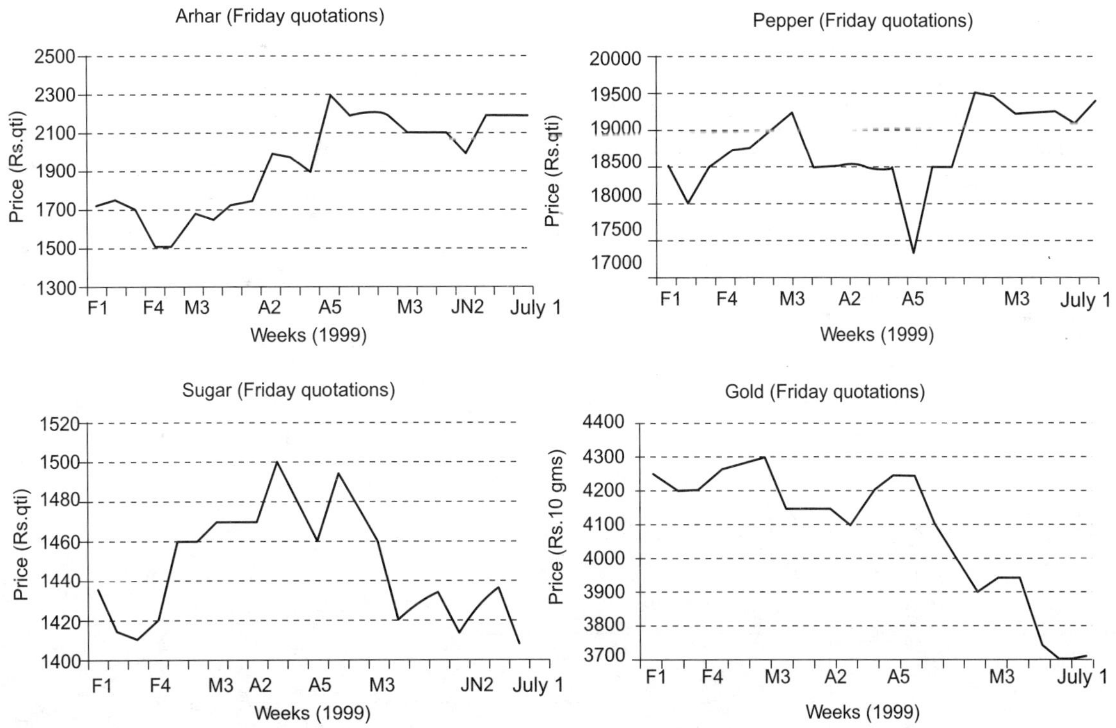

FIGURE 4.10

29. Price change of a commodity is defined as the absolute difference in ending and beginning prices expressed as a percentage of the beginning. What is the commodity with the highest price change?
    (a) Arhar (b) Pepper
    (c) Sugar (d) Gold
30. Price volatility (PV) of a commodity is defined as follows
    PV = (the highest price during the period – the lowest price during the period)/average price during the period.
    Which commodity has the lowest price volatility?
    (a) Arhar (b) Pepper
    (c) Sugar (d) Gold
31. Mr. X. a funds manager with an investment company invested 25 per cent of his funds in each of the four commodities at the beginning of the period. He sold the commodities at the end of the period. His investments in the commodities resulted in:
    (a) 17% profit (b) 5.5% loss
    (c) no profit, no loss (d) 4.3% profit
32. The price volatility of the commodity with the highest PV during the February–July period is approximately equal to:
    (a) 3% (b) 40%
    (c) 20% (d) 12%

Directions for Questions 33 to 35: *Answer the questions on the basis of the data presented in Figure 4.11.*

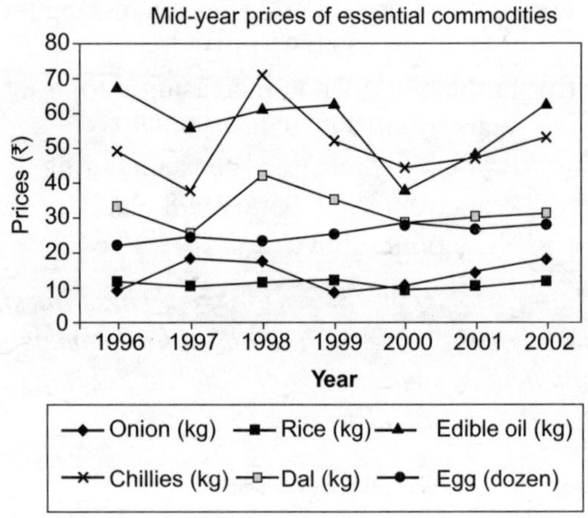

FIGURE 4.11

33. During 1996–2002, the number of commodities that exhibited a net overall increase and a net overall decrease, respectively, were

(a) 3 and 3 (b) 2 and 4
(c) 4 and 2 (d) 5 and 1

34. The number of commodities that experienced a price decline for two or more consecutive years is

(a) 2 (b) 3
(c) 4 (d) 5

35. For which commodities, did a price increase immediately follow a price decline only once in this period?

(a) Rice, Edible oil and Dal
(b) Egg and Dal
(c) Onion only
(d) Egg and Onion

Level of Difficulty 2

Directions for Questions 1 to 2: *On the basis of the data given in Figure 4.12.*

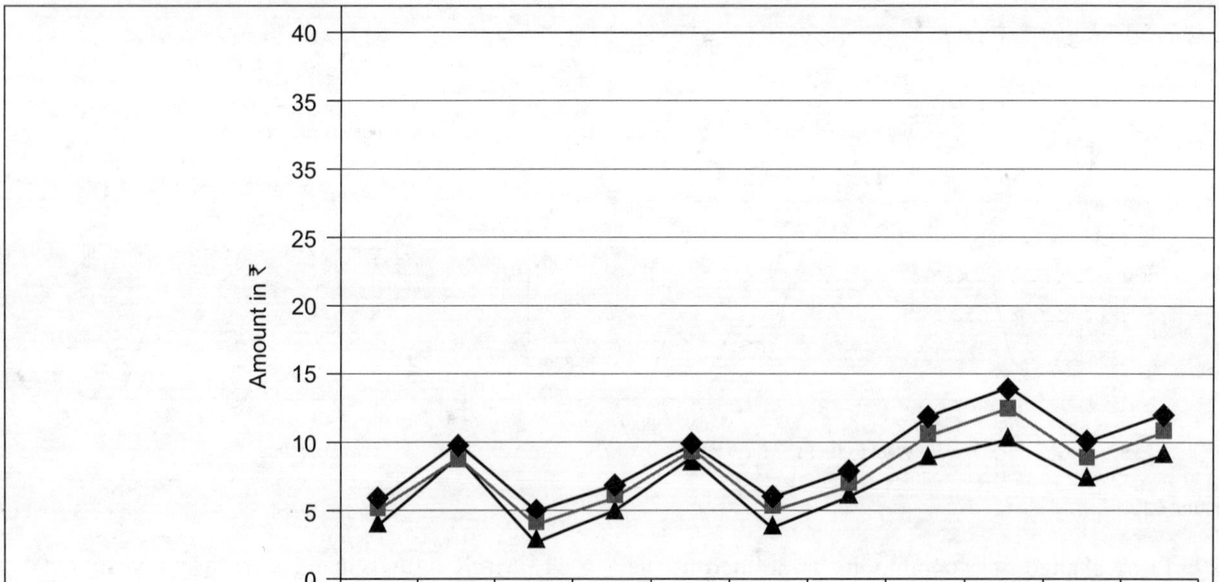

	Paneer Kachouri	Fish Kachouri	Mistisukh	Veg. Pattie	Chicken Pattie	Chicken Titbit	Veg. Pizza	Chicken Pizza	Fish Spring Roll	Cream Roll	Chicken Spring Roll
Prodn. Cost	4	8	3.5	5	8	4	6	9	10	7.5	9
Producer Selling Price	5	8.5	4.2	6	8.5	5	6.8	10.2	12	8.5	10.2
Retailer Selling Price	6	10	5	7	10	6	8	12	14	10	12

FIGURE 4.12

The above chart gives per unit selling prices and costs in rupees of 11 items prepared by a sweet shop. Margins are calculated on percentage basis. Based on the data given, answer the questions that follow:

1. Which of the following conclusions can be made?
   (a) Producer's margin for paneer kachouri is less than retailer's margins.
   (b) Producer's margin for chicken pizza is more than retailer's margins.
   (c) Producer's margin for fish spring roll is more than retailer's margins.
   (d) Producers and retailer's margins are the highest for paneer kachouri alone.
   (e) Retailers made losses in a few products.
2. Which of the following conclusion can be drawn from the diagram?
   (a) Retailers selling price for mistisukh was more than producer's selling price for chicken titbit.
   (b) Difference between retailer's selling price and producer's selling price for fish kachouri was more than that of cream roll.
   (c) There are three types of margins for all items.
   (d) Of all the margins, both for retailer and producer, producer's margin for chicken pizza was the maximum.
   (e) The three lines that connect different points, in the diagram above, are superfluous.

Directions for Questions 3 to 5 *On the basis of the graph given below (Figure 4.13):*

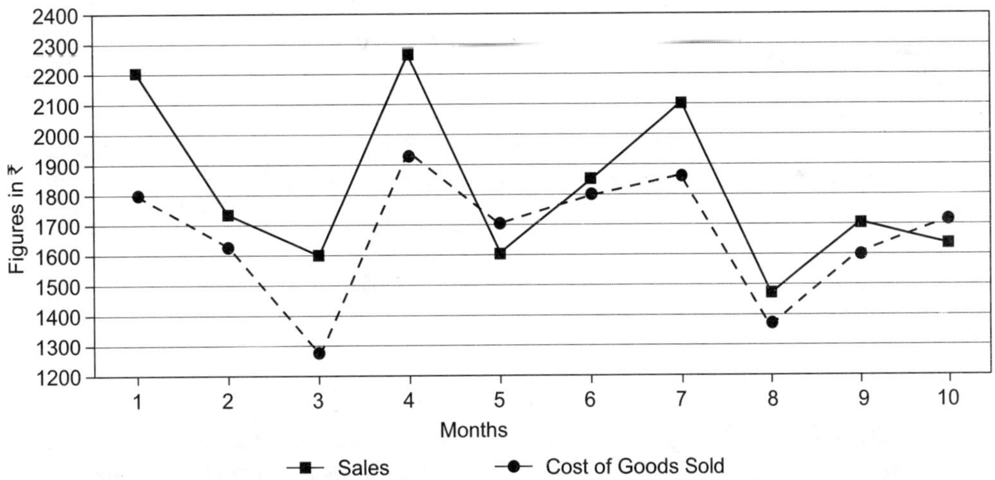

FIGURE 4.13 *Sales and Costs of XYZ Co.*

3. In which month did the company earn maximum profits?
   (a) 5 (b) 4
   (c) 3 (d) 2
   (e) 1
4. In which month did the company witness maximum sales growth?
   (a) 9 (b) 6
   (c) 7 (d) 4
   (e) 1
5. What were average sales and costs figures for XYZ Co. over the period of ten months?
   (a) 1819, 1651 (b) 1919, 1751
   (c) 1969, 1762 (d) 1719, 1601
   (e) 1619, 1661
6. Interpret relationship between the returns of stock X and mutual fund Y based on the following graph, where percentage return of stock X and mutual fund Y are given for sixteen days of a month. (Figure 4.14)
   (a) Returns of stock X are directly proportional to mutual fund Y.
   (b) Average returns from stock X and mutual fund Y are the same.
   (c) Stock X is less volatile than mutual fund Y.
   (d) Stock X is inversely proportional to mutual fund Y.
   (e) Stock X is more volatile than mutual fund Y.

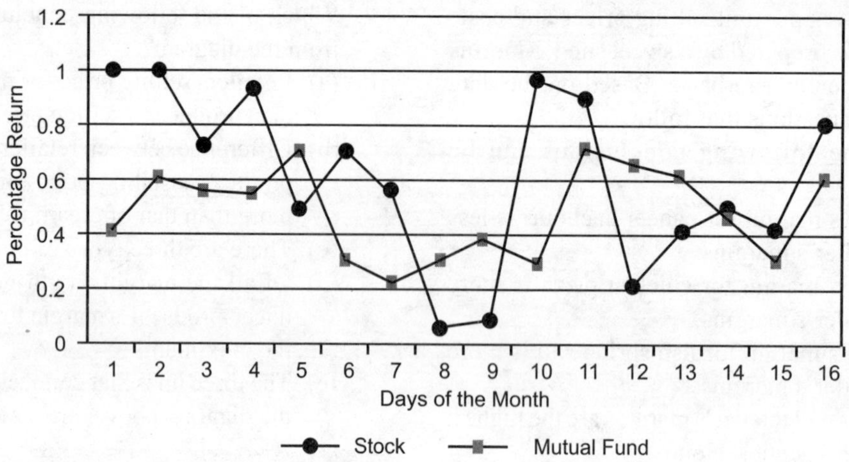

FIGURE 4.14

Directions for Questions 7 to 10: *Based on the following information.*

Figure 4.15 gives the annual data of assets, sales (as percentage of assets) and spending on Corporate Social Responsibility (CSR) (as a percentage of sales), of a company for the period 2004–09.

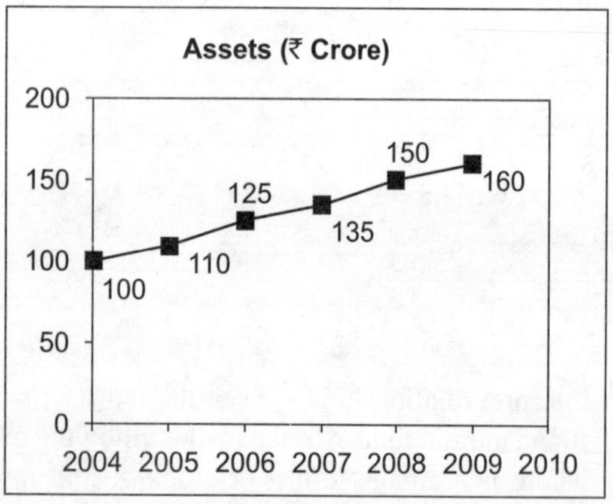

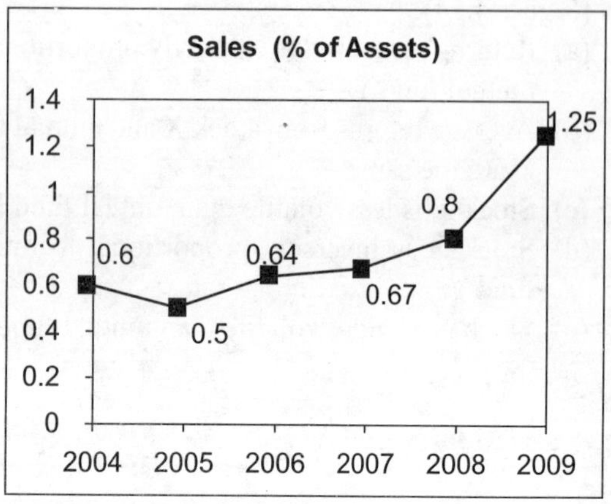

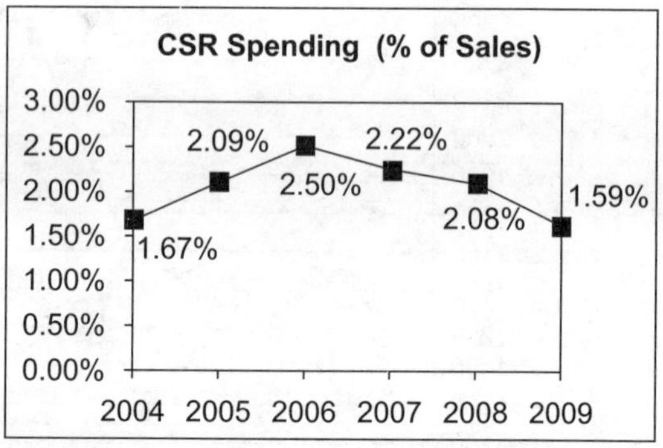

FIGURE 4.15

7. In which year was the increase in spending on CSR, vis-à-vis the previous year, the maximum?
   (a) 2005 (b) 2006
   (c) 2008 (d) 2007
   (e) 2009
8. Of the years indicated below, in which year was the ratio of CSR/assets the maximum?
   (a) 2004 (b) 2006
   (c) 2005 (d) 2007
   (e) 2008
9. What was the maximum value of spending on CSR activities during the period 2004–09?
   (a) ₹0.5 lacs (b) ₹1.0 lac
   (c) ₹2.0 lacs (d) ₹3.18 lacs
   (e) ₹4.0 lacs
10. In which year, did the spending on CSR (measured in ₹) decline as compared to the previous year?
   (a) 2006 (b) 2007
   (c) 2008 (d) 2009
   (e) Never declined

Directions for Questions 11 to 14: *Answer the questions on the basis of the information given below.*

The data points in Figure 4.16 represents monthly income and expenditure data of individual members of the Ahuja family (■), the Bose family (□), the Coomar family (o), and the Dubey family (●). For these questions, savings is defined as Income – Expenditure.

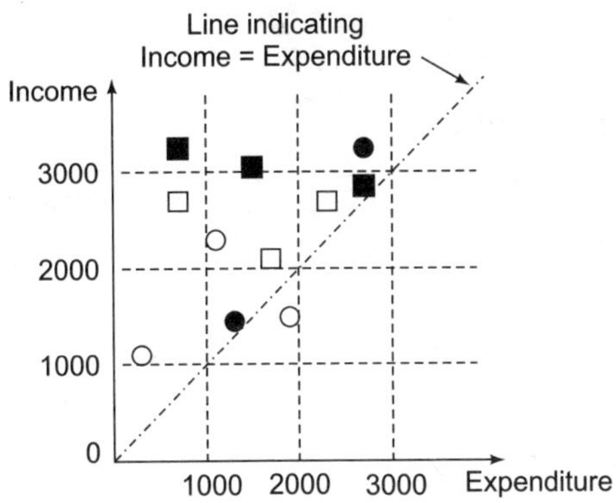

FIGURE 4.16

11. Which family has the highest average expenditure?
    (a) Ahuja (b) Bose
    (c) Coomar (d) Dubey
12. Which family has the lowest average income?
    (a) Ahuja (b) Bose
    (c) Coomar (d) Dubey
13. Which family has the lowest average savings?
    (a) Ahuja (b) Bose
    (c) Coomar (d) Dubey
14. The highest amount of savings accrues to a member of which family?
    (a) Ahuja
    (b) Bose
    (c) Coomar
    (d) Dubey

Directions for Questions 15 to 20: *Answer these questions based on the following information:*

ABC Ltd. produces widgets for which the demand is unlimited and they can sell all of their production. Figure 4.17 describes the monthly variable costs incurred by the company as a function of the quantity produced. In addition, operating the plant for one shift results in a fixed monthly cost of ₹800. Fixed monthly costs for second shift operation are estimated at ₹1200. Each shift operation provides capacity for producing 30 widgets per month.

Note: Average unit cost, AC = Total monthly costs/monthly production, and
Marginal cost, MC is the rate of change in total cost for unit change in quantity produced.

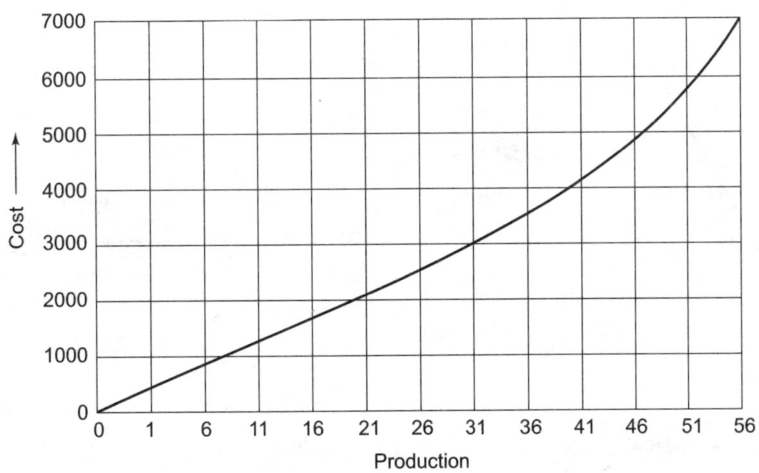

FIGURE 4.17

15. Total production in July is 40 units. What is the approximate average unit cost for July?
    (a) 3600 (b) 90
    (c) 150 (d) 115
16. ABC Ltd. is considering increasing the production level. What is the approximate marginal cost of increasing production from its July level of 40 units?
    (a) 110 (b) 130
    (c) 150 (d) 160
17. From the data provided, it can be inferred that for production levels in the range of 0–60 units,
    (a) MC is an increasing function of production quantity.
    (b) MC is a decreasing function of production quantity.

(c) Initially MC was a decreasing function of production quantity, which attained a minimum and then was an increasing function of production quantity.
(d) None of the above.

18. Suppose that each widget sells for ₹150. What is the profit earned by ABC Ltd. in July? (Profit is defined as the excess of sales revenue over total cost.)
(a) 2400 (b) 1600
(c) 400 (d) 0

19. Assume that the unit price is ₹150 and profit is defined as the excess of sales revenue over total costs. What is the monthly production level of ABC Ltd. at which the profit is the highest?
(a) 30 (b) 50
(c) 60 (d) 40

20. For monthly production level in the range of 0–30 units
(a) AC is always higher than MC.
(b) AC is always lower than MC.
(c) AC is lower than MC up to a certain level and then is higher than MC.
(d) None of the above is true.

Level of Difficulty 3

Directions for Questions 1 to 3: *Answer the questions based on the trend lines from Figure 4.18.*

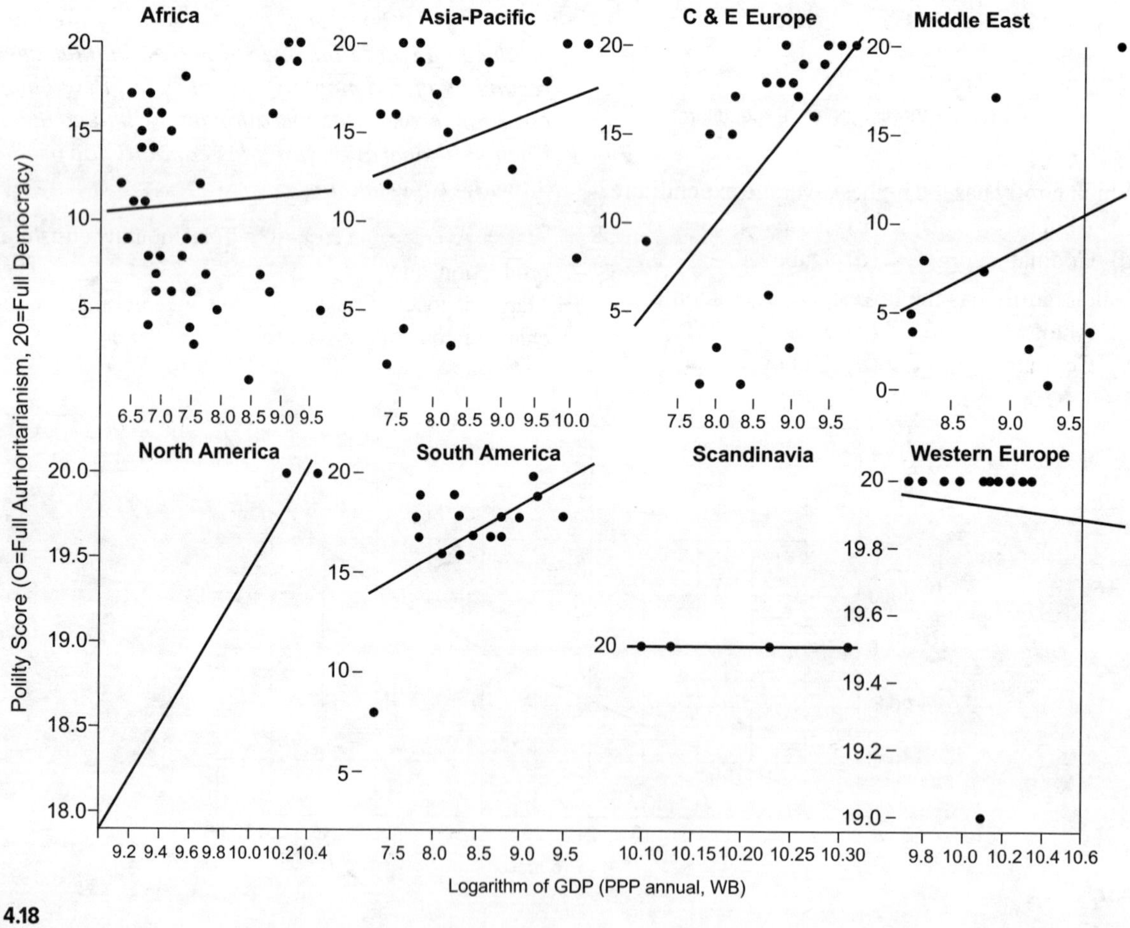

FIGURE 4.18

Note: Left side of X-axis represents countries that are 'poor' and right side of X-axis represents countries that are 'rich', for each region. GDP is based on purchasing power parity (PPP). These are World Bank (WB) estimates.

1. Which of the following could be the correct ascending order of polity score for poor?
(a) North America, C and E Europe, South America, Middle East, Asia Pacific
(b) Scandinavia, Western Europe, Africa, Asia Pacific, Middle East
(c) Scandinavia, Western Europe, North America, C and E Europe, Middle East
(d) C and E Europe, Africa, South America, Western Europe, Scandinavia
(e) Africa, South America, Western Europe, North America, Scandinavia

2. Which region has the highest disparity of democratic participation, between rich and poor?
   (a) North America (b) C and E Europe
   (c) Africa (d) South America
   (e) Western Europe
3. The maximum GDP of African region is higher than the maximum GDP of South American region by factor of:
   (a) 10 (b) 100
   (c) 2 (d) 4
   (e) None of these

Directions for Questions 4 to 8: *Answer the questions based on the following two graphs (Figure 4.19) assuming that there is no fixed cost component and all the units produced are sold in the same year.*

4. In which year is the per unit cost the highest?
   (a) 2002 (b) 2001
   (c) 2005 (d) 2007
5. What is the approximate average quantity sold during the period 2000–10?
   (a) 64 units (b) 70 units
   (c) 77 units (d) 81 units
6. If volatility of a variable during 2000–10 is defined as $\frac{\text{Maximum Value} - \text{Minimum Value}}{\text{Average Value}}$, then which of the following is TRUE?
   (a) Price per unit has the highest volatility
   (b) Cost per unit has the highest volatility
   (c) Total profit has the highest volatility
   (d) Revenue has the highest volatility

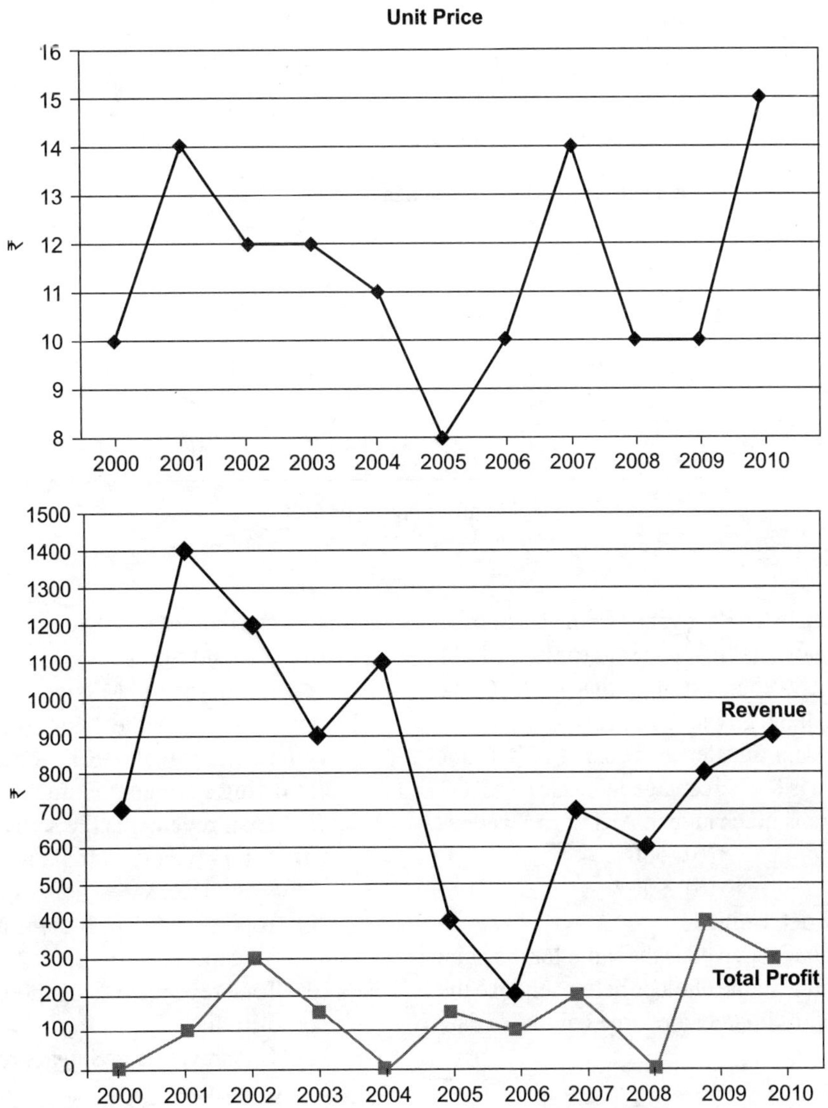

FIGURE 4.19

7. If the price per unit decreases by 20% during 2000–04 and cost per unit increases by 20% during 2005–10, then during how many number of years there is loss?
   (a) 3 years (b) 4 years
   (c) 5 years (d) 7 years
8. If the price per unit decreases by 20% during 2000–04 and cost per unit increases by 20% during 2005–10, then the cumulative profit for the entire period 2000–10 decreases by:
   (a) ₹1650 (b) ₹1550
   (c) ₹1300 (d) ₹1250

Directions for Questions 9 to 11: *Answer the following questions based on the information given below (Figure 4.20).*

Telecom operators get revenue from transfer of data and voice. Average revenue received from transfer of each unit of data is known as ARDT. In the diagram below, the revenue received from data transfer as percentage of total revenue received and the ARDT in US dollars (USD) are given for various countries.

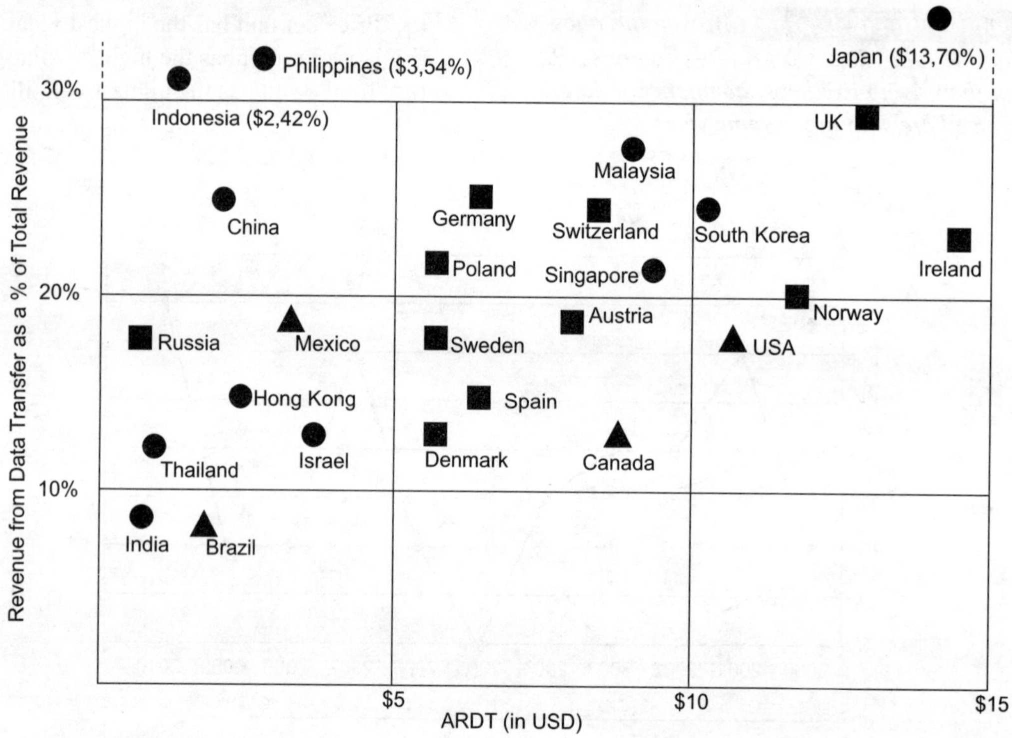

FIGURE 4.20

9. It is expected that by 2010, revenue from data transfer as a percentage of total revenue will triple for India and double for Sweden. Assume that in 2010, the total revenue in India is twice that of Sweden and that the volume of data transfer is the same in both the countries. What is the percentage increase of ARDT in India, if there is no change in ARDT in Sweden?
   (a) 400% (b) 550%
   (c) 800% (d) 950%
   (e) Cannot be determined
10. If the total revenue received is the same for the pairs of countries listed in the choices below, choose the pair that has approximately the same volume of data transfer.
   (a) Philippines and Austria
   (b) Canada and Poland
   (c) Germany and USA
   (d) UK and Spain
   (e) Denmark and Mexico
11. It was found that the volume of data transfer in India is the same as that of Singapore. Then, which of the following statement is true?
   (a) Total revenue is the same in both countries.
   (b) Total revenue in India is about 2 times that of Singapore.
   (c) Total revenue in India is about 4 times that of Singapore.
   (d) Total revenue in Singapore is about 2 times that of India.
   (e) Total revenue in Singapore is about 4 times that of India.

Directions for Questions 12 to 16: *Refer to the data below and answer the questions that follow.*

At the beginning of the year 2030, eight Indian NRIs had planned their budgets, each coming up with their projected income and projected expenses for the year. On 1st January, they recorded the actual figures for the same. Figure 4.21 shows the data they obtained. The incomes are shown with circles and the expenditures with crosses, marked with the respective names of the people involved. The X-coordinate of each point indicates the projected value of that parameter (in thousands of dollars), while the Y-coordinate shows the percentage error (i.e., by what per cent the actual value deviated from the projected one).

Note: Savings = Income – Expenses.

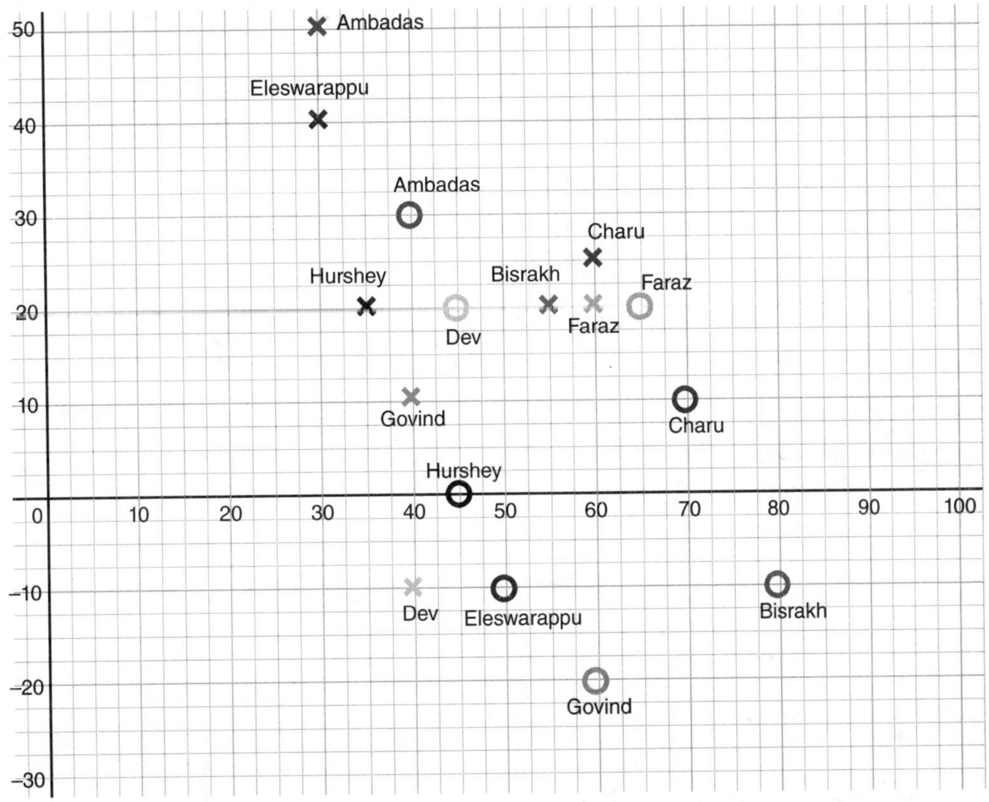

FIGURE 4.21

12. Who ended up with the maximum savings for the year?
    (a) Ambadas (b) Bisrakh
    (c) Charu (d) None of these
13. Which of the following exhibited the minimum percentage change from their projected to actual savings?
    (a) Dev (b) Ambadas
    (c) Faraz (d) None of these
14. For the person who ended up with the maximum actual savings in the year, his actual savings equalled what per cent of his actual expenditure for the year?
15. The actual amount, in dollars, saved by the person who had the least actual income was:
16. What was the numerical value of the difference (in thousands of dollars) between the sum of the actual savings and the sum of the projected savings for all the eight people taken together.

Directions for Questions 17 to 20: *Late in the 22nd century the ICC (International Cricket Commentators) the controlling body of cricket, in the wake of the serious assault on the control of cricket, by the Bankimchandra Cricket Club of IndusInd (BCCI) devised a new tournament, where it made its top eight batsmen in the generation, play a series of innings against the top bowlers of the time, in a specially devised tournament format. The rules of the tournament were such that every one of eight batsmen in the tournament, played a series of innings against the same bowling attack. In order to better judge the performance of the batsmen, the ICC devised a five inning moving average for each batsman's performance. This was defined as:*

M_n, the average score in the last five innings, i.e., innings number (n – 4) to innings number n. (So, for example, a batsman's M_7 would be the average score made by them in the innings number 3, 4, 5, 6 and 7). The following chart shows the value of M_{10} on the X-axis and that of M_{11} on the Y-axis for each of the batsmen. It was observed that all the values on both axes were integers for each of the batsmen. It was also observed, that no batsman was able to score more than 99 runs in any innings during the entire tournament.

Study Figure 4.22 carefully and answer the questions that follow:

17. What could be the maximum possible runs scored by Houghton in the 6th innings?
18. What could be the maximum score of Laxman in the 11th inning?
19. What could be the minimum score of Tendulkar in the 9th inning?
20. What could be the maximum average of all the 8 batsmen in the 6th innings?

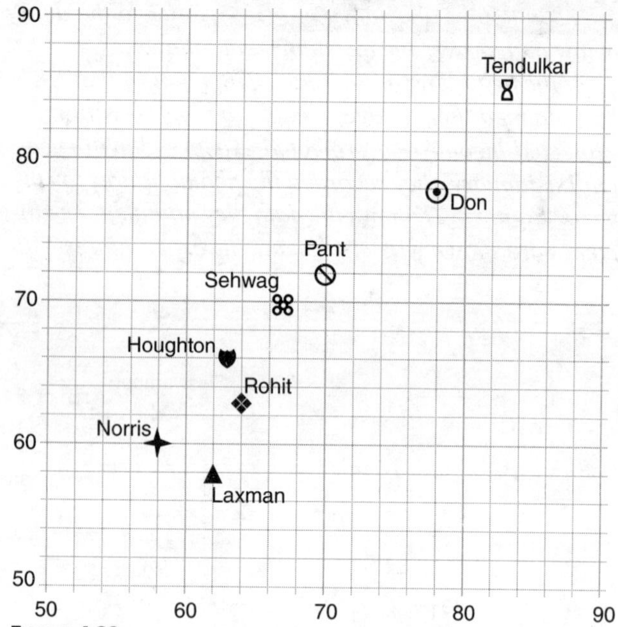

FIGURE 4.22

ANSWER KEY

Level of Difficulty 1

1. (b)	2. (c)	3. (b)	4. (a)	5. (d)	6. (b)	7. (b)
8. (a)	9. (d)	10. (a)	11. (c)	12. (a)	13. (c)	14. (b)
15. (d)	16. (b)	17. (c)	18. (d)	19. (b)	20. (a)	21. (c)
22. (b)	23. (b)	24. (b)	25. (a)	26. (d)	27. (b)	28. (d)
29. (a)	30. (c)	31. (d)	32. (b)	33. (a)	34. (b)	35. (c)

Level of Difficulty 2

1. (c)	2. (e)	3. (e)	4. (d)	5. (a)	6. (e)	7. (b)
8. (e)	9. (d)	10. (e)	11. (d)	12. (c)	13. (d)	14. (a)
15. (c)	16. (b)	17. (a)	18. (d)	19. (a)	20. (a)	

Level of Difficulty 3

1. (d)	2. (b)	3. (e)	4. (b)	5. (b)	6. (c)	7. (c)
8. (b)	9. (c)	10. (d)	11. (e)	12. (d)	13. (c)	14. 50%
15. 3000	16. 56	17. 84	18. 79	19. 29	20. 91.5	

SOLUTIONS

Level of Difficulty 1

1. 145 : 115 = 29 : 23 is the closest to 5 : 4.
2. 55 in 2010 to 30 in 2008. Gives 11 : 6 as the answer.
3. 50% in 2002 to 2009.
4. 33.33% between 2007 and 2008.
5. Visually clear that the graphs are equal at the ages of 2 and 8 months.
6. The required answer = 1700 – 1450 = 250 calories.
7. Add all the values to get 12250.
8. The required change will be 2000/12250 = 16.3%
9. Reverse the calculation for Question 10 and get 12500 as the total calorie requirement per day.
10. It can be seen that the two lines move differently with respect to each other and do not follow any common pattern. Hence, option (a) is correct.
11. 10/25 = 40%.

12. Exports would have increased by 20% of the footwear's value, i.e., by 7 on 35–20%.
13. Solve through options. When you try with 80%, you get 25 + 80% of 25 = 45 + 80% of 45 = 81. Hence the answer is just below 80%.
14. 10 crore/12,000.
15. 25,000 to 17,000.
16. 8333.33 – 3333.33 = 5000
17. Visually see the net revenue line to be maximum for 2002–03.
18. The required ratio is 2900/2100.
19. 300/500.
20. 9.5 for 4th of May
21. This ratio depends on the difference between the two temperatures on a single day as well as on the day temperature of the same day. The lower the difference, the higher the ratio. Also, the data given is such that the day temperatures are in the same range, hence the effect of the same on the ratio will be minimal. For solving this question find out the days which need to be checked and compare the ratios between those days only. 4th of May will give the highest ratio required, since the difference is the lowest on that day.
22. Approximately 40 out of 160 = 25%.
23. Visually checking the options, we get 1978 as the answer.
24. The average speed will be given by the ratio of total distance by the total time.
    The distance covered in any hour will be given by the average speed of the hour.
    Distance covered in first hour = (20 + 0)/2 =10 km.
    Distance covered in second hour = 20 km/hour = 20 km.
    Distance covered in third hour = (20 + 40)/2 = 30.
    Distance covered in fourth hour = (40 + 60)/2 = 50 km.
    Distance covered in fifth hour = (60 + 50)/2 = 55 km.
    Distance covered in sixth hour = 50 km.
    Distance covered in seventh hour = (50 + 0)/2 = 25.
    The required average speed = 240/7 = 34.28 km/hour.

Solutions for Questions 25 to 28

The data presented uses the double Y-axis: On the left Y-axis is shown the sales (with unit markings of 100 crores), while on the right Y-axis we see profit (with unit markings of (b) crore).

25. Visually we can see that the highest percentage increase in sales is in the year 1995–96. Sales have gone up from 100 crores in 1994–95 to around 280 crores in 1995–96—a percentage growth of 180 per cent. No other year shows such a high percentage growth in sales. Hence, option (a) is correct.
26. Profit has also gone up by the highest percentage increase in the year 1995–96 only—it shows a close to 100 per cent increase during this time which is not shown at any other time. Hence, option (d) is correct.
27. Maximum profitability = 7.6/280 (approx values both based on the judgement of the values seen in the graphs) is seen for the year 1997–98. Hence, option (b) is correct.
28. Profitability has shown an up-and-down pattern during the 5-year period. Thus, we cannot say that it is non-decreasing, neither is it non-increasing nor is it constant during the five-year period.
    Thus, we will mark option (d).

Solutions for Questions 29 to 35

Note: All values used are approximations, based on the visualisation in the graphs. We cannot calculate the exact values, since we cannot read the exact values of the numbers in the graphs. In such cases, you are expected to read an approximate value of each number used inside a question and solve approximately. As far as you take the approximations within a certain relevant range, there would only be one option that would be the closest to your calculated answer.

29. The highest price change is seen for Arhar. Can be seen visually from the four graphs.
30. The band of price change is the least for sugar—which means the numerator of the price volatility (PV) ratio is the smallest for sugar. Also looking at the denominator for the same – the average price is dependent on the price band in which the price of the commodity fluctuates. The PV for sugar is around: 90/1440, while for gold it is 500/4000, for arhar it is 800/2000 and for pepper it is 2000/18000. It is clearly evident that PV is least for sugar.
31. Suppose he invested ₹100 in each. Arhar shows a 30% growth, pepper 5% growth, sugar 2% drop and gold 13% drop. Thus, 400 would become equal to 130 + 105 + 98 + 87 = 420 (approximately). The closest answer is a 4.3% profit option (d).
32. From the solution for Question 30, we know that the highest PV is for arhar and at 800/2000 it is close to 40% (approximately).
33. Option (a)
34. Option (b)
35. Option (c)

Level of Difficulty 2

Solutions for Questions 1 and 2:

1. It can be clearly seen that the producer's margin for fish spring roll (20%) is more than the retailer's margin for the same. Hence, option (c) is correct.
2. Looking at each of the 5 options, we can see that the first option is rejected because the retailer's selling price of mistisukh was not more than producer's selling price for chicken titbit as for both of them the price was 5.
   Option (b) is also rejected as we can see that the difference between the retailer's selling price and the producer's selling price was equal.
   Option (c) gets rejected because there are only two types of margins and not three, i.e., retailer's margin and producer's margin.
   Option (d) also gets rejected because there are higher margins than the producer's margins for chicken pizza.
   Hence, Option (e) has to be correct – and it indeed is because if we try to look at the line graphs in the chart, they give no additional information to the values in the table and hence we can call them superfluous.

Solutions for Questions 3 to 5:

3. The maximum profit of 400 can be seen in the very first month itself. Option (e) is correct.
4. The maximum sales growth is observed for month 4. Option (d) is correct.
5. The total sales over the 10 month period is approximately 18200 which means a monthly average of around 1820. Only option (a) matches this value and is hence correct.

Solution for Question 6:

6. Clearly stock X is more volatile than mutual fund Y as there are larger variations in stock X vis-à-vis mutual fund Y.

Solutions for Questions 7 to 10:

7. The conventional way to solve this question would be to calculate all the values for each of the years.

The following numbers would emerge based on the relationships that sales are defined as a percentage of assets while CSR spending is defined as a percentage of sales.

Year	Assets	Sales (in lacs)	CSR Spending (in lacs)
2004	100	60	1
2005	110	55	1.14
2006	125	80	2
2007	135	90.45	2
2008	150	120	2.49
2009	160	200	3.18

From the table it is clear that the highest growth has happened in 2006 and hence option (b) is correct.

However, this process of solving is not feasible to be executed under exam conditions and pressure. Hence, we need to look at an alternative approach for doing the same. The expression for the value of the CSR spending is linearly connected to assets × sales (as % of assets) × CSR spending (as a % of sales) and hence it is a straight multiplicative relationship.

Consequently, in order to spot the probable years when the highest increase in CSR could feasibly occur we can see that the value of CSR in 2004 is ₹1 lac. After this we can see what percentage changes are occurring in each of the parts of the product in order to see how the product would behave from year to year.

In the first year there is a 10% growth in assets, 16.66% drop in sales as a percentage of assets and approx 26% increase in CSR spending as a percentage of sales. Using the percentage change graphic (PCG) for calculating the overall percentage change, we can see that this would mean a 15% (approx) change in the CSR spending.

The second year (2006) obviously becomes the favourite for being the highest increase as it shows a 14% growth in assets, 28% growth in sales as a percentage of assets and approx 21% increase in CSR spending as a percentage of sales – overall a growth of around 75%.

On visual inspection, the only year which needs to be checked against this is 2009 which can be seen to be showing a lower growth than 2006.

Note: While doing this you would need to be careful of making sure that 2006 is greater than 2009 in absolute growth and not just percentage growth – as the base value for 2009 is greater than the base value for 2006 and hence there might be a situation where although the percentage increase in 2006 is higher than in 2009, in terms of absolute growth 2009 is still greater than 2006.

Alternately, you can do the following proxy calculation to see which is the highest:

$100 \times 6 \times 1.67$ compared against $110 \times 5 \times 2.09$ compared against $125 \times 6.4 \times 2.5$ compared against $135 \times 6.7 \times 2.22$ compared against $150 \times 8 \times 2.08$ compared against $160 \times 12.5 \times 1.59 \rightarrow 1000 \rightarrow 1100 \rightarrow 2000 \rightarrow 2000 \rightarrow 2500 \rightarrow 3180$ (approximate values).

8. The highest value as seen from the table above (for the years provided in the options) is for 2008 (2.49/150).
9. The highest value of CSR is 3.18 lacs. Option (d) is correct.
10. It is clear that the CSR spending has never declined during the entire period. Hence, option (e) is clearly the correct answer.

11. The vertical average line would be at the maximum value for the Dubey family. It can be visualised that for all other families, the vertical line representing their average expenditure would be to the left of the line for the Dubey family. Hence, option (d) is the correct answer.
12. The lowest horizontal line (for average income) can be seen to be for the Coomar family option (c).
13. The average of the savings would be the least for the Dubey family option (d).
14. The biggest vertical line from the diagonal would be for the member shown in the figure above.

Solutions for Questions 15 to 18

15. The average cost for 40 units would be given by (Total Cost/No. of units) = (4000 + 800 + 1200)/40 = 6000/40. Answer is 150. We choose option (c) as the closest answer.
16. The variable cost at 40 units production is 4000 and at 46 units it is around 4800 – the graph is almost a straight line between these two points. Thus, the marginal cost of increasing production from 40 units = 800/6 = 130 approximately.
17. It can be seen that the marginal cost is increasing as production quantity is increasing. Thus, option (a) is the correct answer.
18. It is known that for 40 units production cost is 6000 and @ ₹150 per unit, the total revenue would also be ₹6000. Thus the total profit would be 0.
19. Profit would be the highest at 30 units: Revenue (4500) – Cost (2800 + 800) = 900
At 40 units, we have seen that there is no profit.
At 50 units, the profit would be negative and at 60 units, the profit would again be negative. Thus, option (a) is correct.
20. Initially the average cost would be higher than the marginal cost because at 1 unit, the average cost would be above ₹800, while the marginal cost between 0 and 30 units is below 100. Even at 30 units it can be seen that AC > MC. Thus, AC is always greater than MC in the range 0–30 units.

Level of Difficulty 3

1. We can reject Option (a) because, for C and E Europe the polity score for poor nations is clustered below a score of 15, while for North America, the only poor nation is at 18. Thus, the order North America – C and E Europe for ascending order of polity score for poor is incorrect. Options (b) and (c) can be rejected because Scandinavia has a polity score as 20 for all its countries and hence it cannot be at the start of any list with increasing order of polity scores. Option (e) is also rejected because it puts Western Europe (which has perfect democracy as all its countries are at 20) below North America. Only the order in Option (d) obeys ascending order for polity scores. Hence, Option (d) is the correct answer.
2. It can be visually observed to be for C & E Europe as the poor countries in this region are clustered below 10 while the rich countries are clustered around a polity score of 18 to 20.
3. Clearly, the value of the maximum GDP for both the given regions is around 9.5 and hence equal. Hence, Option (e) is the correct answer.

Solutions for Questions 4 to 8:

The sales values and the other variables that can be derived can be first represented on a table as below in order to see the required answers to the questions:

		2000	2001	2002	2003	2004	2005	2006	2007	2008	2009	2010
GIVEN VARIABLES	Price	10	14	12	12	11	8	10	14	10	10	15
	Revenues	700	1400	1200	900	1100	400	200	700	600	800	900
	Profit	0	100	300	150	0	150	100	200	0	400	300
DERIVED VARIABLES	Sales Units	70	100	100	75	100	50	20	50	60	80	60
	Cost	700	1300	900	750	1100	250	100	500	600	400	600

4. The per unit cost is 13 in 2001 and that is the highest value. Option (b) is correct.
5. 765/11 = 70. Option (b) is correct.
6. For total profit the volatility is the greatest as it is above 2 (400/154) which is much higher than the other values.
7. Between 2000 and 2004, there would be a loss in 2000, 2001, 2003 and 2004 as in each of these years the revenue would go down below the cost— if we drop the price by 20% the revenue would also drop by 20% and hence in each of these years there would be a loss.

Between 2005 and 2010, if the cost per unit goes up by 20%, the cost would also go up by 20%. This would result in a loss in the year 2008 as the cost would go above revenues.

8. There would be a drop of 140 + 280 + 240 + 180 + 220 = 1060 in the revenues between 2000 and 2004 and an increase of 50 + 20 +100 + 120 + 80 + 120 = 490 in the cost between the years 2005 and 2010. The total drop in profit would be 1060 + 490 = 1550. Option (b) is correct.
9. According to data given in the question the following conclusions can be drawn:
   (a) Volume of data transfer in India = Volume of data transfer in Sweden.
   (b) Revenue from data transfer as a percentage of total revenue will triple for India and double for Sweden.
   (c) Total revenue of India is twice that of Sweden.

   To calculate percentage change in ARDT of India as compared to Sweden, we have to equate per unit volume of data transfer for both countries which is equal.

   Hence, let revenue of Sweden be 'x', then revenue of India will be '$2x$'.

   ARDT for Sweden from figure can be approximated to \$6,

   $\Rightarrow$ revenue of data transfer = $(2 \times 18\% \text{ of } x)$
   $\Rightarrow$ volume = $(2 \times 18\% \text{ of } x)/6$
   Similarly, let ARDT for India be 'y'.
   $\Rightarrow$ Revenue of data transfer = $(3 \times 9\% \text{ of } 2x)$
   $\Rightarrow$ volume = $(3 \times 9\% \text{ of } 2x)/y$
   Equating we get,
   $\Rightarrow$ $(3 \times 9\% \text{ of } 2x)/y = (2 \times 18\% \text{ of } x)/6$
   $\Rightarrow$ $y = \$9$
   $\Rightarrow$ percentage change = $((9 - 1)/1) \times 100\% = 800\%$. Hence, option (c) is correct.
10. For this question check the volume of data transfer for all pairs. For example,

    For Austria,

    Revenue from data transfer as a percentage of total revenue = 18%.

    Revenue from data transfer = (18/100) × total revenue.

    ARDT = \$8

    Volume of data transfer = (18/100) × (Total revenue/\$8).

    Similarly check for Philippines.

    The only pair that will have equal volume will be UK and Spain option (d).
11. The questions can be solved by calculating the ratio of total revenue of Singapore and India. This will give the result that Singapore's total revenue is four times the total revenue of India.

    The required working out would be: Assume total revenue for India is I and for Singapore is S. Then:

    $(9\% \text{ of } I)/1 = (21\% \text{ of } S)/9 \rightarrow I/S = 1/4$ (approximately).

    Hence, we will mark option (e).

Solutions for questions 12 to 16:

Based on the interpretation of the data, we can come up with the following table for projected, actual savings and expenditure for each person.

Name	Projected Income	Actual Income	Projected Expenditure	Actual Expenditure	Savings = Income-Expenditure (Actual)	Savings (Projected)
Ambadas	40000	52000	30000	45000	7000	10000
Bisrakh	80000	72000	55000	66000	6000	25000
Charu	70000	77000	60000	75000	2000	10000
Dev	45000	54000	40000	36000	18000	5000
Eleswarappu	50000	45000	30000	42000	3000	20000
Faraz	65000	78000	60000	72000	6000	5000
Govind	60000	48000	40000	44000	4000	20000
Hurshey	45000	45000	35000	42000	3000	10000

The answers can be read off the table:

12. The highest savings are seen for Dev. Hence, option (d) is correct.
13. Faraz has a percentage change of only 20% from his projected to actual savings. Hence, option (c) is correct.
14. The person with maximum savings (actual) had a savings that was equal to 50% of his actual expenditure. Hence, the correct answer is 50%.
15. Eleswarappu and Hurshey had the least actual incomes (45000 each). Both of them saved 3000. Hence, the correct answer is 3000.

16. The sum of actual savings is 49000 dollars. The sum of the projected savings for all of them is: 105000 (dollars). The difference, in thousands of dollars is: 56. Hence, the correct answer is 56.

Solutions for questions 17 to 20:

17. Houghton's average for innings 6 to 10 is 63, while his average for innings 7 to 11 is 66. Let S_6 be the number of runs scored by the batsman in the 6th inning, S_7 the number of runs scored in the seventh inning and so on. The following formulae apply in this situation:
$S_6 + S_7 + S_8 + S_9 + S_{10} = 315$
$S_7 + S_8 + S_9 + S_{10} + S_{11} = 330$. Hence, $S_{11} - S_6 = 15$.
Since, it is given to us that the maximum possible score in an innings during the tournament was 99, the maximisation of S_6 will occur, when S_{11} is maximised at 99. Hence, $S_6 = 99 - 15 = 84$.
Hence, the correct answer is 84.

18. M_{10} for Laxman is 62 and M_{11} is 58. Hence, for Laxman:
$S_6 + S_7 + S_8 + S_9 + S_{10} = 310$
$S_7 + S_8 + S_9 + S_{10} + S_{11} = 290$.
Hence, $S_6 - S_{11} = 20$. To maximise S_{11} for Laxman, we need to maximise S_6, which can get maximised only at 99. Hence, S_{11} maximum $= 99 - 20 = 79$.
Hence, the correct answer is 79.

19. Tendulkar has an M_{11} value of 85. Hence, his total score in innings 7 to 11 would be 425. The minimisation of the ninth inning happens, when there is the maximisation of innings 7, 8, 10 and 11. These can all be maximised at 99 each. Hence, he can score 396 runs in innings numbers 7, 8, 10 and 11. Hence, he must have scored a minimum of 29 runs in the ninth inning. There is a doubt that comes to mind in such situations about whether there will be a difference if we think about this using Tendulkar's M_{10} value. It will not matter as we can see in the following explanation:
If we look at the M_{10} value: M_{10} for Tendulkar is 83. Hence, $S_{11} - S_6 = 10$. So, he can score a maximum of 89 runs in S_6. Again, if we see, for Tendulkar: $S_6 + S_7 + S_8 + S_9 + S_{10} = 415$. To minimise S_9, we have to maximise S_6, S_7, S_8 and S_{10}. These maximums are 89, 99, 99 and 99 respectively. So he must score a minimum of $415 - (89 - 99 - 99 - 99) = 29$ runs in his 9th innings.
Hence, the correct answer is 29.

20. We can draw a table for the scores of each of the eight batsmen.

Batsman	Don	Tendulkar	Pant	Sehwag	Rohit	Houghton	Norris	Laxman
M_{10}	78	83	70	67	64	63	58	62
M_{11}	78	85	72	70	63	66	60	58
$S_{11} - S_6$	0	10	10	15	–5	15	10	–20
Maximum S_{11}	99	99	99	99	94	99	99	79
Maximum S_6	99	89	89	84	99	84	89	99

The maximum average in the sixth inning could be: $(99 + 89 + 89 + 84 + 99 + 84 + 89 + 99)/8 = 732/8 = 91.5$
Hence, the correct answer is 91.5

CHAPTER 5

Pie Charts

Outline

Learning Objectives

- Get a first-hand view of how data is presented through its organisation in the form of X-Y charts.
- Get an understanding of the typical data which can be represented through X-Y charts. Also understand the concept of time series as it applies to X-Y charts.
- Get a first-hand feel of what are the typical question types that are asked on the basis of X-Y charts.

Chapter Highlights

- Introduction to pie charts.
- High Quality Solved examples to set you on the way
- Practice exercise at 3 levels of difficulty containing simulated examination level questions.

Pie charts are specific types of data presentation where the data is represented in the form of a circle. In a pie chart, a circle is divided into various sections or segments such that each sector or segment represents a certain proportion or percentage of the total. In such a diagram, the total of all the given items is equated to 360 degrees and the degrees of angles, representing different items, are calculated proportionately. The entire diagram looks like a pie and its components resemble slices cut from a pie. The pie chart is used to show the break-up of one continuous variable into its component parts.

For example, Figure 5.1 shows the distribution of the sales of the car industry amongst six car companies.

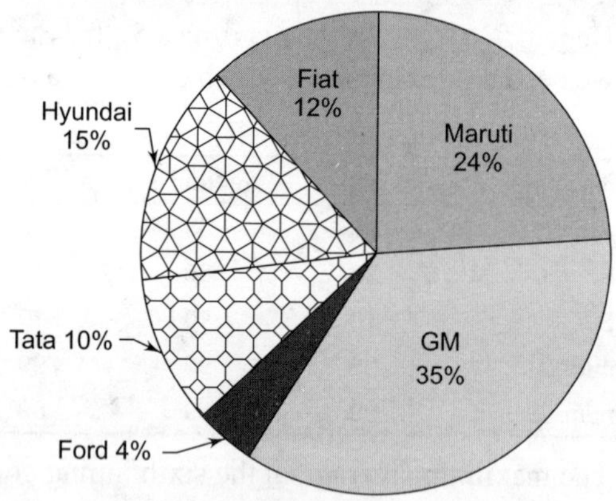

FIGURE 5.1 *Pie Diagram Showing Distribution of Car Sales amongst Six Companies*

Looking at Figure 5.1, we can infer that Maruti accounts for 24 per cent of the market share, while GM accounts for 35 per cent of the market share, Ford for 4 per cent of the market share, Tata for 10 per cent of the market share, Hyundai for 15 per cent of the market share and Fiat for 12 per cent of the market share.

The pie chart encompasses a circle of 360 degrees which represents 100 per cent of the value of the continuous variable. Thus, 3.6 degrees on the pie chart represent 1 per cent of the total value of the continuous variable being represented.

> A single pie diagram can represent only one continuous variable. Hence, in terms of versatility of data representation, pie charts are less versatile than either bar charts, X-Y graphs or tables. However, their utility is in the fact that the representation of data is cleaner and it gives an immediate idea of the relative distribution of the continuous variable amongst different sectors.

Let us now take a look at a couple of sets based on pie-charts, to help you understand how to read and interpret pie chart based questions – especially when a logical element is introduced in them:

EXAMPLE 1

The below multi layered pie chart shows the population for 3 different cities of various states in India after the census of 2011 and 2021. The outer layer shows the population for each city. The middle layer shows the total population of the given cities state-wise and the Inner-most layer represents the census year. While feeding in the data, some of the values went missing. The following information is known about the chart-

(a) The population growth across the state of Maharashtra is constant throughout.

(b) The populations of Muzaffarpur in 2021, Bhagalpur in 2011 and Muzaffarpur in 2011 are in an AP. Meanwhile, the populations of Patna in 2011 and 2021 and Bhagalpur in 2021 are also in an AP.

(c) The population of Lucknow in 2021 was more than that of Prayagraj which was in turn more than that of Moradabad in that particular year.

(d) The populations of the cities of UP in 2021 was the sum of any two cities of the same state in 2011.

(e) There was a population boom of 30% across Jharkhand in 2021 as compared to 2011. However, Dhanbad experienced a drop in population while Ranchi witnessed maximum growth.

(f) Madhya Pradesh witnessed a 50% growth in 2021.

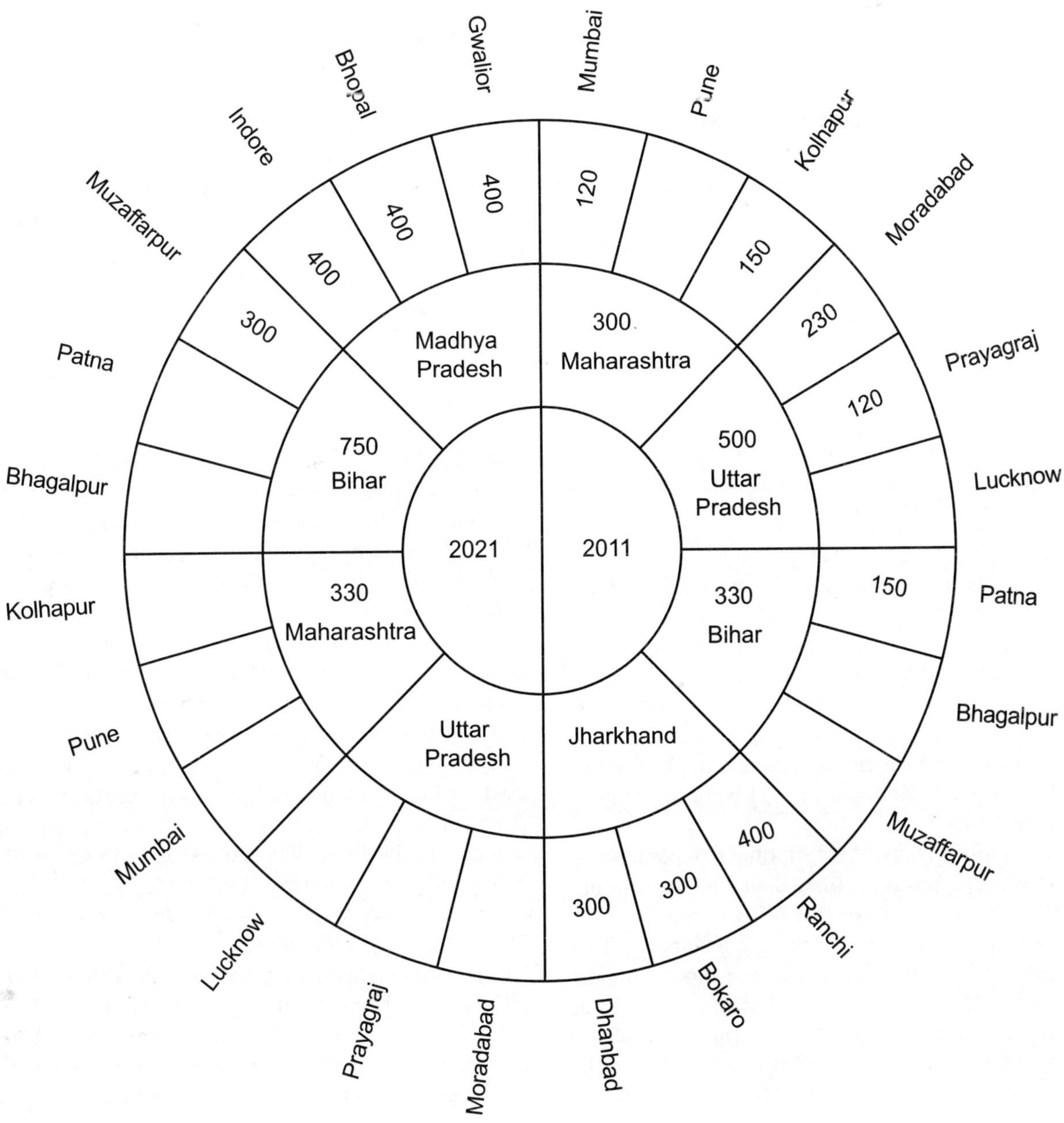

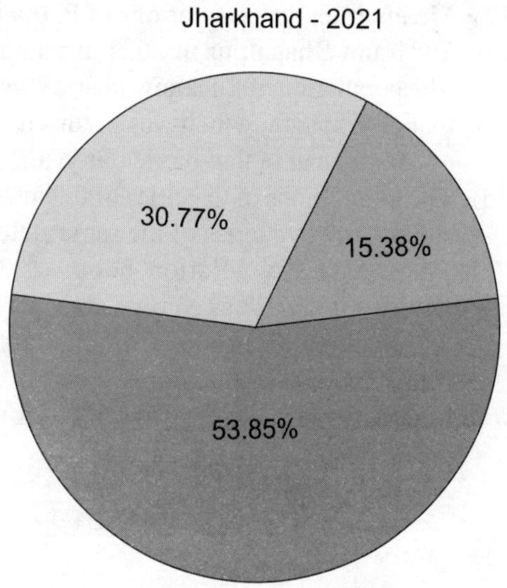

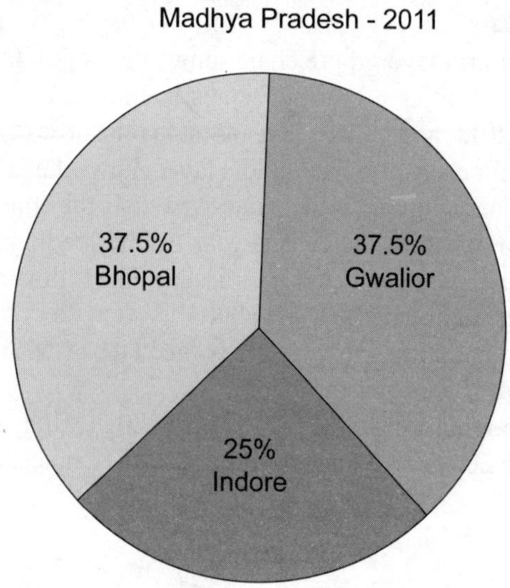

1. What was the population of Dhanbad in 2021? [TITA]
2. What was percentage growth in the population of the three cities of UP from 2011 to 2021?
3. Which state witnessed the maximum growth over the given period?
   (a) UP
   (b) MP
   (c) Bihar
   (d) Cannot be determined
4. How many cities exhibited a population growth of above 50% in 2021 as compared to 2011?
5. By what percentage did the population of Bhagalpur change during the given period?

Solutions:

The set of deductions leading to the solution is as follows:

Deduction 1: From (A), we can see that the population of Pune in 2011 has to be 300 – 120 – 150 = 30. In 2021, since the population growth rate is constant for all cities of Maharashtra, it means that there is a 10% increase in the population of each city. Hence, the populations of Mumbai, Pune and Kolhapur in 2021 were respectively 132, 33 and 165.

Deduction 2: Since, Muzaffarpur's population in 2021 is 300 and the sum of Bhagalpur and Muzaffarpur in 2011 is 180, it follows that Muzaffarpur in 2021 will have the highest of the three populations. This means that their values are in a decreasing Arithmetic Progression. Hence, if we assume Muzaffarpur 2021 as a, then Bhagalpur 2011 and Muzaffarpur 2011 would be a-d and a-2d respectively. Since, a is 300 and the sum of a-d + a – 2d = 180 → d = 140 and the values of Bhagalpur 2011 and Muzaffarpur 2011 would be 160 and 20 respectively.

Deduction 3: Similarly, Patna 2021 and Bhagalpur 2021 can be worked out as 200 and 250 respectively. (Using the information in the second part of clue B). The logic is: Let Patna 2011 be a (=150, given), then Patna 2021 and Bhagalpur 2021 would be (a + d) and (a + 2d) respectively. From the pie chart we can make out that sum of Patna and Bhagalpur in 2021 is 450. Hence, 2a + 3d = 450. Using a = 150, we get d as 50 and hence the values of 200 and 250 respectively.

Deduction 4: (Using Clues C and D): The population of Lucknow in 2011 would be 500 – 230 – 120 = 150. Further, the populations of the three cities of UP in 2021 can be got by summing up the populations 2 cities of UP in 2011. The three values we get are: 150 + 120 = 270; 230 + 120 = 350 and 230 + 150 = 380. These three population values will go for Moradabad, Prayagraj and Lucknow respectively. Hence, Moradabad 2021 = 270; Prayagraj 2021 = 350 and Lucknow 2021 = 380.

Deduction 5: From Clue E The population of Jharkhand in 2021 would be 1300 (30% above the population in 2011). To distribute this in 2021, we will have to look at the Jharkhand pie-chart for 2021 given to us separately. This will get distributed as: 400, 200 and 700. (1300 × 0.3077 = 400; 1300 × 0.1538 = 200; 1300 × 0.5385 = 700). These numbers would go to Dhanbad 200, Bokaro 400 and Ranchi 700, respectively, as per clue E.

Deduction 6: MP's cities have a population of 1200 in 2021. Hence, their population in 2011 would be 100/1.5 = 800. This would be distributed as Bhopal 0.375 × 800 = 300; Indore 0.25×800=200 and Gwalior 0.375 × 800 = 300.

The answers can be worked out from these deductions.

1. 200;
2. 100%
3. Bihar. Option (c) is correct.
4. Prayagraj, Lucknow, Bhagalpur, Muzaffarpur, Ranchi and Indore have shown a greater than 50% growth in population. Hence, the correct answer is 6.
5. Population of Bhagalpur has gone from 160 to 250 – a growth of 56.25%.

EXAMPLE 2

A very intelligent law student, Bhavya was attending one out of many of her compulsory finance related subjects. In the lecture, the teacher, Mr. Shaurya showed a document which contained GDP and Private Consumption of 5 Countries A,B,C,D,E. Because the teacher was not friendly with the students, Mr. Shaurya ended up changing the slide before the students could note down the data fully. As Bhavya is very intelligent, she decided to make two pie charts: the first chart shows the percentage distribution of GDP of each country and the other gives us the Private Consumption Expenditure of each country as a percentage of the country's GDP. The other information is stored in the form of clues which are as follows:

1. The country with the highest percentage of GDP has ₹ 90 Million of Private Consumption Expenditure.
2. The total private consumption is 15% of the GDP of these countries combined.
3. Countries E and D, which numerically have the highest and the third highest Private Consumption Expenditure respectively, both have the same percentage contribution to the total GDP of these countries. Countries D and E also have the 2nd and 3rd maximum Private Consumption Expenditure Contribution to their own GDP (when looked at all 5 countries Private Consumption Expenditure Contribution to their own GDP)
4. The value of a country's contribution to the total GDP of these five countries combined which is also one of the least is ₹ 300 million.
5. Country A and C have the least contribution to the total GDP of the five countries. It is also known that one of them has the second-highest Private Consumption Expenditure
6. Country B and D have the same contribution to the total GDP of the five countries., but country D's Private consumption expenditure is 50% more than C.

Note: In the pie charts given below, the countries are scrambled. i.e., we do not know which of the countries' A,B,C,D,E is country 1, 2, 3, 4 and 5 in the GDP Pie Chart. Also, country 1 of the GDP Chart and Country 1 of the Private consumption Expenditure chart need not be the same country – i.e. across the two pie-charts, which country a particular country number refers to is not fixed.

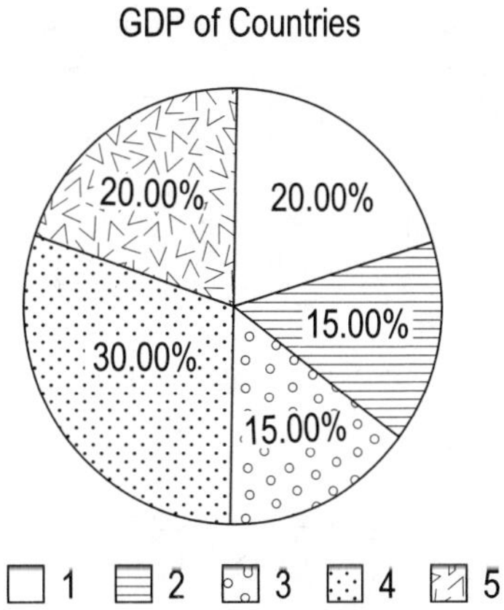

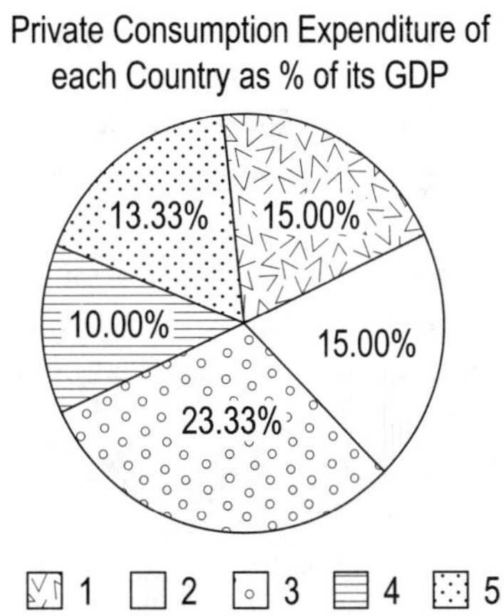

1. What is the value of C's GDP?
   (a) 300 (b) 400
   (c) 600 (d) 500
2. What is the Value of Country B's Private Consumption Expenditure/ GDP?
   (a) 23.33%
   (b) 10%
   (c) 15%
   (d) 13.33%
3. Read the following statements and answer the questions that follow:
   (a) Country B and C have the same value of Private Consumption Expenditure but B has more GDP than C
   (b) Country E contributed the most to the combined GDP of the five countries but country E's PCE contributed the least to it's GDP.

Which of the above statements are true?
(a) A only
(b) B only
(c) A and B both
(d) None of these

4. What is the total contribution of all the countries' Private Consumption Expenditure except country B to the GDP?
(a) 230
(b) 260
(c) 270
(d) 280

Solutions:

Before you start solving this question, you should notice that while the first pie chart adds up to 100%, the second one does not. You should realise that since the second pie chart is giving us the Private Consumption Expenditure (PCE) as a percentage of GDP for the five countries, it need not add up to 100.

Also, you should realise that country names are scrambled in the two pie charts. We cannot make out which of countries 1,2,3,4,5 is Country A, B, C, D and E in the GDP Pie chart. Likewise, we cannot make out the same for the PCE as a percentage of the GDP Pie chart too. Also, between the two charts also there is no country name – country number consistency, which means that if we discover that country 5 in the first pie-chart is country A (for example), it does not mean that country 5 in the second pie chart is also country A.

The following set of deductions will lead us to the answers:

Deduction 1: From clue 4, we get that the total GDP of the five countries taken together is 2000 million and of that the two countries contributing the minimum are 300 million each (15% of the total GDP of the five countries). From Clue 5, we know that these countries have to be A and C. Also from Clue 2, we know that the sum of the private consumption of these 5 countries is 300.

Deduction 2: From Clue 1, we see that the country with the highest GDP has a PCE of 90 million, which means that it has to correspond to a 15% value in the second pie chart. At this stage this country could be B,D or E.

Deduction 3: Countries B and D would have a total GDP of 400 each (from clue 6). This means that the country identified in deduction 2, is country E. After these deductions, we still need to identify the PCE as a percentage of GDP for countries A,B,C and D – and also identify their PCE.

Deduction 4: It is given to us in clue 6 that country D has a PCE of 50% more than C. Correlating with the PCE as a percentage of GDP figures from the second pie-chart, we can make out that this can only occur if we use 13.33% for C and 15% for D, giving us PCE of 40 and 60 respectively for C and D. At this stage we still have to allot a 10% and a 23.33% figure for PCE as a percentage of GDP – between the countries A and B.

Deduction 5: This then means that the reference to the second highest PCE in clue 5, has to be for country A. Thus, country A would have a value of PCE as a percentage of GDP equal to 23.33% and B would have a 10% value for this variable. The completed table of values would now look as follows:

	A	B	C	D	E	Total
GDP	300	400	300	400	600	2000
PCE	70	40	40	60	90	300
GDP (%)	15.000%	20.000%	15.000%	20.000%	30.000%	100%
PCE (%)	23.333%	13.333%	13.333%	20.000%	30.000%	
PC/GDP (Countrywise)	23.33%	10.00%	13.33%	15.00%	15.00%	

The answers can be read off this table:
1. 300. Option (a) is correct.
2. 10%. Option (b) is correct.
3. Only Statement A is correct. Hence, option (a) is correct.
4. The sum of PCE for A, C, D and E is 260. Option (b) is correct.

The following exercise will make the use of pie charts clear to you.

EXERCISE

Level of Difficulty 1

Directions for Questions 1 to 4: *The following pie chart (Figure 5.2) shows the amount of subscriptions generated for India Bonds from different categories of investors.*

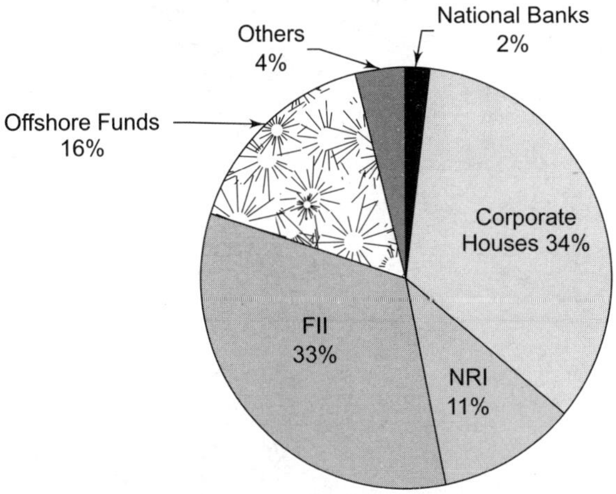

FIGURE 5.2 *Subscriptions Generated for India Bonds*

1. If the investments by NRIs are ₹4,000 crore, then the investment by corporate houses and FIIs together is:
   (a) 24,000 crore
   (b) 24,363 crore
   (c) 25,423.4 crore
   (d) 25,643.3 crore
2. What is the approximate ratio of investment flows into India Bonds from NRIs to corporate houses?
   (a) 1:4 (b) 1:3
   (c) 3:1 (d) Cannot be determined
3. If the total investment flows from FIIs were to be doubled in the next year and the investment flows from all other sources had remained constant at their existing levels for this year, then what would be the proportion of FII investment in the total investment flows into India Bonds in the next year (approximately)?
   (a) 40% (b) 50%
   (c) 60% (d) 70%
4. If the inflow from the FIIs after the doubling (of Question 3) were to the tune of US $500 million, what would be the total investment into India Bonds next year (in US $ millions)?
   (a) 1000 (b) 1500
   (c) 800 (d) Cannot be determined

Directions for Questions 5 to 11: *The following pie charts [Figures 5.3(a) and (b)] exhibit the distribution of the overseas tourist traffic from India. The two charts show the tourist distribution by country and the age profile of the tourists respectively. Study the charts carefully and answer the questions which follow.*

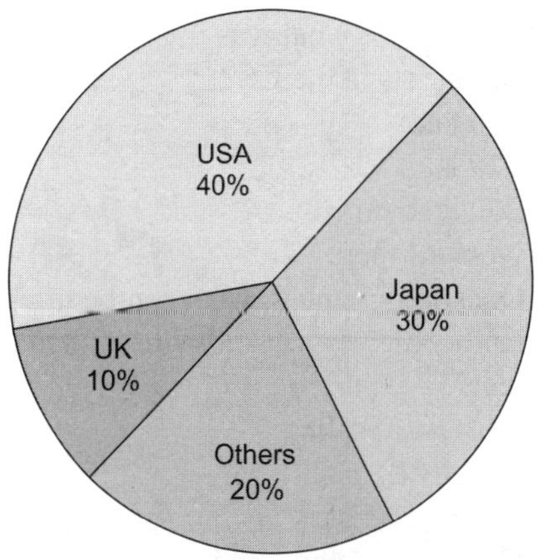

(a)

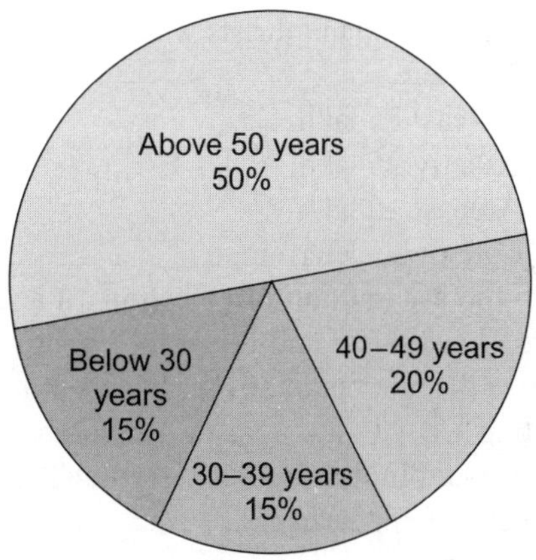

(b)

FIGURE 5.3 *Distribution of Overseas Tourist Traffic from India*

5. What percentage of the Indian tourists went to either USA or UK ?
   (a) 40% (b) 50%
   (c) 60% (d) 70%
6. The ratio of the number of Indian tourists that went to USA to the number of Indian tourists who were below 30 years of age is:
   (a) 2:1
   (b) 8:3
   (c) 3:8
   (d) Cannot be determined

7. If amongst other countries, Switzerland accounted for 25% of the Indian tourist traffic, and it is known from official Swiss records that a total of 25 lakh Indian tourists had gone to Switzerland during the year, then find the number of 30–39-year-old Indian tourists who went abroad in that year.
(a) 18.75 lakh
(b) 25 lakh
(c) 50 lakh
(d) 75 lakh
8. For Question 7, what was the volume of traffic of Indian tourists in the US?
(a) 150 lakh
(b) 125 lakh
(c) 200 lakh
(d) None of these
9. For Questions 7 and 8, what can be inferred about the number of 50+-year-olds who visited UK during the year?
(a) At least 25 lakh
(b) Exactly 25 lakh
(c) At least 10 lakh
(d) Cannot be determined
10. Solve question 9 assuming that the age distribution of overseas Indian tourists was uniform for all the countries.
(a) At least 25 lakh
(b) Exactly 25 lakh
(c) At least 10 lakh
(d) Cannot be determined
11. With the assumption of Question 10 and the data from Questions 7 and 8 taken to be true, find the ratio of the number of 50+-year-olds Indian tourists visiting USA in the year to the number of below 50-year-old Indian tourists visiting UK or Switzerland during the year.
(a) 2:1 (b) 8:3
(c) 3:8 (d) Cannot be determined

Directions for Questions 12 to 14: *The following pie charts [Figures 5.4(a) and (b)] give the information about the distribution of weight in the human body according to different kinds of components. Study the pie charts carefully and answer the questions given.*

12. How much of the human body is neither made of bones nor skin?
(a) 40% (b) 50%
(c) 60% (d) 70%
13. What is the ratio of the distribution of proteins in the muscles to that of the distribution of proteins in the bones?
(a) 2:1 (b) 2:3
(c) 3:2 (d) Cannot be determined
14. What percentage of proteins of the human body is equivalent to the weight of its skin?
(a) 41.66% (b) 43.33%
(c) 44.44% (d) Cannot be determined

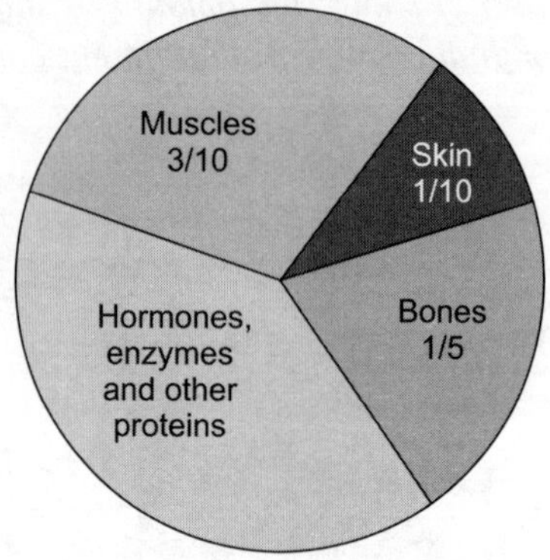

(a)

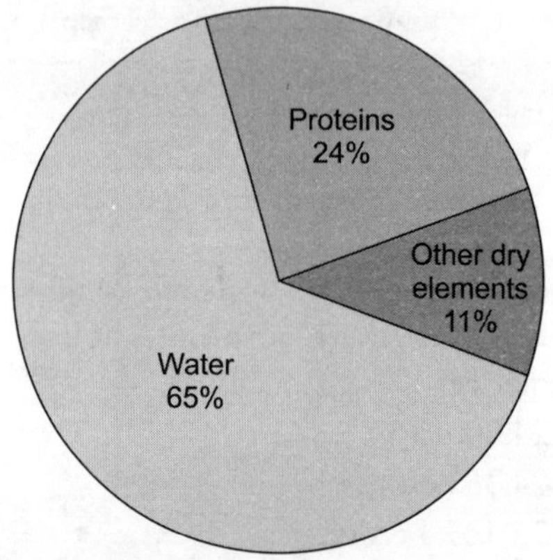

(b)

FIGURE 5.4 *Distribution of Weight in Human Body*

Directions for Questions 15 to 18: *The pie chart given below (Figure 5.5) shows the percentage share of the usage of the income of an individual.*

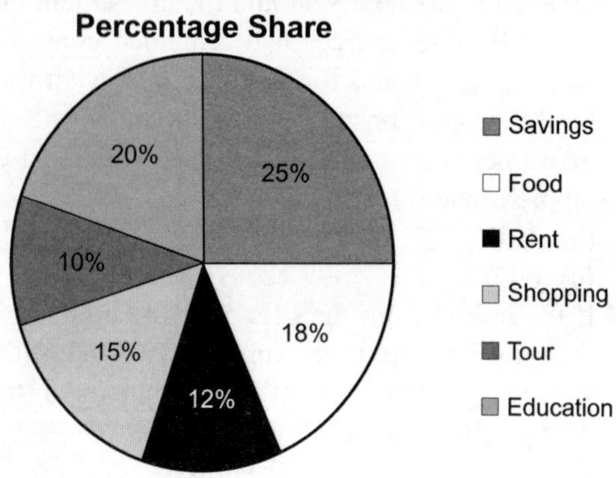

FIGURE 5.5

15. If total income was ₹540000 then find the expenditure on shopping and rent in total.
    (a) ₹92000 (b) ₹194500
    (c) ₹145800 (d) ₹112000
16. If the total amount spend was ₹544000 then find the ratio of expenditure on saving and education together to the expenditure on tour and shopping together.
    (a) 10:9 (b) 9:5
    (c) 3:5 (d) 5:3
17. Find the central angle made by shopping and tour together.
    (a) 136 (b) 90
    (c) 105 (d) 126
18. If the total amount spent is ₹360000 then the amount of food is what per cent of the amount of saving.
    (a) 90% (b) 82%
    (c) 72% (d) 66%

Directions for Questions 19 to 21: *The questions are based on the pie charts given below:*

Chart 1 shows the distribution of twelve million tons of crude oil transported through different modes over a specific period of time. Chart 2 shows the distribution of the cost of transporting this crude oil. The total cost was ₹30 million.

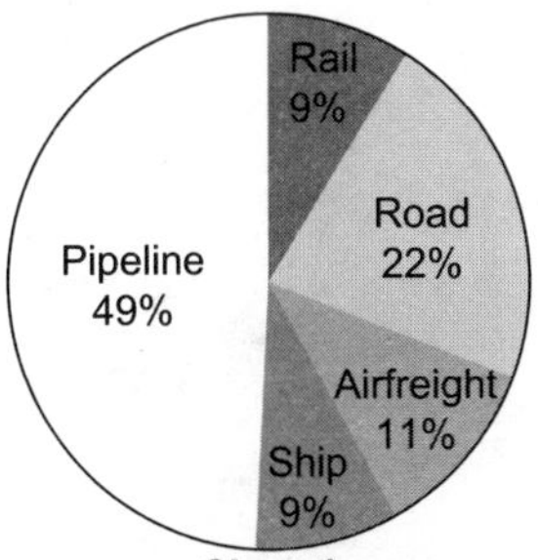

Chart 1

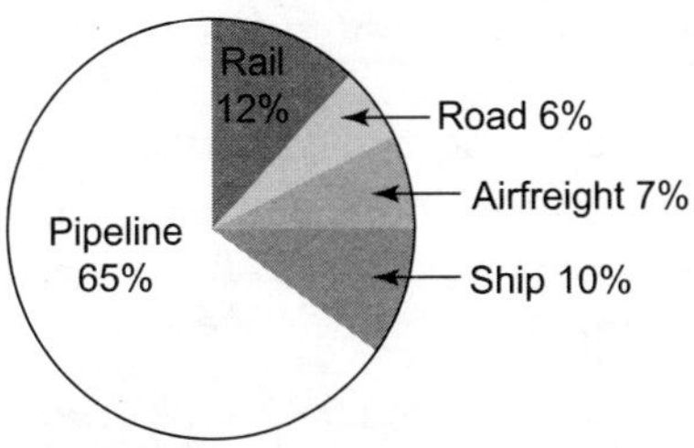

Chart 2

FIGURE 5.6

19. If the cost per tonne of transport by ship, air and road are represented by P, Q and R respectively, which of the following is true?
    (a) R > Q > P
    (b) P > R > Q
    (c) P > Q > R
    (d) R > P > Q
20. The cost in rupees per tonne of oil moved by rail and road happens to be roughly
    (a) 3 (b) 1.5
    (c) 4.5 (d) 8
21. From the charts given, it appears that the cheapest mode of transport is:
    (a) Road (b) Rail
    (c) Pipeline (d) Ship

Level of Difficulty 2

Directions for Questions 1 to 4: *The following is an extract from the placement snapshots at IIT Kharagpur. It depicts the percentage break-up of the number of students opting for a job in particular functional areas. The only functional areas on offer for placements are Civil Engineering, Mechanical Engineering, Computer Science, Information Technology, Electrical Engineering and each student has to opt for only one of these functional area. Also consider that the entire batch was placed, with each student getting exactly one job.*

1. If the number of students opting for a job in Mechanical decreased by 11.11%, by what percentage is the batch strength of 2020 more/less than the strength of 2019?
   (a) increased by 11.11%
   (b) increased by 22.22%
   (c) increased by 88.88%
   (d) Cannot be determined

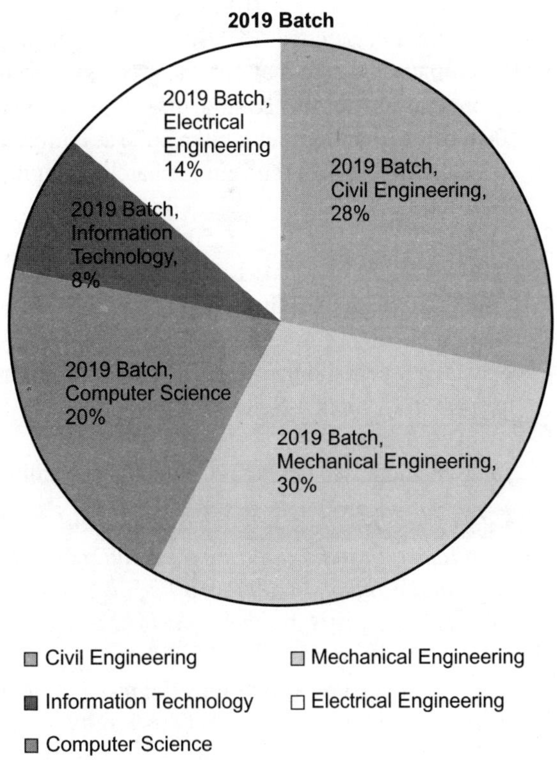

FIGURE 5.7(A)

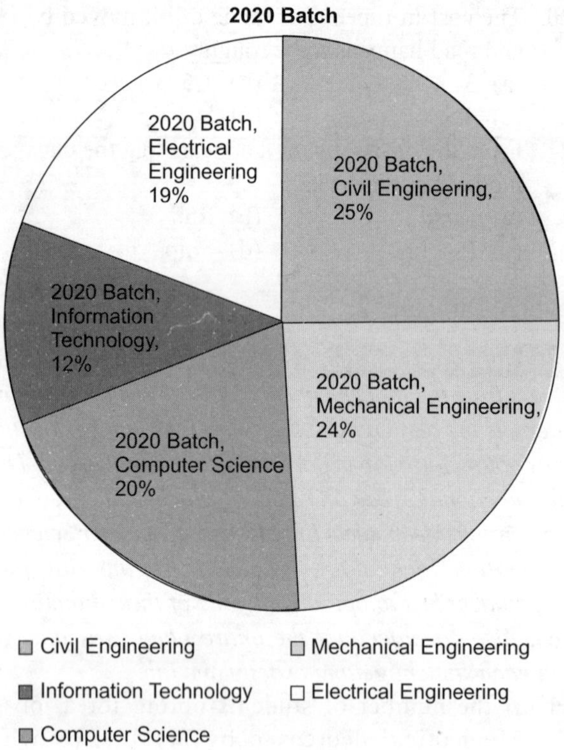

FIGURE 5.7(B)

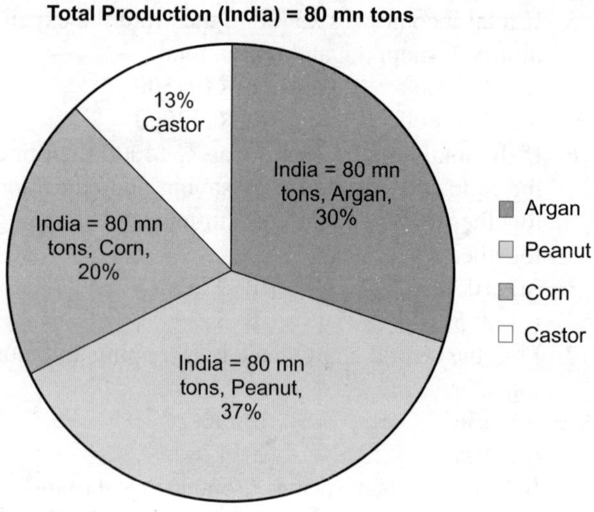

FIGURE 5.8(A)

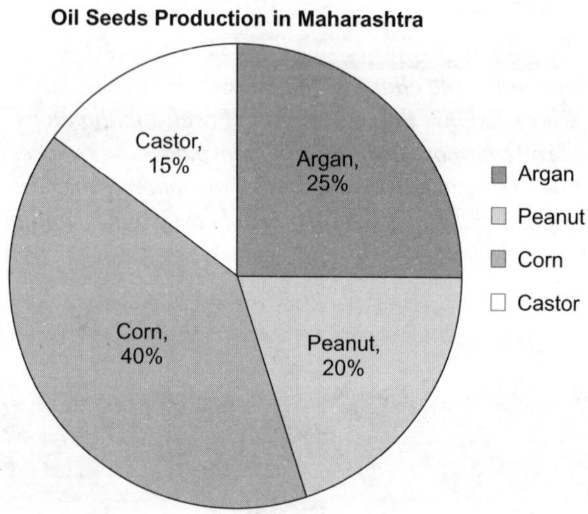

FIGURE 5.8(B)

2. Which functional area saw the greatest decline in the number of students opting for it as a career choice? Assume that atleast one functional area showed a decline in the number of students.
   (a) Civil (b) Mechanical
   (c) Computer Science (d) Cannot be determined
3. If the functional area that saw the greatest percentage increase in number of students opting for it had 100 more students opting for it in 2020 as compared to 2019, find the difference in the batch strength in 2020 and in 2019.
   (a) 30 (b) 50
   (c) 60 (d) Data Insufficient
4. From 2020 to 2019, if the percentage of people not taking up a job in Computer Science grew by 10%, by what per cent did the number of students taking up a job in Computer Science grow by?
   (a) 10% decrease (b) No change
   (c) 10% increase (d) Cannot be determined

Directions for Questions 5 to 8: *The only oil-seeds that are produced in India are argan, peanut, corn and castor. The total production of these oil-seeds in 2020 is 80 mn tons. The first pie chart shows the break-up of this* production across the four varieties. The second pie chart is also the percentage breakup of the total production of oil-seeds across the four varieties, but this is only for the state of Maharashtra.

In all the questions "Rest of India" means all states in India other than Maharashtra.

5. If Maharashtra accounts for 10% of the total production of argan in India, what percentage of the total oil-seed production of India is accounted for by Maharashtra?
   (a) 8% (b) 12%
   (c) 15% (d) Cannot be determined
6. If the production of peanut in Maharashtra is 1.5 mn tons, what percentage of total production of oil-seeds in India is accounted for by Maharashtra?
   (a) 5.5% (b) 8.5%
   (c) 9.375% (d) 12%
7. If the ratio of production of castor in Maharashtra and Rest of India is 1 : 4, then what percentage of the total oil-seed production of the Rest of India is accounted for by castor (approximately)?

(a) 11.3% (b) 12.6%
(c) 17.8% (d) 22.1%

8. If Maharashtra produces 40% lesser corn than Rest of India, find the production of argan in Maharashtra.
(a) 2 mn tons (b) 3.75 mn tons
(c) 5 mn tons (d) 12 mn tons

Directions for Questions 9 to 12: *In the figure below, the first pie chart represents the distribution of total salary of five employees for the month of January 2020 and the second pie chart represents the distribution of expenditure of these five employees for the same month. Total salary = Savings + Expenditure*

Total salary of the five employees = ₹324000

Total expenditure of the five employees = ₹150000

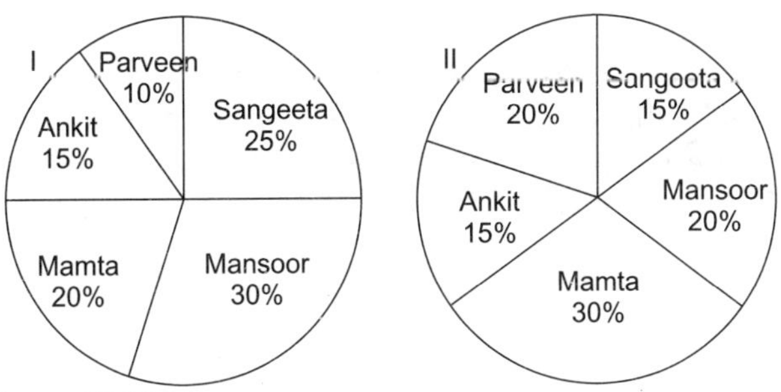

FIGURE 5.8(B)

9. If the person whose expenditure as a percentage of his/her income is the lowest is said to be a spendthrift, then which one of the following persons is a spendthrift person?
(a) Sangeeta (b) Mansoor
(c) Mamta (d) Ankit

10. The approximate difference between the expenditure percentages (expenditure as a percentage of income) of Praveen and Mansoor is:
(a) 46% (b) 27%
(c) 55% (d) 61%

11. What is the difference between the saving of Sangeeta and Praveen?
(a) ₹23700 (b) ₹64800
(c) ₹56100 (d) ₹58300

12. What is the ratio of the expenditure of Sangeeta and Mamta together to the income of Ankit and Praveen together?
(a) 145 : 162 (b) 4 : 7
(c) 5 : 6 (d) 135 : 172

Directions for Questions 13 to 16: *In the first pie chart, the percentage of number of candidates (boys + girls) from five different states – Uttar Pradesh, Delhi, Haryana, Uttarakhand and Punjab who appeared for the CAT exam in the year 2025 is given.*

Total number of candidates (boys and girls) who appeared from the given 5 states = 32400

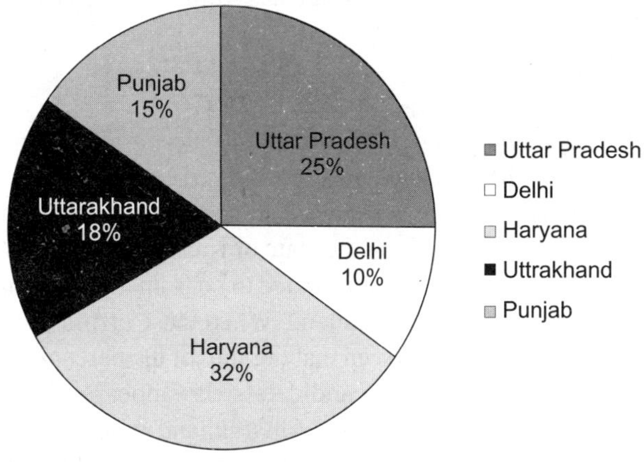

FIGURE 5.9(A)

In the second pie chart, the percentage of the number of girl candidates from the five different states – Uttar Pradesh, Delhi, Haryana, Uttarakhand and Punjab who appeared for the CAT exam in the year 2025 is given.

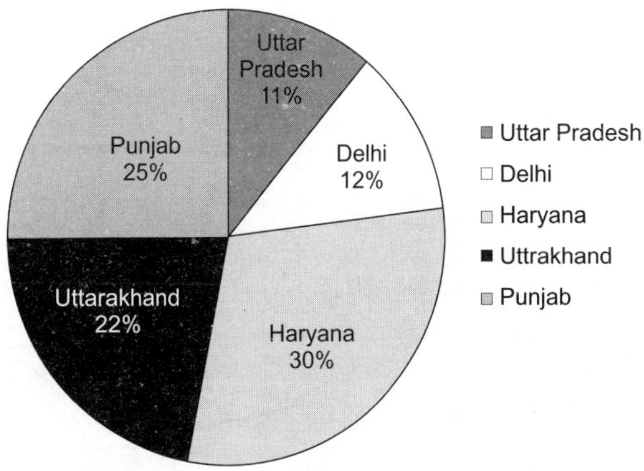

FIGURE 5.9(B)

13. If the total number of girl candidates who appeared from the given 5 states is 12000, then in which state the number of boys is less than the number of girl candidates?
(a) Punjab (b) Uttarakhand
(c) Haryana (d) Delhi

14. In 2026 from the state of Delhi, the number of boy and girl candidates has increased by 37.5% and 25% respectively compared to that from the previous year. If in 2026, the number of boy candidates from Delhi is 110% of the number of girl candidates from Delhi, then the number of girl candidates from Uttarakhand in 2025 is

(a) 2200 (b) 2970
(c) 2640 (d) Cannot be determined

15. If the average number of boy candidates from all the given 5 states is 4000, then what is average of the number of girl candidates from the states Delhi and Haryana?
(a) 1152 (b) 1844
(c) 2046 (d) 2604

16. In a computer glitch found out later, it was found that 520 girl candidates and 480 girl candidates who appeared from the states Haryana and Uttarakhand were actually from the state of Karnataka and mistakenly they were considered to be from the states of Haryana and Uttarakhand. When these errors were corrected, it was seen that the sum of the percentage of number of girl candidates who appeared from the states Haryana and Uttarakhand amongst the given 5 states becomes 46%. It was also checked that there was no other error apart from this. Of all the girl candidates coming from these 5 states, what is the percentage of girls from Delhi?
(a) 10.80% (b) 12%
(c) 10.67% (d) 13.50%

Directions for Questions 17 to 21: *The year is 2018. Ruchi Soya is one of the largest manufacturers of edible oil in India. Seeing the past records of the company Prashnavali Ayurveda wants to acquire it . The CEO of Prashnavali Ayurveda, Logic Bose asked the manager Unlogic Daniels about the sales record of the company for the previous two years (2016 and 2017). Mr. Daniels prepared a multi-layered pie chart (Figure 5.10) and presented it. The outer layer of the graph shows the monthly sales during that period, with each label showing the month followed by sales figure of that month. For some months, the sales figures are not given in the chart. The middle-layer shows the quarter-wise aggregate sales figures (in some cases, aggregate quarter-wise sales numbers are not given next to the quarter). The innermost layer shows the annual sales. It is known that the sales figures during the three months of the second quarter (April, May, June) of 2016 form an arithmetic progression, as do the three-monthly sales figures in the fourth quarter (October, November, December) of that year.*

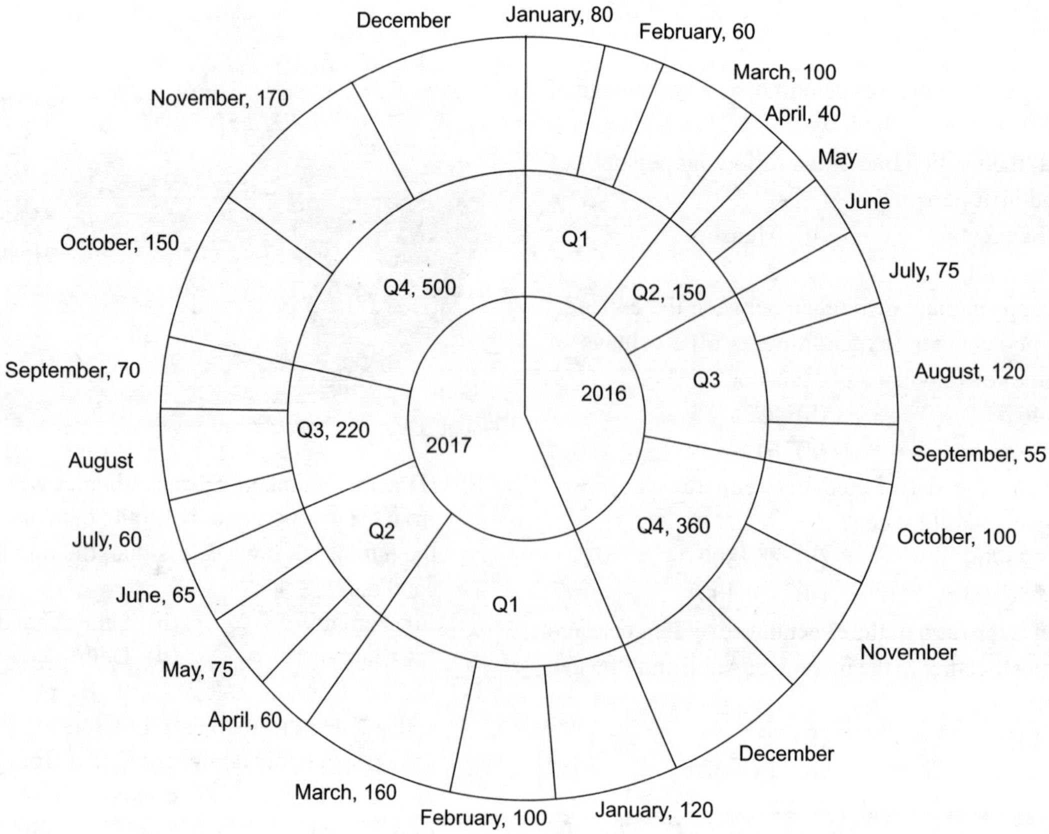

FIGURE 5.10

17. What is the percentage change in sales of Ruchi Soya in August 2017 as compared to the sales in August 2016?
(a) 33.33% increase (b) 33.33% decrease
(c) 25% increase (d) 25% decrease
18. In which quarter of 2017, has Ruchi Soya shown the highest percentage increase in sales from the same quarter of 2016?
(a) Q4 (b) Q1
(c) Q2 (d) Q3
19. What is the number of times that the company shows a drop in monthly sales from the previous month's sales in the period shown.
(a) 8 (b) 9
(c) 10 (d) 11
20. You are asked to find the name of the month, during which the percentage increase in sales from the previous month's sales was the least. Can you name the month?
(a) December of 2017
(b) December of 2016
(c) June of 2017
(d) November of 2017
21. What was the overall percentage increase or decrease in the sales value of Ruchi Soya from 2016 to 2017?
(a) 35 % (b) 25%
(c) 30 % (d) None of these

Level of Difficulty 3

Directions for Questions 1 to 4: *The Following pie charts show the break-up of the students (stream-wise) who appeared in the CAT held once in the years 2016 and 2017.*

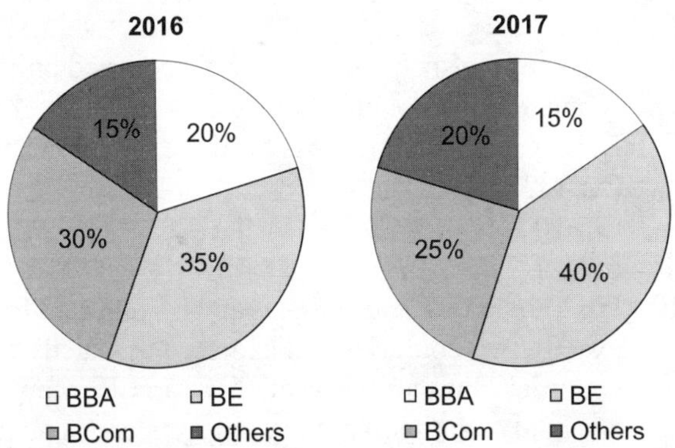

FIGURE 5.11

From amongst the BE students who appeared in the exam in 2016, five per cent students appeared in the exam in 2017 as well. If they had not re-appeared in the exam, then the percentage of BE students in total number of students who appeared in the exam in 2017 would have been 39.

1. What is the ratio of the total number of students who appeared in the exam in 2016 to that in 2017?
(a) 100:107 (b) 400:427
(c) 40:47 (d) Cannot be determined
2. If from the BBA stream, 5% students from those who appeared at the examination in 2016 appear in the exam again in 2017. Also it is known that the total numbers of students who appeared in the exam in 2016 and 2017 were 19000 and 20000 respectively. Then out of those BBA students who appeared in the exam in 2017, what percentage of students were appearing in the exam for the first time in 2017?
(a) 93.66% (b) 93.33%
(c) 92.66% (d) 92.33%
3. If from each stream n% of the students out of those who appeared in the exam in 2016, appeared in the exam again in 2017. Also 70% of the total number of students who appeared in the exam in 2017 appeared in the exam for the first time in 2017. What per cent of the BE students who appeared in the exam in 2017, appeared in the exam in 2017 for the first time?
(a) 26.25% (b) 29.5%
(c) 73.75% (d) Cannot be determined
4. If all the students who appeared in the exam in 2016 appeared in the exam again in 2017 then which of the following is a possible ratio between the total numbers of students who appeared in the exam in 2016 and 2017?
(a) 1:2 (b) 2:1
(c) 4:5 (d) 5:6

Directions for Questions 5 to 8: *Five friends from HEC Paris – Aaron, Bill, Chris, Drake and Elenagovan – invest in a start-up business venture. The percentage of capital invested by each person is represented in the pie chart.*

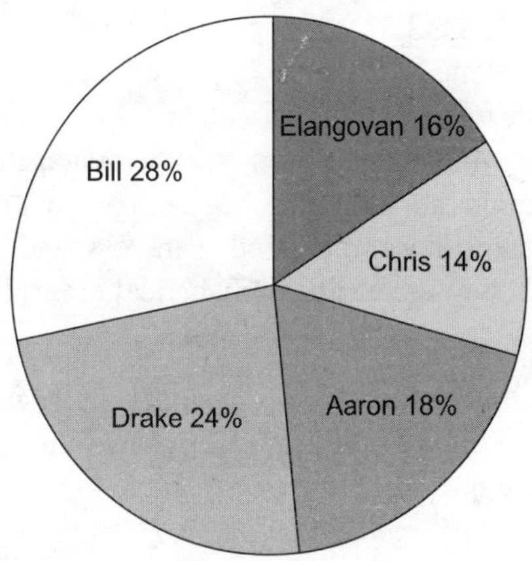

FIGURE 5.12

It is also known that Aaron invested his money for a period of 8 months, while Chris invested his money for 4 months more than Bill invested his money for. Drake's money was invested for 2 months less than Chris, while Elangovan's money was invested for 2 months less than Bill's. The venture turns really successful and at the end of the year their venture earns a big profit. They plan to have a holiday to celebrate the success of their venture after receiving their shares in the profit.

Two of them spend on hotel stays, three of them pay for the food, three for travel and three of them spend on entertainment. Two of them pay for travel along with spending on food and entertainment. Bill receives $28000 as his share in the profit. The one whose profit share is less than Aaron's share spends only on food. All those persons whose share in the profit is more than Chris's share, spend on food. Of the two persons whose share in the profit is less than Bill but more than Elangovan, only one person spends on entertainment and stay, whereas the other one spends on nothing else but travel. Aaron, who receives $18000 as his share in the profit, spends on entertainment. Drake does not spend on stay.

5. Which of the following groups of friends pays for the entertainment?
   (a) Drake, Chris and Elangovan
   (b) Bill, Chris and Drake
   (c) Aaron, Bill and Drake
   (d) Aaron, Chris and Elangovan
6. Who all spend for food, entertainment, travel and stay?
   (a) Only Bill
   (b) Both Bill and Drake
   (c) Both Aaron and Chris
   (d) Nobody spent on all 4.
7. What is the average of the shares in profit of those who received more than $ 15000?
   (a) $25750
   (b) $24250
   (c) $26333.33
   (d) None of these
8. If the total amount spent on travel is 7/20 of Aaron's share in the profit, then what percentage of Chris's share in the profit does he spend on travel expenses (assume those who spend on travel spend in the ratio 1 : 2 : 4 in increasing alphabetical order)?

Directions for Questions 9 to 12: *Six countries, Ambaland (A), Bramaland (B), Curvaland (C), Dratland (D), Enterland (E) and Fineland (F), exported and imported Aluminium only amongst themselves. Any country can both export and import Aluminium. However, no country can export to any country from which it imports and vice versa.*

The following pie charts provides the quantity of aluminium exported and imported by each of the six countries during a particular year:

Aluminium Exported (in mn tonnes)

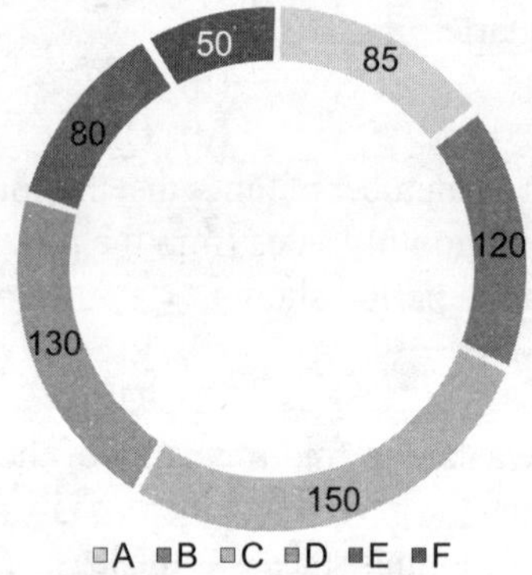

FIGURE 5.13(A)

Aluminium Imported (in mn tonnes)

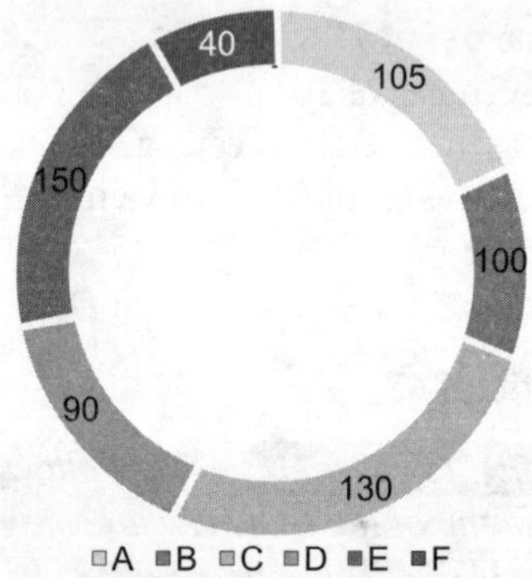

FIGURE 5.13(B)

9. If one of the six countries, say X, exported only to A and another country, say Y, imported only from D, how many distinct possibilities exist for the pair (X, Y)?
   (a) 10 (b) 12
   (c) 14 (d) 15
10. It is known that, each of C, D and E, imported from exactly two countries and exported to exactly two countries. Further, each of C, D and E imported an equal quantity of aluminium from each country from which it imported aluminium and exported an equal quantity of aluminium to each country to which it exported aluminium.
    To which of the following countries did C export aluminium?
    (a) A (b) B
    (c) D (d) F

11. For the conditions stated in Question 10, what is the quantity of aluminium (in million tonnes) that A exported to B?
    (a) 10
    (b) 20
    (c) 15
    (d) A did not export to B
12. For the conditions stated in Question 10, from which of the following countries did B not import aluminium?
    (a) E
    (b) C
    (c) F
    (d) More than one of the above

Directions for Questions 13 to 16: *Consider the information provided in the figure below, relating to India's foreign trade in 1997–98 and the first eight months of 1998–99. Total trade with a region is defined as the sum of exports to and imports from the region. Trade deficit is defined as the excess of imports over exports. Trade deficit may be negative.*

A. USA	*B. Germany*
C. EU	*D. UK*
E. Japan	*F. Russia*
G. Other east Europe	*H. OPEC*
I. Asia	*J. Other LDCs*
K. Others	

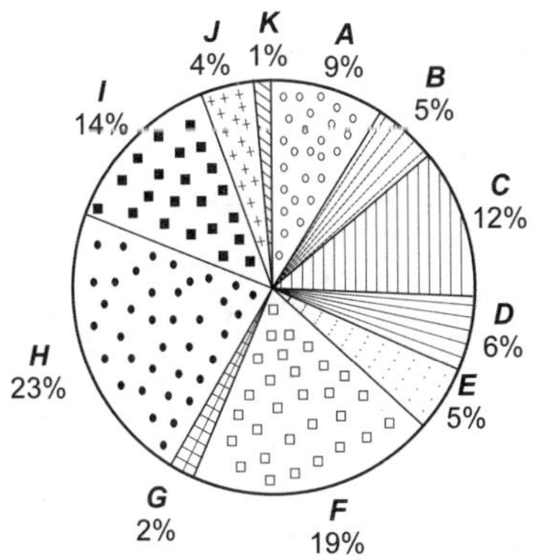

1997–98 Imports into India: $40779 million

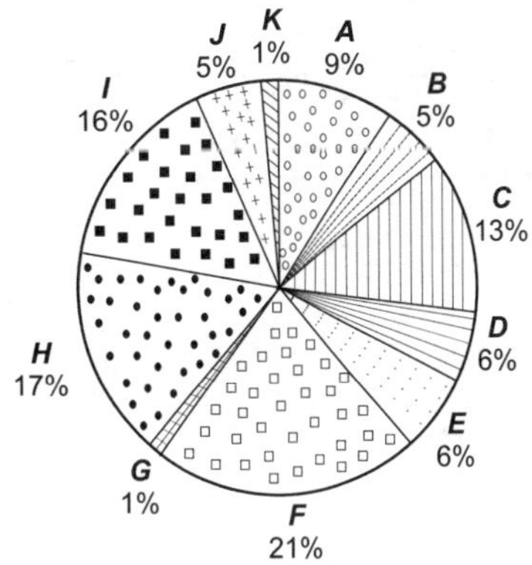

1998–99 Imports into India (April–November): $28126 million

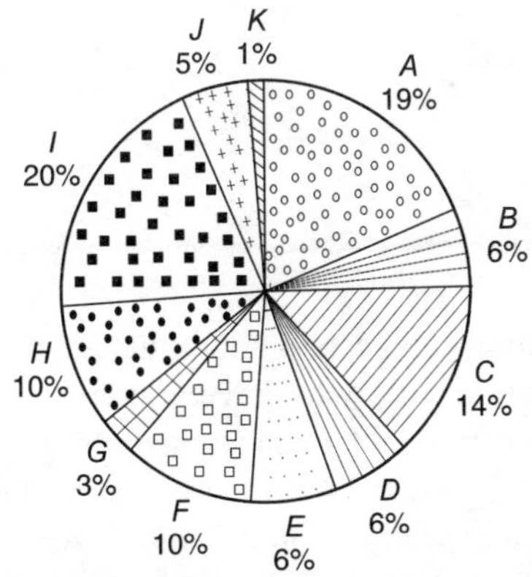

1997–98 Exports from India: $33979 million

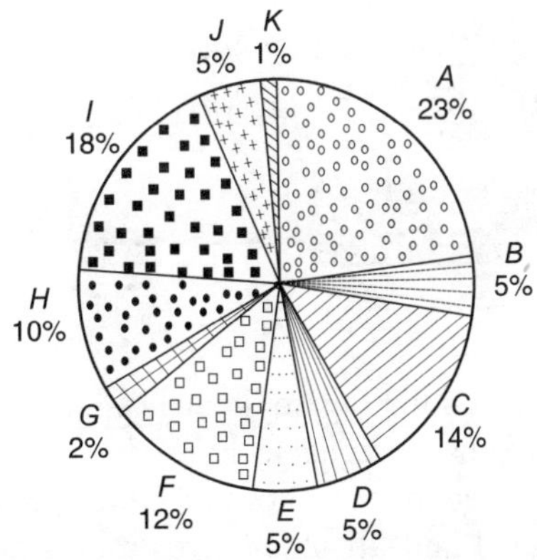

1998–99 Exports from India (April–November): $21436 million

FIGURE 5.14 *Destination of Exports*

13. What is the region with which India had the highest total trade in 1997–98?
    (a) USA (b) EU
    (c) OPEC (d) Others
14. In 1997–98 the amount of Indian exports, in millions US $, to the region with which India had the lowest total trade, was approximately
    (a) 750 (b) 340
    (c) 220 (d) 440
15. In 1997–98, the deficit with respect to India, in billions of US $, for the region with the highest trade deficit with respect to India, was approximately equal to
    (a) 6.0 (b) 3.0
    (c) 4.5 (d) 7.5

16. Which region had the lowest trade deficit with India in 1997–98?
(a) USA
(b) Asia
(c) Others
(d) EU

Directions for Questions 17 and 18: These questions are based on the situation given below.

Assume that the average monthly exports from India and imports to India during the remaining four months of 1998-99 would be the same as that for the first eight months of the year.

17. What is the region to which India exports registered the highest percentage growth between 1997–98 and 1998–99?
(a) Other East Europe
(b) USA
(c) Asia
(d) Exports have declined, no growth

18. What is the percentage growth rate in India's total trade deficit between 1997–98 and 1998–99?
(a) 43
(b) 47
(c) 50
(d) 40

ANSWER KEY

Level of Difficulty 1

1. (b)	2. (b)	3. (b)	4. (a)	5. (b)	6. (b)	7. (d)
8. (c)	9. (d)	10. (b)	11. (b)	12. (d)	13. (d)	14. (a)
15. (c)	16. (b)	17. (b)	18. (c)	19. (c)	20. (b)	21. (a)

Level of Difficulty 2

1. (a)	2. (b)	3. (d)	4. (c)	5. (b)	6. (c)	7. (b)
8. (b)	9. (a)	10. (d)	11. (c)	12. (c)	13. (a)	14. (b)
15. (d)	16. (d)	17. (d)	18. (b)	19. (b)	20. (a)	21. (c)

Level of Difficulty 3

1. (b)	2. (a)	3. (c)	4. (a)	5. (c)	6. (a)	7. (b)
8. 8.57%	9. (a)	10. (b)	11. (b)	12. (a)	13. (c)	14. (b)
15. (b)	16. (b)	17. (b)	18. (b)			

SOLUTIONS

Level of Difficulty 1

1. $(67/11) \times 4000 = 24363$ (approximately).
2. $11:34$ is approximately equal to $1:3$.
3. FIIs currently account for 33 out of 100. If their value is doubled and all other investments are kept constant then their new value would be 66 out of 133 → approximately equal to 50%.
4. 500 million would be approximately 50% of the total investment. Then 1000 will be the total investment.
5. $40 + 10 = 50\%$ (from the first chart)
6. $40:15 = 8:3$
7. 5% corresponds to Switzerland's 25 lakh. Hence 15% will be 75 lakh.
8. US accounts for 40%, i.e., 8 times 5%. Since Switzerland's 5% is 25 lakh, US will be 200 lakh.
9. Nothing can be said about the age break-up of the Indian tourists who have gone to any destination. Hence, cannot be determined.
10. If the age distribution is uniform, then 50+-year-olds will account for 50% of the total Indian tourist traffic in UK, i.e., 5% of the total Indian tourist traffic worldwide will be 50+-year-olds who went to UK, i.e., 25 lakh based on Switzerland's value from Question 10.
11. 50+-year-olds for USA are counted as 50% of 40. 50% of 10 represents the below 50 years olds visiting UK and 50% of 5 represents the below 50 years olds visiting Switzerland. Hence, the required ratio $= 20:(5 + 2.5) = 20:7.5 = 8:3$.
12. $20+10 = 30\%$ is made up of either bones or skin. Hence, 70% is made up of neither.

13. Cannot be determined since the respective distributions are not known.
14. 10/24 = 41.66%.

Solution for Questions 15 to 18

15. Expenditure at shopping and rents = 27 per cent of 540000 = 145800.
16. In solving this question, there is no need to calculate the actual expenditures on the mentioned items. This is so, because we only need the ratios, which can be calculated directly from the percentages.
Thus, expenditures on savings and education = 25 + 20 = 45%.
Expenditures on tour and shopping 10 + 15 = 25%.
Required ratio = 45 : 25 = 9 : 5.
17. Expenditures on shopping and tour = 15 + 10 = 25%. As we know that 100% on a pie chart is equal to 360 degrees, 25% would be equal to 90 degrees.
18. Required percentage according to the question is 18/25 × 100 = 72%.

Solution for Questions 19 to 21

19. Comparing the ratios we get ship (10/9) is the costliest, air (7/11) is the second costliest and road (6/22) is the cheapest. Hence, P > Q > R.
20. 0.18 × 30/0.31 × 12 = 1.45. Hence, option (b) is correct.
21. Road with a ratio of 6:22 is the cheapest.

Level of Difficulty 2

Solutions for Questions 1 to 4:

1. a. When a number reduces by 11.11% it means that the ratio is 8/9. From the charts we get:
$$\frac{0.24 \times y}{0.3 \times x} = \frac{8}{9} \rightarrow \frac{y}{x} = \frac{2.4}{2.16} = \frac{10}{9}$$
This means that the number of students has increased by 11.11%.
Hence, option (a) is correct.
2. In this case, we do not know the value of the total number of students in 2019 and 2020. In such a case, normally we would not have been able to find out if at all there was a decrease in the number of students placed in any area. However, the question tells us one important thing – i.e., that there is a definite decrease in the number of students in at least one area.
Looking through the numbers in the two pie charts, we can see that the greatest percentage decrease in the share is in Mechanical (from 30 to 24).
At the same time, Mechanical also had the largest number of students opting for it in 2019. Thus, both these facts occurring together implies that the decrease in number of students is maximum for Mechanical.
Hence, option (b) is correct.
3. The functional area that showed the maximum percentage increase in the number of students opting for it will be the functional area that showed the greatest percentage increase in its percentage share i.e., Information Technology (from 8% of 2019 students to 12% of 2020 students).
According to the question we are given: 12% of 2020 students, – 8% of 2019 students = 100. If we assume 2020 students as 'y' and 2019 students as 'x' we get the equation: $0.12y - 0.08x = 100$. There is no other information in the question. One should realise that we are in a multiple possibility situation in this question—one equation with two unknowns. Hence, there are multiple values possible for x and y and for their difference. Hence, the correct answer to this question would be 'Data Insufficient'.
Hence, option (d) is correct.
4. From the pie charts, we see that the percentage of students opting for computer science is 20% in both the years 2019 and 2020. This means that the percentage of total students not opting for computer science is the same at 80% in both years. If we assume that the number of students in 2019 and 2020 are x and y respectively, this means that $0.8y/0.8x = 11/10 \rightarrow y/x = 1.1$, which means that the number of students in 2020 (y) is 10% greater than the number of students in 2019 (x).
Hence, option (c) is correct.

Solutions for Questions 5 to 8:

5. 25% of Maharashtra's oil-seed production = 10% of (30% of India's oil-seed production) = 3% of India's oil-seed production.
Thus, Maharashtra's oilseed production = 12% of India's oilseed production. Thus, required percentage = 12%
Hence, option (b) is correct.
6. Since peanut is 1/5th of total oilseed production of Maharashtra, hence total oilseed production of Maharashtra = 7.5 mn tons. Thus, required percentage = 7.5/80 i.e., 9.375%.
Hence, option (c) is correct.
7. b. In such questions, that need to be taken through a series of calculations, in order to be able to get to the answer, it is a good idea to start with the final equation of what the question is asking us to calculate.

In this case, we are asked for the percentage value of the ratio:

$$\frac{\text{Total Castor Production in Rest of India}}{\text{Total Oil Seeds Production in Rest of India}}$$

Total production of castor in entire India = 13% of 80 = 10.4 million tons. This production is divided between Maharashtra and Rest of India in the ratio 1 : 4, i.e., Maharashtra produces 2.08 mn tons of castor.

Hence it produces 2.08 × 100/15 = 13.866 tons of oilseed.

Thus, Rest of India produces 80 – 13.866 = 66.133 tons of oilseeds of which castor is 8.32 mn tons.

Thus, required percentage is

$$\frac{\text{Total Castor Production in Rest of India}}{\text{Total Oil Seeds Production in Rest of India}}$$

$$= \frac{8.32}{66.133} = 12.58\% \text{ (approx)}$$

8. b. Maharashtra produces 40% less corn than the Rest of India – this means that the ratio of corn production in Maharashtra and Rest of India is 3 : 5. Also the total corn production of India is 20% of 80 = 16 (from the first pie chart). Thus, corn production in Maharashtra is 6 mn tons and for the Rest of India it is 10 mn tons.

Further, looking at Maharashtra's pie chart, we can see that this is 40% of its total oilseed production. We need to find 25% of Maharashtra's production. Since 40% is 6, 25% will be 3.75 mn tons.

Solutions for Questions 9 to 12:

Understanding the data: From the data, we see that there are two variables in the data – income and expenditure. From the given percentages in the pie charts, we can come up with the following table for their incomes, expenditures and savings:

	Income	Expenditure	Savings
Sangeeta	81000	22500	58500
Mansoor	97200	30000	67200
Mamta	64800	45000	19800
Ankit	48600	22500	26100
Praveen	32400	30000	2400

9. It can be read off from the table, that the spendthrift person in the group is Sangeeta. Option (a) is correct.
10. Expenditure as a percentage of income for Mansoor is: 30000/97200 ≈ 31%; expenditure as a percentage of income for Praveen is: 30000/32400 ≈ 93%. The required difference is the closest to 61% from the options. Option (d) is correct.
11. The required difference is 58500 – 2400 = 56100. Option (c) is correct.
12. Expenditure of Sangeeta and Mamta together = 45000 + 22500 = 67500;
Income of Ankit and Praveen together = 48600 + 32400 = 81000. The required ratio = 675 : 810 = 135 : 162 = 5 : 6. Option (c) is correct.

Solutions for Questions 13 to 16:

Understanding the data: In this question, the total number of candidates who appeared for the exam from each state is provided (32400). This number is divided into 10 numbers based on boy/girl or UP/Delhi/Haryana/Uttarakhand/Punjab. Hence, the overall 32400 students are divided into 10 types of students leading to an equation like:

$(\text{Boys}_{UP} + \text{Girls}_{UP}) + (\text{Boys}_{Haryana} + \text{Girls}_{Haryana}) + \ldots + \text{Girls}_{Punjab} = 32400.$

Also, from the first pie chart, we can derive the number of students coming from each state. Thus, we can work out: $(\text{Boys}_{UP} + \text{Girls}_{UP})$; $(\text{Boys}_{Haryana} + \text{Girls}_{Haryana})$ and so forth. However, we are not given any information to help us segregate how many boys and how many girls belong to each state. Based on this understanding, we should make the following table:

Let the total number of girls candidate who appeared from the 5 states be 100*n*.

	Number of (Boys +Girls) Candidates	Number of Girl Candidates
Uttar Pradesh	8100	11*n*
Delhi	3240	12*n*
Haryana	10368	30*n*
Uttarakhand	5832	22*n*
Punjab	4860	25*n*

However, as explained above, the number of girl and boy candidates cannot be found from the data given.

13. Total number of girls candidate who appeared from 5 states be = 12000.

	Number of (Boys +Girls)	Number of Girls
Uttar Pradesh	8100	1320
Delhi	3240	1440
Haryana	10368	3600
Uttarakhand	5832	2640
Punjab	4860	3000

We can see that in Punjab, the number of girls is more than the number of boys.

Hence, option (a) is correct.

14. Let the total number of girls candidate who appeared from the 5 states be $100n$.

	Number of (Boys + Girls) Candidates	Number of Girl Candidates
Uttar Pradesh	8100	11n
Delhi	3240	12n
Haryana	10368	30n
Uttarakhand	5832	22n
Punjab	4860	25n

Number of boys in 2026 = $(3240 - 12n) \times 1.375 = 4455 - 16.5n$.
Number of girls candidate in 2026 = $12n \times 1.25 = 15n$.
According to question
$(4455 - 16.5n)/110 = 15n/100$
On solving, $n = 135$
Number of girl candidates in Uttarakhand in 2025= $22n = 22 \times 135 = 2970$.

15. The average number of boys from all the given states is 4000. This means that there are 20000 boys and 12400 girls.
$100n = 12400 \rightarrow n = 124$.
Hence, the average number of girls from Delhi and Haryana = $(12n + 30n) \div 2 = 21n = 2604$.
Hence, option (d) is correct.

16. According to the question, we have the following equation:

$$\frac{(30+22)n - (520+480)}{100n - (520+480)} = \frac{46}{100}$$

On Solving, we get $n = 90$. This means that there are now a total of 8000 girls from these 5 states. Out of these 8000, 12% of 9000 = 1080 girls are from Delhi. So the required percentage = 13.5%.
Hence, option (d) is correct.

Solutions for Questions 17 to 21:

The information given in the pie chart can be represented in a table form as following:

	Month/Sales figure in	2016	2017
	January	80	120
Q1	February	60	100
	March	100	160
	April	40	60
Q2	May	50	75
	June	60	65
	July	75	60
Q3	August	120	90
	September	55	70
	October	100	150
Q4	November	120	170
	December	140	180

These numbers are based on the following deductions:
Now as given sales figure in 2017 Q4 = 500.
So, sales figure in December 2017 = 500 – 150 – 170 = 180.
Total sales in 2017 Q3 = 220.
So, sales in August 2017 = 220 – 60 – 70 = 90.
Similarly, the sales in missing month of 2016 can be obtained as sales in the three months of 2016 Q4 and Q2 are in Arithmetic Progression.

17. Required percentage increase = $\frac{90 - 120}{120} \times 100 = -25\%$.
Hence, option (d) is correct.

18. Comparing Quarter 1, 2, 3 and 4 of 2016 and 2017, we can see that the highest percentage change is exhibited for Quarter 1.
Hence, option (b) is correct

19. From the table obtained we can observe 9 drops for monthly sales when we compare it to previous month's sales in the time period shown.
Hence, option (b) is correct.

20. From the given options, it can be seen that the percentage increase is least for the month of December 2017 (when it grows from 170 to 180) a growth of only 5.9% (approximately). Hence option (a) is correct.

21. Required % increase

$$= \frac{(380+200+220+500) - (240+150+250+360)}{(240+150+250+360)} \times 100 = 30\%$$

Hence, option (c) is correct.

Level of Difficulty 3

Solutions for questions 1 to 4:

1. Suppose,
Total number of students who appeared in the exam in 2016 = $100x$.
Total number of students who appeared in the exam in 2017 = $100y$.
Number of BE students in 2016 = $35x$.
Number of BE students who re-appeared in the exam in 2017 = 5% of $35x = 1.75x$.
Number of BE students in 2017 = $40y$. Of these, the number of fresh BE students (not re-appearing candidates) = $40y - 1.75x$.
Number of students who appeared in 2017 from other disciplines = $60y$.

If these $1.75x$ people had not appeared for the exam in 2017, it would mean that the total number of students appearing in 2017 would be $100y - 1.75x$. It is given to us that:

$$\frac{40y - 1.75x}{100y - 1.75x} = 0.39 \rightarrow 40y - 1.75x = 39y - 0.6825x \rightarrow y = 1.0675x$$

Hence, $x:y = 400:427$.
Hence, option (b) is the correct answer.

2. The total number of BBA students who appeared in the exam in 2016 = 20% of 19000 = 3800.
Total number of BBA students who appeared in the exam in 2017 = 15% of 20000 = 3000.
Out of 3800, the number of BBA students who re-appeared in 2017 = 5% of 3800 = 190.
Hence, the number of BBA students who appeared for the first time in 2017 = 3000 – 190 = 2810. The required percentage will be got by the percentage value of the fraction 2810/3000 → 93.66%.
Hence, option (a) is the correct answer.
3. Let the number of students who appeared for the exam in 2016 be $100a$ and in 2017 be $100b$.
In 2017, the total number of BE students who appeared = $40b$. Total number of students from other disciplines = $60b$. Total number of re-appeared candidates in 2017 = $30b$ (= 30% of the number of candidates who appeared in 2017).
The question also tells us that from the candidates who appeared in 2016, n% from each discipline re-appeared in 2017.
This can be written as an equation as:
$$100a \times \frac{n}{100} = 30b \rightarrow \frac{a}{b} = \frac{30}{n} \rightarrow n = \frac{30b}{a}.$$
Also, $35a$ BE students appeared in 2016. N% of $35a$ appeared again in 2017 $\rightarrow \frac{n}{100} \times 35a = \frac{30b}{100a} \times 35a = 10.5b$. Thus, of the $40b$ BE candidates in 2017, $10.5b$ were repeaters and $29.5b$ were fresh candidates. The required percentage = 29.5/40 = 73.75%. Option (c) is the correct answer.
4. Let the number of students who appeared in 2016 and 2017 be $20a$ and $20b$. Then, from the pie charts we can construct this table.

	Table	BBA	BE	BCom	Others
2016	20*a*	4*a*	7*a*	6*a*	3*a*
2017	20*b*	3*b*	8*b*	5*b*	4*b*

We have to find a possible ratio of $20a$ with $20b$ (or $a:b$), keeping in mind that $3b$, $8b$, $5b$ and $4b$ should be equal to or greater than $4a$, $7a$, $6a$ and $3a$ respectively (since everyone re-appeared, it means that the number of students who appeared from each discipline in 2017, has to be equal to or more than the number of candidates who appeared in 2016). Based on this realisation we can reject option (d) for instance, since if $a:b = 5:6$, then $3b = 18$ and $4a = 20$. $4a > 3b$, which is not possible.
Hence, the correct answer is option (a).

Solutions for Questions 5 to 8:

Let the total amount invested be \$100. Then, the share of profit based on \$ month equivalents would be as follows:

Person	Amount Invested	Months Invested For	$ Equivalent Invested for One Month	Given Shares of Profits
Aaron	18	8	144	18000
Bill	28	*n*	28*n*	28000
Chris	14	*n* + 4	14*n* + 56	21000
Drake	24	*n* + 2	24*n* + 48	30000
Elangovan	16	*n* – 2	16*n* – 32	12000

Profits are distributed on the basis of \$ equivalents. From the information that Aaron got a profit share of 18000, we can workout in the above table that 144 → 18000. Hence, 1\$ equivalent = \$125 of actual profit. Secondly, from Bill's row, we know that $28n$ \$ equivalent = \$28000 in profits. Hence, n \$ equivalent = \$ 1000. Based on these two deductions, we can complete the total amounts of profits for Chris ($14n + 56 = 14000 + 56 \times 125 = 21000$); Drake ($24n + 48 = 24000 + 48 \times 125 = 30000$) and Elangovan ($16n - 32 = 16000 - 32 \times 125 = 12000$). Next, based on the clues about who spent on which activity, we can draw a second table as follows:

Person	Given Shares of Profits	Spends on Entertainment (3)	Spends on Food (3)	Spends on Travel (3)	Spends on Stay (2)
Aaron	18000	Yes	No	No	Yes
Bill	28000	Yes	Yes	Yes	Yes
Chris	21000	No	No	Yes	No
Drake	30000	Yes	Yes	Yes	No
Elangovan	12000	No	Yes	No	No

We can read the answers based on this table:

5. Option (c) is correct.
6. Option (a) is correct.
7. Option (b) is correct.
8. The total amount spent on travel would be \$6300. This would be paid for by B, C and D in the ratio

1:2:4. Chris would spend \$1800 on travel. This would amount to 8.57%

Solutions for Questions 9 to 12:

9. If a country exported only to A, it means its exports have to be greater than the imports of A. From the second pie chart, we can see that the imports of A is 105 million tonnes. There are three countries that are exporting more than 105 million tonnes in total. These are visible as B, C and D (from the first chart). Likewise, D exports 130 million tonnes. There are 4 countries A, B, C and F in the second chart, that can be seen to be importing less than or equal to 130 million tonnes.
Thus, the total possible X, Y pairs are: B- A, C, F; C- A, B, F; D- A, B, C, F. Hence, there are a total of 10 such pairs possible. Hence, option (a) is correct.
10. C imported 130 million tonnes and exported 150 million tonnes. Hence, its import per country would be 65 and export per country would be 75 million tonnes. Likewise, for D and E.

Country	Imports	Exports	Other Countries with Whom Trade Occurs
C	65 + 65(D) = 130	75 + 75(E) = 150	Two of A, B and F
D	45 + 45 = 90	65 + 65(C) = 130	All three of A, B, F
E	75 + 75(C) = 150	40 + 40 = 80	All three of A, B, F

Each of C, D and E, must have been trading (either imports or exports) with four countries – since importing and exporting cannot be done to the same country. Also, since there are only 6 countries A, B, C, D, E, F; each country amongst C, D, E would have to at least do one trade within the other two amongst each other.
Based on this logic, we can make the following conclusions that have been shown in the table:

1. C must have exported to E; E must have imported from C;
2. D must have exported to C and C have must have imported from D. (***Note:*** These are because the number of tonnes of export and import match for these pairs of countries.)

Next set of Deductions from the table above:

E cannot import from F (since E imports 75 mn tonnes and F only exports 50 mn tonnes). Hence, E to F trade must be E exports 40 tonnes to F. Consequently, F must be exporting 45 tonnes to D. Then, C cannot do any of its trades with F. This means that C would be trading only with A and B. The table changes to:

Country	Imports	Exports	Other Countries with Whom Trade Occurs
C	65 + 65(D) = 130	75 + 75(E) = 150	A, B
D	45(F) + 45 = 90	65 + 65(C) = 130	A, B
E	75 + 75(C) = 150	40(F) + 40 = 80	A, B

From this point we have to look at how to spread out the export and import quantities for A and B. A is exporting 85 and importing 105, while B is exporting 120 and importing 100. The only way to fit in the remaining values are:
C must import 65 tonnes from one of A and B. D must import 45 tonnes from one of A and B. E must import 75 tonnes from one of A and B. Hence, two countries (amongst C, D and E) must import from one of the two countries A and B, while one country must import from the other country. Since A is exporting only 85 tonnes, hence A cannot be exporting to two countries amongst C, D, E. Thus, B exports to either C and D or D and E.
In either case, B must export to D. If B is exporting to D, then D must export 65 tonnes to A. C must either export 75 tonnes to or import 65 tonnes from A. A is importing 65 tonnes from D. Hence, it cannot import a further 75 tonnes from C (as it imports only 105 tonnes). Hence, C must import 65 tonnes from A and C must export 75 tonnes to B.
E must export 40 tonnes and import 75 tonnes from A and B in any order.
At this point (after finalising C and D) the spare capacities are:
A exports 20 million tonnes; A imports 40 million tonnes; B exports 75 million tonnes; B imports 25 million tonnes.
The imports of E cannot be met by A's spare export capacity. Hence, B exports 75 million tonnes to E and E exports 40 million tonnes to A. The table evolves to:

Country	Imports	Exports	Other Countries with Whom Trade Occurs
C	65(A) + 65(D) = 130	75(B) + 75(E) = 150	A, B
D	45(F) + 45(B) = 90	65(A) + 65(C) = 130	AB
E	75(B) + 75(C) = 150	40(F) + 40(A) = 80	AB

At this point (after finalising C, D, E) the spare capacities are:

A exports 20 million tonnes; A imports 0 million tonnes; B exports 0 million tonnes; B imports 25 million tonnes. Also, F's spare capacity is export 5 million tonnes, import 0.

Thus, A and F export 20 and 5 million tonnes to B respectively.

From this point we can read off the answers:

10. Option (b) is correct.
11. Option (b) is correct
12. B did not import from D and E. Option (a) is correct.

Solutions for Questions 13 to 16

13. USA = 9% of 40779 + 19% of 33979; EU = 12% of 40779 + 14% of 33979;

    OPEC = 23% of 40779 + 10% of 33979 and others = 1% of 40779 + 1% of 33979.

    This can be approximated as:

    USA = 9% of 41 + 19% of 34; EU = 12% of 41 + 14% of 34;

    OPEC = 23% of 41 + 10% of 34 and others = 1% of 41 + 1% of 34.

    In this case it can be seen that OPEC has the maximum value.
14. India's total trade is minimum with K (others). Thus the answer would be 1 per cent of 33979 = 339.79. Approximately 340.
15. Region with the highest deficit with respect to India, means the region with which India's Trade surplus is maximum. From the charts it can be seen that this is for region A, i.e., USA. USA's trade deficit with respect to India, would be equal to India's trade surplus wrt USA = 19% of 33979 – 9% of 40779. This value works out to 3 billion dollars approximately. Hence option (b) is correct.
16. We are looking for the lowest trade deficit with respect to India for 1997-98. This means we are looking for India's smallest trade surplus with respect to any region. With US, India's trade surplus is quite large. With others as well as with EU India has a trade deficit and not a trade surplus. That leaves us with only Asia as a possible answer. Option (b) is correct.
17. In order to solve this, all you need to look for is the highest percentage increase in the percentage share of a particular region from 1997–98 to 1998–99 (in exports). USA goes from 19 per cent in 1997–98 to 23 per cent in 1998–99. Thus, this would be the largest percentage growth.
18. India's total trade deficit in 1997–98 is: 40779 – 33979 = 6800 millions.

    In 1998–99 the same would be: 1.5 × (28126 – 21436) = 1.5 × 6690 = 10035 millions. A percentage growth of 47% (between 6800 a 10035).

CHAPTER 6

Data Caselets

Outline

Learning Objectives

- Get a first-hand view of how data is presented through cases.
- Get an understanding of typical language used for writing data in the form of language.
- Get a first-hand feel of the question types created on the basis of cases.
- Get an understanding of how difficult questions can be framed on data caselets.

Chapter Highlights

- Introduction to data-based cases
- Practice exercise on cases with 3 levels of Difficulty

INTRODUCTION

The case form of data representation is used by question setters in order to test the student's feel for numbers, for variables and their inter-relationships and his/her ability to convert the information provided into a useful data representation format. Questions and their answers hinge on the student's ability to first spot the variables under consideration and then to inter-relate the given variables in order to make sense of the raw information provided by the case.

A case is nothing but a paragraph/passage which provides information about the values of the variables. Most cases are solved by converting the provided information into a tabular format. The student is advised to follow the following steps while solving data interpretation questions based on cases:

Step 1

During your first reading, identify the variables in the data, the number of instances of the variables provided and the respective inter-relationships amongst the variables.

After having identified these things the student will be in a position to establish a clear picture of the information and the requisite tabular format to solve the given case.

This step is also extremely important from the examination point of view, since it will help you estimate the amount of time required to solve the case. Hence, you will be in a position to make a better decision about whether the case you are pursuing is worth solving under the exam conditions.

Step 2

Chart out the table required and fill in the direct data given in the question into the table. At this stage the objective should not be to complete the table but to get down the direct information provided in the case into the table. It is important to distinguish between the two approaches, since trying to complete the table for the sake of completing the table might result in a lot of unnecessary work on the part of the student (which can easily be avoided). Remember, marks are allotted for the answer to the questions asked, not for filling the table. (Hence, we will do only as much as is asked and not one step more.)

Step 3

With the basic framework of the table ready, the approach of the student should be to identify the required solutions from the questions asked and solve only to get the answer of the question asked.

However, note here that as a rule any intermediate information derived in this process should be directly transferred to the table, since it is quite likely that the calculations you have done for one question might be repeated in the next question. Hence, in order to avoid re-working on things already done once, transfer any information derived during the process of solving one question onto the table so that it is available for all subsequent questions.

EXERCISE

Level of Difficulty 1

Case I George has recently acquired shares of four companies, namely Asian Paintz (AZ), BMZ, ChaeWoo (CW) and Dataman (DT). The financial results of these companies for the financial year ended 2022–23 revealed these interesting facts: Profits of AZ were 10 per cent of its sales, while the profits of BMZ were 20 per cent of its sales. While the profits of CW and DT were the same, the sales of CW were the same as those of BMZ. The total expenses of CW were 400 per cent more than its profits while the sales of DT were 200 per cent more than its profits. The total expenses of CW were ₹10 million and the total expenses of CW were 11.11 per cent more than those of AZ.

1. Which company had the lowest total expenses?
   (a) AZ (b) BMZ
   (c) CW (d) DT
2. Which company had the lowest profits?
   (a) AZ (b) BMZ
   (c) CW (d) DT
3. If next year, the profits of AZ were to equal CW's current profit, then with an increase of 12.5 per cent in sales, what would be the profit of AZ expressed as a percentage of sales next year?
   (a) 17.77 per cent
   (b) 22.22 per cent
   (c) 18.88 per cent
   (d) None of these
4. If profits of DT and BMZ were to be exchanged, what would be the ratio of the profit percentage (expressed as a percentage of sales) for these two companies?
   (a) 7:13 (b) 5:12
   (c) 12:5 (d) 5:13
5. What is the ratio of the highest and the lowest profit?
   (a) 12:5 (b) 7:18
   (c) 5:12 (d) 12:23

Case 2 Not surprisingly the growth of the hotel industry is driven by the increase in the number of people using hotels and the increase in per person use of the hotel. In 2024, it is expected that there will be 200 million hotel users in New Foundland, or about 20 per cent of the population will generate $50 billion in hotel revenues. Industry revenues should expand from $50 billion to $150 billion by 2028, while the number of users should grow to over $560 million or to about half the population of New Foundland in the same period.

6. What is the estimated population of New Foundland in 2024?
   (a) 98 crore
   (b) 100 crore
   (c) 110 crore
   (d) 115 crore
7. What will be the simple average growth rate of population of New Foundland in the given period 2024-28?
   (a) 2%
   (b) 3%
   (c) 4%
   (d) 4.5%
8. What will be the percentage growth in number of hotel users in New Foundland by 2028 with respect to 2024?
   (a) 100%
   (b) 150%
   (c) 180%
   (d) 200%
9. What will be the percentage growth of the revenues of the hotel industry in the given period?
   (a) 200% (b) 230%
   (c) 260% (d) 300%
10. It is believed that if 50% of the population of any country can afford hotel-use, it is economically developed. Can we say that New Foundland will be a developed country by 2027?
   (a) Yes
   (b) No
   (c) Cannot say
   (d) Data inadequate

Case 3 Mindworkzz Inc. is the leader in selling ideas universe wide but its maximum revenue comes from three principal planets only, viz., Earth, Mars and Jupiter. Further, it has three products, viz., CSP, CC and CP. In a particular year, the number of units sold had a distribution as follows: The number of units of CCs sold on Mars was 12 per cent of the number of units of CPs sold on Earth. The number of units of CPs sold on Jupiter was 1000. Total number of CC units sold was 2600. Total number of CP units was 200 higher than that of the total number of units of CCs sold. The number of units of CSP sold on Mars was 10 per cent of the number of units of CP sold on Jupiter. The number of units of CSP sold on Earth was 2000. The number of units of CC sold on Earth was 15 per cent of the number of units of CSP sold on Jupiter.

The prices of the units on the different planets were as follows:

Earth → ₹15 per unit
Mars → ₹10 per unit
Jupiter → ₹8 per unit

The number of units of CSP sold on Jupiter was 300.

The number of units of CP sold on Earth was 600.

11. The number of units of CC sold on Jupiter is:
(a) 1520 (b) 2483
(c) 3423 (d) 600
12. The revenue generated on Earth is greater than that generated on Jupiter by about (to the closest 1000)
(a) ₹8000 (b) ₹9000
(c) ₹10,000 (d) ₹12,000
13. The overall revenue generated is the highest from
(a) CSPs (b) CP
(c) CCs (d) Can't be determined

Directions for Questions 14 to 17: *From the data given below solve the questions:*

Two brothers, Harish and Sanjay bought four acres of land in 1990 and started cultivating it in 1991. They produced 1,000 kg of jowar per acre that year. Being the elder brother, Harish decided the proportion in which the total production would be shared. He retained 1,800 kg and gave the rest to Sanjay. In 1994, when the production was twice that in 1991, Harish gave 60% of the production to Sanjay. Sanjay found that Harish was more considerate in that year than in 1992, when he had received 2,700 kg which was only 200 kg more than what Harish would have retained, had the production been divided equally. In 1995, when the production was twice that of 1993, Harish retained 9,000 kg, which was 75% of the total production in 1995.

14. In 1991 Harish and Sanjay had shared the production in the ratio:
(a) 1:1 (b) 9:11
(c) 11:9 (d) none of the above
15. The increase in production between 1993 and 1994 was:
(a) 1,000 kg (b) 1,500 kg
(c) 2,000 kg (d) 3,500 kg
16. The quantity of jowar received by Harish in 1991 as a ratio of quantity received in 1995 is closer to:
(a) 1:2 (b) 1:3
(c) 1:5 (d) 1:4
17. The quantity received by Sanjay in 1994 was:
(a) four times the production of 1993
(b) one–fourth the production of 1993
(c) twice the production of 1992
(d) 40% of the production of 1995

Level of Difficulty 2

Directions for Questions 1 to 5: *Mr. Hoola Boola is facing a decision problem. He has excellent training products but is not sure about the demand for his products. He wants to set up a training centre to provide training programmes of Sr. Executive, Jr. executive and non-executive level. His financial advisor Mr. Balmas told him that if he wants to set up a non-executive level training centre, the total cost would be on two counts – the first would be a fixed cost which is ₹2 lakh per annum. Besides, it would also entail a variable cost of training per candidate. This would be ₹1,000 per candidate trained. He further estimated that if a training centre is set up for conducting Jr. executive and non-executive level training programmes, the total fixed cost would be ₹3.2 lakh per annum and the cost of training per candidate will be ₹750. Mr. Balmas motivates Mr. Hoola to set up a combined training centre for Sr. executive, Jr. executive and non-executive, the fixed cost of which is ₹5 lakh per annum and the cost of providing training per candidate is ₹500.*

You as a hotshot IIM Ahmedabad MBA, have some decision making abilities. Please help Mr. Hoola Boola by answering the following questions:

1. What would be the volume that Mr. Hoola should train where he would be indifferent between setting up a non-executive level and non-executive and Jr. executive level training centre?
(a) 495 (b) 490
(c) 480 (d) 475
2. What would be the volume that Mr. Hoola should train where he would be indifferent between setting up a training centre for Jr. and non-executive and Sr. Jr. and non-executive level.
(a) 710 (b) 720
(c) 730 (d) 740
3. What would be the volume that Mr. Hoola should train where he could be indifferent between setting up a training centre for non-executive and for all three categories?
(a) 450 (b) 500
(c) 550 (d) 600
4. Assume that Mr. Hoola shares the same vision that Mr. Balmas has and sets up a training centre for all three categories. In the first year he manages to train 1200 candidates at ₹1250 per candidate. What would be his profits?

(a) 3.2 lakh (b) 3.6 lakh
(c) 4 lakh (d) 4.4 lakh

5. In Question 4, what is the profit percentage in the first year of operation?
(a) 27.27% (b) 36.66%
(c) 40% (d) 44.44%

Directions for Questions 6 to 11: *Fabric X has to go through three stages of manufacturing, viz., spinning, weaving and dyeing. In Rimal Fabric Company, there are six spinning machines, ten weaving machines and five dyeing machines. Each machine works for 10 hrs a day. One unit of fabric X needs 40 minutes on a spinning machine, 2 hours on a weaving machine and 30 minutes on a dyeing machine in order to be completed. Similarly one unit of fabric Y needs 60 minutes on a spinning machine, 30 minutes on a weaving machine and 60 minutes on a dyeing machine in order to be completed.*

6. In a day, how many units of fabric Y can be completed at most?
(a) 20 (b) 30
(c) 40 (d) 50

7. If 20 units of fabric Y are made in a day, how many units of fabric X can be completed the same day?
(a) 0 (b) 20
(c) 40 (d) 45

8. If only 30 units of fabric Y are made in a day, how many machine hours will be idle that day?
(a) 120 (b) 130
(c) 135 (d) 150

9. If one more dyeing machine is added, at the most how many more units of fabric X can be made in a day?
(a) 0 (b) 5
(c) 8 (d) 10

10. If only fabric X has to be made, what machines should be bought so that there is a maximum increase in production capacity (only one machine has to be bought)?
(a) spinning machine (b) weaving machine
(c) dyeing machine (d) any one of three

11. If only fabric Y has to be made, what machines should be bought so that there is a maximum increase in production capacity (only one machine has to be bought)?
(a) spinning machine (b) weaving machine
(c) dyeing machine (d) any one of three

Directions for Questions 12 to 14: *Mr. Kunal Dwivedi wants to buy a motorbike which is priced at ₹45,500. The bike is also available at ₹25,000 down payment and monthly installments of ₹1000 per month for 2 years or ₹18,000 down payment and monthly installment of ₹1000 per month for 3 years. Mr. Kunal has with him only ₹12,000. He wants to borrow the balance money of the down payment from a private lender whose terms are:*

If ₹6,000 is borrowed for 12 months, the rate of interest is 20 per cent. The interest will be calculated on the whole amount for the whole year, even though the repayment has to be done in 12 equal monthly installments starting from the first month itself. Thus he will have to repay an amount of ₹600 per month for 12 months to repay ₹6000 (Principal) + ₹1200 (Interest @ 20 per cent).

If ₹10,000 upwards is borrowed for one year, the rate of interest is 30 per cent and is calculated in exactly the same manner as above.

12. If Mr. Kunal is ready to pay either of the down payments which of the installment schemes is the better option of the two? (Assume that Mr. Kunal will pay the installments out of his own earnings and he keeps his savings with himself and earns no interest on the same.) Also assume that instead of borrowing the remaining money for the down payment, he saves the balance before purchase.
(a) ₹1000 for 2 years (b) ₹1000 for 3 years
(c) either of two (d) Data inadequate

13. What is the percentage difference in the total amount paid to the bike dealer, between the two installment schemes (with respect to the total payment of the scheme with ₹25,000 down payment)?
(a) 10.2% (b) 13.5%
(c) 11.4% (d) None of these

14. If Kunal can spare only a total of ₹2000 to be paid to the bike dealer and the money lender from his monthly earnings starting from the first month onwards which scheme should he choose?
(a) ₹1000 for 2 years (b) ₹1000 for 3 years
(c) either of two (d) Data inadequate

Directions for Questions 15 to 20: *It was realised by Mindworkzz that for creating awareness in the market, newspaper advertising is very effective but it should be done consistently. The Times of India (TOI) which claims to have 40 per cent of the total market share brings out a weekly supplement 'Education Times' in which the advertising cost for the range 0–240 sq. cm for 1–2 insertions with a validity period of 30 days is ₹50/cm^2, for 3–5 insertions with a validity period of 60 days is ₹43/cm^2 and 6 onwards insertions with validity period of 90 days is ₹40/cm^2. The cost for size of advertisement 241+ cm^2 for 1–2 insertions with validity period 30 days is ₹50/cm^2 and for 3–5 insertions with validity period 60 days is ₹40/cm^2 and for 6 onwards insertion with validity period* *of 90 days is ₹35/cm². The expected response generation per insertion in TOI in the size 161–200 cm² is 40 and in the size 200+ cm² is 50. Another great market player is Hindustan Times with the weekly supplement 'HT Horizons' and it claims to have 35% of the total market share and the cost of advertising in it for 1–2 insertions with validity period: Number of insertion + one week is ₹40/cm², for 3–6 insertions with validity period: Number of insertions +2 weeks is ₹37/cm² and for 7 insertions onwards with validity period: no. of insertions +3 weeks is ₹34/cm². The expected response generation per insertion is 35 for 160–200 cm² and 45 for 200+ cm² size.*

Please help Mindworkzz with the correct decisions on the following plans.

15. If Mindworkzz looks to generating exactly 95 responses in 2 insertions, which newspaper combination should be selected?
    (a) TOI
    (b) HT
    (c) One TOI and one HT insertion
    (d) Data inadequate
16. Mindworkzz has decided to advertise in TOI but is confused on length between 80 cm and 81 cm but is sure about the width, i.e., 3 cm and 3 insertions. What should be the length?
    (a) 80 cm (b) 81 cm
    (c) either 80 or 81 (d) Data inadequate
17. If Mindworkzz wants to go for two insertions of exactly 80 cm², which newspaper should be selected and what is the percentage difference in the cost differential between the campaign cost between the two newspapers with respect to the lower priced newspaper. (Assume that cost is the only consideration.)
    (a) HT, 20% (b) HT, 25%
    (c) TOI, 20% (d) TOI, 25%
18. If Mindworkzz decides to go in for an advertising campaign of 10 insertions, which will be the best option (in terms of cost) for a size of 243 cm²?
    (a) HT (b) TOI
    (c) either HT or TOI (d) Data inadequate
19. In Question 18, if Mindworkzz is considering its decision only on the basis of validity period which is the best?
    (a) HT (b) TOI
    (c) Either HT or TOI (d) Data inadequate
20. If the only consideration for the choice of the newspaper is the number of responses, then Mindworkzz should run the campaign of Question 19 in:
    (a) HT (b) TOI
    (c) Either HT or TOI (d) Data inadequate

Directions for Questions 21 to 27: *Bihar and Orissa are the most deprived states of India. While they contain one-fifth of India's population, they have almost one-third of India's illiterates. In 1998, only a small fraction of Orissa and Bihar's population was literate versus 85 per cent of Kerala's population. More than two-thirds of the births are not attended by any medical facility, 1/10th of the infants born in Orissa and Bihar die in infancy and an equal number before reaching the age of five. Almost 90 per cent of the under five deaths are due to malnutrition.*

From amongst the lucky kids who have survived for the first five years, 1/3rd of them work as child labourers and only half of the remaining are sent to school. Of those who attend classes, only 40 per cent are able to reach Std V. In India, 30 per cent of the children under 16 work as labourers. Orissa and Bihar contain 1/3rd of the child labourers in India. India has the largest population of child labourers, which is 1/15th of its total population.

In Orissa and Bihar, out of 100 children enrolled in school, 32 are girls. And out of 100 who attend Std X, only 10 are girls. Only 38 out of 100 Indian women are literate versus 57 per cent of males. Even in wealthy states such as Punjab, girls suffer from malnutrition seven times more than boys do. The total population of the country was 90 crore in 1998 and the ratio of male to female in India was 10 to 9.

21. According to the information provided, what percentage of the infants in Orissa and Bihar attend Std V?
    (a) 11.33 (b) 10.66
    (c) 13.33 (d) None of these
22. The number of child labourers in India in 1998 are:
    (a) 15 crore (b) 16 crore
    (c) 12 crore (d) 6 crore
23. In Orissa and Bihar, out of 100 born, approximately how many children work as child labourers?
    (a) 27 (b) 32
    (c) 13 (d) 38
24. What percentage of girl children enrolled in school reach Std X in Orissa and Bihar?
    (a) 10% (b) 32%
    (c) 60% (d) Insufficient data
25. In 1998, the literates in Kerala exceed the literates in UP and Bihar by:
    (a) 30% (b) 35%
    (c) 27% (d) Insufficient data
26. The number of literates in India in 1998 is:
    (a) 16.2 crore (b) 27 crore
    (c) 43.2 crore (d) Insufficient data
27. The number of illiterates in Orissa and Bihar in 1998 is almost:

(a) 18 crore (b) 13.2 crore
(c) 15.6 crore (d) Insufficient data

Directions for Questions 28 to 31: *When the crisis hit, the IMF led the rescue efforts, but it wanted the World Bank to provide $6 billion of the rescue package. The total rescue package was for $22.6 billion. The IMF would provide $11.2 billion of this total. As I stated before; the World Bank would lend $6 billion, and the rest would be provided by the Japanese government. Based on the above information answer the questions that follow.*

28. Which of the following is correct?
    (i) The World Bank paid as much as 111.11% of what the Japanese did not pay of the total rescue package.
    (ii) The IMF paid more than 50% of the total but less than 100% of what the World Bank and the Japanese together paid.
    (iii) The Japanese paid less than the World Bank but more than the IMF.
    (a) (i) only
    (b) (i) and (ii)
    (c) All three
    (d) None of the three are true
29. If Japan had declined to pay 50% of what it actually paid, then how much more would World Bank have to pay? (Assume that the World Bank paid the entire deficit thus created.)
    (i) 45% of its commitment
    (ii) Less than 25% of what IMF did not pay.
    (iii) Less than 25% of what IMF did actually pay.
    (a) (i) only (b) (i) & (ii) only
    (c) (i) & (iii) only (d) All of these
30. How much did Japan not pay?
    (a) More than 300 but less than 320 percent of what it actually paid.
    (b) More than 200 but less than 250 percent of World Bank actually paid.
    (c) 76 percent of what IMF and World Bank together paid.
    (d) Either (b) or (c)
31. If both the World Bank and Japan were to pay equal amounts, with no change in IMF's contribution, then which of the following option is valid?
    (a) The World Bank would have to pay only 5% less than what it actually paid.
    (b) Japan will have to pay 5% more than what it actually paid.
    (c) The percentage drop in World Bank's contribution will be greater than the percentage rise in Japan's contribution.
    (d) None of these.

Level of Difficulty 3

Directions for Questions 1 to 6: *Answer the questions on the basis of the information provided below.*

Mr Sanjay Singh, a prosperous businessman is contemplating on setting up a religious television channel. He has tentatively called it Somvaar. He estimates that with a small investment of ₹3 crore he would be able to set up the channel. His consultants, Mr Pradeep Varma and Miss Reena Singh, tell him that he would require about ₹7 lakh per month as satellite rentals, ₹5 lakh per month in running a transmitting station in Singapore and 15 lakh a month for manpower, offices, studios and other day-to-day costs. The only other cost is interest paid to the bank @ 12% per annum on the initial investment of ₹3 crore. Tax paid to the government is 30% of the profit before tax (PBT).

Unlike the rest of the television business (where the channels pay for the content), on religious channels the religious gurus pay for the content (pravachans), because the religious television channels offer them a faster way to maximise the reach and so gain in terms of donations, etc. On weekdays (Monday to Saturday) the channel charges ₹10,000 for a 30-minute slot between 7:00–9:00 (prime time) in the morning and in the evening.

For 9:00 AM–7:00 PM the charges are half of the charges of prime time and for all other time slots the charges are one fourth of the charges of the prime time. On weekends (Sunday) the charges are double of the normal charges in the weekdays for each category.

*The only other source of revenue is advertisement. Of the 30-minutes slot sold to the religious gurus, the channel actually gives only 25 minutes to the gurus and it uses the rest for advertisement. Its rate is very low as compared to the regular channels like Star Plus and Zee TV. For every 30-second advertisement slot in prime time on weekdays the channel charges ₹1000 and the ratio of charges in different time slots in weekdays and weekends are same as content charges from the gurus. (**Note:** 5th January of 2025 was a Sunday.) Help him with the estimates for the year 2025.*

1. What is the total yearly cost of running *Somvaar*?
   (a) ₹324 lakh (b) ₹360 lakh
   (c) ₹624 lakh (d) ₹660 lakh
2. What will be the estimated total revenue generated by the channel in 2025?
   (a) ₹19.18 crore (b) ₹16.79 crore
   (c) ₹8.39 crore (d) Data insufficient
3. In which month of 2025 can the profit achieve its maximum level?

(a) March (b) June
(c) August (d) Both (a) and (c)

4. What will be the margin percentage for the month of April 2025 achieved by the channel if it got the advertisements and *pravachans* for the period 7:00 AM–9:00 PM only?
(a) 66 (b) 75
(c) 104 (d) 308

5. What will be the ratio of revenue from the slot 7:00 AM–9:00 AM, 9:00 AM–7:00 PM, 7:00 PM–9:00 PM and 9:00 PM–7:00 AM if every slot runs at 100% efficiency?
(a) 4:10:4:5 (b) 4:5:4:5
(c) 4:10:2:5 (d) 5:10:5:5

6. What is the ratio of the effective rate of advertisement per minute and the effective rate of *pravachans* per minute on the channel in the 9:00 AM–2:00 PM slot?
(a) 4:1 (b) 5:1
(c) 6:1 (d) 9:2

Directions for Questions 7 to 9: *On the basis of the following information.*

KK, an aspiring entrepreneur wanted to set up a pen drive manufacturing unit. Since technology was changing very fast, he wanted to carefully gauge the demand and the likely profits before investing. Market survey indicated that he would be able to sell 1 lac units before customers shifted to different gadgets. KK realised that he had to incur two kinds of costs – fixed costs (the costs which do not change, irrespective of numbers of numbers of units of pen drives produced) and variable costs (= variable cost per unit multiplied by number of units). KK expected fixed cost to be ₹40 lac and variable cost to be ₹100 per unit. He expected each pen drive to be sold at ₹200.

7. What would be the break-even point (defined as no profit, no loss situation) for KK's factory, in term of sales?
(a) ₹80 lac (b) ₹100 lac
(c) ₹120 lac (d) ₹140 lac
(e) Cannot be found with the given data.

8. KK was skeptical that per unit variable cost might increase by 10% though the demand might remain same. What will be the expected changes in profit in such a case?
(a) Profit would decrease by 10.33%
(b) Profit will increase will by 15.75%
(c) Profit would decrease by 15.75%
(d) Profit will decrease by 16.67%
(e) Profit will increase by 16.67%

9. He discussed his business with a chartered accountant. KK informed that he was contemplating a loan of 20 lac at simple interest of 10% per annum for starting the business. The chartered accountant informed him that in such a case KK has to pay interest, followed by 30% tax.
By how much does KK's earnings change with 20% growth in sales vis-à-vis the original sales volume, in both cases considering tax and interest on loan?
(a) 20% (b) 16.7%
(c) 25.6% (d) 33.3%
(e) 34.5%

Directions for Questions 10 to 12: *Based on the following information.*

An automobiles company's annual sales of its small cars depends on the state of the economy as well as on whether the company uses some high profile individual as its brand ambassador in the advertisements of its product. The state of the economy is 'good', 'okay', 'bad' with probabilities 0.3, 0.4 and 0.3 respectively. The company may choose a high profile individual as its brand ambassador in TV ads or may go for TV ads without a high profile brand ambassador.

If the company fixes price at ₹3.5 lakh, the annual sales of its small cars for different states of the economy and for different kinds of TV ads are summarised in Table 1. The figures in the first row are annual sales of the small cars when the company uses a high profile individual as its brand ambassador in its TV ads and the ones in the second row are that when the company does not use any brand ambassador in its TV ads, for different states of the economy.

TABLE 1

	'Good'	'Okay'	'Bad'
With brand ambassador	100000	80000	50000
Without brand ambassador	80000	50000	30000

Without knowing what exactly will be the state of the economy in the coming one year, the company will either have to sign a TV ad contract with some high profile individual, who will be the company's brand ambassador for its small car for the next one year, or go for a TV ad without featuring any high profile individual. It incurs a cost of ₹3.45 lakh (excluding the payment to the brand ambassador) to put a car on the road.

When the company's profit is uncertain, the company makes decisions on the basis of its expected profit. If the company can earn a profit x_i with probability p_i (the probability depends on the state of economy), then the expected profit of the company is $\Sigma_i x_i p_i$

10. The maximum that the company can afford to pay its brand ambassador is

(a) ₹10.0 crore (b) ₹10.6 crore
(c) ₹10.8 crore (d) ₹12.0 crore
(e) ₹16.4 crore

11. Mr. Khan a popular film actor, agrees to sign the contract to become the company's brand ambassador for ₹9 crore. As a result, the cost to the company of putting a car on the road also gets escalated. The maximum escalation in cost of putting a car on the road, for which the company can afford to sign the contract with Mr. Khan is
(a) ₹900 (b) ₹967
(c) ₹1250 (d) ₹1267
(e) ₹1300

12. Mr. Khan, a popular film actor, agrees to sign the contract to become the company's brand ambassador for ₹9 crore. The cost to the company of putting a car on the road also gets escalated by ₹1000. If the company signs the contract with Mr. Khan, its profit will
(a) increase by ₹40 lakh
(b) increase by ₹60 lakh
(c) decrease by ₹20 lakh
(d) decrease by ₹40 lakh
(e) decrease by ₹50 lakh

Directions for Questions 13 to 15: *Answer the questions based on the following information.*

Madhubala Devi, who works as a domestic help, received ₹2500 as Deepawali bonus from her employer. With that money she is contemplating purchase of one or more amongst 5 available government bonds – A, B, C, D, and E.

To purchase a bond, Madhubala Devi will have to pay the price of the bond. If she owns a bond she receives a stipulated amount of money every year (which is termed as the coupon payment) till the maturity of the bond. At the maturity of the bond she also receives the face value of the bond.

Price of a bond is given by: $P = \left[\sum_{t=1}^{T} + \frac{C}{(1+r)^t}\right] + \frac{F}{(1+r)^T}$,

where C is the coupon payment on the bond, which is the amount of money the holder of the bond receives annually; F is the face value of the bond, which is the amount of money the holder of the bond receives when the bond matures (over and above the coupon payment for the year of maturity); T is the number of years in which the bond matures; r = 0.25, which means the market rate of interest is 25%.

Amongst the 5 bonds bond A and another two bonds mature in 2 years, one of the bonds matures in 3 years, and bond D matures in 5 years.

The coupon payments on bonds A, E, B, D and C are in arithmetic progression, such that the coupon payment on bond A is twice the common difference, and the coupon payment on bond B is half the price of bond A.

The face value of bond B is twice the face value of bond E, but the price of bond B is 75% more than the price of bond E. The price of bond C is more than ₹1800 and its face value is same as the price of bond A. The face value of bond A is ₹1000.

Bond D has the largest face value amongst the five bonds.

13. The face value of bond E must be
(a) ₹1406.25 (b) ₹1686.25
(c) ₹2250.50 (d) ₹2812.50
(e) ₹3372.50

14. Madhubala Devi purchased one or more of the 5 available bonds from her bonus pay and spent the remainder. She made the purchase decision such that her return from the bonds is maximised. Her return from the bonds is
(a) ₹3000.00 (b) ₹3250.00
(c) ₹3656.25 (d) ₹3906.25
(e) ₹4531.25

15. The price of bond C must be
(a) ₹1825 (b) ₹1874
(c) ₹1925 (d) ₹1976
(e) ₹2342

ANSWER KEY

Level of Difficulty 1

1. (d)	2. (a)	3. (a)	4. (c)	5. (a)	6. (b)	7. (b)
8. (c)	9. (a)	10. (d)	11. (b)	12. (b)	13. (a)	14. (b)
15. (c)	16. (c)	17. (d)				

Level of Difficulty 2

1. (c)	2. (b)	3. (d)	4. (c)	5. (b)	6. (d)	7. (d)
8. (c)	9. (a)	10. (b)	11. (c)	12. (a)	13. (a)	14. (b)

15. (c)	16. (b)	17. (b)	18. (a)	19. (a)	20. (b)	21. (b)
22. (d)	23. (a)	24. (d)	25. (d)	26. (c)	27. (c)	28. (d)
29. (d)	30. (a)	31. (a)				

Level of Difficulty 3

1. (b)	2. (d)	3. (d)	4. (d)	5. (a)	6. (b)	7. (a)
8. (d)	9. (e)	10. (d)	11. (c)	12. (b)	13. (a)	14. (c)
15. (d)						

SOLUTIONS

Level of Difficulty 1

Case 1

The following data table can be formed from the information provided.

Company	Sales	Expenses	Profits
AZ	10	9	1
BMZ	12	9.6	2.4
CW	12	10	2
DT	6	4	2

The values in the table are got through the following process:
Let sales of AZ = x, then its profits = $0.1x$.
Sales of BMZ = sales of CW = y.
Profit of BMZ = 20% of its sales = $0.2y$.
Sales of CW is 400% more than profits of CW. Hence, profit of CW= $0.166y$ = profits of DT.
Sales of DT is 200% more than profits of DT. Hence, sales of DT= $0.5y$.
Also expenses of CW = $y - 0.166y = 0.833y$ = 10 million.
Hence, $y = 12$.
Also, expenses of AZ = $0.9x$ = 9 million. Hence, x = 10 million.

Answers:

1. The lowest total expense = 4 million for DT.
2. The lowest profits = 1 million for AZ.
3. 2/11.25 = 17.77%
4. The respective profit percentages would have been 40% and 16.66%—a ratio of 12:5.
5. The required ratio is 2.4:1 = 12:5.

Case 2

6. 200 million = 20 % of population
   $\Rightarrow$ Population = 200×5 = 1000 million = 100 crore
7. 2004 population = 1000 million
   Population in 2008 or after 4 years = 560×2 = 1120 million
   $\therefore$ Growth rate = $(120 \times 100)/(1000 \times 4) = (12/4)\%$ = 3% per annum simple growth rate.
8. Hotel users in 2004 = 200 million
   Hotel users in 2008 = 560 million
   $\therefore$ Growth in percentage
   $$= \frac{560 - 200}{200} = \frac{360}{200} = 180\%$$
9. Total revenue in 2004 = 50 billion
   Total revenue in 2008 = 150 billion
   $\therefore$ Growth in percentage $= \frac{150 - 50}{50} \times 100 = \frac{100}{50}$ = 200%
10. By 2008 half or 50% of the Indian population will be using hotels.
    We do not have any information about 2007. Hence the data is inadequate.

Case 3

The following table emerges out of the case.

	Earth		Mars		Jupiter		TOTAL	
	Sales	Revenue	Sales	Revenue	Sales	Revenue	Sales	Revenue
CSP	2000	30,000	100	1000	300	2400	**2400**	**33,400**
CC	45	675	72	720	2483	19864	**2600**	**21259**
CP	600	9000	1200	12,000	1000	8000	**2800**	**29,000**
Total		**39,675**		**13,320**		**30,264**		

The answers can be read out of the table itself.

11. 2483
12. 9000
13. CSP

Note: The table structure has to be created according to the information provided and the filling in of the specific values within the table should only be for the questions asked. Hence, the values which were not sought by the questions asked have been left without being calculated for the table.

14. (b) The production in 1991 = 1000 kg per acre. So total = 4000 kgs, so share = 1800 : 2200 = 9 : 11
15. (c) Production in 1993 = 6000 kgs and in 1994 = 8000 kgs, so 2000 kgs increase.
16. (c) Share in 1991 = 1800 and in 1995 = 9000, so ratio = 1800 : 9000 = 1 : 5.
17. (d) Production in 1995 = 12000 kgs and Sanjay's share in 1994 = 4800 kgs, which is 40% of 12000.

Level of Difficulty 2

Solutions for Questions 1 to 5:

1. Let x be the volume. So the cost of training x candidates in both of these should be the same for indifference between the two options,
   i.e., 2 lakh + $1000x$ = 3.2 lakh + $750x$
   $\Rightarrow 250x$ = 1.2 lakh
   $\Rightarrow x = 120{,}000/250 = 480$
2. Let x be the volume.
   3.2 lakh + $750x$ = 5 lakh + $500x$
   $\Rightarrow 250x$ = 1.8 lakh $\Rightarrow x = 720$
3. Let x be the volume.
   2 lakh + $1000x$ = 5 lakh + $500x$
   $\therefore x = 600$.
4. Total sales = 1200 × 1250 = 15 lakh
   Total cost (for all 3 levels) = 5 lakh + 500 × 1200 = 11 lakh
   Thus profit = Total sales – Total cost = ₹15 lakh – ₹11 lakh = ₹4 lakh
5. Total cost = 11 lakh
   Profit = 4 lakh
   ∴ Profit % = (4/11) × 100 = 36.36%

Solutions for Questions 6 to 11:

X	0.66 hours	2 hours	0.5 hours	Time required per unit processed
Y	1 hour	0.5 hours	1 hour	Time required per unit processed
	Spinning	Weaving	Dyeing	
Capacity available	60	100	50	

6. With respect to fabric Y, 60 units can be made in 60 hours on the spinning machine, 200 units can be woven on the weaving machine and 50 units can be made on the dyeing machine. Since, only 50 units can be dyed, only 50 units can be completed in a day.
7. 20 units of fabric Y will consume 20 hours on spinning, 10 hours on weaving and 20 hours on dyeing. Capacity left will be 40 hours of spinning, 90 hours on weaving and 30 hours on dyeing. In this available time 60 units can be spun, 45 units can be woven and 60 units can by dyed. Hence, only 45 units of fabric X can be completed after 20 units of fabric Y are made.
8. 30 units of fabric Y will consume (30 + 15 + 30) = 75 hours totally. 135 hours will remain idle.
9. The capacity constraint for fabric X lies in weaving. Hence, adding any number of dyeing machines is not going to affect the number of units of fabric X that can be produced in a day.
10. As per the logic given for the above question, a weaving machine will be required. Hence, the correct answer is (b).
11. For fabric Y, the constraint lies in the dyeing machine. Hence, if one machine has to be bought and the capacity of fabric Y has to be increased, a dyeing machine should be procured.

Solutions for Questions 12 to 14:

12. Total cost on cash down of 25,000 = 25,000 + 24,000 = ₹49,000.
    Total cost on cash down of 18,000 = 18,000 + 36,000 = ₹54,000.
    ∴ Option (a) is better since it is given that Mr. Kunal does not earn any interest on his money.
13. Total cost on down payment of 25,000 = 25,000 + 24,000 = ₹49,000.
    Total cost on down payment of 18,000 = 18,000 + 36,000 = ₹54,000.
    Required answer = 5000/49,000 is approximately equal to 10.2%.
14. For the second installment scheme he has to borrow ₹6000. Hence, his monthly repayment will be ₹600 per month towards the money lender and ₹1000 per month towards the bike dealer. Hence, the total repayment will be ₹1600 per month.

For the first installment scheme he will have to borrow ₹13000, which will entail a monthly repayment of ₹1408.33 per month to the money lender. (13,000 + 3900 to be repaid in 12 monthly installments.) Besides, he also has to pay ₹1000 per month towards the bike dealer. Hence, the total repayment will be ₹2408.33 per month. This is outside his monthly limit of ₹2000 repayment per month. Hence he has to go for the second scheme.

Solutions for Questions 15 to 20:

15. The required 95 responses will be got by combining 50 through the TOI and 45 through the HT in insertions of size 200+ cm^2.
16. The solution will be got by comparing the cost of the two campaigns against one another. Since the expected response is the same,
Cost of 3 insertions of 240 $cm^2 = 43 \times 240 \times 3 = 720 \times 43$ = ₹30,960
Cost of 3 insertions of $81 \times 3 = 243$ $cm^2 = 40 \times 243 \times 3 = 729 \times 40$ = ₹29,160
Mindworkzz should go for a height of 81 cm since the cost of the campaign is lower.
17. TOI = $50 \times 2 \times 80 = 8000$
HT = $40 \times 2 \times 80 = 6400$
∴ Percentage difference = (1600/6400) = 25%
Since cost is the only consideration, HT should be selected and the required percentage difference is 25% between the two costs over two insertions of 80 cm^2.
18. Cost of campaign in TOI = $243 \times 35 \times 10$.
Cost of campaign in HT = $243 \times 34 \times 10$.
∴ HT is better in terms of cost.
19. Validity Period for HT = 10 + 3 = 13 weeks = 91 days.
Validity Period for TOI = 90 days.
Hence, HT is the better option in terms of validity.
20. TOI will give an expected response of 50×10 = 500 while HT will give an expected response of 45×10 = 450. Hence, TOI will be a better option in terms of numbers of responses.

Solutions for Questions 21 to 27:

21. Born 100 ⇒ 10 die at infancy
90 ⇒ 10 die till age 5
$80 \Rightarrow \frac{2}{3} \times \frac{1}{2} \times 80$ go to school
∴ Who attend Std. V = $80 \times \frac{1}{3} \times 0.4 = 10.66\%$.
22. No. of child labourers in India = $\left(90 \times \frac{1}{15}\right)$ crore = 6 crore.
23. Out of 100 born, 20 die by the age of 5.
Number of child labourers in Orissa and Bihar = $\frac{1}{3} \times 80 \cong 27$.
24. Since we do not know how many children reach Std X, the answer cannot be found. Hence, Option (d).
25. Since we do not know the exact population of Kerala, Orissa and Bihar, the answer cannot be found.
26. Number of female literates = $90 \times \frac{9}{19} \times 0.38 = 16.2$ crore
Number of male literates = $90 \times \frac{10}{19} \times 0.57 = 27$ crore.
∴ Total literates = 16.2 + 27 = 43.2 crore.
27. Total illiterates in India = 90 – 43.2 = 46.8 crore.
∴ No. of illiterates in Orissa and Bihar = $\frac{1}{3} \times 46.8$ = 15.6 crore.
28. None of the three statements is true.
29. WB would have to pay $2.7 billion more. This amounts to 45% of its commitment. All statements are true.
30. Japan paid 5.4 billion out of 22.6 billion. So it did not pay 17.2 billion. Since, 17.2/5.4 is between 3 and 3.2, option (a) is correct.
31. In such a situation, the World Bank and Japan would each pay 5.7 billion. This would reduce the World Bank's payment by 5%. Option (a) is correct.

Level of Difficulty 3

1. The monthly costs are: 7 lakh + 5 lakh + 15 lakh + 3 lakh (monthly interest) = ₹30 lakh.
2. The data is insufficient since we do not know how many slots will be sold and how many will remain unsold.
3. Obviously, since monthly costs are constant, the maximum revenues will be in months with the maximum number of days and the maximum Sundays. Both March and August have 31 days and 5 Sundays.
4. The total revenues for April will be 122.4 lakh against an investment of 30 lakh. Hence profit percentage will be 92.4/30 = 308%.
5. 4:10:4:5. Options (b) and (c) cannot be the answer since the two basic relationships are that the two 7–9 slots would give equal revenues and the ratio of 9–7 day to 9–7 night will be 2:1. Investigate the relationship between the value of 7–9 and 9–7 periods and get (a) as the answer.
6. The rate for *pravachan* is ₹200 per minute (₹5000 for 25 minutes) while the rate for advertisements

is ₹1000 per minute in the time slot 9 –2 (off prime time). Hence, the required ratio is 5:1. Option (b) is correct.

Solutions for Questions 7 to 9:

7. The break-even point would be got by finding the number of units at which there is no profit no loss. It is given by (Total fixed cost/margin per unit) = 4000000/100 = 40000 units. The sales revenue at which the break even occurs would be equal to 40000 × 200 = 80 lacs.
8. The variable cost per unit would go up to 110 and hence the margin per unit would go down to ₹90. Over 1 lac units the profit would be 90 × 1 lacs – 40 lacs = 50 lacs
   The original profit without the increase in variable cost would have been:
   100 × 1 lac – 40 lacs = ₹60 lacs.
   Thus, the reduction in profit is from 60 lacs to 50 lacs = 16.66% drop.
   Option (d) is correct.
9. Under the circumstances his profit would get reduced by the value of the interest and his earnings would get estimated by further reducing by 30% the profit that we get after deduction of interest.
   Scenario 1:
   Sales of 1 lac units:
   Profit before interest deduction = 1 lac × 100 – 40 lacs = 60 lacs
   Interest = 2 lacs
   Profit after interest = 60 – 2 = 58 lacs.
   Tax = 30% of 58 lacs = 17.4 lacs.
   Earnings = 58 – 17.4 lacs = 40.6 lacs.
   Scenario 2:
   Sales of 1.2 lac units:
   Profit before interest deduction = 1.2 lac × 100 – 40 lacs = 80 lacs
   Interest = 2 lacs
   Profit after interest = 80 – 2 = 78 lacs.
   Tax = 30% of 78 lacs = 23.4 lacs.
   Earnings = 78 – 23.4 lacs = 54.6 lacs.
   % difference in profit between the two scenarios = (54.6 – 40.6) × 100/40.6 = 34.5% approx.
   Option (e) is correct.

Solutions for Questions 10 to 12:

10. The maximum the company can afford to pay the brand ambassador is the expected increase in profits due to the use of the brand ambassador.
    The expected increase in sales would be given by the summation of:
    Extra sales for a particular state of the economy × The probability of that state of the economy
    = 20000 × 0.3 + 30000 × 0.4 + 20000 × 0.3 = 24000 units.
    Since the profit per unit is ₹5000 (Sales price being 3.5 lacs and cost per unit being 3.45 lacs)
    The additional profit the company makes due to the use of the brand ambassador is:
    24000 × 5000 = ₹12 crore.
    This is the amount the company can afford to pay to the brand ambassador.
11. The increase in cost that can be afforded should be such that the total extra profit should still be ₹9 crore. Since the expected extra sale is 24000 units, the profit per unit should be = 9 crore/24000 = ₹3750. For a profit of ₹3750, the cost per unit can rise to a maximum of 346250, an increase of ₹1250. Option (c) is correct.
12. The extra profit with an escalation of cost of ₹1000 would be given by 24000 × 4000 = ₹9.6 crore. Out of this since Mr. Khan has to be paid ₹9 crore, the profit will go up by ₹60 lacs. Option (b) is correct.

Solutions for Questions 13 to 15:

There are three key variables in the question: Price of a bond, coupon payment on a bond, face value of a bond besides the number of years to maturity for a bond.

Next, since we know that the coupon payments on A, E, B, D and C are in Arithmetic Progression, we can assume the coupon payments as:

Coupon Payment for A = $a - 2d$,
Coupon Payment for E = $a - d$,
Coupon Payment for B = a,
Coupon Payment for D = $a + d$ and
Coupon Payment for C = $a + 2d$

We also know that the coupon payment on A is two times the common difference

Thus, $a - 2d = 2d \rightarrow a = 4d$ and hence the values of the coupon payments become:

Coupon Payment for A = $2d$,
Coupon Payment for E = $3d$,
Coupon Payment for B = $4d$,
Coupon Payment for D = $5d$ and
Coupon Payment for C = $6d$

Also, since coupon payment for B = half the price of A → Price of A = 2 × coupon payment for B = 2 × $4d$ = $8d$.

Also, since A matures in 2 years and because its face value is 1000 we have:

Price of A = $8d = (2d/1.25) + 2d/1.25^2 + 1000/1.25^2$

$8d = 4.5d/1.25^2 + 1000/1.25^2$

$12.5d - 4.5d = 1000 \rightarrow d = 125$.

Thus, the price of bond A = 8*d* = 1000.

If we now try to tabulate the information we get the following table:

Bond	Coupon	Face Value	Price	Time Period
A	250	1000	1000	2 years
E	375			2 or 3 years
B	500			2 or 3 years
D	625			5 years
C	750			2 or 3 years

From this point we need to use the remaining information to solve the questions.

13. Since the face value of C is the same as price of A, and also using the remaining information we get:

Bond	Coupon	Face Value	Price	Time Period
A	250	1000	1000	2 years
E	375	F_E	P_E	2 or 3 years
B	500	$2F_E$	$1.75P_E$	2 or 3 years
D	625	Highest face value		5 years
C	750	1000	1800+	2 or 3 years

At this point we are in a position to try to calculate the price of C.

If we try to calculate the price of C for 2 years maturity we see that the price of C is:

$P_C = 750[1/1.25 + 1/1.25^2] + 1000/1.25^2$

$= 600 + 480 + 640 = 1720$ which is less than 1800.

Hence, the maturity of C should be 3 years and the maturity of the other bonds B and E should be 2 years.

The face value of E would be:

$P_E = 375[1/1.25 + 1/1.25^2] + F_E/1.25^2$

Also, $P_B = 1.75P_E = 500\ [1/1.25 + 1/1.25^2] + 2F_E/1.25^2$

Using the above two equations together, we get:

$1.75\{375[1/1.25 + 1/1.25^2] + F_E/1.25^2\} = 500[1/1.25 + 1/1.25^2] + 2F_E/1.25^2$

$\rightarrow 1.75\{540 + 0.64F_E\} = 400 + 320 + 1.28F_E$

$0.16F_E = 225 \rightarrow F_E = 1406.25$

Option (a) is correct.

14. In order to complete the table from this point we can complete the remaining calculations and get:

Bond	Coupon	Face Value	Price	Time Period
A	250	1000	1000	2 years
E	375	1406.25	1440	2 years
B	500	2812.5	2520	2 years
D	625	Highest face value		5 years
C	750	1000	1976	3 years

The highest return is given by E and after purchasing 1 unit of E, she can also purchase another unit of A. Thus, she would get back: $1406.25 + 375 \times 2 + 1000 + 250 \times 2 = 3656.25$. Option (c) is correct.

15. The price of bond C would be given by:

$750 \times \{1/1.25 + 1/1.25^2 + 1/1.25^3\} + 1000/1.25^2 = 600 + 480 + 384 + 512 = 1976.$

Option (d) is correct.

CHAPTER 7

Multiple and Miscellaneous Charts

DI ON MULTIPLE CHARTS/GRAPHS AND TABLES

Very often you will see data interpretation questions, that are asked on mixed charts/graphs and tables. The mix used might be a mix of 2 or 3 or sometimes even more figures. The basic process of reading the data in each question remains the same – even in the case of a DI question based on mixed charts/graphs/tables. Follow the following process for the same:

1. Read each chart/graph/table independent of each other.
2. While reading any one graph/table, first identify the variables and the units that are used for those variables.
3. As you read through the multiple charts/tables, extract a clear understanding of all the variables that are given in the charts/tables. List these variables in your mind – as the steps for solving the DI question further would essentially involve the awareness of these variables.
4. Try to look for the interrelationships between the variables that are given and the derived variables that you can find out from the given variables. Have a strong awareness of the derived variables, since the questions asked are quite likely to be about the derived variables.

MISCELLANEOUS GRAPHS

You need to be aware of three more specific data representation pictures that are being commonly used these days.

1. The Spider Graph
2. The Triangular Graph
3. The Candlestick Chart

It is the best to understand these through examples and actual pictures of these.

SPIDER GRAPH AND HOW TO READ IT

Study the graph below carefully in order to understand how a spider graph looks like:

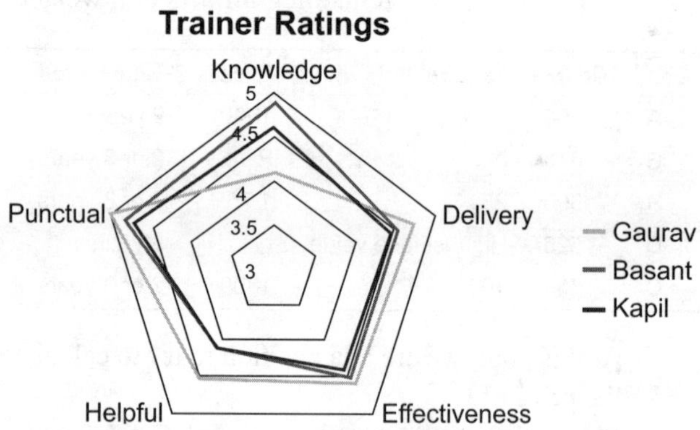

FIGURE 7.1

In the spider chart above, trainers are rated on the basis of five distinct parameters on a scale of 3 to 5. The parameters are: knowledge, delivery, effectiveness, helpfulness and punctuality. Each of the pentagons drawn, represents a specific value of the ratings of each of the three trainers – Gaurav, Basant and Kapil. Gaurav can be seen to have a rating between 4 and 4.5 on knowledge, between 4.5 and 5 on delivery, a rating of 4 on effectiveness, between 3.5 and 4 on helpfulness and a rating of 5 on punctuality. The ratings of the others can be read off similarly.

Why and When are Spider Charts Used?

Spider charts are a neat way to represent data, when you have more than 3 or 4 parameters on which you need to show the ratings for various individuals, companies etc. One of the constraints of a spider chart is that the markings on each axis will be normally same (so for instance, in the above spider graph, if you wanted to include the value of salaries earned by these three trainers, you could not do it, since the values on the chart are limited to ratings between 3 and 5. However, when multiple parameters have to be measured on the same scale – spider charts become very valuable, as they show graphically in one view, what would otherwise require a complete table to tabulate. Thus, for instance, the spider chart shown here shows us 15 data points – 5 data points for each of the three individuals. Also, you should be able to visualise here that in case, we wanted to represent two more individuals here, there would only be two additional lines appearing in the chart and the number of data points exhibited would increase to 25.

Now Let us Take a Look at Triangular Charts

Just like X-Y charts map 2 variables, triangular charts are specifically used for mapping 3 variables/measurements. (The spider graph used in the above example mapped 5 variables.) Again, it's the best to look at how a triangular graph is to be read by looking at a sample triangular graph.

The following graph shows the percentage of gold, silver and bronze in various alloys created at the Great Eastern Alloy Company.

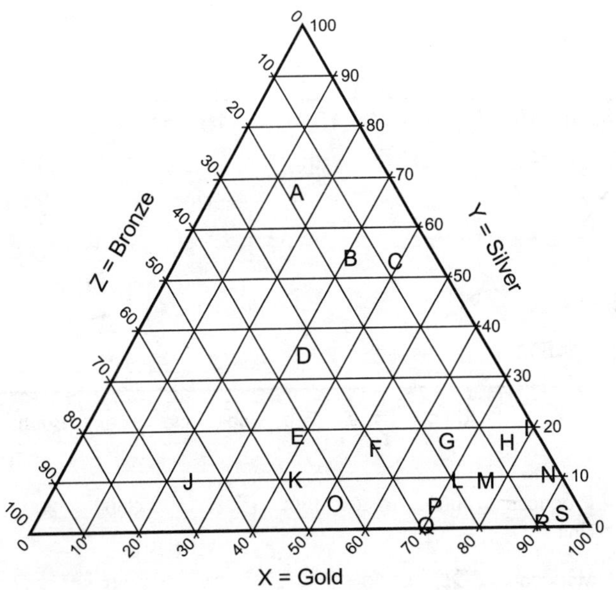

FIGURE 7.2

The key to the interpretation of triangular charts is to understand in which direction to move from any given point in the triangle to read the value of the point. Since, there are 3 Axes, every point will have 3 coordinates. Look at the given figure and understand the following: In order to see that, consider the X = Gold axis. The focus has to be to find the X = 0 line. From the given chart, it is visible that X = 0 is happening along the Z axis (as X moves from 0 at the bottom left to 100 at the bottom right). So, in order to read the value of any point (say E) for it's gold percentage, move parallel to the Z axis in the figure. Hence, X, Gold would have a value of 40. Likewise, the 0 line for the Y (silver) Axis is at the bottom right. This means the reading of the Y axis of any point, would be got by moving parallel to the X axis (i.e. on the horizontal) till you hit the Y axis. Hence, for Point E, the Y axis value = 20. Further, the Z = 0 line is represented by the Y Axis. Hence, The reading of point E on the Bronze (Z) axis, would be 40 (found by moving from Point E, parallel to the Y Axis. Thus, E has the coordinates – (40, 20, 40). Likewise, Point L has the coordinates (70, 10, 20) and so on.

THE CANDLESTICK CHART

A unique kind of chart is used extensively to track stock prices on the stock markets. It is called as a candlestick chart. A sample chart is provided here for your understanding. The X-Axis of the chart represents time and the Y-Axis is the price of the stock being tracked. Each bar in the candle stick represents a certain time period for the stock/index movement. The time period represented can be from as small as 1 second to as large as in months and years. Traders are more interested however in looking at candlestick charts with time periods of between 5 minutes to 1 hour. Each candle (bar) in the graph shows, the starting and closing value of the stock at the start/end of the time period being represented. The bars are color coded to show either a drop in value (dark bars) or an increase in value (light bars). Note: If you see these on a computer screen they will be color coded as red for drop in value and green for rise in value.

For a dark bar, the top of the bar represents the starting price/value at the start of the time period, while the bottom of the bar represents the closing price/value of the stock/index. For the light bar, the starting price is shown by the bottom of the bar, while the ending price is shown by the top of the bar – indicating a rise in price. The wicks in the picture show the highest price/value and the lowest price/value that the stock/index hit during the time period being represented by the candle.

The chart shown gives us the movement of the Nifty Fifty index on 20th Feb 2023, with each candle representing the index value movement in 1 hour time frames. The index opened at 17876 at 9:15 AM and closed the day at 17847.70 at 3:30 the same day.

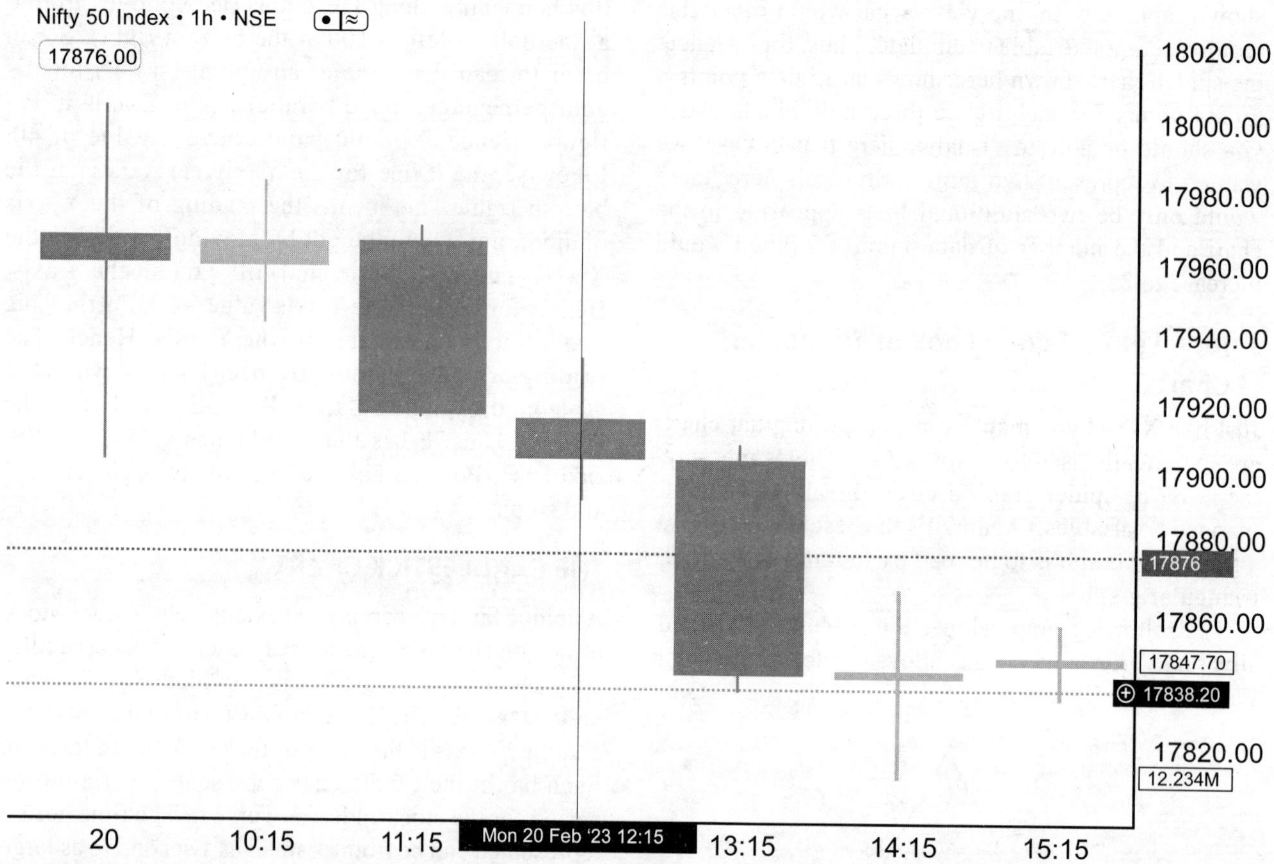

❯ Solved Example

Directions for Questions 1 to 4: *The table given below shows the number of units produced of six different chocolates by a company, the mark-up % on each unit and the discount offered on the marked-up price of each unit in the year 2028. The cost price of all the items is same and fixed at ₹800. The line graph shows the estimated percentage of chocolates sold by the company on the normal discounted price.*

The bar graph shows the percentage of cost price at which the company sold the remaining number of items (means the company sold the remaining number of items at a price lower than the cost price).

TABLE 7.1

	Kitkat	Dairy Milk	Twix	Tobler-one	Galaxy	Bounty
Production Unit	4000	3200	1600	2800	3600	3000
Mark up %	25	30	40	20	30	25
Discount %	10	50	20	30	10	40

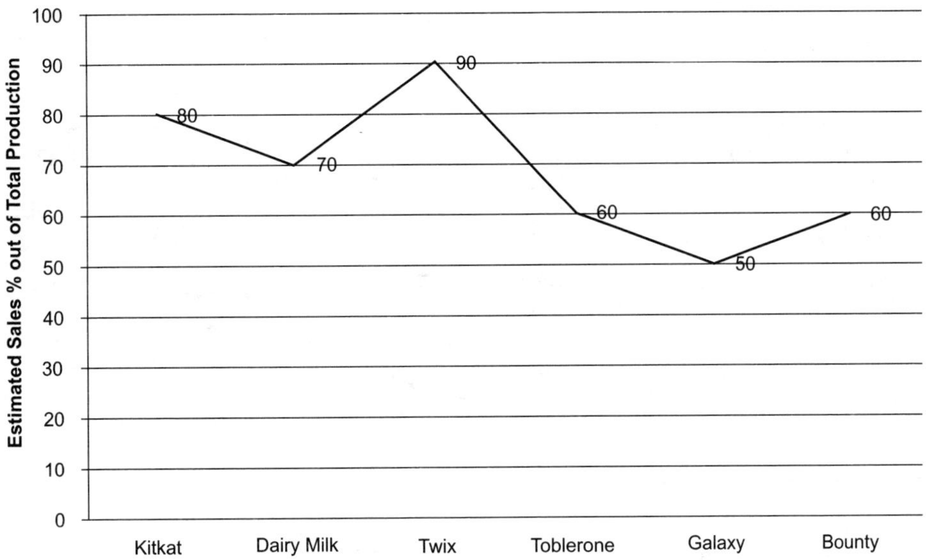

FIGURE 7.3(A)

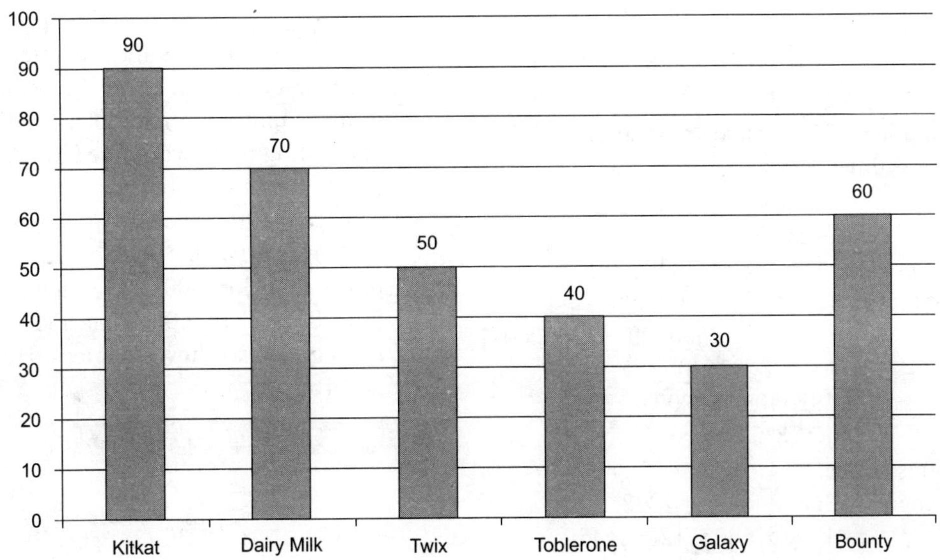

FIGURE 7.3(B)

1. Find profit or loss % of Kitkat and Dairy Milk together in year 2028 if it is known that Dairy Milk sold only 90% of goods of what was actually estimated to sell in the year 2028.
   (a) 33% gain
   (b) 15% loss
   (c) 10.2% gain
   (d) 10.2% loss
2. In the year 2029, Bounty has increased its discount % by 10 basis points and which leads to increase in its estimated sales by 20 basis points. Apart from that everything else remains same. What is the difference in profit/loss for bounty in year 2028–29?
   (a) 144000 (b) 96000
   (c) 88000 (d) 112000
3. What was the average estimated sales (units) for all the brands taken together?
   (a) 2525.33 (b) 2116.66
   (c) 2200.83 (d) 2026.66
4. How many brands have exhibited a profit in the year 2028?
   (a) 1 (b) 2
   (c) 3 (d) 4

Solutions for Questions 1 to 4: *The following table can be drawn in order to develop the basic merged information from the data sources in the question.*

TABLE 7.2

Chocolates	Production (units)	Estimated Sale	Leftover Units	Cost Price	Marked Price	Selling Price	Selling Price of Leftover Units
Kitkat	4000	3200	800	800	1000	900	720
Dairy Milk	3200	2240	960	800	1040	520	560
Twix	1600	1440	160	800	1120	896	400
Toblerone	2800	1680	1120	800	960	672	320
Galaxy	3600	1800	1800	800	1040	936	240
Bounty	3000	1800	1200	800	1000	600	480

1. Estimated sale of Dairy Milk = 2240
   Actual sale = 90% of 2240
   = 2016 (this is given in the question)
   Leftover units = 1184
   Selling price = $2016 \times 520 + 1184 \times 560$
   = 1711360
   Cost price = $3200 \times 800 = 2560000$
   For Kitkat, estimated sale revenue
   = $3200 \times 900 + 800 \times 720$
   = 3456000
   Cost price = $4000 \times 800 = 3200000$
   Total profit/loss = (1711360 + 3456000) – (2560000 + 3200000)
   = loss of 592640
   Loss % = 592640/5760000
   = 10.28% loss.
   Option (d) is correct.
2. Sales revenue for Bounty in year 2028
   = $1800 \times 600 + 1200 \times 420$
   = 1584000
   Cost of Bounty in year 2028
   = $3000 \times 800 = 2400000$
   Loss = 240000 – 1584000 = 816000
   In the year 2029, Bounty would offer a discount of 50% and hence its selling price would become 500. Sales have gone up by 20 basis points. So sales would be 80% = 2400 units. Since, everything else is same, we can assume that production of Bounty was 3000 in 2029 too.
   Therefore new sales revenue of Bounty = $2400 \times 500 + 600 \times 480 = 1488000$.
   Since the cost will remain the same in both cases, we can get the difference in profit/loss by simply getting the difference between the two revenues.
   Required difference = 96000. Option (b) is correct.
3. The required average will be given by: (3200 + 2240 + 1440 + 1680 + 1800 + 1800)/6 = 2026.66
4. The brands that would give a profit would be brands that have an average selling price of more than 800. The average selling price of each brand can be visualised as the weighted average of the normal selling price and the selling price of the leftover units. For example, for Kitkat the average selling price would be $0.8 \times 900 + 0.2 \times 720 > 800$. For Dairy Milk, Toblerone and Bounty, we can see that the average price would be less than 800, since for all the three brands, both their selling prices are below 800. Twix is making a profit, since $0.9 \times 896 + 0.1 \times 400$ is just above 800. Likewise, Bounty is also showing a loss. Hence, option (b) is correct.

Directions for Questions 5 to 8:

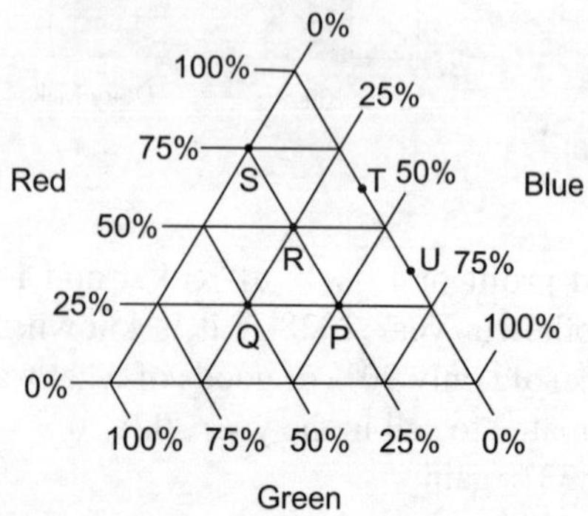

FIGURE 7.4

The triangular graph shows the colour preferences as a percentage of college going students in different streams for the Mindworkzz University. Each student had to choose 1 favourite colour amongst red, blue and green.

P - engineering; total number of students – 160
Q - economics; total number of students – 288

R - politics; total number of students – 240
S - english; total number of students – 200
T - medical; total number of students – 160
U - hotel management; total number of students – 240
The students were asked about their favourite colours out of red, blue and green.

5. Find the number of students in engineering and economics together who like the colour red?
   (a) 96 (b) 144
   (c) 124 (d) 112
6. What is the difference between the number of students in english who prefer green as their favourite colour and the number of students in engineering who like the colour blue?
   (a) 12 (b) 20
   (c) 30 (d) 44
7. The number of students in economics who like the colour red is what percentage of students in politics who like the colour blue?
   (a) 60 (b) 70
   (c) 84 (d) 120
8. Find the total number of students in all the streams who like the colour blue?
   (a) 288 (b) 398
   (c) 460 (d) None of these

Solutions for Questions 5 to 8:

5. Of the 288 people in economics, (Q) 25% = 72 like the colour red. Of, the 160 students in engineering 25% = 40 like red. Hence, the number of people who like the colour red and belong to either engineering or economics = 72 + 40 =112. Option (d) is correct.
6. 25% of english students prefer the colour green (Total = 25% of 200 =50). 50% of engineering students like the colour blue (Total = 50% of 160 = 80). Required difference = 30. Option (c) is correct.
7. The required percentage will be given by: 25% of 288/25% of 240 = 72/60 = 120%. Option (d) is correct.
8. The required addition would be: S (0% = 0); T (37.5% = 60); R (25% = 60); Q (25% = 72); P (50% = 80) and U (62.5% = 150) → 60 + 60 + 72 + 80 + 150 = 422. Hence, option (d) is correct.

Directions for Questions 9 to 12: *The following spider graph, shows the contribution of 2 products out of 4 – apples (A), balls (B), cars (C) and dolls (D) towards the total production in a company. The company compulsorily produces each of these items each year (with a minimum threshold of 1% of total production for each item). Each production value is an integer (as a percentage).*

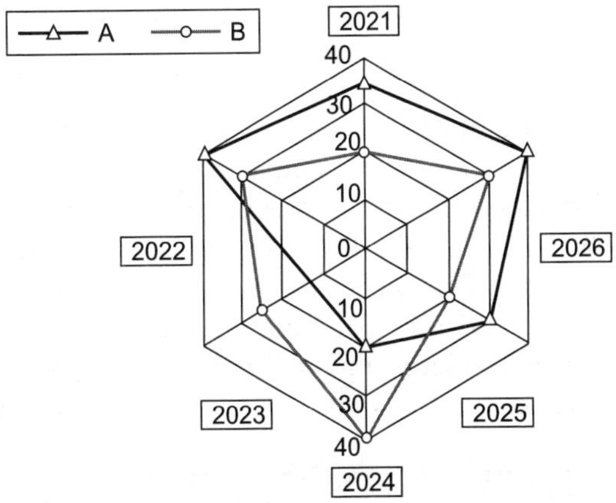

Year	2021	2022	2023	2024	2025	2026
Total Production (in '000s of units)	20	25	30	22	34	40

FIGURE 7.5

9. What is the ratio between the combined sales of cars and dolls in the year 2026 and the combined sales of cars and dolls in 2021?
   (a) 3 : 4 (b) 4 : 3
   (c) 2 : 3 (d) None of these
10. What is the maximum possible change in percentage points in the percentage share of dolls from 2022 to 2024?
   (a) 37 (b) 38
   (c) 40 (d) 10
11. If it is known that dolls' production dipped in year 2025 compared to the previous year, then what can be the maximum drop in its production in 2025?
   (a) 8240 (b) 8340
   (c) 7840 (d) 8800
12. The ratio of apples produced in 2021 to balls produced in 2026 is:
   (a) 3 : 2 (b) 1 : 4
   (c) 4 : 1 (d) 2 : 3

Solutions for 9 to 12:

9. From the spider graph, we see that in 2021, the production of apples accounts for 20% of the total production, while the production of balls accounts for 35% of the total production. This means that the production of cars and dolls would account for 100 – 20 – 35 = 45% of the total production.
   In 2021, production of cars and dolls was 100 – 20 – 35 = 45% of the total. Since the total production is 20000 units, the production of cars and dolls in 2021 would be 9000.
   Similarly, in 2026, the production of cars and dolls would be 30% of 40000 = 12000. Hence,

the required ratio is 3 : 4. Hence, option (b) is correct.

10. In 2022, apples and balls account for 30 + 40 = 70% of the total production. This means that cars and dolls together accounted for 30% of the total production in 2022. Likewise, in 2024, apples and balls account for 40 + 20 = 60% of the total production. This means that cars and dolls together accounted for 40% of the total production in 2024. The largest possible percentage point difference in the production of dolls between 2022 and 2024, would occur if we take dolls as 1% in 2022 and 39% in 2024. This difference would entail a 38-percentage point difference. Hence, option (b) is correct.
11. In order to answer this, you would need to take: maximum possible production of dolls in 2024 – minimum possible production of dolls in 2025 = 39% of 22000 – 1% of 34000 = 8240.
12. 20% of 2000: 40% of 4000 = 4000:16000 = 1 : 4. Option (b) is correct.

Directions for Questions 13 to 15: *The graph represents the opening price, Day's High, Day's Low and Closing price of ITC from 4th Jan to 11th Jan. Each Candlestick represents a 1-day time frame, January 4th has an independent candle and so on. In a light Candle, The opening price is represented by the lower end of the bar, and the closing price is represented by the highest tip of the bar. The wicks represent the highest and lowest price the stock would've reached in the day. In a dark candle, the opening price is represented by the higher end of the bar, and the closing price is represented by the lower end of the bar.*

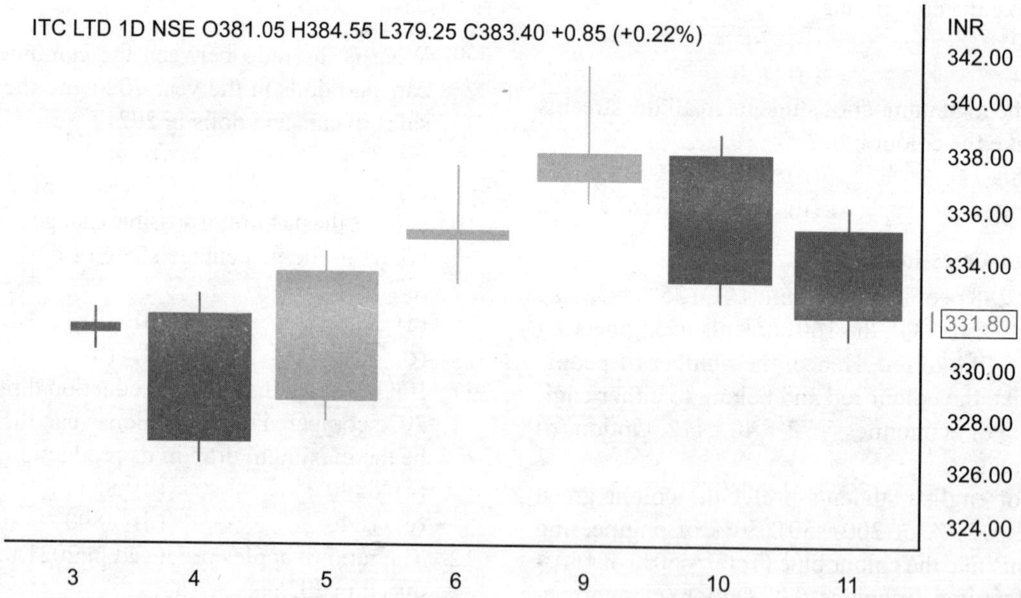

13. What is the approximate percentage increase from the lowest price to the highest price over the 6 days?
(a) 4% (b) 8.25%
(c) 4.75% (d) 10.75%
14. If by 18th January, the stock reached a high of 1.42% based on the closing price of the stock on, 11th Jan, and then closed on +0.86% when compared to 11th Jan, what is the approximate closing price of the stock on 18th Jan 2023?
(a) 334.65 (b) 340
(c) 330 (d) 310
15. A trader decides to buy 150 Quantity of ITC stock on 4th Jan. When the stock reached a high of ₹ 341, he decides to sell 100 Quantity of the stock. Approximately, What could be the minimum and maximum that the trader can gain with the quantity he has left on the day the stock reached a high of 341?
(a) 250 and 800 (b) 180 and 765
(c) 275 and 300 (d) 400 and 500

Solutions for 13 to 15:

13. The lowest price as can be seen from the chart is ₹ 326 on 4th of January. The highest price approximately is 341.5. The percentage change from 326 to 341.5 is 4.75%.
14. The Closing price on 11th jan approximately was 331.8. It is told in the question that the stock closes 0.86% above 11th January's Closing price on 18th January. Hence, the answer is 331.8 × (1.0086) = 334.65

15. Since the trader bought 150 quantity of ITC, sold 100 and was left with 50. We will just use 50 to calculate the profit he can gain as the profit with 100 is already booked. The minimum profit will be when he buys the stock on 4th Jan at the maximum price and sells it on 9th January at the least price. The maximum price approximately was 332.5. on 4th Jan and the minimum price on 9th was approximately 336.10 hence, the minimum profit will be $3.6 \times 50 = 180$. The maximum will be calculated by taking the highest price on 9th jan and the minimum price on 4th jan. The minimum price on 4th jan was 326 and the maximum on 9th jan was approximately 341.3. Hence, the maximum price would be $15.3 \times 50 = 765$. Hence option (b) is the correct answer.

EXERCISE

Level of Difficulty 1

Directions for Questions 1 to 5: The pie chart given below shows the percentage distribution of total students of five colleges of a University – P, Q, R, S and T and the bar graph shows the percentage of students of each of the colleges staying in a hostel during the year 2030.

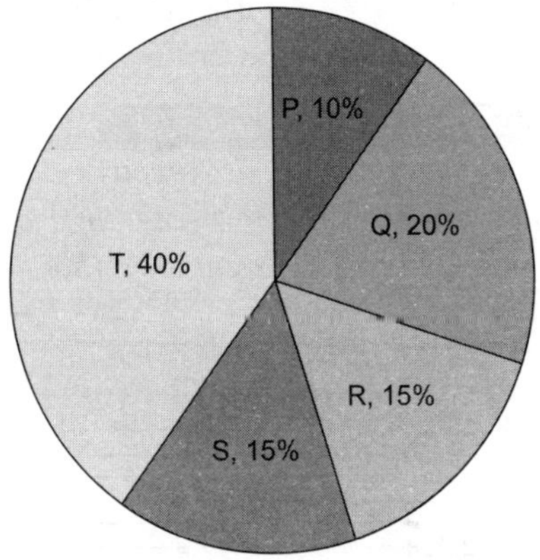

FIGURE 7.6(A)

1. If number of students without hostel in college T in 2030 is 2000, then find the total number of students in College P in 2030?
   (a) 990 (b) 1000
   (c) 1250 (d) 1150

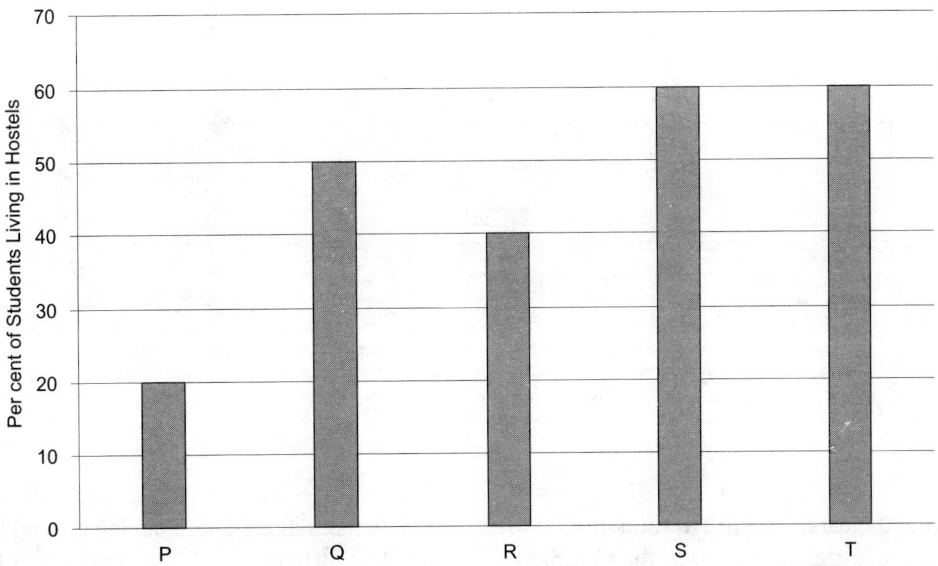

FIGURE 7.6(B)

2. If total number of students in the University was 50000 in 2030, then the total students of college S was how much per cent more than the number of students staying in hostel in college Q?
   (a) 50% (b) 15%
   (c) 13.5% (d) 33.33%

3. If the total population of students in the University is 7500, then find the average of population of students not staying in hostel from sections P, R and T in 2030.
   (a) 825 (b) 800
   (c) 1600 (d) None of these

4. If the total number of students in the University in 2030 was 50000 and in 2031, the number of students of college Q increase by 18% and of college T decreases by 15% then find the difference between total number of students of section Q and section T in 2031.
   (a) 4000 (b) 4500
   (c) 5200 (d) 5000
5. Find the ratio of number of students staying in hostel of section Q and section S together to number of students not staying in hostel of section T and section R together.
   (a) 17:19 (b) 41:32
   (c) 19:25 (d) 13:16

Directions for Questions 6 to 10: *A survey was conducted amongst 50000 prospective car customers. The pie chart shows the percentage of customers interested in buying different cars (Santro, Wagon R, Alto, Swift, Ritz, i10) and the bar graph shows the percentage of women amongst the interested customers for each car.*

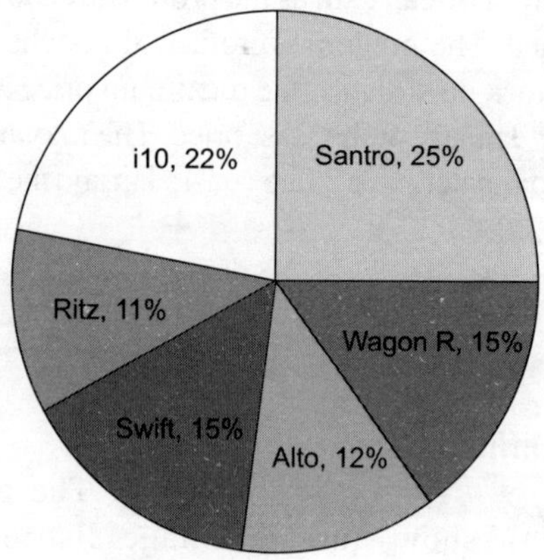

Ratio of Males : Females = 6:4
Total customers = 50,000

FIGURE 7.7(A)

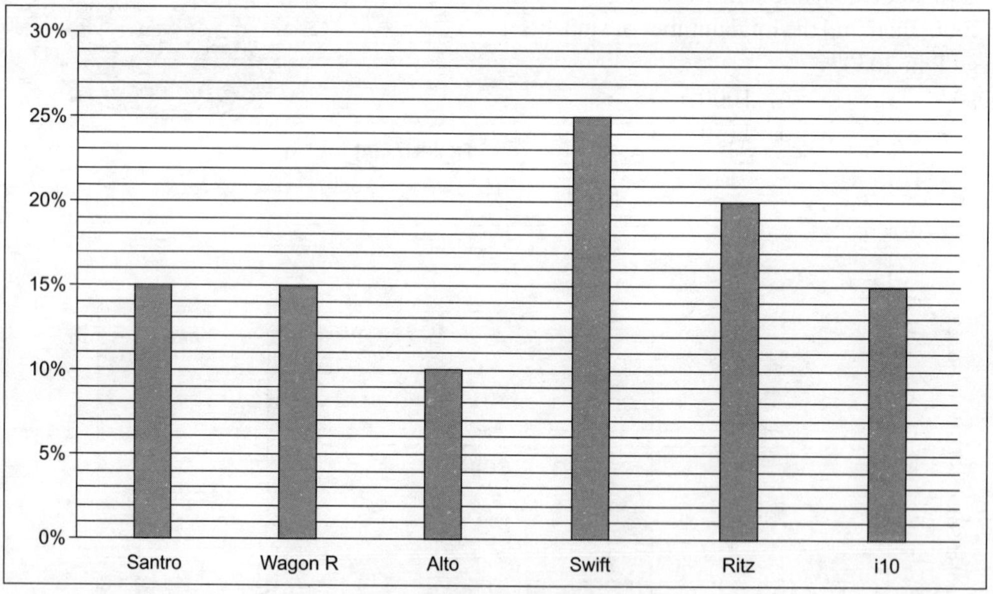

Ratio of Males : Females = 6 : 4
Total Customers = 50,000

FIGURE 7.7(B)

6. For which of the cars, the ratio of total number of customers interested in that car to the number of females interested in that car is minimum?
   (a) Ritz (b) Alto
   (c) Swift (d) None of these
7. What is the difference between the number of females interested in buying Santro and that of Ritz?
   (a) 775 (b) 200
   (c) 670 (d) 440
8. What is the ratio of the number of males interested in Alto and Wagon R together to that of females interested in buying i10 and Swift together?
   (a) 391:141 (b) 471:141
   (c) 235:79 (d) 23:19
9. What is the ratio of the number of customers interested in buying Swift and i10 together to that interested in Santro and Ritz together?
   (a) 37:36 (b) 34:35
   (c) 27:29 (d) None of these
10. Number of females buying Santro and Wagon R together is approximately what per cent of the number of males buying the same car (to the closest percentage)?

(a) 12% (b) 18%
(c) 16% (d) 20%

Directions for Questions 11 to 15: *Analyse the following chart showing the exports and imports of Sono Ltd. and answer the questions based on this chart.*

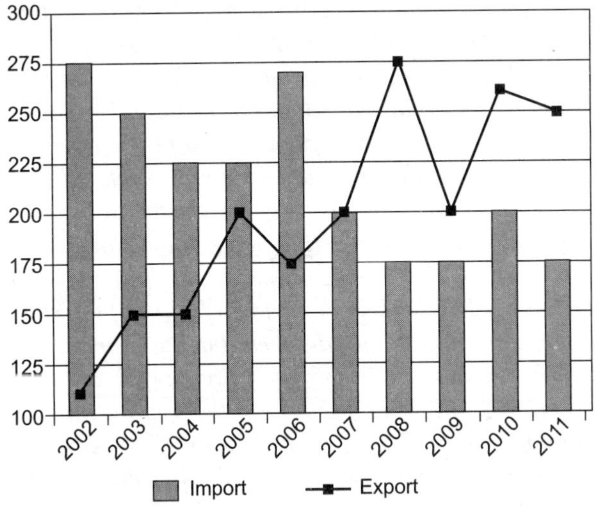

FIGURE 7.8

11. Approximately by what percentage are the total exports greater/smaller than the total imports for the given period?
(a) Greater by 9 per cent
(b) Smaller by 10 per cent
(c) Smaller by 9 per cent
(d) Greater by 10 per cent

12. If the absolute difference between imports and exports are ranked in ascending order, which year gets the 4th rank?
(a) 2010 (b) 2008
(c) 2009 (d) None of the above

13. In which year was the fifth largest annual percentage increase in exports recorded?
(a) 2007 (b) 2005
(c) 2009 (d) None of the above

14. Which year saw the second largest annual percentage increase in imports?
(a) 2010 (b) 2005
(c) 2006 (d) None of the above

15. What is the approximate percentage point difference in the maximum annual percentage increase in export and the minimum annual percentage decrease in imports?
(a) 28 (b) 48
(c) 64 (d) 12

Directions for Questions 16 to 20: *Read the following information on Sectoral Trends in Mergers & Acquisitions in India (2001–02 to 2006–07) given in tables below and answer the questions.*

TABLE 7.3(A) Sector-wise Number of 'Mergers & Acquisitions'

Sectors	2001–02	2002–03	2003–04	2004–05	2005–06	2006–07
Food & Beverage	113	77	77	74	63	61
Textile	57	59	59	64	77	55
Chemicals	134	98	112	99	79	62
Drugs & Pharma	64	60	44	50	60	72
Cement	11	7	8	22	0	0
IT & Telecom	153	114	84	80	109	103
Diversified	15	8	13	4	7	5
Financial Services	194	201	160	116	193	177
Other Services	297	280	287	281	271	293
Misc Manufacturing	31	36	31	35	35	24
Non-Mineral Products	32	24	27	27	47	34

TABLE 7.3(B) Sector-wise Number of 'Mergers'

Sectors	2001–02	2002–03	2003–04	2004–05	2005–06	2006–07
Food & Beverage	17	23	10	19	20	8
Textile	7	7	8	11	21	23
Chemicals	27	15	12	23	24	15
Drugs & Pharma	6	17	14	10	15	12
Cement	0	2	1	3	0	0
IT & Telecom	19	19	13	16	17	12
Diversified	1	0	1	0	0	0
Financial Services	91	107	87	41	75	51
Other Services	90	92	105	81	61	83
Misc Manufacturing	3	13	0	4	11	3
Non-Mineral Products	3	5	1	5	8	11

16. What is the approximate proportion of 'mergers' to 'acquisitions' for the entire period (2001–02 to 2006–07)?
    (a) 26% (b) 36%
    (c) 30% (d) 20%
17. For how many sectors is the proportion of 'mergers' to 'mergers & acquisitions' greater than 20% for the entire period (2001–02 to 2006–07)?
    (a) 2 (b) 3
    (c) 4 (d) 5
18. For how many sectors merger activity (measured by number of mergers) is more in the first 3 years as compared to the last 3 years?
    (a) 7 (b) 3
    (c) 6 (d) 5
19. If the turbulence over a period is defined by the sum of each of the differences (in absolute terms) in number of mergers & acquisitions on a year-on-year basis, then which sector is considered most turbulent for the entire period (2001–02 to 2006–07)?
    (a) Financial Services (b) IT & Telecom
    (c) Food & Beverages (d) Other services
20. In which year maximum sectors have exhibited higher number of acquisitions compared to previous year?
    (a) 2003–04 (b) 2004–05
    (c) 2005–06 (d) 2006–07

Directions for Questions 21 to 25: *The National Stock Exchange of India operates between 9.15 Am and 3.30 Pm. The price of each stock and index is monitored using a candlestick graph. In the chart provided, each candlestick represents the movement of the price of the stock over a 5-minute period. The chart provided maps the price movement of a stock over a 2-day period, starting at 9:15 AM on the first day and closing on the second day. The top and the bottom of the candle rectangles represent the closing and opening price of the stock for a particular five-minute period. A dark candlestick represents a fall in price during the 5 minutes – hence the top of the rectangle represents the starting price of the stock at the start of the 5-minute period, while the lower level of the rectangle represents the closing price of the stock at the end of the 5-minute period being represented. A light candlestick on the other hand represents that the price of the stock went up in the 5-minute period being represented. Hence, the bottom of the rectangle represents the starting price for the 5-minute period, while the top of the rectangle represents the closing price for the 5-minute period being represented by the candle. The wicks at the top and bottom of each candlestick represent the high and low of that stock in that particular interval. Study the chart and answer the questions given below.*

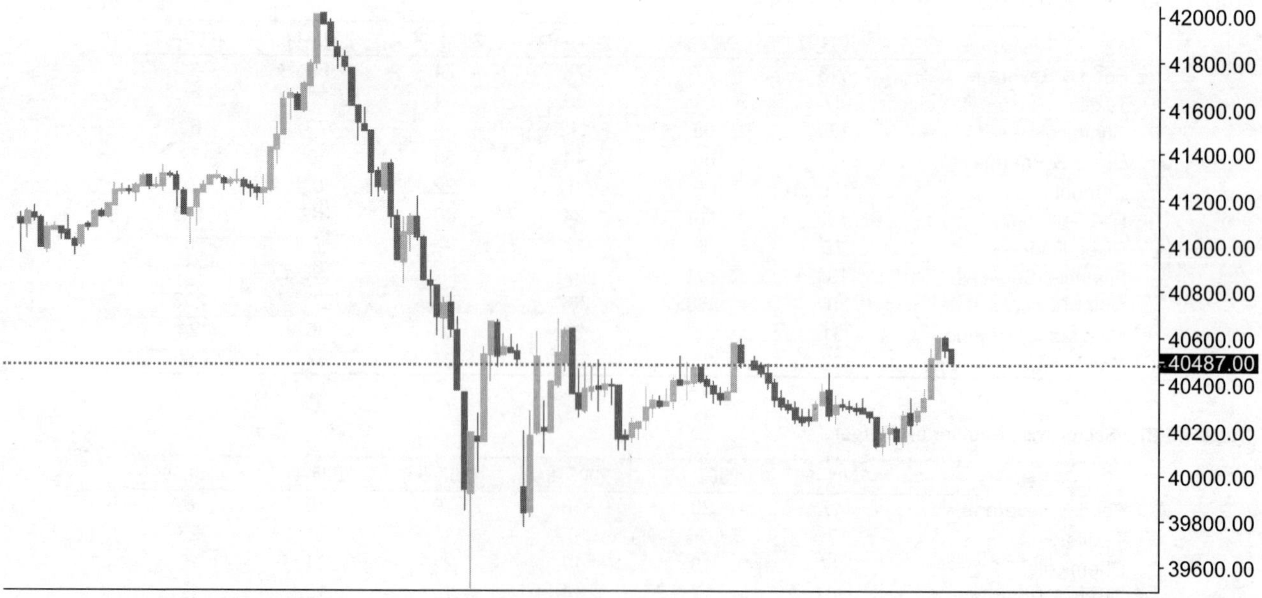

21. What was the highest price(approximately) that the stock hit between 12:46 of the first day and 13:00 of the second day?
    (a) 41500 (b) 42000
    (c) 40000 (d) 38751
22. What is the approximate percentage change in the price between closing of the first day and opening of the second day?
    (a) 3% (b) 1.5%
    (c) 1% (d) 4%

23. If Resistance is defined as an imaginary line at which the stock changes its direction and starts moving downwards, then what is the maximum value of resistance shown on the first day?
    (a) 41300 (b) 42000
    (c) 40600 (d) Cannot be determined
24. In the above question, at what time(approximately) was that price achieved?
    (a) 1300 Hrs (b) 1200 Hrs
    (c) 1100 Hrs (d) 1400 Hrs
25. What was the total fluctuation during the last 25 mins of the second day?
    (a) 350 (a) 500
    (a) 600 (a) Cannot Be Determined

Directions for Questions 26 to 29: *The marks of 5 students, Anirudh, Baldev, Charu, Dhruv and Ekta can be found in the below spider chart. Read the chart and answer the questions following*

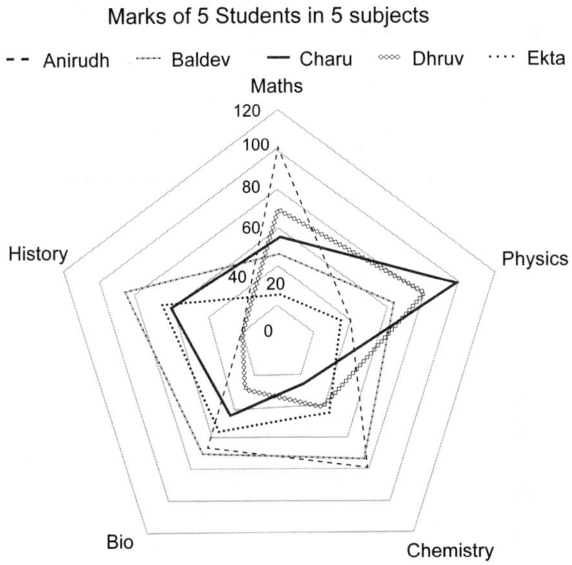

26. Who are the toppers in the subjects Maths, Physics, Chemistry, Bio and History Respectively?
    (a) Anirudh, Charu, Anirudh, Baldev, Baldev
    (b) Anirudh, Baldev, Charu, Dhruv, Ekta
    (c) Anirudh, Charu, Anirudh, Baldev Ekta
    (d) Anirudh, Baldev, Charu, Baldev, Baldev
27. Who has the highest average marks overall in the class?
    (a) Anirudh
    (b) Baldev
    (c) Charu
    (d) Dhruv
28. Which Subjects have the same average per student marks?
    (a) Bio and History
    (b) Physics and Maths
    (c) Bio and Chemistry
    (d) History and Maths
29. If the subject with the highest average marks, was removed, what would the overall class average per subject per student be?
    (a) 53 (b) 53.75
    (c) 54.5 (d) 50.75

Directions for Questions 30 to 34: *The Ministry of Road Transport and Highways, India conducted a survey of the percentage of people preferring different modes of transport such as Cars, Buses and Trains. Each individual was asked to give his preference for his most preferred mode of transport. This survey was conducted across 5 different cities namely Kanpur, Pune, Raisen, Trivandrum and Surat. The total number of people surveyed in the cities are 5000, 6000, 7000, 8000 and 9000 in that order. Study the below chart and answer the questions that follow.*

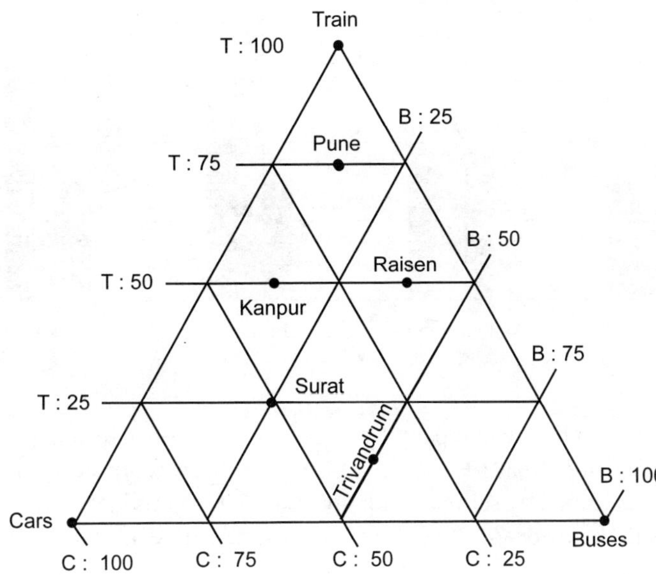

30. What is the total number of people who preferred Cars?
31. What is the total number of people who preferred cars from Pune and Train users from Raisen?
32. By what percentage is the total number of people who preferred trains from Trivandrum more/less than the number of people who preferred buses from Kanpur?
33. What is the maximum percentage difference between any two modes of transportation of any particular city?
34. What is the percentage point difference between the total number of people who preferred Buses to the number of people who preferred trains?

Level of Difficulty 2

Direction for Questions 1- 4: *The following data consists of the details regarding four milk powders Amul, Mother India, Taaza and Verka – manufactured and sold by the company M/s Veeba India Ltd., in the year 2019.*

TABLE 7.4

Product	Cost of Milk (in ₹ per 100 liters of milk)	Quantity of Milk Required to Produce 1 Saleable unit (in liters per unit)	Average Wages Paid to Milkmen (in ₹ per 10 units of saleable milk)	Average Transport Cost (in ₹ per 100 units)	Other Costs (in ₹ per unit)	Profit Percentage Earned on each unit
Amul	500	100	500	5000	50	20%
Mother India	2000	50	1000	1000	50	25%
Taaza	3000	80	1600	8000	80	20%
Verka	1000	150	500	2000	120	10%

Note: Cost per unit = (Cost of Milk + Wages + Transport Cost + Other Costs) per unit

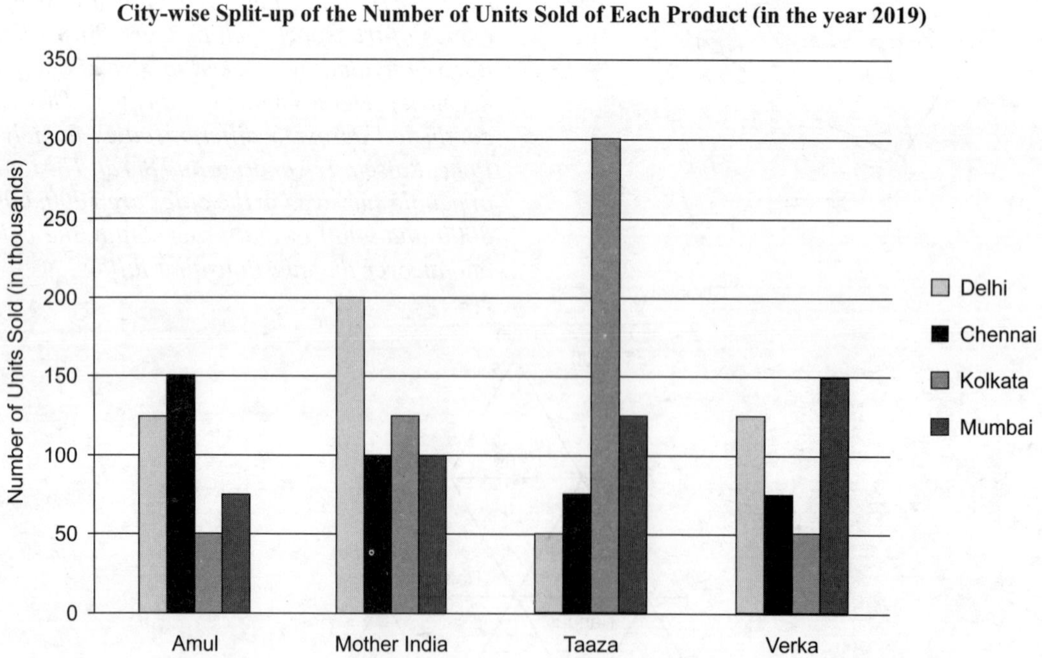

FIGURE 7.9

1. What is the total profit earned by the company by selling Amul milk powder (in ₹) in 2019?
2. What is the ratio of profits earned by selling Amul milk powder and Verka milk powder?
3. What were the average sales revenues (to the closest in ₹ thousands) per City of the Mother India milk powder?
4. Which product earned the maximum revenue from sales in Chennai?

(a) Amul (b) Mother India
(c) Taaza (d) Verka

Direction for Questions 5 to 7: *Aman starts moving along a straight road in the North direction at t = 0 seconds. He travels for a total of 5 minutes. For his first 2.5 minutes, the speed-time graph for him shows the speeds at which he moving for various time periods. The bar chart given shows the distance covered by Aman in the next 2.5 minutes. The speed-time curve for him is a straight line in the time intervals 150–200 seconds, 200–250 seconds and 250–300 seconds.*

5. What is the speed (in m/s) of Aman at t = 150 seconds?
6. What is the average speed (in m/s) of Aman during the entire journey of 300 seconds?
7. What is the average speed (in m/s) of Aman between t = 80 seconds and t = 240 seconds?

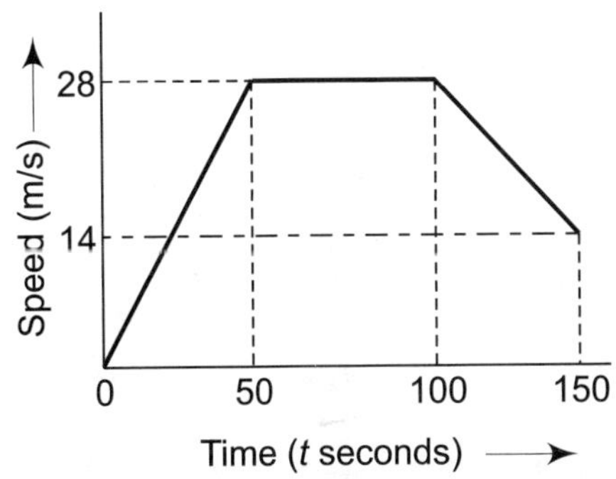

FIGURE 7.10(A)

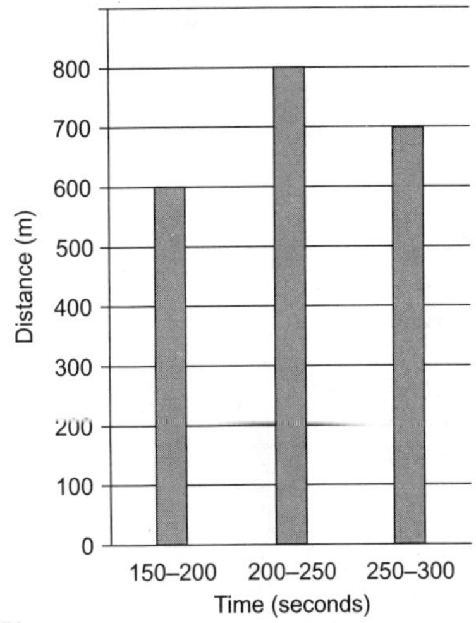

FIGURE 7.10(B)

Direction for Questions 8 and 9: *The graph given below shows the number of books distributed in three cities of India to promote 'The Educated India' mission.*

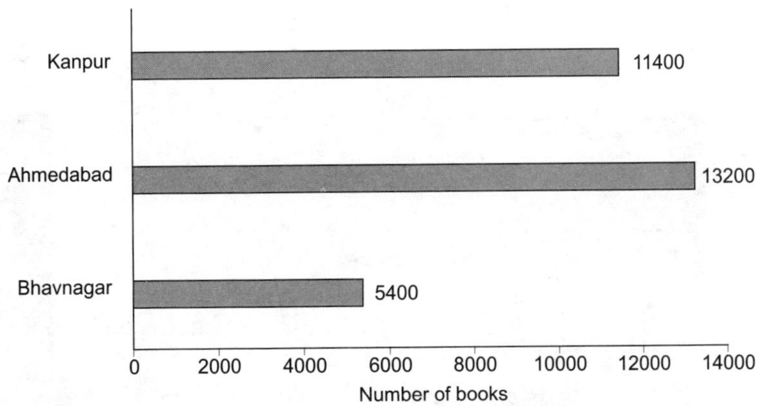

FIGURE 7.11(A)

A book is considered as utilised if it reaches in the hand of deserving student. Some books went unutilised in each city, as they did not reach the deserving students. The pie chart given below shows the number of books utilised in each city as a percentage of the total number of books utilised in the three cities.

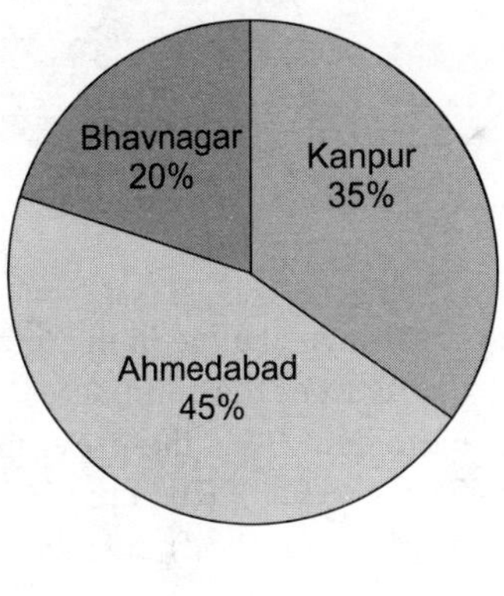

FIGURE 7.11(B)

8. If the total number of books wasted in the three cities is 20% of the total number of books utilised in the three cities, then what is the number of books wasted in Kanpur as a percentage of the total number of books wasted in the three cities?

(a) 28% (b) 53%
(c) 65% (d) None of these

9. The number of books unutilised in Kanpur is thrice the number of books unutilised in Bhavnagar. What is the difference in the number of books unutilised in Ahmedabad and the number of books unutilised in Bhavnagar?
(a) 3500 (b) 3000
(c) 1350 (d) 3010

Direction for Questions 10 and 11: *The bar graph given below shows the total amount (in million $) invested by five different multinationals – A, B, C, D and E – in three fields – R&D, Production and Marketing – in 2019 and 2020. The pie charts given below show the percentage break-up of the total investment (which also includes the three fields mentioned earlier) made by the different companies of USA in 2019 and 2020.*

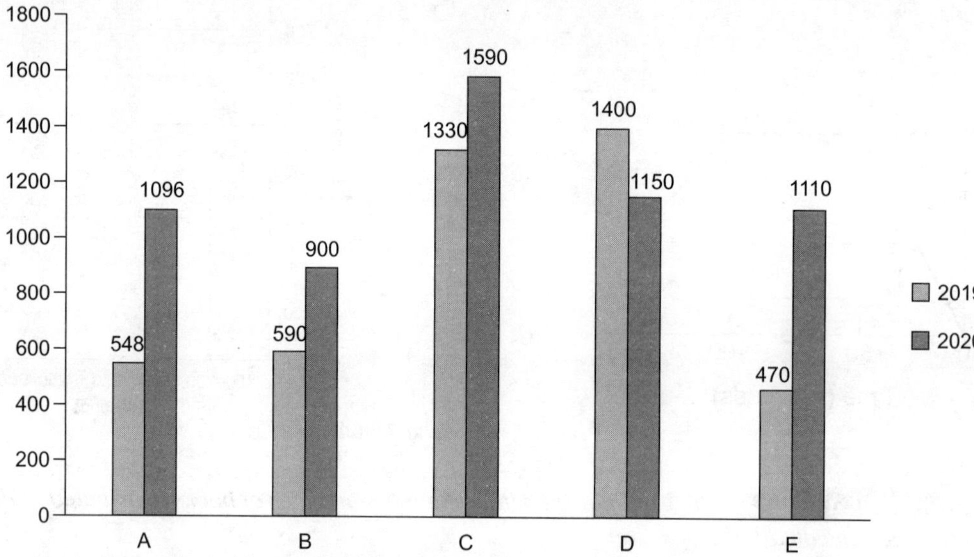

FIGURE 7.12(A)

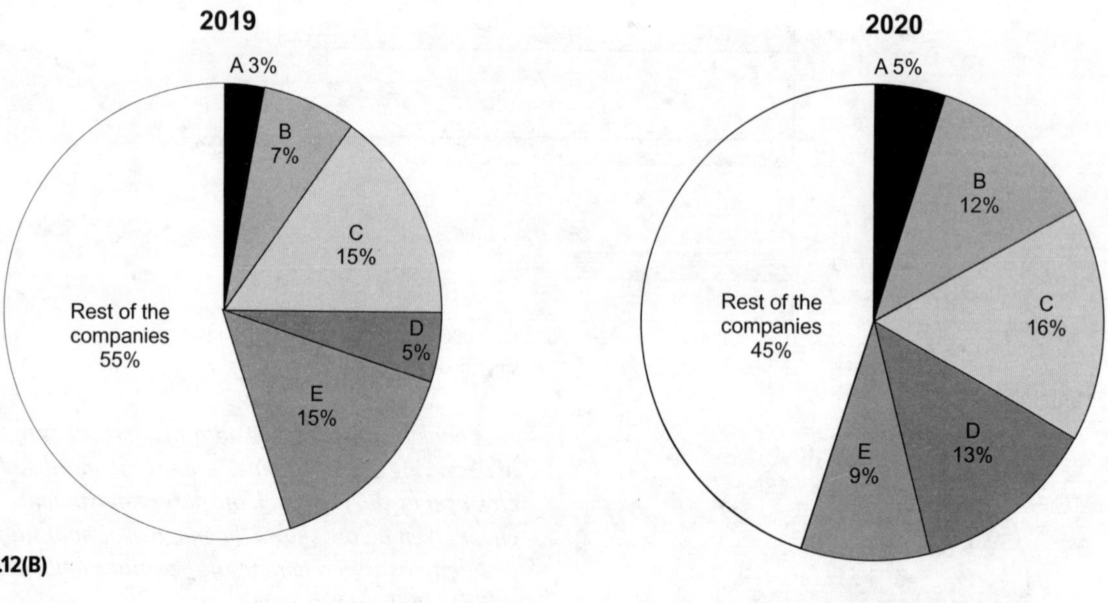

FIGURE 7.12(B)

10. In 2019, D's investment in R&D, Production and Marketing was 56% of its total investments. In 2019, what is the investment made by E (in million $)?
11. In 2020, B's investment in R&D, Production and Marketing was 15% of its total investments. What was the percentage change in the total investment made by the 'Rest of the companies' from 2019 to 2020 (use the data from the previous question)?
(a) 44:47 (b) 11:12
(c) 44:45 (d) 55:45

Directions for Questions 12 to 15: *The line graph indicates the no. of days taken by six male programmers to complete a project. [Fig. 7.13(A)]*

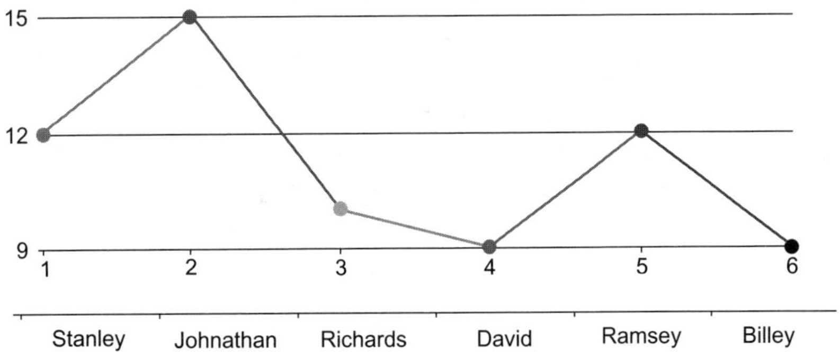

FIGURE 7.13(A)

The chart below shows the number of days taken by six female programmers to complete the same project.

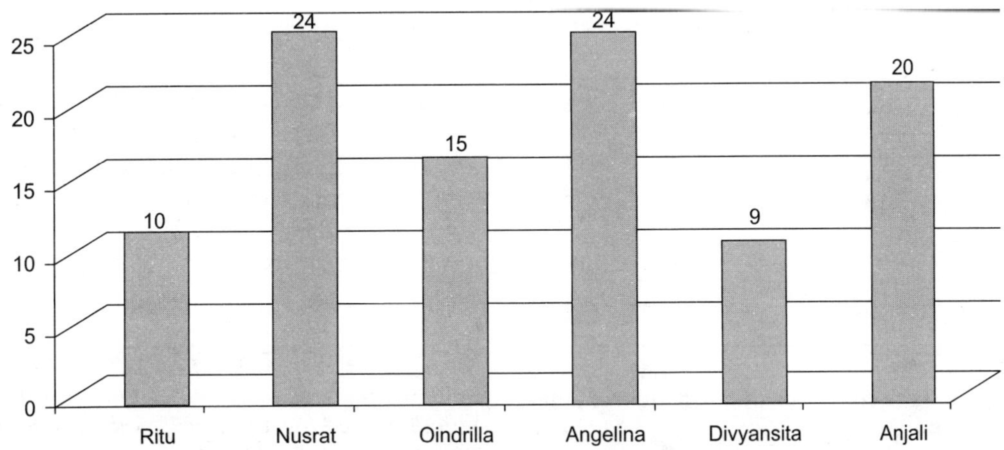

FIGURE 7.13(B)

12. If David and Billey started to work and after 2 days they left and the work was continued by Nusrat, Divyansita and Angelina for the next two days. After the fourth day, what fraction of the work would be left?
    (a) 1/5 (b) 1/6
    (c) 1/12 (d) 1/50
13. If all the male programmers work together, then the time taken by them will be how much less than the time taken by Ritu, Oindrilla, Nusrat and Angelina together to do the work?
    (a) 2.6 days (b) 2.2 days
    (c) 3.4 days (d) 2 days
14. Ramsey and Richards start a work. Ramsey worked at 120% of his efficiency and Richard at 5/6 of his normal routine work. They started work on alternate days starting with Ramsey. How many days will be taken by them to complete the work?
    (a) 54/5 days
    (b) 65/6 days
    (c) 43/4 days
    (d) 44/3 days
15. How many days will it take to complete the work if Stanley does 25% of the work alone and 10% is done by Richard alone and the remaining is done by Anjali, working alone?
    (a) 19 days (b) 16 days
    (c) 13 days (d) 17 days

Directions for Questions 16 to 19: *Given below is a line graph representing number of mobile handsets sold by 4 companies in the years 2012–2016. All values are in thousands. The table shows the profit percentage of each company over the 5 year period. Profit percentage is defined as the profit earned per hundred rupee of cost in producing one mobile handset.*

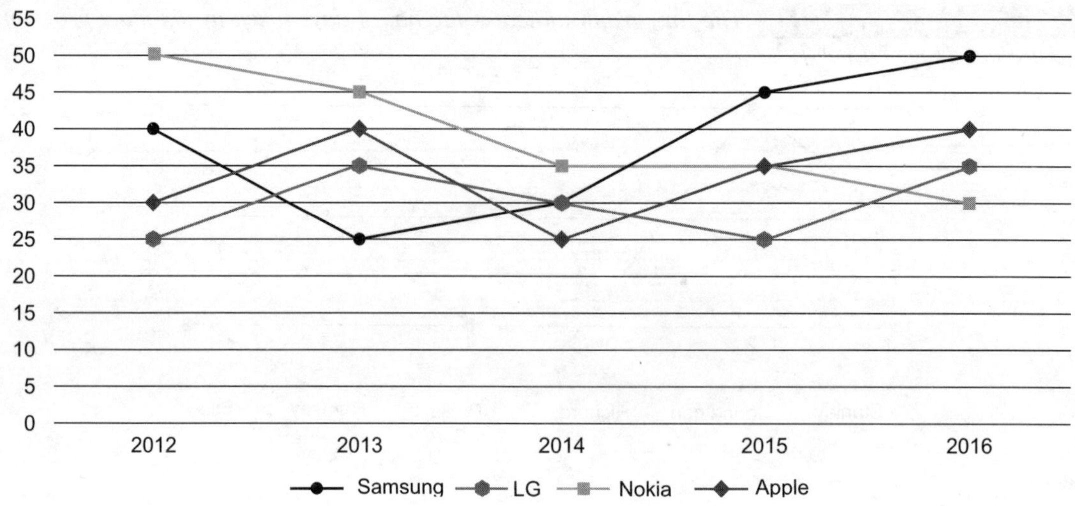

FIGURE 7.14

TABLE 7.5

Company	Profit %				
	2012	2013	2014	2015	2016
Samsung	25%	40%	30%	15%	25%
LG	30%	22%	20%	16%	12%
Nokia	36%	45%	20%	10%	8%
Apple	40%	35%	42%	54%	48%

16. Find the average cost price of one handset manufactured in the year 2014 by Samsung, if the total earnings by selling handsets was ₹45 crores.
(a) ₹12344.60
(b) ₹11538.50
(c) ₹12360.75
(d) ₹11350.60

17. Nokia and LG had two variants each in 2012. Number of handsets sold of variant 1 and variant 2 were in the ratio 3:2 for Nokia and 3:5 for LG. Cost price of variant 1 was ₹8000 and cost of variant 2 was ₹12000 for Nokia. For LG, cost price of variant 2 was ₹27000. Find the cost price of variant 1 for LG if the total profit made by the two companies in 2012 was same.
(a) ₹15840 (b) ₹15640
(c) ₹16840 (d) ₹16440

18. Find the percentage by which the profit made by apple is more or less than the profit made by Samsung in the year 2016, if the average cost price of handset sold by apple was 8% less than the average cost price of Samsung handsets in 2016.
(a) 37.62% (b) 29.92%
(c) 41.312% (d) 36.56%

19. In 2015, Nokia launched 4 handsets which were sold in the ratio 1:3:2:4 respectively. The cost price of the 4 models were in the ratio 6:3:4:2 respectively. If the total profit made in 2015, by Nokia was ₹6.51 crore. Find the cost price of the third model.
(a) 12000 (b) 18000
(c) 22500 (d) 24000

Direction for Questions 20 to 24: *5 students namely, Anshuman, Pallav, Shaurya, Ritika and Kavita appeared for a test in six subjects namely Maths, Physics, English, Chemistry, Computer Science and Physical Education. The maximum marks for these subjects are 100, 100, 120, 150, 200 and 250 in no particular order. The percentage of marks scored by all the students in different subjects is given in the spider chart given below. It is also known that Shaurya's scores in Physics, Chemistry, Computer Science and Physical Education were equal, which was in turn equal to the marks scored by Kavita in Maths. Also, Shaurya scored 66.67% marks in Chemistry, while Kavita scored 83.33% marks in the same subject. Pallav and Shaurya both scored 83.33% marks in Computer Science. Ritika scored 62.5% in Maths and 96% in English. Pallav scored 92 % in English, while Kavita scored 88% in the same. Apart from these scores, all scores of all students were a percentage value ending in 0 or 5.*

Study the graph and answer the questions below.

20. What is the sum of the marks scored by all the students in English?

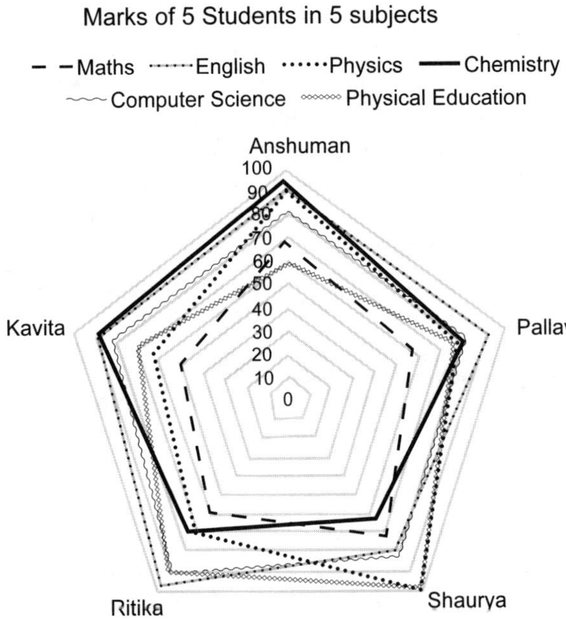

21. What is the difference between the highest score obtained by any student in any subject and the lowest score obtained by any student in any subject?
22. What is the total score of Shaurya in the subjects other than those in which he scored the same marks?
23. What is the sum of scores obtained by Pallav in all the subjects?
24. What is the average percentage of the class?

Directions for Questions 25 to 28: *The figures given below show the amount of work distribution (in operational hours) for a toy manufacturing company having manufacturing plants in Chennai and Kanpur. Each plant carries out six activities. Planned operational cost per hour of Chennai and Kanpur plants are Rs 250 and Rs 300 respectively. However, the actual operational cost per hour is Rs 270 in Chennai and Rs 315 in Kanpur. Cost Difference (in %) =Absolute ((Actual Cost - Planned Cost) / Planned Cost) × 100*

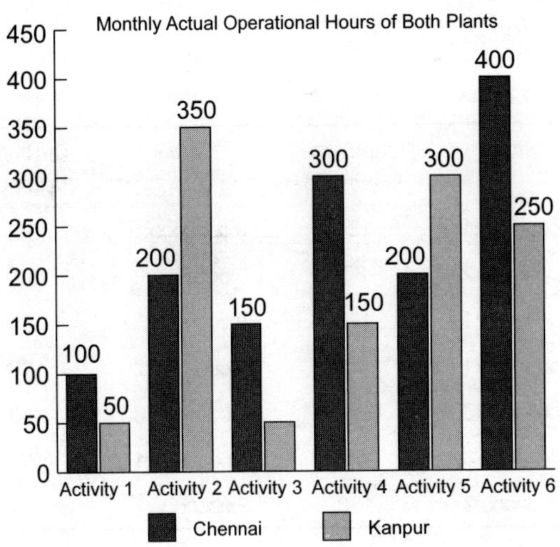

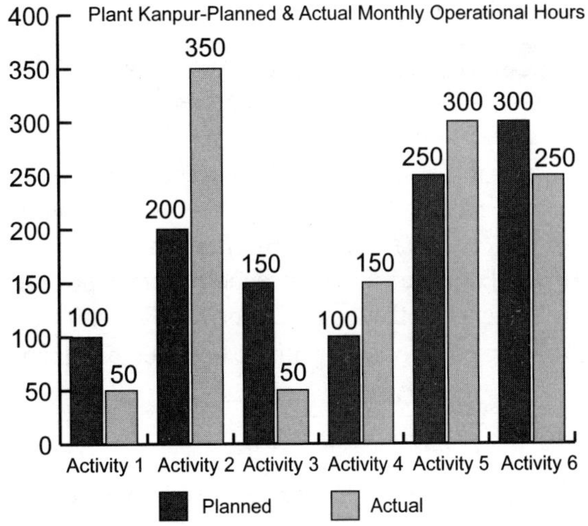

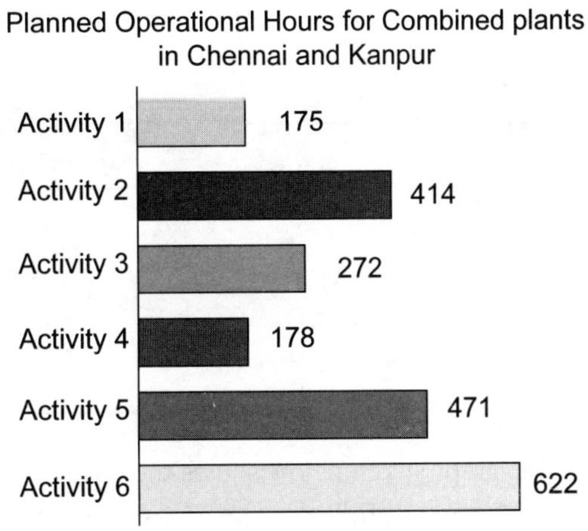

25. What is the overall cost difference in Chennai Plant (Approximately)?
(a) 39% (b) 41%
(c) 65% (d) 70%
26. In how many activities the plant in Chennai could meet at least 50% shortfall in the actual operational hours compared to planned operational hours of plant in Kanpur?
(a) 1 (b) 2
(c) 3 (d) 4
27. Which of the following activities has the maximum cost difference in the Kanpur plant?
(a) Activity 1
(b) Activity 2
(c) Activity 3
(d) Activity 4
28. In how many activities plant in Chennai has higher planned operational hours as compared to the plant in Kanpur?
(a) 1 (a) 2
(a) 3 (a) 4

Level of Difficulty 3

Direction for questions 1 to 3: *YRF, production house sells its movies to various distributors and charges a 'fixed revenue' and 'share in profit'. The 'fixed revenue' is fixed and 'share in profit' is variable, which affects the 'Total income' of the production house. The 'share in profit' is calculated as the difference of two Factors X and Y.*

(i) Total income = Fixed revenue + share in profit/Loss
(ii) Share in profit/Loss = Factor X – Factor Y
(iii) Average income per film (calculated on an annual basis) = $\frac{\text{Total Income}}{\text{Number of Films}}$

The table given below shows the Fixed revenue and the Average Income (per film) for each year from 2015 to 2020. It is known that A < D < B < C < E.

TABLE 7.6

Year	Fixed Revenue (in ₹)	Average Income (per Film) (in ₹)
2015	A	A1
2016	B	A2
2017	C	A2
2018	C	A3
2019	D	A4
2020	E	A5

The line graph given below shows the ratio of Factor X to Factor Y for the production house for each year from 2015 to 2020.

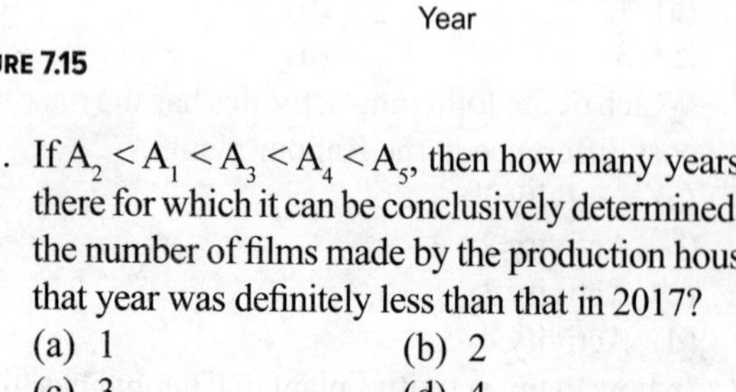

FIGURE 7.15

1. If $A_2 < A_1 < A_3 < A_4 < A_5$, then how many years are there for which it can be conclusively determined that the number of films made by the production house in that year was definitely less than that in 2017?
   (a) 1 (b) 2
   (c) 3 (d) 4
2. If $A_2 < A_1 < A_5 < A_3 < A_4$, for which of the following years can we say that the number of films released will be definitely lower than the number of films released in 2017?
   (a) 2015 (b) 2018
   (c) 2020 (d) None of these
3. Suppose it is known that, the number of films made by the production house increased in each year as compared to the previous year in the period 2016–20. In which of the following pairs of years can the Average Income (per film) of the production house not be equal?
   (a) 2015 and 2016 (b) 2016 and 2017
   (c) 2017 and 2020 (d) 2018 and 2019

Directions for Questions 4 to 7: *Magoo uses a mobile phone of Garuda Network. During a particular week, he made calls to and received calls from only three different numbers, 9xxxxxxxx1, 9xxxxxxxx2 and 9xxxxxxxx3. Each call that he made/received during the week belongs to any one of the following four categories:*

- *Normal incoming call, for which Garuda charges 10 paise per second.*
- *Normal outgoing call, for which Garuda charges 25 paise per second.*
- *Roaming incoming call, for which Garuda charges 50 paise per second.*
- *Roaming outgoing call, for which Garuda charges 125 paise per second.*

For each of the three numbers (mentioned above), there was at least one call that fell into each of the four categories. The following tables and graph give information about the duration of the calls of different categories. The table provides information on the duration (in seconds) of each call made/received by Magoo during the week. The horizontal bar graph provides information on the total duration (in seconds) of calls grouped by category. The second bar graph presents the total cost (in ₹) incurred by Magoo due to calls of all categories from/to each number.

Duration of each call.

TABLE 7.7

Number	Duration (seconds)	Number	Duration (seconds)
9xxxxxxxx1	120	9xxxxxxxx1	10
9xxxxxxxx2	80	9xxxxxxxx2	30
9xxxxxxxx1	120	9xxxxxxxx3	180
9xxxxxxxx1	40	9xxxxxxxx2	100
9xxxxxxxx3	20	9xxxxxxxx3	140
9xxxxxxxx3	50	9xxxxxxxx1	20
9xxxxxxxx2	160	9xxxxxxxx1	110

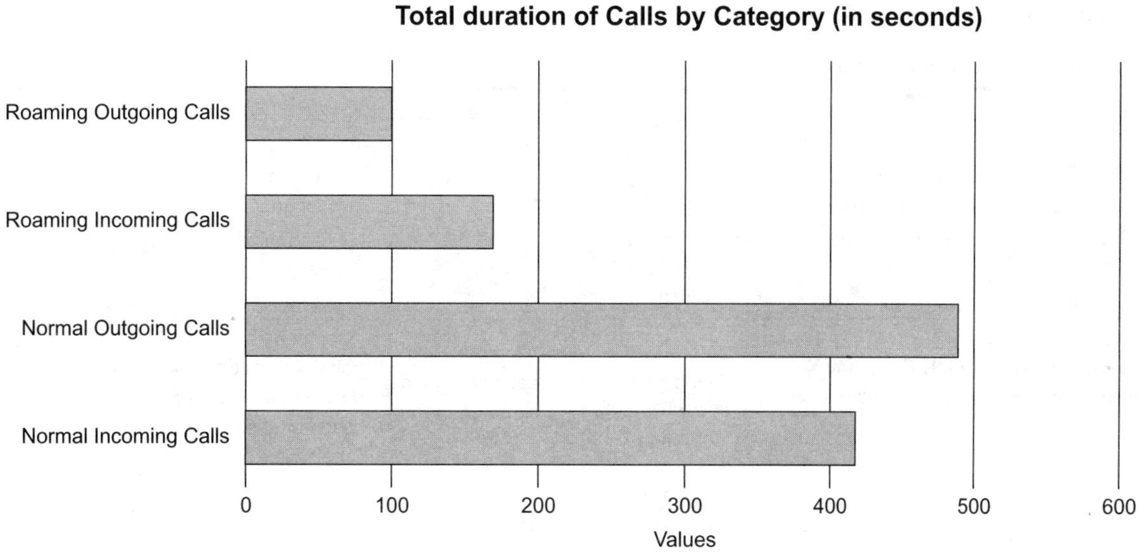

FIGURE 7.16(A)

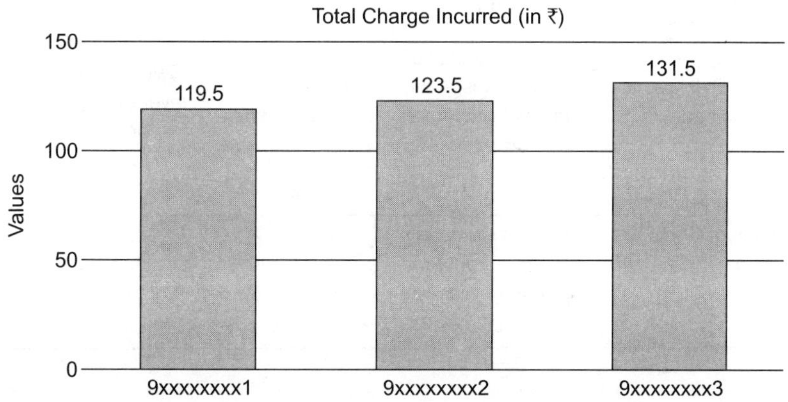

FIGURE 7.16(B)

4. To which category does the call which had a duration of 50 seconds belong?
   (a) Normal incoming call
   (b) Normal outgoing call
   (c) Roaming incoming call
   (d) Roaming outgoing call
5. What is the duration of the normal outgoing calls from the number 9xxxxxxxx2 as a percentage of the total duration of all calls made from or to that number (Correct to 2 decimal places)?
6. What is the average duration in seconds of each roaming incoming call made by Magoo during the week?
7. The average cost incurred per call for all the outgoing calls made by Magoo to 9xxxxxxxx1 was
   (a) ₹20.62
   (b) ₹27.50
   (c) ₹31.25
   (d) ₹29.33

Directions for Questions 8 to 12: *In order to quantify the intangibles and incentives to the multi brand dealers (dealers who stock multiple goods as well as competing brands) and the associated channel members, a company (X) formulates a point score card, called as brand building points. The brand building points are added to the sales target achieved points for redemption. The sales target achieved points are allotted as per the table 7.10 of this question. The sum of brand building points and sales achieved points is the total that can be redeemed by the dealer against certain goods, as shown in the second table.*

The detail of the system is shown in the tables below:

TABLE 7.8 Brands Building Score Card

Brand Building Criteria	Points that are Allotted if Any of the Below is Achieved					
Company (X)'s Signage	Only Company X's signage on main entrance on the store	Company X's signage on the main entrance along with other brands	Company X's signage in the corner of the counter	Company X's signage Outside the counter	No signage of Company (X)'s	Other brands signage only
Points	20	10	5	5	0	–20
Company X's Wall painting in the exterior of the store	Only Company X's painting in the walls of the store	Company X's painting on main entrance with other brands	Company X's painting on the side wall of the store	Company X's painting outside the store on some other structure	No painting of Company X	Other brands painting only
Points	20	5	2.5	2.5	0	–10
Company X's painting in the interior of the store	The interior of the store has only Company X's painting	Company X's painting in the Back side of the counter	Company X's painting on the side wall in the interior	Not painted	Others' painting only	
Points	10	5	2.5	2.5	–10	
POP (point of purchase) display of Company X	All POP display is of company X	The POP display of company X is at the eye level with other brands	Above the eye level with other	Below the eye level with other brands	Store does not have any POP material	Store has only Other brands POP material
Points	25	10	5	5	0	–20
Stacking of Company X goods in the shelves	Goods of Company X's only in the front row	Goods of Company X's share front row with other brands	Company X's goods are only in the back row	Goods of other brands in the front row only		
Points	25	10	0	–20		

TABLE 7.9 Point Redemption Options

Sl. No.	Goods on Offer	Total Points Required for Redemption
1	Umbrella	40
2	Nike Cap	100
3	T-Shirt	200
4	Tupperware Set	600
5	Ray Ban Glasses	800
6	Banarasi Silk Saree	2000
7	Kanjivaram Saree	4000

TABLE 7.10 The Point Calculation on Sales Target Achieved is

Sales Target	Points Assigned
<50% of the Sales Target	0
50–75%	10
75–99%	12
100%	15
Each extra unit sold above the sales target	0.25

There are 10 multi brand dealers in Nasik and the sales that they have achieved at the end of a quarter are:

TABLE 7.11

Dealers	Sales Target (July–Sep) in Units	Actual Sales
Bhoumik Brothers	25,000	24,378
Subhajit Traders	28,000	29,241
Srikrishna Traders	40,000	42,000
Nikil Choudhary & Co	43,000	42,000
M/s Dinesh Kumar	25,000	25,000
Variety Stores	22,000	23,000
Rajib & Co	22,000	22,000
Malling Enterprise	23,000	24,000
Saha H/W	24,000	24,512
Maheswari & Co	50,000	56,241

8. Maheshwari & Company has company X's signage along with other brand's signage at the main entrance of the store, the exterior walls of the store have the painting of only company X's, the side wall in the interior has the painting of company X's.

The POP display of company X's is above the eye level with other brands while the stacking of goods of company X's is in the back row of the shelves. The brand building points when combined with the sales achieved points amount to the total points that a dealer can accumulate in a quarter. The number of Tupperware sets that Maheshwari & Co can redeem after the quarter (July to September) is?

(a) 2 (b) 3
(c) 4 (d) 5

9. Bhowmik Brothers has only other brands signage in the front of the store, and company X's painting on the side wall in the exterior of the store, company X's painting on the side wall in the interior of the store, no POP display of any other company and the goods of company X's are stacked in the front row with other brands. What are the total points Bhowmik Brothers need to accumulate to make them eligible for minimum redemption?

(a) 27 (b) 37
(c) 38 (d) 33

10. The Brand building points of Saha H/W is 85, and Mr. Saha the proprietor of the store wants to redeem a Kanjivaram saree in the next quarter by carrying forward the points accumulated this quarter. The sales target of Saha H/W is 25,000 units in the next quarter. It is assumed that the brand building points for the next quarter is also going to be 85. How many extra units Saha H/W has to sell in order to get the Kanjivaram saree?

(a) 14688 (b) 12668
(c) 13658 (d) 16288

11. Malling Enterprise exhausted all its points while redeeming three Nike caps and an Umbrella. What is its brand building points?

(a) 75 (b) 80
(c) 85 (d) 90

12. If Srikrishna Trader has 80 brand building points then the goods that it can redeem are ____?

(a) Tupperware set, Kanjivaram
(b) Umbrella and Tupperware set
(c) Tupperware set, Nike cap
(d) Nike cap and T-Shirt

Directions for Questions 13 to 16: *Given below is information relating to cost of starting a business and number of days required for specific business activities in select countries.*

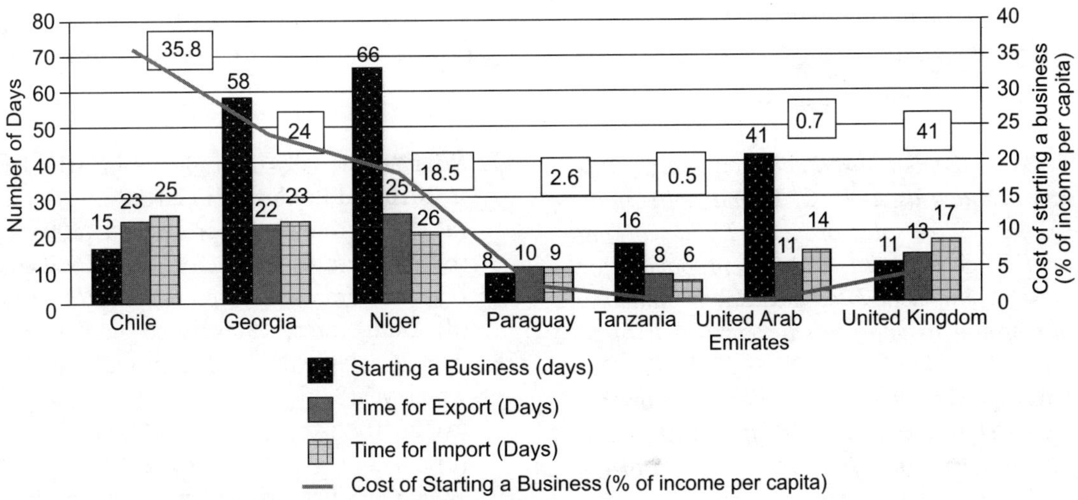

FIGURE 7.17

Answer the questions on the basis of the data in the following figure.

The data labels for the bars are placed above them, while the same for the line graph are placed in boxes. Legend for the bars is given in the order of left bar to right bar.

13. If countries were ranked according to the number of days required to start a business, (with the country requiring least number of days being ranked the highest), which of the top three countries would have the least cost to per capita income ratio?

(a) Chile (b) Tanzania
(c) Paraguay (d) None of the above

14. Ratio of number of days required for export to import is the least for which country?

(a) UK (b) UAE
(c) Chile (d) Georgia

15. Identify the **true** Statement
    (a) In Tanzania, the number of days required for exporting is lower than the number of days required for importing.
    (b) The sum of number of days required for exporting and the number of days required for importing is the third lowest for UK.
    (c) In Paraguay, the number of days required for starting a business is higher than the number of days required for importing.
    (d) In Georgia, the number of days required for exporting is lower than the number of days required for importing.
16. Identify the **false** statement
    (a) The number of days required for starting a business in Chile is lower than the corresponding figure in Tanzania.
    (b) The number of days required for starting a business in UK is equal to the number of days required for exporting in UAE.
    (c) The number of days required for importing in Georgia is higher than the number of days required for exporting in Niger.
    (d) The cost of starting a business as percentage of per capita income in Tanzania is lower than the corresponding figure in UAE.

Directions for Questions 17 to 21: *Read the following information, graph and table and answer the questions that follow.*

Ellen Inc. is a Mumbai-based company which sells five products branded as A, B, C, D and E In India. Anita looks after entire sales of North India working from regional office in Delhi. She was preparing for annual review meeting scheduled next day in Mumbai. She was attempting to analyse sales in North India for the seven year period from 2009 to 2015. She first calculated average sales in rupees of all the five brands and constructed a table exhibiting the difference between average sales of each pair of brands as shown in the following table:

After taking a print out to the above table, she attempted to look at the trend of sales and plotted a graph in MS Excel. Later she took a printout of the graph and left for a meeting. While on her way she figured out that due to some printer cartridge problem sales of Product A in 2013, Product C in 2010 and Product D in 2012 were not visible in the graph as reproduced below. Anita had to make some quick calculations to arrive at the information outlined in the following questions:

TABLE 7.12 Difference between Average Sales of Products for the 7-Year Period 2009-15 in ₹ Crores

	Product A	Product B	Product C	Product D	Product E
Product A	0	214.29	−128.57	142.86	42.86
Product B		0	−342.86	−71.43	−171.43
Product C			0	271.43	171.43
Product D				0	−100
Product E					0

Average Sales of Product A minus Average Sales of Product B

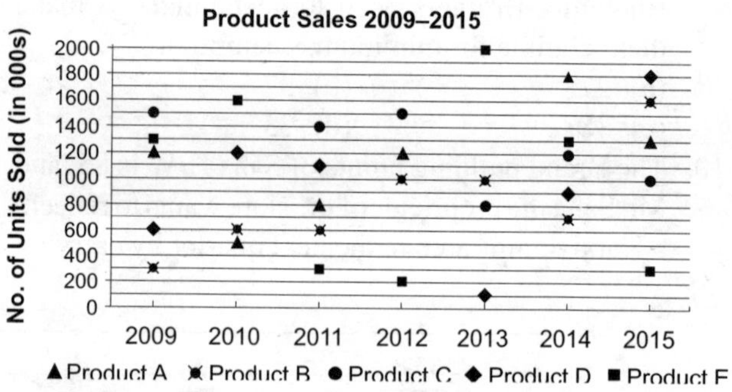

FIGURE 7.18

17. What are the sales of Product A in 2013, Product C in 2010 and Product D in 2012?
    (a) ₹550 crores, ₹800 crores and ₹500 crores
    (b) ₹500 crores, ₹700 crores and ₹600 crores
    (c) ₹500 crores, ₹800 crores and ₹600 crores
    (d) ₹400 crores, ₹800 crores and ₹600 crores
18. Annual sales average of all products is the least in which year?
    (a) 2010 (b) 2011
    (c) 2012 (d) 2013
19. Which product has the least average sales for the seven-year period 2009–15?
    (a) Product A (b) Product B
    (c) Product D (d) Product E
20. The difference between average sales of products for the period 2009–15 is the least for which pair of products?
    (a) Product A and Product B
    (b) Product B and Product C
    (c) Product C and Product D
    (d) Product D and Product E

21. If Year on Year (YoY) Growth is

$$\left\{\frac{\text{Current Year Sales} - \text{Previous Year Sales}}{\text{Previous Year Sales}}\right\}$$

then the YoY growth of combined sales of all products has suffered maximum decline in which year?

(a) 2010 (b) 2011
(c) 2013 (d) 2015

Directions for Questions 22 to 25: *Read the following information and the accompanying graphs to answer the questions that follow.*

www.jay.com spent $5,57,000 during last 12 months for online display advertisements, also called impressions, on five websites (Website A, Website B, Website C, Website D and Website E). In this arrangement, www.jay.com is the destination site, and the five websites are referred to as the ad sites. The allocation of online display advertising expenditure is shown in Graph A. The online display advertisements helped www.jay.com to get visitors on its site. Online visitors, visiting the ad sites, are served display advertisements of www.jay.com and on clicking they land on the destination site (Graph B). Once on the destination site, some of the visitors complete the purchase process (Graph C).

Quality traffic =

$$\frac{\text{No. of site visitors who start purchase on destination site}}{\text{No. of visitors who click the online display advertisement}}$$

Leakage in online buying = 1

$$- \frac{\text{Complete buying on the destination website}}{\text{Start buying on the destination website}}$$

Efficiency of online display advertising expenditure on an ad site =

$$\frac{\text{No. of visitors from the ad site who complete the purchase process}}{\text{Amount spent on the ad site}}$$

22. Which of following ad sites provide facility of least cost per advertisement?

(a) Website A (b) Website B
(c) Website D (d) Website E

23. Which ad site has provided maximum quality traffic?

(a) Website A (b) Website B
(c) Website D (d) Website E

24. Which ad site sent traffic to www.jay.com with maximum leakage?

(a) Website B (b) Website C
(c) Website D (d) Website E

25. On which ad site is the advertising budget spent most efficiently?

(a) Website A (b) Website B
(c) Website C (d) Website E

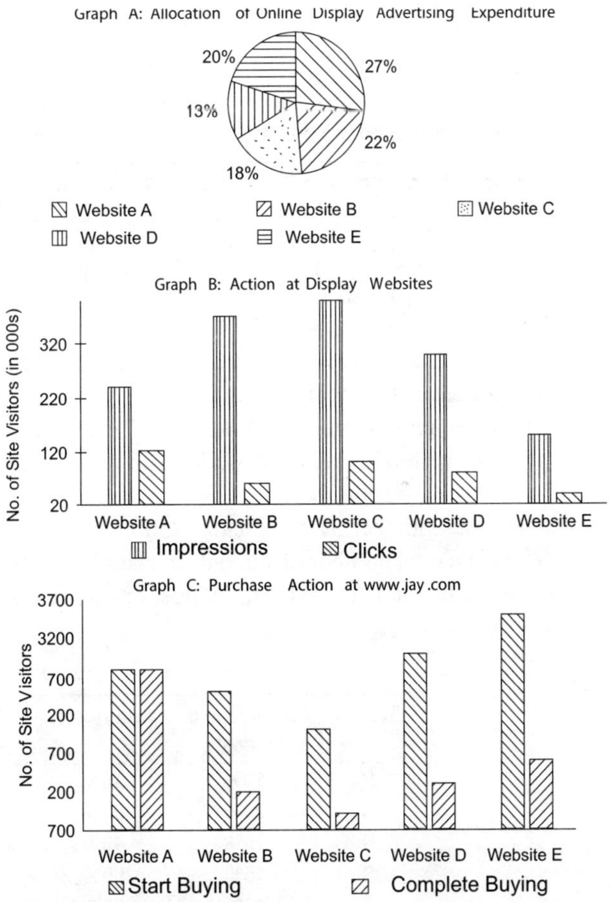

FIGURE 7.19

ANSWER KEY

Level of Difficulty 1

1. (c)	2. (a)	3. (a)	4. (c)	5. (c)	6. (c)	7. (a)
8. (b)	9. (a)	10. (b)	11. (c)	12. (a)	13. (a)	14. (c)
15. (a)	16. (b)	17. (d)	18. (d)	19. (d)	20. (c)	21. (b)
22. (b)	23. (b)	24. (a)	25. (d)	26. (a)	27. (b)	28. (c)
29. (b)	30. 11000	31. 4250	32. 60%	33. 500%	34. 10%	

Level of Difficulty 2

1. 52000	2. 10: 13	3. 190	4. (c)	5. 14	6. 17.5	7. 17.81
8. (b)	9. (b)	10. 7500	11. (d)	12. (b)	13. (b)	14. (b)
15. (d)	16. (b)	17. (d)	18. (c)	19. (b)	20. 1115	21. 180
22. 350	23. 737.5	24. 79%	25. (b)	26. (b)	27. (b)	28. (b)

Level of Difficulty 3

1. (c)	2. (b)	3. (d)	4. (c)	5. 21.62	6. 42.5	7. (b)
8. (a)	9. (d)	10. (a)	11. (a)	12. (d)	13. (b)	14. (a)
15. (d)	16. (c)	17. (c)	18. (b)	19. (b)	20. (d)	21. (b)
22. (c)	23. (d)	24. (c)	25. (a)			

SOLUTIONS

Level of Difficulty 1

Solutions for Questions 1 to 5:

1. For solving questions 1 to 5, we can first tabulate the percentages in the pie and bar charts as follows:

Section	Percentage of Students	With Hostel	Without Hostel
P	10%	20%	80%
Q	20%	50%	50%
R	15%	40%	60%
S	15%	60%	40%
T	40%	60%	40%

40% of total students in T = 2000.
Therefore total number of students in T = 5000.
40% of the total number of students in all classes is in class T = 5000.
Then total number of students = 12500.
Then, the total number of students in class P = 10% of the total students = 1250. Hence, option (c) is correct.

2. Total students of class S = 15% of 50000 = 7500. Taking cues from the table above, if total number of students in the school is 50000, the number of students in sections Q and S becomes 10000 and 7500 respectively. The number of students of class Q staying in the hostel becomes 5000 (50% of its total students). Therefore percentage of students in S is more than students in hostel in section Q = (7500 – 5000)/5000 = 2500/5000 = 50%. Hence, option (a) is correct.

3. Solution
The number of students in P = 750 of which 80% do not stay in hostels = 600; The number of students in R = 15% of 7500 = 1125, of which 60% do not stay in hostels = 675; The number of students in T = 40% of 7500 = 3000, of which 40% do not stay in hostels = 1200.
Average number of students from P, R, T who do not stay in hostels = (600 + 675 + 1200)/3 = 825. Hence, option (a) is correct.

4.

Section	Percentage of Students	With Hostel	Without Hostel	Number of Students (2030)	Number of Students (2031)
P	10%	20%	80%	5000	
Q	20%	50%	50%	10000	11800
R	15%	40%	60%	7500	
S	15%	60%	40%	7500	
T	40%	60%	40%	20000	17000
				50000	

Of 50000 students, Q will have 10000 students and T will have, 20000 students in 2030. In 2031, Q will have 11800 students (after an 18% increase), while T will have 17000 students (after a 15% drop). Hence, the required difference = 17000-11800 = 5200. Hence, option (c) is correct.

5. Let there be 100 students in the University. Students in hostels in Q and S = 50% of 20% of 100 + 60% of 15% of 100 = 10 + 9 = 19.
Students not in hostel in R and T = 60% of 15% of 100 + 40% of 40% of 100 = 9 + 16.
Hence, the required ratio is 19:25. Option (c) is correct.

Solutions for Questions 6 to 10:

For answering questions 6 to 10, it would be a good idea to make the following table depicting the number of customers interested in each car and the number of female and male customers amongst the total customers interested in buying each car.

Cars	Total Customers	Female	Male
Santro	12500	1875	10625
Wagon R	7500	1125	6375
Alto	6000	600	5400
Swift	7500	1875	5625
Ritz	5500	1100	4400
I10	11000	1650	9350

6. This question can be answered without any calculations – as the required ratio would be minimum for the car that has the highest percentage value in the bar graph. Swift with 25% of its total customers being female, would give us a constant ratio of 100/25 =4, for the ratio of total customers interested in buying the car to the female customers. Hence, option (c) is correct.
7. Santro – Ritz =1875 – 1100 = 775. Hence, option (a) is correct.
8. Ratio = 11775 : 3525
   = 471 : 141. Hence, option (b) is correct.
9. The required ratio = 18500 : 18000 =37:36. Hence, Option (a) is correct.
10. Females buying Santro and Wagon R = 3000.
    Males buying the same = 17000.
    3/17% = approx 17.68%; option (b) is the closest.

Questions 11 to 15:

11. The total exports for the period is 1970, while the total imports for the given period is 2170. Thus, exports is lower than imports by $(200 \times 100) \div 2170$ % = 9.2% approx. Option (c) is the correct answer.
12. The absolute difference can be seen to be the least visually for the year 2007 (200–200). 2005 and 2009 rank joint second (in ascending order) as the difference is exactly 25 for each of these years. The fourth rank would go to the year 2010, and hence Option (a) is the correct answer.
13. There are exactly 5 years in which there has been a growth of exports. In 2007, the percentage growth is $(25 \times 100 \div 175)\% = 14.28\%$ which happens to be the least percentage growth amongst the five years where there is growth recorded. The percentage growth in the other years can be seen to be lower than this. Hence, Option (a) is the correct answer.
14. There are only two years when there is an increase in imports *viz.* 2006 and 2010. For the year 2010, the percentage growth in imports is $(25 \times 100 \div 175)\%$ = 14.28%. This is the second highest recorded percentage growth in imports (as the highest can be seen for the year 2006). 225 to 270 represents a 20% increase in the imports for that year.
15. The maximum annual percentage increase in export is 37.5% (for 2008) and the minimum annual percentage decrease in import is 9.09% (for 2003). The approximate percentage point difference between these two values is 28. Hence, Option (a) is correct.

Solutions for Questions 16 to 20:

16. To find the proportion of 'mergers' to 'acquisitions' for the entire period, we need to add up the total M & A table and the total Mergers table. The remaining would correspond to the number of acquisitions.

    The number of mergers and acquisitions row-wise are:

    465; 371; 584; 350; 48; 643; 52; 1041; 1709; 192; 191 = 5646.

    The number of mergers row-wise is:

    97; 77; 116; 74; 6; 96; 2; 452; 512; 34; 33 = 1499.

    The number of acquisitions would be: 5646 – 1499 = 4147.

    So the required percentage $= \dfrac{\text{Total Merger} \times 100}{\text{Total Acquisitions}}$

    $\dfrac{1499}{4147} \times 100 = 36\%$. Hence, option (b) is correct.
17. From the sector-wise sums we have calculated for the previous question, we can see that the values of 97/465; 77/371; 74/350; 452/1041 and 512/1709 are all above 20%. There are a total of 5 such sectors. Hence, option (d) is correct.
18. It can be visually verified from the second table that the sum of the first three columns is greater than the sum of the last 3 columns in the table in 5 cases. Hence, option (d) is correct.
19. Since the turbulence is defined as sum of the differences between the number of mergers and number of acquisitions from 2001–02 to 2006–07, we need to realise that difference is always a positive value. So if M > A, the difference would be M – A, while if A > M, then the turbulence would be given by A – M.

    Mathematically this can be written by taking the absolute values of the subtraction between mergers and acquisitions for any particular year: Turbulence = |Number of mergers in 2001–02 – Number of acquisitions in 2001–02| + |Number of mergers in 2002–03 – Number of acquisitions in 2002–03| + … + |Number of mergers in 2006–07 – Number of acquisitions in 2006–07.

    Turbulence for financial services = (103 – 91) + (107 – 94) + (87 – 73) + (75 – 41) + (118 – 75) + (126 – 51) = 12 + 13 + 14 + 34 + 43 + 75 = 191.

Turbulence for other services = (207 – 90) + (198 – 92) + (182 – 105) + (200 – 81) + (210 – 61) + (210 – 83) = 117 + 106 + 77 + 119 + 149 + 127 = 685.

It can be seen that for the other two options, the value of turbulence is below 685. Option (d) is the correct answer.

20. By observing the two tables, it can be seen that in 2005–06 the maximum number of sectors exhibited higher number of acquisitions compared to the previous year.
Hence, option (c) is the correct answer.

Questions 21 to 25:

21. The statement says that the market opens at 9:15 am and each candle represents a 5 min interval. So from the graph, It is clear that the 12:46pm candle will be two candles before the one which touches an all time high of 42000. Therefore the answer is 42000.
22. The stock closed at around 40500 on the first day and opened at around 39950. This indicates a fall of around 550 points. The percentage change would be calculated as (550/40500) × 100 ≈1.5%
23. According to definition, the price at which the movement reverses its direction is called resistance. The maximum price at which the resistance is shown is approximately 42000.
24. According to the graph, The price of 42000 was achieved in the 12:55-1300 Hrs interval.
25. Total Fluctuation is defined as the difference between highest and lowest price achieved in the given interval. It is given that the day ends at 3:30 pm but the graph given above represents price till around 2:00pm. So we do not know what the price was in the last 25 mins of the trading session.

Questions 26 to 29:

The answers can be read off this table

	Maths	Physics	Chemistry	Bio	History	Average Marks Per student
Anirudh	100	40	80	65	20	61
Baldev	45	65	75	70	85	68
Charu	55	100	25	45	60	57
Dhruv	70	80	40	30	20	48
Ekta	25	35	45	55	65	45
Average Marks per subject	59	64.000	53.000	53.000	50.000	55.800

26. As we can see from the table, Anirudh has topped in Maths and Chemistry, Charu has topped in Physics, And Baldev has topped in Bio and History, Hence the answer is Option (a).
27. As can be seen from the table, Baldev has the highest average marks per student. Hence, option (b) is correct.
28. As can be seen from the table, Chemistry and Bio have the same Average marks per student hence, Option (c) is the answer
29. If Physics was removed as it is the subject with the highest average marks per student, The average would then be (59+53+53+50)/4 = 53.75. Hence, Option (b) is the correct answer.

Questions 30 to 34:

From the triangular graph given in the question, we can conclude the following table:

	Cars	Buses	Trains	Total
Kanpur	1875	625	2500	5000
Pune	750	750	4500	6000
Raisen	875	2625	3500	7000
Trivandrum	3000	4000	1000	8000
Surat	4500	2250	2250	9000
Total	11000	10250	13750	35000

30. 11000. From the above table we can see that the total number of people who use cars as their preferred mode of transport is 11000.
31. 4250. Car users from Pune=750
Train users from Raisen=3500
Total=4250
32. Train users from Trivandrum=1000, Bus users from Kanpur=625.
Percentage difference= 60%

33. 500%. If we look at the table carefully, we see that the number of people who preferred trains from Pune are 6 times the number of those who prefer buses as also 6 times those who prefer cars. So the maximum percentage difference is 500%.
34. 10%. Total number of people who preferred buses account for 29.28% of the total population. Meanwhile, the total number of users who preferred trains is 39.28 of the the total population. Therefore the percentage point difference between the two is 10%. Alternately, the absolute difference between the two is 13750-10250=3500. This represents 10% of the total population.

Level of Difficulty 2

Solutions for Questions 1 to 4:
Based on the information in the table, we can create a cost per unit and profit per unit table as shown below:

Product	Cost of Milk per unit (in ₹)	Average Wages Paid to Milkmen per unit (in ₹)	Average Transport Cost per unit (in ₹)	Other Costs (in ₹ per unit)	Total Cost per unit (in ₹)	Profit % Earned on each unit	Profit (in ₹)	Selling Price (in ₹) per unit
Amul	500	50	50	50	650	20	130	780
Mother India	1000	100	10	50	1160	25	290	1450
Taaza	2400	160	80	80	2720	20	544	3264
Verka	1500	50	20	120	1690	10	169	1859

1. In 2019 total units of Amul milk powder sold by the company in 2019 = 125 + 150 + 50 + 75 = 400 units.
   Total profit (in ₹) = 130 × 400 = 52000.
2. Required ratio = (125 + 150 + 50 + 75) × 130 : (125 + 75 + 50 + 150) × 169 = 10: 13.
3. Average sales per city of Mother India milk powder = [(200 + 100 + 125 + 100) × 1450]/4 = 190312.50 or 190 thousands.
4. Revenue earned by Amul in Chennai = 150 × 780 = 117000.
   Revenue earned by Mother India in Chennai = 100 × 1450 = 145000.
   Revenue earned by Taaza in Chennai = 75 × 3264 = 244800.
   Revenue earned by Verka in Chennai = 75 × 1859 = 139425.
   Hence, the correct answer is Taaza.
   Option (c) is correct.

Solutions for Questions 5 to 7:

5. From the first graph it is clear that speed of Aman at $t = 150$ seconds = 14 m/s.
6. Total distance covered by Aman in first 150 seconds $= \frac{1}{2} \times 28 \times 50 + 50 \times 28 + (\frac{1}{2} \times (28 + 14) \times 50)$
   = 700 + 1400 + 1050 = 3150 meters.
   Total distance covered in 300 seconds = 3150 + 600 + 800 + 700 = 5250 m.
   Required speed (in m/s) = 5250/300 = 17.5 m/s.
7. Total distance covered between $t = 80$ seconds and $t = 150$ seconds $= (20 \times 28 + (\frac{1}{2} \times (28 + 14) \times 50)$
   = 560 + 1050 = 1610 meters.
   As the distance time curve for the interval 150–200 and 200–240 seconds is linear then we can use the formula, $s = vt$.
   Total distance covered by Aman in 150–200 seconds time period = 600 meters.
   Total distance covered by Aman in 200–240 seconds.
   Time period $= \frac{800}{50} \times 40 = 640$ meters.
   Total distance by Aman for period $t = 80$–240 seconds = 1610 + 600 + 640 = 2850 meters.
   Required speed in (m/s) = 2850/160 = 17.81 m/s.

Solutions for Questions 8 and 9:

8. If the total number of books utilised in the three cities is $100x$, then $20x$ books were unutilised.
   Total number of books = $100x + 20x = 120x$ = 11400 + 13200 + 5400 = 30000
   On solving we get, $x = 250$.
   Total utilised books = $100x$ = 25000.
   Total utilised books in Kanpur = 35% of 25000 = 8750.
   Total unutilised books in Kanpur = 11400 – 8750 = 2650.
   Total unutilised books = $20x$ = 5000.
   Required percentage $= \frac{2650}{5000} \times 100 = 53\%$.
   Hence, option (b) is correct.

9. Let the number of utilised books is $100x$.
Total utilised books in Kanpur = $35x$.
Total unutilised books in Kanpur = $11400 – 35x$.
Total utilised books in Bhavnagar = $20x$.
Total unutilised books in Bhavnagar = $5400 – 20x$.
According to the question: $11400 – 35x = 3 \times (5400 – 20x)$.
On solving the above equation we get, $x = 192$.
Total unutilised books in Ahmedabad = $13200 – 45x = 13200 – (45 \times 192) = 4560$.
Total unutilised books in Bhavnagar = $5400 – 20x = 1560$.
Required difference = 4560 – 1560 = 3000.
Hence, option (b) is correct.

Solutions for Questions 10 to 11:

10. Let the total investment made by all the companies in 2019 be $100x$.
Investment made by $D = 5x$.
According to the question: 56% of $5x = 1400$.
$$\frac{56}{100} \times 5x = 1400$$
$$x = 500$$
Investment made by E (in million \$) in 2019 = $15x = 7500$.

11. Let the total investment made by all the companies in 2020 is ₹$100y$.
Investment made by company B = $12y$.
$$15\% \text{ of } 12y = 900$$
$$y = 500.$$
Since, $x = y = 500$, the total investment made by all the five companies is same in 2019 and 2020 (at 50000 million \$).
Ratio of the investment made by 'Rest of the Companies' = $55x : 45y = 55 : 45$.
Hence, option (d) is correct.

Solutions for Questions 12 to 15: For all these questions assume that the total work is 360 units.

12. Let work 360 units. (Work is taken as such that total work is divisible by the time taken to do the work, for each of the workers involved.)
David's 1 day's work = 360/9 = 40 units
Billey's 1 day's work = 40 units
Nusrat's 1 day's work = 15 units
Angelina's 1 day's work = 15 units
Divyansita's 1 day's work = 40 units
Billey and David worked for 2 days. In two days they would do: $(40 + 40) \times 2 = 160$ units of work.
Therefore remaining work = 200.
Now for 2 days, Nusrat, Diyansita and Angelina would do $(15 + 15 + 40) \times 2 = 140$ units of work.
So, the remaining work = 360 – 160 – 140 = 60.
Hence, the remaining work is 1/6th of the total work. Hence, option (b) is correct.

13. Work rate of all the men: Stanley = 30 units/day; Jonathan = 24 units/day; Richard = 36 units/day; David = 40 units/day; Ramsey = 30 units/day and Billey = 40 units/day.
All the male programmers together do = 30 + 24 + 36 + 40 + 30 + 40 = 200 units/day.
Time taken to complete the project by all the male programmers = 360/200 days = 1.8 days.
For the women mentioned: Ritu = 36 units/day; Nusrat = 15 units/day; Oindrilla = 24 units/day; Angelina = 15 units/day.
The total work per day these female programmers can do = 36 + 15 + 24 + 15 = 90 units.
Time taken to complete the project by Ritu, Oindrilla, Nusrat and Angelina = 360/90 days = 4 days.
The answer = 4 – 1.8 days = 2.2 days. Hence, option (b) is correct.

14. Ramsey's one day's work = 360/12 = 30 units.
Richard's one day's work = 360/10 = 36 units.
Now, Ramsey works at 120% of 30 = 36 units per day.
Richard at 5/6 of 36 = 30 units per day.
Ramsey + Richard's 2 days work = 66.
In 10 days = $66 \times 5 = 330$ units.
On the 11th day, Ramsey will be working and the Remaining work = 360-330 = 30 units.
Ramsey does 36 units a day. So to do 30 units he will take 5/6 days.
Therefore total time taken = (10 + 5/6) days = 65/6 days. Hence, option (b) is correct.

15. Stanley's 1 day's work = 30 units.
So to do 25% work = 90 units he will = take 3 days.
To do 10% work, i.e., 36 units Richard will take 1 day.
The remaining work = 360 – 126 = 234.
Since, Anjali can do 18 units of work per day, in order to do 234 units of work, Anjali will take 234/18 = 13 days (Anjali's 1 day's work = 360/20 = 18 units).
Total days = 3 + 1 + 13 = 17 days. Hence, option (d) is correct.

Solutions for Questions 16 to 19:

16. From the line graph, Number of mobile handsets sold by Samsung in 2014 = 30000
Given, total earnings by selling handsets was ₹45 crores. Average selling price of 1 handset = 450000000/30000 = ₹15000.
From the table, % profit made by Samsung in 2014 = 30% Let the average cost price of 1 handset be

'a' $a + 30\%$ of $a = 15000$.

$1.3a = 15000$.

Hence, a = ₹11538.46. The closest answer is option (b).

17. From the line graph.

Total number of handsets sold by Nokia in 2012 = 50000. Total number of handsets sold by LG in 2012 = 25000.

Given, number of handsets sold of variant 1 and variant 2 were in the ratio 3 : 2 for Nokia and 3 : 5 for LG, we can deduce that Nokia sold 30000 and 20000 handsets of variant 1 and 2 respectively. Also, LG sold 9375 and 15625 handsets of variant 1 and 2 respectively.

Now, cost price of variant 1 was ₹8000 and cost of variant 2 was ₹12000 for Nokia. For LG, cost price of variant 2 was ₹27000.

Total cost incurred by Nokia = $30000 \times 8000 + 20000 \times 12000$ = 48 crores.

Let the cost price of variant I handset of LG be 'a'.

Total cost incurred by LG = $9375a + 15625 \times 27000 = 9375 \times a + 421875000$.

From the table,

Profit% made by Nokia in 2012 = 36%. Profit% made by LG in 2012 = 30%.

Given, total profit made by the two companies in 2012 was same.

(36% of 480000000) = 30% of ($9375 \times a + 421875000$).

$5760000000 = 9375 \times a + 421875000$.

$9375 \times a = 154125000$.

A = ₹16440. Option (d) is correct.

18. From the graph,

Total number of handsets sold by Samsung in 2016 = 50000. Total number of handsets sold by apple in 2016 = 40000.

From the table, profit percentage of Samsung in 2016 = 25% and profit percentage of apple in 2016 = 48%.

Let the average cost price of handset sold by Samsung be a. Then the average cost price of handsets sold by apple would be $0.92a$ (it's cost price being 8% less than Samsung's).

Total profit earned in 2016 by apple = 48% of 40000 $\times 0.92a = 17664a$.

Total profit earned in 2016 by Samsung = 25% of $50000 \times a = 12500a$.

Thus, profit earned by apple is higher percentage by which the profit made by apple is more than the profit made by Samsung in the year 2016:

$$\frac{17664 - 12500}{12500} \times 100 = 41.312\%$$

Hence, option (c) is correct.

19. We can see from the graph that the total number of handsets sold by Nokia in 2015 = 35000. Hence, the four models launched sold: 3500, 10500, 7000 and 14000 units respectively. (We get this by dividing 35000 in the ratio of 1 : 3 : 2 : 4.)

Let the cost price of the 4 models be $6a$, $3a$, $4a$ and $2a$ respectively.

Total cost price of all models = $3500 \times 6a + 10500 \times 3a + 7000 \times 4a + 14000 \times 2a = 108500a$

From the table, profit percentage of Nokia in 2015 = 10%

Given, profit made in 2015 by Nokia was ₹6.51 crore, we get that 10% of $108500a$ = 6.51 crore.

$\rightarrow a$ = ₹6000

Cost price of model 2 = $3a$ = ₹18000. None of the options match, answer is (b).

Questions 20 to 24:

From the graph, we can frame this table. However, the values mentioned are the percentage of marks scored in the respective subjects. We do not know the maximum marks of each subject. As given in the set, the maximum marks are 100,100, 120, 150, 200 and 250 in no particular order. In order to identify which subject has how many maximum marks, you would need to use the clue that Shaurya's score in Physcis, Chemistry, Computer Science and Physical Education are equal and also equal to the marks of Kavita in Maths.

	Maths	English	Physics	Chemistry	Computer Science	Physical Education
Anshuman	65	90	90	90	75	60
Pallav	60	92	80	85	83.333	80
Shaurya	75	80	100	66.667	83.333	100
Ritika	62.5	96	70	75	90	90
Kavita	50	88	60	83.333	80	70

First of all, when we look at Shaurya's percentages and the possibility of the scores he could have in various subjects, we see that the only score where he could score equally in 4 different subjects would be if his two 100%s are amounting to 100 marks each, his 83.33% score is out of 120 and his 66.667% score is out of 150. Thus, Physics and Physical education must be out of 100 marks each, while Chemistry and Computer Science would be out of 150 and 120 marks respectively. Kavita's Maths score can then be equal to 100 only if Maths is out of 200 and hence, English would be out of 250.

The final scores of the five students subject wise can then be tabulated as:

	Maths (200)	English (250)	Physics (100)	CS (120)	Chemistry (150)	P. Ed(100)
Anshuman	130	225	90	90	135	60
Pallav	120	230	80	100	127.5	80
Shaurya	150	200	100	100	100	100
Ritika	125	240	70	108	112.5	90
Kavita	100	220	60	96	125	70

Using the above table, we get the answers to our questions.

20. 1115
21. 180.
    Highest marks is 240 which is scored by Ritika in English while the lowest marks is 60 which is obtained by Kavita and Anshuman in Physics and P. Ed respectively. Therefore the difference is 240-60=180.
22. 350.
    Shaurya scored 150 in Maths and 200 in English. So, the total marks is 350.
23. 737.5.
    Pallav has scored 120, 230, 80, 100, 127.5 and 80 in the subjects given. The total marks for would be 737.5
24. 79%.
    The average percentage of the class would be (Sum of all the scores/total of maximum marks) × 100. Total score = 625 + 1115 + 400 + 494 + 600 + 400 = 3634. Total possible marks = 920 × 5 = 4600. This works out to 79%.

Questions 25 to 28:

25. (b) From the charts given above, we can form the table given below

	Chennai		Kanpur	
	Planned	Actual	Planned	Actual
Activity 1	75	100	100	50
Activity 2	214	200	200	350
Activity 3	122	150	150	50
Activity 4	78	300	100	150
Activity 5	221	200	250	300
Activity 6	322	400	300	250

    Planned cost for Chennai= 1032 × 250= Rs 258000
    Actual Cost for Chennai = 1350 × 270= Rs 364500
    Percentage cost difference= 41%(approximately.
    Option (b) is correct.
26. (b)
    From the above table, we have to analyse different activities 1 by 1 to arrive at a conclusion.
    In Activity 1, Shortfall of Planned and Actual in Kanpur plant is 50. 50% of this is 25. Excess in chennai plant is 25. So we will consider this activity.
    In Activity 2, There is no shortfall. Therefore we will not take this activity into consideration.
    In Activity 3, The shortfall in the Kanpur Plant is 100. 50% of this is 50, The excess in the chennai Plant is only 28. Therefore this activity is not to be considered.
    In Activity 4, There is no shortfall.
    In Activity 5, There is no shortfall.
    In Activity 6, The shortfall is 50, 50% of which is 25. The excess in Chennai is 78. Therefore this activity will be counted.
    So, in total we have 2 activities which satisfy the conditions mentioned in the questions. Therefore our answer is option (b).
27. (b) The cost difference has two components – The excess hours over the planned hours and the excess cost per hour (which goes up from 300 to 315, a growth of 5%). The total cost is the product of the number of hours and the cost per hour. Hence, the effect of the excess cost per hour will have the same percentage effect in all the activities. Thus to see the maximum cost differ-

ence, we just need to see the activity that has the maximum percentage difference between Planned and actual hours. It can be seen that Activity 2 shows the maximum percentage change from planned to actual hours for Kanpur and hence, the correct answer is option (b).

28. (b)
If we look at the above table, We see that in activities 2&6 Chennai has more planned operational hours when compared with that of Kanpur Plant.
Therefore the answer is Option (b).

Level of Difficulty 3:

Solutions for 1 to 3:

We are given that A < D < B < C < E.

The average income per film for the year 2015 will be given by the formula:

$$\frac{\text{Fixed revenue} + \text{Share in profit/Loss}}{N_{2015}}$$

Where N_{2015} = number of films released in 2015. From the line graph, we can only make out the ratio of Factor X and Factor Y. Hence, we can only deduce that if X/Y > 1, there will be an increment in the numerator. For instance, we can see that YRF will get a positive share in profit in 2015, 2017 and 2020; while for 2016 and 2019 the share in profit would reduce the revenue as X < Y in those years. In 2018, X = Y since X/Y = 1 and the share in profit/loss would be 0. We can deduce that

$$A_1 = \frac{A + ??}{N_{2015}}$$

Based on this understanding and the understanding that there will be similar equations for A_2, A_3, A_4 and A_5, we can move to the questions.

1. For this question we are given that: $A_2 < A_1 < A_3 < A_4 < A_5$ and we already know that: A < D < B < C < E. We are asked to work out how many years the number of films (*N*) was definitely less than N_{2017}. The following thought process gives us the required answer:

(a) Comparing 2017 and 2016: $A_2 = \dfrac{C + ??}{N_{2017}}$ **and** $A_2 = \dfrac{B - ??}{N_{2016}}$. Since we know that B < C, it follows that the numerator of the first of these ratios is greater than the numerator of the second ratio. Also, since the value of both these ratios are same, which means that $N_{2017} > N_{2016}$.

(b) Comparing 2017 and 2015: $A_2 = \dfrac{C + ??}{N_{2017}}$ **and** $A_1 = \dfrac{A + ??}{N_{2015}}$. C > A and $A_1 > A_2$ and also the values of the additions in both the numerators being unknown, tells us that we cannot determine a relationship between the N_{2017} and N_{2015}. This is because, we cannot conclude which numerator is larger (as it will depend on the additions in the numerators).

Note: The best way to think is that if C + ?? = 100 + 20 and N_{2017} = 20, we get A_2 as 6. If A + ?? = 40 + 20, then since $A_1 > A_2$, the value of A_1 should be greater than 6 – which shows us that N_{2015} is < 10. In such a case we get $N_{2017} > N_{2015}$. However, if we change the value of *A* + ?? to 40 + 960 = 1000, then N_{2015} has to be less than 166.66. Since N_{2017} is 20, in this case, N_{2015} can be greater than, equal to and even less than N_{2017}. Hence, we cannot deduce a relationship between N_{2015} and N_{2017}.

(c) Comparing 2017 and 2018: $A_2 = \dfrac{C + ??}{N_{2017}}$ **and** $A_3 = \dfrac{C}{N_{2018}}$. It follows that the numerator of the first of these ratios is greater than the numerator of the second ratio. Also, since the value of $A_2 < A_3$, it means that $N_{2017} > N_{2018}$.

(d) Comparing 2017 and 2019: $A_2 = \dfrac{C + ??}{N_{2017}}$ **and** $A_4 = \dfrac{D - ??}{N_{2019}}$. Since we know that D < C, it follows that the numerator of the first of these ratios is greater than the numerator of the second ratio. Also, since the value of $A_2 < A_4$, it means that $N_{2017} > N_{2019}$.

(e) Comparing 2017 and 2020: $A_2 = \dfrac{C + ??}{N_{2017}}$ and $A_5 = \dfrac{E + ??}{N_{2020}}$. In this case again we do not know which numerator is larger, even though we know that E > C (since the value of the numerator would depend on the value of the additions created by X – Y). Also, $A_5 > A_2$, does not allow us to determine a unique relationship between N_{2017} and N_{2020}.

Hence, we can definitely say that there are 3 years when the number of films is less than the number of films in 2017. (Viz: 2016, 2018 and 2019). Hence, option (c) is correct.

2. The question can be answered on the same logic of the previous question. The correct answer is option (b).

Note: It makes no difference that the inequalities between A_3, A_4 and A_5 are changed here, since when we compare them to the 2017 figure of A_2, the inequalities pairwise between A_2 and A_3; A_2 and A_4 and A_2 and A_5 do not change. Hence, the analysis of the previous question would hold here too.

3. We know the following equations:

$$A_1 = \frac{A + ??}{N_{2015}};\ A_2 = \frac{B - ??}{N_{2016}};\ A_2 = \frac{C + ??}{N_{2017}};$$

$$A_3 = \frac{C}{N_{2018}};\ A_4 = \frac{D - ??}{N_{2019}} \text{ and } A_5 = \frac{E + ??}{N_{2020}}$$

It is known that A < D < B < C < E.

Also, since the number of films has consistently increased for all the years, it means that:

$$N_{2015} < N_{2016} < N_{2017} < N_{2018} < N_{2019} < N_{2020}.$$

We will now need to compare and check scenarios for each option.

We can see that 2015 and 2016, A_1 and A_2 can be same, as $N_{2015} < N_{2016}$, but the relationship between the numerators is unknown. Only in the case of 2018 and 2019, we can deduce that the numerator for 2019 is lower (as D < C, hence D-?? < C). Also, the denominator for 2019 is larger than the one for 2018. Hence, the values of the average income per film cannot be equal for 2018 and 2019. Option (d) is correct.

Solutions for Questions 4 to 7:

4. The first thing to do is collect the calls and durations for each number independently.

Number	Call 1	Call 2	Call 3	Call 4	Call 5	Call 6
9xxxx1	120	120	40	10	20	110
9xxxx2	80	160	30	100		
9xxxx3	20	50	180	140		

It is given to us that each phone number had at least 1 call of each category. This means that the calls for the numbers 9xxx2 and 9xxx3 → must be distributed in one call for each category. From the bar chart we know that the total timings for the four call categories are:

Roaming Outgoing (RO) = 100; Roaming Incoming (RI) = 170; Normal Outgoing (NO) = 490 and Normal Incoming (NI) = 420.

Based on matching this data, we can make out that for 9xxx3, the 180 and 140 second calls are normal calls, while the 20 and 50 second calls are roaming calls.

We now need to fit in the total cost of 131.5 to this situation.

The only combination that fits is:

180 × 0.25 + 140 × 0.1 + 50 × 1.25 + 20 × 0.5 = 45 + 14 + 62.5 + 10 = 131.5.

For 9xxx2, the total cost is 123.5, which can be rationalised as: 80 × 0.25 + 160 × 0.1 + 30 × 1.25 + 100 × 0.5 = 123.5.

From this point, we can see that the time left for Normal Incoming is 120 seconds, Normal Outgoing is 490 – 180 – 80 = 230; Roaming Incoming = 170 – 20 – 100; Roaming Outgoing = 100 – 50 – 30 = 20.

The calls of 9xxx1, can be allocated as shown in the table.

	Normal Incoming (420) Cost 0.1	Normal Outgoing (490) Cost 0.25	Roaming Incoming (170) Cost 0.5	Roaming Outgoing (100) Cost 1.25
9xxx3	140	180	20	50
9xxx2	160	80	100	30
9xxx1	120	120,110	40,10	20

The correct option is (c).

5. From the above explanation we can say that the duration of incoming calls from 9xxxxxxxx2 = 80 seconds.

Required percentage = (80/370) = 21.62%.

The correct answer is 21.62

6. From the above explanation we can say that the total duration of roaming incoming calls = 20 + 100 + 40 + 10 = 170.

Average duration of each call = 170/4 = 42.5 seconds.

The correct answer is 42.5.

7. From the above explanation we can say that the total cost incurred due to outgoing calls made to 9xxxxxxxx1 (20 × 1.25) + (120 × 0.25) + (110 × 0.25) = 82.5.

Average cost of each call = 82.5/3 = ₹27.5.

The correct option is (b).

Questions 8 to 12:

8. The main points earned by Maheshwari and Company will be for the sales above the target. Since it sells 6241 units above the target, it would earn 6241 × 0.25 = 1560.25 points for

the excess sales. Apart from the points the other things would contribute small number of points for redemption and do not have the potential to cross 1800 points when a third Tupperware set can be redeemed. Thus, Maheshwari & Co. can redeem 2 Tupperware sets. Hence, option (a) is the correct answer.

9. The points got by Bhowmick Brothers would be $12 - 20 + 2.5 + 2.5 + 10 = 7$. It would need at least 33 more points to reach the minimum number of points required for redemption. Thus, option (d) is correct.
10. The total points for Saha H/W carried forward would be 85 + 15 (for achieving 100% of target) + 512×0.25. Besides it expects to get another 85 +15 points in the next quarter. Thus, the total points it would have for redemption would be 328. It would need to get another 3672 points by achieving sales over the target values. For 3672 points through excess sales, Saha H/W would need to sell $3672 \times 4 = 14688$ units above the target.
Option (a) is correct.
11. Malling Enterprise would have redeemed $100 \times 3 + 40 = 340$ points. Out of these, they would generate 15 points for achieving the target and $1000 \times 0.25 = 250$ points for excess sales.
Thus, the remaining 75 points would be got through brand building points.
Option (a) is correct.
12. Srikrishna Trader would have $2000 \times 0.25 = 500$ points for sales over the target, plus 15 points for 100% target achievement. After adding the brand building points (80) as given in the question, the trader would have a total of 595 points, which would not be sufficient for redemption to get a Tupperware set. Thus, none of the first three options can be the goods that can be redeemed. Option (d) is the only possible set of items that Srikrishna Traders can redeem.
Thus, option (d) is correct.

Questions 13 to 16:

13. The three countries with the least number of days required to start a business are Paraguay, Tanzania and United Kingdom. Of these, the least cost to per capita income ratio would be for Tanzania. Hence, Option (b) is correct.
14. We need to find the least ratio amongst 13/17 (UK); 11/14 (UAE); 23/25 (Chile) and 22/23 (Georgia). Amongst these 13/17 is the least ratio. Hence, option (a) is the correct answer.
15. The first three options can be rejected as:
Option (a) is incorrect because in Tanzania the number of days required for exporting is higher than the number of days required for importing.
Option (b) is incorrect because the sum is the 4th lowest for United Kingdom (after Tanzania, Paraguay and UAE).
Option (c) is incorrect as in Paraguay the number of days required for starting a business is lower than the number of days required for importing.
Only Option (d) is correct and hence it is the correct answer.
16. The statement in Option (c) can be identified as false. Hence, Option (c) is correct.

Questions 17 to 21:

17. Average sales of product
$$B = \frac{300+600+600+1000+1000+700+1600}{7}$$
$= 828.57$
Average sales of A = 214.29 + 828.57 = 1042.86
Total sales of A = $1042.86 \times 7 = 7300$
Let the sales of A in 2013 be x.
$1200 + 500 + 800 + 1200 + 1800 + 1300 + x = 7300$
X = ₹500 crores.
Using similar method we can calculate that the sales of C in 2010 was ₹800 crores and sales of D in 2012 was ₹600 crores. Hence, option (c) is correct.
18. Average sales of all product in 2010 = ₹940 crores.
Average sales of all product in 2011 = ₹840 crores.
Average sales of all product in 2012 = ₹900 crores.
Average sales of all product in 2013 = ₹880 crores.
Hence, the required answer is 2011. Hence, option (b) is correct.
19. Option (b).
20. By checking the options we can see that the difference between average sales of D and E is minimum. Option (d) is correct.
21. YoY growth in 2010 = $\frac{4700 - 4900}{4700} \times 100$
$= -4.08\%$
YoY growth in 2011
$$= \frac{4200 - 4700}{4700} \times 100 = -10.63\%$$
YoY growth in 2013 = $\frac{4400 - 4500}{4500} \times 100 = -2.2\%$
YoY growth in 2015 = $\frac{6000 - 5900}{5900} \times 100 = +1.69\%$
Maximum decline was in 2011. Hence, option (b) is correct.

Questions 22 to 25:

22. Cost/advertisement for
    A = 27% of 557000/240000 = 0.63
    B = 22% of 557000/370000 = 0.33
    D = 13% of 557000/300000 = 0.24
    E = 20% of 557000/150000 = 0.74
    Option (c) is correct.
23. Quality traffic:
    A: 2800/120000= 0.023
    Similarly by calculating the quality traffic for B, D and E we get E had maximum quality traffic.
24. Leakage:
    For B = 1 – 1200/2500 = 1 – 0.48 = 0.52.
    Similarly by calculating for other options we get D had maximum leakage. Option (c) is correct.
25. ***Note:*** For this question, since the amount spent on the ad site would be a percentage of 557000 and that would be constant for each of the four options-based calculations, we can actually ignore that part of the calculation (since we are only comparing the efficiencies of the four options). Thus, we can see which ad site would give the highest efficiency, simply by the proxy calculations shown below:
    A = 2700/27 = 100
    B = 1200/22 = 54.54
    C = 900/18 = 50
    E = 1600/20 = 80
    Option (a) is correct.

PART 2

HOW TO THINK IN TRADITIONAL DATA INTERPRETATION

IN THIS PART YOU WILL LEARN:

- To identify the Mathematical Structures on which Traditional DI questions are framed
- To improve your ability to read, understand and anticipate DI questions in Traditional DI sets
- To improve your line by line understanding of various kinds of DI sets
- To improve your calculations, by learning the best processes for the typical kinds of calculations you would expect to see in Traditional DI Questions

CHAPTER 1

Introduction to Traditional Data Interpretation & Mathematical Constructs in Traditional Data Interpretation

As you must have read in the preface, this book is divided into two sections – Traditional Data Interpretation (DI) & Logical DI. This distinction has not been formally made or announced by any exam conducting body – but has become obvious by looking at the various questions being asked in the latest CAT and XAT papers. It is self-evident in the sense that the skills required to master both these question types are very different from each other – you might as well be studying two different subjects. Hence, in order to master aptitude exams like the CAT and the XAT, you need to master both Traditional and Logical DI.

For the time being, our focus is on Traditional DI.

WHAT IS TRADITIONAL DATA INTERPRETATION?

A typical question on Traditional DI would consist of some data in the form of graphs/charts/text which would be clearly given to you, followed by questions based on the same. Questions would mostly involve heavy calculations and would be based on one of the principal structures listed in the list below.

Since we are currently in the section of Traditional DI, I will first take you through some important thought structures that you need to develop for Traditional DI.

If you were to take a historical look at the DI questions that have been asked in most examinations, the mathematical constructs of the questions on DI can be broken down into the following quantitative divisions:

The main mathematical structures used in DI:

1. DI based on Averages and Alligations
2. DI based on Percentages
3. DI based on Ratio and Proportions
4. DI based on Mixed concepts of the above
5. DI based on Numerical Logic
6. DI based on Set Theory
7. DI sets based on miscellaneous concepts

Almost every DI set that has appeared in any exam (CAT, XAT, Bank PO) over the past decade and more has been based on these mathematical concepts. The key factor in understanding and solving a set in DI is dependent on the ability to identify this mathematical construct – during your first reading. What essentially occurs is that every DI set gives rise to questioning possibilities – possibilities of the kinds of questions that can be asked on the set. The questioning possibilities that emerge out of a data set are essentially dependent on this mathematical construct of the set.

Obviously, if you get good at identifying the construct of a set, your ability to pre-assess the difficulty level of the question would automatically improve. This in turn would help you identify the easier DI question sets that you should target to solve in the exam. Of course, if you change your DI to your strength you would want to solve all the DI sets as a matter of strategy in every question paper you would be given – in which case identification of easy and difficult sets might not be an important issue for you.

From the opposite perspective, the identification of the mathematical construct of a DI set is critical because there are only two reasons one is not able to handle a DI set:

(a) Inability to understand the data set – This happens mainly because the solver is unable to identify the mathematical construct of the question;
(b) Inability to calculate – This would normally only occur with the unprepared student. Calculations in DI are very repetitive in nature and hence not being prepared for a particular calculation, or being slow

at a particular calculation would only be an excuse that could be given by an under-prepared student. I would like to take this opportunity to tell you once again that while solving this book, whatever calculation situations you face – you should focus on creating a strategy/process/technique to get to the answer accurately and quickly. Throughout this book, in various parts of the solutions to the sets given, I have explained to you the best techniques available when you reach a particular calculation situation. I would once again encourage you to identify those situations and rework the best methods to handle those situations, so as to fortify your mind with the best techniques possible for these calculation situations. This is crucial because you are not going to face any new calculation situations inside the CAT, XAT or any other aptitude exam. Everything (calculation-wise) that would happen in DI is predictable and hence can be prepared for.

This leaves us with only one variable that we need to control in order to reach a belief level in DI – 'I can solve anything in DI'. Once you reach that level of belief, the entire DI section opens up.

So let us now move onto looking at some of these mathematical structures as used in Data Interpretation. In this discussion, I have chosen random questions asked in previous year's papers that are based on the above mathematical structures – and shown you how to think while solving such questions.

Key Concepts in Data Interpretation

1. Averages

Average is one of the most elementary concepts in mathematics. It is one of the measures of central tendency (along with median and mode), but is much more popular than the other two. It is used in most statistical analysis and for comparisons. So, one is always interested in knowing about averages of all kinds in various situations – the batting average of a cricket batsman, the bowling average of a bowler, the average price of a commodity, the average sales per territory for a product, the average speed of a car in a journey – and so many other situations.

Mathematical Concept: The average for a group of numbers is simply the sum of the numbers divided by the number of numbers.

Useful for DI: *The assumed average approach to calculate Averages:*

One of the most common situations that you would come across in DI based on averages is the one where you have to estimate the average of a group of numbers. The assumed average approach explained here is the most powerful approach for handling such situations.

Let's try to look at an example to understand the assumed average approach:

Suppose you have to find the average of 6 numbers. Let us start with an easy set of numbers to understand the process.

Suppose the 6 numbers are 12, 17, 8, 22, 15 and 34. Since the calculation of the average is about finding a measure of the central tendency, the first step in this process, as the name itself suggests is to assume an average. Let's say we try to assume the average as 22. The following process shown in the table is self-explanatory and explains what the assumed average approach is all about:

Numbers	Deviation from the Assumed Average of 22	Net Deviation = Sum of All the Deviations	Average Deviation = Net Deviation/ Number of Numbers
12	–10	–10 – 5 – 14 – 7 + 12 = –24	–24/6 = –4
17	–5		
8	–14		
22	0		
15	–7		
34	12		

The correct average would be: Assumed average + Average deviation = 22 – 4 =18.

The best part of this process is that (the correct answer would be got) irrespective of the value you take of the assumed average. For instance, if you were to take the assumed average as 8, the working would go as follows:

Numbers	Deviation from the Assumed Average of 8	Net Deviation = Sum of All the Deviations	Average Deviation = Net Deviation/ Number of Numbers
12	4	4 + 9 + 0 + 14 + 7 + 26 = 60	60/6 = 10
17	9		
8	0		
22	14		
15	7		
34	26		

Thus, the correct average would be Assumed average + Average deviation = 8 + 10 =18.

Obviously, you do not need this technique in this situation since you could have easily added these numbers and got the average automatically by yourself.

And it is not for these simple average calculation situations that I am advocating this process here. The assumed average approach becomes a killer thought in many DI situations where you would need to calculate the average or the total of a set of numbers. Let us take a look at a couple of such situations:

Let us suppose you are required to make the average of 5 numbers 98, 95, 95.5, 95 and 1 missing number equal to 96. To find the missing number, your thought could be the following:

If we assume the average of the 5 numbers to be 96, the individual deviations are: +2, –1 – 0.5, –1 and 1 unknown value. Since, the net deviation should be zero in this case, we need the deviation of the final number to be 0.5. Hence, the final number would be 96.5.

Note: This thought has been asked in CAT and you can look at the question set 15 to 19 in the exercise that follows. (Specifically look at question 15)

The other situation where the Assumed average approach would help you would be in finding the average of large numbers. Suppose, you needed to find the average of five five-digit numbers – say: 37484, 52776, 81447, 93829 and 78561.

The first step would be to find the average of 37, 52, 81, 93 and 78 (the left most two digits of each of the above numbers). Using the Assumed average approach: Assuming an average of 70 the average of these would come to: 70 – 9/5 = 70 – 1.8 = 68.2.

68.2 here means a value of 68200 (since we had taken 37000 as 37 and 52000 as 52 for the calculation of 68.2 in the first place). So, at this point we know that our answer is '68200 + something'. The something here refers to the average of the last three digits in each of the five numbers that we had ignored. A quick glance across the numbers would show us that the minimum of these ignored last three digits is 447 (in the number 81447) and the maximum is 829 (in the number 93829). Thus, the minimum value of this something would be 447 and the maximum value would be 829. So at this point using this minimum and maximum we know that the average of these five numbers comes out to:

Minimum: 68200 + 447 = 68647; **Maximum:** 68200 + 829 = 69029.

So the average of the numbers: 37484, 52776, 81447, 93829 and 78561 lies between 68647 and 69029.

In my experience in most such situations that you are likely to face in DI (based on over 20 years of trend and difficulty analysis), I can tell you that this range would be quite sufficient to answer the given question. However, in case you need to get a closer answer the additional effort required is just to find the average of the third digit in the five numbers: The third digits are – 4, 7, 4, 8 and 5 respectively and the average of these five numbers is 28/5= 5.6. Since, these digits are the hundreds digit of the numbers, an average of 5.6 means an average of 560. Thus, the average of the numbers evolves to:

68200 + 560 + average of the last two digits of the five numbers =

68760 + average of the last two digits of the five numbers.

Also, since the least of the last two digits is 29 and the largest is 84, we can work out a minimum average of: 68760 + 29 = 68789 and a maximum average of 68760 + 84 = 68844.

I would encourage the reader to practice more of these situations.

2. Alligations

The Alligation situation and how to think in such a situation:

Very often we come across quantitative situations where the concept of weighted average comes into the picture. Weighted average is nothing but a situation where multiple groups with their own averages are getting mixed to form a composite group with a single composite average. The number of units in each group is the weightage that is attached to each average and it plays a role in determining the overall average of the composite group.

Thus, if you were to drive your car at three different speeds, over three different time periods, you would get a single average speed for the entire time period you have traveled for. Similarly, if you have three different sections of students having their own numbers of students in each section, scoring three different averages in an exam – the merging of the three groups would create 1 composite average for the entire group.

The formula for the weighted average situation can be understood by the following situation:

If you have a city A with an average literacy of 80% and a population of 1 lac, city B with an average literacy of 90% and a population of 2 lac and city C with an average literacy of 70% and a population of 3 lac, the weighted average of the three cities would be given by the formula:

$$A_w = \frac{n_1 A_1 + n_2 A_2 + n_3 A_3}{n_1 + n_2 + n_3}$$

So, in this case the value would turn out to be:

$$\frac{80 \times 1 + 90 \times 2 + 70 \times 3}{1 + 2 + 3} = \frac{470}{6} = 78.33$$

Note: Here, that the value of the weighted average is not dependent on the actual values of the populations, but on the ratio of the populations. Thus, if you were to change the population to 2 lacs, 4 lacs and 6 lacs respectively, the answer would still remain the same. In fact, as far as you would keep the ratio of the numbers equal to 1 : 2 : 3, the weighted average of the groups shown above would remain the same.

Note: In each of the following cases, the same formula would apply:

(a) You drive a car at 80 kmph for 1 hour, 90 kmph for 2 hours and 70 kmph for 3 hours and you want to find out your average speed.
(b) You mix 1 liter of liquid costing 80 ₹/liter, 2 liters of liquid costing 90 ₹/liter and 3 liters of liquid costing 70 ₹/liter and you want to find out the average price of the mixture.
(c) You mix three diet formulations—one having 80% protein, another with 90% protein and a third with 70% protein in the ratio 1 : 2 : 3 and you want to work out the average protein percentage in the mixture.

As you can well realise the weighted average formula can work for two, three, four or even more groups. What we need to move to now is to the weighted average formula for 2 groups. In this case, the entire structure of thinking to get to the required answer gets encapsulated into a visual picture – which can be termed as 'alligation'.

The alligation situation:

Suppose you mixed two diet formulations with 80% protein and 90% protein respectively in the ratio 2:3, and you want to work out the average protein percentage in the total mixture. You can of course solve this through the weighted average formula, but since this is a case of mixing of two groups, the situation can also be solved using the alligation structure on the number line.

Consider the following structures of thinking. There are essentially three cases for alligations to be used. Let A_1 and A_2 be the averages of the two groups being mixed, n_1:n_2 be the ratio of the mixing and Aw be the weighted average. Then we have the following cases:

Case 1: When we know the values of A_1, A_2 and A_w and want to know the ratio of n_1:n_2.

Case 2: When we know the values of A_1, A_2, the ratio of n_1:n_2 and we want to know the value of A_w

Case 3: When we know the ratio of n_1:n_2 and we know A_w and the value of one of the two averages. In this situation we would need to find out the second average, i.e., if A_1 is known we would need to find out A_2, while if A_2 is known we would need to find A_1.

The following illustrations will give you a clear idea of how to use Alligation to think in each of these situations.

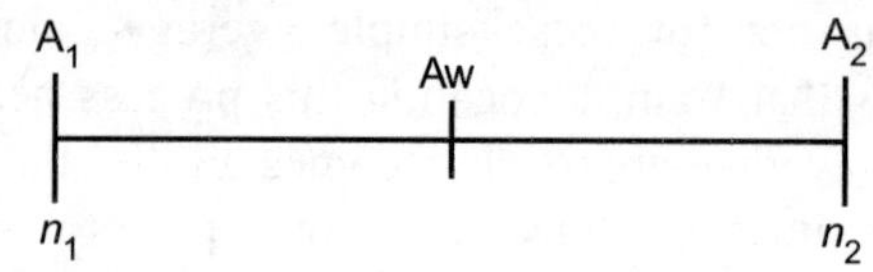

Visualise this as a fragment of the number line with points A_1, *Aw* and A_2 in that order from left to right. Then,

(a) n_2 is responsible for the distance between A_1 and *Aw* or n_2 corresponds to $Aw - A_1$
(b) n_1 is responsible for the distance between *Aw* and A_2 or n_1 corresponds to $A_2 - Aw$
(c) $(n_1 + n_2)$ is responsible for the distance between A_1 and A_2 or $(n_1 + n_2)$ corresponds to $A_2 - A_1$.

The processes for the 3 cases illustrated above can then be illustrated below:

Illustration 1

On mixing two classes of students having average marks 25 and 40 respectively, the overall average obtained is 30 marks. Find

(a) the ratio in which the classes were mixed.
(b) the number of students in the first class if the second class had 30 students.

Solution:

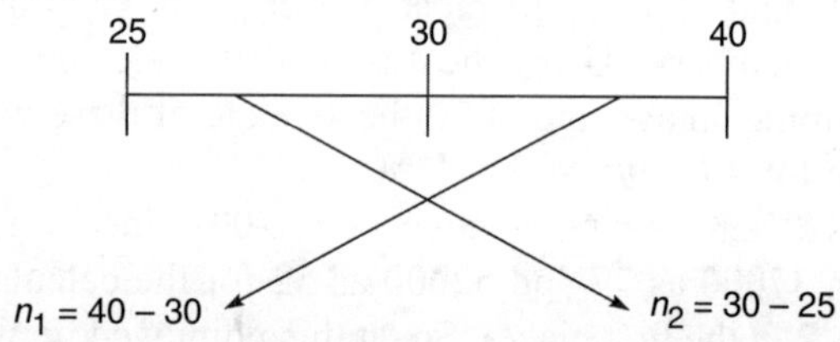

Hence, ratio is 2 : 1, and the first class has 60 students.

Case 2 A_1, A_2, n_1 and n_2 are known; *Aw* is unknown.

Illustration 2

4 kg of rice at ₹5 per kg is mixed with 8 kg of rice at ₹6 per kg. Find the average price of the mixture.

Solution:

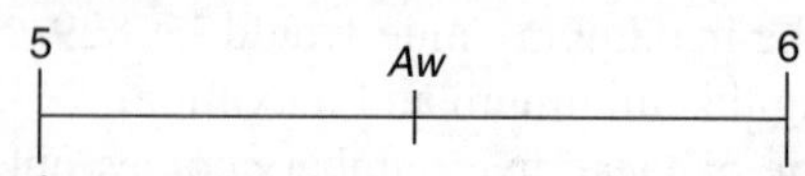

is the same as

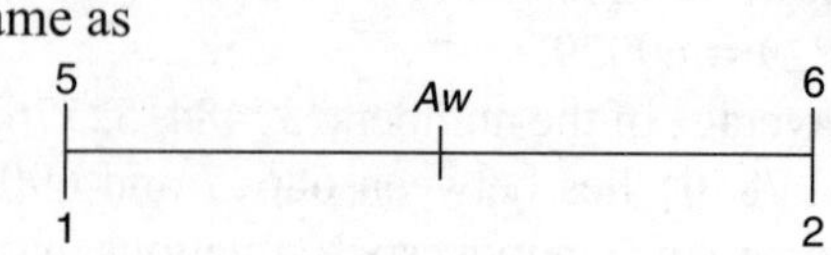

Then, by unitary method:

$n_1 + n_2$ corresponds to $A_2 - A_1$
$\rightarrow 1 + 2$ corresponds to $6 - 5$

That is, 3 corresponds to 1

$\therefore$ n_2 will correspond to $\dfrac{(A_2 - A_1) \times n_2}{(n_1 + n_2)}$

In this case (1/3) × 2 = 0.66.

Hence, the required answer is 5.66.

Case 3: A_1, Aw, n_1 and n_2 are known; A_2 is unknown.

Illustration 3

5 kg of rice at ₹6 per kg is mixed with 4 kg of rice to get a mixture costing ₹7 per kg. Find the price of the costlier rice.

Using straight line method:

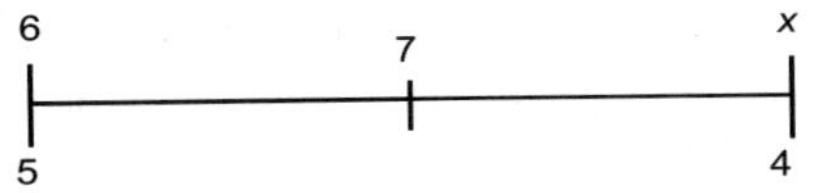

4 corresponds to 7 – 6 and 5 corresponds to x – 7.

The thought process should go like:

$$4 \rightarrow 1$$

$$\therefore \quad 5 \rightarrow 1.25$$

Hence, $x - 7 = 1.25$

and $x = 8.25$

3. Percentages

There are two basic structures of percentage calculations that are repeatedly used in DI. These are illustrated below:

A. Percentage Calculations

Percentage Rule for Calculating Percentage Values through Additions

We have already discussed this method in the previous part of this book, when we discussed Divisions, Percentages and Ratio Comparisons. I would request you to continue your practise of the same.

B. Percentage Change in a Product

PCG applied to Product Change

Suppose you have a product of two variables say 10 × 10.

If the first variable changes to 11 and the second variable changes to 12, what will be the percentage change in the product? [***Note:*** There is a 10% increase in one part of the product and a 20% increase in the other part.]

The formula given for this situation goes as: (a + b + ab/100).

Hence, required % change = $10 + 20 + \dfrac{10 \times 20}{100}$

(Where 10 and 20 are the respective percentage changes in the two parts of the product. This is being taught as a shortcut at most institutes across the country currently.)

However, a much easier solution for this case can be visualised as:

$100 \xrightarrow[+20]{20\%\uparrow} 120 \xrightarrow[+12]{10\%\uparrow} 132$. Hence, the final product shows a 32% increase.

Similarly suppose 10 × 10 × 10 becomes 11 × 12 × 13.

In such a case the following PCG will be used:

$$100 \xrightarrow[+30]{30\%\uparrow} 130 \xrightarrow[+26]{20\%\uparrow} 156 \xrightarrow[+15.6]{10\%\uparrow} 171.6$$

Hence, the final product sees a 71.6 percent increase

(Since, the product changes from 100 to 171.6).

Note: You will get the same result irrespective of the order in which you use the respective percentage changes.

Also note that this process is very similar to the one used for calculating successive percentage change.

Application for DI:

Suppose you have two pie charts as follows:

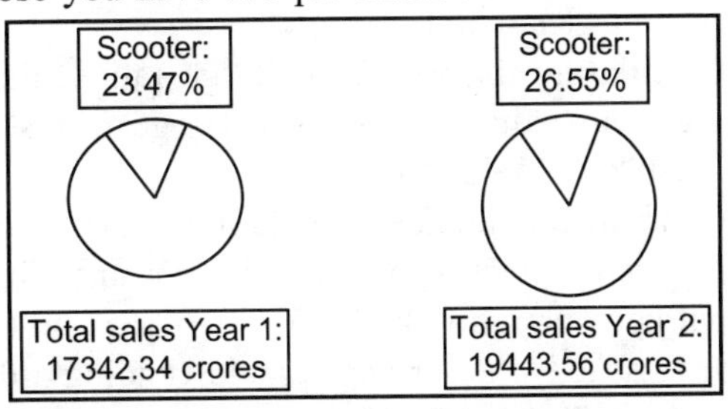

If you are asked to calculate the percentage change in the sales revenue of scooters for the company from year one to year two, what would you do?

The formula for percentage change would give us:

$$\frac{(0.2655 \times 19443.56) - (0.2347 \times 17342.34) \times 100}{(0.2347 \times 17342.34)}$$

i.e., $\dfrac{\text{New Sales Revenue} - \text{Original Sales Revenue}}{\text{Original Sales Revenue}} \times 100$

Obviously this calculation is easier said than done. However, the product change application of PCG allows us to execute this calculation with a lot of ease comparatively. Consider the following solution:

Product for year one is: 0.2347 × 17342.34

Product for year two is: 0.2655 × 19443.56

These can be approximated into:

234 × 173 and 265 × 194 respectively (***Note:*** By moving into three digits we do not end up losing any accuracy. We have elaborated this point in the note on Ratio and Proportions.)

The overall percentage change depends on two individual percentage changes:
234 increases to 265: A % change of 31/234 = 13.2 % approx. This calculation has to be done using the percentage rule for calculating the percentage value of the ratio.

173 increases to 194 – A percentage change of approximately 12%.

Thus PCG will give the answer as follows:

$$100 \xrightarrow[+13.2]{13.2\%\uparrow} 113.2 \xrightarrow[+13.56]{12\%\uparrow} 126.76$$

Hence, 26.76% increase in the product's value. (***Note:*** The value on the calculator for the full calculation sans any approximations is 26.82 %, and given the fact that we have come extremely close to the answer—the method is good enough to solve the question with a great degree of accuracy.)

4. Ratios

There are three essential situations that you repeatedly face with respect to ratios when you are doing data interpretation. These are:

1. Calculating the values for large ratios; finding the ratio value for two very large ratios like: 41738876/94372258.
2. Comparison of ratios: Comparing ratios and placing them in increasing order. For instance finding out how the ratios 45/52, 51/59, 57/65 and 63/71 are stacked when arranged in descending order.

In order to solve both these situations efficiently, the fundamental ratio concept to be utilised can be explained as below. Suppose, you have a situation where you have a ratio of 10/20. Let us say that you add 1 in the numerator and 2 in the denominator. What happens to the ratio? It becomes 11/22 and the value off 11/22 is equal to the value of 10/20. Why does this occur?? Because, the ratio of the additions in the numerator and the denominator is equal to the original ratio!! In such a case, the final ratio (in this case 11/22) would be equal to the original ratio (10/20). It would happen in all such cases and can be seen in the following:

244/366 = 200/300 because when we add 44 in the numerator and 66 in the denominator of 200/300, the ratio of the additions (44/66 in this case) is equal to the original ratio.

So, the first conclusion we draw is that if the ratio of the additions is equal to the original ratio, then the value of the new ratio is equal to the original ratio.

Once you have realised this, the next thing to understand is that if the ratio of the additions in the numerator and the denominator is greater than the original ratio, the result would be that the new ratio would be greater than the original ratio. For instance:

To the ratio 10/20, if we add 2 in the numerator and 3 in the denominator, the ratio would become 12/23. We can easily see that 12/23 > 10/20. The reason for the same is that 2/3 > 10/20 (i.e., the ratio of the additions to the numerator and denominator is greater than the original ratio).

Similarly, in case the ratio of the additions in the numerator and the denominator is smaller than the original ratio, the result would be that the new ratio would be smaller than the original ratio. For instance:

To the ratio 10/20, if we add 2 in the numerator and 7 in the denominator, the ratio would become 12/27. We can easily see that 12/27 < 10/20. The reason for the same is that 2/7 < 10/20 (i.e., the ratio of the additions to the numerator and denominator is smaller than the original ratio).

This concept can be used in a certain way in order to handle both the above situations. Let us take a look at how we do so now one by one.

Calculating a ratio like:
41738876/94372258

The first thing you need to understand is that if the decimal value of the given 8 digit divided by 8 digit number is 0.abcdefgh, and change your calculation to a 3 digit divided by 3 digit calculation, you would by and large be maintaining the accuracy of the answer in the first three digits. The following table shows you how much accuracy you lose if you start ignoring digits from the right while calculating such ratios.

Ratio	Value	Answer Reliable Till
41738876/ 94372258	0.44227908	
4173887/ 9437225	0.44227905	7 digits after decimal.
417388/ 943722	0.44227852	6 digits after decimal (the change in the 6th digit after decimal is essentially a carry-over change that has occurred due to the change in the 7th digit after decimal in this case).
41738/ 94372	0.442270075	5 digits after decimal—Note that you have lost accuracy after 5 digits after decimal.
4173/9437	0.44219561	4 digits after decimal—Note that you have lost accuracy after 4 digits after decimal. Also note that the change in the 4th digit of the answer is largely because of the carry-over change from the 5th digit of the answer.

Ratio	Value	Answer Reliable Till
417/943	0.44220572	The accuracy seems to be till 4 digits after decimal here, but actually this is accurate only till 3 digits after decimals. The fourth digit coming out to be correct has occurred accidentally.

The point I am trying to make here is that you would never need to calculate anything more than 3 digits divided by 3 digits, even if you are faced with an 8 digit divided by 8 digit ratio.

Hence, when you are faced with the ratio 41738876/94372258, we need to just calculate the ratio 417/943. Or in the most challenging cases, you might have to go till 4173/9437. In order to do so, first calculate the percentage value of 41/94 (using the percentage rule explained above).

41/94 = 43.6% approximately.

Hence, the decimal value of 41/94 = 0.436.

But we are faced with a situation where we need to calculate 4173/9437.

The value of 4100/9400 would remain 0.436 and if we can adjust this answer for the last two digits we would get a very accurate answer.

The above ratio can be looked at as:

$$\frac{4100+73}{9400+37}$$

If this ratio had been such that the addition ratio had been equal to the original ratio, the answer of 0.436 would have been the correct value for this calculation. However the addition ratio will normally differ from the original ratio. The process for the adjustment for the value of the addition ratio can be done, by thinking as follows:

For a denominator addition of 37, if the numerator addition had been such that the ratio of additions had been 0.436 in this case, the answer for the 4 digit ratio would have remained at 0.436. So, first try to see how much addition there should have been in the numerator, if the addition in the denominator of 37 had been fixed, so that there would be no change in the ratio necessitated.

Think: $\frac{x}{37} = 43.6\%$ So x = ? In order to find x, we can do an approximate back of the hand calculation and see that 43% of 37 is 3.7 + 3.7 + 3.7 + 3.7 + 0.37 + 0.37 + 0.37 = 15.91. Thus, approximately, if the numerator addition had been 16, with a denominator addition of 37, there would be no need to change the ratio.

So we think as follows from here:

$$\frac{4100+16}{9400+37} = 0.436 \text{ (as no change would be necessitated in the answer)}$$

But we have to calculate:

$$\frac{4173}{9437} = \frac{4116+57}{9437} = 0.436 + \frac{57}{9437}$$

= 43.6% + the percentage value of 57/9437.

The percentage value of 57/9437 can be seen as approximately 0.6 (since 9.4 added 6 times gets us close to 57).

Hence, the correct answer to $\frac{4173}{9437} = 0.442 = 44.2\%$.

That's it!! The beauty of this process is that you have done nothing but two digit ratio calculations and got to the answer.

I would encourage you to practice this extensively as you are likely to face many such situations in your examination while solving data interpretation.

Handling the Ratio Comparison Situation:

In the previous part of this book, we have discussed a few methods for handling the ratio comparison calculation. Let me now explain to you one more method, which is perhaps the most powerful method to compare ratios.

In any ratio comparison situation, we are faced with four fundamental situations.

1. Numerator increases, denominator decreases – The ratio would go up. You do not need any calculations to identify this.
2. Numerator decreases, denominator increases – The ratio would go down. Again, no calculations required.
3. Numerator increases, denominator increases.
4. Numerator decreases and denominator decreases.

Note: *Both of these are opposite cases to each other. So if you know how to do the numerator increases, denominator increases ratio comparison case, you can do the numerator decreases and denominator decreases case by just reversing the ratios. What I mean to say here is that if you are trying to compare 53/62 to 46/53 – where both numerator and denominator are decreasing, you can compare 46/53 with 53/62 – and look at it as a case of both numerator and denominator increasing.*

In this case, the numerator increase would increase the ratio, but the denominator increase would decrease the ratio. Naturally, whether the ratio increases or decreases, would depend on how much force of change the numerator exerts vis-à-vis how much force of change the denominator is exerting.

In such a situation, we can use the logic of the ratio of the additions to compare two ratios. A little bit of practice in the following logic would show you that even in extremely close situations, finding which ratio is larger and which is smaller is normally a no-brainer.

Lets' see how: Suppose you are comparing 46/53 and 53/62.

The calculator will give you values of 0.8679 and 0.8548—values that are quite close to each other.

Using the additions in the ratio logic we see this situation as:

$$\frac{46+7}{53+9} = \frac{53}{62}$$

In this case, it can be easily seen that the value of 46/53 is above 80%, while the value of 7/9 being 77.77% is below 80%. Since, the ratio of the additions is smaller than the original ratio, the new ratio would be smaller.

This process is by far the best ratio comparison process available. I would encourage you to practice more of these in order to make sure that you make this your default thinking. Ratio comparisons is a repetitive theme in data interpretation and getting good at it will take you a long way in getting stronger at DI solving.

We will now move directly to looking at some traditional DI questions and trying to experience situations that DI throws at us and understanding how to think in such situations.

CHAPTER 2

How to Think in Traditional Data Interpretation

Directions for Questions 1 to 4: *(Set based on Averages)*

Answer the questions on the basis of the information given below.

The data points in the figure below represent monthly income and expenditure data of individual members of the Ahuja family (■), the Bose family (□), the Coomar family (○) and the Dubey family (●). For these questions, savings is defined as

Savings = Income – Expenditure

(Your first focus after reading this text that introduces the table below is to note that inside the graph you would be looking at members of the four families marked with their respective signs.)

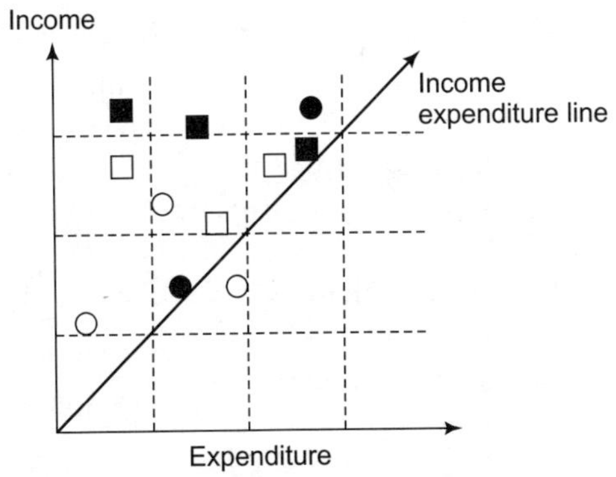

FIGURE 2.1 *Monthly Income and Expenditure Data*

While 'reading' the graph, your focus should be on understanding the meaning of the points in the graph. The axes represent 'Expenditure' on the X-axis and 'Income' on the Y-axis. As already mentioned in the text above, savings can be calculated for any individual using the equation: Savings = Income – Expenditure. The other thing you need to understand is the significance of the Income = Expenditure line. Any point on that line obviously signifies Income and Expenditure being equal—hence zero savings. But what you need to also understand is that the points lying above this line would mean Income > Expenditure and hence positive savings. Likewise, a point on the graph that is below the Income = Expenditure line would represent negative savings since for these points Expenditure is greater than Income. Also, you need to be able to work out during your first glance at the graph that the vertical distance from the Income = Expenditure line would signify the savings for any individual. With this understanding you are now ready to face the questions that follow:

1. Which family has the lowest average income?
   (a) Ahuja (b) Bose
   (c) Coomar (d) Dubey

   Average income can be estimated by visualising a horizontal line that should be drawn for the members of a family, such that the sum of the vertical deviations for points above the line and the sum of the vertical deviations for points below the horizontal line should be equal.

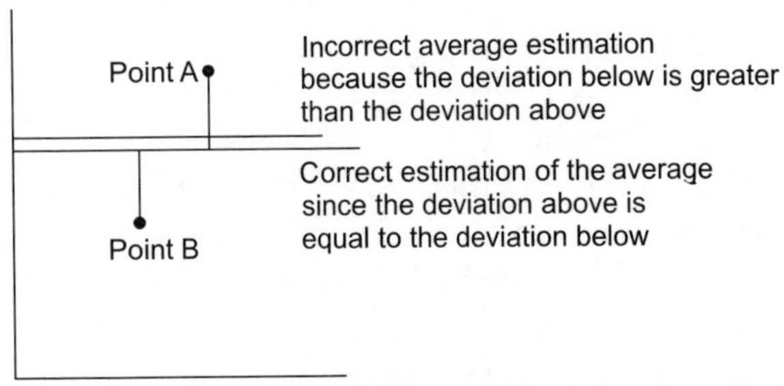

FIGURE 2.2(A) *Finding Average for Two Points on The Y-Axis*

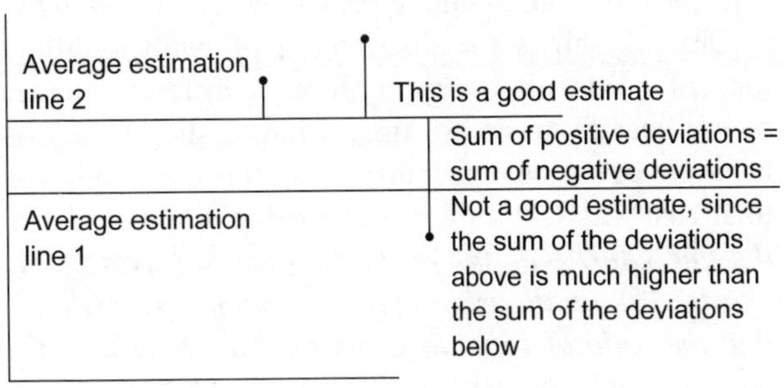

FIGURE 2.2(B) *Finding Average for Three Points on The Y-Axis*

In this fashion, if you were to estimate the average incomes for each of the three families by estimating a horizontal line to signify the average income, you can easily visualise in the figure above that the average income would be least for the Coomar family.

2. Which family has the highest average expenditure?
   (a) Ahuja (b) Bose
   (c) Coomar (d) Dubey

The highest average expenditure can be estimated in the same way by visualising a vertical line to signify the average – in this case the deviations would be to the right and the left of the vertical line, and the correct average estimation would be on the vertical line that has the sum of deviations to the right equal to the sum of deviations to the left. Clearly, the Dubey family has the highest average expenditure as its estimated vertical line for the average expenditure would be to the right most, when it is compared to the estimated vertical lines of the other families.

3. Which family has the lowest average savings?
   (a) Ahuja (b) Bose
   (c) Coomar (d) Dubey

The savings is estimated by the vertical distance from the Income = Expenditure line. The average savings would be equal to the average vertical distance for all the members of any family. In the given figure it is clear that the average height from the I = E line is least for the Dubey family.

4. The highest amount of savings accrues to a member of which family?
   (a) Ahuja (b) Bose
   (c) Coomar (d) Dubey

The savings is estimated by the vertical distance from the Income = Expenditure line. The maximum such distance is exhibited by a member of the Ahuja family.

Directions for Questions 5 to 7: *(Set Based on Percentages and Ratios)*

The questions based on the pie charts are given below:

Chart 1 shows the distribution of twelve million tons of crude oil transport through different modes over a specific period of time. Chart 2 shows the distribution of the cost of transporting this crude oil. The total cost was ₹30 million. *(The situation presented in this pie chart pair is one of the common uses of pie charts. The relationship between volume and value is that the ratio of value to volume would determine the value per unit volume – which would in effect represent the unit cost.)*

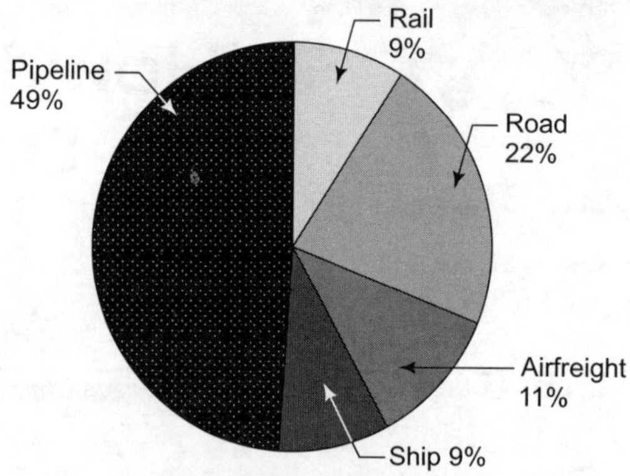

Chart 1

FIGURE 2.3(A) *Distribution of Twelve Million Tons of Crude Oil Transport Through Different Modes*

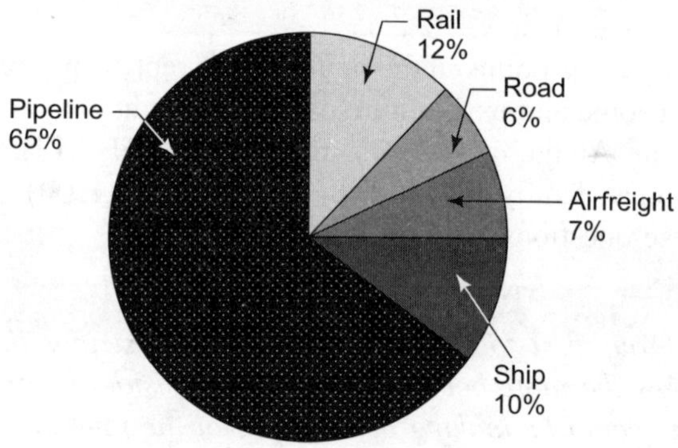

Chart 2

FIGURE 2.3(B) *Distribution of the Cost of Transporting The Crude Oil*

5. If the cost per ton of transport by ship, air and road are represented by P, Q and R respectively, which of the following is true?
   (a) $R > Q > P$ (b) $P > R > Q$
   (c) $P > Q > R$ (d) $R > P > Q$

(The actual calculation for each of the three would have been:

$$\text{Cost per ton by ship} = \frac{10\% \text{ of } 30 \text{ million}}{9\% \text{ of } 12 \text{ million}} = \frac{0.1 \times 30 \text{ million}}{0.09 \times 12 \text{ million}}.$$

If we had to work out the actual cost of transportation per ton for each of the modes of transport, this would have to be the calculation we would need to do. Likewise the values for air would be

$$= \frac{7\% \text{ of } 30 \text{ million}}{11\% \text{ of } 12 \text{ million}} = \frac{0.07 \times 30 \text{ million}}{0.11 \times 12 \text{ million}};$$

For road it would be

$$= \frac{6\% \text{ of } 30 \text{ million}}{22\% \text{ of } 12 \text{ million}} = \frac{0.06 \times 30 \text{ million}}{0.22 \times 12 \text{ million}}.$$

However, in this question, we do not need to find out the exact values for the cost per ton transported. The only calculation required in order to place in descending order the cost per ton transported by various means would be the ratio of the two percentages for that mode of transport. Thus, we just need to compare the ratio of percentages of value/volume for each of the three modes being asked for. The value/volume ratio is 10/9 for ship, 7/11 for air and 6/22 for road. The highest ratio is for ship > air > road. So it is $P > Q > R$. Option (c) is correct. ***Note:*** In this case, we do not need to consider the actual values of the total cost of goods transported or the total volume of the total crude transported.)

6. The cost in rupees per ton of oil moved by rails and road happens to be roughly
   (a) 3 (b) 1.5
   (c) 4.5 (d) 8
   Total value = 18% of 30 million = 5.4 million. Total volume = 31% of 12 million = 3.72 million. Approximately 1.5.
7. From the charts given, it appears that the cheapest mode of transport is:
   (a) Road (b) Rail
   (c) Pipeline (d) Ship
   Again we need to consider the least ratio for the value/volume. It is clearly for road at 6/22.

Directions for Questions 8 to 10: *(Set based on Percentages)*

Answer these questions based on the data given below.

There are six companies, 1 through 6. All of these companies use six operations, A through F. The graph shows the distribution of efforts put in by each company in these six operations. *(A quick glance at the bar chart below, shows us that the chart gives us the break down of 100% of effort, distributed between operations A through F. There is nothing more to do at this point than perhaps understand and make sense of a couple of values in the charts. So, what we could explain to ourselves before moving into the questions could be perhaps that a value like 15.7 means that for company 1, the effort in operation F is 15.7% of its entire effort. With this understanding, you are now in a position to move onto the questions on the data.)*

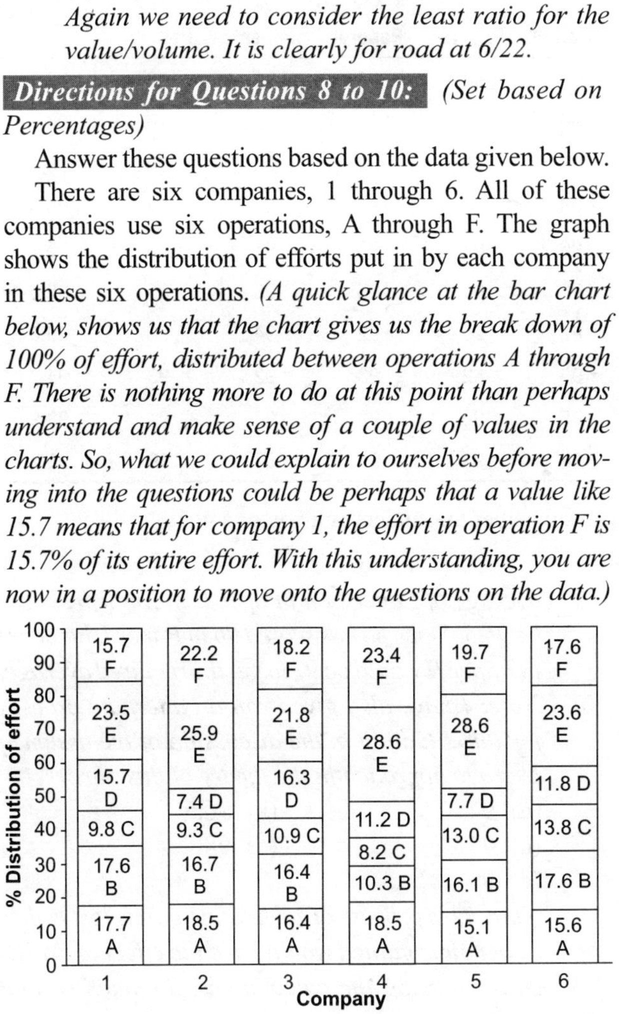

8. Suppose effort allocation is inter-changed between operations B and C, then C and D, and then D and E. *(The effect of this change is going to be that the effort in operation B would become the effort for operation E. Also the efforts of operation E would become the effort of operation D, D would become C and C would become B. In effect, the effort of B would go up by three levels, while the efforts of C, D and E would come down by one each.)* If companies are then ranked in ascending order of effort in operation E, *(we would need to just look at the ascending order of effort involved in operation B in the given chart. The ascending order would be 4, 5, 3, 2, 1 and 6 tied)* which company would be at third rank *(company 3 has ranked 3rd)*?
   (a) 2 (b) 3
   (c) 4 (d) 5
9. Suppose the companies find that they can remove operations B, C and D and re-distribute the effort released equally amongst the remaining operations. *(Releasing the efforts of B, C and D would mean that the sum of the efforts of B, C and D would be released and then the effort thus released is to be equally distributed amongst operations A, E and F. For instance for company 1, the effort released would be equal to 17.6 + 9.8 + 15.7 = 43.1. When this effort is re-distributed equally amongst A, E and F it would mean that the effort in A would become 17.7 + 43.1/3 = 17.7 + 14.36 = 32.06. Similarly, effort in E would become 23.5 + 14.36 = 37.86 and effort in F would become 15.7 + 14.36 = 30.06.* ***Note:*** *You might not do all these calculations at this point in time because you still have not been asked to do these calculations. You would just create the mental template of what has to be done at this point and move onto what the question has asked you to do.)* Then, which operation will show the maximum across all companies and all operations *(given the options, you are just looking at which of the given operations would become the maximum. E for company 1, is 23.5, while it is 28.6 in each of 4 and 5. You can reject F for company 5—option 'c' because it is lower than E for company 5, the addition to both being the same)*?
   (a) Operation E in company 1
   (b) Operation E in company 4
   (c) Operation F in company 5
   (d) Operation E in company 5

   A quick glance at the numbers shows us that operation E in company 5, would get a larger allocation than operation E in company 4, since the value released in company 5 is greater than the operation released in company 4. So, the answer is either option (d) or option (a). E in company 5 = 28.6 + 36.8/3 ≈ 40 to 41 which is higher than 23.6 + 14.3 ≈ 38.

10. A new technology is introduced in company 4 such that the total effort for operations *B* through *F* gets evenly distributed amongst these. *(Equal distribution of effort for operations B through F would mean a re-distribution of 81.5 in 5 equal parts. Thus, each operation B through F would become equal to 81.5/5 = 16.3.)* What is the change in the percentage of effort in operation *E (the effort in operation E would go down from 28.6 to 16.3, a reduction of 12.3)*?
(a) Reduction of 12.3 (b) Increase of 12.3
(c) Reduction of 5.6 (d) Increase of 5.6

Directions for Questions 11 to 15: *(Set based on Averages)*

In a Class X Board examination, ten papers are distributed over five Groups – PCB, Mathematics, Social Science, Vernacular and English. Each of the ten papers is evaluated out of 100. The final score of a student is calculated in the following manner. First, the group scores are obtained by averaging marks in the papers within the group. The final score is the simple average of the group scores. The data for the top ten students are presented below. *(A quick glance at the table gives us that the group score for any group being the simple average of the papers within the group – the group score for PCB would be obtained by dividing the total score in Physics, Chemistry and Biology by 3, while for Social Science, Vernacular and English groups it would be divided by 2, and for Mathematics group since the only paper is Mathematics itself, the score in that paper would itself be the group score for the Mathematics group.)* (Dipan's score in English Paper II has been intentionally removed in the table.)

Name of the Student	PCB Group			Mathematics Group	Social Science Group		Vernacular Group		English Group		Final Score
	Phy.	Chem.	Bio.		Hist.	Geo.	Paper I	Paper II	Paper I	Paper II	
Ayesha (G)	98	96	97	98	95	93	94	96	96	98	96.2
Ram (B)	97	99	95	97	95	96	94	94	96	98	96.1
Dipan (B)	98	98	98	95	96	95	96	94	96	??	96.0
Sagnik (B)	97	98	99	96	96	98	94	97	92	94	95.9
Sanjiv (B)	95	96	97	98	97	96	92	93	95	96	95.7
Shreya (G)	96	89	85	100	97	98	94	95	96	95	95.5
Joseph (B)	90	94	98	100	94	97	90	92	94	95	95.0
Agni (B)	96	99	96	99	95	96	82	93	92	93	94.3
Pritam (B)	98	98	95	98	83	95	90	93	94	94	93.9
Tirna (G)	96	98	97	99	85	94	92	91	87	96	93.7

Note: *B* or *G* against the name of a student respectively indicates whether the student is a boy or a girl

11. How much did Dipan get in English Paper II? *(Dipan's final score is 96, which means that he has lost a total of 20 points out of 500 when his final score is calculated. If we go over the row in which Dipan's scores are mentioned we can easily see that since his average in PCB is 98, he has lost 2 points in PCB. In Mathematics he has lost 5 points, 4.5 points in Social Science and 5 points in Vernacular. Thus, over the first four groups he has lost a total of 16.5 points. This means that he must have lost another 3.5 points in the English group. To lose 3.5 points in the English group, his group score viz. the average of Paper I and Paper II in English should be 96.5. Since he has scored 96 in Paper I, his score in Paper II would be 97 to get the required average.* ***Note:*** *I have also given you an alternate process for this situation in the discussion of the assumed average approach in the theory of this part.)*
(a) 94 (b) 96.5
(c) 97 (d) 98
(e) 99

Note: *This process of calculating points lost rather than points gained would have the effect of drastically reducing the calculations. So much so that* *it would actually make the whole solution to this problem visual and mental, rather than one involving extensive calculations.*

12. Students who obtained group scores of at least 95 in every group are eligible to apply for a prize. Amongst those who are eligible, the student obtaining the highest group score in Social Science group is awarded this prize. The prize was awarded to:
(a) Shreya (b) Ram
(c) Ayesha (d) Dipan
(e) no one from the top ten
This question has to be solved visually again. A look through the Vernacular group for the bottom 6 students in the table would show you that there is nobody eligible between Sanjiv and Tirna as they score less than 95 in the group score for the Vernacular group. Ram loses out because of the Vernacular group again, while Ayesha loses out because of the Social Science group where she is scoring only 94. Dipan gets the prize.

13. Amongst the top ten students, how many boys scored at least 95 in at least one paper from each of the groups?
(a) 1 (b) 2
(c) 3 (d) 4
(e) 5
Ram fails because he does not score 95 in either paper of the Vernacular group. Sagnik, Agni and Pritam are not to be counted because of the English group where they have not scored 95 or more in any of the two papers. Joseph and Sanjiv are not to be counted because they have failed to score 95 or more in the Vernacular group. Only Dipan scores 95 in at least 1 paper in each group. So there is only 1 boy who satisfies this criteria. Option (a) is correct.

14. Each of the ten students was allowed to improve his/her score in exactly one paper of choice with the objective of maximising his/her final score. Everyone scored 100 in the paper in which he or she chose to improve. After that the topper amongst the ten students was:
(a) Ram (b) Agni
(c) Pritam (d) Ayesha
(e) Dipan
Looking through the options, we can see that the five names to be considered are Ram, Agni, Pritam, Dipan and Ayesha. In order to solve this question, you first need to understand the equation you are dealing with here. The correct equation of the

$$\text{Average score} = \frac{\frac{Physics + Chemistry + Biology}{3} + \frac{Mathematics}{1} + \frac{History + Geography}{2} + \frac{Vern\,Paper\,1 + Vern\,Paper\,2}{2} + \frac{English\,Paper\,1 + Paper\,2}{2}}{5}$$

Now, from this equation, it is clear that if a student raises his/her score by 1 mark in any of the papers of the PCB group, it would mean an increment of 1/15 = 0.06666 in the final score. An increment of 1 mark in Mathematics would increase the final score of the student by 1/5 = 0.2 marks. In the same manner an increment of 1 mark in any of the papers of the other three groups would result in an increase of 1/10 = 0.1 in the final score.

With this understanding, if you were to check the five students one by one, you realise that for Ayesha, her maximum score improvement potential is available if she improves on her score in Geography. Thus, Ayesha would increase her score to 96.2 + 0.7 = 96.9 by improving her Geography score to 100 from 93. Likewise, Ram can increase his score to a maximum of 96.1 + 0.6 by either improving his Mathematics by 3 marks, or his score in any of the Vernacular group papers by 6 marks. In either case, his final score would go up by 0.6 to 96.7. Dipan on the other hand could improve his score by 1, by improving his marks in Mathematics from 95 to 100. Thus, Dipan's final score would reach 96 +1 = 97. The other two students, Agni and Pritam would be able to reach—Agni = 94.3 + 1.8 = 96.1, by improving Vernacular paper I to 100 from 82, Pritam = 93.9 + 1.7 = 95.6, by improving History to 100 from 83. Thus, Dipan would be the new topper in this case, since his score of 97 would be the maximum amongst all students.

15. Had Joseph, Agni, Pritam and Tirna each obtained group score of 100 in the Social Science group, then their standing in decreasing order of final score would be:
(a) Pritam, Joseph, Tirna, Agni
(b) Joseph, Tirna, Agni, Pritam
(c) Pritam, Agni, Tirna, Joseph

(d) Joseph, Tirna, Pritam, Agni
(e) Pritam, Tirna, Agni, Joseph

By obtaining a score of 100 in Social Science group, Joseph would improve his final score to 95 + 4.5/5 = 95 + 0.9 = 95.9. I would encourage you to work out why the change in his score would come to 4.5/5 in this case.

For Agni, the score would be 94.3 + 4.5/5 = 95.2; For Pritam, it would be 93.9 + 11/5 = 93.9 + 2.2 = 96.1; For Tirna, it would be 93.7 + 10.5/5 = 93.7 + 2.1 = 95.8. The required decreasing order would be Pritam, Joseph, Tirna and Agni. Option (a) is the correct answer here.

Directions for Questions 16 to 21: *(Set based on percentages)*

Answer these questions based on the two graphs. Figure 2.4(A) shows the amount of work distribution, in man-hours for a software company between offshore and onsite activities. Figure 2.4(B) shows the estimated and actual work effort involved in the different offshore activities in the same company during the same period. (***Note:*** Onsite refers to work performed at the customer's premise and offshore refers to work performed at the developer's premise.)

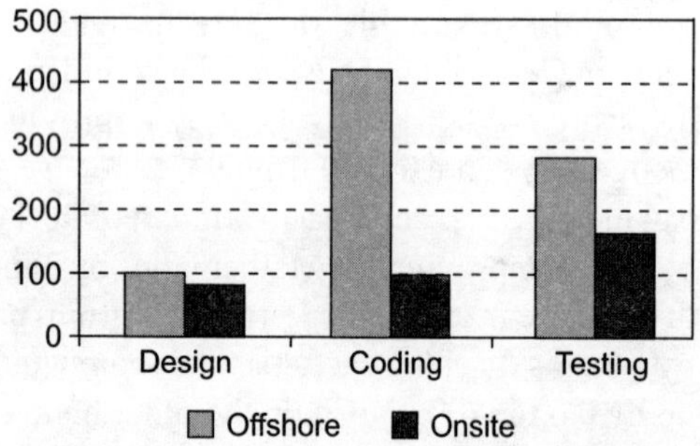

FIGURE 2.4(A) *The Amount of Work Distribution (in man-hours)*

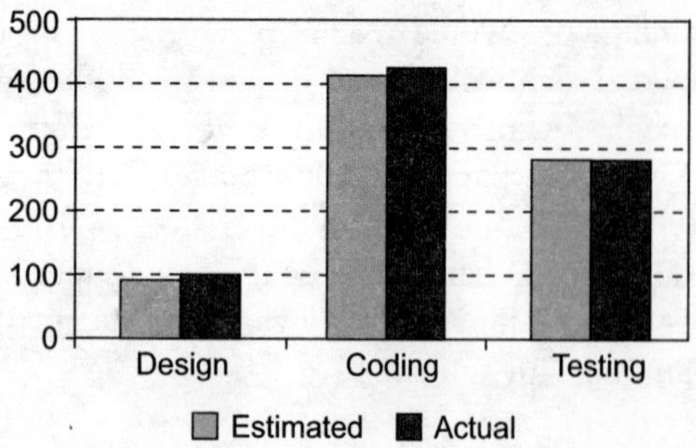

FIGURE 2.4(B) *The Estimated and Actual Work Effort Involved in the Different Offshore Activities*

The first thing you should do for this question is to identify what the bar charts are telling you. The first bar chart, as mentioned in the text above, gives us the break-up of the work in terms of man-hours, distributed between offshore and onsite activities. For instance, 410 man-hours of coding is done off-shore and 100 man-hours of coding is done onsite. The second bar chart tells us the estimated and actual man-hours of offshore activities for the software company. What you need to spot right at this time is that the value of the actual man-hours of design, coding and testing seen in the second bar chart, would be equal to the number of offshore manhours of Designing, Coding and Testing in the first bar chart.

16. If 50 per cent of the offshore work were to be carried out onsite, with the distribution of effort between the tasks remaining the same, which of the following is true of all work carried out onsite? *(You need to identify first that this question would be solved from the first bar chart. In order to make any conclusions about the number of man-hours of work carried out onsite after the shift of 50% offshore work to onsite, you would first need to transfer 50% of the offshore work to onsite for each of the activities of design, coding and testing. When you do that, the values would be: Onsite design = 80 + 50 = 130; Onsite coding = 100 + 205 = 305; Onsite testing = 160 + 140 = 300.* ***Note:*** *We only estimate the fresh values of the onsite activities because the question is pointedly asking us about onsite activities only.)*
    (a) The amount of coding done onsite, is greater than that of testing. *(Can be seen to be just about correct. However, since you have only visual estimates of the individual values of the charts, you would need to be careful before you mark this as the correct answer. Move on to check the other options and ensure that they get rejected.)*
    (b) The amount of coding done onsite is less than that of design done onsite. *(Rejected)*
    (c) The amount of design carried out onsite is greater than that of testing. *(Rejected)*
    (d) The amount of testing carried out offshore is greater than that of total design. *(Rejected)*
    Hence option (a) would be correct.
17. Roughly what percentage of total work is carried on site? *(For this question, you would need to overlook the changes you made to the chart by shifting half the offshore to onsite for the previous question. You would just need to look at the amount of onsite activities total as a percentage of the total work as given in the first bar chart. Total offshore = 100 + 410 + 280 = 790; Total onsite = 90 + 100 + 160 = 350. Percentage of work done onsite = 350/1140 ≈ 30 per cent. Option (c) is correct.)*
    (a) 40 (b) 20
    (c) 30 (d) 50

18 The total effort in hours onsite is the nearest to which of the following? *(From our calculations for the previous question, we know that the total effort in hours onsite = 350. We have to check which of the given options works out the closest to 350 man-hours.)*
   (a) Sum of estimated and actual effort for offshore design *(100 + 90, not close enough to 350)*
   (b) The estimated man-hours of offshore coding *(around 400; better but we will need to see)*
   (c) The actual man-hours of offshore testing *(280)*
   (d) Half the no. of estimated man-hours of offshore coding *(205)*
   Looking at these values, we can clearly see that the closest to 350 is option (b).

19. If the total working hours were 100 which of the following tasks will account for approx. 50 hours? *(We need to see which of the given options accounts for half the total hours. The total hours we have already calculated as 790 + 350= 1140 in a previous question. We need to see which of the given options comes the closest to half of 1140, i.e., 570.)*
   (a) Coding *(510)*
   (b) Design *(190)*
   (c) Offshore testing *(280)*
   (d) Offshore testing plus design *(380)*
   (Option (a)is correct.)

20. If 50 per cent of the offshore work is to be carried out onsite, with the distribution of effort between the tasks remaining the same, the percentage of testing carried out offshore would be *(Total testing = 280 + 160 = 440; After half the offshore testing is shifted onsite, we get offshore testing as 140 out of 440. This is the closest to 30%. Option 2 is correct.)*
   (a) 40% (b) 30%
   (c) 50% (d) 70%

21. Which of the work requires as many man-hours as that spent in coding? *(Total hours spent in coding = 410 + 100 = 510. Offshore design and coding is clearly equal to the same value. Hence, option (a) is correct.)*
   (a) Offshore, design and coding
   (b) Offshore coding
   (c) Testing
   (d) Offshore testing and coding.

Directions for Questions 22 to 29: *(Set based on Ratios and Percentages)*
Answer these questions based on the following table.

The following table shows the revenue and expenses in millions of Euros (European currency) associated. REPSOL YPF company's oil and gas activities in operations in different parts of the world for the year 1998–2000.

REPSOL YPF'S Operations of Oil and Gas Producing Activities

	Year	Total World	Spain	North Africa and Middle East	Argentina	Rest of Latin America	Far East	North Sea	Rest of the World
Revenues	1998	916	70	366	281	34	82	78	5
	1999	3374	55	666	2006	115	301	140	91
	2000	8328	394	1290	5539	482	603	0	20
Operating Costs	1998	668	39	255	187	57	63	52	15
	1999	1999	48	325	1168	131	204	65	58
	2000	3709	43	530	2540	252	311	0	33
Income before Taxes and Charges	1998	248	31	111	94	–23	19	26	–10
	1999	1375	7	341	838	–16	97	75	33
	2000	4619	351	760	2999	230	292	0	–13
Taxes and Charges	1998	152	6	104	33	–3	9	6	–3
	1999	561	3	169	338	–6	39	21	–3
	2000	1845	126	404	1150	61	103	0	1
Income after Taxes and Charges	1998	96	25	7	61	–20	10	20	–7
	1999	814	4	172	500	–10	58	54	36
	2000	2774	225	356	1849	–169	189	0	–14

(Since there is no introductory text in this question, it is best to move straight to the table and understand the numbers given in the table. ***Note:*** *In data heavy question sets, it is advisable to spend a bit of time – as much as required – to understand the data given in the table.)*

Note on interpretation of the table: *First get a grip of what the rows are telling you, then look through the column headings anchoring your eyes and mind onto individual values in the table in order to understand the information given in the table. For instance, looking down the third column gives us a complete grip of the information in the table. 916 is the total revenues of the company in 1998. Looking further down we can make out that 668 is the operating cost and the subtraction of 916 – 668 = 248 is the value of the income before taxes and charges. Further, from 248 if you subtract taxes and charges (152) – you are left with 96 which is the value for income before taxes and charges in 1998. The other relationship you should be able to identify during the reading of the table is the fact that the total world revenue equals the sum of the revenues of the seven operations of the company.*

Based on the table above, answer the following questions:

22. How many operations (Spain, North Africa and Middle East...) of the company accounted for less than 5% of the total revenue earned in the year 1999? *(The first thing you should do to solve this is to calculate an approximate value of 5% of 3374 ≈ 167–168. Naturally, we need to look for operations with revenues less than 167–168. Spain, Rest of Latin America, North Sea and Rest of the world are the four operations that satisfy this criterion.)*
    (a) 2 (b) 3
    (c) 4 (d) None of these
23. How many operations (Spain, North Africa and Middle East...) of the company witnessed more than 200% revenue growth from the year 1999 to 2000? *(200% revenue growth means trebling of revenues. Looking at the relevant part of the table as shown below, we see that trebling of revenues is occurring in Spain and Rest of Latin America from 1999 to 2000. Hence, option (b) is correct.)*

Year	1999	2000
Total World	3374	8328
Spain	55	394
North Africa and Middle East	666	1290
Argentina	2006	5539
Rest of Latin America	115	482
Far East	301	603
North Sea	140	0
Rest of the World	91	20

(a) 1 (b) 2
(c) 3 (d) None of these

24. How many operations registered a sustained yearly increase in income before taxes and charges from 1998 to 2000? *(The relevant part of the table to look at for this would be:*

	Income before taxes and charges		
Year	1998	1999	2000
Total World	248	1375	4619
Spain	31	7	351
North Africa and Middle East	111	341	760
Argentina	94	838	2999
Rest of Latin America	–23	–16	230
Far East	19	97	292
North Sea	26	75	0
Rest of the World	–10	33	–13

Sustained yearly increase from 1998 to 2000 is seen to occur in North Africa and Middle East, Argentina, Rest of Latin America and Far East. Option (b) is correct.)
    (a) 3 (b) 4
    (c) 5 (d) None of these
25. Ignoring the loss making operations of the company in 1998 *(We will need to ignore Rest of Latin America and Rest of the world for the purpose of this question)*, for how many operations was the percentage increase in net income before taxes and charges higher than the average from 1998 to 1999? *(First create a benchmark value for the average percentage increase in net income before tax and charges from 1998 to 1999 – The total world's percentage increase can be estimated in the form of the multiplier that has been applied on the 1998 value to get the 1999 value. When 248 has grown to 1375, the multiplier is approximately 5.5. In order to find the answer to this question, we need to look at the profit making operations for 1998 and see*

how many of those had a multiplier greater than 5.5. Only two operations come into the picture – with Argentina being comfortably higher than 5.5 (838/94 – clearly above 7); while Far East at 97/19 would be comfortably below 5.5. Thus there is only one operation that satisfies this requirement. Option (b) is correct.)

(a) 0 (b) 1
(c) 2 (d) None of these

26. If profitability is defined as the ratio of net income after taxes and charges to expenses, which of the following statements is true?
   (a) The Far East operations witnessed its highest profitability in 1998.
   (b) The North Sea operations increased its profitability from 1998 to 1999.
   (c) The operations in Argentina witnessed a decrease in profitability from 1998 to 1999.
   (d) Both (b) and (c) are true.

The relevant aspects of the table to look at, is given below. This question moves into the domain of ratio comparisons. Testing the statement given in option 'a', we get that we need to compare the value of 10/63 – i.e., the profitability for 1998 and see whether it is the highest amongst the three years for the Far East. In 1999 itself, the profitability for this operation goes up to 58/204 and hence we can reject this option at this point itself. Testing the second option, we need to see whether the North Sea operations have indeed increased their profitability from 1998 to 1999? We observe from the table that the profitability ratio has gone up from 20/52 to 54/65, which is a definite increase. Thus, the statement of this option is correct. However, we cannot mark this as the answer since the 4th option talks about both (b) and (c) being true. Testing option (c), we see that the operations in Argentina went from a profitability ratio of 61/187 to 500/1168 – i.e., from below 1/3 to above 1/3. This is not a decrease and hence this option is not true. Thus, we reject options (c) and (d) and choose option (b) as the correct answer.

27. In the year 2000, which amongst the following countries had the best profitability? *[The ratios to compare would be 356/530 (is <1 for North Africa and Middle East), 225/43 (is >5 for Spain), we can ignore Rest of Latin America and realise that Far East is again below 1 and hence does not challenge for the highest profitability. Option (b) is correct.]*
   (a) North Africa and Middle East
   (b) Spain
   (c) Rest of Latin America
   (d) Far East

	Year	Total World	Spain	North Africa and Middle East	Argentina	Rest of Latin America	Far East	North Sea	Rest of the World
Operating Costs	1998	668	39	255	187	57	63	52	15
	1999	1999	48	325	1168	131	204	65	58
	2000	3709	43	530	2540	252	311	0	33
Income after Taxes and Charges	1998	96	25	7	61	–20	10	20	–7
	1999	814	4	172	500	–10	58	54	36
	2000	2774	225	356	1849	–169	189	0	–14

28. If efficiency is defined as the ratio of revenue to expenses, which operation was the least efficient in the year 2000?
   (a) Spain (b) Argentina
   (c) Far East (d) None of these

The effective part of the table we need to look at for this question is given here. Since there is a 'None of these' option, it might be better not to look for individual values of the options in the table. Just move to the table and create your own calculations for trying to find out the least efficient operation.

	Year	Total World	Spain	North Africa and Middle East	Argentina	Rest of Latin America	Far East	North Sea	Rest of the World
Revenues	2000	8328	394	1290	5539	482	603	0	20
Operating Costs	2000	3709	43	530	2540	252	311	0	33

As you move into the table to check for the least efficient operation you start from left to right. Spain starts off at 394/43 >9, Middle East and Argentina at 1290/530 and 5539/2540 respectively are both >2, Rest of Latin America and Far East both are >1, while Rest of the World is <1 and hence is the least profitability. Option (d) is correct.

29. Of the following statements which one is not true?
    (a) The operations in Spain had the best efficiency in 2000.
    (b) The Far East operations witnessed an efficiency improvement from 1999 to 2000.
    (c) The North Sea operations witnessed an efficiency improvement from 1998 to 1999.
    (d) In the year 1998, the operations in Rest of Latin America were the least efficient.

Looking at the options again, we realise that this question is also about efficiency. So we would need to look at only the relevant parts of the table viz. Revenues and Operating Costs

The relevant part of the table you need to look at for this question is given here:

Statement 1, operations in Spain have the best efficiency in 2000, is clearly true. Remember, we are looking for what is not true. For Far East, efficiency in 1999 was 301/204, while in 2000 it was 603/311. While the first ratio is lower than 1.5, the second one is clearly quite close to 2, hence definitely above 1.5. Thus, there is indeed an efficiency improvement from 1999 to 2000 for the Far East. Testing statement in option (c), we see that the efficiency of the North Sea operation has gone from 78/52 to 140/65, which is clearly an improvement. This is also clearly true. Only option (d) is left as a feasible answer and hence must be the correct answer, in that the statement must be false. A quick check (though unnecessary here) reveals that the Rest of the World's efficiency in 1998 is much lower than for the Rest of Latin America. Hence, option (d) is not true and hence the correct answer.

	Year	Total World	Spain	North Africa and Middle East	Argentina	Rest of Latin America	Far East	North Sea	Rest of the World
Revenues	1998	916	70	366	281	34	82	78	5
	1999	3374	55	666	2006	115	301	140	91
	2000	8328	394	1290	5539	482	603	0	20
Operating Costs	1998	668	39	255	187	57	63	52	15
	1999	1999	48	325	1168	131	204	65	58
	2000	3709	43	530	2540	252	311	0	33

Directions for Questions 30 to 33: *(Set based on Averages)*

Bankatlal works x hours a day and rests y hours a day. This pattern continues for 1 week, with an exactly opposite pattern next week, and so on for four weeks. Every fifth week he has a different pattern. When he works longer than he rests, his wage per hour is twice what he earns per hour when he rests longer than he works. The following are his daily working hours for the weeks numbered 1 to 13.

	Ist week	5th week	9th week	13th week
Rest	2	3	4	—
Work	5	7	6	8

A week consists of six days and a month consists of 4 weeks.

(The data here is pretty simple to understand, the values of x and y are changing after every 4 weeks. Hence, there is nothing to be done in this case)

30. If Bankatlal is paid ₹20 per working hour in the 1st week, what is his salary for the 1st month?
    (a) ₹1760 (b) ₹1440
    (c) ₹1320 (d) ₹1680

The first thing you should do in this situation is to make a table for the number of hours he has worked and rested each week, with the rates per hour mentioned along with. A suitable table to create is the most important decision while solving this question. The following tabular structure might be a good one to make for the first 4 weeks in order to solve the first question:

	Week 1	Week 2	Week 3	Week 4
Rest	2 hours	5	2 hours	5
Work	5 hours	2	5 hours	2
Total Work Hours	$5 \times 6 = 30$	$2 \times 6 = 12$	$5 \times 6 = 30$	$2 \times 6 = 12$
Wage Rate Per Hour	₹ 20	₹ 10	₹ 20	₹ 10
Total Wages	$30 \times 20 = 600$	$12 \times 10 = 120$	$30 \times 20 = 600$	$12 \times 10 = 120$

The total wages earned in the first month = 1440. Option (b) is correct.

31. Referring to the data given in Q.30, Bankatlal's average monthly salary at the end of the first four months will be
(a) ₹1780 (b) ₹2040
(c) ₹1830 (d) ₹1680

In the first month he has earned ₹1440. In the second month, he would earn 7 × 6 × 20 = ₹840 each in the 5th and 7th weeks, while he would earn 3 × 6 × 10 = ₹180 each in weeks 6 and 8. His total income in the second month would be 2040. In the third month his income would be 2 × 6 × 6 × 20 + 2 × 4 × 6 × 10 = ₹1920. In the fourth month his income would be 2 × 8 × 6 × 20 = ₹1920. Thus, his average income for the four months would be given by:

$$\frac{1440 + 2040 + 1920 + 1920}{4} = 1830$$

Option (c) is correct.

32. The new manager Khushaldas stipulated that ₹5 be deducted for every hour of rest and ₹25 be paid per hour starting 9th week, then what will be the change in Bankatlal's salary for the 3rd month? (Hourly deductions are constant for all weeks starting 9th week)
(a) ₹540 (b) ₹480
(c) ₹240 (d) ₹120

Bankatlal's salary under the new scheme for the third month would be:

6 × 6 × 25 – 4 × 6 × 5 = ₹ 780 each for weeks 9 and 11. Thus a total of 1560;

4 × 6 × 25 – 6 × 6 × 5 = ₹420 per week for weeks 10 and 12. Thus, his total earning for month 3 would be 2400. This is an increase of 2400 – 1920 = ₹480 on his salary based on the earlier scheme of payment. Option (b) is correct.

33. Using the data in the previous questions, what will be the total earning of Bankatlal at the end of sixteen weeks.
(a) ₹7320 (b) ₹7800
(c) ₹8400 (d) ₹9600

His total income would be as follows:

Weeks 1 and 3: 2 × (5 × 6 × 25 – 2 × 6 × 5) = 1380

Weeks 2 and 4: 2 × (2 × 6 × 25 – 5 × 6 × 5) = 300

Weeks 5 and 7: 2 × (7 × 6 × 25 – 3 × 6 × 5) = 1920

Weeks 6 and 8: 2 × (3 × 6 × 25 – 7 × 6 × 5) = 480

Month 3, his income is ₹2400 (as calculated for the previous question).

Month 4: Weeks 13 and 15: 2 × (8 × 6 × 25 – 0) = 2400.

Weeks 14 and 16: Negative income of 2 × 8 × 6 × 5 = 480.

Total income for the 4 months = ₹8400.

Directions for Questions 34 to 36: *Answer these questions with reference to the table given below:*

INFORMATION TECHNOLOGY INDUSTRY IN INDIA (FIGURES ARE IN MILLION US DOLLARS)

	1994–95	1995–96	1996–97	1997–98	1998–99
Software Domestic	350	490	670	950	1250
Exports	485	734	1083	1750	2650
Hardware Domestic	590	1037	1050	1205	1026
Exports	177	35	286	201	4
Peripherals Domestic	148	196	181	229	329
Exports	6	6	14	19	18
Training	107	143	185	263	302
Maintenance	142	172	182	221	236
Networking and Others	36	73	156	193	237
Total	2041	2886	3807	5031	6052

34. The total annual exports lay between 35 and 40 per cent of the total annual business of the IT industry in the years
(a) 1997–98 & 1994–95
(b) 1996–97 & 1997–98
(c) 1996–97 & 1998–99
(d) 1996–97 & 1994–95

Sol. *(b) The requisite percentage range is occurring in the years 1996–97 and 1997–98. It is below 35% in the first two years, while in the last year (1998–99) it is above 40%.*

35. The highest percentage growth in the total IT business relative to the previous year was achieved in
(a) 1995–96 (b) 1996–97
(c) 1997–98 (d) 1998–99

Sol. *(a) 1995–96 exhibits a growth rate of over 40% (see this as 204 to 288 to 380 to 503 to 605). It is evident that the highest growth rate happens between 1994–95 and 1995–96.*

36. Which one of the following statements is correct?
(a) The annual software exports steadily increased but annual hardware exports steadily declined during 1994–99.

(b) The annual peripheral exports steadily increased during 1994–1999.
(c) The business in training during 1994–1999 was higher than the total IT business in maintenance during the same period.
(d) None of the above statements is true.

Sol. *(c) The statement in Option (c) is correct and can be verified by looking at the gap between the two values in every year and aggregating. Training vis-a-vis Maintenance would be – 35 – 29 + 3 + 42 + 66 a positive value.*
Option (a) is wrong as hardware exports have not shown a steady decline over the period. Option (b) is wrong as peripheral exports cannot be said to have steadily increased during the period.

Directions for Questions 37 to 38: *For any activity, A, year X dominates year Y if IT business in activity A, in the year X, is greater than the IT business, in activity A, in the year Y. For any two IT business activities, A & B, year X dominates year Y if*
(i) the IT business in activity A, in the year X, is greater than or equal to the IT business, in activity A in the year Y,
(ii) the IT business in activity B, in the year X, is greater than or equal to the IT business in activity B in the year Y, and
(iii) there should be strict inequality in the case of at least one activity.

37. For the hardware business activity which one of the following is not true?
(a) 1997–98 dominated 1996–97
(b) 1997–98 dominated 1995–96
(c) 1997–98 dominated 1998–99
(d) None of these

Sol. *(d) Each of the first three options is seen as correct. Since we are looking for not true – the correct answer would be option (d).*
Option (a) is true because 1997–98 (1406) dominates 1996–97 (1336).
Option (b) is true because 1997–98 (1406) dominates 1995–96 (1072).
Option (c) is true because 1997–98 (1406) dominates 1998–99 (1030).

38. For the two IT business activities hardware and peripherals which one of the following is true?
(a) 1996–97 dominated 1995–96
(b) 1998–99 dominates 1995–96
(c) 1997–98 dominates 1998–99
(d) None of these

Sol. *(d) In order to solve this question, the following tabular format might prove useful:*

	Column 1	Column 2	Column 3	Column 4	Column 5
	1994–95	1995–96	1996–97	1997–98	1998–99
Hardware	767	1072	1336	1406	1030
Peripherals	154	202	195	248	347

To test option (a), compare columns 3 and 2. The inequalities are 1072 < 1336 and 202 > 195. So neither year dominates the other.
To test option (b), compare columns 5 and 2. The inequalities are 1072 > 1030 and 202 < 347. So neither year dominates the other.
To test option (c), compare columns 4 and 5. The inequalities are 1406 > 1030 and 248 < 347. So neither year dominates the other.
Thus, the correct answer is option (d), i.e., None of the given options is true.

Directions for Questions 39 to 43: *Answer these questions based on the data provided in the table below.*

Sector	Factories	Employment	Fixed Capital	Gross Output	Value Added
Public	7.0	27.7	43.2	25.8	30.8
Central Govt.	1.0	10.5	17.5	12.7	14.1
State/Local Govt.	5.2	16.2	24.3	11.6	14.9
Central & State/Local Govt.	0.8	1.0	1.4	1.5	1.8
Joint	1.8	5.1	6.8	8.4	8.1
Wholly Private	90.3	64.6	46.8	63.8	58.7
Others	0.9	2.6	3.2	2.0	2.4
	100	100	100	100	100

39. Suppose the average employment level is 60 per factory. The average employment in wholly private factories is approximately:
(a) 43 (b) 47
(c) 50 (d) 54

Sol. *(a) The average employment per factory is Total employment/Total factories = x/y (say). This implies that, the average employment per factory in wholly private factories would be 0.646x/0.903y = approximately 0.7 times x/y. The closest answer is 43.* ***Note:*** *x/y = 60 is given to us.*

40. Amongst the firms in different sectors value added per employee is the highest in
    (a) Central Government
    (b) Central and State/Local Governments
    (c) Joint sector
    (d) Wholly private

Sol. *(b) The required ratio is the highest for Central and State/Local Government (1.8/1).*

41. Capital productivity is defined as the gross output value per rupee of fixed capital. The three sectors with the higher capital productivity arranged in descending order are:
    (a) Joint, Wholly private, Central and State/Local
    (b) Wholly private, Joint, Central and State/Local
    (c) Wholly private, Central and State/Local, Joint
    (d) Joint, Wholly private, Central

Sol. *(b) We have to compare the ratios for Wholly private (63.8/46.8), joint (8.4/6.8) and Central and State Local (1.5/1.4). In this context, 63.8/46.8 > 8.4/6.8 > 1.5/1.4.*

42. A sector is considered "pareto efficient" if its value added per employee and its value added per rupee of fixed capital is higher than those of all other sectors. Based on the table data the pareto efficient sector is
    (a) Wholly private
    (b) Joint
    (c) Central and state/local
    (d) Others

Sol. *(c) Since we already know that the sector with the highest value added per employee is the Central and State/Local Government (from answering question 141), and we are in a situation where there are close ended options, i.e., one of the 4 options has to be the correct answer, it follows that none of the options (a), (b) or (d) can be the pareto-efficient sector. Thus, we can choose option (c) as the answer to this question on the basis of this logic without calculating anything.*

43. The total value added in all sectors is estimated at ₹140,000 crore. Suppose that the number of firms in the joint sector is 2700. The average value added per factory in ₹ crore in the Central Government is
    (a) 141 (b) 14.1
    (c) 131 (d) 13.1

Sol. *(d) The number of factories in the Joint sector = 1.8% of the total number of factories = 2700. There must be 1,50,000 factories. This means that the number of factories in the Central Government is 1500 and the value added in Central Government factories is 14.1% of the total value added = 0.141 × 140000 crore = 19740. Thus, value added per factory in this sector would be 19740/1500 = 13.1*

Directions for Questions 44 to 49: Answer these questions based on the tables given below.

There are six refineries, seven depots and nine districts. The refineries are BB, BC, BD, BE, BF and BG. The depots are AA, AB, AC, AD, AE, AF and AG. The districts are AAA, AAB, AAC, AAD, AAE, AAF, AAG, AAH, and AAI. Table A gives the cost of transporting one unit from refinery to depot. Table B gives the cost of transporting one unit from depot to a district.

TABLE A

	BB	BC	BD	BE	BF	BG
AA	928.2	537.2	567.8	589.9	589.9	800.1
AB	311.1	596.7	885.7	759.9	759.9	793.9
AC	451.1	0	320.1	780.1	720.7	1000.1
AD	371.1	150.1	350.1	750.1	650.4	980.1
AE	1137.3	314.5	0	1157.7	1157.7	1023.4
AF	617.1	516.8	756.5	1065.9	1065.9	406.3
AG	644.3	299.2	537.2	1093.1	1093.1	623.9

TABLE B

	AA	AB	AC	AD	AE	AF	AG
AAA	562.7	843.2	314.5	889.1	0	754.8	537.2
AAB	532.7	803.2	284.5	790.5	95.2	659.6	442
AAC	500.7	780.2	0	457.3	205.7	549.1	331.5
AAD	232.9	362.1	286.2	275.4	523.6	525.3	673.2
AAE	345.1	268.6	316.2	163.2	555.9	413.1	227.8
AAF	450.1	644.3	346.2	372.3	933.3	402.9	379.1
AAG	654.5	0	596.7	222.7	885.7	387.6	348.5
AAH	804.1	149.6	627.2	360.4	1035.3	537.2	498.1
AAI	646	255	433.5	137.7	698.7	112.2	161.5

44. What is the least cost of sending one unit from any refinery to any district?
    (a) 95.2 (b) 0
    (c) 205.7 (d) 284.5

Sol. *(b) BC-AC-AAC would cost 0. Hence, option (b) is the correct answer.*

45. What is the least cost of sending one unit from any refinery to district AAB?
    (a) 0 (b) 284.5
    (c) 95.2 (d) None of these

Sol. (c) *Looking first at the AAB row of the second table, it is clear that the least cost is 95.2 (through AE). Next looking at the AE row in the first column, it is clear that BD-AE is no cost. Hence, the least cost would be given by 95.2 + 0 = 95.2.*

46. What is the least cost of sending one unit from refinery BB to any district?
(a) 284.5 (b) 311.1
(c) 451.1 (d) None of these

Sol. (b) *The least cost from BB to any depot is 311.1 and this is supplemented by AB to AAG which costs 0. Hence, the required answer is 311.1.*

47. What is the least cost of sending one unit from refinery BB to district AAA?
(a) 765.6 (b) 1137.3
(c) 1154.3 (d) None of these

Sol. (a) *Looking at the AAA row in the second table and matching it with the BB column of the first table; adding the value of the column with the corresponding value of the row we would get BB-AC-AAA with the total cost of 765.6.*

48. How many possible ways are there for sending one unit from any refinery to any district?
(a) 63 (b) 42
(c) 54 (d) 378

Sol. (d) *There are 6 refineries, 7 depots and 9 districts. Number of ways would be given by* $6 \times 7 \times 9 = 378$.

49. The highest cost of sending one unit from any refinery to any district is
(a) 2172.6
(b) 2193.0
(c) 2091.0
(d) None of these

Sol. (b) *The maximum cost is the combination of the two highest costs—BF-AE-AAH which gives us 2193.*

Directions for Questions 50 to 53: *Answer the following questions based on the information given below.*

The bar chart below shows the revenue received, in million US Dollars (USD), from subscribers to a particular internet service. The data covers the period 2003–07 for the United States (US) and Europe. The bar chart also shows the estimated revenues from subscription to this service for the period 2008–10.

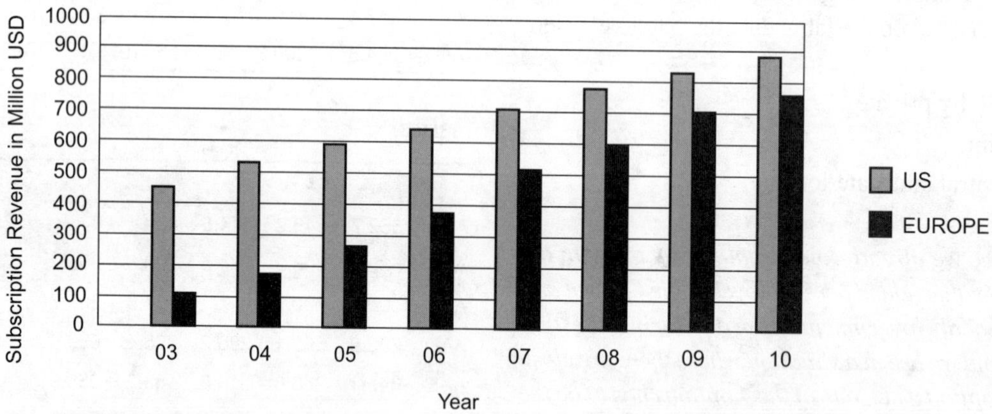

FIGURE 2.5 *Revenue Received, in Million US Dollars (USD)*

50. In 2003, 60 per cent of subscribers in Europe were men. Given that women subscribers increase at the rate of 10 per cent per annum and men at the rate of 5 per cent per annum, what is the approximate percentage growth of subscribers between 2003 and 2010 in Europe? The subscription prices are volatile and may change each year.
(a) 62 (b) 15
(c) 84 (d) 78
(e) 50

Sol. (a) *In 2003,*
60 men + 40 women

In 2008, men would go up by:

60 5%↑ 5%↑ 5%↑ 5%↑ 5%↑ 5%↑ 5%↑

An increase of approximately 24.

*(**Note:** For a detailed description of how to handle this calculation quickly, please go through compound interest in my book 'QA for CAT'.)*

Also, 40 women would become

40 10%↑ 10%↑ 10%↑ 10%↑ 10%↑ 10%↑ 10%↑

An increase of approximately 38.

Thus, the net percentage increase would be 62 per cent approximately (option (a).

51. Consider the annual per cent change in the gap between subscription revenues in the US and Europe. What is the year in which the absolute value of this change is the highest?
    (a) 2003–04
    (b) 2005–06
    (c) 2006–07
    (d) 2008–09
    (e) 2009–10

Sol. *(d) Visually this can be seen for 2008–09 (option (d).*

52. While the subscription in Europe has been growing steadily towards that of the US, the growth rate in Europe seems to be declining. Which of the following is the closest to the per cent change in growth rate of 2007 (over 2006) relative to the growth rate of 2005 (over 2004)?
    (a) 17 (b) 20
    (c) 35 (d) 60
    (e) 100

Sol. *(c) Growth rate in 2007 → 380 to 500 gives (120/500) × 100 = 31% approx*
Growth rate in 2005 → 180 to 270 gives (90/180) × 100 = 50%
Percentage change from 50 to 31 = (19/50) × 100 = 35% approx.
The closest value of the percentage change is 35% (option (c)).

53. The difference between the estimated subscription in Europe in 2008, and what it would have been if it were computed using the percentage growth rate of 2007 (over 2006), is the closest to:
    (a) 50 (b) 80
    (c) 20 (d) 10
    (e) 0

Sol. *(a) The growth rate in 2007 (as seen for the previous question) is around 31%.*
With this growth rate, the value of European subscription would be approximately 650.
The actual prediction for 2008 is 600.
Thus, the closest option would be 50 (option (a)).

PART

3

MOCK TEST PAPERS (BASED ON THE LATEST CAT PATTERN)

IN THIS PART YOU WILL LEARN:

- To solve simulated DI tests under time pressure and get an actual feel of the examination.
- To tackle CAT like simulated tests of the DI part of the QA and DI section.
    - To further improve the depth of your understanding and interpretation of data
    - To further improve your anticipation of questions when you see a data set
    - To improve the depth and breadth of your exposure to DI questions as well as your DI problem-solving skills
    - To improve your accuracy while solving DI questions
    - To further improve your speed of solving and understanding of DI questions

THIS PART CONTAINS:

- Mock Test Papers containing good quality examination-level questions that cover the breadth and depth of questions that could be asked in Traditional Data Interpretation.
- Total 26 Mock test Papers based of different difficulty levels to help you solve with more accuracy and speed:

Level of Difficulty (LOD) 1

- MTP 1
- MTP 2
- MTP 3
- MTP 4
- MTP 5
- MTP 6
- MTP 7

Level of Difficulty (LOD) 2

- MTP 8
- MTP 9
- MTP 10
- MTP 11
- MTP 12
- MTP 13
- MTP 14
- MTP 15
- MTP 16
- MTP 17
- MTP 18
- MTP 19
- MTP 20
- MTP 21
- MTP 22
- MTP 23
- MTP 24
- MTP 25
- MTP 26

1. For each test in
LOD 1, first take the test under
a strict thirty minute time frame.
Ideally, you should be able to complete the
paper in thirty minutes.
2. For the LOD 2 tests, set a strict time limit of forty minutes.

2. AFTER YOU FINISH SOLVING A TEST:

(a) Check your errors and closely analyse the reasons for these errors. You would need to work on eliminating the error sources to become better at DI.

(b) In case there are many unsolved questions and/or questions that you have not understood, go back and solve these questions.

(c) Keep a chart of your scores as you progress through the tests in this part.
Your score would be given by:
No. of correct answer × 3 - numbers of wrong answers.

(d) Because, each test consists of 20 questions, each paper is out of 60 marks.
You would be guided by the following numbers:
Net Score: 40+ You are doing really well and just need to make sure that you execute the same in the actual exams;
Net Score: 30–40 → There is room for improvement.
Work on improving your understanding, your analysis and your speed and accuracy while solving DI.
Net Score: Below 30: Clearly DI is not proving to be your strength.
Focus on learning what errors you are making while solving. Think about how you can improve your speed and accuracy while solving. Focus on improving your understanding of data and try to push yourself first in the 30–40 category and finally in the 40+ category.

1 Mock Test Paper

Directions for Questions 1 to 5: *Ghosh Babu surveyed his companies and obtained the following data (Table 1.1). Income tax is paid on profit before tax and the remaining amount is apportioned to dividend and retained earnings. The retained earnings were accumulated into reserves. The reserves at the beginning of 2001 were ₹80 lakh.*

TABLE 1.1 Select Data Pertaining to Ghosh Babu's Firms

(in Lakhs)

Figure	2004	2003	2002	2001
Sales	6730	5130	2810	3370
Profit before Tax	840	730	230	330
Dividends	150	80	40	40
Retained Earnings	450	320	80	155

1. In which year was the tax per rupee of profit before tax highest?
   (a) 2001 (b) 2002
   (c) 2003 (d) 2004
2. In which year was the sales per rupee of share capital least?
   (a) 2001 (b) 2002
   (c) 2003 (d) Cannot be determined
3. In which year the profit before tax per rupee of sales was the least?
   (a) 2001 (b) 2002
   (c) 2003 (d) 2004
4. In which year was the percentage addition to reserves over previous year reserves the highest?
   (a) 2001 (b) 2002
   (c) 2003 (d) 2004
5. Amount of the reserves at the end of 2004 is:
   (a) ₹885 lakh (b) ₹1085 lakh
   (c) ₹1125 lakh (d) None of these

Directions for Questions 6 to 10: *Study Figures 1.1(A) and 1.1(B) and answer the questions following that.*

Operating Profit ₹ 320 lakh in 2002–03

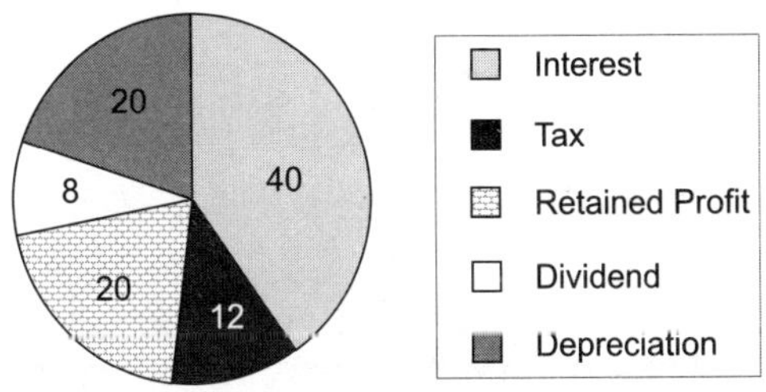

FIGURE 1.1 (A) *Data Pertaining to a Select Industrial Firm*

Operating profit 2001–02 (₹ 260 lakh)

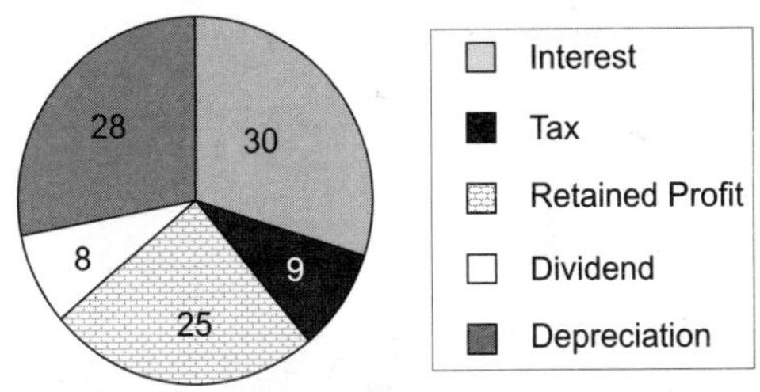

FIGURE 1.1 (B) *Data Pertaining to a Select Industrial Firm*

6. The interest in 2002–03 increased over that in 2001–02 by:
   (a) 68% (b) 58%
   (c) 44% (d) 64%
7. The interest burden in 2002–03 was higher than that in 2001–02 by:
   (a) ₹50 lakh (b) ₹25 lakh
   (c) ₹80 lakh (d) None of these
8. If on an average, 10 per cent rate of interest was charged on borrowed funds, then the total borrowed funds used by this company in the given two years amounted to:
   (a) ₹1220 lakh (b) ₹2060 lakh
   (c) ₹880 lakh (d) none of these
9. The dividend in 2002–03, as compared to that in 2001–02 was:
   (a) Higher by 23% (b) Higher by 12 lakh
   (c) Higher by 32% (d) None of these

10. The equity base of these companies remained unchanged. Then the total dividend earning by the share-holders in 2001–02 is:
(a) ₹104 lakh (b) ₹10.4 lakh
(c) ₹20.8 lakh (d) None of these

Directions for Questions 11 to 13: Figure 1.2 shows the distribution of twelve million tonnes of crude oil transported through different modes over a specific period of time. Figure 1.3 shows the distribution of the cost of transporting this crude oil. The total cost was ₹ 30 million.

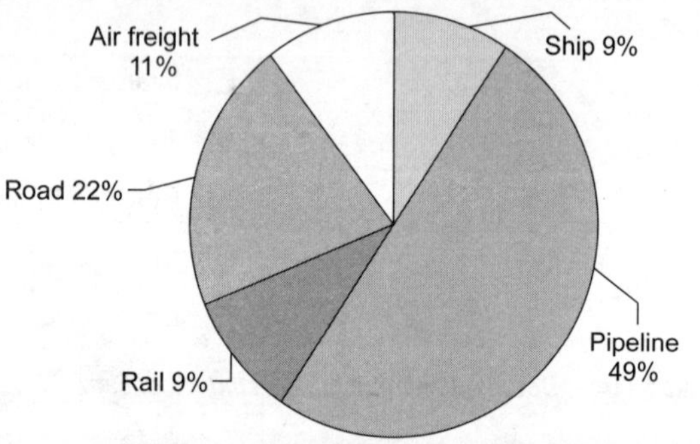

FIGURE 1.2 *Volume of Crude Oil Transported Over a Specific Period*

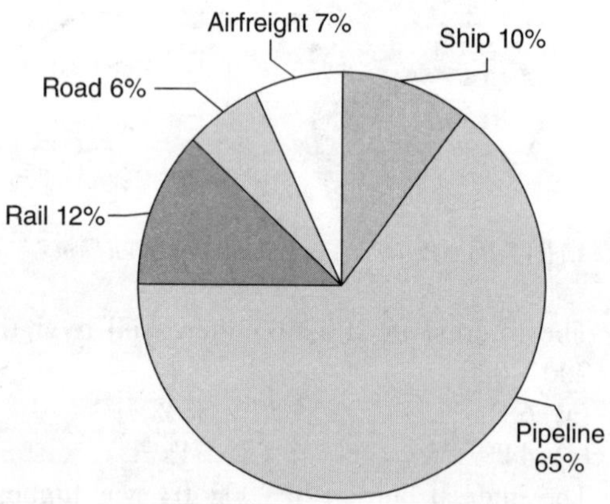

FIGURE 1.3 *Distribution of Cost of Transported Crude Oil*

11. The cost in rupees per tonne of oil moved by air-freight and ship happens to be roughly:
(a) 3 (b) 2.125
(c) 2.23 (d) Cannot be determined

12. From the charts given, it appears that the costliest mode of transport is:
(a) road (b) rail
(c) pipeline (d) ship

13. If the costs per tonne of transport by pipeline, air and rail are represented by P, Q and R respectively, which of the following is true?
(a) R > Q > P (b) P > R > Q
(c) P > Q > R (d) R > P > Q

Directions for Questions 14 to 16: The following table (Table 1.2) gives the data about the models of shoes produced in various factories of the Nike Shoe Company.

TABLE 1.2 Models of Shoes

Model-1	Men	F1, F2, F3, F4, F5
	Women	F6, F7, F8
	Children	F9, F10, F11
Model-2	Men	F5, F8, F12
	Women	F9, F13
	Children	F6
Model-3	Men	F2, F6, F7, F13
	Women	F3, F9, F11
	Children	F1, F4
Model-4	Men	F3, F10, F11
	Women	F1, F2, F4
	Children	F9, F5

Note: F1 to F13 represent 13 factories of the Nike Shoe Company which produce shoes.

14. How many factories produce model-1 or model-2 for women and model-3 for children?
(a) 0 (b) 1
(c) 2 (d) 3

15. Which of the following is true?
(a) All women's model-2 producing factories also produce men's model-3 shoes.
(b) All men's model-1 producing factories also produce women's and children's model-4 shoes.
(c) There are exactly four model-3 producing factories, which also produce model-4 but not model-2.
(d) Some model-3 producing factories produce model-1, but not men's model-2.

16. How many factories producing children's model-1 shoes either produce men's model-4 shoes or women's model-3 shoes?
(a) 1 (b) 2
(c) 3 (d) 0

Directions for Questions 17 to 20: Ghosh Babu has a manufacturing unit. The following graph (Figure 1.4) gives the cost for various numbers of units. Given that profit = revenue – variable cost. The fixed cost remains constant up to 349 units after which additional investment is to be done on fixed assets. In any case, production cannot exceed 500 units.

Note: The fixed cost was ₹600 for upto 349 units and it changed to ₹ 1000 for values above and equal to 350.

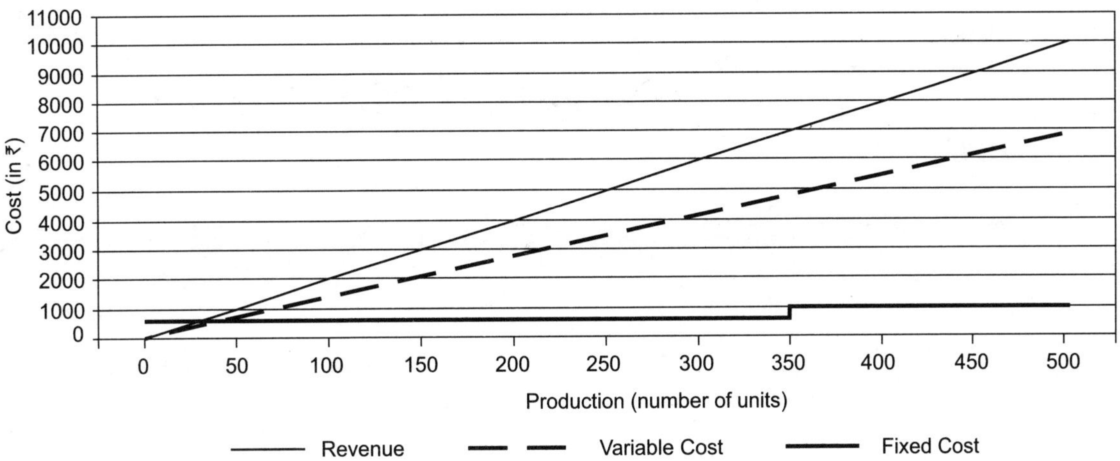

FIGURE 1.4 *Individual Cost of Various Units in a Manufacturing Firm*

17. What is the minimum number of units that need to be produced to make sure that there was no loss?
    (a) 50
    (b) 100
    (c) 250
    (d) Cannot be determined
18. How many units should be manufactured such that profit was at least ₹600?
    (a) 200 (b) 340
    (c) 450 (d) 300
19. If at the most 400 units can be manufactured, then what is the number of units that can maximise profit per unit?
    (a) 400 (b) 349
    (c) 350 (d) 250
20. If the production cannot exceed 450 units, then what is the number of units that can maximise profit per unit?
    (a) 400 (b) 349
    (c) 450 (d) 350

2 Mock Test Paper

Directions for Questions 1 to 5: *Study table (Table 2.1) below and answer the questions that follow:*

TABLE 2.1 Market Share of Mosquito Repellent in Four Metropolitan Cities

Period/ Product	Mumbai 2003–04	Kolkata 2003–04	Delhi 2003–04	Chennai 2003–04
Baygon	20–15	35–30	20–15	20–30
Finit	20–25	30–15	15–10	20–20
Hit	45–40	25–35	35–35	10–10
Mortein	15–20	10–20	10–10	50–40

1. The maximum percentage increase in market share is:
   (a) 60% (b) 50%
   (c) 80% (d) 100%
2. The city in which minimum number of products decreased their market shares in 2003–04 is:
   (a) Mumbai (a) Delhi
   (c) Kolkata (d) Chennai
3. The market shares of which product did not increase in any city between the years 2003 and 2004?
   (a) Baygon (b) Finit
   (c) Hit (d) None of these
4. The number of cities where the four brands taken together did not account for 100 % market share for any of the two given years is:
   (a) 0 (b) 1
   (c) 2 (d) 3
5. The number of products which had constant market shares in one or more cities is:
   (a) 0 (b) 1
   (c) 2 (d) 3

Directions for Questions 6 to 8: Study the following table (Table 2.2) and answer the questions that follow:

TABLE 2.2 Information Technology Industry in India

(Figures are in million US dollars)

		1994–95	1995–96	1996–97	1997–98	1998–99
Software	Domestic	350	490	670	950	1250
	Exports	485	734	1083	1750	2650
Hardware	Domestic	590	1037	1050	1205	1026
	Exports	177	35	286	201	4
Peripherals	Domestic	148	196	181	229	329
	Exports	6	6	14	19	18
Training		107	143	185	263	302
Maintenance		142	172	182	221	236
Networking and Others		36	73	156	193	237
Total		2041	2886	3807	5031	6052

6. The total annual exports lay between 30 and 40 per cent to the total annual business of the IT industry. In the years:
   (a) 1994–95 and 1997–98
   (b) 1994–95, 1996–97 and 1997–98
   (c) 1996–97 and 1998–99
   (d) None of these
7. The lowest percentage growth in the total IT business, relative to the previous year was achieved in:
   (a) 1995–96 (b) 1996–97
   (c) 1997–98 (d) 1998–99
8. Which one of the following statements is correct?
   (a) The annual software exports and the annual hardware exports steadily increased during 1994–99.

(b) The annual peripheral domestic business steadily increased during 1994–99.
(c) The IT business in maintenance during 1994–99 was higher than the total IT business in training during the same period.
(d) None of the above.

Directions for Questions 9 and 10: For any activity A, year X dominates year Y if the IT business in activity A, in the year X, is greater than the IT business, in activity A, in the year Y. For any two IT business activities, A and B, year X dominates year Y if:

I. the IT business in activity A, in the year X, is greater than or equal to the IT business, in activity A in the year Y,
II. the IT business in activity B, in the year X, is greater than or equal to the IT business in activity B in the year Y and
III. there should be strict inequality in the case of at least one activity.

9. For the IT software business activity, which one of the following is not true?
(a) 1997–98 dominates 1996–97
(b) 1997–98 dominates 1995–96
(c) 1995–96 dominates 1998–99
(d) 1998–99 dominates 1996–97
10. For the two IT business activities, software and peripherals, which one of the following is true?
(a) 1996–97 dominates 1995–96
(b) 1998–99 dominates 1995–96
(c) 1997–98 dominates 1998–99
(d) None of these

Directions for Questions 11 and 12: The pie charts [Figure 2.1(A) and (B)] give the data about a motorcycle manufacturing unit producing five different models of motorcycles. The total sales value is ₹3860 crore and the total number of units sold is 0.1023 crore.

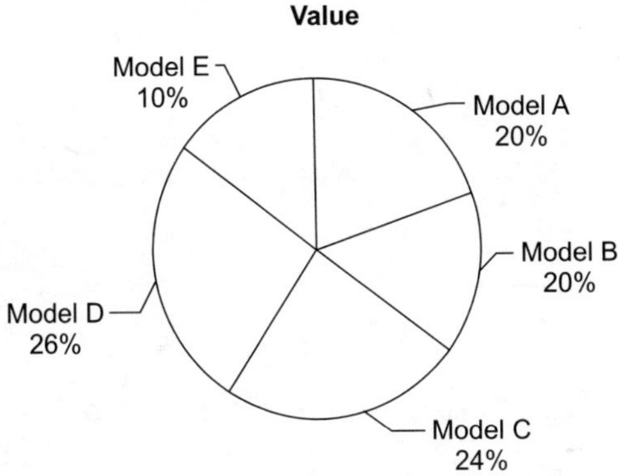

FIGURE 2.1 (A) *Value*

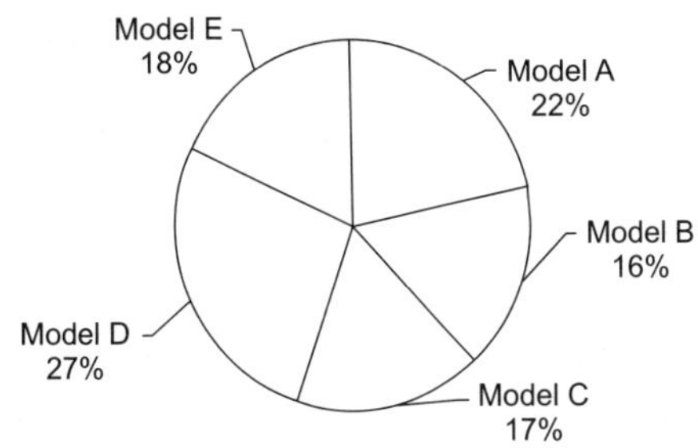

FIGURE 2.1 (B) *Quantity*

11. Which of the models of motorcycles sold by the company is sold at the highest price?
(a) Model C (b) Model A
(c) Model B (d) Model D
12. What is the price in thousands of ₹ for Model C?
(a) 53.2 (b) 37.4
(c) 45.5 (d) None of these

Directions for Questions 13 to 16: Refer the following table (Table 2.3) and answer the questions that follow.

TABLE 2.3 Market Share in Metros

	Mumbai		Kolkata		Delhi		Chennai	
Year	1993	1994	1993	1994	1993	1994	1993	1994
Product								
HD	15	20	30	35	20	15	20	30
CO	25	20	40	45	15	10	20	15
BN	40	45	5	10	30	35	10	10
MT	20	15	25	10	5	10	50	45

13. Which product's market share did not deteriorate between 1993 and 1994 in any city?
(a) HD (b) CO
(c) BN (d) None of the products
14. The number of products which doubled their market share in one or more cities between 1993 and 1994 was:
(a) None (b) 1
(c) 2 (d) 3
15. The largest percentage drop in market share between 1993 and 1994 was:
(a) 60 (b) 33.3
(c) 50 (d) 20
16. The city where the number of products losing market share between 1993 and 1994 was minimum was:
(a) Mumbai (b) Kolkata
(c) Delhi (d) Both (a) and (b)

Directions for Questions 17 to 20: Consider Table 2.4 and answer the questions given below that.

TABLE 2.4 Top Ten Law Firms

(By Number of Lawyers)

Name/Country	1995			Today		
	Tot. No. of Lawyers	No. of Lawyers Abroad	No. of Offices	Tot. No. of Lawyers	No. of Lawyers Abroad	No. of Offices
Clifford Chance/UK	1382	432	23	3543	2208	29
Baker & McKenzie/US	1742	1,319	49	3019	2442	61
Fresh Fields/UK	780	215	16	2014	1168	30
Allen & Overy/UK	640	115	15	1734	838	26
Linklaters/UK	640	136	10	1600	1300	24
SkaddenArps/US	1035	80	11	1565	156	11
Jones Day/US	1100	59	19	1550	325	26
White & Case/US	664	239	27	1423	879	38
Eversheds/UK	715*	403	13	1310	219	20
Lovells/UK	446	81	10	1302	653	26

17. The highest growth rate in terms of the number of lawyers has been shown by:
    (a) Allen & Overy/UK
    (b) Lovells/UK
    (c) Fresh Field/UK
    (d) None of these
18. Which law firm has exhibited the highest percentage increase in terms of number of offices between the two time periods?
    (a) Baker & McKenzie
    (b) Lovells/UK
    (c) Fresh fields/UK
    (d) None of these
19. How many firms consistently had less than 50% of their lawyers abroad (on both dates).
    (a) 3 (b) 4
    (c) 5 (d) 6
20. How many firms showed a higher percentage increase in the number of offices as compared to the percentage increase in the number of offices of all firms put together?
    (a) 3 (b) 4
    (c) 5 (d) 6

3 Mock Test Paper

Directions for Questions 1 to 3: *Answer the questions on the basis of the following charts.*

Per Capita Availability of Tea (gms) Chaidesh

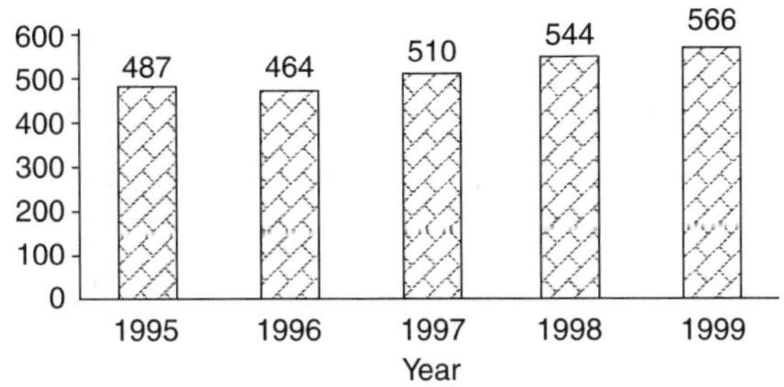

FIGURE 3.1

Note: Availability is defined as production less export.

Production and Export of Tea (Chaidesh)

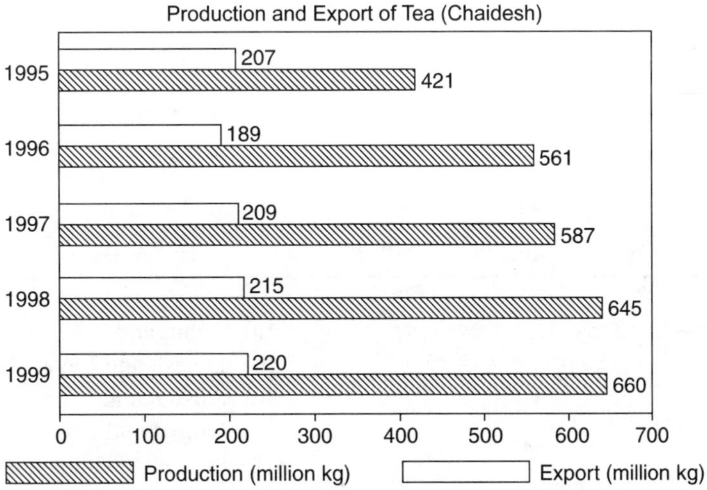

FIGURE 3.2

1. In which year during the period 1996–99 was Chaidesh's export of tea, as a proportion of tea produced, the highest?
   (a) 1996 (b) 1997
   (c) 1998 (d) 1999
2. In which of the following years was the population of Chaidesh the lowest?
   (a) 1995 (b) 1996
   (c) 1997 (d) 1999
3. The area under tea cultivation continuously decreased in all four years from 1996 to 1999, by 10%, 7%, 4% and 1%, respectively. In which year was tea productivity (production per unit of area) the highest?
   (a) 1999 (b) 1998
   (c) 1997 (d) 1996

Directions for Questions 4 to 6: *The table below reports the gender, designation and age-group of the employees in an organisation. It also provides information on their commitment to projects coming up in the months of January (Jan), February (Feb), March (Mar) and April (Apr), as well as their interest in attending workshops on: Business Opportunities (BO), Communication Skills (CS) and E-Governance (EG).*

TABLE 3.1

Sl. No.	Name	Gender	Designation	Age Group	Committed to Projects During	Interested in Workshop On
1.	Anshul	M	Mgr	Y	Jan, Mar	CS, EG
2.	Bushkant	M	Dir	I	Feb, Mar	BO, EG
3.	Charu	F	Mgr	I	Jan, Feb	BO, CS
4.	Dinesh	M	Exe	O	Jan, Apr	BO, CS, EG
5.	Eashwaran	M	Dir	O	Feb, Apr	BO
6.	Fatima	F	Mgr	Y	Jan, Mar	BO, CS
7.	Gayatri	F	Exe	Y	Feb, Mar	EG
8.	Hari	M	Mgr	I	Feb, Mar	BO, CS, EG
9.	Indira	F	Dir	O	Feb, Apr	BO, EG
10.	John	M	Oir	Y	Jan, Mar	BO
11.	Kalindi	F	Exe	I	Jan, Apr	BO, CS, EG
12.	Lavanya	F	Mgr	O	Feb, Apr	CS, EG
13.	Mandeep	M	Mgr	O	Mar, Apr	BO, EG
14.	Nandlal	M	Dir	O	Jan, Feb	BO, EG
15.	Parul	F	Exe	Y	Feb, Apr	CS, EG
16.	Rahul	M	Mgr	Y	Mar, Apr	CS, EG
17.	Sunita	F	Dir	Y	Jan, Feb	BO, EG
18.	Urvashi	F	Exe	I	Feb, Mar	EG
19.	Yamini	F	Mgr	O	Mar, Apr	CS, EG
20.	Zeena	F	Exe	Y	Jan. Mar	BO, CS, EG

M = Male, F = Female; Exe = Executive, Mgr = Manager, Dir = Director; Y= Young, I = In - between, O = Old.

For each workshop, exactly four employees are to be sent, of which at least two should be Females and at least one should be Young. No employee can be sent to a workshop in which he/she is not interested in. An employee cannot attend the workshop on

- *Communication Skills, if he/she is committed to internal projects in the month of January;*
- *Business Opportunities, if he/she is committed to internal projects in the month of February;*
- *E-governance, if he/she is committed to internal projects in the month of March.*

4. Assuming that Parul and Hari are attending the workshop on Communication Skills (CS), then which of the following employees can possibly attend the CS workshop?
   (a) Rahul and Yamini
   (b) Dinesh and Lavanya
   (c) Anshul and Yamini
   (d) Fatima and Zeena
5. How many Executives (Exe) cannot attend more than one workshop?
   (a) 2
   (b) 3
   (c) 15
   (d) 16
6. Which set of employees cannot attend any of the workshops?
   (a) Anshul, Charu, Eashwaran and Lavanya
   (b) Anshul, Bushkant, Gayatri and Urvashi
   (c) Charu, Urvashi, Bushkant and Mandeep
   (d) Anshul, Gayatri, Eashwaran and Mandeep

Directions for Questions 7 to 12: *Answer the questions based on the graph (Figure 3.3).*

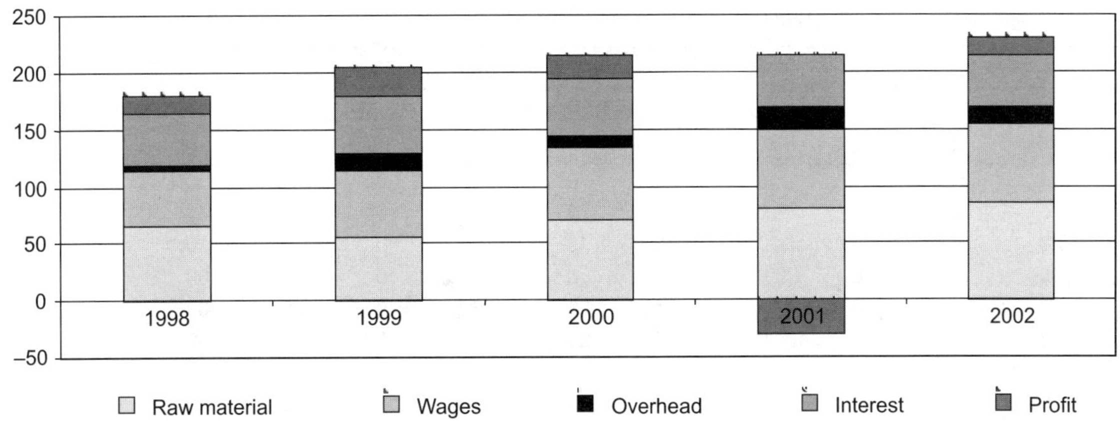

FIGURE 3.3 *Break-up of Costs of a Select Manufacturing Firm*

7. In which year was the percentage increase in the raw material maximum?
   (a) 1999
   (b) 2000
   (c) 2001
   (d) 2002
8. In which of the following time periods was the change in the level of profit the maximum?
   (a) 1998–2000
   (b) 1999–2000
   (c) 1999–2001
   (d) 2001–2002
9. Which component of the cost of production has remained more or less constant over the period?
   (a) Interest
   (b) Overheads
   (c) Wages
   (d) Raw material
10. In which year were the overheads, as a percentage of the raw material, maximum?
    (a) 2002
    (b) 2001
    (c) 1999
    (d) 2000
11. Approximately what per cent of the costs did the profits form over the period?
    (a) 3% (b) 5%
    (c) 8% (d) 11%
12. If the interest component is not included in the total cost calculation, which year would show the minimum profit per unit costs (excluding interest)?
    (a) 1998 (b) 1999
    (c) 2000 (d) 2002

Directions for Questions 13 to 16: Study Table 3.2 and answer the questions given below that.

TABLE 3.2 **Projected Food Grain Requirements—Global and US**
(Demand in billion kilogram)

	2005		2015		2025	
	World	America	World	America	World	America
Wheat	100.0	8	140	20	160	30
Rice	60.0	1	80	5	100	10
Gram	100.0	8	120	10	150	20
Corn	20.0	1	40	2	50	2.6
Pulses	20.0	2	20	3	40	4.0
Total	300.0	20	400	40	500	66.6

13. The proportion of which food grain in total food demand has decreased continuously over the period 2005 to 2025?
    (a) Rice (b) Gram
    (c) Corn (d) None of these
14. Which is the grain whose proportion in the total food demand remained constant over the period 2005–2025, but whose proportion increased in the total food demand of America?
    (a) Gram (b) Corn
    (c) Pulses (d) Rice
15. Which two grains meet more than 60% of the total food demand of the both world and America in 2005 to 2025?
    (a) Wheat and Rice (b) Wheat and Gram
    (c) Rice and Pulses (d) None of the above
16. The proportion of which grains demand increased over the period 2005 and 2015 and decreased over the period 2015 to 2025 for both the world and America?
    (a) Wheat (b) Rice
    (c) Gram (d) None of these

Directions for Questions 17 to 20: *The following table (Table 3.3) describes garments manufactured based upon the colour and size for each lay. There are four sizes : S-Small, M-Medium, L-Large and XL-Extra Large. There are three colours: brown, blue and green.*

TABLE 3.3 Select Data Pertaining to a Garment Unit

Lay	Number of Garments											
	Brown				Blue				Green			
Lay No.	S	M	L	XL	S	M	L	XL	S	M	L	XL
1	14	14	7	0	0	0	0	0	0	0	0	0
2	0	0	0	0	0	0	0	0	42	42	21	0
3	20	20	10	0	18	18	9	0	0	0	0	0
4	20	20	10	0	0	0	0	0	30	30	15	0
5	0	0	0	0	24	24	12	0	30	30	15	0
6	22	22	11	0	24	24	12	0	32	32	16	0
7	0	24	24	12	0	0	0	0	0	0	0	0
8	0	20	20	10	0	2	2	1	0	0	0	0
9	0	20	20	10	0	0	0	0	0	22	22	11
10	0	0	0	0	0	26	26	13	0	20	20	10
11	0	22	22	11	0	26	26	13	0	22	22	11
12	0	0	2	2	0	0	0	0	0	0	0	0
13	0	0	0	0	0	0	0	0	0	0	20	20
14	0	0	0	0	0	0	0	0	0	0	22	22
15	0	0	10	10	0	0	2	2	0	0	22	22
16	0	0	0	0	1	0	0	0	1	0	0	0
17	0	0	0	0	0	5	0	0	0	0	0	0
18	0	0	0	0	0	32	0	0	0	0	0	0
19	0	0	0	0	0	32	0	0	0	0	0	0
20	0	0	0	0	0	5	0	0	0	0	0	0
21	0	0	0	18	0	0	0	0	0	0	0	0
22	0	0	0	0	0	0	0	26	0	0	0	0
23	0	0	0	0	0	0	0	0	0	0	0	22
24	0	0	0	8	0	0	0	1	0	0	0	0
25	0	0	0	8	0	0	0	0	0	0	0	12
26	0	0	0	0	0	0	0	1	0	0	0	14
27	0	0	0	8	0	0	0	2	0	0	0	12
Production	76	162	136	97	67	194	89	59	135	198	195	156
Order	75	162	135	97	67	194	89	59	135	197	195	155
Surplus	1	0	1	0	0	0	0	0	0	1	0	1

17. How many lays are used to produce blue fabrics?
    (a) 10 (b) 11
    (c) 15 (d) 16
18. How many lays are used to produce small fabrics?
    (a) 15
    (b) 16
    (c) 17
    (d) None of these
19. How many lays are used to produce medium blue or small green fabrics?
    (a) 8 (b) 9
    (c) 10 (d) None of these
20. For how many varieties of fabrics, has the order been exactly matched?
    (a) 9 (b) 8
    (c) 7 (d) 6

4 Mock Test Paper

Directions for Questions 1 to 2: *Answer the questions on the basis of the data presented in the figure below.*

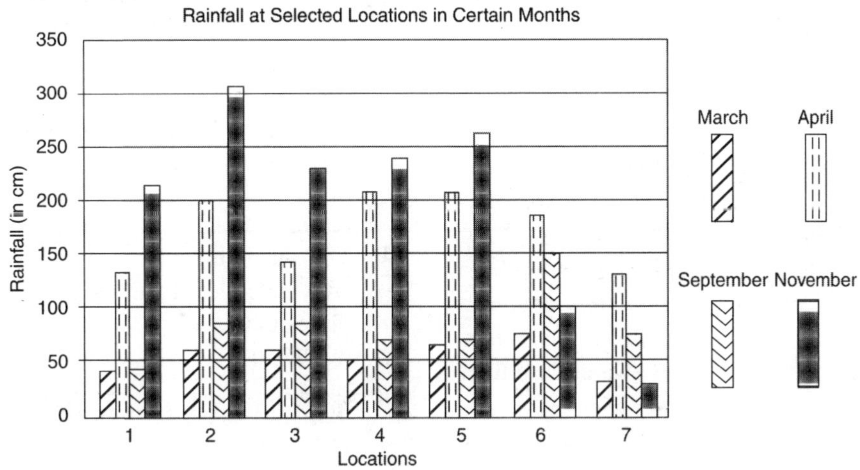

FIGURE 4.1

1. Which of the following statements is correct?
   (a) November rainfall exceeds 100 cm in each location.
   (b) September rainfall exceeds 50 cm in each location.
   (c) March rainfall is lower than September rainfall in each location.
   (d) None of the above.

2. Locations 6 and 7 differ from all the rest because only in these two locations,
   (a) April rainfall exceeds March rainfall.
   (b) Peak rainfall occurs in April.
   (c) November rainfall is lower than March rainfall.
   (d) April rainfall is less than 200 cm.

Directions for Questions 3 to 5: *Answer the questions on the basis of the data presented in the figure below.*

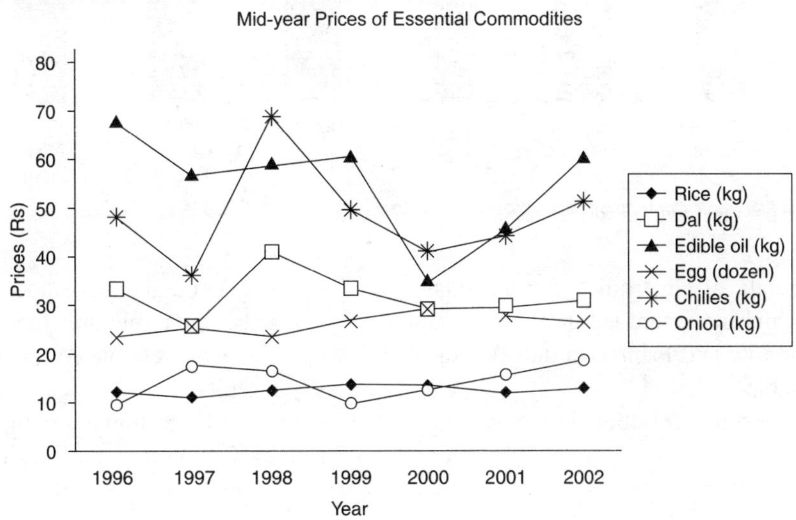

FIGURE 4.2

3. During 1996–2002, the number of commodities that exhibited a net overall increase and a net overall decrease, respectively, were
   (a) 3 and 3 (b) 2 and 4
   (c) 4 and 2 (d) 5 and 1
4. The number of commodities that experienced a price decline for two or more consecutive years is
   (a) 2 (b) 3
   (c) 4 (d) 5
5. For which commodities did a price increase immediately follow a price decline only once in this period?
   (a) Rice, Edible oil and Dal
   (b) Egg and Dal
   (c) Onion only
   (d) Egg and Onion

Directions for Questions 6 to 9: *A survey of movie goers from five cities—A, B, C, D and E is summarised below. The second column gives the percentage of viewers in each city who watch less than one movie a week. The third column gives the total number of viewers who view one or more than one movie per week.*

6. How many viewers in the city C watch less than one movie a week?
   (a) 2040 (b) 13600
   (c) 1600 (d) 3600

TABLE 6.4

City		
A	60	2400
B	20	3000
C	85	2400
D	55	2700
E	75	8000

7. Which city has the highest number of viewers who watch less than one movie a week?
   (a) City E (b) City D
   (c) City B (d) City C
8. The city with the second lowest number of movie watchers is
   (a) City E (b) City D
   (c) City B (d) City C
9. The total number of all movie goers in the five cities who watch less than one movie per week is
   (a) 50000 (b) 36000
   (c) 18500 (d) 45250

Directions for Questions 10 to 13: *Study the following chart carefully and answer the questions.*

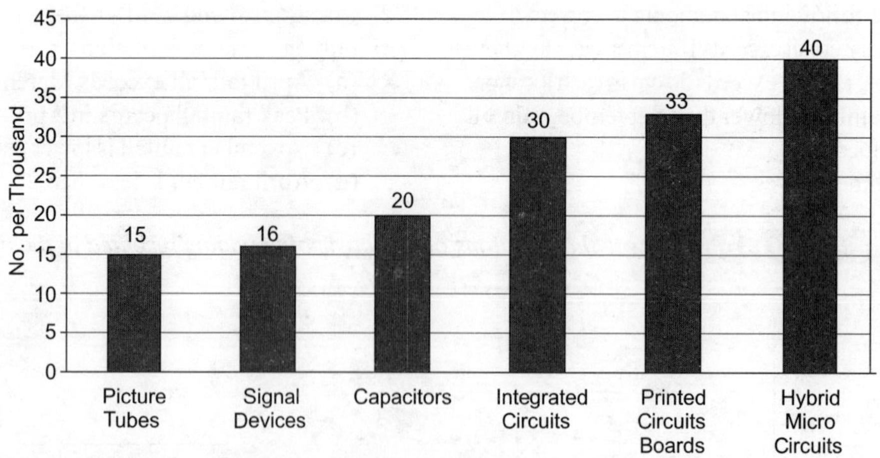

FIGURE 4.3 *Failure Rates of Electronic Components*

10. From the failure data of electronics components presented here, which statement is true?
    (a) Integrated circuits and Printed circuit boards are more reliable.
    (b) Capacitors are more reliable than pictures tubes.
    (c) Higher number of components' failures is likely to be due to pictures tubes.
    (d) The least reliable component is Hybrid Micro circuits.
11. Which of the following components has a failure rate 25% more than that of signal devices?

(a) Pictures tubes
(b) Capacitors
(c) Integrated circuits
(d) Printed Circuits boards.

12. The lowest priority for investing in any changes or additions to the component manufacturing units, in the company's investment plans, may be given to the following:
(a) Printed circuits boards and hybrid micro circuits.
(b) Capacitors and integrated circuits.
(c) Pictures tubes and signal devices
(d) Signal devices and capacitors

13. For the equipment using Integrated circuit Board: 400, Capacitors: 240 and Printed circuits boards: 120 to run with minimum downtime, how many spares should be kept in the store respectively?
(a) 12, 4, 3 (b) 12, 5, 4
(c) 5, 12, 4 (d) 12, 4, 4

Directions for Questions 14 to 16: *The table given below reports annual statistics related to rice production in select states of India for a particular year.*

TABLE 4.1

State	Total Area (in million hectares)	% of Area Under Rice Cultivation	Production (in million tonnes)	Population (in millions)
Himachal Pradesh	6	20	1.2	6
Kerala	4	60	4.8	32
Rajasthan	34	20	6.8	56
Bihar	10	60	12.0	83
Karnataka	19	50	19.0	53
Haryana	4	80	19.2	21
West Bengal	9	80	21.6	80
Gujarat	20	60	24.0	51
Punjab	5	80	24.0	24
Madhya Pradesh	31	40	24.8	60
Tamil Nadu	13	70	27.3	62
Maharashtra	31	50	48.0	97
Uttar Pradesh	24	70	67.2	166
Andhra Pradesh	28	80	112.0	76

14. How many states have a per capita production of rice (defined as total rice production divided by its population) greater than Gujarat?
(a) 3
(b) 4
(c) 5
(d) 6

15. An intensive rice producing state is defined as one whose annual rice production per million of population is at least 400,000 tonnes. How many states are intensive rice producing states?
(a) 5
(b) 6
(c) 7
(d) 8

16. Which two states account for the highest productivity of rice (tonnes produced per hectare of rice cultivation)?
(a) Haryana and Punjab
(b) Punjab and Andhra Pradesh
(c) Andhra Pradesh and Haryana
(d) Uttar Pradesh and Haryana

Directions for Questions 17 to 20: *Answer the questions on the basis of the information given below.*

The following bar graph gives the production, exports and per capita consumption of rice in country A, for the five years from 2006 to 2010.
Consumption = Production – Exports
Per Capita Consumption = (Consumption) ÷ (Population)

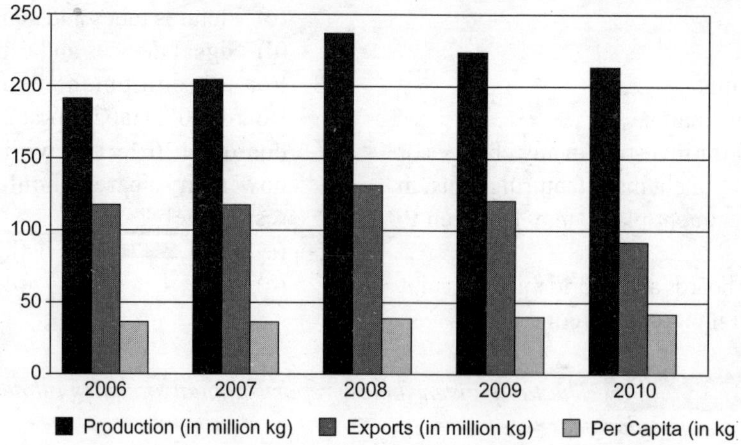

FIGURE 4.4

17. In which year was the percentage increase in the consumption of rice over the previous year, the highest?
    (a) 2007 (b) 2008
    (c) 2009 (d) 2010
18. What is the population of country A in the year 2008 (in million)?
    (a) 1.64 million (b) 2.72 million
    (c) 2.79 million (d) 3.15 million
19. The ratio of exports to consumption in the given period was the highest in the year
    (a) 2006 (b) 2007
    (c) 2008 (d) 2009
20. In which of the given years was the population of country A, the highest?
    (a) 2007 (b) 2008
    (c) 2009 (d) 2010

5 Mock Test Paper

Directions for Questions 1 to 3: *Answer the questions on the basis of the table given below.*

TABLE 5.1 Sex Ratio (Number of females per 1000 males) of Selected States in India: 1901–2001

	1901	1911	1921	1931	1941	1951	1961	1971	1981	1991	2001
AP	985	992	993	987	980	986	981	977	975	972	978
Assam	919	915	896	874	875	868	869	896	910	923	932
Bihar	1061	1051	1020	995	1002	1000	1005	957	948	907	921
Goa	1091	1108	1120	1088	1084	1128	1066	981	975	967	960
Gujarat	954	946	944	945	941	952	940	934	942	934	921
Haryana	867	835	844	844	869	871	868	867	870	865	861
HP	884	889	890	897	890	912	938	958	973	976	970
J&K	882	876	870	865	869	873	878	878	892	896	900
Karnataka	983	981	969	965	960	966	959	957	963	960	964
Kerala	1004	1008	1011	1022	1027	1028	1022	1016	1032	1036	1058
MP	972	967	949	947	946	945	932	920	921	912	920
Maharashtra	978	966	950	947	949	941	936	930	937	934	922
Orissa	1037	1056	1086	1067	1053	1022	1001	988	981	971	972
Punjab	832	780	799	815	836	844	854	865	879	882	874
Rajasthan	905	908	896	907	906	921	908	911	919	910	922
TN	1044	1042	1029	1027	1012	1007	992	978	977	974	986
UP	938	916	908	903	907	998	907	876	882	876	898
WB	945	925	905	890	852	865	878	891	911	917	934
India	**972**	**964**	**955**	**950**	**945**	**946**	**941**	**930**	**934**	**927**	**933**

1. Each of the following statements pertain to the number of states with females outnumbering males in a given census year. Which of these statements is NOT correct?
   (a) This number never exceeded 5 in any census year.
   (b) This number registered its sharpest decline in the year 1971.
   (c) The number of consecutive censuses in which this number remained unchanged never exceeded 3.
   (d) Prior to the 1971 census, this number was never less than 4.
2. The two states which achieved the largest increases in sex ratio over the period 1901–2001 are
   (a) Punjab and HP
   (b) HP and Kerala
   (c) Assam and J&K
   (d) Kerala and J&K
3. Amongst the states which have a sex ratio exceeding 1000 in 1901, the sharpest decline over the period 1901–2001 was registered in the state of
   (a) Goa (b) TN
   (c) Bihar (d) Orissa

Directions for Questions 4 to 7: *Answer the following questions based on the following bar diagram.*

The diagram gives us Country XX's Monthly Outward Investment Flows to various countries and the world. The FDI figures are given in US $ Million.

4. What is the compound average growth rate of Country XX's Overall Outward Investment during the period January to May 2021?
   (a) 6 per cent (approx.)
   (b) 3.5 per cent (approx.)
   (c) 5.75 per cent (approx.)
   (d) None of the above

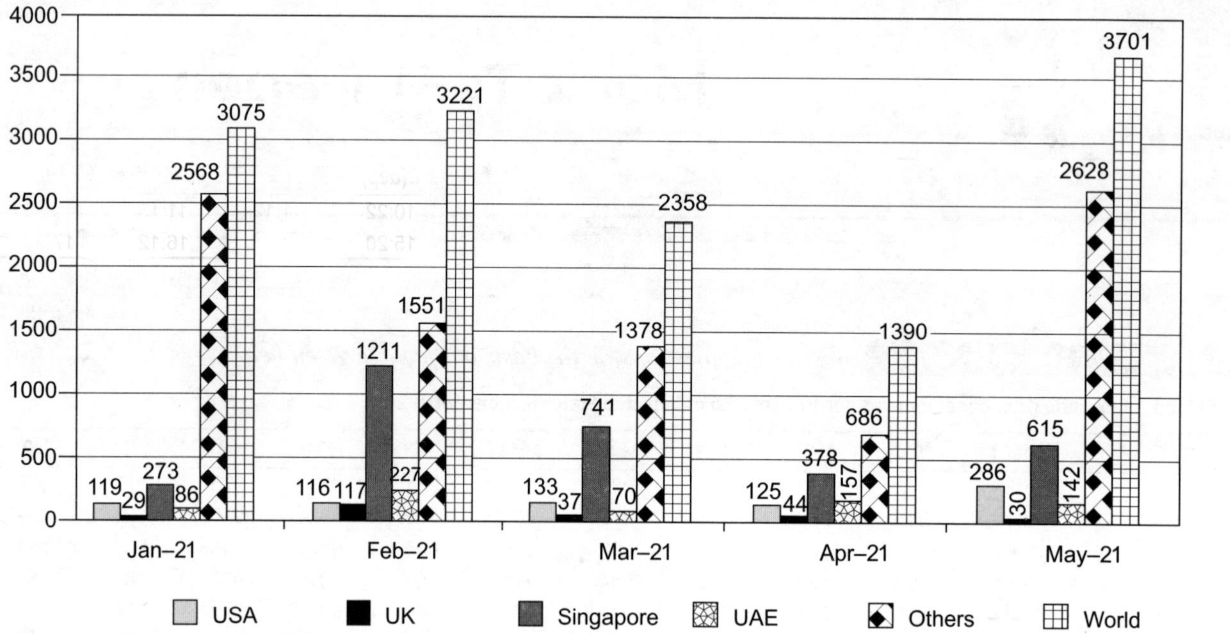

FIGURE 5.1

5. In which month there was a maximum drop in Country XX's Outward Investment to Singapore and what is the 'month on month' growth in that period?
   (a) April, approximately negative growth of 39 per cent
   (b) March, approximately negative growth of 49 per cent
   (c) April, approximately negative growth of 49 per cent
   (d) None of the above
6. Of its total investment in the world, what is the share of Country XX's Outward Investment together in USA and UK in February 2021?
   (a) 7.24 per cent (b) 8.30 per cent
   (c) 6.79 per cent (d) None of the above
7. In which month did the share of Country XX's Total Outward Investment together in Singapore and UAE achieve the highest level and what is the value?
   (a) April, 40 per cent (b) February, 45 per cent
   (d) March, 45 per cent (d) None of the above

Directions for Questions 8 to 10: *The following graph (Figure 5.2) shows the speed at which a motorist drove from Indore to Jhansi and beyond, on his way to an unknown destination. Answer the questions below, after going through the line chart. Note that he starts from the rest at time t = 0.*

Assume the distance between Indore to Jhansi is 400 kms.

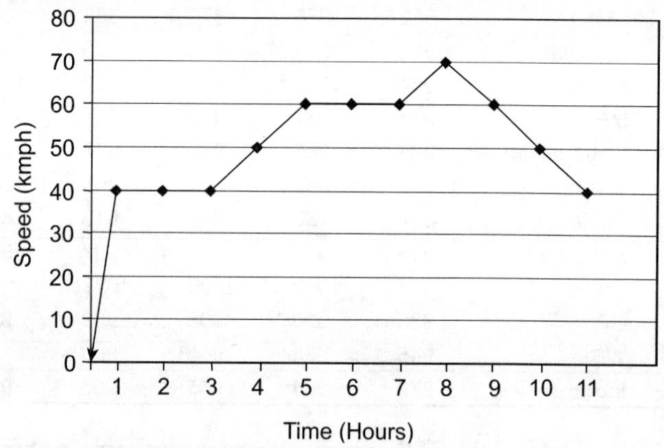

FIGURE 5.2 *Speed Time Graph*

8. If he were to ride at speeds shown in the reverse direction(riding in the first hour at speed attained after the 11th hour, in the second hour at speed attained in the 10th hour, and so on...), how much time would he have taken to reach Jhansi?
   (a) 6.27 hrs (b) 5.67 hrs
   (c) 4.83 hrs (d) None of these
9. What is the difference between the average speed in the first five hours and that in the last five hours?
   (a) 12.5 kmph (b) 18 kmph
   (c) 14.5 kmph (d) 15.5 kmph
10. What is the ratio of the distance covered in the first four hours to the distance covered in the next six hours? (approximately)
    (a) 0.41 : 1 (b) 0.37 : 1
    (c) 0.39 : 1 (d) 0.42 : 1

Directions for Questions 11 to 14: *Answer the following questions on the basis of the information given in Table 5.2 below. This distance between X and Y is 288 km and a, b, c & d are the intermediate stations. (arr) stands for arrival, (dep) stands for departure.*

TABLE 5.2 Timetable of Two Trains Running between Stations X and Y

Section	X	A(arr)	A(dep)	B(arr)	B(dep)	C(arr)	C(dep)	D(arr)	D(dep)	Y
Train 1	08:30	08:40	08:42	09:30	09:35	10:18	10:22	11:12	11:15	12:35
Train 2	13:30	13:40	13:42	14:20	14:27	15:18	15:20	16:07	16:12	17:30

11. By how much is the faster train faster than the slower train?
(a) 0.94 kmph (b) 0.92 kmph
(c) 1.47 kmph (d) None of these
12. Between which stretch is the ratio of the speeds of Train 1 and Train 2 1 : 1?
(a) *d* to Y (b) *a* to *b*
(c) *b* to *c* (d) X to a
13. What is the percentage difference between the maximum speed of Train 1 and minimum speed of Train 2?
(a) 29% (b) 39%
(c) 49% (d) Cannot be determined
14. In which stretch of the journey is the difference between the speeds of the two trains the minimum?
(a) X to A (b) A to B
(c) B to C (d) D to Y

Directions for Questions 15 to 17: *Based on the following information.*

Five years ago, *Maxam Glass Co.* had estimated its staff requirements in the five levels in their organisation as: Level-1: 55, Level-2: 65, Level-3: 225, Level-4: 255 and Level-5: 300. Over the years the company had recruited people based on ad-hoc requirements, in the process also selecting ex-defence service men and ex-policemen. The following graph shows actual staff strength at various levels as on date.

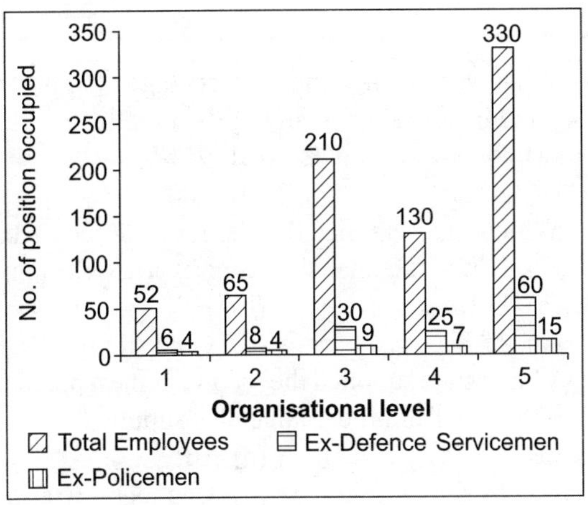

FIGURE 5.3

15. The level in which the Ex-Defence Servicemen are the highest in percentage terms is:
(a) 1 (b) 2
(c) 3 (d) 4
(e) 5
16. If the company decides to abolish all vacant posts at all the levels, which level would incur the highest reduction in percentage terms?
(a) 1 (b) 2
(c) 3 (d) 4
(e) 5
17. Amongst all levels, which level has the lowest representation of Ex-policemen in percentage terms?
(a) 1 (b) 2
(c) 3 (d) 4

Directions for Questions 18 to 20: *Jaspy starts a stationary shop in the year 2000, his revenue in the first year of operations being ₹25000, which incidentally is also his cost in the following year. The amounts of profit, however, remain constant for both these years. In 2002, the revenue increased by ₹7500 over the previous year but the profit could increase by only 50% from the profit of last year. The revenue for the year 2003 could increase by only 20% over the previous year, the cost following the same absolute increase. The revenue for 2001 was ₹30000.*

18. In which year was the percentage increase in profit the maximum?
(a) 2001 (b) 2003
(c) 2002 (d) None of these
19. The percentage cost was the highest in the year:
(a) 2001 (b) 2003
(c) 2002 (d) 2001 & 2003
20. Which of the following is True?
(a) The highest profit earned is one and a half times the lowest profit earned.
(b) The second lowest cost is four times the lowest profit earned.
(c) The second highest revenue equals the third highest cost.
(d) The simple annual growth rate of the revenue and cost are in the ratio of 1 : 1.

6 Mock Test Paper

Directions for Questions 1 to 5: *Answer the questions based on the following information (Table 6.1), which gives data about certain packaged atta products in India.*

TABLE 6.1 Data on Packaged Atta Products

	Production ('000 tonnes)	Capacity Utilisation (%)	Sales ('000 tonnes)	Total Sales Value (₹ in crore)
Annapoorna	3.01	77.50	2.65	32.15
Basuri	2.52	72.20	2.13	27.75
Chetakar	1.68	65.80	1.36	16.25
Dhanpura	1.58	60.35	1.57	18.45
Total (including others)	11.80	62.30	11.17	137.80

1. What is the maximum production capacity (in '000 tonnes) of Chetakar for packaged atta?
(a) 3.03 (b) 2.65
(c) 2.34 (d) 2.53
2. Which company out of the four companies mentioned above has the maximum unutilised capacity ('000 tonnes)?
(a) Chetakar (b) Basuri
(c) Annapoorna (d) Dhanpura
3. What is the approximate total production capacity (in '000 tonnes) of packaged atta in India?
(a) 18 (b) 20
(c) 18.9 (d) Data insufficient
4. The lowest price for atta per kilogram is for:
(a) Basuri
(b) Dhanpura
(c) Chetakar
(c) Data insufficient
5. What percentage of the total market share (by sales value) is controlled by 'others'?
(a) 60% (b) 31%
(c) 67% (d) Data insufficient

Directions for Questions 6 to 11: *Table 6.2 gives the quantity of apples (in tonnes) arriving at New Delhi market from various states in a particular year. The month, in which demand was more than supply, the additional demand was met by the stock from cold storage.*

TABLE 6.2 Select Data Pertaining to Apple Trade in Delhi

Month	State			Cold Storage	Total
	HP	UP	J & K		
April	13	0	7	63	83
May	18	1	0	0	19
June	8,765	267	8,123	0	17155
July	71,559	0	19,560	0	91119
August	78,135	0	19,887	0	98022
September	54,935	0	58,445	0	113380
October	13,986	0	81,213	28	95227
November	3,590	0	42,872	46	46508
December	1,843	0	14,631	20	16494
January	319	0	10,934	205	11458
February	41	0	11,638	80	11759
March	0	0	723	89	812

6. What was the maximum percentage of apples supplied by any state in any of the months?
(a) 99% (b) 95%
(c) 88% (d) 100%
7. Which state supplied the maximum apples over the first half of the financial year? (April to September)
(a) UP (b) HP
(c) J&K (d) Cold storage
8. Which state supplied the second highest percentage of apples from the total apples supplied?
(a) UP (b) HP
(c) J&K (d) Cannot be determined

9. In which of the following months was the supply greater than the demand?
   (a) October, November, January, March
   (b) June–October
   (c) May–September
   (d) Cold storage
10. If the yield per tree was 40 kg, then from approximately how many trees were the apples supplied to New Delhi (in million) during the year? (approximately)
   (a) 11.5
   (b) 12.5
   (c) 13.5
   (d) Cannot be determined
11. Using the data in the question above, if there were 250 trees per hectare, then how many hectares of land was used? (approximately)
   (a) 9,400 (b) 48,000
   (c) 50,000 (d) 60,000

Directions for Questions 12 to 15: *Refer to Table 6.3 below and answer the questions that follow.*

TABLE 6.3 Reduced Holding Dilution of Equity Stakes by Promoters in the Financial Year 2001–02

Companies	Holding on 31/03/01	Holding on 31/03/02	Company	Holding on 31/03/01	Holding on 31/03/02
Vital communication	91.96	8.04	Aditya International	68.8	55.31
Rajesh Strips	89	20.8	Boot & Crompton Engg	89.98	77.13
Gleitlager (India)	76	24	Welspun Syntex	34.06	21.26
ICICI Bank	46.99	0	Neocure Therapeutics	24.78	12.21
Ruby Mills	73.8	30.37	KPIT Infosystems	52.79	40.35
Design Auto Systems	41.33	1.28	Prime Securities	27.64	15.7
Aryan Pesticides	68.76	29.49	Murudesh Ceramics	55.84	44.07
Global Capital	52.36	15.26	Balaji Distilleries	69.4	57.99
Belsund Sugar	59.83	22.83	Flex Industries	41.28	29.9
IndusInd Bank	56.62	49.86	MP Glychem Industries	30.34	24.41
Himachal Futuristic Comm.	26.9	20.22	S S Organics	59.18	53.51
Nav Bharat Refineries	72.54	66.11	Ganesh Benzoplast	37.69	32.15
Cybermate Infotek	27.14	20.73	Softpro Systems	62.47	56.95
Wellwin Industries	9.76	3.53			

12. The highest percentage dilution of stake has been for
   (a) Vital Communications
   (b) Gleitlager (India)
   (c) Design Auto Systems
   (d) None of these
13. The number of companies in which the promoters have diluted over 50% of their initial stake is:
   (a) 10 (b) 9
   (c) 11 (d) 1
14. In terms of the absolute value of the dilution of equity stake, rank the following in ascending order.
   (i) IndusInd Bank
   (ii) S.S. Organics
   (iii) Prime Securities
   (iv) Murudesh Ceramics
   (v) Flex Industries
   (a) (ii), (i), (iv), (v), (iii)
   (b) (i), (ii), (v), (iv), (iii)
   (c) (ii), (i), (iii), (iv), (v)
   (d) (ii), (i), (v), (iv), (iii)
15. From the data provided, it is clear that the highest monetary benefits of the dilution of equity stakes has occurred for the promoters of:
   (a) Vital Communications
   (b) ICICI Bank
   (c) Rajesh Strips
   (d) Can't be determined

Directions for Questions 16 to 19: *The following table provides certain information about surpluses and deficits of SEBs in 1990. Answer Questions 9–12 based on the information provided in Table 6.4.*

TABLE 6.4 Surplus/Deficit of SEBs

Period	Surplus/Deficit (with Subsidy)	Revenue Subsidies and Grants as in Accounts	Surplus/Deficit (without Subsidy)
1991–92	153.65	3293.64	–3139.99
1992–93	766.27	3709.69	–2943.42
1993–94	1117.48	4136.93	–3018.91
1994–95	1125.36	5486.64	–4360.80
1995–96	1382.59	8140.57	–6757.98
1996–97	833.03	8419.11	–7586.08
1997–98	1434.76	9871.42	–8436.66
1998–99	887.23	11793.82	–10906.59

16. The highest percentage increase in deficit without subsidy is:
(a) 60% (b) 55%
(c) 11% (d) 6%
17. Which year can be said to be an improvement in overall fiscal performance of SEBs over the previous year?
(a) 1992–93 (b) 1993–94
(c) 1995–96 (d) Cannot be determined
18. The greatest percentage change in subsidy is approximately:
(a) 48.5% (b) 50%
(c) 52.3% (d) 46.2%
19. What percentage of the total subsidies granted over the period shown, pertains to the last four years
(a) 69.4% (b) 69.7%
(c) 70% (d) 70.3%

Direction for Question 20: *Answer Question 13 based on the following table.*

TABLE 6.5

Relative Sweeteners of Different Substances			
Lactose	0.16	Maltose	0.32
Glucose	0.74	Sucrose	1.00
Saccharin	675.00		

20. What is the ratio of glucose to lactose in a mixture as sweet as maltose?
(a) 8:21 (b) 1:3
(c) 3:2 (d) 16:9

7 Mock Test Paper

Directions for Questions 1 to 4:

TABLE 7.1

Market	Jan. 1984 (Kshs/kg)	Nov. 1984 (Kshs/kg)	Province
Kalandu	2.50	9.31	Eastern
Mwingi	2.50	9.00	Eastern
Kiambu	2.14	5.30	Central
Machakos	2.40	5.76	Eastern
Iciara	2.53	5.94	Eastern
Limuru	2.02	4.19	Central
Runyenjes	2.57	4.70	Eastern
Thika	2.86	4.91	Central
Kandara	2.84	4.76	Central
Embu Town	2.92	4.89	Eastern
Eldoret	2.00	2.92	Riftvalley
Kitale	1.51	2.11	Riftvalley
Bondo	2.50	3.33	Nyanza
Ahero	2.51	3.19	Nyanza
Sondu	2.31	2.73	Nyanza
Mumais	2.35	2.69	Western
Luanda	2.71	2.57	Western

1. Which of the following provinces witnessed both positive and negative percentage change in the price between Jan. and Nov.?
   (a) Eastern (b) Western
   (c) Central (d) None of these
2. Which of the following provinces witnessed the maximum percentage change in price in any one market? Each province has a number of markets within it, each market witnessing percentage change in the price.
   (a) Eastern (b) Central
   (c) Riftvalley (d) Western
3. Only one market witnessed a negative percentage change in its price. What was the magnitude of that change? (approximately)
   (a) 20 (b) 15
   (c) 10 (d) 5
4. How many markets whose name starts with 'K' witnessed at least a 2 digit percentage increase in the price?
   (a) 1 (b) 2
   (c) 3 (d) 4

Directions for Questions 5 to 7: *The following line graph shows the ratio of wheat production to rice production of a state in India over a period of 7 years from the 1999–2006. Answer the questions based on provided in the graph.*

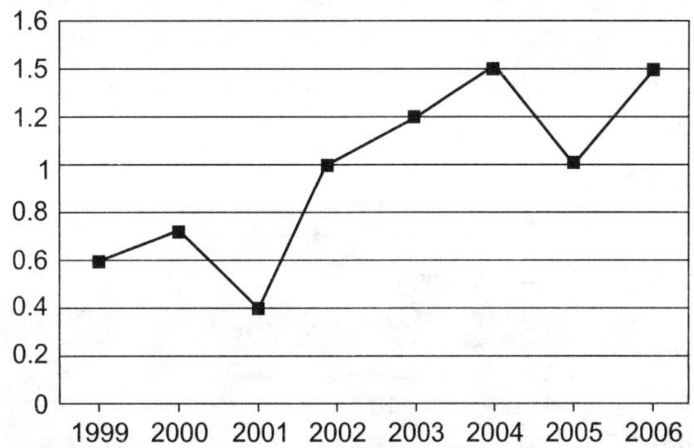

FIGURE 7.1

5. If the rice production in 2003 was 4 lakh tons what was its wheat production during 2003?
   (a) 1.2 lakh tons (b) 3.6 lakh tons
   (c) 4.8 lakh tons (d) 5.0 lakh tons
6. In how many years wheat production was more than the rice production?
   (a) 2 (b) 3
   (c) 4 (d) 5
7. If the total annual grain requirement (wheat and rice together) of the state is 5 lakh tons and if the rice production during 2001 was 3 lakh tons, how much grain had to be imported from another state of India to fulfill the requirement?
   (a) 2.00 lakh tons (b) 1.55 lakh tons
   (c) 1.05 lakh tons (d) 0.8 lakh tons

Directions for Questions 8 to 10: *The following table gives the speed of a train over a 3-hour period. The time count does not begin from starting of train.*

TABLE 7.2

Time (Minutes)	0	30	45	60	90	120	150	180
Speed at Given Time (in km/hour)	40	45	47.5	50	55	60	65	70

8. During the three-hour period shown in the table, the speed of the train increased by:
(a) 25% (b) 100%
(c) 75% (d) 125%

9. At time t, measured in minutes after the beginning of the time period, which of the following gives the speed of the train in accordance with the table?
(a) $t/6$ (b) $6t$
(c) $40 + t$ (d) $40 + t/6$

10. How fast was the train traveling 2½ hours after the beginning of the time period?
(a) 50 km/hr (b) 55 km/hr
(c) 60 km/hr (d) 65 km/hr

Directions for Questions 11 to 13: *The following table gives cost data of select stock prices on 3rd Dec. 2003 in two markets, BSE of India and NQE of Kya Kya island. Closing stock refers to the price at the close of trading hours and opening stock to the price at the beginning of the day. The currency of Kya Kya is # and the exchange rate is # = ₹11.*

TABLE 7.3

	3rd Dec 2003			
	Closing		Opening	
	BSE (₹)	NQE (in #)	BSE (₹)	NQE (in #)
SIFY	247	22	232	21
INFY	115	10.5	105	9.5
WIPRO	65	6.5	60	5.5
TCS	444	40	450	40.5

11. Which share and which market showed the highest percentage increase on 3rd Dec. 2003?
(a) SIFY on BSE (b) INFY on NQE
(c) WIPRO on NQE (d) TCS on NQE

12. Arbitrage means buying in one market and selling simultaneously in another market. If Mr. Ghosh Babu were to buy a share at the opening price on one exchange and was able to sell it at the closing price on the other exchange on which share does he make maximum percentage profit?
(a) SIFY (b) INFY
(c) WIPRO (d) TCS

13. In an M & A deal, SIFY is purchased by its parent company SATYAM which purchases 15% of SIFY's equity shares. SIFY's total equity shares are 1 million. How much does Satyam pay in ₹ for the stake if 50% of its purchases were on BSE's opening price and balance on BSE's closing price?
(a) 36 million (b) 3.5 million
(c) 363 million (d) 217 million

Directions for Questions 14 to 17: *The following pie-charts give the percentage distribution of employees in different departments in XYZ Company Ltd. during the years 2025 and 2026. Answer the questions using this data.*

A-Administration; B-Operations; C-Sales & Marketing; D-Finance & Accounts; E-Corporate HQ

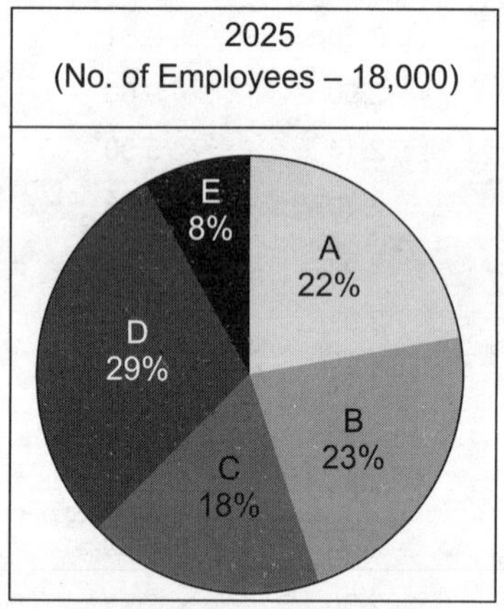

FIGURE 7.2(A)

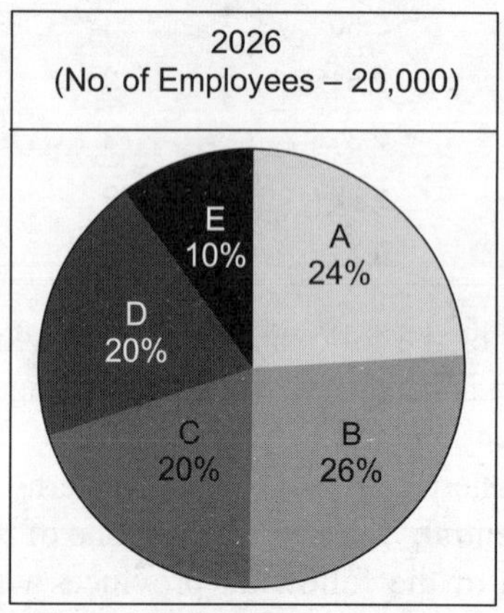

FIGURE 7.2(B)

14. If the average monthly salary of employees in Administratioxn was ₹12,000 in 2025, what was the approximate total salary expense of Administration in 2025?
(a) ₹57 crores (b) ₹4.7 crores
(c) ₹66 crores (d) ₹66 lacs

15. What is the percentage increase in the number of employees in Sales & Marketing?
(a) 2% (b) 2.34%
(c) 23.45% (d) None of these

16. In which department is the variation in strength the maximum in 2026?
(a) A (b) B
(c) D (d) E

17. If 300 employees left Operations at the end of 2025, how many joined in 2026?
(a) 480
(b) 960
(c) 1360
(d) None of these

Directions for Questions 18 to 20: *The questions are based on the following graph (Figure 7.3), which give the value of the total marks scored in the given years by the candidates appearing for the CAT as also the number of candidates (Figure 7.4).*

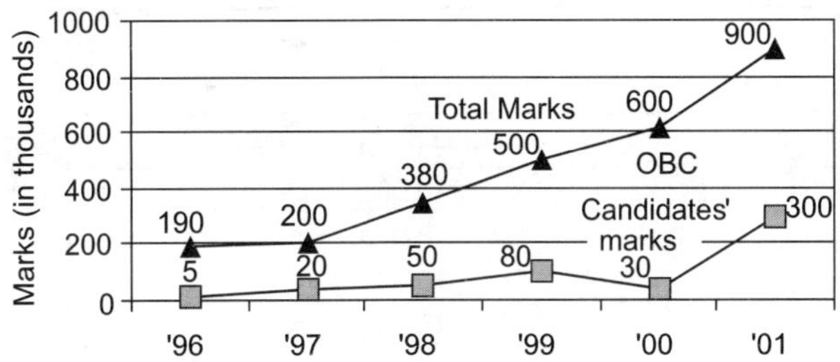

FIGURE 7.3 *Value of Total Marks*

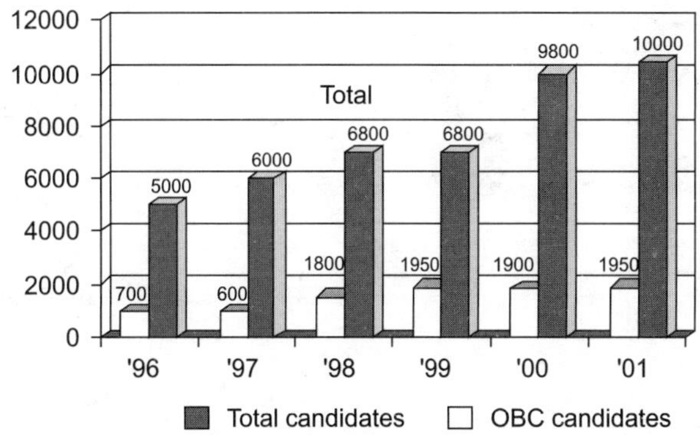

FIGURE 7.4 *Number of Candidates*

18. What is the average marks per candidate in the CAT in 2001?
(a) 91 (b) 84
(c) 77 (d) Cannot be determined

19. The average marks per candidate of CAT from 1996 to 2001:
(a) has remained almost the same
(b) has increased
(c) has decreased
(d) has almost doubled

20. What were the average marks in 1998 of candidates other than the OBC candidates (approx.)?
(a) 55 (b) 65
(c) 75 (d) 85

LEVEL OF DIFFICULTY – 2

8 Mock Test Paper

Directions for Questions 1 to 4: *Refer to the following tables [Tables 8.1(A), (B) and (C)]:*

TABLE 8.1 (A) Manpower Costs for a Building Project in Narhi (All costs in ₹)

Project Phase	Managers	Engineers	Skilled Workers	Unskilled Workers	Supervisors
Design	1	3	–	–	–
Foundation	1	2	5	23	2
Construction	1	2	12	43	4
Finishing (internal)	1	3	15	31	6
Painting	1	0	5	23	3

TABLE 8.1 (B) Cost per Month for Select Category of Workers

Manpower	Cost (in ₹)
Managers	₹10,000
Engineers	₹8,000
Supervisors	₹5,000
Skilled workers	₹3,000
Unskilled workers	₹1,800

TABLE 8.1 (C) Estimated Time and the Actual Time Required for Each Phase of the Project (in months)

	Design	Foundation	Construction	Finishing	Painting
Actual	5	3	8	4	2
Estimated	3	2	6	3	2

1. What was the phase in which there was the highest absolute increase between the estimated and the actual cost?
   (a) Foundation (b) Design
   (c) Construction (d) Cannot be determined
2. For which phase of the project was there the highest percentage increase in cost (as compared to the estimated cost).
   (a) Foundation (b) Design
   (c) Construction (d) Cannot be determined
3. What is the value of the percentage overflow in costs during construction? (approximately)
   (a) 50% (b) 33.33%
   (c) 66.66% (d) None of these
4. If internal finishing and painting can be started simultaneously at the end of construction, then what is the overflow of the project as a percentage of the estimated total time of completion of the project?
   (a) 27.27% (b) 33.33%
   (c) 42.85% (d) Cannot be determined

Directions for Questions 5 to 8: *Ravan on his death bed gave 4 trunks full of gold coins to his four sons – Raman, Shaleen, Tarun and Ujjwal. He then told them, 'Each of the trunks has a few lakh gold coins. In all, there are 20 lakh gold coins and Raman being the eldest, has got the maximum number of gold coins while Ujjwal being the youngest, has the least number of gold coins. Also, Shaleen has got one lakh more gold coins than Tarun'. He dies at this juncture. His brother Kumbhakaran awakes at this very instant and tells Shaleen – 'I know for a fact that no one has got less than 3 lakh gold coins. Can you open your trunk and count the number of gold coins you have and tell me the number of gold coins each of you has got'? Shaleen does so, counts the number of gold coins in his trunk and answers, 'Yes'. Kumbhakaran then asks Raman the following questions as a test for becoming the new king. Raman being logically* *sound, answers all questions correctly without anybody else opening their trunks. Can you identify the answers Raman gave to secure his right to the throne?*

5. The number of coins received by Raman is:
   (a) 7 lakh (b) 8 lakh
   (c) 9 lakh (d) 10 lakh
6. The number of coins received by Shaleen is:
   (a) 6 lakh (b) 5 lakh
   (c) 4 lakh (d) None of these
7. The number of coins received by Tarun is:
   (a) 5 lakh (b) 4 lakh
   (c) 3 lakh (d) None of these
8. The number of coins received by Ujjwal is:
   (a) 3 lakh (b) 2 lakh
   (c) 4 lakh (d) None of these

Directions for Questions 9 to 12: *The table (Table 8.2) shows trends in external transactions of the Indian corporate sector during the period 2003–04 to 2007–08. In addition, the following definitions hold good:*

$Sales_i$, $Imports_i$ and $Exports_i$ respectively denote the Sales, imports and exports in year i.
Deficit for year 1, is denoted by $Deficit_i$.

TABLE 8.2 Trends in External Transactions of Indian Corporate Sector

(All figures in per cent)

Year	2007–08	2006–07	2005–06	2004–05	2003–04
Export intensity *	7.2	6.2	5.9	5.6	5.4
Import Intensity *	12.2	14.2	13.3	11.6	10.2
Imported Raw Material/Total Cost of Raw Material	17.2	16.2	14.5	13.4	14.0
Imported Capital Goods/Gross Fixed Assets	15.6	7.8	9.7	14.3	17.3

* Ratio of Exports (or imports) to sales.

9. The highest growth rate in deficit intensity was recorded in:
   (a) 2004–05 (b) 2005–06
   (c) 2006–07 (d) 2007–08
10. The value of the highest growth rate in deficit intensity is:
    (a) 20% (b) 22.5%
    (c) 33.33% (d) 25%
11. In 2005–06, the total cost of raw materials is estimated as 50% of sales of that year. The turnover of gross fixed assets, defined as the ratio of sales to gross fixed assets, in 2005–06, is approximately:
    (a) 0.62
    (b) 1.6
    (c) 0.33
    (d) Not possible to determine
12. Which of the following statements can be inferred to be true from the given data?
    (a) During the 5-year period between 2003–04 and 2007–08 exports have increased every year.
    (b) During the 5-Year period between 2003–04 and 2007–08, imports have decreased every year.
    (c) Deficit in 2007–08 was lower than that in 2004–05 and 2006–07.
    (d) Deficit intensity has increased every year between 2003–04 and 2006–07.

Directions for Questions 13 to 15: *The following graph represents the cost per square feet of four retailers from the financial years 2004 to 2012. The expected cost per square feet for the years 2010, 2011 and 2012 are forecasted figures.*

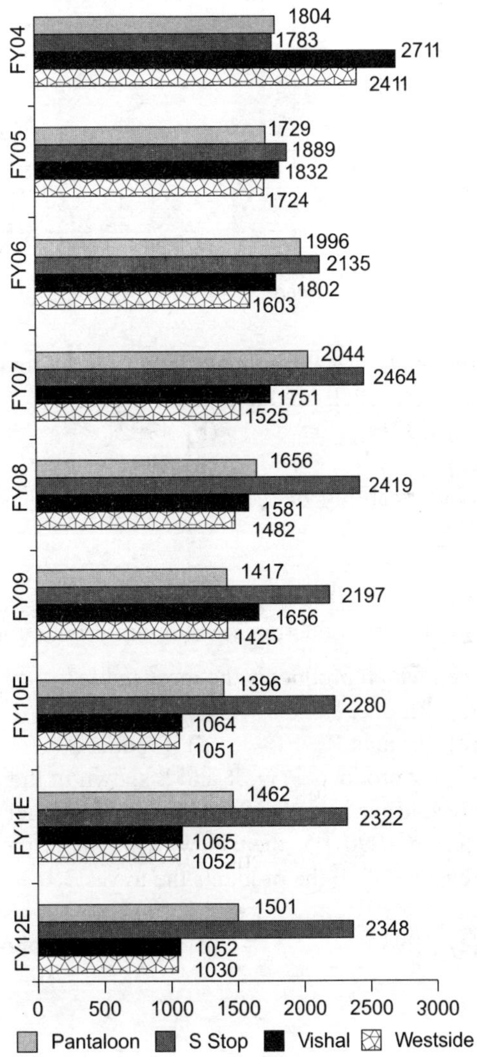

13. Which retailer shows the sharpest decline in cost per square feet and in which year?
    (a) Westside, 2005 (b) Pantaloon, 2008
    (c) S. Stop, 2009 (d) Vishal, 2010
14. Which retailer has shown the maximum increase in its cost per square feet and in which year?
    (a) S. Stop, 2006 (b) S. Stop, 2007
    (c) Pantaloon, 2006 (d) Vishal, 2006
15. What is the average rate of change in the cost per square feet of the retail sector, if the sector is represented by the above four retailers in the period FY07 to FY10E?
    (a) –8.12 (b) –10.86
    (c) –6.73 (d) None of these

Directions for Questions 16 to 20: *Answer the question based on the following graph.*

Production of P, Q, R and S (1990–95)

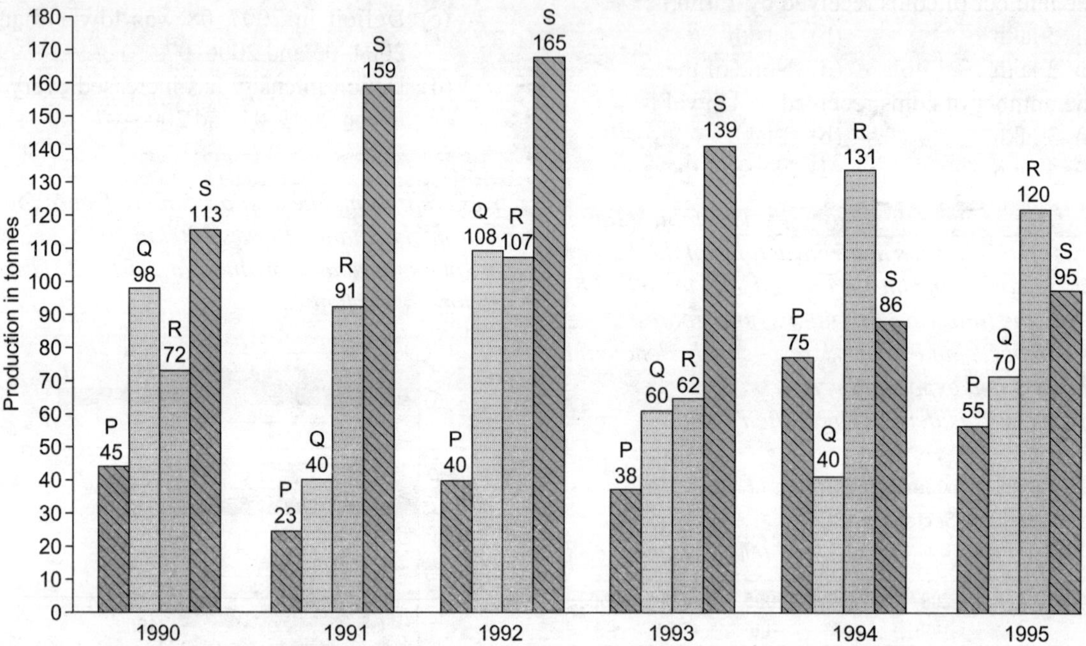

16. In which year the annual growth rate of total production (of all products) is the highest?
    (a) 1991 (b) 1992
    (c) 1993 (d) 1995
17. If the stability of the production during 1990 to 1995 is defined as,

$$\frac{\text{Average Production}}{\text{Maximum Production} - \text{Minimum Production}}$$

then which product is the most stable?
    (a) Product P (b) Product Q
    (c) Product R (d) Product S
18. If four products P, Q, R and S shown in the graph are sold at a price of ₹9, ₹4, ₹13 and ₹3 respectively during 1990–95, then in which year is the total revenue of all the products the lowest?
    (a) 1991 (b) 1992
    (c) 1993 (d) None of the above
19. Individual revenue of P, Q, R and S for the entire period (1990–95) is calculated based on the price of ₹9, ₹4, ₹13 and ₹3 respectively. Which product fetches the lowest revenue?
    (a) Product P (b) Product Q
    (c) Product R (d) Product S
20. Four products P, Q, R and S shown in the graph are sold at price of ₹9, ₹4, ₹13 and ₹3 respectively during 1990–95 .Which of the following statements is True?
    (a) Product R fetches the second highest revenue across products in 1991.
    (b) Sum of revenue of P, Q and S is more than the revenue of R in 1994.
    (c) Cumulative revenue of P and Q is more than the revenue of S in 1993.
    (d) None of the above

9 Mock Test Paper

Directions for Questions 1 to 4: *Maruti Udyog Ltd. produces two models of cars – Maruti 800 and Maruti Zen. The factory employs three spray painters, six assemblers and two quality control executives, each of them working for exactly 10 hours a day. Whereas each Maruti 800 car requires 20 mins for spray painting, 1 hour for assembling and 15 minutes for quality checking, the Maruti Zen model requires 30 mins. 1 hour and 30 mins, respectively for these activities.*

1. What is the maximum number of Maruti Zen cars that can be produced in a day?
   (a) 20 (b) 30
   (c) 40 (d) 50
2. What is the maximum number of Maruti 800 cars that can be produced in a day?
   (a) 90 (b) 60
   (c) 80 (d) 70
3. If on 1st of January, the factory has produced 30 Maruti 800s, what is the maximum number of Maruti Zens that can be produced?
   (a) 25 (b) 6
   (c) 10 (d) None of these
4. If Maruti Udyog decides to hire one more employee of any of the three categories, what is the maximum number of Maruti 800s that can be produced in a day?
   (a) 90 (b) 60
   (c) 80 (d) 70

Directions for Questions 5 to 8 *Based on the following information.*

In the beginning of the year 2010, Mr. Sanyal had the option to invest ₹ 800000 in one or more of the following assets – gold, silver, US bonds, EU bonds, UK bonds and Japanese bonds. In order to invest in US bonds, one must first convert his investible fund into US Dollars at the ongoing exchange rate. Similarly, if one wants to invest in EU bonds or UK bonds or Japanese bonds, one must first convert his investible fund into Euro, British Pound and Japanese Yen respectively at the ongoing exchange rates. Transactions were allowed only in the beginning of every month. Bullion prices and exchange rates were fixed at the beginning of every month and remained unchanged throughout the month. Refer to the table titled 'Bullion Prices and Exchange Rates in 2010' for the relevant data.

TABLE 9.1 Bullion Prices and Exchange Rates in 2010

Date	Gold Prices	Silver Prices	US$	€	£	¥
	₹/10 gram	₹/10 gram	₹/ US$	₹/€	₹/£	₹/¥
January 1	20000	300	40	60.0	70.0	0.50
February 1	20100	302	41	61.5	71.0	0.51
March 1	20250	307	41	62.0	71.0	0.52
April 1	20330	310	42	62.0	71.0	0.52
May 1	20400	312	42	62.5	72.0	0.53
June 1	20500	318	42	62.5	72.0	0.54
July 1	20650	330	44	63.0	73.0	0.55
August 1	20720	335	45	63.0	73.0	0.55
September 1	20850	340	47	64.0	74.0	0.57
October 1	20920	342	49	65.0	74.0	0.58
November 1	20950	345	50	65.0	74.5	0.59
December 1	21000	350	50	65.0	75.0	0.60

Interest rates on US, EU, UK and Japanese bonds are 10%, 20%, 15% and 5% respectively.

5. Mr. Sanyal invested his entire fund in gold, US bonds and EU bonds in January 2010. He liquefied his assets on 31st August 2010 and gained 13% on his investments. If instead he had held his assets for an additional month he would have gained 16.25%, which of the following options is correct? (*3 marks*)
   (a) Mr. Sanyal invested less than 40% in gold and more than 40% in EU bonds.
   (b) Mr. Sanyal invested less than 40% in each of gold and US bonds.
   (c) Mr. Sanyal invested less than 40% in gold, and less than 25% in US bonds.
   (d) Mr. Sanyal invested more than 40% in gold, less than 25% in EU bonds.
   (e) Mr. Sanyal invested more than 40% in each of US bonds and EU bonds.

6. At the beginning of every month, by sheer luck, Mr. Sanyal managed to correctly guess the asset that gave maximum return during that month and invested accordingly. If he liquefied his assets on 31st December 2010, how much was the percentage gain from his investments? (*2 marks*)
   (a) 34.64%
   (b) 46.71%
   (c) 47.5%
   (d) 49.15%
   (e) 49.96%
7. Mr. Sanyal adopted the following investment strategy. On 1st January 2010 he invested half of his investible fund in gold and the other half in fixed deposit of an Indian bank that offered 25% interest per annum. At the beginning of every quarter he liquefied his assets to create his investible fund for that quarter. Every quarter he invested half of his fund in the bullion that gave maximum return in the previous quarter and the other half in the foreign bond that gave maximum return in the previous quarter. However, if in any quarter none of the foreign bonds gave a better return than the fixed deposit of his Indian bank, he invested half of his investible fund in the fixed deposit for the next quarter. On 31st December 2010, Mr. Sanyal liquefied his assets and realised that all of the following options are true except, (*2 marks*)
   (a) By investing the entire amount in US bonds, he would have gained an additional ₹118395.
   (b) By investing the entire amount in UK bonds, he would have gained an additional ₹65035.
   (c) By investing the entire amount in EU bonds, he would have gained an additional ₹65035.
   (d) By investing the entire amount in Japanese bonds, he would have gained an additional ₹38395.
   (e) None of these is correct.
8. Advisors were asked to prepare an investment strategy that involved US Bonds, EU Bonds and Japanese Bonds keeping at least 20% of the initial fund in each of these assets for the entire year, and allowing exactly four additional transactions in the course of the year. On 2nd January 2011, while comparing five different recommendations that he had received from his financial advisors in the beginning of 2010, Mr. Sanyal referred to the table 'Bullion Prices and Exchange Rates in 2010'. One transaction is defined as the buying or selling of an asset. Which of the recommendation out of the following was the best one?
   (a) Two additional transactions each during the month of June and November.
   (b) Two additional transactions each during the month of June and October.
   (c) Two additional transactions each during the month of May and June.
   (d) Two additional transactions each during the month of March and November.
   (e) Two additional transactions each during the month of March and October.

Directions for Questions 9 to 13: *Given below are the shares of sectoral FDI inflow to India in different years (figures in percentage). Answer the questions on the basis of the following data.*

TABLE 9.2

Sector	2007	2008	2009	2010	2011	2012
Services Sector	18.2	24.3	20.8	16.8	4.9	20.8
Construction Development	7.6	8.1	12.2	11.7	5.9	10.5
Telecommunications	5.5	8.3	9.4	7.2	6.6	0.4
Drugs and Pharmaceuticals	1.4	0.8	0.7	1	9.1	2.7
Computer Software and Hardware	12.8	5.6	2.5	4.7	2	2.8
Chemicals (other than Fertilizers)	1.3	1.9	1.7	2.1	16.6	1.5
Automobile Industry	1.9	3.4	5.1	5.9	2.5	4.9
Power	1.3	3.9	5.8	5.1	4.9	3.2
Metallurgical Industries	2.5	4.5	1.8	4.9	4.7	6.9
Hotel and Tourism	1.3	1.6	2.2	2.4	2.6	14.9

9. Amongst the four sectors mentioned below, the increase in share of FDI inflows between the terminal years 2007 and 2012 has been the highest for
   (a) Services Sector
   (b) Construction Development
   (c) Automobile Industry
   (d) Power
10. Over 2007 to 2012, the simple average share of FDI inflows has been the second lowest for
   (a) Chemicals (Other than Fertilizers)
   (b) Automobile Industry
   (c) Metallurgical Industries
   (d) Hotel and Tourism
11. Identify the false statement from the following sentences:
   (a) During 2009 to 2012 the percentage share of FDI inflow in power sector has witnessed a continuous decline.
   (b) During 2007 to 2009 the percentage share of FDI inflow in drugs and pharmaceuticals sector has witnessed a continuous decline.
   (c) During 2009 to 2011 the percentage share of FDI inflow in hotel and tourism sector has witnessed a continuous increase.
   (d) During 2007 to 2010 the percentage share of FDI inflow in chemicals (other than fertilizers) sector has witnessed a continuous increase.
12. Identify the True alternative from the given options based on the following statements:
   (i) In 2011, the construction development sector was ranked fifth in terms of percentage share of FDI inflow in the country.
   (ii) In 2009, the computer software and hardware sector was ranked sixth in terms of percentage share of FDI inflow in the country.
   (iii) In 2012, the drugs and pharmaceuticals sector was ranked the fourth lowest from the bottom in terms of percentage share of FDI inflow in the country.
   (a) Statement (ii) only
   (b) Both statements (i) and (ii)
   (c) Statement (iii) only
   (d) All three statements
13. Mark the highest figure amongst the following options
   (a) Increase in FDI inflow percentage share for telecommunications sector between 2007 and 2008
   (b) Increase in FDI inflow percentage share for computer software and hardware sector between 2009 and 2010
   (c) Increase in FDI inflow percentage share for automobile sector between 2011 and 2012
   (d) Increase in FDI inflow percentage share for power sector between 2007 and 2008

Directions for Questions 14 to 17: *Given below are the detailed characteristics of select Indian industries. Answer the questions on the basis of the following data.*

TABLE 9.3

	Industry 1	Industry 2	Industry 3	Industry 4	Industry 5	Industry 6	Industry 7
Number of Factories	65	110	32	30	78	39	300
Number of Workers	9066	877	5656	1099	7508	3333	15670
Total Number of Persons Engaged	9466	1255	6830	1330	9088	4271	19159
Wages to Workers (₹ Lakh)	1875	420	3706	596	5800	3117	6966
Total Emoluments (₹ Lakh)	2095	747	6479	1024	9284	6084	15053
Fuels Consumed (₹ Lakh)	88	762	10817	1384	14790	6461	32178
Material Consumed (₹ Lakh)	2519	4135	57275	34027	327400	123275	106233
Total Inputs (₹ Lakh)	3256	5990	80238	41037	371605	138780	171246
Depreciation (₹ Lakh)	41	149	6667	1044	25674	3515	11246
Net Value Added (₹ Lakh)	3178	2284	23640	5831	71739	42434	72290
Profit (₹ Lakh)	816	913	9356	3990	34943	31219	45392

14. If total managerial wage bill is defined as the difference between total emoluments and total wage to workers, and total managerial staff is defined as the difference between total persons engaged and total number of workers, then average managerial wage would be the **highest** for:
   (a) Industry 5 (b) Industry 6
   (c) Industry 3 (d) Industry 7
15. Profit expressed as a ratio of net value added is the **highest** for
   (a) Industry 6 (b) Industry 7
   (c) Industry 4 (d) Industry 5

16. If gross value added is defined as the sum of net value added and depreciation, then the difference in gross value added per worker is the maximum between which of the following pairs?
    (a) Industry 6 and Industry 3
    (b) Industry 7 and Industry 1
    (c) Industry 5 and Industry 2
    (d) Industry 6 and Industry 4
17. Expense on fuel consumption as a percentage of input cost has been the **highest** for
    (a) Industry 3 (b) Industry 7
    (c) Industry 2 (d) Industry 6

Directions for Questions 18 to 20: *Read the following information and Tables and answer the questions.*

Bhubaneswar, Chennai, Kanyakumari, Kochi, Mumbai and Vizag are 6 major Indian cities. For some reason people use only a certain mode of transport between a pair of cities. The modes of transport are provided in Table 9.4, while in Table 9.5 the distances between different pairs of cities are given. Table 9.6 provides the speed of the mode of transport and the cost associated with each of them.

TABLE 9.4 Mode of Transport between Cities

	Destination					
Origin	**Bhubaneswar**	**Chennai**	**Kanyakumari**	**Kochi**	**Mumbai**	**Vizag**
Bhubaneswar	–	Ship	Train	Airplane	Bus	Train
Chennai	Ship	–	Train	Ship	Ship	Train
Kanyakumari	Train	Train	–	Train	Bus	Ship
Kochi	Airplane	Ship	Train	–	Train	Airplane
Mumbai	Bus	Ship	Bus	Train	–	Airplane
Vizag	Train	Train	Ship	Airplane	Airplane-	–

TABLE 9.5 Distance between Cities (KM)

	Destination					
Origin	**Bhubaneswar**	**Chennai**	**Kanyakumari**	**Kochi**	**Mumbai**	**Vizag**
Bhubaneswar	–	950	700	798	701	1002
Chennai	950	–	999	901	1000	300
Kanyakumari	700	999	–	1100	950	250
Kochi	798	901	1100	–	300	600
Mumbai	701	1000	950	300	–	500
Vizag	1002	300	250	600	500	–

TABLE 9.6 Mode of Transport and Cost

Mode of Transport I	KMPH	Cost per KM (in ₹)
Airplane	60	5
Bus	40	2
Ship	30	1.5
Train	25	2.5

18. For which of the following options, travel time is the least?
    (a) Mumbai - Kanyakumari
    (b) Bhubaneswar - Chennai
    (c) Chennai - Kochi
    (d) Mumbai - Chennai
19. Mr. Ranjith lives in Mumbai and wants to travel to KOCHI. However, the train services are on halt due to laying of track for bullet trains across the country. In this scenario, which of the following is the least cost route to reach Kochi?
    (a) Mumbai - Bhubaneswar - Kochi
    (b) Mumbai - Chennai - Kochi
    (c) Mumbai - Kanyakumari - Kochi
    (d) Mumbai - Vizag - Kochi
20. A school in Chennai is planning for an excursion tour for its students. They want to show them Kanyakumari, Vizag, and Bhubaneswar, not necessarily in the same order. What is the minimum travel cost (in ₹) the school should charge from each of the student for the entire tour?
    (a) ₹4300 (b) ₹5000
    (c) ₹7500 (d) ₹6800

10 Mock Test Paper

Directions for Questions 1 to 6: *The Bhartiya Petrol Company produces two varieties of petrol, viz., Normal and Premium. It refines its petrol at six refineries. The refined petrol is sent from the refinery to any one of seven depots and then onwards onto any one of eight districts. The refineries are XA, XB, XC, XD, XE and XF. The depots are DA, DB, DC, DD, DE, DF and DG. The districts are ZA, ZB, ZC, ZD, ZE, ZF, ZG and ZH. Table 10.1 gives the cost of transporting 1000 litres of petrol from the refinery to the depots, while Table 10.2 gives the cost of transportation of 1000 litres of petrol from a depot to a district.*

TABLE 10.1 Cost of Transporting Petrol from Refinery to Depot

(All figures in 000s of rupees)

	XA	XB	XC	XD	XE	XF
DA	928.2	537.2	567.8	589.9	589.9	800.1
DB	311.1	0.0	885.7	759.9	759.9	793.9
DC	451.1	602.3	320.1	780.1	720.7	1000.1
DD	371.1	211.1	350.1	750.1	650.4	980.1
DE	1137.3	324.5	5.0	1157.7	1173.6	1023.4
DF	617.1	506.4	756.5	1065.9	1065.9	406.3
DG	644.3	303.2	537.2	1093.1	1093.1	623.9

TABLE 10.2 Cost of Transporting Petrol from Depot to District

(All figures in 000s of rupees)

	DA	DB	DC	DD	DE	DF	DG
ZA	562.7	843.2	314.5	889.1	0.0	754.8	537.2
ZB	532.7	803.2	284.5	790.5	93.1	659.6	442.0
ZC	500.7	780.2	0.0	457.3	205.7	549.1	331.5
ZD	232.9	362.1	286.2	275.4	523.6	525.3	673.2
ZE	345.1	268.6	316.2	163.2	555.9	413.1	227.8
ZF	450.1	644.3	346.2	372.3	933.3	402.9	379.1
ZG	654.5	0.0	596.7	222.7	885.7	387.6	348.5
ZH	804.1	149.6	627.2	360.4	1035.3	537.2	498.1

1. What is the least cost to transport one litre of petrol from any refinery to any district?
   (a) 95.2 (b) 0
   (c) 205.7 (d) 284.5
2. What is the minimum cost of transportation of one litre of petrol from any refinery to district ZB?
   (a) 0 (b) 284.5
   (c) 98.1 (d) None of these
3. What is the minimum cost of transportation of one litre of petrol from refinery XB to district ZA?
   (a) 324.5 (b) 843.2
   (c) 1154.3 (d) None of these
4. What is the maximum cost of transportation of one litre of petrol from any refinery to any district?
   (a) 2172.6 (b) 2193.0
   (c) 2208.9 (d) None of these
5. In how many ways can you transfer the petrol from any of the refinery to any of the district?
   (a) 56 (b) 63
   (c) 72 (d) None of these
6. What is the minimum cost of transportation from refinery XD to district ZC?
   (a) 527.3 (b) 780.1
   (c) 750.1 (d) None of these

Directions for Questions 7 to 11: *Table 10.3 below presents data on the percentage of population covered by electricity and roads in selected third world countries.*

TABLE 10.3 Population Covered by Electricity and Roads

(Percentage coverage)

	Electricity			Roads		
	Urban	Rural	Total	Urban	Rural	Total
India	42.5	39.5	40.5	35.0	7.0	14.0
Myanmar	49.5	48.0	48.5	39.5	22.0	24.0
Malaysia	48.5	28.0	33.5	37.0	3.5	12.0
Thailand	41.0	34.5	37.0	38.5	17.0	23.5
Pakistan	46.0	40.0	43.0	44.0	33.0	38.5
Iran	39.5	27.0	31.0	36.5	20.0	25.5
UAE	44.0	26.0	28.5	34.0	31.0	31.5
Nepal	44.0	30.0	31.5	29.0	6.0	9.0

Note: Country A is said to dominate B or A > B, if A has a higher percentage in total coverage for both electricity and roads. In such a case Country B is said to be dominated by A, or B < A.

A country is said to be on the coverage frontier if no other country dominates it. Similarly, a country is not on the coverage frontier if it is dominated by at least one other country.

7. Which are the countries on the coverage frontier?
   (a) India and Malaysia
   (b) UAE and Iran
   (c) Myanmar and Pakistan
   (d) Thailand and Nepal
8. Which of the following statements is/are true?
   A. India > Thailand and India > Iran
   B. India > Malaysia and India > Nepal
   C. UAE > Malaysia
   D. Malaysia > Nepal
   (a) A and D (b) B and D
   (c) A, B and D (d) B and C
9. Analysing the data presented under road facilities, it can be concluded that rural population in India as a percentage of its total population is approximately:
   (a) 75 (b) 70
   (c) 67 (d) Cannot be determined
10. Putting to use the data under the roads columns sequence India, Myanmar and Pakistan in the ascending order of their rural population as percentage of their respective total population. The correct order is:
    (a) India, Pakistan, Myanmar
    (b) India, Myanmar, Pakistan
    (c) Myanmar, India, Pakistan
    (d) Pakistan, India, Myanmar
11. India is not on the coverage frontier because:
    A. India is lower than Myanmar in terms of coverage of electricity facilities.
    B. It is lower than UAE in terms of coverage of roads.
    C. It is lower than Thailand in terms of coverage of roads.
    D. It is dominated by Pakistan.
    (a) A and B (b) A and C
    (c) D (d) None of these

Directions for Questions 12 to 15: *Study the following graph carefully and answer the questions which follow. Assume that all the values end in either 0 or 5.*

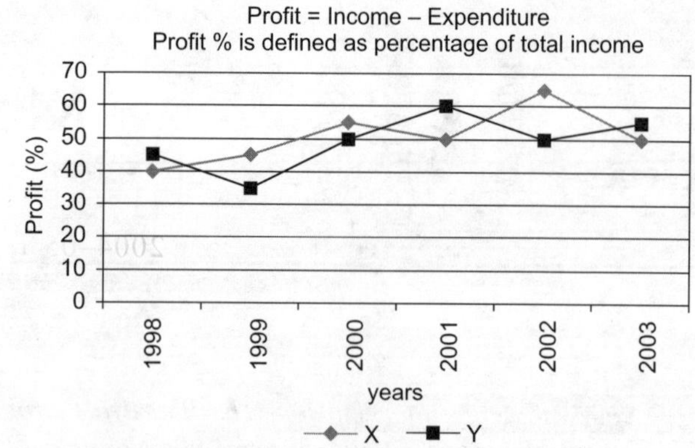

FIGURE 10.1 *Profits for Companies X and Y*

12. If the profit of company Y in the year 1999 was ₹108,000, what was its approximate expenditure in that year?
    (a) ₹900,000 (b) ₹80,000
    (c) ₹185,000 (d) ₹200,000
13. If company X spent ₹350,000 in the year 2000, the income of company X in that year was approximately equal to:
    (a) ₹542,500 (b) ₹525,000
    (c) ₹525,800 (d) None of these
14. If the expenditures of both the companies X and Y in the year 2002 were equal, then what was the ratio between the incomes of company X and company Y?
    (a) 5:4 (b) 10:7
    (c) 16:5 (d) 15:6
15. In which of the following years was the second highest percentage change in profit percentage over the previous year in the case of company X?
    (a) 2002 (b) 2000
    (c) 2001 (d) None of these

Directions for Questions 16 to 20: *Given below are the shares of India's export basket to different regions (figures in percentage). Answer the questions on the basis of the following data.*

TABLE 10.4

Region	2002–2003	2003–2004	2004–2005	2005–2006	2006–2007	2007–2008	2008–2009	2009–2010	2010–2011	2011–2012
EU countries	22.55	22.74	21.85	22.53	21.21	21.17	21.32	20.16	18.33	17.17
West Africa	2.02	1.99	1.98	1.80	1.93	2.13	1.84	1.76	1.71	2.12
East Africa	1.20	1.35	1.37	1.39	2.33	2.58	2.40	1.97	2.13	2.17
North Africa	1.28	1.21	1.62	1.55	1.47	1.63	1.84	1.75	1.59	1.54
North America	22.49	19.61	17.96	18.25	16.23	13.85	12.57	11.89	10.98	12.48
Latin America	2.06	1.40	2.15	2.47	2.95	3.11	2.96	3.13	3.72	4.00
ASEAN	8.76	9.12	10.09	10.10	9.98	10.05	10.29	10.16	10.21	12.00
West Asia-Gulf Cooperation council (GCC)	9.32	11.07	11.75	11.42	12.96	13.35	17.21	17.06	16.90	14.85
West Asia (Other than GCC)	3.68	3.68	3.67	3.26	3.81	3.66	3.32	3.22	3.09	3.12
North East Asia	14.92	14.70	15.83	15.74	15.33	16.23	13.80	16.12	14.83	14.86
South Asia	5.28	6.73	5.51	5.38	5.12	5.90	4.62	4.69	4.64	4.37

16. Amongst the four options mentioned below, export share of India witnessed the highest year-to-year decline in absolute terms in which of the region-period combinations?
    (a) In ASEAN region from 2005–06 to 2006–07
    (b) In South Asian region from 2004–05 to 2005–06
    (c) In West Asia (GCC) region from 2008–09 to 2009–10
    (d) In North African region from 2009–10 to 2010–11
17. Amongst the four options mentioned below, for which region have the export shares declined the maximum number of times in a year-on-year basis?
    (a) South Asia (b) North Africa
    (c) North America (d) West Africa
18. Between 2009–10 and 2010–11, the annual growth rate in India's (percentage) export share has been the lowest for
    (a) North Africa (b) North East Asia
    (c) North America (d) EU Countries
19. Mark the highest figure from the following options:
    (a) India's simple average export share to North Africa during 2008–09 and 2009–10
    (b) India's simple average export share to East Africa during 2004–05 and 2007–08
    (c) India's simple average export share to Latin America during 2002–03 and 2004–05
    (d) India's simple average export share to West Africa during 2007–08 and 2010–11
20. Identify the false statement
    (a) In 2011–12, South Asia was ranked sixth in India's export basket.
    (b) The export share of North Africa in India's export basket has been the lowest for the maximum number of years
    (c) In 2004–05, Latin America was ranked fourth from the bottom in India's export basket
    (d) Between 2002–03 and 2003–04, the annual growth rate in India's (percentage) export share has been the highest for West Asia (GCC) market.

11 Mock Test Paper

Directions for Questions 1 to 6: *The following figures (Figure 11.1) represent the annual growth rates, expressed as the percentage change relative to the previous year, in the sales of four two-wheeler models of the Balal scooter works. The figures are for the years during the 9-year period from 1990 to 1998. Assume that the index of the sale of the two-wheeler model for each of the four models is set at 100 in 1989. Further, the four models namely: Model A, Model B, Model C and Model D, respectively, constituted 20%, 15%, 10% and 15% of total sales for 1989.*

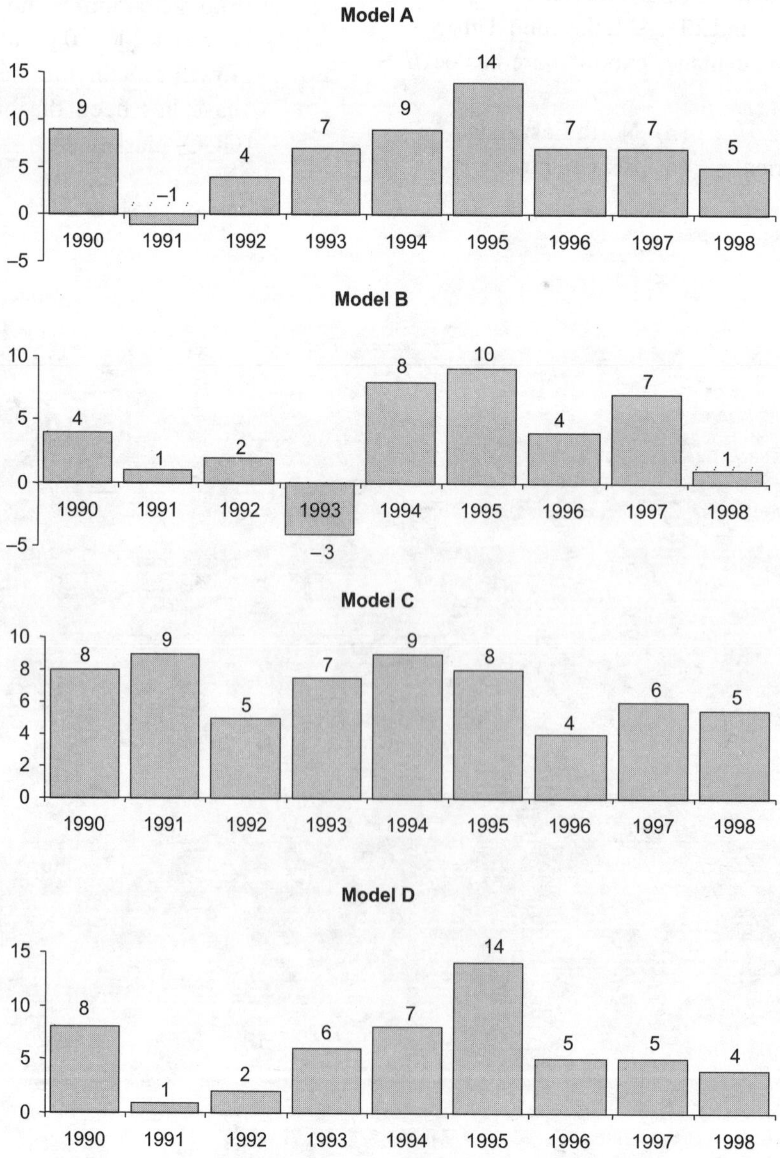

FIGURE 11.1 *Annual Growth Rate of Four Two-Wheeler Models*

1. Which is the model with the highest growth during the period 1989 to 1998?
(a) Model A (b) Model B
(c) Model C (d) Model D
2. The overall growth rate in 1991 of the four models together is approximately:
(a) 10% (b) 1%
(c) 2.5% (d) 1.5%
3. When was the highest level of production achieved for Model C during the 9-year period 1990–98?
(a) 1998 (b) 1995
(c) 1990 (d) Cannot be determined
4. When was the lowest level of production of the Model A achieved during the nine-year period 1990–98?
(a) 1996 (b) 1991
(c) 1990 (d) Cannot be determined
5. The percentage increase of production in the four models, taken together in 1994 relative to 1989 is approximately:
(a) 25 (b) 20
(c) 50 (d) 40
6. It is known that the total production in 1994 was 50% more than in 1989. Then, the percentage increase in production between 1989 and 1994 in models other than the four listed above is:
(a) 57.5 (b) 87.5
(c) 127.5 (d) 47.5

Directions for Questions 7 and 8: *These relate to Table 11.1 with the provision that the gap between the percentage of population covered by roads and electricity in any sector (viz: urban or rural) is a measure of the disparity of coverage of roads versus electricity for the sector.*

TABLE 11.1 Population Covered by Electricity and Roads

(Percentage coverage)

	Electricity			Roads		
	Urban	Rural	Total	Urban	Rural	Total
India	42.5	39.5	40.5	35.0	7.0	14.0
Myanmar	49.5	48.0	48.5	39.5	22.0	24.0
Malaysia	48.5	28.0	33.5	37.0	3.5	12.0
Thailand	41.0	34.5	37.0	38.5	17.0	23.5
Pakistan	46.0	40.0	43.0	44.0	33.0	38.5
Iran	39.5	27.0	31.0	36.5	20.0	25.5
UAE	44.0	26.0	28.5	34.0	31.0	31.5
Nepal	44.0	30.0	31.5	29.0	6.0	9.0

7. The country with the least disparity in the coverage of the rural sector is:
(a) India (b) Myanmar
(c) Nepal (d) None of these
8. The country with the most disparity in the coverage of the urban sector is:
(a) India (b) Thailand
(c) Pakistan (d) None of these

Directions for Questions 9 to 12: *Read the following information and tables and answer the questions that follow.*

Torrent Enterprises sells air conditioners of Eagle Brand in the retail market of Delhi. The month-wise total number of Window Air Conditioner (WAC) units sold by Torrent during April 2014 to March 2015 are shown below in Table 11.2 A. Table 11.2B shows the share of different types of WACs in total monthly sales for the said period.

Number of Units Sold by Torrent Enterprises During the Period April 14 to March 15

TABLE 11.2(A)

Month	Units Sold	Month	Units Sold	Month	Units Sold
Apr-14	1266	Aug-14	1296	Dec-14	1300
May-14	1268	Sep-14	1296	Jan-15	1330
Jun-14	1272	Oct-14	1298	Feb-15	1340
Jul-14	1292	Nov-14	1300	Mar-15	1350

TABLE 11.2(B)

WAC Type (Tonnage)	April, May & Sep	Jun, Jul & Dec	Aug, Feb & Mar	Oct, Nov & Jan
Two Ton	20.00%	25.00%	31.00%	25.00%
One & Half Ton	19.00%	33.00%	19.00%	33.00%
One Ton	14.00%	12.00%	34.00%	26.00%
Half Ton	47.00%	30.00%	16.00%	16.00%

Performance measures are as follows:

Half Yearly Sales Performance:

$$\frac{\text{Oct 14 to Mar 15 Average Sales} - \text{April 14 to Sep 14 Average Sales}}{\text{April 14 to Sep 14 Average Sales}}$$

Monthly Sales Performance:

$$\frac{\text{Current Month Sales} - \text{Previous Month Sales}}{\text{Previous Month Sales}}$$

Sales Volatility:

$$\frac{\text{Maximum Monthly Sales} - \text{Minimum Monthly Sales}}{\text{Average Monthly Sales}}$$

9. What is the closest average number of 1½ ton Window ACs sold by Torrent Enterprises during April 2014–March 2015?
   (a) 342 (b) 338
   (c) 350 (d) 330
10. The absolute difference between average annual sales (in units) of which pair of WACs type is the highest?
   (a) 1 Ton and ½ Ton
   (b) 1 Ton and 2 Ton
   (c) 2 Ton and ½ Ton
   (d) 1 ½ Ton and ½ Ton
11. Which type of WAC has performed the second best in Half Yearly Sales Performance?
   (a) ½ Ton (b) 1 Ton
   (c) 1 ½ Ton (d) 2 Ton
12. In which of the months given below, the total WAC Monthly Sales Performance was the highest?
   (a) May 2014 (b) June 2014
   (c) October 2014 (d) February 2015

Directions for Questions 13 and 17: *Instructions [11 - 15] Given below are the detailed characteristics of select India industries. Answer the question on the basis of the following data.*

	Industry 1	Industry 2	Industry 3	Industry 4	Industry 5	Industry 6	Industry 7
Number of Factories	65	110	32	30	78	39	300
Number of Workers	9066	877	5656	1099	7508	3333	15670
Total Number of Person Engaged	9466	1255	6830	1330	9088	4271	19159
Wages to Workers (₹ Lakh)	1875	420	3706	596	5800	3117	6966
Total Emoluments. (₹ Lakh)	2095	747	6479	1024	9284	6084	15053
Fuels consumed (₹ Lakh)	88	762	10817	1384	14790	6461	32178
Material consumed (₹ Lakh)	2519	4135	57275	34027	327400	123275	106233
Total Inputs (₹ Lakh)	3256	5990	80238	41037	371605	138780	171246
Depreciation (₹ Lakh)	41	149	6667	1044	25674	3515	11246
Net Value Added (₹ Lakh)	3178	2284	23640	5831	71739	42434	72290
Profit (₹ Lakh)	816	913	9356	3990	34943	31219	45392

13. If the total managerial wage bill is defined as the difference between total emoluments and total wage to workers, and total managerial staff is defined as the difference between the total person engaged and the total number of workers, then the average managerial wage would be HIGHEST for:
   (a) Industry 5 (b) Industry 6
   (c) Industry 3 (d) Industry 7
14. Profit expressed as a ratio of net value added is HIGHEST for
   (a) Industry 6 (b) Industry 7
   (c) Industry 4 (d) Industry 5
15. If gross value added is defined as the sum of net value added and depreciation, then the difference in the gross value added per worker is maximum between which of the following pairs?
   (a) Industry 6 and Industry 3
   (b) Industry 7 and Industry 1
   (c) Industry 5 and Industry 2
   (d) Industry 6 and Industry 4
16. Expense on fuel consumption as a percentage of input cost has been HIGHEST for
   (a) Industry 3 (b) Industry 7
   (c) Industry 2 (d) Industry 6
17. Identify the TRUE statement
   (a) Number of worker's per factory is third highest for industry 6
   (b) Expense on Material consumption expressed as a percentage of input cost is second highest for industry 4
   (c) Profit earned expressed as a percentage of emolument is second highest for Industry 7
   (d) Emoluments expressed as a percentage of net value added is lowest for Industry 5

Directions for Questions 18 and 20: *Given below is the time table for a trans-continental train that cuts across several time zones. All timings are in local time in the respective cities. The average speed of the train between any two cities is the same in both directions.*

local time arrival	local time departure		City		local time arrival	local time departure
—	6:00 AM	↓	Zut		12:40 PM	—
7:45 AM	7:50 AM	↓	Yag	↑	10:50 AM	10:55 AM
2:45 PM	2:50 PM	↓	Vaq	↑	11:50 PM	11:55 PM
7:40 PM	7:45 PM	↓	Sab	↑	12:55 PM	1:00 PM
10:40 PM	—	↓	Raz	↑	—	8:00 AM

18. Which of the following pairs of cities are in the same time zone?
    (a) Yag and Vaq
    (b) Vaq and Sab
    (c) Zut and Yag
    (d) No pair of cities are in the same time zone.
    (e) Sab and Raz
19. What is the total time taken in minutes by the train to go from Zut to Raz?
    (a) 22 hours, 40 minutes
    (b) 28 hours, 40 minutes
    (c) 16 hours, 40 minutes.
    (d) 20 hours, 40 minutes
    (e) 24 hours, 40 minutes
20. What time is it in Yag when it is 12:00 noon at Sab?
    (a) 5:00 pm (b) 12:00 noon
    (c) 9:30 am (d) 7:00 am
    (e) 2:30 pm

12 Mock Test Paper

Directions for Questions 1 to 6: *Mindworkzz produces mobile phones. They have a revolutionary new technology due to which the demand for the product is unlimited, i.e., they are in a position to sell all of their production. The graph (Figure 12.1) below describes the monthly variable cost incurred by the company as a function of the quantity produced. In addition to this, operating the plant for one shift results in a fixed monthly cost of ₹8000. Fixed monthly cost for second shift operation are estimated at ₹12000. Each shift of operation provides capacity for producing 300 mobile phones per month.*

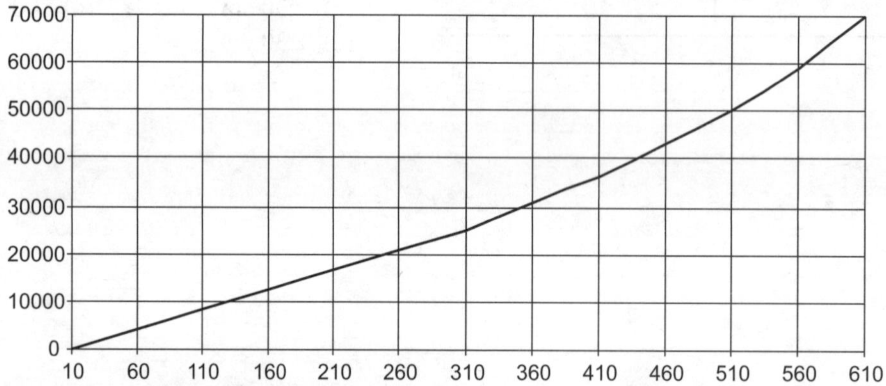

FIGURE 12.1 *Monthly Variable Cost Incurred by a Mobile Phone Company*

Note: Average unit cost, AC = Total monthly cost/monthly production and Marginal Cost (MC) is the rate of change in total cost for unit change in quantity produced.

1. The total production in June 2017 was 400 units. What was the approximate average unit cost for the month?
   (a) 130 (b) 120
   (c) 140 (d) 150
2. Mindworkzz is considering increasing the production level. What is the approximate marginal cost of increasing production from its June level of 400 units?
   (a) 110 (b) 130
   (c) 150 (d) 160
3. From the data provided it can be inferred that, for production levels in the range of 0 to 300 units:
   (a) MC increases as the production quantity increases.
   (b) MC decreases as the production quantity decreases.
   (c) Initially MC is decreases with increase in the production quantity, attains a minimum and then it increases with the increase of production quantity.
   (d) None of these.
4. Suppose that each mobile phone sells for ₹200. What is the profit earned by Mindworkzz in June for production of 400 units?
   (a) 25,000 (b) 16,000
   (c) 4000 (d) None of these
5. Assume that the unit price is further dropped to ₹160 and profit is defined as the excess of sales revenue over total costs. What is the monthly production level of Mindworkzz at which the profit is the highest?
   (a) 310 (b) 510
   (c) 610 (d) 410
6. For monthly production level in the range of 0 to 300 units:x
   (a) AC is always higher than MC.
   (b) AC is always lower than MC.
   (c) AC is lower than MC up to a certain level and then is higher than MC.
   (d) None of the above.

Directions for Questions 7 to 12: *From the data given in Table 12.1, solve the questions given below that.*

TABLE 12.1 Present and Past Users of Different Toilet Soaps.

Present Users (Number of people)

PAST USERS (NUMBER OF PEOPLE)	Lux	Liril	Dove	Nivea	No Soap Usage	
Lux	300	75	90	60	45	570
Liril	60	240	45	60	30	435
Dove	90	45	90	15	00	240
Nivea	135	30	00	60	30	255
No soap usage	210	15	00	30	210	465
	795	405	225	225	315	1965

7. The percentage increase in the number of people using any kind of soap is:
   (a) 10% (b) 15%
   (c) 20% (d) Cannot be determined
8. How many brands of soap have shown a decrease in their market shares?
   (a) One (b) Two
   (c) Three (d) Four
9. If from the present users, the total soap usage increases by 20% and Lux users increase by 25%, approximately what per cent of the soap using market would be Lux users?
   (a) 39% (b) 47%
   (c) 50.2% (d) 55%
10. If a consumer uses 1.5 kg of soap a month (on an average), what is the present soap usage amongst the consumers surveyed?
    (a) 22 tonnes/month
    (b) 22.5 tonnes/month
    (c) 24.75 tonnes/month
    (d) Cannot be determined
11. What is the decrease in the usage of Liril as a percentage of the total present soap users from the sample population?
    (a) 1.7% (b) 1.81%
    (c) No change (d) 18.1%
12. If a new brand Palmolive is introduced into the market, and the brand shift to Palmolive from the present users is Lux 10%, Liril 10%, Dove 8% and Nivea 6%, how many users will Palmolive have (round off all decimal values of number of people to the higher integer)?
    (a) 151 (b) 152
    (c) 153 (d) 154

Directions for Questions 13 to 16: *Four newspapers were evaluated on four parameters and their scores listed (Table 12.2). The net score, on which the rankings are based is calculated as a weighted average of the four scores. Read the data carefully and answer the questions that follow. Assume equal weightages unless otherwise stated.*

TABLE 12.2 Score Card

	Price	International	Sports	Political
HT	5	7	6	7
TOI	8	6	5	5
Telegraph	7	7	6	6
Indian Express	6	7	7	5

13. What would be HT's rank if equal weightages were given to all the four parameters?
    (a) 2nd (b) 1st
    (c) 4th (d) Cannot be determined
14. If a new newspaper offers sports like TOI, price like Indian Express, international news as good as Telegraph and political news equal to that of HT, then what would be its rank?
    (a) 2nd (b) 3rd
    (c) 4th (d) 5th
15. Which newspaper was ranked the second best?
    (a) HT (b) Indian Express
    (c) Telegraph (d) Both (a) and (b)
16. If price is not a consideration and equal weights are given to the other parameters, which newspaper should be chosen?
    (a) HT (b) TOI
    (c) Telegraph (d) Both (a) and (b)

Directions for Questions 17 to 20: *Read the following information and graph, and answer the questions that follow.*

An International Organisation produces a Competitive Index of countries every two years based on eight factors (Institutions, Infrastructure, Macroeconomic Environment, Higher Education, Market Efficiency, Technological Readiness, Business Sophistication and Innovation). The last three indices were developed in 2010, 2012 and 2014. The scores for all eight factors of XYZ country are shown in the graph below:

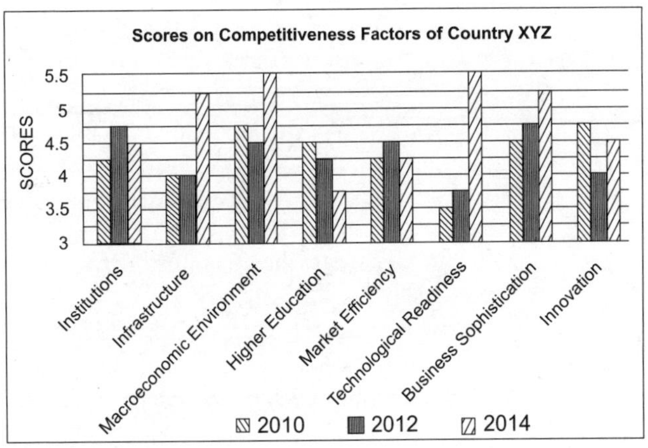

FIGURE 12.2

17. If Factor Performance is measured as 0.30 × Factor Score in 2014 + 0.35 × Factor Score in 2012 + 0.35 × Factor Score in 2010, then which of the following has the best Factor Performance?
    (a) Innovation
    (b) Business Sophistication
    (c) Infrastructure
    (d) Macroeconomic Environment
18. If Factor Performance is measured as

$$\left\{\frac{\text{Factor Score 2014} - \text{Factor Score 2012}}{\text{Factor Score 2010}}\right\}$$

then which of the following has the best Factor Performance?
    (a) Innovation
    (b) Business Sophistication
    (c) Infrastructure
    (d) Macroeconomic Environment
19. Which of the following factors has the highest average score across indices 2010, 2012 and 2014?
    (a) Infrastructure
    (b) Institutions
    (c) Technological Readiness
    (d) Market Efficiency
20. Which amongst the following factors had the least growth rate in 2014 versus scores of 2010?
    (a) Business Sophistication
    (b) Institutions
    (c) Technological Readiness
    (d) Infrastructure

13 Mock Test Paper

Directions for Questions 1 to 5: *Machine M1 as well as machine M2 can independently produce either LG or Samsung air conditioners. The time taken by machines M1 and M2 (in minutes) to produce one unit of LG and Samsung are given in the table in minutes (Each machine works 10 hours per day).*

TABLE 13.1 Data

System	M1	M2
LG	12	10
Samsung	8	8

1. What is the maximum number of units that can be manufactured in one day?
   (a) 150 (b) 160
   (c) 130 (d) 135
2. If M2 works at half its normal efficiency, what is the maximum number of units produced, if at least one unit of each must be produced?
   (a) 105 (b) 110
   (c) 111 (d) 112
3. What is the least number of machine hours required for producing 30 LG and 25 Samsung A/c's respectively?
   (a) 6 hr. 40 min (b) 7 hr. 30 min.
   (c) 6 hr. 50 min. (d) None of these
4. If for every three units of LG one unit of Samsung is produced, what is the maximum idle time that can remain unutilised to maximise the total units manufactured?
   (a) 0 min. (b) 30 min.
   (c) 45 min (d) None of these
5. If equal quantities of both are to be produced, then out of the four choices given below, the least efficient way would be:
   (a) 48 of each with 4 min idle
   (b) 64 of each with 40 min idle
   (c) 54 of each with 60 min idle
   (d) 75 of each with 12 min idle

Directions for Questions 6 to 10: *Karuna sold 10 acres of land to Kaku and Chikoo who paid him the total amount in the ratio 2 : 3. Kaku invested a further ₹3 lakh in the land for the purpose of planting coconut and lemon trees in the ratio 4:1. These trees were planted on equal areas of land. There were a total of 200 lemon trees. The sale price of one coconut was ₹10 in 2033. The crop took 7 years to mature and when the crop was reaped in 2033, the total revenue generated was 50% of the total initial amount put in by Kaku and Chikoo together. The revenue generated from the coconut and lemon trees was in the ratio 5:4 and it was shared equally by Kaku and Chikoo as the initial amount spent by them were equal.*

6. How many coconuts were reaped?
   (a) 24,000 (b) 50,000
   (c) 25,000 (d) None of these
7. What was the value of output per acre of lemon trees planted?
   (a) 0.8 lakh per/acre
   (b) 4 lakh per/acre
   (c) 2.4 lakh per/acre
   (d) Cannot be determined
8. What was the amount received by Kaku in 2033?
   (a) ₹3 lakh (b) ₹4.5 lakh
   (c) ₹6 lakh (d) None of these
9. What was the value of output per tree for coconuts?
   (a) ₹360 (b) ₹625
   (c) ₹650 (d) None of these
10. What was the ratio of yield per acre of land for coconuts and lemons (in terms of number of lemons and coconuts)?
    (a) 3 : 2 (b) 2 : 3
    (c) 1 : 1 (d) Cannot be determined

Directions for Questions 11 to 15: *Dataman Infosys, before selling a package to its clients, follows the given schedule (Table 13.2).*

TABLE 13.2 Schedule followed by Dataman Infosys

Month	Stage	Cost (₹ '000 per man/month)
1–2	Specification	20.0
3–4	Design	10.0
5–8	Coding	5.0
9–10	Testing	7.5
11–15	Maintenance	5.0

The number of people employed in each month is:

TABLE 13.3 Number of People Employed by Dataman Infosys

Month	1	2	3	4	5	6	7	8	9	10	11	12	13	14	15
Number of People Employed	4	6	8	6	8	10	10	8	8	2	6	6	2	2	2

11. Due to an overrun in design, the design stage took three months, i.e. months 3, 4 and 5 instead of only two months. The number of people working on design in the fifth month was 5. Calculate the percentage change in the cost incurred in the fifth month. (Due to improvement in coding technique, this stage was completed in months 6–8 only.)
(a) 20% (b) 30%
(c) 25% (d) 10%
12. With reference to the above question, what is the cost incurred in the new coding stage? (under the new technique 4 people work in the sixth month and 5 in the eighth.)
(a) ₹95,000 (b) ₹90,000
(c) ₹1,40,000 (d) ₹1,10,000
13. What is the difference in cost between the old and the new techniques? (Assume data in question 11 to be true)
(a) ₹60,000 (b) ₹25,000
(c) ₹70,000 (d) None of these
14. Under the new technique, which stage of software development is most expensive for Dataman Infosys?
(a) Testing (b) Specification
(c) Coding (d) Design
15. Which five consecutive months have the lowest average cost per man/month under the old technique?
(a) 1.5 (b) 9–13
(c) 11–15 (d) None of these

Directions for Questions 16 to 20: *Namaste Exports produces five types of trousers—A, B, C, D and E, using cloth of three qualities – high, medium and low, and dyes of three qualities – high, medium and low. One trousers require 3 m of cloth. The following table (Table 13.4) gives specific information about the production in Quarter 3 of 2025. It gives information about:*
1. *The number of trousers (of each category) produced, in thousands.*
2. *The percentage distribution of cloth quality in each type of trousers and*
3. *The percentage distribution of dye quality in each type of trousers.*

16. What is the total requirement of cloth?
(a) 300,000 m (b) 450,000 m
(c) 600,000 m (d) None of these
17. How many metres of medium quality cloth is consumed?
(a) 264,000 m (b) 288,000 m
(c) 312,000 m (d) None of these
18. How many metres of low-quality cloth is consumed by C-type trousers?
(a) 24,000 m (b) 48,000 m
(c) 60,000 m (d) None of these
19. What is the ratio of the three qualities of dyes in high-quality cloth ?
(a) 2 : 3 : 4 (b) 1 : 3 : 6
(c) 7 : 8 : 12 (d) Cannot be determined
20. What is the ratio of low-quality dye used for A-type to that used for B-type trousers?
(a) 1 : 3 (b) 3 : 8
(c) 1 : 2 (d) 4 : 9

TABLE 13.4 Namaste Exports: Q3 Cloth Production

			Distribution of Cloth (%)				Distribution of Dye (%)		
Trousers Type	Number in Thousand	Trousers type	High	Medium	Low	Trousers Type	High	Medium	Low
A	40	A	70	30	–	A	60	20	20
B	60	B	20	50	30	B	30	40	30
C	60	C	–	60	40	C	–	70	30
D	20	D	–	70	30	D	–	30	70
E	20	E	–	20	80	E	–	10	90

14 Mock Test Paper

Directions for Questions 1 to 4: *Consider the information provided in Figures 14.1 and 14.2 below relating to the Republic of Fantasia's foreign trade in 1897–98 and the first eight months of financial year 1898–99. Total trade with a region is defined as the sum of exports and imports from that region. Trade deficit is defined as the excess of imports over exports. Trade deficit may be negative.*

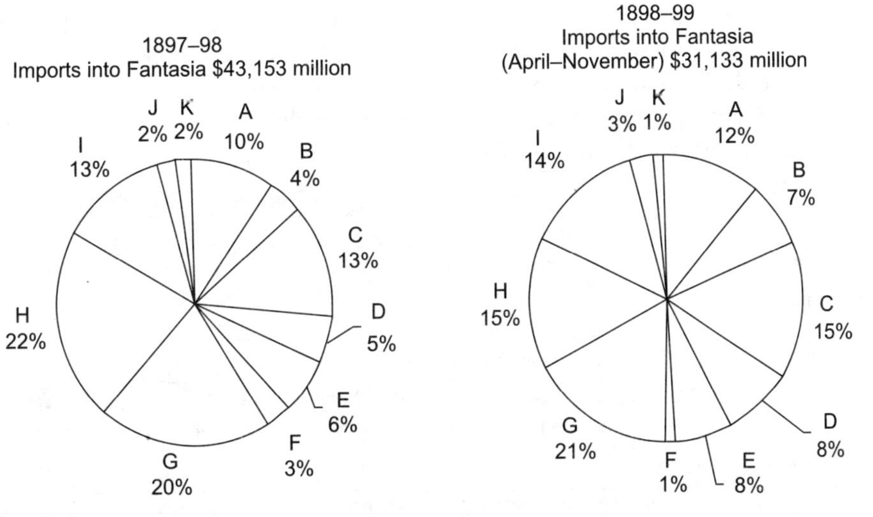

FIGURE 14.1 *Destination of Imports*

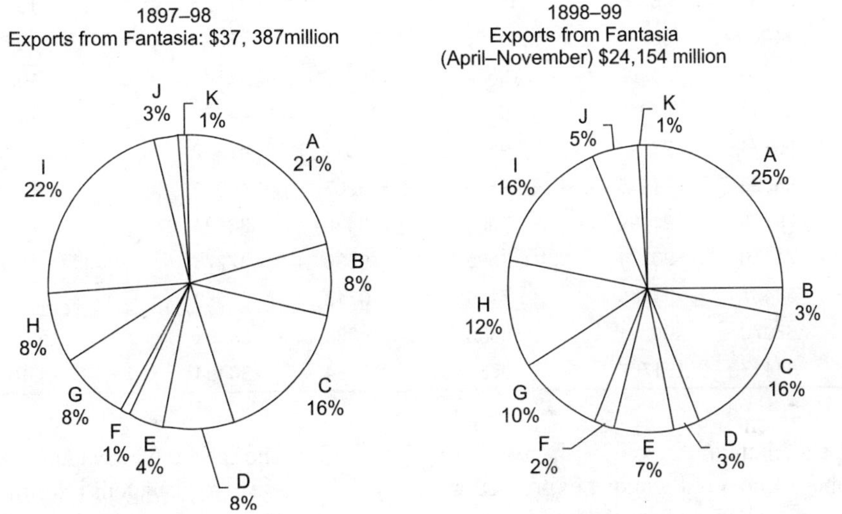

FIGURE 14.2 *Destination of Exports*

Refer to the nomenclature below for the name of the countries:

A. USA *B. Germany* *C. Other EU*
D. UK *E. Japan* *F. Russia*
G. Other East Europe *H. OPEC* *I. Asia*
J. Australia *K. Others*

1. What is the region with which Fantasia had the highest total trade in 1897–98?
(a) USA (b) Other EU
(c) OPEC (d) Asia
2. In 1897–98, the amount of exports from Fantasia in millions of dollars, to the region with which Fantasia had the lowest total trade, is approximately:
(a) 750 (b) 373
(c) 220 (d) 440
3. In 1897–98, the trade deficit with respect to Fantasia in billions of US dollars, for the region with the highest trade deficit with respect to Fantasia, is approximately equal to:
(a) 6.0 (b) 3.5
(c) 4.5 (d) 7.5
4. Amongst the region having a trade deficit with respect to Fantasia, the region with the lowest trade deficit with respect to Fantasia in 1897–98 is:
(a) USA (b) Asia
(c) Others (d) Australia

Directions for Questions 5 and 6: *Assume that the average monthly exports from Fantasia and imports to Fantasia during the remaining four months of 1898–99 financial year would be the same as that for the first eight months of the year.*

5. What is the region to which Fantasia's exports registered the highest percentage growth between 1897–98 and 1898–99?
(a) Japan (b) Australia
(c) Asia (d) Russia
6. What is the percentage growth rate in Fantasia'stotal trade deficit between 1897–98 and 1898–99 ?
(a) 22% (b) 44%
(c) 82% (d) 66%

Directions for Questions 7 to 12: *Answer the questions based on the following table.*

TABLE 14.1 Growth Trend in Rail Wagons

Year	Total Wagons Number	Covered Wagons Number	Open High Sided Wagons Number	Open Low Sided Wagons Number	Departmental Wagons Number	Special Type Wagons Number	Total Wagon Capacity (Million Tonnes)	Average Wagon Capacity (Tonnes)
1993	337562	157581	105469	12221	12009	50282	11.79	34.9
1994	312405	138642	101160	11922	11473	49208	11.32	36.2
1995	291360	121946	98795	11507	11185	47927	10.76	36.9
1996	280791	114065	98297	11196	11008	46225	10.62	37.8
1997	272127	106634	98906	10601	10645	45341	10.64	39.1
1998	263981	102217	97616	9726	10569	43853	10.69	40.5
1999	252944	96371	95613	9106	9612	42242	10.7	42.3
2000	234397	86024	91415	7735	8907	40316	10.26	43.8
2001	222193	75768	91099	7999	8443	38884	10.19	45.9
2002	216717	71950	90371	7585	9536	37275	10.09	46.6
2003	214760	68467	90765	7160	10718	37650	9.98	46.5
2004	227752	67870	100211	8882	11388	39401	10.66	46.8
2005	222379	64417	101757	8787	10964	36454	10.6	47.7

7. Find the True statement:
(a) The number of covered wagons expressed as a percentage of total wagons declined consistently from 1993 to 2002, but increased marginally in 2003 as compared to the previous year's level.
(b) The special type wagons expressed as a percentage of total wagons is the maximum during 2003.
(c) The open high sided wagons expressed as a percentage of total wagons increased during 1994 to 2001, but declined from the 2001 level in 2002.
(d) None of the above.

8. The special type wagons expressed as a percentage of total wagons were at almost same level during the following pair of years:
(a) 1995 and 2001 (b) 1998 and 2004
(c) 2000 and 2002 (d) 1993 and 1994
9. The departmental wagons expressed as a percentage of total wagons was the maximum during:
(a) 2002 (b) 2005
(c) 2004 (d) 2003
10. Find out the lowest annual growth rate amongst the following
(a) Annual growth rate of total wagons in 1999.
(b) Annual growth rate of covered wagons in 1998.
(c) Annual growth rate of special type wagons in 2002.
(d) Annual growth rate of total wagon capacity in 2000.
11. Find out the False statement:
(a) The annual growth rate of covered wagons in 1996 was higher than the same in 2000.
(b) The annual growth rate of open high sided wagons in 1997 was higher than the same in 2003.
(c) The annual percentage growth rate of average wagon capacity has been the maximum in 1999.
(d) None of the above.
12. Find out the highest annual growth rate amongst the following
(a) Annual growth rate of total wagons in 1995.
(b) Annual growth rate of covered wagons in 2002.
(c) Annual growth rate of open low-sided wagons in 1998.
(d) Annual growth rate of departmental wagons in 2000.

Directions for Questions 13 to 16: *Read the following information on Sectoral Trends in Mergers & Acquisitions in India (2001–02 to 2006–07) given in tables below and answer the questions.*

TABLE 14.2 Sector wise Number of 'Mergers & Acquisitions'

Sectors	2001–02	2002–03	2003–04	2004–05	2005–06	2006–07
Food & Beverage	113	77	77	74	63	61
Textile	57	59	59	64	77	55
Chemicals	134	98	112	99	79	62
Drugs & Pharma	64	60	44	50	60	72
Cement	11	7	8	22	0	0
IT & Telecom	153	114	84	80	109	103
Diversified	15	8	13	4	7	5
Financial Services	194	201	160	116	193	177
Other Services	297	280	287	281	271	293
Misc Manufacturing	31	36	31	35	35	24
Non Mineral Products	32	24	27	27	47	34

TABLE 14.3 Sector wise Number of 'Mergers'

Sectors	2001–02	2002–03	2003–04	2004–05	2005–06	2006–07
Food & Beverage	17	23	10	19	20	8
Textile	7	7	8	11	21	23
Chemicals	27	15	12	23	24	15
Drugs & Pharma	6	17	14	10	15	12
Cement	0	2	1	3	0	0
IT & Telecom	19	19	13	16	17	12
Diversified	1	0	1	0	0	0
Financial Services	91	107	87	41	75	51
Other Services	90	92	105	81	61	83
Misc Manufacturing	3	13	0	4	11	3
Non Mineral Products	3	5	1	5	8	11

13. What is the approximate proportion of 'mergers' to 'acquisitions' for the entire period (2001–02 to 2006–07)?
(a) 26% (b) 36%
(c) 30% (d) 20%

14. For how many sectors is the proportion of 'mergers' to 'mergers & acquisitions' greater than 20% for the entire period (2001–02 to 2006–07)?
(a) 2 (b) 3
(c) 4 (d) 5

15. For how many sectors merger activity (measured by number of mergers) is more in the first 3 years as compared to the last 3 years?
(a) 7 (b) 3
(c) 6 (d) 5

16. If the turbulence over a period is defined by the sum of each of the differences (in absolute terms) in number of mergers & acquisitions on a year-on-year basis, then which sector is considered the most turbulent for the entire period (2001–02 to 2006– 07)?
(a) Financial Services (b) IT & Telecom
(c) Food & Beverages (d) Other services

Directions for Questions 17 to 20: *On the basis of the data given below:*

TABLE 14.4

Area/Month		January	February	March
Sale in Bistupur				
	Television	900	1050	1200
	iPods	15750	16800	17850
Sales in Sakchi				
	Television	1800	2100	2400
	iPods	9450	10080	10710
Sales in Kadma				
	Television	6300	7350	8400
	iPods	6300	6720	7140

Units ordered = Units Sold + Ending Inventory – Beginning Inventory
All sales figures are in Rupees thousand.
All other things are constant
All Rupees figures are in thousands

17. In the period from January to March, Jamshedpur Electronics sold 3150 units of televisions having started with a beginning inventory of 2520 units and ending with an inventory of 2880. What was the value of order placed (in ₹ thousand) by Jamshedpur Electronics during the three month period? [Profits are 25% of cost price, uniformly.]
(a) 28080 (b) 2808
(c) 26325 (d) 22320
(e) 25200

18. What was the total value of surcharge paid (in ₹ thousand) – at the rate of 14% of sales value – by Jamshedpur Electronics, over the period of three months?
(a) Cannot be calculated
(b) 18522 (c) 18548
(d) 18425 (e) 18485

19. 10% of sales price of iPods and 20% of sales price of televisions contribute to the profits of Jamshedpur Electronics. How much profit did the company earn in the month of January from Bistupur and Kadma from the two products?
(a) 513 (b) 4410
(c) 3645 (d) 5230
(e) 5350

20. In the period from January to March, consider that Jamshedpur Electronics ordered 7560 units of iPods for all three areas put together. What was the unit sales price of an iPod during the period? The ending inventory was 6120 units and the beginning inventory stood at 5760.
(a) 14.00 (b) 14.65
(c) 14.80 (d) 13.00
(e) 13.60

15 Mock Test Paper

Directions for Questions 1 to 5: *Table 15.1 presents data on percentage population covered by schools and colleges in selected underdeveloped countries of the world.*

TABLE 15.1 Percentage of Population covered by Schools and Colleges in some Underdeveloped Countries

	Percentage Covered Schools			Percentage Covered Colleges		
	Urban	Rural	Total	Urban	Rural	Total
Nigeria	77	61	64	52	48	49
India	98	69	77	64	62	63
Pakistan	86	46	63	67	53	59
Ghana	47	38	41	43	36	38
Sri Lanka	72	52	57	70	68	69
Indonesia	88	59	68	50	46	47
Nepal	73	68	69	48	44	45

Note: A person is said to be covered by a school if there is a school within 10 kms of his place of normal residence and he is said to be covered by a college if he has a college in a radius of 100 kms from the place of residence.

(1) Country A is said to dominate country B (A > B) if A has a higher percentage in total coverage for both schools and colleges.

(2) Country A is said to dominate country B ($A_U > B_U$) if A has a higher percentage in urban coverage for both schools and colleges.

(3) Country A is said to dominate Country B ($A_R > B_R$) if A has a higher percentage in rural coverage for both schools and colleges.

(4) A country is said to be on the development frontier if no other country dominates it in total coverage.

(5) A country is similarly said to be on the development frontier urban if no other country dominates it in urban coverage.

(6) A country is similarly said to be on the development frontier rural if no other country dominates it in rural coverage.

1. The countries on the Development Frontier are:
   (a) India and Ghana
   (b) Nigeria and Sri Lanka
   (c) India and Indonesia
   (d) None of these
2. Which of these countries are on the Development Frontier Urban?
   (a) India and Sri Lanka
   (b) India and Pakistan
   (c) India, Pakistan and Sri Lanka
   (d) None of these
3. Using the above data, and looking at only the college columns, it can be concluded that the urban population in Ghana as a percentage of its total population is:
   (a) 27.55%
   (b) 31.22%
   (c) 28.56%
   (d) Cannot be determined
4. Which of these represents the correct sequence of ascending order of rural population as a percentage of urban population?
   (a) India, Nigeria, Ghana
   (b) Ghana, India, Nigeria
   (c) India, Ghana and Nigeria
   (d) Cannot be determined
5. Which of these countries are not on the Development Frontier Rural?
   (a) Nigeria, India and Nepal
   (b) Nigeria, Pakistan, Ghana, Indonesia and Nepal
   (c) Nigeria, Pakistan, Ghana Indonesia and Nepal
   (d) Nigeria, Pakistan, Ghana and Nepal only

Directions for Questions 6 to 8: *Answer the questions on the basis of the following line graph (Figure 15.1).*

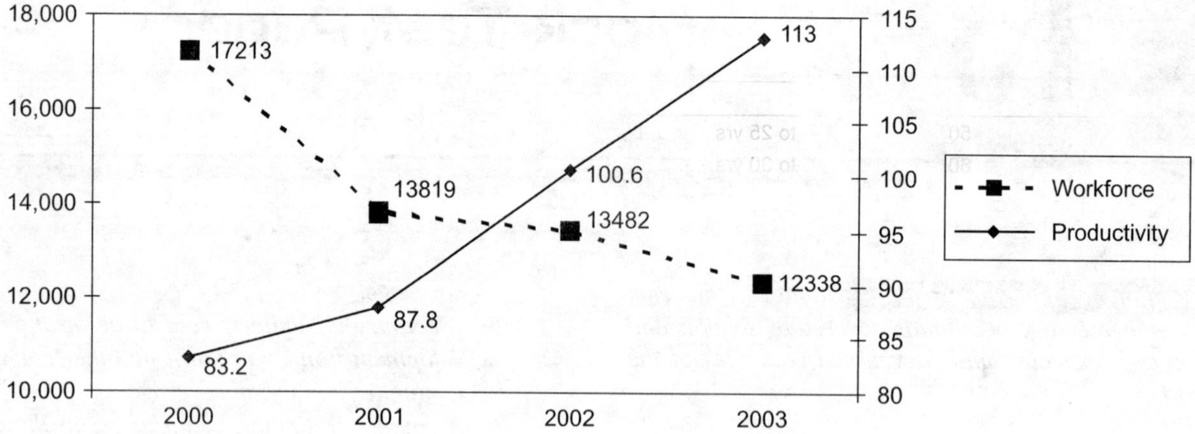

FIGURE 15.1 *The Change in Workforce and Productivity of Bajaj Auto for the Period 2000–03 (Vehicles Per Employee)*

6. By how much percentage has production changed (approximately) in 2003 as compared to its value for 2000?
   (a) –3 % (b) +5%
   (c) 0 % (d) +7%
7. The percentage change in which of the mentioned areas is the highest over the period 2000–03?
   (a) Workforce (b) Productivity
   (c) Production (d) (a) and (c) both
8. Which two variables have moved in the same direction in the mentioned period?
   (a) Workforce and productivity
   (b) Workforce and production
   (c) Production and productivity
   (d) None of these

Directions for Questions 9 to 13: *Refer to the following table (Table 15.2).*

TABLE 15.2 Real Estate Values

Location	Rental Value (Apt) (₹/month)	Capital Value (₹/sq. ft.)	Location	Rental value (Apt) (₹/month)	Capital Value (₹/sq. ft.)
Vasant Vihar (Grade A)	1 lakh–1.75 lakh	7000–10,000	Cuffe Parade, Churchgate	60,000–1.25 lakh	7000–15,000
Jor Bagh, Sunder Nagar	1.25 lakh–2 lakh	10,000–12000	Malabar Hill, Breach Candy	80,000–1.5 lakh	10,000–18,000
Kalkaji	10000–15000	2000–2500	Bandra, Juhu	45,000–1 lakh	6500–10000
Gurgaon (Grade A)	25,000–35,000	2200–3000	Powai	15,000–45000	2750–4500
Noida (Grade A)	15,000–25,000	1400–2000	Andheri	18,000–45000	3000–5000

9. How many areas amongst those shown, will Mr Vinay Srivastava be able to purchase a 1000 sq. ft flat if he wants to invest upto ₹25 lakh. (He has a saving of ₹25 lakh on retirement.)
   (a) 1 (b) 6
   (c) 7 (d) None of these
10. For Question 8, if Mr Vinay Srivastava decides to take a loan of 75% of the value of the property apart from his personal investment of ₹25 lakh, in how many areas of Mumbai or Delhi will it still be possible that a 1000 sq. ft. flat might cost above his budget?
   (a) 1 (b) 2
   (c) 3 (d) 4
11. The ratio of the highest possible rent/sq ft to the lowest possible rent/sq ft from amongst the areas exhibited is:
   (a) 25 (b) 20
   (c) 15 (d) Cannot be determined
12. The highest possible value of the rent/sq. ft. is for:
   (a) Cuffe Parade, Churchgate
   (b) Malabar Hill, Breach Candy
   (c) Vasant Vihar (Grade A)
   (d) Cannot be determined
13. Mr Vijay Srivastava bought a 2000 sq. ft. flat for ₹ 4,800,000. How many possible areas could he have bought the flat in:
   (a) 1 (b) 2
   (c) 3 (d) 4

Directions for Questions 14 to 16: *Refer to the following table (Table 15.3).*

TABLE 15.3 Term Life Insurance

Policy/Insurance	Max. Age of Entry	Tenures Possible	Max. Age at Expiry	Min. Sum Assured	For Life Cover of ₹ 10 lakh Premium in ₹ (Entry Age/Coverage Period in Yrs)			
					(30/25)	(40/20)	(50/10)	(55/10)
ICICI Prudential	50	5 to 25 yrs	65	₹1 lakh	3043	5110	8197	N.A.
HDFC Standard Life	60	5 to 30 yrs	65	₹1 lakh	3050	5130	8320	12,600
Max New York Life	55	5,10,15,20,25 yrs	60	₹2.5 lakh	3220	5650	10,000	12,150
Birla Sunlife	55	5,10,15,20,25 yrs	70	₹2 lakh	3160	5150	8790	13,100
LIC Anmol Jeevan	50	5 to 25 yrs	60	₹5 lakh	3860	7010	11,450	N.A.

14. The maximum that a 50-year-old individual can hope to insure his life for is:
(a) 10 yrs (b) 15 yrs
(c) 20 yrs (d) Cannot be determined
15. From the table above, if a 50-year-old individual wants to buy a life insurance cover of ₹ 10 lakh, (for a coverage period of 10 yrs) then his best option is:
(a) ICICI prudential
(b) HDFC Standard Life
(c) Max New York Life (till 60 yrs.)
(d) Cannot be determined
16. From the table, how many life insurance options are available for a 51-year-old who wants 6 years of coverage:
(a) 1 (b) 2
(c) 3 (d) None of these

Directions for Questions 17 to 20: *The rate of taxation has the following slabs in New Foundland:*

Taxable Income	*Tax Rate*
0–50,000	*Exempt*
50,000–60,000	*10%*
60,000–150,000	*20%*
150,000+	*30%*

For salaried employees having salaries below 150,000 p.a., a standard deduction of 30,000 is available to salaried employees, which is reduced from the total income. Besides, a rebate is available on investments in various saving schemes like Provident Fund, Infrastructure Bonds, Post office savings, etc. The rebate is calculated at 20% of the total investment in these savings instruments. Thus, if a person has invested 10,000 in some saving instruments, he gets 2,000 rebate on his net tax liability.

Note: all the numbers are in the local currency.

However, if the salary increases above ₹150,000 p.a., the standard deduction is reduced to ₹25,000 and the rebate on investments is calculated at the rate of 15% of the total investment. Thus, a person saving ₹20,000 will get a rebate of 3,000 on his liability. Besides, a tax surcharge of 10% is added on the total tax liability for all tax payers. Also, working women have a further rebate of ₹5,000 available to them on their total tax liability.

Based on the above information, answer questions 5 to 8.

17. What will be the total tax liability of Mr Rajiv Srivastava, who has a salary of 150,000 p.a. [assume he saved 40,000 in the year].
(a) 5,000 (b) 5,500
(c) 1,000 (d) Data insufficient
18. For the question above, if Mr Srivastava's salary increases by 5,000 p.a., what will be the change in his net income after tax [assuming that he again saves 40,000 in the year]
(a) Increase of 1,000
(b) Decrease of 800
(c) Increase of 600
(d) Increase of 5,000
19. Mrs Shruti Srivastava who works in the same firm, earns a salary of 150,000 p.a. How much must she save to pay no tax for the year?
(a) 41,000 (b) 40,000
(c) 30,000 (d) 60,000
20. Prakash Purti has a salary income of 144,000. Besides he has earned 35,000 as consultancy income. He has saved 70,000 for the year in tax savings instruments. How much tax will he have to pay?
(a) 18,800 (b) 14,800
(c) 4,800 (d) None of these

16 Mock Test Paper

Directions for Questions 1 to 4 *There are 16 boxes in a grid. Each of the 16 boxes has a number as shown below. The value of the box is the number on the box.*

Four friends Amar, Biren, Chandan and Deepak are playing a game, where the objective is to make the maximum addition of the boxes. Each person has exactly 4 boxes with him at all points of time.

TABLE 16.1

	1	2	3	4
A	22	12	30	6
B	10	16	24	20
C	32	2	28	14
D	18	4	26	8

1. *Amar did not own any of the boxes in the A-row.*
2. *Biren's highest number is A-3.*
3. *B-2 & C-1 belong to someone other than Chandan.*
4. *Chandan doesn't own any of the boxes in the 1-column.*
5. *In the last round of the game, Amar traded B-4 for B-1.*
6. *D-2, A-2 and D-3 all belong to the same player.*
7. *C-1 B-3 and 4-D all belong to the same player.*
8. *Deepak's score was 8 higher than Biren's who has three boxes in the A row.*
9. *Amar has just one box in the B-row, which is B-1.*

Based on the information above answer the questions which follow:

1. Who has the lowest total?_
   (a) Amar (b) Biren
   (c) Chandan (d) Deepak
2. To whom does C-4 belong at the end of the game?
   (a) Amar (b) Biren
   (c) Chandan (d) Deepak
3. What is the difference between the total of Deepak and Chandan?
   (a) 4 (b) 8
   (c) 14 (d) 18
4. Who has the highest total at the end of the game?
   (a) Amar (b) Biren
   (c) Chandan (d) Deepak

Directions for Questions 5 to 9: *Answer the questions based on the following information.*

Ms. Vandana Surana, a farming consultant has been posed with a business decision problem by Mr. Dipak Jhunjhunwala. He has 5 acres of land suitable to grow rice or dal or both, 64 man days of human labour and ₹1600 as working capital. The alternative available to him is to invest in the production of rice or dal or a combination of the two crops. The labour requirement to produce rice and dal in an acre is 8 man days and 16 man days respectively while the cash requirements to grow the crop in an acre is ₹400 and ₹200 respectively. The price ratio of produce per of rice and dal is 1 : 2 and in the worst alternative to Mr. Dipak profit is zero. The cropping season is about to begin and Mr. Dipak is puzzled.

5. Which of the following combination of production is possible?
   (a) Rice (4 acre) and dal (1 acre)
   (b) Rice (1 acre) and dal (4 acre)
   (c) Rice (2.5 acre) and dal (2.5 acre)
   (d) None of these.
6. Which of the following is the best alternative to Mr. Jhunjhunwala in terms of profit?
   (a) Rice (3 acre) and dal (2 acre)
   (b) Rice (4 acre) and dal (0 acre)
   (c) Rice (2 acre) and dal (3 acre)
   (d) Data insufficient
7. What is the margin percentage in the rice (2 acre) and dal (3 acre) production alternative?
   (a) 75%
   (b) 100%
   (c) 50%
   (d) Can't be determined
8. At dal (3 acre) and rice (2 acre) production alternative which resource(s) are idle?
   (a) Capital only
   (b) Land and capital only
   (c) Labour and capital
   (d) Land and labour

9. Which of the following is definitely true?
   (a) There are exactly two points at which the positive profits are maximised.
   (b) At the maximum profit levels for option A above, both labour and capital are being utilised fully.
   (c) To maximise his returns Mr. Jhunjhunwala can put half of his working capital in bank without compromising the maximum possible profit from the production of the crops.
   (d) None of these

Directions for Questions 10 to 16: *A pond has three types of fishes—Big, Medium & Small. On the 31st of July there were 100 Big, 500 Medium and 4000 Small fishes.*

Every day, the number of small fishes becomes double its value of the previous day. However, 3 small fishes are eaten by each Medium fish every day. Thus the doubled number of Small fishes is reduced by the number of small fishes eaten by medium fishes to get the tally at the end of the day. The day's end value is doubled the next day.

The medium fishes are incremented by 250 every day, and the incremented number of medium fishes eats three small fishes every day. However, the number of medium fishes are reduced after that due to big fishes eating up one medium fish every day.

The number of big fishes increased by 25 each day (by the birth of 25 big fishes daily). Big fishes have a life span of 10 days, little fishes have 20 days and medium fishes have a lifespan of 15 days.

The questions below are concerned with the goings on of the first week of August. Assume that on 31st July all fishes in the pond are 0 day's old.

10. What is the maximum value of the number of medium fishes as of end of day on any day during the period?
    (a) 1100 (b) 1125
    (c) 875 (d) 850
11. On which day will this maximum get achieved?
    (a) 6th August (b) 7th August
    (c) 5th august (d) 5th and 6th August
12. What is the number of small fishes at the end of 7th August?
    (a) 192050 (b) 188675
    (c) 96025 (d) 99400
13. What is the total number of small fishes eaten during the period?
    (a) 18000 (b) 19000
    (c) 20000 (d) 21000
14. What will be the number of small fishes in the pond at the end of August?
    (a) 194250 (b) 208425
    (c) 416850 (d) Infinite
15. What is the total number of fishes in the pond at the end of 4th August?
    (a) 27550 (b) 26500
    (c) 27350 (d) None of these
16. What is the ratio of the number of medium fishes eaten to the number of small fishes eaten between 1st and 7th August?
    (a) 1: 18 (b) 1: 20
    (c) 1:15 (d) 1:12

Directions for Questions 17 to 20: *The following table (Table 16.2) shows the comparison between Malaysia and India on certain parameters. Study the table and answer questions 1–4.*

TABLE 16.2 India and Malaysia: Peer-to-Peer Evaluation on Select Parameters

EPF Malaysia	Parameter	EPF India
11% by employee, 12% by employer	Contribution	12% by both employee and employer
3 accounts; 60% in retirement, 30% in housing, 10% in healthcare	Fund channelled into	2 accounts; 65.3% into provident fund, 34.7% into pension scheme
$50.5 billion	EPF assets	$33.47 billion
53.10%	EPF assets as % of GDP	7%
$4886.60	Average balance per member	$1242
Twice a year	Account statement to members	Once a year
Yes	Educating members on EPF benefits	No
1983–2001	Average annual rate of return	1986–2000
7.62%	Nominal	11.80%
2.94%	Inflation (CPI)	9.00%
4.66%	Real	2.70%

17. The ratio of India's GDP to Malaysia's GDP is the closest to:
(a) 6 : 1 (b) 5 : 1
(c) 4 : 1 (d) Cannot be determined

18. Assuming that there is an equal amount of service period put in by all members of the EPF, nearly which of these will represent the ratio of salary income in US$ in Malaysia to that in India? (Assume equal withdrawals.)
(a) $\dfrac{4886.6 \times 0.24}{1242 \times 0.23}$ (b) $\dfrac{4886.6 \times 0.23}{1242 \times 0.24}$
(c) $\dfrac{4886.6}{1242}$ (d) Cannot be determined

19. Based on the value of EPF assets and the average balance per member, what can be concluded about the number of EPF members in Malaysia to the number of EPF members in India: (Assume that the value of the EPF assets is equal to the total balance of all members of the EPF.)
(a) It is greater
(b) It is smaller
(c) Both are equal
(d) No conclusion can be made

20. Which of the following statements is/are not true?
(i) The real value of 1$ invested in Malaysia in 1983 will be greater than the real value of 1$ invested in India in 1986 by the year 2000.
(ii) The inflation in India is over 300% more than the inflation in Malaysia.
(iii) The real rate of return for the period shown for India is over 50% of the real rate of return for the period shown for Malaysia.
(a) All of these (b) (i) and (iii)
(c) (ii) only (d) (ii) and (iii) only

17 Mock Test Paper

Directions for Questions 1 to 10: *Mr Keshri, the CEO of Keshri Foods Inc. is facing a vital business decision. His company has two exciting new inventions of mango varieties. The company has the option to go in for further development of either of these two varieties—Alphonso Superior and Langda Inferior. He estimates that the development cost of Alphonso Superior would be $750,000, while Langda Inferior would cost $250,000. The salaries of scientists' would constitute 28% of the cost while the research equipment and development facilities would account for 39%, irrespective of the variety of mango developed. Patenting cost would be $30,000 each while the rest of the budget would be accounted for by overheads. Mr Keshri calculates that the country wise patent license fees for Alphonso Superior would be $7500 per year per territory in developed countries and $2500 per year per territory in an under developed country. The country wise patent license fees in developed and underdeveloped countries for Langda Inferior would be $1250 per year per territory. The latest UN statistics showed that there were 150000 territories in the world, which could be classified as developed territories and 250000 territories were underdeveloped territories.*

1. The scientist's salaries for Alphonso Superior & Langda Inferior would respectively be:
   (a) $150000 & $70000 (b) $100000 & $45000
   (c) $210000 & $70000 (d) $105000 & $36000
2. Patenting cost would constitute what percentage of the total cost for Alphonso Superior?
   (a) 12% (b) 4%
   (c) 6% (d) 8%
3. What is the overhead cost for Alphonso Superior?
   (a) $112450 (b) 108750
   (c) 105000 (d) None of these
4. If the product was to be distributed in only 35% of the developed countries territories and 25% of the underdeveloped countries territories, then what would be the earnings (in$'000) through the distribution of Alphonso Superior variety in two years?
   (a) 8800000 (b) 1200000
   (c) 1000000 (d) None of these
5. The license fee of Langda Inferior if it were licensed to all the available territories for a period of one year would amount to (in $'000):
   (a) 480000 (b) 550000
   (c) 500000 (d) None of these
6. If the cost of developing the Alphonso Superior variety is actually 40% higher than the estimated cost due to a terrible miscalculation on Mr Keshri's part, then the scientist's fees in $ 000 is (assume % share remains same):
   (a) 2940 (b) 29.4
   (c) 294 (d) None of these
7. If the development blueprint of Alphonso Superior could be sold at $20000 per territory, then what would be the revenue from such sales (in $ '000) assuming that Mr Keshri is able to sell the development blueprints in only 130 territories of developed countries and 113 territories of underdeveloped countries?
   (a) 243000 (b) 2430
   (c) 243 (d) 4860
8. If the license fee rates for Langda Inferior in the developed and underdeveloped countries were to go up by 20%, then the revenue earned in one year in all the available territories would be (in $ '000)
   (a) 4,00,000 (b) 50,00,000
   (c) 60,00,000 (d) 6,00,000
9. If the patenting cost for Langda Inferior decreases by 35%, then what would be the patenting cost as a percentage of the total cost for developing Langda Inferior? Assume that there is no change in the other components of the cost.
   (a) 6% (b) 8.8%
   (c) 7.8% (d) 8.14%
10. If the cost of research equipment & development facilities for Alphonso Superior goes up by 25%, then the increase in the cost of developing & patenting Alphonso Superior would be:
    (a) $365625 (b) $37455.75
    (c) $34456.5 (d) None of these

Directions for Questions 11 to 15: *Answer the questions based on the following information. The following table (Table 17.1) shows the capacity to do a work in different work centres of Dataman Infosys Private Limited at different times of the day.*

It is given that:

- *A product passes through work centres A-B-C-D-E in sequence and when it comes out of department E it is said to be the Final Product or Output and it is transferred to the warehouse.*
- *Transfers of semi-processed parts occur at the end of every 30-minute shifts and it takes no time.*
- *Each work center completes its work on the raw material it receives in a maximum period of 30 minutes.*
- *The unprocessed parts at the work centres are called inventories.*
- *The work is done normally on the 'first come first serve' basis.*
- *Every time work centre A has raw material equal to its capacity to be processed in the next half hour.*

The other work centres work according to the availability of raw materials based on the completion of work in previous work centres.

At 9:00 work centres A, B, C, D and E had 2, 6, 4, 1 and 1 unit respectively to process.

TABLE 17.1 **Work Capacity of Dataman Infosys Private Limited**

Time	A	B	C	D	E	Output
9:00	2	6	4	1	1	
9:30	6	1	3	6	3	
10:00	4	5	2	3	4	
10:30	2	2	2	5	2	
11:00	5	5	5	1	5	
11:30	3	4	6	2	4	
12:00	6	6	5	2	6	
12:30	4	3	2	1	5	
13:00	5	3	6	3	4	
13:30	2	5	6	5	3	
14:00	2	5	3	4	4	
14:30	6	3	3	6	5	
15:00	5	1	5	3	5	
15:30	2	6	2	2	6	
16:00	4	2	2	5	4	
16:30	1	3	1	6	5	
17:00	2	3	4	4	3	

11. What is the total output of the day?
    (a) 46 (b) 40
    (c) 50 (d) 48
12. Which work centre will show any inventory first?
    (a) A (b) B
    (c) D (d) E
13. If at 10:00 the company got an urgent order of processing 10 units of special material for mathapacchi.com Limited, when will the company be able to deliver the material at the earliest? (It is given that the special material doesn't take any extra time to process at any work centre.)
    (a) 15:30 (b) 14:30
    (c) 15:00 (d) 16:00
14. What will be the total output at 11:30?
    (a) 11 (b) 14
    (c) 16 (d) None of these
15. Which work centre is running at minimum level of efficiency for the period 9:00–11:00?
    (a) B (b) C
    (c) D (d) E

Directions for Questions 16 to 20: *The data given below in Table 17.2 shows the money supply and interest rates in different countries on different types of bonds. Answer the questions that follow based on the information provided.*

TABLE 17.2 Money and Interest Rates in Different Countries

	Money Supply* % Change on Year Ago		Interest Rates % p.a. (May 19th 2024)					
			3-Month's Money Market		2-Years	10-Year Govt Bonds		Corporate
	Narrow	Broad	Latest	Year Ago	Govt. Bonds	Latest	Year Ago	Bonds
Australia	+8.0	+13.9 Mar	5.49	4.71	5.28	6.88	4.9	6.88
Britain	+7.1	+7.7 Mar	4.5	3.56	4.82	5.14	4.03	5.92
Canada	+11.6	+8.9 Mar	2.02	3.20	3.11	5.14	4.62	6.32
Denmark	+8.1	+10.6 Mar	2.25	2.60	2.64	4.48	3.91	5.65
Japan	+4.1	+1.9 Apr	0.02	0.02	0.13	1.5	0.58	1.58
Sweden	+0.5	+2.2 Mar	1.95	3.16	2.97	4.69	4.16	3.13
Switzerland	+9.9	+4.1 Apr	0.26	0.28	1.22	2.72	2.16	2.56
United States	+6.8	+4.9 Apr	1.09	1.20	2.58	4.78	3.38	6.16
Euro Area	+11.4	+6.3 Mar	2.09	2.37	2.55	4.28	3.687	4.14

*Narrow: M1 except Britain & Sweden MO, broad: M2 or M3 except Britain M4, Germany for bonds. Benchmarks: US 30-yrs. 5.48%, Japan No. 2591.49%. Central Bank rates: US fed funds 1.00%, ECB refinancing 2.00%, BOJ overnight call 0.001%, BOE repo 4.25%. Sources: Commerzbank, Danske Bank, J.P. Morgan Chase, Royal Bank of Canada, Stockholmsborsen, UBS, Global insite, Westpac, Thomson Detastream. Rates cannot be construed as banks' offers.

16. How many countries have shown a single direction in their interest rates over each of the two types of bonds (3 month money market) and 10 year govt. bonds?
    (a) 1
    (b) 2
    (c) 3
    (d) 4
17. For the 9 countries shown above, what is the average % increase in the value of the money supply (narrow) from a year ago?
    (a) 7.1
    (b) 7.3
    (c) 7.5
    (d) Cannot be determined
18. The highest interest rates are available for which category?
    (a) 10-yrs govt bond, latest
    (b) 10-yrs govt bond, year ago
    (c) Corporate bonds
    (d) either a or c
19. The highest % change in the % rate of interest between 2 yrs. govt. bonds for a country and the latest value of 10 yrs. govt. bonds is approximately:
    (a) 123% (b) 153%
    (c) 1054% (d) None of these
20. The country with the second lowest rate of interest across all categories is:
    (a) Japan
    (b) Sweden
    (c) Switzerland
    (d) There is no such country

18 Mock Test Paper

Directions for Questions 1 to 4: *Refer to Table 18.1 and answer the questions that follow.*

TABLE 18.1 Data Pertaining to Fixed Assets *(₹ in crore)*

Sl. No.	Particulars	Gross Block				Depreciation				Net Block	
		As at 31.03.23	Additions and/or Transfers	Deductions and/or Transfers	As at 31.03.24	Upto 31.03.23	Deductions and/or Transfers	For the Year	Upto 31.03.24	As at 31.03.24	As at 31.03.23
1	Freehold Land	64.12	5.78	0.01	69.89	–	–	–	–	69.89	64.12
2	Leasehold Land	52.89	0.13	2.72	50.3	2.87	0.08	1.3	4.09	46.21	50.02
3	Buildings	441.97	25.47	0.24	467.2	74.87	0.03	10.48	85.32	381.88	367.1
4	Workers' Quarters Under Government Subsidised Schemes	0.55	–	–	0.55	0.47	–	–	0.47	0.08	0.08
5	Railway Sidings	101.25	1.5	–	102.75	23.82	–	4.97	28.79	73.96	77.43
6	Plant and Machinery	4311.7	248.44	21.49	4538.7	1889	14.66	219.5	2094	2444.64	2422.49
7	Ships	108.23	-	44.11	64.12	32.16	13.83	4.54	22.87	41.25	76.07
8	Furniture, Fittings and Office Equipment	142.48	10.63	4.42	148.69	73.33	2.98	11.45	81.8	66.89	69.15
9	Livestock	0.01	–	–	0.01	–	–	–	–	0.01	0.01
10	Vehicles Etc.	25.99	21.09	3.14	43.94	11.31	1.5	2.93	12.74	31.2	14.68
		5249.2	313.04	76.13	5486.1	2108	33.08	255.1	2330.1	3156.01	3141.15
	Previous Year	5246.2	236.71	233.74	5249.2	2009	153.78	253	2108.1		
	Capital Work-in-progress								89.02	102.9	
	(including Advances and Pre-operative Expenses)									3245.03	3244.05

1. The asset category for which the maximum depreciation has been claimed (as a percentage of its purchase value) is:
   (a) Furniture, fittings and office equipment
   (b) Ships
   (c) Plant and Machinery
   (d) None of these
2. Approximately what % of the gross block has been depreciated (upto 31.03.02)?
   (a) 40.2% (b) 41.3%
   (c) 42.4% (d) None of these
3. The highest % increase in net block was for?
   (a) Freehold Land (b) Ships
   (c) Vehicles etc. (d) None of these
4. The highest % addition to the gross block was?
   (a) Buildings
   (b) Plant and machinery
   (c) Vehicles
   (d) None of these

Directions for Questions 5 to 8: *The famous Pack & Chew Restaurant in Interlaken Switzerland, increased its sales of samosas by 20% in 2006. This increase in sales* *was exactly equal (in terms of increase in units) as that in 2008. However, 2007 having been an unusually poor year, the value of the decrease in the sales of samosas in 2007 was equal to half the value of the increase in 2008 (or for that matter in 2006).*

Due to an anticipated increase in the salaries of his cooks, the proprietor Monsieur Jean Nitin Francard had increased the sales price of the samosas by 1 Euro in 2006. However, the increase occurred only in 2007, and the value of this increase was double the value of the increase in sales price in 2008 (on a per samosa basis).

The cost of making a samosa prior to the increase in wages was 6 Euros, while the profit saw an increase of 80% in 2006 (when it became 14400 Euros).

The selling price was consistently incremented by 1 Euro every year from 2006 to 2008.

5. What is the total cost of the restaurant in 2005? (in Euros)
   (a) 23000 (b) 24000
   (c) 25000 (d) 26000
6. How many samosas were sold in 2008?
   (a) 4900 (b) 4800
   (c) 5000 (d) None of these
7. The sales value in 2007 is (in Euros):
   (a) 43200 (b) 32000
   (c) 44000 (d) 57200
8. Which of the following statements is/are true?
   (i) The margin has always improved (margin = S.P. – Cost).
   (ii) The profits have increased every year.
   (iii) The number of years in which sales exceeded the average sales in the 4 year period, bears to the number of years in which sales was less than the average sales for the 4 year period, a ratio of 1:1.
   (a) (i) only (b) (i) & (iii) only
   (c) (ii) only (d) (iii) only

Directions for Questions 9 to 13: *The following table (Table 18.2) gives details regarding the total earning of 15 employees and the number of days they have worked on complex, medium and simple operations in the month of June 2024. Note that payments are made on the basis of achievement of a minimum level of efficiency. In case that level of output is not met there is no payment to the employee.*

TABLE 18.2* **Total Earnings and Work Days of Employees in a Firm**

Employee Code	Total Earning (In $)				Total Days			
	Complex	Medium	Simple	Total	Complex	Medium	Simple	Total
EC22147	82.98		636.53	719.51	3	0	23	26
EC22148	51.53		461.73	513.26	3.5	1.67	16	21
EC22149	171.71		79.10	250.81	5.5	4	8.5	18
EC22150	100.47		497.47	597.95	6	4.67	7.33	18
EC22151	594.43	159.64		754.06	9.67	13.33	0	23
EC22156	89.70			89.70	8	0	1	9
EC22158	472.31	109.73	213.67	582.04	1.39	9.61	1	12
EC22164	402.25	735.22		1351.14	5.27	12.07	0.67	18
EC22170	576.57			576.57	21	0	0	21
EC22171	286.48	6.10		292.57	8.38	4.25	0.38	13
EC22172	512.10	117.46		629.56	10	8.5	3.5	22
EC22173	1303.88			1303.88	25.5	0	.5	26
EC22174	1017.94			1017.94	26	0	0	26
EC22179	46.56	776.19		822.75	2	19	0	21
EC22180	116.40	1262.79		1379.19	5	19	0	24

* You are likely to find errors of rounding off in the table.

9. How many employees are getting more than $25 per day in complex work?
   (a) 8 (b) 9
   (c) 10 (d) 11
10. How many specific instances of employees not meeting their required level of output (minimum) can be seen in the table?
    (a) 8 (b) 7
    (c) 9 (d) 10
11. Which employee has received the maximum salary per day in complex operation?
    (a) EC22180
    (b) EC22164
    (c) EC22158
    (d) None of these
12. How many employees have 75% attendance and earn more than $800 in the month of June which

consists of 25 working days (some might be coming on overtime too) ?
(a) 5 (b) 7
(c) 4 (d) 6

13. Amongst the employees who were engaged in complex and medium operation, the number of employees whose average earning per day in medium operation is more than the average earning per day in complex operation is?
(a) 7 (b) 2
(c) 5 (d) 3

Directions for Questions 14 to 18: *Study Table 18.3 and answer the questions given below that.*

TABLE 18.3 Factory Sector by Type of Ownership

(All figures in the table are in per cent of the total for the corresponding column)

Sector	Factories	Employment	Fixed Capital	Gross Output	Value Added
Public	7	27.7	43.2	25.8	30.8
Central Government	1	10.5	17.5	12.7	14.1
State Local Government	5.2	16.2	24.3	11.6	14.9
Central and State Local Government	0.8	1.0	1.4	1.5	1.8
Joint:	1.8	5.1	6.8	8.4	8.1
Wholly Private	90.3	64.6	46.8	63.8	58.7
Others	0.9	2.6	3.2	2.0	2.4
Total	100	100	100	100	100

14. Suppose the average employment level is 80 per factory. The average employment in public factories is approximately:
(a) 244 (b) 316
(c) 324 (d) 310

15. Amongst the firms in different sectors, the gross output per employee is the highest in:
(a) central government
(b) central and state/local governments
(c) joint sector
(d) wholly private

16. Capital productivity is defined as the gross output value per rupee of fixed capital. The three sectors with the lowest capital productivity, arranged in ascending order are:
(a) others, central government and state local government.
(b) state local government, others and central government.
(c) state local government, central government and others.
(d) joint, wholly private, central.

17. The efficiency of a sector is considered on the basis of its value added per employee and its value added per rupee of fixed capital . The higher these values the better the rank of the sector. Further, it is known that if there is a tie between the two sectors, it is resolved on the basis of superiority in value added per employee. Based on the table data, the most efficient sector is:
(a) wholly private
(b) joint
(c) central and state/local
(d) none of these

18. The total value added in all sectors is estimated at ₹225,000 crore. Suppose the number of factories in the joint sector is 3000. The average value added per factory, in ₹ crore, in the central government is:
(a) 20.11 (b) 201.1
(c) 19.03 (d) 191.1

Directions for Questions 19 to 20: *Based on the following information.*

TABLE 18.4

Income-Tax Rates for Financial year 2009–10		
Individual & HUF Below Age of 65 Years	**Women Below Age of 65 Years**	**Tax Rates**
Income up to ₹1,60,000	Income up to ₹1,90,000	Nil
₹1,60,001 to ₹3,00,000	₹1,90,001 to ₹3,00,000	10%
₹3,00,001 to ₹5,00,000	₹3,00,001 to ₹5,00,000	20%
Above ₹5,00,001	Above ₹5,00,001	30%

Total income tax payable is obtained by adding two additional surcharges on calculated income tax.

- *Education Cess*: An additional surcharge called 'Education Cess' is levied at the rate of 2% on the amount of income tax.
- *Secondary and Higher Education Cess*: An additional surcharge called 'Secondary and Higher Education Cess' is levied at the rate of 1% on the amount of income tax.

19. Sangeeta is a young working lady. Towards the end of the financial year 2009–10, she found her total annual income to be ₹3,37,425. What percentage of her income is payable as income tax?

(a) 5.64 (b) 6.82
(c) 7.38 (d) 8.10
(e) None of the above

20. Mr. Madan observed his tax deduction at source, done by his employer, as ₹3,17,910. What was his total income (in ₹) if he neither has to pay any additional tax nor is eligible for any refund?

(a) 13,48,835 (b) 14,45,522
(c) 14,47,169 (d) 15,70,718
(e) None of the above

19 Mock Test Paper

Directions for Questions 1 to 5: *The following table (Table 19.1) shows the tax incidence and TDS calculations. Ms Parul Jaiswal works for Mindworkzz and is paid ₹240,000 p.a. out of which she saves ₹60,000 in tax saving instruments u/s 88.*

The following additional information is available:

The tax incidence is calculated as per the following slabs:

(a) Income between ₹50,000 and ₹60,000, tax charged at the rate of 10%

(b) Income between ₹60,000 and ₹150,000, tax charged at the rate of 20%

(c) Income ₹150,000 + tax charged at the rate of 30%

(d) All perquisites are taxable

TABLE 19.1 How TDS is Calculated for Ms Parul Jaiswal

Estimated salary for financial year ending 31 March 2004 including all	₹240,000
perquisites after subtracting standard deduction	
Tax on the above is	₹46,000
Less: Rebate under section 88, say, 15% of ₹60,000 (saving)	₹9,000
Less: Rebate under section 88c in case of women	₹5,000
Total tax payable	₹32,000
TDS deducted every month (32,000/12)	₹2,667

1. What component of the total incidence on Ms Parul Jaiswal's salary is charged under the highest tax slab: (approximately)
   (a) 63%
   (b) 59%
   (c) 53%
   (d) Cannot be determined
2. What will be the TDS amount per month for a person earning ₹170,000 as take home salary and ₹30,000 as allowance for car and house rent?
   (a) 25,000 (b) 2833.33
   (c) 34,000 (d) Cannot be determined
3. If due to a war between India and Pakistan, the government decides to add a 5% surcharge on tax incidence above ₹60,000, what will be the TDS amount per month for Ms Parul Jaiswal (including the surcharge)?
   (a) 3270.833 (b) 2854.166
   (c) 3054.66 (d) None of these
4. If disposable income is defined as the total salary including perquisites less the savings u/s 88 less the TDS amount, what would be the annual disposable income of Ms. Parul Jaiswal?
   (a) ₹208,000 (b) ₹203,000
   (c) ₹148,000 (d) ₹143,000
5. What would be the TDS per month on Ms. Parul Jaiswal, if her annual income is ₹200,000 and she saves ₹40,000 u/s 88 (assume no surcharge)?
   (a) 2333.33 (b) 2833.33
   (c) 3333.33 (d) Cannot be determined

Directions for Questions 6 to 9: *Prof. Qazi gives Maths test once a week. There are five students in his class whose names start with the letter A, viz. Arun, Amit, Ankur, Amritesh and Arjit. Unfortunately, he forgets to record some of the scores of these students. All scores are out of 100. Find the missing numbers in the table, and answer the questions that follow. Besides, we also know that Prof. Qazi grades his students according to their score as under:*

Grade	*Score*
A	*60% plus*
B	*56–60%*
C	*50–55%*
D	*Below 50%*

TABLE 19.2 Student Score

	1	2	3	4	5	6	7	8	9
Arun	46	55	87	33	74	38	40		95
Amit	48	60		51	85	46	37	19	85
Ankur	38	70	90		100	48	38	20	97
Amritesh	38		93	49	93	50	46	20	100
Arjit	42	66	84	44	84		38	20	98

(1) Amit's missing score is equal to the average score of the topper excluding Ankur and himself..

(2) The total of all the scores is 2626.

(3) Ankur got 70% in test 2. Amritesh got 1% less.

(4) The missing score on test 8 is 27. On test 6 it is 55.

6. Who is the topper amongst these students?
   (a) Arun (b) Amit
   (c) Arjit (d) Amritesh
7. If an A grade gets 4 points and a B grade gets 3 points, a C gets 2 and a D gets 1 point, what is the grade point average of the class? (approximately)
   (a) 2.6 (b) 1.5
   (c) 1.2 (d) 2.3
8. The least difference between any two missing scores is:
   (a) 7 (b) 6
   (c) 5 (d) None of these
9. Who is ranked in the middle amongst these students?
   (a) Arun (b) Amit
   (c) Arjit (d) Amritesh

Directions for Questions 10 to 16: *The following table (Table 19.3) shows the revenue and expenses in millions of dollars associated with Shell Oil Company's operations in different parts of the world for the years 2022 -24. Answer Questions 1–7 on the basis of the information provided in the table.*

TABLE 19.3 **Revenue and Expenses of Shell Oil Company**

Item	Year	Total World	Spain	North Africa & Middle East	Argentina	Rest of Latin America	Far East	North Sea	Rest of World
1. Income	2022	891	48	364	278	44	86	66	5
	2023	3235	34	643	1889	99	306	142	122
	2024	8091	334	1277	5143	663	554	0	120
2. Expenses	2022	620	37	244	164	57	51	45	22
	2023	1931	54	325	1098	133	223	45	53
	2024	3900	55	458	2734	313	302	0	38
3. Income before Tax & Charges(1–2)	2022	271	11	120	114	–13	35	21	–17
	2023	1304	– 20	318	791	–34	83	97	69
	2024	4191	279	819	2409	350	252	0	82
4. Tax & Charges	2022	154	4	94	44	–3	11	7	– 3
	2023	539	–2	149	320	–6	44	19	12
	2024	1747	112	384	1054	63	112	0	22
5. Net Income after Tax & Charges(3–4)	2022	117	7	26	70	–10	24	14	–14
	2023	765	–18	169	471	–28	39	78	57
	2024	2444	167	435	1355	287	140	0	60

10. How many operations of the company accounted for more than 4% of the total revenue earned in the year 2023?
    (a) 3 (b) 4
    (c) 2 (d) None of these
11. How many operations of the company witnessed more than 200% growth from the year 2023 to 2024?
    (a) 1 (b) 2
    (c) 3 (d) None of these
12. How many operations did not register a sustained yearly increase in income before tax and charges from 2022–24?
    (a) 4 (b) 5
    (c) 3 (d) None of these
13. If income to expenses ratio is defined as efficiency, which operation has the least efficiency for the year 2024?
    (a) Spain (b) Africa
    (c) Far East (d) None of these
14. Ignoring the loss making operations of the company in 2022, for how many operations was the percentage increase in net income before taxes and charges higher than the average from 2022–23?
    (a) 0 (b) 1
    (c) 2 (d) None of these
15. If profitability is defined as the ratio of net income after taxes and charges to expenses, which of the following statement is true?
    (a) The far-east operation witnessed its highest profitability in 2022.
    (b) The north sea operations increased its profitability from 2022 to 2023.
    (c) The operation in Argentina witnessed an increase in profitability from 2022 to 2023.
    (d) All three are true.

16. In 2023 which amongst the following regions has the best profitability?
   (a) North Africa & Middle East
   (b) North Sea
   (c) Argentina
   (d) Far East

Directions for Questions 17 to 20: *The table represents the information collected by TRAI about the Service Area wise Access of (Wireless + Wire line) subscribers in India. On the basis of the information provided in the table answer the questions that follow.*

TABLE 19.4

Service Area	Subscribers (in Millions)		Service Area	Subscribers (in Millions)	
	Dec 2019	March 2020		Dec 2019	March 2020
U.P. (E)	39.68	45.53	Orissa	13.57	15.89
Bihar	33.17	38.36	Mumbai	27.21	29.43
Karnataka	35.5	39.91	Kerala	25.69	27.65
Andhra Pradesh	44.99	48.09	Punjab	20.03	21.7
TN (Chennai Included)	53.17	57.26	Delhi	29.38	31.01
Madhya Pradesh	29.89	33.65	Haryana	13.59	14.96
Maharashtra	43.02	46.53	Kolkata	16.55	17.87
U.P(W)	28.47	31.97	Assam	8.11	9.06
West Bengal	22.68	26.07	North East	4.94	5.64
Gujarat	31.37	34.43	Jammu and Kashmir	5.22	5.78.
Rajasthan	32.22	35.27	Himachal Pradesh	4.83	5.34

17. Which service area has observed the maximum rate of change from Dec 2019 to March 2020 (in percentage)?
   (a) U.P (E) (b) Bihar
   (c) Orissa (d) Haryana
18. As a result of the decision to allow only two or three telecom operators in a particular service area, TRAI allocates R-Com and Vodafone to operate only in the east of India and Idea and Airtel to operate only in south. R-Com has got 28% subscribers in the east while Vodafone has 72% subscribers; similarly Idea has 48% subscribers in the south while Airtel has 52% subscribers. How many subscribers do these four players have in 2020?
   (a) R-Com-28.03, Vodafone-73.22, Idea-86.22 Airtel-89.5
   (b) R-Com-30.03, Vodafone-72.82, Idea-85.03, Airtel-80.04
   (c) R-Com 28.03, Vodafone-76.25, Idea-84.01, Airtel-85.76
   (d) R-Com-30.03, Vodafone-77.22, Idea-82.99, Airtel-89.91
19. Due to operability issues early in 2020, Madhya Pradesh and entire UP were added to the eastern telecom circle. The telecom operators in Madhya Pradesh and entire UP namely R-Com, Vodafone and Idea had 28%, 40% and 32% subscribers respectively. What is the percentage of subscribers that each player has in the newly formed eastern circle in March 2020?
   (a) R-Com-30.01%, Vodafone-55.72%, Idea 14.27%
   (b) R-Com-32.01%, Vodafone-53.72%, idea 14.27%
   (c) R-Com-28%, Vodafone-55.72%, Idea-16.27%
   (d) None of these
20. The all India rate of change in number of subscribers from December 2019 to March 2020 is?
   (a) 10.7%
   (b) 10.5%
   (c) 11.8%
   (d) 12.4%

20 Mock Test Paper

Directions for Questions 1 to 4: *Study the data given in Table 20.1 and answer questions 1–4.*

TABLE 20.1 Key Financials of Select Private Sector Banks

	Dep	Adv	Res	Eq	NP	EPS	CMP
HDFC Bank	579.41	257.68	39.13	3.20	5.22	26.10	840
Stanchart	425.78	203.72	11.72	2.13	3.30	13.58	445
Citi bank	2568.57	1444.85	23.15	2.80	20.24	112.44	1620
ICICI Bank	741.24	386.16	19.09	3.26	2.55	11.33	470
UTI Bank	2533.08	1297.34	58.51	12.09	17.86	16.10	280
Canara Bank	283.40	131.94	4.72	4.40	0.11	0.32	77

Note: ICICI Bank figures relate to 2023–24. All other figures relate to 2022–23.

Dep — Deposit (₹ crore) NP — Net Profit (₹ crore)
Adv — Advance (₹ crore)
EPS — Earnings per share ₹ Res — Reserve (₹ crore)
CMP — Current market price ₹
Eq — Equity (₹ crore) P/E — Price earnings ratio

1. Which bank has the highest reserves to net profit ratio?
   (a) ICICI Bank (b) UTI Bank
   (c) Canara Bank (d) Stanchart
2. What is the share of deposits accrued by ICICI Bank in the net deposits of all banks in the year 2022–23?
   (a) 15% (b) 35%
   (c) 10% (d) Cannot be determined
3. What is the premium on each share of HDFC Bank? (Premium = Current Market Price – Base Price) [(Base Price = Equity/ (No. of shares)] (No. of shares = Net Profit/EPS)
   (a) 600 (b) 1790
   (c) 200 (d) None of these
4. Which bank has the highest Current Market Price (CMP) to EPS ratio?
   (a) ICICI Bank (b) UTI Bank
   (c) Canara Bank (d) Stanchart

Directions for Questions 5 to 7: *Refer to the following table (Table 20.2) and answer the questions that follow.*

The table shows Mr Cheekoo's estimation of probabilities of how the stock market will behave, and his fund manager Mr Kaku's projections about the returns that will be generated in three mutual funds A, B and C based on what happens in the stock markets.

TABLE 20.2 Returns Probability

Event	Probability	Returns		
		A	B	C
5% Decline	20%	–5%	0%	5%
Flat	30%	+10%	+10%	+10%
5% Increase	40%	+25%	+20%	+15%
10% Increase	10%	+35%	+30%	+25%

5. If Mr Cheekoo wants to maximise his actual expectation what should he do? (Assume he has ₹100 crore to invest and he has only these three options.)
   (a) Invest in A (b) Invest in B
   (c) Invest in C (d) Can't be determined
6. If Mr Cheekoo invests all his amount in Fund B, then his expected return will be to the tune of (Assume ₹100 crore invested):
   (a) 30 crore (b) 20 crore
   (c) 11 crore (d) 14 crore
7. If Mr Cheekoo has invested 50% in Fund A, 30% in Fund B and 20% of his money in Fund C, then his expected return is?
   (a) 14.45%
   (b) Better than his expected return from Fund B and C invested 1 : 1
   (c) Both (a) and (b)
   (d) None of these

Directions for Questions 8 to 11: *If Mr Kaku's market research suggests that the respective probabilities for each of the four events are:*

5% decline	*25%*
Flat	*25%*

5% increase *30%*
10% increase *20%*

8. The percentage difference in the maximum expectations of Mr Kaku with respect to the maximum expectations of Mr Cheekoo is nearly:
(a) 1.4% (b) 1.5%
(c) 1.6% (d) 1.7%
9. The highest percentage difference between Mr Cheekoo's expectation and Mr Kaku's expectations will be for:
(a) Fund A (b) Fund B
(c) Fund C (d) Can't be determined
10. Based on the event probabilities assigned by Mr Kaku and Mr Cheekoo, which of the following conclusions can be made:
(i) Kaku is more optimistic than Cheekoo
(ii) Kaku is more pessimistic than Cheekoo
(iii) Kaku's expected returns are higher than Cheekoo's expected returns
(iv) Kaku expects more volatility is the stock market than Cheekoo
(a) (i), (iii) and (iv) (b) (ii), (iii) and (iv)
(c) (iii) only (d) (iii) and (iv)
11. If the investment pattern is 50% in Fund A, 30% in Fund B and 20% in Fund C, then the absolute difference between expectations of Kaku and Cheekoo (on an investment of ₹ 100 crore) is:
(a) ₹45 million (b) ₹4.25 million
(c) ₹52.5 million (d) None of these

Directions for Questions 12 to 15: *The following chart (Figure 20.1) shows the performance of the students of St. Xavier's High School Patna in the Tenth standard board examinations. Refer to it and answer the following questions. It is assumed that St-Xavier's High School, Patna, has 799 students in total and the number remained constant over the period.*

Points scored = No. of students passed – No. of students failed.

Assume that a student is allowed to attempt the board examination under the school's name only once. If he fails he is no longer allowed to take the exam under the school's banner.

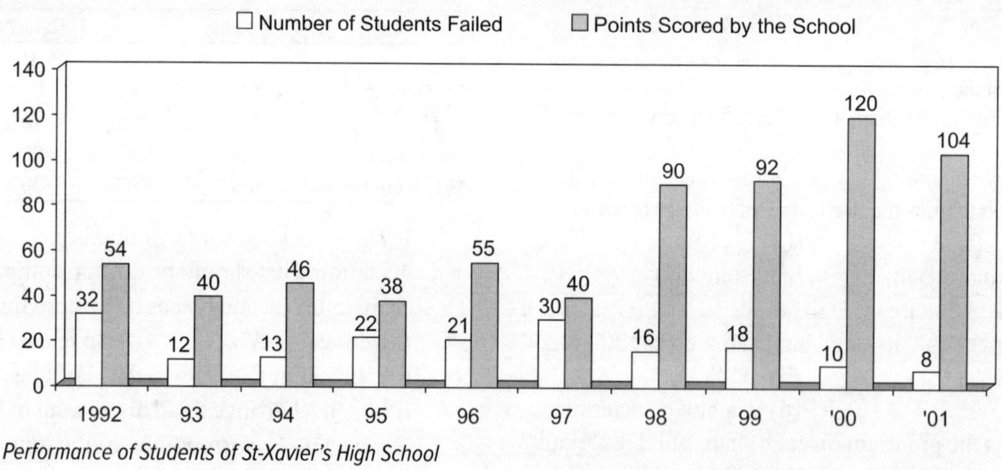

FIGURE 20.1 *Performance of Students of St-Xavier's High School*

12. SXAA stands for St. Xavier's Alumni Association. Find the students (in %) who could not become a member of SXAA in the years 1992 to 2001?
(a) 11% (b) 9%
(c) 7% (d) 21%
13. If pass percentage is the best indication of the school's performance, in which year did the school have its best performance?
(a) 1999 (b) 2000
(c) 2001 (d) Cannot say
14. Suppose that in the year 1995, the students who failed were allowed to take their exams again the next year (against the normal trend of the school) and 50% of the students who repeated the exam in 1996 failed again, then what would have been the percentage of students passing in 1996 if no repeaters had been allowed?
(a) 86.66% (b) 80%
(c) 85% (d) Data insufficient
15. In 1994, the principal of the school decided not to throw out the failed students but to give them one more chance. It was then decided that the performance of those students would not be counted for the score of the school. If all those students passed next year, then what would have been the score of the school if their results had been included in the final tally?
(a) 22 (b) 16
(c) 12 (d) None of these

Directions for Questions 16 to 20: *Mr. Praveen, an intelligent farmer, is facing a dilemma. He has three enterprises in which he can invest his money —dairy, poultry and crops. Apart from this he can either put the money in the bank or simply keep the money in his hand. The investment in any enterprise should be in multiples of $10,000. He collected the data about returns (revenue) from the different enterprises at different level of investments given in the following table (Table 20.3). After getting all these data he is puzzled—where should he put his money? Any money that he does not invest in an enterprise he keeps in the bank (whose returns are defined in the table). Further, he can invest in a single enterprise only once, i.e., if he invests $20,000 in poultry he cannot invest $10,000 twice and his return will get limited to $27,500, and not 15,000 × 2.]*

TABLE 20.3 Returns from Various Investments

Amount of Capital Used	Crop	Dairy	Poultry	Bank
10,000	13,000	14,000	15,000	11,000
20,000	26,000	26,000	27,500	22,000
30,000	38,000	37,000	38,500	33,000
40,000	50,000	46,000	48,500	44,000
50,000	61,000	54,000	57,500	55,000

16. If Mr Praveen wants to invest $50,000 in any alternative or a combination of alternatives, then what will be the maximum percentage return that he will be able to generate on the amount invested?
(a) 22% (b) 35%
(c) 30% (d) None of these
17. What is the highest possible profit percentage that can be achieved?
(a) 35% (b) 22%
(c) 50% (d) Can't say
18. If he has just $30,000 available to him, where should he invest the money?
(a) All in poultry
(b) $20,000 in poultry and the rest in dairy
(c) $20,000 in poultry and the rest in crop
(d) Equal amounts in crop, dairy and poultry
19. After which level of investment in crop, dairy and poultry taken together, bank deposit is an equally good alternative?
(a) 80,000 (b) 90,000
(c) 110,000 (d) Never
20. After what investment level would putting more money in dairy not be a good business decision?
(a) 30,000 (b) 40,000
(c) 20,000 (d) 50,000

21 Mock Test Paper

Directions for Questions 1 to 4: *Refer to the following tables (Tables 21.1(A) and (B)) and answer the questions that follow:*

TABLE 21.1 (A) Rate of Growth of Gross State Domestic Product

	1980–81 to 1990–91 (per cent per year)	1991–92 to 1998–99 (per cent per year)
1 Bihar	4.66	2.88
2 Rajasthan	6.60	5.85
3 Uttar Pradesh	4.95	3.58
4 Orissa	4.29	3.56
5 Madhya Pradesh	4.56	5.89
6 Andhra Pradesh	5.65	5.20
7 Tamil Nadu	5.38	6.02
8 Kerala	3.57	5.61
9 Karnataka	5.29	5.87
10 West Bengal	4.71	6.97
11 Gujarat	5.08	8.15
12 Haryana	6.43	5.13
13 Maharashtra	6.02	8.01
14 Punjab	5.32	4.77
Combined GSDP of 14 states	5.24	5.90
GDP (National Accounts)	5.47	6.50

TABLE 21.1 (B) Growth Rates of Per Capita Gross State Domestic Product

	1980–81 to 1990–91 (per cent per year)	1990–91 to 1998–99 (per cent per year)
1 Bihar	2.45	1.27
2 Rajasthan	3.96	3.48
3 Uttar Pradesh	2.60	1.28
4 Orissa	2.38	2.08
5 Madhya Pradesh	2.08	3.67
6 Andhra Pradesh	3.34	3.67
7 Tamil Nadu	3.87	4.78
8 Kerala	2.19	4.35
9 Karnataka	3.28	4.08
10 West Bengal	2.39	5.14
11 Gujarat	3.08	6.73
12 Haryana	3.86	2.85
13 Maharashtra	3.58	6.19
14 Punjab	3.33	2.93
Combined GSDP of 14 states	3.03	4.02

1. How many states had an increase in their rate of growth of gross state domestic product, as well as an increase in the growth rates of per capita gross state domestic product?
   (a) 4 (b) 5
   (c) 6 (d) 7
2. Performance of the 14 states shown, with respect to the performance of the national economy, it can be said that these states have
   (a) Out performed (b) Under performed
   (c) Performed at par (d) Nothing can be said
3. Which state has shown the lowest growth rate of population between 1980–81 and 90–91?
   (a) Orissa (b) Tamil Nadu
   (c) West Bengal (d) None of these
4. The population growth rate over the entire period for the 14 states combined is nearly
   (a) 2.8% (b) 3.6%
   (c) 5.1% (d) None of these

Directions for Questions 5 to 8: *Refer to the following chart (Figure 21.1) and table (Table 21.2)*

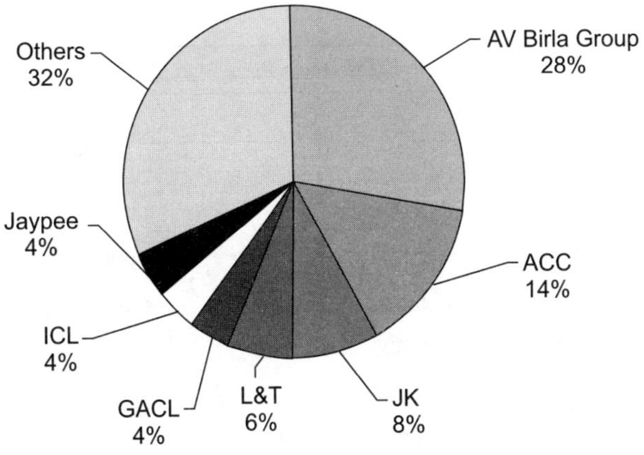

FIGURE 21.1 *Market Shares of Indian Cement Companies (2018–19)*

5. Which of these companies had the maximum profit before tax in the year 2018–19?
   (a) ACC (b) GACL
   (c) ICL (d) Birla
6. Which of these companies spent the maximum in advertising in the year 2018–19?
   (a) ICL (b) GACL
   (c) ACC (d) Birla
7. If in the future, ICL merges with L & T, what profit before tax does this union generate if ₹100 worth of cement is being bought in the year. (Assume that the market shares remain constant)
   (a) 0.46275 (b) 0.76275
   (c) 0.9178 (d) 0.36275

TABLE 21.2 Cost per Rupee of Sale in Cement Companies

	ACC	Birla	GACL	ICL	L&T	Others
Fixed Expenses	22.25	21.14	27.07	24.57	22.40	24.10
Wages & Salaries	6.43	9.91	2.79	6.83	7.07	5.04
Repairs & Maintenance	4.82	1.93	1.53	3.09	2.13	1.56
Other Expenses	3.14	2.48	5.41	3.54	6.58	2.51
Interest	4.70	4.19	8.86	5.81	3.61	7.61
Depreciation	3.15	2.64	8.47	5.29	3.22	7.39
Variable Expenses	74.27	78.08	58.82	65.49	68.92	57.54
Raw Materials	19.05	26.34	10.07	12.54	32.33	18.92
Energy	22.14	23.21	24.62	25.41	6.67	22.27
Other Mfg. Expenses	1.07	1.61	1.27	3.06	16.01	0.00
Indirect Taxes	14.85	13.61	13.25	12.49	6.45	1.94
Excise	13.52	13.44	13.16	10.62	5.91	0.00
Advertising	0.77	0.38	1.13	0.63	0.49	1.21
Marketing	2.08	0.68	0.48	4.89	0.37	0.37
Distribution	14.31	12.24	8.00	6.47	6.60	12.84
Profit Before Tax	3.48	0.77	14.12	9.94	8.67	18.36

8. With every passing year, cement companies are generating more profits per rupee of sale. This is occurring due to improved efficiencies of working. ICL follows this trend in 2019–20 and increases its profit before tax per rupee of sale by 10% over the previous year. Part of the reason for this profit figure is since its fixed expenses dropped to 10% of the sales value in 2019–20. But there is also some simultaneous change in the variable expenses. Identify the change.
   (a) Increases by around 24%
   (b) Decreases by around 24%
   (c) Increases by around 20%
   (d) Decreases by around 20%

Directions for Questions 9 to 12: *Answer the questions based on the following information.*

Mr. Hulla Bulla has collected the following details (Table 21.2) about the rental values and purchasing prices in different areas of the city of Hoola Boola. The rental values are given for the apartment and the purchasing price is given in terms of ₹/sq. ft for the finished apartment ready to rent. The area of apartments of grade A is 2500 sq. ft and that of grade B is 1800 sq. ft for all the locations mentioned in the table. The only cost involved in the purchase of the property is the purchase price cost and if it is an investment, then the depreciation in the value of the property can be assumed to be equal to the rise in the price of the property, i.e., loss due to depreciation is zero and the only gain from the investment is from the rental value of the property. Rent is paid monthly which is kept in the bank giving interest at the rate of 5% any additional cash in hand is also kept in the bank.

TABLE 21.3 Rental and Capital Values for Delhi and Mumbai

Location	Rental Values (Apartments) ₹/month		Purchase Price ₹/sq. ft	
	A	B	A	B
West End	175,000	100,000	10,000	7,000
Nariman Point	80,000	60,000	5,000	4,000
Colaba	175,000	100,000	10,000	7,000
Khar	80,000	60,000	5,000	4,000
Kalkaji	15,000	10,000	2,500	2,000
CR Park	21,000	15,000	2,500	2,000
Goregaon I	35,000	25,000	3,000	2,200
Goregaon II	20,000	10,000	1,800	1,400
Vashi I	25,000	15,000	2,000	1,400

9. Which of the following locations in the Grade A category gives the maximum return per rupee invested?
   (a) West End (b) Khar
   (c) Vashi I (d) Goregaon I
10. If Mr. Hulla Bulla has ₹1 crore with him, then in how many locations can he purchase an apartment?
   (a) 4 (b) 8
   (c) 5 (d) 7
11. Mr. Hulla Bulla invested 1 crore in buying an A category apartment in Colaba by taking a loan from the bank (for the balance amount). The bank charges him 10% per annum interest rate. What is his annual profit or loss from the investment? (Ignore interest on rent)
   (a) ₹600,000 gain (b) ₹100,000 gain
   (c) ₹400,000 loss (d) None of these
12. If Hulla Bulla treats each grade in a location as a different zone, then how many zones will give him a monthly percentage return of more than 1.25%?
   (a) 6 (b) 4
   (c) 2 (d) None

Directions for Questions 13 to 16: *Consider Table 21.4 and answer the questions given below that.*

TABLE 21.4 Top Ten Law Firms

(By Number of Lawyers)

Name/Country	1995			Today		
	Tot. No. of Lawyers	No. of Lawyers Abroad	No. of Offices	Tot. No. of Lawyers	No. of Lawyers Abroad	No. of Offices
Clifford Chance/UK	1382	432	23	3543	2208	29
Baker & McKenzie/US	1742	1,319	49	3019	2442	61
Fresh Fields/UK	780	215	16	2014	1168	30
Allen & Overy/UK	640	115	15	1734	838	26
Linklaters/UK	640	136	10	1600	1300	24
SkaddenArps/US	1035	80	11	1565	156	11
Jones Day/US	1100	59	19	1550	325	26
White & Case/US	664	239	27	1423	879	38
Eversheds/UK	715*	403	13	1310	219	20
Lovells/UK	446	81	10	1212	653	26

13. The highest growth rate in terms of the number of lawyers has been shown by:
    (a) Allen & Overy/UK
    (b) Lovells/UK
    (c) Fresh Field/UK
    (d) None of these
14. Which law firm has exhibited the highest percentage increase in terms of number of offices between the two time periods?
    (a) Baker & McKenzie
    (b) Lovells/UK
    (c) Fresh fields/UK
    (d) None of these
15. How many firms consistently had less than 50% of their lawyers abroad (on both dates).
    (a) 3 (b) 4
    (c) 5 (d) 6
16. How many firms showed a higher percentage increase in the number of offices as compared to the percentage increase in the number of offices of all firms put together?
    (a) 3 (b) 4
    (c) 5 (d) 6

Directions for Questions 17 to 20: *Thandawala, the masala cold drink maker has a number of mixed masala cold drinks to offer to his customers. The details of these drinks are as follows. He makes a soda lime by mixing soda and lime in the ratio of 1 : 2, cola orange by mixing cola and orange in the ratio of 1 : 3, he makes orange soda by mixing soda and orange in the ratio 1 : 1, cola lime is made by mixing cola& lime in the ratio 11 : 1 and soda cola by mixing cola and soda in the ratio of 4 : 3.*

Answer the following questions on the basis of the information provided in Table 21.5.

TABLE 21.5 Various Flavours of Mixed Masala Cold Drinks Offered by Thandawala

Flavour	₹/Bottle
Cola	9.00
Orange	7.00
Lime	11.00
Soda	8.00
Mango	10.00

17. If he sells each drink at a profit of 20% of the cost, which drink gives the highest profit per bottle?
    (a) Mango (b) Cola soda
    (c) Cola orange (d) Lime
18. Which of the following would be the cheapest to manufacture?
    (a) Orange soda (b) Soda lime
    (c) Cola soda (d) Cola Lime
19. The cost of manufacturing of which of the following is equal?
    (a) 4 Mango and 3 Orange soda
    (b) 3 soda cola and 2 Orange soda
    (c) 2 Soda lime and 2 Cola orange
    (d) None of these
20. Arrange the masala drinks in the descending order of their cost of manufacture.
    (1) Soda lime (2) Orange soda
    (3) Cola lime (4) Soda cola
    (a) 1234 (b) 2341
    (c) 2413 (d) 1342

22 Mock Test Paper

Directions for Questions 1 to 5: *Refer to Table 22.1 and answer Questions 1–5.*

TABLE 22.1 Growth Trends in Key Segments (*All figures in percentage*)

	1994–95	1995–96	1996–97	1997–98	1998–99	1999–2000
GDP at factor cost	7.0	7.3	7.5	5.0	6.8	6.4
Industrial Production Index	8.9	13.1	6.1	6.6	3.8	8.1
Agricultural Production	4.5	–2.1	9.5	–6.2	8.2	–1.9
Exports	8.2	9.0	8.7	8.6	8.1	8.3
Imports	8.9	10.4	10.2	10.2	10.1	10.4

1. The highest percentage change in the value between 1999–2000 and 1994–95 was exhibited by which segment?
   (a) Imports
   (b) Exports
   (c) Industrial Production
   (d) GDP at factor cost
2. The maximum change in the trade deficit (defined as Imports–Exports) was shown for which year? [Assume that in 1993–94 imports were at ₹10,383 crore and exports were at 5,427 crore.]
   (a) 1996–97
   (b) 1998–99
   (c) 1999–2000
   (d) Cannot be determined
3. How many segments have shown a greater than 50% increase in their values in 1999–2000 over 1994–95?
   (a) 2 (b) 3
   (c) 4 (d) 5
4. What would have been the answer for Question 3, if the figure shown in the graphs were all simple annual growth rates?
   (a) 1 (b) 2
   (c) 3 (d) 4
5. If the ratio of imports to exports had been 1.8:1 in 1993–94, then what would be this ratio at the end of 1996–97?
   (a) 1.8 : 1 (b) 1.86 : 1
   (c) 2.1 : 1 (d) 1.91 : 1

Directions for Questions 6 to 9: *Refer to the following table (Table 22.2) and answer Questions 6–9:*

TABLE 22.2 Pan Indian Railways

Description	Unit	Year 1	Year 2
Plant & Equipment:			
Capital-at-Charge	₹ in crore	*36,829.34	@39,772.06
Total Investment	,,	53,657.55	58,353.66
Route Length	km.	62,809	62,759
Locomotives	Nos.	7,429	7,517
Passenger Services Vehicles	,,	35,650	36,510

Description	Unit	Year 1	Year 2
Other Coaching Vehicles	,,	5,338	4,838
Wagons	,,	252,944	244,419
Railway Stations	,,	6,896	6,867
	,,		
Operations:			
Passenger: Train kms.	Millions	434.1	445.7
Vehicle kms	,,	11,022	11,699
Freight Train kms	,,	246	261
Wagon kms.	,,	25,240	27,003
Volume of Traffic:			
Passenger Originating	Millions	4,411	4585
Passenger kms	,,	403,884	430,666
Tonnes Origination	,,	441.58	478.18
Tonne kms	,,	284,270	303,039
Employment and Wages:			
Regular Employees	Thousand	1,578.4	1,577.2
Wage Bill of Regular Employees	₹ in crore	1,5610.6	16,288.7
Average Annual Wage per Regular Employee	Rupee	54387.3	61211.8
Financial Results:			
Revenues	₹ in crore	29,619.46	32,938.81
Expenses	,,	27,834.60	30,843.99
Misc. Transactions	,,	356.30	64.85
Net Revenue (before dividend)	,,	2,141.16	2,735.67
Rate of Return on Capital	Percentage	5.81	6.88
Dividend on Capital	₹ in crore	1,742.08	1,889.78
Shortfall (–)/Excess (+)	,,	(+) 399.08	(+) 845.89

* Includes investment (₹9,516.50 crore) from Capital Fund.
@ Includes investment (₹10,116.75 crore) from Capital Fund.

6. The ratio of the number of specific items that have shown an increase to the number of specific items that have shown a decrease between year 1 and year 2 is:
   (a) 18: 8 (b) 21:5
   (c) 20:6 (d) 19:7
7. The highest percentage decrease has been shown by:
   (a) Route length
   (b) Other coaching vehicles
   (c) Misc. transactions
   (d) None of these
8. The highest percentage increase has been shown by:
   (a) Net Revenue (before dividend)
   (b) Excess
   (c) Vehicle kms
   (d) None of these
9. On an average, in year 2, how many kms did one passenger who boarded the train travel for?
   (a) 93.9 (b) 98.1
   (c) 95.7 (d) Can't be determined

Directions for Questions 10 to 13: *The following figures (Figure 22.1) gives the information about the production for different varieties of foodgrains: (Rice + Pulses + Wheat + Coarse Cereals = Foodgrains). Refer to them for answering Questions 10-13.*

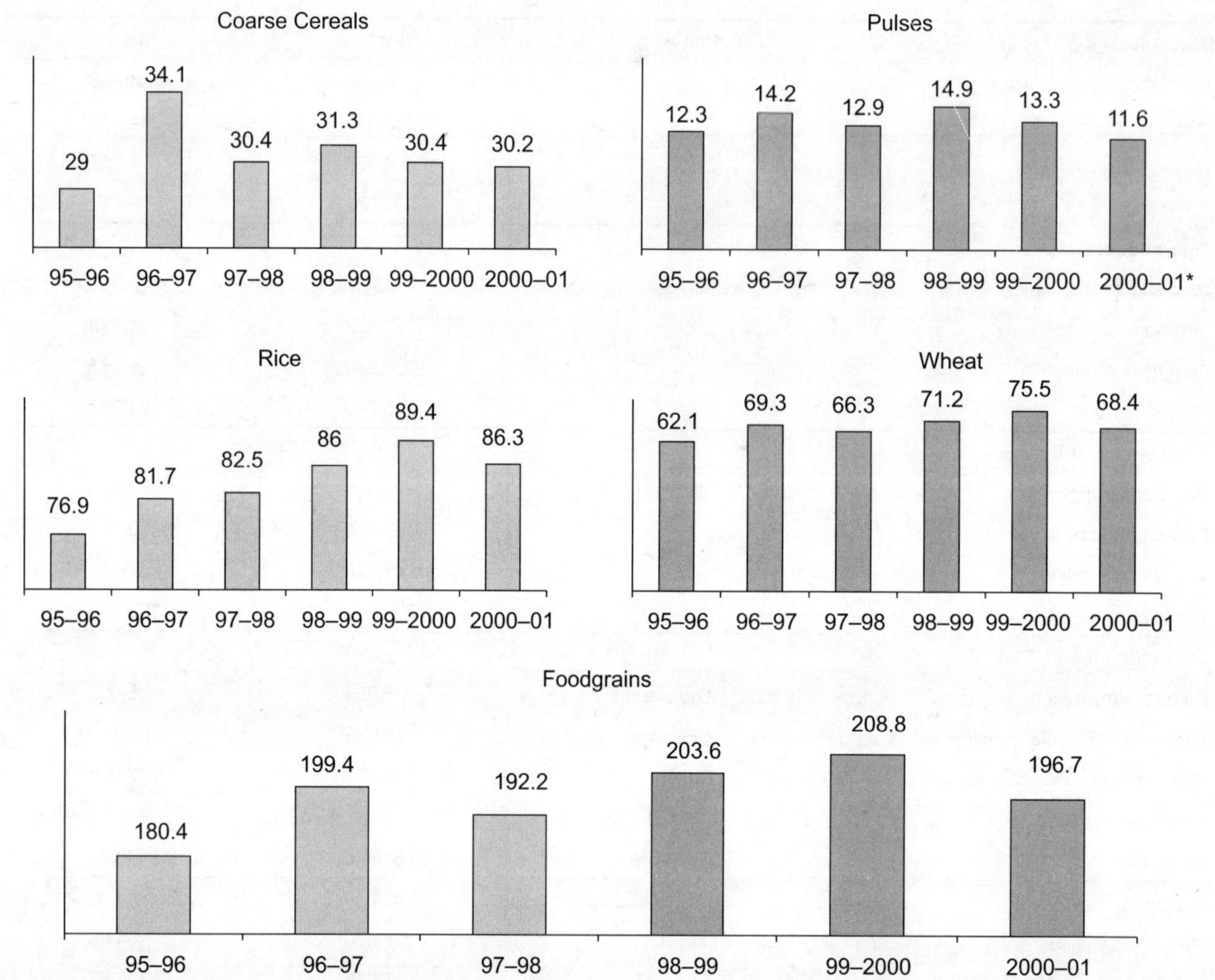

FIGURE 22.1 *Information Pertaining to Select Foodgrain Items*

10. Which foodgrain can be said to have displayed an identical trend in its production as the total foodgrain production over the entire period?
    (a) Rice (b) Coarse cereals
    (c) Pulses (d) Wheat
11. For which year was the percentage contribution of wheat to the total food grain production the highest?
    (a) 1997–98 (b) 1998–99
    (c) 1999–2000 (d) 2000–01
12. Which of the following statements is/are true?
    (i) Except 1997–98, rice and wheat production have followed identical trends
    (ii) Pulses production can be expected to increase in 2001–02
    (iii) The highest percentage increase in coarse cereals production between two successive years over the period was higher than the same figure for pulses.
    (iv) Production of coarse cereals has remained the least volatile over the period except for 96–97.
    (a) (i) and (iii) (b) All except (ii)
    (c) (iii) and (iv) only (d) All 4
13. 1996–97 was the best year in terms of percentage growth of production for which of these.
    (a) Rice and pulses
    (b) Wheat
    (c) Coarse cereals, rice and pulses
    (d) All food grains

Directions for Questions 14 to 16: *Based on the information given below.*

The retail prices of flowers, consumer's expenditure on flowers and sales of flowers for the calendar year 2022, in Phoolgaon, a small town with a population of 70000, is summarised in Table 22.3.

TABLE 22.3

Month	Price (Retail) of Roses (`/dozen)	Average Consumer Expenditure on Roses and Carnations (₹)	Total Consumer Expenditure on Roses (₹)	Sales of Carnations (Dozens)
Jan	99.0	47.4	1136916	13848
Feb	112.5	51.9	1051650	20486
Mar	135.0	49.5	1137915	12928
Apr	130.5	51.6	1315310	14021
May	126.0	59.4	1116612	18774
Jun	157.5	55.8	979020	17579
Jul	144.0	56.4	1188432	17521
Aug	117.0	54.0	940446	20355
Sep	162.0	55.5	1287900	16031
Oct	126.0	55.2	772884	22897
Nov	189.0	52.8	597240	19128
Dec	166.5	56.4	977688	18859

14. Compared to January, the total expenditure on carnations in March
    (a) increased by 6.27%
    (b) decreased by 6.64%
    (c) increased by 6.69%
    (d) decreased by 7.11%
    (e) did not change
15. Compared to January, the sales of roses in July
    (a) decreased by 39.15%
    (b) decreased by 28.13%
    (c) increased by 4.53%
    (d) increased by 4.33%
    (e) did not change
16. Compared to January, the price of carnations in December
    (a) increased by 26.57%
    (b) increased by 28.12%
    (c) increased by 36.19%
    (d) increased by 38.16%
    (e) did not change

Directions for Questions 17 to 20: *Power Plant P produces certain amount of electricity, which it distributes equally to substations Q and R. They further distribute the obtained electricity equally to the different mini stations downstream. Thus, R splits it's received electricity equally between mini stations H and I. Likewise, Q, splits it's electricity received equally between A,D and G. Further, the mini station passes on it's electricity downstream (after it retains 50% of the total electricity it received). Thus, D splits what it need to pass on equally between E and F, while A passes on what it needs to pass on to mini station B. It is assumed that after the sub-stations, the wire loses 10% of the original electricity it is carrying for every kilometer, i.e., if 10 A is sent through a wire, after 1 km it will have 9 A and after 2 kms it will have 8 A and so on.*

Further it is known that every mini-station retains 50% of the electricity that it receives (after the losses) and passes on the remainder 50% of the electricity that it receives to the stations down the line.

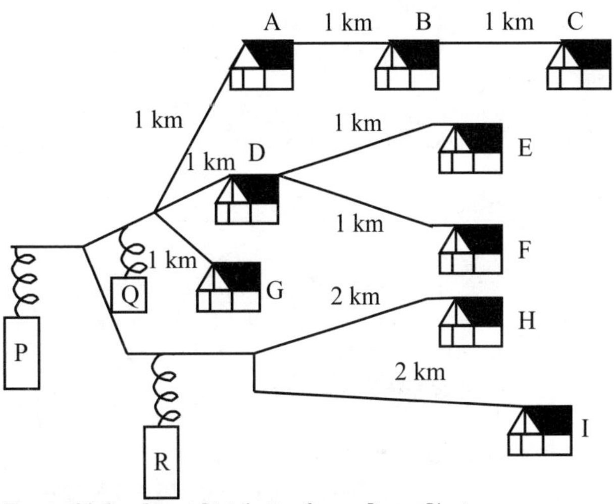

FIGURE 22.2 *Power Distribution from a Power Plant*

17. If mini-station I is receiving 10 A, then how much is mini-station 'A' receiving?
    (a) 7.5 A (b) 8.2 A
    (c) 10.5 A (d) None of these
18. Approximately how much should P produce so that C can get 10 A of current?
    (a) 230 A (b) 300 A
    (c) 330 A (d) 360 A
19. Mini-station H is using a device which decreases the current losses on the transmission route directly connected to it to 75%. If H is receiving 34 A, then how much is G receiving?
    (a) 80 A (b) 26.66 A
    (c) 24 A (d) None of these
20. If E is using the same device that H is (for Question 19), then the ratio of current used by E and G is. (Assume that E receives 37.)
    (a) 160:37 (b) 37:160
    (c) 80:37 (d) 37:80

23 Mock Test Paper

Directions for Questions 1 to 4: *Table 23.1 below shows the tax incidents and TDS calculations. Mrs. Vinay Shrivastava works for AMS Inc. and is paid ₹240,000 p.a out of which he saves ₹60,000 in tax saving instruments u/s 88.*

TABLE 23.1 Tax Incidents and TDS Calculations of Mrs Vinay Shrivastava

How TDS is Calculated	
Estimated salary for financial year ending 31 March 2004 including all perquisites after standard deduction	2,40,000
Tax on the above is	46,000
Less: Rebate under Section 88, say, 15% of ₹60,000 (Saving)	9,000
Less: Rebate under Section 88c in case of women	5,000
Total tax payable	32,000
TDS deducted ever month (32,000/1b)	2,667

The following additional information is available:

Tax incidence is calculated as per the following slabs:

(1) Income between ₹50000 and ₹60000, Tax charged at the rate of 10%

(2) Income between ₹60000 and ₹150000, Tax charged at the rate of 20%

(3) Income ₹150000+, Tax charged at the rate of 30%

(4) All perquisites are taxable

1. What component of the total tax incidence on Mrs Vinay Shrivastava's salary is charged under the highest tax slab: (Approximately)
   (a) 63% (b) 59%
   (c) 53% (d) Cannot be determined
2. What will be the TDS amount per month for a person earning ₹1,70,000 as take home salary and ₹30,000 as allowance for car and house rent?
   (a) 25000 (b) 2833.33
   (c) 34000 (d) Cannot be determined
3. If due to a war between India and Pakistan, the government decides to add a 5% surcharge on the tax incidence on an income of above ₹60,000, what will be the TDS amount per month for Mrs Vinay Shrivastava (including the surcharge)?
   (a) 3270.833 (b) 2854.166
   (c) 3054.66 (d) None of these
4. If disposable income is defined as the total salary including perquisites less the savings less the TDS amount, what would be the annual disposable income of Mrs Vinay Shrivastava?
   (a) ₹ 208000 (b) 203000
   (c) 148000 (d) 143000

Directions for Questions 5 to 8: *Refer to the following table (Table 23.2).*

TABLE 23.2 Figures Relating to Select Items from Synthetic Industry

In '000 tonnes		1997–98		1998–99		1999–2000	
		C	P	C	P	C	P
I. Polymers							
	LDPE	200	187.29	200	185	200	190
	LLDPE/HDPE	540	528.10	860	550	1445	1000
	PP	550	501.13	550	540	760	625
	PS	@144	120.06	@144	125	@144	130
	PVC	780	679.90	780	700	780	750
	Total	2214	2016.47	2454	2100	3328	2695

In '000 tonnes		1997–98		1998–99		1999–2000	
		C	P	C	P	C	P
II. Synthetic Fibre							
	Acrylic Fibre (AF)	105	79.51	105	80	105	80
	Nylon Filament Yarn (NFY)	*22	29.98	*22	30	*22	30
	Tyre Cord (TY)	*44	46.58	*44	50	*44	55
	Polyester Filament Yarn (PSY)	$832	659.73	$848	700	$848	770
	Polyester Staple Fibre (PSF)	575	430.65	591	500	591	530
	Total	1578	1246.45	1610	1360	1610	1458
III. Elastomer							
	SBR	45	27.52	84	30	84	30
	PBR	50	33.88	50	35	50	40
	Total	95	61.40	134	65	134	70
IV. Synthetic Detergent Intermediate							
	LAB	274	250.85	274	260	274	270

* Independent Capacities; $ include 101 kt broad banded capacity.
@ Includes 20 kt broad banding with ABS; C: Capacity; P: Production.

Note: Capacity utilisation is defined as the production as a percentage of the total capacity.

5. How many specific instances of over 100% capacity utilisation are visible from the table?
   (a) 4 (b) 5
   (c) 6 (d) None of these
6. The number of products which have continuously shown a capacity utilisation greater than 80% is
   (a) 7 (b) 8
   (c) 9 (d) 10
7. The total addition to installed capacity over the entire time period is:
   (a) 1185 kt (b) 118,500 tonnes
   (c) 2370 k (d) 237,000 tonnes
8. How many product categories have exhibited a consistent yearly growth in capacity as well as a consistent yearly growth in production?
   (a) 4 (b) 3
   (c) 2 (d) None of these

Directions for Questions 9 to 12: *Refer to the following table (Table 23.3) and answer the questions that follow:*

TABLE 23.3 Percentage of Population in Poverty

	1983	1987–88	1993–94	1999–2000
1 Bihar	52.22	52.13	54.96	42.60
2 Rajasthan	34.461	35.15	27.41	15.28
3 Uttar Pradesh	47.07	41.46	40.85	31.15
4 Orissa	65.29	55.58	48.56	47.15
5 Madhya Pradesh	49.78	43.07	42.52	37.43
6 Andhra Pradesh	28.91	25.86	22.19	15.77
7 Tamil Nadu	51.66	43.39	35.03	21.12
8 Kerala	40.42	31.79	25.43	12.72
9 Karnataka	38.24	37.53	33.16	20.04
10 West Bengal	54.85	44.72	35.66	27.02
11 Gujarat	32.79	31.54	24.21	14.07
12 Haryana	21.37	16.64	25.05	8.74
13 Maharashtra	43.44	40.41	36.86	25.02
14 Punjab	16.18	13.20	11.77	6.16
All 14 states	43.8	39.92	36.25	26.43
All India	44.48	38.86	35.97	26.10

Note: Rankings are to be done in reverse order, i.e., the lower the poverty percentage, the higher the rank. (e.g., Maharashtra will be ranked 8th in 1983).

9. If states are ranked on the basis of least poverty levels and the best state is ranked at No. 1, while the worst state is ranked at No. 14; which state will rank at No. 7 in the year 1993–94?
   (a) Karnataka
   (b) UP
   (c) Haryana
   (d) Tamil Nadu
10. Cumulative poverty rating is defined as the sum of the ranks of a state over the four time periods shown. Which state shows the highest cumulative poverty rating over the period?

(a) Bihar
(b) MP
(c) Punjab
(d) Orissa

11. The state which has the best poverty alleviation record in terms of percentage change in the number of poor people in the state in 1983 to 1999–2000 is:
(a) Punjab
(b) Haryana
(c) Tamil Nadu
(d) Can't be determined

12. State A is said to dominate state B, if it has a better percentage of population in poverty as compared to state B. By how many states is Bihar dominated for all the four years shown in the table?
(a) 11 (b) 12
(c) 0 (d) 1

Directions for Questions 13 to 16: *The cumulative bar chart (Fig. 23.1) below gives us the production of four products A, B, C & D for four years. It is known that the total production increases @ 20% over its value in the previous year. The difference between C's production in 2023 and A's production in 2021 is 2640 units.*

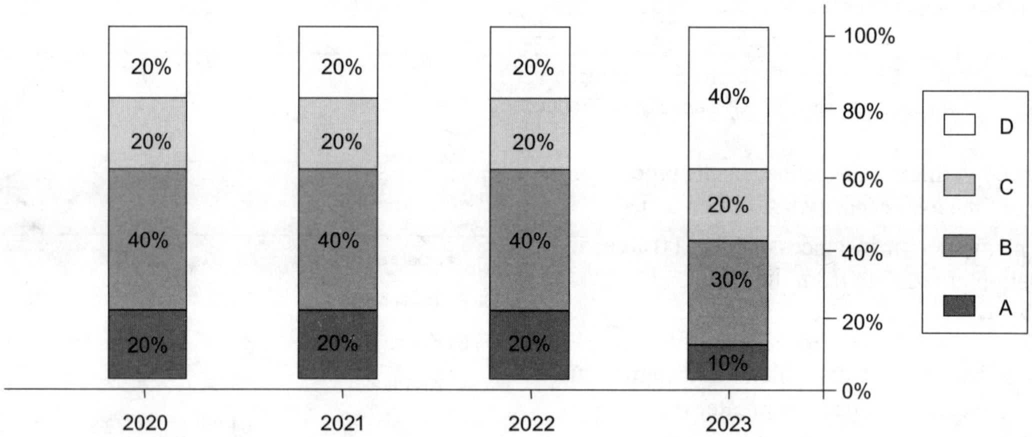

FIGURE 23.1 *Production of A, B, C and D*

13. If the price of B in 2021 is ₹125 per unit, what is the sales revenue in the same year due to sale of B (in ₹ lakhs)?
(a) 15
(b) 12.5
(c) 20
(d) None of these

14. Assuming no pile up of inventory at the beginning or the end of the year, what is the ratio of the number of units of C produced in these four years?
(a) 120:175:260:228
(b) 125:135:240:224
(c) 125:165:270:216
(d) None of these

15. If the price of the four products is in the ratio of 3:5:7:8, what is the ratio of the revenue generated by these products in 2022?
(a) 6:15:21:16
(b) 4:10:14:9
(c) 9:16:24:20
(d) 3:10:7:8

16. Which of the following is Not true?
(a) In the given period, the maximum number of units produced was that of B.
(b) In 2023, the number of units of B produced was the second highest for B in the given period.
(c) The only product that does not show an increasing trend is A.
(d) None of these.

Directions for Questions 17 to 20: *Answer the following questions based on the following bar diagram.*

The diagram gives us Country XX's Monthly Outward Investment Flows to various countries and the world. The FDI figures are given in US $ Million.

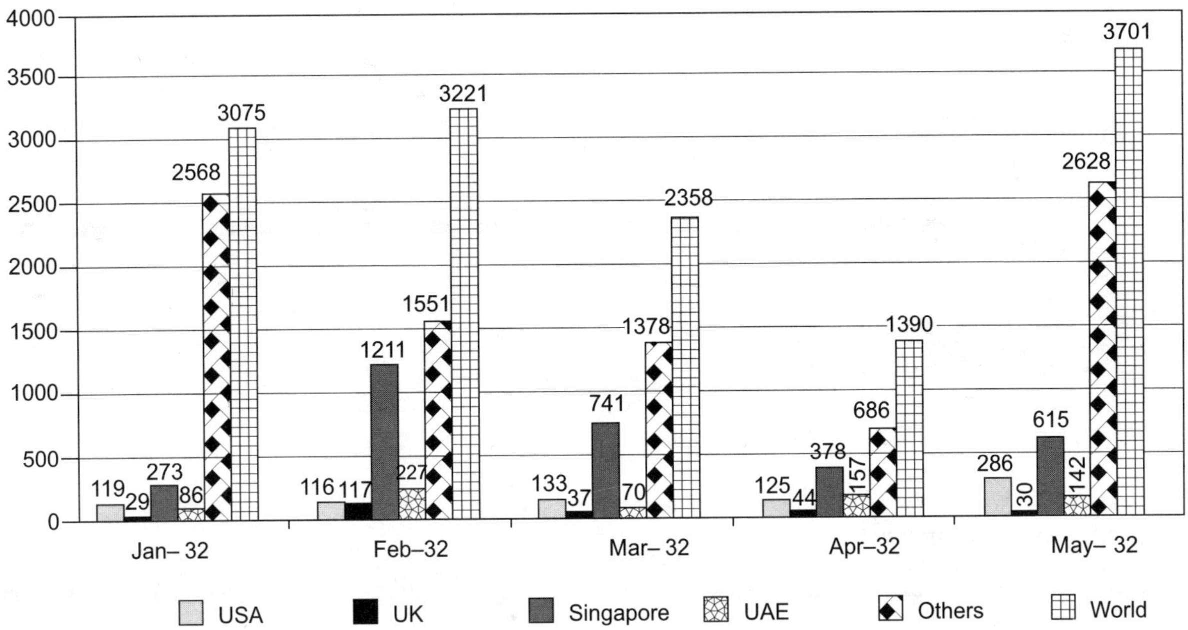

FIGURE 23.2

17. What is the compound average growth rate of Country XX's Overall Outward Investment during the period January to May 2032?
    (a) 6 per cent (approx.)
    (b) 3.5 per cent (approx.)
    (c) 5.75 per cent (approx.)
    (d) None of the above

18 In which month there was a maximum drop in Country XX's Outward Investment to Singapore and what is the 'month on month' growth in that period?
    (a) April, approximately negative growth of 39 per cent
    (b) March, approximately negative growth of 49 per cent
    (c) April, approximately negative growth of 49 per cent
    (d) None of the above

19. Of its total investment in the world, what is the share of Country XX's Outward Investment together in USA and UK in February 2032?
    (a) 7.24 per cent
    (b) 8.30 per cent
    (c) 6.79 per cent
    (d) None of the above

20. In which month did the share of Country XX's Total Outward Investment together in Singapore and UAE achieve the highest level and what is the value?
    (a) April, 40 per cent
    (b) February, 45 per cent
    (d) March, 45 per cent
    (d) None of the above

24 Mock Test Paper

Directions for Questions 1 to 4: *Answer the following questions based on the information given as follows:*

The proportion of male students and the proportion of vegetarian students in a school are given below. The school has a total of 800 students, 80% of whom are in the Secondary Section and rest equally divided between Class 11 and 12.

TABLE 24.1

	Male (M)	Vegetarian (V)
Class 12	0.600	
Class 11	0.550	0.50
Secondary Section		0.55
Total	0.475	0.53

1. What is the percentage of male students in the secondary section?
   (a) 40
   (b) 45
   (c) 50
   (d) 55
   (e) 60
2. In the Secondary Section, 50% of the students are vegetarian males. Which of the following statements is correct?
   (a) Except vegetarian males, all other groups have same number of students.
   (b) Except non-vegetarian males, all other groups have same number of students.
   (c) Except vegetarian females, all other groups have same number of students.
   (d) Except non-vegetarian females, all other groups have same number of students.
   (e) Data inconsistent.
3. What is the percentage of vegetarian students in Class 12?
   (a) 40
   (b) 45
   (c) 50
   (d) 55
   (e) 60
4. In Class 12, twenty five per cent of the vegetarians are male. What is the difference between the number of female vegetarians and male non-vegetarians?
   (a) less than 8
   (b) 10
   (c) 12
   (d) 14
   (e) 16

Directions for Questions 5 to 9: *On the basis of the data given in the two charts.*

Sodium carbonate, also called as soda ash is an important ingredient for glass, soaps and detergents, and many other products. There were two ways producing soda ash. The first is producing soda ash from trona obtained naturally. The second method was producing soda ash from common salt through Solvay process. Soda ash produced thus was called synthetic soda ash. Tata Chemicals was one of the largest producers of soda ash. The first chart shows production by Tata Chemicals and the second chart shows the global soda ash production of two varieties of soda ash in the world.

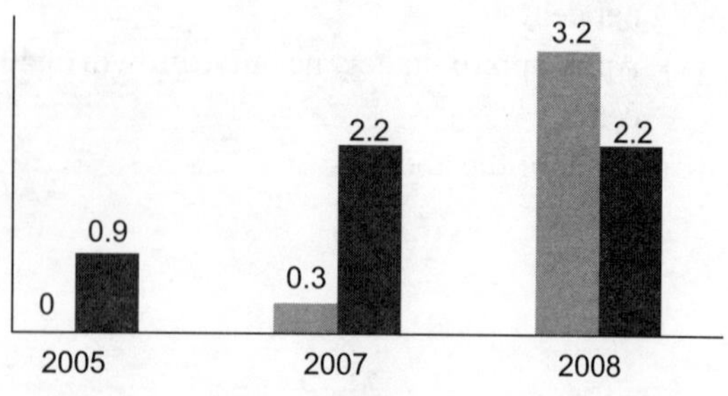

FIGURE 4.3(A) *Tata Chemicals Soda Ash Production (MT)*

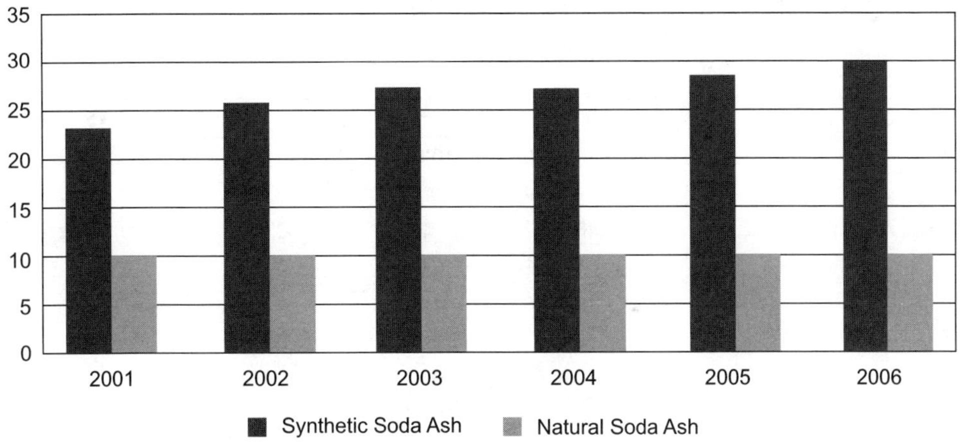

FIGURE 4.3(B) *Global Soda Ash Production (MT)*

5. It was expected that global soda ash production would be same for 2006, 2007 and 2008 (only for this question). What could be a possible reason for different patterns of production in Tata Chemicals and the world?
   (a) Tata Chemicals built new plants of 2.2 MT natural soda ash capacity in 2007.
   (b) Tata Chemicals built 3.2 MT of natural soda ash capacity from 2005 to 2008.
   (c) Tata Chemicals produced 2.7% of total soda ash in the world.
   (d) Tata Chemicals might have acquired 0.3 MT of natural soda ash facility in 2007.
   (e) None of above conclusion could possibly be drawn.
6. Suppose the total global production increased (year on year) from 2005 to 2008 by the amount Tata Chemicals' synthetic production (year on year) increased in the same period. By what percentage did the total global production increase from 2007 to 2008?
   (a) Cannot be calculated at all from the given charts.
   (b) Increased by 10.16%.
   (c) Increased by 9.48%.
   (d) Did not increase at all.
   (e) Increased by 8.64%.
7. Which of the following statements are true?
   (1) Proportion of natural soda ash to synthetic soda has decreased from 2001 to 2006 globally.
   (2) Proportion of natural soda ash to synthetic soda ash has increased from 2001 to 2006 globally.
   (3) Proportion of synthetic soda ash to total soda ash has decreased for Tata chemicals from 2005 to 2007.
   (4) Proportion of synthetic soda ash to total soda ash has increased for Tata chemicals.
   (a) 1 and 3
   (b) 1 and 4
   (c) 2 and 4
   (d) 2 and 3
   (e) 1, 2 and 3 only
8. What is Tata Chemicals' share of global production in 2008?
   (a) 12.86%
   (b) 17.42%
   (c) 59.34%
   (d) Incomplete data
   (e) None of the above
9. Suppose total global production of soda ash in 2008 was 40 MT and Tata Chemicals was the second highest producer of soda ash globally after another company called Solvay. FMC Wyoming was the third highest producer. Two Indian giants, Tata Chemicals and Nirma have a combined production capacity of 8.8 MT. Which of the following statements are right?
   (1) Solvay's market share was more than 20.66%
   (2) Solvay's market share was more than 13.5%
   (3) FMC's market share was less than 10.33%
   (4) FMC's market share was less than 13.5%
   (5) Nirma, which was the sixth largest producer, had a share of less than 8.5%
   Choose the right option.
   (a) 1 and 3
   (b) 1 and 5
   (c) 2 and 4
   (d) 1, 3 and 5
   (e) 2, 4 and 5

Directions for Questions 10 to 13: *Refer to the following table (Table 24.2).*

TABLE 24.2 Short-Term Plans—Growing Day-by-Day

Scheme (₹ in Cr) as on on 30/08/02	Fund Size 30/08/02	Nav (in ₹) as	7 days	15 days	30 days
Zurich (I) HIF–STP	1028.79	10.5866	0.1675	0.2775	0.8795
Tata ST Bond	134.49	10.1150	0.1396	0.2955	0.8756
Templeton (I) ST Inc	481.357	10.58	0.1978	0.3275	0.8693
Birla Bond Plus	480.62	10.7020	0.1347	0.2698	0.8386
Grindlays SSI–ST	1039.56	11.5896	0.1824	0.2908	0.8230
HDFC STP	1335.32	10.5014	0.1478	0.2798	0.8034
JM ST Fund	284.67	10.2314	0.1556	0.3118	0.7980
Pru ICICI STP	1508.23	10.8414	0.1598	0.3072	0.7921
IL&FS Bond–STP	196.17	10.5647	0.1479	0.2810	0.7890
Alliance ST Fund	312.66	10.3572	0.1334	0.2934	0.7814
IDBI-PRIN Inc–STP	321.81	10.3548	0.1528	0.2808	0.7708
K Bond STP	418.89	10.3366	0.1444	0.2638	0.7466
Chola Freedom Inc ST	100.04	16.6492	0.1456	0.2807	0.7284

10. If the ratio of fund size to NAV gives the value for the number of units of the mutual fund, then the lowest number of units is for:
    (a) Tata ST Bond
    (b) Templeton (I) St Inc
    (c) Pru ICICI STP
    (d) none of these
11. The fund having the highest number of units is:
    (a) Pru ICICI STP (b) HDFC STP
    (c) Zurich (I) HIF–STP (d) None of these
12. The number of units of Chola Freedom Inc ST is the closest to
    (a) 5 crore (b) 6 crore
    (c) 60 lakh (d) None of these
13. How many funds have more than 80 crore units?
    (a) 3 (b) 4
    (c) 5 (d) 6

Directions for Questions 14 to 17: *On the basis of the data given in Table 24.3.*

A cake chain manufactures two types of products—'cakes/pastries/gateaux' and savouries. The chain was concerned about high wastage (in terms of leftover) and wanted to reduce it. Table Table 24.3 provides information about sales, costs and wastage for both products.

TABLE 24.3 Revenue statement

Year	Cakes/Pastries/Gateaux			Savouries		
	Sales in ₹ lac	Costs in ₹ lac	Leftover as %age of Sales	Sales in ₹ lac	Costs in ₹ lac	Leftover as %age of Sales
1993	81.47	80.06	1.52	41.79	41.07	9.38
1994	171.42	168.03	1.58	80.69	79.09	10.61
1995	326.95	323.7	1.43	146.88	145.42	10.08
1996	591.77	576.52	1.23	220.96	215.26	10.45
1997	667.1	657.89	2.06	516.23	509.10	8.43
1998	936.52	928.95	1.74	468.39	464.60	11.04
1999	978.69	966.97	1.19	528.31	521.98	6.98
2000	752.09	743.20	1.50	637.63	630.09	5.61
2001	713.46	687.83	1.83	694.42	669.47	5.96
2002	885.29	845.83	1.76	869.15	830.40	5.66
2003	1071.81	1014.87	1.81	913.68	865.14	6.72
2004	1225.00	1163.75	2.78	1075.00	1021.25	6.14

14. Which of the following statement(s) is (are) right?
    (1) The worth of leftover for cakes/pastries/gateaux increased continuously from 1993 to 2004.
    (2) The worth of leftover for cakes/pastries/gateaux kept on fluctuating, many a times, between 1993 and 2004.
    (3) The worth of leftover for savouries and cakes/pastries/gateaux was the highest in 2004.
    (4) The worth of leftover for savouries kept on fluctuating, many a times, between 1993 and 2004.

    Choose the right combination from the following:
    (a) 1 and 4
    (b) 3 and 4
    (c) 1 and 2
    (d) Only 3
    (e) 2 and 3
15. Maximum decline in amount of leftover of cakes/pastries/gateaux occurred in the year:
    (a) From 1997 to 1998
    (b) From 1996 to 1997
    (c) From 1998 to 1999
    (d) There was always an increase in worth of leftover.
    (e) Cannot be calculated from the data.
16. If profit = sales – cost – leftover. In which year was the cakes chain was in losses?
    (1) 1993 (2) 1997
    (3) 1998 (4) 2000

    Choose the right option:
    (a) 1, 2, 3, 4 (b) 3, 4
    (c) 2, 3 (d) 1, 2, 3
    (e) It was always in profit.
17. After implementing a waste reduction policy in 1996, the restaurant managed to reduce its wastage by 10% in each subsequent year. How much money(in lacs) did the restaurant save during that period?
    (a) 19
    (b) 20
    (c) 16
    (d) 15

Directions for Questions 18 to 20: *Refer to the following table (Table 24.4) and answer the questions that follow.*

TABLE 24.4 Model Investment Chart for Vinay Srivastava

Holding In Debt-based Mutual Funds					Equity Holding		
Year	Value at the Beginning of the year (₹)	Return for the Year (₹)	Withdrawals (₹)	Value at the End of the Year (₹)	Value at the Beginning of the Year (₹)	Return for the Year (₹)	Value at the End of the Year (₹)
2014	1,000,000	70,000	180,000	890,000	600,000	84,000	684,000
2015	890,000	62,300	180,000	772,300	684,000	95,760	779,760
2016	2,572,300	180,061	180,000	2,572,361	779,760	109,166	888,926
2017	2,772,361	194,065	180,000	2,786,426	8,88,926	124,450	1,013,376
2018	2,986,426	209,050	180,000	3,015,476	1,013,376	141,873	1,155,249

18. What is the percentage of the initial funds in debt-based mutual funds that has been invested at the end of year 2015 by the investor in debt-based mutual funds?
    (a) 140% (b) 180%
    (c) 133.16% (d) None of these
19. Of the total amount invested by Vinay Srivastava, what is the percentage amount invested at the start of 2014 in debt-based mutual funds?
    (a) 23.41% (b) 28.43%
    (c) 26.31% (d) 33.31%
20. The highest percentage growth in the value of the portfolio at the beginning of the year is shown for:
    (a) 2015 (b) 2016
    (c) 2017 (d) 2018

25 Mock Test Paper

Directions for Questions 1 to 4: Answer the following questions based on the information given below:

The following table shows the break-up of actual costs incurred by a company in last five years (year 2002 to year 2006) to produce a particular product:

The production capacity of the company is 2000 units. The selling price for the year 2006 was ₹125 per unit. Some costs change almost in direct proportion to the change in volume of production, while others do not follow any obvious pattern of change with respect to the volume of production and hence are considered fixed. Using the information provided for the year 2006 at the basis for projecting the Figures for the year 2007, answer the following questions:

TABLE 25.1

	Year 2002	Year 2003	Year 2004	Year 2005	Year 2006
Volume of Production and Sale (units)	1000	900	1100	1200	1200
Costs (₹)					
Material	50,000	45,100	55,200	59,900	60,000
Labour	20,000	18,000	22,100	24,150	24,000
Consumables	2,000	2,200	1,800	1,600	1,400
Rent of Building	1,000	1,000	1,100	1,100	1,200
Rates and Taxes	400	400	400	400	400
Repair and Maintenance Expenses	800	820	780	790	800
Operating Cost of Machines	30,000	27,000	33,500	36,020	36,000
Selling and Marketing Expenses	5,750	5,800	5,750	5,800	5800

1. What is the approximate cost per unit in rupees, if the company produces and sells 1400 units in the year 2007?
   (a) 104 (b) 107
   (c) 110 (d) 115
   (e) 116
2. What is the minimum number of units that the company needs to produce and sell to avoid any loss?
   (a) 313 (b) 350
   (c) 384 (d) 747
   (e) 928
3. If the company reduces the price by 5 per cent, it can produce and sell as many units as it desires. How many units the company should produce to maximise its profit?
   (a) 1400 (b) 1600
   (c) 1800 (d) 1900
   (e) 2000
4. Given that the company cannot sell more than 1700 units, and it will have to reduce the price by ₹5 for all units, if it wants to sell more than 1400 units, what is the maximum profit, in rupees, that the company can earn?
   (a) 25,400 (b) 24,400
   (c) 31,400 (d) 32,900
   (e) 32,000

Directions for Questions 5 to 8: The following table presents the data collected for an on-line job portal infinite Jobs.com. For each question, there are two statements, each of which could be either True or False. Choose one of the following options as an answer.

(a) Only [X] is True
(b) Only [Y] is True
(c) Both [X] and [Y] are true
(d) Neither [X] nor [Y] is True

TABLE 25.2

Year	Category	Number of Registrations	Number of Candidates who Posted their CV's	Number of Candidates Shortlisted by Employers	Number of Jobs Offered
2024	Technical	61,205	59,981	684	181
	Managerial	19,236	15,389	138	48
2025	Technical	63,298	60,133	637	115
	Managerial	45,292	40,763	399	84

5. **Statement X:** The percentage increase in number of Registrations from 2024 to 2025 is higher for Managerial candidates than for Technical candidates

   Statement Y: The overall Registrations have grown by more than 25%

6. **Statement X:** The percentage of drop-outs (from Registration stage to posting (CV's) had decreased from 2024 to 2025 for Managerial category

   Statement Y: The percentage of drop-out was higher for Technical than for Managerial category in 2025

7. **Statement X:** The success rate of candidates getting shortlisted based on CV's is higher for Managerial category than for technical category in 2025.

   Statement Y: The success rate of candidates getting shortlisted based on CV's is better for Managerial category in 2025 than in 2024.

8. **Statement X:** In 2024, the number of candidates offered jobs as a proportion of the number of CV's posted was higher for Technical than for Managerial candidates

   Statement Y: In 2024, amongst those shortlisted by Employers, the technical category had a higher success rate in securing jobs than the Managerial category.

Directions for Questions 9 to 10: *The following pie-chart gives the sectorwise sales of a group of companies for the financial year 2019–2020. Study the chart and answer the following questions.*

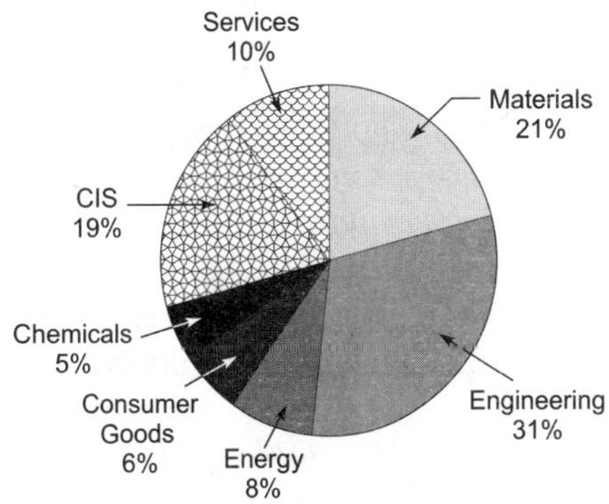

FIGURE 25.1 *Sectorwise Sales 2019–20*

TABLE 25.3

Sectors	(₹ million)	% Share
Materials	164,430	21.0
Engineering	244,830	31.2
Energy	62,990	8.0
Consumer Goods	47,880	6.1
Chemicals	35,510	4.5
Communications and Information Systems	148,160	18.9
Services	78,950	10.1
Total	782,750	

* Sales turnover was US $17.4 billion (₹78,274 crore) representing a year-on-year growth of 30.3 per cent in dollar terms and 27.4 per cent in rupee terms.

* Sales figures shown are net of excise duty.

9. This group of companies operates in multiple sectors. The holding company has decided to closely monitor minimum number of sectors (not exceeding 5) contributing together a major part (at least 80%) of sales of the group. Identify the correct set of sectors.

(a) Engineering, Services, CIS and Consumer Goods
(b) Engineering, Services, CIS, Energy and Consumer Goods.
(c) Engineering, Material, Services and CIS
(d) Engineering, Material, CIS and Energy

10. The average profit against the sales across the sectors is 10% while the profit margin of engineering is 12% and CIS 20%. What is the average profit across the remaining sectors?
(a) 5.87% (b) 7.6%
(c) 4.96% (d) 8.9%

Directions for Questions 11 to 14: *Answer the following questions based on the information given below:*

A health-drink company's R and D department is trying to make various diet formulations, which can be used for certain specific purposes. It is considering a choice of 5 alternative ingredients (O, P, Q, R and S), which can be used in different proportions in the formulations. The table below gives the composition of these ingredients. The cost per unit of each of these ingredients is O: 150, P: 50, Q: 200, R: 500, S: 100.

TABLE 25.4

Ingredient	Composition			
	Carbohydrate %	Protein %	Fat %	Minerals %
O	50	30	10	10
P	80	20	0	0
Q	10	30	50	10
R	5	50	40	5
S	45	50	0	5

11. In what proportion P, Q and S should be mixed to make a diet having at least 60% carbohydrate at the lowest per unit cost?
(a) 2:1:3 (b) 4:1:2
(c) 2:1:4 (d) 3:1:2
(e) 4:1:1

12. The company is planning to launch a balanced diet required for growth needs of adolescent children. This diet must contain at least 30% each of carbohydrate and protein, no more than 25% fat and at least 5% minerals. Which one of the following combinations of equally mixed ingredients is feasible?
(a) O and P (b) R and S
(c) P and S (d) Q and R
(e) O and S

13. For a recuperating patient, the doctor recommended a diet containing 10% minerals and at least 30% protein. In how many different ways can we prepare this diet by mixing at least two ingredients?
(a) One (b) Two
(c) Three (d) Four
(e) None

14. Which amongst the following is the formulation having the lowest cost per unit for a diet having 10% fat and at least 30% protein? The diet has to be formed by mixing two ingredients.
(a) P and Q (b) P and S
(c) P and R (d) Q and S
(e) R and S

Directions for Questions 15 to 18: *Refer to the Bar Chart (Figure 25.2). The following additional information is available:*

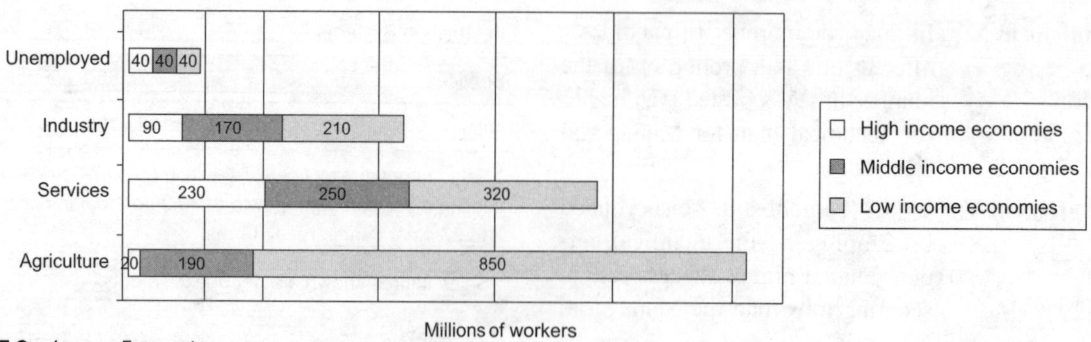

FIGURE 25.2 *Income Economies*

Total worldwide working population: 2.5 billion (2500 million)
Working population in low income economies: 1400 million
Working population in middle income economies: 660 million
Working population in high income economies: 440 million
Total unemployed population: 120 million

The following definitions hold true:
Poor or low income economies: Annual per capita income less than $695
Rich or high income economies: Annual per capita income more than $8626

15. Approximately what percentage of the poor economies total workforce is in agriculture?
    (a) 43% (b) 52%
    (c) 61% (d) 78%
16. Approximately what percentage of the middle income economies total workforce is in services?
    (a) 23% (b) 38%
    (c) 49% (d) 62%
17. Which of the following statements is/are not true ?
    (i) Of the total workforce in services, over 50% do not come from the poor economies
    (ii) Poor economies account for nearly one-third of the total unemployed workers in the world
    (iii) High income economies account for over 25% of the total industrial work force
    (iv) Middle income economies account for nearly one-third of the total services sector employees in the world.
    (a) All of the above (b) (iii) only
    (c) (iii) and (iv) (d) None of these
18. Which of the following statements is true?
    (a) Unemployed workforce accounts for approximately 7% of the world's total working population.
    (b) For both high and middle income economies, the services sector is the highest provider of employment
    (c) Low income economies contribute a higher proportion of the total workforce engaged in the services sector than either the high or the middle income economies, yet the services sector is not the biggest provider of jobs in the low income economies.
    (d) Both (b) and (c)

Directions for Questions 19 to 20: *Table 25.5 contains figures relating to trends in the jute industry.*

TABLE 25.5 Growth in Capacity in the Organised Mill Sector—JUTE

Year Ending March	No. of Mills			Installed Capacity		
	Spinning	Composite	Total	Spindles (Mn.)	Rotors ('000)	Looms ('000)
1994	909	266	1175	28.60	139	150
1995	1148	268	1416	30.70	185	139
1996	1294	275	1569	31.75	226	132
1997	1438	281	1719	33.15	276	124
1998	1504	278	1782	33.88	313	124
1999	1543	281	1824	34.72	383	123
2000	1565	285	1850	35.10	392	123
Dec. 2000	1561	281	1842	35.41	395	123

19. Based on the relative trends of movement in the number of mills and the installed capacity for various types of production machines, which of the following statements can be inferred?
    (i) The role of spindles in the production of jute has declined over the period
    (ii) The role of looms in the production of jute has declined over the period
    (iii) The role of rotors in the production of jute has declined over the period
    (a) All of these (b) (i) and (ii)
    (c) (ii) only (d) (ii) and (iii)
20. If the capacity of production of 1 million spindles is equivalent to the capacity of 1000 rotors, and the capacity of 1 rotor is equivalent to the capacity of 5 looms, then which year showed the highest percentage change in the installed capacity of jute?
    (a) 1995 (b) 1996
    (c) 1997 (d) Can't be determined

26 Mock Test Paper

Directions for Questions 1 to 4: *Answer the questions on the basis of the information given below.*

A study was conducted to ascertain the relative importance that employees in five different countries assigned to five different traits in their Chief Executive Officers. The traits were compassion (C), decisiveness (D), negotiation skills (N), public visibility (P) and vision (V). The level of dissimilarity between two countries is the maximum difference in the ranks allotted by the two countries to any of the five traits. The following table indicates the rank order of the five traits for each country.

TABLE 26.1

Rank	Country				
	India	China	Japan	Malaysia	Thailand
1	C	N	D	V	V
2	P	C	N	D	C
3	N	P	C	P	N
4	V	D	V	C	P
5	D	V	P	N	D

1. Which amongst the following countries is most dissimilar to India?
   (a) China (b) Japan
   (c) Malaysia (d) Thailand
2. Which of the following pairs of countries are most dissimilar?
   (a) China & Japan (b) India & China
   (c) Malaysia & Japan (d) Thailand & Japan
3. Three of the following four pairs of countries have identical levels of dissimilarity. Which pair is the odd one out?
   (a) Malaysia & China (b) China & Thailand
   (c) Thailand & Japan (d) Japan & Malaysia
4. Which of the following countries is least dissimilar to India?
   (a) China (b) Japan
   (c) Malaysia (d) Thailand

Directions for Questions 5 to 8: *Answer the following questions based on the information given below:*

The bar chart below shows the revenue received, in million US Dollars (USD), from subscribers to a particular internet service. The data covers the period 2003 to 2007 for the United States (US) and Europe. The bar chart also shows the estimated revenues from subscription to this service for the period 2008 to 2010.

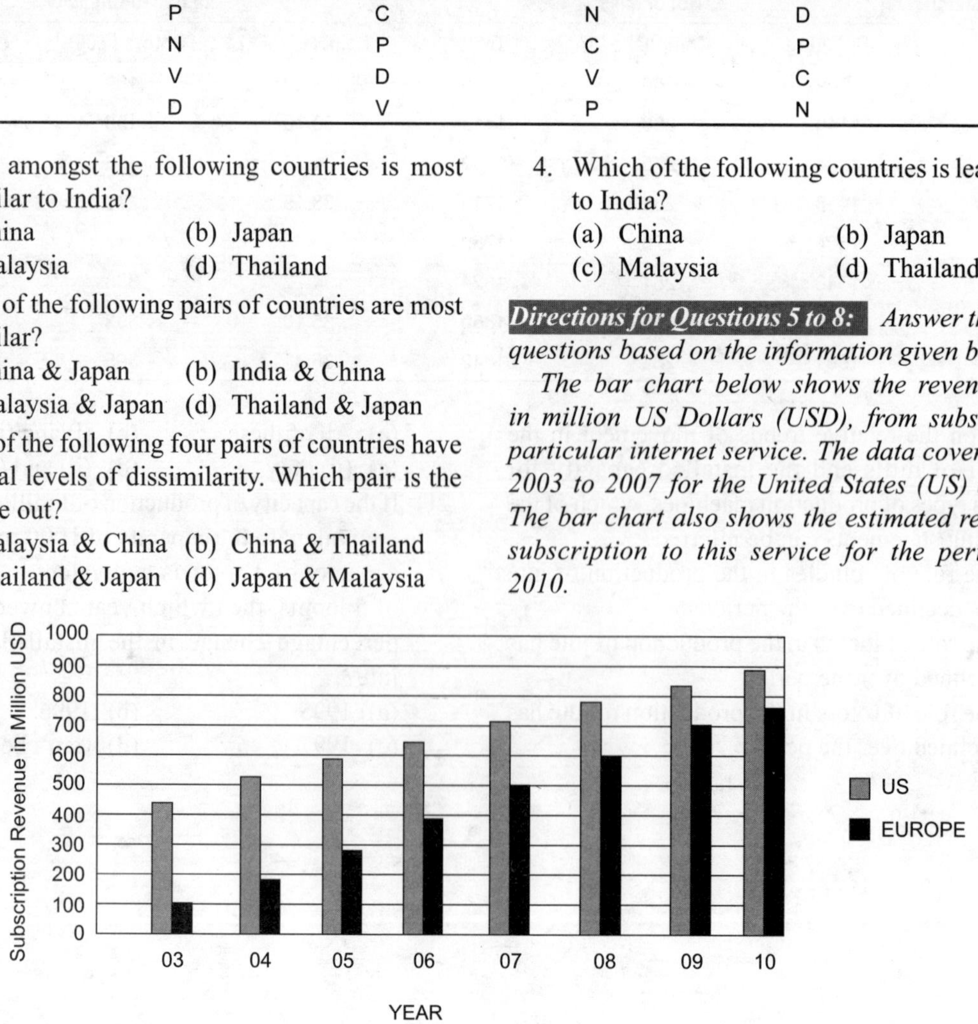

FIGURE 26.1

5. In 2003, 60 per cent of subscribers in Europe were men. Given that women subscribers increase at the rate of 10 per cent per annum and men at the rate of 5 per cent per annum, what is the approximate percentage growth of subscribers between 2003 and 2010 in Europe? The subscription prices are volatile and may change each year.
(a) 62 (b) 15
(c) 84 (d) 78
(e) 50
6. Consider the annual per cent change in the gap between subscription revenues in the US and Europe. What is the year in which the absolute value of this change is the highest?
(a) 03–04 (b) 05–06
(c) 06–07 (d) 08–09
(e) 09–10
7. While the subscription in Europe has been growing steadily towards that of the US, the growth rate in Europe seems to be declining. Which of the following is the closest to the percentage change in growth rate of 2007 (over 2006) relative to the growth rate of 2005 (over 2004)?
(a) 17 (b) 20
(c) 35 (d) 60
(e) 100
8. The difference between the estimated subscription in Europe in 2008 and what it would have been if it were computed using the percentage growth rate of 2007(over 2006), is the closest to:
(a) 50 (b) 80
(c) 20 (d) 10

Directions for Questions 9 to 11: *On the basis of the following data.*

TABLE 26.2

	Drop-Out Rates, in percentage, at Primary, Elementary and Secondary Classes in India								
	Primary (I - V) Classes			Elementary (I-VIII) Classes			Secondary (I- X) Classes		
Year	Boys	Girls	Total	Boys	Girls	Total	Boys	Girls	Total
1996–97	39.7	40.9	40.2	54.3	59.5	56.5	67.3	73.7	70.0
1997–98	37.5	41.5	39.2	53.8	59.3	56.1	66.6	73.0	69.3
1998–99	40.9	41.3	41.5	54.2	59.2	56.3	64.5	69.8	66.7
1999–00	38.7	42.3	40.3	52.0	58.0	54.5	66.6	70.6	68.3
2000–01	39.7	41.9	40.7	50.3	57.7	53.7	66.4	71.5	68.6
2001–02	38.4	39.9	39.0	52.9	56.9	54.6	64.2	68.6	66.0
2002–03	35.8	33.7	34.8	52.3	53.5	52.8	60.7	65.0	62.6
2003–04	33.7	28.6	31.5	51.9	52.9	52.3	61.0	64.9	62.7
2004–05	31.8	25.4	29.0	50.4	51.2	50.8	60.4	63.8	61.9

Gender bias is defined as disproportion in percentage of drop-out rate of the two genders.

9. Based on the data above, choose the true statement from the following alternatives:
(a) Gender bias in primary education has consistently decreased over the years.
(b) Gender bias decreases as students move from primary to secondary classes.
(c) Total drop-out rate decreased consistently for primary classes children from 1996–97 to 2004–05
(d) Gender bias was consistently the highest for secondary classes.
(e) None of the above.
10. Assume that girls constituted 55% of the students entering school. In which year, as compared to the previous year, number of boys in secondary education would be more than the number of girls for the first time?
(a) 1997–98 (b) 1996–97
(c) 2000–01 (d) 1998–99
(e) 2001–02
11. Suppose, every year 7,000 students entered Class I, out of which 45% were boys. What was the average number (integer value) of girls, who remained in educational system after elementary classes, from 1996–97 to 2004–05?
(a) 1475 (b) 1573
(c) 1743 (d) 1676

Directions for Questions 12 to 15: *Refer to the following tables [Tables 26.3(A) and (B)].*

TABLE 26.3 (A) Production of Inorganic Chemicals

Description	Production (tonnes)	
	20013–14	2012–13
Bleaching Powder	60,043	51,434
Aluminium Chloride	31,908	31,176
Sodium Tripoly Phosphate	60,639	60,041
Sodium Bi-carbonate	61,615	72,895
Calcium Carbonate	143,980	142,125
Chlorine and Liquid Chlorine	717,220	718,530
Calcium Carbide	83,445	83,388
Titanium Oxide	30,422	19,624

TABLE 26.3 (B) Production of Organic Chemicals

Description	Production (tonnes)	
	2012–13	2013–14
Ethylene Glycol	327,387	454,371
Formaldehyde	140,384	145,590
Fatty Acids	99,320	113,851
Aniline	44,273	39,340
Acetone	45,657	44,500
Acetic Acid	208,921	212,319
Phthalic Anhydride	127,318	125,959
Benzene	329,000	373,000
Xylenes	147,288	156,000
Phenol	69,281	66,210

12. The ratio of the number of organic chemicals for which the production has fallen to the number of inorganic chemicals for which production has fallen is:
(a) 6:5 (b) 3:2
(c) 2:3 (d) 2:1
13. Of all the chemicals shown, the highest percentage increase in production has been exhibited for:
(a) Fatty acids
(b) Ethylene glycol
(c) Aniline
(d) Sodium bicarbonate
14. If productive volatility is defined as the percentage change in production, and it is known that any chemical whose productive volatility is greater than 5% is classified as highly volatile, then how many chemicals are not highly volatile (amongst organic chemicals)
(a) 4 (b) 5
(c) 6 (d) None of these
15. The ratio of highly volatile organic chemicals to inorganic chemicals which are not highly volatile is:
(a) 1:1 (b) 5:6
(c) 6:5 (d) None of these

Directions for Questions 16 to 19: *Consider the additional information provided in the following table (Table 26.4) and answer the questions that follow.*

TABLE 26.4 User Industries

Description	Production (tonnes)	
	2012–13	2013–14
Dyes and Pigments	2,398	2,236
Perfumes	358	379
Paints and Varnishes	2,740	3,081
Printing Inks	432	553
Hair Oils	266	287
Dental Hygiene Products	2,249	2,853
Industrial Explosives	1,100	1,100
Plastic Floor Covering	151	121
Pesticides	4,336	4,801

16. What is the average price per tonne of chemical in 2012–13 (approximate):
(Assume that the production shown is fully consumed in the user industries shown, and the user industries use only organic and inorganic chemicals)
(a) ₹48,000 (b) ₹4800
(c) ₹54,000 (d) Cannot be determined
17. Assuming that there is an equivalent proportionate increase in the value of the total raw materials used for each of the user industries as for the chemicals

used, then which user industry has the maximum percentage change in its quantity of raw materials used?

(a) Printing inks
(b) Dental hygiene products
(c) Hair oils
(d) Cannot be determined

18. For Question 17, the maximum change in the value of the raw materials used is for:

(a) Pesticides
(b) Printing inks
(c) Dental hygiene products
(d) Cannot be determined

19. The percentage change in the average price per tonne for chemical used in all the user industries shown was: (Assuming that the production shown has been fully consumed in the user industries shown).

(a) 15% (b) 18%
(c) 23% (d) Cannot be determined

Directions for Question 20: *Answer the question on the basis of the following information.*

20. Seventy per cent of the employees in a multi-national corporation have VCD players, 75 per cent have microwave ovens, 80 per cent have ACs and 85 per cent have washing machines. At least what percentage of employees has all four gadgets?

(a) 15 (b) 5
(c) 10 (d) Cannot be determined

Answer Key

LEVEL OF DIFFICULTY – 1

MOCK TEST PAPER 1

1. (b)	2. (d)	3. (b)	4. (a)	5. (b)	6. (d)	7. (a)
8. (b)	9. (a)	10. (c)	11. (b)	12. (b)	13. (d)	14. (a)
15. (d)	16. (c)	17. (b)	18. (a)	19. (b)	20. (b)	

MOCK TEST PAPER 2

1. (d)	2. (d)	3. (d)	4. (b)	5. (d)	6. (b)	7. (d)
8. (d)	9. (c)	10. (b)	11. (a)	12. (a)	13. (c)	14. (c)
15. (a)	16. (b)	17. (b)	18. (b)	19. (b)	20. (c)	

MOCK TEST PAPER 3

1. (b)	2. (a)	3. (a)	4. (a)	5. (b)	6. (b)	7. (b)
8. (c)	9. (a)	10. (b)	11. (b)	12. (d)	13. (d)	14. (d)
15. (b)	16. (a)	17. (d)	18. (d)	19. (d)	20. (b)	

MOCK TEST PAPER 4

1. (c)	2. (b)	3. (c)	4. (d)	5. (d)	6. (b)	7. (a)
8. (b)	9. (d)	10. (d)	11. (b)	12. (c)	13. (b)	14. (b)
15. (d)	16. (a)	17. (a)	18. (c)	19. (a)	20. (d)	

MOCK TEST PAPER 5

1. (c)	2. (b)	3. (c)	4. (d)	5. (d)	6. (a)	7. (b)
8. (d)	9. (b)	10. (a)	11. (c)	12. (d)	13. (d)	14. (a)
15. (d)	16. (d)	17. (c)	18. (c)	19. (d)	20. (a)	

MOCK TEST PAPER 6

1. (d)	2. (d)	3. (c)	4. (b)	5. (b)	6. (a)	7. (b)
8. (b)	9. (c)	10. (b)	11. (c)	12. (d)	13. (c)	14. (d)
15. (d)	16. (b)	17. (a)	18. (a)	19. (b)	20. (a)	

MOCK TEST PAPER 7

1. (b)	2. (a)	3. (d)	4. (d)	5. (c)	6. (b)	7. (d)
8. (c)	9. (d)	10. (d)	11. (c)	12. (c)	13. (a)	14. (a)
15. (c)	16. (c)	17. (c)	18. (a)	19. (b)	20. (b)	

LEVEL OF DIFFICULTY – 2

MOCK TEST PAPER 8

1. (c)	2. (b)	3. (b)	4. (c)	5. (b)	6. (b)	7. (b)
8. (a)	9. (a)	10. (d)	11. (b)	12. (d)	13. (a)	14. (b)
15. (d)	16. (b)	17. (d)	18. (c)	19. (b)	20. (c)	

MOCK TEST PAPER 9

1. (c)	2. (b)	3. (a)	4. (d)	5. (d)	6. (b)	7. (e)
8. (c)	9. (c)	10. (b)	11. (d)	12. (a)	13. (a)	14. (b)
15. (a)	16. (c)	17. (b)	18. (a)	19. (b)	20. (a)	

MOCK TEST PAPER 10

1. (b)	2. (c)	3. (a)	4. (c)	5. (a)	6. (b)	7. (c)
8. (b)	9. (a)	10. (d)	11. (c)	12. (d)	13. (d)	14. (b)
15. (d)	16. (d)	17. (c)	18. (a)	19. (c)	20. (d)	

MOCK TEST PAPER 11

1. (c)	2. (c)	3. (a)	4. (b)	5. (a)	6. (b)	7. (d)
8. (d)	9. (b)	10. (a)	11. (c)	12. (d)	13. (b)	14. (a)
15. (c)	16. (b)	17. (d)	18. (c)	19. (a)	20. (a)	

MOCK TEST PAPER 12

1. (c)	2. (a)	3. (a)	4. (a)	5. (b)	6. (a)	7. (a)
8. (c)	9. (c)	10. (c)	11. (b)	12. (c)	13. (a)	14. (a)
15. (d)	16. (a)	17. (d)	18. (c)	19. (b)	20. (b)	

MOCK TEST PAPER 13

1. (a)	2. (d)	3. (d)	4. (a)	5. (b)	6. (b)	7. (a)
8. (b)	9. (b)	10. (d)	11. (c)	12. (a)	13. (b)	14. (b)
15. (c)	16. (c)	17. (b)	18. (d)	19. (d)	20. (d)	

MOCK TEST PAPER 14

1. (d)	2. (b)	3. (a)	4. (b)	5. (d)	6. (c)	7. (b)
8. (c)	9. (c)	10. (a)	11. (c)	12. (c)	13. (b)	14. (d)
15. (d)	16. (d)	17. (a)	18. (b)	19. (c)	20. (a)	

MOCK TEST PAPER 15

1. (d)	2. (c)	3. (c)	4. (d)	5. (c)	6. (a)	7. (b)
8. (b)	9. (d)	10. (c)	11. (d)	12. (d)	13. (b)	14. (c)
15. (a)	16. (a)	17. (b)	18. (c)	19. (b)	20. (d)	

MOCK TEST PAPER 16

1. (a)	2. (b)	3. (d)	4. (d)	5. (c)	6. (d)	7. (d)
8. (a)	9. (d)	10. (c)	11. (d)	12. (b)	13. (d)	14. (d)
15. (a)	16. (c)	17. (b)	18. (a)	19. (b)	20. (b)	

MOCK TEST PAPER 17

1. (c)	2. (b)	3. (d)	4. (d)	5. (c)	6. (c)	7. (d)
8. (d)	9. (d)	10. (d)	11. (d)	12. (b)	13. (b)	14. (a)
15. (c)	16. (b)	17. (d)	18. (d)	19. (c)	20. (c)	

MOCK TEST PAPER 18

1. (d)	2. (a)	3. (c)	4. (c)	5. (b)	6. (d)	7. (c)
8. (d)	9. (c)	10. (a)	11. (c)	12. (c)	13. (b)	14. (b)
15. (c)	16. (b)	17. (c)	18. (c)	19. (a)	20. (a)	

MOCK TEST PAPER 19

1. (b)	2. (d)	3. (d)	4. (c)	5. (d)	6. (d)	7. (d)
8. (a)	9. (c)	10. (b)	11. (b)	12. (c)	13. (c)	14. (b)
15. (d)	16. (b)	17. (c)	18. (d)	19. (d)	20. (b)	

MOCK TEST PAPER 20

1. (c)	2. (d)	3. (d)	4. (c)	5. (a)	6. (d)	7. (c)
8. (c)	9. (c)	10. (d)	11. (b)	12. (d)	13. (c)	14. (a)
15. (d)	16. (b)	17. (c)	18. (d)	19. (a)	20. (c)	

MOCK TEST PAPER 21

1. (d)	2. (b)	3. (b)	4. (d)	5. (b)	6. (c)	7. (c)
8. (c)	9. (a)	10. (d)	11. (b)	12. (d)	13. (b)	14. (b)
15. (a)	16. (c)	17. (d)	18. (a)	19. (d)	20. (d)	

MOCK TEST PAPER 22

1. (a)	2. (c)	3. (b)	4. (b)	5. (b)	6. (c)	7. (c)
8. (b)	9. (a)	10. (d)	11. (c)	12. (b)	13. (d)	14. (c)
15. (b)	16. (e)	17. (a)	18. (c)	19. (c)	20. (b)	

MOCK TEST PAPER 23

1. (b)	2. (d)	3. (b)	4. (c)	5. (c)	6. (a)	7. (a)
8. (d)	9. (a)	10. (d)	11. (d)	12. (a)	13. (a)	14. (d)
15. (d)	16. (c)	17. (d)	18. (d)	19. (a)	20. (b)	

MOCK TEST PAPER 24

1. (b)	2. (e)	3. (a)	4. (e)	5. (d)	6. (d)	7. (a)
8. (d)	9. (c)	10. (d)	11. (a)	12. (b)	13. (b)	14. (d)
15. (c)	16. (a)	17. (c)	18. (b)	19. (c)	20. (b)	

MOCK TEST PAPER 25

1. (b)	2. (c)	3. (e)	4. (a)	5. (c)	6. (a)	7. (b)
8. (d)	9. (c)	10. (c)	11. (e)	12. (e)	13. (a)	14. (d)
15. (c)	16. (b)	17. (b)	18. (d)	19. (b)	20. (a)	

MOCK TEST PAPER 26

1. (b)	2. (d)	3. (d)	4. (a)	5. (a)	6. (d)	7. (c)
8. (a)	9. (e)	10. (b)	11. (d)	12. (d)	13. (b)	14. (b)
15. (a)	16. (d)	17. (a)	18. (d)	19. (d)	20. (c)	

Solutions

LEVEL OF DIFFICULTY – 1

MOCK TEST PAPER 1

Questions 1 to 5:

	2004	2003	2002	2001
Profit before tax	840	730	230	330
Dividends + Earnings	600	400	120	195
So, tax	240	270	110	135

1. (b) In 2002 tax per rupee of profit is the highest which is = $\frac{230-120}{230}\times 100 \approx 48\%$
2. (d) It cannot be determined because the value of share capital is not known.
3. (b) In 2002, it is the least which is = $\frac{230}{2810}\times 100 \approx$ 8%
4. (a) It is maximum for the year 2001, which is = $\frac{155}{80}\times 100 \approx 194\%$
5. (b) Amount in reserves after 2004 will be = 80 + 155 + 80 + 320 + 450 = 1085 lakh.

Questions 6 to 10:

Operating profit in 2002–03 (320 lakh)

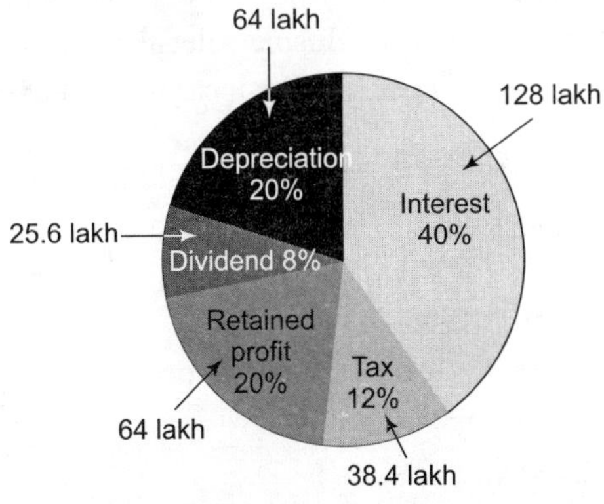

Operating Profit in 2001–02 (260 lakh)

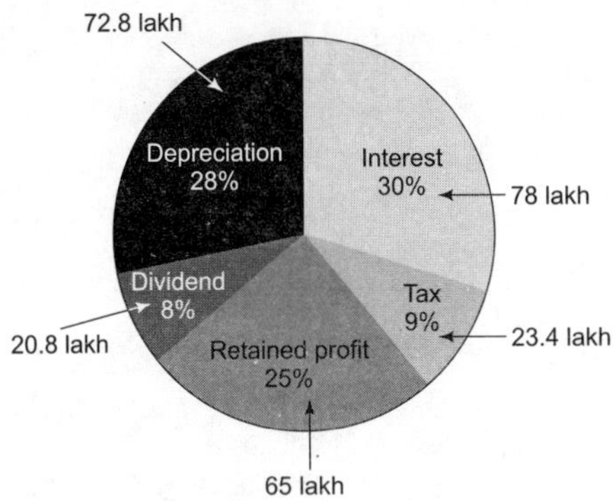

6. (d) Increase = $\frac{128-78}{78}\times 100 = 64\%$
7. (a) Difference = 128 – 78 = 50 lakh
8. (b) For 2001, let borrowed fund = x
   $\Rightarrow$ 10% of $x = 78 \Rightarrow x = 780$
   For 2002, let borrowed funds = y
   $\Rightarrow$ 10% of $y = 128 \Rightarrow y = 1280$
   $\Rightarrow$ Total borrowed funds = 2060 lakh
9. (a) In 2001, dividend = 20.8 lakh
   In 2002, dividend = 25.6 lakh
   $\Rightarrow$ Dividend is higher by $\frac{25.6-20.8}{20.8}\times 100$ = 23%
10. (c) Dividend = ₹20.8 lakh

Questions 11 to 13:

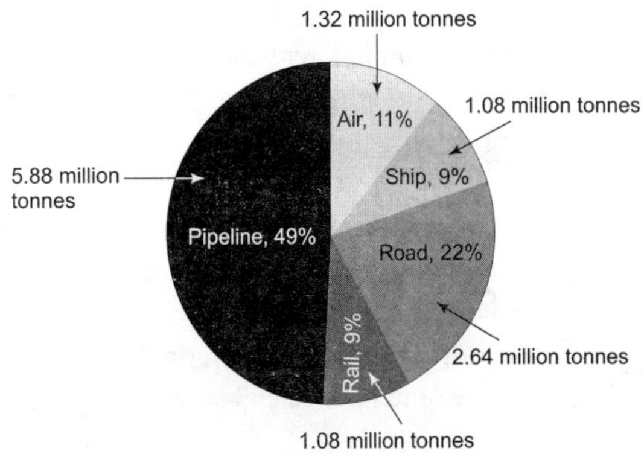

FIGURE 1.2 *Volume*

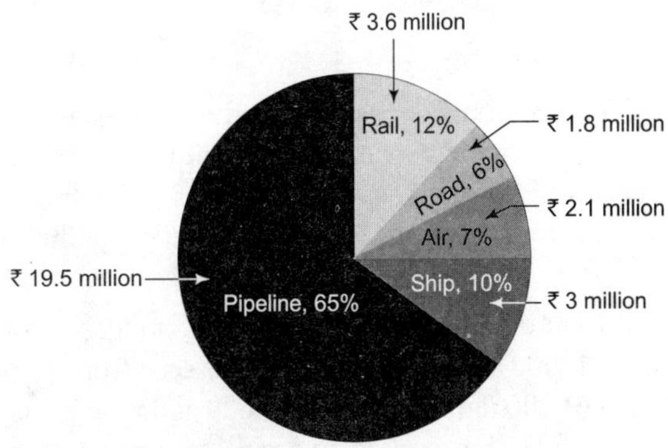

FIGURE 1.3 *Distribution Cost*

11. (b) 2.125
    $\therefore$ cost/tonne = $\frac{2.1+3}{1.32+1.08}$
    = 2.125

12. (b) Looking at the percentage ratios we see that for rail 12/9 is the greatest ratio. (Pipeline's cost per tonne would be lower than that of rail since 65/49 < 12/9.)
13. (d) Cost/tonne is
    (P) Pipeline = 19.5/5.88 = 3.31
    (Q) Air = 2.1/1.32 = 1.59
    (R) Rail = 3.6/1.08 = 3.33
    $\Rightarrow$ R > P > Q (d)

Questions 14 to 16:

	Model 1	Model 2	Model 3	Model 4
Men	F_1, F_2, F_3, F_4, F_5	F_5, F_8, F_{12}	F_2, F_6, F_7, F_{13}	F_3, F_{10}, F_{11}
Women	F_6, F_7, F_8	F_9, F_{13}	F_3, F_9, F_{11}	F_1, F_2, F_4
Children	F_9, F_{10}, F_{11}	F_6	F_1, F_4	F_9, F_5

14. (a) Let Model 1 or Model 2 for women include
    Factories – $F_6, F_7, F_8, F_9, F_{13}$ = A
    And Model 3 for children – F_1, F_4 = B
    $\Rightarrow$ A and B = 0.
15. (d) Some Model 3 producing factories produce Model 1 $\Rightarrow$ Model 3 $\cap$ Model 1
    = $F_2, F_6, F_7, F_3, F_9, F_{11}, F_1, F_4$
    and none is common with men's Model 2 producing. Men's Model 2 producing factories, which are – F_5, F_8, F_{12}
    So (d) is true.
16. (c) 3
    $\therefore$ Children's Model 1 producing factories included = F_9, F_{10}, F_{11},
    And factories either producing men's Model 4 shoes or women's Model 3 shoes include:
    = F_3, F_{10}, F_{11}, F_9
    So common factories are:
    F_{10}, F_9, F_{11} = 3.

Questions 17 to 20:

Note: For these questions you need to understand that the per unit variable cost is ₹14 per unit (since the variable cost at 0 units is 0 and at 500 units is 7000 and it moves in a straight line); Also, the revenue per additional unit is ₹20.

17. (b) At 100 units, we have no profit, no loss. Cost = ₹2000 and revenue = ₹2000 as seen from graph.
18. (a) At 200 units fixed cost = ₹600 and variable cost = ₹2800 as seen from graph, so profit = ₹600
19. (b) After 349 units, we get a profit of 1500 which gives us a per unit profit of 1494/349 = 4.28. The profit at 400 units is 1700, but the profit per unit is lower as the number of units is higher.
20. (b) The profit per unit at 349 units = 1494/349 = 4.28. Profit per unit at 450 units = 1700/450 = 3.777. Hence, the maximum profit per unit is got at 349 units. Option (b) is the correct answer.

MOCK TEST PAPER 2

Questions 1 to 5:

1. (d) 100% increase for Mortein in Kolkata from 2003 to 2004, i.e. from 10% to 20%
2. (d) In Chennai only Mortein decreased its market share by 10%
3. (d) Shares of all companies have either increased or decreased from 2003 to 2004 in some city.
4. (b) 1 – only in Delhi
5. (d) 3 – Finit in Chennai, Hit in Chennai, Mortein in Delhi

Questions 6 to 8:

6. (b)

Total Export In	Total Figure	%
1994–95 = 668	2041	32.7
1995–96 = 775	2886	26.8
1996–97 = 1383	3807	36.3
1997–98 = 1970	5031	39.2
1998–99 = 2672	6052	44.2

7. (d) 1998–99
   The lowest per cent growth = 20.3%
8. (d) None of these
   Because in (a) – Hardware exports decreased
   In (b) – Business decreased in 1996–97
   In (c) – IT Business in maintenance = 945
   In training = 1000

Questions 9 to 10:

9. (c) $\therefore$ in 1995–96, software business is lower than that of 1998–99
10. (b) $\therefore$ software business and IT peripherals is greater in 1998–99 than 1995–96.

Questions 11 to 12:

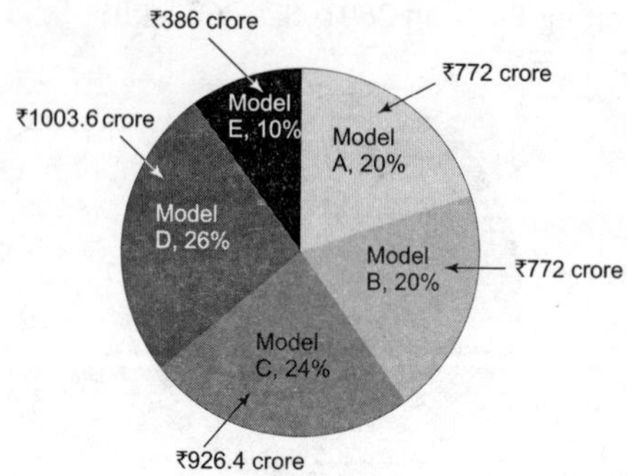

FIGURE 2.1 (A) *Value*

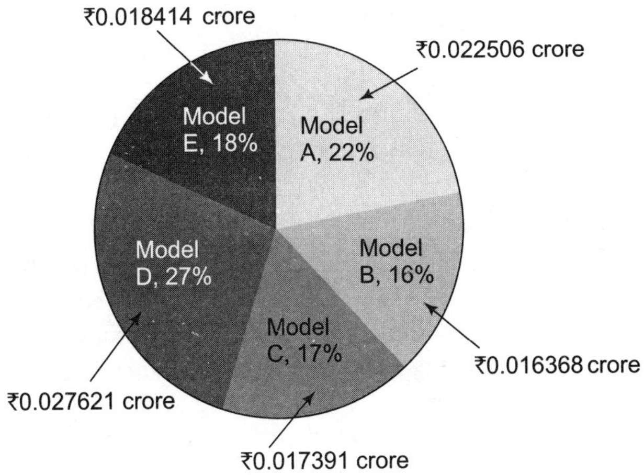

FIGURE 2.1 (B) *Quantity*

Total sales value = ₹3860 crore
Total number of units sold = 0.1023 crore
Costs per bike are: (approx)
Model A = ₹34,301
Model B = ₹47,615
Model C = ₹53,269
Model D = ₹36,334
Model E = ₹20,962

11. (a) Model C = ₹53,269. Note, C being the highest is also calculable by taking the ratio of % of value divided by % of volume. This ratio is the highest or Model C.
12. (a) ₹53.2

Questions 13 to 16:

13. Visual scanning gives us BN as the answer.
14. Doubling of market shares has been exhibited by BN & MT.
15. 60% drop for MT in Kolkata is the highest drop.
16. Kolkata shows only one product losing market share.

Questions 17 to 20:

17. Lovells UK and Allen & Overy UK are very close to each other in this respect—Lovells being marginally higher than Allen & Overy (1% calculation range needed).
18. Clearly Lovells UK from 10 to 26.
19. Allen & Overy, Skadden, Jones Day and Lovells meet the condition.
20. There is approximately a 51% growth in the number of offices over all. This is exceeded by five law firms.

MOCK TEST PAPER 3

Questions 1 to 3:

1. Comparing the four ratios in the option, 209/587 (1997) is the correct answer.
2. The values to be compared based on availability per capita are:
   (421 – 207)/487 for 1995 i.e. 214/487.
   372/464 for 1996
   378/510 for 1997
   and 440/566 for 1999.
   Looking at these four ratios it is quite clear that the ratio is below 1/2 only for one year i.e. 1995. This year would account for the lowest population amongst the given years. Hence, option (a) is correct.
3. Obviously 1999. Hence Option (a). [Since area has continuously decreased and production has continuously increased.]

Questions 4 to 6:

4. Only Lavanya, Rahul and Yamini are eligible to attend the workshop on communication skills. Hence, Option (a) is correct.
   For doing this, eliminate the people who are not interested in CS and the people who are committed to internal projects in January.
5. There are a total 6 executives, out of which three can attend up to 2 workshops (Parul, Kalindi and Dinesh.) Hence, the required answer is 3. Hence, Option (b) is correct.
6. While solving the previous question, you would have identified that Gayatri and Urvashi cannot attend a single workshop. Hence, Option (b) is correct.

Questions 7 to 12:

7. (b) In 2000, the maximum increase can be visualised.
8. (c) This question can be solved visually. In 1999–2001, it is maximum as seen from the bar graph – profit goes from + ve in 1999 to–ve in 2001 – so you can just add the two chunks of the bar chart which shows profit in 1999 and loss in 2001. For none of the other year's pairs given in the problem do we get the difference between profits higher than the year 1999 and 2001.
9. (a) Interest is almost constant throughout.
10. (b) In 2001, this percentage can be seen to be maximum.
11. (b) The profits total around 45 (approximately) while the costs total between 900 and 950 for the 5 years. Hence, the answer would be the closest to 5%. Option (b) is correct.

12. (d) It can be observed for 2002, since the (raw material + wages) for that year is the highest. At the same time for that year, the profit is at a minimum. Hence, Option (d) is correct.

Questions 13 to 16:

13. (d) For rice the percentage has remained constant while for gram the percentage has decreased and then remained constant. For corn from 2005 to 2015, the percentage has actually gone up. Hence, Option (d) is correct.
14. (d) Amongst all the given options, it is only for rice that the proportion in the total food demand of the world has remained constant, while its proportion of the total demand in America has gone up.
15. (b) For wheat and gram it can be seen clearly from the data in the table that the portion is more than 60% for both the years.
16. (a) It can be seen to be for Wheat.

Questions 17 to 20:

17. (d) Lay No. : 3, 5, 6, 8, 10, 11, 15,16, 17, 18, 19, 20, 22, 24, 26, 27
    So 16.
18. (d) None of these → 7
19. (d) None of these → 13
20. (b) Brown – (M)(XL)
    Blue – S, M, L, XL
    Green – S, L . A total of 8 fabrics

MOCK TEST PAPER 4

Questions 1 to 2:

The answers to these questions can be seen visually.

1. We can see that option (c) is correct.
2. Option (b).

Questions 3 to 5:

3. Except Edible Oil and Dal, all other commodities have shown an increase. Hence, option (c) is correct.
4. Except for edible oil all other commodities have exhibited this. Hence, the correct answer is 5. Option (d) is correct.
5. There is only one such instance exhibited by the commodities Egg and Onion. Hence, option (d) is correct.

Questions 6 to 9:

6. Since 2400 represents the number of viewers who watched 1 or more than 1 movie a week in City C, we can say that this value would be equal to 15% of the City C viewers (as 85% of the viewers in this city watch less than a movie a week – as seen from the second column in the table.)
   Thus, the number of viewers in City C who watched less than a movie a week would be given by:
   2400 × 85/15 = 13600. Option (b) is correct.
7. Using calculation similar to the previous question, (we get the table given below). It can be seen that the highest number of viewers who watched less than 1 movie a week were from City E – and this value would be 24000. Option (a) is correct.

8.

City	% of Viewers Who Watch Less than 1 Movie a Week	% of Viewers Who Watch 1 or >1 Movie per Week	Number of Viewers Who Watch 1 or >1 Movie per Week	Number of Viewers Who Watch Less than 1 Movie a Week	Total Number of Movie Goers
A	60	40	2400	3600	6000
B	20	80	3000	750	3750
C	85	15	2400	13600	16000
D	55	45	2700	3300	6000
E	75	25	8000	24000	32000

In the above table the third column (% of Viewers Who Watch 1 or >1 Movie Per Week) is derived by 100—the value from the second column. Also, the calculation for the 5th column (Number of Viewers Who Watch Less than 1 Movie a Week) is based on unitary method as follows:

For city A: 60 × 2400/40 = 3600.

It can be seen from the above table, that the second lowest value of the total number of movie goers is for City D. Option (b) is correct.

9. The sum of the 5th column in the table for the previous question would give us the answer for this question. This sum = 3600 + 750 + 13600 + 3300 + 24000 = 45250. Option (d) is correct.

Questions 10 to 13:

10. Option (d) is the correct option and it can be directly inferred from the bar chart in the figure that Hybrid Micro circuits would have the least reliability.
11. Since signal devices have a failure rate of 16%, we are looking for something which has a failure rate of 25% more than signal devices. In other words we are looking at the component which has a failure rate of

20%. It can be seen from the bar chart that Capacitors is the correct answer. Hence, we choose Option (b).

12. The lowest priority in fresh investment plans should be for the most reliable components. Since picture tubes and signal devices have the most reliability, they should be placed on the lowest priority for fresh investment. Option (c) is correct.
13. Integrated circuit boards have a failure rate of 30 per thousand which translates to 3%. Thus, for an equipment using 400 of these, we need to keep 3% spare. 3% of 400 = 12. Thus, we should keep a total of 12 integrated circuit boards as spare.
By the same logic, for capacitors we need 2% spares, for 240 we need a back-up of 4.8 capacitors, which gets rounded off to 5 capacitors. Option (b) can be selected at this point as the correct answer.

Questions 14 to 16:

14. The required states are Haryana, Punjab, Maharashtra and Andhra Pradesh. Hence, the answer is 4, i.e. Option (b).
15. 400000 tonnes means 0.4 million tonnes. Hence, we are looking for a ratio of production to population greater than 0.4 in order to identify the states that need to be counted. As we move down the table, starting from Haryana, then excluding West Bengal all the other 7 states that are after West Bengal in the table have a ratio greater than 0.4 Hence, the correct answer is 8. Option (d) is correct.
16. Haryana and Punjab both show a productivity of 4.8 (19.2/4 for Haryana and 24/5 for Punjab). Hence, option (a) is correct.

Questions 17 to 20:

17. The respective values of consumption are approximately: 70, 90, 110, 110 and 125. The highest percentage growth can be seen between 70 and 90 which means that it is for the year 2007.
Option (a) is correct.
18. Taking approximate values for 2008, we have production = 240, consumption = 130 and per capita consumption = 40. Thus, 110/40 = 2.75 million. But there are two options close to 2.75 one on either side. So we need to take a call about thinking more closely about the numbers for production, consumption and per capita consumption. It can be seen that the bar for per capita consumption is lower than the 40 mark and hence the value of the ratio would be higher than 2.75. Thus, we select option (c) as the correct answer.
19. The ratios are: 110/70, 110/90, 130/110 and 120/100. The highest ratio is for 2006 – the first year. Option (a) is correct.
20. Visual inspection shows us that the ratio of consumption/per capita consumption is the highest for the year 2010 (it is around 3 for that year) and hence, the population would be the highest in that year. Option (d) is thus correct.

MOCK TEST PAPER 5

Questions 1 to 3:

Questions are also solvable visually. The answers are:

1. Option (c) is the correct option as we can see that between 1971, 1981, 1991 and 2001, for four consecutive censuses, the number of states where females outnumber men was 1. Hence, option (c) is correct.
2. Himachal Pradesh has grown from 884 to 970 – a growth of 86 and this can be seen as the highest growth. Kerala, with a growth of 54, has the second highest growth amongst the states. Hence, option (b) is correct.
3. 'Sharpest decline' can be understood as the highest percentage decline. Bihar has dropped from 1061 to 921 – a drop of close to 13-14% and this is the highest percentage decline of the sex ratio amongst all the five states that had a 1000+ sex ratio in 1901.

Questions 4 to 7:

4. We need to solve this by checking the options and seeing whether any of the values in the options match the given data. Checking for option (c), @ 3.5%, 3075 would become 3182, 3182 would become 3293, 3293 would become 3408 and 3408 would reach somewhere in the 3500s after the fourth time period. Thus, 3.5% is too low a value for the compound average growth rate. Checking similarly for 6% and 5.75%, you can see that the numbers do not work out at this rate.
Thus, option (d) is correct.
5. The maximum drop can be seen to have happened during March from 1211 to 741; a drop of 470 on a starting value of 1211. This is close to 39% of the value. None of the three options matches this and hence Option (d) is correct.
6. The required percentage would be given by the percentage value of the ratio of: 233/3221 = 7.24%. Option (a) is correct.
7. The highest value is for February @ (1211 + 247) out of 3221 which is approximately 45%.
Option (b) is correct.

Questions 8 to 10:

8. His travel would have been: $20 + 45 + 55 + 65 + 65 + 60 + 60 = 370$. Hence the time taken will be over 7 hours. Hence (d).

9. $$\frac{\left[\begin{array}{c}\text{Distance travelled in first 5 hours} - \\ \text{Distance in last 5 hours}\end{array}\right]}{5}$$

$= |200 - 290|/5$

10. Total distance traveled in first 4 hours $= 20 + 40 + 40 + 45 = 145$. Total distance traveled in next 6 hours $= 55 + 60 + 60 + 65 + 65 + 55 = 360$. Required ratio $=145/360 = 0.40$. Option (a) is the closest answer.

Questions 11 to 14:

11. The faster train takes 4 hours to travel 288 km, while the slower train takes 4 hours and 5 minutes.
12. Visual inspection shows X to A.
13. Data is not available to answer this question.
14. Obviously X to A

Questions 15 to 17:

15. The highest percentage of ex-defence servicemen is for the ratio 25/130 which is for level 4. Option (d) is correct.
16. Level 4 would lose the maximum as it would incur a reduction of 125 out of the original estimation of 255 posts. No other level is close to this value in percentage terms. Option (d) is correct.
17. The closest comparisons are 9 out of 210 (level 3) and 15 out of 330 (level 5). 9 out of 210 is a lower percentage as compared to 15 out of 330. Option (c) is correct.

Questions 18 to 20:

We can make the following table from the given information:

Year	Revenues	Cost	Profit
2000	25000	20000	5000
2001	30000	25000	5000
2002	37500	30000	7500
2003	45000	37500	7500

The answers can be read off the table:

18. The increase in profit is maximum for 2002. Option (c) is correct.
19. We can see that the cost is 5/6th of revenues or 83.33% for both 2001 and 2003. Hence, option (d) is correct.
20. Option (a) can be seen to be true and is the correct answer.

MOCK TEST PAPER 6

Questions 1 to 5:

1. (d) With 65.8% utilisation, production = 1.63

   So with 100% utilisation, product $= \frac{1.68 \times 100}{65.8}$

   $= 2.53$
2. (d) Dhanpura has a production of 1.58 and with a capacity utilisation of 60.35%, it would have a total capacity of 2.61 approximately. The unutilised capacity would be 1.03 which is higher than of the other companies.
3. (c) With 62.3% use, production = 11.8

   So with 100% use, production $= \frac{11.8 \times 100}{62.3} = 18.9$
4. (b) Price = Total Sales Value/Sales which is the lowest for Dhanpura at 11.75
5. (b) Total sales including others is given = 137.80 crore

   Total sales for packaged atta of the given companies = 32.15+27.75+16.25+18.45 = 94.6

   ⇒ Percentage of market share with others =

   $$\frac{137.80 - 94.6}{137.8} \times 100 = 31\%$$

Questions 6 to 11:

6. (a) In February, J&K supplies 11,638 tonnes out of 11759 tonnes ≈ 99%, which is the highest.
7. (b) From April–September, HP provided the maximum amount of apples as seen from the table.
8. (b) Amount supplied by HP = 233204

   Amount supplied by J&K = 268033.
9. (c) Months with '0' in cold storage value indicates the supply was more than demand. So May–September
10. (b) Amount by HP = 233204

    J&K = 268033

    UP = 268

    ⇒ Total apples supplied = 501505 tonnes

    501505000 kgs

    ⇒ Number of trees = 501505000/40

    = 12.5 million
11. (c) Land used = 12.5 million/250

    = 50,000

Questions 12 to 15:

12. The highest percentage dilution is for ICICI Bank (100%).

13. There are 11 such companies. Option (c) is correct.
14. The correct order is (ii), (i), (v), (iv), (iii). Option (d) is correct.
15. The market value/the value at which the equity stake was divested is not available. Neither is the data about the number of shares divested by each company available. Hence, it cannot be determined.

Questions 16 to 19:

16. Visual inspection will show that it occurs between 1994–95 and 1995–96. The value will be given by:
$$\frac{(675-436)\times 100}{436}$$
i.e., the percentage equivalent of 239/436.

Note: Negative surplus means deficit.

17. The overall fiscal performance is measured through surplus/deficit without subsidy. 1992-93 is the only year when there is a drop in deficit.
18. Visual inspection will show that this occurs between 1994–95 and 1995–96.
Calculate: $\frac{(814-548)\times 100}{548}$
i.e., the percentage equivalent of the ratio 266/548 = 48.5% (approximately)
19. $\frac{\text{Subsidy for last four years}}{\text{Total subsidy over the period}} = 38223/54847 =$ 69.7% (approximately)

Question 20:

20. A mixture as sweet as maltose should have a sweetness of 0.32. Mixing lactose (0.16) and glucose (0.74) in the ratio 21 : 8 would give us a mixture containing sweetness of 0.32.
Option (a) is correct.

MOCK TEST PAPER 7

Questions 1 to 4:

1. Visual inspection shows western province.
2. The highest percentage change is seen in Eastern province in Kalandu.
3. Luanda 14/271 = 5% approx.
4. Visual inspection show us 4 markets viz: Kalandu, Kiambu, Kandara and Kitale.

Questions 5 to 7:

5. In 2003 the wheat production is 1.2 times the rice production and hence the wheat production would be $4 \times 1.2 = 4.8$ lakh. Option (c) is correct.
6. The ratio wheat production to rice production is more than 1 in three years. Hence, Option (b) is correct i.e. Wheat production was greater than rice production in 3 years over the period.
7. The wheat production in 2001 would be 0.4×3 lakh = 1.2 lakh tons and hence the total grain availability would be 4.2 lakh tons. The remaining would have to be imported. Thus, the import requirement is 0.8 lakh tons.

Questions 8 to 10:

8. The speed of the train at the start of the 3 hour period was 40 kmph and it was 70 kmph at the end of the 3 hour period. This means that there was a growth of 75% in the speed of the train in the 3 hour period. Option (c) is correct.
9. Looking at the values it is evident that they obey the expression 40+t/6 where t is in minutes. Option (d) is correct.
10. After 2 ½ hours, the train's speed can be seen to be 65 kmph. Option (d) is correct.

Questions 11 to 13:

11. Clearly WIPRO on NQE has shown the highest percentage increase. Option (c) is correct.
12. If he buys WIPRO on BSE @ ₹ 60 and sells WIPRO on NQE, he would be selling effectively at $6.5 \times 11 =$ 71.5, a profit percentage of close to 20%. Option (c) is correct.
13. The total purchase would be 1.5 lakh shares and hence the purchase would be 75000 shares at 232 and 75000 shares at 247. Total cost would be $75000 \times 232 + 75000 \times 247$, which in million terms can be taken as: $7.5 \times 2.32 + 7.5 \times 2.47$ which is close to 36 million.

Questions 14 to 17:

14. The total monthly salary expense for Administration would be given by $0.22 \times 18000 \times 12000 = 3960 \times 12000 = 4.7$ crore. Thus, the annual cost would be $4.7 \times 12 = 57$ crore. Option (a) is correct.
15. The number of employees in Sales and Marketing was 18% of 18000 = 3240 in 2025 while it was 20% of 20000 which is equal to 4000. From 3240 to 4000 it represents a 23.45% increase. Option (c) is correct.
16. For Administration, the variation is from 3960 to 4800.
For Operations the variation is from 4140 to 5200
For Sales and Marketing the variation is from 3240 to 4000
For Finance and Accounts the variation is from 5220 to 4000

For Corporate HQ the variation is from 1440 to 2000. The maximum variation in strength is for Finance and Accounts. Hence, Option (c) is correct.

17. The number of joinees would be given by: 5200 – (4140 – 300) = 1360. Option (c) is correct.

Questions 18 to 20:

18. The average marks are approximately 900000/10000 = 90. Option (a) is the closest.

19. Here the safest answer is option (b). Since it can be seen that the marks per student has actually grown.

20. Average marks = $\frac{380-50}{6800-1800} \times 1000 = 66$

The closest option is (b).

LEVEL OF DIFFICULTY – 2

MOCK TEST PAPER 8

Questions 1 to 4:

1. The cost overflow depends on two things – time overflow and the per day cost of running that phase. We can easily see that a time overflow of 2 days occurs in design and construction both. However, construction obviously has a much higher cost of running it per day - hence the biggest cost increase would be in construction. Option (c) is correct.
2. Since the cost per day is the same, the highest percentage increase would occur for the phase that had the highest percentage change in the number of days. Design moves from an estimated 3 days to an actual 5 days – a percentage increase of 66.66% and this represents the highest value of the percentage increase. Hence, option (b) is correct.
3. Construction goes from 6 days to 8 days – a growth of 33.33%. This would also be the percentage change in the cost, since the per day costs of running a phase is constant for all phases.
4. Estimated total time would be 3 + 2 + 6 + 3 = 14 days. Actual time would be: 5 + 3 + 8 + 4 = 20. Percentage growth in time = 6/14 = 42.85%.

Questions 5 to 8:

Solve all 4 questions simultaneously through the options to meet the constraints, i.e. everybody should have more than or equal to 3 lakh gold coins, Shaleen should get 1 lakh more than Tarun, while Raman + Shaleen + Tarun + Ujjwal = 20 lakhs. The only set of answers that fit all these constraints together is: (8 + 5 + 4 + 3)

Questions 9 to 12:

9. (a) The deficit intensity can be calculated as the difference between Import Intensity and Export Intensity. The values for the deficit intensity are as follows:

Year	2003–04	2004–05	2005–06	2006–07	2007–08
Deficit Intensity	4.8	6	7.4	8	5

The growth in Deficit Intensity is 25%, which is the highest in 2004–05.

10. (d) From the solution to the above question we can see that this growth percentage is 25% (from 4.8 to 6).
11. (b) We need the ratio of sales to gross fixed assets. Let the total cost of raw material be 100 for the year 2005–06. This means that the value of Imported raw material is 14.5.

    Then, the total sales for the year is 200 (since the problem says that the total cost of raw materials is 50% of sales for the year).

    The total imports would be given by:

    13.3% of 200 = 26.6 (since import intensity is 13.3)

    Total Imports = Imported raw materials + Imported Capital goods → 26.6 = 14.5 + Imported Capital Goods → Imported Capital Goods = 12.1

    We also know that the Imported Capital Goods represents 9.7% of the gross fixed assets. Thus: 12.1 × 100 ÷ 9.7 = 124.74 ≈125.

    The ratio of sales to gross fixed assets ≈ 200 ÷ 125 = 1.6.

    Hence, Option (b) is correct.
12. (d) Statement (d) is true since the deficit intensity has always grown between 2003–04 and 2006–07. This can be seen from the table in the solution to Question 9.

Solutions for questions 13 to 15:

13. Checking the four options it can be clearly seen that the maximum percentage drop is for Westside which goes from 2411 to 1724 which can be seen as a proxy calculation using 241 to 172 – a drop of 69 on 241 which is close to 29%. (***Note:*** The sharpest decline also means the largest percentage drop.) Hence, Option (a) is correct.
14. Shoppers Stop in 2007 has grown by 329 which is the highest increase amongst the four options. Hence, Option (b) is correct.
15. We do not have information about the cost per square feet of the entire retail sector – even if the 4 retailers

represent the entire retail sector we still would need to know the respective retail space that each of them has in 2007 and in 2010 in order to be able to calculate the retail cost per square feet for the retail sector. Hence, option (d) is the correct answer.

Solutions for questions 16 to 20:

16. The highest growth rate is clearly for 1992 as the value grows from around 313 to 420 in that year – which is much higher in terms of percentage terms than the other percentage changes for the years 1991 (where the total production changes from 328 to 313 – a negative change), 1993 (420 to 299 again a negative change) and 95 (332 to 340— a small change in comparison to the change in 1992).
Option (b) is thus the correct answer.
17. Based on the table below the highest stability is for S (126/79)

	90	91	92	93	94	95
Total	328	313	420	299	332	340
P	45	23	40	38	75	55
Q	98	40	108	60	40	70
R	72	91	107	62	131	120
S	113	159	165	139	86	95

18. The total revenue would be given by the following formula:
Number of units of P × 9 + Number of units of Q × 4 + Number of units of R × 13 + Number of units of S × 3.
In 1991 the value is: 23 × 9 + 40 × 4 + 91 × 13 + 159 × 3 = 207 + 160 + 1183 + 477 = 2027
In 1992 the value is: 40 × 9 + 108 × 4 + 107 × 13 + 165 × 3 = clearly greater than 1991 – so we do not need to calculate this.
In 1993 the value is: 38 × 9 + 60 × 4 + 62 × 13 + 139 × 3 = 342 + 240 + 806 + 417 = 1805
In 1990, 1994 and 1995 the value is greater than 1805 and hence 1993 would give us the least revenues.
Option (c) is correct.
19. The total revenue of the four products would depend on:
Average sale × revenue per unit × 6
For Product P = 46 × 9 × 6 = 414 × 6
For Product Q = 69.33 × 4 × 6 = 277.33 × 6
For Product R we do not need to check for least revenue because both the sales and also the price are high.
For Product S = 126.16 × 3 × 6 = 378.5 × 6
Clearly Product Q has the least revenue over the period.
Option (b) is correct.
20. The statement in Option (c) is clearly true as the revenue of P & Q is greater than the revenue of S in 1993 (through visual inspection this aspect is clear).

MOCK TEST PAPER 9

Questions 1 to 4:

1. The no. of Maruti Zen that can be:
Spray painted = 30/0.5 = 60
Assembled = 60/1 = 60
Quality checked = 20/0.5 = 40
∴ Quality checking is the bottleneck resource.
2. Solve as above for Maruti 800.
3. Since 30 Maruti 800 cars have been produced, capacity left is 20 hours of spray painting, 30 hours of assembly and 12.5 hours of Quality checking . Where only 25 cars can be completed.
4. Hiring 1 assembler will raise Maruti 800 capacity to 70 cars.

Questions 5 to 8:

5. Between January to August, for the 8 month period— the returns in gold are 3.6%. In US bonds it would be equivalent to 8 months interest plus the appreciation of the dollar vis-a-vis the rupee. In this case, the interest is 6.66% (2/3rd of the year @ 10% per annum) and the dollar appreciation is from 40 to 45 which is an 12.5% growth. Since, it is a multiplicative relationship between the two, the actual growth would be: 100 would grow to 100 × 1.125 × 1.0666 = 20 %.
Similarly, the growth in EU bonds would be equivalent to 8 months interest plus the appreciation of the Euro vis-à-vis the rupee. In this case, the interest is 13.33% (2/3rd of the year @ 20% per annum) and the Euro appreciation is from 60 to 63 which is a 5% growth. Since, it is a multiplicative relationship between the two, the actual growth would be: 100 would grow to 100 × 1.1333 × 1.05 = 19%.
You need to observe that the percentage returns on US bonds and EU bonds are almost the same and the weighted average of returns between these two instruments would lie somewhere in between 19 and 20%. Hence 13% is effectively the weighted average between 3.6% (return in gold) and 19.xx% (weighted average return in US and EU bonds). It can be seen that the investment in gold is close to 40% and is greater than 40% if we take the weighted average return for US and EU bonds closer to 20% (the extreme case is 7/16.4 = 42.68%) while it goes lower than 40% if we take this weighted average closer to 19% (the extreme case being 6/15.4 = 38.96%)
If we assume equal investments in EU and US bonds, their weighted average return would be

19.5%. At 19.5% the investment in gold would be 6.5/15.9 = 40.88%

We still have to use the other information in this case. If sold in September we are given that the returns become 16.25%. If we take a look at the respective returns for January to September for the three instruments we get:

Gold = 4.25%

US Bonds = 100 grows to 100 × 1.075 × 1.175 = 126.31 which means a 26.3% return

EU Bonds = 100 grows to 100 × 1.15 × 1.0666 = 122.66 which means a 22.66% return

The weighted average for these three returns is 16.25%.

From this point we need to move to trial and error for finding the ratio of the investments between EU bonds and US bonds and consequently their weighted average. Suppose we assume a 1 : 1 ratio of investment between these two, we get a weighted average return between EU and US bonds as 24.5% approx. At this value, we also realise that the weighted average of all 3 being 16.25%, the relative investments between gold and the two bonds would be such that we get a weighted average between 4.25 and 24.5 as 16.25 – which gives us approximately 40.7% investment in gold. Since there is a gap between 40.7% here and 40.88% got earlier assuming a 1 : 1 ratio of investment we need to close this gap. In order to do so we would need to increase the investment in US bonds slightly.

At this point we can conclude that the investment in gold is approximately 40.7 to 40.8% of his initial investment while the remaining investment is shared equally between EU and US bonds and would be 29.6% each (approx.) with EU bonds at a lower value than 29.6. If we now look at the options, the fourth option is the only one which gives us an investment in gold of over 40% and hence is the correct answer.

Option (d) is correct.

On a serious note, how do the XAT question setters expect a student to do so much mental processing? Frankly it beats me – and this question set is definitely one to be left.

6. In order to decide which is the asset class which is giving the highest return in each month we need to first build the following table mainly comparing US, EU and UK bonds.

		US Bonds (Monthly Return 0.83%)	EU Bonds (Monthly Return 1.66%)	UK Bonds (Monthly Return 1.25%)	Japanese Bonds (Monthly Return 0.4166%)
% RETURNS DUE TO CURRENCY RATE FLUCTUATIONS (approx values)	February	2.5	2.5	1.42	2
	March	0	0.81	0	1.96
	April	2.44	0	0	0
	May	0	0.80	1.41	1.92
	June	0	0	0	1.88
	July	4.76	0.8	1.4	1.85
	August	2.27	0	0	0
	September	4.44	1.58	1.4	3.63
	October	4.25	1.56	0	1.75
	November	2.04	0	0.7	1.72
	December	0	0	0.7	1.69

The asset class for investment would be:

Month	Best Asset Class	Value of an Initial Investment of ₹100
Jan to Feb (Feb)	EU bonds	104.2
March	EU Bonds	106.8
April	US Bonds	110.31
May	UK bonds	113.27
June	Silver	115.44
July	US bonds	121.94
August	US bonds	125.75
September	US bonds	132.43
October	US bonds	139.21
November	US bonds	143.23
December	Japanese bonds	146.26%

Thus, option (b) is the closest answer and hence is correct.

Again a question that you cannot feasibly do inside the examination as the minimum time required to solve this given the intricate calculations and the mind blowing length of the question is somewhere between 10 minutes and 15 minutes for the aspirants who are the fastest at calculations.

7. The question was incorrect in the XAT 2011 examination.

In this case, Mr. Sanyal's investment and return track would be something like what is given in the following table:

	Bullion Invested in	Amount	Bond/Fixed Deposit Invested in	Amount	Total Valuation
Initial investment in January	Gold	400000	Indian FD	400000	800000
Valuation on 1st April at the end of the first quarter		406600		425000	831600
Investment on 1st April	Silver	415300	EU Bonds	415300	
Valuation on 1st June at the end of the second quarter		442093		443098	885191
Investment on 1st July	Silver	442595	US Bonds	442595	
Valuation on 1st October at the end of the third quarter		458689		505212	963900
Investment on 1st October	Silver	481950	US Bonds	481950	
Valuation on 31st December at the end of the last quarter		499475		504080	1003555

From the options all the options are seen to be incorrect based on this value of what his initial investment of 800000 has become.

This can be further verified if we look at what each asset would have returned in terms of the valuation at the end of the year in case the entire amount was invested in that asset.

The valuation of ₹800000 invested for a year in US bonds would be 1100000

The valuation of ₹800000 invested for a year in EU bonds would be 1040000

The valuation of ₹800000 invested for a year in UK bonds would be 985714

The valuation of ₹800000 invested for a year in Japanese bonds would be 1008000

The valuation of ₹800000 invested for a year in FD would be 1000000.

Even from these values and working backwards from the options we can see that all 4 options give us different values of his investment valuation at the end of the year.

Hence, Option (e) is correct.

8. The best recommendation would be the ones which would give the maximum variance in the returns as against not transacting. In order to spot the best recommendation months we need to look at the months where converting an investment from one asset class to another would give us the maximum impact in terms of returns.

The months to be considered from the options are:

June, November, October , May and March.

Based on the following table we can see the respective returns for US, EU and Japanese bonds in these months:

		US Bonds (Monthly Return 0.83%)	EU Bonds (Monthly Return 1.66%)	Japanese Bonds (Monthly Return 0.4166%)
% RETURNS DUE TO CURRENCY RATE FLUCTUATIONS (approx. values)	February	2.5	2.5	2
	March	0	0.81	1.96
	April	2.44	0	0
	May	0	0.80	1.92
	June	0	0	1.88
	July	4.76	0.8	1.85
	August	2.27	0	0
	September	4.44	1.58	3.63
	October	4.25	1.56	1.75
	November	2.04	0	1.72
	December	0	0	1.69

From the above table we can derive the following table for the return estimates comparisons for EU, US and Japanese bonds for all the months of 2010.

	US bonds (Monthly Return 0.83%)	EU bonds (Monthly Return 1.66%)	Japanese bonds (Monthly Return 0.4166%)
February	3.35%	4.2%	2.42%
March	0.83%	2.49%	2.38%
April	3.3%	1.66%	0.4166%
May	0.83%	2.48%	2.34%
June	0.83%	1.66%	2.30%
July	5.63%	2.48%	2.27%
August	3.12%	1.66%	0.4166%
September	5.31%	3.27%	4.06%
October	5.11%	3.25%	2.17%
November	2.89%	1.66%	2.14%
December	0.83%	1.66%	2.11%

From this table it is clear that the more funds we park in US bonds from July to December the greater would be our return. Hence, the best recommendation of all must have recommended shifting all the excess money into US bonds before June. (By excess money we mean the money beyond the minimum of 20% of the initial funds which have to be kept compulsorily in each bond).
Thus, option (c) would be the best recommendation – 2 transactions each during May and June viz: convert EU bonds to US bonds in May end and convert Japanese bonds to US bonds in June end.

Questions 9 to 13:

9. The increase can be seen to be: 2.6 for Services Sector (20.8 – 18.2); 2.9 for Construction Development (10.5 – 7.6); 3 for Automobile Industry (4.9 – 1.9) and 1.9 for Power (3.2 – 1.3). It can be clearly seen that it is the maximum for Automobile Industry. Hence, Option (c) is the correct answer.
10. The simple average of FDI inflows can be ranked directly on the basis of the additions of the individual FDI inflows for the values across the 6 years for any sector. We thus calculate the individual FDI inflow totals for each of the four options. We see that the totals are:
Chemicals = 25.1; Automobile = 23.7.
Metallurgical Industries = 25.3 & Hotel and Tourism = 25.
However, the question has asked us for the second lowest overall (and not the second lowest amongst the given options). Hence, if we look through the other sectors in the table, we can see that the total for Drugs and Pharmaceuticals is the least. Hence, we will select Automobiles (@23.7 that sector is the second lowest after Drugs and Pharmaceuticals @14.7). Hence, Option (b) is the correct answer.
11. The fourth statement is clearly false, since during 2007 to 2010 we do not see a continuous rise for Chemicals (other than fertilizers).
12. Statement (i) can be seen as false since the value of construction development in 2011 was ranked fourth and not fifth. Statement (iii) is also false, since in 2012 Drugs and Pharmaceuticals was ranked the third lowest from the bottom and not the fourth lowest from bottom.
Statement (ii) is correct as Computer software and hardware was indeed ranked sixth in 2009. Hence, Option (a) is the correct answer.
13. The figures for the given options would be: (a) = 2.8; (b) = 2.2; (c) = 2.4 and (d) = 2.6. The highest amongst these is Option (a).
Hence, Option (a) is the correct answer.

Questions 14 to 17:

14. For Industry 3, the ratio would be 2773/1174, for Industry 5 it would be 3484/1580, for Industry 6 2967/938 and for Industry 7 8087/3489. The ratio is the highest for Industry 6 as the value of 2967/938 is >3 and all the other ratios are <3. Hence, Option (b) is the correct answer.
15. Again, for this question, since the options are close ended we need to consider only the ratios for the four industries given in the options. The ratios to be compared to get the highest value are: Industry 4:3990/5831; Industry 5: 34943/71739, Industry 6: 31219/42434 & Industry 7: 45392/72290. The highest amongst these ratios is 31219/42434, which is > 0.7 while all the other ratios are <0.7. Hence, Option (a) is correct.
16. The respective ratios are:

Industry	1	2	3	4	5	6	7
Gross value added	3219	2433	30307	6875	97413	45949	83536
Number of workers	9066	877	5656	1099	7508	3333	15670
Gross value added per worker							

Based on the above table, if we start comparing the industry pairs as given in the options we get:
Option (a) 45949/3333 – 30307/5656 ≈ 459.4/33.33 – 303/56 ≈ 13.7 – 5.4 ≈ 8.3
Option (b) 83536/15670 – 3219/9066 ≈ 835/156 – 32/90 ≈ 5.36 – 0.35 ≈ 5.01
Option (c) 97413/7508 – 2433/877 ≈ 974/75 – 24/8.7 ≈ 12.99 – 2.7 ≈ 10.29
Option (d) 45949/3333 – 6875/1099 ≈ 459.4/33.33 – 68.75/11 ≈ 13.7 – 6.25 ≈ 7.45
From the above approximate calculations we can make out that the difference between Industry 5 and Industry 2 is the maximum. Hence, Option (c) is the correct answer.
17. The required ratios are: Industry 2 – 762/5990, Industry 3 – 10817/80238, Industry 6 – 6461/138780 and Industry 7 – 32178/171246. The values can be compared basis their percentage values where 762/5990 is around 12–13%, 10817/80238 is also around 13%, 6461/138780 is below 10% while 32178/171246 is

also over 10% but close to 20%. Hence, Industry 7 exhibits the highest percentage for this parameter. Hence, Option (b) is the correct answer.

Questions 18 to 20:

18. The travel time would be given by distance/speed. In order to solve this question, we need to find the least travel time amongst the given options.

The following ratios need to be compared:

Mumbai- Kanyakumari = $\frac{950}{40}$, Bhubaneshwar-Chennai = $\frac{950}{30}$, Chennai-Kochi = $\frac{901}{30}$, Mumbai – Chennai = $\frac{1000}{30}$

Mumbai–Kanyakumari has a ratio of <24, while the time for each of the other journeys is >30. Clearly, the Mumbai–Kanyakumari journey takes the minimum amount of time amongst the given options. So option (a) is correct.

19. The cost of travel would be given by the product of the distance and the cost per km of each of the four alternatives provided in the options for Mr. Ranjith.

Considering the cost of travel in each option.

The cost of each of the options can be worked out as under:

Mumbai-Bhubaneswar-Kochi	Mumbai-Chennai-Kochi	Mumbai-Kanyakumari- Kochi	Mumbai-Vizag-Kochi
(701 × 2) + (798 × 5)	(1000 × 1.5) + (901 × 1.5)	(950 × 2) + (1100 × 2.5)	(500 × 5) + (600 × 5)

Looking across the table, it is quite evident that the Mumbai-Chennai-Kochi route is the cheapest.

Hence, option (b) is the correct answer.

20. There are multiple ways in which this movement can be organised. However, blindly checking all possible routes would be a wrong thing to do, as it is likely to lead to a very tedious solution. We should realise to start with that the cost would essentially depend on two aspects – the mode of travel and the distance that is to be traveled on a particular route. In terms of cost of travel the increasing order of costs is:

Ship < Bus < Train < Airplane

Also, the route would involve a round trip to Chennai and can be visualised as:

Chennai – city 1 – city 2 – city 3 – Chennai

A brief look at the relevant distances gives us:

Chennai-Bhubaneswar = 950 (ship);
Chennai-Vizag = 300 (train);
Chennai-Kanyakumari = 999 (train);
Bhubaneswar-Vizag = 1002 (train);
Bhubaneswar-Kanyakumari = 700 (train);
Vizag-Kanyakumari = 250 (ship)

Looking through the above options, the Chennai- Vizag-Kanyakumari-Bhubaneswar-Chennai route (Route 1) or the Chennai-Bhubaneswar-Kanyakumari-Vizag-Chennai route (Route 2) would be the best. The cost of both these would be the same since the legs of the journey are the same:

Cost of Route 1: 300 × 2.5 + 250 × 1.5 + 700 × 2.5 + 950 × 1.5 = 4300

Hence, option (a) is correct.

MOCK TEST PAPER 10

Questions 1 to 6:

1. (b) Least cost is from
XB → DB → ZG which is 0.
2. (c) If we move from
XC → DE → ZB →, minimum cost comes out as 98.1
3. (a) Moving as XB → DE → ZA
Minimum cost = ₹324.5
4. (c) Maximum cost is on the way from XE → DE → ZH = 2208.9
5. (a) ∵ From one refinery we can go in 7 ways to the depots and from 7 depots we can go to 8 districts/depots. Forming a tree we will get 56 ways of transporting the petrol.

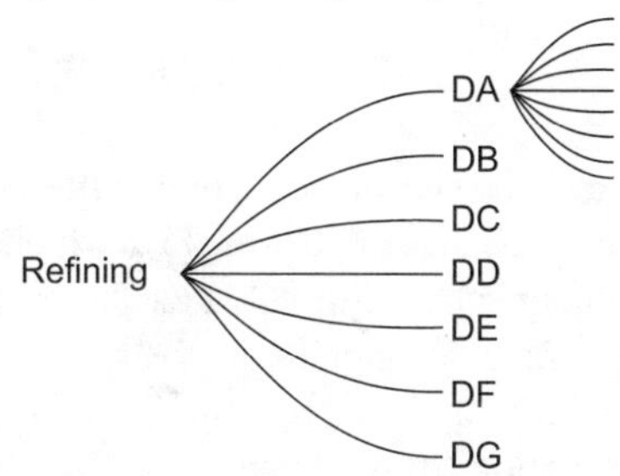

6. (b) Moving as XD → DC → ZC
We come to minimum cost of transportation = ₹780.1

Questions 7 to 11:

7. (c) From all countries, given in the options, Myanmar and Pakistan form a coverage frontier.
8. (b) B and D
India clearly does not dominate Thailand—hence statement A is not true. At the same time UAE also does not dominate Malaysia and hence Statement C is also not true.
Hence, Option (b) is correct.
9. (a) This can be solved using alligation for weighted average of rural and urban coverage. For 35%

urban and 7% rural coverage, the average of 14% requires a 1 : 3 ratio between urban and rural population. This means that the percentage of rural population is 75% for India.

10. (d) For India percentage of rural = 75%
    For Pakistan, the average of 33 and 44 being 38.5, the ratio of urban to rural population comes out as 1 : 1. Thus, Pakistan's rural population is 50%. For Myanmar, similarly, the rural population percentage is 87%. Hence,
    ⇒ Rank = Pakistan, India, Myanmar.
11. (c) It is dominated by Pakistan in terms of both electricity and road facilities.

Questions 12 to 15:

12. Profit of company Y = ₹108000
    Suppose income = x
    $35x/100 = x - 108000 \rightarrow x = 08571.42$
    Expenditure = income – profit
    = 308571.42 – 108000
    = 200571... the closest option is (d).
13. Suppose income of company X = x
    $55x/100 = x - 350000$
    x = ₹777777. Hence option (d) is correct.
14. Assume the expenditure of both X and Y = E
    Suppose income of X = I_1 and income of Y = I_2.
    $$\frac{65I_1}{100} = I_1 - E \text{ and } \frac{50I_2}{100} = I_2 - E$$
    So $E = 0.35\ I_1$ and $E = 0.50I_2$
    $0.35I_1 = 0.50I_2$
    $I_1/I_2 = 50/35 \rightarrow 10/7$. Hence option (b) is the correct answer.
15. The year 2000 shows the second highest percentage change—a change of 10% on 45% which represents a percentage change of 22.22%. This is lower than the percentage change in the year 2002. However, 2003 exhibits a higher percentage change than this. Hence, option (d) is correct.

Questions 16 to 20:

16. The respective year-to-year absolute declines for the given options are:
    Option (a) ASEAN 2005–06 to 2006–07 → 10.1 to 9.98 = 0.12;
    Option (b) South Asia 2004–05 to 2005–06 → 5.51 to 5.38 = 0.13;
    Option (c) West Asia (GCC) from 2008–09 to 2009–10 → 17.21 to 17.06 = 0.15;
    Option (d) North Africa 2009–10 to 2010–11 → 1.75 to 1.59 = 0.16.
    Clearly the value for North Africa is the highest amongst the four mentioned options. Hence, Option (d) is the correct answer.
17. The export shares have declined six times each for South Asia, North Africa and West Africa. For North America it has declined 7 times. Hence, Option (c) is the correct answer.
18. If we look at the values of the annual growth rate for the regions given in the options, we can clearly see that there is negative growth for each of the four regions given in the options. Since we are looking for the lowest annual growth rate amongst the given options, we will need to look for the highest percentage reduction. The reductions can be seen to be:
    (a) North Africa – from 1.75 to 1.59 → –9.14%;
    (b) North East Asia – from 16.12 to 14.83 → –8%
    (c) North America – from 11.89 to 10.98 → –7.65%
    (d) EU countries – from 20.16 to 18.33 → –9.07%.
    Option (a) is the correct answer.
19. Since each of the options is an average of 2 numbers, we can do this by comparing the sums of the two given numbers and looking for the highest sum to get the highest average.
    (a) North Africa 2008–09 & 2009–10 = 1.84 + 1.75 = 3.59
    (b) East Africa 2004–05 & 2007–08 = 1.37 + 2.58 = 3.95
    (c) Latin America 2002–03 & 2004–05 = 2.06 + 2.15 = 4.21
    (d) West Africa 2007–08 & 2010–11 = 2.13 + 1.71 = 3.84.
    The value is the highest for Latin America's two given years. Hence, Option (c) is the correct answer.
20. The statements in Options (a), (b) and (c) are clearly true as:
    For Option (a) we can see that South Asia was ranked sixth in India's export basket in 2011–12;
    For Option (b) we can see that North Africa's share of India's export basket was least for 7 of the ten years and hence would be the least for the maximum number of years.
    For Option (c) we can see that in 2004–05 Latin America was indeed ranked fourth from bottom in India's export basket with a share of 2.15 %, as there are exactly three regions with a lower market share than 2.15. These are East Africa (1.37), North Africa (1.62) and West Africa (1.98). Option (d) has to be false and can be marked without any calculations.
    Hence, Option (d) is the correct answer.

MOCK TEST PAPER 11

Questions 1 to 6:

1. (c) If we add the individual growth percentages of each of the models, the total addition is equal for Model A and Model C. However, this being a compounded growth construct, we need to see which of the products has a higher growth: Model A $1.09 \times 0.99 \times 1.04 \times 1.07 \times 1.09 \times 1.14 \times 1.07 \times 1.07 \times 1.05$ Model C: $1.08 \times 1.09 \times 1.05 \times 1.07 \times 1.09 \times 1.08 \times 1.04 \times 1.06 \times 1.05$
2. (c) Overall growth will be the weighted average of –1 (weight 20), + 1 (weight 15), + 1 (weight 10) & + 9 (weight 15).
   Assume the initial values for the four models to be 20, 15, 10 and 15 respectively in the year 1990. (These would be approximately correct weightages since we know the weights to be 20:15:10:15 for the year 1989 and the four models have approximately grown by similar percentages in 1990.)
   After the changes for the year 1991 are incorporated into these values, the total value of the sales of the four models would be:
   $19.8 + 15.15 + 10.1 + 16.35 = 61.4$.
   The percentage growth is $(61.4 - 60) \times 100 \div 60 \approx 2.5\%$
   Option (c) is correct.
3. (a) 1998, since C has always shown a positive growth trend.
4. (b) 1991, { Sales for A dipped during that year.
   9 & 10 have to be solved using the combination of options, which fits the information.
   The only combination that fits for the overall growth to be 50% is
5. (a) 25%.
6. (b) 87.5%

Questions 7 to 8:

7. (d) UAE has the least disparity.
8. (d) Nepal has the highest disparity.

Questions 9 to 12:

Based on the two tables, we can make a consolidated table with sales of each type of air conditioner in each month. The following values would come out (based on rounding off to the nearest integer:

	2 Tons	1.5 tons	1 ton	0.5 ton
April	253	241	177	595
May	254	241	177	596
June	318	420	152	381
July	323	426	155	387
August	402	246	440	207
September	259	246	181	609
October	324	428	337	207
November	325	429	338	208
December	325	429	156	390
January	332	439	346	213
February	415	254	455	214
March	418	256	459	216
Average sales (approx.)	329	338	282	352

9. 338. Option (b).
10. From the solution table we have constructed, we can see that the largest difference in average sales is between 1 ton and 0.5 ton ACs. Hence, option (a) is correct.
11. Use the formula for half yearly sales performance given in the question to calculate. You can see that the required calculation is highest for 1 ton and second highest for 1.5 tons. Hence, option (c) is correct.
12. According to the question, monthly sales performance is defined as the relative increase with respect to the previous month. Amongst the given options February 2015 grows the highest with respect to January 2015. Hence, option (d) is correct.

Questions 13 to 17:

13. The correct answer is B. As mentioned in the question that the Total managerial wage bill is defined as the difference between total emoluments and total wage to workers, and total managerial staff is defined as the difference between total person engaged and total number of workers.
    Hence, the average managerial wage = Total managerial wage bill/total managerial staff
    = (total emoluments – total wage to workers)/(total person engaged – total number of workers) Now we have to find the highest average managerial wage amongst industries 3, 5, 6, and 7. Industry 3 = (6479 – 3706) lakhs/ (6830 – 5656) = 2773/1174 lakhs = 2.36 lakhs Industry 5: (9284 – 5800) / (9088 – 7508) = 3484/1580 = 2.20 lakhs /
    Industry 6 = (6084 – 3117) / (4271 – 3333) ⇒ 2967/938 = 3.16 lakhs
    Industry 7 = (15053 – 6966) lakhs / (19159 – 15670) ⇒ 8087/3489 = 2.31 lakhs As we can see, the Average Managerial Wage for industry 6 is the highest amongst all.
14. The correct answer is A. Solving by options we can see that for Option A: industry 6 has a Net

value added of ₹42434 lakhs Profit of ₹31219 lakhs. Required ratio is (31219/ 42434) × 100 = 73.57% For Option B, Industry 7 has a Net value added of ₹72290 lakhs and a Profit of ₹45392 lakhs. The Required ratio will be (45392/72290) × 100 = 62.79 %For Option C, industry 4 has a Net value added of ₹5831 and a Profit of ₹ 3990 lakhs lakhs. Hence, the Required ratio is (3990/5831) × 100 = 68.42 % For Option D, industry 5 has a Net value added = 71739 lakhs and Profit of ₹34943 lakhs hence, the required ratio is = (34943/= 71739) × 100 = 48.70%. As we can see, Industry 6 has the highest profit percentage of 73.57%. Hence, A is the correct answer.

15. The Correct answer is C. As given in the question that Gross value added = net value added+Depreciation. The Gross value added per worker would be Gross value added/Number of workers
Industry 1: (3178+41)/9066 = ₹0.35 lakhs
Industry 2: (2284+149)/877 = ₹2.77 lakhs
Industry 3: (23640 + 6667)/5656 = ₹5.35 lakhs
Industry 4: (5831+1044)/1099 = ₹6.25 lakhs
Industry 5: (71739+25674)/7508 = ₹12.97 lakhs
Industry 6: (42434+3515)/3333 = ₹13.78 lakhs
Industry 7: (72290+11246)/15670 = ₹ 5.33 lakhs
Now the difference will be calculated by subtracting the two industries mentioned in the options. Option A Industry 6 – Industry 3 = 13.78 - 5.35 = ₹8.43 lakhs Option B Industry 7 – Industry 1 = 5.33 – 0.35 = 4.98 lakhs Option C Industry 5 – Industry 2 = 12.97 – 2.77 = 10.2 lakhs Option D Industry 6 – industry 4 = 13.78 – 6.25 = 7.53 lakhs As the difference between industry 2 and 5 is maximum, amounting to ₹10.2 Lakhs, hence option c is the correct answer.

16. The calculation will be (Fuel Consumed/Input cost) × 100. For Option A, Industry 3 has Fuel consumed of ₹10817 lakhs and Total inputs cost at ₹80238 lakhs. The Required percentage would be = (10817/ 80238) × 100 = 13.48 % for Option B, Industry 7 has Fuel consumed of ₹ 32178 lakhs and Total inputs cost at ₹171246 lakhs. The Required percentage is (32178/ 171246) × 100 = 18.79 % for Option C, industry 2 has Fuel consumed of ₹ 762 lakhs and Total inputs cost at ₹ 5990 lakhs. The Required percentage is (762/5990) × 100 = 12.72 % for Option D, industry 6 has Fuel consumed at ₹ 6461 lakhs and Total inputs cost at ₹ 138780 lakhs. The Required Percentage is (6461 /138780) × 100 = 4.65 % As the question asks us which industry has the highest expense on fuel consumption as percentage of input cost, Option B is the correct answer.

17. Statement 1: Number of worker's per factory is third highest for industry 6 The calculation for each industry will be → Number of Workers / Number of factories number of worker's per factory in industry 1 is 9066/65 = 139.47 number of worker's per factory in industry 2 is 877/110 = 7.97 number of worker's per factory in industry 3 is 5656/32 = 176.75 number of worker's per factory in industry 4 is 1099/30 = 36.63 number of worker's per factory in industry 5 is 7508/78 = 96.25 number of worker's per factory in industry 6 is 3333/39 = 85.46 number of worker's per factory in industry 7 is 15670/300 = 52.23 we can clearly see that the 3rd highest number of workers per factory is for industry 7, hence this is a false statement. Statement 2: Expense on Material consumption expressed as a percentage of input cost is 2nd highest for industry 4. The calculation for each industry will be → (Expense on Material's consumed/ Input cost) × 100
For industry 1: 2519/3256 = 77.36%
For industry 2: 4135/5590 = 73.90% For industry 3: 57275/80238 = 71.38% For industry 4: 34027/41037 = 82.91% For industry 5: 327400/371605 = 88.10% For industry 6: 123275/138780 = 88.82% For industry 7: 106233/171246 = 62.03%
While calculating the percentages, We only need to consider decimals for Industry 5 and 6 as their percentages are close. As we can see, Industry 4 is third highest, hence statement 2 is incorrect. Statement 3: Profit earned expressed as a percentage of emolument is second highest for Industry 7 The calculation for each industry will be → (Profit/ Total Emoluments) × 100 For industry 1: 816/2095 = 38.94% For industry 2: 913/747 = 122.22% For industry 3: 9356/6479 = 144.47% For industry 4: 3990/1024 = 389.64% For industry 5: 34943/9284 =376.37% for industry 6: 31219/6084 = 513.13% for industry 7: 45392/15053 = 301.01%
As it is visible Clearly, Profit earned expressed as a percentage of emolument is second highest for Industry 6 which makes statement c false. Now we have only 1 statement left which has to be true.

Questions 18 to 20:

If we look at the table the time taken to reach different station are as follows
Zut(z) to Yag(y)=1hr 45min
Yag(y) to Vaq(v)=6hr 55min
Vaq(v) to Sab(s)=4hr 50min
Sab(s) to Raz(r)=2hr 55min
While returning, the timings were as follows
R to S= 4hr 55min
S to V= 10hr 50min
V to Y= 10hr 55min
Y to Z= 1hr 45min

The cities between which the journey time is the same would be in the same time zone.

For cities where the time taken going and coming is different it indicates that there is a time zone shift. To understand how to work it out, consider the Y to V and V to Y journeys. Y-V time = 6 hours 55 mins; V-Y time 10 hours 55 minutes. This means that the actual time going from Y-V or V-Y is 8 hours 55 minutes (average of the two) and that going from V to Y, since the time taken on the clocks is 10 hours 55 minutes, it means that Y is 2 hours ahead of V in terms of the time zone. Likewsie V is 3 hours ahead of S.

So, according to the above data, we see that Zut & Yag lie in the same timezone. And for the remaining cities the time difference is as follows:

Station	
Zut	Base time zone
Yag	Base time zone
Vaq	2 hours behind base time zone
Sab	3 hours behind Vaq, 5 hours behind base time zone.
Raz	1 hour behind Sab, 6 hours behind base time zone.

18. As mentioned above, Zut and Yag lie in the same time zone. Option (c) is correct.
19. From the table we see that it takes a total of 16hrs 40mins to reach from Zut to Raz, considering the times given in the table in the question. However, a total of 6 hrs needs to be added to this, since when it is 10:40 PM local time at Raz, it is 4:40 AM of the next day at Zut. Therefore the answer would be 16:40 +6 hrs= 22 hrs 40 mins. Hence, option (a) is correct.
20. Yag is 5 hours ahead of Sab. Hence, if it is 12 noon in Sab, then it would be 5 PM at Yag. Option (a) is correct.

MOCK TEST PAPER 12

Questions 1 to 6:

1. (c) From the graph, at 400 units the variable cost = ₹35,000
   $\Rightarrow$ Total cost = ₹55,000
   So average unit cost = 55000/400 = ₹137.5
   The closest option is 140.
2. (a) Cost of providing 300 units = ₹24000
   Cost of producing 400 units = ₹35000
   $$\text{So MC} = \frac{35000 - 24000}{100} = 110$$
3. (a) Graph shows that with increase in number of units, variable cost increases, so rate of change also increases, hence MC will increase with increase in production quantity.
4. (a) Total cost incurred = ₹55000
   Total sales revenue = ₹200 × 400 = ₹80,000
   $\Rightarrow$ Profit = ₹25,000
5. (b) At 310, total sales = 310 × 160 = 49600
   Cost of production = 44000
   Profit = ₹5600
   At 410, sales = 410 × 160 = 81600
   Production cost = 70,000
   $\Rightarrow$ Profit = ₹10,600
   At 510, sales = 510 × 160 = 81600
   Production cost = 70,000
   $\Rightarrow$ Profit = ₹11,600
   At 610, sales = 610 × 160 = 97600
   Production cost = 90000
   Profit = ₹7600.
6. (a) The marginal cost is constant at Rs. 80 per unit or thereabouts, while the Average cost is larger since the fixed cost has to be added to the total cost.

Questions 7 to 12:

7. Present users of all the soaps — 795 + 405 + 225 + 225 = 1650. Past users of all the soaps – 570 + 435 + 240 + 255 = 1500. Percentage increase = (1650 – 1500) × 100/1500 = 10%. Option (a) is correct.
8. From the table we can see that market shares of Liril, Dove and Nivea have decreased. Option (c) is correct.
9. 20% increase in total soap users (795 + 405 + 225 + 225 = 1650) = 1980.
   25% increase in Lux users = 993.75. So we get 993.75 × 100/1980 = 50.2%. Option (c) is correct.
10. 1650 × 1.5/100 = 24.75 tonnes per month. Option (c) is correct.
11. The decrease in usage of Liril = $\frac{435 - 405}{1650} \times 100$ = 1.81%. Option (b) is correct.
12. Palmolive will have = 10% of 795 + 10% of 405 + 8% of 225 + 6% of 225 = 153. Option (c) is correct.

Questions 13 to 16:

13. HT's score is 5 + 7 + 6 + 7 = 25 which is the second highest score. Option (a) is correct.
14. Score of that new newspaper = 6 + 7 + 5 + 7 = 25. Rank is 2nd. Option (a) is correct.
15. Indian Express and HT got the second best rank with score = 25. Option (d) is correct.
16. HT got the maximum point in this case 7 + 7 + 6 = 20. Option (a) is correct.

Solutions for questions 17 to 20:

17. Factor performance of innovation
    = 0.3 × 4.5 + 0.35 × 4 + 0.35 × 4.75 = 4.4125

Factor performance of business sophistication
$= 0.3 \times 5.25 + 0.35 \times 4.75 + 0.35 \times 4.5 = 4.8125$
Factor performance of infrastructure
$= 0.3 \times 5.25 + 0.35 \times 4 + 0.35 \times 4 = 4.375$
Factor performance of macroeconomic environment
$= 0.3 \times 5.5 + 0.35 \times 4.5 + 0.35 \times 4.75 = 4.8875$
Option (d).

18. Factor performance of innovation $= \frac{4.5 - 4}{4.75} = 0.105$

Factor performance of business sophistication
$= \frac{5.25 - 4.75}{4.5} = 0.11$

Factor performance of infrastructure
$= \frac{5.25 - 4}{4} = 0.3125$

Factor performance of macroeconomic environment
$= \frac{5.5 - 4.5}{4.75} = 0.21$

Option (c).

19. Average score of Infrastructure
$= \frac{4 + 4 + 5.25}{3} = 4.416$

Similarly by calculating the averages for other parameters as well we can see that option (b), Institutions had the highest average score.

20. Option (b).

MOCK TEST PAPER 13

Questions 1 to 5:

1. (a) The maximum number of units would get produced if we produce only Samsung on both machines (as Samsung takes less time to manufacture). Hence, the required answer = 600/8 + 600/8 = 150 units.
2. (d) In order to meet the constraint of at least 1 unit of each, produce only units of Samsung on Machine 1 and produce 1 unit of LG on Machine 2. The rest of the time available on Machine 2, can be used for additional Samsung units. The number of units produced = [600/8] + [580/16] + 1 = 75 + 36 + 1 = 112.
3. (d) The least time would be given by: 30 × 10 + 25 × 8 = 500 minutes = 8 hours 20 minutes. Option (d) is correct.
4. (a) A 3 : 1 ratio can be maintained by making 60 units of LG on M2, followed by 20 units of Samsung on M1. This will leave us with 440 minutes on M1. This can be used to make exactly 30 units of LG and 10 units of Samsung, leaving us with no idle time. Option (a) is correct.
5. (b) It is possible to make 64 units of each with 40 minutes idle. The pattern would be: 64 units of Samsung on M1 with 4 units of LG on M1 and 60 units of LG on M2. This would utilise 560 minutes on M1 and 600 minutes on M2, leaving 40 minutes idle on M1
None of the other options is possible to be achieved with the exact idle time as specified in the options.

Questions 6 to 10:

Let amount spent by Kaku and Chikoo = $2x$ and $3x$
Kaku spends further 3 lakhs and amount invested by both is equal
$\Rightarrow 2x + 300000 = 3x \Rightarrow 300000$
⇒ Kaku and Chikoo invested 9 lacs each
Revenue = 50% of amount invested = 9 lacs
Revenue share amongst lemon tree and coconut tree = 4 : 5 = 4 lacs and 5 lacs.

6. (b) ∵ Revenue = 5 lacs, cost of one coconut = ₹10
⇒ Number of coconuts reaped = 50,000
7. (a) In 5 acre 200 lemon trees are planted that generated a revenue of 4 lacs ⇒ output/acre = 4/5 = 0.8
8. (b) Amount received = 50% of revenue (i.e., 50% of 9 lacs)
= 4.5 lacs
9. (b) Number of coconut trees = 800
Revenue = 5 lacs
⇒ Revenue output per tree = 500000/800 = ₹625
10. We cannot determine the answer to this question, as we do not know the exact number of lemons yielded.

Questions 11 to 15:

11. (c) In normal case in 5th month, cost increased = ₹ 5000 × 8 = ₹40,000
Here, 5 people are working for designing
⇒ So cost increased to = ₹50000
⇒ Percentage change = 25%
12. (a) In new technique cost incurred in new coding stage will be
= 4 × 5000 + 10 × 5000 + 5 × 5000
= 95000
13. (b) The difference in cost under the old technique and the new technique would be essentially due to the difference in the costs during months 5 to 8. So to solve this question we can just look at the difference in costs for these 4 months.
Under the old technique the total cost during

these months = (8 + 10 + 10 + 6) × 5000 = ₹170000

In the new technique, cost incurred during this phase = 5×10000 + 4 × 5000 + 10 × 5000 + 5 × 5000 = ₹145000

⇒ Change = ₹25000

14. (b) Most expensive stage will be the specification phase that costs = 4 × 20000 + 6 × 20000 = 200000.
15. (c) Average cost for months 11–15 is ₹5000 as only the maintenance phase is running during this time – and maintenance has the least cost per man month. Hence, the correct answer is Option (c).

Questions 16 to 20:

16. (c) Total trousers = 200000
 So cloth required = 200000 × 3
 = 600000
17. (b)Total medium quality cloth that is required
 = [40(0.3) + 60(0.5) + 60(0.6) + 20(0.7) + 20(0.2)] × 3
 = 96000 mts × 3
 = 288000 m
18. (d) Low quality cloth required in type C = 60000 × 3 × 0.4 mts
 = 72,000 mts
19. (d) No relationship amongst quality and dye is provided.
20. (d) ratio and low quality dye in A and B type
 = 40000(0.20) : 60000(0.3)
 = 80 : 180 = 4 : 9.

MOCK TEST PAPER 14

Questions 1 to 4:

1. (d) In 1897–98, imports with
 Asia = 13% of $43,153 mn
 $ 5609.89 mn
 Exports = 22% of $37,387 mn
 = $8225.14 mn
 Total trade = $13,835.03 mn which is the highest amongst all.
2. (b) K – Others have the lowest total trade. In terms of exports the exports from Fantasia to Others is = 1% of $37,387 mn
 = $ 373 mn
3. (a) In 1897–98, Fantasia has the highest trade deficit with OPEC nations (H), which is
 22% of $43,153 mn – 8% of $37,387 mn ≈ $6 billion
4. (b) We can check the four options to check which of the four have the least trade deficit. Trade deficit for any region with respect to Fantasia = Trade Surplus for Fantasia with respect to that region. We can begin by writing down the trade surplus of Fantasia with the regions in each of the four options as follows:
 USA – 10% of 43153 – 21% of 37387 → Trade-deficit for Fantasia, which means that USA has a trade surplus with Fantasia and hence cannot be the region with the lowest trade deficit for Fantasia.
 Asia – 13% of 43153 – 14% of 37387 → Fantasia's trade surplus = 375.71
 Others – 2% of 43153 – 1% of 37387 → Fantasia's trade surplus = 489.19
 Australia – 2% of 43153 – 3% of 37387 → Fantasia has a trade deficit and hence Australia would have a trade surplus with respect to Fantasia.
 The least trade deficit is for Asia

Questions 5 to 6:

For these questions the value of imports and exports in 1898–99 can be calculated for the full year by multiplying the given values for 8 months by 1.5 (to get the pro-rata values for 12 months).

5. (d) Growth of Fantasia's exports to Russia is the highest as it can be seen to have almost doubled from 1% of 37387 = 373 to 2% of 24154 × 1.5 = 724. No other region has shown this kind of percentage growth. Hence, Option (d) is the correct answer.
6. (c) Trade deficit is Imports – Exports.
 In 1897–88 is
 = $43153 mn – $37387 mn
 = $5766 mn
 Trade deficit in 1898–99 is
 = $46699.5 mn – $36231 mn
 = $10,468.5 mn
 ⇒ Per cent increase = $\frac{10468.5 - 5766}{5766} \times 100$ = 82%

Solutions for questions 7 to 9:

7. It can be clearly seen that the number of covered wagons as a percentage of total wagons has decreased even from 2002 to 2003 – hence, the statement in Option (a) is incorrect.
 The statement in option (c) can be similarly rejected because the ratio 90371/216717 is higher than the ratio 91099/222193.
 Option (b) is correct because the ratio 376/214 (which is an approximation of the ratio 37650/214760) is substantially higher than the other ratios.
8. 37275/216717 is almost the same value as 40316/234397.
 Option (c) is correct.

9. The only ratio amongst 2002, 2003, 2004 and 2005 which is above 5% is for 2004. Hence, Option (c) is correct.

Note: In order to check the value of the numbers as to which ratio is above 5%, you need to multiply the numerator by 20 in order to see whether the multiplication is greater than the denominator or not. If the multiplication by 20 is greater than the denominator the ratio is greater than 5%. In this case 11388×20 is greater than 227752 and hence we can confirm that the ratio for 2004 is greater than 5%. For the other years the ratio can be seen to be below 5% by the same logic.

Questions 10 to 12:

10. There is a 4.18% drop in the total wagons in 1999 which is the least growth rate as in terms of growth rate this value would be – 4.18 %. The other drops are lesser than 4.18% and hence their values in terms of percentage growth would be higher than – 4.18%. Option (a) is thus the correct answer.
11. Option (c) is clearly the correct answer as the annual percentage growth rate of average wagon capacity has been the maximum not in 1999 but clearly in 2004. Since we are looking for the false statement, this statement is clearly false and hence is the correct answer.
12. Annual growth rate of open low-sided wagons is the highest as it has dropped by just around 1% while the others have dropped by more than that. Option (c) is correct.

Questions 13 to 16:

13. To find the proportion of 'mergers' to 'acquisitions' for the entire period, we need to add up the total M&A table and the total Mergers table. The remaining would correspond to the number of acquisitions.

    The number of mergers and acquisitions row-wise are:

    465; 371; 584; 350; 48; 643; 52; 1041; 1709; 192; 191 = 5646

    The number of mergers row-wise is:

    97; 77; 116; 74; 6; 96; 2; 452; 512; 34; 33 = 1499

    The number of acquisitions would be: 5646 – 1499 = 4147.

    So the required percentage $= \dfrac{\text{Total Merger} \times 100}{\text{Total Acquisitions}}$

    $\dfrac{1499}{4147} \times 100 = 36\%$. Hence, option (b) is correct.

14. From the sector-wise sums we have calculated for the previous question, we can see that the values of 97/465; 77/371; 74/350; 452/1041 and 512/1709 are all above 20%. There are a total of 5 such sectors. Hence, option (d) is correct.
15. It can be visually verified from the second table that the sum of the first three columns is greater than the sum of the last 3 columns in the table in 5 cases. Hence, option (d) is correct.
16. Since the turbulence is defined as sum of the differences between the number of mergers and number of acquisitions from 2001–02 to 2006–07, we need to realise that difference is always a positive value. So if $M > A$, the difference would be $M - A$, while if $A > M$, then the turbulence would be given by $A - M$.

    Mathematically this can be written by taking the absolute values of the subtraction between mergers and acquisitions for any particular year: Turbulence = |Number of mergers in 2001–02 –Number of acquisitions in 2001–02| + |Number of mergers in 2002–03 – Number of acquisitions in 2002–03| + ... + |Number of mergers in 2006–07 – Number of acquisitions in 2006–07|

    Turbulence for financial services = (103 – 91) + (107 – 94) + (87 – 73) + (75 – 41) + (118 – 75) + (126 – 51) = 12 + 13 + 14 + 34 + 43 + 75 = 191.

    Turbulence for other services = (207 – 90) + (198 – 92) + (182 – 105) + (200 – 81) + (210 – 61) + (210 – 83) = 117 + 106 + 77 + 119 + 149 + 127 = 685.

    It can be seen that for the other two options, the value of turbulence is below 685. Option (d) is the correct answer.

Questions 17 to 20:

17. The total sales revenue for the shop during the period from January to March resulting out of televisions sales = ₹31500000.

    Since, the total sales quantity is given as 3150 units it means that the per unit price of television sets is ₹ 31500000/3150 = ₹10000 (sale price).

    The question also tells us that there is a profit of 25% of cost price uniformly for Jamshedpur Electronics. This means that the cost price of a television set would be: ₹8000.

    Further, the number of units ordered would be:

    Closing inventory + Sales – Starting inventory = Order

    Thus, Order = 2880 + 3150 – 2520 = 3510 units

    Value of order (in rupees thousands) = 3510 × 8 = 28080.

    Option (a) is correct.

18. The total sales value over the three month period is got by adding the sales of all the three shops for both televisions and iPods. This value comes out to be ₹ 132300 thousand. 14% of the sales value is the value of the surcharge. Value of surcharge = 0.14 × 132300 thousand = 18522 thousand. Option (b) is correct.

19. Profits in January from Bistupur and Kadma = 10% of (15750 + 6300) + 20% of (900 + 6300) = 2205 + 1440 = 3645. Option (c) is correct.
20. The total sales value for iPods over the three month period = 100800 thousand (***Note:*** This value is got by adding all the individual values of iPod sales in the table).
    Total unit sales = 7560 + 5760-6120 = 7200
    Per unit price = 100800/7200 = 14.
    Option (a) is correct.

MOCK TEST PAPER 15

Questions 1 to 5:

1. India and Sri Lanka are on the development frontier.
2. India, Pakistan and Sri Lanka.
3. Alligation usage will give us a ratio of 2 : 5. Hence, 28.56%. This is because, if we look at the colleges coverage, we see that the percentage of population covered is 43% for rural, while it is 36% for urban. At the same time the overall country's college coverage is 38% for Ghana. 36 & 43 giving a weighted average of 38, would mean a 2 : 5 ratio between rural and urban populations.
4. This cannot be answered since whether the calculation has to be done on the basis of College or Schools is not defined.
5. Option (c) is correct as it can be seen that India and Sri Lanka are the only countries that are on the development frontier rural. Hence, all other countries: Pakistan, Ghana, Nigeria, Indonesia and Nepal are not on the development frontier rural.

Questions 6 to 8:

6. The percentage drop is approximately three per cent.
7. Productivity has grown by over 30% while the other mentioned variables have shown a less than 30% change.
8. Both workforce and production have dropped.

Questions 9 to 10:

9. Kalkaji, Gurgaon Grade A and Noida Grade A are the three options possible.
10. His budget will now become ₹1 crore. With this budget it is possible that he might not be able to buy a flat at Malabar Hill, Cuffe Parade or Jor Bagh. Hence, the required answer is 3.

Questions 11 to 12:

There is no information about the rent value per square feet. Hence, these questions cannot be answered.

Question 13

13. Kalkaji or Gurgaon since the rate per square feet is ₹2400.

Questions 14 to 16

14. The maximum age at expiry is 70 years (Birla Sunlife). Hence a 50-year-old can insure his life for a maximum of 20 years.
15. ICICI prudential offers the least premium for the required profile. Hence, it is the correct option.
16. ICICI, HDFC and LIC are three options offering a 6 year tenure. However, only HDFC standard life allows entry age above 50 years. Hence, there is only one option possible. Option (a) is correct.

Questions 17 to 20

17. Rajiv Shrivastava's tax liability
    10% of 10000 + 20% of 60000 = 13000
    13000–8000 (Rebate on savings) = 5000
    Hence, total tax liability = 5000 × 1.1 = 5500.
18. At ₹155000, his standard deduction becomes ₹25000.
    Hence, total taxable income = 130000
    Tax = 10% of 10000+ 20% of 70000 = 15000.
    Rebate = 15% of 40000 = 6000
    Total tax = 1.1 × 9000 = 9900
    Net income = 155000 – 9900 = 145100.
    Hence, increase of ₹600 (as his previous net income was 144500).
19. Being a woman she gets a rebate of ₹5000 on the total tax liability. Hence if she follows Rajiv Shrivastava's saving pattern (₹40000), she will pay no tax.
20. His total taxable income would be 144000 + 35000 – 25000 (standard deduction) = 154000.
    His tax liability would be 1000 + 18000 + 1200 = 20200. He will get a tax rebate of 14000 due to savings. So net tax payable = 6200 + 10% surcharge = 6820. Option (d) is correct.

MOCK TEST PAPER 16

Questions 1 to 4:

Go through a comprehensive analysis of the 16 possibilities for each of the 4, using direct and indirect clues. The following table will emerge:

Amar	10	18	2	28	Total
	B1	D1	C2	C3	58
Biren	30	22	6	14	72
	A3	A1	A4	C4	
Chandan	12	4	26	20	62
	A2	D2	D3	B4	
Deepak	16	24	32	8	80
	B2	B3	C1	D4	

Solutions for Questions 5 to 9.

5. Only a production of 2.5 acres of rice and dal each is possible. Option (A) is infeasible due to constraint of working capital, while option (B) is infeasible due to constraint of man days available.
6. The data is insufficient since the sale price of the item is not available.
7. No comments can be made about the profits. Hence, (d) is correct.
8. ₹1400 is required for the given production level as working capital. Hence, ₹200 of capital is unutilised.
9. No comments can be made about the profits. Hence, (d) is the correct option.

Questions 10 to 16:

Create a table based on the following formulae for the number of each type of fishes:

Number of big fish = Number of big fish at the end of the previous day + 25 – number of big fishes that die each day (Note that the number of big fishes that would die on 10th of August – when they become 10 days old would be 100, while the number of big fishes that would die subsequently would be 25 every day. Also, since the number of big fishes being added is 25 per day too, from the 11th of August the number of big fishes would be constant. Thus, the pattern for the number of big fishes would be:

1st Aug	2nd Aug	3rd Aug	4th Aug	5th Aug	6th Aug	7th Aug	8th Aug	9th Aug	10th Aug	11th Aug	12th Aug
125	150	175	200	225	250	275	300	325	250	250	250

Create similar number strings for the other fishes to solve the question.

So on any particular day, the number of medium fishes = Number of medium fishes on the previous day +250 – number of big fishes on that day × 1.

Likewise, the number for the smaller fishes = Number of small fishes on the previous day × 2 – Number of medium fishes after incrementing the medium fishes for that day × 3.

Questions 17 to 20:

17. The value of EPF assets and the EPF assets as a percentage of GDP are provided.

$$\text{Malaysia's GDP} = \frac{50.5 \times 100}{53.1}$$

$$\text{India's GDP} = \frac{33.47 \times 100}{7}$$

The required ratio is approximately 5 : 1.

18. The PF in Malaysia represents 23% of the salary while in India it is 24% of the salary. Assuming equal service periods and equal withdrawals we can directly correlate the average balance per member to the salary per member.

The answer will be (a).

19. The number of members

$$= \frac{\text{Value of EPF assets}}{\text{Average balance per member}}$$

Malaysia's ratio is smaller than India's. Hence, (b) is the correct answer.

20. (i) and (iii) are both true.

MOCK TEST PAPER 17

Questions 1 to 10: The following table details the data:

	Development Cost	Salaries	Research	Patent	Overheads
Alphonso Superior	750000	210000	292500	30000	217500
Langda Inferior	250000	70000	97500	30000	52500

1. Read directly from the table.
2. 30000/750000 = 4%
3. 217500 from the table.
4. $0.35 \times 150000 \times 7500 + 0.25 \times 250000 \times 2500$ $= 393750000 + 156250000 = 550000000 = 5.50000$ = 5.5 lakh ($ '000s)
5. 4 lakh × 1.25 = 5 lakh
6. 2.1 lakh × 1.4 = 2.94 lakh = 294 ($ '000s)
7. 243 × 20 = 4860 thousand.
8. 4 lakh × 1.5 = 6 lakh
9. $\frac{0.65 \times 30000 \times 100}{(250000 - 0.35 \times 30000)} = 8.14\%$
10. 0.25 × 292500 = 73125

Questions 11 to 15:

You will have to follow the completion of materials in each work centre in each half hour. Based on the completion of the units in A, the availability of the raw material in B will be defined. Similarly, for other work centres.

Thus from 9 to 9:30, A will complete 2 units but will only transfer 1 unit to B since there is only 1 unit capacity available in B.

Complete the following table to get all answers.

Time	A			B		C		D		E		Output
	Capacity & Comp.		Retained In A	Cap	Ret in B	Cap	Ret in C	Cap	Ret in	Cap	To Output	
9	2	2	0	6	0	4	0	1	0	1	1	
9:30	6	6	0	1	1	3	3	6	0	3	1	
10:00	4	4	0	5								
10:30	2	2	0	2								
11:00	5	5	0	5								
11:30	3	3	0	4								
12:00	6	6	0	6								
12:30	4	4	0	3								
13:00	5	5	0	3								
13:30	2	2	0	5								
14:00	2	2	0	5								
14:30	6	6	0	3								
15:00	5	5	0	1								
15:30	2	2	0	6								
16:00	4	4	0	2								
16:30	1	1	0	3								
17:00	2	2	0	3								

11. It can be seen that since B is not lacking raw materials, it's output till it's 14:30 to 15:00 slot will all get produced as output (we also see that there is no production constraint for B's output in C, none of C's output in D and likewise no constraint for D's output in E.) Hence, the total output is $6 + 1 + 5 + 2 + 5 + 4 + 6 + 3 + 3 + 5 + 5 + 3 = 48$.
12. Work Centres B and C will first show inventory as seen from the table above. However, C is not in the options. Hence, option (b) is correct.
13. The first ten units that are started after 10 will get completed by 14:30.
14. Add the total output by 11:30 ($1 + 1 + 4 + 2 + 3$).
15. On completing the above table you will see that there is a lack of complete supply to D between the time periods mentioned.

Questions 16 to 20:

16. Australia and Britain are the only countries exhibiting the same trend.
17. The answer will be the weighted average of the percentage increase. Since, original values are unknown, this cannot be solved.
18. Either corporate bonds or 10 year govt. bonds give the highest interest rates.
19. This is visible in the case of Japan.
20. Visually, Switzerland.

MOCK TEST PAPER 18

Questions 1 to 4:

1. The highest depreciation has been for Workers quarters under government subsidised schemes (0.47/0.55). Hence, option (d) is correct.
2. The ratio to look at is 2108/5249.2 = 40.2% approx. Option (a) is correct.
3. The net block for vehicles has more than doubled and hence option (c) is correct.
4. Again visual inspection will yield that the answer is vehicles.

Questions 5 to 8:

5. Total cost in 2005 = 24000. Hence, option (b) is correct.
6. 1.3X = 5200. Hence, option (d) is correct.
7. 44000. Hence, option (c) is correct.
8. Only the third statement is true. Hence, option (d) is correct.

Questions 9 to 13:

9. (c) Number of employees getting more than \$25 per day in complex work = 10.
10. (a) 8 → EC22148, EC22149, EC22150, EC22156, EC22164, EC22171, EC22172 and EC22173
11. (c) EC22158 = 472.31/1.39 = 339.8
12. (c) 4 – EC22173, EC22174, EC22179 and EC22180.
13. (b) 2 – EC22179 & EC22180

Questions 14 to 18:

14. (b) Average employment level in public factories

$$= \frac{\left(80 \times 100 \times \frac{27.7}{100}\right)}{7} = 316$$

15. (c) Ratio of gross output to employment is maximum in joint sector which is 8.4/5.1 = 1.63

16. (b) Capital Productivity for
Other = 2/3.2 = 0.625
State = 11.6/24.3 = 0.477
Central = 12.7/17.5 =0.726
Joint = 8.4/6.8 = 1.235
Wholly = 63.8/46.8 = 1.36
⇒ State is less than other which is less than central.
17. (c) Amongst all options, value of central and state/local is the highest, i.e. 1.8
So option (c)
18. (c) Total value added = ₹ 225,000 crore
So value added in central government is = 225,000 crore × 0.141 = 31725 crore
and average value added / factory

$$= \frac{31725}{\frac{3000 \times 100}{1.8}} = 19.03$$

Questions 19 to 20:

19. The tax Sangeeta would have to pay would be under the following structures:
10% on income between 190001 and 300000
And 20% on income from 300001 to 337425
Her income tax liability would be: 10% of 110000 + 20% of 37425 = 11000 + 7485 = 18485
Her total tax liability would be calculated by adding 3% to her income tax as calculated above.
Thus, her total tax liability = 1.03 × 18485 = 19039.
This is 5.64% of her income.
Thus, Option (a) is correct.
20. Solve through options. For Option (a), total tax liability would be:
103% of [14000 + 40000 + 30% of 848835] = 317910.
Hence, Option (a) is correct.

MOCK TEST PAPER 19

Questions 1 to 5:

1. 27,000/46,000 = 59% (approx).
2. Cannot be determined since the value of the standard deduction available is not provided.
3. Ms Parul Jaiswal has a tax incidence below 60,000. Hence, no surcharge will be applicable. Hence, her TDS will be at the rate of ₹2667 per month.
4. 240,000 – 60,000 – 32,000 = 148,000
5. Standard deduction value is not available. Hence, the answer is (d).

Questions 6 to 9:

Complete the table based on the information in statements (1) to (4)
Arun's missing score is 27, Arjit's is 55, while Amritesh's is 69.
Identify the topper between Arun, Arjit and Amritesh to find Amit's missing score.
Then Ankur's missing score will be got by: 2626–Sum of all other scores.
All questions are routine calculation-based questions once you have the table.

Questions 10 to 16:

10. (b) ∵ Only in North Africa and Middle East, Argentina, Far East and North Sea, the ratio of individual incomes to total income for 2003, is greater than 4%.
11. (b) Only Spain and the rest of Latin America.
12. (c) 3–Spain, the rest of Latin America and North Sea
13. (c) For Far East the ratio is the least = 554 : 302 = 1.83
14. (b) Average = 4.81 which is only for Argentina so 1 is the answer
15. (d) All three are true, because for Far-East, profitability in 2002 was 47.1% was the highest, also North Sea increased its profitability from 2002–03 as 31.11% to 173.33% and, operation in Argentina witnessed increase in profitability from 2002–03 as 42.7% to 42.9%, so Option (d) holds correct.
16. (b) North Sea, for which profitability was 173.33% and is the highest.

Questions 17 to 20:

17. Checking the four options it can be seen that the maximum rate of growth is for Orissa from 13.57 to 15.89 which is a growth of over 17%.
Option (c) is correct.
18. Since the market shares for R-Com and Vodafone refer to the same regions, the ratio of number subscribers for Vodafone to the number of subscribers for R-Com should be 72/28 = 18/7 = 2.57.
Looking at the options, only the first and the fourth options give us a ratio of around 2.5–2.6 between the number of subscribers for Vodafone and the number of subscribers for R-Com. Thus, we can reject options (b) and (c). Also, based on the same logic, the ratio between Airtel and Idea should be 52/48 = 13/12. In other words, the number of subscribers for Airtel should be 8.33% more than the number of subscribers for Idea.
In option (a) the value of Airtel (89.5) is just about 4-5% more than the value for Idea and we can reject this as the correct answer. Thus, option (d) is correct.
19. We are not aware of the market shares in the other states of the Eastern telecom circle and hence cannot find this out. Option (d) is hence correct.

20. The number of subscribers have grown from 562.08 to 621.30 (in millions). This implies a 10.5% increase approximately.
Option (b) is correct.

MOCK TEST PAPER 20

Questions 1 to 4:

1. It can be seen to be occurring for Canara Bank. Hence, option (c) is correct.
2. We cannot determine this since the values are given for different years for ICICI Bank and the other banks. Hence, option (d) is correct.
3. Base Price = $3.2/n$
$n = 5.22/26.1 = 0.2$ crores.
∴ Base price = ₹16.
∴ Premium = 840 – 16 = 824.
4. Compare: 470/11.33, 280/16.1, 77/0.32 and 445/13.58. Canara Bank's 77/0.32 is the highest ratio. Hence, option (c) is correct.

Questions 5 to 7:

Expectation is given by the summation of (return × probability of return).
Thus, expectation from fund A is:
$0.2 \times (-5) + 0.3 \times 10 + 0.4 \times 25 + 0.1 \times 35 = 15.5\%$
Similarly, Expectation from Fund B = 14%
Expectation from Fund C = 12.5%

5. Hence, invest in A.
6. 100 crore invested in B will yield 14%, i.e., 14 crore
7. $0.5 \times 15.5 + 0.3 \times 14 + 0.2 \times 12.5 = 14.45$
Also $14.45\% > 0.5 \times 14 + 0.5 \times 12.5$
Hence both (a) and (b)

Questions 8 to 11:

8. Maximum expectation of Kaku will be from fund A = $0.25 \times (-5) + 0.25 \times 10 + 0.3 \times 25 + 0.2 \times 35 = 15.75\%$
Hence, the required answer will be given by the percentage equivalent of the ratio $\frac{15.75 - 15.5}{15.5}$ = 1.6% (approx)
9. Fund C has the highest percentage difference
10. (iii) and (iv) are true while nothing can be said about either (i) or (ii).
11. The resultant answer will be:
₹(14.875 – 14.45) crore
= 0.425 crore = ₹ 4.25 million.

Questions 12 to 15:

12. The answer will be given by the ratio of the number of students failed to the number of students passed = 182/861 = 21% (approximately). Hence, option (d) is correct.
13. The best performance is visibly in 2001.
14. Out of 22 students who retook the exam, 11 must have failed and 11 passed. Hence, without these repeaters, the ratio would have been 65:10, i.e., 86.66% would have passed.
15. 13 students failed in 1994. These students passed in 1995 but they were not counted amongst the successful students of the school. If they had been, the number of successful students would have gone up by 13 – hence, the score of the school would have been 38 + 13 = 51. Hence, option (d) is correct.

Questions 16 to 20:

16. The maximum return structure on investing \$50,000 will be if he breaks up the investment into 20,000,10,000 and 20,000 respectively on each of crops, dairy and poultry. The return will be 26,000, 14,000 and 27,500 respectively and equal \$67,500 a return of 35% on 50,000.
17. The highest possible profit percentage will be for an investment of \$10,000 in poultry which will give him a return of 50%.
18. Compare the four alternatives given. Obviously, equal amounts in each of the three ventures will give him the maximum returns.
19. He should invest \$40,000 in crops + \$20,000 in dairy + \$20,000 in poultry. After this in each of these categories the return is 10% or \$11,000 on an investment of \$10,000.
20. The return on investment on dairy after 20,000 is 11,000 for the next 10,000.

MOCK TEST PAPER 21

Questions 1 to 4:

1. There are 7 such states. Option (d) is correct.
2. The overall growth of GDP (national accounts) is greater than the growth of GSDP of 14 states. Hence, option (b) is correct.
3. The lowest ratio between Growth rate of Gross State Domestic Product to Growth rate of per capita gross State Domestic product is an indicator of population growth. The lower this ratio, the lower the population growth. In the table, for the years 1980-81 to 1990-91, the least ratio is seen for Tamil Nadu.

Note: Develop the skill for visual comparison.

4. Assume GSDP of 14 states to be 100 in 1980. Increase it using compounded growth rate of 5.24% for 11 years. Then increase it consecutively by using 5.90% for 8 years (compounded). Repeat the same process by using 3.03% and 4.02% over 11 years and 8 years respectively.

Then divide the final value of GSDP and per capita GSDP to get the total population growth over 19 years. Now, estimate the compound annual growth rate (CAGR) value that can be substituted for the percentage growth over 19 years. This will give the answer.
Needless to say, such a question cannot be and should not be attempted in the exam.

Questions 5 to 8:

5. The profit will be got by: percentage profit × sales. Since sales have been given as a percentage (in terms of market share) and since we do not need to find out the individual values we need to make no adjustments and can directly multiply the profit before tax (given as a percentage of the sale value) by the market share. The highest multiplication for the options given will give the answer.
GACL is clearly the highest profit value.
6. Look for maximum value of the multiplication of advertising by market share. ACC has the highest value.
7. If sales is worth ₹100, ₹6 will go to L&T of which the profits will be worth 8.67%. Similarly for ICL. Hence, the calculation 8.67% of 6 + 9.94% of 4 will yield the answer. The value is 0.9178.
8. Profit before tax per rupee of sale has risen by 10%. Thus, this value will become: 9.94 × 1.1 = 10.93. Thus, the total cost would be: 89.07 = Fixed expenses + Variable expenses.
Also, fixed expenses have become 10%, hence variable expenses should be 79.07% → a rise of 13.58 on 65.49 = 20.73% increase

Questions 9 to 12:

9. Look at the ratio of the rental values to the purchase price. This can be done since the investment is directly proportional to the purchase price and the annual return is directly proportional to the rental values per month.
10. Calculations will show that there is a possibility for purchasing property in seven locations.
11. The costs will be: 5 lakh interest loss (for not keeping 1 crore in bank) + 15 lakh interest cost for loan = 20 lakh.
Revenues = 175,000 × 12 = 21 lakh. Hence, profit is ₹100,000.
12. The monthly percentage return of 1.25% means a return of 15% per annum. Calculate the investment in each location and each category and find the percentage return of each category.
For example, the investment in West End A is 2.5 crore. The required return of 15% per annum means a rent value of 37.5 lakh. However, the rental value is only 21 lakh per year. Hence, West End A is not to be counted. Similarly calculate for all other locations.

Questions 13 to 16:

13. Lovells UK and Allen & Overy UK are very close to each other in this respect—Lovells being marginally higher than Allen & Overy (1% calculation range needed).
14. Clearly Lovells UK from 10 to 26.
15. Allen & Overy, Skadden and Jones Day meet the condition.
16. There is approximately a 51% growth in the number of offices over all. This is exceeded by five law firms.

Questions 17 to 20:

Calculate the cost of making each drink. Organise your data in the form of a table to get all answers directly. The per bottle cost of manufacturing would be: Soda Lime = 10; Cola orange = orange soda = 7.5; Cola Lime = 9.166 and Soda Cola = 59/7 = 8.4285.

17. Lime would give the maximum profit amongst the options listed since lime is the costliest variety. Option (d) is correct.
18. Orange soda would cost the least at 7.5 per bottle.
19. The cost is not the same for any of these. Option (d) is correct.
20. 1342 is the order required. Option (d) is correct.

MOCK TEST PAPER 22

Questions 1 to 5:

1. The highest percentage change is for Imports. Hence, option (a) is correct.
2. As the CAGR is successfully applied, the values of both imports and exports keep increasing. The higher the value, the higher will be the effect of the CAGR. Further, the value of the deficit increase also depends on the relative values of the percentage increase in imports and exports for the year being considered. The higher the positive difference in between import percentage change and export percentage change, the higher will be the change in the deficit. In this case, both these factors favour 1999–2000 to be the maximum change in trade deficit. Hénce, 1999–2000 is the answer.
3. Imports and exports both have a greater than 50% growth even if simple annual growth rate was considered. You will need to check closely for

GDP at factor cost and industrial production index. Of these industrial production index has grown by over 50%, while GDP at factor cost has not. Hence, option (b) is correct.

4. Obviously, only imports and exports would have grown by 50% +.
5. The answer will be given by:

$$\frac{1.8 \times 1.089 \times 1.104 \times 1.102}{1 \times 1.082 \times 1.09 \times 1.087} = 1.86$$

Questions 6 to 9:

6. Six items out of 26 have shown a decrease in value.
7. Misc. Transactions shows the highest percentage decrease. Option (c) is correct.
8. Excess has grown by over 100% and no other category shows such a high percentage increase. Hence, option (b) is correct.
9. 430666/4585, i.e., Passenger kms/Passengers = 93.9 (approx.)

Questions 10 to 13:

10. Visual inspection gives us wheat as the correct option. Option (d) is correct.
11. The highest percentage is around 37% in 1999–2000. Hence, option (c) is correct.
12. Statements (i), (iii) and (iv) can be verified to be true.
13. It can be verified visually that 1996–97 is the best year in terms of growth for all the four food grain categories.

Questions 14 to 16:

14. In January the total expenditure on roses and carnations was 70000 × 47.4 = 33.18 lacs out of which the expense on Roses was 1136916. Thus, the expenditure on carnations was 3318000 – 1136916 = 2181084. The same values for March were: total expenditure on roses and carnations = 70000 × 49.5 = 3465000 while expenditure on roses only was 1137915. So expenditure on carnations in March = 3465000 – 1137915 = 2327085. The percentage change from 2181084 to 2327085 is an increase of 6.69%. Thus, option (c) is correct.
15. The sales of roses in January = 1136916/99 = 11484, Sales of roses in July = 1188432/144 = 8253. The percentage drop from 11484 to 8253 is 28.13%.
16. January price of carnations = total revenue on carnations/ sales of carnations = 2181084/13848 = 157.5 Also, total revenue on carnations in December = 70000 × 56.4 – 977688 = 3948000 – 977688 = 2970312
December price of carnations = total revenue on carnations/ sales of carnations = 2970312/18859 = 157.5.
Thus, there is no change in the price of carnations in January when compared to the price in December.

Questions 17 to 20:

17. If I is receiving 10 A then H will also receive 10 A. Hence, substation R will receive 25 A and substation Q will also receive 25 A. The 25 A that Q receives will be distributed equally into A, D and G – 8.33 A each. With a 10% loss for 1 km, A would receive 7.5 A.
18. For C to receive 10 A, B should send 11.11 A to C. If C receives 10 A, B will have received 22.22 A (since B will retain half and send forward half the electricity it receives). That means A should send 24.7 A to B (approx.). Thus A receives (24.7 × 2) = 49.4 A. Thus substation Q sends 55 A to A. So Q must have received 55 × 3 = 165 A. Hence, P must have produced 330 A.
19. R must be sending 40 A to H. Thus, R receives 80 A and so will Q. Q will send forward towards G 80 A/3 = 26.66 A. 10% of this will be lost on the way and G will receive 24 A.
20. If E receives 37, D must be sending 40 A each to E and F. Since D will retain half the current it gets, this means that D must be getting 160 A. Since D and G are identical, G must be receiving 160 A. Hence, the ratio E to G will be 37 : 160.

MOCK TEST PAPER 23

Questions 1 to 4:

1. The total tax incidence would be: 10% of amount between 50000 and 60000 = 1000; 20% of amount between 60000 and 150000 = 18000 and 30% of amount between 150000 and 240000 = 27000. Required percentage = 27000/46000 = 59% (approx). Hence, option (b) is correct.
2. Net income = 170000 + 30000 = 200000.
Tax = 1000 + 18000 + 15000 = 34000
However, data about savings and sex is unavailable. Hence cannot be answered.
3. $$\frac{(45000 \times 1.05 + 1000 - 9000 - 5000)}{12} = 2854.166$$
4. 240000 – 60000 – 32000 = 148000.

Note: Her total tax is 46000 – 9000 – 5000 = 32000, which will also be her TDS amount during the year.

Questions 5 to 8:

5. Nylon filament yarn and tyre cord for the entire period.
6. Do not confuse products with product categories. Hence, although polymers and synthetic fibres both show a greater than 80% capacity utilisation, they are not to be counted. There are seven such products, that have shown 80% plus value of capacity utilisation for the entire period.
7. Look at the following values to be added: 1114 for polymers, 32 for synthetic fibres and 39 for elastomers (All capacities are in kt).
8. The only product category that exhibits this amongst the four is polymers.

Questions 9 to 12:

9. No. 7 rank in 1993–94 will go to Karnataka as it has the 7th lowest poverty percentage (or the 8th highest).

Note: Lower the poverty percentage, the better it is.

10. Orissa has the highest overall cumulative poverty rating, 14 + 14 + 13 + 14 if you have ranked from the lowest to the highest. On the other hand if you have ranked the highest poverty as 1, you can do: $(15-1)+(15-1)+(15-2)+(15-1)$. Understand this clearly as it is used very often.
11. The populations of the states are unknown. Hence, cannot be determined.
12. Bihar is dominated by all except Orissa, West Bengal and of course itself. Hence, 11 states and the answer is option (a).

Questions 13 to 16:

Assume the total production of the first year as 10000, second year becomes 12000, third year 14400 and fourth year 17280. Then $0.2 \times 17280 - 0.2 \times 12000 = 1056$. But this difference is given as 2640. Hence, the values of production will be; 25000, 30000, 36000 and 43200 respectively for the 4 years.

13. $125 \times 0.4 \times 30000 = 15$ lakhs. Hence, option (a) is correct.
14. $0.2\times25000 : 0.2\times30000 : 0.2\times36000 : 0.2\times43200$. None of the ratios in the first three options matches this. Hence, option (d) is correct.
15. $2\times3:4\times5:2\times7:2\times8 = 6:20:14:16 = 3:10:7:8$. Hence, option (d) is correct.
16. Statement (c) is not true, since both A and B have not shown an increasing trend.

Questions 17 to 20:

17. We need to solve this by checking the options and seeing whether any of the values in the options match the given data. Checking for option (c), @3.5%, 3075 would become 3182, 3182 would become 3293, 3293 would become 3408 and 3408 would reach somewhere in the 3500s after the fourth time period. Thus, 3.5% is too low a value for the compound average growth rate. Checking similarly for 6% and 5.75%, you can see that the numbers do not work out at this rate.
    Thus, option (d) is correct.
18. The maximum drop can be seen to have happened during March from 1211 to 741; a drop of 470 on a starting value of 1211. This is close to 39% of the value. None of the three options matches this and hence Option (d) is correct.
19. The required percentage would be given by the percentage value of the ratio of: 233/3221 = 7.24%. Option (a) is correct.
20. The highest value is for February @ (1211 + 247) out of 3221 which is approximately 45%. Option (b) is correct.

MOCK TEST PAPER 24

Questions 1 to 4:

You will be able to make the following deductions. Note this was an original CAT question with a wrong question in the set. Question 2 we have reproduced here exactly like what was asked in the CAT – and you should have been able to identify that there was something wrong there and hence skipped that question while taking the test – as you would be required to do whenever there is a such an error in the CAT.

	Males (%) (Numbers)	Females (%) (Numbers)	Vegetarians (%) (Numbers)	Non-vegetarians (% of that Class) (Numbers)
Class 12	60% – 48	**40% – 32**	**40% – 32**	**60% – 48**
Class 11	55% – 44	**45% – 36**	50% – 40	50% – 40
Secondary Section	**45% – 288**	**55% – 352**	**55% – 352**	45% – 288
Total	47.5% – 380	52.5% – 420	53% – 424	**47% – 376**

Note: In the above table the values given in bold are calculated Figures while the ones in normal fonts are given directly.

Hence, the answers are:

1. (b)
2. The data in this question is inconsistent since, 50% of the students cannot be male vegetarians as there are only 45% males in the secondary section.

3. (a)
4. If 25% of the vegetarians are male, it means that out of 32 vegetarians there are 8 male vegetarians and 24 female vegetarians. Also, there are 40 male non vegetarians in class 12. Hence, the correct answer is 16(40–24). Option (e).

Questions 5 to 9:

5. From the two graphs it is evident that the global soda ash production for natural soda ash has always been stagnant at 10 MT. At the same time it can be seen that Tata Chemicals has increased its natural soda ash production from 0 to 0.3 MT between 2005 and 2007—which obviously means that Tata Chemicals must have acquired 0.3 MT of soda ash production facility in 2007.
Thus, option (d) is a conclusion we can draw from the graphs by looking at the patterns of production for Tata Chemicals and the world.
6. It can be seen that the increase in Tata Chemicals' Synthetic soda ash production between 2007 and 2008 was 0. Hence, there would be no increase in the global soda ash production also. Option (d) is correct.
7. The proportion of natural soda ash to synthetic soda ash was 10/34 in 2001 and it became 10/40 in 2006. Thus, it has decreased. Thus statement 1 is correct. Statement 2 is the opposite of statement 1 and hence has to be false.
Statement 3 is also seen to be true as the proportion of synthetic soda ash for Tata Chemicals' was 0.9/0.9 in 2005 and it reduced to 2.2/2.5 in 2007.
Thus, Statements 1 and 3 are correct and hence option (a) is correct.
8. We do not have information about the global production in 2008 and hence we should mark that the data is incomplete.
Option (d) is correct.
9. Since Tata Chemicals has a production of 5.4 MT (13.5% of the total market share) we can conclude that Nirma has a production of 3.4 MT (8.5% of the total market share.
Thus, since Solvay produced more than Tata Chemicals, its market share would be more than 13.5%. Similarly, FMC's market share has to be less than 13.5% (as it is lower than Tata Chemicals' market share). Thus, Statements 2 and 4 are correct. Hence, Option (c) is the correct answer.

Questions 10 to 13:

10. The lowest ratio is for Chola Freedom Inc ST (approximately 100/16 → 6. No other fund comes close for minimum. Hence, option (d) is correct.
11. Obviously, the comparison is between HDFC STP and Pru ICICI STP. Amongst them, HDFC STP is 1335/10.5, which would be between 120 and 130, while for Pru ICICI STP it would be above 130.
12. 100.04 crore/16.64 = 6 crore (approx). Hence, option (b) is correct.
13. $\frac{\text{Fund size}}{\text{NAV}} > 80$. Check the ratio for each fund.

Note: Take the number from the NAV, multiply it roughly by 80 and check if the outcome is below the fund size. If so, then that fund has to be counted. We can see 4 funds satisfying this in the table. Hence, option (b) is correct.

Questions 14 to 16:

14. In order to solve this question we need to take a look at the behaviour of the actual leftover values (as a % of sales) for both cakes/pastries as well as for savouries.

The following visual observations can be made about the leftover amount for cakes/pastries:

Year	Sales of Cakes/ Pastries/Gateaux	Leftover as % of Sales for Cakes/Pastries/ Gateaux	Hence, Actual Leftover Amount for Cakes/Pastries/Gateaux
1994	Grows	Grows	Grows
1995	Grows close to 90%	Reduces about 10%	Grows
1996	Grows 80-90%	Reduces 10-20%	Grows
1997	Grows	Grows	Grows
1998	Grows over 40%	Reduces 10-20%	Grows
1999	Grows about 5%	Reduces by over 30%	Reduces
2000	Grows	Grows	Grows
2001	Reduces 5%	Grows over 20%	Grows
2002	Grows over 20%	Reduces around 5%	Grows
2003	Grows	Grows	Grows
2004	Grows	Grows	Grows

From the table of conclusions about the direction that the leftover of cakes/pastries/gateaux is taking— we can see that both statements 1 and 2 are incorrect because we cannot say that the worth of leftover for cakes, etc. increased continuously from 1993 to 2004 and neither can we say that the worth of leftover kept fluctuating many a times.
We can definitely conclude that the worth of leftover for cakes/pastries/gateaux would have been the highest in 2004. In order to test the remaining two statements we need to see the behaviour of leftovers for savouries:

Year	Sales of Savouries	Leftover as % of Sales for Savouries	Hence, Actual Leftover Amount for Savouries
1994	Grows	Grows	Grows
1995	Grows 80%	Reduces 5%	Grows
1996	Grows	Grows	Grows
1997	Grows over 100%	Reduces about 20%	Grows
1998	Reduces about 10%	Grows about 30%	Grows
1999	Grows about 13%	Reduces more than 30%	Reduces
2000	Grows about 20%	Reduces about 20%	Very close call
2001	Grows	Grows	Grows
2002	Grows about 20-30%	Reduces about 5-10%	Grows
2003	Grows	Grows	Grows
2004	Grows 17-18%	Reduces about 10%	Grows

Looking at this table of values about leftovers for savouries we can conclude that the value for this would be highest in 2004. Thus, statement 3 is completely correct.

At the same time we can reject statement 4 too, as the worth of leftovers for savouries was not fluctuating all the time.

Thus, only statement 3 is correct and hence we choose option (d) as the correct answer.

15. From our table of conclusions about the leftovers for cakes/pastries/gateaux we can see that the only year when there is a decrease in its value is from 1998 to 1999 and hence option (c) is the correct answer.

16. In order to solve this question we need to test the values of profit/loss for the cake chain in the years 1993, 1997,1998 and 2000.

In 1993, the value of profit/loss would be given by: (81.47 + 41.79) – (80.06 + 41.07) – (1.52% of 81.47 + 9.38% of 41.79)

= 123.46 – 121.13 – (1.52% of 81.47 + 9.38% of 41.79)

= 2.33 – (1.52% of 81.47 + 9.38% of 41.79)

This can clearly be seen to be a negative value and hence there is a loss in 1993.

Once we have this conclusion that the chain was in losses in 1993 we look at the options and see that there are only two feasible choices – Option (a) or Option (d) as Options (b), (c) and (e) are effectively telling us that the chain made profits in 1993 and hence can be rejected.

To choose between Options (a) and (d) we need to check for the year 2000.

In 2000, the value of profit/loss would be given by:

= 1389.72 – 1373.29 – (1.5% of 752.09 + 5.61% of 637.63)

= 16.43 – (1.5% of 752.09 + 5.61% of 637.63)

This can clearly be seen to be a negative value and hence there is a loss in 2000.

17. Since the restaurant managed to save 10% each year from 1996, The leftover value would be 90% of the original value. Therefore, the amount saved would be 1/9 of the leftover value.

	Sale (in lacs)	Leftover % age	Leftover Value (in lacs)	Amount Saved (in lacs)
1996	591.77	1.23	7.28	0.81
1997	667.1	2.06	13.74	1.53
1998	936.52	1.74	16.3	1.81
1999	978.69	1.19	11.65	1.3
2000	752.09	1.5	11.28	1.25
2001	713.46	1.83	13.06	1.45
2002	885.29	1.76	15.58	1.73
2003	1071.81	1.81	19.4	2.16
2004	1225	2.78	34.06	3.78

Therefore, the total amount saved= 0.81+1.53+1.81+1.3+1.25+1.45+1.73+2.16+3.78=15.82

The closest option is 16. Option C

18. The closing value of the debt-based mutual funds at the end of the year 2015 will be given by: Starting value + Return for the year – Withdrawal for the year. This value comes to 772,300 at the end of the year 2015. However, the starting value of 2016 is 2,572,300. This means that there must be an increment of 1,800,000 at the end of the year 2015. This represents a 180% value of the initial investment. Hence, Option (b) is correct.

19. The total amount invested is 1,000,000 + 600,000 (Start of 2014 in debt-based + equity-based funds) + 1,800,000 (start of 2016 in debt-based funds) + 200,000 + 200,000 (start of 2017 and 2018 respectively in debt-based mutual funds). Hence, the required answer will be the percentage equivalent of the ratio 10/38 = 26.31%.

20. Portfolio means the net value of the debt-based mutual funds + the value of the equity holdings. The maximum percentage growth in this value is clearly for 2016 from 2015.

MOCK TEST PAPER 25

Questions 1 to 4:

By observing the table we can make out that the following costs are variable: Material, Labour and Operating cost of Machines.

At the same time, the following costs are fixed: Consumables , Rent of Building, Rates and Taxes, Repair and Maintenance expenses

And Selling and Marketing expenses.

Based on this we can make the following deductions:

1. Total cost for 1400 units = 70000 + 28000 + 1400 +1200 + 400 + 800 + 42000 + 5800 = 149600.
   Hence, the per unit cost = 149600/14 = 107.
2. The total fixed costs for the company are: 1400 +1200 + 400 + 800 + 5800 = 9600, the selling price is 125 and the variable cost per unit is– 50 (for materials) + 20 (for labour) + 30 (for Operating cost of machines) = 100.
   Hence, the margin per unit is ₹25. Thus the number of units for avoiding any loss (i.e. Break Even Point) = 9600/25 = 384. Hence, option (c) is correct.
3. In order to maximise profit it would have to produce and sell 2000 units.
4. Profit at 1400 units → 125 × 1400 – 107 × 1400 = 25200 (an approximate value).
   Profit at 1700 units will depend on fixed cost per unit at 1700 units. This would be 100 (variable cost per unit) + 8600/1700 (fixed cost per unit) = 105.06 (approximately × Hence, the profit at 1700 units would be 120 × 1700 – 105.06 × 1700 = 14.94 × 1700 = 25400.
   Hence, Option (a) is correct.

Questions 5 to 8:

5. Option (c) is correct because both the statements X and Y can be seen to be true.
   In the case of X, we can see that while managerial registrations have increased from 19000 to 45000, technical registrations have grown from 61000 to 63000. Clearly, registrations of managerial candidates have grown more than that for technical candidates.
   Similarly Y is also true because the overall growth in registrations is from 80000 to 108000 (we have taken approximate values here) which is clearly over 25%.
6. Statement X is true as the percentage of drop-outs in 2004 can be estimated as the % reduction from 192 to 153 – a reduction of 39 on a base value of 192 which means approximately 20%. In 2025, this drop is only from 452 to 407 – approximately 10%. Thus, the percentage drop-outs have reduced in 2025 from 2024.
   Statement Y is not true because the percentage of drop-outs was only about 5% for technical candidates while it was seen as around 10% for managerial candidates. Thus, the percentage drop-out for technical candidates was lower and not higher than the percentage drop-out for managerial candidates in 2025.
   Hence, since only Statement X is true, we choose option (a).
7. Statement X is false as 399 out of 40763 is lower than 637 out of 60133.
   Statement Y is true as 399 out of 40763 is a higher rate of success than 138 out of 15389.
   Thus, option (b) is the correct answer.
8. 181 out of 59981 is lower than 48 out of 15389. Thus, statement X is false.
   Similarly Statement Y is also false as 181 out of 684 is a lower success rate than 48 out of 138.

Questions 9 to 10:

9. Monitoring Engineering (31%), Materials (21%), CIS (19%) and Services (10%) would account for over 80% of the group sales while using the minimum number of sectors.
   Option (c) is correct.
10. Using the technique of alligation, we know that the average profit for CIS and engineering would be 15.04% based on the thought given below:

12% profit		20% profit
Engineering	31:19	CIS

weighted average = 12 + 19 × 8/50 = 15.04%

Further, since CIS and Engineering account for exactly 50% of the sales, the remaining 50% sales comes from the other sectors. Thus the required answer would be got by using the alligation process to the situation below:

??	Weighted average 10%	15.04%
Remaining sectors	1:1	CIS & Engg

The profit margin in the remaining sectors should be 4.96% using a 1:1 ratio.

Questions 11 to 14:

For solving this question first of all you should write down all the costs (of each ingredient alongside the table)

11. Solve by options:
Option (a) gives us the carbohydrate percentage as– $(2\times 80+1\times 10+3\times 45)/6 = 305/6 < 60\%$. Hence, this is not a valid mixture.
Similarly,
Option (b) gives us $420/7 = 60\%$, while Option (e) gives us a concentration of
$(4\times 80+1\times 10+1\times 45)/6 > 60\%$.
Options (c) and (d) do not satisfy the 60% condition. Also between the mixture created in Option (b) and the one created in Option (e), the mixture used in Option (e) is clearly cheaper since the proportion of P (which is the cheapest ingredient) is maximised and the other two are minimised. Hence, Option (e) is correct.
12. Option (a): O and P do not give us 30% of protein.
Option (b): R and S mixed 1:1 will not give us 30% carbohydrates.
Option (c): P and S mixed 1:1 will not give us 5% minerals
Option (d): Q and R mixed 1:1 will not give us 30% carbohydrates.
Option (e) satisfies all conditions and hence is the answer.
13. To ensure 10% minerals, we just have one possibility i.e. O and Q. Hence, option (a) is correct.
14. With Option (a) (P and Q) we cannot create 30% protein With Option (b) (P and S) we cannot create 10% fat.
With Option (c) (P and R) we need a mixing ratio of 3 : 1 to get exactly 10% fat as required by the question. The cost per unit would become 1550/4 = 387.5 With Option (d) (Q and S) the mixing ratio required is 1 : 4 to get exactly 10% fat as required by the question. The cost per unit would become 600/5 = 120
With Option (e) (R and S) the mixing ratio required is 1 : 3 to get exactly 10% fat as required by the question. The cost per unit would become 800/4=200. Hence, option (d) being the cheapest is the correct answer.

Questions 15 to 18:

15. 850/1400 = 61% (approximately). Notice here that the values of the options are so far away from the answer that you do not need to estimate an exact value for the numerator here.
16. 250/660. Again note that no other option is in contention for being the correct answer apart from option (b).
17. The proportion of high income economies in the industrial workforce is seen to be less than 20%. Hence, (iii) is not true. The other statements can be seen to be true. Hence, option (b) is correct.
18. Both (b) and (c) are true.

Questions 19 to 20:

19. The number of spindles per mill as well as number of looms per mill has gradually declined over the period. Hence both (i) and (ii) are correct.
20. The percentage change will have the highest weightage when it comes from a change in number of spindles and the number of rotors. For both of these, the percentage change is the highest during the period ended March 1995.

MOCK TEST PAPER 26

Questions 1 to 4:

You need to understand the meaning of the variable: level of dissimilarity (lod) the highest difference in the ranks allotted to any of the 5 traits by the two countries.

1. India – China (lod 2 due to Ranking of N)
India – Japan (lod 4 due to D)
Lod cannot exceed 4, Hence answer is Option (b).
2. The lod's are:
China – Japan 3(due to ranking of D)
Thailand – Japan 4(due to ranking of D)
Hence answer is Option (d).
3. Malaysia–China, China–Thailand and Thailand–Japan have lod 4. Hence answer is Option (d).
4. China – 2, Japan – 4, Malaysia and Thailand lod 3 each. Hence answer is Option (a).

Questions 5 to 8:

5. In 2003,
60 men + 40 women
In 2010, men would go up by:

$60 \xrightarrow{5\%\uparrow} \xrightarrow{5\%\uparrow} \xrightarrow{5\%\uparrow} \xrightarrow{5\%\uparrow} \xrightarrow{5\%\uparrow} \xrightarrow{5\%\uparrow} \xrightarrow{5\%\uparrow}$

An increase of approximately 24.

Note: For a detailed description of how to handle this calculation quickly, please go through compound interest in my book Quantitative Aptitude for the CAT.

Also, 40 women would become

$40 \xrightarrow{10\%\uparrow} \xrightarrow{10\%\uparrow} \xrightarrow{10\%\uparrow} \xrightarrow{10\%\uparrow} \xrightarrow{10\%\uparrow} \xrightarrow{10\%\uparrow} \xrightarrow{10\%\uparrow}$

An increase of approximately 38.
Thus, net percentage increase would be 62 per cent approximately.

6. Visually this can be seen for 2008–09.
7. Growth rate in 2007 →
 380 to 500 gives (120/500) × 100 = 31% approx.
 Growth rate in 2005 →
 180 to 270 gives (90/180) × 100 = 50%
 Percentage change from 50 to 31 = (19/50)× 100 = 35 per cent approx.
 The closest value of the percentage change is 35 per cent.
8. The growth rate in 2007 (as seen for the previous question) is around 31 per cent
 With this growth rate, the value of European subscription would be approximately 650.
 The actual prediction for 2008 is 600.
 Thus, the closest option would be 50.
 Option (a)

Questions 9 to 11:

9. Each of the first four statements can be seen to be false. Hence, Option (e) is correct.
10. It can be seen that for 1996–97, if the number of girls started with 55 then in the secondary classes we would have $0.327 \times 45 = 14.715$ (because there is a 67.3% drop out rate in secondary classes boys it means that only 32.7% of the boys who joined school would reach the secondary classes.
 Similarly, the girls would be $0.263 \times 55 = 14.465$
 The boys would outnumber girls in the very first year and hence 1996–97 is the correct answer.
11. The average drop-out rate for girls till elementary classes over the years is 56.46%.
 This means that 43.533% of girls remained in education after elementary classes.
 Number of girls = $7000 \times 0.55 \times 0.43533 = 1676$

Questions 12 to 15:

12. There are exactly four organic and two inorganic chemicals for which the production has fallen. So, the required answer is 2 : 1.
13. The percentage increase in Ethylene Glycol is from 327 to 454 (considering only the first three digits of the numbers) – a growth of close to 40%. None of the other chemicals in the options is close to this percentage growth. Hence, the correct answer is Ethylene Glycol. Option (b) is correct.
14. Formaldehyde, acetone, acetic acid, phthalic anhydride and phenol are not highly volatile.
15. There are five organic chemicals whose percentage change in production is greater than 5%. There are also five inorganic chemicals whose percentage change in production is less than 5%. Hence, the answer is 5 : 5 = 1 : 1. Option (a) is correct.

Questions 16 to 19:

16. We cannot determine the answer to this question, as we do not have any idea of the value of the chemicals.
17. The highest percentage change in value of raw materials used is shown either in printing inks or in dental hygiene products. The comparison is (553 – 432)/432 against (2853 – 2249)/2249 i.e., 121/432 against 604/2249. It can be seen that for Printing inks, the percentage is higher. Hence, option (a) is correct.
18. Since we don't know the composition of the relative usage of different raw materials in the user industries we cannot comment on the total use of raw materials nor can we make any conclusion about the absolute change of the value of the total raw materials consumed.
19. Again in this question, we have no idea of the price per tonne of any chemical and hence we cannot determine the answer.

Question 20:

20. The approach to such questions is based on minimising the interference between the various sets. In order to do so think of the people as numbered 1 to 100. Assume 1 to 70 have VCDs, then 71 to 100 and 1 to 45 can be given microwave ovens - and in such a case, the number of people with both microwave ovens and VCD players is 45. Next, avoid giving the ACs to these 45 people, as much as possible. In order to do so, let 46 to 100 have ACs. Then, from 1 to 45, you would need to give ACs to a minimum of 25 people (to complete the 80 for ACs). Let these people be 1 to 25. At this stage, we have people 1 to 25 having VCD, Microwave ovens and ACs. Next, we move to allocating washing machines amongst the 100 people. Again, if we want to minimise the percentage of people with all four gadgets, we would need to avoid people 1 to 25 having a washing machine. In order to do so, we should first allocate washing machines to 26 to 100. This would account for 75 washing machines. However, since the number of washing machines is 85 – we need to add 10 more to the washing machines – this can get done by people 1 to 10 having washing machines. In this case 10 people (viz: 1 to 10) have all the four gadgets. Hence, the required answer is 10%. Option (c) is correct.

SECTION

II LOGICAL DATA INTERPRETATION

PART 1

HOW TO THINK IN LOGICAL DATA INTERPRETATION

IN THIS PART YOU WILL LEARN:

- To identify the Mathematical Structures on which DI questions are framed
- To improve your ability to read, understand and anticipate DI questions in DI sets of various parts
- To improve your line by line understanding of various kinds of DI sets.
- To get an understanding of Logical Data Interpretation
- To improve your thought processes and solving abilities while solving Logical Data Interpretation

CHAPTER 1 Introduction to Logical Data Interpretation

INTRODUCTION TO LOGICAL DATA INTERPRETATION

We have already seen in the Section One of this book various mathematical constructs on Data Interpretation and also learnt 'How to think in Traditional Data Interpretation'. As you know, this book is divided into two sections:

Section I: Traditional Data Interpretation (dominant theme – Data extraction and calculations);

Section II: Logical Data Interpretation (dominant theme – reasoning, logic and analysis).

This distinction between different kinds of data interpretation questions is not something that is explicitly defined by examinations or exam conducting bodies. However, as a trainer helping students prepare for the CAT and other aptitude exams, I have always felt the need to look at problem solving from a functional point of view. By that, I mean, for all aptitude areas, preparation processes become more robust if you start looking at a question from the perspective of 'what it got your mind to do' rather than from the plain theoretical perspective of which chapter to slot a question into. It is in this context, that over the past 15 years I could clearly sense that the CAT was moving its Data Interpretation questions away from what I now call as 'Traditional Data Interpretation' to questions that tested your logical thinking, your reasoning abilities and your analytical skills. The trend started off from the CAT 2003 paper with the introduction of one or two sets that would test these skills. As the years rolled by, however, the Data Interpretation questions being asked started becoming increasingly logical and reasoning based, so much so that if you were to look at the papers of the last few years, you would find no calculation oriented sets – and the Data Interpretation questions are completely logical and reasoning oriented in nature. In fact, this trend has reached such an extreme over the past few years, that sometimes while solving a data interpretation question, it is difficult to understand whether you are solving a DI or a reasoning question! (In fact, even the XAT exam has moved in the same direction- though you still see the DI questions in the XAT as a mixture of traditional and logical DI.

Clearly, the skills you need to learn and equip yourself with for such questions are very different than those that were required to master traditional Data Interpretation. However, most aspirants I see struggle to solve these questions, since they have not developed the clarity and analytical ability to handle the challenges posted by this section. Students and aspirants across the country are at a loss to understand how to prepare for this make or break section of the exam. Thus, was born the need to train on and write content related to Logical Data Interpretation.

It is in this context, that I clearly felt the need to divide Data Interpretation questions and in fact this whole book into two separate sections – where we segregate questions and question sets based on the need to cater to these dual mind development requirements. In Section One of this book, you have seen traditional Data Interpretation and its thought structures extensively. In this Section of the book, we shift our focus to Logical Data Interpretation. All the question sets in this section of the book, would have a dominant theme of reasoning, analysis and logic. The design of this section is to take you through a learning process that equips your mind to tackle the CAT in the current avatar. In fact, I have a strong belief that if you were to get to know and understand each question set in this section, you would be adequately prepared for whatever the CAT throws at you. This is because, even though initially while solving the first few sets in this section, you might feel that every set of questions is different and hence required distinct skills – the actual fact is that you would start to see and experience a sameness to the logic across the sets, once you are done with solving and learning through a significant number of logical DI question sets.

This section of the book is divided into:

- Introduction to Logical Data Interpretation (including: the write up that follows – 'How to think in Logical Data Interpretation'
- 12 minute test papers
- Mock Test Papers based on Logical Data Interpretation

Together these contain a gamut of varied questions and situations that would help you learn the skills required to master this question type during your CAT Prep journey.

What you would need to do would be to get to first solve and learn on your own from each and every set across this section – followed by looking at the solutions (if required).

You should now move on to 'How to think in Logical Data Interpretation' but before you do that I may suggest that you go back to the Traditional DI part of this book and review the Mathematical constructs in Data Introduction.

CHAPTER 2

How to Think in Logical Data Interpretation

Directions for Questions 1 to 4: *Set based on Averages* on the basis of the information given below

A management institute was established on January 1, 2000 with 3, 4, 5 and 6 faculty members in the Marketing, Organisational Behaviour (OB), Finance and Operations Management (OM) areas respectively, to start with. No faculty member retired or joined the institute in the first three months of the year 2000. In the next four years, the institute recruited one faculty member in each of the four areas. All these new faculty members, who joined the institute subsequently over the years, were 25 years old at the time of their joining the institute. All of them joined the institute on April 1st. During these four years, one of the faculty members retired at the age of 60. *(All this is preliminary information that has to be understood only in the context of the bar chart that follows. Once we move to the bar chart we would need to interpret each of these)* The following diagram gives the area-wise average age (in terms of number of completed years) of faculty members as on April 1st of 2000, 2001, 2002 and 2003.

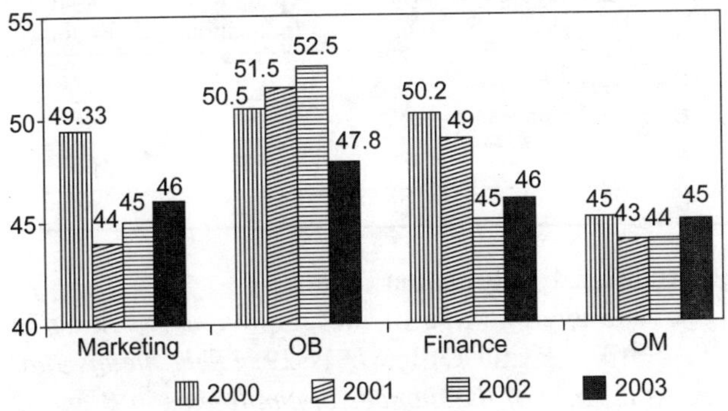

FIGURE 2.1

When you reach the bar chart and start to look at the individual values of the bars, you can start connecting to the information provided in the textual form at the start of the question. For instance when we look at the bars for Marketing, we can analyse that initially marketing had 3 faculty members with an average age of 49.33. Next year, the average age dropped to 44. If the faculty team were constant between 2000 and 2001, the expected average age would have just increased by 1 year from the previous year. However, a drop in the average age could mean one of two things would have happened. An inclusion of a new 25-year old faculty in the team, or the retirement of a 60-year old faculty from the team. In both the events, there would be a drop of the average age of the group (and you can see that since the starting average age is below 60 and above 25 for all the departments, the recruitment of a new faculty or the retirement of an older faculty would have the effect of reducing the average age of the departments' faculty team). A look through the bar chart after gaining this understanding, shows us that the areas of Marketing, OB and OM all have one drop in the average age, while the department of finance is exhibiting a drop in the average age on two occasions. Since, the starting text of this data set has told us that there is one recruitment in each department during the period shown, and there is also one retirement during this time from one of the four departments, we can correlate that the drops in Marketing, OB and OM must be due to the recruitments in those departments, while the two drops in the finance area means that there must be one recruitment and one retirement in the finance area. The other thing to note is that the ages are always counted in whole number of years and the average age calculations are with reference to the date of 1st April for each year. With this analysis we are ready to move into the questions of the set.)

1. From which area did the faculty member retire?
   (a) Finance (b) Marketing
   (c) OB (d) OM

This is something that we have already analyzed while looking at the bar chart. It is clearly evident that the retirement must have been from the finance department.

2. Professors Naresh and Devesh, two faculty members in the Marketing area, who have been with the Institute since its inception, share a birthday, which falls on 20th November. One was born in 1947 and the other one in 1950. (*Reaction: Naresh would be 52 years old on 1st April 2000, Devesh would be 49 years old on that day. Since the average of the three faculty members in Marketing is 49.33, on 1st April 2000, it means that the sum of the three ages would be 49.33 × 3 = 148 years. So, the third faculty members age would be 148 – 52 – 49 = 47 years on 1st April 2000.*) On April 1st 2005, what was the age of the third faculty member, who has been in the same area since inception (*5 years later he would be 47 + 5 = 52 years old*)?
   (a) 47 (b) 50
   (c) 51 (d) 52

(You got an answer to this question through your reactions to the information provided in the question.)

3. In which year did the new faculty member join the Finance area?
   (a) 2000 (b) 2001
   (c) 2002 (d) 2003

There are two alternate possible scenarios to analyse here. Since the finance department is witnessing two years where the average age of the finance department is reducing, we have already concluded that the finance department has had one recruitment and one retirement. Scenario 1 is that the retirement occurred in 2001 and the recruitment occurred in 2002. Scenario 2 is the opposite of this. The only way to identify correctly as to which of these scenarios is true, would be to work out the numbers and see which scenario fits the given numbers in the bar chart.

Analysing scenario 1: The retirement occurred in 2001 and the recruitment occurred in 2002: Finance initially has 5 members with an average age of 50.2 on 1st April 2000. Total age of the finance department faculties on 1st April 2000 = 50.2 × 5 = 256. Their total age on 1st April 2001 = 251 + 5 = 256. If there was a retirement from one of these five faculties, it would mean that the total age of 4 members remaining on 1st April 2001 would be 256 – 60 = 196. The average age of the 4 members would be 49. This number confirms with what is given in the bar chart and hence we can conclude that the retirement occurred in 2001 and the new faculty member joined the finance area in 2002.

Note: *If you try to reverse this, you would find that the numbers do not match for recruitment in 2001. The following working would give you that it is not working: Finance initially has 5 members with an average age of 50.2 on 1st April 2000. Total age of the finance department faculties on 1st April 2000 = 50.2 × 5 = 256. Their total age on 1st April 2001 = 251 + 5 = 256. If there is a recruitment in 2001, the total age of 6 people would be 256 + 25 = 281. Average age of 6 people with total age as 281 = 281/6 = 46.833 ≠ 49. Hence, we can conclude that the recruitment did not occur in 2001 and must have occurred in 2002.*

4. What was the age of the new faculty member, who joined the OM area, as on April 1st 2003?
   (a) 25 (b) 26
   (c) 27 (d) 28

   The recruitment has happened in OM in 2001, on 1st April 2001 to be precise. Naturally, the new faculty member would have been 25 years old on that day. 2 years later on 1st April 2003, he would be 27 years old. Option (c) is the correct answer.

Directions for Questions 5 to 7: *(Set based on Averages)*

Answer the questions on the basis of the information given below. Fifty four employees of a company called MJF are spread across four different offices, with each employee working in exactly one office. The table given below shows the office-wise distribution of employees, their average age, their average salary and their average login hours.

TABLE 2.1

Office	Number of Employees	Average Age (Years)	Average Salary (in ₹ thousands)	Average Login Hours
A	13		40	100
B		42		46
C		30	36	80
D		28	42	60

Additional Information:

- The average age of the employees working in Office *B* and Office *D* is 29. *(This means that the ratio of the number of employees in B and D is 1 : 13 – using the concept of alligation. This in effect means that the number of employees in Office B and Office D are 1 and 13 or 2 and 26 respectively. It obviously cannot be 3 and 39 because in that case the total number of employees would cross 54.)*

- The average salary of the fifty four employees is ₹39200. (*This would help us calculate the average salary for Office B – once we can sort out how many people are there in each department.*)
- At least 2 employees work in each office of the company. (*This fixes the number of employees in each of the offices as: A = 13, (given); B = 2; D = 26 and C = 54 – 13 – 2 – 26 = 13.*)
- The average age of the employees working in each office is an integer.

5. Out of the total employees in Office *A*, '*x*' are transferred to Office *B* and the remaining to Office *D*. The average age of the employees working in Office *B* and Office *D* increases by 3 and 10 respectively. What is the average age of the employees working in Office *A*?
(a) 58 (b) 59
(c) 60 (d) Data Insufficient

The information we have is that the average of B has gone up to 45 years, while the average age of Office D has gone up to 38. The possible scenarios of what has actually occurred would depend on the value of x as given in the question—which is a variable.

We can build the following tabular structure to understand what is happening:

TABLE 2.2

If x is:	1	2	3	4	5
Total age of Office B	3 × 45	4 × 45	5 × 45	6 × 45	7 × 45
Total age of Office D	38 × 38	37 × 38	36 × 38	35 × 38	34 × 38
Addition of age to the total age of Office B (original total 2 × 42 = 84)	51	96	141	186	231
Addition of age to the total age of Office D (Original total = 26 × 28 = 728)	716	678	640	602	564
Total age addition to Offices B and D = Total age originally of 13 Office A employees	767	774	781	788	795
Average age of Office A	= 767/13 = 59	= 774/13 is not integral	Not integral	Not integral	Not integral

As we can observe from the above, the values of x from 2 to 5 give us an average age of Office A that is not an integer. This contravenes the conditions of the problem and hence is not possible. For x = 6 to x = 13, we will get 802/13, 809/13, 816/13, 823/13, 830/13, 837/13, 844/13 and 851/13 respectively. Each of these values is not integral in nature. Hence, the average age of Office A has only one possibility = 59. Option (b) is correct.

6. What is the average salary of the employees working in Office B?
(a) ₹44600 (b) ₹30200
(c) ₹18400 (d) ₹24400

This is a calculation intensive question on the surface. But if you look closely at the numbers and use alligation to solve this, it might not be such. The information we have to start with can be seen in the table below:

TABLE 2.3

Office	Number of Employees	Average Salary (in ₹ thousands)
A	13	40
B	2	
C	13	36
D	26	42

The average salary of Offices A and C would be 38000 (since the number of employees in both the offices are the same). This 38000 would be the average salary for 26 employees of Offices A and C. Now, if we incorporate the employees of Office D into this average, we again face a situation of 26 people with average 42000 being added to 26 people with an average of 38000. The average salary for these 52 employees of departments A, C and D would be equal to 40000. Since the average salary of the 54 employees is 39200, we will get the average salary of the 2 employees from Office B using alligation as follows:

??? 39200 40000
2 52

Solving this, we will get the value of 18400 as the average of Office B. Option (c) is correct.

Note: This was a case of a situation where if you were not able to recognise the use of alligation, it would hurt you badly in terms of the time and effort required to solve a question of this type. The only alternate calculation there would have involved solving the equation:

54 × 39200 = 13 × 40000 + 2 × Average of *B* + 13 × 36000 + 26 × 42000.

You can yourself imagine the calculation effort required in solving this, in order to find the average of *B*.

7. How many employees work in Office C?
(a) 13 (b) 14
(c) 26 (d) Cannot be determined

We worked this out while analysing the basic information of the question – there are 13 employees in Office C. Option (a) is correct.

Directions for Questions 8 to 10: *(Set based on Averages and Alligation)*

Answer the following questions on the basis of the information given below. A retailer has some chocolates in five different boxes T1, T2, T3, T4 and T5. Table 2.4 provides the data about the number of chocolates (N), the average weight per chocolate in grams (AWG) and the average selling price per chocolate in ₹ (SPR) for each of the five boxes. Table 2.5 shows the relationship between AWG and the customer satisfaction index (CSI).

TABLE 2.4

Box	N	AWG	SPR
T1	8	90	15
T2	24	45	12
T3	16	70	11
T4	32	65	18
T5	20	85	17

TABLE 2.5

AWG	CSI
AWG ≤ 50	60
50 < AWG ≤ 60	70
60 < AWG ≤ 70	80
70 < AWG ≤ 80	90
80 < AWG	100

On reading the information in the tables, we notice that the variables provided in the first table have the following relationships: AWG × N = total weight of the chocolates in the box; N × SPR = total revenue from the box. Looking through the second table we see that the CSI is increasing with an increase in the AWG, i.e., the higher the AWG, the higher the CSI.

8. All the chocolates of box T2 are to be mixed with all the chocolates of exactly one of the other four boxes. Which box should be chosen to maximise the CSI of the mixture? *(We need to mix the chocolate boxes in such a way that the AWG for the mixed boxes is highest – since higher the AWG, higher the CSI.)*
(a) T5 (b) T3
(c) T1 (d) T4

The AWG of the mixture would be the weighted average of the AWG of Box T2 and the AWG of the Box being mixed with T2. On the surface, Box T1 having the highest AWG would seem to be the best bet, but if you look at the value of N for box T1, you realise that there would be a lower AWG for the mixture, than if you were to mix T2 with T5. A mixture of T2 and T5 would give us an average AWG of over 60, while T2 and T1 would lead to an AWG of below 60. These calculations can be visualised through alligation.

9. If the retailer wants to keep the CSI of the mixture at least 70 and the SPR between 13 and 17, which of the following combinations should he make?
(a) T1, T2 and T3 (b) T2, T3 and T4
(c) T3, T4 and T5 (d) T1, T4 and T5

You can again visualise utilising multiple alligation structures here. For T1, T2 and T3, first the mixing of T2 and T3 would lead to an average SPR of 11.6 for 40 chocolates (Individual SPRs of 11 and 12 mixed in the ratio of 16 : 24 or 2 : 3). Next mixing 40 chocolates with average SPR of 11.6, and 8 chocolates of T1 with average SPR of 90 would give us an average SPR of 15, would result in an average SPR of below 13. Hence, this mixture is not feasible.

The visualisations for the above would look as follows:

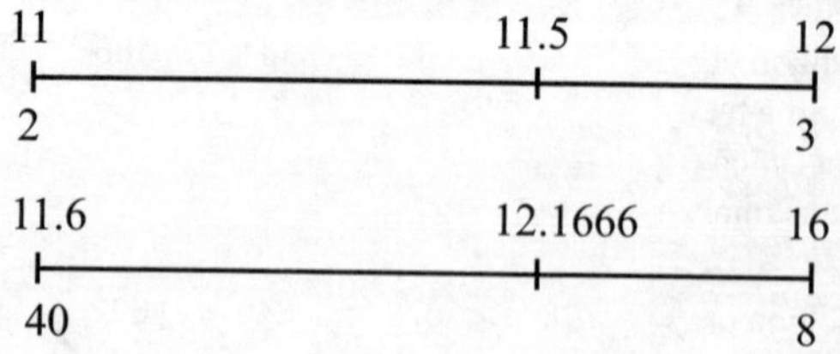

Looking at option (b) it is clear that the AWG for T2, T3 and T4 can never be above 70 since the AWGs of each of the three is below or equal to 70.

Option (d) is also rejected since the average SPR is coming out to be above 17 in the case of T1, T4 and T5. Option (c) would satisfy the given constraints and is hence the correct answer.

10. If 4 chocolates of box T1 are mixed with 3 chocolates of box T2, then what is the CSI of the mixture?
(a) 90 (b) 80
(c) 70 (d) Cannot be determined

The average AWG of the 7 chocolates would be over 70. Hence, the CSI of the mixture would be 90. Option (a) is correct.

Directions for Questions 11 to 13: *(Set based on Percentages)*

Answer the questions on the basis of the information given below.

Each point in the graph below shows the profit and turnover data for a company.

Each company belongs to one of the three industries: textile, cement and steel.

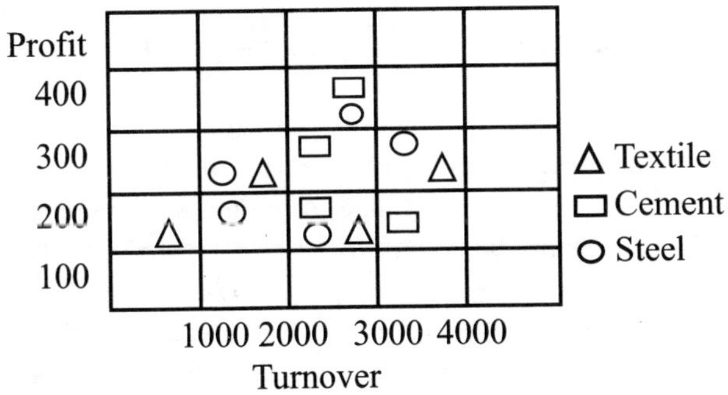

FIGURE 2.2

11. For how many companies does the profit exceed 10% of turnover?
    (a) 8 (b) 7 (c) 6 (d) 5

This is a question that needs to be solved visually. For profit to exceed 10% of turnover, if the turnover is above 3000, the profit should be above 300. Looking at the chart, we see that there are no companies that exhibit this trend. For turnover between 2000 and 3000, the profit above 300, would definitely be greater than 10%. The company that has a profit of just below 300 and turnover above 2000 and below 3000 can also be seen to have a profit exceeding 10% of turnover – since the turnover of that company is just above 2000, while the profit is just below 300. Thus, there are 3 companies with turnover between 2000 and 3000, which exhibit a profit of over 10%. Next, there are 2 companies with turnover between 1000 and 2000 and profit above 200. These companies too would have profit exceeding 10%. The company that has a profit of just below 200 and turnover above 1000 and below 2000 can also be seen to have a profit exceeding 10% of turnover – since the turnover of that company is just above 1000, while the profit is just below 200. Thus, there are 3 companies with turnover between 1000 and 2000, which exhibit a profit of over 10%. Finally, there is one company more that needs to be counted – the company that has a turnover less than 1000, but whose profit exceeds 100. Thus, there are 7 companies that satisfy the profit exceeds 10% of turnover criterion. Option (b) is correct.

12. An investor wants to buy stock of only steel or cement companies with a turnover more than 1000 and profit exceeding 10% of turnover. How many choices are available to the investor? *(Steel and Cement, means either the circles or the squares in the figure. This question is easy because, we have already identified the 7 companies that have a profit exceeding 10% of turnover. With turnover between 2000 and 3000, we had identified 3 companies having profit above 10%. On going back to the figure, we see that all these three are either squares or circles. Also, for turnover between 1000 and 2000, we see that of the three companies with over 10% profit, there are two circles and 1 triangle. The triangle is not a feasible option in this case – as we are looking at only circles and squares. Thus, the investor would have a total of 3 + 2 = 5 options.)*
    (a) 4 (b) 5 (b) 6 (d) 7
13. For how many steel companies *(circles on the graph)* with a turnover of more than 2000 is the profit less than 300? *(Visually you can see that there are 2 circles above 2000 on the x-axis and below 300 on the y-axis. Option (c) is correct.)*
    (a) 0 (b) 1 (c) 2 (d) 7

Directions for Questions 14 to 17: *(Set based on Percentages)*

Answer the questions on the basis of the following information.

The following is the wholesale price index (WPI) of a select list of items with the base year of 1993–94. In other words, all the item prices are made 100 in that year (1993–94). Prices in all other years for an item are measured with respect to its price in the base year. For instance, the price of cement went up by 1% in 1994–95 as compared to 1993–94. Similarly, the price of power went up by 3% in 1996–97 as compared to 1993–94. (*A quick glance at the table at this point of time would give you the logic. So if we first look at the legends down the first column we get that the first legend in the first column is the 'All Items' legend—whose growth essentially would be expected to be the weighted average of the growths of the individual items like cement, limestone etc. The other thing we notice is that the value for the year 1993–94 has been set as the base year for each of the items and the growth in the costs till the year 2002–03 has been given for each of the items*).

TABLE 2.6

	1993–94	1994–95	1995–96	1996–97	1997–98	1998–99	1999–00	2000–01	2001–02	2002–03
All Items	100	102.0	102.5	104.00	103.00	105.00	106.0	108.00	107.0	106.0
Cement	100	101.0	100.5	103.00	102.50	103.50	103.1	103.80	103.7	104.0
Limestone	100	102.0	102.5	102.75	102.25	103.00	104.0	105.00	104.5	105.0
Power	100	101.5	102.5	103.00	103.50	104.00	106.0	107.00	107.5	108.0
Steel	100	101.5	101.0	103.50	104.00	104.25	105.0	105.50	106.0	105.5
Timber	100	100.5	101.5	102.00	102.50	102.00	103.0	103.50	104.0	104.5
Wages	100	101.5	103.0	103.50	104.00	104.25	104.0	104.75	104.9	105.3

14. Let us suppose that one bag of cement (50 kg) consumes 100 kg of limestone and 10 units of power. The only other cost item in producing cement is in the form of wages. During 1993–94, limestone, power and wages contributed, respectively, 20%, 25% and 15% to the cement price per bag. (*Your reaction at this point of time should be that a total of 20 + 25 + 15 = 60% of the price of the cement bag in 1993–94 comes from these three items—and that these are the only items used in producing cement, which in turn means that the operating profit for cement in 1993-94 is 40%.*) The average operating profit (% of price per cement bag) earned by a cement manufacturer during 2002–03 is closest to:

(a) 40% (b) 39.5%
(c) 38.5% (d) 37.5%

The price of a cement bag would increase by 4% from 1993–94 to 2002–03. Thus a bag priced at 100 in 1993–94 would be priced at 104 in 2002–03. Further, the individual cost components of the cement bag would also increase. Checking the percentage increases on each of the items that are used in making cement and applying the percentage growth to them, we get that the cost of limestone would grow by 20 to 21 – a 5% increase, cost of power would increase by 8% – so it would go from 25 to 27. Similarly wages would grow from 15 to 15.795 – an increase of 5.3%. The total cost for a cement bag priced at 104 would be 21 + 27 + 15.795 = 63.795. The profit per cent, i.e., % of price per bag would be given by the percentage value of the ratio 40.2/104 – which works out closest to 38.5%. Option (c) is correct.

15. Steel manufacturing requires the use of iron ore, power and man power. The cost of iron ore has followed the All Items index. During 1993–94 power accounted for 30% of the selling price of steel, iron ore for 25%, and wages for 10% of the selling price of steel. Assuming the cost and price data for cement as given in the previous question, the operating profit (% of selling price) of an average steel manufacturer in 2002–03:

(a) is more than that of a cement manufacturer.
(b) is less than that of a cement manufacturer.
(c) is the same as that of a cement manufacturer.
(d) cannot be determined

Steel's price has gone up by 5.5% during the period, from a base value of 100 to 105.5. In 1993–94 the base price had 30% cost for power, which has grown by 8% to 32.4 in 105.5. Similarly, the 25% component of the base price that was accounted for by iron ore, has grown by 6%. This would mean that it would have increased to 26.5. Similarly, wages would have increased from 10 to 10.53. Thus, the total cost component in the selling price of 105.5 for steel in 2002–03 would be 'Cost of Power + Cost of Iron Ore + Cost of Wages' = 32.4 + 26.5 + 10.53 = 69.43. This means a profit per cent equal to the percentage value of the ratio (105.5 – 69.43)/105.5 = 36.07/105.5. Compared to the profit per cent of a cement manufacturer, this is obviously lower. Hence, the correct answer is option (c).

16. Which item experienced continuous price rise during the ten-year period?

1. Power 2. Cement
3. Wages 4. Limestone

This is a visual question and the only thing you need to check for this is for a continuous increase in the WPI of the items given in the options. Clearly, power is the correct answer as it exhibits a continuous price increase over the given period – i.e., its WPI numbers are always increasing.

17. Which item(s) experienced only one decline in price during the ten-year period? (*This is again a visual question and can be easily seen that steel shows two declines, so the first two options can be rejected forthwith. Looking at the third and fourth options, Timber is there in both. Hence, even without looking at the table we can easily understand that Timber must be*

exhibiting the required property. Checking for wages, we can see that wages has declined only once during the given period—the decline is seen between 1998–99 and 1999–2000. Hence, option (d) is correct.)

(a) Steel and Limestone (b) Steel and Timber
(c) Timber (d) Timber and Wages

Directions for Questions 18 to 21: *(Set based on Averages)*

Answer the following questions on the basis of the information given below.

The performance of six students of a class in five subjects is evaluated on a 9-point grading system. Each student is awarded a grade and grade points in each of the five subjects based on the marks obtained by him in that subject (See Table 2.7). Table 2.8 shows the marks obtained by each student in the five subjects. A student's GPA (Grade Point Average) is the average of the grade points awarded to him in the five subjects.

TABLE 2.7

Marks Range	Grade	Grade Points
91–100	A1	10
81–90	A2	9
71–80	B1	8
61–70	B2	7
51–60	C1	6
41–50	C2	5
31–40	D	4
21–30	E	3
0–20	F	2

(The reaction to the table giving us the grade points is that the Grade and the grade points are both directly dependent on the range of marks scored by a student. When you look at the table giving us the subject-wise marks scored, we see that there are some missing values, denoted by the letters X, Y and Z in the table. Obviously, the information provided after the table must be to help us work out those numbers.)

TABLE 2.8

	Subject-wise Marks Scored				
	English	Hindi	Maths	Science	S. Sc.
Abhishek	56	67	92	97	51
Saral	88	79	87	Z	88
Himanshu	X	81	82	89	81
Puneet	83	93	91	78	79
Vijay	74	65	Y	67	77
Sanjay	73	88	93	60	76

Additional Information: 363, 403 to 412; 333 + 91 to 100; 421; 283 + 81 to 90; 400

- The sum of the GPAs of Saral and Puneet is equal to the sum of the GPAs of Himanshu and Sanjay.
- The GPAs of Abhishek and Vijay are equal.
- Saral, Himanshu, Puneet and Sanjay get distinct GPAs.
- Though the total marks (the sum of the marks obtained in the five subjects) of Himanshu are not the highest, his GPA is the highest amongst the six students.
- The sum of the marks obtained by the six students in Science is more than the sum of the marks obtained by the six students in exactly three of the other four subjects.

The first thing you should do is to change the subject-wise total and write down the grade points for every score in that table. This is how the grade-wise table would look:

TABLE 2.9

	English	Hindi	Maths	Science	S.Sc.	GPA
Abhishek	6	7	10	10	6	7.8
Saral	9	8	9	Z'	9	(35 + Z')/5
Himanshu	X'	9	9	9	9	(36 + X')/5
Puneet	9	10	10	8	8	9
Vijay	8	7	Y'	7	8	(30 + Y')/5
Sanjay	8	9	10	6	8	8.2

From the information about GPAs of Abhishek and Vijay being equal we get that Y' must be 9. From the information that Himanshu has the highest GPA, we can conclude that his GPA must be above 9. This is only possible if X' is 10. This information would change the solution table to:

TABLE 2.10

	English	Hindi	Maths	Science	S. Sc.	GPA
Abhishek	6	7	10	10	6	7.8
Saral	9	8	9	Z'	9	(35 + Z')/5
Himanshu	10	9	9	9	9	9.2
Puneet	9	10	10	8	8	9
Vijay	8	7	9	7	8	7.8
Sanjay	8	9	10	6	8	8.2

Now using the information that the sum of the GPAs of Saral and Puneet is equal to the sum of the GPAs of Himanshu and Sanjay, we can work out that:

GPA of Saral + 9 = 9.2 + 8.2 → GPA of Saral = 8.4. This means that Z' must be 7. The final table would look as follows:

TABLE 2.11

	English	Hindi	Maths	Science	S. Sc.	GPA
Abhishek	6	7	10	10	6	7.8
Saral	9	8	9	7	9	8.4
Himanshu	10	9	9	9	9	9.2
Puneet	9	10	10	8	8	9
Vijay	8	7	9	7	8	7.8
Sanjay	8	9	10	6	8	8.2

18. Which grade is awarded to Saral in Science?
    (a) A1 (b) A2
    (c) B1 (d) B2
    The answer can be read off the final solution table. Since he got 7 grade points in Science, Saral should have got a grade of B2 in Science.
19. Who gets the second highest GPA amongst the six students?
    (a) Saral (b) Puneet
    (c) Vijay (d) Sanjay
    The second highest GPA is for Puneet. Option (b) is the correct answer.
20. What is the sum of the marks obtained by Saral in the five subjects?
    (a) 422 (b) 432
    (c) 426 (d) Cannot be determined
    Saral's score in science is something we cannot work out exactly. He has got between 61 and 70 marks in Science but we cannot determine his exact score.
21. How many values are possible for X?
    (a) 1 (b) 10
    (c) 8 (d) None of these
    Since Himanshu cannot be getting the highest total marks his total must be less than 421. However, if we take a closer look at this, Himanshu's total is $333 + X = 424$ to 433. The only total marks in that range are for Puneet, who has scored a total of 424. Since Himanshu's score cannot be greater than 424, he must have got 91 in English. X thus has only 1 value possible.

Directions for Questions 22 to 25: *(Set based on Numerical Logic and Percentages)*
Answer the questions on the basis of the information given below.

Coach John sat with the score cards of Indian players from the 3 games in a one-day cricket tournament where the same set of players played for India and all the major batsmen got out. John summarised the batting performance through three diagrams, one for each game. In each diagram, the three outer triangles communicate the number of runs scored by the three top scorers from India, where K, R, S, V and Y represent Kaif, Rahul, Saurav, Virender and Yuvraj respectively. The middle triangle in each diagram denotes the percentage of total score that was scored by the top three Indian scorers in that game. (*At this point in the text, we have enough information to look at the charts given. It is clear that in the first game against Pakistan, Virender scored 130, while Kaif scored 28 and Yuvraj scored 40. Thus the top three scorers in the first game scored a total of 198 runs. From the middle triangle it is evident that the top three scored 90% of India's total score in that game. Naturally, India must have scored a total of 220 runs in that game. Similar working out can be done for the other two triangles too, but we will not do these at this point since we are not required to find out the values for all three games at this point of time. We would get to those when we reach a question necessitating the calculation. Note that the Pakistan calculation was for understanding the data and whether the equation used in the question is understood by us.*) No two players score the same number of runs in the same game. John also calculated two batting indices for each player based on his scores in the tournament; the R-index of a batsman is the difference between his highest and lowest scores in the 3 games while the M-index is the middle number, if his scores are arranged in a non-increasing order. (*Naturally the R-Index would be calculable exactly only for a batsman whose highest and least scores are known. Likewise, the M index would only be calculable for a batsman whose middle score would be available.*)

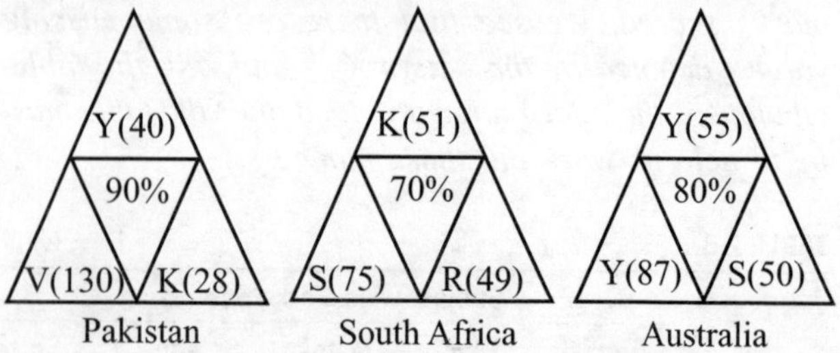

FIGURE 2.3

22. Amongst the players mentioned, who can have the lowest R-index from the tournament?
    1. Only Kaif, Rahul or Yuvraj
    2. Only Kaif or Rahul
    3. Only Kaif or Yuvraj
    4. Only Kaif

(This question requires us to look at the values of the individual scores of the five batsmen in the three matches. You should also realise that there are a total of 5 × 3 = 15 scores, but the triangles only reveal 9 scores. Thus, for the remaining 6 scores we would need to make a possibility range in order to handle questions based on R-Index and M-Index of the batsmen. It might be good at this point to make a table encapsulating the data for easier reading–since a quick glance at the upcoming questions shows that all the questions are about R-Index and M-Index only. Before we make the table for the individual batsmen we should take out the total runs made by the team in each match.)

Match 1 against Pakistan (we have already worked this out during our initial understanding of the set): Total runs = 220, V + Y + K = 130 + 40 + 28 = 198. Remaining runs = 220 – 198 = 22

Match 2 against South Africa: Total runs = 250, S + K + R = 75 + 51 + 49 = 175. Remaining runs = 250 – 175 = 75

Match 3 against Australia: Total runs = 240, Y + R + S = 87 + 55 + 50 =192. Remaining runs = 240 – 192 = 48.

The following table can then be constructed:

TABLE 2.12

Name	Match 1	Match 2	Match 3	R-Index	M-Index
Virender	130	0–48	0–48	82–130	0–48
Yuvraj	40	0–48	87	47–87	40–48
Kaif	28	51	0–48	23–51	28–48
Rahul	0–22	49	55	33–55	49
Saurav	0–22	75	50	53–75	50

(From the table it can be seen that the least R-Index can be for Kaif, Yuvraj or Rahul. Under no circumstance can Saurav or Virender claim the least R-Index.)

23. How many players amongst those listed definitely scored less than Yuvraj in the tournament?
(a) 0 (b) 1
(c) 2 (d) More than 2

Taking the scores derived in the table for the first question we get:

TABLE 2.13

Name	Match 1	Match 2	Match 3	Total Runs
Virender	130	0–48	0–48	130–226
Yuvraj	40	0–48	87	127–175
Kaif	28	51	0–48	79–127
Rahul	0–22	49	55	104–126
Saurav	0–22	75	50	125–147

Yuvraj has scored a minimum of 127 runs. Only Rahul has definitely scored less than Yuvraj. Hence, option (b) is correct.

24. Which of the players had the best M-index from the tournament?
(a) Rahul (b) Saurav
(c) Virender (d) Yuvraj

Going back to the table drawn while answering the first question, we get that the best M-index must be for Saurav. Option (b) is correct.

25. For how many Indian players is possible to calculate the exact M-index?
(a) 0 (b) 1
(c) 2 (d) More than 2

Going back to the table drawn while answering the first question, we get that the best M-index can be calculated for Saurav and Rahul, i.e., for two players. Hence, option (c) is correct.

Directions for Questions 26 to 29: Answer these questions based on the data provided in the figure below.

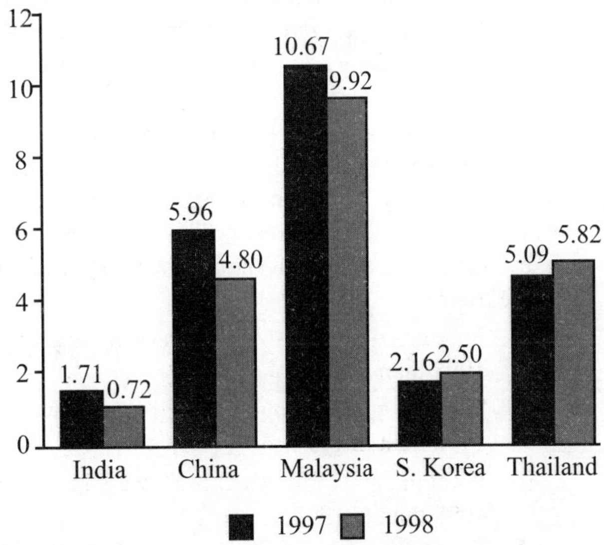

FIGURE 2.4

FEI for a country in a year, is the ratio (expressed as a percentage) of its foreign equity inflows to its GDP. The following figure displays the FEIs for selected Asian countries for the years 1997 and 1998.

26. The country with the largest change in FEI in 1998 relative to its FEI in 1997 is
(a) India (b) China
(c) Malaysia (d) Thailand

Sol. *(a) The largest relative change (which should be interpreted as the largest percentage change here) can be seen visually to be for India – 1.71 to 0.72 which is a change of over 50 per cent of its original value. No other country's percentage change (relative change) is as high as this.*

27. Based on the data provided it can be concluded that
    (a) Absolute value of foreign equity inflows in 1998 was higher than that in 1997 for both Thailand and South Korea.
    (b) Absolute value of foreign equity inflows was higher in 1998 for Thailand and lower for China than corresponding values in 1997.
    (c) Absolute value of foreign equity inflows was higher in 1998 for both Thailand and China than their corresponding values in 1997.
    (d) None of the above can be inferred.

Sol. *(d) Before you solve this question, you should realise that we are only given the values of the FEI ratios (Foreign Equity inflows/GDP) for each of these countries for 2 years. Hence, we are not in any position to comment on the absolute changes in the Foreign Equity Inflows for any country. Since all the three options are talking about absolute value changes in the Foreign Equity Inflows–we cannot make any of those conclusions. Thus, option (d) is the correct answer.*

28. It is known that China's GDP in 1998 was 7 per cent higher than its value in 1997, while India's GDP grew by 2 per cent during the same period. The GDP of South Korea, on the other hand, fell by 5 per cent. Which of the following statements are true?
    I. Foreign equity inflows to China were higher in 1998 than in 1997.
    II. Foreign equity inflows to China were lower in 1998 than in 1997.
    III. Foreign equity inflows to India were higher in 1998 than in 1997.
    IV. Foreign equity inflows to South Korea decreased in 1998 relative to 1997.
    V. Foreign equity inflows to South Korea increased in 1998 relative to 1997.
    (a) I, III & IV (b) II, III & IV
    (c) I, III & V (d) II & V

Sol. *(d) Since India's GDP has gone up by 2 per cent the effect on the FEI ratio for India would be that the denominator would grow by 2 per cent. A 2 per cent increase in the denominator would mean approximately 1.8 per cent decrease in the ratio. But the ratio for India has fallen from 1.71 to 0.72 – a drop of almost 57–58 per cent approximately. This can only happen if the numerator has also gone down. i.e., India's Foreign Equity Inflows in 1998 were lower than the corresponding value in 1997. Thus, statement III is false.*

A similar analysis for China shows that since the GDP of China has gone up by 7 per cent, we expect a 6.7 per cent (approx) decrease in its FEI ratio due to the denominator alone. However, looking at the FEI ratio values for China in 1997 and 1998 we see that the values have gone down from 5.96 to 4.80 a drop which is greater than a 6.7 per cent drop – this implies a drop in the numerator i.e., Foreign Equity inflows for China in 1998 were lower than the corresponding value in 1997. Thus, statement II is true and statement I is false.

At this stage we can conclude from the options that the correct answer to the question would be option (d).

For South Korea, you can check by a similar logic that the Foreign equity inflows for South Korea actually increased from 1997 to 1998.

29. China's foreign equity inflows in 1998 were 10 times that into India. It can be concluded that:
    (a) China's GDP in 1998 was 40 per cent higher than that of India.
    (b) China's GDP in 1998 was 70 per cent higher than that of India.
    (c) China's GDP in 1998 was 50 per cent higher than that of India.
    (d) No inference can be drawn about relative magnitudes of China's and India's GDPs.

Sol. *(c) Let India's Foreign Equity Inflows = x, then China's Foreign Equity Inflows = 10x.*

Then: $FEI_{1998(India)} = 0.72 = y/GDP_{1998(India)}$ *and*

$FEI_{1998(China)} = 4.8 = 10y/GDP_{1998(China)}$

$FEI_{1998(India)}/FEI_{1998(China)} = 0.72/4.8 = GDP_{1998(China)}/10\ GDPIndia \rightarrow GDP_{1998(China)}/GDP_{1998(India)} = 7.2/4.8 = 1.5$

Thus, we can conclude that China's GDP in 1998 was 50 per cent higher than India's GDP in that year.

Directions for Questions 30 to 33: Answer these questions based on the table below:

The table shows trends in external transactions of Indian corporate sector during the period 1993–94 to 1997–98. In addition, the following definitions hold good:

Sales, Imports and Exports, respectively denote the sales, imports and exports in year *i*.

Deficit in year *i*, Deficit = Imports – Exports

Deficit Intensity in year *i*, $DI_i = Deficit_i/Sales$

Growth rate of deficit intensity in year i, $GDI_i = (DI - D_{i-1})/DI_{i-1}$

Further, note that all imports are classified as either raw material or capital goods.

TABLE 2.14 Trends in External Transactions of Indian Corporate Sector (All figures in %)

Year	1997–98	1996–97	1995–96	1994–95	1993–94
Export Intensity*	9.2	8.2	7.9	7.5	7.3
Import Intensity*	14.2	16.2	15.5	13.8	12.4
Imported raw material/Total cost of raw material	20.2	19.2	17.6	16.3	16.0
Imported capital goods/ Gross fixed assets	17.6	9.8	11.8	16.3	19.5

*Ratio of Exports (or Imports) to Sales

30. The highest growth rate in deficit intensity was recorded in:
    (a) 1994–95
    (b) 1995–96
    (c) 1996–97
    (d) 1997–98

Sol. *(a) The Deficit Intensity would be (Import Intensity - Export Intensity).*
The series of values for the same would be: 1993–94 = 5.1, 1994–95 = 6.3, 1995–96 = 7.6, 1996–97 = 8 and 1997–98 = 5.
The highest growth rate in the same is seen in the year 1994–95 (over 23 per cent) and is higher than 1995–96 (20-21 per cent). In the other two years the values are either too small or negative and hence, need not be calculated.

31. The value of the highest growth rate in deficit intensity is approximately:
    (a) 8.45% (b) 2.15%
    (c) 33.3% (d) 23.5%

Sol. *(d) We have already done this calculation in the previous question. 5.1 → 6.3 = growth rate of 23.5 per cent approx.*

32. In 1997–98 the total cost of raw materials is estimated as 50 per cent of sales of that year. The turnover of gross fixed assets, defined as the ratio of sales to gross fixed assets, in 1997–98 is, approximately
    (a) 33
    (b) 4.3
    (c) 0.33
    (d) Not possible to determine

Sol. *(b) For the year 1997–98, the following thought process would give the required answer:*
Imported Raw Material/Total Cost of Raw Materials = Imported Raw Material/0.5 Sales = 20.2 →
Imported raw material = 10.1 Sales (1)
The Import intensity = Import/Sales = 14.2 →
Import = 14.2 Sales (2)
But we are given that Import = Imported Raw Material + Imported Capital Goods = 14.2% of Sales
14.2 = 10.1 Sales + Imported Capital Goods →
Imported Capital Goods = 4.1% of Sales.
Then we are given that, Imported Capital Goods/ Gross Fixed Assets = 17.6 → 4.1 Sales/Gross Fixed Assets =17.6 → Sales/Gross Fixed Assets = 17.6/4.1 = 4.3 (required answer)

33. Which of the following statements can be inferred to be true from the given data?
    (a) During the five year period between 1993–94 and 1997–98, exports have increased every year.
    (b) During the five year period between 1993–94 and 1997–98, imports have decreased every year.
    (c) Deficit in 1997–98 was lower than that in 1993–94.
    (d) Deficit intensity has increased every year between 1993–94 and 1996–97.

Sol. (d) It is clear from the given data, that since we only know ratios, we are not in a position to answer any questions about absolute value changes for any individual component of the ratio. Thus, we are not in a position to conclude anything about the increase/ decrease in exports or imports or Deficits. Hence, we can safely delete options (a), (b) and (c). From the values of deficit intensity calculated for question 76, we see that deficit intensity has grown every year from 1993–94 to 1996–97. Thus, option (d) is correct.

Directions for Questions 34 to 39: Answer these questions based on the data given below:

The figures below present annual growth rate, expressed as the percentage change relative to the previous year, in four sectors of the economy of the Republic of Reposia during the 9-year period from 1990 to 1998. Assume that the index of production for each of the four sectors is set at 100 in 1989. Further, the four sectors are set at 100 in 1989. Furthermore, the four sectors: Manufacturing, Mining and Quarrying, Electricity and Chemicals, respectively, constituted 20 per cent, 15 per cent, 10 per cent and 15 per cent of total industrial production in 1989.

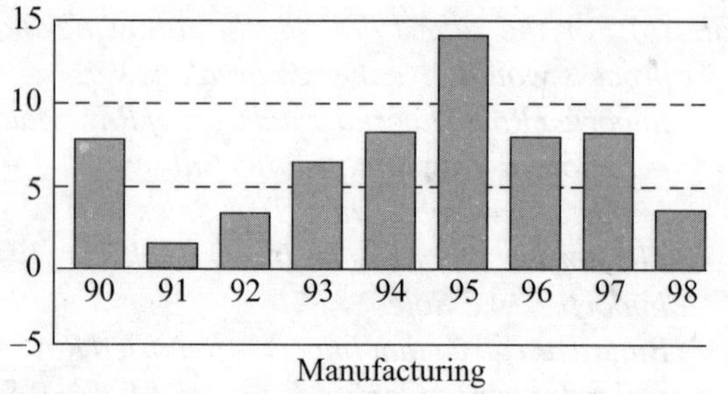

FIGURE 2.5(A)

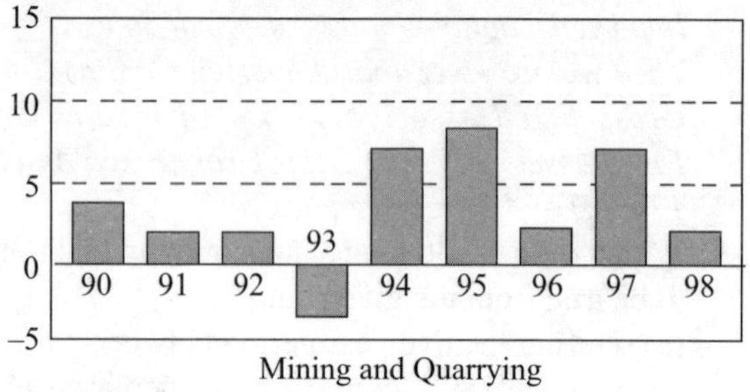

FIGURE 2.5(B)

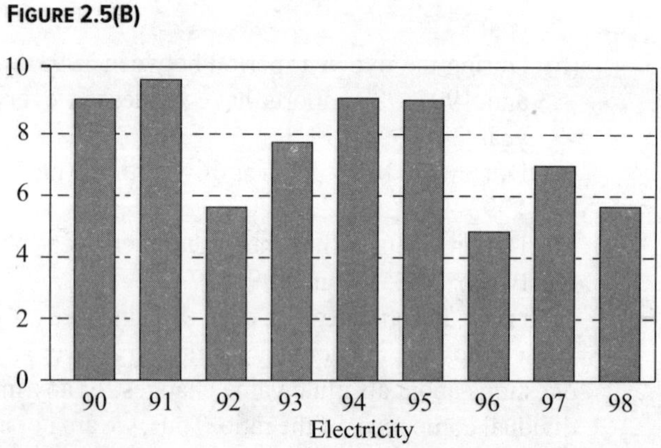

FIGURE 2.5(C)

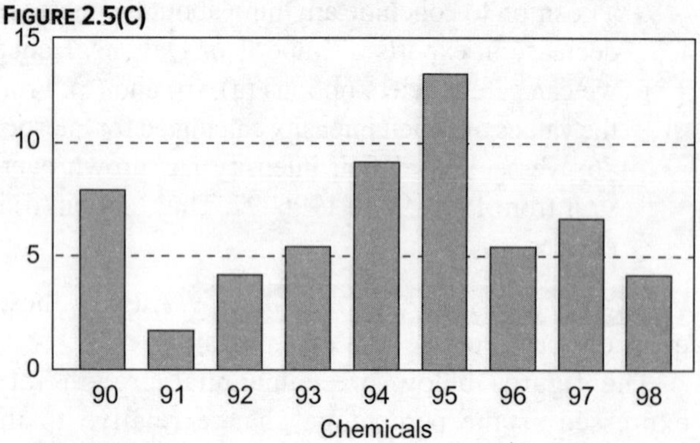

FIGURE 2.5(D)

34. Which is the sector with the highest growth during the period from 1989 to 1998?
(a) Manufacturing
(b) Mining and Quarrying
(c) Electricity
(d) Chemicals

Sol. *(c) It is evident from a visual inspection of the four charts given in the question that the highest growth rate is in the Electricity sector.*

35. The overall growth rate in 1991 of the four sectors together is approximately:
(a) 10% (b) 1%
(c) 5% (d) 1.5%

Sol. *(d) The overall growth rate of the four sectors would be given by:*
$0.2 \times 1 + 0.15 \times 1 + 0.1 \times 9 + 0.15 \times 1 = 1.5\%$

36. When was the highest level of production in the manufacturing sector achieved during the nine-year period 1990–1998?
(a) 1998 (b) 1995
(c) 1990 (d) Cannot be determined

Sol. *(a) Since the manufacturing sector has always grown year on year, it is obvious that the highest level of production in this sector in the given period would be seen in the last year, i.e., 1998.*

37. When was the lowest level of production of the mining and quarrying sector achieved during the nine year period 1990–1998?
(a) 1996 (b) 1993
(c) 1990 (d) Cannot be determined

Sol. *(c) If we assume production of the Mining and Quarrying sector in 1989 to be 100, then it grows by 4% approximately in 1990, then by 1%, then by 2% and then goes down by approximately 4% in 1993. After that it consistently increases. It is obvious that the least level of production would be in 1990.*

38. The percentage increase of production in the four sectors, namely, manufacturing, mining & quarrying, electricity and chemicals, taken together, in 1994, relative to 1989, is approximately:
(a) 25 (b) 20
(c) 50 (d) 40

39. It is known that the index of total industrial production in 1994 was 50 per cent more than that in 1989. As a result, the percentage increase in production between 1989 and 1994 in sectors other than the four listed above is:
(a) 57.5 (b) 87.5
(c) 127.5 (d) 47.5

Sol. *38 and 39. In order to solve question 38, we would need to calculate the individual growths of each of the 4 sectors over the 5 year period – using compounding and then take a weighted average of the 4 growths thus obtained—definitely something you should not solve, since the amount of calculations involved in this question is almost impossible. (It might take you 4–5 minutes to do it with a calculator.)*

However, if you look at what the next question is asking and try to match the two questions, you realise that the entire industrial production in 1989 would be divided into two broad parts—60% comprising these four sectors (@ 20%, 15%, 10% and 15% respectively as given in the data) and 40% comprising others.

Thus, 100% (total Industrial Production) = 60% (4 given sectors) + 40% (Others)

We also know that between 1989 and 1994, the growth in the total industrial production is 50% (given in question 39).

Thus, the vision we should have is:

100 = 60 + 40

150 = ?? + ??

The two values represented by question marks in the above equation, would help us find the percentage growth in the 4 sectors combined between 1989 and 1994 (answer to question 38) and the percentage growth in the other sectors during the same period (answer to question 39).

From this realisation, we can move to the options:

Checking option 1 from question 38: If there is 25 per cent growth in these four sectors combined-

TABLE 2.15(A)

Year	Total	Four Listed Sectors	Other Sectors
1989	100	60	40
1994	150	75	75
Growth Rate	50%	25% (from option 1)	Calculated as 87.5% – option (b) in question 39.

If you were to check for any of the other three options for question 38, you would not get a matching value in the options for question 39 and hence we can conclude that the answers are:

38. *1*
39. *2*

For example if we check for option (b) of question 38, i.e., 20% growth in the four listed sectors combined.

TABLE 2.15(B)

Year	Total	Four Listed Sectors	Other Sectors
1989	100	60	40
1994	150	72	78
Growth Rate value is not	50%	20% (from option (a) of question 38)	Calculated as 95% – This is not present in the options for question 39.

Thus, we reject option (b).

Similarly option (c) can be rejected through the following calculation:

TABLE 2.15(C)

Year	Total	Four Listed Sectors	Other Sectors
1989	100	60	40
1994	150	90	60
Growth Rate value is not	50%	50% (from option (c) of question 84)	Calculated as 50% – This is not present in the options for question 85.

Thus, we reject option (c).

For Option (d) of question 38:

TABLE 2.15(D)

Year	Total	Four Listed Sectors	Other Sectors
1989	100	60	40
1994	150	84	66
Growth Rate value is not	50%	40% (from option (d) of question 38)	Calculated as 65%–This is not present in the options for question 39.

Thus, option (d) is also rejected.

Directions for Questions 40 to 47: Answer these questions based on the table given below.

The following table shows the revenue and expenses in millions of Euros (European currency) associated with REPSOL YPF company's oil and gas activities in operations in different parts of the world for the year 1998–2000.

TABLE 2.16 REPSOL YPF'S Operations of Oil and Gas Producing Activities

	CATEGORY								
	Year	World Total	Spain	North Africa & Middle East	Argentina	Rest of Latin America	Far East	North Sea	Rest of the World
Revenue	1998	916	70	366	281	34	82	78	5
	1999	3374	55	666	2006	115	301	140	91
	2000	8328	394	1290	5539	482	603	0	20
Expenses	1998	668	39	255	187	57	63	52	15
	1999	1999	48	325	1168	131	204	65	58

CATEGORY									
	Year	World Total	Spain	North Africa & Middle East	Argentina	Rest of Latin America	Far East	North Sea	Rest of the World
	2000	3709	43	530	2540	252	311	0	33
Income	1998	248	31	111	94	−23	19	26	−10
Before Tax	1999	1375	7	341	838	−16	97	75	33
and Charges	2000	4619	351	760	2999	230	292	0	−13
Taxes and	1998	152	6	104	33	−3	9	6	−3
charges	1999	561	3	169	338	−6	39	21	−3
	2000	1845	126	404	1150	61	103	0	1
Income	1998	96	25	7	61	−20	10	20	−7
After Taxes	1999	814	4	172	500	−10	58	54	26
and Charges	2000	2774	225	356	1849	−169	189	0	−14

40. How many operations (Spain, North Africa and Middle East, ...) of the company accounted for less than 5 per cent of the total revenue earned in the year 1999?
(a) 2 (b) 3
(c) 4 (d) none of these

Sol. *(c) The benchmark value (5 per cent of total world in 1999) would be around 166. There are 4 operations below this value.*

41. How many operations (Spain, North Africa and Middle East, ...) of the company witnessed more than 200 per cent revenue from the year 1999 to 2000?
(a) 1 (b) 2
(c) 3 (d) none of these

Sol. *(b) We are looking for operations whose revenue went up by more than 200 per cent, which means that we are looking for revenue which is three times the original revenue. There are only two operations – Spain and Rest of Latin America.*

42. How many operations registered a sustained yearly increase in income before taxes and charges from 1998 to 2000?
(a) 3 (b) 4
(c) 5 (d) none of these

Sol. *(c) There are five such operations.*

43. Ignoring the loss making operations of the company in 1998, for how many operations was the percentage increase in net income before taxes and charges higher than the average from 1998 to 1999?
(a) 0 (b) 1
(c) 2 (d) none of these

Sol. *(b) It is only true for one operation Argentina.*

44. If profitability is defined as the ratio of net income after taxes and charges to expenses, which of the following statements is true?
(a) The Far East operations witnessed its highest profitability in 1998.
(b) The North Sea operations increased its profitability from 1998 to 1999.
(c) The operations in Argentina witnessed a decrease in profitability from 1998 to 1999.
(d) Both b and c are true.

Sol. *(b) It can be easily seen that the North Sea operation has gone up from 20/52 to 54/65 from 1998 to 1999.*

45. In the year 2000, which amongst the following countries had the best profitability?
(a) North Africa and Middle East
(b) Spain
(c) Rest of Latin America
(d) Far East

Sol. *(b) Profitability as defined in the previous question is highest for Spain in 2000 (225/43).*

46. If efficiency is defined as the ratio of revenue to expenses, which operation was the least efficient in the year 2000?
(a) Spain (b) Argentina
(c) Far East (d) None of these

Sol. *(d) The rest of world operation can be seen to be the least efficient (20/58).*

47. Of the following statements which one is not true?
(a) The operations in Spain had the best efficiency in 2000.
(b) The Far East operations witnessed an efficiency improvement from 1999 to 2000.
(c) The North Sea operations witnessed an efficiency improvement from 1998 to 1999.
(d) In the year 1998, the operations in Rest of Latin America were the least efficient.

Sol. *(d) In 1998, the Rest of the World operations are more inefficient than Rest of Latin America. Hence, the fourth option is not true.*

Directions for Questions 48 to 52: Answer the questions on the basis of the following information.

Recently, the answers of a test held nationwide were leaked to a group of unscrupulous people. The investigative agency has arrested the mastermind and nine other people A, B, C, D, E, F, G, H and I in this matter. Interrogating them, the following facts have been obtained regarding their operation. Initially the mastermind obtains the correct answer-key. All the others create their answer-keys in the following manner.

They obtain the answer key from one or two people who already possess the same. These people are called his/her 'sources'. If the person has two sources, then he/she compares the answer-keys obtained from both sources. If the key to a question from both sources is identical, it is copied, otherwise it is left blank. If the person has only one source, he/she copies the source's answers into his/her copy. Finally, each person compulsorily replaces one of the answers (not a blank one) with a wrong answer in his/her answer-key.

The paper contained 200 questions; so the investigative agency has ruled out the possibility of two or more of them introducing wrong answers to the same question. The investigative agency has a copy of the correct answer key and has tabulated the following data. This data represents question numbers.

TABLE 2.17 Answer Key

Name	Wrong Answer(s)	Blank Answer(s)
A	46	----
B	96	46, 90, 25
C	27, 56	17, 46, 90
D	17	------
E	46, 90	------
F	14, 46	92, 90
G	25	------
H	46, 92	------
I	27	17, 46, 90

Sol. *The first thing you need to understand while trying this question is that there are essentially two ways of forming an answer key:*

1. ***If you have one source*** *– All you do is carry forward that source's answer key and introduce 1 error from your own side in it. Thus, if the mastermind is your key then you would have 1 error in your answer key – which you would have introduced yourself. (**Note:** this is the only way of someone having an answer key with no blanks and 1 wrong answer only)*

   Similarly, if a person had a source who had 1 wrong answer in his answer key – you would have 2 wrong answers – 1 carried over and another one introduced by you.

   Thus, in essence you would carry forward the entire answer key of your source (blanks and wrongs as it is) and add one wrong answer of your own.

2. ***If you have two sources –***

   (a) ***Blank introduced*** *– If you have two different answers for the same question in the answer keys of the two sources. This means that if for one answer, one of the two sources had a right answer and the other had a wrong answer, then a blank would be introduced. Even if one of them had a blank and the other one had a correct or a wrong answer, it would still be a blank.*

   (b) Wrong answer carried forward: If both sources had the same wrong answer, that wrong answer would be carried forward.

   And according to the basic situation of the question, one new wrong answer of his own would also be carried forward.

The following table shows the first set of deductions:

TABLE 2.18(A)

Name	Wrong Answer(s)	Blank Answer(s)	Deduction About Source	Deduction About Wrong Answer Introduced
A	46	—	Mastermind	46
B	96	46, 90, 25		
C	27, 56	17, 46, 90		
D	17	—	Mastermind	17
E	46, 90	—	Single Source A	90
F	14, 46	92, 90		
G	25	—	Mastermind	25
H	46, 92	—	Single Source A	92
I	27	17, 46, 90		

We now need to think of the remaining people in the group:

B—His answer key is possible if his sources are E and G. In such a case, he would get blanks for 25, 46 and 90 (since the answers would be different for these questions in both the sources).

New wrong answer introduced would be 96.

F—His answer key is possible if his sources are E and H. This would give us blank answers as 90 and 92, the wrong answer 46 would be carried forward and 14 would be the new wrong answer introduced by him.

The table would now look like:

TABLE 2.18(B)

Name	Wrong Answer(s)	Blank Answer(s)	Deduction About Source	Deduction About Wrong Answer Introduced
A	46	—	Mastermind	46
B	96	46, 90, 25	Two Sources: E and G	
C	27, 56	17, 46, 90		
D	17	—	Mastermind	17
E	46, 90	—	Single Source A	90
F	14, 46	92, 90	Two Sources E and H	
G	25	—	Mastermind	25
H	46, 92	—	Single Source A	92
I	27	17, 46, 90		

We, now, need to think about C and I.

Looking at C and I's answer keys, it is evident that C would have I as a source.

I's answer key can be explained as: Two sources D and E.

TABLE 2.18(C)

Name	Wrong Answer(s)	Blank Answer(s)	Deduction About Source	Deduction About Wrong Answer Introduced
A	46	—	Mastermind	46
B	96	46, 90, 25	Two Sources: E and G	96
C	27, 56	17, 46, 90	Single source I	56
D	17	—	Mastermind	17
E	46, 90	—	Single Source A	90
F	14, 46	92, 90	Two Sources E and H	14
G	25	—	Mastermind	25
H	46, 92	—	Single Source A	92
I	27	17, 46, 90	Two sources D and E	27

The answers can be read off the table.

48. Which one amongst the following must have two sources?
   (a) A (b) B
   (c) C (d) D

Sol. (B (Option b).)

49. How many people (excluding the mastermind) needed to make answer-keys before C could make his answer-key?
   (a) 2
   (b) 3
   (c) 4
   (d) 5

Sol. (c) For C to make his answer key, I has to make this answer key. For I, D and E have to make their answer key. For E to make his answer key, A should make his answer key before that. Thus, A, D, E and I should make their answer keys before C makes his. Thus, option 3 is correct.

50. Both G and H were sources to
   (a) F
   (b) B
   (c) 1
   (d) none of the nine

Sol. (d) None of the nine (Option d).

51. Which of the following statements is true?
   (a) C introduced the wrong answer to question 27.
   (b) E introduced the wrong answer to question 46.
   (c) F introduced the wrong answer to question 14.
   (d) H introduced the wrong answer to question 46.

Sol. *(c) F introduced the wrong answer to question 14 (Option c).*

52. Which of the following two groups of people had identical sources?
   (I) A, D and G (II) E and H
   (a) Only (I)
   (b) Only (II)
   (c) Neither (I) nor (II)
   (d) Both (I) and (II)

Sol. (d) A, D and G's source was the mastermind. E and H's source was A. Thus, option (d) is correct.

Directions for Questions 53 to 56: Answer the questions on the basis of the following table that lists countries region-wise. Each region-wise list is sorted, first by birth rate and then alphabetically by name of country. We now wish to merge the region-wise list into one consolidated list and provide overall rankings to each country, based first on birth rate and then on death rate. Thus, if some countries have the same birth rate, then the country with a lower death rate will be ranked higher. Further, countries having identical birth and death rates will get the same rank. For example, if two countries are tied for the third position, then both will be given rank 3, while the next country (in the ordered list) will be ranked 5.

TABLE 2.19

Rank	Country	Birth Rate	Death Rate	Region	Rank	Country	Birth Rate	Death Rate	Region
1	South Africa	36	12	Africa	1	Germany (FRG)	12	12	Europe
2	Egypt	39	13	Africa	2	Austria	12	13	Europe
3	Cameroon	42	22	Africa	3	Belgium	12	12	Europe
4	Mozambique	45	18	Africa	4	Germany (DRG)	12	14	Europe
5	Zaire	45	18	Africa	5	Sweden	12	11	Europe
6	Ghana	46	14	Africa	6	Switzerland	12	9	Europe
7	Angola	47	23	Africa	7	UK	12	12	Europe
8	Madagascar	47	22	Africa	8	Netherlands	13	8	Europe
9	Morocco	47	16	Africa	9	France	14	11	Europe
10	Tanzania	47	17	Africa	10	Italy	14	10	Europe
11	Ethiopia	45	23	Africa	11	Greece	16	9	Europe
12	Ivory Coast	43	23	Africa	12	Bulgaria	17	10	Europe
13	Rhodesia	48	14	Africa	13	Hungary	18	12	Europe
14	Uganda	48	17	Africa	14	Spain	18	8	Europe
15	Nigeria	49	22	Africa	15	USSR	18	9	Europe
16	Saudi Arabia	49	19	Africa	16	Yugoslavia	18	8	Europe
17	Sudan	49	17	Africa	17	Czech Republic	19	11	Europe
18	Algeria	50	16	Africa	18	Portugal	19	10	Europe
19	Kenya	50	14	Africa	19	Romania	19	10	Europe
20	Upper Volta	50	28	Africa	20	Poland	20	9	Europe
1	Japan	16	6	Asia	1	USA	15	9	N. America
2	Korea (ROK)	26	6	Asia	2	Canada	16	7	N. America
3	Sri Lanka	26	9	Asia	3	Cuba	20	6	N. America
4	Taiwan	26	5	Asia	4	Mexico	40	7	N. America
5	Malaysia	30	6	Asia	1	Australia	16	8	Pacific
6	China	31	11	Asia	2	Philippines	34	10	Pacific
7	Thailand	34	10	Asia	3	Indonesia	38	16	Pacific
8	Turkey	34	12	Asia	1	Argentina	22	10	S. America
9	India	36	15	Asia	2	Chile	22	7	S. America
10	Burma	38	15	Asia	3	Colombia	34	10	S. America
11	Iran	42	12	Asia	4	Brazil	36	10	S. America
12	Vietnam	42	17	Asia	5	Venezuela	36	6	S. America
13	Korea (DPRK)	43	14	Asia	6	Guatemala	40	14	S. America
14	Pakistan	44	12	Asia	7	Peru	40	13	S. America
15	Nepal	46	20	Asia	8	Ecuador	42	11	S. America
16	Bangladesh	47	19	Asia					
17	Syria	47	14	Asia					
18	Iraq	48	14	Asia					
19	Afghanistan	52	30	Asia					

Sol. *In order to solve this question, you need to understand the process for making the consolidated list. The logic, as explained in the question is, that while making the consolidated list, we would first take the least birth rate as the first criteria. In the case of two or more countries having the same birth rate, then we would look at the death rates in those countries to act as a tie breaker – the country with the least death rate getting the lowest rank amongst the countries which are tied for rankings on the basis of their birth rates. Note that the usage of the death rate is only a tie breaker – in the event of countries tying on the basis of birth rates.*

The other thing you need to take into account is that if there is a tie between two or more countries on the basis of both the birth rate and the death rate—then, they share the same rank and the next rank is not given to any country.

53. In the consolidated list, what would be the overall rank of the Philippines?
    (a) 32 (b) 33
    (c) 34 (d) 35

Sol. *(b) The Philippines has a birth rate of 34 and a death rate of 10. Thus, in order to find the position of Philippines in the consolidated list – we should first look at the countries which have a birth rate of less than 34. There are 20 countries in Europe, 3 in N America, 0 in Africa, 6 in Asia, 1 in Pacific and 2 in S. America which have birth rates below 34. (A total of 32 countries). For the 33rd rank we need to check between Philippines (34, 10), Colombia (34, 10), Thailand (34, 10) and Turkey (34, 12). It is evident that there would be a tie between Colombia, Philippines and Thailand for the 33rd position (Option b).*

54. In the consolidated list, how many countries would rank below Spain and above Taiwan?
    (a) 9 (b) 8
    (c) 7 (d) 6

Sol. *(a) Spain (18, 8) would be ranked 17th jointly with Yugoslavia, while Taiwan (26, 5) would be ranked 28th. Thus, there would be 9 countries below Spain and above Taiwan in the consolidated list (Option a).*

55. In the consolidated list, which country ranks 37th?
    (a) South Africa (b) Brazil
    (c) Turkey (d) Venezuela

Sol. *(d) We already know that Philippines, Colombia and Thailand jointly stand 33rd (34,10) and Turkey would be 36th (34,12). The next country would be Venezuela (37th) (Option d).*

56. In the consolidated list, how many countries in Asia will rank lower than every country in South America, but higher than at least one country in Africa?
    (a) 8 (b) 7
    (c) 6 (d) 5

Sol. *(a) The lowest country in S. America is at 42,11. Thus we need to look at countries in Asia below 42,11. Starting from Iran (42,12) there are 9 such countries. However, out of these 9, Afghanistan does not satisfy the condition of being higher than at least one of the African countries. (Option 8).*

Directions for Questions 57 to 59: Answer the questions on the basis of the following information.

In a Decathlon, the events are 100 m, 400 m, 100 m hurdles, 1500 m, High jump, Pole vault, Long jump, Discus, Shot Put and Javelin. The performance in the first four of these events is consolidated into Score 1, the next three into Score 2 and the last three into Score 3. Each such consolidation is obtained by giving appropriate positive weights to individual events. The final score is simply the total of these three scores. The athletes with the highest, second highest and the third highest final scores receive the gold, silver and bronze medals, respectively. The table below gives the scores and performances of 19 top athletes in this event.

TABLE 2.20

Name	Country	Final Score	Score 1	Score 2	Score 3	100 M	High Jump	Pole Vault
Eduard Hamalainen	BLS	8802	491	5322	2989	10.74	2.08	4.8
Michael Smith	CAN	8855	174	5274	3407	11.23	1.97	4.9
Tomas Dvorak	CZE	8796	499	5169	3128	10.63	1.91	4.7
Uwe Frimuth	DDR	8799	441	5491	3124	11.06	1.97	4.8
Torsten Voss	DDR	8880	521	5234	2868	10.69	2.10	5.1
Erki Nool	EST	8768	408	5553	2808	10.71	1.99	5.4
Christian Plaziat	FRA	8775	563	5430	2781	10.72	2.10	5.0
Jurgen Hingsen	FRG	8792	451	5223	3033	10.95	2.00	4.9
Siegfried Wentz	FRG	8856	470	5250	3137	10.85	2.05	4.8
Guido Kratschmer	FRG	8861	575	5308	3064	10.58	2.00	4.6
Daley Thompson	GBR		582		3003	10.55	2.11	4.6
Frank Busemann	GER	8905	568	5392	2945	10.60	2.04	4.8
Alexandr Apaichev	SOV	8803	492	5370	3115	10.92	1.95	4.8
Grigory Degtyarov	SOV	8823	339	5196	3114	11.05	2.08	4.9
Robert Zmelik	TCH	8832	494	5455	2883	10.78	2.06	5.1
Dave Johnson	USA	8811	366	5370	3114	10.78	2.10	5.0
Steve Fritz	USA	8827	427	5163	3119	10.75	2.04	5.0
Bruce Jenner	USA	8846	483	5280	3200	10.94	2.03	4.8
Dan O'Brein	USA	8897	408	5331	3120	10.36	2.09	4.8

57. The athletes from FRG and USA decided to run a 4×100 m relay race for their respective countries with the country having three athletes borrowing the athlete from CZE. Assume that all the athletes ran their stretch of the relay race at the same speed as in Decathlon event. How much more time did the FRG relay team take as compared to the USA team?
    (a) 0.18
    (b) 0.28
    (c) 0.78
    (d) 0.00

Sol. *(a) From the table, it is clear that the FRG team has 3 athletes, while the USA team has 4. Thus, the FRG team would borrow a runner from the CZE team. The FRG team would take 10.95 + 10.85 + 10.58 + 10.63 second, while the USA team would take 10.78 + 10.75 + 10.94 + 10.36 seconds. The difference in time is equivalent to + 17 + 10 – 36 + 27 to be written as + 0.17 + 0.10 – 0.36 + 0.27 seconds = 0.18 seconds: (Option a).*

58. What is the least that Daley Thomson must get in Score 2 that ensures him a bronze medal?
    (a) 5309
    (b) 5296
    (c) 5271
    (d) 5270

Sol. *(b) In order to get a bronze medal, Daley Thomson should get an aggregate of at least 8881 (>Torsten Voss). Daley Thomson's score is 582 + 3003 + Unknown Score 2. This sum should be equal to 8881 at least, for him to get a bronze medal. Hence, 8881 – 3585 = 5296 (option b).*

59. At least how many competitors (excluding Daley Thompson) must Michael Smith have out-jumped in the long jump event?
    (a) 1
    (b) 2
    (c) 3
    (d) 4

Sol. *(d) Michael Smith scores 5274 in Score 2 (which is formed on the basis of high jump, pole vault and long jump). His high jump is of 1.97m and pole vault of 4.9m. In order to find the number of athletes who he must have out-jumped in long jump, we need to look for athletes who had greater values in high jump and pole vault than Michael Smith, yet who got a lower overall score than Michael Smith in Score 2. Thus, we are looking for athletes who had less than 5274 in Score 2 and greater than or equal to 1.97 in high jump and 4.9 in pole vault.*

In visual terms, this can be represented as: Score 2 < 5274; High Jump > 1.97, Pole vault > 4.9

Torsten Voss, Jurgen Hingsen, Gregory Degtyarov and Steve Fritz satisfy all these conditions. Thus, the answer is four athletes (Option d).

Directions for Questions 60 to 63: Answer the questions on the basis of the information given below.

Purana and Naya are two brands of kitchen mixer-grinders available in the local market. Purana is an old brand that was introduced in 1990, while Naya was introduced in 1997. For both these brands, 20 per cent of the mixer-grinders bought in a particular year are disposed off as junk exactly two years later. It is known that 10 Purana mixer-grinders were disposed off in 1997. The following figure shows the number of Purana and Naya mixer-grinders in operation from 1995–2000 at the end of the year.

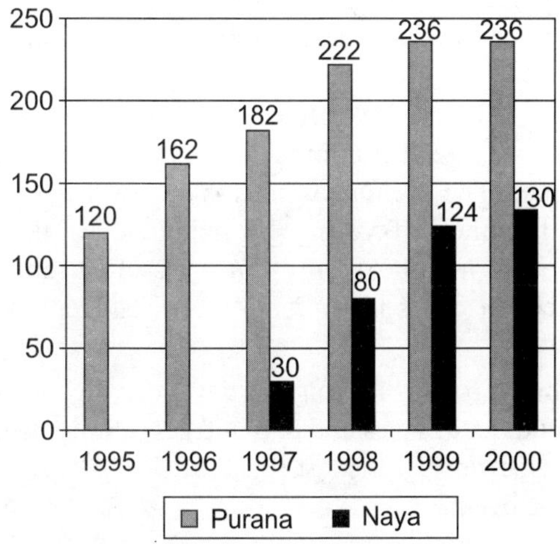

FIGURE 2.6

60. How many Naya mixer-grinders were disposed off by the end of 2000?
    (a) 10
    (b) 16
    (c) 22
    (d) Cannot be determined from the data

Sol. *(b) 20% of 1997 will be disposed off in 1999 and 20% of 1998 will be disposed off in 2000. Hence, 6 + 10 = 16*

61. How many Naya mixer-grinders were purchased in 1999?
    (a) 44
    (b) 50
    (c) 55
    (d) 64

Sol. *(b) 50 (As in 124 – 80 + 6)*

62. How many Purana mixer-grinders were disposed off in 2000?
    (a) 0
    (b) 5
    (c) 6
    (d) Cannot be determined from the data

Sol. *(d) Cannot be determined since this is asking the value for an even year.*

63. How many Purana mixer-grinders were purchased in 1999?
    (a) 20
    (b) 23
    (c) 50
    (d) Cannot be determined from the data

Sol. *(a) 20 (from the table and the logic 222 – 6 + purchases in 1999 = 236)*

Directions for Questions 64 to 67: Answer questions 64–67 on the basis of the information given below.

The year is 2089. Beijing, London, New York and Paris are in contention to host the 2096 Olympics. The eventual winner is determined through several rounds of voting by members of the IOC with each member representing a different city. All the four cities in contention are also represented in IOC.

- In any round of voting, the city receiving the lowest number of votes in that round gets eliminated. The survivor after the last round of voting gets to host the event.
- A member is allowed to cast votes for at most two different cities in all rounds of voting combined. (Hence, a member becomes ineligible to cast a vote in a given round if both the cities (s)he voted for in earlier rounds are out of contention in that round of voting.)
- A member is also ineligible to cast a vote in a round, if the city (s)he represents is in contention in that round of voting.
- As long as the member is eligible, (s)he must vote and vote for only one candidate city in any round of voting.

The following incomplete table shows the information on cities that received the maximum and minimum votes in different rounds, the number of votes cast in their favour and the total votes that were cast in those rounds.

TABLE 2.21

Round	Total Votes Cast	Maximum Votes Cast		Eliminated	
		City	No. of Votes	City	No. of Votes
1		London	30	New York	12
2	83	Paris	32	Beijing	21
3	75				

It is also known that:

- All those who voted for London and Paris in round one, continued to vote for the same cities in subsequent rounds, as long as these cities were in contention. Seventy five per cent of those who voted for Beijing in round one, voted for Beijing in round two as well.
- Those who voted for New York in round one, voted for either Beijing or Paris in round two.
- The difference in votes cast for the two contending cities in the last round was one.
- Fifty per cent of those who voted for Beijing in round one, voted for Paris in round three.

Sol. for 64 to 67: When you read the initial set of instructions, you would have realised that there are essentially two rules which are operating here in order to change the eligibility of a country's representative from voting.

From the language, "A member is allowed to cast a vote for at most two different cities in all rounds of voting combined" we can infer the following rule:

***Rule 1:** Making an eligible member ineligible: This would occur when a member votes for 1 city in the first round, and another in the second round and both these cities get eliminated before the third round. Looking at the table—an eligible member would become ineligible to vote only in case he has voted for New York in the first round and Beijing in the second round. This is the only way of making an eligible member ineligible to vote and hence, would only occur for some of those voters who voted for New York in the first round but shifted their votes to Beijing in the second round.*

This rule, when it is applied, would naturally reduce the number of voters who voted in a particular round, from the number who voted in the previous round. Also, the third round is the first time this rule would apply.

Rule 2: *Making an ineligible member eligible: This rule can be inferred from the language 'A member is also ineligible .....in that round of voting'. This obviously means that if I am a member whose city is in contention—then I cannot vote. However, if my city gets eliminated from the fray, then I would become eligible to vote.*

This rule would obviously apply only to the member from New York in the second round (as he would become eligible to vote in the second round) and to the member from Beijing in the third round as these are the only two cities that are becoming eligible from being ineligible.

Based on these deductions, we derive the following table:

TABLE 2.22

Round	Total Votes Cast	Maximum Votes Cast		Eliminated			
		City	No. of Votes	City	No. of Votes		
1	82	London	30	New York	12	Paris	Beijing
2	83	Paris	32	Beijing	21	London(30)	
3	75						

The following deductions can be drawn:

In the first round, the number of votes cast must be 82 (as in the second round the member from New York has become eligible to vote).

This means that Paris + Beijing must be 40 (for the first round).

Now, from the first clue we realise that since 75 per cent of the Beijing voters continued to vote for Beijing in the second round—the inference is that Beijing's number in the first round must be a multiple of 4. (Otherwise 75 per cent would not be an integer).

This gives us the following possibilities for Paris and Beijing in the first round:

TABLE 2.23

	Paris	Beijing
Possibility 1	24	16
Possibility 2	20	20
Possibility 3	16	24

At this point of time, you should also realise that the change from 83 votes cast in the second round and 75 votes cast in the third round would be due to two things:

The member from Beijing becoming eligible (thus, increasing the number of eligible voters to 84) and the members who shifted out of New York to Beijing becoming ineligible to vote in the third round. $83 + 1 - x = 75$. Thus, nine New York voters must have shifted to Beijing in the second round.

We also know that the London voters continued to vote for London – so London must have found no new voters. This means that Paris must have got three of the New York voters from the first round – voting for it in the second round.

We need to now try to fit in one of the above three possibilities to see which of them gives us the correct situation.

We also know that 75 per cent of Beijing's first round voters continued to vote for Beijing in the second round – thus 25 per cent of Beijing's first round voters must have shifted out of Beijing.

In the second round – there are a total of 12 New York voters, one member from New York and 25 per cent of Beijing's first round voters who are free to vote.

Since, Beijing got 21 votes, the only way this could have happened would be if Possibility 1 was correct in the above case. In such a case – the following numbers would work out:

London – 30 voters in first round, all carry over to the second round.

Beijing – 16 voters in the first round, of which 75 per cent (12) voted again for them + 9 voters who voted for New York in the first round shifted to Beijing in the second round = A total of 21 votes in the second round.

Paris – 24 votes in the first round + 4 voters who voted for Beijing in the first round voted for Paris in the second + 3 voters who voted for New York in the first round voted for Paris in the second + 1 member from New York who was not eligible to vote in the first round and becomes eligible to vote in the second round = A total of 32 votes in the second round.

In the third round, since there are 75 votes and the difference between the votes cast for the two cities was 1, it must be that the two cities got 38 and 37 votes respectively. What we need to see is, which city had how many votes?

For this purpose, we first need to understand how many free votes there are. An analysis of the second round would give us that.

Out of the 21 voters for Beijing in the second round, 9 have become ineligible to vote. So, there must be 12 free votes from there.

Also, the member from Beijing would be eligible to vote in the third round.

Thus, there would be a total of 13 free votes in the third round.

We need to match this deduction with the clues we are left with.

For this purpose, we have the last clue – 50 per cent of those who voted for Beijing in the first round voted for Paris in Round 3.

This means that Paris must have got an additional 4 voters from Beijing (as it already got four voters in the second round – and those four cannot move to London, as they have already voted for two cities in the first two rounds).

Thus, out of the 12 free votes available from Beijing's voters, 4 have gone to Paris and 8 must have shifted to London. Thus, London reaches 38 and consequently Paris must have got the member from Beijing to vote for it.

So, London = 30 votes in round 2 + 8 Beijing voters = 38 votes.

Paris = 32 votes in round 2 + 4 Beijing voters + 1 member from Beijing = 37 votes

64. What percentage of members from among those who voted for New York in round one, voted for Beijing in round two?
    (a) 33.33 (b) 50
    (c) 66.67 (d) 75

Sol. (d) 9 out of 12 = 75% (option d).

65. What is the number of votes cast for Paris in round one?
    (a) 16 (b) 18
    (c) 22 (d) 24

Sol. (d) 24 (option d).

66. What percentage of members from amongst those who voted for Beijing in round two and were eligible to vote in round three, voted for London?
    (a) 33.33 (b) 38.10
    (c) 50 (d) 66.67

Sol. (d) 8 out of 12 = 66.66% (option d).

67. Which of the following statements must be true?
    1. IOC member from New York must have voted for Paris in round two.
    2. IOC member from Beijing voted for London in round three.

    (a) Only (1)
    (b) Only (2)
    (c) Both (a) and (2)
    (d) Neither (1) nor (2)

Sol. (a) A is true but B is not. Hence, option (a) is correct.

Directions for Questions 68 to 71: Answer questions 68–71 on the basis of the information given below:

The table below presents the revenue (in million rupees) of four firms in three states. These firms, Honest Ltd., Aggressive. Ltd, Truthful Ltd. and Profitable Ltd. are disguised in the table as A, B, C and D, in no particular order.

TABLE 2.24(A)

States	Firm A	Firm B	Firm C	Firm D
UP	49	82	80	55
Bihar	69	72	70	65
MP	72	63	72	65

Further, it is known that:

- In the state of MP, Truthful Ltd. has the highest market share.
- Aggressive Ltd.'s aggregate revenue differs from Honest Ltd.'s by ₹5 million.

Sol. for 68 to 71

The basic info contained in this question gives us that there are four companies – Honest Ltd. (H), Aggressive Ltd. (A), Truthful Ltd. (T) and Profitable Ltd. (P) disguised in the table as A, B, C and D, in no particular order.

TABLE 2.24(B)

States	Firm A	Firm B	Firm C	Firm D
UP	49	82	80	55
Bihar	69	72	70	65
MP	72	63	72	65
Total	190	217	222	185

Using the additional information given in the question—

- *In the state of MP, Truthful Ltd. has the highest market share.*

  We can see that T has to be either Firm A or Firm C.

- *Aggressive Ltd.'s aggregate revenue differs from Honest Ltd.'s by ₹5 million.*

This means that Aggressive and Honest can be distributed in a random order between Firms A and D or Firms B and C.

Based on our interpretations of the above two statements, we can make the following possibilities structure for the four firms:

TABLE 2.25

	Possibility 1	Possibility 2	Possibility 3	Possibility 4
A	Truthful	Truthful	Aggressive	Honest
B	Aggressive	Honest	Profitable	Profitable
C	Honest	Aggressive	Truthful	Truthful
D	Profitable	Profitable	Honest	Aggressive

Based on this Possibility table, we can work out the questions that follow.

68. What can be said regarding the following two statements?

Statement 1: Profitable Ltd. has the lowest share in MP market.

Statement 2: Honest Ltd.'s total revenue is more than Profitable Ltd.

(a) If Statement 1 is true then Statement 2 is necessarily true.
(b) If Statement 1 is true then Statement 2 is necessarily false.
(c) Both Statement 1 and Statement 2 are true.
(d) Neither Statement 1 nor Statement 2 is true.

Sol. *(b) For this question, we have to consider the truth/false nature of the following two statements:*

***Statement 1:** Profitable Ltd. has the lowest share in MP market.*

If this statement is true, we are referring to the situation where Profitable is firm B. This is true in Possibilities 3 and 4 only.

***Statement 2:** Honest Ltd.'s total revenue is more than Profitable Ltd.*

It can be seen that in both Possibilities 3 and 4, this statement is false.

Hence, if the first statement is true, the second has to be necessarily false. Option (b) is correct.

69. What can be said regarding the following two statements?

Statement 1: Aggressive Ltd.'s the lowest revenues are from MP.

Statement 2: Honest Ltd.'s the lowest revenues are from Bihar.

(a) If Statement 2 is true then Statement 1 is necessarily false.
(b) If Statement 1 is false then Statement 2 is necessarily true.
(c) If Statement 1 is true then Statement 2 is necessarily true.
(d) None of the above.

Sol. *(c) For this question, we have to consider the truth/false nature of the following two statements:*

***Statement 1:** Aggressive Ltd's the lowest revenues are from MP.*

For this statement to be true, Aggressive should be Firm B. This takes us to Possibility 1 in the possibility table above.

***Statement 2:** Honest Ltd.'s the lowest revenues are from Bihar.*

In Possibility 1, Honest becomes Firm C—and it can be seen that its lowest revenues would indeed come from Bihar.

Thus, we can say that if Statement 1 is true, then Statement 2 is necessarily true. Option (c) is the correct answer.

70. What can be said regarding the following two statements?

Statement 1: Honest Ltd. has the highest share in the UP market.

Statement 2: Aggressive Ltd. has the highest share in the Bihar market.

(a) Both statements could be true.
(b) At least one of the statements must be true.
(c) At most one of the statements is true.
(d) None of the above.

Sol. *(c) For this question we have to consider the truth/false nature of the following two statements.*

***Statement 1:** Honest Ltd. has the highest share in the UP market.*

In this case, Honest becomes B and we go to Possibility 2.

***Statement 2:** Aggressive Ltd. has the highest share in the Bihar market.*

In this case, Aggressive becomes Firm B – which means possibility 1.

It is clear that at most one of these can be true at a time. Hence, option (c) is correct.

71. If Profitable Ltd.'s the lowest revenue is from UP, then which of the following is true?

(a) Truthful Ltd.'s the lowest revenues are from MP.

(b) Truthful Ltd.'s the lowest revenues are from Bihar.
(c) Truthful Ltd.'s the lowest revenues are from UP.
(d) No definite conclusion is possible.

Sol. *(c) If Profitable Ltd.'s the lowest revenue is from UP, then Profitable must be Firm D. In such a case, Truthful becomes Firm A (as both possibilities 1 and 2 give us the same thing). It can be seen that in such a case Truthful's least revenues would be from UP. Option (c) is correct.*

Directions for Questions 72 to 75: Answer questions 72–75 on the basis of the information given below.

Help Distress (HD) is an NGO involved in providing assistance to people suffering from natural disasters. Currently, it has 37 volunteers. They are involved in three projects: Tsunami Relief (TR) in Tamil Nadu, Flood Relief (FR) in Maharashtra and Earthquake Relief (ER) in Gujarat. Each volunteer working with HD has to be involved in at least one relief work project.

- A maximum number of volunteers are involved in the FR project. Amongst them, the number of volunteers involved in FR project alone is equal to the volunteers having additional involvement in the ER project.
- The number of volunteers involved in the ER project alone is double the number of volunteers involved in all the three projects.
- Seventeen volunteers are involved in the TR project.
- The number of volunteers involved in the TR project alone is one less than the number of volunteers involved in ER project alone.
- Ten volunteers involved in the TR project are also involved in at least one more project.

Sol. *for 72 to 75*
The figure has been made on the following deductions and facts which can be deduced based on the following clues:

- *The number of volunteers involved in the ER project alone is double the number of volunteers involved in all the three projects.*
- *Seventeen volunteers are involved in the TR project.*
- *The number of volunteers involved in the TR project alone is one less than the number of volunteers involved in ER project alone.*
- *Ten volunteers involved in the TR project are also involved in at least one more project.*

1. *TR is given as 17 (overall) out of which 10 are involved in at least 1 more project apart from TR. Hence, only TR would be 7.*
2. *ER alone is one more than TR alone. So, ER alone would be eight. Also, all three is half of ER alone – so, all three should be four.*

At this point of analysis we have the figure as shown below:

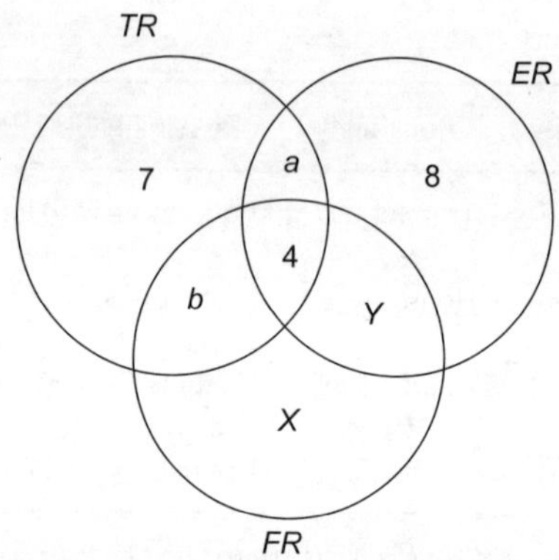

FIGURE 2.7

At this point we also know—
$x + y = 12$ and $a + b = 6$
At this point of our analysis, the only clue we need to further interpret is the first one – a maximum number of volunteers are involved in the FR project. Amongst them, the number of volunteers involved in FR project alone is equal to the volunteers having additional involvement in the ER project.
From the second statement in this clue we can deduce that, since FR only has to be equal to the number having additional involvement in ER – X must be 8 and Y must be 4.

Note: *There was an interpretation based confusion which test-takers had while thinking about this clue in the exam. The confusion was – what does additional involvement in ER mean? Does it mean FR and ER only or does it include both the areas viz., FR and ER only as well as FR, ER and TR.*

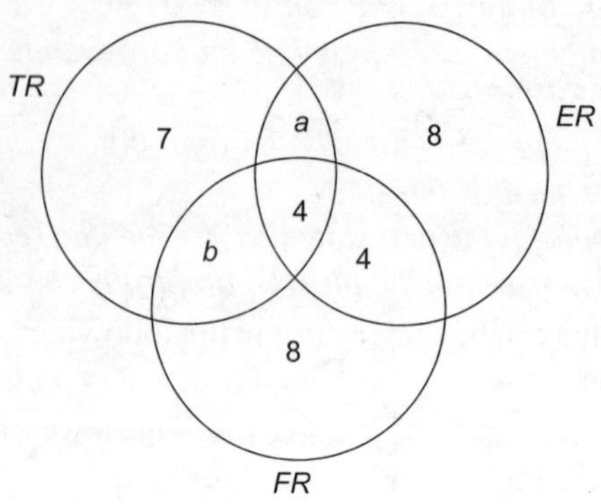

FIGURE 2.8

A little bit of clear thinking would tell you that when we say – FR with additional involvement of ER, we are not referring to any third (or for that matter fourth) category. Hence, the four people in all three, would also be counted in this category.

Thus, the new figure evolves to:

Now, we know that a + b = 6.

This leads to the following possibility matrix:

TABLE 2.26

		TR	FR (A Maximum)	ER	
			16+b	16+a	
Possibility 1	a=6,b=0	17	16	22	Not possible
Possibility 2	a=5,b=1	17	17	21	Not possible
Possibility 3	a=4,b=2	17	18	20	Not possible
Possibility 4	a=3,b=3	17	19	19	Possible
Possibility 5	a=2,b=4	17	20	18	Possible
Possibility 6	a=1,b=5	17	21	17	Possible
Possibility 7	a=0,b=6	17	22	16	Possible

Note here: *There was huge confusion in the minds of test-takers – as must be in yours as you read this. FR is given as 'A maximum'. So, does this condition allow us to take a = 3 and b = 3 as a possible distribution of 6 between a and b (as shown in possibility 4 above).*

As you can see, at these values, we get FR = ER = 19 [and FR is not a unique maximum].

And, that is exactly what you perhaps need to understand – The language used in the question 'A maximum' means literally 'one of the maximums', i.e., it allows for more than one maximum simultaneously. Hence, interpreting that FR is a unique maximum in this situation is an error.

Based on the above tabular analysis, we can get the answers to the question asked.

72. Based on the information given above, the minimum number of volunteers involved in both FR and TR projects, but not in the ER project is:
    (a) 1
    (b) 3
    (c) 4
    (d) 5

Sol. (b) The minimum value of (b) is asked for. From the table, it is 3. Option (b) is correct.

73. Which of the following additional information would enable us to find the exact number of volunteers involved in various projects?
    (a) Twenty volunteers are involved in FR.
    (b) Four volunteers are involved in all the three projects.
    (c) Twenty-three volunteers are involved in exactly one project.
    (d) No need for any additional information.

Sol. (a) The first option is the correct answer as we know that FR = 20, then we know the value of b = 4 and we get all the values in the given situation. Notice that the information carried in statements of options (b) and (c) are already known to us.

For 74 and 75, the following changes would take place:

TABLE 2.27

		TR (one person opted out of TR)	FR =14+b	ER = 15+a	
Possibility 1	a=3,b=3	16	17	18	Possible
Possibility 2	a=2,b=4	16	18	17	Possible
Possibility 3	a=1,b=5	16	19	16	Possible
Possibility 4	a=0,b=6	16	20	15	Possible

We have deleted the values of a = 4, 5 and 6, as we had ruled those values out for the previous questions' analysis.

74. After some time, the volunteers who were involved in all the three projects were asked to withdraw from one project. As a result, one of the volunteers opted out of the TR project, and one opted out of the ER project, while the remaining ones involved in all the three projects opted out of the FR project. Which of the following statements, then, necessarily follows?
    (a) The lowest number of volunteers is now in TR project.
    (b) More volunteers are now in FR project as compared to ER project.
    (c) More volunteers are now in TR project as compared to ER project.
    (d) None of the above

Sol. (d) It can be seen that option (a) is not true (rejected by possibility 4 where ER has the least number of volunteers).

Option (b) can be rejected, as possibility 1 has ER>FR.

Option (c) is rejected due to possibilities 1, 2 and 3.

Hence, the correct answer is none of these.

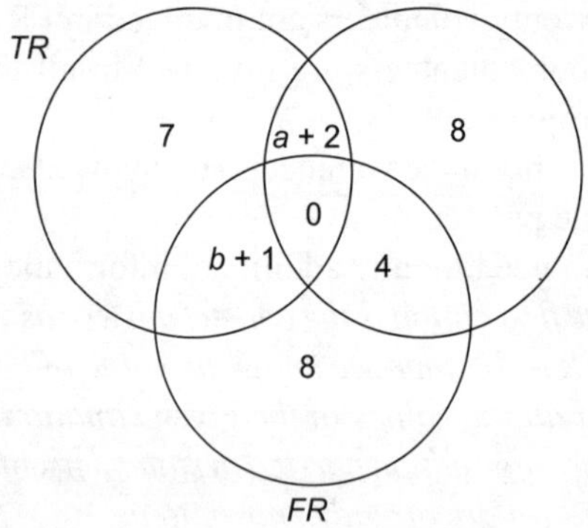

FIGURE 2.9

75. After the withdrawal of volunteers, as indicated in Question 130, some new volunteers joined the NGO. Each one of them was allotted only one project in a manner such that, the number of volunteers working in one project alone for each of the three projects became identical. At that point, it was also found that the number of volunteers involved in FR and ER projects was the same as the number of volunteers involved in TR and ER projects. Which of the projects now has the highest number of volunteers?
(a) ER
(b) FR
(c) TR
(d) Cannot be determined

Sol. *(a) For FR & ER to be same as TR + ER, it means $a + 2 = 5$. Hence, $a = 3$ and $b = 3$.*
Then the numbers become:
$TR = 16 + m + 1 = 17 + m$
$ER = 18 + m$
$FR = 17 + m$
Where, m is the number of volunteers inducted into ER alone and FR alone. (m + 1 being the number inducted into TR alone).
Clearly, ER would have the highest number of volunteers [option (a)].

Directions for Questions 76 to 80: Answer questions 76–80 on the basis of the information given below.

Mathematicians are assigned a number called Erdos number (named after the famous mathematician, Paul Erdos). Only Paul Erdos himself has an Erdos number of zero. Any mathematician who has written a research paper with Erdos has an Erdos number of 1. For other mathematicians, the calculation of his/her Erdos number is illustrated below:

Suppose that a mathematician X has co-authored papers with several other mathematicians. From amongst them, mathematician Y has the smallest Erdos number. Let the Erdos number of Y be y. Then X has an Erdos number of $y + 1$. Hence, any mathematician with no co-authorship chain connected to Erdos has an Erdos number of infinity.

In a seven day long mini-conference organised in memory of Paul Erdos, a close group of eight mathematicians, call them A, B, C, D, E, F, G and H, discussed some research problems. At the beginning of the conference, A was the only participant who had an infinite Erdos number. Nobody had an Erdos number less than that of F.

On the third day of the conference, F co-authored a paper jointly with A and C. This reduced the average Erdos number of the group of eight mathematicians to three. The Erdos numbers of B, D, E, G and H remained unchanged with the writing of this paper. Further, no other co-authorship amongst any three members would have reduced the average Erdos number of the group of eight to as low as three.

- At the end of the third day, five members of this group had identical Erdos numbers while the other three had Erdos numbers distinct from each other.
- On the fifth day, E co-authored a paper with F, which reduced the group's average Erdos number by 0.5. The Erdos numbers of the remaining six were unchanged with the writing of this paper.
- No other paper was written during the conference.

Sol. for 76–80:

In order to solve this question (and in fact most questions of this nature where you have a long data/info filled passage), the key is to be able to decode the language step by step. So instead of getting bogged down by the surfeit of information which you have – focus on reacting to the language of the information sentence by sentence.

So let us now go through the information sentence by sentence and see how one should react in this question.

Mathematicians are assigned a number called Erdos number (named after the famous mathematician, Paul Erdos). [Reaction: The question is introducing a variable called 'Erdos Number']. Only Paul Erdos himself has an Erdos number of zero. Any mathematician who has written a research paper with Erdos has an Erdos number of 1. For other mathematicians, the calculation of his/her Erdos number is illustrated below:

Suppose that a mathematician X has co-authored papers with several other mathematicians. From amongst them, mathematician Y has the smallest Erdos number. Let the Erdos number of Y be y. Then, X has an Erdos number of y + 1. Hence, any mathematician with no co-authorship chain connected to Erdos has an Erdos number of infinity. [Reaction: We now have a process for assigning the value of the Erdos number—from the co-authors to an individual whose Erdos number you want to find, choose the co-author with the smallest Erdos number. The required Erdos number would be got by adding 1 to this least number. A-ha point: If an individual x has a co-author list with the following Erdos numbers – 2, 4, 6, 3, 8, then x would have an Erdos number of 2 + 1 = 3 – since 2 is the least value in his list of co-authors.]:

In a seven day long mini-conference organised in memory of Paul Erdos [Reaction: Paul Erdos is dead – he would not be a part of the group.] , a close group of eight mathematicians, call them A, B, C, D, E, F, G and H, discussed some research problems. At the beginning of the conference, A was the only participant who had an infinite Erdos number. Nobody had an Erdos number less than that of F.

Reaction:

TABLE 2.28(A)

Person	A	B	C	D	E	F	G	H
Erdos Number	Infinite	b	c	d	e	f(least Erdos number)	g	h

Note here that 'f' is the least value but not necessarily the single such least value, i.e., there can be more than 1 person having the same number. At this point of time the only conclusion we can make is that there is nobody else with an Erdos number less than f – but that does not guarantee the fact that there cannot be anybody with a number equal to f.

On the third day of the conference F co-authored a paper jointly with A and C.

Reactions:

A's Erdos number would come down to f + 1.

For C's Erdos number, there could be three specific cases

CASE 1: C's number would come down to f + 1 from a higher number. Obviously, this would happen if C had a higher Erdos number earlier.

CASE 2: C's Erdos number was f + 1 earlier. In such a case, his number would not change and would remain f + 1 again.

CASE 3: C's Erdos number was f earlier. In such a case his number would not change and remain at f.

TABLE 2.28(B)

Person	A	B	C	D	E	F	G	H
Erdos Number	f+1	b	f or f+1	d	e	f (least Erdos number)	g	h

This reduced the average Erdos number of the group of eight mathematicians to 3. The Erdos numbers of B, D, E, G and H remained unchanged with the writing of this paper.

Reaction: The sum of the eight numbers must be 8 × 3 = 24.

Further, no other co-authorship amongst any three members would have reduced the average Erdos number of the group of eight to as low as 3.

Reaction: Since the effect of A and C co-authoring with F is to bring the average of the group to the lowest possible, this clearly means that C's starting Erdos number must have been the second highest amongst all the values (after A). This can be understood further by the fact that if someone other than C (say H) had the second highest Erdos number in the group initially, then the least possible average would have been got by co-authoring F with A and H.

Thus, we can conclude that C must have had the second highest Erdos number in the group – in which case we can also reject Case 3 above and conclude that C's new Erdos number must be f + 1.

We also know that C's number must have fallen to f + 1 – It could not have been f + 1 earlier – since, C's new number must represent the largest drop apart from A's drop in value.

Thus the table would evolve to:

TABLE 2.28(C)

Person	A	B	C	D	E	F	G	H
Erdos Number	f + 1	b	f + 1	d	e	f (least Erdos number)	g	h

At the end of the third day, five members of this group had identical Erdos numbers while the other three had Erdos numbers distinct from each other.

Reaction: Since we know that A and C both have f + 1 as their values, it is clear from this statement that there must be five people having f + 1 as their

Erdos numbers. For the other three there should be unique values for each of them. One of them being f, the other two should be distinct values (say m and n).

Thus, we can create the equation:

$5(f + 1) + f + m + n = 24$

The issue now is to try to fix the value of f. If we take the value of f as 2, then the following would happen to the equation above:

$5x3 + 2 + m + n = 24 \rightarrow 17 + m + n = 24.$

We now realise that the sum of m and n (i.e., m + n) would be equal to 7. Also, since f + 1 is 3, the least values of m and n can be 4 and 5 respectively. This is not possible in this situation.

It is also easily seen that if we change the value of f, (from 2) we cannot take it further up – as that would only worsen the situation. Thus, the only possibility left would be the value of f is 1.

Then the equation,

$5(f + 1) + f + m + n = 24$, would transform to $5 \times 2 + 1 + m + n = 24$, giving us the sum of m and n as 13.

The sum of m and n as 13 can happen through four possibilities as:

(i) 3 + 10,

(ii) 4 + 9,

(iii) 5 + 8 or

(iv) 6 + 7.

Thus, the table would evolve to:

TABLE 2.29(A)

Person	A	B	C	D	E	F	G	H
Erdos Number	2	b	2	d	e	1	g	h

and we also know that amongst b, d, e, g and h three have to be equal to 2 and the remaining two would be taking the values of m and n. At this point, however, we do not know which one is which.

On the fifth day, E co-authored a paper with F which reduced the group's average Erdos number by 0.5. The Erdos numbers of the remaining six were unchanged with the writing of this paper.

Reactions: If E co-authors with F, E's value would reduce to 2. Also, since the average is reducing by 0.5, it would mean that there is a drop in the total by 4. ($0.5 \times 8 = 4$). Thus, E's value right through in each of the above tables would have been 6 and would go down to 2 after the fifth day. Thus, the value for m + n which would fit, would be possibility iv (6 + 7) above.

Thus the table would evolve to:

TABLE 2.29(B)

Person	A	B	C	D	E	F	G	H
Erdos Number	2	b	2	d	2	1	g	h

Out of b, d, g and h, three would have a value of 2 and one would have a value of 7.

No other paper was written during the conference. We are now ready to answer the questions which were asked.

76. The person having the largest Erdos number at the end of the conference must have had Erdos number

(a) 5 (b) 7
(c) 9 (d) 14
(e) 15

Sol. (b) Obviously 7. Hence, option (b) is the right answer.

77. How many participants in the conference did not change their Erdos number during the conference?

(a) 2 (b) 3
(c) 4 (d) 5
(e) Cannot be determined

Sol. (d) It would be better to look at how many changed their numbers. We know that A, C and E have changed their numbers and also that the others have not changed. Hence, the option (d) is correct.

78. The Erdos number of C at the end of the conference was:

(a) 1 (b) 2
(c) 3 (d) 4
(e) 5

Sol. (b) C's number at the end of the conference would be 2. Hence, option (b) is correct.

79. The Erdos number of E at the beginning of the conference was:

(a) 2 (b) 5
(c) 6 (d) 7
(e) 8

Sol. (c) C's number at the beginning of the conference would be 6. Hence, option (c) is correct.

80. How many participants had the same Erdos number at the beginning of the conference?

(a) 2 (b) 3
(c) 4 (d) 5
(e) Cannot be determined

Sol. (b) After A and C's Erdos number went down to 2, there were 5 people with the same Erdos number. Hence, before that only 3 people must have had the same Erdos number (option b).

Let us now go through the inferences for the next question set of questions 137 to 141.

Directions for Questions 81 to 85: Answer questions 81–85 on the basis of the information given below.

Two traders, Chetan and Michael, were involved in the buying and selling of MCS shares over five trading days. At the beginning of the first day, the MCS share was priced at ₹100, while at the end of the fifth day it was priced at ₹110. At the end of each day, the MCS share price either went up by ₹10, or else, it came down by ₹10. Both Chetan and Michael took buying and selling decisions at the end of each trading day. The beginning price of MCS share on a given day was the same as the ending price of the previous day. Chetan and Michael started with the same number of shares and amount of cash, and had enough of both. Below are some additional facts about how Chetan and Michael traded over the five trading days.

- Each day if the price went up, Chetan sold 10 shares of MCS at the closing price. On the other hand, each day if the price went down, he bought 10 shares at the closing price.
- If on any day, the closing price was above ₹110, then Michael sold 10 shares of MCS, while if it was below ₹90, he bought 10 shares, all at the closing price.

Sol. for 81–85:

Two traders, Chetan and Michael, were involved in the buying and selling of MCS shares over five trading days. At the beginning of the first day, the MCS share was priced at ₹100, while at the end of the fifth day it was priced at ₹110. At the end of each day, the MCS share price either went up by ₹10, or else, it came down by ₹10.

Reaction: This clearly means that there must have been 3 increases of ₹10 each and two drops of ₹10 each. At this point, of course we are in no condition to comment on the order they are going to take – but a little bit of permutation and combination thinking would give you that there can be ${}^5C_3$= 10 ways of ordering the increases and the decreases.

Both Chetan and Michael took buying and selling decisions at the end of each trading day. The beginning price of MCS share on a given day was the same as the ending price of the previous day. Chetan and Michael started with the same number of shares and amount of cash, (Reaction: Take a note of this at this point.) and had enough of both. Below are some additional facts about how Chetan and Michael traded over the five trading days.

- *Each day if the price went up, Chetan sold 10 shares of MCS at the closing price. On the other hand, each day if the price went down, he bought 10 shares at the closing price.*

  Reaction: Chetan must have sold 10 shares thrice and bought 10 shares twice during this period. Thus, obviously it means that he must have been a net seller of 10 shares during this period. Obviously, this would have a positive effect on his cash balance and it would go up by around 1000 to 1200 rupees due to offloading 10 of his shares. Of course, he might gain or lose some value due to the profit/loss he might have made in the other buying and selling transactions he might have made.
- *If on any day, the closing price was above ₹110, then Michael sold 10 shares of MCS, while if it was below ₹90, he bought 10 shares, all at the closing price.*

  Reaction: Michael's buying trigger—price of 80

  Michael's selling trigger—Price of 120 or 130.

  It is obvious at this point that if we consider Michael's activity, it is not possible for him to both buy and sell under any conditions. This is because, if the price hits 120 on any of the 5 days, it cannot have gone to 80 during the 5 days under consideration as we have only 2 decreases of ₹10 each in price. So from 120 the minimum level the price can reach is 100. Similarly, if the price had hit 80, it could not have gone up to 120 in the same 5 day cycle as we have only a maximum of 3 increases of ₹10 each – giving an upper limit of price reaching to 100 if it had hit 80 during the time under consideration.

  Thus, if during a 5 day cycle, a sell trigger is activated for Michael, then a buy trigger cannot occur in that cycle and vice versa.

Obviously, we have to move directly into the questions and react to what has been written there – in terms of the conditions mentioned.

81. If Chetan sold 10 shares of MCS on three consecutive days, while Michael sold 10 shares only once during the five days, what was the price of MCS at the end of day 3?

(a) ₹90
(b) ₹100
(c) ₹110
(d) ₹120
(e) ₹130

Sol. *(c) If Chetan sold 10 shares of MCS on three consecutive days, (Reaction: Since Chetan sells everytime there is a price increase, this obviously means that the price must have increased on three consecutive days, i.e., the three price rises on the five days must have happened on consecutive days. These can happen in three cases:*

***Case 1:** Price goes up on first three days and falls on fourth and fifth days – 110, 120, 130, 120, 110*

***Case 2:** Price goes up on second to fourth days and falls on the first and fifth days – 90, 100, 110, 120, 110.*

***Case 3:** Price goes up on the last three days and falls on the first two days – 90, 80, 90, 100, 110) while Michael sold 10 shares only once during the five days (Reaction: Michael's selling trigger of ₹120 must have got activated only once in the five days under consideration. From the above reaction, it can be easily seen that this condition is fulfilled only by Case 2), what was the price of MCS at the end of day 3? (Reaction: In case 2, price at the end of day 3 is 110).*

Option (c) is the correct answer.

82. If Michael ended up with ₹100 less cash than Chetan at the end of day 5, what was the difference in the number of shares possessed by Michael and Chetan (at the end of day 5)?
(a) Michael had 10 shares less than Chetan.
(b) Michael had 10 shares more than Chetan.
(c) Chetan had 10 shares more than Michael.
(d) Chetan had 20 shares more than Michael.
(e) Both had the same number of shares.

Sol. *(e) If Michael ended up with ₹100 less cash than Chetan at the end of day five, (Reaction: We know that Chetan is a net seller of 10 shares, so obviously we expect his cash balance to have gone up from his initial level. Now, if we further know that Michael ended up with just ₹100 cash difference from Chetan, then his cash balance would also have gone up by almost the same amount as Chetan's. This can only happen if Michael is also a net seller of 10 shares overall.) What was the difference in the number of shares possessed by Michael and Chetan (at the end of day 5)? (Reaction: Obviously the number of shares possessed by both of them at the end of day 5 would be equal – as they started with equal amount of shares and cash at the start of the 5 day period).*

Option (e) is the correct answer. Note that this is 100% safe thought logic to arrive at this answer. In case, you do not get it I would suggest that you try to see the cash and share balance of both under each of the 10 possible conditions of price rise and fall. You would discover that whenever there is a difference in the number of shares, the cash balance would also vary distinctly.

83. If Chetan ended up with ₹1300 more cash than Michael at the end of day 5, what was the price of MCS share at the end of day 4?
(a) ₹90 (b) ₹100
(c) ₹110 (d) ₹120
(e) Not uniquely determinable

Sol. *(b) If Chetan ended up with ₹1300 more cash than Michael at the end of day 5, (Reaction: Since Chetan is a net seller of 10 shares, Michael must not have sold or bought any shares. If you make Michael buy shares, the difference in the number of shares would be 20 and the difference in cash balance would be around ₹2000. On the other hand if Michael had sold shares, there would not be such a gap in the cash balance.) What was the price of MCS share at the end of day 4? (Reaction: Michael neither sells nor buys. So the price does not hit either 80 or 120. So on day 4, the price can only be ₹100 – if the price was 120, Michael's sell trigger would have occurred.)*

Option (b) is the correct answer. If you are not confident of your answer – try it out.

The pricing would have been: 90, 100, 110, 100, 110 (in order for Michael not to have a sell or buy trigger).

In such a case, the cash balance of Chetan would get affected as shown below:

Day 1 – price 90, buy 10 shares, cash balance –900.

Day 2 – price 100, sell 10 shares, cash balance +100,

Day 3 – Price 110, sell 10 shares, cash balance +1200,

Day 4 – Price 100, buy 10 shares, cash balance +2000,

Day 5 – Price 110, sell 10 shares, cash balance +1300. Goes to confirm the line of thought I was talking about in the reactions to this question.

84. What could have been the maximum possible increase in combined cash balance of Chetan and Michael at the end of the fifth day?
(a) ₹3700 (b) ₹4000
(c) ₹4700 (d) ₹5000
(e) ₹6000

Sol. *(d) For maximum possible increase in cash balance, the condition that should be met is that the maximum number of shares should be sold. Since Chetan's transactions are largely fixed in that, we know definitely that he has sold 10 shares net, Michael should have sold the maximum number of shares. For this to happen, the price must have been over 110 for the maximum time. This happens in the case of:*

TABLE 2.30

Day	1	2	3	4	5	Net effect
Price	110	120	130	120	110	
Chetan	Sells	Sells	Sells	Buys	Buys	
Effect on Chetan's cash	+1100	+1200	+1300	-1200	-1100	+1300
Michael	No action	Sells	Sells	Sells	No action	
	0	+1200	+1300	+1200	0	+3700

So, the combined increase in cash balance is ₹5000 (option d).

85. If Michael ended up with 20 more shares than Chetan at the end of day five, what was the price of the share at the end of day three?
(a) ₹90 (b) ₹100
(c) ₹110 (d) ₹120
(e) ₹130

Sol. *(a) If Michael ended up with 20 more shares than Chetan at the end of day 5, (Reaction: Share wise, we know that Chetan is –10, so obviously Michael must be +10 shares in order for him to have 20 more shares than Chetan. This means that Michael must have bought once. For that to happen the price of the share must have gone down to ₹80. The only way that occurs is if we take the price down on both the first two days. Thus, the price string would be 90, 80, 90, 100, 110) what was the price of the share at the end of day 3? (Reaction: Obviously 90).*
Hence, option (a) is correct.

Directions for Questions 86 to 90: Answer questions 86–90 on the basis of the information given below.

A significant amount of traffic flows from point S to point T in the one-way street network shown below. Points A, B, C and D are junctions in the network, and the arrows mark the direction of traffic flow. The fuel cost in rupees for travelling along a street is indicated by the number adjacent to the arrow representing the street.

Motorists traveling from point S to point T would obviously take the route for which the total cost of traveling is the minimum. If two or more routes have the same least travel cost, then motorists are indifferent between them. Hence, the traffic gets evenly distributed amongst all the least cost routes.

The government can control the flow of traffic only by levying appropriate toll at each junction. For example, if a motorist takes the route S-A-T (using junction A alone), then the total cost of travel would be ₹14 (i.e., ₹9 + ₹5) plus the toll charged at junction A.

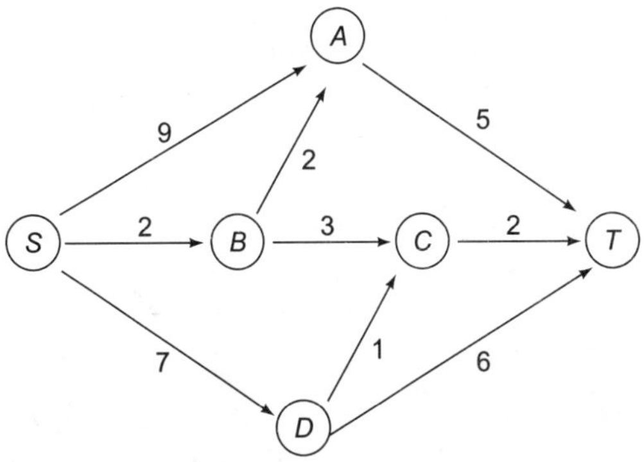

FIGURE 2.10

Sol. for 86–90:
Reaction: Possible routes
(1) SAT – Cost 14 + A
(2) SBAT – Cost 9 + A + B
(3) SBCT – Cost 7 + B + C
(4) SDCT – Cost 10 + C + D
(5) SDT – Cost 13 + D

86. If the government wants to ensure that all motorists travelling from S to T pay the same amount (fuel costs and toll combined) regardless of the route they choose and the street from B to C is under repairs (hence unusable), then a feasible set of toll charged (in rupees) at junctions A, B, C and D respectively to achieve this goal is:
(a) 2, 5, 3, 2 (b) 0, 5, 3, 1
(c) 1, 5, 3, 2 (d) 2, 3, 5, 1
(e) 1, 3, 5, 1

Sol. *(b)/(c) If the government wants to ensure that all motorists travelling from S to T pay the same amount (fuel costs and toll combined) (Reaction: The question is asking us to fix toll charges in such a way that the total cost on all feasible routes is equal.) regardless of the route they choose and the street from B to C is under repairs (hence, unusable) (Reaction: Route SBCT is closed), then a feasible set of toll charged (in rupees) at junctions A, B, C and D respectively to achieve this goal is:*

Reaction: To equate SDCT cost with SDT cost, C should be 3. This leaves only options b and c. Checking option 2, SAT = 14, SBAT = 14, SDCT = 14 and SDT = 14 (feasible as all 4 routes cost is equated).

Checking option (c), SAT = 15, SBAT = 15, SDCT = 15 and SDT = 15 (feasible again as all 4 routes' cost is equated). This question is clearly giving 2 answers. Mark either one and move ahead. [Note—this question was neglected from the final score calculations].

87. If the government wants to ensure that no traffic flows on the street from D to T, while equal amount of traffic flows through junctions A and C, then a feasible set of toll charged (in rupees) at junctions A, B, C and D respectively to achieve this goal is:

(a) 1, 5, 3, 3 (b) 1, 4, 4, 3
(c) 1, 5, 4, 2 (d) 0, 5, 2, 3
(e) 0, 5, 2, 2

Sol. *(e) If the government wants to ensure that no traffic flows on the street from D to T, (Reaction: SDT has to be made infeasible) while equal amount of traffic flows through junctions A and C, (Reaction: There are 2 routes each through A and C. In order to make an equal amount of traffic flow through each junction A and C respectively, we need to ensure either of two things: 1. All four routes SAT, SBAT, SBCT and SDCT should be the same least cost, OR 2. One route through A and one route through C should be the least cost. At the same time SDT should not be the least cost route.) then a feasible set of toll charged (in rupees) at junctions A, B, C and D respectively to achieve this goal is:*

Reaction: Looking at the options, four of the five options give the value of B as 5. We can clearly see that if B is 5, SAT and SBAT give the same cost. In such a case, the two routes through C should also give the same least cost. Also for SBCT to be equal to SBAT, C should exceed A by 2. This is occurring in option (a) and (e). From this point checking for option (a) and (e) it is evident that option (e), is the correct solution as SAT = SBAT = SDCT = SBCT = 14.

88. If the government wants to ensure that all routes from S to T get the same amount of traffic, then a feasible set of toll charged (in rupees) at junctions A, B, C and D respectively, to achieve this goal is:

(a) 0, 5, 2, 2 (b) 0, 5, 4, 1
(c) 1, 5, 3, 3 (d) 1, 5, 3,1
(e) 1, 5, 4, 2

Sol. *(d) If the government wants to ensure that all routes from S to T get the same amount of traffic, then a feasible set of toll charged (in rupees) at junctions A, B, C and D respectively to achieve this goal is:*

Reaction: We need to equate all 5 routes. Thus, looking at the equations for total cost on each route, we see the following:

For SAT = SBAT, B should be 5 (All options have this).

For SAT = SDT, D should be 1 more than A (Only options (b) and (e) have this).

For SDT = SDCT, C should be 3. Only option (e) has this. Hence, we will mark option (e).

89. If the government wants to ensure that the traffic at S gets evenly distributed along streets from S to A, from S to B and from S to D, then a feasible set of toll charged (in rupees) at junctions A, B, C and D respectively to achieve this goal is:

(a) 0, 5, 4, 1 (b) 0, 5, 2, 2
(c) 1, 5, 3, 3 (d) 1, 5, 3, 2
(e) 0, 4, 3, 2

Sol. *(a) If the government wants to ensure that the traffic at S gets evenly distributed along streets from S to A, from S to B and from S to D, then a feasible set of toll charged (in rupees) at junctions A, B, C and D respectively to achieve this goal is:*

Reaction: Since SA has only 1 route going through it, there should be exactly 3 least distance cost routes— 1 each through SA, SB and SD. Further, SAT has to be one of the least cost routes. In Option (a), (b) and (e), SAT would cost 14 while in options (c) and (d), SAT would cost 15. On checking Option (a) gives:

SAT = SBAT = SDT = 14 while SBCT (16) and SDT (15) would not be least cost routes. The traffic would get evenly distributed between SAT, SBAT and SDT as required by the question.

Hence, we will mark option (a).

90. The government wants to devise a toll policy such that the total cost to the commuters per trip is minimised. The policy should also ensure that not more than 70 per cent of the total traffic passes through junction B. The cost incurred by the commuter travelling from point S to point T under this policy will be:
(a) ₹7 (b) ₹9
(c) ₹10 (d) ₹13
(e) ₹14

Sol. *(c) The government wants to devise a toll policy such that the total cost to the commuters per trip is minimised. The policy should also ensure that not more than 70 per cent of the total traffic passes through junction B. (Reaction: There should be at least 1 least cost route which is not passing through B.) The cost incurred by the commuter travelling from point S to point T under this policy will be:*
Reaction: The minimum cost on a route not passing through B is 10, hence options (a) and (b) are not feasible. The issue to look out for is, whether we can create a total cost of 10 and have the 70 per cent condition met.
Looking at the cost equations, it is clear that if we want SDCT to cost 10 totally, C and D should be toll free. Then, SBCT should also cost 10 at least to share the least cost route with SDCT. Thus, the toll at B should be 3. In such a case, SDCT = 10 = SBCT and the other routes cost more than 10. Hence, the traffic would get divided 50-50 between SDCT and SBCT and 10 would represent the least cost you would need to get the value required (option c).

Directions for Questions 91 to 93: Answer the following questions based on the information given below.

There are 100 employees in an organisation across five departments. The following table gives the department-wise distribution of average age, average basic pay and allowances. The gross pay of an employee is the sum of his/her basic pay and allowances.

TABLE 2.31

Department	Number of Employees	Average Age (years)	Average Basic Pay (₹)	Allowances (% of Basic Pay)
HR	5	45	5000	70
Marketing	30	35	6000	80
Finance	20	30	6500	60
Business Development	35	42	7500	75
Maintenance	10	35	5500	50

There are limited number of employees considered for transfer/promotion across departments. Whenever a person is transferred/promoted from a department of lower average age to a department of higher average age, he/she will get an additional allowance of 10 per cent of basic pay over and above his/her current allowance. There will not be any change in pay structure if a person is transferred/promoted from a department with higher average age to a department with lower average age.

Sol. for 91 to 93
Before you start solving the questions in this set, you need to understand the following:
a. Interpretation of the values in the table:
The table gives us department-wise four pieces of information—
1. *The number of employees in the department.*
2. *The average age of these employees, thus, you can get the total age of any department by multiplying the average age & the number of employees of that department.*
3. *The average basic pay—gives us again the average basic pay of the department employees. We do not have any particular information about a single employee, but we have only aggregate information about the department.*
4. *The allowances as percentage of basic pay, would also be fixed within a department and would be fixed for all employees within the department.*

However, since we do not know the basic pay of individual employees, we cannot find out the allowance given to an individual employee. Thus, we conclude that the allowances date is also on aggregate that can be calculated as on average.
b. Transfer conditions:
When an employee is transferred from one department to another, his allowance would increase if the transfer is from lower average age department to a higher average age department. In any other case this would not occur.

Questions below are independent of each other.

91. There was a mutual transfer of an employee between Marketing and Finance department and transfer of one employee from Marketing to HR. As a result, the average age of the Finance department increased by one year and that of Marketing department remained the same. What is the new average age of the HR department?

(a) 30 (b) 35
(c) 40 (d) 45
(e) Can't be determined

Sol. *(c) The net result is that there would be 1 person less in the marketing department and one person more in HR. However, the number of people in the Finance department would remain the same.*
The normal way a student and most instructors would approach this problem would be as follows:
Initial total age of the three departments = Final total age of the three departments.
$\rightarrow 5 \times 45 + 30 \times 35 + 20 \times 30 = 6 \times A + 29 \times 35 + 20 \times 31.$
Solving, we would get the value of A as 40. However, this would be a very cumbersome process as it would involve tedious calculations and the minimum time would range between 45 secs and 2 mins depending on the calculation speed of the individual solver.
A much superior way to do this would be as follows:
Net change in total age should be zero.
Thus,
Change in total age of Marketing + Change in total age of Finance + change in total age of HR = 0
$\Rightarrow -1 \times 35 + 20 \times 1 + x = 0$
$\Rightarrow x = 15$ *= change in total age of HR department*
Thus, the total age of the HR department would increase from 45 × 5 = 225 to 240 for 6 people.
Thus, the new average age of HR = 40 (option (c).

92. What is the approximate percentage change in the average gross pay of the HR department due to transfer of a 40-year old person with a basic pay of ₹ 8000 from the Marketing department?
(a) 9% (b) 11%
(c) 13% (d) 15%
(e) 17%

Sol. *(c) This can be calculated by:*
Total gross pay of HR before the transfer = 8500 × 5 = 42500.
(₹8500 from 5000 + 3500)
Total gross pay of HR after the transfer
= 42500 + 8000 + (90% of 8000)
= 42500 + 15200 = 57700.
Average gross pay = 57700/6 = 9616.66
The change in average gross pay can be calculated by calculating the percentage change in the value from 8500 to 9616.66 which is approximately 13% (option (c).

93. If two employees (each with a basic pay of ₹6000) are transferred from Maintenance department to the HR department and one person (with a basic pay of ₹8000) was transferred from Marketing department to the HR department, what will be the percentage change in the average basic pay of HR department?
(a) 10.5% (b) 12.5%
(c) 15% (d) 30%
(e) 40%

Sol. *(b) Initial average = 5000*
Initial total = 25000 (5000 × 5)
New total = 25000 + 6000 + 6000 + 8000 = 45000
New average = 45000/8 = 5625
Percentage change = 12.5%
Hence, option (b) is the correct option.

Directions for Questions 94 to 96: Answer the following questions based on the information given below.

Abdul, Bikram and Chetan are three professional traders who trade in shares of a company XYZ Ltd. Abdul follows the strategy of buying at the opening of the day at 10 am and selling the whole lot at the close of the day at 3 pm. Bikram follows the strategy of buying at hourly intervals: 10 am, 11 am, 12 noon, 1 pm and 2 pm; and selling the whole at the close of the day. Further he buys an equal number of shares in each purchase. Chetan follows a similar pattern as Bikram but his strategy is somewhat different. Chetan's total investment amount is divided equally amongst his purchases. The profit or loss made by each investor is the difference between the sale value at the close of the day less the investment made in purchase. The 'return' for each investor is defined as the ratio of the profit or loss to the investment amount expressed as a percentage.

Sol. for 94 to 96
The following set of questions is based on your understanding of the concept of weighted averages. The simplest one to understand is the one about Abdul. Abdul will make a profit if the price goes up and loss if the price goes down.
Further, his percentage profit /loss would be exactly the same as the percentage increase/decrease of the share price.
Before you hit the question, you need to understand clearly the difference between Bikram and Chetan's strategies.
Since, Chetan invests an equal amount at every hour, the no. of shares he has bought would be dependent on the price fluctuation. For example, if

the prices are going down on a particular day, he would end up purchasing more shares at the lower price. In fact, his strategy of inverting an equal amount every hour ensures that he buys a higher number of shares at the lower prices irrespective of the fluctuation. Thus, his average purchase price per share would be the weighted average of all the prices with higher weights allocated to the lowest one during the day.

For Bikram on the other hand, his investment would always be in buying an equal no. of shares every hour. Thus, his average purchase price would always be the simple average of his 5 purchase prices.

Naturally, on any fluctuation prices day, Bikram's average price would be greater than Chetan's average price. As Chetan's average price would be the weighted average of the 5 price (@ 10, 11, 12, 1 & 2) with higher weights attached to the lower prices.

***Note:** What you need to have clear in your mind is that weighted average with higher weights attached to the lower prices would always have a lower value than a simple average.*

However, if the prices are flat the whole day (i.e., there is no change in prices throughout the day) the weighted average and simple average both would be equal to that single price.

94. Which one of the following statements is always true?
    (a) Abdul will not be the one with minimum return.
    (b) Return for Chetan will be higher than that of Bikram.
    (c) Return for Bikram will be higher than that of Chetan.
    (d) Return for Chetan cannot be higher than that of Abdul.
    (e) none of the above

Sol. *(e) We can solve this by looking at and eliminating individual options. Option (a) cannot be true as Abdul would have the minimum return if the price is highest at 10 am and continuously drops till 3 pm.*

Option (b) would normally 'have been true, but is not always true because if the price remains constant at 10, 11, 12, 1 & 2, Chetan would have the same return as Bikram.

Option (c) is also eliminated as we have seen that most of the time Chetan has a higher return than Bikram.

Option (d) can be eliminated on the basis of the thought that it is easily possible that Chetan has higher return than Abdul. For example, on a day of consistently reducing prices, Abdul has the least return.

Thus, option (e) is correct.

95. On a 'boom' day, the share price of XYZ Ltd. keeps rising throughout the day and peaks at the close of the day. Which trader got the minimum return on that day?
    (a) Bikram (b) Chetan
    (c) Abdul (d) Abdul or Chetan
    (e) cannot be determined

Sol. *(a) Abdul would get the maximum return on that day, since his purchase price (average) would be the least. Also, between Chetan and Bikram, we know that Bikram's average purchase price is higher and hence he would have the least returns.*

Hence, we will mark option (c).

96. On a day of fluctuating market prices, the share price of XYZ Ltd. ends with a gain, i.e., it is higher at the close of the day compared to the opening value. Which trader got the maximum return on that day?
    (a) Bikram (b) Chetan
    (c) Abdul (d) Bikram or Chetan
    (e) Cannot be determined

Sol. *(e) The maximum return could be for Abdul or Chetan. But, between the two we cannot determine who gained more because in order to get that we would need to know the exact price at each hour, starting from 10 am.*

Hence, we will mark option (e).

Directions for Questions 97 and 98: One day two other traders, Dane and Emily joined Abdul, Bikram and Chetan for trading in the shares of XYZ Ltd. Dane followed a strategy of buying equal number of shares at 10 am, 11 am and 12 noon, and selling the same numbers at 1 pm, 2 pm and 3 pm. Emily, on the other hand , followed the strategy of buying shares using all her money at 10 am and selling all of them at 12 noon; and again buying the shares for all the money at 1 pm and again selling all of them at the close of the day at 3 pm. At the close of the day, the following was observed:

(a) Abdul lost money in the transactions.
(b) Both Dane and Emily made profits.

(c) There was an increase in the share price during the closing hour compared to the price at 2 pm.
(d) Share price at 12 noon was lower than the opening price.

Before solving 153 and 154 we need to logically work out what happened with respect to prices on that day.

(a) Since Abdul lost money, price at 3 pm < price at 10 am, i.e., $P_3 < P_{10}$
(b) Dane made profits means $P_{10} + P_{11} + P_{12} < P_1 + P_2 + P_3$
(c) Emily made profits means $P_{10} + P_1 < P_{12} + P_3$
(d) $P_2 < P_3$
(e) $P_{12} < P_{10}$
(f) From (c) & (e) above, we know that $P_3 > P_1$.
(g) Also, from (c) we have $P_{10} - P_{12} < P_3 - P_1$. and from (b) & (g) we have: $2P_{10} + P_{11} < 2P_3 + P_2$ $\rightarrow P_{11} < P_2$

97. Which of the following is necessarily false?
(a) Share price was at its lowest at 2 pm.
(b) Share price was at its lowest at 11 am.
(c) Share price at 1 pm was higher than the share price at 2 pm.
(d) Share price at 1 pm was higher than the share price at 12 noon.
(e) None of the above

Sol. *(e) None of the four options (a – d) can be said to be necessarily false. As:*
Option (a) (share price least at 2 pm) can happen.
Option (b) (share price least at 11 am) can also happen.
In terms of equalities, what we know is:
$P_{10} - P_{12}, P_{10} < P_3, P_3 > P_1$ & $P_3 > P_2$ & $P_2 > P_{11}$
Option (c) and option (d) could also be true in some cases and hence are not necessarily false.

98. Share price was at its highest at:
(a) 10 am (b) 11 am
(c) 12 noon (d) 1 pm
(e) Cannot be determined

Sol. *(a) From the above, we have:*
$P_{10} > P_{12}, P_{10} > P_3$ *& since* $P_3 > P_1$ *and* $P_3 > P_2$, *it follows that* $P_{10} > P_{11}$ *and* $P_{10} > P_{11}$ *would also be true.*
Thus, the highest price would definitely be at 10 am (option (a).

PART II

TWELVE MINUTE TESTS

PART 2

TWELVE MINUTE TESTS

Twelve Minute Tests 1–30

IN THIS PART YOU WILL LEARN:

- To solve difficult reasoning-based questions in Data Interpretation in the format of a mock test.
- Not only to tackle the DI section more effectively but also by solving this part you would
  - Improve your ability to handle new unknown situations and unforeseen twists in a DI question
  - Improve your anticipation/recognition of novelties in DI question sets
  - Improve the depth and breadth of your exposure to DI questions as well as your DI problem solving skills
  - Improve your ability to make earlier decisions about whether you are going to be able to solve a question set or not
  - Improve your ability to work around hurdles in advanced DI problems
  - Improve your ability to work around hurdles in advanced DI problems
  - Increase your confidence level to take on any challenge thrown at you in a DI question paper

THIS PART CONTAINS:

- 30 Mock Tests, where you would be expected to solve 1 DI set in 12 minutes.
- In case you are not able to solve a particular set in 12 minutes, take additional time and try to solve the set on your own. Do keep track of the time you take to solve each set in this way. Once you finish the set (with or without the complete solution), head over to the solution and see how you could have modified your approach to help you solve the question or to become more efficient in the solution.

Twelve Minute Tests

Outline

Learning Objectives

- A unique collection of questions to test your mettle, your guts and your intelligence

Chapter Highlights

- Question sets of advanced reasoning based on Data Interpretation.

This part contains 30 Twelve-minute tests. These tests have been designed in such a way that they will test your solving prowess of Logical Data Interpretation. The Twelve-minute time limit has been set since, in order to crack the DI-lR section of the CAT with a high 99+ percentile, you would need to solve 2–3 sets in 40 minutes. (as I have explained in the preface of the book).

For each of these sets, you are expected to first solve the set in a strict 12 minute time frame. Each of the tests in this part contains 1 high quality set based on Logical DI. If you are able to do the set in that time then you are clearly heading to a good percentile in the CAT - however, you might still need to ask yourself the question of how you can reduce your time further - since 100 percentile would be breached only if you solve 3+ sets in 40 minutes (meaning around 10–11 minutes per set).

If you are not able to solve the set in 12 minutes your focus should be to first make sure that you can solve the same beyond the time limit and learn to identify what you were missing in the solving of the questions. It is imperative to first try to do it on your own – since that is going to be crucial to make sure that you extract maximum learning from each question. Hence, after the 12 minute time limit, don't bother about how much more time you take – and how many times you have to try the question, but it is important to stick to trying to solve on your own. After sufficient trial (that might include trying the set 5-10 times) if you are not done with the set by yourself, you can then try to check the solutions and try to identify what it is that you were not able to see in the question, due to which you weren't able to solve the question. You will be expected to use the same process for every set contained in Part 3 (Mock Test Papers of Logical DI) of this Section. Have a great learning experience!

LEVEL OF DIFFICULTY 3

1 Test

Direction for Question 1 to 4: Zaffran is a famous street food joint serving four items: fried rice, noodles, chips and ice creams. It has three employees Vijay, Bhola and Palan who prepare the items ordered by the customers. Preparation time is 12 minutes for fried rice, 8 minutes for noodles and 3 minutes for an order of ice cream and. An employee can prepare only one of these items at a time. The chips are prepared in an automatic fryer which can prepare up to 3 portions of chips at a time, and takes 5 minutes irrespective of the number of pieces. The fryer does not need an employee to constantly attend to it, and we can ignore the time taken by an employee to start and stop the fryer; thus, an employee can be engaged in preparing other items while the frying is on. However, chips cannot be prepared in anticipation of future orders. Zaffran wishes to serve the orders as early as possible. The individual items in any order are served as and when ready; however, the order is considered to be completely served only when all the items of that order are served. The table below gives the orders of five customers and the times at which they placed their orders:

Customer No.	Time	Order
1	11:00	1 Fried Rice, 3 portions of chips, 1 ice cream
2	11:05	1 Noodle, 2 portions of chips, 2 ice cream
3	11:07	1 Fried Rice, 1 Noodle and 1 portion of chips
4	11:11	1 Fried Rice, 2 portions of chips and 1 Noodle
5	11:17	1 ice cream, 2 Noodles and 1 Fried Rice

1. If they all take the most optimal decisions based on the constraints above, at what time would customer 5 get his complete order served?
   (a) 11:35 (b) 11:36
   (c) 11:38 (d) 11:40
2. If they all take the most optimal decisions based on the constraints above, at what time would customer 4 get his complete order served?
   (a) 11:30 (b) 11:26
   (c) 11:28 (d) 11:32
3. Assume that only one customer's order can be processed at any given point of time. So, Vijay, Bhola and Palan cannot start preparing a new order while a previous order is being prepared. At what time is the order placed by customer 5 completely served?
   (a) 11:58 (b) 11:55
   (c) 11:56 (d) 11:52
4. Assume that only one customer's order can be processed at any given point of time. So, Vijay, Bhola and Palan cannot start preparing a new order while a previous order is being prepared. What is the total idle time for the three workers starting from 11:00 AM to the time when the last order was served?
   (a) 58 minutes (b) 68 minutes
   (c) 67 minutes (d) 99 minutes

2 Test

Directions for Questions 1 to 4: A public poll was conducted to find the cleanest city of India in the year 2020. The public poll was conducted in five rounds namely Round I, Round II, Round III, Round IV and Round V in that particular order. The same group of 40000 people voted in each of the five rounds. The nominees for the most popular city award were P, Q, R, S, T and U. The following table provides information about the number of votes received by each of these six cities in the given rounds. One person could vote for only one city in the given rounds.

	Round-1	Round-2	Round-3	Round-4	Round-5
P	6800	7800	8600	5800	6800
Q	5200	7800	6200	7000	5800
R	10400	6400	8600	7200	8200
S	4200	6800	5600	5800	5600
T	8600	8600	7200	7000	8800
U	4800	2600	3800	7200	4800

Additional Information Given:

(i) People, who voted for P in any round, voted for either S or T in the following round.

(ii) Only those people, who voted for Q or U in any round, voted for P in the following round.

(iii) People, who voted for T in any round, voted for either R or U in the following round.

(iv) People who voted for S in round 1, voted for S in each of the next three rounds.

1. The Montmorency number for a city is defined as the number of cities who have got lesser number of votes than it in exactly two rounds. What is the sum total of all the Montmorency numbers of all the 6 cities in the table?
(a) 0 (b) 1
(c) 2 (d) 3

2. Out of the number of people who voted for P in any round, the minimum number of people who voted for S in the next round (counting for all the five rounds) is at least:
(a) 2200 (b) 600
(c) 1600 (d) 1100

3. The number of people who were retained by Q or U across the rounds of voting was at most:
(a) 7400 (b) 8200
(c) 14800 (d) 15600

4. What is the maximum number of voters that U could have retained in round 2?
(a) 2600 b) 2200
(c) 1300 (d) 400

3 Test

Directions for Questions 1 to 4: Answer the questions on the basis of the information given below.

In a Maori village of New Zealand elections are held every 5 years for the local elected representatives. The rules of voting are very strict – i.e., only those who are at least 18 years of age are allowed to vote – and unlike a lot of democracies voting is compulsory if you are eligible. The elections are always held on the 1st of May – which is the beginning of their calendar year. The following table gives the number of people of different age groups, who have cast their votes in the five elections from 1999 through 2019. During this period, in every election, every person who is eligible to vote casts his/her vote. Assume that during this time nobody left the village and nobody came into the village from outside.

	1999	2004	2009	2014	2019
18 Age < 38 years	438	380	384	440	450
38 Age < 58	472	500	400	440	432
58 Age	410	400	500	440	460

1. What is the least possible number of people who died between 1999 and 2019?
   (a) 422 (b) 96
   (c) 428 (d) 432
2. What is the maximum possible number of people who cast their votes in the year 1999 cast their votes in 2014 as well?
   (a) 1220 (b) 1192
   (c) 1200 (d) 892
3. If exactly 1100 people who cast their votes in 1999, cast their votes in 2004 also, then what is the maximum possible number of people whose age is between 38 and 43 in 2004?
   (a) 238 (b) 218
   (c) 138 (d) 28
4. What is the minimum possible number of people who cast their votes in both 1999 and 2009?
   (a) 800 (b) 850
   (c) 880 (d) 900

4 Test

Directions for Question 1 to 4: Four golfers Tiger, Shubhankar, Jeev and Els took some shots on the green in order to test their putting form. The following table gives the number of successful putts made by the four during the day on four different holes of the golf course – viz., Hole 1, Hole 2, Hole 3 and Hole 4.

	Hole 1	Hole 2	Hole 3	Hole 4
Tiger	7 or 8	5 or 6	3 or 4	5 or 6
Shubhankar	3 or 4	5 or 6	5 or 6	7 or 8
Jeev	6	3 or 4	7 or 8	3 or 4
Els	3 or 4	7 or 8	5 or 6	5 or 6

It is further known that:

1. No golfer putted the same number of putts on any two holes.
2. No two golfers putted the same number of putts on any hole.
3. The aggregate of the number of putts on the four holes, for each golfer was different.
4. The aggregate of the number of putts done by the four golfers was different across the four holes.

1. What is the total number of successful putts by the four golfers on Hole 1?
   (a) 21 (b) 19
   (c) 20 (d) Cannot be determined
2. On which of the following holes can the total number of putts by all the four golfers never be the maximum?
   (I) Hole 2
   (II) Hole 3
   (III) Hole 4
   (a) I only (b) II only
   (c) III only (d) II and III
3. The aggregate total number of putts for all four golfers put together is?
   (a) 83 (b) 84
   (c) 85 (d) 86
4. The aggregate putts successfully made by Tiger, if Shubhankar putted 7 times on Hole 4 was?
   (a) 24 (b) 23
   (c) 21 (d) 22

5 Test

Directions for Question 1 to 5: A group of 5 students- Pawan, Qazi, Ram, Shravan and Tarun participated in the National Management competition 2019. The competition consists of four exams of different subjects Verbal Ability (VA), Data Interpretation (DI), Logical Reasoning (LR) and Quantitative Aptitude (QA).

The tables given below show the marks of all the candidates on different subjects and the total marks of all students on a given subject.

TABLE A Students and Their Scores on Different Subjects

Student	VA	DI	LR	QA
Pawan		300		159
Qazi	264	195		156
Ram			330	
Shravan	216	225	60	168
Tarun	180		234	

TABLE B

Subject	Combined Score of All Students
VA	810
DI	900
LR	720
QA	600

In Table A each column has two missing values which are the least two scores on that subject and none of the missing values is more than 10% of the total marks scored by all the candidates together in that subject. Also assume that all the missing numbers in the table are integers.

1. What are the Maximum possible marks of Qazi in LR?
   (a) 24 (b) 12
   (c) 16 (d) None of these
2. What is the maximum possible percentage contribution of Ram in the total marks obtained by all the students in all the subjects?
   (a) 19.33 (b) 18.51
   (c) 24.47 (d) None of these
3. If the absolute difference between the total marks obtained by Pawan and Ram in the four subjects is minimum possible then what is the absolute difference between total marks obtained by Shravan and Tarun?
4. The student with the highest total marks in all the four subjects got 1st rank and student with the lowest total marks got 5th rank and it is known that no two students got same number of total marks then what rank did Ram get?
   (a) 3rd (b) 4th
   (c) 5th (d) Cannot be determined
5. In the previous question what rank did Qazi get if his total score in all the four subjects is a prime integer and his score in LR has more than four factors?

6 Test

Directions for Questions 1 to 4: MS, MBA and M.Tech are the three most sought after professional degree programmes in each of the five countries, viz., India, US, UK, Australia and Singapore. To complete any of these degrees, students can choose to study in any of these five countries. After the completion of their degrees, these students become professionals employable in all the five countries. The following table lists the total Expenses Incurred (EI) on these professional degrees and the Annual Incomes (AI) earned by the professionals, in their first job after the completion of their degrees, in each of these five countries in the local currencies.

Expenses Incurred (EI) and Annual Incomes (AI)

	India		US (USD)		UK (GBP)		Australia (AUD)		Singapore (SGD)	
	EI	AI	EI	AI	EI	AI	EI	AI	EI	AI
Humanities	300000	300000	52000	56000	40000	36000	50000	45000	60000	70000
MBA	1200000	1800000	90000	100000	56000	50000	60000	90000	65000	110000
M Tech	400000	620000	70000	80000	40000	40000	40000	50000	50000	75000

Using the following table, the EI and the AI figures of different countries can be compared in terms of Indian Rupees.

1 USD = 68.65 INR

1 GBP = 90.81 INR

1 AUD = 48.68 INR

1 SGD = 50.76 INR

Assume that the data given above is valid for every year. Also assume that professionals receive no increment in their salaries, unless specified.

1. Studying in which of these five countries, a student gets the best return on the expense incurred by him, at the end of the first year of his first job, if he completes any of the courses and works in the same country?
   (a) India (b) US
   (c) Singapore (d) Australia
2. Harshit works in Australia for an Australian company. The company sponsors him an interest free loan of 75% of the total expense on his MBA degree in UK. In return, he has to serve the company for three consecutive years in Australia after completing his MBA. The annual salary, net of deductions, that the company can pay Harshit, when employing him again, for full recovery of the loan amount over the period of three years should be closest to? (Assume that the salary payable is the same as the average income for an MBA in Australia.)
   (a) 84600 AUD (b) 64100 AUD
   (c) 77700 AUD (d) 192300 AUD
3. Mukul Sharma lives in India. In a few days, he will leave for UK to pursue a one year MBA degree. Airfare from India to UK is INR 22500 and that from UK to India is GBP 340. Before completing his degree, he wishes to visit India. Before allocating money for his expenses on his MBA degree in UK, his total Budget for tuition and travel is INR 2340000 only. How many times, from UK, can he make a return trip to India?
   (a) Only once (b) Only twice
   (c) Only thrice (d) Only four times
4. Parikshit and Shwetank completed their degrees in M Tech from Singapore and US respectively. Their M Tech was funded through a zero interest loan taken and to be refunded in Indian rupees. After completion of their degrees, Parikshit started working in US and Shwetank started working in Singapore. It is also known that Shwetank's placement in Singapore was at a salary that was 50% higher than the normal Singapore salary for M.Tech degree holders. Taking into account, their expenditures on degrees and their salaries only, the difference in the income available to be spent for them after repaying their study loans, at the end of first year of their jobs is approximately: (Assume the total loan has to be finished off in 3 years for both).
   (a) INR 544000 (b) 3100 USD
   (c) INR 422000 (d) INR 318000

7 Test

Directions for Questions 1 to 4: Answer the questions on the basis of the information given below.

The used car market in India is dominated by five major companies – Udhar, Sudhar, Sutradhar, Bhrashtachar and Sishtachar – and three minor companies – Mindtree, Lemontree and Boringtree. Each of these eight companies sold only Sedans. In all the years from 2019 onwards, each minor company had a sales value less than that of each major company, but the sales value of all the minor companies put together was at least as much as that of the least selling major company (by value). The table below, gives the percentage market shares (by value) of the top three selling major companies (by value), in each year from 2020 to 2023.

	Udhar	Sudhar	Sutradhar	Bhrashtachar	Sishtachar	Mindtree	Lemontree	Boringtree	Total Sales Value in ₹ Crore
2020		30%	20%	24%					1200
2021	23%		32%		25%				1500
2022	25%	22%			28%				2000
2023	24%			22%	20%				3000

It is also known that in each of the given years, the percentage shares of the eight companies were distinct natural numbers.

1. In how many numerical combinations of percentage distributions can we possibly distribute the remaining percentages for the year 2020?
2. The approximate percentage increase in the sales value of the sedans of major companies from 2020 to 2023, is at most:

   (a) 158% (b) 159%
   (c) 161% (d) 162%
3. The number of years in which each of the given eight companies had a sales value of more than ₹50 crore, is at most:
4. The total sales value (in ₹ crore) of Sutradhar in the given four years, was at least:

8 Test

Directions for Questions 1 to 3: Answer the questions on the basis of the information given below.

In the diagram given below, all the routes of going from Kanpur to Lucknow are shown by the help of arrows. Each route passes through some of the seven villages called A, B, C, D, E, F and G. The number given in brackets along with the name of a village represents the number of people staying in that village.

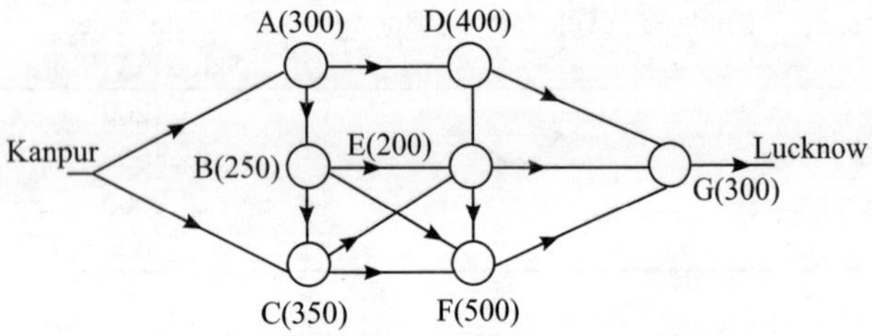

It is also known that:

(i) An Indian oil tanker is loaded with kerosene oil at Kanpur. It takes one of the possible routes to Lucknow and distributes oil cans amongst the people staying in all the villages along its route.

(ii) Each person staying in a village is given an oil can of 1.5 litres. A tanker is allowed to pass through a village on its route only after each person staying in the village gets the oil can.

1. How many different routes can a tanker loaded with 2100 liters of oil take from Kanpur to Lucknow such that it can give oil cans to all the people staying in villages along that route?
   (a) 4 (b) 6
   (c) 10 (d) 8
2. A tanker loaded with 2100 liters of oil is barely able to give oil cans to all the people staying in villages along its route and is left with no oil when it reaches Lucknow. How many villages fall in the route taken by the tanker?
   (a) 5
   (b) 4
   (c) 3
   (d) Cannot be determined
3. A pair of two routes on which the quantity of oil that needs to be distributed by a tanker is exactly the same is called a 'Perfect-pair'. How many Perfect-pairs are there amongst the different routes from Kanpur to Lucknow?
   (a) 0 (b) 1
   (c) 2 (d) 3
4. A tanker was sent from Kanpur to Lucknow on three successive days, such that it went through only 3 intermediate villages on each day. What is the total oil quantity dispensed on these three days?

9 Test

Directions for Questions 1 to 4: Answer the questions on the basis of the information given below.

A group of 5 students Aman, Bendre, Charwak, Denboo and Elangovan participated in an interschool science quiz, the quiz had four different rounds (1 to 4). The following table gives partial information about their individual points and the total points scored by the team in each round.

Each column has two values missing. These are the points scored by the two lowest scorers in that round. None of the two missing values is more than 10% of the total points scored in that round.

	Round-1	Round-2	Round-3	Round-4
Aman		200		106
Bendre	176	130		104
Charwak			226	
Denboo	144	150	40	112
Elangovan	120		150	
TOTAL	540	600	480	400

1. What is the minimum possible percentage contribution of Aman in the total points scored in the quiz?
   (a) 18.66% (b) 19.2%
   (c) 18.1% (d) None of these
2. If the absolute difference between the total points scored by Aman and Charwak in the four rounds is minimum possible then what is the absolute difference between total points scored by Ben and Elanin the quiz?
   (a) 70 (b) 34
   (c) 72 (d) Cannot be determined
3. If the difference between the total points scored by Aman and Charwak in the four rounds is the maximum possible then what is the difference between the difference of the total points scored by Aman and Charwak and the difference between the total points scored by Bendre and Elangovan?
4. The students are ranked 1 to 5 on the basis of the total points scored by them in the quiz, with the highest scorer getting rank 1. If it is known that no two students scored the same number of total points, how many students are there whose ranks can be exactly determined?

10 Test

Each of three companies, X, Y and Z, sells a different car amongst Falcon, Gauntlet and Prize, not necessarily in the same order. The companies did not sell any other products apart from these three cars.

The pie chart below provides, for the year 2018, the number (in '000) of cars sold by each of the three companies.

The table provides the price at which each car was sold (price/unit) in 2018.

Number (in '000) of Cars Sold

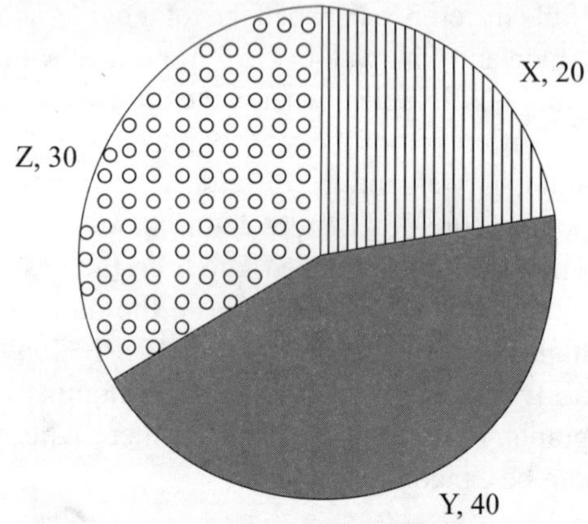

Cars	Price/Unit (in ₹)
Falcon	20000
Gauntlet	40000
Prize	30000

Note: The market share of a company is calculated as the revenue of the company as a percentage of the revenues of the three companies combined.

1. If it is known that the market share of none of the three companies was greater than 40%, which company sold Prize?
   (a) Y
   (b) X
   (c) Z
   (d) Cannot be determined
2. What is the lowest possible market share of any of the three companies, approximately?
   (a) 13.8%
   (b) 14.3%
   (c) 21.4%
   (d) 23.1%
3. If the company that sells Prize has more than 45% market share, what is the market share of the company that sells Falcon?
   (a) 30.8%
   (b) 27.4%
   (c) 31.2%
   (d) 23.1%
4. What is the approximate highest possible difference between the highest market share of any company and the second-lowest market share of any company?
   (a) 41.4%
   (b) 42.8%
   (c) 37.9%
   (d) 48.3%

LEVEL OF DIFFICULTY 3

11 Test

Arun wanted to get a new phone number, which comprises eight non-zero digits. He chose a phone number which satisfied all the following conditions, with the digits being referred to as first to eighth, starting from the leftmost digit:

(i) The last digit was greater than the third digit, while the fourth digit and the fifth digit, taken in that order, comprised (i.e., formed) a prime number.

(ii) The sixth and the third digits, taken in that order, comprised an even number greater than 40, while the first and the second digits are not the same.

(iii) The sum of the fourth digit and the third digit was the same as the fifth digit.

(iv) The sum of the fifth and the sixth digits was exactly 9, while the sixth and the seventh digits, taken in that order, comprised a prime number.

(v) The second and the eighth digits, taken in that order, comprised a number which was four more than the number comprised by the first and the second digits, taken in that order.

1. In how many ways could Arun have chosen the phone number?
   (a) 1 (b) 2
   (c) 4 or 5 (d) 8
2. Which of the following is the seventh digit of the phone number?
   (a) 3 (b) 6
   (c) 1 or 7 (d) None of these
3. Which of the following is the number comprised by the fifth and the third digits off the phone number, taken in that order?
   (a) 72 (b) 32
   (c) 39 (d) 59
4. What is the difference between the first and the sixth digit of the phone number?
   (a) 2 (b) 6
   (c) 8 (d) 3

12 Test

Three panel members, A, B and C, interviewed four candidates – P, Q, R and S. Each panel member scored each of the four candidates on four parameters – P1, P2, P3 and P4. The following tables provide partial information about the score given by each panel member to each candidate in each parameter:

Panel Member: B

	P1	P2	P3	P4
P		7		
Q				5
R				
S		8		

Panel Member: A

	P1	P2	P3	P4
P	1			
Q				
R				
S	4			

Panel Member: C

	P1	P2	P3	P4
P				4
Q				
R				
S				5

The following information is known about the scores given by each panel member:

(i) In each parameter, A gave a different score to each candidate and, for each candidate, A gave a different score in each parameter.

(ii) In each parameter, B gave a different score to each candidate and, for each candidate, B gave a different score in each parameter.

(iii) The scores that A gave to any candidate in any parameter was a positive integer less than 5.

(iv) The scores that B gave to any candidate in any parameter was an integer less than 9 and greater than 4.

(v) The score given by C to any candidate in any parameter was the average of the scores given by A and B to that candidate in that parameter.

(vi) The score given by C to any candidate in any parameter was an integer.

1. What is the score given by B to R in P3?
2. What is the score given by A to Q in P4?
3. What was the highest composite score in P3?
4. How many candidates received a higher composite score in P2 as compared to that in P3?

13 Test

Exactly 60 employees work in an office. During each of eight consecutive days, from Day 1 through Day 8, each of these 60 employees drank exactly one drink amongst Fanta, Pepsi and Sprite. On Day 1, an equal number of employees drank Fanta, Pepsi and Sprite.

The following table provides, for each day, starting from Day 2, the number of people who switched from Pepsi to Fanta, from Pepsi to Sprite, from Fanta to Pepsi, from Fanta to Sprite, from Sprite to Pepsi and from Sprite to Fanta as compared to the previous day.

	Day 2	Day 3	Day 4	Day 5	Day 6	Day 7	Day 8
Pepsi to Fanta	5	3	4	6	9	7	5
Pepsi to Sprite	4	2	6	4	5	2	7
Fanta to Pepsi	8	3	3	4	2	7	1
Fanta to Sprite	6	6	8	2	3	1	6
Sprite to Pepsi	7	2	5	4	6	3	1
Sprite to Fanta	2	5	2	2	8	3	4

1. How many employees drank Sprite on Day 6?
2. What is the average number of employees who drank Fanta per day during the given period?
3. During the given period, on how many days did at least 16 employees drink each of the three drinks?
4. What is the maximum number of employees that could have had Sprite on each of the 8 days?

14 Test

Seven persons – P through V – are standing in a line, from left to right, all facing the same direction. Amongst the seven persons, Q, S, T and U are girls, while the remaining are boys. Starting from the left, each person declared the number of persons standing adjacent to him/her who are not of the same gender as him/her. The numbers that each person declared, from left to right, are 1, 1, 1, 2, 2, 2 and 1 respectively.

Further, it is known that Q is standing adjacent to neither P nor R, while S is standing to the immediate right of V. Also, R is standing to the immediate left of T, who, in turn was not standing at the extreme right.

1. How many girls are standing to the right of Q?
   (a) 0 (b) 1
   (c) 2 (d) 3
2. Who amongst the following is standing adjacent to P?
   (a) S (b) V
   (c) T (d) R
3. Amongst the seven persons, exactly two persons exchanged their places and each of them as again declared the number of persons standing adjacent to him/her who are not of the same gender as him/her.
   If the maximum number of persons declared the highest possible number, who amongst the following exchanged his/her place?
   (a) R (b) S
   (c) U (d) Q
4. Amongst the seven persons, exactly two persons exchanged their places and each of them as again declared the number of persons standing adjacent to him/her who are not of the same gender as him/her.
   If, starting from the left, seven persons declared the same number, who amongst the following exchanged his/her place?
   (a) P (b) Q
   (c) V (d) None of these

15 Test

Shikha, an assistant to the dean of a college, was given a task to tabulate the courses taken by the students in the college. The students can take any number of courses amongst ME, CV, CH, AE, CS, EC and TL. She prepared a table comprising eight columns, with the students' names mentioned in the first column and the remaining seven columns, i.e., the second column to the eighth column, representing the seven courses, in the same order, from left to right, as mentioned above. In the row corresponding to every student, Shikha marked every cell corresponding to a course that the student took with a tick and every cell corresponding to a course that the student did not take with a cross.

After preparing the table, she made the following observations:

(i) The student in the first row of the table took all the courses.

(ii) The student in the second row took all the courses except for the courses in the second and eighth columns.

(iii) The student in the third row took all the courses except for the courses in the second, third, seventh and eighth columns.

(iv) The student in the fourth row took all the courses except for the courses in the second, third, fourth, sixth, seventh and eighth columns.

(v) The students in the fifth, sixth and seventh rows took the same courses as the students in the third, second and first rows respectively.

(vi) This pattern mentioned from (i) through (v) repeats, starting from the seventh row for all the students in the table, and continues repeating until the last row.

1. If the number of students who took at least three courses was 243, how many students are there in the college?
   (a) 291 (b) 292
   (c) 290 (d) Cannot be determined
2. If exactly 59 students in the college took CS, how many students are there in the college?
   (a) 69 (b) 71
   (c) 70 (d) Cannot be determined
3. If there were 93 students in the college, how many students took CS but not CV?
   (a) 33 (b) 30
   (c) 31 (d) 32
4. How many students could possibly take EC, if only 43 students took ME?
   (a) 127 (b) 126
   (c) 125 (d) 130

16 Test

Professor Kumar gave five assignments – a, b, c, d and e – to five of his students – Rajiv, Dinesh, Max, Rishi and Anand, as part of a group assignment. The following table shows the times (in hours) taken by each of the students to complete the assignments:

Student	a	b	c	d	e
Rajiv	2	5	1.5	3	5
Dinesh	4	2	3	1	4
Max	1	3	4	2	1.5
Rishi	1.5	2.5	3.5	3	3
Anand	5	4	3.5	2	4

In a group assignment, all the assignments given must be completed and it is not necessary that every person does each and every assignment. At a time only one student can work on a given assignment.

1. Prof. Kumar decided to form a group of Dinesh, Max and Rishi to complete all the 5 assignments What is the minimum time required by the group?
2. What is the minimum cumulative time spent by all the students in completing the group assignment given that each student completed an assignment?
3. What is the maximum cumulative time spent by all the students in completing the group assignment given that each student completed an assignment?
4. What is the average cumulative time taken by the 5 students to complete the assignment?

17 Test

Exactly three persons, Rajeev, Dev and Kabeer, participated in a weightlifting competition, comprising three rounds, in which each person lifts a weight exactly once in each of the three rounds. After the three persons participate in the three rounds, the Combined Total Weight, which is defined as the sum of the heaviest two weights lifted in any round by a person, is calculated for each of the three persons. The three persons are then ranked, from 1 to 3, in the descending order of their Combined Total Weights. No person lifted the same weight across any two rounds and the Combined Total Weight for each person was distinct. Further, the weight (in kg) that each person lifted was an integer.

Kabeer lifted 17 kg more in the first round than Dev did in that round, while Rajeev lifted the same weight in the second round as Dev did in the third round. Also, the round in which a person lifted his least weight was distinct for the three persons. The difference in the weight lifted by Dev in the first round and that by Kabeer in the third round was 20 kg, while the difference in the weights lifted by Kabeer in the first round and Rajeev in the third round was 18 kg. Dev lifted 25 kg more in the second round than Rajeev did in the first round. The Combined Total Weight for Rajeev was calculated using the weights that he lifted in the first and second rounds. Further, Kabeer lifted 15 kg more in the second round than Dev did in the third round.

1. If Kabeer was ranked first in the competition, then what is the maximum difference (in kg) in the weights lifted by Rajeev in the first round and Dev in the first round?
2. If Dev is ranked first in the competition, what is the minimum difference (in kg) between the highest weight that any person lifted in any round and the lowest weight that any person lifted in any round?
3. If Rajeev was ranked second in the competition, what is the minimum difference (in kg) between the weight that Dev lifted in the second round and the weight that Kabeer lifted in the second round?
4. If the weights lifted by each person in the second round were all distinct integral multiples of 15, what is the minimum combined total weight (in kg) of the person who was ranked first?

18 Test

On a particular day, six persons, P through U, got into and got down a train at seven different train stations – S1 through S7. The train stopped at the seven stations in the same order as mentioned above. The first table below provides the persons who got into and got down the train at each station and the second table provides the duration (in minutes) for which each person was in the train:

Train Station	Persons Who Got Into the Train	Persons Who Got Out of the Train
S1	P, U	–
S2	T	–
S3	S	–
S4	Q	P, T
S5	R	S, U
S6	–	Q
S7	–	R

Person	Duration in Train (in minutes)
P	41
Q	16
R	23
S	17
T	29
U	47

Assume that the duration for which the train stops at any station is negligible.

1. How many minutes did it take to reach S5 from S4?
2. For how many minutes were both P and S in the train?
3. For how many minutes were there at least two persons in the train?
4. For how many minutes were there four persons in the train?

19 Test

Two football teams, A and B, from the same college play against each other frequently. During a particular year, the two teams played exactly 100 matches against each other. It is also known that the number of goals scored in any match was at most 4; the number of goals scored by A in any match was at least 1; the number of goals scored by B in any match was at least 1. The following information is known about the number of goals scored by the two teams in each match:

(i) The number of matches that A won was 27 more than the number of matches in which B scored at least 2 goals.

(ii) The number of matches that ended as a draw was the same as the number of matches in which A scored exactly 1 goal.

(iii) The number of matches in which the difference in the number of goals scored by the two teams was at least 2 was twice the number of matches in which 3 goals were scored in total.

(iv) The sum of the number of matches that A did not win and those it won by at most 1 goal was 15 more than the number of matches that it won.

(v) The number of matches in which one team scored exactly one goal more than the other team was 20 less than the number of matches in which one team scored exactly two goals more than the other team.

1. How many matches ended in a win for A?
2. How many goals did B score in all the matches it played against A during the year?
3. In how many matches did B score 2 goals more than A?
4. What is the goal difference (goals for – goal against) of A for all the matches it played against B?

20 Test

A sales representative, Rishi Agarwal, deals with only six drugs – P, Q, R, S, T and U. He purchases the drugs from the company at ₹120, ₹400, ₹160, ₹320, ₹640 and ₹140 per unit respectively and sells them to pharmacies at ₹184, ₹460, ₹256, ₹352, ₹720 and ₹196 per unit respectively. He sells each drug only in packs of 100 units.

1. On a certain day, if he sold a total of 200 units, then which of the following cannot be his total profit on that day?
   (a) ₹8,800 (b) ₹12,800
   (c) ₹14,600 (d) ₹17,600
2. On a day on which he sold all the six drugs, selling 100 units of each drug, what was his total profit (in ₹)?
3. On a given day Rishi attained a profit percentage of 12.8%. Which of these drugs did he definitely sell?
   (a) Q (b) S
   (c) T (d) Cannot be determined
4. Rishi wanted to maximise his revenue on a given day. On that day he sold 600 units of drugs. It is known that he sold at least 3 drugs on that day. What is the maximum revenue he can make on that day?

21 Test

Utkarsh, the manager of a retail shop, tracks the number of customers of different ages who visited the shop on 15 days, from February 10th to February 24th. He observed that no customer whose age is 10 years or less visited the shop during the given time.

He made the following line graph which provides the number of customers of different age groups who visited the shop on each of the 15 days:

1. On one of the 15 days, Anjali, a 36-year-old beautician visited the shop. On which of the following days did she definitely not visit the shop.
   (a) 14th Feb (b) 22nd Feb
   (c) 18th Feb (d) None of these
2. What is the minimum possible average age of all the persons that visited the shop on one of the 15 days? (To one decimal point.)
3. On one of the days, 12 teenagers visited the shop along with 12 customers with ages between 30 and 40. Also, at least 15 customers over the age of 40 visited the shop. On how many of the 15 days could this happen?
4. What is the mean age of all the customers that visited the shop in these 15 days?
   (a) 24.67 (b) 28.72
   (c) 25 (d) Cannot be determined

LEVEL OF DIFFICULTY 2

22 Test

Directions for Questions 1 to 4: Answer the questions on the basis of the following charts.

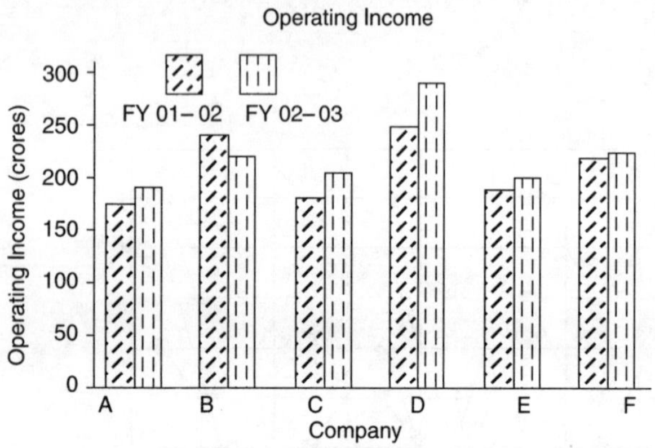

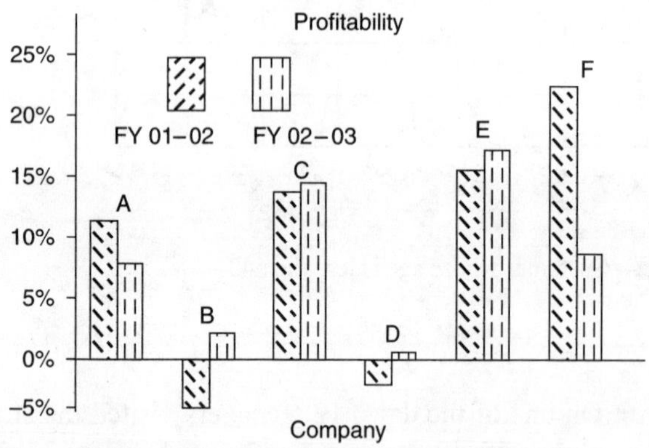

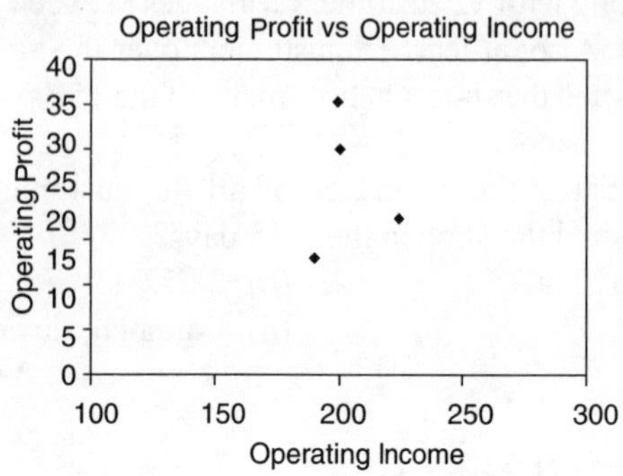

The profitability of a company is defined as the ratio of its operating profit to its operating income, typically expressed in percentage. The following two charts show the operating income as well as the profitability of six companies in the Financial Years (F.Y.s) 2001–02 and 2002–03.

The operating profits of four of these companies are plotted against their respective operating income figures for the F.Y. 2002–03, in the third chart given above.

1. What is the approximate average operating profit, in F.Y. 2001–02, of the two companies excluded from the third chart?
   (a) –7.5 crore (b) 3.5 crore
   (c) 25 crore (d) Cannot be determined
2. Which company recorded the highest operating profit in F.Y. 2002–03.
   (a) A (b) C
   (c) E (d) F
3. Which of the following statements is NOT true?
   (a) The company with the third lowest profitability in F.Y. 2001–02 has the lowest operating income in F.Y. 2002–03.
   (b) The company with the highest operating income in the two financial years combined has the lowest operating profit in F.Y. 2002–03.
   (c) Companies with a higher operating income in F.Y. 2001–02 than in F.Y. 2002–03 have higher profitability in F.Y. 2002–03 than in F.Y. 2001–02.
   (d) Companies with profitability between 10% and 20% in F.Y. 2001–02 also have operating incomes between 150 crore and 250 crore in F.Y. 2002–03.
4. The average operating profit in F.Y. 2002–03, of companies with profitability exceeding 10% in F.Y. 2002–03, is approximately:
   (a) 17.5 crore (b) 25 crore
   (c) 27.5 crore (d) 32.5 crore

23 Test

Directions for Questions 1 to 4: Answer the questions on the basis of the information given below.

Prof. Singh has been tracking the number of visitors to his homepage. His service provider has provided him with the following data on the country of origin of the visitors and the university they belong to:

Number of Visitors

	Day		
Country	**1**	**2**	**3**
Canada	2	0	0
Netherlands	1	1	0
India	1	2	0
UK	2	0	2
USA	1	0	1

Number of Visitors

	Day		
University	1	2	3
University 1	1	0	0
University 2	2	0	0
University 3	0	1	0
University 4	0	0	2
University 5	1	0	0
University 6	1	0	1
University 7	2	0	0
University 8	0	2	0

1. University 1 can belong to
   (a) UK (b) Canada
   (c) Netherlands (d) USA
2. To which country does University 5 belong?
   (a) India or Netherlands but not USA
   (b) India or USA but not Netherlands
   (c) Netherlands or USA but not India
   (d) India or USA but not UK
3. Which amongst the listed countries can possibly host three of the eight listed universities?
   (a) None (b) Only UK
   (c) Only India (d) Both India and UK
4. Visitors from how many universities from UK visited Prof. Singh's home page in the three days?
   (a) 1 (b) 2
   (c) 3 (d) 4

LEVEL OF DIFFICULTY 2

24 Test

Directions for Questions 1 to 4: Answer the questions on the basis of the information given below.

The Dean's office recently scanned student results into the central computer system. When their character reading software cannot read something, it leaves that space blank. The scanner output reads as follows:

In the grading system, A, B, C, D and F grades fetch 6, 4, 3, 2 and 0 grade points respectively. The Grade Point Average (GPA) is the arithmetic mean of the grade points obtained in the five subjects. For example, Nisha's GPA is (6 + 2 + 4 + 6 + 0)/5 = 3.6.

Some additional facts are also known about the students' grades. These are:

Name	Finance	Marketing	Statistics	Strategy	Operations	GPA
Aparna		B	F		C	1.4
Bikas	D	D	F	F		
Chandra		D	A	F	F	2.4
Deepak	A	B		D	D	3.2
Fazal	D	F	B		D	2.4
Gowri	C	C	A	C	B	3.8
Hari		B	A		D	2.8
Ismet			B		A	
Jagdeep	A	A	B		C	3.8
Kunal	F		A	F	F	1.8
Leena	B	A		B	F	3.2
Manab			A	B	B	
Nisha	A	D	B	A	F	3.6
Osman	C		B	B	A	4.6
Preeti	F	D		D		3.2
Rahul	A	C	A		F	4.2
Sameer		C	F	B		
Tara	B					2.4
Utkarsh			F	C	A	3.0
Vipul	A		C	C	F	2.4

(a) *Vipul obtained the same grade in Marketing as Aparna obtained in Finance and Strategy.*

(b) *Fazal obtained the same grade in Strategy as Utkarsh did in Marketing.*

(c) *Tara received the same grade in exactly three courses.*

1. In Operations, Tara could have received the same grade as:
   (a) Ismet (b) Hari
   (c) Jagdeep (d) Manab

2. What grade did Preeti obtain in Statistics?
   (a) A (b) B
   (c) C (d) D

3. In Strategy, Gowri's grade point was higher than that obtained by:
   (a) Fazal (b) Hari
   (c) Nisha (d) Rahul

4. What grade did Utkarsh obtain in Finance?
   (a) B (b) C
   (c) D (d) F

25 Test

Directions for Questions 1 to 4: Answer the questions on the basis of the information given below.

The year was 2006. All six teams in Pool A of World Cup Hockey, play each other exactly once. Each win earns a team three points, a draw earns one point and a loss earns zero points. The two teams with the highest points qualify for the semifinals. In case of a tie, the team with the highest goal difference (Goal For - Goals Against) qualifies.

In the opening match, Spain lost to Germany. After the second round (after each team played two matches), the pool table looked as shown below.

In the third round, Spain played Pakistan, Argentina played Germany and New Zealand played South Africa. All the third round matches were drawn. The following are some results from the fourth and fifth round matches

(a) *Spain won both the fourth and fifth round matches.*

(b) *Both Argentina beat and Germany won their fifth round matches by 3 goal to 0.*

(c) *Pakistan won both the fourth and fifth round matches by 1 goal to 0.*

Pool A							
Teams	Games Played	Won	Drawn	Lost	Goals For	Goals Against	Points
Germany	2	2	0	0	3	1	6
Argentina	2	2	0	0	2	0	6
Spain	2	1	0	1	5	2	3
Pakistan	2	1	0	1	2	1	3
New Zealand	2	0	0	2	1	6	0
South Africa	2	0	0	2	1	4	0

1. Which one of the following statements is true about matches played in the first two rounds?
   (a) Pakistan beat South Africa by 2 goals to 1.
   (b) Argentina beat Pakistan by 1 goal to 0.
   (c) Germany beat Pakistan by 2 goals to 1.
   (d) Germany beat Spain by 2 goals to 1.
2. Which one of the following statements is true about matches played in the first two rounds?
   (a) Germany beat New Zealand by 1 goal to 0.
   (b) Spain beat New Zealand by 4 goals to 0.
   (c) Spain beat South Africa by 2 goals to 0.
   (d) Germany beat South Africa by 2 goals to 1.
3. Which team finished at the top of the pool after five rounds of matches?
   (a) Argentina (b) Germany
   (c) Spain (d) Cannot be determined
4. If Pakistan qualified as one of the two teams from Pool A, which was the other team that qualified?
   (a) Argentina (b) Germany
   (c) Spain (d) Cannot be determined

26 Test

Directions for Questions 1 to 4: Venkat, a stockbroker, invested a part of his money in the stock of four companies – A, B, C and D. Each of these companies belonged to different industries, viz., Cement, Information Technology (IT), Auto, and Steel, in no particular order. At the time of investment, the price of each stock was ₹100. Venkat purchased only one stock of each of these companies. He was expecting returns of 20%, 10%, 30%, and 40% from the stock of companies A, B, C and D, respectively. Returns are defined as the change in the value of the stock after one year, expressed as a percentage of the initial value. During the year, two of these companies announced extraordinarily good results. One of these two companies belonged to the Cement or the IT industry, while the other one belonged to either the Steel or the Auto industry. As a result, the returns on the stocks of these two companies were higher than the initially expected returns. For the company belonging to the Cement or the IT industry with extraordinarily good results, the returns were twice that of the initially expected returns. For the company belonging to the Steel or the Auto industry, the returns on announcement of extraordinarily good results were only one and a half times that of the initially expected returns. For the remaining two companies, which did not announce extraordinarily good results, the returns realised during the year were the same as initially expected.

1. What is the minimum average return Venkat would have earned during the year?
   (a) 30% (b) 31¼% (c) 32½ % (d) Cannot be determined
2. If Venkat earned a 35% return on average during the year, then which of these statements would necessarily be true?
   I. Company A belonged either to Auto or to Steel Industry.
   II. Company B did not announce extraordinarily good results.
   III. Company A announced extraordinarily good results.
   IV. Company D did not announce extraordinarily good results.
   (a) I and II only (b) II and III only
   (c) III and IV only (d) II and IV only
3. If Venkat earned a 38.75% return on average during the year, then which of these statement(s) would necessarily be true?
   I. Company C belonged either to Auto or to Steel Industry.
   II. Company D belonged either to Auto or to Steel Industry.
   III. Company A announced extraordinarily good results.
   IV. Company B did not announce extraordinarily good results.
   (a) I and II only (b) II and III only
   (c) I and IV only (d) II and IV only
4. If Company C belonged to the Cement or the IT industry and did announce extraordinarily good results, then which of these statement (s) would necessarily be true?
   I. Venkat earned not more than 36.25% return on average.
   II. Venkat earned not less than 33.75% return on average.
   III. If Venkat earned 33.75% return on average, Company A announced extraordinarily good results.
   IV. If Venkat earned 33.75% return on average, Company B belonged either to Auto or to Steel Industry.
   (a) I and II only (b) II and IV only
   (c) II and III only (d) III and IV only

27 Test

Directions for Questions 1 to 4: In the following table is the listing of players, seeded from the highest (#1) to the lowest (#32), who are due to play in an Association of Tennis Players (ATP) tournament for women. This tournament has four knockout rounds before the final, i.e., first round, second round, quarterfinals, and semi-finals. In the first round, the highest seeded player plays the lowest seeded player (seed #32) which is designated match No. 1 of first round; the 2nd seeded player plays the 31st seeded player which is designated match No. 2 of the first round, and so on. Thus, for instance, match No. 16 of first round is to be played between the 16th seeded player and the 17th seeded player. In the second round, the winner of match No. 1 of first round plays the winner of match No. 16 of first round and is designated match No. 1 of second round. Similarly, the winner of match No. 2 of first round plays the winner of match No. 15 of first round, and is designated match No. 2 of second round. Thus, for instance, match No. 8 of the second round is to be played between the winner of match No. 8 of first round and the winner of match No. 9 of first round. The same pattern is followed for later rounds as well.

Seed #	Name of Player	Seed#	Name of Player	Seed	Name of Player
1.	Maria Sharapova	12.	Mary Pierce	23.	Silver Farina Elia
2.	Lindsay Davenport	13.	Anastasia Myskina	24.	Tatiana Golovin
3.	Amelie Mauresmo	14.	Alicia Molik	25.	Shinobu Asagoe
4.	Kim Clijsters	15.	Nathalie Dechy	26.	Francesca Schiavone
5.	Svetlana Kuznetsova	16.	Elena Bovina	27.	Nicole Vaidisova
6.	Elena Dementieva	17.	Jelena Jankovic	28.	Gisela Dulko
7.	Justine Henin	18.	Ana Ivanovic	29.	Flavia Pennetta
8.	Serena Williams	19.	Vera Zvonareva	30.	Anna Chakvetadze
9.	Nadia Petrova	20.	Elena Likhovtseva	31.	Ai Sugiyama
10.	Venus Williams	21.	Daniela Hantuchova	32.	Anna-lena Groenefeld
11.	Patty Schnyder	22.	Dinara Safina		

1. If Elena Dementieva and Serena Williams lose in the second round, while Justine Henin and Nadia Petrova make it to the semi-finals, then who would play Maria Sharapova in the quarterfinals, in the event Sharapova reaches quarterfinals?
   (a) Dinara Safina (b) Justine Henin
   (c) Nadia Petrova (d) Patty Schnyder
2. If the top eight seeds make it to the quarterfinals, then who, amongst the players listed below would definitely not play against Maria Sharapova in the final, in case Sharapova reaches the final?
   (a) Amelie Mauresmo (b) Elena Dementieva
   (c) Kim Clijsters (d) Lindsay Davenport
3. If there are no upsets (a lower seeded player beating a higher seeded player) in the first round, and only match Nos. 6, 7, and 8 of the second round result in upsets, then who would meet Lindsay Davenport in quarter finals, in case Davenport reaches quarter finals?
   (a) Justine Henin (b) Nadia Petrova
   (c) Patty Schnyder (d) Venus Williams
4. If, in the first round, all even numbered matches (and none of the odd numbered ones) result in upsets, and there are no upsets in the second round, then who could be the lowest seeded player facing Maria Sharapova in semi-finals?
   (a) Anastasia Myskina (b) Flavia Pennetta
   (c) Nadia Petrova (d) Svetlana Kuznetsova

LEVEL OF DIFFICULTY 2

28 Test

Directions for Questions 1 to 4: The table below shows the comparative costs, in US Dollars, of major surgeries in USA and a select few Asian countries.

Procedure	Comparative Costs in USA and Some Asian Countries (in US Dollars)				
	USA	India	Thailand	Singapore	Malaysia
Heart Bypass	130000	10000	11000	18500	9000
Heart Valve Replacement	160000	9000	10000	12500	9000
Angioplasty	57000	11000	13000	13000	11000
Hip Replacement	43000	9000	12000	12000	10000
Hysterectomy	20000	3000	4500	6000	3000
Knee Replacement	40000	8500	10000	13000	8000
Spinal Fusion	62000	5500	7000	9000	6000

The equivalent of one US Dollar in the local currencies is given below:

1 US Dollar Equivalent		
India	40.928	Rupees
Malaysia	3.51	Ringgits
Thailand	32.89	Bahts
Singapore	1.53	S Dollars

A consulting firm found that the quality of the health services were not the same in all the countries above. A poor quality of a surgery may have significant repercussions in future, resulting in more cost in correcting mistakes. The cost of poor quality of surgery is given in the table below.

Procedure	Comparative Costs of Poor Quality in USA and Some Asian Countries (in US Dollars '000)				
	USA	India	Thailand	Singapore	Malaysia
Heart Bypass	0	3	3	2	4
Heart Valve Replacement	0	5	4	5	5
Angioplasty	0	5	5	4	6
Hip Replacement	0	7	5	5	8
Hysterectomy	0	5	6	5	4
Knee Replacement	0	9	6	4	4
Spinal Fusion	0	5	6	5	6

1. Approximately, what difference in amount in Bahts will it make to a Thai citizen if she were to get a hysterectomy done in India instead of in her native country, taking into account the cost of poor quality? It costs 7500 Bahts for one-way travel between Thailand and India.
   (a) 235000 (b) 40500
   (c) 57500 (d) 67500
2. Taking the cost of poor quality into account, which country/countries will be the most expensive for knee replacement?
   (a) India (b) Thailand
   (c) Malaysia (d) Singapore

3. A US citizen is hurt in an accident and requires an angioplasty, hip replacement and a knee replacement. Cost of foreign travel and stay is not a consideration since the government will take care of it. Which country will result in the cheapest package, taking cost of poor quality into account?
   (a) India (b) Thailand
   (c) Malaysia (d) Singapore

4. The rupee value increases to ₹35 for a US Dollar, and all other things including quality, remain the same. What is the approximate difference in cost, in US Dollars, between Singapore and India for a Spinal Fusion, taking this change into account?
   (a) 1700 (b) 2500
   (c) 4500 (d) 8000

29 Test

Directions for Questions 1 to 5: Answer the following questions based on the information given below:

A low-cost airline company connects ten India cities, A to J. The table below gives the distance between a pair of airports and the corresponding price charged by the company. Travel is permitted only from a departure airport to an arrival airport. The customers do not travel by a route where they have to stop at more than two intermediate airports.

1. What is the lowest price, in rupees, a passenger has to pay for travelling by the shortest route from A to J?
   (a) 2275 (b) 2850
   (c) 2890 (d) 2930
   (e) 3340
2. The company plans to introduce a direct flight between A and J. The market research results indicate that all its existing passengers travelling between A and J will use this direct flight if it is priced 5% below the minimum price that they pay at present. What should the company charge approximately, in rupees, for this direct flight?
   (a) 1991 (b) 2161
   (c) 2707 (d) 2745
   (e) 2783
3. If the airports C, D and H are closed down owing to security reasons, what would be the minimum price, in rupees, to be paid by a passenger travelling from A to J?
   (a) 2275 (b) 2615
   (c) 2850 (d) 2945
   (e) 3190
4. If the prices include a margin of 10% over the total cost that the company incurs, what is the minimum cost per kilometer that the company incurs in flying from A to J?
   (a) 0.77 (b) 0.88
   (c) 0.99 (d) 1.06
   (e) 1.08
5. If the prices include a margin of 15% over the total cost that the company incurs, which amongst the following is the distance to be covered in flying from A to J that minimises the total cost per kilometer for the company?
   (a) 2170 (b) 2180
   (c) 2315 (d) 2350
   (e) 2390

Sector	Airport of Departure	Airport of Arrival	Distance between the Airports (km)	Ticket Price (Rs)
1	A	B	560	670
2	A	C	790	1350
3	A	D	850	1250
4	A	E	1245	1600
5	A	F	1345	1700
6	A	G	1350	2450
7	A	H	1950	1850
8	B	C	1650	2000
9	B	H	1750	1900
10	B	I	2100	2450
11	B	J	2300	2275
12	C	D	460	450

Sector	Airport of Departure	Airport of Arrival	Distance between the Airports (km)	Ticket Price (Rs)
13	C	F	410	430
14	C	G	910	1100
15	D	E	540	590
16	D	F	625	700
17	D	G	640	750
18	D	H	950	1250
19	D	J	1650	2450
20	E	F	1250	1700
21	E	G	970	1150
22	E	H	850	875
23	F	G	900	1050
24	F	I	875	950
25	F	J	970	1150
26	G	I	510	550
27	G	J	830	890
28	H	I	790	970
29	H	J	400	425
30	I	J	460	540

30 Test

Directions for Questions 1 to 3: Answer the following questions based on the information given as follows:

Abdul, Bikram and Chetan are three professional traders who trade in shares of a company XYZ Ltd. Abdul follows the strategy of buying at the opening of the day at 10 a.m. and selling the whole lot at the close of the day at 3 p.m. Bikram follows the strategy of buying at hourly intervals: 10 a.m., 11 a.m., 12 noon, 1 p.m. and 2 p.m., and selling the whole at the close of the day. Further, he buys an equal number of shares in each purchase. Chetan follows a similar pattern as Bikram but his strategy is somewhat different. Chetan's total investment amount is divided equally amongst his purchases. The profit or loss made by each investor is the difference between the sale value at the close of the day less the investment in purchase. The 'return' for each investor is defined as the ratio of the profit or loss to the investment amount expressed as a percentage.

1. Which one of the following statement is always true?
   (a) Abdul will not be the one with minimum return.
   (b) Return for Chetan will be higher than that of Bikram.
   (c) Return for Bikram will be higher than that of Chetan.
   (d) Return for Chetan cannot be higher than that of Abdul.
   (e) None of the above.
2. On a 'boom' day, the share price of XYZ Ltd. keeps rising throughout the day and peaks at the close of the day. Which trader got the minimum return on that day?
   (a) Bikram (b) Chetan
   (c) Abdul (d) Abdul or Chetan
   (e) Cannot be determined
3. On a day of fluctuating market prices, the share price of XYZ Ltd. ends with a gain, i.e., it is higher at the close of the day compared to the opening value. Which trader got the maximum return on that day?
   (a) Bikram (b) Chetan
   (c) Abdul (d) Bikram or Chetan
   (e) Cannot be determined

Directions for Questions 4 to 5: One day two other traders, Dane and Emily joined Abdul, Bikram and Chetan for trading in the shares of XYZ Ltd. Dane followed a strategy of buying equal number of shares at 10 a.m., 11 a.m., and 12 noon, and selling the same numbers at 1 p.m., 2 p.m. and 3 p.m. Emily, on the other hand, followed the strategy of buying shares using all her money at 10 a.m. and selling all of them at 12 noon and again buying the shares for all the money at 1 p.m. and again selling all of them at the close of the day at 3 p.m. At the close of the day, following observations were made:

(A) Abdul lost money in the transactions.
(B) Both Dane and Emily made profits.
(C) There was an increase in the share price during the closing hour compared to the price at 2 p.m.
(D) Share price at 12 noon was lower than the opening price.

4. Which of the following is necessarily false?
   (a) Share price was at its lowest at 2 p.m.
   (b) Share price was at its lowest at 11 a.m.
   (c) Share price at 1 p.m. was higher than the share price at 2 p.m.
   (d) Share price at 1 p.m. was higher than the share price at 12 noon.
   (e) None of the above
5. Share price was at its highest at:
   (a) 10 a.m. (b) 11 a.m.
   (c) 12 noon (d) 1 p.m.
   (e) Cannot be determined

Answer Key

TEST 1
1. (b) 2. (c) 3. (c) 4. (b)

TEST 2
1. (c) 2. (a) 3. (d) 4. (d)

TEST 3
1. (c) 2. (a) 3. (a) 4. (d)

TEST 4
1. (c) 2. (b) 3. (d) 4. (d)

TEST 5
1. (d) 2. (b) 3. 108 4. (c)
5. 2

TEST 6
1. (c) 2. (b) 3. (c) 4. (a)

TEST 7
1. 32 2. (c) 3. 2 4. 920

TEST 8
1 (d) 2. (a) 3. (c) 4. 4500

TEST 9
1. (a) 2. (c) 3. 36 4. 3

TEST 10
1. (c) 2. (a) 3. (d) 4. (b)

TEST 11
1. (b) 2. (c) 3. (b) 4. (a)

TEST 12
1. 6 2. 1 3. 18 4. 1

TEST 13
1. 23 2 16.25 3. 3 4. 11

TEST 14
1. (c) 2. (a) 3. (a) 4. (a)

TEST 15
1. (d) 2. (b) 3. (c) 4. (a)

TEST 16
1. 3.5 2. 8.5 3. 21
4. 14.8 hours

TEST 17
1. 10 2. 38 3. 46 4. 65

TEST 18
1. 6 2. 11 3. 57 4. 11

TEST 19
1. 49 2. 126 3. 4 4. 70

TEST 20
1. (c) 2. 38800 3. (b)
4. 369200

TEST 21
1. (d) 2. 17.6 3. 3 4. (d)

TEST 22
1. (a) 2. (c) 3. (a) 4. (d)

TEST 23
1. (c) 2. (a) 3. (a) 4. (b)

TEST 24
1. (d) 2. (a) 3. (b) 4. (c)

TEST 25
1. (b) 2. (d) 3. (c) 4. (d)

TEST 26
1. (a) 2. (b) 3. (c) 4. (b)

TEST 27
1. (d) 2. (c) 3. (d) 4. (a)

TEST 28
1. (d) 2. (a) 3. (c) 4. (b)

TEST 29
1. (a) 2. (b) 3. (c) 4. (b)
5. (d)

TEST 30
1. (e) 2. (a) 3. (e) 4. (e)
5. (a)

Solutions

TEST 1

The most optimal decisions would involve the following (assuming that they work in the order Vijay, Bhola and Palan):

Person					
Vijay	11 to 11:12 FR for (1)	11:12 to 11:20 N for (3)	11:20 to 11:28 N for (4)	11:28 to 11:36 N for (5)	
Bhola	11 to 11:03 I for 1	11:05 to 11:13 N for (2)	11:13 to 11:25 FR for (4)	11:25 to 11:33 N for (5)	11:33 to 11:36 I for 5
Palan	11:05 to 11:08 I for (2)	11:08 to 11:11 I for (2)	11:11 to 11:23 FR for (3)	11:23 to 11:35 FR for (5)	
Fryer for Chips	11 to 11:05 3 portions for (1)	11:05 to 11:10 2 portions for (2)	11:10 to 11:15 1 portion for (3)	11:15 to 11:20 2 portions for (4)	

1. Customer 5 gets served at 11:36. Option (b) is correct.
2. Customer 4 gets served at 11:28. Option (c) is correct.

For questions 3 and 4, the table would change to the following:

Person					
Vijay	11 to 11:12 FR for (1)	11:20 to 11:32 FR for (3)	11:32 to 11:44 FR for (4)	11:44 to 11:56 FR for (5)	
Bhola	11 to 11:03 I for 1	11:12 to 11:18 2 Ice Creams for (2)	11:20 to 11:28 N for (3)	11:44 to 11:52 N for (5)	11:52 to 11:55 I for (5)
Palan	11:12 to 11:20 N for (2)	11:32 to 11:40 N for (4)		11:44 to 11:52 N for (5)	
Fryer for Chips	11 to 11:05 3 portions for (1)	11:12 to 11:17 2 portions for (2)	11:20 to 11:25 1 portion for (3)	11:32 to 11:37 2 portions for (4)	

3. Customer 5 is completely served at 11:56 when his fried rice is served. Option (c) is correct.
4. It can be seen from the above table that Vijay's idle time is: 8 minutes, Bhola's idle time is (9 + 2 + 16 + 1 = 28 minutes) & Palan's idle time is (12 + 12 + 4 + 4 = 32 minutes). Hence, the total idle time is: 8 + 28 + 32 = 68 minutes. ***Note:*** For questions 3 and 4 you can change the work definition of the three people, yet the overall outcome for these questions would not change. Also note that we are not supposed to add the idle time for the fryer during this time.

TEST 2

1. R with respect to T & S with respect to U are the only cases where we see a city having lesser votes than another city in exactly 2 rounds. Thus, there are 2 instances in the table. Option (c) is correct.
2. We need to minimise the number of people who voted for S from those who voted for P in the previous round. In order to do this, the following is required:

   Round 1 to 2: People who voted for P: 6800, Shifted to T in Round 2 = 6800 (maximise this to minimise those who shift to S); Voted for S = 0;
   Round 2 to 3: People who voted for P: 7800, Shifted to T in Round 3 = 7200 (maximise this to minimise those who shift to S); Voted for S in Round 3 = 600;
   Round 3 to 4: People who voted for P: 8600, Shifted to T in Round 4 = 7000 (maximise this to minimise those who shift to S); Voted for S = 1600;
   Round 4 to 5: People who voted for P: 5800, Shifted to T in Round 4 = 5800 (maximise this to minimise those who shift to S); Voted for S = 0;
   Thus, the required answer is 600 + 1600 = 2200. Option (a) is correct.

Questions 3 to 4:

3. The shifts in the table are defined as: P to S; P to T; Q to P; U to P; T to R and T to U. In order to maximise the number of retentions, we would need to shift a voter only if he/she really needs to be shifted.

According to the problem:
Voters retained by P = 0; P's second round 7800 has to come from Q or U's first round voters. For this to occur – the total requirement of 7800 has to be serviced from the 5200 + 4800 of Q and U. Thus, Q and U have to transfer 7800 votes to P in round 2. Thus, the combined retention of Q and U would be 2200 at the maximum. Likewise, this number for round 3, would be: 7800 + 2600 – 8600 = 1800; for round 4 = 6200 + 3800 – 5800 = 4200 and for round 5 = 7000 + 7200 – 6800 = 7400. Thus, the total votes retained by Q or U would be a maximum of: 2200 + 1800 + 4200 + 7400 = 15600. Option (d) is correct.

4. Voters retained by P = 0; Voters retained by Q and U (maximum) = 15600; Voters retained by T = 0 (according to the 3rd clue).
Also, since voters of T shift to R or U in the next round, we can see that:
Round 1 to round 2: 8600 voters of T, have to shift to R or U (who have 6400 and 2600 votes respectively in round 2). Thus, of the total of 9000 votes that R and U got in round 2, 8600 must come from T. The minimum U would have received from T, would be 2200 and thus out of its 2600 voters in round 2, U could have retained a maximum of 400 voters. Hence, the correct answer would be 400.
Option (d) is correct.

TEST 3

1. The key to solve this is to look at the fact, that all the below 38 voters (18 to 38 age group) of the 1999 elections, would be between the age groups of 38 and 58 in 2019. Since, there are 438 voters below 38 in 1999 and there are only 432 voters in 2019 in the 18 to 38 age group, it must mean that a minimum of 6 voters who were between 18 and 38 in 1999 must have died. Likewise, those who were between 38 and 58 in 1999, were all above 58 in 2019. Since there are 472 voters in the 38 to 58 category, and only 460 in the 58 + category, it means that there were a minimum of 12 deaths in this category. Further, if we assume that all the 460 above 58 voters in 2019, were from the 38 to 58 category of 1999, it follows that all the 410 voters who were above 58 years of age in 1999 were dead by 2019. Thus it follows that there must be a minimum of 410 + 12 + 6 = 428 deaths between 1999 and 2019. Option (c) is correct.

2. In order to solve this question, you need to consider how many of each of the groups can at maximum vote in each of the years 1999, 2004, 2009 and 2014. Between 1999 and 2004, there is a minimum transfer of 28 people into the 38–58 category from the 18 to 38 category. Also, a maximum of 380 people can be retained in the voters of the 18 and 38 age group. Thus, of, the 438 people in the 18–38 category, who voted in 1999, 380 + 28 = 408 could have also voted in 2004. In 2009, all these 380 could possibly continue in the 18 and 38 category. Also, in 2014, a minimum of 40 from these 380 people would have to come into the 38 and 58 category. Thus, a maximum of 340 would continue to be in the 18 and 38 age group. Thus, from the 438 people in the first age group, 28 + 340 + 40 = 408 people could have possibly voted in all the three elections.
A similar analysis of the second category would show us that a maximum of 372 people could possibly continue to vote in this category through the four elections. [***Note:*** The numbers break up could be seen as: 1999 election: 472; 2004 election: 472 (retained) + 28 (coming from the first category); 2009 election – 100 transferred out from the second to the third category: 372 (retained) + 28 (retained) and 100 transferred out to the third category. 2014 election: 372 (retained) + 28 (retained) + 40 (coming in from the first age category into this category for the 2014 election). We have already added the 28 and 40 in the addition for the first group. We will need to see what happens to the 100 who moved to the third category when we consider the numbers in the third category. So, we get 372 people that we should count from here.
We now turn our attention to the numbers in the third group:
1999: 410; 2004: 400 (retained) 10 died; 2009: 400 (retained) + 100 coming in from the second age category as detailed above; 2014: 440 retained and 60 died from the 2009 list. So we need to add 440 from this group.
The required answer = 408 + 372 + 440 = 1220.
Option (a) is correct.

3. In order to maximise the number of people who were between 38 and 43 years of age in 2004, we need to maximise the number of people who got transferred from the 18 to 38 age category to the 38

to 58 age category, between 1999 and 2004. Also, we can see that the total number of voters in 1999 is 1320. So, out of these 1320 voters if only 1100 are voting in 2004, it means that there are 220 deaths in all the groups combined. Of these, 10 deaths must have happened in the 58 + age category. We will get the required maximum, when we assume that all the remaining 210 deaths occurred from amongst the 472 people in the 38 to 58 category. If we assume that, of the 472 people 210 deaths have occurred, it means that the 38 to 58 age category would only be retaining 262 people. Thus, 238 people must have come into this category from the first category between 1999 and 2004. Thus, a maximum of 238 people would be aged between 38 and 43 in 2004. Option (a) is correct.

4. The minimum retentions between 1999 and 2009 would occur under the following conditions:
Assume we minimise the number of people retained in the first group – i.e., of the 438 people in group 1, everybody shifted out to group 2 in 2004. This means that group 2 can retain at maximum only 62 people. In this situation, the 380 people in group 1 in 2004 must be all fresh 18 year olds who became eligible to vote in the interim. Thus, in the first group's 384 voters in 2009, none of them would have voted in 1999. Now, if we look at the second group in 2004, its construct would be: 438 (coming in from group 1) + 62(retained). Now, if we look at the numbers of groups 2 and 3 in 2004, we realise that a minimum of 100 need to be transferred into the third group from the second group between 2004 and 2009. But, this is not possible – since the second group in 2004 has only 62 retentions. Thus, the second group needs to have at least 100 retentions for the table to adhere to the logic. Thus, the story of the numbers would be as:
Group 1: 1999: 438; 2004: 400 (moved to group 2), 38 retained & 342 fresh first time voters who became 18 years old during 1999 to 2004; 2009: 342 retained + 42 new voters, 38 deaths.
Group 2: 1999:472; 2004: Retained 100 + 400 (Coming from Group 1); 2009: 400 who had come in from group 1 in 2004 would be retained. 100 would get transferred out to group 3.
Group 3:1999: 410; 2004: 10 died and 400 (retained); 2009: 400 retained + 100 (coming from group 2).
The minimum number of people who voted in 1999 and 2009 both = 0 + 400 + 500 = 900. Option (d) is correct.

TEST 4

Questions 1 to 4:

Based on the information provided in the table and the further conditions of the problem, we can deduce the following table of possibilities:

	Hole 1	Hole 2	Hole 3	Hole 4
Tiger	7 or 8	5/6	3 or 4	6/5
Shubhankar	3/4	6/5	5/6	7 or 8
Jeev	6	3/4	7 or 8	4/3
Els	4/3	7 or 8	6/5	5/6
TOTALS	Numbers with Shubhankar 3 and Els 4: 7 + 3 + 6 + 4 = 20 OR 8 + 3 + 6 + 4 = 21 Numbers with Shubhankar 4 and Els 3: 7 + 4 + 6 + 3 = 20 OR 8 + 4 + 6 + 3 = 21	Numbers with Tiger as 5 and Shubhankar as 6: 5 + 6 + 3 + 7 = 21 OR 5 + 6 + 3 + 8 = 22 OR 5 + 6 + 4 + 7 = 22 OR 5 + 6 + 4 + 8 = 23 Numbers with Tiger as 6 and Shubhankar as 5: 6 + 5 + 3 + 7 = 21 OR 6 + 5 + 3 + 8 = 22 OR 6 + 5 + 4 + 7 = 22 OR 6 + 5 + 4 + 8 = 23	Numbers with Shubhankar as 5 and Els as 6: 3 + 5 + 7 + 6 = 21 OR 3 + 5 + 8 + 6 = 22 OR 4 + 5 + 7 + 6 = 22 OR 4 + 5 + 8 + 6 = 23 Numbers with Shubhankar as 6 and Els as 5: 3 + 6 + 7 + 5 = 21 OR 3 + 6 + 8 + 5 = 22 OR 4 + 6 + 7 + 5 = 22 OR 4 + 6 + 8 + 5 = 23	Numbers with Tiger as 6 and Els as 5: 6 + 7 + 4 + 5 = 22 OR 6 + 7 + 3 + 5 = 21 OR 6 + 8 + 4 + 5 = 23 OR 6 + 8 + 3 + 5 = 22 Numbers with Tiger as 5 and Els as 6: 5 + 7 + 4 + 6 = 22 OR 5 + 7 + 3 + 6 = 21 OR 5 + 8 + 4 + 6 = 23 OR 5 + 8 + 3 + 6 = 22

Note the following things about the above table:

Deduction 1: On Hole 2, Tiger could be 5 or 6. If we put Tiger as 5 on hole 2, then the following chain happens:
Tiger is 6 on Hole 4; Shubhankar is 6 on Hole 2; Shubhankar is 5 on hole 3; Els is 6 on Hole 3 and Els is 5 on Hole 4.

On the other hand, if we put Tiger as 6 on hole 2, then the following chain happens:

Tiger is 5 on Hole 4; Shubhankar is 5 on Hole 2; Shubhankar is 6 on hole 3; Els is 5 on Hole 3 and Els is 6 on Hole 4.

Deduction 2: We have similar logic on Hole 1 between Shubhankar and Els → If Shubhankar is 3 on Hole 1, then Els would be 4 on hole 1. On the other hand if Shubhankar is 4 on Hole 1, then Els would be 3 on Hole 1. Please note, that this two way choice between Shubhankar and Els on hole 1 is not connected to the chain of 5's and 6's described above.

Deduction 3: Similarly, for Jeev, 3 and 4 have to be shared between Hole 2 and Hole 4. Thus, if Jeev is 3 on Hole 2, then he is 4 on Hole 4, and vice versa. Again, this chain for Jeev's numbers on hole 2 and hole 4 is not connected to the other chains mentioned above.

Hence, there are a total of 8 possible scenarios for the numbers in the table.

Deduction 4: It is given to us that the sum of the number of putts on each hole is different. (The aggregate of the number of putts done by the four golfers was different across the four holes.) If we look through the possibilities, we see that the sum of the first hole is 20 or 21. The sums of the second, third and fourth hole are 21 or 22 or 23. This necessarily means that the sums of 21,22 and 23 would necessarily be shared between Holes 2, 3 and 4. Thus, Hole 1 cannot have a 21. Hence, Hole 1 would be 20. This also means that Tiger's number of putts on hole 1 would be necessarily 7. The table would then look as follows:

	Hole 1	Hole 2	Hole 3	Hole 4
Tiger	7	5/6	3 or 4	6/5
Shubhankar	3/4	6/5	5/6	7 or 8
Jeev	6	3/4	7 or 8	4/3
Els	4/3	7 or 8	6/5	5/6
Possible Sums for each hole:	20	21/22/23	21/22/23	21/22/23

1. The required total is 20. Option (c) is correct.
2. From this point we can move forward to the second question. In order to solve the second question, we need to consider the sums of the putts for each golfer.

	Hole 1	Hole 2	Hole 3	Hole 4	Possible Sums for Each Golfer
Tiger	7	5/6	3 or 4	6/5	21 or 22
Shubhankar	3/4	6/5	5/6	7 or 8	21 or 22 or 23
Jeev	6	3/4	7 or 8	4/3	20 or 21
Els	4/3	7 or 8	6/5	5/6	21 or 22 or 23
Possible Sums for each hole:	20	21/22/23	21/22/23	21/22/23	

In the sums column for the number of putts made by each golfer, we can see that the number of putts is 21 or 22 for Tiger, 21/22/23 for Shubhankar and Els. This means that 21 cannot belong to anyone outside these three – since if you tried to make Jeev as 21, the numbers for Tiger, Shubhankar and Els would not be distinct from each other.

Thus, Jeev cannot have a total of 21 and hence his total is 20. This also means that Jeev's Hole 3 score cannot be 8. Hence, his Hole 3 score must be 7. Thus, 23 is ruled out as the sum of Hole 3. Hence, Hole 3 cannot have the largest number of putts. Option (b) is correct.

3. The total number of putts for the four holes would be the addition of 20 (hole 1) + 21 + 22 + 23 (Holes 2 to 4 in no particular order) = 20 + 21 + 22 + 23 = 86 putts. Option (d) is correct.
4. To the current table if we add the fact that Shubhankar has a 7 on Hole 4, the following chain of deductions emerge: We already know that Jeev is 7 on Hole 3. The sum of hole 3 would be between 21 and 22. Likewise, the sum of hole 4 (after inserting 7 for Shubhankar as stated in the question) would be 21 or 22. This means that Hole 2 has to be 23. If you continue this chain of thought to its logical concluding point, the table that emerges from these conclusions would look as follows:

	Hole 1	Hole 2	Hole 3	Hole 4	Possible Sums for Each Golfer
Tiger	7	5/6	4	6/5	22
Shubhankar	3	6/5	5/6	7	21
Jeev	6	4	7	3	20
Els	4	8	6/5	5/6	23
Possible Sums for each hole:	20	23	22	21	

In this situation, we can clearly see that Tiger's aggregate putts was 22.

Hence, option (d) is correct.

TEST 5

We can make the following table to understand the total value of the missing numbers to be allocated to each subject:

	VA	DI	LR	QA
Total Score	810	900	720	600
Total of top three scores given	660	720	624	483
Total Score of the last two missing numbers	150	180	96	117
10% limit	81	90	72	60
Third scorer's limit	180	195	60	156

1. The total marks in LR are equal to 720. Out of this, 624 marks have been scored by Ram, Shravan and Tarun. This leaves a total of 96 marks left to be scored by Pawan and Qazi. Also, both of them should score a maximum of 59 marks – as they have to score below Shravan's score of 60. So, the maximum possible score for Qazi in LR is 59. Hence, option (d) is correct.
2. Ram's maximum contribution would occur if he gets the maximum possible marks in the 3 subjects for which his score is missing. In VA it is 81, in DI it is 90, and in QA it is 60. So his total score (maximum possible) would be: 81 + 90 + 330 + 60 = 561 out of a total of 3030. It works out to 18.51%.

   Hence, option (b) is correct.
3. With the given numbers in the table, Pawan has an advantage of 129 marks over Ram. In order to make the difference between their scores the minimum, we would need to ensure that Ram's score catches up as much as possible with Pawan's. For this to happen, Ram should be given the maximum possible score in the three subjects whose scores are missing and Pawan should be given the minimum score in the two scores that are missing. The allocations would be: VA: Ram = 81 and Pawan = 69; DI: Ram = 90; LR: Pawan = 37 and QA: Ram = 60. The table of values would look as follows with these allocations:

Student	VA	DI	LR	QA
Pawan	69	300	37	159
Qazi	264	195	59	156
Ram	81	90	330	60
Shravan	216	225	60	168
Tarun	180	90	234	57

   In this situation, the difference between Shravan and Tarun is 108 marks.
4. We can draw the following table with the limits for the missing values inserted and the totals for each person.

Student	VA	DI	LR	QA	Totals	Range for Total
Pawan	a (= 69 to 81)	300	b (37 to 59)	159	459 + a + b	565 to 599
Qazi	264	195	c (37 to 59)	156	615 + c	652 to 674
Ram	d (= 69 to 81)	90	330	F (57 to 60)	420 + d + f	546 to 561
Shravan	216	225	60	168	669	669
Tarun	180	90	234	h (57 to 60)	504 + h	561 to 564

Note: A sample thought used to create the total above is that for VA – the total of the two missing scores (a + d) should be 150. Also, the maximum that anyone of a or d can take is 81. Hence, the minimum that one of them would have to take is 150 – 81 = 69. Thus, the values of a and d must range between 69 and 81. For DI the residual value of 180 has to be equally divided between Ram and Tarun. Likewise, for b and c (the missing value for LR) the maximum score is limited to 59 and hence the minimum score would be 96 – 59 = 37.

Based on the ranges for the total, we can see that the first two ranks would be shared by Qazi and Shravan. Pawan would definitely get the third rank. Tarun and Ram would have different scores, hence a tie is not possible between them. Thus, Tarun would be 4th and Ram 5th. Hence, option (c) is correct.

5. Qazi's totals could be any prime integer between 652 and 674. The prime numbers between these numbers are: 653, 659, 661, 667 and 673. To score a total of 673 marks, he would need to get 58 in LR. But 58 has only 4 factors (1,2,29,58), which is not allowed in the question. Hence, he must have scored less than 669 (Shravan's score). Hence, Qazi must have got the second rank. Thus, the correct answer is the number 2.

TEST 6

1. The highest return on investment is clearly is for an MBA in Singapore, as the return in the first year itself is 45000 on an investment of 65000 SGD – a return of over 60%.
2. The company would finance a value of 42000 GBP. Since, conversions are given only in terms of India Rupees, we would need to assume that converting the value of the GBP into AUD using the go through of the INR rates for the two currencies, would lead to the same result as using the direct rate between the GBP and the AUD.

   So, the loan is worth:

   $\frac{42000 \times 90.8}{48.7} \approx 42000 \times 1.85 \approx 77700$ AUD.

   Since, this loan has to be recovered in 3 years, and the annual salary to Harshit should be 90000 AUD – it follows that in 3 years out of the total salary of 270000 AUD, there should be a deduction of 77700 AUD. Hence, the net payout in 3 years should be 192300. Annual payout would be 192300/3 = 64100 AUD. Hence, option (b) is correct.
3. The cost of a UK MBA is 56000 GBP. That would cost ₹5085000 in Indian Rupees. His first trip from India to UK would cost him ₹22500. Thus he would be left with a balance of 5300000 – 5085000 – 22500 = 192500. A return trip from UK to India and back would cost him 340 × 90.8 + 22500 ≈ 53372. He would be able to make 3 return trips to India and back from the UK. Option (c) is correct.
4. The cost for Parikshit would be 50000 × 50.76 = 2538000 while for Shwetank the cost would be 70000 × 68.65 ≈ 4800000. Parikshit's salary would be 80000 × 68.65 ≈ 5490000 while Shwetank's salary would be 75000 × 1.5 × 50.76 ≈ 5700000. If they are paying off their loans in 3 years, then Parikshit would repay 846000 per year. His disposable annual income would be 5490000 – 846000 = 4644000. Shwetank's disposable income would be: 5700000 – 1600000 = 4100000. The difference in their annual disposable income would be: 544000 in Indian Rupees. Option (a) is correct.

TEST 7

If we were to look at the values for 2020, we see that a total of 26% of the market share has to be distributed amongst 2 major companies and 3 minor companies. The conditions we have to adhere to, in order to distribute the 26% market share are: (i) The two major companies should get a higher percentage value than any particular minor company. (ii) The share of the three minor companies should be at least equal to the share of the lowest major company. (iii) All numbers should be distinct integers. The following table would give us the combinations possible:

4th Major Company's Share	5th Major Company's Share	3 Minor Companies Share	Possibility Count
19	3	4	No possibility
18			No possibility
17			No possibility
16	4	6 (1,2,3)	1 possibility
15	5	6 (1,2,3)	1 possibility
14	5	7 (1,2,4)	1 possibility
14	6	6 (1,2,3)	1 possibility
13	6	7 (1,2,4)	1 possibility
13	5	8 (1,3,4)	1 possibility
12	7	7 (1,2,4)	1 possibility
	6	8 (1,2,5), (1,3,4)	2 possibilities
	5	9 (2,3,4)	1 possibility
11	7	8 (1,2,5); (1,3,4)	2 possibilities
	6	9 (1,3,5); (2,3,4)	2 possibilities
10	8	8 (1,2,5); (1,3,4)	2 possibilities
	7	9 (1,2,6); (1,3,5); (2,3,4)	3 possibilities
	6	10 (1,4,5); (2,3,5)	2 possibilities
9	8	9 (1,2,6); (1,3,5);(2,3,4)	3 possibilities
	7	10(1,3,6); (1,4,5); (2,3,5)	3 possibilities
	6	11 (2,4,5)	1 possibility
8	7	11 (1,4,6); (2,3,6); (2,4,5)	3 possibilities
	6	12 (3,4,5)	1 possibility
			32 possibilities

2. The highest percentage increase in the sales value would occur if the combined percentage of the major companies for the year 2020 is the least, while at the same time the combined percentage of the major companies in 2023 should be the maximum. The minimum percentage value for 2020 for the 5 major companies is: 74 + 8 + 6 = 88% (as seen from the table we have drawn for the first question). The maximum percentage value for 2023 would occur when the last two major companies are allocated percentage shares of 19 and 7 respectively. This would give the 5 major companies a total market share of 92%. The required percentage change would be got by calculating the percentage change from 88% of 1200 (= 1056) to 92% of 3000 (= 2760). The closest approximation of the percentage value is 161%. Hence, option (c) is correct.
3. For all the companies to have a sales value of above 50 crore, for 2020 each of the companies should

have a market share of 5% or above. We have already seen in the solution to the first question above, that this is not possible. Likewise, in 2021 we can see again that it would not be possible to allocate the residual 20% of the market share amongst the 5 remaining companies so that each company has a share of greater than 4% (because in 2021, we need each company to have a market share of at least 4% to cross a sales value of 50 crore). In 2022, since the total market size is 2000 crore, we need a possible distribution where the smallest minor company gets 3%. Since, in 2022, the residual percentage is 25%, this can be done by distributing the value in 7, 6 and 3, 4, 5. Thus in 2022 it is possible. Likewise, it is possible for 2023 (when we allocate 10, 9, 4, 5 and 6 to the five companies for instance). Hence, it is possible for 2 years.

4. The required minimum value would be when we allocate the 5th position in the major companies to Sutradhar and also make the percentage allocation to the 5th position company as the least amongst all the possible values. For 2022, this would be at 4% (with a distribution of 15, 4, 1, 2, 3). For 2023, this would occur at 6% (at 26, 4, 1, 2, 3). Thus, the least total sales value for Sutradhar would be: 20% of 1200 + 32% of 1500 + 4% of 2000 + 4% of 3000 = 240 + 480 + 80 + 120 = 920.

TEST 8

The table given below lists all the possible routes, the number of villages covered in a route and the total number of people staying across all the villages covered in a route.

S. No.	Route	The Number of Villages Covered	The total Number of People
1	Kanpur – A – D – G – Lucknow	3	1000
2	Kanpur – A – D – E – G – Lucknow	4	1200
3	Kanpur – A – D – E – F – G – Lucknow	5	1700
4	Kanpur – A – B – E – G – Lucknow	4	1050
5	Kanpur – A – B – E – F – G – Lucknow	5	1550
6	Kanpur – A – B – F – G – Lucknow	4	1350
7	Kanpur – A – B – C – E – G – Lucknow	5	1400
8	Kanpur – A – B – C – E – F – G – Lucknow	6	1900
9	Kanpur – A – B – C – F – G – Lucknow	5	1700
10	Kanpur – C – E – G – Lucknow	3	850
11	Kanpur – C – E – F – G – Lucknow	4	1350
12	Kanpur – C – F – G – Lucknow	3	1150

1. As the tanker contains 2100 liters of oil supply and everybody is given an oil can of 1.5 L, the tanker can deliver oil to at most 2100/1.5 = 1400 people in a trip. There are eight routes on which the total number of people are either less than or equal to 1400.
2. The only route along which exactly 1400 people stay in the villages is Kanpur – A – B – C – E – G – Lucknow. The number of villages covered is 5.
3. The two Perfect – pairs are:
   (i) 1350 people – Kanpur – C – E – F – G – Lucknow and Kanpur – A – B – F – G – Lucknow.
   (ii) 1700 people – Kanpur – A – D – E – F – G – Lucknow and Kanpur – A – B – C – F – G – Lucknow.
4. There are only three routes that have 3 villages en route.
   The total population encountered on these 3 days would be 850 + 1000 + 1150 = 3000. The total oil distributed would be 4500 liters.

TEST 9

The given table of values can be completed based on the possible ranges of the incomplete scores as follows:

	Round 1	Round 2	Round 3	Round 4	
Aman	46 TO 54	200	25 TO 39	106	306 + 71 to 93
Bendre	176	130	39 TO 25	104	410 + 25 to 39
Charwak	54 TO 46	60	226	38 TO 40	280 + 84 to 94
Denboo	144	150	40	112	446
Elangovan	120	60	150	40 TO 38	336 + 38 to 40
Total	540	600	480	400	2020
Sum of Missing Values	100	120	64	78	
Ten Per cent Limit	54	60	48	40	
Third Highest Scorers' Limit	120	130	40	104	

We can then use the above table to find the answers to the questions asked.

1. Aman's minimum contribution would occur if he scores 306 + 46 + 25 = 377. Out of a total score of 2020, this means 377/2020 ≈ 18.66%.
2. It can be seen that the score of Aman is 306 + two missing numbers for rounds 1 and 3. For Charwak, the scores is 286 + two missing numbers for round 1 and 4. Since, Charwak's score is below Aman's score for the two rounds for which their scores are known, we need to cover this gap in order to make the difference between the two minimised. For this to occur – we should give Charwak as high a possible score for round as allowed, while minimising Aman's score. Thus, we will allocate 46 to Aman and 54 to Charwak. This makes the scores as: Aman = 352 + Round 3 score; Charwak = 340 + Round 4 score. At this point we still notice that Aman has a higher score (by 12) over Charwak. With one score for each unknown, we should allocate this score in such a way that their scores get equated (if possible) or the difference between their scores is minimised. We can easily see that in the event we allocate
   Case i) 40 to Charwak in round 4 & Aman 28 in round 3, their scores are equated. Likewise Case ii) 39 for Charwak and 27 for Aman also has the same effect – their difference becomes 0.
   Case iii) 38 for Charwak and 26 for Aman also minimises their difference to 0.
   In these three cases Bendre gets: 36, 37 and 38 respectively in his Round 3 score, while Elangovan gets 38, 39 or 40 in his round 4 scores.
   There are three cases for Bendre's total: Case i) 410 + 36 = 446; Case ii) 410 + 37 = 447 and Case iii) 410 + 38 = 448.
   In these three cases, Elangovan's totals are:
   Case i) 336 + 38 = 374; Case ii) 336 + 39 = 375; Case iii) 336 + 40 = 376. In each case, it can be seen that their difference is always 72. Hence, option (c) is correct.
3. If the difference between Aman and Charwak is the maximum, we need to think exactly opposite to the thought for the previous question in allocating the missing numbers amongst them. Since Aman's score is: 306 + (46 to 54) + (25 to 39) while Charwak's score is 286 + (46 to 54) + (38 to 40), for maximising their difference, we should take the following scenario:
   Aman = 306 + 54 + 39 = 399. Charwak = 286 + 46 + 38 = 370. In this case their difference is maximised at 29.
   In such a case, Bendre scores 410 + 25 = 435; while Elangovan scores 330 + 40 = 370. The difference between Bendre and Elangovan is 65 points. The required difference is the difference between these two differences. Hence, the required answer is 65 – 29 = 36.
4. The respective scores for the five people are:

Student	Total Range	Rank
Aman	377 to 399	3rd
Bendre	435 to 449	Cannot be determined
Charwak	370 to 380	4th
Denboo	446	Cannot be determined
Elangovan	368 to 370	5th

Hence, the correct answer is 3.

TEST 10

1. Since there are three unique products (F, G, P) and three companies (X, Y, Z), there are 6 possible ways of associating the products with the company. They are:

Company	Case 1	Case 2	Case 3	Case 4	Case 5	Case 6
X	F	F	G	G	P	P
Y	G	P	F	P	F	G
Z	P	G	P	F	G	F

The revenue of the companies in the all the cases are (in millions):

Company	Case 1	Case 2	Case 3	Case 4	Case 5	Case 6
X	400	400	800	800	600	600
Y	1600	1200	800	1200	800	1600
Z	900	1200	900	600	1200	600
Total	2900	2800	2500	2600	2600	2800

Only in case 3 is the revenue of all the companies less than 40%.
So, the answer is (c) Z.

2. The market share of each company in all the six cases is given below:

Company	Case 1	Case 2	Case 3	Case 4	Case 5	Case 6
X	13.8	14.3	32	30.8	23.1	21.4
Y	55.2	42.9	32	46.2	30.8	57.1
Z	31	42.9	36	23.1	46.2	21.4

The lowest market share was of company X in Case 1.

So, the answer is (a) 13.8%.

3. As from the table in the above answer, the market share of the company selling Prize is more than 45% only in Case 4. The market share of the company selling Falcon in case 4 is 23.1%. So, the answer is (d) 23.1%
4. The highest market share of any company = 57.1% for Y in Case 6, and the second lowest market share of any company = 14.3% for company X in case 2. The difference between the two values = 42.8% So, the answer is (b) 42.8%.

TEST 11

1. We know that 4th and 5th digit taken together forms a prime number, so the 5th digit is an odd number ≠ 5. The 6th digit is ≥ 4 and the 3rd digit is even. As the sum of 5th and 6th digit = 9, therefore, the 5th digit is either 1 or 3, but as 4th + 3rd = 5th, 5th cannot be 1, hence the 5th digit = 3. Hence, from (iv) 6th digit = 6.
From (ii) & (iii) 3rd digit = 2 and the 4th digit = 1. As 6th and 7th digit together comprised a prime number, 7th digit = 1 or 7.
As the 1st and 2nd digit is not the same and according to (v), 2nd digit is 1 more than the 1st digit. Also, the difference between 2nd and 8th digit = 6. As the 8th digit is greater than the 3rd digit and ≤ 4, the 8th digit = 3. Hence, the 2nd digit = 9 and the 1st digit = 8.

Position	1st	2nd	3rd	4th	5th	6th	7th	8th
Digit	8	9	2	1	3	6	1 or 7	3

So, Arun could have chosen the sets in 2 ways. Hence, the answer is (b).
2. From the table in the above solution, the 7th digit of the number could be either 1 or 7. Hence, the answer is (c).
3. From the table in the first answer of this set, the number comprised by the fifth and the third digits off the phone number, taken in that order is 32. Hence, the answer is (b).
4. From the table in the first answer of this set, the difference between the first and the sixth digit of the phone number = 8 – 6 = 2. Hence, the answer is (a).

TEST 12

From (i) & (iii), the score given by panel member A ranges from 1 to 4. From (ii) & (iv). The score given by panel member B ranges from 5 to 8.

Also, from (v), score given by panel member C = (A + B)/2, i.e., 2C = A + B. And as score given by C is always an integer (vi), so score given by A and B for the same candidate and the same parameter are either both even or both odd.
From the tables provided, the value for score given by B to P in P4 can only be 6 and as A + B = 8 and 5 and 7 cannot be the score. Therefore, the value for score given by A to P in P4 = 8 – 6 = 2.
Similarly, the value for score given by B to S in P4 = 7 and value for score given by A to S in P4 = 10 – 7 = 3.
Also, the value for score given by A to Q in P4 = 1 (both odd), and value for score given by C to Q in P4 = 3.
So on and so forth, we are able to find the scores given by all the panel members to all the candidates in all the parameters. The result is as follows:

Panel Member: A

	P1	P2	P3	P4
P	1	3	4	2
Q	2	4	3	1
R	3	1	2	4
S	4	2	1	3

Panel Member: B

	P1	P2	P3	P4
P	5	7	8	6
Q	8	6	7	5
R	7	5	6	8
S	6	8	5	7

Panel Member: C

	P1	P2	P3	P4
P	3	5	6	4
Q	5	5	5	3
R	5	3	4	6
S	5	5	3	5

1. The score given by B to R in P3 = 6. Hence, the answer is 6.
2. The score given by A to Q in P4 = 1. Hence, the answer is 1.
3. The highest composite score in P3 was received by P. And the total composite score received by P in P3 = 4 + 8 + 6 = 18. Hence, the answer is 18.
4. As can be seen from the table, only S got a higher composite score in P2 as compared to P3. Hence, the answer is 1.

TEST 13

1. The number of employees that drink Sprite on Day 6 = 20 + No. of employees that have shifted to sprite in the 7 days – No. of employees that have shifted away from Sprite in the 7 days.
   = 20 + (P to S) + (F to S) – ((S to P) + (S to F))
   = 20 + 21 + 25 – (24 + 19)
   = 20 + 46 – 43 = 23.
   Hence, the answer is 23.
2. It would be easier to solve this question and the questions to follow, if we make a table of the number of employees that consume each beverage on each of the 8 days. To find the no. of employees consuming a drink on any specific day, use the calculation as shown in the previous question.

Beverage	Day 1	Day 2	Day 3	Day 4	Day 5	Day 6	Day 7	Day 8
Fanta	20	13	12	7	9	21	23	25
Pepsi	20	26	26	24	22	16	17	7
Sprite	20	21	22	29	29	23	20	28

   Average no. of employees that drank Fanta per day = 130/8 = 16.25. Hence, the answer is 16.25.
3. As can be seen from the table, on 3 days at least 16 employees drank each of the three drinks. Hence, the answer is 3.
4. As 9 employees switch from Sprite to other beverages on Day 1, therefore, 11 employees drank sprite on the 1st and the 2nd day. Also, these 11 employees can be drinking Sprite also on all the 8 days, as the number of employees leaving on each of the 8 days is less than the total number of employees who have switched to sprite in the previous days, keeping the 11 employees constant. Hence, the answer is 11.

TEST 14

As the numbers declared by each person from left to right is 1, 1, 1, 2, 2, 2, 1, therefore 1 and 2 or of different gender. Also, 2 and 3 are of the same gender. 3, 5 and 7 are of the same gender. As there are 4 women and 3 men, therefore, women occupy positions 2, 3, 5 and 7 and men occupy positions 1, 4 and 6.
As Q is not standing adjacent to either P or R and S is standing to the immediate right of V, therefore, Q is to the immediate left of V. From the above statement, it is clear that Q, V and S occupy positions 3, 4 and 5 respectively. As T is not standing at extreme right, therefore, U occupies the 7th position. As R is to the immediate left of T, R can only be at 1st position, meaning T is at the 2nd position and P occupies the 6th position.

The order is as follows:

1st	2nd	3rd	4th	5th	6th	7th
R	T	Q	V	S	P	U

1. As can be seen from the analysis above, S and U are the only 2 girls standing to the right of Q. Therefore, the answer is (c).
2. As can be seen from the analysis above, S is standing adjacent to P. Hence, the answer is (a).
3. If R and T exchange their places then 5 people will have to declare the number 2 as the number of people of different gender standing adjacent to them. Thus, the answer is (a).
4. As only 5 people can declare the number 2 at max, therefore, 7 people must have declared number 1. For this to happen, 5th and 6th position must have interchanged their places, i.e., P and S must interchange their places for 7 people to have the same number. Hence, the answer is (a).

TEST 15

According to the data in the set, following table can be prepared:

Student	ME	CV	CH	AE	CS	EC	TL
1	Yes	Yes	Yes	Yes	Yes	Yes	Yes
2	No	Yes	Yes	Yes	Yes	Yes	No
3	No	No	Yes	Yes	Yes	No	No
4	No	No	No	Yes	No	No	No
5	No	No	Yes	Yes	Yes	No	No
6	No	Yes	Yes	Yes	Yes	Yes	No
7	Yes	Yes	Yes	Yes	Yes	Yes	Yes
8	No	Yes	Yes	Yes	Yes	Yes	No

For all the answers in this set we will be using the help of the table.

1. As is evident from the table, the pattern of the first 6 rows keeps on repeating for other students. So, out of the first 6 rows (students), 5 have taken at least 3 subjects. If the number of students taking at least 3 subjects = 243 then the total number of students approximately = 243 × 6/5 = 291.6.
   If the total number of students were 291, then there would be 48 batches of 6 students along with 3 extra students. No. of students who have taken at least 3 subjects would be equal to 48 × 5 = 240. And as the next 3 students will also have taken at least 3 subjects so, for 243 students to take at least 3 subjects, at least 291 students must be there in the college.

But, if the 4th student of the 49th batch is added (292nd student), then also the number of students who have taken at least 3 subjects will remain 243. Therefore, the answer is (d).

2. As is evident from the table, the pattern of the first 6 rows keeps on repeating for other students. In the first six rows, CS courses were opted for by 5 students. Therefore, for 59 students to opt for CS, 11 batches of 6 students should be present where 5 students opt for CS and 4 students from the 12th batch must have opted for CS. This can only be done if there are 5 students in the 12th batch. Hence, the total number of students = 11 × 6 + 5 = 71. So, the answer is (b).
3. From the table, there are 2 students out of every 6 six students, who take CS but not take CV. If there are 93 students in total, then it will form 15 sets of 6 students and 3 students in the 16th set. In each of the first 15 sets there will be 2 students that select CS but not CV. And in the 16th set, there will be 1 student who opts for CS but not CV. Number of students who took CS but did not take CV = 15 × 2 + 1 = 31. Hence, the answer is (c).
4. If 43 students took ME, then that means there are 42 complete sets of 6 students and there are more than 1 student in the 43rd set. As there are 3 students who took EC in each set, therefore there are 42 × 3 = 126 students in the first 42 sets and 1 to 3 students who have opted for EC in the 43rd set. So, the number of students who opted for EC is in the range of 127 to 129. As 127 is the only value from this range in the option set, hence, the answer is (a).

TEST 16

1. If Dinesh, Max and Rishi handle the 5 assignments, then the minimum taken by the three will occur when Max completes assignment a & e, Dinesh completes assignment b & d and Rishi completes assignment c. In this scenario, the total time taken will be equal to 3.5 hrs. (The time taken by Rishi to complete assignment c, as Max and Dinesh will finish their assignments before that.) So, the answer is 3.5.
2. As Rajiv takes the minimum time to complete assignment c by a long margin, so he is assigned that assignment. Max takes the minimum time to complete assignment e by a long margin, so he is assigned that assignment. As out of the remaining students Rishi takes the minimum time to complete assignment a, therefore he is assigned a. Between Dinesh and Anand the minimum cumulative time will occur when Dinesh does assignment b and Anand does assignment d. So, the minimum cumulative time taken by the group to complete the task = 1.5 + 1.5 + 1.5 + 2 + 2 = 8.5 hrs. Hence, the answer is 8.5.
3. Maximum cumulative time will occur in the following case–
   a – Anand – 5
   b – Rajiv – 5
   c – Max – 4
   d – Rishi – 3
   e – Dinesh – 4
   So, the maximum cumulative time taken = 21 hr and the answer is 21.
4. Time taken by each student to complete the assignment –
   Rajiv – 16.5; Dinesh – 14; Max – 11.5; Rishi – 13.5; Anand – 18.5
   Average cumulative time taken to complete the assignment = 74 / 5 = 14.8 hrs.

TEST 17

First solve the set as much as possible and then answer the questions:

Let the weights lifted by Dev in the 1st round be a, weights lifted by Rajeev in 2nd round be b and weights lifted by Rajeev in the first round be c, then from the information provided we can create the following table:

Round	Rajeev	Dev	Kabeer
1	c	a	a + 17
2	b	c + 25	b + 15
3	a + 17± 18	b	a ± 20

In the 3rd round, Kabeer cannot have the minimum weights that he lifted, as Rajeev has his minimum weights lifted in that round. So, weights lifted by Kabeer in the 3rd round will be a + 20 (as a – 20 will be lesser than both b + 15 and a + 17).

Weights lifted by Rajeev in round 3 cannot be a + 35, as in that case b > a + 35 and that would mean that both Dev and Kabeer will have their minimum weights lifted in the 1st round (which is not possible). So, the weights lifted by Rajeev in the 3rd round = a – 1.

We know that b > a – 1 and as a and b cannot be the same, therefore b > a. This means that Dev will have his minimum weights lifted in round 1 and Kabeer will have his minimum weights lifted in round 2, i.e., b + 15 < a + 17. This will only happen when b = a + 1.

After these conclusions, the following picture emerges:

Round	Rajeev	Dev	Kabeer
1	c	a	a + 17
2	a + 1	c + 25	a + 16
3	a – 1	a + 1	a + 20
Combined Total Weight	c + a + 1	c + a + 26	2a + 37

1. If Kabeer was first, then, $2a + 37 > c + a + 26$, i.e., $c < a + 11$ or $c – a < 11$. Therefore, the maximum difference between the weights lifted by Rajeev and Dev in the 1st round can be 10 kg. So, the answer is 10.
2. If Dev was first, then $c + a + 26 > 2a + 37$, i.e., $c > a + 11$. The highest weight anybody lifted in the competition = c + 25 kg and the lowest weight lifted = a – 1 kg. As $c > a + 11$, therefore, the lowest value c can take is a + 12. The minimum difference between the highest and the lowest weight lifted in the competition will be: $a + 12 + 25 – (a – 1) = 38$ kg. Hence, the answer is 38.
3. If Rajeev was ranked second in the competition, then $c + a + 1 > 2a + 37$, i.e., $c > a + 36$. The lowest value c can take is: a + 37. The minimum difference between the weight that Dev lifted in the second round and the weight that Kabeer lifted in the second round = $a + 37 + 25 – (a + 16) = 46$ kg. Hence, the answer is 46.
4. To minimise the combined total weight of the first ranked person, a must be 14, b (a + 1) must be 15 and c must be 20. Putting these values in the table, we obtain the following results:

Round	Rajeev	Dev	Kabeer
1	20	14	31
2	15	45	30
3	13	15	34
Combined Total Weight	35	60	65

Therefore, the answer is 65.

TEST 18

We can make out the following with respect to the total time required between stations:

Travel Between Stations	Time Taken
S1–S2	12
S2–S3	18
S3–S4	11
S4–S5	6
S5–S6	10
S6–S7	13

The answers can be read off from the above table:

1. It takes 6 minutes to reach S5 from S4.
2. They were both in the train between stations S3 and S4 – a total of 11 minutes.
3. There were at least two people in the train between S1 and S6 – a total time of: $12 + 18 + 11 + 6 + 10 = 57$ minutes.
4. 4 persons were in the train between S3 and S4 – a total of 11 minutes.

TEST 19

The following are the possible scores in the matches:

Number of Matches	Goals Scored by A	Goals Scored by B	Result
D	1	1	Draw
E	2	2	Draw
F	2	1	A wins
G	3	1	A wins
H	1	2	B wins
J	1	3	B wins

According to the clues:

CLUE V: $F + H + 20 = G + J$ (i)

CLUE IV: $D + E + H + J + F – 15 = F + G$ (ii)

CLUE III: $G + J = 2(F + H)$ (iii)

CLUE II: $D + E = D + H + J \rightarrow E = H + J$ (iv)

CLUE I: $F + G = E + H + J + 27$ (v)

Also we know that $D + E + F + G + H + J = 100$ (vi)

From (iv), (v) and (vi), we get: $F + G = 2(H + J) + 27 \rightarrow D + 4(H + J) = 73$ (vii)

From, (ii) and (v) we have: $D + E + H + J + F – 15 = F + G$ & $F + G = E + H + J + 27 \rightarrow D + F + G – 27 + F – 15 = F + G \rightarrow D + F = 42$ (viii)

From (vii), we know that since: $D + 4(H + J) = 73$, D can only take such values that 4(H + J) should be a multiple of 4. Thus, values possible for D = 1, 5, 9, 13, 17… etc. However, from (viii) we know that since D + F = 42, D can only take the values of 1, 5, 9, … 41. In these cases, F would be 41, 37, 33 … 1 respectively. We can start to form the following table of possible values:

Possibility No:	D	E	F	G	H	J	H + J
1	1	18	41	22	Infeasible		18
2	5	17	37	24	Infeasible		17
3	9	16	33	26	Infeasible		16
4	13	15	29	28	Infeasible		15
5	17	14	25	30	Infeasible		14
6	21	13	21	32	1	12	13
7	25	12	17	34	4	8	12
8	29	11	13	36	7	4	11
9	33	10	9	38	10	0	10
10	37	9	5	40	Infeasible		9
11	41	8	1	42	Infeasible		8
		Since E = H + J		G will be got by subtracting the sum of all known values from 100			H + J's value is derived from D + 4(H + J) = 73

At this stage, we also know that: G + J = 2(F + H). If we try to fit in possibilities 1 to 5 with this equation, we will get an infeasible situation in each of these cases. Possibilities 10 and 11 are also not feasible since we cannot create a situation where G + J = 2(F + H). For possibilities 6 to 9, the values of H and J such that this equation is satisfied are shown in the table.

Checking the other equations with this table, we can see that only possibility 8 satisfies equation (i): F + H + 20 = G + J. Hence, we get the final table of values for each match outcome:

Hence, the final values are:

Possibility No:	D	E	F	G	H	J	H + J
8	29	11	13	36	7	4	11

We can derive the answers from the table:

1. F + G = 13 + 36 = 49.
2. B would have scored: 29 × 1 + 11 × 2 + 13 × 1 + 36 × 1 + 7 × 2 + 4 × 3 = 126 goals.
3. J = 4
4. We already know that B scored 126 goals. A would have scored: 29 × 1 + 11 × 2 + 13 × 2 + 36 × 3 + 7 × 1 + 4 × 1 = 196 goals. Goal difference = 196 – 126 = 70.

TEST 20

We can make the following table for getting a sense of the information:

Drug Name	Purchase Price	Selling Price	Profit Per Unit	Profit Per 100 Units
P	120	184	64	6400
Q	400	460	60	6000
R	160	256	96	9600
S	320	352	32	3200
T	640	720	80	8000
U	140	196	56	5600

1. We can see that the values in options (a), (b) and (d) are possible – if he sells 100 units each of S & U (8800); 100 units each of R & S (12800) and 100 units each of R & T (17600). Only the value in option (c) cannot be made as a profit. Hence, the correct answer is option (c).
2. His total profit would be: 6400 + 6000 + 9600 + 3200 + 8000 + 5600 = 38800.
3. The only drug that gives a profit percentage of below 12.8% is S. All other drugs are giving Rishi a profit percentage greater than 12.8%. Hence, if his profit percentage is only 12.8%, it follows that there is definitely some sale of S. Hence, option (b) is the correct answer.
4. The maximum revenues with the sale of three drugs would occur if he sold 400 units of T, 100 units of Q and 100 units of S. The total revenue would be: 288000 + 46000 + 35200 = 369200.

TEST 21

Date	Number of Customers Above 10 (A)	Number of Customers Above 30 (B)	Number of Customers Below 40 (C)	Number of Customers Between 10 and 30 (D = A – B)	Number of Customers Between 30 and 40 (E = C – D)	Number of Customers Above 40 (F = B – E)
10th Feb	40	25	30	15	15	10
11th Feb	60	30	40	30	10	20
12th Feb	70	40	30	30	0	40
13th Feb	50	20	40	30	10	10
14th Feb	30	10	30	20	10	0
15th Feb	80	50	50	30	20	30
16th Feb	40	30	20	10	10	20
17th Feb	80	60	60	20	40	20
18th Feb	60	40	30	20	10	30
19th Feb	80	30	60	50	10	20
20th Feb	30	10	20	20	0	10
21st Feb	70	50	40	20	20	30
22nd Feb	50	30	30	20	10	20
23rd Feb	40	20	30	20	10	10
24th Feb	80	70	50	10	40	30

From the table we can read off the answers to the questions:

1. Since she is a 36 year old, she would be counted in the 30–40 category. There are two days, viz., 12th February and 20th February when nobody in that age group visited the shop. On all other days it is possible for a 36 year old to visit the shop. Since the options given to us in this question are 14th, 18th and 22nd February, the correct answer is none of these.
2. The minimum average age would be on 14th February when nobody aged 40 + would have come to the shop. The average on 14th February is $(20 \times 11 + 10 \times 31) \div 30 = 530 \div 30 = 17.6$.
3. This can happen when the number of customers between 11 and 30 are greater than 12, the number of customers between 31 and 40 are greater than 12 and the number of customers above 40 is greater than 15. Such a situation is seen on three days – viz., 15th February, 17th February and 21st February. Hence, the correct answer is 3 days.
4. We cannot determine the answer to this since we do not know the exact ages of each of the customers. Hence option (d) is correct.

TEST 22

In order to solve these questions you need to find out the operating profit of each of the six companies and then identify the points represented on the third chart to the correct company.

From the first and third chart it is very obvious that company D is excluded from the third chart. (why? Think!). Also, one of B and F must have been excluded. This is so evident from the first and third charts. You will realise that B and D are excluded.

The answers are:

1. Option (a).
2. Option (c).
3. Option (a).
4. Option (d).

TEST 23

Start solving from Day 3. You can deduce that university 4 is from UK and 6 is from USA. From Day 2, University 8 belongs to India and university 3 to Netherlands. Adding the clues from Day 1 to the above deduction, the following possibilities table emerges:

University 1	Netherlands/India
University 2	Canada/U.K.
University 3	Netherlands
University 4	U.K.
University 5	India/Netherlands
University 6	USA
University 7	UK/Canada
University 8	India

Note: University 2 and 7 have to be distributed amongst Canada and UK, while University 1 and 5 go to India and Netherlands.

Hence answers are:

1. Option (c) the Netherlands is the correct Option.
2. Option (a) is the correct Option.
3. Option (a) is the correct Option.
4. Option (b) is the correct Option.

TEST 24

Partially complete the table at the relevant places by using the 3 clues given.

1. Tara must have obtained either a B or F. Hence, Option (d) is the correct option.
2. Must have obtained an A in both unknown subjects since she has to have a total of 16 points.
3. Gauri got a C in strategy, Fazal got a B, Nisha and Rahul got an A. While Hari got a D. Hence Option (b) is the correct option.
4. Fazal gets a B in Strategy. So does Utkarsh (as per clue 2). Hence, Utkarsh gets a D in Finance.

TEST 25

(Detailed solution to this question is provided in my book—*How to Prepare for Logical Reasoning for CAT*)
The table of matches in the first two rounds will look like:

Round 1:

Germany beat Spain 1–0,
Argentina beat New Zealand 1–0
Pakistan beat South Africa 2–0

Round 2:

Germany beat SA 2–1
Spain beat New Zealand 5–1
Argentina beat Pakistan 1–0

Round 3:

Germany drew with Argentina
Spain drew with Pakistan
New Zealand drew with South Africa

1. Argentina beat Pakistan 1–0 is true. Hence, Option (b) is correct.
2. Germany beat SA 2–1 is true. Hence, Option (d) is correct.
3. Spain will finish on top after 5 rounds. Hence, Option (c) is correct.
4. This cannot happen since at least Spain and Germany will have a higher goal difference than Pakistan. Besides, all the teams except South Africa and New Zealand will score 10 points. Hence (d).

TEST 26

1. For the minimum possible average return, extraordinary good results should be in company A (1.5 times) and company B (2 times). The average return will be: $\frac{30+20+30+40}{4} = 30\%$
   Hence Option (a) is correct.
2. In order to visualise this, draw a table as below.

Company	Normal	1.5 times	2 times
A	20	30	40
B	10	15	20
C	30	45	60
D	40	60	80

   When you try out the various combinations to make a total of 140 (since 140/4 = 35), you will also need to take care that there should be exactly 2 companies showing extraordinary results; one with 1.5 times, and the other with 2 times. Also, there should be exactly 2 companies with normal returns. The required answer will be got with company A producing 2 times the returns and D producing 1.5 times the returns. It can also occur if C gets 2 times return and A gets 1.5 times return.
   Hence, II and III are correct. Option (b) is correct.
3. For 38.75% returns, your combination should add up to 155.
   From the table we drew for solving question 2, it is clear that total of 155 can only be achieved by:
   20 (A) + 10 (B) + 45 (C) + 80 (D).
   This means that C got 1.5 times the normal return, while D got 2 times the normal return. Hence, C must belong to the Auto or Steel industry, while B did not announce extraordinarily good results. Hence, Option (c) is correct (i.e., statements I and IV).
4. As per the condition and the table above, company C gave 60% returns. With this the maximum possible returns are 150% giving an average of 37.5%. Hence statement I is wrong. [***Note:*** This occurs at 20 (A) + 10 (B) + 60 (C) + 60 (D)].
   However, on the lower side, the minimum return will be for the following conditions:
   20 (A) + 15 (B) + 60 (C) + 40 (D) = 135.
   In this case the average returns will be 33.75. This means that statements II and IV are true. Option (b) is correct.

TEST 27

Visualise the rounds as:

First Round	Second Round	Quarters	Semis	Final
1–32	1–16	1–8	1–4	1–2
2–31	2–15	2–7	2–3	
3–30	3–14	3–6		
4–29	4–13	4–5		
5–28	5–12			
6–27	6–11			
7–26	7–10			
8–25	8–9			
9–29				
10–23				
11–22				
15–18				
16–17				

1. In the quarters, Maria Sharapova is seeded to play the 8th seed (Serena Williams). But Serena Williams loses in the second round (where she must have played either the 9th or the 24th seed). But it can be seen that the 9th seed Nadia Petrova reaches the semis. Hence, Maria Sharapova must play Nadia Petrova in the Quarter finals. Option (d) is correct.
2. Maria Sharapova is seeded to meet the 8th seed in the quarters and the 4th/5th seed in the semis. Neither of them can play her in the final, since they have to meet in the earlier rounds. Amongst these only Kim Clijsters name figures in the options. Hence Option (c) is correct.
3. Davenport being the 2nd seed is scheduled to play the winner of match 7 of the second round in the quarters. As per the question Match 7 has resulted in an upset in the second round. This means that Venus Williams won the Match 7 and will play Davenport in the quarters. Hence, Option (d) is correct.
4. According to this question seeds 1, 3, 5, 7, 9, 11, 13, 15, 17, 19, 21, 23, 25, 27, 29 and 31 will reach the second round. In such a case, 4th seed is replaced by 29th seed. The second round match between 13 and 29, does not have an upset. Hence, 13 moves ahead and plays 5 in the quarters. The lowest seeded player who could play Maria Sharapova in the semi finals is Seed 13. Option (a) is correct.

TEST 28

1. In India a hysterectomy would cost 3000 + 5000 = 8000 dollars, while in Thailand it costs her 4500 + 6000 = 10500 dollars. Thus the difference would be equivalent to an advantage of 2500 × 32.89 bahts out of which she would lose 15000 bahts for two way travel giving her a net saving of apporx. 67500 bahts.
2. For knee replacement, costs are: India 17500
   Thailand 16000
   Malaysia 12000
   Singapore 17000.
   Hence, India is the costliest
3. India's cost for the package would be:
   [11000 + 5000] (angioplasty) + [9000 + 7000] (hip replacement) + [8500 + 9000] (knee replacement) = 49500.
   Similarly, other countries would cost:
   Thailand: 51000
   Singapore: 51000
   Malaysia: 47000
   USA: 140000.
   Hence, Malaysia is the cheapest.
4. Spinal fusion in India costs $5500 while in Singapore it costs $9000. We can ignore the cost of poor quality here since there is no difference in costs in the same. The current exchange rate, which is equivalent to ₹5500 × 40.928 and at the new rate it would be equivalent to US $ 5500 × 40.928/35 = $ 6430 approx., while the cost in Singapore is equal to $ 9000.
   Hence, the difference is 2500 dollars approximately.
   Note: You do not need to calculate costs of poor quality because they are not cash costs, that you paid for in the respective countries.

TEST 29

1. The possible routes for A to J with one intermediate stop are: ABJ, ADJ, AFJ, AHJ and AIJ.
   There are many more routes possible with two intermediate stops but these would not be considered because the costs would become very high (as can be seen from the table).
   The shortest route would be between AHJ and the cost would be ₹2275. Hence, Option (a) is correct.
2. 2275 × 0.95 = 2161. Hence, option (b) is correct
3. AFJ will then become the cheapest route and its cost would be 1700 + 1150 = 2850.
4. The cheapest route for the airline (even on a per kilometre basis) continues to be AHJ. ***Note:*** This can be spotted by the fact that the AH route is the only one which has a per kilometer cost below 1. Hence, the required answer would be given by 0.9 × 2275/2350 = 0.88 (approx).

5. As we have seen for the above question AHJ minimises the total kilometers. This value comes out to be 1950 + 400 = 2350.

TEST 30

1. We can solve this by looking at and eliminating individual options. Option (a) cannot be true as Abdul would have the minimum return if the price is the highest at 10 a.m. and continuously drops till 3 p.m.
   Option (b) would normally have been true, but is not always true because if the price remains constant at 10, 11, 12, 1 and 2, Chetan would have the same return as Bikram.
   Option (c) is also eliminated as we have seen that most of the time Chetan has a higher return than Bikram. Option (d) can be eliminated on the basis of the thought that it is easily possible that Bikram got the least return. Thus, option (e) is correct.
2. Abdul would get the maximum return on that day since his purchase price (average) would be least. Also, between Chetan and Bikram, we know that for Bikram, average purchase price is higher and hence he would have the least returns.
3. The maximum return could be for Abdul or Chetan but between the two we cannot determine who gains more because in order to get that we would need to know the exact price at each hour starting from 10 a.m.

Before solving 4 and 5 we need to logically work out what happened with respect to prices on that day.

(a) Since Abdul lost money, price at 3 p.m. < price at 10 a.m., i.e., $P_3 < P_{10}$
(b) Dane made profits means $P_{10} + P_{11} + P_{12} < P_1 + P_2 + P_3$
(c) Emily made profits means $P_{10} + P_1 < P_{12} + P_3$
(d) $P_2 < P_3$
(e) $P_{12} < P_{10}$
(f) From (c) & (e) above, we know that $P_3 > P_1$
(g) Also, from (c) we have $P_{10} - P_{12} < P_3 - P_1$ & from (b) & (g) we have: $2P_{10} + P_{11} < 2P_3 + P_2 \rightarrow P_{11} < P_2$

4. None of the four options (a) to (d) can be said that it has to be necessarily false. As:
   Option (a) (share price least at 2 p.m.) can happen.
   Option (b) (share price least at 11 a.m.) can also happen.
   In terms of equalities what we know is:
   $P_{10} - P_{12}$, $P_{10} < P_3$, $P_3 > P_1$ & $P_3 > P_2$ & $P_2 > P_{11}$
   Option (c) and option (d) could also be true in some cases and hence are not necessarily false.
5. From the above we have:
   $P_{10} > P_{12}$, $P_{10} > P_3$ and since $P_3 > P_1$ & $P_3 > P_2$ it follows that $P_{10} > P_{11}$
   & $P_{10} > P_{11}$ would also be true.
   Thus, the highest price would definitely be at 10 a.m.

PART 3

MOCK TESTS ON LOGICAL DATA INTERPRETATION (MOCK TEST PAPERS 1-28)

IN THIS PART YOU WILL LEARN:

- To solve difficult reasoning based questions in Data Interpretation in the format of a mock test.
- Not only to tackle the DI section more effectively but also by solving this part you would
  - Improve your ability to handle new unknown situations and unforeseen twists in a DI question
  - Improve your anticipation/recognition of novelties in DI question sets
  - Improve the depth and breadth of your exposure to DI questions as well as your DI problem solving skills
  - Improve your ability to make earlier decisions about whether you are going to be able to solve a question set or not
  - Improve your ability to work around hurdles in advanced DI problems
  - Increase your confidence level to take on any challenge thrown at you in a DI question paper

THIS PART CONTAINS:

- 28 Mock Tests on the latest pattern of the CAT Paper, where you would be expected to solve 4 DI sets in 40 minutes.

1.
For each test first try to solve the test within a strict time limit of 40 minutes. If you want to compete against the 100 percentilers in CAT, you should be able to solve a minimum of 13-14 questions in the stipulated time (of course all correct). The 99 percentiler would be able to solve around 10-11 questions on average out of 20 in these tests in the stipulated time.

2.
After you finish a test , go through the provided solution for each question set to see what you are missing (in case you you were not able to solve the question) or how you could have seen things faster.

3.
For sets you were not able to solve in the stipulated time period, do not jump to the solutions, since doing that would cut short your learning from those questions. Naturally there would be two kinds of question sets that you did not solve during the time limit.

(a) Sets you did not reach: For these try to adhere to a strict 12 minute time limit while trying to solve the same after the test. If you can solve it in 12 minutes, then you can proceed to look at the solution provided to see if you can learn something more.

(b) Sets you tried but could not solve: For these sets as I have mentioned in the introduction to Part 2 of this section, I would prefer you to first try the unsolved questions. Your focus should be to first make sure that you can solve the same beyond the time limit and learn to identify what you were missing in the solving of the questions. It is imperative to first try to do it on your own – since that is going to be crucial to make sure that you extract maximum learning from each question. Hence, after the 12 minute time limit, don't bother about how much more time you take – and how many times you have to try the question, but it is important to stick to trying to solve on your own. After sufficient trial (that might include trying the set 5-10 times) if you are not done with the set by yourself, you can then try to check the solutions and try to identify what it is that you were not able to see in the question, due to which you weren't able to solve the question.

Mock Tests on Logical Data Interpretation

Outline

Learning Objectives

- A unique collection of questions to test your mettle, your guts, and your intelligence
- Question sets of advanced reasoning based on Data Interpretation.

This part consists of 28 Mock Tests divided between Level of Difficulty 2 (Tests 1 to 8) and Level of Difficulty 3 (Tests 9 to 28). containing Logical DI questions, designed on the latest pattern of CAT – with each test consisting of 20 questions to be solved in 40 minutes (which is what you would be exactly required to face in the actual CAT exam).

The logic of solving each of these tests in a strict time limit of 40 minutes comes essentially from what you have to do in the CAT.

For each of these tests, you are expected to first solve the test as if you are solving the actual CAT – so during the solving of the test, your approach would be to solve in such a way so that you can maximize your score (+3 for every correct answer, –1 for every option based question whose answer went wrong and 0 marks for a wrong answer to a TITA question). Needless to say, you should try to solve any sets you have not been able to solve during the time of the test, as well as those you got wrong. While doing this, for any untouched set, try to solve first in a 12 minute time period – and if not solved in that time, then just focus on solving it without time limits. Remember, most of your learning in Data Interpretation would occur while solving and learning through tough sets.

The following is an indicative score assessment algorithm, which would indicate to you the approximate percentile you can expect on different net scores in these tests.

Net Score	Percentile Expected	Suggested Action
45+	100	None – just maintain your score. You would be very close to the top.
35-45	99.5+	You are doing great. Continue your learning journey, try to reduce your time taken to solve each set, improve your selection and try to improve your
28-35	99 to 99.5	There is scope for improvement. Try to identify your personal scope of improvement – think about how can you improve your learning quality, selectively go back to questions that you have already solved, re-do them, identify repetitive processes, work on reducing the amount of time you use to read a set of questions. You might also want to take a look at your question selection and think about how you could improve the same.
20 to 28	90 to 99	
14 to 20	80–90	
<14	<80	You would need to do all the above, plus you need to re-do everything you have done and improve the quality of your learning through each question you have already solved and also through the questions that you would do in the future.

1 Mock Test Paper

Directions for Questions 1 to 5: *In a science quiz of a school five students were asked to name the Nobel prize winners in physics from 2010 to 2014. As the anchor gave them a hint that the winners for the five years were Alex, Bob, Chris, Denial and Elina not necessarily in that order. After getting the hint the contestants gave their respective orders as follows:*

Students	2010	2011	2012	2013	2014
Pulkit	Chris	Denial	Alex	Elina	Bob
Qasim	Bob	Chris	Alex	Denial	Elina
Rahim	Chris	Denial	Alex	Bob	Elina
Sahir	Elina	Alex	Chris	Bob	Denial
Taufiq	Bob	Chris	Alex	Elina	Denial

If a student names the winner of all the five years correctly then he will get 100 marks. If a student names the winner of only k years correctly (where $k < 5$), he will get $10k + 10$ marks. Further, it was found that each of the student got different marks.

1. Which of the following could be the winner of 2010 physics Nobel prize?
   (a) Bob (b) Alex
   (c) Denial (d) Elina
2. Which of the following students can get 100 marks in the quiz?
   (a) Pulkit (b) Rahim
   (c) Sahir (d) Taufiq
3. Who won the physics noble prize in 2012?
   (a) Chris (b) Alex
   (c) Bob (d) Either (a) or (b)
4. How many students predicted the winner of 2011 correctly?
5. What is the maximum possible difference between the marks scored by Pulkit and Sahir?

Directions for Questions 6 to 10: *The diagram given below is a connector network for current supply between nine electrical nodes A, B, C, D, E, F, G, H and I. The current carried in some of the connectors and the requirement of some of the nodes is also mentioned. Electricity is only supplied from node A – It is the source node and it does not have any requirement of its own but it supplies the requirement of all the other nodes.*

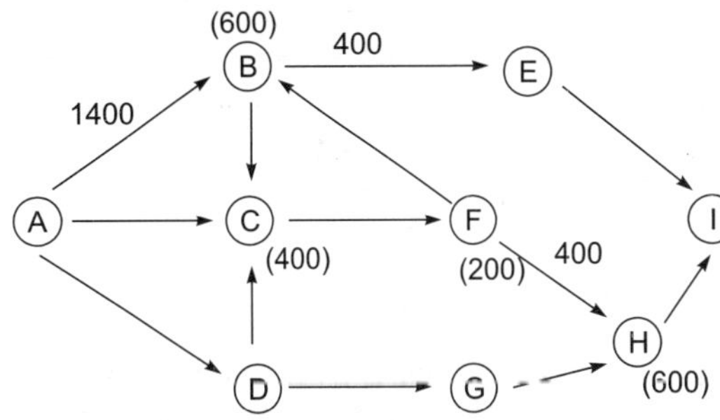

The following information is also known:

1. The maximum capacity of any connector between 2 nodes is 2000 amperes.
2. No two connectors directly connected to the same node carry the same amount of current.
3. The current transfer through none of the above connectors shown is zero.
4. The current requirement at any node except nodes A and I is equal to the current transported by exactly one of the connectors directly connected to it.

6. Find the current requirement at the node E?
7. What is the amount of current in the connector F-B?
8. What is the amount of current in the connector D-C?
9. What is the total requirement that should be supplied by C?
10. What is the amount of current in the connector F-H?

Directions for Questions 11 to 13: *During commando training in NSG a recruit has to complete 12 stages successfully, O to Z. The following table gives the time required to complete each stage, and the necessary stages that should be completed before that stage can be started.*

Stages	Stages Required to be Completed Before Starting the Stage	Time Required to Complete the Stage (in months)
O	None	4
P	O	15
Q	O	12
R	Q	9
S	P, R	2
T	P	3

Stages	Stages Required to be Completed Before Starting the Stage	Time Required to Complete the Stage (in months)
U	T	5
V	S	7
W	R	9
X	U, V	17
Y	V, W	11
Z	Y	7

Any stage cannot be stopped before its completion once it is started. However it is possible that the recruit can be trained under more than one stage simultaneously.
A recruit is said to be trained if all the 12 stages (from O to Z) are completed. Assume that the training started on 1 January, 2022.

11. Stage X cannot be started before
    (a) November, 2024 (b) October 2024
    (c) September, 2024 (d) December, 2024
12. After completing stage S, at least how many more months are required to complete the training?
13. If the training is to be completed in least possible number of months, then after the completion of stage T, at least how many more months are required to complete the training?

Directions for Questions 14 to 15: *After completing the above mentioned training, the recruits have to undergo another two training sessions (Session M and Session N) same as the above training but this time no stage could be implemented simultaneously at a time in both the trainings.*

14. What is the least time required, from the start of these new trainings, to complete the stage U in both the training sessions M & N??
15. What is the least time required, from the start of these new trainings, to complete the stage R in both the trainings?

Directions for Questions 16 to 20: *Answer the questions on the basis of the information given below.*

The following tables show the batting performance of the Indian Cricket Team in the final match of the Asia Cup 2008. Table A gives the runs scored by the 11 batsmen and the order in which they appeared in the batting line up. Table B indicates the score of the team at the fall of each wicket (from 1 to 10).

TABLE A

S. No.	Batsman	Runs Scored
1	Sachin	40
2	Sehwag	29
3	Gautam	11
4	Yuvraj	0
5	Kohli	25
6	Dhoni	6
7	Raina	18
8	Harbhajan	5
9	Ashwin	1
10	Bhuvi	10
11	Zaheer	5

TABLE B

Fall of Wickets	Total Score
1	35
2	54
3	62
4	87
5	97
6	122
7	128
8	133
9	144
10	150

The batsmen came on the field as per the order given in table A. E.g. Sachin and Sehwag opened the innings and if any one of them gets out, the no. 3 batsman (Gambhir) took his place. It is known that Kohli was the sixth wicket to fall.

16. How many batsmen lost their wickets between Sachin's and Dhoni's dismissal?
    (a) 0 (b) 1
    (c) 2 (d) 3
17. How many runs were scored by the batsman who was the 7th to be dismissed?
    (a) 1 (b) 8
    (c) 5 (d) Cannot be determined
18. Any run which is not scored by the batsman but credited to the batting team's score (because of any error of fielding side) can be considered as extra run. Find the total extra runs given to the Indian team.
    (a) 0 (b) 1
    (c) 2 (d) Cannot be determined.
19. If India's total comprised only 'Singles', 'Doubles' and 'Sixes', then find the maximum number of sixes scored by India.
20. How many combinations are possible for the batsmen who got out 9th and 10th in the innings?
    (a) 1 (b) 2
    (c) 4 (d) 8

2 Mock Test Paper

Directions for Questions 1 to 4: *Answer these questions on the basis of the information given below (Table 2.1).*

In the recent past, the world has witnessed a mass transition to ATM enabled services. The following table shows the costs incurred by any bank, in Rupees per transaction, when a customer of that bank uses an ATM of any of the banks.

For example, when ABN AMRO customer uses an ABN AMRO ATM, then the cost incurred by ABN AMRO is ₹9 per transaction. When he uses a Bank of Baroda ATM, the cost incurred by ABN AMRO is ₹30 per transaction and when he uses a Canara Bank ATM, the cost incurred by ABN AMRO is ₹36 per transaction.

TABLE 2.1

ATM Of → Customer Of ↓	ABN AMRO	Bank of Baroda	Canara Bank	Dena Bank	Eastern Cooperative Bank	Federal Bank	Gujarat Cooperative Bank	HDFC Bank	ICICI Bank	J & K Bank
ABN AMRO	9	30	36	18	24	45	60	18	45	60
Bank of Baroda	36	6	63	21	27	57	33	42	51	66
Canara Bank	48	30	15	42	30	42	27	51	57	54
Dena Bank	21	36	48	18	33	54	48	63	24	42
Eastern Cooperative Bank	24	30	42	60	12	48	33	15	54	24
Federal Bank	66	33	36	24	51	24	36	24	33	42
Gujarat Cooperative Bank	39	24	36	39	66	51	33	75	39	60
HDFC Bank	33	27	36	42	48	66	48	24	72	39
ICICI Bank	84	48	51	66	66	69	51	54	48	45
J & K Bank	42	42	51	30	51	81	42	39	33	27

* Transaction costs (Transaction costs* in ₹) from January 2008 to June 2008.

From the month of July 2008 onwards, the banks in list formed two alliances – **RUMMY** and **KITTY**, where Dena Bank and Eastern Cooperative Bank are part of the RUMMY alliance while the remaining banks belong to the KITTY alliance. Members of the RUMMY alliance get a 25% discount on transaction costs incurred for all transactions among themselves and similarly members of KITTY alliance get a 20% discount on all transactions among themselves.

Transaction costs among members belonging to RUMMY alliance and those belonging to KITTY alliance continue as per the above (i.e. without any discounts).

1. If in a particular month in 2008, the customers of ABN AMRO bank made a total of 3 million ATM transactions of which 75 per cent were transacted through ABN AMRO's own ATMs and the remaining through Dena Bank ATMs then what is the total expenditure incurred on ATM transactions by ABN AMRO in that month?
   (a) ₹5.3 million (b) ₹12.25 million
   (c) ₹28.5 million (d) ₹33.75 million
   (e) Cannot be determined
2. After the alliances are formed, for how many banks is it still profitable to use their own ATMs instead of another bank's ATM?
   (a) 3 (b) 7
   (c) 5 (d) 4
   (e) 6
3. If in June 2008, ICICI Bank incurred a total expenditure of ₹252 lakh on account of its customers transacting through ATMs and of this, 50 per cent was on account of transactions through ICICI Bank ATMs then what is the maximum possible number of ATM transactions by the customers of ICICI Bank in June 2008?
   (a) 6.1 lakh (b) 12.5 lakh
   (c) 7.3 lakh (d) 63 lakh
   (e) None of these

4. If in the month of March 2008, all the banks had an equal number of transactions each through their own ATMs then which bank would incur the maximum additional expenditure in case its ATMs were blocked by a computer virus in March 2008 and its customers transacted through the ATMs of the next cheapest alternative bank?
   (a) ABN AMRO
   (b) Bank of Baroda
   (c) ICICI Bank
   (d) Eastern Cooperative Bank
   (e) None of these

Directions for Questions 5 to 6: *Crap is a popular game in which you throw a pair of dice one or more times until you either win or lose.*

There are two ways to win in this game. You can throw the dice once and obtain a score of 7 or 11 in the first throw, or you can obtain a 4, 5, 6, 8, 9, or 10 on the first throw and repeat the same score on the subsequent throw before you obtain a 7.

There are two ways to lose. You can throw the dice once and obtain a 2, 3 or 12, or you can obtain a 4, 5, 6, 8, 9, or 10 on the first throw and then obtain a 7 on a subsequent throw before you have repeated your original score.

5. What is the probability that a person wins on the 2nd throw?
   (a) 100/1296 (b) 50/1296
   (c) 100/216 (d) 50/216
   (e) None of these
6. What is the probability that a person loses on the 2nd throw?
   (a) 100/1296 (b) 120/1296
   (c) 144/1296 (d) 72/1296
   (e) None of these

Directions for Questions 7 to 11: *Three persons A, B, and C play the game continuously without knowing the exact rules. They obtain a set of 10 scores as given below:*

A = {6, 4, 10, 9, 8, 6, 7, 12, 9, 2}
B = {8, 5, 7, 12, 6, 3, 2, 9, 8, 3}
C = {2, 7, 3, 12, 7, 6, 5, 4, 6, 3}

Later on, they are told the exact rules. Now they count their wins or losses. If they win or lose at any of the score obtained, they consider it as end of one game and again start counting wins or losses from the next score. For example if a person D scores 7 in the first score he wins and counts it as the end of one game. In the entire set of 10 scores if he wins 2 times and loses 3 times with the final win or loss at the 10th score he considers it as 1 game. In case the last game does not decide a win or a loss, then the last unfinished game is terminated at the tenth throw and the number of games is incremented by 1.

7. Which of the following statement/s is/are correct?
   (i) A is the first person to win on any of the score.
   (ii) B is the first person to lose on any of the score.
   (iii) C has a maximum number of losses.
   (a) Only (iii) (b) (i) and (ii)
   (c) (ii) and (iii) (d) All
   (e) None of these
8. Who plays the maximum number of games?
   (a) A (b) B
   (c) C
   (d) Both A and B have played the maximum number of games
   (e) Both A and C have played the maximum number of games
9. How many times does A lose in the entire game?
   (a) 1 (b) 2
   (c) 3 (d) 4
10. For C, the number of losses minus the number of wins is
    (a) 1 (b) 0
    (c) 3 (d) 2
    (e) None of these
11. How many games are played overall by all three combined?
    (a) 6 (b) 7
    (c) 12 (d) 10
    (e) 14

Directions for Questions 12 to 16: *There are 16 boxes in a grid. Each of the 16 boxes has a number as shown below. The value of the box is the number on the box.*

Four friends Amar, Biren, Chandan, and Deepak are playing a game, where the objective is to make the maximum addition of the boxes. Every person has exactly 4 boxes with him at all points of time.

	1	2	3	4
A	22	12	30	6
B	10	16	24	20
C	32	2	28	14
D	18	4	26	8

1. *Amar did not own any of the boxes in the A-row.*
2. *Biren's highest number is A-3.*
3. *B-2 and C-1 belong to someone other than Chandan.*
4. *Chandan doesn't own any of the boxes in the 1-column.*
5. *In the last round of the game, Amar traded 4-B for B-1.*
6. *D-2, A-2, and D-3 all belong to the same player.*
7. *C-1, B-3, and D-4 all belong to the same player.*

8. *Deepak's score was 8 higher than Biren's.*
9. *Amar has just one box in the B-row, which is B-1.*
10. *Biren has three boxes in the A-row.*

Based on the information above answer the questions which follow with respect to the end of the game.

12. Who has the lowest total?
    (a) Amar
    (b) Biren
    (c) Chandan
    (d) Insufficient Information
13. To whom does C-4 belong at the end of the game?
    (a) Amar (b) Biren
    (c) Chandan (d) Deepak
14. What is the difference between the total of Deepak and Chandan?
    (a) 4 (b) 8
    (c) 18 (d) Cannot be determined
15. Which of the following could be Amar's total at the end of the game?
    (a) 58
    (b) 50
    (c) 76
    (d) All the three are possible
16. Who has the D1 Box at the end of the game?
    (a) Amar (b) Biren
    (c) Chandan (d) Deepak

Directions for Questions 17 to 20: *Prof. Qazi takes a Maths test once a week. There are five students in his class whose names start with the letter A viz: Arun, Amit, Ankur, Amritesh, and Arjit. Unfortunately, he forgets to record some of the scores of these students. All scores are out of 200. Find the missing numbers in Table 2.2 and answer the questions that follow.*

Besides, we also know that Prof. Qazi grades his students according to their average score as under:

Grade	***Score***
A	*60% plus*
B	*56-60%*
C	*50-55%*
D	*Below 50%*

TABLE 2.2

	1	2	3	4	5	6	7	8	9
Arun	92	110	174	66	148	76	80		190
Amit	96	120		102	170	92	74	38	170
Ankur	76	140	180		200	96	76	40	194
Amritesh	76		186	98	186	100	92	40	200
Arjit	84	132	168	88	168		76	40	196

1. *Amit's missing score is equal to the average score of the topper (who is not Ankur).*
2. *The total of all the scores is 5252*
3. *Ankur got 70% in test 2. Amritesh got 1% less*
4. *The missing score on test 8 is 54 and on test 6 it is 110.*

17. Who is the topper amongst these students?
    (a) Arun (b) Amit
    (c) Arjit (d) Amritesh
    (e) Ankur
18. If an A grade gets 4 points and a B grade gets 3 points, a C gets 2 and a D gets 1 point, what is the grade point average of the class (approximately)?
    (a) 2.6 (b) 1.5
    (c) 1.2 (d) 2.3
    (e) 1.4
19. The least difference between any two missing scores is:
    (a) 14 (b) 24
    (c) 20 (d) 44
    (e) None of these
20. The highest GPA as per data from question 18 is shown by:
    (a) Arun (b) Arjit
    (c) Ankur (d) Amritesh
    (e) Both Amritesh and Arjit

3 Mock Test Paper

Directions for Questions 1 to 2: *A computer assembly unit produces computers. The production of the factory over one week is provided in the data given below.*

Mon	Tues	Wed	Thurs	Fri	Satur	Sun
128	156	64	150	72	150	120

The finished goods are transported to the market using a truck capacity carrying 500 computers at one time. The initial starting stock was of 50 computers. The cost of keeping stock of 1 computer for 1 night is ₹5. The cost of hiring the truck is ₹1000.

1. If the total cost has to be minimised, on which day should the company hire the truck?
   (a) Tuesday, Thursday, and Saturday
   (b) Tuesday, Friday, and Sunday
   (c) Tuesday and Saturday
   (d) None of these
2. What is the minimum total cost for the week?
   (a) ₹4000 (b) ₹4270
   (c) ₹5170 (d) ₹4170

Directions for Questions 3 to 7: *Refer to the data given below (Table 3.1) and answer the questions that follow:*

The Management entrance scenario has undergone a drastic change in the last 200 years. In the current year (2222) an MBA course is essentially a six year course consisting of MBA 1, MBA 2, MBA 3, MBA 4, MBA 5, and Internship Year (following which students pass out of their B Schools.

Table 1.1 gives the number of students in Indian School of Management, Ahmedabad in each year of the MBA program. The years are 2222 and 2223 respectively.

Entrance examinations being very tough (an estimated 23 lac students appeared for the entrance in 2221), the school only admits students in MBA 1 and no student leaves the B-School without passing out through his internship program. Students who fail have to repeat the year completely, and are only promoted if they satisfactorily pass their exams.

TABLE 3.1

Class	Students in the Year 2222	Students in the Year 2223
MBA 1	360	420
MBA 2	252	300
MBA 3	216	210
MBA 4	192	180
MBA 5	144	168
MBA Internship Year	108	162

3. If no student of MBA 5 failed in the year 2222, then what is the pass percentage of MBA Internship Year for the year 2222?
   (a) 22.66% (b) 16.66%
   (c) 83.33% (d) 77.77%
4. If the new joiners in the year 2223 were 228, then the number of students failed in MBA Internship Year in the year 2222?
   (a) 30 (b) 42
   (c) 24 (d) 48
4. For the above question, how many students would have failed in MBA 5?
6. How many students of MBA 3 failed in the year 2222, if no student of MBA 5 failed in the year 2222?
   (a) 36 (b) 24
   (c) 30 (d) None of these
7. If 192 students of MBA 1 failed in the year 2222, then what is the total number of students who failed in the year 2222?
   (a) 450 (b) 546
   (c) 585 (d) 492

Directions for Questions 8 to 12: *Answer the questions based on the information given below.*

India is known around the world for its large reserves of precious stones. India mainly produces four precious stones, Diamond, Ruby, Pearl, and Emerald. The number of units of production, domestic sales and exports for each of the precious stones is given in the following bar chart (Figure 3.1) for the four quarters of the fiscal year 2019-20.

For these questions, all ratios have to be calculated till the second digit after decimal.

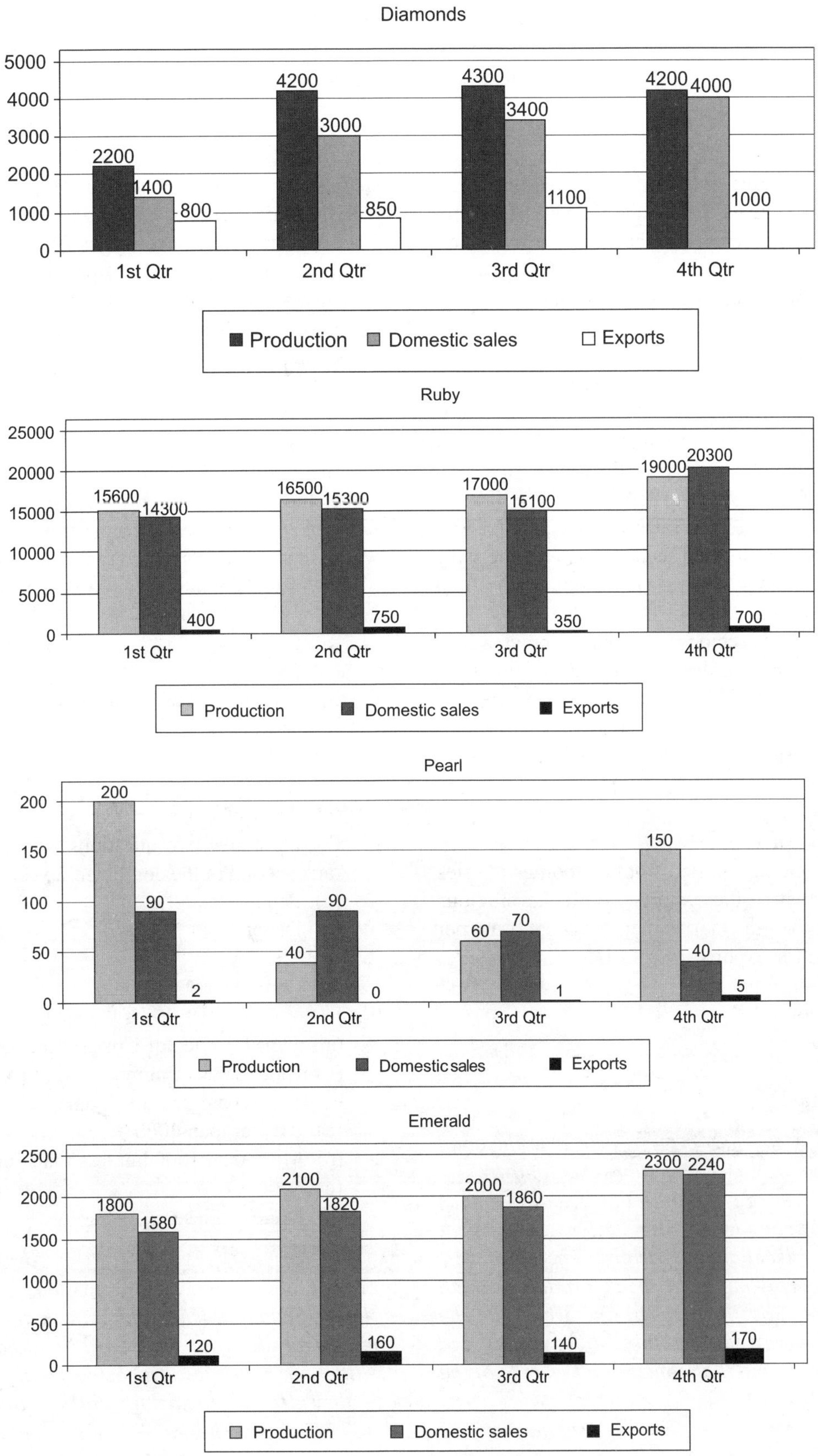
Diamonds
5000
4000
3000
2000
1000
0
2200
1400
800
4200
3000
850
4300
3400
1100
4200
4000
1000
1st Qtr
2nd Qtr
3rd Qtr
4th Qtr
Production
Domestic sales
Exports
Ruby
25000
20000
15000
10000
5000
0
15600
14300
400
16500
15300
750
17000
16100
350
19000
20300
700
1st Qtr
2nd Qtr
3rd Qtr
4th Qtr
Production
Domestic sales
Exports
Pearl
200
150
100
50
0
200
90
2
40
90
0
60
70
1
150
40
5
1st Qtr
2nd Qtr
3rd Qtr
4th Qtr
Production
Domestic sales
Exports
Emerald
2500
2000
1500
1000
500
0
1800
1580
120
2100
1820
160
2000
1860
140
2300
2240
170
1st Qtr
2nd Qtr
3rd Qtr
4th Qtr
Production
Domestic sales
Exports

FIGURE 3.1

8. The ratio of total sales (Exports + Domestic) to total production is minimum for:
   (a) Diamond
   (b) Ruby
   (c) Pearl
   (d) Emerald
9. Which among the following shows the maximum percentage increase in the ratio of total sales to production for a given particular quarter over the last quarter
   (a) Diamond: 2nd Quarter to 3rd Quarter
   (b) Pearl: 1st Quarter to 2nd Quarter
   (c) Emerald: 3rd Quarter to 4th Quarter
   (d) Ruby: 1st Quarter to 2nd Quarter
10. On a quarter-to-quarter basis, for each stone, how many instances of a drop in the ratio of total sales to production do we see over the time period?
11. Consider the following statements:
    (i) The ratio of the Total sales to production for Emerald for the first and second quarter is the same
    (ii) The percentage decrease in the ratio of the Total sales to production for Diamonds is 10%
    (iii) None of the Precious stones have shown a continuous increase/decrease in ratio of the Total sales to production over all the four quarters

    Which of the above statements is true?
    (a) (i) and (ii)
    (b) (ii) and (iii)
    (c) All of these
    (d) (i) and (iii)
12. If the revenue generated from the domestic sales is twice that of the exports for all the precious stones in the 4th Quarter then the ratio of the per unit price for exports to that of domestic sales is the maximum for:
    (a) Diamonds
    (b) Ruby
    (c) Pearl
    (d) Emerald

Directions for Questions 13 to 17: *Refer to the data given below and answer the questions that follow:*

Summer beverages manufacture cold drinks named Pep, Miran, Fant, Slic, Dewy, Cok, Sprit, and 12 other miscellaneous drinks. The sales volumes of 5 top ranking cold drink products which belong to Fant, Slic, Pep, Sprit, and Dewy for the year 2018–19 were 5500, 13000, 18000, 16000, and 7500 respectively and that contributed to 75% of the total sales volume.

The sales in the next fiscal year hiked spectacularly by 56.25%. Slic contributed to 10.8% of the total sales volume in 2019-20. Pep, Dewy, Miran, and Cok contributed 14%, 4%, 16.8%, and 14.4% of the total sales volume in 2019-20. The sales mentioned above are for the top five rated products in the year 2019-20. In 2018-19, the sales of the miscellaneous categories was 15% of the total sales The sales of each of the drinks in the miscellaneous category was lower than the sales of the seven indvidual drinks mentioned here.

13. If the increase in the sales of Miran in the year 2019–20 is 400% with respect to the previous year then what is the rank of Cok in the year 2018–19? (Consider the sales of the number of miscellaneous categories are equal)
    (a) 6th
    (b) 7th
    (c) 8th
    (d) 9th
14. If the products for the two years combined are ranked in the decreasing order of their sales, which of these products would rank 6th? (The products in the miscellaneous category were not among the top 7 for both the years)
    (a) Sprit (b) Dewy
    (c) Fant (d) Slic
15. In the above ranking which of these would rank 5th
    (a) Miran
    (b) Cok
    (c) Sprit
    (d) Cannot be determined
16. For the above two questions, which drink would rank second in the combined 2 year ranking?
    (a) Pep
    (b) Dewy
    (c) Slic
    (d) Cannot be determined
17. In the year 2018–19, if the sales of Miran ranked 6th then the sales of Cok in that year would be? (Consider sales of number of products in the miscellaneous category are equal)
    (a) Greater than 4000
    (b) More than 1000 but less than 4000
    (c) 4000
    (d) None of these

Directions for Questions 18 to 20: Answer the questions that follow the given information.

Rohit, Shyam, Karan, and Manish are four friends. They travel all around the world and collect stamps of different countries. Once when they all were in US, they decided to identify facts about the collections. These are the facts they have claimed during the conversation,

Rohit said, "We have collected 200 stamps altogether."

Shyam said, "None of us have collected less than 20 stamps."

Karan said, "Each of us has collected an even number of stamps."

Together, all of them said, "Each one of us has collected a different number of stamps."

18. The friend who collected the most number of stamps could not have exceeded:
    (a) 134 (b) 132
    (c) 130 (d) 120
19. One of the four friends collected 116 stamps and he was not Shyam. If Karan collected two more than double the number collected by Manish, then how many stamps did Shyam collect?
    (a) 20 (b) 22
    (c) 24 (d) Indeterminable
20. If the friend with the maximum number of coins, had exactly 116 coins, then in how many ways (numerically) can the remaining coins be distributed amongst the other three friends?

Note: For the purpose of this question, you do not need to count the same numerical distribution more than once. For instance, a distribution of 20, 38, 42 will be counted only once (and does not need to be counted for who got how many coins).

4 Mock Test Paper

Directions for Questions 1 to 4: *Refer to the following graph and pie chart (Figure 4.1) to answer these questions:*

Given here is the data of the company AMS Ltd. The company publishes five books. The productions in its entire array of five books (in ₹ Crore). Quant (A), DI (B), Reasoning (C), English (D), and General awareness (E) and its total turnover over a period of five years (from 2003 to 2007) is shown in the bar charts. The distribution of the turnover for each year, for each of the five products is shown in the pie charts (as %) (Figure 4.1).

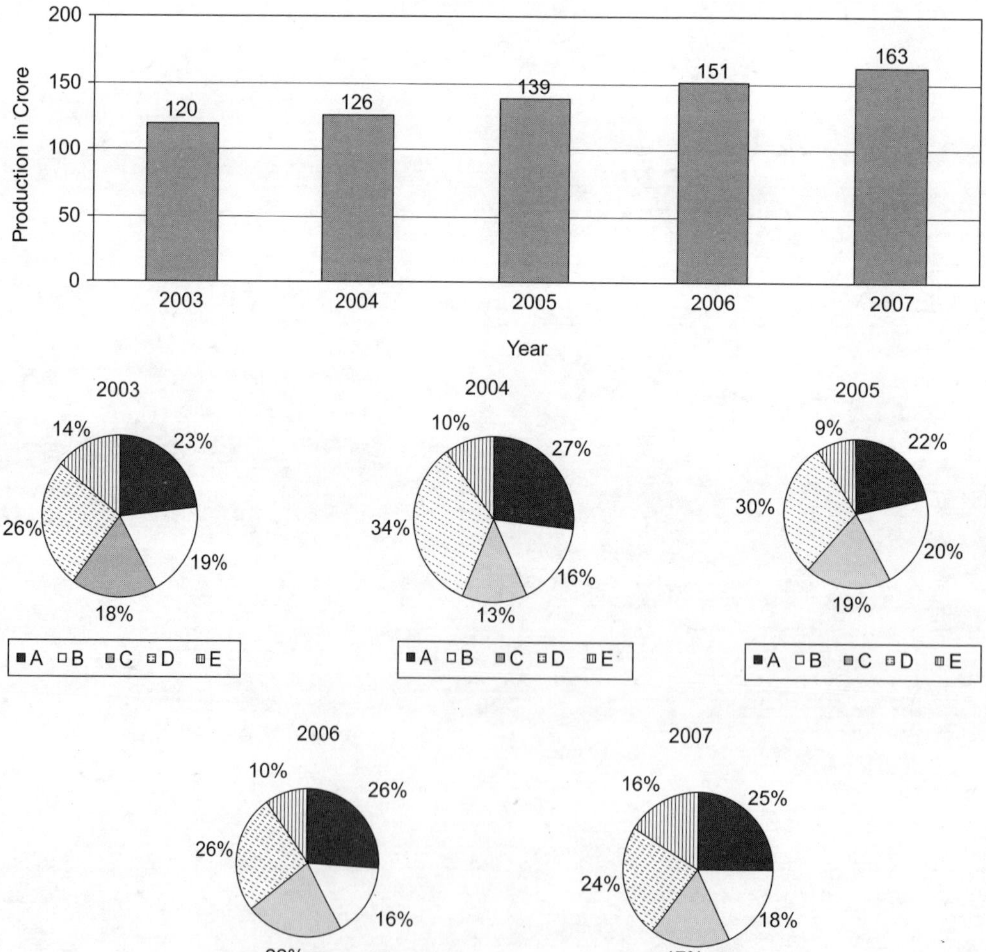

FIGURE 4.1

1. If we assume that the book on English maintained y% share on an average every year in the company's productions then what is the value of y? (round off your answer to the closest integer.)
   (a) 26%
   (b) 27%
   (c) 28%
   (d) Cannot be determined

2. If for two consecutive years, the highest growth in percentage terms of the company's productions between two successive years be b % then the average compounded annual growth rate over the given period is c % then what is the value of the difference between the two is:
   (a) 2.35% (b) 2.40%
   (c) 2.30% (d) 2.75%
3. How much more is the combined turnover of Quant and Reasoning books in 2006 to that of the combined turnover of DI and English in 2007.
   (a) ₹3.9 cr. (b) ₹3.8 cr.
   (c) ₹4.5 cr. (d) ₹4 cr.
4. Which of the following is not true?
   (a) For the given 5 year period the average of the production of the company is more than the third years production
   (b) B's production has been fluctuating in the given period
   (c) The maximum percentage increase in the turnover of the individual of products is 72% in between any two consecutive years
   (d) None of these

Directions for Questions 5 to 8: *Refer to the given data (Table 4.1) to answer the questions given below. The following table gives the performance of the players of the team Cuppy Vs the team Cake in the world cup cricket 2007. The first column of the table (Table 4.1) gives the name of the bowler of the Cake team vs the Batsman of the Cuppy team who was facing them.*
To interpret the above table, the following guidelines may be used:

For ZK vs AS:
Number of balls faced by AS = 9 + 1 = 10
Score of AS = 1 × 4 = 4
Strike rate of AS = score/balls × 100 = 4/10 × 100 − 40%
AS was dismissed by ZK and RS in two innings and the modes of dismissal were Lbw and Caught respectively

TABLE 4.1

Bowler of Team Cake Vs. Batsman of Team Cuppy	0s	1s	2s	3s	4s	6s	Dismissal
ZK Vs. KP	15	0	0	0	1	0	Lbw
RP Vs. AC	16	5	2	1	0	0	
RS Vs. IB	12	3	1	1	3	0	
AK Vs. AC	37	2	0	0	0	1	Bowled
RS Vs. KP	4	2	0	0	1	1	Bowled
ZK Vs. MV	14	1	2	0	1	0	Caught
ST Vs. IB	7	1	2	0	1	1	
SS Vs. MV	6	0	1	0	0	1	Bowled
SG Vs. PC	2	3	0	0	0	0	
SS Vs. IB	12	2	0	2	0	0	Lbw
SS Vs. KP	5	0	0	0	1	0	
ZK Vs. PC	16	2	1	0	1	1	Caught
ZK Vs. IB	2	0	1	0	0	0	
SS Vs. AC	25	2	3	0	2	0	
SS Vs. PC	9	1	0	0	0	0	Bowled
RS Vs. AS	4	0	0	1	0	0	Caught
SG Vs. IB	5	0	1	0	0	0	
RS Vs. PC	10	3	2	2	3	0	
SG Vs. AC	16	1	2	0	1	0	Lbw
ZK Vs. AC	15	1	0	1	3	0	
AK Vs. IB	3	2	1	0	0	0	Caught
ZK Vs. AS	9	0	0	0	1	0	Lbw

5. For how many batsmen-bowler combinations is the strike rate equal to 125%?
   (a) 2 (b) 3
   (c) 4 (e) 5
   (e) None of these
6. Which batsman of the Cuppy team scored the maximum runs?
   (a) AS (b) AC
   (c) MV (d) KP
   (e) IB

7. Let x = number of batsmen a bowler has bowled to as a percentage of the total runs given by a bowler, then what is the percentage difference among the bowlers with the highest value of x and lowest value of x?
   (a) 14.76% (b) 16.32%
   (c) 16.26% (d) 16.13%
   (e) 16.84%
8. Which of the following bowlers gave away the maximum number of runs to all the six batsmen put together?
   (a) AK (b) ZK
   (c) ST (d) RS
   (e) SG

Directions for Questions 9 to 13: *From the data (Figure 4.2), derive the appropriate answers.*

Mr. Sharma, a graduate in electronics engineering and an MBA from IIM Bangalore, decided to open an entrepreneurial venture. He decided to run an electronics workshop and manufacture Field effect transistors. The manufacturing required three simultaneous processes: Substrating, Masking, and Etching. Electronica Ltd and Electrica Ltd. gave orders of 15 units and 10 units per day respectively. The profit made by Mr. Sharma on 1 unit for Electronica Ltd. is ₹75 and for 1 unit of Electrica Ltd. is ₹100. The working hours were 0900 hours to 1700 hours. The workshop has two machines for Substrating, four for Masking, and three for Etching.

The bar chart (Figure 4.2) gives the time required for each machine per unit(in minutes)

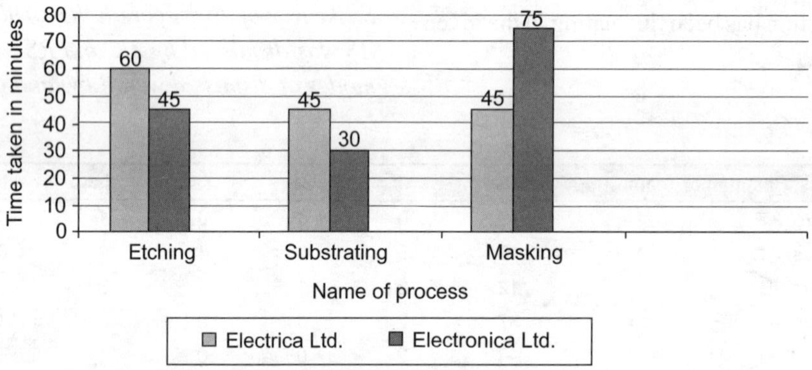

FIGURE 4.21

9. After supplying both the companies, Mr. Sharma might conclude that:
   (a) Mr. Sharma can make one more unit for Electrica Ltd.
   (b) Out of the two machines of process Substrating, one has an idle time of 30 minutes and the other has an idle time of 15 minutes
   (c) Machines of process Masking have no idle time left
   (d) Mr. Sharma can make two more units for Electronica Ltd.
   (e) None of the above conclusions can be drawn
10. Ignoring Mr. Sharma's commitments to Electrica Ltd., the maximum number of units that Mr. Sharma can make for Electronica Ltd. is:
    (a) 24 (b) 25
    (c) 26 (d) 27
    (e) 28
11. If Mr. Sharma has the flexibility to manufacture anyone of the two products, what is the maximum profit that he can make on any given day and for which product?
    (a) ₹2400, Electrica Ltd.
    (b) ₹2100, Electronica Ltd.
    (c) ₹1800, Electronica Ltd.
    (d) ₹2000, Electrica Ltd.
12. Mr. Sharma decided to install one more machine for each process. With the existing commitments, in order to maximise his profits, what should he produce so that he gets the best deal (Both the companies will levy no extra production)
    (a) 6 more units for Electronica Ltd. and 7 more units for Electrica Ltd.
    (b) 7 more units for Electronica Ltd. and 6 more units for Electrica Ltd.
    (c) 5 more units for Electronica Ltd.
    (d) 10 more units of Electrica Ltd.
13. What is the total idle time available on the machines as a percentage of total time?
    (a) 12.5%
    (b) 8.33%
    (c) 13.2%
    (d) 15.5%

Directions for Questions 14 to 17: *Refer to the following data (Table 4.2) to answer the questions that follow:*

As per the JP Organ survey of the companies in India, the table that is given below shows the number of Indian companies from the year 1997 to 2007. Sources at JP Organ revealed that the total number of companies in the year 1997–98 were 1,76,800.

Assuming that all companies are into only particular business, the following bar graph (Figure 4.3) gives the percentage of all the companies in the various sectors, i.e. Oil (O), Food (F), Power (P), and Energy (E). It may be noted that companies are of either small scale, medium scale, or large scale,.

TABLE 4.2

Year	1997–98	1998–99	1999–20	2000–01	2001–02	2002–03	2003–04	2004–05	2005–06	2006–07
Number of Indian Companies.	31745	33600	30600	33800	35480	54600	54600	66800	75570	79600

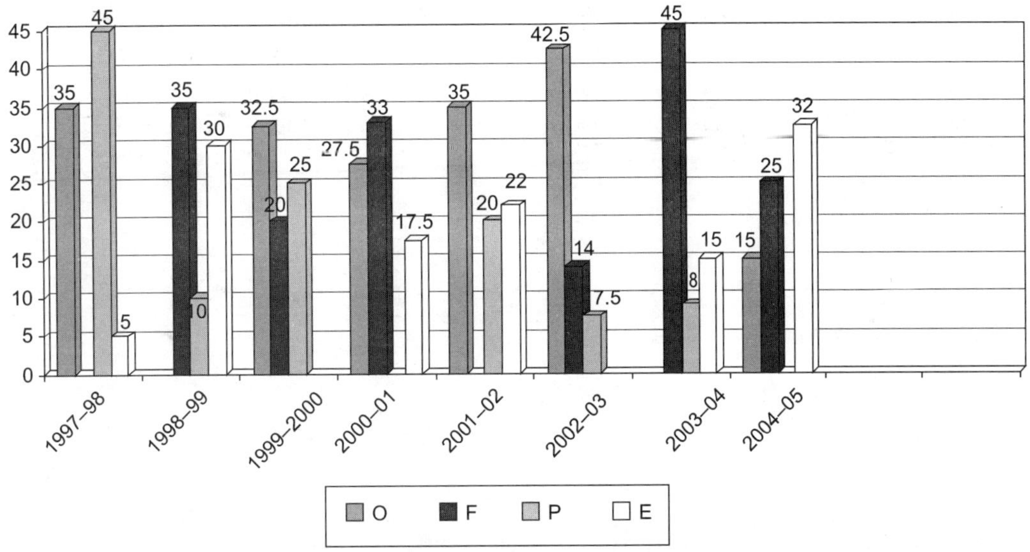

FIGURE 4.3

14. Find the ratio of the number of Indian companies who are into the Oil business in 1998–99 to that of those who are in the Power business in 2004–05:
    (a) 75/167 (b) 83/162
    (c) 76/167 (d) 85/162
15. If the total number of companies was increased by 15% in the year 1998–99 as compared to the previous year then find the number of multinational companies in the year 1998–99.
    (a) 169720 (b) 1,71,580
    (c) 1,71,570 (d) Data insufficient
16. Find the number of Indian companies in the Oil business in the year 2003-04.
    (a) 15702 (b) 16882
    (c) 17472 (d) None of these
17. If in the year 2006–07 the number of companies who grew to become large scale companies was 79%, which is 8% more than that of the previous year and the number of small scale companies is 17% which is 9% less than that for the year 2005–06, then how many Indian companies were there apart from the small scale companies and the large scale companies, i.e. the medium scale?
    (a) 2894 (b) 3184
    (c) 2478 (d) Data insufficient

Directions for Questions 18 to 20: *There are three tables given. Table 4.4 gives the monthly production capacity of five different farmers. Table 4.5 gives monthly consumption of four different families. Table 4.6 gives the transportation cost involved in transporting grains from different farmers to different families.*

TABLE 4.4

Farmer's Name	Total Production Per Month (in tons)
Piku	20
Qadir	60
Ramu	20
Sonu	60
Tinku	40

TABLE 4.5

Family	Consumption Per Month (in tons)
A	80
B	60
C	20
D	40

TABLE 4,6

Farmer	Transportation Cost Per Ton (in INR)			
	A	B	C	D
Piku	200	150	300	50
Qadir	250	150	300	100
Ramu	300	200	200	50
Sonu	150	200	350	200
Tinku	100	150	200	100

Assume that only these five farmers are the source of food for these four families and production of grains at any month is transported to the family on only one day in a month such that monthly demand of the families is met.

18. In a given month what is the minimum possible value (in INR) of sum of transportation costs paid by all the farmers to transport the grains to all the families?
19. If due to some transportation problems, Qadir cannot supply grains to family B and D, then the monthly cost of transportation of grains to all the families is at least:
20. The transportation cost for which of the following is least?
    (a) Piku supplies 20 tons to A.
    (b) Piku supplies 20 tons to B.
    (c) Qadir supplies 20 tons to A.
    (d) Tinku supplies 20 tons to D.

5 Mock Test Paper

Directions for Questions 1 to 5: *Refer to the data given below and answer the following questions*

Three friends Aishwarya, Bebo, and Chiranjeevi together have 25 marbles together, when they go to a fair. Aishwarya has 10 marbles and Chiranjeevi has one more marble than Bebo. Mithilesh is a magician who has the ability to change the number of marbles that any person gives him by putting the marbles into his hat. This he does by making them undergo one of 4 distinct processes – He either halves (PROCESSNAME-DIVIDEBY2), doubles (PROCESSNAME-MULTIPLYBY2), triples (PROCESSNAME-MULTIPLYBY3) or quadruples (PROCESSNAME-MULTIPLBY4) the number of marbles. In the game which consists of three consecutive rounds, each of Aishwarya, Bebo, and Chiranjeevi puts marbles in the hat of the magician in each of the 3 consecutive rounds.

You know the following additional things about the game:

1. *In every round, the process on the marbles of the friends is different i.e. in any particular round, no two friends can have their marbles halved. The same rule applies to other processes of doubling, tripling or quadrupling also.*
2. *In no two rounds can any person have the same process done on his marbles. For example, if the process DIVIDEBY2 is used with Aishwarya in the first round, then in subsequent rounds the DIVIDEBY2 process cannot be used again for Aishwarya. The same rule applies to each of the other processes (viz: MULTIPLYBY2, MULTIPLYBY3, and MULTIPLYBY4).*

An observer to the game also points out to you, "At any point in the game the number of marbles with any friend lies between 5 and 100 (both inclusive)." It is also known that each of the friends puts in all the marbles he had in the hat of the magician in each round.

1. How many combinations of processes on Aishwarya's marbles in the three rounds, will lead to the minimum possible number of marbles with Aishwarya at the end of the game?

   (a) $2! \times 2$ (b) $3!$
   (c) $0!$ (d) $2!$

2. What can be the highest total number of marbles with all the three friends in the second round of the game?

   (a) 78 (b) 88
   (c) 68 (d) 98

3. At the end of the game, what is the absolute difference between the maximum possible marbles with Aishwarya to minimum possible number of marbles with Chiranjeevi?

   (a) 2!.3 (b) 3!.2
   (c) 3! (d) 36

4. What can be the lowest total number of marbles with all the three friends at the end of the game?

   (a) 58 (b) 75
   (c) 25 (d) 102

5. At the end of the game, what is the ratio of maximum possible number of marbles with Chiranjeevi and Bebo combined to the minimum possible number of marbles with Aishwarya?

   (a) 2:1 (b) 4:1
   (c) 5:2 (d) 3:1

Directions for Questions 6 to 10: *Refer to the data given below and answer the following questions:*

International paper sizes table: The 'A' series is based on A0 (841 × 1189 mm) which is equivalent to a square metre in area, and each smaller size A1, A2, etc. is equal to half the area of the preceding larger size.

Size	Millimetres
2A	1189 x 1682
A0	841 x 1189
A1	594 x 841
A2	420 x 594
A3	297 x 420
A5	___ x ___
A6	x ___
A7	___ x ___
A8	___ x ___
A9	___ x ___
A10	26 x 37

'C' series is the series of envelopes or folders suitable for enclosing stationery in the A sizes.

Size	Millimetres
C3	324 x 458
C4	229 x 324
C5	___ x ___
C6	___ x ___
C7	___ x ___
DL	110 x 220

Based on the above, answer the following:

6. What is the size of A8 papers?
   (a) 105 × 210 (b) 52 × 74
   (c) 74 × 26 (d) 26 × 52
7. 8 sheets of A1 paper is cut into A7 size papers. How many A7 papers can be obtained?
   (a) 1024 (b) 64
   (c) 128 (d) 2048
8. In the envelop of size C3 how many type of different size papers of series can be placed without folding the paper :
   (a) 6 (b) 7
   (c) 8 (d) 9
9. What is the size of the C6 envelop?
   (a) 55 × 110 (b) 55 × 81
   (c) 81 × 114 (d) 114 × 162
10. The approximate sum of areas of all different papers equal to or larger than A9 is?
   (a) $37 \times 52 \times [2^{11}–1]$
   (b) $37 \times 52\ [2^{10}–1]$
   (c) $37 \times 52 \times [2^{9}–1]$
   (d) $37 \times 52\ [2^{8}–1]$

Directions for Questions 11 to 15: *Refer to the following data (Figure 5.1) to answer the questions that follow: The following figure gives the number of students in St. Francis' college in the year 2007 and 2008 from class 7th to class 12th. It may also be noted that new students joined the school only in class 7th unless otherwise stated and no student leaves school before class 12th. Obviously, the students who failed in a particular class had to repeat the same class again.*

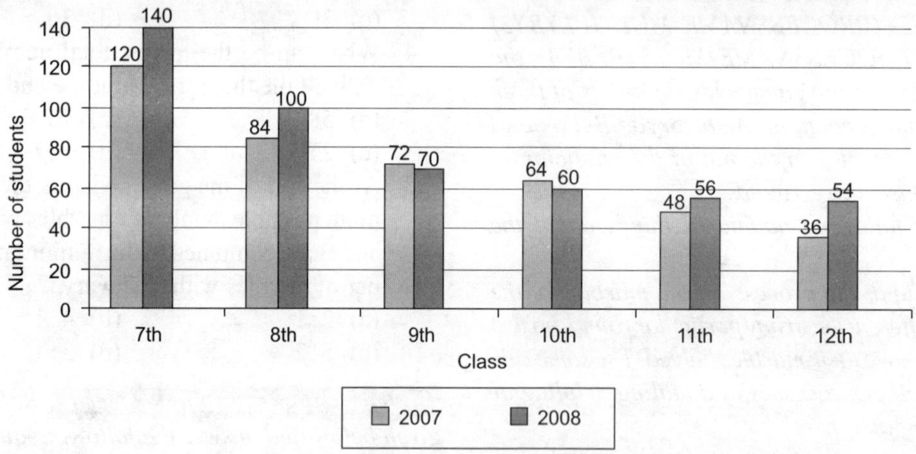

FIGURE 5.1

11. How many students in class 9th failed in the year 2007 if no students of class 11th failed in the 2007?
   (a) 12 (b) 15
   (c) 18 (d) 20
12. If it is known that the school was opened in the year 2007 itself and 14 students of class 10th failed in that year, what is the percentage increase/decrease in the number of new students joining the school from 2007 to 2008?
   (a) 100/3% (b) 100/6%
   (c) 100/9% (d) 100/11%
13. If no student of class 11th failed in the year 2007, then what is the pass percentage of class 12th for the year 2007?
   (a) 82(1/3)% (b) 81(1/3)%
   (c) 80(1/3)% (d) None of these
14. If no student of class 11th failed in the year 2007, then what is the total number of students of the school who failed in that year?
   (a) 120 (b) 121
   (c) 122 (d) 123
15. If exactly 5 students failed in class 12th in 2007, then what is the number of students who failed in Class 7th in that year?
   (a) 5 (b) 2
   (c) 12 (d) This is not possible

Directions for Question 16 to 20 *Answer the questions on the basis of the table and the pie-charts given below.*

The following table gives the amount (in crores) of loan disbursed by banks in India during 2001–2005. The bank, which disburses the maximum amount in a particular year, is considered to be the market leader.

The pie-chart shows the distribution of the loans disbursed by all the banks that are part of others in 2005

Name of Bank	2001	2002	2003	2004	2005
SBI	80	92	112	143	167
FBI	98	78	79	80	120
CBI	82	88	82	82	82
BoI	98	102	105	105	109
Others	34	25	67	76	80
Total	**392**	**385**	**445**	**486**	**558**

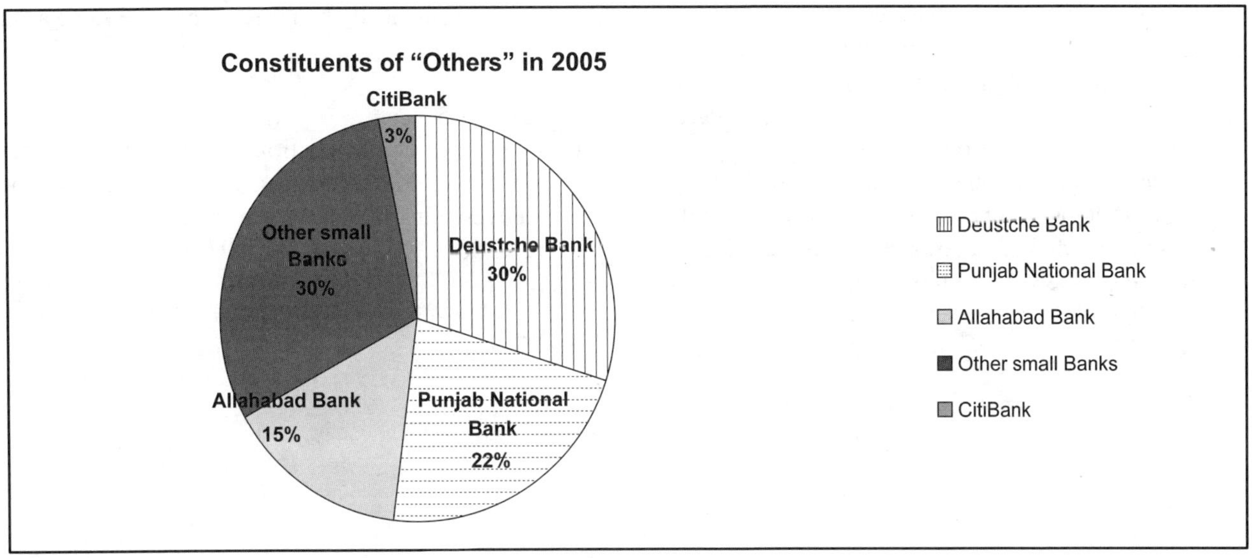

The pie-chart given below shows the distribution of the loans disbursed by "Other smaller banks" in 2005

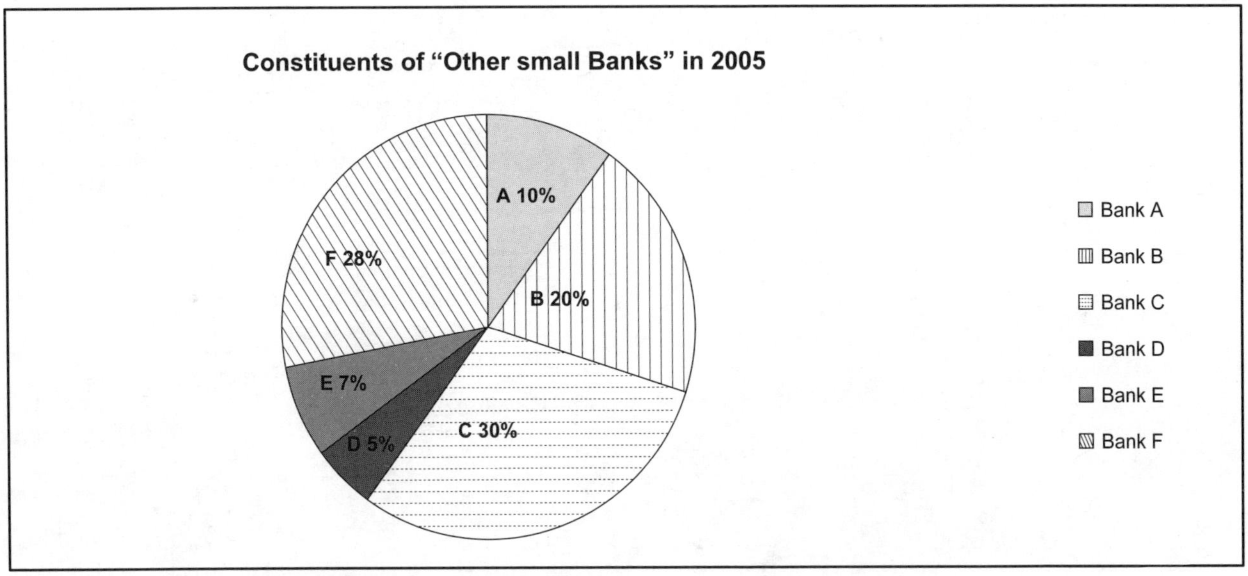

16. In 2002, all banks had the same percentage share in Housing Finance as their respective shares in loan disbursement. By what amount (approximately in crore INR) was the share of SBI Bank greater than the share of FBI, if the total Housing Finance market was ₹150 crore INR?
(a) 14 (b) 3.6
(c) 20.26 (d) 5.45

17. Recession was round the corner and banks unaware of the global errors kept catering to increasing loan requirements of customers in 2006. Indian banking regulatory authorities realized something bad is inevitable and declared a notice that only those banks that have loans disbursed of more than 7 crore INR can continue their operations and rest should halt their operations by 1st January 2007 until next notice. How many banks had to halt their operations? (Assume the same figures and data for 2006 as for 2005 above)
(a) 6 (b) 7
(c) 8 (d) 9
18. 2008 brought along recession with it and only 30% of the loans disbursed in 2007 were recovered in 2008. If loan disbursement had been aggressive and growing at the rate of 10% year by year since 2005 until 2007, what amount of loans (in crore INR) was not recovered by banks in 2008? (Assume 0 disbursements in the year 2008). Round off the value to next integer.
(a) 203 (b) 675
(c) 473 (d) 202
19. Recession of 2008 was disastrous and all banks under category "Others" had to shut down due to bad recovery. This means no amount of loan they disbursed in 2007, was recovered by them in 2008. Also in 2008 the banks, which somehow managed to survive the blow, could not recover more than 50% of the loan disbursements made by them in 2007. What is the amount recovered in 2008 by all banks put together? (in crore INR)
    - Consider data from the previous question
    - Assume that the percentage share of loan disbursements by banks remained the same as in 2005

(a) 97 (b) 578
(c) 337.5 (d) 289
20. In the previous question, approximately what amount of loan disbursed in 2007 could not be recovered in 2008 at all? (in crore INR)
(a) 386 (b) 97
(c) 289 (d) 0

6 Mock Test Paper

Directions for Question 1 to 5: *Answer the questions on the basis of information below.*

Sneakers and Boots are 2 types of shoes of brand Quma available in the local market. Boots were introduced by Quma in 2007 while Sneakers in 2011. For both these types, 30% of the shoes bought in any given year are disposed off 2 years later. It is known that 20 Boots were disposed off in 2011. The following figures show the Number of Boots and Sneakers being used by customers from 2009 through 2014, as in the end of that year.

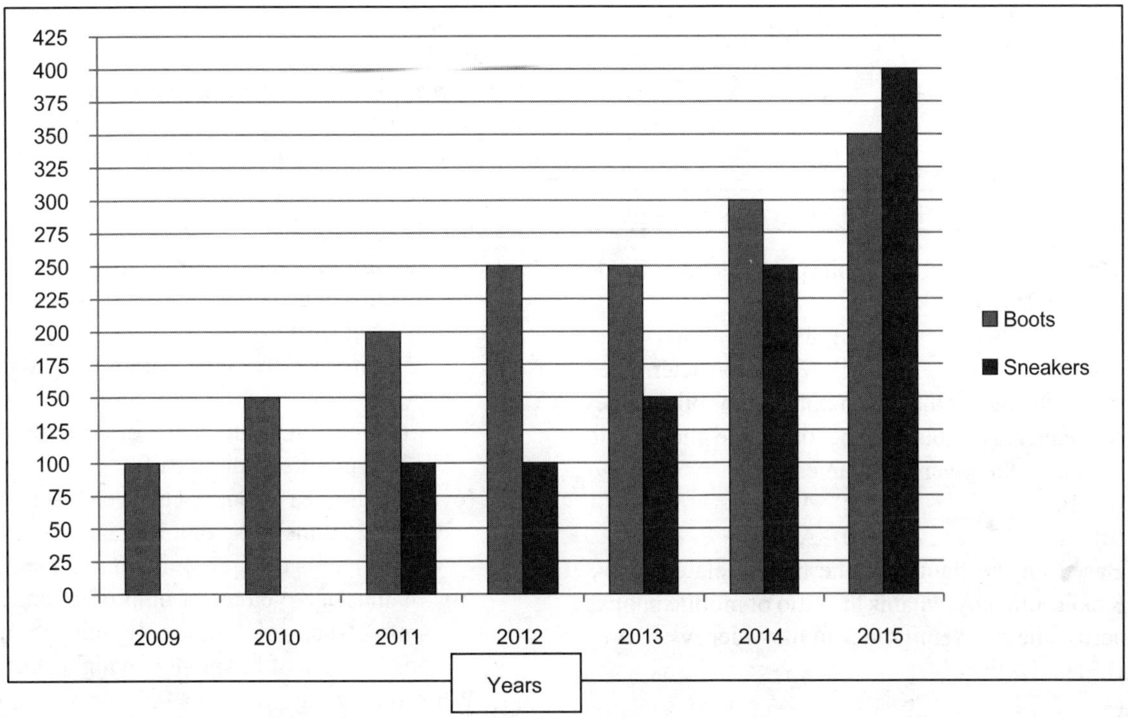

1. How many Sneakers were purchased in 2013?
   (a) 50 (b) 80
   (c) 100 (c) Cannot be determined
2. How many sneakers were disposed off by the end of 2015?
   (a) 54 (b) 84
   (c) 75 (d) 45
3. How many boots were disposed off in 2013?
   (a) 15 (b) 6
   (c) 21 (d) Cannot be determined
4. How many boots were bought in 2012?
   (a) 80 (b) 50
   (c) 70 (d) Cannot be determined
5. How many Boots were purchased in 2013?
   (a) 0 (b) 21
   (c) 16 (d) Cannot be determined

Directions for Question 6 to 9: *Answer the questions on the basis of information below.*

The following tables show the sales of 5 Mobile phone companies: TTC, Bokorola, Kokia, Hi-Phone and Mony across various grades of mobile phones in India

Table 6.1 gives percentage break up of sales of different grades of mobile phones across different companies

Table 6.2 gives percentage break up of sales of mobile phones of various companies across different grades

TABLE 6.1

		Grade				
		A++	A+	A	B+	B
Company	TTC	20	21	20	10	23
	Bokorola	18	09	20	15	27
	Kokia	22	21	20	25	01
	Hi-Phone	17	31	20	30	23
	Mony	23	18	20	20	26
		100	100	100	100	100

TABLE 6.2

		Company				
		TTC	Bokorola	Kokia	Hi-Phone	Mony
Grade	A++	01	82	01	09	11
	A+	08	04	02	09	01
	A	08	08	20	09	09
	B+	07	03	01	09	09
	B	76	03	76	64	70
		100	100	100	100	100

6. What is the number of Mobile phones sold in Grade A++ by Bokorola?
(a) 100 (b) 89
(c) 189 (d) Cannot be determined
7. In which grade is the total number of mobile phones sold equal to the total number of mobile phones sold by one of the given companies?
(a) B (b) A+
(c) A (d) A++
8. Based on the figures in the tables related to the Kokia company, what is the ratio of mobile phones across the different grades in the order A++ , A +, B+ and B?
(a) 22:21:1:25:76
(b) 1/22:2/21:1:1/25:23/21
(c) 1/22:2/21:1:1/25:76
(d) Cannot be determined
9. If Kokia company sold 55,000 phones in total, what is the total number of phones sold of Grade A++ of all the brands put together?
(a) 2500 (b) 550
(c) 12100 (d) Cannot be determined

Directions for Questions 10 to 14: *Refer to the data given below (Table 6.3) and answer the questions that follow:*

Praveen Kumar Tiwari has a factory which manufactures Kryptonite, Arsonite, and Liptonite. All these are manufactured by processing Ramena 55. Kryptonite requires 2 kg/unit, Arsonite requires 4 kg/unit, and Liptonite requires 5 kg per unit of Ramena 55, which costs ₹4 per kilogram. The total availability of Ramena 55 is 700 kilograms. The processing is done on a machine having a production capacity of 324 hours per month in the day shift and 364 hours per month in the night shift. The time required per unit production for each product is different for each shift and is as follows:

TABLE 6.3

Product	Day Shift	Night Shift
Kryptonite	4 hours	5 hours
Arsonite	6 hours	8 hours
Liptonite	2 hours	3 hours

The machine costs ₹2 per hour.

The sales price for Kryptonite, Arsonite, and Liptonite are ₹16 per Unit, ₹24 per Unit, and ₹7 per Unit respectively. At least 50 units of Kryptonite have to be produced and at the most 150 units of Liptonite can be produced.

10. Which of the following is possible?
(a) 75 units of Kryptonite, 4 units of Arsonite in day shift,manufacture 40 units of Arsonite I and 40 units of Liptonite and 10 units of Kryptonite in night shift.
(b) 75 units of Kryptonite I, 4 units of Arsonite I, in the day shift, manufacture 40 units of Arsonite and 40 units of Liptonite and 5 units of Kryptonite in night shift.
(c) 74 units of Kryptonite, 4 units of Arsonite in day shift. 25 units of Arsonite, 10 units of Liptonite and 20 units of Kryptonite in night shift.
(d) 74 units of Kryptonite, 4 units of Arsonite in day shift. 25 units of Arsonite, 10 units of Liptonite and 20 units of Kryptonite in night shift.
11. What percentage of the available raw material is utilised if 100 units of Kryptonite, 40 units of Arsonite, and 10 units of Liptonite are produced?
(a) 50% (b) 58%
(c) 68% (d) 78%
12. If Praveen Kumar Tiwari spends initially 300 machine hours in the day shift to manufacture Liptonite, 20 hours to manufacture Kryptonite, and in the night shift manufactures 53 units of Liptonite and spends the rest of the night shift to manufacture Kryptonite. What will be his profit/loss?
(a) loss of ₹65
(b) profit ₹65
(c) loss of ₹165
(d) This manufacturing pattern is not possible

13. If the minimum possible manufacturing requirement for Kryptonite is met and the remaining raw material is utilised for the manufacture of the other 2 products then
    (a) 10 units of Arsonite can be manufactured
    (b) 0 units of Arsonite can be manufactured
    (c) 5 units of Arsonite can be manufactured
    (d) Any of these
14. If in the day shift, 65 units of Kryptonite, 4 units of Arsonite , 15 units of Liptonite and in the night shift 20 units of Arsonite, 40 units of Liptonite and 10 units of Kryptonite are manufactured then which of the following is true?
    I. 5 hours of machine time is unutilised
    II. Total cost of production is ₹540
    III. More than 20% of the available raw material is unutilised
    (a) Only I (b) Only II
    (c) I and III (d) Only III

Directions for Questions 15 to 18: *Refer to the data given below (Table 6.4) and answer the following questions:*

The Indian Premier League is a hockey tournament organised every year on the lines of its more famous counterpart – The IPL cricket league. There are five teams in the IPL hockey tournament. Delhi Daredevils, Chennai Superkings, Mumbai Indians, Kolkata Knight Riders, and Kings Eleven Punjab. In the year 2017, the IPL was keenly contested and fought. The following data gives the results of that tournament.

The tournament is played as a round robin league where in each team plays each other exactly twice on a home and away basis. Table 6.4 gives us information about the results of the first leg of matches.

Here, Chennai Superkings 4-2 means Chennai Superkings scored 4 goals and the other team 2 goals.

The winning team gets 3 points and if the game is a draw, then both the teams get 1 point each. Losing teams do not get any points. The team with maximum number of points at the end of the tournament wins the cup.

Also, team performance ratio is defined as the ratio of the number of goals for to the number of goals against. Lesser the ratio, lower the performance.

TABLE 6.4

1.	Chennai Superkings (CSK)	3–1	2–0	1–1	4–2
2.	Mumbai Indians (MI)	1–0	0–2	1–3	1–1
3.	Kolkata Knight Riders (KKR)	3–1	2–2	1–2	1–1
4.	Kings Eleven Punjab (KEP)	1–3	1–1	2–2	1–1
5.	Delhi Daredevils (DD)	1–1	0–1	2–1	2–4

15. The only match that Delhi Daredevils had drawn was with
    (a) Mumbai Indians
    (b) Chennai Superkings
    (c) Kolkata Knight Riders
    (d) Kings Eleven Punjab
16. The only match which KEP lost was with
    (a) Chennai Superkings
    (b) Mumbai Indians
    (c) Delhi Daredevils
    (d) Kings Eleven Punjab
17. In terms of performance ratio which is the worst team
    (a) Chennai Superkings
    (b) Mumbai Indians
    (c) Kings Eleven Punjab or Delhi Daredevils
    (d) Chennai Superkings or Mumbai Indians
18. In the second leg of the tournament, what is the minimum number of matches to be played in order for the team second in standing, to take over the 1st ranked team pool?
    (a) 2
    (b) 3
    (c) 4
    (d) 5

Directions for Question 19 to 20: *The graph shown at the bottom of the next page shows the total salary of the employees of Mindworkzz with respect to the total number of units sold by them. Each employee gets two types of salary: Fixed salary and Variable salary.*

Total salary of the employee = Fixed salary+ Variable salary

Average salary per unit = Total salary/Total units sold

Year	20 < Age < 40 years	40 ≤ Age < 60	Age ≥ 60
1995	329	346	315
2000	300	360	310
2005	302	310	360
2010	330	330	330
2015	335	326	340

Variable salary continuously increases with number of units sold by the employee (as shown in the diagram below) and fixed salary varies in discrete levels. For 1st 4000 units his fixed salary is 4 lakh rupees. If the number of units sold by the employee is more than 4000 and less than or equals to 7000 then his fixed salary will be 5 lakh rupees. If the number of units sold by the employee is more than 7000 and less than 12000 then the fixed salary will be 6 lakh rupees.

19. If average salary per unit sales of an employee is the maximum, then how many units has that employee sold?
    (a) 7000
    (b) 6000
    (c) 8000
    (d) 1000

20. Which of the following statement is true?
    (a) From 1000 to 12000 units average salary per unit sold of an employee first decreases then increases then decreases.
    (b) From 1000 to 12000 units average salary per unit sold of an employee first increases then decreases then increases.
    (c) From 1000 to 12000 average salary per unit sold of an employee first increases then decreases.
    (d) None of these.

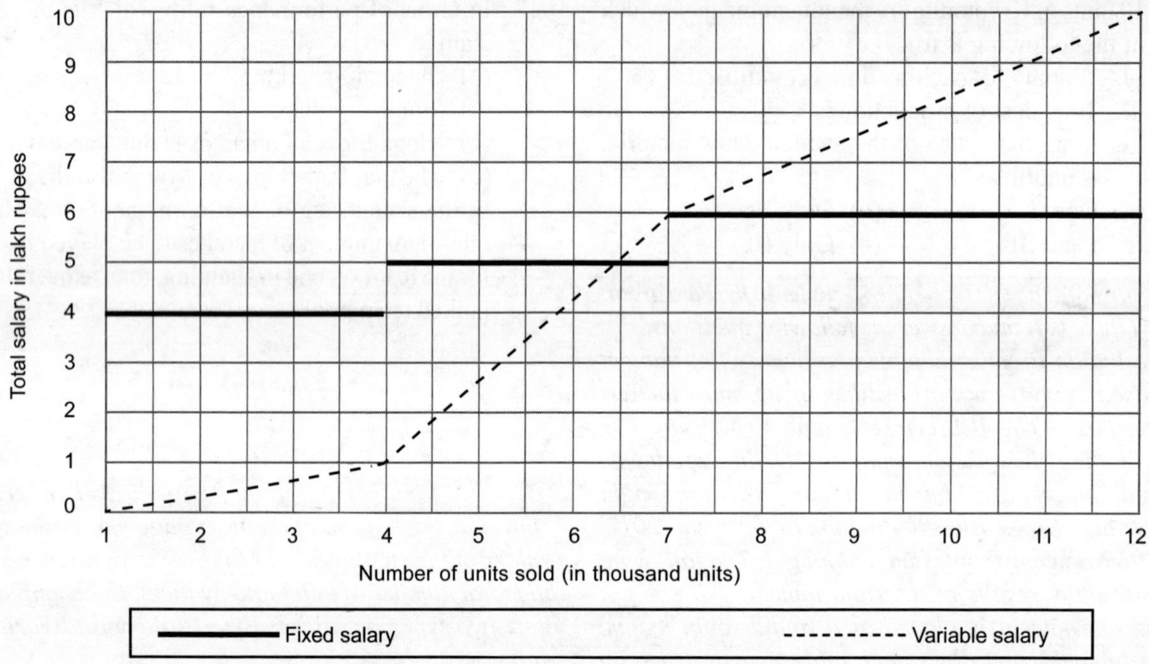

7 Mock Test Paper

Directions for Questions 1 to 4: *The graph given shows the profit of a company XYZ in terms of its' total production profit and its total distribution profit at different sales volumes.*
Total Profit = Production profit + Distribution profit

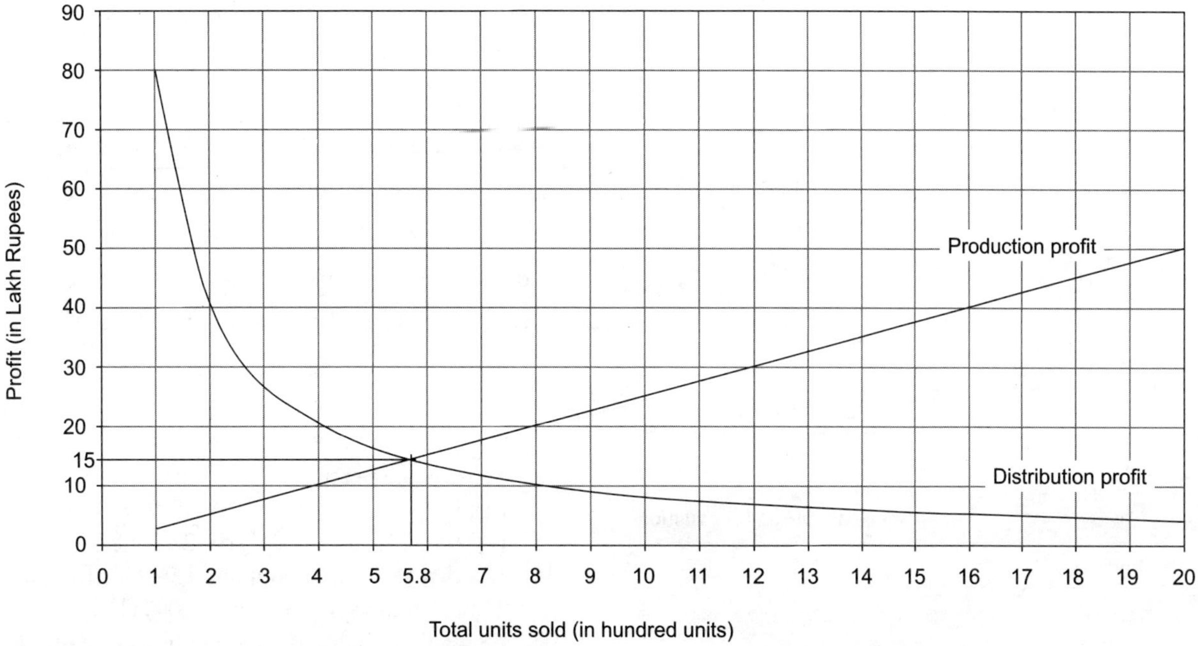

1. If company made a total profit of 'X' by selling 'n' units and '3X' by selling '$3n$' units then how many values of n are possible?
   (a) 0
   (b) 1
   (c) 2
   (d) Infinite values are possible
2. What is the minimum possible total profit (in lakh rupees) of the company if it is known that total units sold by the company is between 200 to 1200 units?
   (a) 12
   (b) 15
   (c) 25
   (d) None of these
3. What is the value of the total units sold by the company for which the total profit is least?
4. Consider the following statements:
   (i) The total profit initially decreases between 1 to 580 units sold, reaches a minimum at 580 units of sales and then starts to increase till 2000 units of sales.
   (ii) After 580 units, the rate drop in distribution profit is lower than the rate of increase in Production profit
   (iii) The production profit varies linearly with the number of units sold and moves in inverse proportion to the number of units sold.

   Which of the above statements is/are true?
   (a) i & iii
   (b) i & ii
   (c) ii & iii
   (d) all of these

Directions for Question 5 to 8: *In Kuwait eleven major oil companies A, B, C, D, E, F, G, H, I, J and K produce all the crude oil. In July 2013 Kuwait produced exactly 1000 tons crude oil. The table-A given below gives total oil production of these companies in July 2013. These 11 companies owned by 5 business tycoons Parizad, Qadir, Rahim, Sakib and Taufiq. Table B gives the percentage production share of these five business tycoons of total production in July 2013.*

TABLE A

Company	Total Production (in tons)
A	100
B	80
C	70
D	110
E	70
F	120
G	120
H	140
I	80
J	60
K	50

TABLE B

Owner	Percentage Share in Total Production
Parizad	20%
Qadir	26%
Rahim	22%
Sakib	18%
Taufiq	14%

5. Find the difference between the maximum and minimum number of companies which can be owned by Taufiq.
6. If each owner owned more than a single company, then at most how many companies did Parizad own?
   (a) 2 (b) 3
   (c) 4 (d) None of these.
7. If Sakib and Taufiq sold all of their companies to Rahim, then find the minimum number of companies owned by Rahim.
8. If each owner owned at least two companies in such a way that no owner owned any two companies with same production quantity, then for how many of the given owners can the companies owned by them be uniquely determined?
   (a) 0 (b) 1
   (c) 2 (d) 4

Directions for Question 9 to 13: *Answer the questions on the basis of the information given below.*

The following table provides partial information about the composition of six different Gujarati sweet dishes namely – A, B, C, D, E and F. Each of these six dishes contains five ingredients namely Sugar, Milk, Saffron, Cardamom and Gram flour. Another dish – "Gujarati cocktail", ingredients of which are not given in the table, contains dishes A, B and C in the ratio 2 : 1 : 3. It is also known that in Gujarati cocktail – Milk, Sugar and Gram flour are present in an equal quantity.

DISH	Cardamom	Milk	Sugar	Gram flour	Saffron
A	10%	40%	8.666	31.333	10%
B	25%	15%	50%	5%	5%
C	15%	10.55	20%	19.45	35%
D	20%	25%	15%	30%	10%
E	5%	50%	25%	5%	15%
F	40%	10%	5%	30%	15%

9. What is the percentage of Gram flour in Dish A?
   (a) 95/6 (b) 92/9
   (c) 95/3 (d) 25/3
10. If a dish X, which contains 15% Saffron, at least 15% Cardamom and at most 20% Gram flour, is to be made, how many combinations of exactly two of the six mentioned dishes can be used to make it?
    (a) 2 (b) 1
    (c) 3 (d) 4
11. Which of the following can be a value of the ratio in which dishes A, E and F need to be mixed to get at least 12% Sugar in the resulting mixture?
    (a) 1:2:3 (b) 4:3:5
    (c) 3:2:3 (d) 4:1:1
12. If a dish Z, which contains at least 8.25% Saffron, is to be made by using the dishes mentioned in the table, the percentage of dish B in dish Z cannot be more than?
    (a) 95.46%
    (b) 83.16%
    (c) 85.17%
    (d) 89.16%

13. What is the percentage of gram flour in Dish C?
    (a) 95/9% (b) 185/9%
    (c) 95/3% (d) 175/9%

Directions for Question 14 to 17: *Answer the questions on the basis of information below.*

Grocers Pvt. Ltd. is a grocery delivery service company that uses three delivery modes for its services – Bicycle, Motorbike and Auto-Rickshaw delivery. Following pie charts show the distribution of Total number of deliveries (Chart 1), Revenue generated (Chart 2) and Total cost incurred (Chart 3) for the mentioned different modes of transport in the year 2015. Assume that only cost involved was that incurred on travel.

Values represent degrees out of 360°.

14. If Grocers makes 50% profit in the year 2015, what is the profit percentage on deliveries sent by Motorbike?
    (a) 50% (b) 33.33%
    (c) 66.67% (d) 240%
15. Through which mode of transport does Grocers make maximum profit in the year 2015?
    (a) By Auto-Rickshaw
    (b) By Motorbike
    (c) By Bicycle
    (d) Data insufficient
16. Which mode of delivery offers the least Cost of transport per delivery in 2015 for Grocers?
    (a) Motorbike (b) Bicycle
    (c) Auto-Rickshaw (d) Data insufficient
17. If the Revenue generated from delivery by Auto-Rickshaw is 10 INR and Cost incurred from delivery by it is 20 INR, what is the ratio of Cost incurred to Revenue generated by delivery on Bicycle?
    (a) 5/2
    (b) 2/3
    (c) 2/5
    (d) Cannot be determined

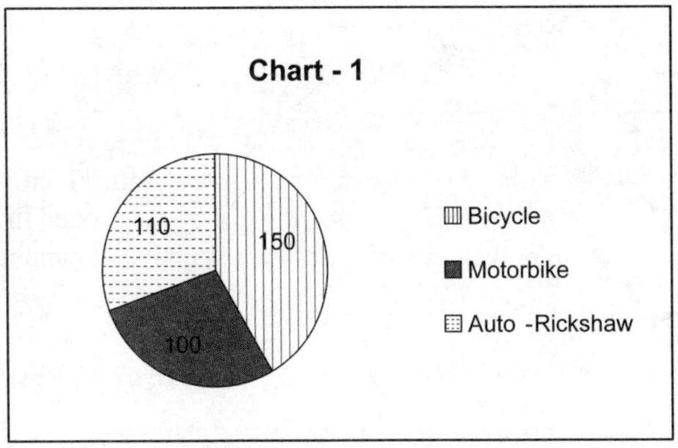

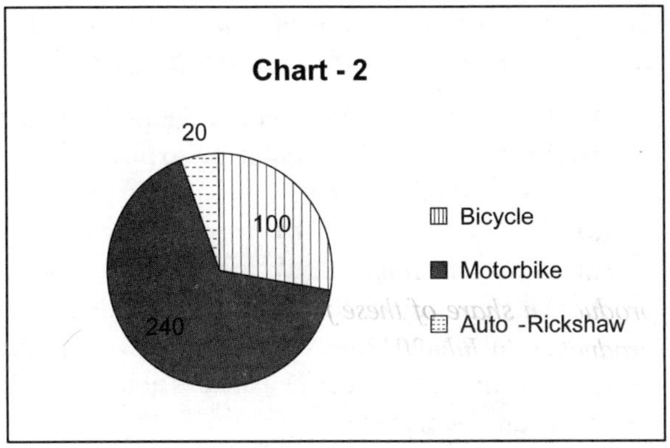

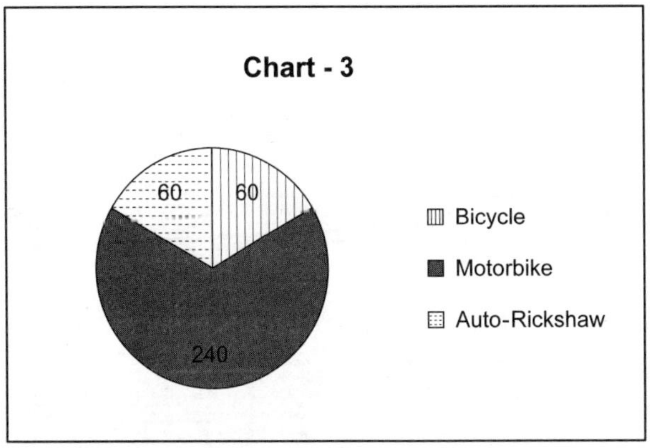

Directions for Questions 18 to 20: *Refer to the data given below and answer the following questions.*

Two jewellers (a British and an American) go to buy newly designed weights from the trade fair. In the shop they visit, the salesman asks their limits of weighing at a time. Both of them tell the salesman that their limit of weighing required is 120 grams at a time and also mention that they are required to measure jewellery in such a way that the number is always an integer. The salesman shows them the price list as:

Any weight less than and including 10 grams – $10 per piece

More than 11 grams but less than 50 grams – $20 per piece More than 51 grams but less than 100 grams –$30 per piece. More than 100 grams $50 per piece.

The two jewellers, however, have a difference in their requirements in the sense that the British has a weighing scale which allows him to put weights on both sides of the scale.

For example: If one wants to measure a weight of 7 grams, then you could put 10 grams on weight side and put 3 grams on the goods side.

However, the American shopkeeper does not have this facility in the weighing balance that he uses and hence, needs to put the weights only on the weight side and cannot put any weight on the goods side.

18. What is the minimum number of weights the British jeweller would require to purchase so that he incurs the least cost of purchase?
    (a) 8 (b) 10
    (c) 5 (d) 4
19. If the American jeweller has to buy weights, what is the minimum number of weights he would need to buy at the lowest cost so that he is able to satisfy his requirements?
    (a) 5 (b) 7
    (c) 10 (d) 8
20. One of them needed as much more amount as the other has left after purchase. Suppose both of them left their home with the same amount. Who borrowed and what amount was borrowed?
    (a) British Jeweller borrowed $30
    (b) American jeweller borrowed $30
    (c) American jeweller borrowed $15
    (d) None of these

8 Mock Test Paper

Directions for Questions 1 to 2: *Refer to the data given below and answer the following questions:*

A certain perfume is available at a duty-free shop at the Bangkok international airport.

It is priced in the Thai currency Baht but other currencies are also acceptable.

In particular, the shop accepts Euro and US Dollar at the following rates of exchange:

US Dollar 1 = 41 Bahts

Euro 1 = 46 Bahts

The perfume is priced at 1040 Bahts per bottle. After one bottle is purchased, subsequent bottles are available at a discount of 30%. Three friends Shaurya, Raghav, and Nehal together purchase three bottles of the perfume, agreeing to share the cost equally. Raghav pays 4 Euros, Nehal pays 8 Euros and 54 Thai Bahts, and Shaurya pays the remaining amount in US Dollars.

1. How much does Nehal owe to Shaurya in US Dollars?
   (a) 6 (b) 8
   (c) 10 (d) 12
   (e) 18
2. How much does Raghav owe to Shaurya in Thai Baht?
   (a) 856 (b) 716
   (c) 668 (d) 648
   (e) 632

Directions for Question 3 to 7: *Answer the questions on the basis of information below.*

Liverpool, Chelsea, ManU, Real Madrid, Arsenal and ManCity take part in European Football League. In the first round, each team plays each of the other teams exactly once. At this stage 2 points are awarded for a win, 1 point for a draw and 0 points for a loss. After all the matches are played, the top 2 teams, in terms of points scored advance to Finals.

In case 2 or more teams end up with same number of points, the team with a better goal difference/better performance is placed higher

3. The total number of matches played in the tournament is:
4. What is the minimum number of points with which a team can advance to finals?
5. What is the maximum number of points that can be scored by a team, which failed to advance to the finals?
6. What is the maximum number of points a team can score in order to win the tournament?
7. If the tournament rules are changed to make two groups of 3 teams each, such that each team plays the other team in it's group twice and teams in the other group once – followed by the top 4 teams advancing to the semifinals. The semifinals are plated as a knockout round, with the winners playing the best of three finals. In order to maximise television revenues, on a single day only one match is held. What is the minimum number of days in which the tournament can get concluded?

Directions for Question 8 to 12: *Answer the questions on the basis of the information given below.*

The following table shows business details of a company Grocers Pvt. Ltd.

Division	Sub Division	Annual Sales (in INR)	Margin	Number of Employees	Annual salary Per Employee (in INR)
Services	Online	3 crores	42	25	2,00,000
	On call	5 crores	54	56	3,00,000
Inventory	Online	7 crores	67	78	3,00,000
	On call	5 crores	68	68	1,00,000

Margin= Profit/Sales × 100

8. If the salary of each "Inventory–Online" employee is increased by 50%, what is the new margin percentage of Grocers? (All other factors remain same)
   (a) 60.25% (b) 54.40%
   (c) 66.10% (d) Cannot be determined

9. If the annual salary of a Services Online employee is made equal to a Services on Call employee, on call, what is the percentage increase/decrease in Services–online margin? (approximately)
   (a) 80% (b) 20%
   (c) 60% (d) Cannot be determined
10. If in each sub division, annual sales increases by 15%, what is the new profit of the company approximately, in crore INR? (Assume that margin remains same)
   (a) 12.05 (b) 14.77
   (c) 13.8 (d) 10.09
11. Due to increasing orders each day on Grocers, a new division – "Phone requests" was introduced that'd take care of customer issues on phone. This division will also generate revenue (sales) by charging the customer for the call made to Grocers. If the margin is set to be at 10% and Annual Sales are estimated to be 10 Lakh INR, what should be the salary of each employee in Phone requests division if it is decided to employ 10 employees in this division?
   (a) 10,000 INR (b) 1,000 INR
   (c) 100 INR (d) Cannot be determined
12. What is the difference in the percentage value of employee salary expressed as a percentage of profits between the services division and the Inventory division?

Directions for Questions 13to 16: *Refer to the pie charts below and answer the questions that follow.*
The pie charts (Figure 8.1) represent the sale of Cold drinks in the year 2007 for the company ABC Ltd.

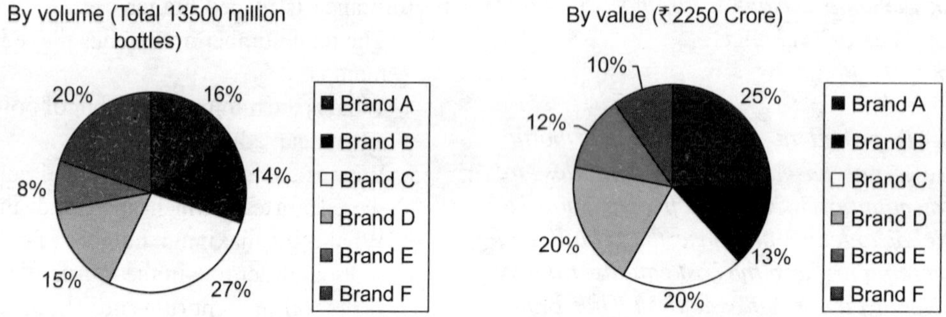

FIGURE 8.1

13. The costliest brand of Cold Drinks in 2007 for the company ABC Ltd. was priced at:
   (a) ₹2.6 (b) ₹2.7
   (c) ₹2.8 (d) ₹2.9
14. Find the ratio of prices of the cheapest brand to the costliest brand for the company in 2007 is closest to:
   (a) 4:15 (b) 4:13
   (c) 2:15 (d) 2:17
15. If The manufacturing cost of a Cold Drink of Brand C was 93 paisa per bottle then what was the total profit of the company for the brand C?
   (a) ₹97.47 crore
   (b) ₹100 crore
   (c) ₹104.8 crore
   (d) ₹109.35 crore
16. Say the consumers of brand E change over to brand A and D in the ratio of 2:3 respectively because brand E suffered A loss and withdrew from the market then what will be the new percentage share of brand A in value sales? (approximately)
   (a) 28% (b) 29%
   (c) 30% (d) 31%

Directions for Questions 17 to 20: *Refer to the graphs given on the next page (Figure 8.2) and answer the questions that follow.*

Note: Productivity of wheat in India = Total wheat production/Area under wheat production

17. The population of India in 2003–04 was:
   (a) 750 million (b) 770 million
   (c) 790 million (d) 800 million
18. Say the area under production was reduced by 10% in 2004–05 as compared to that of 2003–04 then the rate of increase/decrease in the productivity of wheat in 2004–05 was:
   (a) 13% decrease (b) 14% decrease
   (c) 13.2% increase (d) 13.6% increase
19. The ratio of the average wheat that is exported to that of the wheat produced from 2000–01 to 2004–05 is:
   (a) 0.30 (b) 0.32
   (c) 0.36 (d) 0.38
20. The average of per capita availability of wheat in the given period was:
   (a) 514 gm (b) 469 gm
   (c) 501 gm (d) 536 gm

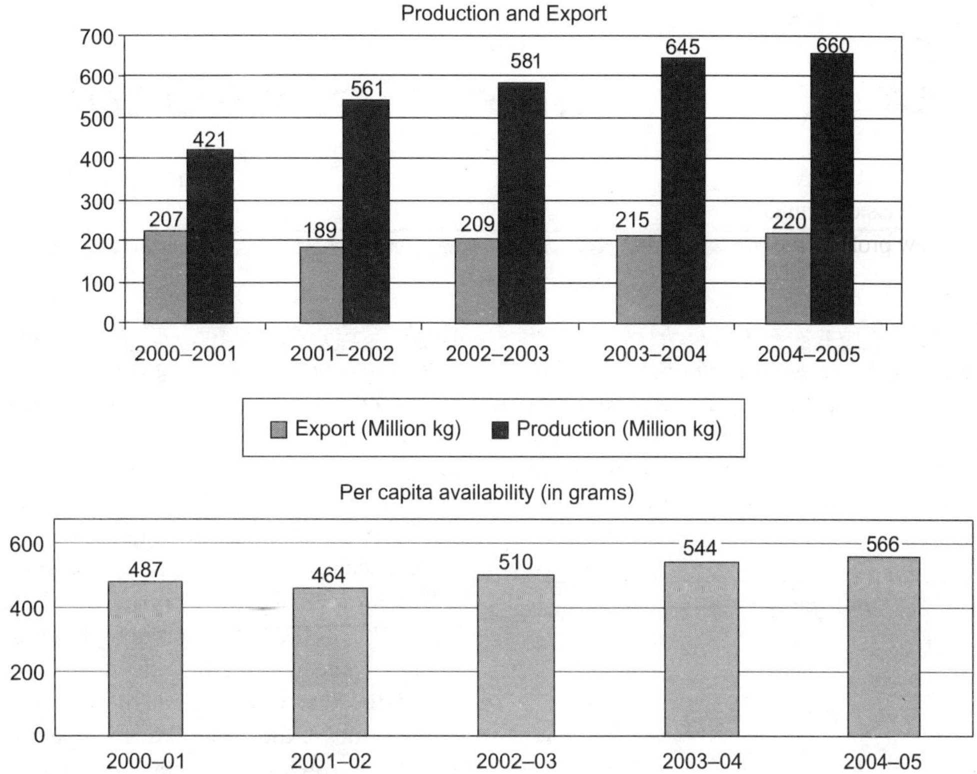

FIGURE 8.2 *Wheat Production in India*

9 Mock Test Paper

Directions for Questions 1 to 5: *In a high school exam the rank of the candidate is decided on the basis of his score in each of the four subjects – Physics, Chemistry, Biology and Maths. The weightage of these subjects in the final result is 20%, 40%, 20% and 20% respectively. The following are the scores and the rank of the ten students of the class.*

Name	Physics	Chemistry	Biology	Maths	Total	Rank
A	40	45	45			10
B	70	65		60	62	7
C	60	60	80	85	69	5
D	45		75	90		1
E	55	75	55	60	64	6
F	70	65	80	95	75	2
G	50	45	55			8
H	75	50		85		4
I	45	40	60	70	51	9
J	65	65	75		72	3

The maximum possible score for each subject was 100 and the maximum marks any of these ten students obtained in any subject was 95. If two or more students got the same total marks then they are all awarded the same rank.

1. Find the marks scored by B in Biology?
2. If the score obtained by G in Maths was 'p' then which of the following is a possible value of p?

   (a) 45 (b) 72
   (c) 60 (d) 54
3. The minimum number of students who scored less than H in Biology?
4. Maximum possible marks obtained by D is?
5. How many students definitely obtained more marks than A in Maths?

Directions for Questions 6 to 9: *Answer the questions on the basis of information given below:*

10 contestants namely Ashok, Bilal, Chetan, Danish, Esha, Fatima, Garima, Hatim, Imran, Jai contested for the post of President . In Round 1, if any candidate gets more than 50% of the total number of votes cast in that round, he/she is declared the winner, else top five candidates based on number of votes move to Round 2. In Round 2, if any candidate gets more than 50% of the total number of votes cast in that round, he/she is declared the winner, else top three candidates based on number of votes move to Round 3. In Round 3, the candidate who gets the maximum number of votes out of total votes cast in that round is declared the winner.

Also note that:

1. In any round, no two candidates get the same number of votes.
2. Total number of votes cast in any round is independent of the votes cast in other rounds i.e. total number of votes cast in these 3 rounds may/may not be different.

Table below shows number of votes received by these 10 candidates in Round 1 of the election.

Name of Candidate	Number of Votes Received in Round 1
Ashok	4501
Bilal	4523
Chetan	4499
Danish	4498
Esha	4300
Fatima	4651
Garima	4444
Hatim	4455
Imran	4419
Jai	5000

6. If 45000 votes were cast in Round 2, then the value of the sum of the number of votes received by the candidate who got the maximum votes and the number of votes received by the candidate who got minimum votes in that round could not be less than:
7. If the winner was decided after Round 3 and 20,000 votes were cast in each of Round 2 and Round 3, then total number of votes received, in the three rounds put together, by a candidate who was not the winner could not be more than:
   (a) 24999
   (b) 25000
   (c) 0
   (d) 45000
8. If 48000 votes were cast in Round 2 and 51000 votes were cast in Round 3, then the total number of votes received, in the three rounds put together, by the candidate who won the election could not be less than:
   (a) 21303 (b) 21502
   (c) 21301 (d) 37300
9. The number of votes received, in all the 3 rounds put together, by a candidate who reached Round 3 but did not win the election could not be less than:
   (a) 4300 (b) 4302
   (c) 4501 (d) 8097

Directions for Questions 10 to 13 *The IIT-JEE 2035 exam consists of six different exams. Table 9.1 gives the information regarding the percentage distribution of 2 marks and 4 marks questions in IIT JEE 2035 exams and table 9.2 gives the marks distribution of Piyush in the IIT JEE 2035 exam. There were a total of 1000 questions asked in the exam and there was no negative marking for any wrong answer. There are a total of 160 questions asked in the Chemistry I section.*

TABLE 9.1 Percentage Distribution of 2 Marks and 4 Marks Questions Among Different Sections in IIT JEE 2035

Section	2 Marks Questions	4 Marks Questions
Math I	20%	15%
Math II	20%	30%
Chemistry I	15%	20%
Chemistry II	10%	5%
Physics I	20%	10%
Physics II	15%	20%

TABLE 9.2 Marks Obtained by Piyush in Different Sections

Subject	Marks
Math I	60
Math II	180
Chemistry I	240
Chemistry II	120
Physics I	300
Physics II	300

10. Find the maximum 2 marks questions correctly attempted by Piyush.
11. Find the minimum possible percentage of marks Piyush scored if only his 4 mark questions were counted?
12. Find the minimum number of questions that Piyush could attempt in Chemistry II?
13. If Piyush attempted 'x' 4 marks questions correctly in Chemistry II and he also attempted 'y' 4 marks questions in Physics II, then which of the following options is correct? Assume he solved the minimum number of questions in both sections.
    (a) $x < y$ (b) $x > y$
    (c) $x = y$ (d) $x \geq y$

Directions for Questions 14 to 16: *The following table gives the partial information about the marks obtained by 5 students in the four different sections of CAT 2015 exam. Each column has two missing values. It is also given that none of these two missing values is more than 10% of the total score of all the five students for the QA and DI sections. Similarly, for the LR sections none of the two missing values is less than 10% or greater than 15% of the total score of all the five students. For the VA section, the missing values are not less than 10% and not greater than 14% of the total score of all the five students.*

Name of Student	QA	LR	DI	VA
Pulkit		100		63
Qasim	98	55		62
Rohan			110	
Sameer	72	85	30	65
Taskin	70		80	
Total	280	320	270	250

14. The students are ranked A to E according to the total marks obtained by them in CAT-2015 exam, with the highest scorer getting rank A. If marks of all the students are different, then how many

students are there whose ranks can be exactly determined?

15. If the absolute difference between the total marks scored by Pulkit and Rohan is the minimum possible, then what is the absolute difference between the total marks scored by Taskin and Qasim?
16. Find the maximum possible percentage contribution of Pulkit in the total score of all the five students in the CAT-2015 paper.

Directions for Questions 17 to 20: *An investigation was conducted on the total grain produced by the farmers of two different villages – A and B. The result of the investigation is represented in the following table:*

Range of Production (p) (in tons)	Number of Farmers of Village A	Number of Farmers of Village B
$p < 20$	5 (900–1500)	4 (1100–1500)
$20 \le p < 28$	8 (700–1100)	7 (750–1400)
$28 \le p < 36$	10 (600–900)	11(700–1100)
$36 \le p < 44$	6 (450–750)	6 (600–1000)
$44 \le p < 60$	3 (400–600)	4 (500–800)

In the above table, for every range of production the value inside the bracket in each cell gives the minimum and the maximum area (in square meters) of the farms of any farmer in the corresponding village (i.e. village A and B) in that production range. For example the 3rd column of the first row shows that there are 4 farmers in village B with a production less than 20 tons and of these four farms, the minimum area was 1100 square meters and the maximum area was 1500 square meters.

17. The minimum number of farmers with farm area not more than 1000 square meters but the production capacity less than 30 tons is?
18. Any farm with a production whose numerical value was not less than 0.04 times of the numerical value of its area was termed to be 'fertile'. The maximum total number of fertile farms in the two villages is?
19. Find the maximum possible number of farmers of village B with the farm area of more than 750 square meters and production of more than 34 tons.
20. Find the maximum possible value of the average production of all the farmers.

10 Mock Test Paper

Directions for Questions 1 to 4: *Answer the questions on the basis of information below.*

There are 2700 students in first year of Amethi University. They belong to one of the four courses – MBBS, B.Tech, BA and B.Com. All courses have different number of students. The tables 10.1 and 10.2 give partial information about the sets of books bought by the students of first year. A set of books contains all the subject books corresponding to the course of the student. Two different books are available for each subject and a student can choose any one of the two.

Table 10.1 shows the percentage of students buying different books (e.g. 'p' percent of students in the MBBS course buy book type – B1 for Biology).

Table 10.2 shows the total number of the sets of books bought by the students of each course.

Additional information given is:

TABLE 10.1

	Biology		Maths		Indian Politics		English	
	B1	B2	M1	M2	P1	P2	E1	E2
MBBS	*p*	*q*	*n*	*s*	*o*	*r*	*m*	*t*
B.Tech	XX	XX	*p*	*r*	*n*	*t*	*o*	*s*
BA	XX	XX	XX	XX	*q*	*r*	*p*	*s*
B.Com	XX	XX	XX	XX	XX	XX	*q*	*s*

TABLE 10.2

Total Sets of Books Bought in Various Courses			
MBBS	B.Tech	BA	B.Com
972	648	378	162

1. 'XX' means that the subject is not studied in that course
2. Percentage of students who buy books in each stream is a multiple of 10.
3. Percentage of students is different for all 4 courses
4. At least one student in each course does not buy the set of books
5. Number of students in each stream is a multiple of 10. It is also known that the number (or percentage) of students of a particular course who buy books for any of the subjects for which they have to purchase books are equal. In other words, for the MBBS course for instance, in the table $p + q = n + s = o + r$ and so on.

1. What is the total number of Indian Politics books bought by students?
   (a) 666 (b) 1998
   (c) 2430 (d) 2700
2. How many students are there in BA course of Amethi college?
   (a) 378 (b) 810
   (c) 540 (d) 630
3. Which is the book bought by the maximum number of students in the MBBS course?
   (a) E1 (b) E2
   (c) M1 (d) P2
4. What is difference between the number of students of Amethi University who buy E1 and those who buy P1?
   (a) 328 (b) 99
   (c) 324 (d) 297

Directions for Question 5 to 8: *Answer the questions on the basis of the information below.*

A Shopkeeper has some marbles in five different boxes B1, B2, B3, B4 and B5. Table 10.3 provides the data about the Number of marbles (N), Average weight per marble (AWPM) and Average Selling Price per marble (ASPPM) for each of the 5 boxes. Table 10.4 shows the relationship between AWPM and Ease of Selling Index (ESI)

TABLE 10.3

Box	N	AWPM	ASPPM
B1	16	180	15
B2	48	90	12
B3	32	140	11
B4	64	130	18
B5	40	170	17

TABLE 10.4

AWPM	ESI
<= 100	6.5
100 < and <=120	7.5
120 < and <= 140	8
140 < and <=170	9
> 170	10

5. If 5 marbles of Box B1 are mixed with 10 marbles of Box B2, then what is the ESI of the mixture?
   (a) 7.5 (b) 6.5
   (c) 8 (d) Cannot be determined
6. All the marbles of Box B2 are to be mixed with all the marbles of exactly one of the other four boxes. Which box should be chosen to maximize the ESI of the mixture?
   (a) B1 (b) B4
   (c) B3 (d) B5
7. If the retailer wants to keep the ESI of the mixture at least 7.5 and the ASPPM between 13 and 15, which of the following combinations should he make?
   (a) B1, B2 and B3
   (b) B2, B3 and B4
   (c) B3, B4 and B5
   (d) B1, B4 and B5
8. If the retailer wants to keep the ESI of the mixture at least perfect 10 and the ASPPM between 12 and 18, which of the following combinations should he make?
   (a) B1, B4 and B5 (b) B2, B3 and B4
   (c) B3, B4 and B5 (d) None of these

Directions for Question 9 to 12: *Answer the questions on the basis of information below.*

The bar chart below shows mock tests performance of 2 students Bhavuk and Pulkit while studying for three different sections of CAT – Verbal, Quants, LR & DI from three different groups of CAT experts. Ratings given to these teachers are C, B and A, with C being the lowest and A being the highest.

The bar chart also gives numbers, which are the percentage marks obtained by Bhavuk and Pulkit in these 3 sections. Each section carries 100 marks. A student always gets integral marks, which are multiples of 5 in each section. For example: If Bhavuk studies all the three sections from a group of teachers such that all 3 have a rating of A, then he scores 85% marks of total marks of the 3 sections put together. In this case, Pulkit scores 90% of total marks of the 3 sections put together and so on.

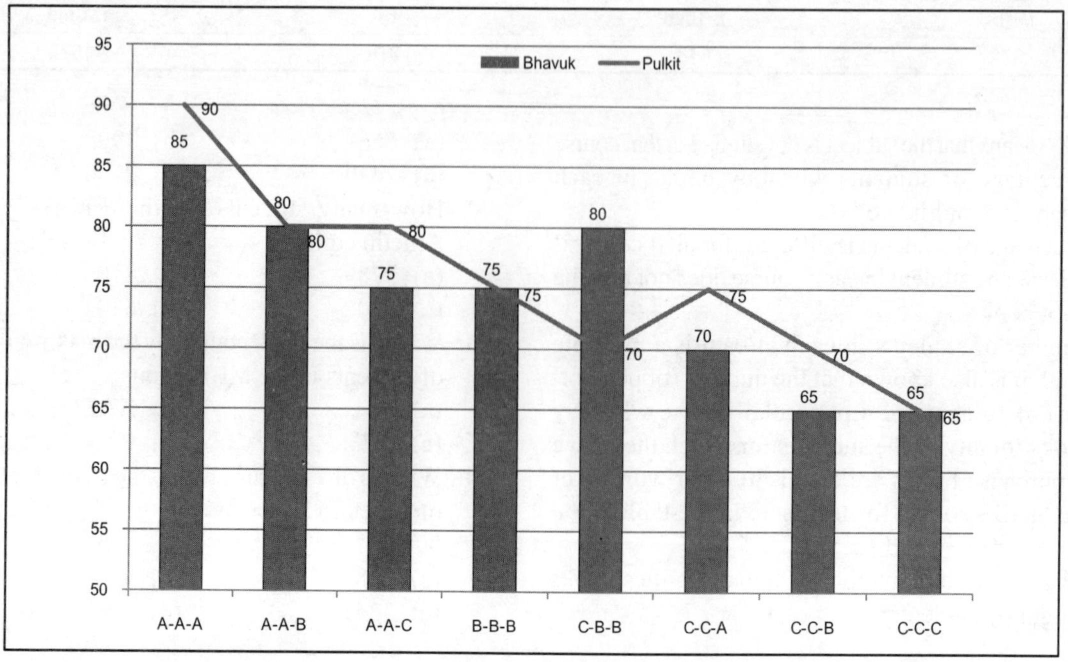

9. Clearly Bhavuk performs his best when he is taught the 3 sections, all by A rated teachers. However this combination costs him a lot and since he has left his job for CAT preparation he cannot pay that amount anymore. Thus he decided he'd compromise on any one teacher with a lower rating. What is the maximum change (in percentage) his total score will go through due to this decision?
   (a) 5.88% (b) 17.64%
   (c) 11.76% (d) None of these
10. What is the lowest possible score in any section Pulkit can achieve if he decides to take coaching from all B rated teachers?
   (a) 0 (b) 25
   (c) 75 (d) Cannot be determined
11. Combination of teachers is called "manageable" if average score of all 3 sections of Bhavuk and Pulkit is equal to or more than 70% and individual percentage (of all 3 sections per individual) is greater than or equal to 75%. How many combinations from those mentioned are manageable?
   (a) 3 (b) 5
   (c) 6 (d) 4
12. A student is inherently smart if his average percentage of percentages of all the possible combinations as mentioned above is greater than or equal to 74%. Who is inherently smart amongst Bhavuk and Pulkit?
   (a) Only Bhavuk (b) Only Pulkit
   (c) Both are smart (d) None is smart

Directions for Questions 13 to 16: *Answer the questions on the basis of information below.*

The table below provides information about the number of experienced and non-experienced faculty in each of the four coaching institutes – Lime, Mindworkzz, Career Lander and ITS as a percentage of the total number of professors in that institute.

	Lime-C-R	Mindworkzz-D-S	Career Lander- B-Q	ITS-A-P
Percentage of Experienced faculty members	80%	60%	70%	90%
Percentage of Non-experienced faculty members	20%	40%	30%	10%

Number of Non-experienced faculty members in institutes Lime, Mindworkzz, Career Lander and ITS is R, S, Q, P. Also, the number of experienced faculty members in Lime, Mindworkzz, Career Lander and ITS are C, D, B and A respectively.

13. What is the number of Non-experienced faculty members in Lime institute?
   (a) 3200 (b) 1600
   (c) 3000 (d) 2800
14. What is the absolute difference between number of experienced faculty members in ITS and non-experienced members in Mindworkzz?
   (a) 11200 (b) 11400
   (c) 5400 (d) 6900

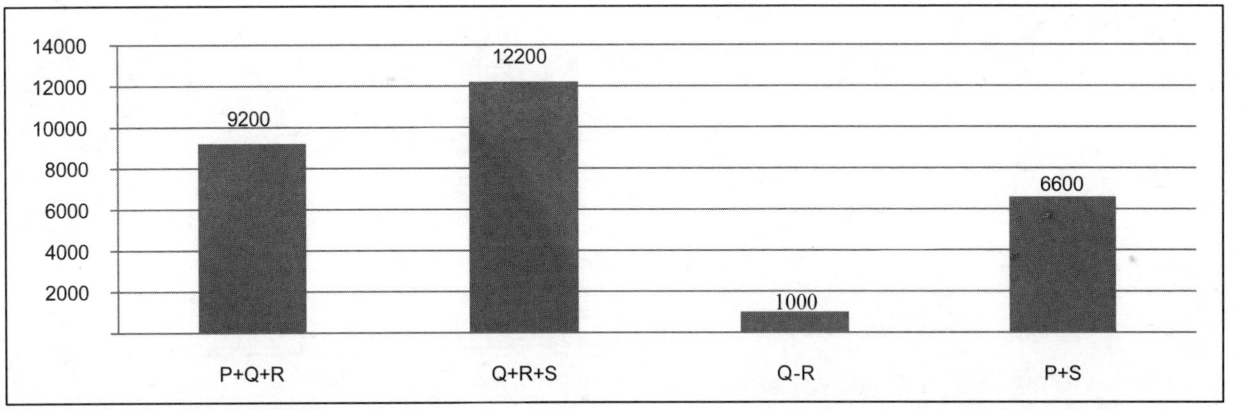

15. What is the ratio of the total number of faculty members in Mindworkzz to the number of experienced faculty members in Lime?
   (a) 4:5
   (b) 3:4
   (c) 15:16
   (d) 16:15
16. If ITS shut down due to some reasons, and all faculty members of ITS joined Lime, Mindworkzz and Career Lander in equal number (irrespective of their experience), then number of faculty members in Mindworkzz increased by what percentage?
   (a) 25% (b) 40%
   (c) 60% (d) 50%

Directions for Question 17 to 20: *The following table (on the start of the next page) gives us the data of the total number of employees of Mindworkzz of different age group. The data is given for years from 1995 to 2015, for different years at 5-year intervals. The data is recorded on the 1st of April of each of the given years. A few employees left the job during these years. According to the company policy employees above 25 years are categorized as permanent employees. It is also known that Mindworkzz only hires new employees below 25 years of age but this condition was relaxed during the period 1st April 2010 to 1st April 2015 as some experienced people had come to the company seeking employment during this time.*

17. If exactly 900 employees who were under the permanent employees list in 1995 also fall in the same list in 2000 as well, then the maximum possible number of employees whose age was more than 40 and less than 45 in 2000 was? (Assume no new recruitments between 1995 and 2000)
18. What is the minimum possible number of employees who moved from the 20 to 40 age group, to the 40 to 60 age group during this time?
19. Least possible number of employees who left the job between 1995 and 2015?
20. What is the minimum number of recruitments that must have taken place during the period 1995 to 2015?

Year	20 < Age < 40 years	40 ≤ Age < 60	Age ≥ 60
1995	329	346	315
2000	300	360	310
2005	302	310	360
2010	330	330	330
2015	335	326	340

11 Mock Test Paper

Directions for Questions 1 to 6: *Answer the questions on the basis of information below.*

The table below shows what Bhavuk observed about the fuel consumption of his bike when he drives from Delhi to Leh via Kurukshetra, Mandi and Debring.

Place	Distance to Leh (in Km)	Km/L	Range	Fuel Filled?
Delhi (D)	1000			Yes
Kurukshetra (K)	860	14	560	?
Mandi (M)	580	21		?
Debring (Deb)	120	23		?

Some more information is given below:

(a) Whenever Bhavuk fills the bike tank with fuel, he resets the trip meter to zero

(b) Range is the distance that the fuel will last, at the current fuel efficiency

(c) "Km/L" is the fuel efficiency of Bhavuk's bike for the distance he covered from the time the trip meter was reset

1. What is the fuel efficiency of Bhavuk's bike (in Km/L) between Kurukshetra (K) and Mandi (M)?
   (a) 17.5 (b) 20
   (c) 28 (d) Cannot be determined
2. How much fuel (approximately) was consumed (in L) in the entire trip from Delhi to Leh?
   (a) 38 L (b) 43.5 L
   (c) 53 L (d) Cannot be determined
3. How much fuel did the bike start with?
   (a) 50 L (b) 40 L
   (c) 53 L (d) Cannot be determined
4. If Bhavuk could not find an active fuel station in Kurukshetra because of a bandh called all across Haryana, where should he get his bike refueled next to ensure hassle free ride to Leh?
   - Note that Bhavuk gets his bike refueled only from registered fuel stations at the stops mentioned above (D, K, M, Deb and Leh)
   - Mandi, Debring and Leh are not in Haryana and the fuel stations there are active
   - Bhavuk is a miser and likes to refuel only if he thinks that he actually needs to. Every time he stops at a stop, he analyzes his immediate fuel efficiency and calculates if he can leave without refueling and save on money
   - Bhavuk cannot predict his bike's fuel efficiency from the point he is at till the next planned stop

   (a) Mandi (b) Debring
   (c) Bhavuk did not feel the need to refuel
   (d) Cannot be determined
5. If stations at Kurukshetra were open, would Bhavuk get refuel done there? (Consider all data from previous question)
   (a) Definitely Yes (b) Definitely No
   (c) May be Yes, but he can do without it
   (d) Can't say
6. If the average fuel efficiency for each of the three segments Delhi to Kurukshetra, Kurukshetra to Mandi and Mandi to Debring is calculated separately and then the simple average of these three fuel efficiencies is calculated, then the final value would come out as:

Directions for Questions 7 to 11: *In the ICC Champions Trophy, held across 4 continents, every team played 1 match on each of the four continents viz: Australia, Asia, Europe and Africa. All matches held in Asia were held in India, for Europe were held in England, for Africa were held in South Africa. In the Australian continent, of course, the matches were all held in Australia. At the end of the fiercely fought tournament, the best batsman was decided on the basis of runs scored by him in the four countries – Australia, India, England and South Africa. The weightage for the runs in each of the countries was 20%, 20%, 40% and 20% respectively.*

Note: *Runs in England were weighted higher since that particular year, the conditions in England were particularly humid and the ball swung a lot. The following are the runs scored and the ranks of the top 10 batsmen of the tournament (based on their weighted total scores). Some information is missing in the table.*

It is known that no batsman scored more than 190 in any innings during the tournament. If two or more batsmen scored the same total runs, they are awarded the same place in the rankings.

Player's Name	Australia	England	India	South-Africa	Weighted Total Score	Rank
Sachin	130	130	150		144	3
Younis	140	130		120	124	7
Adam	120	120	160	170	138	5
Saurav	90		150	180		1
Lance	110	150	110	120	128	6
Srikant	140	130	160	190	150	2
Neel	100	90	110			8
Hamish	150	100		170		4
Rahul	90	80	120	120	102	9
Damian	80	90	90			10

7. The minimum possible number of batsmen who scored more than Hamish in India is?
8. If Neel scored '*k*' runs in South Africa, then how many different values are possible for k?
9. How many players definitely scored more than Damian in South Africa?
10. Find the maximum possible total weighted score of Saurav.
11. What is the minimum number of runs Saurav scored in England?

Directions for Questions 12 to 16: *Refer to the data given (Table 11.4) and answer the following questions :*

In a cycle rally in the international Interschool Games, six schools from the Indian city of Lucknow participated.

There are 4 cyclists from each team and cyclists are given penalty points based on their timings in the race. The performance of some of the four players of all six teams is given in the table along with some missing values. The final standings of a team are considered on the basis of the sum of the penalty points earned by all 4 players. The team which gets the least penalty points wins the rally.

Cyclist I of National gets 52.27 penalty points, while Cyclist II of National in turn gets 48.55 penalty points & so on. Following additional informations are also known:

TABLE 11.4

	Cyclist I	Cyclist II	Cyclist III	Cyclist IV	Final Standing
National	52.27	48.55		55.00	
Loreto	53.43	45.29	55.45	44.77	5
Colvin Taluqdars	43.35			48.50	
St. Francis	46.79		44.63	50.06	
St. Fidelis	43.40			44.91	
St. Anthony	51.40	45.27	44.56		

1. *Before this tournament, the International Inter school games record of 400 metres was 43.19 penalty points.*
2. *Before this tournament, the Team Record for the rally was 178.21 penalty points combined for all 4 members of a team.*
3. *None of the cyclists of any team got less than 40.15 penalty points.*
4. *The worst score (maximum penalty points) in this event is recorded by Cyclist III of Loreto.*
5. *There is no tie (same penalty points) between any 2 teams for the complete race.*

12. If St. Fideles secured 6th and Colvin Taluqdars secured the 4th place in the overall standings, then what can be said about these statements?

    Statement I: At least 1 Cyclist breaks the individual record in this event.

    Statement II: At Most 3 Cyclists break the individual record in this event.

    (a) I is true while II is false
    (b) II is true while I is false
    (c) Both I and II are false
    (d) Both I and II are true
13. If two of the teams managed to break the team record, then what can be said about these statements?
    I. At least 1 Cyclist of Colvin Taluqdars breaks the individual record for the rally.
    II. 1 Cyclist of St. Fideles breaks the individual record for the rally.

    (a) I is true while II may be true
    (b) II is true while I may be true
    (c) Both I and II are false
    (d) Both I and II are true
14. If St. Anthony's secured the first position in the event where Cyclist IV of St. Anthony gets 44.30 penalty points, then what can be the maximum

number of cyclists (of all 6 teams) who can break the individual record mentioned above?

(a) One (b) Two
(c) Three (d) Four

15. If St. Francis secured the first place with Cyclist II of St. Francis getting 43.16 penalty points and was the only Cyclist to break the individual record of 400 meters in all the 6 teams then which of the following statements is definitely false?
(a) St. Fideles secured Second Place
(b) St. Anthony secured Second Place
(c) Colvin Taluqdars secured Fourth Place
(d) National secured Third Place

16. How many teams could possibly be the winner of the tournament?

Directions for Questions 17 to 20: *Refer to the data given below (Table 11.5) and answer the following questions:*

The GMAT for the year 2056 came as an altogether surprise for the students as the pattern of the paper was completely changed. Instead of the normal 3 sections, the paper consisted of only two sections – English(Section-I) and Reasoning (Section-II).

Results of four batches of Mindworkzz (an MBA training institute) at it's Kapurthala Centre namely Microsoft, GE, Apple, and Compaq is given below in terms of percentiles in the English section (Section-I), Reasoning section (Section-II) and Overall (Aggregate of section I & II). Table 11.5 shows the number of students who fell into each of four demarcated categories of percentile ranges:

The following additional information is available to Mr. Subhasis Mazumdar, CEO about the table:

1. *In the table, for each percentile range the higher end of the spectrum is included, while the lower end of the spectrum is not included. i.e. for the 60+ to 80 percentile range, those students who have a percentile of more than 60 and less than equal to 80 are included in this range*
2. *For all the batches shown, the overall percentile secured by any student from any batch is always less than his percentile in any individual section unless specifically stated.*
3. *Each student of the Microsoft and Compaq batches has secured a lower percentile in English than in Reasoning.*
4. *Each student of the GE and Apple batches has secured a lower percentile in Reasoning than in English.*

TABLE 11.5

	English				Reasoning				Overall			
	0 – 30	30 + TO 60	60 + TO 80	80 + TO 100	0 – 30	30 + TO 60	60 + TO 80	80 + TO 100	0 – 30	30 + TO 60	60 + TO 80	80 + TO 100
Microsoft	40			12	36	32	32	20	48	28	36	8
G.E.	36	48	56	40	38	82			82	50	32	16
Apple	10	26	100	34			82	10	60	96		
Compaq	52	10	30	18	38	22	32	18			6	2

17. What is the difference between the minimum possible value of 30+ to 60 percentile in English for Microsoft batch and the minimum possible value of 60+ to 80 percentile in reasoning for the GE batch?
(a) 12 (b) 16
(c) 24 (d) 14

18. What is the difference between maximum possible number of students in 30+ to 60 for Compaq to the minimum possible numbers in the 0–30 percentile range for Compaq?
(a) 50 (b) 52
(c) 2 (d) 4

19. What is the sum of the minimum possible number of students who secured an overall percentile of 60+ to 80 category for Apple and the minimum possible number of students who secured an overall percentile in 0-30 category for Compaq?
(a) 48 (b) 50
(c) 42 (d) 56

20. What is the sum of the maximum and minimum possible number of students in 60+ to 80 percentile category in Reasoning for GE?
(a) 52 (b) 78
(c) 68 (d) 64

12 Mock Test Paper

Directions for Questions 1 to 3: *The state of AmpaZampa consists of 12 districts – all rich in minerals – especially bauxite. In each of the twelve districts, there are a certain number of companies operational in Bauxite mining. The following table gives for each of the 12 districts, the highest production and the least production of any company (in metric tons). It is also known that the production of each company (in metric tons) is a distinct integer and the total production in each of the given district is 100 metric tons. Also, it is known that no two companies produce the same amount of bauxite in any district.*

District	Highest Production (in metric tons)	Lowest Production (in metric tons)	Number of Companies in the District
A	30	8	6
B	40	14	4
C	24	6	6
D	32	16	4
E	34	12	5
F	34	12	4
G	30	8	5
H	30	20	4
I	45	11	4
J	35	9	5
K	40	5	6
L	35	10	6

1. Find the maximum number of districts possible in which there are at least two companies with production greater than 32 metric tons for each company.
2. Find the maximum possible number of districts in which the production of the company with the second highest production could be more than thrice the production of the company with second lowest production?
3. Find the maximum possible number of districts in which less than half the number of companies produce more than half of the total production of the district.

Directions for Questions 4 to 8: *Answer the questions on the basis of the information given below (Table 21.1):*

Twenty Indian states were chosen (A through T). The following table gives the difference in cities among any two states of India. It is assumed that each state has a unique, distinct number of cities.

4. How many states have more cities than each of states M and N or less cities than each of M and N?
   (a) 14
   (b) 15
   (c) 16
   (d) Cannot be determined
   (e) None of these
5. Which of the following cannot be the total number of cities with states J, K, L, M and N together?
   (a) 200
   (b) 80
   (c) 100
   (d) Cannot be determined
   (e) None of these
6. If state P has 15 cities, what is the total number of cities with states A and C put together?
   (a) 51
   (b) 52
   (c) 53
   (d) Cannot be determined
   (e) None of these
7. Which of the following groups can have 80 cities in total?
   (i) A, B, and C (ii) P, Q, and R
   (iii) G, H, and I (iv) K, L, and M
   (a) Both (i) and (ii)
   (b) Both (ii) and (iv)
   (c) Both (i) and (iii)
   (d) Both (ii) and (iii)
   (e) Both (iii) and (iv)
8. What is the number of states who have cities between B and R?

TABLE 21.1

A	A	B	C	D	E	F	G	H	I	J	K	L	M	N	O	P	Q	R	S
B	8																		
C	13	5																	
D	6	2	7																
E	7	1	6	1															
F	21	13	8	15	14														
G	1	9	14	7	8	22													
H	7	15	20	13	14	28	6												
I	9	1	4	3	2	12	10	16											
J	12	4	1	6	5	9	13	19	3										
K	5	3	8	1	2	16	6	22	4	7									
L	2	10	15	8	9	23	1	5	11	14	7								
M	11	3	2	5	4	10	12	18	2	1	6	13							
N	19	11	6	13	12	2	20	26	10	7	14	21	8						
O	20	12	7	14	13	1	21	27	11	8	15	22	9	1					
P	17	9	4	11	10	4	18	24	8	5	12	19	6	2	3				
Q	27	19	14	21	20	4	28	34	18	15	22	28	16	8	7	10			
R	25	17	12	19	8	4	26	32	16	13	20	27	14	6	5	8	2		
S	23	15	10	17	16	2	24	30	14	11	18	25	12	4	3	6	4	2	
T	22	14	9	16	15	1	23	29	13	10	17	24	11	3	2	5	5	3	1

For example, the difference in between the number of cities of states C and D is 7

Directions for Questions 9 to 12: *Answer the questions on the basis of the information and the data given below:*

The Indian Institutes of Technology conduct the Joint Entrance Examination (JEE) for admission to their under graduate engineering program every year. The three subjects that are tested are physics, chemistry, and mathematics. The following table gives the cumulative score of the students, i.e. if the cumulative number of students who got 99 marks is 90, then it means that a total of 90 students got less than 99 marks in a particular test. If the test takers are arranged in ascending/descending order for physics then it may be assumed that the arrangement for chemistry and mathematics are also same respectively. Also the overall score for a student is his total score in all the three examinations.

Score	Cumulative Number of Students in Physics	Cumulative Number of Students in Chemistry	Cumulative Number of Students in Mathematics
>= 0	100	100	100
>= 10	82	75	69
>= 20	68	60	50
>= 30	52	50	40
>= 40	50	35	30
>= 50	30	25	20
>= 60	12	12	8
>= 70	5	7	4
>= 80	3	3	1
>= 90	2	1	0
=100	1	0	0

For the purpose of the questions assume that a person who scores higher than another in Physics, would also score higher than that person in Chemistry as well as in Mathematics.

Scores of all students are in multiples of 10, unless otherwise stated.

9. If 50% of the students who took JEE cleared the cutoff of the test, then which of the following is the cutoff for each of the three tests? The cutoff is the minimum marks a student must get to pass in the examination
   (a) 50 marks (b) 60 marks
   (c) 70 marks (d) Cannot be determined

10. Find the number of students who scored more than 60 marks in each of the three sections.
    (a) 5 (b) 6
    (c) 7 (d) 4
11. What is the overall score of the topper of JEE?
    (a) 240 (b) 250
    (c) 260 (d) 270
12. Consider the following statements:-
    (i) 2 students secured a minimum of 10 marks in each of the three examinations
    (ii) 7 students secured 60 marks in Physics.
    (iii) Two students secured more than 70 marks in each of the three examinations
    (iv) 10 students secured 0 marks in each of the three examinations

    Which of the above statements is false?
    (a) (i), (ii) and (iii) (b) (ii), (iii) and (iv)
    (c) (i), (iv) (d) (i), (iii) and (iv)

Directions for Questions 13 to 16: *Refer to the data in the table (Table 12.1) to answer the questions that follow:*

Table 12.1 gives the number of Engineers and Doctors of several countries. Due to shortage of technology in various countries, countries often outsource professionals to other countries. In turn, the countries that are in shortage of technology and need services requisition these professionals from countries that have professionals in excess. If a country outsources because it has a surplus of talent, the country can outsource to only one country. The deficit of a certain country in talent can be fulfilled by requisitioning professionals from at the most three countries.

TABLE 12.1

Country ↓	Doctors Out-sourced	Engineers Out-sourced	Doctors Requisi-tioned	Engineers Requisi-tioned
Egypt	57	78	48	123
Germany	86	83	86	67
Bangladesh	56	37	86	26
India	67	87	53	122
Argentina	76	64	57	64
Japan	52	76	47	99
Holland	58	66	47	43
Denmark	89	54	73	46
Finland	79	96	104	63
Kazakhstan	37	81	56	69

* The number of Doctors/Engineers mentioned in the table are in million.

13. From which of the following countries does Bangladesh requisition doctors (if it is known that any country having a deficit of doctors is required to requisition from at least two countries)?
    (a) Holland, India, and Japan
    (b) Denmark and India
    (c) Argentina and Holland
    (d) Both (a) and (c)
14. To nullify its deficit in Engineers, how many countries does India requisition Engineers from?
    (a) 4 (b) 3
    (c) 2 (d) 0
15. If the country having the highest deficit in Doctors was to requisition, how many different possible countries will it have to requisition from?
    (a) 4 (b) 5
    (c) 6 (d) 7
16. Which of the following countries can requisition Doctors from maximum number of countries?
    (a) Finland (b) Kazakhstan
    (c) Bangladesh (d) India

Directions for Questions 17 to 20: *Refer to the data in the table given below (Table 12.2) to answer the following questions:*

Bankrupt Airlines started its new air route from North Pole to South Pole so that Eskimos from both worlds could exchange culture. Five aircrafts were dedicated to this noble cause. Bankrupt airlines outlined the following guidelines to the captains of these five aircrafts while they traversed from North Pole to South Pole:

(b) A, B, C, D, E, F, G, H are the eight stop over points (cities) in between North Pole and South Pole where each of the five aircrafts stop for a fixed time as decided by Bankrupt airlines. The stop over time for the aircrafts might not be the same

(c) All the five aircrafts start from the North pole at the same time but may or may not reach the South pole at the same time

(d) Each of the five aircrafts take five different routes. No two aircrafts traverse the same route

(e) The table given above gives the time taken to traverse from one city to another in hours. All the aircrafts traveling on the same path have the same traversal time

(f) The time taken by an aircraft to traverse from North pole to South Pole is equal to the sum of the flying time in between various stop over points after starting from North pole and the sum of the stop over time in each stop over point

TABLE 12.2

		TO									
		North pole	A	B	C	D	E	F	G	H	South pole
	North pole	–	–	–	–	–	6	8	–	–	–
	A	–	–	–	–	–	–	–	–	–	10
	B	–	–	–	–	1	–	–	4	–	–
	C	–	–	–	–	–	–	–	–	–	8
From	D	–	–	–	–	–	–	–	3	–	–
	E	–	–	–	–	–	–	–	–	3	–
	F	–	–	–	–	–	–	–	6	–	–
	G	–	–	–	2	–	–	–	–	–	–
	H	–	4	3	–	4	–	–	–	–	–
	South pole	–	–	–	–	–	–	–	–	–	–

17. If bankrupt airlines decides to have an equal stop over time in every intermediate stop over point of 2 hours each, then what is the difference in between the time taken to reach South Pole by the aircraft that reaches first and the one that reaches last?
    (a) 9 hours (b) 10 hours
    (c) 8 hours (d) None of these
18. Bankrupt Airlines brought a more powerful aircraft than its existing fleet of aircrafts and as a result the travelling time in between city B and G was reduced to 3 hours. If the stop over time due to the new fleet of aircrafts be 7, 2, 0, 1, 1, 5, 1, 1 hours for each of the intermediate stop over cities A to H respectively, then which of the following statements stand true?
    (a) All the aircrafts reach South Pole at the same time
    (b) Three air routes have the same traversal time of 35 hours to reach the destination
    (c) Four air routes have a traversal time of 30 hours
    (d) None of these
19. Bankrupt airlines decides to chart its traversal and stop over time in such a fashion such that all aircrafts reach South Pole in the same time. To this effect, if the stopover time of cities C, E, G, and H be 2 hours each, then what is the total time taken by any aircraft to traverse its path?
    (a) 32 hours (b) 33 hours
    (c) 34 hours (d) None of these
20. Which of the following cannot be a stop over time at the eight cities respectively if exactly four aircrafts reach the South Pole simultaneously?
    (a) 3, 2, 0, 0, 1, 3, 4, 4
    (b) 3, 2, 1, 0, 2, 5, 4, 4
    (c) 5, 1, 4, 5, 1, 0, 4, 2
    (d) None of these

13 Mock Test Paper

Directions for Questions 1 to 4: *Answer the questions on the basis of information below.*

Advent of Mr. Narendra Modi as the Prime Minister of India in 2014 brought along a lot of awareness campaigns to promote various causes within India. The table below gives you the information about four of these campaigns, their star campaigners and the fee they charge per campaign. No celebrity, other than the eight mentioned, has worked in these campaigns. Each of the celebrities has worked in exactly two of the four campaigns. Table also gives you partial information about the celebrities who have worked in a particular campaign.

Additional information given: Fee paid to celebrities (star campaigners) is exactly 25% of the total budget of that campaign.

	Fee Charged Per Campaign (in INR)	Digital India	Give It Up India	Startup India	Swachh Bharat Abhiyaan
Total budget for the campaign (in Lakh INR) Star campaigner		176	144	192	288
Mohli	20		Yes		
Imran	16	Yes			
Sairukh	10	Yes	No	No	Yes
Moni	12			Yes	
Kajal	12			Yes	
Anshika	10				
Hansika	14				Yes
Amir	6		Yes		

1. In which of the following campaigns has Kajal worked?
   (a) Give It Up India
   (b) Digital India
   (c) Swachh Bharat Abhiyaan
   (d) Cannot be determined
2. Which celebrity has not worked with Sairukh in any of the given campaigns?
   (a) Mohli (b) Anshika
   (c) Hansika (d) Amir
3. What is the absolute difference (in Lakh INR) in the total budget of the campaign released in which Mohli has worked and total budget of the campaigns in which both Moni and Kajal have worked?
   (a) 192 (b) 48
   (c) 64 (d) 240
4. Disappointed with the kind of fee these celebrities charge for such noble national causes, PM Narendra Modi bans all the campaigns from appointing any celebrity whosoever. He instead decided to use the amount that was previously kept aside for celebrities from all campaigns put together to start a new campaign called Make In India to finance Small and Medium sized Indian manufacturing enterprises. He also announced that whatever the amount sums up to for Make In India, he'd add 20% of it more from the National treasure to facilitate this campaign. However, this campaign requires 23 Paise to be spent on banners and ads for every 1 INR invested in it. How much money (in Lakhs INR) was spent on banners and ads in Make In India campaign?
   (a) 55.2 (b) 46.46
   (c) 23.2 (d) 185.8

Directions for Questions 5 to 8: *In Charlie's chocolate factory, one day there are 10 children visiting. Let's call them – A, B, C, D, E, F, G, H, I, J. Charlie distributes a certain number of chocolates to these 10 children. He has given them chocolates in packs of 4 chocolates each, or 6 chocolates each or as single chocolates. The table 13.1 shows the percentage of the total number of chocolates that Charlie distributed and that each child has. The second table shows the percentage distribution of the total number of chocolates each child has got – in terms of 4 and 6 chocolate packs. The total number of chocolates distributed by Charlie is less than 375 and no two children have got the same number of chocolates except A and D.*

TABLE 13.1

Child	Percentage of Total Chocolates
A	25
B	30
C	10
D	25
Others (E, F, G, H, I, J)	10

TABLE 13.2

Player	Percentage of Total Chocolates in 4 Chocolate Packs	Percentage of Total Chocolates in 6 Chocolate Packs
A	13.33333	40
B	22.22222	11 1111
C	66.6666	33.3333
D	40	20
Others(E–J)	33.3333	33.3333

5. If B has got a total of 'n' chocolates then n = ?
6. If D has a total of 'x' 6-chocolate packs then x = ?
7. Find the total number of 4-chocolate packs given by Charlie.
8. At most how many children could not have any chocolate?

Directions for Questions 9 to 12: *Answer the questions on the basis of information below.*

Saimukh Khan is one of the biggest actors of Bollywood and has been cast in more than 50 Bollywood movies. In 2019 alone, he was cast in 8 movies. In a survey conducted to get the reviews of these 8 movies, 10 people were interviewed. They either Liked or Disliked a movie. These 8 movies were: Dilwale, Gharwale, Dil me, Gatekeeper, Bodyguard, Junoon, Delhiites, Salam Bombay

Additional information:

- The Bar-Chart given provides details about the number of people (10 surveyed) who liked the movies Dilwale, Gharwale, Dil me, Gatekeeper, Bodyguard, Junoon and Delhiites.
- Details about the movie – Salam Bombay is not provided in the chart
- The given table gives the information about the number of movies Not liked by each of the 10 people

Name of Person	Bijoy	Pulkit	Kanu	Sanju	Guddu	Neha	Bhavye	Charu	Shanky	Dimpy
No. of Movies Not Liked	5	4	5	4	1	2	6	7	0	3

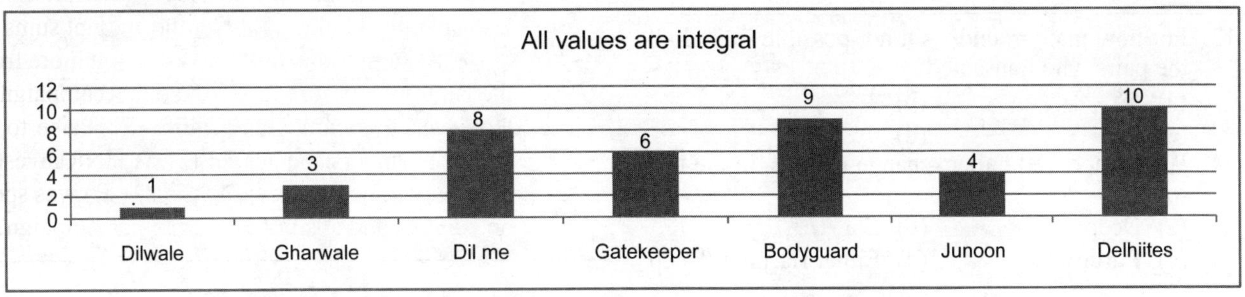

9. How many people did not like the movie – Salam Bombay?
   (a) 9 (b) 2
   (c) 8 (d) 7
10. Which of the following movies is not liked by Dimpy?
   (a) Salam Bombay (b) Delhiites
   (c) Bodyguard (d) Dil me
11. Out of the given 8 movies, how many movies are liked by Pulkit but not by Charu?
   (a) 4 (b) 2
   (c) 3 (d) 1
12. Out of the given 8 movies, how many movies are not liked by Kanu but liked by Neha?
   (a) 4 (b) 3
   (c) 5 (d) 6

Directions for Questions 13 to 16: *Refer to the data given below (Table 13.3) and answer the following questions:*

Six friends Arun, Barun, Charan, Deep, Ela, and Faiz play a Unique game every Sunday. Each of them started with some initial no. of Marbles. In each round every player transacted marbles with exactly one person. At the end of the 5th round it was observed that each person had exchanged marbles with every other person. Refer to Table 13.3 and answer the questions that follow:

TABLE 13.3

	Arun	Barun	Charan	Deep	Ela	Faiz
Initial No. of Marbles	160	130	150	180	150	200
No. of Marbles at the end of 1st round	140	150	180	160	170	170
No. of Marbles at the end of 2nd round	150	140	190	190	140	160
No. of Marbles at the end of 3rd round	170	130	170	200	–	150
No. of Marbles at the end of 4th round	180	120	180	190	–	170
No. of Marbles at the end of 5th round	–	–	–	–	–	–

13. For how many rounds is it not possible to find all the pairs who transacted?
   (a) 5 (b) 4
   (c) 3 (d) 0
14. With whom did Faiz exchange marbles in the last round?
   (a) Deep (b) Ela
   (c) Barun (d) Either Barun or Deep
15. In the 5th round, if those who transacted with Charan and Deep gave them half the numbers of the marbles they had with them, then what would be the difference between the number of marbles of Charan and Deep?
   (a) 35 (b) 20
   (c) 30 (d) 2
16. With whom did Arun transact in the fourth round?
   (a) Deep (b) Barun
   (c) Faiz (d) Charan

Directions for Questions 17 to 20: *100 students of five different countries France, UK, USA, India, China participated in an International science Olympiad. In the competition each student took 10 exams of different subjects with a maximum marks of 500 marks for each subject.*

It was observed that only 9 students – A, B, C, D, E, F, G, H, I scored 100 or more marks in at least one subject.

Table X gives the detail of number of instances in which a student from the given country scored 100 to 199 marks, 200 to 299 marks, 300 or more.

Table Y gives the detail of number of subjects in which each of these nine students scored 100 or more marks, 200 or more marks, 300 or more marks.

TABLE X

Country/Marks	100 to 199	200 to 299	300+
UK	1	2	2
USA	3	1	2
INDIA	1	2	1
CHINA	2	0	1
FRANCE	1	1	2

TABLE Y

Student/Marks	100+	200+	300+
A	3	2	2
B	2	2	1
C	4	3	2
D	1	1	0
E	4	2	1
F	2	2	0
G	2	1	1
H	3	1	1
I	1	0	0

17. Which of the following student is from India?
    (a) E (b) F
    (c) B (d) H
18. Out of these nine students, the maximum number of students, belong to which country?
    (a) India (b) USA
    (c) China (d) UK
19. Which of the following student belongs to the same country as G?
    (a) F (b) B
    (c) E (d) None of these.
20. How many students (among these nine students) came from France?

14 Mock Test Paper

Directions for Questions 1 to 5: *Refer to the following charts and solve the questions based on them: Following charts show currency ratio from 11th May to 15th May*

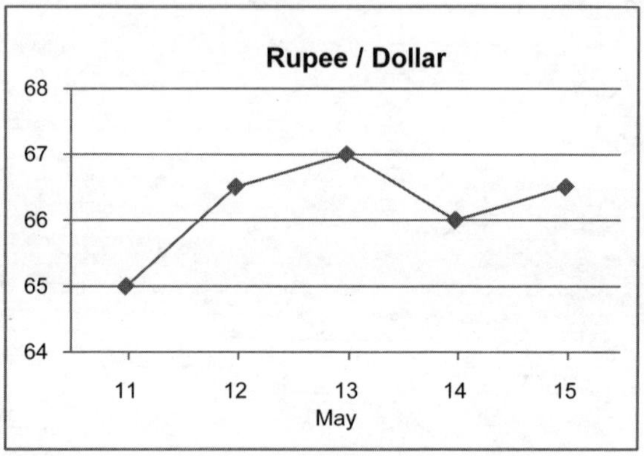

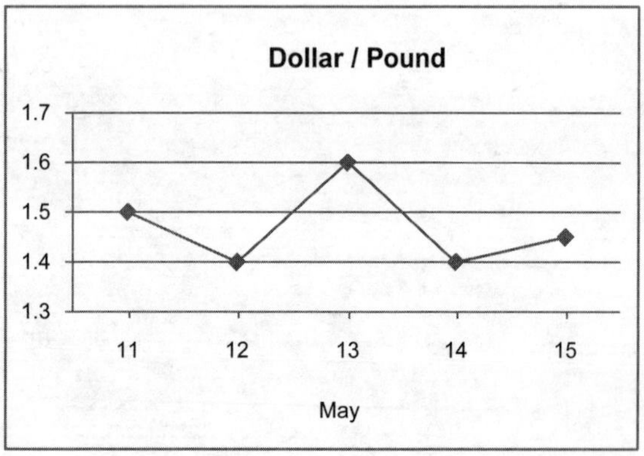

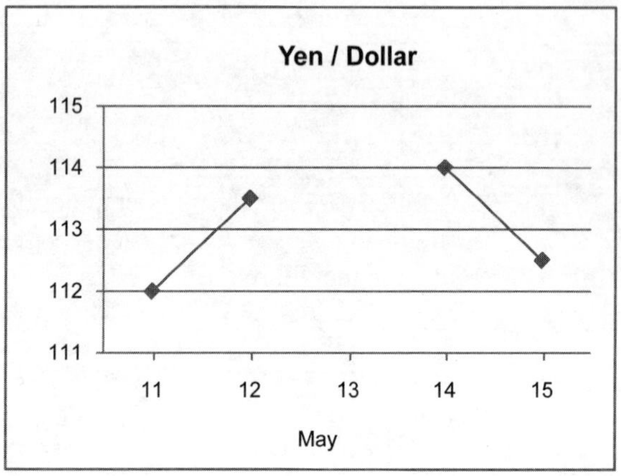

Conversion ratio of Yen/Dollar on 13th May is NOT mentioned deliberately.

If needed, let the currency symbols be $ for dollar, INR for Indian Rupee, ¥ for Yen and £ for Pound

1. On May 14th, how much Yen did INR 4,000 yield approximately? (Rounded off to nearest integer)
   (a) 6020 (b) 6910
   (c) 2316 (d) 30096
2. On 15th May, Bhavuk went to a local market in Los Angeles, USA and liked a watch worth $300. Being a frequent traveler, he carries different currencies of different amounts on him. For now, he only has INR 19,500; £200 and ¥34,250 on him. Being in a local market, the shopkeeper there won't agree on accepting any foreign currency, however with relentless effort Bhavuk could convince him to sell the watch in a single foreign currency for this transaction. What currency would Bhavuk offer to buy this watch in? Consider currency exchange charges as NIL for this question and the fact that the shopkeeper gets the received currency exchanged for dollars on the same day.
   (a) Yen
   (b) Pound
   (c) Indian Rupee
   (d) Bhavuk cannot buy this watch with a single currency
3. If Bhavuk had visited this market on 13th May, which currency would he have offered to buy this watch in?
   (a) Yen (b) Pound
   (c) Indian Rupee (d) Cannot be determined
4. China, which has Yen as its official currency, learnt that the Yen is overvalued in global markets. Thus on 16th May it depreciated its currency by 2.22% of its value on 15th May against the dollar as a measure to boost exports. How many dollars will 56000 Yen yield on 16th May? (Rounded off to nearest Integer)

   Note: When a currency is depreciated, it gets cheaper and you can buy more of that currency against another currency now.

   (a) 487 (b) 500
   (c) 467 (d) 115

5. By what percent did the Indian Rupee appreciate/depreciate against Yen on 16th May over 15th May after the devaluation measure taken by China for Yen? Given that fluctuation of Indian Rupee was negligible on 16th May.
   (a) 2.22% appreciated (b) 2% depreciated
   (c) 2.22% depreciated (d) 4.44% appreciated

Directions for Questions 6 to 10: *A group of 5 students – Pulkit, Qasim, Rahim, Shaan, Tejas participated in the National Science competition 2019. The competition consists of four exams of different subjects – Physics, Chemistry, Biology, Maths.*

The tables given below show the marks of all candidate on different subjects (Table 14.1) and the total marks of all students in a given subject (Table 14.2).

In table 14.1 each column has two missing values which are the least two scores on that subject and none of the missing values is more than 10% of the total marks scored by all the candidates together in that subject.

6. The maximum possible marks of Pulkit in Physics is:
   (a) 34.5 (b) 36.5
   (c) 39.5 (d) None of these.
7. What is the maximum possible percentage contribution of Rahim in the total marks obtained by all the students in all the subjects?
   (a) 19.33 (b) 18.51
   (c) 24.47 (d) None of these.
8. If the absolute difference between the total marks obtained by Pulkit and Rahim in the four subjects is the minimum possible, then what is the absolute difference between the total marks obtained by Qasim and Tejas?
9. The student with the highest total marks in all the four subjects got the 1st rank and the student with the lowest total marks got 5th rank and it is known that no two students got the same number of total marks. What rank did Pulkit get?
   (a) 1st (b) 2nd
   (c) 3rd (d) cannot be determined
10. In the previous question what rank did Qasim get, if his total score in all the four subjects is a prime integer?

TABLE 14.1 Students and Their Scores on Different Subjects

Student	Physics	Chemistry	Biology	Math
Pulkit		150		79.5
Qasim	132	97.5		78
Rahim			165	
Shaan	108	112.5	30	84
Tejas	90		117	

TABLE 14.2

Subject	Combined Score of All Students
Physics	405
Chemistry	450
Biology	360
Math	300

Directions for Questions 11 to 15: *Answer the questions on the basis of information below.*

128 players participate in the Australian Open Tennis tournament. The tournament is scheduled to be held over 7 rounds and each round is a knock out round, where in any match between 2 players, the winner advances to the next round and the loser is eliminated from the tournament. There are no draws or byes in the tournament. Players who take part are seeded from 1 to 128, with seed 1 being the highest seed, 2 the next and so on. Matches are scheduled in such a way that in any round, assuming there are no upsets, the highest seeded player plays against the lowest seeded player at that point, the next highest seeded player plays against the next lowest seeded player and so on. An upset is said to happen when a lower seeded player beats a higher seeded player. The schedule of matches in the next rounds remains unchanged in case of an upset in a round, with the only difference being that the player who caused the upset advances to the next round and takes the designated place of the player he upset.

11. In case of no upsets throughout the tournament, in which round would the player seeded-8 face a player seeded higher than him?
    (a) 1st round (b) 4th round
    (c) 5th round (d) 6th round
12. In case of no upset, how many players in the tournament won exactly 2 matches?
    (a) 32 (b) 16
    (c) 17 (d) None of these
13. If the player seeded 16 won the tournament, then a minimum of how many upsets would have happened in the tournament?
    (a) 3 (b) 2
    (c) 4 (d) 5
14. With no information given on the number of upsets, which of the following players could have faced the player seeded 15 in the 4th round?
    (a) Seed 34 (b) Seed 1
    (c) Seed 128 (d) Seed 8
15. Assuming no upsets, which player beats Seed 25?
    (a) Seed 26 (b) Seed 24
    (c) Seed 9 (d) Seed 8

Directions for Questions 16 to 20: *Refer to the data and the two tables given below (Tables 14.3 and 14.4) and answer these questions.*

People of the Hippie land have their Olympics called "Hippie". Hippie consists of four tournaments, namely the HI-HI, HE-HE, HA-HA, and HO-HO. Each of these four tournaments contain one or more of the several games A, B, C ... M. Table 14.3 gives the individual points scored by the players in the respective games in the year 2023. Points which a player secures in a particular given tournament are of the rounds up to which the player has reached.

Table 14.4 gives the total prize money and the points awarded to each level in the various tournaments.

The rules for the sharing of the prize money are that the prize money of any tournament is distributed in the ratio 20:14:18:20 among the winners, the runner-up, two semifinalists, and four quarter finalists. The two semifinalists get an equal amount of money and same goes for the quarterfinalists as well. Each match is played between only two players and there is no draw in any of the matches. Winners of R64 play R32, winners of R32 play R16 and so on and so forth; winners of semifinals play in the final.

W: Points awarded to the winner of the tournament

F: Points awarded to the runner up of the tournament

SF: Points awarded to the loser in semifinals, i.e. semifinalist

QF, R16, R32, and R64 are the points awarded to the players who lost in the quarter finals, round of 16, round of 32, and round of 64. All the tournaments are played with 64 players at the starting of the tournament

TABLE 14.3

	H	F	B	L	A	D	I	E	J	K	C	G	M
Scrooge	50	12	15	45	50	5	7	1	5	50	7	30	1
Shaggy	0	12	7	1	15	27	25	12	1	1	15	30	25
Mickey	140	1	45	1	90	5	1	3	42	1	1	7	45
Johny	0	3	7	15	7	15	25	3	1	7	7	140	1
Scooby	0	1	25	0	50	3	70	22	0	140	45	1	0
Bluto	7	1	15	100	30	60	100	50	1	15	70	200	100
DD	30	22	15	15	30	42	1	35	5	50	7	30	1
Donald	0	5	15	70	7	1	1	5	3	15	15	1	70
Dupey	200	50	100	0	90	1	0	1	60	200	100	90	0
Dexter	90	0	70	0	140	15	1	0	27	90	15	0	0
Scrappy	50	5	15	25	15	15	1	22	15	15	7	15	1
Simpson	7	35	1	15	50	27	15	5	15	7	1	90	25
Jetson	15	22	7	0	200	15	0	7	27	0	7	30	0

TABLE 14.4

Name of Tournament	R 16	R 32	R 64	QF	SF	F	W	Prize
HO-HO	5	3	1	12	22	35	50	17,700
HE-HE	15	7	1	25	45	70	100	36,000
HI-HI	30	15	7	50	90	140	200	72,000
HA-HA	5	3	1	15	27	42	60	21,600

16. The total prize money earned by runners up in all the tournaments is:
    (a) 106283 (b) 106280
    (c) 106286 (d) 106289
17. Which of the following players have possibly played against each other in the quarter finals of the tournament in which the K game is played?
    (a) Scrooge and DD
    (b) Dexter and Scrooge
    (c) Dupey and Scooby
    (d) Scrappy and Simpson
18. What is the total prize money earned by Donald from all the given tournaments?
    (a) 12000 (b) 13000
    (c) 11000 (d) 14000
19. Which of the following is a possible combination for the semifinals of the given tournament?
    (a) Dexter and Jetson in I
    (b) DD and Shaggy in F
    (c) Scrooge and Jetson in H
    (d) Bluto and Scooby in C
20. Who has won the maximum number of tournaments?
    (a) Scrooge
    (b) Bluto
    (c) Dupey
    (d) Both (b) and (c)

15 Mock Test Paper

Directions for Questions 1 to 4: *Answer the following questions on the basis of the data and the line chart (Figure 15.1) given below:*

There are four reputed coaching institutes of India that offer preparation classes for various MBA examinations. For each of these four institutes W, X, Y, and Z, the following graph gives the cost incurred by the institute (Preparation cost) in the study material that they provide to each of their students in ₹ With respect to the fees that they take from each student in ₹ (Tuition cost). The study material provided by each of these four institutes is in four subjects, i.e. Quant (E), English (F), Reasoning (G), and Data Interpretation (H) respectively. For each of the four study materials, the preparation cost is in ascending order. Assume all numbers in the graph are in perfect 000's.

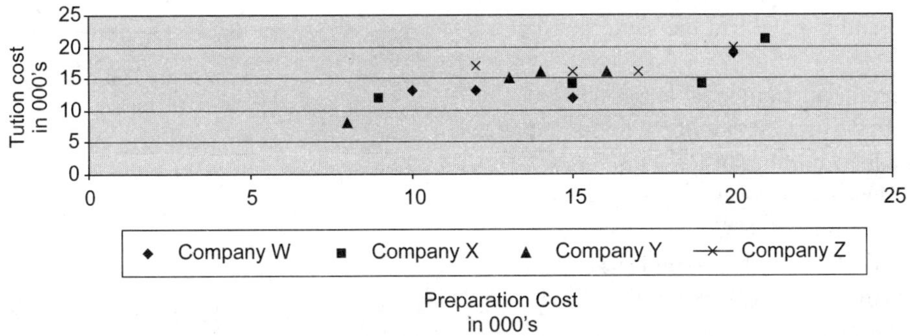

FIGURE 15.1

1. In which of the following ratios should coaching W prepare the units of products E, F, G, and H to make an overall profit? Assume the number of units prepared to be equal to the number of units sold to the students for each product
   (a) 3 : 1 : 5 : 7 (b) 5 : 6 : 8 : 2
   (c) 1 : 2 : 3 : 4 (d) 2 : 1 : 1 : 2
2. The company X prepared and sold 10, 20, 30, and 40 units of the respective products E, F, G, and H in some random order then its maximum overall profit could be? (in 000's)
   (a) ₹40 (b) ₹45
   (c) ₹50 (d) ₹35
3. The difference between the total number of profit making products and the total number of products that incur a loss to the coaching institutes is
   (a) 5 (b) 4
   (c) 3 (d) 2
4. If coaching Y sold a total of 100 units of all the products combined, it suffered a loss of ₹20,000. Which of the following could have been the total number of units of products F and G sold by company Y?
   (a) 25 (b) 30
   (c) 35 (d) 40
   (e) None of these

Directions for Questions 5 to 8: *Answer the questions on the basis of the information given below (Table 15.1):*

In the six nation mini world cup football, each country played another country exactly once. The table given below gives the position of the countries with respect to their total points, i.e. the team with maximum points is ranked first. Each win gets a team 3 points, a draw gives 1 point while a loss gives 0 points. It is also known that Country C beat country D and no two teams finished with the same number of points. Some of the cells have been intentionally kept blank.

TABLE 15.1

Position	Country	Won	Draw	Lost	Goals For	Goals Against	Total Points
1	A				17	5	15
2	B				9	6	10
3	C					2	8
4	D				2	5	
5	E				7	11	2
6	F				8	16	

5. Consider the following statements:
   (i) The total points of team F are 1
   (ii) The total points of team D are 5
   (iii) The difference between the total points of team D and team F is 5
   Which of the above statements cannot be determined?
   (a) (i) and (iii) (b) (i) and (ii)
   (c) (ii) and (iii) (d) All of the above
   (e) None of these
6. Consider the following statements:
   (i) Team B and C have had the same number of draws
   (ii) The difference in number of losses between the team with the highest number of losses and that with the least number of losses is 5
   (iii) Team E has had 4 losses
   Which of the above is false?
   (a) (i) and (iii) (b) (i) and (ii)
   (c) (ii) and (iii) (d) All of the above
   (e) None of these
7. Consider the following statements:
   (i) Two teams have the same number of wins as the number of losses
   (ii) The number of wins, draws, and losses for team D cannot be determined
   (iii) The number of draws of team C and E each is two more than the number of draws of team B and F each
   Which of the above statement is true?
   (a) (i) and (iii) (b) Only (ii)
   (c) (ii) and (iii) (d) All of the above
   (e) None of the above
8. Consider the following statements:
   (i) The number of wins of at the most one pair of two teams is the same
   (ii) The difference in between the number of wins of team A and C is 3
   (iii) The difference in between the number of draws of B and losses of E is 0
   (iv) The goals for team C is more than 2 but less than 9
   (v) The product of the number of wins of C and losses of team D is an even number
   If the above statement are True (T), False (F), or Cannot Be Determined (CBD) then match the appropriate statement to its condition
   (a) (i) –T, (ii) – F, (iii) – CBD, (iv) – CBD, (v) – T
   (b) (i) – F, (ii) – F, (iii) – T, (iv) – CBD, (v) – T
   (c) (i) – CBD, (ii) – T, (iii) – T, (iv) – F, (v) – F
   (d) (i) –T, (ii) – CBD, (iii) – T, (iv) – T, (v) – F
   (e) (i) –F, (ii) – T, (iii) – F, (iv) – F, (v) – T

Directions for Questions 9 to 12: *On the basis of the information given below (Table 15.2), answer the questions that follow:*

The Industry Today group reviews and ranks the companies in India on the basis of twenty parameters. These parameters are ranked Good (G), Satisfactory (Y), and Below satisfactory (B). There are six industries it reviewed and rewarded them 3 points for Good, 2 for Satisfactory, and 1 for Below satisfactory. It also awarded them total points which were the sum of the points obtained for each of Good (G), Satisfactory (Y), and Below satisfactory (B) points. The ranking of the industries was done in descending order of their total points. If the total points were equal then a higher rank was given to the industry with higher 'Good' points. If the 'Good' points were also equal then ranking was done on the basis of 'Satisfactory' points. Higher the points meant better the rank. Some cells are intentionally left blank. For each question, you can use the data of the previous questions.

Note: Each Industry might also be rated poor, and a poor rating would lead to 0 points.

TABLE 15.2

Rank	Industry	Good	Satisfactory	Below Satisfactory	Total
3	C	4		5	
1	A	6			24
5	E	3			19
4	D	2		5	
2	B		5	2	
6	F		1		

9. Which of the following is the total points scored by Industry B?
   (a) 19 (b) 24
   (c) 23 (d) Either of (a) or (c)
10. If D has 6 satisfactory ratings, how many satisfactory ratings did C have?
   (a) 2 (b) 3
   (c) 4 (d) Either (a) or (b)
11. If you were to build a table for the possible ways in which the points structure for the situation described with respect to the number of Good, Satisfactory and Below Satisfactory ratings could be allotted to the first 5 ranked industries, how many possibilities exist for building the table between A to E?
   (a) 48 (b) 84
   (c) 96 (d) 192
12. Which of the following statements is definitely true?
   (a) The Satisfactory points won by C cannot be determined
   (b) The below satisfactory points of D can be determined
   (c) The Satisfactory points of D cannot be determined
   (d) Both (a) and (c)

Directions for Questions 13 to 16: *Refer to the following data (Table 15.3) to answer the questions that follow:*

In a dog show, 20 dogs were made to sit in a row facing north for people to view. Each dog was given a tag number 1 through 20 and was supposed to be called by the same number as the number on its tag. The owners of the dogs were told the name (or tag number) so that they could recognise their dog after the show. However, the curator messed up with the tags and now every dog has a different tag than what the name of the dog is. The following table could be (Table 15.3) drawn by the curator at the end of the show. A (+x) suggests that the dog with a particular tag is sitting x places to the left of the dog with the same name and a (–y) suggests that the dog with a name is sitting y places to the left of the dog with that tag.

As an example, consider row 1, column 1. A +6 suggests that the dog with name 1 is seated 6 places to the right of the dog having the tag 1 on him.

***Example**: The dog with name 20 is sitting +3 places (that is 3 places right) to the dog that is labelled with the tag 4*

TABLE 15.3

Name of dog	Tag number																			
	1	2	3	4	5	6	7	8	9	10	11	12	13	14	15	16	17	18	19	20
1	+6	+3	–13																	
2				–9	–4	–1														
3							–3	–7	–9											
4										+7	+9	+6	+3							
5					–5												–13	–11		
6		+4											–1							–6
7												+8	+5						+3	
8								–4												
9									–8											
10				–6							+6									
11							–11													
12														–7			–17			
13	+2													–5						
14								–13								–8				
15							+2													+1
16			0												+18					
17											+13				+14					
18		+15																		
19	+16																–1			
20				+3					–1							+6				

13. How many dogs are seated to the left of 16?
   (a) 11 (b) 12
   (c) 13 (d) None of these
14. Consider the following statements:
   (i) The dog named 13 has tag 10 on him
   (ii) The dog with tag 14 is seated in position 7
   (iii) The dog with name 1 is tagged 7
   (iv) The dog with tag 1 is seated in position 1
   (v) The dog with name 8 has a tag 7 and is seated in position 13

Which of the above statements is true?
(a) All of the above
(b) None of these
(c) Cannot be determined
(d) (iv) and (v)
(e) All but (iv) and (v)

15. The dog tagged 4 has which dog seated to the right of him (name) and what is his tag number and position? (name-tag-position)
(a) 17-18-16 (b) 18-17-16
(c) 17-19-16 (d) Cannot be determined
(e) None of these

16. Consider the following statements:
(i) The dog with tag 6 is seated 6 places left to the dog with name 14.
(ii) The dog with name 13 is seated two places right of the dog with tag 15.
(iii) The difference in the tags of the dog seated in position 18 and the dog with name 5 is 6.
(iv) The dogs with name 12 and 17 have the same tag number as their position number.
(v) The dog with tag 7 is 8 places right of the dog with name 8.
Which of the above is true?.
(a) (i), (iii), and (v) (b) (ii), (iv), and (v)
(c) (i), (iii), and (iv) (d) None of these

Directions for Questions 17 to 20: *Refer to the data given below to answer the questions that follow:*

Two Physicists, Mr. Nerdy and Mr. Geeky, have recently discovered four new sub atomic particles. They decide to name these particles Atron, Btron, Ctron, and Dtron. While discovering them they also found that the mean life (the time over which the sub atomic particle is in stable state) was probabilistically distributed and could be at best 100 nano seconds (ns) and at the minimum 0 nano seconds.

Mr. Nerdy and Mr. Geeky recorded the following data in their log book:
(a) The expected mean life of the four particles Atron, Btron, Ctron and Dtron is 60, 90, 80, and 75 nano seconds respectively
(b) Upon observation it was found that the mean life of either of Atron or Btron is 10% higher than the expected results
(c) Similarly, upon observation it was found that the mean life of either of Ctron or Dtron is 20% higher than the expected results
(d) Also, the observed results of the mean life of one of the sub atomic particles is 10% lower than the expected mean life and of another sub atomic particle is 20% less than the expected

Expected mean life is the mean life that the two Physicists expect from their prior knowledge without performing any experiments. Practical mean life is the mean life obtained upon performing practical experiments

17. If the sum of the practical mean life of Btron and Ctron is 195 nano seconds, then the sum of the mean life of all the four sub atomic particles cannot be:
(a) equal to 310 ns (b) less than 310 ns
(c) more than 310 ns (d) None of the above

18. If the sum of the mean life of all the four sub atomic particles is 309 ns then which of the following statements is definitely true?
(i) The practical mean life of Atron is more than its expected mean life
(ii) The practical mean life of Btron is less than its expected mean life
(iii) The practical mean life of Ctron is more than its expected mean life
(iv) The practical mean life of Dtron is less than its expected mean life
(a) (i), (ii), and (iv)
(b) (ii), (iii), and (iv)
(c) (i), (iii), and (v)
(d) None of these

19. A new study revealed that when the four sub atomic particles are subjected to radiation then the sum of their expected mean life increases or decreases by 20%. What is the maximum difference of the sum of the new mean life and the sum of the old expected life?
(a) 60.5 (b) 62.5
(c) 66.5 (d) Cannot be determined

20. If the practical mean life of two out of the four sub atomic particles is the same then which of the following statements is definitely true?
(i) The practical mean life of Atron is 66 ns
(ii) The practical mean life of Btron is 66 ns
(iii) The practical mean life of Ctron is 72 ns
(iv) The practical mean life of Dtron is 90 ns
(v) The sum of the practical mean life of all the four sub atomic particles is 301.5 ns
(a) All but (i) and (ii) (b) All but (i), (ii), and (iii)
(c) All but (ii) and (v)
(d) Cannot be determined

16 Mock Test Paper

Directions for Questions 1 to 4: *Answer the questions on the basis of the information given below:*

Five cricket teams are playing against each other. Each team played with the other team at the most once and no match has ended in a draw. The following rules are applicable to the game:

(i) Each of the two participating teams put an equal amount of money in before the match. The team that wins the match takes away the total money that was put before the match while the looser gets nothing.

(ii) The total money won by any team at the end of all the matches is called the teams GAIN while the money lost by a team is called its LOSS.

(iii) No two teams won or lost the same number of matches.

(iv) For any team, the money put in before the match for any two matches is different.

(v) Team E won ₹17 against A and the total money involved in the match of C and D is ₹4.

(vi) The GAIN of A is equal to the LOSS of D.

(vii) The amount of money chipped in by any team is an integral amount in rupees and is not less than ₹4 or greater than ₹21.

(viii) The sum of all the money put in by each of the five teams is 55, 37, 40, 55, and 53 respectively

(ix) Neither the GAIN of any team that won at least one match nor the LOSS of any team that lost at least one match is less than ₹20 or more than ₹40.

(x) The number of matches won by D is equal to the number of matches lost by A. Similarly the number of matches lost by C is more than the number of matches lost by D.

1. The total money involved in the match in between B and C is?
   (a) 6 (b) 7
   (c) 8 (d) Cannot be determined
   (e) None of these
2. The team that won the maximum number of matches is
   (a) B (b) C
   (c) D (d) Cannot be determined
   (e) None of these
3. What is the total monetary loss of team A?
   (a) ₹35 (b) ₹36
   (c) ₹37 (d) Cannot be determined
   (e) None of these
4. The team that won the same number of bets as it lost is?
   (a) A (b) B
   (c) D (d) Cannot be determined
   (e) None of these

Directions for Questions 5 to 8: *Refer to the data given below (Table 16.1) to answer the following questions.*

The timetable of the second semester students of the year 2022 of an engineering institute is given

TABLE 16.1

Code of Course	Room	L&T	Lab Slots Slots	(Lecture) L	(Tutorial) T	(Practical) p	Credits
MA009	214	5a,5b,5c		2	1	0	8
MA006	213	4a,4b,4c		2	1	0	6
SI001	164	2a,2b,2c		3	1	0	8
MA002	213	3a,3b,3c		2	1	0	6
CS002	CSE	–	9b,8b,7b	0	1	3	5
MA001	213	2a,2b,2c		3	1	0	8
MA014	215	2a,2b,2c		3	1	0	8
SI003	113	1a,1b,1c		2	1	0	6
MA007	216	1a,1b,1c		2	1	0	6

Code of Course	Room	L&T	Lab Slots Slots	(Lecture) L	(Tutorial) T	(Practical) p	Credits
SI002	105	3a,3b,3c		3	1	0	8
MA008	216	6a,6b,6c		3	1	0	8
MA010	214	6a,6b,6c		2	1	0	6
MA011	215	5a,5b,5c		2	1	0	8
SI004	113	2a,2b,2c		3	1	0	8
MA004	214	1a,1b,1c		2	1	0	6
MA015	215	1a,1b,1c		3	0	0	6
EE001	EED	4a,4b,4c		2	1	0	6
SI005	113	3a,3b,3c		2	1	0	6
MA012	113	6a,6b,6c		2	1	0	6
SI006	113	5a,5b,5c		2	1	0	8
MA005	213	5a,5b,5c		3	1	0	8
MA013	113	4a,4b,4c		2	1	0	6
SI007	CSE	–	7a,8a,9a	0	0	3	3
CS001	CSE	–	7a.8b,9a	0	1	3	5
MA003	214	4a,4b,4c		2	1	0	6

Here the day slot a, b, c indicates 3 days in a week. The courses for which student opt must not clash with each other. Columns L, T, and P give the number of contact hours per week for each of Lecture, Tutorials, and Practicals. Columns credits indicate the number of credits given for each course. The structure of the academics is such that out of the above 25 courses, 3 are lab courses. A student taking admission in the institute has to choose 7 courses of which at least one will be a lab course. L and T slots are given by AB where A indicates the time slot and B indicates the day (Example: 2a indicates a time slot 2 and day a)

5. Ms. Dumbo wants to take the maximum possible number of lab courses, how much minimum credit can be earned in a given particular semester?
   (a) 37 (b) 38
   (c) 39 (d) 40
6. Mr. Weirdo takes MA012, MA004, and MA003 along with two lab courses, so which of the following two courses can he not take simultaneously?
   (a) MA007 and SI003
   (b) SI001 and MA009
   (c) SI001 and MA011
   (d) MA009 and SI007
7. Mr. Fool selects his courses with a minimum number of contact hours per week, so find the minimum number of contact hours the student needs to attend.
   (a) 22 hrs (b) 23 hrs
   (c) 24 hrs (d) 25 hrs
8. Mr. Dodo has taken MA004, MA001, MA002, MA006, MA005, MA008, and SI007. What will be true about him?
   (a) He has to attend a total of 24 hrs per week
   (b) He will earn 45 credits
   (c) He has to attend 15 hrs of lecture per week
   (d) All of the above

Directions for Questions 9 to 14: *The Indian Railways ran three types of trains between Bengaluru and Chennai on 12th January 2030. The trains were either Mail Trains, Passenger Trains or Express Trains. They are further classified by the Number of People the trains can carry, Namely Small Trains, Medium Trains, and Large Trains. It was found that of the 10000 People who rode these trains on that day, 40% went in Mail Trains, 52% in Passenger Trains while the rest went in Express Trains. The 10000 people are further divided into people who have a Bachelor's Degree, or who don't. The Ratio of the people in Small: Medium: Large Trains is 7:19:14 The table below gives information about the people traveling in these trains and those who don't have a Bachelor's Degree.*

	Mail Train	Passenger Train	Express Train	Total
Small	500	150	350	1000
Medium	800	2125	75	3000
Large	1200	725	75	2000
Total	2500	3000	500	6000

i. Of the People commuting in Large Trains, 70% of the surveyed people were in the Mail Train. Moreover, in Large Trains, all surveyed People who had completed a bachelor's degree were in either train Mail Trains or Express Trains.

ii. Among the people travelling in the Small Express Train, the number of people who had a bachelor's degree was 10% of the people who did not have a bachelor's degree.

iii. Among the people travelling in small Mail trains, The ratio of the people who had a bachelor's degree to those who did not was 1:5.

9. Out of The People travelling in Medium Trains who had completed their Bachelor's Degree, education, how many people were travelling in the Express Train?
(a) 30 (b) 120
(c) 150 (d) 15

10. The number of People who have a Bachelor's Degree and ride in Small Trains are what percentage of the total number of people?
(a) 7.5% (b) 10%
(c) 15% (d) 6.66%

11. The number of People who have a Bachelor's Degree and ride in Medium and Large Mail Trains are what percentage of the total number of people?
(a) 12% (b) 14%
(c) 16% (d) 18%

12. To commemorate the 1-year anniversary of the train journeys, the same route was followed for the exact same set of people. Nobody who did not have a bachelor's degree earlier had one now. The Small trains had been Discontinued due to low demand. The people who were in the small express and small mail trains earlier now travel in large passenger trains (both bachelor and non-bachelor degree people). Also, for both people with and without a bachelor's degree, 1/3rd of the people in the small passenger trains were split into 5 trains equally namely Large Mail, Large Express, Medium Mail, Medium Passenger and Medium Express trains.
The rest of the people who would travel in Small passenger Trains started travelling in new size Jumbo Trains, which are only available in Express Trains (for both bachelor and non-bachelor people)
What is the total number of people who are traveling in Medium Passenger trains?

13. To commemorate the 1-year anniversary of the train journeys, the same route was followed for the exact same set of people. Nobody who did not have a bachelor's degree earlier had one now. The Small trains had been Discontinued due to low demand. The people who were in the small express and small mail trains earlier now travel in large passenger trains (both bachelor and non-bachelor degree people). Also, for both people with and without a bachelor's degree, 1/3rd of the people in the small passenger trains were split into 5 trains equally namely Large Mail, Large Express, Medium Mail, Medium Passenger and Medium Express trains.
The rest of the people who would travel in Small passenger Trains started travelling in new size Jumbo Trains, which are only available in Express Trains (for both bachelor and non-bachelor people)
What is the difference between people with bachelor's degree traveling in Medium passanger trains and people without bachelors degree traveling in Large mail trains?

14. The very next day, the same passengers again traveled on the same route. However, the jumbo trains developed a fault and all the passengers of the Jumbo express trains were accomodated in passenger trains – either medium or large. What is the number of people who traveled in Passenger trains that day?

Directions for Questions 15 to 20: *In the heart of Bangalore, Mindworkzz has recently opened its new counseling office to boost the company's sales. To begin its operations, Mindworkzz hired a bunch of female employees and 210 male employees for different roles and positions. However these employees need to commute to the office on a daily basis. The HR team at Mindworkzz circulated a form to get data about its employees which included the distance of their residence from the office and the sport they liked. The HR team reviewed the employees data and figured that a lot of the employees reside within the 5 km radius from the office. Further it is known that few employees did not fill the form. The distance from the office for such employees was found to be greater than 5 kms. The head of HR Team, Mr Arun Chaturvedi, divided the employees in three categories on the basis of how far they live from the office, namely- 3 km radius, 4 km radius and 5 km radius. Employees were also asked whether they were cricket fans or football fans or neither. Nobody was a fan of cricket as well as football. Of those who answered, there were 70 cricket fans out of which 20 were women. Also, there were 130 football fans in the office out of which 100 were men. It is also assumed that those who did not fill the form didn't like any of the sports.*

Further, it known about the employees that-

i. The employees who live within 3 kms will also fall under the 4km & 5km bracket. Similarly, those who live within 4 km will also fall under the 5 km bracket.

ii. Few of the male employees that Mindworkzz hired live within the 5 km radius but do not fall in the 4 km radius. Some of the other men live under 4 kms but not under 5 kms.

iii. The number of cricket fans living within 4 kms is 45 more than the number of football fans living within 4 kms.

iv. 40% of the women who live within 4 kms did not mention their choice of sport. Also 50% of the men who live within 4 kms also did not mention their favorite sport.

v. All of the male employees live more than 3 kms away from the office. All the women cricket fans and 10 of the football fans live within 3 kms.

vi. All the men and two-thirds of women live within 5 kms of the office. Half of the women are living within 4 kms of the office.

vii. The number of women who filled the survey form and were fans of neither cricket nor football was seen to be a two-digit number.

15. How many female employees did Mindworkzz hire?
16. Which of the following information cannot be determined?
    (a). Number of female employees living within the 5km radius who did not mention their sport
    (b). Number of male employees living within the 4km radius who did not mention their sport
    (c). Number of female employees living within the 3km radius who did not mention their sport
    (d). Number of male cricket fans living within the 4km radius
17. What percentage of employees live within the 4km radius?
18. What is the number of female football fans who live within the 4 km radius?
19. How many male football fans live within 4 kms of Mindworkzz office?
20. What is the number of Males within the 5 km radius who are fans of neither cricket nor football?

17 Mock Test Paper

Directions for Questions 1 to 5: *Palak, Qusum, Rashmi, Shreya, Tanya, Umesh & Vivek are 7 friends who are connected on different social media platforms such as Facebook, Instagram, and LinkedIN. A pair is connected to each other on only one of these platforms – i.e. if two of them are connected on Linkedin with each other, then they are not connected on facebook or on instagram. The following information represents the number of connections they have amongst themselves.*

Palak has 1 follower on Instagram and 4 connections on LinkedIN. Rashmi has 1 follower on Instagram. Moreover it is known that Shreya, Tanya and Vivek are connected with 2,1, and 2 members respectively on LinkedIN. Meanwhile, Umesh has 1 friend on Facebook and Vivek has 3 followers on Instagram. Assume that all connections are two-way connections: i.e. if for instance A follows B on Instagram, B will also follow A on Instagram. Likewise friendships on Facebook are mutual and connections on LinkedIn are also mutual.

The following facts are also known about the above people:

1. Palak, Qusum and Rashmi are connected with each other on LinkedIN.
2. Palak, Shreya, and Umesh are friends with Tanya on Facebook.
3. Rashmi and Vivek are friends on Facebook.
4. Everyone who is a friend of Palak on Facebook follows Qusum on Instagram and every Instagram follower of Qusum is friends with Palak on Facebook.
5. Every Facebook friend of Qusum follows Palak on Instagram and every Instagram follower of Palak is a facebook friend of Qusum.

1. Who are Vivek's connections on Instagram?
   (a) Palak, Qusum and Umesh
   (b) Shreya, Tanya and Umesh
   (c) Palak, Shreya and Umesh
   (d) Qusum, Shreya and Tanya
2. Which of the following pairs are connected on the same platform?
   (a) (Qusum, Rashmi) and (Shreya,Tanya)
   (b) (Rashmi,Tanya) and (Shreya,Vivek)
   (c) (Palak,Vivek) and (Tanya,Umesh)
   (d) (Qusum,Tanya) and (Umesh,Vivek)
3. Who is a connection of Palak on Instagram?
   (a) Shreya
   (b) Tanya
   (c) Umesh
   (d) Vivek
4. How many FB connections does Tanya have?
5. Who is a connection of Rashmi on Instagram?
   (a) Tanya
   (b) Qusum
   (c) Umesh
   (d) Shreya

Directions for Questions 6 to 10: *Mindworkzz wanted to publish its latest mock test for students preparing for CAT. Three faculties Pallav, Shaurya, and Anshuman are tasked with selecting questions from a pool of 13 questions (Q1 to Q13). Questions can be created by Arun Sharma or by one of the three faculties. Each of the faculties either approves or disapproves a question that is shown to them. Their decisions lead to eventual acceptance or rejection of the question in the manner described below.*

If a question is created by Arun Sharma, it is reviewed first by Pallav, and then by Shaurya. If both of them approve the question, then the question is accepted and is not reviewed by Anshuman. If both disapprove the question, it is rejected and is not reviewed by Anshuman. If one of them approves the question and the other disapproves it, then the question is reviewed by Anshuman. Then the question is accepted only if he approves it.

A question created by one of the faculties is decided upon by the other two. If a question is created by Pallav, then it is first reviewed by Shaurya. If Shaurya approves the question, then it is accepted. Otherwise, it is reviewed by Anshuman. The question is then accepted only if Anshuman approves it. A similar process is followed for questions created by Shaurya, whose questions are first reviewed by Anshuman, and then by Pallav only if Anshuman disapproves it. Questions created by Anshuman are first reviewed by Pallav, and then, if required, by Shaurya.

The following facts are known about the review process after its completion.

A. Q2, Q6, Q9, Q11, and Q12 were rejected and the other questions were accepted.
B. Pallav reviewed only Q2, Q3, Q4, Q6, Q8, Q10, Q11, and Q13.
C. Shaurya reviewed only Q2, Q4, Q6 through Q9, Q12, and Q13.
D. Anshuman reviewed only Q1 through Q5, Q7, Q8, Q9, Q11, and Q12.

6. How many questions were definitely created by Pallav?
7. How many questions were definitely created by Anshuman?
8. How many questions were definitely created by Arun Sharma?
9. How many questions were definitely rejected by Shaurya?
10. What is the maximum possible number of questions created by Anshuman & Shaurya?

Directions for Questions 11 to 15: *Few counselors of Mindworkzz are tasked to enroll students for its CAT preparation program. To meet their monthly targets for February, Ritika, offline sales head at Mindworkzz, gives her subordinates, Fatima, Kavita and Jyoti two days to enroll the students. They are supposed to call the leads generated through different mediums and explain to them the benefits of the course. On a particular day, each of them can call any number of students. However, if the student reports the number as spam then that counselor will not be able to call any other student on that particular day. The counselors need to update the remarks of students on the company database. The conversion rate of a counselor is the number of enrollments as a percentage of the number of students called.*

A. All the counselors made an equal number of calls over the two days and enrolled 20 students each. Moreover, Jyoti made an equal number of calls on both days along with getting equal enrolments.
B. The first call Kavita made after being assigned this task was reported as spam.
C. Since Fatima decided to work from home on the second day, she was able to make 30 more calls because of increased efficiency.
D. Being more experienced than any other counselor, Fatima's conversion rate was double that of Jyoti on the first day. However her conversion rate was 75% of that of Jyoti on the second day.

11. What was the total number of calls made by counselors over the two days?
12. What was the average conversion rate of the less experienced counselors?
13. Who had the best conversion rate on any of the days?
14. Who showed maximum growth in their conversion rate over the two days?
15. How many students did Fatima enroll on the second day?

Directions for Questions 16 to 20: *There are five major Stock baskets that investors use for their investment/ Trading purposes. These stock baskets invest in different companies and give the shareholders a good return on their investment. During a week, three such investors, Shaurya, Pallav and Shubuti decided to make use of these baskets to earn themselves a good deal of money. Buying of the baskets takes place only at the start of the session at 9:15 am and can only be sold at the end of the session at 3:30 pm. Also, the opening price on a day of a stock is the same as the closing price of that stock on the previous day.*

The following are the stock baskets that these investors use:

Basket Name	Stocks in the Basket
Reliance SB (RB)	Reliance Ent, Coal India
Adani SB (AB)	Adani Ent, Coal India
Tata SB (TB)	Tata Steel, Coal India
Mixed SB (MB)	RelianceEnt, Adani Ent, Tata Steel,Coal India
Invesco (IB)	Reliance Ent, Adani Ent, Tata Steel

The following information is also known:

A. The value of Coal India on the opening of day 1 is 500 and Reliance is 60% of that of Coal India. Adani Ent and Tata Steel are two-thirds and one-thirds of that of Reliance in no particular order.
B. Closing price of all the stocks on the first two days is an integer.
C. Coal India showed a growth of 4% on 1st day and 5% on the second day. Meanwhile, Reliance Ent showed a 5% growth on the 1st day and 20% on the second day. Adani Ent showed 10% growth on all three days. Tata steel showed 20% growth on the first day and a dip of 5% on the second day. Because of data released by RBI, The stock market went up by 10% on the third day and this growth was uniform.

The amount received at the end of the day for each person is given below:

Day	Shaurya	Pallav	Shubhuti
1	1575	1830	1830
2	1448	1394	2068
3	2134	2274.8	1883.2

16. How many different types of baskets were traded on the first day?
17. What was the sum of opening price of Adani Ent and Tata Ent on the second day?
18. What is the percentage growth of the Reliance Basket over the three day period?
19. What was the basket combination for Pallav on the third day?
    (a) Adani Basket + Reliance Basket
    (b) Tata Basket + Reliance Basket
    (c) Adani Basket + Mixed Basket
    (d) Tata Basket + Invesco
20. Which basket had the maximum participation?
    (a) AB & TB
    (b) AB & MB
    (c) MB & TB
    (d) AB only

18 Mock Test Paper

Directions for Questions 1 to 3: *Refer to the data given below and answer the following questions:*

The captain of a ship played a trick on the sailors. He claimed that he can predict the future. He has three caskets with him and in each casket there are three plates with a single non-zero digit inscribed on each plate. No two plates have the same number and no casket contains two plates with digits totaling ten. Further, the total of three cards in the first casket is greater by two than the total in the second casket and by four than that of third casket. When any sailor asks for his prediction, the captain tells him to randomly pick a plate from the three caskets. Before making the prediction, the captain totals the digits on the three plates and charges the same amount from the sailor. On a day sailor paid seven rupee for his prediction.

1. What is the lowest payment possible?
   (a) ₹5 (b) ₹7
   (c) ₹6 (d) ₹8
2. What is the maximum possible amount that anyone can pay?
   (a) ₹22 (b) ₹23
   (c) ₹24 (d) ₹25
3. Which of the following payments can never be made by any customer?
   (a) ₹19 (b) ₹16
   (c) ₹17 (d) ₹23

Directions for Questions 4 to 8: *Refer to the data given below (Table 18.1) and answer the following questions:*

In an Inter School meet six schools from a city participated in "PIN POCKET TOURNMENT" where in only one candidate from each school participated in the tournament. The rules of the game are as follows:

TABLE 18.1

Blue	Black	Pink	Yellow	Green	Purple	Indigo	White	Violet	Red
11	12	13	14	15	16	17	18	19	20

In the game 'PIN POCKET' ten different coloured balls are used to play on board with six pockets. If a Player manages to pocket a ball in any of these pockets then such a shot is known as G-Pots. If a Player manages to pocket 2 balls then it is said that he has made 2 G-Pots. A player uses a stick to pocket the balls in G-Pot.

Table 18.1 shows the number assigned to different color balls.

Special feature of this game is that balls are further hit in a particular sequence by the first ball depending upon the number of the ball which is hit first. Sequences are given as follows:

1. *If a Prime numbered ball is hit first, then all prime numbered balls are hit in an increasing sequence followed by balls which are numbered in a sequential order. For example: If ball number 13 is hit first then it follows the sequence 13-17-19-11-12-14-15-16-18-20.*
2. *If a composite numbered ball is hit first, then balls with a composite number are hit first in an increasing sequential order For example: If ball number 16 is hit first then the sequence followed is: 16-18-20-12-14-15-17-19-11-13*
3. *The ball numbered 11 has a special property. If the ball numbered 11 is hit first then all balls with a number which are a perfect square, or a perfect square +1 or a perfect square –1 are hit first in an increasing order, followed by balls numbered in an increasing sequential order from the last number hit.*

TABLE 18.2

Player's Name	1st Ball Hit	Number of G-Pots Made	G-Pot Number	Ball	Total Hit	Balls	Total	Points
Rahul	12	1	15		4			
Tarun		2			2		56	
Akhil	14	2			4		97	
Samar	18	2	12,?		5		106	
Ritesh	11	1			10		168	
Mahim	11	2	19,?				188	

Example: *If the first ball hit is 11 then the sequence followed is: 11-15-16-17-18-19-20-12-13-14.*

A player scores points in this game depending upon the number of the balls he has hit and the balls he is able to pocket in any of the 6 G-Pots. Total points scored by a player is the sum of the number of the balls he managed to hit plus the bonus points of ball numbers which he manages to pocket in the G-Pot. Suppose that he hits ball number 15 first and a total of 5 balls (i.e. sequence of balls would be 15-16-18-20-12. Further he managed to pocket ball number 18 and 20 in G-Pot. Then total points scored by that player = 15 + 16 + 18 + 18 + 20 + 20 + 12 =119 points.

In the above example, first ball hit is ball number 15, Number of G-Pots made is 2, G -Pot ball numbers are 18 and 20. Total balls hit is 5 and total points scored is the sum of number of balls hits and balls among them which are pocketed (G-pot) as bonus points.

A player is given only one chance to hit the ball and he can hit a maximum of 10 balls which are on board. Table 18.2 above shows the overall performance of the players in a tournament of 'PIN POCKET'. A player cannot G-pot a ball more than once.

4. Which of the following ball can be G-pocketed twice considering the overall performance of six players in the tournament?
   (a) Blue
   (b) Black
   (c) Violet
   (d) Pink
5. Which of the following balls do maximum number of players in the tournament hit?
   (a) White
   (b) Red
   (c) Pink
   (d) Green
6. What is the sum of the total points scored by all six players excluding the person whose name begins and ends with the same alphabet?
   (a) 509
   (b) 489
   (c) 499
   (d) Indeterminable
7. What is the colour of the second ball that Mahim has potted?
   (a) Green
   (b) Indigo
   (c) White
   (d) Yellow
8. What is the difference between the total points between the second highest scorer and the second lowest scorer?
   (a) 90
   (b) 92
   (c) 96
   (d) 71

Directions for Questions 9 to 12: *Refer to the data given below (Figures 18.1 and 18.2) to answer the questions that follow:*

Bar chart 1 (Figure 18.1) gives the number of Transponders (T) in each Satellite (S) of the INSAT 2C geostationary satellite. Bar chart 2 (Figure 18.2) given below gives the number of Transponders in a Sister Satellites (SS). Each Sister Satellite is made up of a combination of satellites such that the number of satellites used for each sister satellite is not more than five. Each sister satellite can contain more than one satellite of the same type.

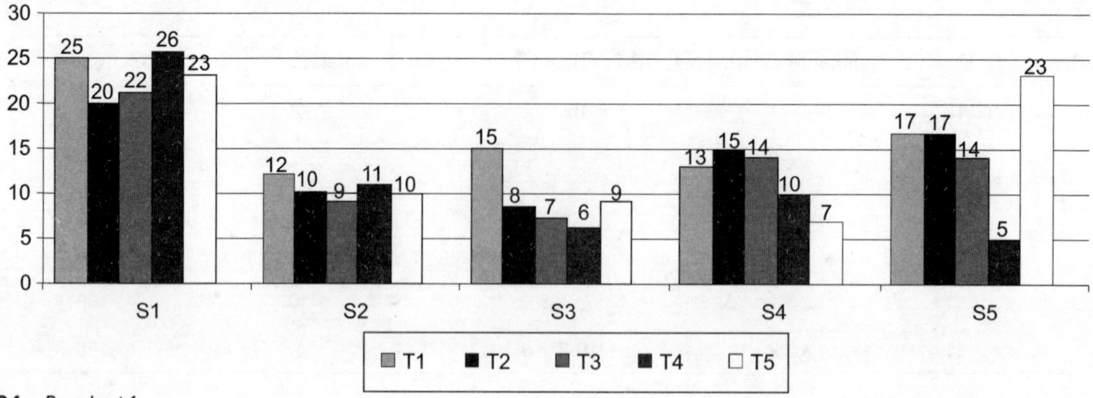

FIGURE 18.1 *Bar chart 1*

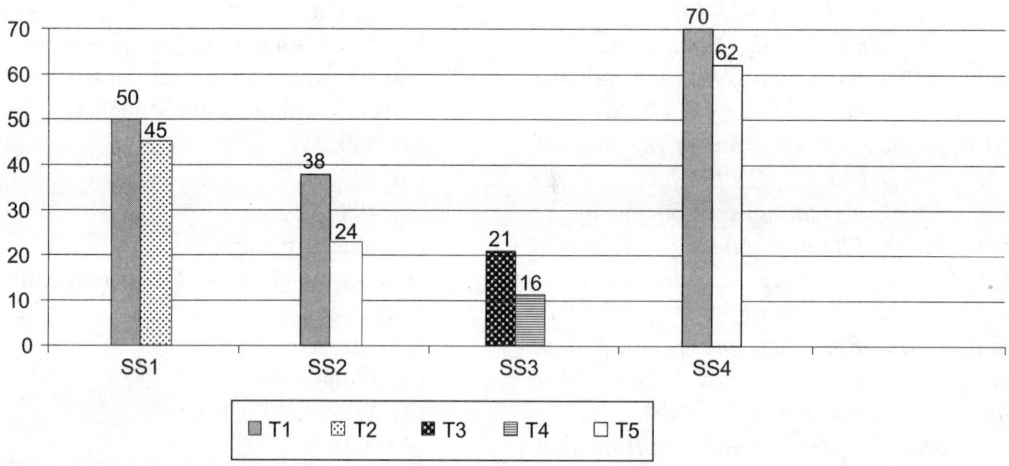

FIGURE 18.2 *Bar chart 2*

9. For a particular Transponder, if Sister Satellite 1 and Sister Satellite 2 are used then how many satellites are used in the transponder?
   (a) 1
   (b) 2
   (c) 3
   (d) 4
10. What types of Satellites are used in Sister Satellite 3?
   (a) S3 and S5
   (b) S3 and S4
   (c) S2 and S5
   (d) S1 and S2
11. In transponders consisting of SS3 and SS4, what is the total number of T2 used?
   (a) 79
   (b) 80
   (c) 81
   (d) 83
12. If a particular system contains 63 T4s and less than 80 T5s. Which of these can be the possible combination of satellites used?
   (a) S2, S3, and S5
   (b) S1, S2, and S5
   (c) S2, S3, and S4
   (d) Both (b) and (c) but not (a)

Directions for Questions 13 to 16: *Answer the questions on the basis of the information and the figures given below:*

McD is a leading fast food chain. It sells four fast food products, Veggie (A), Chicken (B), Salsa (C), and Fishy (D). 4, 5, 6, and 7 man-hours are respectively required to dish out the four products. McD Lucknow has 6 workers P, Q, R, S, T, and U and the working days are Sunday through Saturday, eight hours each. All the production started on Sunday and finished on Saturday. Also, once a worker took up a job, he did not leave it, transfer it, take a break or do anybody else's job until his job was complete. Chart A (Figure 18.3) given below gives the number of units produced on any given day and chart B (Figure 18.4)gives the number of man hours required to complete the corresponding units of work on that particular day.

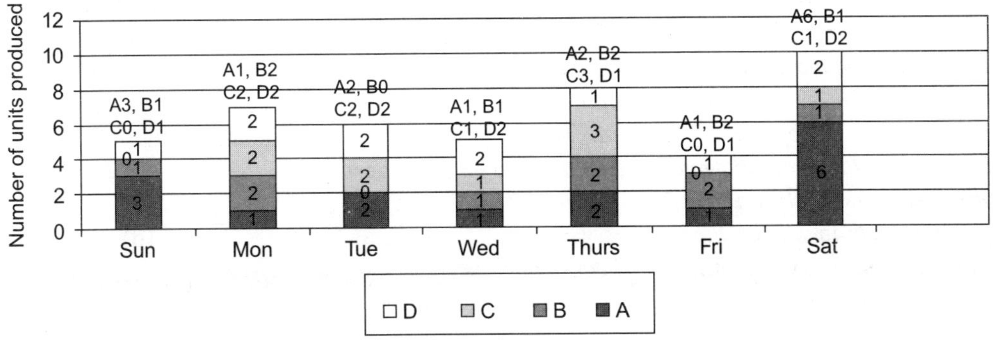

FIGURE 18.3 *Chart A*

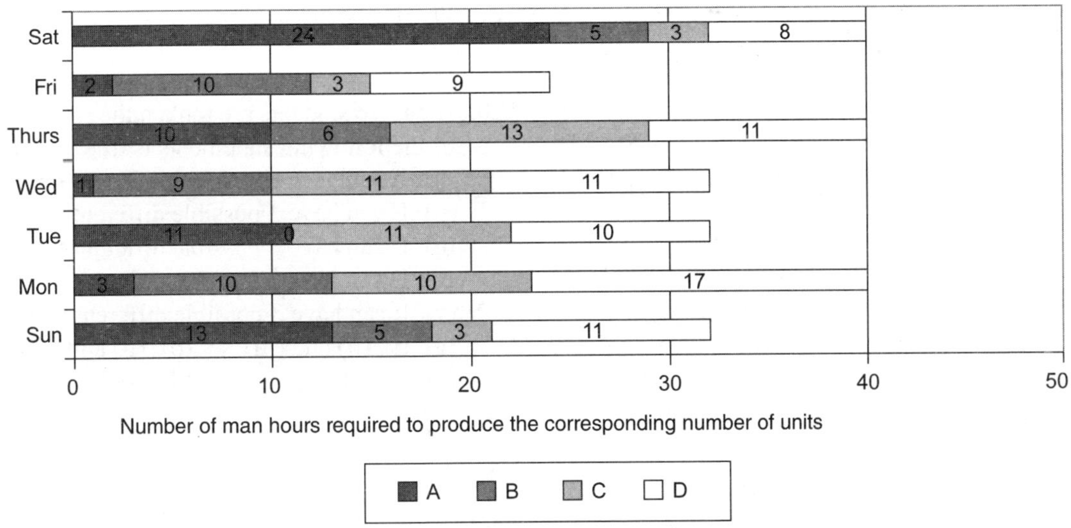

FIGURE 18.4 *Chart B*

The following graphs are to be read as follows: Say for product A, we need to find the number of units produced on Sunday and the number of hours that went into producing it. Then chart A gives the number of units of A produced on Sunday, i.e. 3 and chart B gives the corresponding number of hours required to produce those 3 units, i.e. 13 man hours.

Since it is not humanly possible to work for all seven days, the following data gives the leave record of the six workers:

P	Q	R	S	T	U
Tue	Sun	Mon	Sun	Tue	Wed
Fri	Thurs	Wed	Fri	Fri	Sat

13. On which product did R work on Thursday if he worked only on product D on Saturday
    (a) A and B (b) A and D
    (c) A and C (d) Cannot be determined
    (e) None of these
14. If T and P completed the production of units of A and B respectively at the end of Thursday then on which other product did T work on that day?
    (a) A (b) D
    (c) C (d) Cannot be determined
    (e) None of these
15. If Q did not work on product C on Tuesday then find the product(s) on which S worked on Monday. (You may use data from the previous question)
    (a) A and C (b) C and D
    (c) A and D (d) Cannot be determined
    (e) None of these
16. How many units in all did P manufacture in the given week (You may use data from the previous question)
    (a) 5 (b) 6
    (c) 7 (d) 8
    (e) None of these

Directions for Questions 17 to 20: *Refer to the given data (Table 18.3) to answer the questions that follow:*

Prof. Sharma is the head of the department of Electronics and Communication Engineering at a reputed engineering college in India. He wanted to rank six students on the basis of their total marks obtained in engineering in their second, third, and fourth year such that the student with the higher total in all the three years combined got a higher rank. The following table (Table 18.3) gives the marks of the six students, A, B, C, D, E, and F in each of the three years and also the average of all the six students in a particular year. While compiling the results, Prof. Sharma noted that all the six students had marks that were distinct integers, different from each other in all the three years. Some cells in the following table have intentionally been left blank. All marks were out of 100.

TABLE 18.3

Students	Marks Obtained in Each Term		
	2nd year	3rd year	4th year
A	100		
B	98	96	93
C	88	99	94
D	92		97
E		87	
F		91	95
Average =>	91	90	93

17. If the rank of A and D is the same then the difference in the score of E and F in the second year is:
    (a) 2 (b) 3
    (c) 4 (d) Cannot be determined
18. Which student among the following is ranked the lowest?
    (a) A (b) F
    (c) B (d) E

Additional information: The score of E and F differ by 4 in the 2nd year.

19. If the total score of four students is equal then how many possible number of scores are there for all the six students?
    (a) 5 (b) 6
    (c) 7 (d) None of these
20. If no two students are ranked the same then which of the following statements is true?
    (i) A can have possible 3 different total scores
    (ii) B can have 3 possible different total scores
    (iii) C can have 3 possible different total scores
    (iv) D can have 3 possible different total scores
    (v) E can have 3 possible different total scores
    (a) (i), (ii) and (iii) (b) (ii) and (iii)
    (c) Only (i) (d) (i), (iv) and (v)

19 Mock Test Paper

Directions for Questions 1 to 5: *The following table gives us the information about the weight carried by the six tourists Aman, Binay, Charu, Dinesh, Ervin and Fahim at four different airports Mumbai, Delhi, Chennai and Bangalore. Maximum permissible weights in these airports are 40a, 50b, 60c and 80d respectively, where a, b, c, d are real numbers. It is also given that weight carried by Aman at the Mumbai airport is not less than that carried by him at the Delhi or Chennai airports but not more than that carried by him at the Bangalore airport. This holds true for the weights carried by Binay, Charu, Dinesh, Ervin and Fahim.*

	Mumbai	Delhi	Chennai	Bangalore
Aman	10a	20b	8c	25d
Binay	20a	10b	16c	15d
Charu	25a	15b	20c	20d
Dinesh	10a	18b	25c	30d
Ervin	20a	32b	10c	10d
Fahim	30a	12b	20c	35d

1. If Aman carried equal weights at the Delhi and Chennai airports, then find the ratio of weight carried by Aman at the Delhi airport and weight carried by Charu at the Chennai airport.
2. A passenger is said to be a light weight carrying passenger, if he carried 30% or less weight of the maximum permissible weight at that airport. Out of these six passengers how many passengers are considered as light weight group passenger in at least two airports?
3. If Dinesh carried 30 kg weight at the Bangalore airport, then the maximum possible weight that Aman could carry at the Mumbai airport is = _ kg.
4. The difference between the weight carried by Binay at the Mumbai and the Delhi airports is D.
   How many passengers (among these six passengers) definitely carried lesser weight than D at the Delhi airport?
5. If the value of D, mentioned in the previous question was equal to 120, then how many passengers definitely carried a weight less than 75 kg at the Delhi airport?

Directions for Questions 6 to 8: *In Encore, there were four events organized by the institute Dancing, Robotics, Singing, Bike riding. The graph given below shows the number of students of two different disciplines – EC and CS who participated in an event and number of students who participated only in that event.*

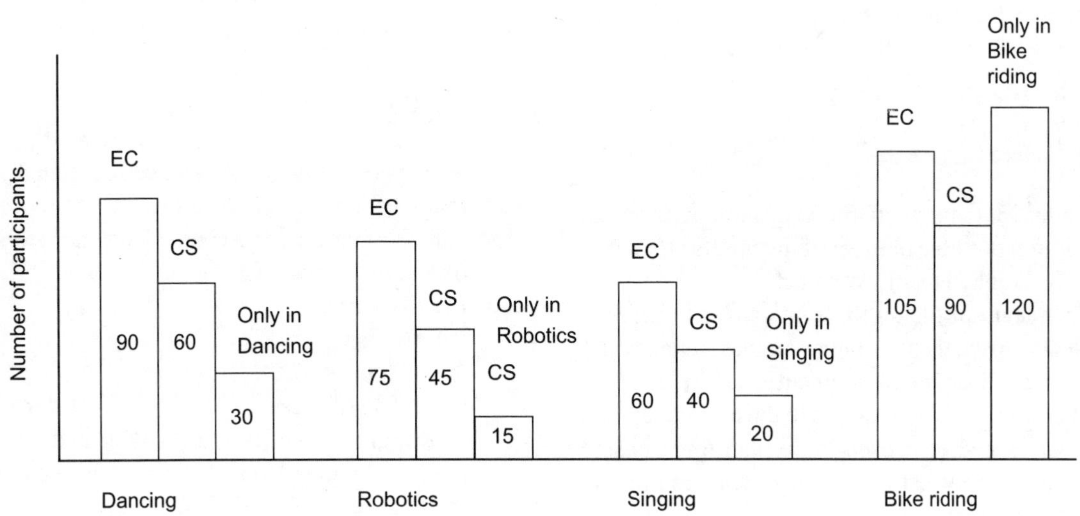

6. What can be the minimum number of students of EC branch who participated in Encore?
   (a) 100
   (b) 120
   (c) 110
   (d) Cannot be determined.
7. What can be the maximum number of students of EC branch who participated in Encore?
8. The Minimum number of CS students who participated in Encore.

Directions for Questions 9 to 12: *64 teams participated in the FIFA World Cup 2050. There were a total of six rounds in the tournament–I, II, III, IV, semifinals, final. Each round was knock out in nature, which means that the winner advanced to the next round and the loser got eliminated from the tournament. The draw of the matches in the tournament were as follows:*

1st round: 1st match was played between the 1st ranked team and the 64th ranked team. 2nd match was played between the 2nd highest team and 63rd number team and so on. The 32nd match of the first round was the match between the 32nd ranked team and the 33rd ranked team. 2nd round: The 1st match was played between the winner of the 1st match of the 1st round and the winner of the 32nd match of the first round, the second match of the 2nd round was played between the winner of the 2nd match and the winner of the 31st match of the first round team and and so on.

A similar pattern was followed for the matches of the next rounds as well.

If a lower ranking team beat a higher ranking team in any match of any round then it was called an 'upset'. In the tournament the 1st ranked team was considered to be the highest ranked team and so on.

9. If the rank 1 team was the winner of the tournament then, which among the following could be the team it beat in the final of the tournament?
   (a) 22
   (b) 56
   (c) 4
   (d) 13
10. If rank 23 team won the tournament then the minimum possible number of the upsets created by the 23rd ranked team would be?
11. If each team of the tournament caused or faced at least one upset, then the highest ranked team, which could have won the tournament, was?
12. If there were only four upsets in the tournament and no team faced or caused more than three upsets, then find the lowest ranked team who could have won the tournament.
    (a) 16 (b) 32
    (c) 64 (d) 33

Directions for Questions 13 to 16: *The IIM Lucknow management was assessing the performance of the top five students in last five class tests . Abhay, Balwinder, Chetan, David and Faraz are the top five students of the class. For each of the five tests, the table below gives the names of the three highest scoring students in that test, along with their respective scores in that test, mentioned in the brackets alongside. The last column gives the percentage of the total class score made by the given three students together. The management also observed that in a particular test the scores of no students are equal. There are a total 10 students in the class.*

The college management has the following two parameters to judge the performance of each student:

A. Consistency value (C.V.) which is the median of all the five scores of the concerned student.
B. Intelligence value (I.V.) which is the sum of the highest and the lowest scores of the concerned student.

Test	Highest Marks	Second Highest Marks	Third Highest Marks	Percentage of Total Score
1.	Abhay (90)	Balwinder (55)	Chetan (58)	70
2.	David (60)	Faraz (56)	Abhay (40)	65
3.	Balwinder (75)	Faraz (52)	David (27)	70
4.	David (66)	Abhay (54)	Faraz (36)	65
5.	Chetan (70)	Balwinder (62)	Abhay (50)	70

13. Which of the following student had the highest value of C.V.?
    (a) Chetan (b) David
    (c) Abhay (d) Balwinder
14. The exact value of C.V. can be calculated for how many of the given five students?
15. Which of the students cannot have the lowest value of I.V. in the five tests?
    (a) Balwinder
    (b) Chetan
    (c) David
    (d) None of these
16. In the given five tests Balwinder and Chetan together accounted for at most what percentage of the total score of the class?

(a) 31.2% (b) 39.36%
(c) 34.5% (d) 33.6%

Directions for Questions 17 to 20: *Answer the questions on the basis of the information given below.*

There is a group of 200 students, where each student studies one or more of the three subjects among Aeronautics, Biotechnology, and Cryogenics. The number of students studying Cryogenics is more than the number of students studying Aeronautics, which, in turn, is more than the number of students who study Biotechnology, which, in turn, is more than the number of students who study exactly two of the three subjects, which, in turn, is more than the number of students who study all the three subjects. It is known that at least one student studies all the three subjects.

17. What is the maximum number of students who study Biotechnology?
(a) 166 (b) 165
(c) 150 (d) 149
18. What is the minimum number of students who study Biotechnology?
(a) 67 (b) 68
(c) 69 (d) 70
19. If it is known that exactly half the students study Cryogenics, what is the maximum number of students who study all the three?
(a) 30 (b) 31
(c) 32 (d) 33
20. What is the maximum number of students who study only Aeronautics?
(a) 100 (b) 99
(c) 98 (d) 97

20 Mock Test Paper

Directions for Questions 1 to 4: *Answer the questions based upon the information given below (Figure 20.1)*

Mr. Sharma's home was full of rats. The rat kingdom consisted of five provinces (Mr. Sharma's five rooms in his home). The Rat kingdom decided to have a rat race to decide who the fastest rat was. As per the rat rules, the fastest rat was the heir to the throne of the rat king. Ten rats were called from the five different provinces in Mr. Sharma's home to contest for the race. The ten rats were given the tag of R1, R2, R3, and so on till R10. Similarly the province that they belonged to was tagged as P1, P2, P3, P4, and P5. Rat 1, 2 belonged to P1, rat 3, 4 belonged to P2, and so on till P5. A total of three races were held. The rats that finished 1st, 2nd, 3rd, and so on till 10th were rewarded 10, 9, 8, and so on till 1 point respectively in every race. No two rats got the same points in any race. The total of all the three races for the two rats of each province is shown in the bar chart above:

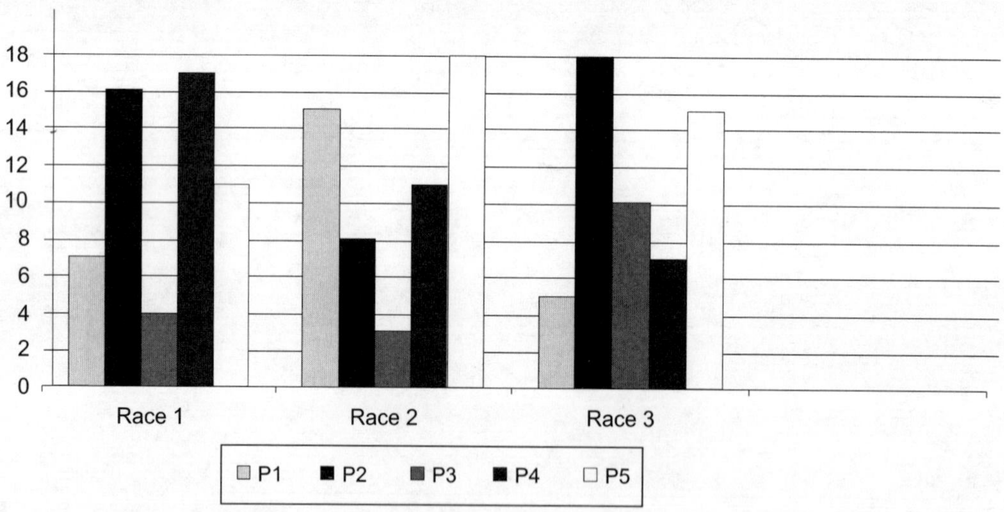

FIGURE 20.1

1. Which of the following rats might have finished third in race 1?
   (a) R7
   (b) R8
   (c) R9
   (d) Either of (a) or (b)
2. If in race 1, R1 finished before R5 but after R6 while R3 finished before R9 but after R10 then which of the following statements is definitely false?
   (i) R1 secured 8th position
   (ii) R2 secured 7 points
   (iii) R3 secured 5th position
   (iv) R4 secured 9 points
   (v) The winner of race 1 was R5

   (a) (i), (ii) and (iv)
   (b) (i), (ii) and (iii)
   (c) (i), (ii) and (v)
   (d) All but (iii)
3. Which of the following statements is true? (Take into consideration the data from the previous question.)
   (a) The exact position of R7 cannot be determined
   (b) The exact points secured by R8 cannot be determined
   (c) Both of the above
   (d) None of the above
4. If no rat finished at the same position in any of the three races then which of the following statements is true?

(a) R6 finished 9th in race 2 while R5 finished 8th in race 1
(b) R1 finished 6th in race 1 while R5 finished 4th in race 3
(c) R5 finished 10th in race 1 while R6 finished 4th in race 3
(d) Both (a) and (b)

Directions for Questions 5 to 8: *On the basis of the information given below (Table 20.1), answer the questions that follow:*

A railway traffic scheduler has to schedule train timings from 0800 hrs from Lucknow to Pune, Kanpur, Agra, and back. The rules for the railway signaling are as given below:

(i) No train arrives at Lucknow or departs on days 1/3/5/7 at 0845 hrs apart from train number AMS005
(ii) The train from the same origin and to the same destination should be maintained with a difference of at least one hour
(iii) There is only one train arriving or departing at 1215 hrs. If we go directly from Lucknow to Kanpur, the time taken is less than two hours but more than one hour.
(iv) Train number AMS008 reaches Lucknow after train number AMS006 and before train number AMS011
(v) Time taken for a train to travel between any two cities is the same in both directions

Due to a technical snag, some data was lost from the railway traffic scheduler and the following table could be extracted from the computer:

TABLE 20.1

Train Number	Origin	Destination	Via	Departure	Arrival	Time Taken in Hours	Days Operated
AMS008	Kanpur	Lucknow	Jaipur	0530			Daily
AMS001	Lucknow	Kanpur	Jaipur	0800			Daily
AMS015	Kanpur	Lucknow	Udaipur	0635		3:55	Daily
AMS003	Pune	Lucknow	Raipur	0415	0830	4:15	Daily
AMS006	Agra	Lucknow	Bangalore	0555	0900	3:05	Daily
AMS022	Lucknow	Agra	Hyderabad	1245	1630	3:45	Daily
AMS009	Lucknow	Agra	Bangalore	0945	1250	3:05	Daily
AMS010	Lucknow	Pune	Nagpur	1000	1405	4:05	Daily
AMS002	Lucknow	Agra	—	—	1000	—	1/3/5/7
AMS007	Pune	Lucknow	—	—	0930	—	1/3/5/7
AMS011	Agra	Lucknow	—	—	1015	—	1/3/5/7
AMS012	Lucknow	Kanpur	—	—	1125	—	2/4/6
AMS004	Kanpur	Lucknow	—	—	0815	—	2/4/6
AMS014	Lucknow	Pune	—	—	13:35	—	1/3/5/7
AMS016	Pune	Lucknow	—	0810	—	—	2/4/6
AMS018	Lucknow	Kanpur	Udaipur	1130	1525	3:55	Daily
AMS005	Lucknow	Pune	—	0845	—	—	2/4/6
AMS019	Lucknow	Pune	Raipur	1200	1615	4:15	Daily
AMS020	Agra	Lucknow	—	1030	—	—	2/4/6
AMS013	Agra	Lucknow	Hyderabad	0730	1115	3:45	Daily
AMS021	Pune	Lucknow	Nagpur	0825	1230	4:05	Daily
AMS023	Kanpur	Lucknow	—	1105	—	—	1/3/5/7
AMS017	Lucknow	Agra	—	1100	—	—	2/4/6
AMS024	Lucknow	Kanpur	—	1300	—	—	2/4/6

1-Monday 2-Tuesday 3-Wednesday 4-Thursday 5-Friday 6-Saturday 7-Sunday

Railway traffic control data sheets tell that at the Lucknow station the time difference between any two arrivals/departures or in between any arrival and departure is 15 minutes.

5. At what time will the train from Lucknow to Kanpur via Jaipur reach its destination?
(a) 1000 hrs (b) 1145 hrs
(c) 1130 hrs (d) 1200 hrs
(e) Cannot be determined

6. What time the train AMS017 from Lucknow shall reach Agra?
(a) 1405 hrs (b) 1145 hrs
(c) 1245 hrs (d) 1300 hrs
(e) Cannot be determined

7. When does train number AMS012 depart from its place of origin? (Assume some trains are delayed on the day)
(a) 0830 hrs (b) 0845 hrs
(c) 0930 hrs (d) None of these

8. Find out the time when train number AMS016 from Pune reaches Lucknow.
   (a) 0945 hrs (b) 1005 hrs
   (c) 1030 hrs (d) 1045 hrs

Directions for Questions 9 to 12: *Refer to the data (Tables 20.2 and 20.3) to answer the questions:*

Bell computers manufacture computers and peripherals. Due to their latest induction into the Indian market, they have just one showroom where they sell their products. It may be noted that not all computers manufactured are put for sale in the showroom and not all computers that are put in the showroom are sold. If a computer is not sold in a particular month then it continues to be displayed in the showroom until it is sold out. Table 20.2 gives the partial data from the month of January through September.

The table (Table 20.3) gives the sales figures from January through September with respect to its month of manufacture. A '#' symbol in the table indicates that no computers remain to be sold in that particular month as the stock has been exhausted in an earlier month.

Assume: All computers manufactured during Jan to April are put up for sale. Also, January was the first month when the company started its operations.

TABLE 20.2

Month	Computers Manufactured	Computers Put in Showroom	Computers Sold	Computers Unsold
Feb	1478		1542	268
Sept	1753		1440	
Aug	1545			
May		2182		
Jan	1563	1563		
June	1467			
Mar		1421		373
July	1254		1077	
Apr	1496			459

TABLE 20.3

		Months in which Computers are Sold								
		Jan	Feb	Mar	Apr	May	June	July	Aug	Sept
Month of manufacture of computer	Jan	1231		136	19		1	#	#	#
	Feb	—	1389		41	4	3		2	1
	Mar	—	—	875		86	49	23	6	#
	Apr	—	—	—	1236	131	78	26	21	3
	May	—	—	—	—	1548	107	45	17	0
	June	—	—	—	—	—	1353	9	0	
	July	—	—	—	—	—	—	973	146	63
	Aug	—	—	—	—	—	—	—	1327	79
	Sept	—	—	—	—	—	—	—	—	1243

9. What is the number of unsold computers in the outlet after April?
   (a) 777 (b) 780
   (c) 782 (d) Cannot be determined
   (e) None of these

10. If the selling price of one computer in the month of its manufacture is ₹500, and it increases by 10% every month thereafter due to inflation; what is the revenue earned from the sales of computers in April?
    (a) 718140 (b) 718142
    (c) 718136 (d) 718149
    (e) 718149.5

11. How many computers manufactured in Jan. were sold in May?
    (a) 23
    (b) 17
    (c) 26
    (d) 19
    (e) None of these

12. How many computers manufactured in Feb remained unsold in Mar?
    (a) 71 (b) 64
    (c) 68 (d) 52
    (e) 48

Directions for Questions 13 to 16: *Answer the questions on the basis of the information given below:*

The following table gives the time in minutes taken by five people, Adam, Barbie, Chandler, Dopey, and Estella, to complete five different questions in data interpretation, 1, 2, 3, 4, and 5. Any person can do any of the above mentioned questions but one person can do only one question.

TABLE 20.4

	Question				
	1	2	3	4	5
Adam	38	44	29	57	28
Barbie	31	42	53	24	39
Chandler	42	53	51	27	36
Dopey	25	36	38	33	49
Estella	38	39	41	47	45

13. If no two persons can work simultaneously and there is no time gap in between two consecutive work sessions, then how much time will it take to complete all the questions in the worst case?
(a) 4 hr 10 min (b) 4 hr 15 min
(c) 4 hr 20 min (d) Cannot be determined
14. Keeping all the conditions of the above question same, how little time will be taken to complete the five questions in the best case?
(a) 2 hr 31 min (b) 2 hrs 33 min.
(c) 2 hr 35 min (d) Cannot be determined

Additional information Different people can solve different questions simultaneously with the same efficiency but every student can solve only one question at a given time

15. What is the minimum working time required to the closest minute to complete all the questions if all the students start together?
(a) 20 min (b) 25 min
(c) 30 min (d) Cannot be determined
16. If only three out of the five people do the five questions, what is the minimum time taken to complete the questions. Use data from the previous questions if necessary (approximately)
(a) 40 min (b) 45 min
(c) 51 min (d) 55 min

Directions for Questions 17 to 20: *Each question is followed by two statements, A and B. Answer each question using the following instructions:*

Choose a if the question can be answered by using statement A alone but not by using B alone.

Choose b if the question can be answered by using statement B alone but not by using A alone.

Choose c if the question can be answered by using both statements together.

Choose d if the question cannot be answered by using both the statements together.

Choose e if the question can be answered by using either statement alone.

17. In a cricket match, the 'man of the match' award is given to the player scoring the highest number of runs. In case of a tie, the player (out of those locked in the tie) who has taken the higher number of catches is chosen. Even thereafter if there is a tie, the player (out of those locked in the tie) who has dropped fewer catches is selected. Aakash, Biplab and Chirag who were contenders for the award dropped at least one catch each. Biplab dropped 2 catches more than Aakash did, scored 50, and took 2 catches. Chirag got two chances to catch and dropped both. Who was the 'man of the match'?
A. Chirag made 15 runs less than both Aakash and Biplab.
B. The catches dropped by Biplab are 1 more than the catches taken by Aakash.
18. Four friends, A, B, C and D got the top four ranks in a test but A did not get the first, B did not get the second, C did not get the third and D did not get the fourth. Who secured which rank?
A. Neither A nor D were amongst the first 2.
B. Neither B nor C was third or fourth.
19. The members of a local club contributed equally to pay ₹600 towards a donation. How much did each one pay?
A. If there had been five fewer members, each one would have paid an additional ₹10.
B. There were at least 20 members in the club, and each one paid no more than ₹30.
20. A family has only one kid. The father says 'after "*n*" years, my age will be 4 times the age of my kid.' The mother says 'after "*n*" years, my age will be 3 times that of my kid.' What will be the combined ages of the parents after "n" years?
A. The age difference between the parents is 10 years.
B. After '*n*' years the kid is going to be twice as old as she is now.

21 Mock Test Paper

Directions for Question 1 to 4: *Answer the questions on the basis of information below*

Ampa Loompa is an ethical hacker and wants to hack computer servers of Internet Cafes to gather logged in users' details. He decides to hack into servers of eight Cafes (Cafe1, Cafe2…….Cafe8) in five areas – Shalimar Bagh, Ashok Vihar, Rohini, Pitampura and Haiderpur. However to start with he decided that he'd only fetch the information on the number of visitors in the above-mentioned cafes over a period of 3 days. The tables on the next page provide details of cafes and the areas they belong to.

NUMBER OF VISITORS

AREA	DAY		
	Day 1	Day 2	Day 3
Shalimar Bagh	4	0	0
Ashok Vihar	2	6	0
Rohini	2	9	0
Pitampura	4	0	1
Haiderpur	2	0	7

NUMBER OF VISITORS

CAFE	DAY		
	Day 1	Day 2	Day 3
Café 1	2	0	0
Café 2	4	0	0
Cafe 3	0	6	0
Café 4	0	0	1
Café 5	2	0	0
Café 6	2	0	7
Café 7	4	0	0
Café 8	0	9	0

1. How many Cafés are there in Haiderpur area?
   (a) 2 (b) 1
   (c) 7 (d) 3
2. Café 1 can belong to which of the following areas?
   (a) Rohini (b) Pitampura
   (c) Shalimar Bagh (d) Haiderpur
3. To which area does Café 2 belong to?
   (a) Pitampura or Ashok Vihar but not Shalimar Bagh
   (b) Shalimar Bagh or Rohini but not Haiderpur
   (c) Shalimar Bagh or Pitampura but not Ashok Vihar
   (d) Only Pitampura
4. How many of the below listed areas can have 3 cafes?
   (a) Only Ashok Vihar
   (b) Only Shalimar Bagh
   (c) Both Pitampura and Shalimar Bagh
   (d) None

Directions for Questions 5 to 8: *Refer to the following data (Table 21.2) to answer the questions that follow:*

TABLE 21.2

Round	Total Votes	Minimum Votes For		Maximum Votes For	
		Candi-date	Votes	Candi-date	Votes
1		D	24	A	60
2	163	C	39	B	64
3	147				

The G8 is an association of South East Asian countries to resolve their trade disputes. Every year, the 24 countries elect their chairperson. For this, several rounds of voting are done, the details of which is given below:-

(i) *For the post of chairperson, only member countries of the G8 can nominate at the most one candidate per country*
(ii) *For the post of chairperson for the year 2023–2024, four people, Audi, Boxer, Coffee, and Dimply, are contending*
(iii) *In each round of voting, the candidate with the minimum number of votes is eliminated such that the person with the maximum votes at the last of the voting process is designated the chairperson of G8*
(iv) *While voting, the member countries whose members are in the contention can caste a vote and for only one member in contention*
(v) *A member country is eligible to vote for at the most two candidates in the entire voting process*

(vi) Candidates Audi and Boxer retain their votes from all the previous rounds as long as they were in contentions for the post of the chairperson

(vii) 25% of those who voted for Coffee in round 1 voted for Boxer in round 2

(viii) Those who voted for Dimply in round 1 voted for either Boxer or Coffee in round 2

(ix) Half of those who voted for Coffee in round 1 voted for Boxer in round 3

(x) All countries whose candidates are in contention voted for their own candidates as long as they were in contention

The Table 21.2 gives some more information regarding the voting pattern in different rounds of voting that happened.

5. Which of the following statements is necessarily true?
   (i) 16 candidates who voted for Dimply in round 1 voted for Coffee in round 2
   (ii) Audi won the election in round 3 by a margin of 3 votes
   (a) Only (i) (b) Only (ii)
   (c) Both of the above (d) None of the above
6. How many countries who voted for Dimply in round 1 voted for Boxer in round 2?
   (a) 8 (b) 7
   (c) 9 (d) Cannot be determined
7. What is the number of votes cast for candidate Coffee in round 1?
   (a) 28 (b) 29
   (c) 30 (d) 32
8. Among the members who voted for Coffee in round 2 and were still eligible to vote in round 3, what percentage voted for Audi in round 3?
   (a) 64.8% (b) 66.7%
   (c) 65.9% (d) 65.2%

Directions for Questions 9 to 12: *Each question is followed by two statements, A and B. Answer each question using the following instructions:*

Mark (a) if the question can be answered by using the statement A alone but not by using the statement B alone.

Mark (b) if the question can be answered by using the statement B alone but not by using the statement A alone.

Mark (c) if the question can be answered by using either of the statements alone.

Mark (d) if the question can be answered by using both the statements together but not by either of the statements alone.

Mark (e) if the question cannot be answered on the basis of the two statements.

9. Thirty per cent of the employees of a call centre are males. Ten per cent of the female employees have an engineering background. What is the percentage of male employees with engineering background?
   A. Twenty five per cent of the employees have engineering background.
   B. Number of male employees having an engineering background is 20 per cent more than the number of female employees having an engineering background.
10. In a football match, at the half-time, Mahindra and Mahindra Club was trailing by three goals. Did it win the match?
    A. In the second-half Mahindra and Mahindra Club scored four goals.
    B. The opponent scored four goals in the match.
11. In a particular school, sixty students were athletes. Ten amongst them were also amongst the top academic performers. How many top academic performers were in the school?
    A. Sixty per cent of the top academic performers were not athletes.
    B. All the top academic performers were not necessarily athletes.
12. Five students Atul, Bala, Chetan, Dev and Ernesto were the only ones who participated in a quiz contest. They were ranked based on their scores in the contest. Dev got a higher rank as compared to Earnesto, while Bala got a higher rank as compared to Chetan. Chetan's rank was lower than the median. Who amongst the five got the highest rank?
    A. Atul was the last rank holder.
    B. Bala was not amongst the top two rank holders.

Directions for Questions 13 to 16: *Refer to the following data (Table 21.3) to answer the questions that follow. The financial detail of 12 Indian companies is listed below in the following table. The details have been obtained from the Department of Commerce, Government of India for the year 2021–22. Each of the 12 companies belongs to one of the sector of Polyester industry, Agriculture industry, Machinery industry, or Communication industry. It is also known that there are at least two companies in each industry mentioned above out of the 12 companies. All the values except Liquidity Ratio are in ₹ crore.*

The following information was also found from the Department of Commerce, Government of India:

(i) For any two Communication industry based companies A and B, if the liquidity ratio of A is less than B then the net profit of A is more than B

(ii) *For every Communication industry based company, the 'other incomes' is more than ₹1000 crore*

(iii) *For any two Agriculture industry based companies A and B, if the expenditure of A is less than B then the Liquidity ratio of A is more than B*

(iv) *For every Agriculture industry based company, the net profit is more than ₹700 crore*

(v) *For any two Machinery industry based companies A and B, if the sales of A is more than B then the 'other incomes' of A is less than B*

(vi) *For every Machinery industry based company, the Liquidity ratio is more than 1.6*

(vii) *For any two Polyester industry based companies A and B, if the 'other incomes' of A is more than B then the net profit of A is more than B*

(viii) *For every Polyester industry based company, the sales is more than ₹ 5000 crore*

TABLE 21.3

Company	Expenditure	Liquidity Ratio	Other Incomes	Net Profit	Sales
1	6230	1.80	740	1020	7820
2	5840	1.40	1100	480	6200
3	4790	1.75	920	450	5490
4	3680	1.45	1130	550	4500
5	1980	1.73	980	800	2100
6	2790	1.40	380	350	5800
7	3800	1.48	1350	950	3800
8	2140	1.44	1020	850	3420
9	2680	1.62	1240	180	6400
10	4230	1.36	650	720	4500
11	2200	1.75	940	525	3680
12	5460	1.33	1460	650	6500

13. Say if there are four companies in industry X then which among the following could be X?
    (a) Agriculture and Communication
    (b) Polyester and Agriculture
    (c) Polyester and Machinery
    (d) Cannot be determined

14. Consider the following statements:
    (i) Company 3 is either machinery or Agriculture based industry
    (ii) Companies 7 and 11 are Agriculture based companies
    (iii) It cannot be decided which industry does company 5 belong to
    (iv) Communication industry for certain has companies 2, 8, and 9
    (v) It cannot be decided for certain which industry do companies 3 and 5 fall into
    Which of the following combinations is correct?
    (a) (i) – true, (ii) – false, (iii) – false, (iv) – true, (v) – true
    (b) (i) – false, (ii) – false, (iii) – true, (iv) – false, (v) – true
    (c) (i) – false, (ii) – false, (iii) – true, (iv) – true, (v) – false
    (d) None of these

15. If all the four industries have the same number of companies then which of the following statements is true?
    (i) 3 is a Polyester company
    (ii) 5 is a Machinery company
    (iii) 12 is a communication company
    (a) (i) and (ii) (b) (ii) and (iii)
    (c) All of the above (d) None of these

16. Which among the following is a communication industry based company?
    (a) 9 (b) 10
    (c) 11 (d) None of these

Directions for Questions 17 to 20: *Answer the questions on the basis of the information given below:*

Mindworkzz Centre for Management Studies has three branches in India, i.e. at Patna, Lucknow, and Jamshedpur. The number of faculty members in each centre may vary depending upon the intake capacity of students. The following information was obtained from reliable sources:

(i) *At times, a specialist of a subject of one city may visit a centre at another city to teach for a few days. Each faculty teaches at at least one city and may or may not teach at another city.*

(ii) *Some of the faculty members are teaching at exactly two centres and the number for various possible combinations is in the ratio of 1 : 2 : 3 respectively.*

(iii) 10 faculty members teaching at Patna centre are also teaching at a minimum of one other centre.

(iv) 24 Faculty members teach at the Patna centre

(v) The number of faculty members in Lucknow alone is twice the number of those who visit all the three cities to teach their respective specialisations.

(vi) Number of faculty members teaching at Jamshedpur centre alone is four more than the number of faculty members teaching at all the three centres.

(vii) The number of faculty members for Patna and exactly one more centre is 4.

17. Based upon the information given above, how many total faculty members are employed at Mindworkzz?
    (a) 43 (b) 44
    (c) 45 (d) 48

18. Which of the following additional information will enable us to find the exact number of faculty members involved in each centre?
    (i) Six faculty members teach at all the three centre.
    (ii) Twenty one teachers work at Lucknow centre.
    (iii) Twenty one teachers work at Jamshedpur centre.
    (a) (i) and (ii) (b) (i) and (iii)
    (c) (ii) and (iii) (d) (i), (ii), and (iii)

Additional information *Due to over burden on faculty members it was decided by the Mindworkzz management that every faculty could teach at at the most at two centers. Hence any faculty who was associated with all the three cities had his duties withdrawn from exactly one of the centre (randomly or as decided by the management) and reinstated with responsibilities of two centres only. The number of teachers withdrawn from Lucknow centre are two less than the number that are withdrawn from the Patna centre which is 4 more than the number withdrawn from the Jamshedpur centre. It is also known that the number of people working at Patna and Jamshedpur only is greater than the number working at Patna and Lucknow only.*

19. Which of the following statements is/are definitely false
    (a) Number of faculty members working at Patna centre is less than 15
    (b) Number of faculty members working at Jamshedpur centre is more than 23
    (c) Both of the above
    (d) None of these

20. In addition to the previous question, some new faculty members were inducted into the Mindworkzz team who joined only one center. They were distributed across the three centers in such a fashion that after the distribution, the number of faculty members at all the three centres became identical. What is the minimum number of faculty members required to satisfy the given condition?
    (a) 4 (b) 3
    (c) 2 (d) None of these

22 Mock Test Paper

Directions for Questions 1 to 5: *In the biggest school in Bertfordshire, the teachers follow a particularly peculiar academic process in awarding marks in practical exams based on the marks one has got in a paired theory paper. One of the pairings they have is for the theory marks of thermal physics and the practical marks of thermodynamics. Table 22.1 provides data about the theory marks in thermal physics and the corresponding increase in the practical marks in thermodynamics. Table 22.2 gives the marks in viva of thermodynamics and its corresponding marks in the practical of thermodynamics and corresponding and the associated average marks in the IQ test of the student. Table 22.3 gives us the grades of the students and their corresponding marks in the practical of thermodynamics.*

TABLE 22.1

Theory Marks in Exam of Thermal Physics	Increase in the Practical Marks in Thermodynamics
1–10	2
11–20	3
21–30	2
31–40	4
41–50	1
51–60	3
61–70	2
71–80	4
81–90	2
91–100	1

TABLE 22.2

Marks in Viva of Thermodynamics	Practical Marks in Thermodynamics	Marks in IQ Test
0	12	0
1	15	1
2	17	3
3	21	4
4	22	5
5	25	6
6	27	7
7	31	9
8	33	10
9	34	11

TABLE 22.3

Practical Marks in Thermodynamics	Grade
12	A
15	B
17	C
21	D
22	E
25	F
27	G
31	H
33	I
34	J

Practical marks in thermodynamics is 10 for 0 marks in theory exam of thermal physics. If theory marks in thermal physics is greater than 0 the practical marks is calculated according to the Table 22.1.

1. If the marks in theory exam of thermal physics varies from 25 to 76 then what is the range over which the marks in IQ test can vary?

   (a) 1–7 (b) 3–9
   (c) 4–11 (d) None of these.

2. Which of the following is not a possible theory score when the grade is either C, D, E, F or G?

   (a) 72 (b) 64
   (c) 34 (d) 56

3. What is the percentage increase in marks in viva if theory marks has increased from 19 to 63?

   (a) 400 (b) 333.33
   (c) 500 (d) None of these.

4. It was seen that Amit had a grade J, while his friend grade Anand had a grade I. What is the maximum

possible difference in the theory marks between the two friends?

5. What is the minimum possible increase of theory marks required for an A grader to become a G grader?

Directions for Questions 6 to 8: *The table given below shows the total budget of the four defence research projects released in the year 2022 and the fee charged per project by eight foreign scientists. Each of the eight scientists has worked in exactly two of the four projects. The table also gives partial information about the scientist who has worked in a particular project. It is known that the total fee paid to the scientists who have worked in a particular project is exactly 1/8th of the total budget of that project.*

	Fee Per Project (in Crore ₹)	A	B	C	D
Total Budget (in Crores ₹)		352	288	384	576
P	20		Y		
Q	16	Y			
R	10	Y	N	N	Y
S	12			Y	
T	12			Y	
U	10				
V	14				Y
W	6		Y		

Y Scientist worked on that project, N Scientist did not work on that project.

6. What is the absolute difference (in crores of rupees) in the total budgets of the projects in which P has worked and the total budgets of the projects in which both S and T have worked?
7. In which of the following projects has S worked definitely?
   (a) B (b) D
   (c) A (d) Either A or D
8. Which scientist has not worked with R in any of the four projects in the year 2022?
   (a) P (b) U
   (c) V (d) W

Directions for Questions 9 to 12: *The following table gives some information about the points scored by Sudhir in five different CAT Mock tests (from 1 to 5). The question paper is of objective type.*

Mock Tests	Total Number of Problems	Attempted Problems	Correct Attempts	Incorrect Attempts	Total Score
1	60				
2	70	58			
3	70	34		12	
4	80				132
5	90		60		

It is also known that:

A. For every correct answer Sudhir gets 6 marks and for every incorrect attempt he loses 2 marks. He loses 1 mark for every unattempted problem.
B. Sudhir's total marks in test 3 is ½ of his marks in test 1.
C. The number of incorrect attempts in test 4 is 1/6th of his incorrect attempts in all the tests and is twice of that in test 1.
D. In all the tests together, Sudhir attempted total 250 problems and scored 804 marks.

9. Find the total marks scored by Sudhir in Mock test 1.
10. Find the total marks Sudhir lost in test 2 because of unattempted problems.
11. Find the total marks scored by Sudhir in Mock test 5.
12. If passing marks for any of these five mock tests is 140, then in how many tests Sudhir scored more than passing marks?

Directions for Questions 13 to 16: *In a target shooting competition, the target has ten circles. The innermost circle is called the bull's eye (and has 10 points associated with it.), the next circle has 9 points, the third 8, and so on till the outermost which has 1 point. No points are awarded for shooting outside the ten circles.*

Each round of shooting consists of two shots. The following rules apply for awarding bonus points.

1. *In case of a shot hitting the bull's eye, the shooter is awarded as many points as he scores in the next 2 shots. If less than two shots are left in the day, the bonus points will only be for the shots left. Any bulls eye hit during these 2 shots will not trigger off another set of bonus points. These bonus points are called primary bonus points.*
2. *In case, the total in a given round is > 10, the shooter is awarded as many bonus points as the first shot in the next round. In case there is no round*

left no bonus points are awarded. These are called secondary bonus points.

3. *The total for the competition is the sum of points of all rounds of shooting plus the primary bonus points plus the secondary bonus points. The shooter with highest total score wins gold medal.*

Three shooters Rathore, Russell, and Bindra took part in the competition for Olympic Gold. Details to their scores are provided below.

Read the data and information provided below carefully and try to answer the questions.

Round	Rathore	Russell	Bindra
First	10/?	8/3	8/5
Second	?/3	?/10	9/?
Third	9/1	6/4	7/2
Fourth	10/?	3/10	6/5
Fifth	4/5	?/6	4/?
Sixth	10/0	4/7	3/3
Seventh	2/8	2/8	9/2

None of the three missing scores of Rathore was less than 4.

The following additional information was available

	Primary Bonus Points	Secondary Bonus Points
Rathore	23	>13 & <22
Russell	>22	22
Bindra	15	>20

- *Russell gets 4 secondary bonus points in the fifth round.*
- *Neither of the two missing scores for Russell is zero.*
- *Rathore hit a 5 in the second of the fourth round.*
- *None of three missing scores of Rathore was less than 4.*

13. The difference between the shooters (in total points) who came first and last was
    (a) 2 points (b) 5 points
    (c) 12 points (d) Indeterminate
14. What is the value of the total number of bonus points scored by Russell?
    (a) 48 (b) 42
    (c) 44 (d) Indeterminate
15. The highest total of missing values was for
    (a) Rathore (b) Russell
    (c) Bindra (d) Indeterminate
16. Who won the competition?
    (a) Rathore (b) Russell
    (c) Bindra (d) Indeterminate

Directions for Questions 17 to 20: *Six students (A, B, C, D, E, and F) of a class get difficult scores in an aptitude examination based on the CAT. It is known that the scores were in the order A > B > C > D > E > F.*

It is also known that when seven teachers of their school were quizzed about the totals, they had this to say:

The English Teacher said: "Exactly five of them scored a total of 232."

The Math Teacher said: "Exactly five of them scored a total of 238."

The Biology Teacher said: "Exactly five of them scored a total of 244."

The Geography Teacher said: "Exactly five of them scored a total of 245."

The Marathi Teacher said: "Exactly five of them scored a total of 250."

The Hindi Teacher said: "Exactly five of them scored a total of 256".

The History Teacher said: "Exactly five of them scored a total of 235"

It is known that exactly one of the seven teachers is lying about the total of five of the six students. Based on this information, try to answer the following questions:

17. The difference between the highest and the lowest score is:
    (a) 21 (b) 24
    (c) 18 (d) Cannot be determined
18. The second highest score is:
    (a) 55 (b) 56
    (c) 55 or 56 (d) Cannot be determined
19. Which of the following is the least possible score?
    (a) 34 (b) 35
    (c) 37 (d) Cannot be determined
20. If it is known that the sum of the two lowest scores is 80, then which of these could be the sum of two of the scores?
    (a) 93 (b) 104
    (c) 112 (d) 102

23 Mock Test Paper

Directions for Questions 1 to 3: *Answer the questions on the basis of the information given below.*

In the data given below, Table-23.1 indicates the number of movies watched by six students in three different multiplexes – PVR, Big Cinemas and INOX. Table 23.2 shows the number of movies of each of the six genres in these three multiplexes. It is also known that:

- The person who watched exactly one horror movie in INOX had also watched horror movies in PVR and Big Cinemas.
- D did not watch a Sci-fi movie in Big Cinemas.
- From among A, D and F exactly two people watched the same type of movie(s) in Big Cinemas and INOX as they watched in PVR.
- In any given multiplex, each of them watched only one type of movie.

TABLE 23.1

Name	PVR	BIG CINEMAS	INOX
A	4	4	1
B	2	1	2
C	2	1	4
D	1	1	1
E	2	1	1
F	2	2	1

TABLE 23.2

Genre	PVR	BIG CINEMAS	INOX
Action	2	0	0
Sci-Fi	2	2	0
Comedy	4	4	1
Dance based	2	2	1
Romance	1	1	1
Horror	2	1	7

1. For how many students can the number of movies watched of each type be conclusively determined?
2. What can be the maximum number of dance based movies watched by F in all the three multiplexes collectively?
3. Who watched horror movies in all the three multiplexes?
   (a) D (b) E
   (c) E or F (d) D or E

Directions for Questions 4 to 8: *Five students at AMS Learning Systems' Mindworkz program were put through a rigorous testing schedule in their preparation for the tough CAT paper. The students were Aroon, Baroon, Caroon, Daroon, and Earon. They took a total of 60 tests, where each test was taken by all the five students. The tests were organised in groups of ten tests each and a consolidated position board was maintained and updated after every ten tests. In any test, the student who secured the 1st, 2nd, 3rd, 4th, and 5th, ranks got 8, 6, 4, 2, and 0 points respectively. The testing system was structured in such a way that no two persons would secure the same rank in any test. Also no student scored the same number of points in any three consecutive tests.*

TABLE 23.3

End of the First	Person				
	Aroon	Baroon	Caroon	Daroon	Earon
10 tests	60	60	40	20	20
20 tests	100	110	100	40	40
30 tests	150	170	130	60	90
40 tests	190	200	200	80	130
50 tests	240	240	220	140	16
60 tests	300	260	260	180	200

The table (Table 23.3) shows the consolidated position board in terms of the points scored by each of the five students at the end of each set of ten tests from the beginning.

4. At least how many times did Aroon secure the 1st rank in the 60 tests?
   (a) 2 (b) 3
   (c) 4 (d) 5
   (e) None of these
5. If Caroon secured 2nd rank exactly three times in the first 20 tests, at most how many times did he secure 3rd rank in the first 20 tests?
   (a) 9 (b) 10
   (c) 11 (d) 12
   (e) None of these

6. At most how many times did Daroon secure the last rank in the 60 tests?
   (a) 31 (b) 32
   (c) 35 (d) 34
   (e) None of these
7. At least how many times did Daroon secure the last rank in the 60 tests?
   (a) 6 (b) 7
   (c) 8 (d) 9
   (e) None of these
8. At least how many times did Earon secure 2nd rank in the first 30 tests, if he got two pointers exactly two times in each of the first, second, and third sets of ten tests each?
   (a) 0 (b) 1
   (c) 2 (d) 3
   (e) None of these

Directions for Questions 9 to 12: *A jailor decided to play a game with five of his prisoners who were extremely adept at logical analysis.*

The prisoners were Aristotle, Bach, Coutin, Dell, and Einstein. He gave them each a box of money and announced, "Each of you have received a box of currency. All boxes look identical from outside." The jailor then asked each prisoner to secretly open the boxes and look at the currency inside. He then said, " Three of you have a box containing Indian Rupees, two of you have a box containing US Dollars. I shall now give each one of you a chit containing information about the box of exactly one other person." He did so and asked them to open the chit and see the information provided to them. "No one of you will be able to tell the exact currency of any third prisoner," he then said and further announced, "Bach has a box containing Indian Rupees." Aristotle immediately said, "I know the currency of all 5 people." On hearing this Einstein also said, "So do I, now."
Assume: *A prisoner speaks up as soon as he is able to deduce the currency of all five prisoners.*
Answer the following questions:

9. Apart from Bach, the prisoners with Indian currency were:
   (a) Einstein and dell
   (b) Aristotle and Einstein
   (c) Coutin and Dell
   (d) None of these
10. The prisoners given US Dollars were:
    (a) Coutin and Dell
    (b) Dell and Einstein
    (c) Aristotle and Einstein
    (d) None of these
11. Whose currency was written in the chit Aristotle received?
    (a) Bach (b) Einstein
    (c) Dell (d) None of these
12. Einstein did not receive a chit containing the currency of.
    (a) Aristotle (b) Bach
    (c) Dell (d) Coutin

Directions for Questions 13 to 16: *Answer the questions on the basis of the information given below.*

The following table (Table 23.4) shows the seedings of different tennis players before the start of the World Tennis Cup tournament in the year 2090

TABLE 23.4

Player	Seeding
Federer (Fed)	1
Nadal (Nad)	2
Sampras (Sam)	3
McEnroe (Mc)	4
Lendl (Ldl)	5
Agassi (Aga)	6
Leander(Lee)	7
Roddick (Rod)	8
Becker (Beck)	9
Edberg (Ed)	10
Connors (Con)	11
Stich (Sti)	12

Note: In the above table, Seed 1 is the favourite

Note:

(i) The tournament is a single round robin format. Each player plays the other exactly once.
(ii) The table gives the matches played in their reverse chronological order. That is, the match at the top left corner was the last match of the tournament, while the second last and the third last matches were both played by Sampras against Federer and Nadal respectively. Further, the fourth last match was played by McEnroe against Federer and so on till the first match of the tournament, which was played by Stich against Connors.
(iii) The outcome of a match is considered as a
Thwack – if the lower seed wins in straight sets.
Shack – if the lower seed wins in three sets (i.e. loses one set)
Brick – if the higher seed wins in straight sets.
Track – if the higher seed wins in three sets (i.e. loses one set)
These four are the only possible outcomes of any match.

Vs	Fed										
Nad	Thwack	Nad									
Sam	Thwack	Shack	Sam								
Mc	Shack	Brick	Thwack	Mc							
Ldl	Brick	Thwack	Shack	Track	Ldl						
Aga	Shack	Brick	Thwack	Shack	Track	Aga					
Lee	Thwack	Thwack	Track	Thwack	Track	Thwack	Lee				
Rod	Brick	Track	Shack	Thwack	Track	Thwack	Shack	Rod			
Beck	Track	Thwack	Brick	Track	Thwack	Track	Shack	Brick	Beck		
ED	Brick	Thwack	Track	Thwack	Thwack	Brick	Track	Shack	Brick	ED	
Con	Brick	Thwack	Track	Shack	Thwack	Brick	Shack	Track	Track	Shack	Con
Sti	Thwack	Shack	Thwack	Shack	Shack	Track	Thwack	Shack	Brick	Track	Thwack

FIGURE 23.1 *Result of all the matches played in the Honda World Cup Tennis Cup (In the year 2090)*

The final of the tournament is played between the two players with the maximum number of points. In case of a tie, the player with the maximum number of wins qualifies. If there is still a tie, the player with the maximum number of straight set wins qualifies.

(iv) Players are awarded points as follows:
   (a) For every match won in straight sets, the winner gets 5 points while the loser gets 0 points.
   (b) For every match won in 3 sets, the winner gets 4 points while the loser gets 1 point.

13. Who among the following won the least number of matches in the tournament?
    (a) Federer (b) Nadal
    (c) Sampras (d) Lendl
    (e) Agassi
14. What is the total number of points scored by Agassi in the series?
    (a) 21 (b) 31
    (c) 32 (d) 36
15. Between which two players is the final of the tournament played.
    (a) Stich-Agassi (b) Stich-Roddick
    (c) Stich-Becker (d) Agassi-Becker
16. The player who ended up with the least points is?
    (a) Nadal (b) McEnroe
    (c) Connors (d) Leander

Directions for Questions 17 to 20: *Refer to the data below (Table 23.5) to answer the questions that follow. The number of matches won by the top six cricket playing nations in the world against each other at home and abroad is given in the following table. The numbers in the table show the number of matches the respective team won against each other while being at home or away from home. Also note that no match has ended in a draw.*

TABLE 23.5

Country ↓		Country Played Against (total number of matches played at home)					
		Aus (85)	Ind (90)	NZ (70)	SA (80)	Pak (85)	SL (89)
Aus	Home	X	15	20	5	3	15
	Away	X	25	18	12	1	25
Ind	Home	20	X	12	23	6	8
	Away	12	X	28	15	32	9
NZ	Home	15	8	X	22	6	9
	Away	13	20	X	11	23	15
SA	Home	12	7	3	X	32	21
	Away	8	19	16	X	11	9
Pak	Home	8	23	19	8	X	12
	Away	5	15	21	9	X	13
SL	Home	21	17	6	12	13	X
	Away	13	12	12	19	22	X

17. A neutral ground is one where both the teams participating against each other are not on their respective home grounds. For at least how many matches did NZ won against SA on a neutral ground?
(a) 5 (b) 6
(c) 7 (d) Cannot be determined
18. Consider the following statements:
(i) Aus has had 27 losses at home ground
(ii) The number of losses Ind has had at home is 12 more than the losses NZ has had at home
(iii) The number of wins and number of losses of SL differ by 49
(iv) The number of losses NZ has had at home is twice the number of losses SA has had at home
Which of the above statements is true?
(a) (i), (ii), and (iii) (b) (i) and (iii)
(c) (i) and (iv) (d) Cannot be determined
19. How many matches in between NZ and Pak were played on neutral ground, if it is known that for any match played at NZ or Pak, the team of that country is one of the participating teams?
(a) 11 (b) 12
(c) 13 (d) 19
20. Find the maximum number of teams possible that have won all their matches played in Aus and against Aus, if no matches are played in Aus without Aus being one of the contending teams
(a) 0 (b) 1
(c) 2 (d) None of these

24 Mock Test Paper

Directions for Questions 1 to 5: *Eight mobile companies A, B, C, D, E, F, G and H sell their mobile phones in one or more countries among 5 different countries P, Q, R, S and T.*

Two companies are said to be competitors of each other, if there is at least one country where both companies sell their mobile phones. The following table provides information about the number of competitors of seven of these eight companies (from B to H).

Company	Number of Competitors
B	3
C	1
D	6
E	4
F	7
G	6
H	3

1. Which of the following statement is correct?
   (a) A has more competitors than D.
   (b) A has more competitors than E.
   (c) A has more competitors than B
   (d) Cannot be determined.
2. Find the average number of competitors per company.
3. The maximum number of companies selling their mobile phones in one country is?
4. The maximum number of countries in which company C sells its mobile phones.
5. In the previous question if country P has highest number of competitors then maximum possible value of number of mobile companies in country P is = ?

Directions for Questions 6 to 8: *Answer the following questions on the basis of information given below:*

The following table shows the marks obtained by four students in Gate exam from 2012 to 2014. The four students Ajay, Mohanish, Peter and Faraz are disguised as P, Q, R and S not necessarily in the same order.

	P	Q	R	S
Gate-2012	94		102	106
Gate-2013		124	118	20
Gate-2014	144	50	56	
Total marks	w	x	y	z

It is also known that:

A. The maximum possible marks in each Gate exam were 150.
B. Ajay's total score is more than Peter's total score.
C. Ajay scored the lowest marks in Gate-2012 and Faraz scored the highest marks in Gate-2013 among the four students.
D. In each Gate exam, a correct answer carried +6 marks and an incorrect answer carried – 2 mark.
E. Mohanish's total score is less than Peter's total score.
F. P's total score is a multiple of 12.

6. How many different total scores are possible for Mohanish?
   (a) 101 (b) 97
   (c) 98 (d) 100
7. What is the name of the person disguised as Q?
   (a) Ajay (b) Faraz
   (c) Peter (d) Mohanish
8. How many different values are possible for 'w'?
   (a) 7 (b) 8
   (c) 9 (d) 15

Directions for Questions 9 to 12: *Answer the questions on the basis of the information given below (Table 24.1).*

The following is the table of points drawn at the end of all the matches in a six-nation Football Tournament, in which each country played with every other country exactly once. The table gives the positions of the countries in terms of their respective total points scored (i.e. in the decreasing order of their total points). Each win was worth three points, each draw one point, and there were no points for a loss. Due to a problem with the computer in which the data was stored, some of the data went missing. A computer expert was called in to retrieve the data but he was only partially successful. The table below (Table 24.1) gives the information that was retrieved by the computer expert. The results of none of the individual matches are known except that Spain beatEngland and no two teams finished with the same number of points.

TABLE 24.1

Position	Country	Won	Drawn	Lost	Goals For	Goals Against	Total Points
1	Argentina				17	5	15
2	Brazil				9	6	10
3	Spain				2		8
4	England				2	5	
5	France				7	11	2
6	Cameroon				8	16	

9. Which of the following matches was a draw?
   (a) England vs Brazil
   (b) England vs France
   (c) Cameroon vs France
   (d) Brazil vs France
   (e) Cameroon vs Brazil
10. The total number of points won by England is
    (a) 7 (b) 4
    (c) 1 (d) 6
    (e) cannot be determined
11. The total number of goals scored in the match between Brazil and Spain is
    (a) 1 (b) 9
    (c) 0 (d) 6
    (e) cannot be determined
12. The number of goals scored by Argentina against England is at most
    (a) 2 (b) 3
    (c) 4 (d) 5
    (e) cannot be determined

Directions for Questions 13 to 16: *Answer the questions on the basis of the information given below:*

The President of Nicaragua is elected through a special system, which consists of several rounds of voting by the representatives of the different state legislatures.

For the President's post, only member states can nominate candidates (and each member state can nominate a maximum of 1 candidate per state.)

Four candidates – Amarjeet Singh, Birender Singh, Charanjeet Singh, and Daler Singh (Denoted as A, B, C, and D respectively in the table below) – are in the fray.

In each round of voting, the candidate getting the least number of votes is eliminated. The President elected is the person getting the maximum number of votes in the final round of voting. While voting, in each round, each of the eligible member states has to vote for exactly one candidate in contention. But the states whose nominees are in contention are eligible to vote only as long as their nominees are still in the fray.

The following table (Table 24.2) shows some of the information regarding the voting pattern in the different rounds of voting that happened:

TABLE 24.2

Round	Total Votes	Maximum Votes For		Minimum Votes For	
		Candidate	Votes	Candidate	Votes
1		A	90	B	24
2	223	C	94	D	39
3	207				

1. *A member state is eligible to vote for at most two candidates in all the rounds combined. This means (in other words) that if a member state has voted for 2 different candidates in the first 2 rounds and none of these two candidates is in contention in round 3, then that state is ineligible to vote as it is not allowed to vote for a third candidate.*
2. *A and C retained their votes from all previous rounds as long as they were in contention.*
3. *25% of those who voted for D in round 1, voted for C in round 2.*
4. *Those who voted for B in round 1, voted for either C or D in round 2.*
5. *50% of those who voted for D in round 1, voted for C in round 3.*
6. *All states whose nominees are in contention voted for their nominees as long as they were in contention. i.e. there was no cross voting.*

13. What is the number of votes cast for C in round 1?
    (a) 78 (b) 82
    (c) 74 (d) 70
    (e) None of these

14. How many voters who voted for candidate D in round 1, voted for candidate C in round 2?
    (a) 7 (b) 10
    (c) 8 (d) 9
    (e) None of these
15. Among the members who voted for D in round 2 and were still eligible to vote in round 3, what percent voted for A in round 3?
    (a) 68.5% (b) 95.2%
    (c) 66.68% (d) 65.2%
    (e) 79.5%
16. Which of the following statements must be true?
    I. Candidate A won the election in round 3 by a margin of three votes.
    II. 16 candidates who voted for B in round 1, voted for D in round 2.
    (a) Only II (b) neither I nor II
    (c) Both I and II (d) Only I
    (e) Cannot be determined

Directions for Questions 17 to 20: *Answer the questions on the basis of the information given below (Table 24.3)*

The Indian cricket team had just finished a five-match one day series with Australia. The team management was assessing the performance of the top five batsmen in the series – Sachin, Viru, Rahul, Laxman, and Jaffer. All these batsmen played each of the five matches and each of them was out in each of the five innings they played in.

In a departure from tradition each of the five matches was played for 100 overs per team.

The table below (Table 1.1) gives the names of three highest scoring batsmen in that match, along with their respective scores, mentioned in the brackets alongside. The last column gives the percentage of the total team score made by the given three players together.

The team management has devised the following two indices to judge the performance of each player:

I. The Median Index (M.I.), which is the middle number, if all the five scores of the concerned player in the series are arranged in the increasing order.

II. The Differential Index (D.I.), which is the difference between the highest and the lowest scores of the concerned player in the series.

Further, it is also observed that in any match, the scores of no two players who batted are equal.

17. Which of the players had the lowest value of M.I. for the series?
    (a) Sachin
    (b) Jaffer
    (c) Laxman
    (d) Rahul
    (e) Viru
18. Sachin and Rahul together accounted for at most what percentage of India's total score in the series, approximately?
    (a) 35% (b) 52%
    (c) 40% (d) 35%
    (e) 45%
19. The exact value of M.I. can be calculated for how many of the given players?
    (a) 0 (b) 3
    (c) 4 (d) 5
    (e) 2
20. Among the players mentioned, who can have the lowest value of D.I. in the series?
    (a) Only Sachin, Rahul, Laxman, or Jaffer
    (b) Only Jaffer, Rahul, or Laxman
    (c) Only Jaffer or Laxman
    (d) Only Jaffer, Laxman, or Sachin
    (e) Only Jaffer

TABLE 24.3

Match	Highest	Second Highest	Third Highest	Percentage of Total Score
1	Sachin (194)	Viru (126)	Rahul (112)	80
2	Laxman (170)	Jaffer (130)	Sachin (60)	75
3	Viru(250)	Jaffer (124)	Laxman (74)	70
4	Laxman (154)	Sachin (124)	Jaffer (96)	85
5	Rahul (160)	Viru (144)	Sachin (120)	80

25 Mock Test Paper

Directions for Questions 1 to 2: *Answer the questions on the basis of the information given (Table 25.1):*

In the recently played Twenty20 tournament, 6 teams participated. The schedule of the tournament was such that every team had to play every other team 12 times. Points were awarded for W (Wins), L (Loss), and T (Tie). The following chart gives the number of matches won, lost, and tied by different teams.

TABLE 25.1

Team	W	L	T
India	26	30	04
Pakistan	14	36	10
Sri Lanka	24	30	06
South Africa	P	Q	R
Bangladesh	20	32	08
Canada	18	30	12

1. How many W, L, and T combinations are possible for team SOUTH AFRICA?
   (a) 3 (b) 4
   (c) 1 (d) 2
   (e) None
2. If 5 points are awarded for each win, –3 points for each loss, and 2 points for each tie, then what is the maximum possible difference between the third team and the second last team, if we will rank them according to their points in descending order?
   (a) 14 (b) 12
   (c) 13 (d) 18
   (e) None of these

Directions for Questions 3 to 5: *(1) Nine years from now Amit will be twice as old as Vishal was when Vikas was nine times as old as Amit.*
(2) Eight years ago , Vikas was half as old as Vishal will be when he is one year older to Amit will be at the time when Vikas will be five times as old as Amit will be two years from now.
(3) When Amit was one year old, Vikas was three years older to what Amit will be when Vishal is three times as old as Vikas was six years before the time when Vishal was half as old as Amit will be when Vikas will be ten years older to Vikas was when Vishal was one third as old as Amit will be when Vikas will be three times as old as he was when Vishal was born.(Assume all ages are whole nos.)

3. How old is Amit ?
   (a) 3 (b) 7
   (c) 4 (d) Cannot be determined
4. How old is Vishal ?
   (a) 8 (b) 14
   (c) 3 (d) Cannot be determined
5. How old is Vikas ?
   (a) 4 (b) 3
   (c) 15 (d) Cannot be determined

Directions for Questions 6 to 9: *Refer to the data given below to answer the questions that follow:*

The World Health Organization recently conducted a research to find the most hazardous cities in the world in terms of pollution. The three kinds of pollution under consideration were air, water, and sound pollution. In its research drive in India, WHO initially shortlisted ten urban cities that had the highest levels of pollution in stage 1. WHO gave these cities tokens on the basis of the level of pollution in them for each of the three variables, i.e. air, water, and sound pollution. The pollution level in either variables could be one of "Ultra Hazard Level" (UHL), "Medium Hazard Level" (MHL), and "Low Hazard Level" (LHL). A total of four tokens were given to each city in stage 1 and a total of three tokens were given to each city in stage 2. There are 'Token Points' associated with each token. A UHL token is worth 5 token points, a MHL token is worth 2 token points, and a LHL token is worth 0 token points. Each city could be given more than one token of UHL, MHL, or LHL for any of the three variables depending upon the gravity of the situation as decided by the scientists at WHO. Obviously, the city with the maximum number of token points was the most polluted. The four cities with the highest levels of pollution in stage 1 were then again taken into consideration in stage 2. A reevaluation was done and again the same token system was fol-

lowed. However the tokens from the first stage did not carry forward to the second stage. At the end of the research, the city with the highest number of token points was declared the most hazardous city of India.

Table 25.2 was made available by the scientists at WHO and gives the number of tokens given to the various cities (some cells have intentionally been left blank):

TABLE 25.2

City	Number of UHL Tokens	Number of MHL Tokens	Number of LHL Tokens
	Stage 1		
A			2
B			1
C		1	
D	0		
E		3	
F		3	
G			0
H			2
I	0		
J			
	Stage 2		
City 1	0		
City 2			
City 3			1
City 4		3	

Further, the following information was also provided:

(i) In stage 1, City A through E got a total of 7, 0, 12, 17, and 11 token points (data not necessarily in the same order as the cities listed)

(ii) Similarly in stage 1 itself, cities F through J received 4, 20, 6, 9, and 7 token points (data not necessarily in the same order as the cities listed)

(iii) The cities that secured 11, 17, 12, and 20 token points in stage 1 were the ones to move onto stage 2 of the research and secured 7, 2, 6, and 12 token points respectively

6. Which of the following cities was declared the second most hazardous city in India?
   (a) A (b) E
   (c) I (d) C
7. Which city was ranked ninth in pollution level after the first stage?
   (a) B (b) D
   (c) F (d) None of these
8. Which city was declared the most hazardous city of India?
   (a) E (b) G
   (c) H (d) Cannot be determined
9. Consider the following statements:
   (i) In stage 1, the number of cities which had token points greater than 10 were equal to the number of cities that token points less than 10
   (ii) The total number of UHL tokens points in stage 1 is 65
   (iii) The number of MHL tokens in stage 1 is equal to the UHL tokens given in the same stage
   (iv) City D is the least polluted city in India among the cities taken into consideration by WHO
   (v) In stage 1, the number of MHL tokens of the first five cities is more than the number of LHL tokens of the last five cities (order as given in the table above)

   Which of the above statements is/are false?
   (a) (ii) and (v) (b) (i), (ii), (iv), and (v)
   (c) (i), (ii), and (iii) (d) (i), (iii), and (v)

Directions for Questions 10 to 13: *Answer the questions on the basis of the information given below:*

Mr. Arun Sharma, the CEO of AMS Centre for Management Studies, wished to find some details regarding ten students who took coaching at his institute. For the purpose of CAT, each of the 10 students appeared in a mock paper called the Arun Sharma CAT Challenge consisting of four sections, English, Quant, DI, and Reasoning. Apart from this, Mr. Sharma also graded the students on the basis of their GD/PI sessions. The following table (Table 25.3) gives the details of the relevant data.

Due to computers overload certain errors have crept into the Table 25.3 in the grades and marks. The following information is also known so that Mr. Sharma can retrieve the original, correct data:

(i) All marks are whole numbers and the maximum marks possible in any subject is 100

(ii) There are only 4 grades – A, B, C, and D – that the students got

(iii) If a student got a C grade in GD/PI or scored less than 50 marks in English then he got more than 60 marks in DI

(iv) If a student got more than 80 marks in DI, he got a B grade.

(v) If a student got a A grade in GD/PI then he scored less than 50 marks in quant, more than 50 marks in reasoning and less than 70 marks in English.

TABLE 25.3

Name of Student	Grade in GD/PI	Marks Obtained In			
		English	Quant	DI	Reasoning
A	C	10	40	20	30
B	B	40	50	30	70
C	A	60	40	88	50
D	B	70	50	60	60
E	A	50	80	70	40
F	B	80	30	90	40
G	B	40	50	80	70
H	C	40	60	50	80
I	A	40	30	60	50
J	C	90	85	40	90

10. What are the minimum number of errors that crept into the table?
    (a) 5 (b) 6
    (c) 7 (d) None of these
11. If all the grades mentioned in the above table are correct for all students and also the least possible number of mistake have occurred while tabulating the marks then the total marks scored by C in all the four sections together can be at maximum
    (a) 275 (b) 280
    (c) 285 (d) Cannot be determined
12. What is the least possible total score of any student in all the four sections put together? (You may use data from the previous questions, if needed)
    (a) 160 (b) 200
    (c) 150 (d) 141
13. At the most how many students could have scored more than 320 marks as their grand total? (You may use data from the previous questions, if needed)
    (a) 1 (b) 2
    (c) 3 (d) Cannot be determined

Directions for Questions 14 to 16: *On the island of Gibraltor, the Indian Air Force has installed an airbase. The Gibraltor island being the only island on the sea filled Kryptol planet, all planes make sorties & come back. One fine day, Air Chief Marhsal Chitnis decided that one plane had to fly across the planet to see the amount of wear & tear on the plane caused by flying non stop across the planet. But since the fuel capacity of all the planes is such that the plane can only fly halfway across the planet he has hired the great logician Sherry to advise him. Sherry learns that all planes have the facility to be refueled in mid air by another plane. Help Sherry answer the following questions assuming that all planes have to be safely back.*

14. The minimum number of planes required to help complete one full round across the world for a plane which starts flying clockwise is:
    (a) 2 (b) 3
    (c) 4 (d) 5
15. The minimum number of flights required to help complete one full round across the world for a plane which starts flying clockwise is:
    (a) 4 (b) 5
    (c) 6 (d) 7
16. What is the minimum number of planes required to be sent from the Gibraltor island base anticlockwise to meet the incoming planes coming into the base clockwise?
    (a) 1 (b) 2
    (c) 3 (d) Any of these

Directions for Questions 17 to 20: *Refer to the following table (Table 25.4)to answer the questions that follow.*

Time division multiple access is often used as a method to divide a minute of occupancy time of a CDMA communication link to process N number of mobile users queued. An engineer decides to come out with a few conclusions regarding the performance of the CDMA communication link. He finds out from the technical sheets that each minute is equally divided into five slots and each user occupies one time slot to connect his call. To connect one user to another, each user is connected to a slot. Users 1, 2, 3, 4, and 5 are the hosts of the slots 1, 2, 3, 4, and 5 respectively. The algorithm that CDMA communication link follows is given below:

1. *For each slot during the first second, the link checks if the host of that slot has a job.*
2. *If the host has a job, the link is left idle for the next second*
3. *If no job is there then the link checks for the pending jobs of some other user*
4. *The pending job will be processed according to the priority of the users, i.e. user 1 has the highest priority while user 5 has the lowest priority*

A job is defined as the actual time used by host to complete his job, i.e. the time beyond the first two seconds of any slot that are used by the communication link to check whether an active host exists or there is a pending host. Only one job is done in one time slot. The engineer gathers the following statistics (Table 25.4) from the computer's memory:

***T**: Time at which the user asks for a connection to be established*

***S**: Actual time needed in seconds by the host to complete the job, i.e. the time beyond the first two seconds*

TABLE 25.4

Computers	JOB 1		JOB 2	
	T	S	T	S
User 1	7:59:58	10	9:02:10	20
User 2 ⇩	8:00:08	13	9:02:27	13
User 3	8:00:07	32	9:02:29	31
User 4	8:00:06	18	9:02:47	11
User 5	8:00:22	11	9:02:13	15

17. If the CDMA communication link is idle before job 1 is given to it, then in which of these slots will the job of user 3 will be finished if no jobs by user 2 are given as yet
    (a) Slot 1 (b) Slot 2
    (c) Slot 3 (d) Slot 4
18. Which of the following users did not get access to any of the slots in the first minute of job 2?
    (a) User 2 (b) User 3
    (c) User 4 (d) User 5
19. Which of these users completes its job utilising only the slots assigned to him in job 2?
    (a) User 2 (b) User 3
    (c) User 4 (d) No user
20. Of all the slots required for the completion of job 2, for how much time was the link idle?
    (a) 53 seconds
    (b) 54 seconds
    (c) 55 seconds
    (d) Cannot be determined

26 Mock Test Paper

Directions for Questions 1 to 5: *There is a method of ascription known as Caeser cipher: if a letter in the plain text is the Nth letter in the alphabet, it is replaced by the (N + K)th letter in the alphabet where K is some fixed integer. (Caeser used K = 3). The table below shows how a message is encrypted using this method with K = 1*

Plain text	:	*ATTACK AT DAWN*
Cipher text	:	*BUUBDLABUAEBXO*

One way to make this type of message more difficult is to use more than one table. An extension of Caeser cipher is called the Vegenere cipher: in this a small repeated key is used to determine the value of K for each letter. At each step the key letter index is added to the plain text letter index to determine the cipher text letter index. One simple example with the key ABC, is encrypted as below:

Key	:	*ABCABCABCABCAB*
Plain text	:	*ATTACK AT DAWN*
Cipher text	:	*BVWBENBCWBFDXP*

1. A message, "WE ARE ONE", is encrypted in Caeser cipher with K = –3. Which of the following represents the encrypted message?
   (a) ZHDDUHDRQH (b) TBXXYOBXLKB
   (c) VDZQDZNPD (d) TBXXOBXMKB
   (e) TBXXOBXLKB
2. A French term, CARTE BLANCHE, is encrypted in the Vegenere cipher with the key, "ABCDABCD.." Which encrypted message represents that French word?
   (a) DCUXFCEPBPFLF
   (b) DCUXEBFPCQGLE
   (c) DCUXDBEQCPFLE
   (d) DCUXFCEPBPFLG
   (e) None of these
3. If two key types, ABC and ABCD in Vegenere cipher are added to make a new key type, which encrypted message will represent "SECRET" [*Hint:* (B + B = D)]
   (a) UJKWHY (b) UIIVGY
   (c) UIIWGY (d) None of these
   (e) UIIVGX
4. A message is encrypted with
   A B C D E F G H I J K L M N O P Q R S T U V W X Y Z &
   T H E Q U I C K R O W N F X J M P D V R L A Z Y G B
   What will be the encrypted message for "ATTAC AT DAWN"?
   (a) HVVHOTHPTQHAF
   (b) HVVHOTHVTQHBF
   (c) HVVHOTHVTQHAF
   (d) HVVHOTNVTQBHG
   (e) None of these
5. In Vegenere cipher if two keys ABCD and ABCDE are added to make a new key, what will be the new key?
   (a) BDFHE (b) BDEHE
   (c) BDFHG (d) BDFFE
   (e) None of these

Directions for Questions 6 to 10: *The diagram below shows the letters A, B, C, & D, each of which is surrounded, can be 'flipped over' the letter itself either horizontally or vertically.*

1	*4*	*6*	*9*	*11*	*14*	*16*	*19*	*21*
2	*A*	*7*	*B*	*12*	*C*	*17*	*D*	*22*
3	*5*	*8*	*10*	*13*	*15*	*18*	*20*	*23*

Thus, if we were to flip this diagram vertically around B, the figure would become:

1	*4*	*11*	*9*	*6*	*14*	*16*	*19*	*21*
2	*A*	*12*	*B*	*7*	*C*	*17*	*D*	*22*
3	*5*	*13*	*10*	*8*	*15*	*18*	*20*	*23*

Arjit, a naughty boy, flips over the original diagram around the letters A, B, C, & D in the order vertically, horizontally, horizontally, & vertically. From the final position obtained, answer the questions that follow:

6. How many numbers will not change their position?
   (a) 5 (b) 3
   (c) 7 (d) 8
   (e) None of these

7. Into the position of which number will the number 17 go?
   (a) 12 (b) 22
   (c) 18 (d) 7
   (e) None of these
8. The highest percentage numerical loss is exhibited by which position?
   (a) 3rd column 3rd row
   (b) 5th column 1st row
   (c) 6th column 3rd row
   (d) 4th column 2nd row
   (e) None of these
9. How many positions have exhibited an absolute change of 1 in their numerical value?
   (a) 2 (b) 3
   (c) 4 (d) 6
   (e) 5
10. The increase in the sum of the number around C is:
   (a) 15 (b) 12
   (c) 9 (d) 10
   (e) None of these

Directions for Questions 11 to 15: *Nine horses participated in a horse tournament. Five races were held in this tournament. The winner of a race gets 5 points, 2nd gets 3, and the 3rd gets 1.*

1. The table gives the points tally at the end of the races.

Horse	A	B	C	D	E	F	G	H	I
Points	5	5	8	2	5	6	4	10	0

One race is held between five horses. The first race is held among the first 5 horses from the left in the above table. In the next race, out of these horses, A drops out of the race and a new horse F enters into the race. In the next race, B drops out and G enters and so on. It is also given that H is the only horse that scored in 2 consecutive races.

11. What was the position of horse F in race 4?
   (a) 4th (b) 2nd
   (c) 3rd (d) 1st
12. What is the ratio of the points scored by G and E in race 5?
   (a) 1:3 (b) 3:1
   (c) 1:5 (d) Cannot be determined
13. The first 3 rankers of race 3 are:
   (a) C, E, G (b) D, E, F
   (c) C, G, E (d) Either (a) or (c)
14. D could have come third in which of the following races?
   (a) Race 1 (b) Race 3
   (c) Race 4 (d) Race 5
15. Suppose C had 6 points and E had 7 points while the points of the rest of the horses remain unchanged. Then E could have come second in ...
   (a) One race
   (b) Two races
   (c) At most one race
   (d) At most two races

Directions for Questions 16 to 20: *Refer to the data given below and answer the following questions:*

Arun, Barun, Charan, Deep, and Eahsan are five brothers who are ancestors to the royal family of Kaluchistan. They have assets in the form of palaces and cash only. Together they have 9 palaces and each brother has at least 1 palace. Value (in terms of rupees) of all palaces is equal and constant. Cash with each brother is an integral multiple of ₹1 crore. The amount of cash with Barun is just enough to buy one more palace, all the other brothers have cash less than that of Barun. Eahsan has got the maximum number of palaces. Number of palaces with Arun = sum of number of palaces with Barun and Charan.

Amount of cash with Barun is double of that with Deep and Deep has got assets worth ₹200 lakhs more than that of Barun.

16. What is the value of the nine palaces?
   (a) ₹27 crore (b) ₹45 crore
   (c) ₹36 crore (d) ₹18 crore
   (e) Cannot be determined
17. What can be the maximum possible value of assets of Arun?
   (a) ₹9 crore (b) ₹10 crore
   (c) ₹11crore (d) ₹12 crore
   (e) ₹13 crore
18. What is the ratio of the maximum possible value of assets of Eahsan to minimum possible of assets value of Charan?
   (a) 10:4 (b) 20:5
   (c) 10:5 (d) 6:2
   (e) 6:9
19. Which of these can be a possible value of the assets of all the brothers taken together?
   (a) ₹54 crore (b) ₹48 crore
   (c) ₹55 crore (d) ₹52 crore
   (e) ₹43 crore
20. For how many brothers the exact value of their total assets can be found?
   (a) 1 (b) 2
   (c) 3 (d) 4
   (e) 5

27 Mock Test Paper

Directions for Questions 1 to 5: *7 teams A, B, C, D, E, F, and G participate in the Mindworkzz Premiere League (MPL), a very unfair tournament. There were a Total of 200 Players who had to join 1 Team amongst these 8. There was no limitation on the maximum number of players each team hired in the auction. After the players were selected during the auction, Team G was disqualified from the league by the organisers, as it was found that they had participated in auction rigging. Because of the disqualification, the organisers had to conduct a second auction. In this auction, the organisers allowed the players who had been chosen by Team G, to be re-auctioned into the 6 remaining teams. All the players were chosen again – since team G had hired the best players in the original auction. Also, the players who were previously a part of a team also were put back into the auction – and while some of them were retained by their original teams, others were selected by the other teams. To be transparent with the teams, the MPL decided to share the details of the shuffle with every team, however, the person uploading the files missed some details while uploading. Some sketchy details of the number of players chosen by each team in the original auction and those chosen by each team in the new auction are shown in the table. The table also captures the retention/movement of the players from one team to another in the second auction. The details are given in the table below.*

		List of final selections in the second auction (number of players)					
List of original selections in the first auction (number of players)		A	B	C	D	E	F
	A	3	7	10	1	4	
	B		10	8	8	3	3
	C	2	6	11		1	
	D			2	10	1	5
	E		11	1		10	
	F	1	7	3		10	8
	G	4	12	11	5	5	11

Further, the following are known:

A. C had 1 more player than D before the change process, and after the shuffle, C had 21 more than D.

B. The number of players in F before the change process was even and 1 more than what it is now.

C. Before the change process, Team E had 11 less players than they have now. A lost a total of 14 players after the auction. The total number of players in A before the change process is an even number.

D. If you double B's number of players before the change process, it will be 10 more than what they have after the change process.

E. The missing numbers in the entire table are either 0 or 1.

1. How many players went from Team D to B?
2. How many players did D gain or lose because of the shuffle?
3. The team which gained/lost the highest number of players after the shuffle?
   (a) C
   (b) B
   (c) F
   (d) E
4. The teams which had the 2nd least and 3rd highest number of players before the shuffle?
   (a) A, D
   (b) C, A
   (c) F, E
   (d) C, F
5. What is the correct increasing order of the Teams as per the total number of players after the second auction?
   (a) D, C, E, A, F, B
   (b) A, D, E, C, F, B
   (c) A, D, F, E, C, B
   (d) B, C, E, F, D, A

Directions for Questions 6 to 10: *Anshuman works in a school as a part time faculty. His salary is ₹5000 for each student taught. After each class, the students have to give an exam of four subjects, Physics, Chemistry, Data Science and English. Each subject has a total of 10 marks, and the students get at least 1 mark in each of the four subjects.*

If a student's total marks obtained in the four subjects is more than 30, Anshuman is given a bonus of ₹2000 by the management.

Also, the students may tip the teacher for his expertise, the amount is either ₹500 or ₹200.

On 4th of Feb, 2033, he took a class wherein he taught all the four subjects to Pragyan, Qusum, Richa and Sherry and received a salary of 25,200 including tips and bonuses.

The following facts are also known:

A. The total marks received by all the four students was the highest in English and amounted to 34.

B. In physics, the total marks was 27 and 3 of the four students received the same number of marks.

C. The students scored distinct marks in Data science adding upto 24 marks, the lowest of all. The students also score distinct marks in English, and this was the only subject wherein a student scored full marks.

D. Amongst all the students, Pragyan scored the highest in Physics, Qusum in Chemistry and Data Science (with the same number of marks), and Sherry in English.

E. The lowest marks scored was by Richa in Chemistry. She also scored the lowest overall marks, 19.

F. It is known that Richa's marks in Data Science is 3/4th of Sherry's marks.

G. If the students have to be ranked on the marks obtained in a subject, then Pragyan's rank in English is the same as Richa's rank in Chemistry, and Qusum's rank in English is the same as Sherry's rank in Data Science.

H. One of the students who received the overall highest marks did not give a tip. Also the student who scored the least marks gave the lowest tip.

I. Pragyan and Qusum both scored overall equal marks, and the total marks obtained by all the four students, was 111

J. Sherry's marks in Chemistry was 100% more than that of Data Science.

6. Anshuman received the bonus because of which of his students?
   (a) Qusum and Sherry
   (b) Qusum and Pragyan
   (c) Richa and Sherry
   (d) Sherry and Pragyan
7. Which of the following students gave ₹500 as a tip to Anshuman?
   (a) Only Pragyan
   (b) Only Qusum
   (c) Sherry and one among Pragyan and Qusum
   (d) Richa
8. How many marks did Qusum score in Chemistry?
   (a) 9 (b) 8
   (c) 10 (d) 7
9. By how many marks was Sherry short of Pragyan's score overall?
   (a) 4 (b) 8
   (c) 5 (d) 7
10. Anyone scoring 8 or more marks in a subject received an A grade in that subject. How many A grades were awarded to these 4 students?

Directions for Questions 11 to 15: *At the National Sports Academy, Bengaluru, all the players train primarily for two sports, cricket and football. Each cricket player has to go to two different fitness tests, Yoyo Test and Beep Test, before he is given the green signal to participate in any tournament (i.e. he is cleared to play only is he passes both the tests). Each football player has to appear for only one of the two mentioned fitness tests. Any player who fails any test is deemed unfit to play. Players are given different grades, Best (B), Good (G), Average (A) and Fail (F) based on their performance in different tests.*

The following information is also known about the players and the grades they obtained:

A. The number of football players who appeared for the Yoyo and Beep Test were in the ratio 1:2.

B. The number of football players who appeared for either of the tests was equal to the number of cricket players.

C. The total number of football players who were not cleared to participate in the tournament was equal to the number of cricket players who got an A grade in their Beep Test. Moreover, the number of football players who failed their respective tests was equal in numbers.

D. In the Beep test, 45.45% of players who cleared the test got a Good grade.

E. The number of players who got B and A grade in the Yoyo Test were in the ratio 9:11. However, this number for the Beep Test was in the ratio 5:7.

F. All the cricket players passed their Yoyo Test and none of the football players got a B grade in the Yoyo Test.

G. The number of cricket players who got best, good and average grades in the Yoyo Test were in the ratio 3:5:2 and that for the Beep test was 3:7:4.

H. The ratio of the number of football players who were not cleared to participate to that of cricket players was 4:1

I. 60 players could not participate in any tournament because of their performance in the beep test.

11. If all the cricket and football players are different from each other, what is the total number of players who cannot participate in any tournament?
12. What is the total number of players at the National Sports Academy, Bengaluru?
    (a) 300 (b) 600
    (c) 900 (d) Cannot be determined
13. What is the maximum number of cricket players who got the best grade in at least 1 test?
14. If all the cricket and football players are different from each other, in total how many players received an average grade in their report cards (assume every cricket player who is average in the Yoyo Test is also average in the Beep test)?
15. After training for a year, all the average football players upgraded to the best grade in their respective tests. There was no change in the grades of the cricket players. If all the cricket and football players are different from each other, then what is the total number of best cricket and football players in the Yoyo Test one year later?

Directions for Questions 16 to 20: *3 Digital Marketing Companies, A, B, C took up a marketing assignment for companies X, Y, Z respectively. The project had Companies X, Y, Z generate leads for A, B, C and then convert those leads. The leads which were converted are called conversions, and the leads which were not converted are called as Lost Leads.*

Companies X, Y and Z then sell products to these converted leads at ₹ 150 per unit. The costs incurred are ₹20 per lead and ₹60 if you convert that lead.

Lead to conversion rate is defined as the percentage of leads that company converted in that year. Profits are Defined as Revenue-Cost Incurred.

Company D, a survey company which publishes reports for companies' performance, while compiling the data, ended up losing some of the numbers. This led to missing bars in Chart 1 and 2.

Chart 1 Shows Distribution of Revenue and Costs incurred for Companies X, Y and Z from 2019 to 2022. Note: The value of Y's revenue in 2019 is 3750, while the value of X's cost incurred in 2021 is 3120. All other values in this bar graph are in multiples of 100.

Chart 1: Distribution of Company X, Y and Z Revenue and Cost Over 2019-2021

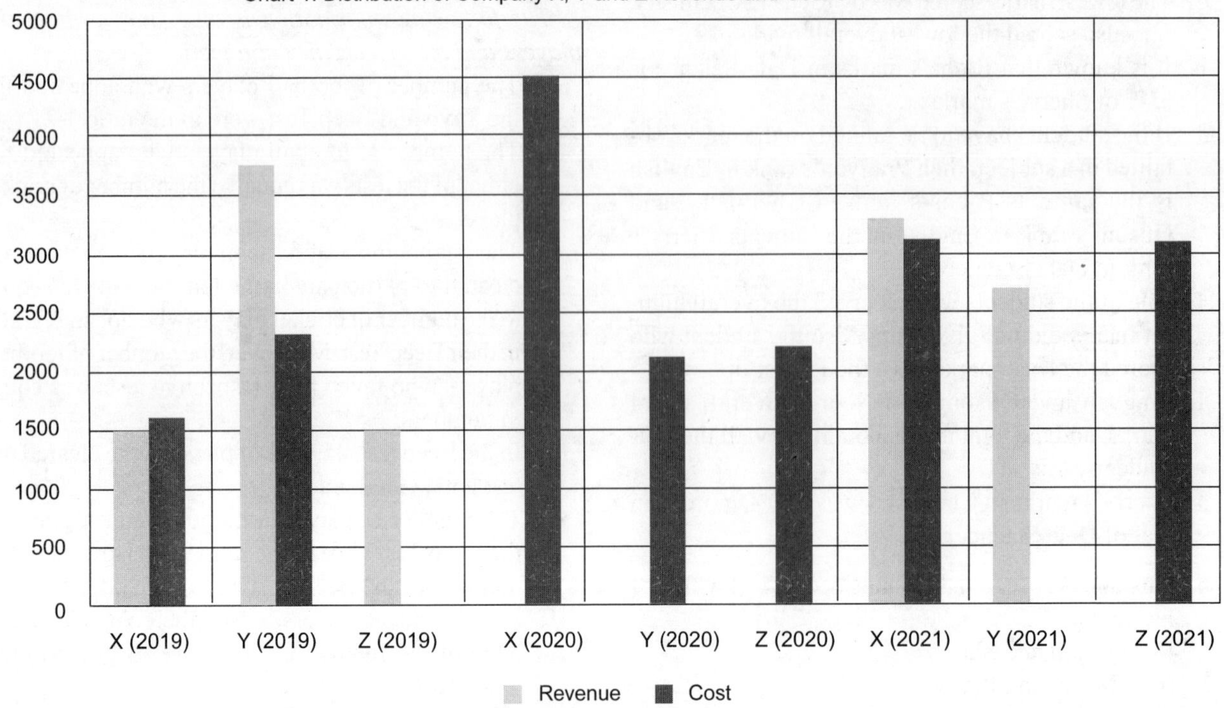

Chart 2 shows Distribution of Leads and Conversions for companies A, B and C From 2019-2021. B's leads and conversions in 2021 are 28 and 18 respectively. All the remaining values in this chart are multiples of 5.

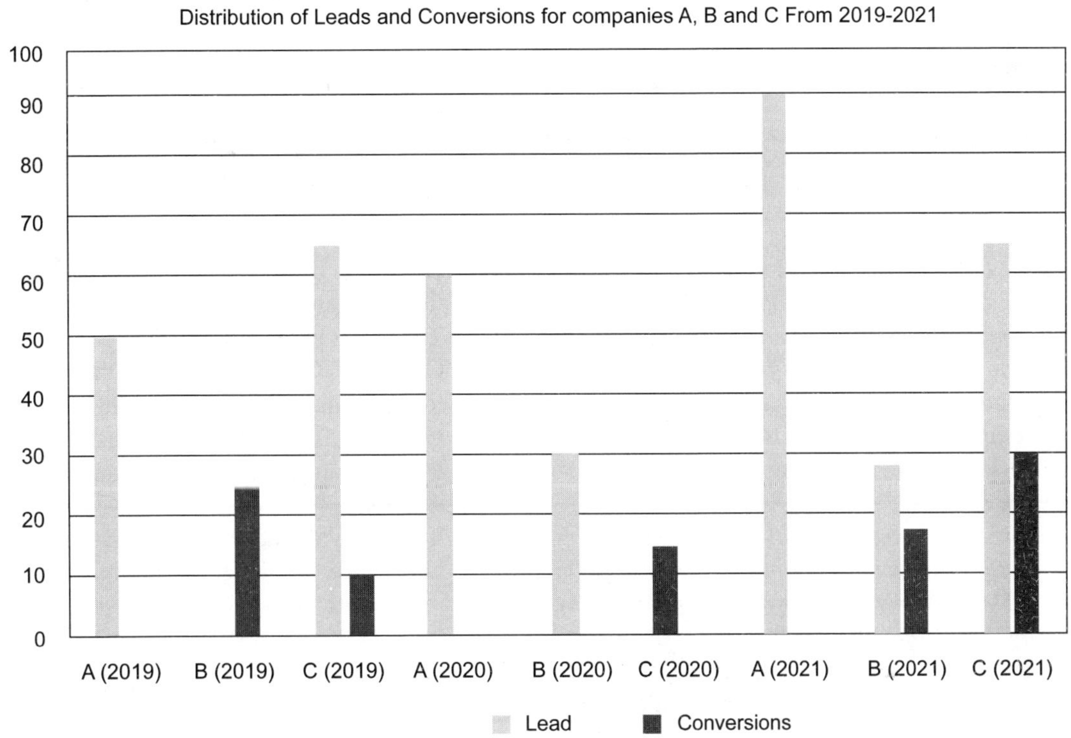

The following additional facts are known.

A. Each converted lead buys exactly 1 unit of the product being sold.
B. A had a 91.66% lead conversion rate in a particular year, the highest amongst its peers for all the years.

16. Which Company had the maximum Overall Profit?
    (a) X (b) Y
    (c) Z (d) Both X and Y
17. Which company had the least overall Profit?
    (a) X (b) Y
    (c) Z (d) None of these
18. Which company had the highest Lost Leads in 2021?
    (a) Company C
    (b) Company A
    (c) Company B
    (d) None of these
19. Which company had the highest lead to conversion ratio in 2021?
    (a) Company C
    (b) Company A
    (c) Company B
    (d) None of these
20. If the Net profit margin ratio is defined as the ratio of Profit and Revenue, which company had the highest NPM and in which year?
    (a) Company X, 2020
    (b) Company Y, 2020
    (c) Company Z, 2021
    (d) None of these

28 Mock Test Paper

Directions for Questions 1 to 5: *P, Q, R, S, T, U are 6 high net worth individuals who go to Ocean restaurant in Mumbai, (one of the fanciest restaurants in India) to eat dinner. After dining at the restaurant, they award tips to the waiter serving them. At least 2 of them dine together. In one month, they went to the restaurant on 5 different days and were served by 5 different waiters A, B, C, D and E.*

It is not necessarily true that all 5 of the customers went to the Restaurants on all the days. For example, On Day 1 it could be that only P and Q went, were served by A and they left him a tip collectively.

The tips are values which are in the multiples of 2, 3, 5, 11, 17 and 19. To determine the numerical value of the tip, the numbers are written on a chit and jumbled in a box. After the meal is over, each customer dining on that day picks out a random chit and they collectively tip the waiter based on the chit drawn. Once a chit is drawn, it is removed from the box and assigned to that person. The next time that person comes to dine, his contribution to the tip will be the same as the number drawn previous time he/she came to dine. The value of the tip is ₹20 × (the product of the face values of all the chits of the people dining on that day). For example, On Day 1 P and Q went to the restaurant, and they were served By A. After dining, P picks up a chit and gets the number 5. This chit is now removed from the box. Now Q picks up a chit and gets number 2. The total tip given to A would be 2 × 5 × 20 = 200. On day 2, If P and S come to the restaurant, They will be served by someone other than A. Let's say C served them, now the tip received by C would be ₹20 × 5 (5 is P's chit which he drew on day 1) × (the chit drawn by S). If S draws 11, then the tip amount would be 20 × 5 × 11 = 1100.

The Product of the face value of the chits on the dining days were 30, 7106, 114, 418 and 34 in some random order.

The following facts are also known.

A. On Day 1, P and S were amongst some of the customers who tipped ₹600 to A.
B. On Day 2, B served 4 customers and received the maximum tip.
C. On day 3, D served 3 customers. It is also known that Q, T and 1 more individual dined with them. The total tip value was ₹8360
D. On Day 4, C served P and 2 other customers. The total tip value amounted to 2280.
E. On day 5, E served the least customers.
F. P is the only individual to have tipped all the waiters.
G. It is known that R was not served by B.
H. U because of budget constraints, only visited the restaurants on one of the first three days and the last day.

1. If it is known that S's chit value is the first odd prime number, what is the Value of the chit R picked?
   (a) 5 (b) 3
   (c) 2 (d) 11
2. If it is known that the sum of R and T's chit values is 14, then what are the values of the chits of Q and S?
   (a) 3 and 11 b. 19 and 5,
   (c) 11 and 5 d. 17 and 2
3. If it is known that R visited the restaurant instead of Q on the 2nd day, and T has the 3rd highest chit value amongst all, then which of the following can be true?
   (1) the total product of all the chits used for the tips on the 2nd day is 1870
   (2) The total sum of all the chits used for the tips on the 2nd day is 33.
   (3) The total tip value is ₹22,440.
   (a) only 1 (b) Only 2
   (c) 1, 2 and 3 (d) Both 2 and 3
4. If R likes to dine with Q and decides to go on the days Q went, who amongst all the waiters will he definitely give a tip to?
   (a) A, B and D (b) A, B, C, D
   (c) A, B, C (d) A and B only
5. If it is known that C received a tip by T along with the others who were giving him a tip, what is the value of T's chit?
   (a) 2 (b) 19
   (c) 3 (d) 5

Directions for Questions 6 to 10: *The FSSAI is responsible for grading restaurants on the basis of their Food Quality (FQ), Dining Experience (DE), Location (LC), Kitchen Cleanliness (KC) and Quality of Drinks (DQ) The ratings in these five parameters are used to calculate the overall rating of a restaurant. In each parameter, there are five possible grades which carry different points, A, B, C, D and F. The values of the ratings are 100, 80, 60, 40 and 0 respectively. The overall rating is calculated as the sum of points scored across different parameters. The weightage of different parameters are 0.1, 0.2, 0.3, 0.4 and 0.5 as given in the brackets in the table below.*

FSSAI conducted random assessments at 8 different restaurants and gave ratings as given below.

	FQ (0.5)	DE (0.2)	LC (0.1)	KC (0.4)	DQ (0.3)
Tamasha	A			D	C
McDonalds	B	F	D		A
GolaSizzlers	A	C	C	A	D
Local	D	B	A	B	
Privee		A	D		A
MyBarHQ	C	B	D		
Harlequin	B	C	C	B	C
38Barracks		D	A		C

Based on their overall scores, FSSAI released the following information:

A. Only Privee and McDonalds got F in at least one of the parameters.

B. Tamasha had a similar score in DE & LC, Privee had similar score in FQ & KC, 38 Barracks had similar score in FQ & KC, My Bar HQ had similar score in KC & DQ

C. Local & MyBarHQ had similar ratings in at least 2 of the 5 parameters. Meanwhile, Tamasha & McDonalds had a similar rating in one of the 5 parameters.

Answer the following questions based on your understanding of the set:

6. In total how many Fs were there?
7. Which restaurant got the maximum overall score?
8. Which restaurant performed the worst?
9. What is the maximum difference between the overall scores of any 2 restaurants?
10. What is the sum of the overall ratings of Tamasha and Privee?

Directions for Questions 11 to 14: *Mindworkzz has an offline center at Connaught Place, New Delhi. They have a total of 800 boys and girls in total enrolled with them per year. 60% of which study in Section 3, and the rest equally divided between Section 1 and Section 2. It is also known that the boys are 50% of the total students in section 2 and football players are 50% of the total students in Section 2. The students either play football or cricket but nobody plays both. 42% of the total students are boys.*

Distribution of Students (Gender and Sport-Wise)

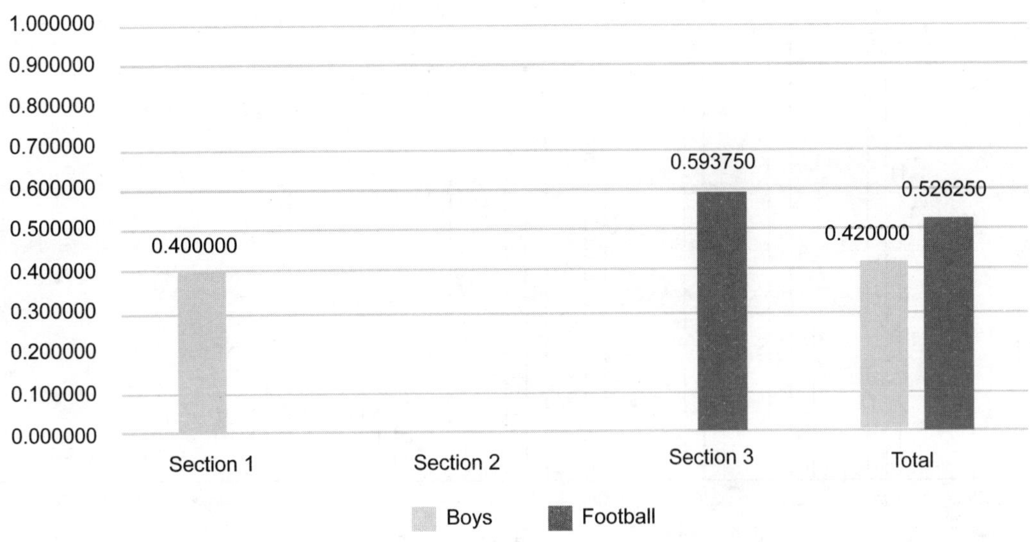

11. How many students studying in section 1 play Football?
    (a) 56
    (b) 80
    (c) 285
    (d) 300
12. The percentage of students who study in Section 1 and do not play Cricket?
    (a) 35%
    (b) 20%
    (c) 25%
    (d) 40%
13. If in Section 1, there are 54 girl cricket players, then what is the number of boy football players in that section?
14. If in section 3, 70 football players are boys, then what is the percentage value of the ratio of number of girl cricket players to the number of boy cricket players in that section?

Directions for Questions 15 to 20: *KIIT, an engineering college in Bhubaneswar, conducted an IQ Championship in partnership with Mindworkzz. The scores were calculated and the top four candidates qualified for the final round. The championship consisted of an MCQ Test with 3 sections- Logical reasoning (LR), Verbal Ability (VA) and Quantitative Aptitude (QA) -of 20 marks each. A final score was calculated out of 80 by doubling the score in LR and adding it to remaining scores. Students who fail to secure 70% marks in two or more sections were disqualified. From the remaining students, the top 4 were selected for the final round. If less than 4 students qualify, all those who qualify moved to the final round.*

While feeding the values in the database, the typist at KIIT made a huge blunder and jumbled all the data. Later, in the review meeting he admitted to the mess up and put forward the following data that he remembered from the main sheet.

A. The marks for the following students, Palak & Qadir, Ritika & Sagar, Tanya & Urvashi, Vivek & Wriddhi, Xavier & Yash, were clubbed together. The name of the sections were correct throughout the graph but the exact scores of the students were missing.
B. Also, no two students had the same composite score.
C. Among the four students who moved to the finals, Vivek had the lowest composite score.
D. Sagar, Wriddhi and Xavier score the same marks in QA.
E. Tanya had consecutive multiples of a number in at least 2 different sections and Yash scored 14 marks in QA.
F. The sectional scores of Palak, Sagar, and Xavier were equal in one or more sections.
G. Qadir scored 2 less marks in LR than in QA. Ritika's Score in one section and Sagar's Score in another section were consecutive multiples of a prime number.
H. Wriddhi, Vivek and Urvashi in that order had consecutive scores in distinct sections.
I. Xavier qualified for the final round.
J. Xavier and Yash scored 100% in exactly one section and Yash's composite score was 10 more than that of Xavier.

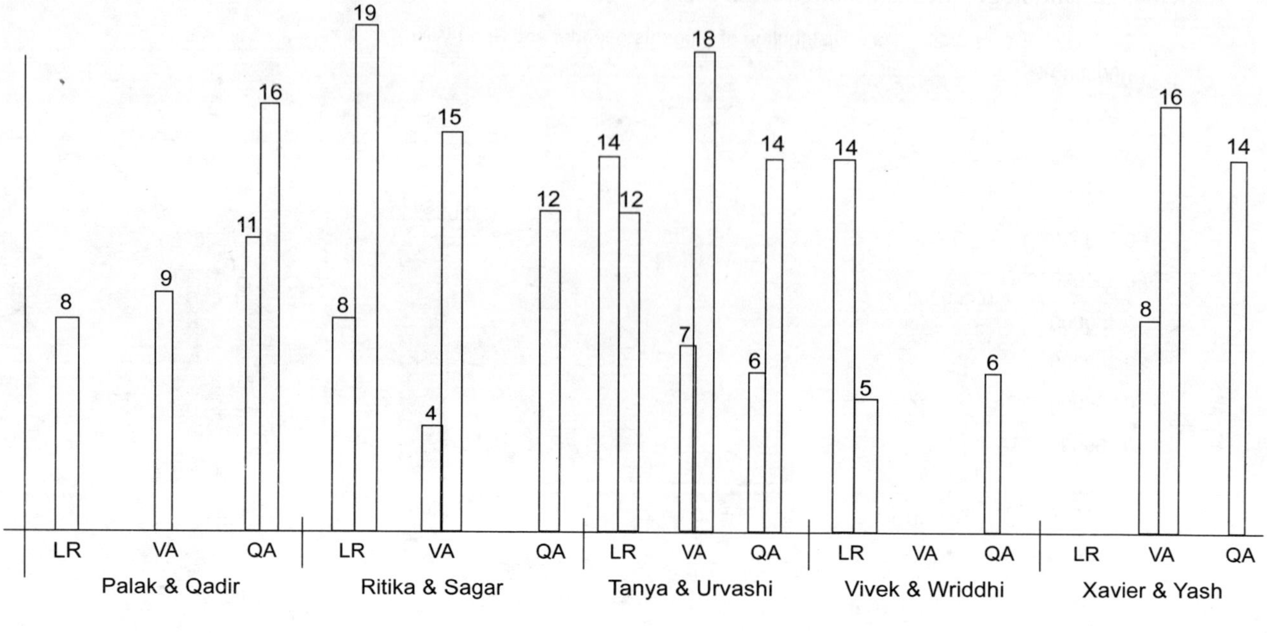

15. Which of the following statements MUST be true?
    1. Yash's composite score was more than that of Sagar.
    2. Xavier scored less than Ritika in LR.
    3. Yash scored more than Xavier in QA.

    (a) Only 2 (b) Both 2 and 3
    (c) Only 1 (d) Both 1 and 2

16. Which of the following statements MUST be FALSE?
    (a) Qadir scored same as Yash in LR
    (b) Qadir's composite score was less than that of Tanya
    (c) Ritika scored more than Qadir in LR
    (d) Wriddhi's composite score was less than that of Urvashi

17. If Qadir scored more than Palak in QA, then what is the maximum he could have scored in VA?

18. What is the score of Vivek in VA?
    (a) 12
    (b) At least 12
    (c) 16
    (d) At least 16.

19. Who amongst Palak, Qadir and Wriddhi had the maximum composite score?
    (a) Palak
    (b) Qadir
    (c) Wriddhi
    (d) Cannot be determined.

20. What is the maximum number of instance of scores in excess of 15 that have been scored by the students?

Answer Key

LEVEL OF DIFFICULTY 2

MOCK TEST PAPER 1

1. (a) 2. (a) 3. (b) 4. 2 5. 90 6. 200 7. 200
8. 200 9. 800 10. 400 11. (a) 12. 25 13. 22 14. 42
15. 36 16. (a) 17. (c) 18. (a) 19. 17 20. (c)

MOCK TEST PAPER 2

1. (d) 2. (c) 3. (e) 4. (b) 5. (a) 6. (c) 7. (a)
8. (c) 9. (a) 10. (a) 11. (e) 12. (a) 13. (b) 14. (c)
15. (a) 16. (a) 17. (d) 18. (d) 19. (a) 20. (e)

MOCK TEST PAPER 3

1. (a) 2. (c) 3. (c) 4. (d) 5. 30 6. (d) 7. (b)
8. (c) 9. (b) 10. 4 11. (d) 12. (b) 13. (b) 14. (b)
15. (d) 16. (c) 17. (b) 18. (a) 19. (b) 20. 10

MOCK TEST PAPER 4

1. (c) 2. (a) 3. (d) 4. (d) 5. (a) 6. (b) 7. (a)
8. (b) 9. (e) 10. (a) 11. (d) 12. (d) 13. (c) 14. (a)
15. (a) 16. (c) 17. (b) 18. 26000 19. 34000 20. (d)

MOCK TEST PAPER 5

1. (b) 2. (a) 3. (d) 4. (b) 5. (d) 6. (b) 7. (d)
8. (c) 9. (d) 10. (a) 11. (d) 12. (a) 13. (d) 14. (c)
15. (d) 16. (d) 17. (a) 18. (c) 19. (d) 20. (a)

MOCK TEST PAPER 6

1. (b) 2. (a) 3. (c) 4. (d) 5. (b) 6. (d) 7. (c)
8. (c) 9. (a) 10. (c) 11. (b) 12. (d) 13. (d) 14. (d)
15. (d) 16. (a) 17. (b) 18. (a) 19. (d) 20. (a)

MOCK TEST PAPER 7

1. (a) 2. (d) 3. 580 4. (b) 5. 1 6. (b) 7. 5
8. (a) 9. (c) 10. (a) 11. (a) 12. (d) 13. (d) 14. (a)
15. (d) 16. (b) 17. (c) 18. (c) 19. (b) 20. (c)

MOCK TEST PAPER 8

1. (c) 2. (d) 3. 16 matches 4. 4 points 5. 8 points 6. 10 points 7. 26
8. (b) 9. (b) 10. (c) 11. (d) 12. 17.72 13. (a) 14. (b)
15. (d) 16. (c) 17. (c) 18. (d) 19. (d) 20. (a)

LEVEL OF DIFFICULTY 3

MOCK TEST PAPER 9

1. 50
2. (b)
3. 9
4. 80
5. 5
6. 11252
7. (a)
8. (b)
9. (c)
10. 570
11. 2.5%
12. 50
13. (a)
14. 2
15. Cannot be determined.
16. 19.46%
17. 3
18. 38
19. 18
20. 36

MOCK TEST PAPER 10

1. (b)
2. (c)
3. (a)
4. (d)
5. (d)
6. (d)
7. (b)
8. (d)
9. (c)
10. (b)
11. (d)
12. (c)
13. (a)
14. (b)
15. (c)
16. (d)
17. 239
18. 34
19. 324
20. 61

MOCK TEST PAPER 11

1. (c)
2. (d)
3. (a)
4. (c)
5. (a)
6. 21.06
7. 0
8. 70
9. 5
10. 160
11. 166
12. (d)
13. (a)
14. (c)
15. (d)
16. 5
17. (b)
18. (c)
19. (d)
20. (d)

MOCK TEST PAPER 12

1. 3
2. 5
3. 7
4. 11
5. (c)
6. (b)
7. (a)
8. (e)
9. (c)
10. (d)
11. (d)
12. (d)
13. (c)
14. (b)
15. (b)
16. (c)
17. (a)
18. (d)
19. (c)
20. (d)

MOCK TEST PAPER 13

1. (d)
2. (b)
3. (d)
4. (a)
5. 108
6. 3
7. 27
8. 1
9. (c)
10. (a)
11. (c)
12. (b)
13. (d)
14. (c)
15. (a)
16. (b)
17. (c)
18. (a)
19. (c)
20. 1

MOCK TEST PAPER 14

1. (b)
2. (a)
3. (d)
4. (a)
5. (a)
6. (d)
7. (b)
8. 56
9. (c)
10. 2nd Rank
11. (c)
12. (b)
13. (c)
14. (a)
15. (d)
16. (a)
17. (b)
18. (d)
19. (d)
20. (d)

MOCK TEST PAPER 15

1. (d)
2. (c)
3. (d)
4. (a)
5. (e)
6. (d)
7. (e)
8. (e)
9. (b)
10. (b)
11. (c)
12. (d)
13. (d)
14. (d)
15. (a)
16. (d)
17. (a)
18. (d)
19. (c)
20. (c)

MOCK TEST PAPER 16

1. (e)
2. (a)
3. (a)
4. (e)
5. (d)
6. (a)
7. (a)
8. (d)
9. (d)
10. (a)
11. (b)
12. 3761
13. 415
14. 5981
15. 150
16. (c)
17. 48.61%
18. 25
19. 0
20. 60

MOCK TEST PAPER 17

1. (b)
2. (d)
3. (a)
4. 3
5. (c)
6. 3
7. 1
8. 3
9. 4
10. 7
11. 150
12. 40%
13. Fatima
14. Kavita
15. 12
16. 4
17. 340
18. 27.05%
19. (c)
20. (b)

MOCK TEST PAPER 18

1. (c)	2. (c)	3. (d)	4. (d)	5. (d)	6. (c)	7. (a)
8. (c)	9. (c)	10. (b)	11. (d)	12. (d)	13. (c)	14. (c)
15. (b)	16. (d)	17. (c)	18. (d)	19. (d)	20. (c)	

MOCK TEST PAPER 19

1. 0.4	2. 4	3. 5 kgs	4. 5	5. 4 passengers	6. (b)	7. 250
8. 90	9. (a)	10. 0	11. 33	12. (a)	13. (d)	14. 2
15. (d)	16. (b)	17. (b)	18. (a)	19. (c)	20. (b)	

MOCK TEST PAPER 20

1. (d)	2. (d)	3. (c)	4. (d)	5. (b)	6. (c)	7. (c)
8. (d)	9. (c)	10. (e)	11. (a)	12. (d)	13. (a)	14. (b)
15. (c)	16. (c)	17. (c)	18. (e)	19. (a)	20. (a)	

MOCK TEST PAPER 21

1. (b)	2. (a)	3. (c)	4. (d)	5. (b)	6. (a)	7. (d)
8. (d)	9. (c)	10. (e)	11. (a)	12. (d)	13. (c)	14. (b)
15. (d)	16. (a)	17. (d)	18. (c)	19. (c)	20. (b)	

MOCK TEST PAPER 22

1. (b)	2. (a)	3. (c)	4. 19	5. 51	6. 480	7. (d)
8. (b)	9. 144	10. 12	11. 312	12. 3	13. (c)	14. (a)
15. (c)	16. (b)	17. (b)	18. (c)	19. (a)	20. (b)	

MOCK TEST PAPER 23

1. 3	2. 3	3. (b)	4. (c)	5. (d)	6. (d)	7. (c)
8. (b)	9. (b)	10. (a)	11. (b)	12. (a)	13. (b)	14. (c)
15. (a)	16. (b)	17. (b)	18. (c)	19. (d)	20. (d)	

MOCK TEST PAPER 24

1. (c)	2. 4.25	3. 5	4. 2	5. 5	6. (b)	7. (b)
8. (a)	9. (c)	10. (d)	11. (c)	12. (b)	13. (a)	14. (c)
15. (d)	16. (d)	17. (d)	18. (c)	19. (e)	20. (b)	

MOCK TEST PAPER 25

1. (a)	2. (e)	3. (b)	4. (b)	5. (c)	6. (b)	7. (d)
8. (b)	9. (d)	10. (d)	11. (b)	12. (d)	13. (a)	14. (a)
15. (b)	16. (b)	17. (a)	18. (c)	19. (d)	20. (b)	

MOCK TEST PAPER 26

1. (e)	2. (a)	3. (e)	4. (e)	5. (a)	6. (c)	7. (b)
8. (a)	9. (c)	10. (a)	11. (b)	12. (d)	13. (d)	14. (c)
15. (d)	16. (c)	17. (d)	18. (d)	19. (b)	20. (b)	

MOCK TEST PAPER 27

1. 1	2. 5	3. (a)	4. (d)	5. (c)	6. (b)	7. (c)
8. (a)	9. (a)	10. 9	11. 100	12. (d)	13. 150	14. 190
15. 140	16. (b)	17. (c)	18. (b)	19. (c)	20. (a)	

MOCK TEST PAPER 28

1. (a)	2. (b)	3. (c)	4. (a)	5. (b)	6. 3	7. Gola Sizzlers
8. Privee	9. 66	10. 154	11. (a)	12. (a)	13. 42	14. 59.83%
15. (d)	16. (a)	17. 3	18. (c)	19. (d)	20. 11	

Solutions

LEVEL OF DIFFICULTY 2

MOCK TEST PAPER 1

Questions 1 to 5:

If a student named four of the scientists correctly then definitely he named the fifth scientist correctly. It is given that the five contestants got different marks hence these five students named 5, 3, 2, 1, 0 scientists correctly in any order.

Now let's assume Pulkit named all of them correct. Then Qasim, Rahim, Sahir, Taufiq named 1, 3, 0, 2 of them correctly. This means that this is a possibility for the 5 winners – since we have got all the number of correct answers corresponding to different numbers of students. Similarly, if we check for Qasim getting all 5 answers correct, we would see that Pulkit, Rahim, Sahir and Taufiq get 1, 2, 0 and 3 answers correct respectively – thus satisfying the condition. However, if we check the table for Rahim getting all answers correct, we see that there is no one with 0 answers correct (as we get Qasim and Taufiq both getting 1 answer correct). Hence, Rahim getting all answers correct is not a possibility. Similar thinking would give us that, Sahir and Taufiq as all answers correct would also not be possible.

Thus, based on the answers of Pulkit and Qasim we get the following two possibilities:

Year	Possibility-1 Pulkit All Correct Scientist Name	Possibility-2 Qasim All Correct Scientist Name
2010	Chris	Bob
2011	Denial	Chris
2012	Alex	Alex
2013	Elina	Denial
2014	Bob	Elina

1. Bob could be a winner of 2010 physics Noble prize. Option (a).
2. Pulkit and Qasim can get 100 marks in the quiz. From the given options only option (a) is correct.
3. Alex. Option (b).
4. In both the possible cases, two students predicted the winner correctly.
5. Maximum possible marks scored by Pulkit = 100 (Possibility-1)
   In either of the possible arrangements, Sahir got none of the scientists in the correct order.
   Hence, marks scored by Sahir = $10 \times 0 + 10 = 10$.
   Required difference = $100 - 10 = 90$.

Questions 6 to 10:

Deduction 1: From statements 2, 3, and 4 either G-H or H-I must carry 600 amperes. If G-H carries 600 amperes then H-I must carry 400 amperes, which is not possible because it violates the statement 2.
Hence, H-I must carry 600 amperes and G-H must carry 800 amperes.

Deduction 2: D-G should carry 800 amperes more than the requirement of G. G's requirement is equal to the requirement of G-H.

Hence, requirement of G = 800 amperes and connector D-G carries the 800 + 800 = 1600 amperes of current.

Deduction 3: The current in the connector E-I and requirement of E both are same and equals to 200 amperes. Therefore the requirement of node I = 200 + 600 = 800 amperes.

Deduction 4: The current transfer in the node F-B and requirement of F both are same and equals to 200 amperes.

Deduction 5: Current in the connector C-F = 200 + 200 + 400 = 800 amperes.

Similar analysis for the other nodes would lead us to the following diagram:

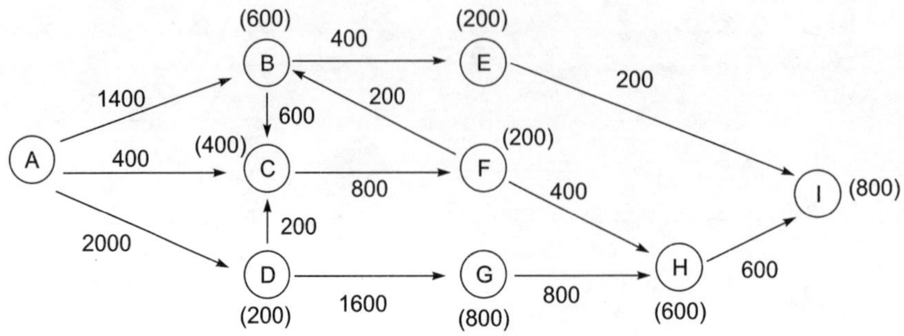

6. 200 amperes.
7. 200 amperes.
8. 200 amperes.
9. 800 amperes.
10. 400 amperes.

Questions 11 to 13:

Stages	Earlier Stage	Time Required to Complete the Stage from Beginning (in months)
O	None	4
P	O	15 + 4 = 19
Q	O	12 + 4 = 16
R	Q	9 + 16 = 25
S	P, R	2 + 25 = 27
T	P	3 + 19 = 22
U	T	5 + 22 = 27
V	S	7 + 27 = 34
W	R	9 + 25 = 34
X	U, V	17 + 34 = 51
Y	V, W	11 + 34 = 45
Z	Y	7 + 45 = 52

11. Stage X depends upon U and V. Stage U takes 27 months and stage V takes 34 months.

    ∴ X can start in the 35th month. So, X can start in November, 2024.
12. After stage S, number of months required to complete the training = 52 – 27 = 25 months.
13. Stages U and X follow stage T. U requires 5 months and X requires 17 months. Since the training requires a minimum 52 months, it means that there are at least 5 + 17 = 22 monhts that are required to be available after completion of T.

Questions 14 to 15:

14. O → P → T → U

Stages	Session M	Session N
O	1–4	5–8
P	5–19	20–34
T	20–22	35–37
U	23–27	38–42

The least required time is 42 months.

15. O → Q → R

O	1–4	5–8
Q	5–16	17–28
R	17–25	29–36

The least required time is 36 months.

Questions 16 to 20:

Table B states that the first wicket falls at score 35. As Sachin himself scored 40, as 40 > 35, we can conclude that Sehwag was the first to get out. At that time Sachin must have scored 35 – 29 = 6 runs. From doing the similar analysis for other batsmen we can get the following result:

Fall of Wickets	Total Score	Runs Scored by the Batsmen to Get Out	Runs Scored by the Batsman Who is Not Out/Batting.	Partnership
1	35	Sehwag (29)	Sachin (6)	35
2	54	Gautam (11)	Sachin (8)	19
3	62	Yuvraj (0)	Sachin (8)	8
4	87	Sachin (18)	Kohli (7)	25
5	97	Dhoni (6)	Kohli (4)	10
6	122	Kohli (14)	Raina (11)	25
7	128	Harbhajan (5)	Raina (1)	6
8	133	Ashwin (1)	Raina (4)	5
9	144	Bhuvi (10)/ Raina (2)	Raina (1) / Bhuvi (9)	11
10	150	Raina (1)/Zaheer (5) or Bhuvi (1)/ Zaheer (5)	Zaheer (5)/Raina (1) or Zaheer (5)/ Bhuvi (1)	6

16. (a) 0
17. (c) 5
18. (a) Total runs scored by all the batsmen of India is equal to the total score of the team, so there is no extra runs in the Indian team's score.
19. For the first wicket: Sehwag can hit maximum four sixes and Sachin can hit maximum one six. Similarly for the 2nd wicket Gautam can hit maximum one six and Sachin can hit maximum one six.

Fall of Wickets	Maximum Possible 6's
1	5
2	2
3	1
4	4
5	1
6	3
7	0
8	0
9	1
10	0

Maximum possible number of sixes = 17 sixes.

20. From the solution table we can see that the 9th -10th wicket could be Bhuvi-Raina; Bhuvi-Zaheer or Raina-Bhuvi or Raina-Zaheer. So a total of 4 combinations are possible. Option (c) is correct.

MOCK TEST PAPER 2

Questions 5 to 6:

5. The win on the second throw would happen under the following cases:
   4 & 4 or 5 & 5 or 6 & 6 or 8 & 8 or 9 & 9 or 10 & 10.
   The required probability will be (3/36 × 3/36 + (4/36 × 4/36) + (5/36 × 5/36)+(5/36 × 5/36)+ (4/36 × 4/36) + (3/36 × 3/36) = 100/1296
6. The loss on the second throw would happen under the following cases:
   4 & 7 or 5 & 7 or 6 &7 or 8 &7 or 9 & 7 or 10 & 7
   The required probability will be (3/36 × 6/36) + (4/36 × 6/36) + (5/36 × 6/36) + (5/36 × 6/36) + (4/36 × 6/36) + (3/36 × 6/36) = 144/1296
   The series of wins/losses can be summarised in the table below:

Player ↓				
A	6, 4, 10, 9, 8, 6 (win)	7 win	12 loss	9,2 no result
B	8, 5, 7 loss	12 loss	6, 3, 2, 9, 8, 3 no result	
C	2 Loss, 7 Win, 3 Loss, 12 Loss, 7 Win, 6, 5, 4, 6 Win, 3 Loss			

Only statement (iii) is correct.

Questions 7 to 11:

7. Statement (iii) is correct. Hence, option (a) is correct.
8. Option (c) is correct.
9. A has lost only once. Hence, option (a).
10. Option (a) 4 losses – 3 wins = 1.
11. 4 + 3 + 7 = 14 games. Hence option (e).

Questions 12 to 16:

From the given clues, the following table can be deduced:

	1	2	3	4
A	Biren	Chandan	Biren	Biren
B	Amar	Deepak	Deepak	Chandan
C	Deepak	Amar	Amar	Biren
D	Amar	Chandan	Chandan	Deepak

Totals	Amar	Biren	Chandan	Deepak
	10	30	4	32
	18	22	12	24
	2	6	26	8
	28	14	20	16
Total	58	72	62	80

12. Amar
13. Biren
14. 80 – 62 = 18
15. 58
16. Amar

MOCK TEST PAPER 3

Questions 1 to 2:

1. Monday stock = 128 + 50 = 178 → Cost of keeping stock = 178 × 5 = 890.
   Tuesday stock = 178 +156 = 334 → Cost of keeping stock = 334 × 5 = 1670. It's better to hire the truck on Tuesday. In the same manner we can see that the truck should be hired on Thursday and Saturday too.
2. 890 + 1000 + 320 + 1000 + 360 + 1000 + 600 = 5170

Questions 3 to 7:

3. If no student failed in MBA 5, then all 144 get promoted, which means that exactly 18 (162 – 144) fail in their Internship. Hence, the pass percentage is 83.33%.
4. If 228 new students joined MBA 1 in 2223, then 192 students from MBA 1 would have failed in the year 2222. Consequently, 360 – 192 = 168 students passed MBA 1 in 2222. These 168 would be part of the 300 students of 2223 who were in MBA 2. Thus, 300 – 168 = 132 students would have failed MBA 2 in 2222. So 120 students passed MBA 2 in 2222 and 90 students failed MBA 3 in 2222. So, 126 students passed MBA 3 in 2222 and 54 students failed MBA 4 in 2223. So 192–54 = 138 students passed MBA 4 in 2222 and 30 students failed MBA 5 in 2222. So, 114 students passed MBA 5 in 2222 and 48 students failed MBA Internship Year in 2222. Hence, option (d) is correct.
5. From the analysis for the previous question, we can see that this number is 30.
6. If no student of MBA 5 failed in 2222, it means that all the 168 students of MBA 5 in 2223, must have come from students who were in MBA 4 in 2222. Thus, 24 students of MBA 4, failed in 2222. So, 156 students of MBA 3 passed in 2222 and 60 students of MBA 3 would have failed in 2222. Hence, option (d) is correct.
7. Total failures = 192 + 132 + 90 + 54 + 30 + 48 = 546

Questions 8 to 12:

8. *Diamond:* 15550 / 14900 = 1.04
   Ruby: 67200 / 68100 = 0.98
   Pearl: 298 / 450 = 0.66
   Emerald: 8090 / 8200 = 0.98
   Clearly, Pearl has the minimum ratio. Hence (c).

9. It is best to draw a table which shows the ratio of the total sales to production for all the quarters.

	Ratio of Total Sales to Production			
	1st Quarter	2nd Quarter	3rd Quarter	4th Quarter
Diamond	1	0.91	1.04	1.19
Ruby	0.94	0.97	0.9	1.1
Pearl	0.46	2.25	1.18	0.3
Emerald	0.94	0.94	1	1.04

Clearly, the maximum change in ratio can be observed for Pearl from 1st quarter to 2nd quarter. The % increase $= (2.25 - 0.46)/0.46 \times 100 = 3891.3$ %. Hence (b).

10. From the table we drew for the previous question, we can make out that Diamond has dropped once, Ruby once and Pearl has dropped twice. Hence, there are 4 instances.
11. All the three statements can be verified from the table of the ratio of the Total sales to production. Statement (i) and (iii) are true while statement (ii) is false. Hence (d).
12. The revenue from domestic sales = 2 × revenue from exports as given. Let the per unit price for domestic sales and exports for Diamonds be ₹a and ₹b respectively.
Then, $4000a = 2 \times 1000b \Rightarrow b/a = 2$.
Similarly the ratio for the others comes out to be 14.5, 4 and 6.6 respectively. Hence (b) is the correct answer.

Questions 13 to 17:

13. Total number of products sold in 2018–19 = $60000/0.75 = 80000$
Total number of products sold in 2019–20 = $1.5625 \times 80000 = 125000$
Products sold in the category of Miran in the year 2019–20 = $125000 \times 0.168 = 21000$. Hence sales of products in the category of Miran in 2018–19 = $21000/5 = 4200$
Hence sales of products in the category of Cok in 2018–19 = $0.85 \times 80000 - 60000 - 4200 = 3800$.
Similarly sales of products in the miscellaneous category = $12000/12 = 1000$. Thus sales of products in the category of Cok ranks 7th. Hence (b).
14. From the given data, we have the total sales of the following category in two years.
Pep ⇒ $18000 + 17500 = 35500$
Dewy ⇒ $7500 + 5000 = 12500$
Slic ⇒ $13000 + 13500 = 26500$
Now we know the ranks of the top five sales volume of the range in the respective year, we can find the range of sales of the remaining category. Since the sales of Miran in 2019–20 is 21000 and as sales of category which ranked 5th (Fant) i.e. 5500, we have sales of Miran ranging from $21000 <$ Miran ≤ 26500.
Similarly we have $18000 \leq$ Cok ≤ 23500
$16000 \leq$ Sprit ≤ 21000
$5500 \leq$ Fant ≤ 10500
The drinks in the category of Miran, Cok and Sprit could have either of 3rd, 4th or 5th rank. Now as Dewy's sales are higher than Fant, it ranked 6th. Hence (b).
15. From the above discussion it can be concluded that the correct option is (d).
16. From the previous discussion, we can see that Slic would rank second.
17. The total number of drinks in category Miran and Cok are 8000. As Miran ranks 6th, Cok has to be 7th. Thus the Miran has more units than 4000 and the Cok category less than 4000. Hence (b).

Questions 18 to 20:

18. The maximum someone can collect would occur if you give three people the minimum number of stamps.
Thus, $20 + 22 + 24 + 134 = 200$. Hence, the maximum stamps possible for one friend is 134. Option (a) is correct.
19. If one friend collected 116, the other three have to collect 84, with the given condition. It can only be done if, Manish has 20 stamps, Karan has 42 stamps and Shyam has 22 stamps. Option (b) is correct.
20. $20 + 22 + 24 = 66$. The remaining 18 can be distributed as: 2,4,12 (4 ways); 2,6,10 (4 ways); 4,6,8 (2 ways). This can be thought of as:

Base Value	20	22	24	
Additions (for 2,4,12)	+2 = 22	+4 = 26	+12 = 36	
	+2 = 22	+12 = 34	+4 = 28	
	+4 = 24	+12 = 34	+2 = 26	
	+4 = 24	+2 = 24	+12 = 36	not to be counted as there is a repetition of values
	+12 = 32	+2 = 24	+4 = 28	
	+12 = 32	+4 = 26	+2 = 26	not to be counted as there is a repetition of values

Base Value	20	22	24	
Additions (for 2,6,10)	+2 = 22	+6 = 28	+10 = 34	
	+2 = 22	+10 = 32	+6 = 30	
	+6 = 26	+2 = 24	+10 = 34	
	+6 = 26	+10 = 32	+2 = 26	not to be counted as there is a repetition of values
	+10 = 30	+2 = 24	+6 = 30	not to be counted as there is a repetition of values
	+10 = 30	+6 = 28	+2 = 26	

Base Value	20	22	24	
Additions (for 4,6,8)	+4 = 24	+6 = 28	+8 = 32	
	+4 = 24	+8 = 30	+6 = 30	not to be counted as there is a repetition of values
	+6 = 26	+4 = 26	+8 = 32	not to be counted as there is a repetition of values
	+6 = 26	+8 = 30	+4 = 28	
	+8 = 28	+4 = 26	+6 = 30	Repetition of previous case – hence not to be counted
	+8 = 28	+6 = 28	+4 = 26	not to be counted as there is a repetition of values

Hence, there are a total of 10 ways in which the stamps can be distributed.

MOCK TEST PAPER 4

Questions 1 to 4:

1. The company's combined turnover = 120 + 126 + 139 + 151 + 163 = 699. D's share = 0.26 × 120 + 0.34 × 126 + 0.30 × 139 + 0.26 × 151 + 0.24 × 163 = 194.12.
   Hence required %age = 194.12/699 × 100 = 27.8%.
   Hence (c)
2. Highest growth rate is in between 2004–2005 and it is (139 – 126)/126 × 100 = 10.31%
   Compounded average annual growth rate = $[(163 - 120/120)^{1/4} - 1] \times 100 = 7.96\%$
   The difference is 2.35%. Hence (a).
3. In 2006, (A+ C)'s turnover = (26 + 22)% of 151 = ₹72.48 cr. In 2007, (B + D)'s turnover = (18 + 24)% of 163 = ₹68.46 cr. Hence approx difference is ₹4 cr. Hence (d).
4. (a) is true as the average turnover is 699/5 = 139.8 crore.
   (b) is true because B's turnover has continuously increased and decreased.
   (c) is true as E has recorded the highest jump in between 2006–2007.
   Hence (d).

Questions 5 to 8:

5. There are two pairs that satisfy a strike rate of 125: ST vs IB and RS vs PC. Hence, option (a) is correct.
6. It would be in the best interests of the students to make a table corresponding to the number of balls faced and runs scored by each batsman Vs each bowler to save time in this questions (Activity left for students to complete)
   It is clear from the given table that AC scored a maximum of 61 runs. Hence (b).
7. x can be calculated for each of the bowlers. As an example, for SG, $x = \frac{3}{14} \times 100 = 21.42\%$ (highest) and for ST, $x = 1/15 \times 100 = 6.66\%$ (lowest). The difference in between the two is 21.42 – 6.66 = 14.76%. Hence (a).
8. ZK gave away a maximum of 49 runs to all the batsman put together. Hence (b).

Questions 9 to 13:

9. It will be useful to make the following table which depicts spare time on each machine after meeting the commitments to each of the two companies

	Machine 1	Machine 2	Machine 3	Machine 4
Process: Substrating	30 minutes (15 units for Electronica Ltd)	30 minutes (10 units for Electrica Ltd)	–	–
Process: Masking	30 minutes (6 units for Electronica Ltd.)	30 minutes (6 units for Electronica Ltd)	4 hours 15 minutes (3 unit for Electronica Ltd)	30 minutes (10 units for Electrica Ltd)
Process: Etching	30 minutes (10 units for Electronica Ltd)	2 hours 15 minutes (5 units for Electronica Ltd and 2 units for Electrica Ltd)	No spare time (8 units for Electrica Ltd)	–

Using the above table, option (e) is correct.

10. The bottleneck for Electronica Ltd is obviously process masking as can be observed from the table. The maximum number of units each process masking machine can make is 6. Hence the maximum possible number units of Electronica Ltd. are 24; the other two processes not being any constraint. Hence (a).
11. Profit made by manufacturing only for Electronica Ltd. = 24 × 75 = ₹1800
    Profit made by manufacturing only for Electrica Ltd = 20 × 100 = ₹2000
    Hence (d).
12. From the given options, the most profitable one is (d) as it generates ₹1000 in profits. Hence (d) is the correct option.
13. The total time available for production is 8 hours multiplied by 9 machines = 72 hours. Out of this, as can be seen in the solution table, the idle time available is: 9 hours 30 minutes. The required percentage is approximately 13.2%. Hence, option (c) is correct.

Questions 14 to 17:

14. The percentage of industries in the Oil sector in the year 1998–99 was [100 – (35 + 10 + 30)] = 25%. Similarly the percentage of Industries in Power sector in the year 2004–2005 was [100 – (15 + 25 + 32)] = 28%
    Hence the ratio is (25 × 33600)/(28 × 66800) = 75/ 167.
    Hence (a)
15. The total number of industries in 1997–1998 was 176800. Number of industries in the year 1998–1999 = 176800 × 1.15 = 203320. Hence the number of multinational companies in the year 1998–1999 was 203320 – 33600 = 169720. Hence (a).
16. The percentage of industries in the Oil sector in the year 2003–2004 was [100 – (45 + 8 + 15)] = 32%. Hence the number of industries in the Oil business = 32 × 54600/100 = 17472. Hence (c) is the correct option.
17. The number of medium scale companies would be 4% of 79600 = 3184. Hence, option (b) is correct.

Questions 18 to 20:

18. The lowest cost of transportation occurs when the grains are transported along the cheapest routes available, which are shown below:
    Piku – D: 20 × 50 = 1000
    Ramu – D: 20 × 50 = 1000
    Qadir – B: 60 × 150 = 9000
    Tinku – A = 20 × 100 = 2000
    Sonu – A: 60 × 150 = 9000
    Tinku – C: 20 × 200 = 4000
    Total = 1000 + 1000 + 9000 + 2000 + 9000 + 4000 = 26000 INR
19. The minimum cost of transport when Qadir cannot supply grains to B and D would be:
    Qadir – C: 20 × 300 = 6000
    Qadir – A: 40 × 250 = 10,000
    Ramu – D: 20 × 50 = 1000
    Piku – D: 20 × 50 = 1000
    Sonu – B: 60 × 200 = 12,000
    Tinku – A: 40 × 100 = 4000
    Total = 6000 + 10,000 + 1000 + 1000 + 12000 + 4000 = 34000 INR
20. Transportation cost when Piku supplies 20 tons grain to A: 200 × 20 = INR 4000
    When Piku supplies 20 tons to B = 20 × 150 = INR 3000
    When Qadir supplies 20 tons to A = 250 × 20 = INR 5000
    When Tinku supplies 20 tons to D = 100 × 20 = INR 2000
    Hence, option (d) is correct.

MOCK TEST PAPER 5

Questions 1 to 5:

1. (b) There are $3C_2$x3! possible combinations for Aishwarya, out of which only 6 give the minimum possible number of marbles i.e. 30.
   (***Note:*** DIVIDEBY2 will have to be used for all three, if we have to maintain the constraint of their values being lower than 100)
2. The three of them start with 10, 7 and 8 marbles respectively. The maximum condition in the second round would be 10 × 4 + 7 × 2 + 8 × 3 = 78
3. (d) There are $3C_2$ × 3! possible combinations for Aishwarya, out of which the maximum number of marbles at the end could only be 60 when a combination of DIVIDEBY2, MULTIPLYBY3 and MULTIPLYBY4 are used:
   Further, for Chiranjeevi the minimum number would be if we use a combination of DIVIDEBY2, MULTIPLYBY2 & MULTIPLYBY3- In such a case his value would end up at 24 (whichever way you look at it).
   8, 16, 8, 24. Hence, the difference is 36.
4. Lowest total will occur if we use a combination of DIVIDEBY2, MULTIPLYBY2 & MULTIPLYBY3 for each of the three. Hence, this total will be 75.

5. (d) Maximum possible with Chiranjeevi is got by using a combination of DIVIDEBY2, MULTIPLYBY3 & MULTIPLYBY4.
   This makes a starting value of 8 into 48.
   Similarly for Bebo 7 would become 42
   For Aishwarya, the minimum possible value is 30.
   Thus the ratio is 90 : 30 = 3 : 1

Questions 6 to 10:

Size	*Millimeters*
2A	1189 × 1682
A0	841 × 1189
A1	594 × 841
A2	420 × 594
A3	297 × 420
A4	210 × 297
A5	148 × 210
A6	105 × 148
A7	74 × 105
A8	52 × 74
A9	37 × 52
A10	26 × 37

'C' series is the series of envelopes or folders suitable for enclosing stationary in the A sizes.

Size	*Millimeters*
C3	324 × 458
C4	229 × 324
C5	162 × 229
C6	114 × 162
C7	81 × 114
DL	110 × 220

Hence, the answers are:

6. (b) A8 = 52 × 74
7. (d) From 1 A1 paper, we can get 16 × 16 = 256 A7 papers. Hence, from 8 sheets we can obtain 2048.
8. (c) We can insert paper sizes from A3 to A10 in a C3 envelope. Hence, 8 possible solutions.
9. (d) From the table above it is 114 × 162
10. (a) We need the sum of the geometric series:
    37 × 52 + 37 × 52 × 2 + 37 × 52 × 4 upto 11 terms which is given by the sum of the geometric series: $a(r^n - 1)/(r - 1) = 37 \times 52 \times (2^{11} - 1)$

Questions 11 to 15:

11. As no class 11th student fails, hence all the 56 students of class 11th of 2008 are from class 10th of the year 2007. In class 10th the number of students failed in class 10th of 2007 = 64 – 56 = 8. Hence in class 9th the number of students who failed = 72 – 60 + 8 = 20. Hence (d).
12. 14 students of class 10th failed. Hence number of students of class 9th who failed in the year 2007 is 72 – 60 + 14 = 26. Hence number of students from class 8th who failed = 84 – 70 + 26 = 40. Hence number of failed students of class 7th = 120 – 100 + 44 = 64. Hence out of 140 students studying in class 7th in 2008, 64 are those who failed in the year 2007. Hence number of students newly joined = 140 – 64 = 76. Hence percentage decrease from 2007 to 2008 is (120 – 76)/120 × 100 = 36.66%. Hence (a).
13. As no student failed in class 11th in the year 2007, there must be 48 students in class 12th in the year 2008. Since there were 54 students, hence 54 – 48 = 6 students failed in class 12th in 2007. Hence the pass percentage = 30 / 36 × 100 = 83 (1/3) %. Hence (d) is the correct option.
14. Number of students who failed in class 8th = 34. Hence number of students who failed in class 7th = 120 – 100 + 34 = 54. Hence the total number of failed students (as derived from the other questions as well) = 6 + 8 + 20 + 34 + 54 = 122. Hence (c) is the correct option.
15. It can be seen that if 5 students fail in Class 12th in 2007, then the 2008 composition of 54 students in 2008, would require 54-5-49 students coming from class 11 of 2007. However, Class 11 in 2007, has a strength of only 48. Thus, it is not possible to complete the number of 54 for Class 12 in 2008. Hence, option (d) is correct.

Questions 16 to 20:

16. In 2002:
    Market share of SBI in loan segment = 92/385 × 100 = 23.89%
    Market share of FBI in loan segment = 78/385 × 100 = 20.26%
    Difference in share = 23.89 – 20.26 = 3.63%
    Housing finance market in 2002 = 150 crore INR
    3.63% of 150 crore = 5.45 crore INR
    Answer is option (d)
17. Banks affected are:
    Citibank = 3% of 80 crore = 2.4 crore INR
    Bank A, B, D, E and F.
    C had a market share of 30% of 30% of 80 crore INR
    = 7.2 crore INR, hence it continued its operations.
    Therefore, 6 banks had to halt their operations
    Answer is option (a)
18. Loan disbursement in 2006 = 110% of 558 = 613.80 crore INR
    Loan disbursement in 2007 = 110% of 613.80 = 675.18 crore INR

Loan recovered in 2008 = 30% of 675.18 = 202.55 crore INR

Bad loan or amount NOT recovered = 675.18 – 202.55 or 70% of 675.18

= 472.63

≈ 473 crore INR

Answer is option (c)

19. Taking data from previous question, loan disbursement in 2007 = 675 crore INR

Percentage share of "Others" = 80/558 × 100 = 14.34% (Because percentage share is the same in consecutive years after 2005)

Now in 2008:

Amount NOT recovered = 14.34% of 675

= 96.80 crore INR

Share of banks that survived recession = 578.2 crore INR

Amount recovered by these banks = 50% of their share

= 50% of 578.2 = 289.05

≈ 289 crore INR

Therefore only 289 crore INR was recovered in 2008.

Answer is option (d)

20. 675 – 289 = 386 crore INR

Answer is option (a)

MOCK TEST PAPER 6

Questions 1 to 5:

1. Sneakers purchased in the year 2011 = 100

Sneakers disposed off in the year 2013 = 30% of 100 = 30

Sneakers purchased in the year 2013 = 50 + 30 = 80

Answer is option (b)

2. Sneakers bought in 2011 = 100, thus sneakers disposed off in 2013 = 30% of 100 = 30

Sneakers bought in 2012 = 0, thus sneakers disposed off in 2014 = 0

Sneakers bought in 2013 = 50 + 30 = 80, thus sneakers disposed off in 2015 = 30% of 80 = 24

Therefore total sneakers disposed off till 2015 = 30 + 0 + 24 = 54

Answer is option (a)

3. In the question it is given that 20 Boots were disposed off in 2011, so new boots bought were = 50 + 20 = 70 (new boots were bought in 2011.)

Now 2 years later, in 2013, 30% of 70 boots bought in 2011 will be disposed off

= 21 boots are disposed off in 2013

Answer is option (c)

4. This will depend on the number of boots bought in 2010 which would also include the boots bought in 2008 and disposed off in 2010, however no such information is given about the year 2008, hence we cannot determine the answer.

Answer is option (d)

5. In the question it is given that 20 Boots were disposed off in 2011, so new boots bought were = 50 + 20 = 70 new boots were bought in 2011.

Now from the graph, Boots bought in 2013 = 0 + 30% of boots bought in 2011 = 0 + 21 = 21 boots were bought in 2013

Answer is option (b)

Questions 6 to 9:

6. Since only the percentage break up is given, number of mobile phones sold cannot be determined.

Answer is option (d)

7. 20% of Kokia = 20% of Grade A

Hence, mobile phones sold by Kokia = Mobile phoncs sold of Grade A

Answer is option (c)

8. We can compare the percentage breakup of Kokia with different grades.

Grade A++:

1% of total sales of Kokia (K) = 22% of total sales of A++

K = 22 × A++

A++ = K/22

Grade A+:

2% of K = 21% of A+

A+ = (2/21)K

Grade A:

20% of K = 20% of A

A = K

Grade B+:

1% of K = 25% of B+

B+ = (1/25)K

Grade B:

76% of K = 1% of B

B = 76K

Therefore, required ratio of A++ : A+ : A : B+ : B = 1/22 : 2/21 : 1 : 1/25 : 76

Answer is option (c)

9. Given that, 1% of Kokia Phones is of grade A++

1% of 55,000 = 550 Phones of Kokia are of Grade A++

Now, Kokia A++ contribute 22% of the total A++ phones available in the market

22% of total number of A++ phones = 550

Total number of A++ phones = 2500 phones

Answer is option (a)

Questions 10 to 14:

10. (c)
11. (b)

12. (d)
13. (d)
14. (d)

Questions 15 to 18:

CSK's results:

CSK – DD 4 – 2 (Since there is only one 4 – 2 result)
CSK – MI 2 – 0 (Since there is only one 2 – 0 result)
Then, CSK's 3 – 1 result must have come against KEP.
Hence, CSK-KKR was a 1 – 1 draw.

MI's results:

0 – 2 to CSK, 1-3 to KKR, 1 – 1 KEP & 1 – 0 DD

KKR's results:

CSK 1 – 1, MI 3 – 1, KEP 2 – 2 and DD 1 – 2

KEP's results:

CSK 1 – 3, MI 1 – 1, KKR 2 – 2 and DD 1 – 1

And DD's results:

CSK 2 – 4, MI 0 – 1, KKR 2 – 1 and KEP 1 – 1

Hence, the answers are:

15. (d) Kings Eleven Punjab
16. (a) Chennai Super Kings
17. (b) Mumbai Indians has a performance ratio of 3/6 which is lower than all others.
18. (a) KKR has 5 points from it's first leg of matches. If it wins it's first two matches in the second leg it would end up with 11 points and would reach the top of the table. Hence, 2 matches are required.

Questions 19 to 20:

19. Average salary per unit will be maximum when the employee sells exactly 1000 units. Option (d).
20. (a)

MOCK TEST PAPER 7

Questions 1 to 4:

1. The Production profit varies linearly with the total units sold. Therefore, when the total units sold increases by three times the production profit also increases by three times. Distribution profit decreases with the total units sold so when the total units sold increases by three times the distribution profit reduces. Therefore the situation given in the question cannot be fulfilled by any real value of '*n*'. Option (a) is correct.
2. Production profit increases with number of units sold and distribution profit decreases with number of units sold. It can be seen from the graph that the rate of decrease of distribution profit is greater than the rate of increase of production profit to the left of the intersection point. After the intersection point, the rate of decrease of distribution profit becomes slower than the rate of increase of the production profit. Hence, after the intersection point, the total profit would go up. Therefore, from the graph it is clear that total profit will be minimum at the intersection point (Production profit and distribution profit). Therefore the minimum possible total profit = 15 + 15 = 30 lakh rupees. Option (d) is the correct answer.
3. Required value of total units sold = 580 units
4. It can be seen that the statements (i) and (ii) are correct and hence, option (b) is correct.

Questions 5 to 8:

5. Taufiq has a production share of 14% that means the total production of the companies owned by Taufiq is 140 tons, it is possible only when Taufiq owned C and E or I and J or J and B or H, therefore maximum number of companies owned by Taufiq is 2 while the minimum number of companies owned by Taufiq is 1. Therefore the required difference = 2 – 1 = 1.
6. If each person owned more than one company then Taufiq could not own company H, he could own J and I or J and B or C and E. In each of the cases, Parizad owned at most three companies. Option (b) is correct.
7. Minimum number of companies owned by Sakib, Taufiq and Rahim were 2, 1, 2 respectively. Therefore after buying all the companies of Sakib and Taufiq, Rahim owned total 2 + 1 + 2 = 5 companies.
8. There are multiple possibilities to get the numbers for each of the five people. Hence, we cannot uniquely determine the companies for any of the five owners. Hence, the correct answer would be 0. Option (a) is correct.

Questions 9 to 13:

9. The given information can be tabulated as:

DISH	Cardamom	Milk	Sugar	Gram Flour	Saffron
A	10%	40%	(a)%	(40-a)%	10%
B	25%	15%	50%	5%	5%
C	15%	(b)%	20%	(30-b)%	35%
D	20%	25%	15%	30%	10%
E	5%	50%	25%	5%	15%
F	40%	10%	5%	30%	15%

In Gujarati Cocktail, percentage of:
Milk = $(3b + 95)/6$
Sugar = $(2a + 110)/6$
Gram flour = $(175 - 2a - 3b)/6$
Now, $(3b + 95) = (2a + 110) = (175 - 2a - 3b)$
$a = 25/3$ and $b = 95/9$
Therefore, percentage of Gram flour in dish A = $(40 - a) = (40 - 25/3) = 95/3$
Answer is option (c)

10. From above table, we see that there are 2 possible ways in which dish X can be prepared. These 2 ways are: Mixing (E and F) or mixing (B and C)
    Answer is option (a)
11. Percentage of sugar in A, E and F is 25/3%, 25% and 5% respectively
    Checking options:
    (a) Percentage of sugar in mixture
    $$= \frac{\frac{1\times 25}{3}+2\times 25+3\times 5}{6} = \frac{110}{9}\% > 12\%$$
    Answer is option (a)
12. Because the percentage of Saffron in dish B and dish Z is 5% and 8.25% respectively, to maximize the percentage of B in Z, we need to choose a dish in which Saffron is much more than 8.25% and better if it's the maximum amongst the given dishes, so we choose dish C
    Let the percentage of dish B in dish Z be x%
    Thus, $5x + 35(1 - x) = 8.25$
    $x = 89.16\%$
    Answer is option (d)
13. From our solution of the first question in this set, we know that the value of b (which represents the milk percentage in Dish C) is 95/9. Hence, Gram flour in Dish C would be (30-95/9) =175/9.

Questions 14 to 17:

14. Let the Total cost be 100 units, then to gain 50% profit, revenue should be 150 units.
    From Chart 2, Revenue generated by delivery on Motorbike = (240/360) × 150 = 100 units
    From Chart 3, Cost incurred by delivery on Motorbike = (240/360) × 100 = 66.67 units
    Profit earned by delivery on Motorbike = (100 – 66.67) = 33.33 units
    Profit percentage on deliveries done on Motorbike = 33.33/66.67 = 50%
    Answer is option (a)
15. Let the total cost be = 360C
    Let the total revenue be = 360R
    Then, Profit generated by:
    Motorbike = 240R – 240C
    Bicycle = 100R – 60C
    Auto Rickshaw = 20R – 60C
    As we can see that Profit is a function of R and C, which is not known in the question.
    OR
    To calculate the actual profit, we need to know the numbers and not just percentage contribution. Therefore we cannot calculate this and need more information.
    Answer is option (d)
16. Let the total number of deliveries be 360N and total cost incurred be 360C in 2015 by Grocers
    So the cost per delivery for:
    Auto-Rickshaw = 60C/110N = .545 × (C/N)
    Motorbike = 240C/100N = 2.4 × (C/N)
    Bicycle = 60C/150N = 0.4 × (C/N)
    Here the ratio (C/N) remain constant throughout, thus the relative values for the cost per delivery can be worked out in terms of which one is costlier and which is cheaper. Bicycle offers least Cost per delivery for Grocers.
    Answer is (b)
17. Total revenue generated would be = 10 × 360/20 = 180 INR
    Total Cost incurred would be = 20 × 360/60 = 120 INR
    Cost incurred by delivery on Bicycle = 60 × 120/360 = 20 INR
    Revenue generated by delivery on bicycle = 100 × 180/360 = 50 INR
    Required ratio = 20/50 = 2/5
    Answer is option (c)

Questions 18 to 20:

18. (c) He should buy weights with values of 1, 3, 9, 27 and 81 grams. If he does so, he would be able to weigh any value from 1 to 121 grams.
    Note: All values are in powers of 3
19. (b) He should buy weights with values of 1, 2, 4, 8, 16, 32 and 64. If he does so, he would be able to weigh any value from 1 to 127 grams.
    Note: All values are in powers of 2
20. (c) The cost for the British jeweller is: 10 + 10 + 10 + 20 + 30 = $80
    The cost for the American jeweller is: 10 + 10 + 10 + 10 + 20 + 20 + 30 = $110.
    Hence, the American borrows $15 from the British.

MOCK TEST PAPER 8

Questions 1 to 2:

1. (c) There is a total payment of 1040 + 728 + 728 = 2496 Thai Bahts to be made (832 Bahts per person) and out of this Raghav has paid 4 × 46 = 184 bahts while Nehal has paid 8 × 46 + 54 = 422 Bahts. Hence, there would be an additional payment of 410 Bahts or 10 dollars that Nehal owes Shaurya.
2. (d) There is a total payment of 1040 + 728 + 728 = 2496 Thai Bahts to be made (832 Bahts

per person) and out of this Raghav has paid 4 × 46 = 184 bahts. Hence, there would be an additional payment of 648 Bahts that Raghav owes Shaurya.

Questions 3 to 7:

3. Total number of matches played is = 5 + 4 + 3 + 2 + 1 = 15 in Round 1 where each team played 5 matches against any other team.
   And 1 match in the final round
   = 15 + 1 = 16 matches are played
   Answer is = 16 matches
4. Total number of points available is = (15 matches × maximum 2 points per match) = 30 points
   Let's consider that the top team won all matches, thus this first team to reach finals would have scored = 5 × 2 = 10 points
   Now the second team could have scored as much as other teams left in the group, however it was selected based on its performance for final round. Thus all other 5 teams scored = 4 points each
   Hence total points exhausted = 10 + 4 × 5 = 10 + 20 = 30 points
   Therefore minimum points scored by any team that reached finals = 4 points
   Answer is = 4 points
5. Consider the following case:

	Against Liverpool	Against ManU	Against Chelsea	Against Arsenal	Against ManCity	Against Real Madrid
Liverpool plays	X	Won	Lost	Won	Won	Won
ManU plays	Lost	X	Won	Won	Won	Won
Chelsea plays	Won	Lost	X	Won	Won	Won
Arsenal plays	Lost	Lost	Lost	X	Won	Won
ManCity plays	Lost	Lost	Lost	Lost	X	Won
Real Madrid plays	Lost	Lost	Lost	Lost	Lost	X

**** Liverpool plays against ManU → Won means that team Liverpool won the match it played against team ManU**

As we can see in the above case 3 teams- Liverpool, ManU and Chelsea scored 8 points each; Arsenal scored 4 points; ManCity scored 2 points and Real Madrid scored 0 points, thus total points exhausted = 30 points
Now out of top 3 only 2 teams will advance to finals and one will not, this one will be rejected on basis of worse performance than top 2.
Therefore, maximum points any team score yet not reach finals is = 8 points
Answer is = 8 points

6. Winner can win all matches in Round 1 and the final round
   Thus maximum points are = 5 × 2 =10 points.
   Note: Points are only awarded in the first stage.
   Hence, even when the team wins the final it would get only ten points at the maximum.
   Answer is = 10 points
7. During the round-robin phase of the tournament: Intra-Group matches = $^3C_2$× 2× 2 (groups) = 12. Intergroup matches: 3 × 3=9. Semifinals = 2 matches, Finals = 3 matches. Hence, the total number of matches = 12 + 9 + 2 + 3 = 26. The minimum number of days required for the tournament would be 26.

Questions 8 to 12:

8. Profit of Grocers Pvt. Ltd. from various divisions=
   Services – Online = 3 × 42/100 = 1.26 crore INR
   Services – On call = 5 × 54/100 = 2.7 crore INR
   Inventory – Online = 7 × 67/100 = 4.69 crore INR
   Inventory – On call = 5 × 68/100 = 3.40 crore INR
   Therefore, total profit = 12.05 crore INR
   Now, salary of Inventory – Online employees is increased by 50% that is by 1,50,000 INR each
   Increase in total salary is = 78 × 1,50,000 = 1,170,000 = 1.17 crore INR
   Thus, new net profit = 12.05 – 1.17 = 10.88 crore INR
   Therefore, new margin percentage = New net Profit/ Total Sales × 100 =
   = 10.88/20 × 100
   = 54.40%
   Answer is option (b)

9. Services – Online:
When no change:
Margin = 42
Annual Sales = 3 crore INR
Net Profit = 42 × 3/100 = 1.26 crore INR
After change:
Increase in cost = (3,00,000 – 2,00,000) × 25 = 25 Lakhs INR
Earlier net profit = 1.26 crore
New net profit = (1.26 – .25) = 1.01 crore INR
% decrease in Services- Online margin

$$= \frac{\frac{.25}{3}}{\frac{1.26}{3}} \times 100 = 19.84 \approx 20\%$$

Answer is option (b)

10. New profit in Services – Online = 42% of (115% of 3 crore) = 1.45 crore INR
New profit is Services – On call = 54% of (115% of 5 crore) = 3.11 crore INR
New profit in Inventory – Online = 67% of (115% of 7 crore) = 5.30 crore INR
New profit in Inventory – On call = 68% of (115% of 5 crore) = 3.91 crore INR
Hence, new total profit = 13.77 ≈13.8 crore INR
Answer is option (c)

11. Salary of each employee cannot be deduced from the available information.
Answer is option (d)

12. Employee salary as a percentage of profits for Services Division =

$$\frac{\text{Total Salary of services division}}{\text{Total Profit services division}} \times 100$$

$$= \frac{25 \times 200000 + 56 \times 300000}{39600000} \times 100 - 55.05\%$$

Employee salary as a percentage of profits for Inventory Division

$$= \frac{\text{Total Salary of inventory division}}{\text{Total Profit inventory division}} \times 100$$

$$= \frac{78 \times 300000 + 68 \times 100000}{80900000} \times 100 = 37.33\%$$

Required difference = 55.05 – 37.33 = 17.72.

Questions 13 to 16:

13. The price per unit of Brand A: $(0.25 \times 2250 \times 10^7)/(0.16 \times 13500 \times 10^6) = 562.5/216 = 2.6$
Price per unit of brand B = (0.13 × 2250)/(0.14 × 1350) = 1.55
Similarly price per units of Brand C, D, E and F are ₹1.23, ₹2.22, ₹2.5 and ₹0.83 respectively. Hence brand A is the costliest which is ₹2.6 per bottle. Hence (a).

14. The cheapest brand cost ₹0.83 and the costliest brand's price is ₹2.6. Hence the required price ratio is 4 : 13. Hence (b).

15. The profit for one bottle of brand C is 1.23 – 0.93 = 0.3
Hence the total profit of brand C = $0.3 \times 0.27 \times 13500 \times 10^6 = 109.35$ crore. Hence (d).

16. Percentage share of brand A in value sales = 25 / (2 / 5 × 12) = 30%
Hence (c).

Questions 17 to 20:

17. For the period of 2003–2004 quantity of wheat (in million kg) which was not exported was 645 – 215 = 430 million kg
Hence total population = 430/0.544 = 790 million
Hence (c).

18. Say the area under the productivity in the year 2003-2004 be 'z' hectare
Productivity in 2003–2004 = $645/z$
Productivity in 2004-2005 = $660/0.9z = 733/z$ (approx).
Hence rate of increase in productivity in 2004–2005 = $[(733/z) - (645/z)]/(645/z) \times 100 = 88/645 \times 100 = 13.6\%$
Hence (d).

19. The average wheat exported is (207 + 189 + 209 + 215 + 220)/5 = 208 million kg
The average wheat production is (421 + 561 + 581 + 645 + 660)/5 = 573.6 million kg
Hence the required ratio is 220/573.6 = 0.38
Hence (d).

20. Average of per capita availability = (487 + 464 + 510 + 544 + 566)/5 = 514.2 g
Hence (a).

LEVEL OF DIFFICULTY – 3

MOCK TEST PAPER 9

Questions 1 to 5:

1. Let B scored 'x' marks in Biology.
According to the question:

$$70\times\frac{20}{100}+65\times\frac{40}{100}+x\times\frac{20}{100}+60\times\frac{20}{100}=62$$

By solving the above equation we get: $x = 50$.

Note: The solution can be thought off much faster as follows:

20% of 70 + 40% of 65 + 20% of x + 20% of 60 = 62 → 14 + 26 + 12 + 20% of x = 62 → 20% of x = 10, hence x = 50.

2. G's rank is 8, hence he should have scored more than 51 marks and less than 62 marks in Maths.

$$\therefore \quad 51<0.2p+10+18+11<62$$

$$\rightarrow \quad 51<0.2p+39<62$$

$\Rightarrow 12<0.2p<23$ or $60<p<115$. However, the question has mentioned that the value of p cannot be greater than 95. Hence, $60<p\leq 95$. Hence only option (b) is correct.

3. H got the 4th rank. His total marks must be more than 69 (Marks scored by C who got 5th rank in the exam). If he scored x marks in Biology then according to the question:

$$75\times\frac{20}{100}+50\times\frac{40}{100}+x\times\frac{20}{100}+85\times\frac{20}{100}>69$$

$15+20+0.2x+17>69$

$x>85$

Hence, H scored more than everybody else in biology. Hence, the required answer must be 9.

4. D is the topper of the exam hence he must have scored more than 75. To maximize his total score his marks in chemistry should be the highest possible.
If he scored 95 marks in chemistry, then his total score

$$= 45\times 0.2+95\times 0.4+75\times 0.2+90\times 0.2=80.$$

5. Let A scored 'x' marks in Maths.

$$\therefore\ 40\times 0.2+45\times 0.4+45\times 0.2+x\times 0.2<51$$

By solving we get: $x < 80$.
Hence, at least 5 students (C, D, H, F, J) scored more marks than A in Maths. (***Note:*** Working out for J, we see that he should have scored 90 marks in Maths).

Questions 6 to 9:

6. The sum of required number of votes will be minimum when the number of votes for top four candidates is as close as possible and the fifth candidate gets no vote (= 0).
Now just for calculation purpose, let's assume that they all get equal votes i.e. = 45000/5 = 9000 votes each.
Now as we concluded that the 5th one with minimum number of votes will get no vote i.e. = 0 votes, therefore this 9000 votes will be equally distributed amongst top 4 candidates.
⇒ 9000/4 = 2250 added to each.
Top 4 now have = 9000 + 2250 = 11250 votes each
But question says that no 2 candidates can have same number of votes, therefore separating them so that they remain as close as possible, we get:
1st candidate = 11252 votes
2nd candidate = 11251 votes
3rd candidate = 11249 votes
4th candidate = 11248 votes
And 5th candidate = 0 votes
Hence, the sum = 11252 + 0 = 11252 votes.
Answer is 11252

7. Sum will be maximum for the candidate who got maximum number of votes in Round 1 + not more than 50% votes in Round 2 (Because 1 more than 50% in Round 2 will make him the winner and this is not the case) + just one less than 50% votes in Round 3 (Because this candidate is not the winner and assuming that the winner got exactly 50% votes in Round 3)
This person is Jai and his total votes are in this case =:
5,000 + 10,000 + 9,999 = 24,999
Answer is option (a) 24,999 votes

8. If this candidate got the least number of votes amongst the candidates who moved to Round 2 then he should be number 5th from the top. This candidate is Chetan. His Round 1 score from the table given is = 4499 votes which is 5th highest.
Now Round 2 has 48,000 votes and Chetan qualifies Round 2, however he'd receive least number of votes amongst top 3 qualifiers, therefore

bottom two should have received 0 and 1 votes (Both cannot be = 0 votes because in the question, condition is mentioned that all candidates received unique number of votes every time in each round) and Chetan should have received 2 votes in Round 2. This makes him stand 3rd and a qualifier of Round 2.

Now Round has 51,000 votes and if Chetan won the election he should have received the maximum number of votes amongst all candidates, however this score should be as low as possible to satisfy the requirement of the question. Therefore 3 candidates received following number of votes:

1st = 17,001 (Winner) This is also the least number of votes the winner has to receive in order to win this round

2nd = 17,000

3rd = 16,999

Now as we know Chetan moved on to become the winner, his total number of votes (from all 3 rounds put together) should be at least =

4499 + 2 + 17001 = 21,502 votes

Answer is option (b) 21,502

9. The total can be minimum for Chetan who qualified Round at 5th rank with 4499 votes and qualified Round 2 with 2 votes and reached Round 3. He did not win the election hence to make the sum minimum we can consider that he received 0 votes in Round 3

Therefore total number of votes received by Chetan = 4499 + 2 + 0 = 4501 votes

Answer is option (c)

Questions 10 to 13:

Let the total number of 2 marks question be 'a' and the total number of 4 marks questions be 'b'.

$a + b = 1000$ .....(1)

$0.15a + 0.20b = 160$ .....(2)

By solving equation 1 and equation 2 we get: $a = 800$, $b = 200$. This will give us the following table:

Section	2 Marks Questions	4 Marks Questions
Math I	160	30
Math II	160	60
Chemistry I	120	40
Chemistry II	80	10
Physics I	160	20
Physics II	120	40

10. From the above discussion we can form the following table for the maximum number of 2 marks questions possible for Piyush:

Subject	Maximum Possible 2 Marks Questions
Math I	30
Math II	90
Chemistry I	120
Chemistry II	60
Physics I	150
Physics II	120

Hence the required answer = 30 + 90 + 120 + 60 + 150 + 120 = 570

11. Maximum possible marks in the exam = 800 × 2 + 200 × 4 – 2400

From the solution of the previous question minimum possible 4 marks question attempted by Piyush = 15

Therefore the required percentage

$$= \frac{60}{2400} \times 100 = 2.5\%$$

12. To minimize the number of attempts in Chemistry II exam he had to attempt maximum number of 4 marks questions. Therefore he should have attempted all the ten four marks questions and in this case he attempted total 10 + 80/2 = 10 + 40 = 50 questions.

13. Option (a).

Questions 14 to 16:

Let us analyse the scores in QA first:

Marks scored by Qasim, Sameer and Taskin = 98 + 72 + 70 = 240

Hence, marks obtained by Pulkit and Rohan = 280 – 240 = 40

Pulkit and Rohan can score maximum 28 marks in the subject (10% of 280).

Hence, marks range for Pulkit in QA = 12 – 28, and subsequently marks range for Rohan in QA = 28 – 12.

By doing the similar analysis for rest of the three sections, we can get the following data:

In LR section: Marks obtained by Rohan = 32 – 48
Marks obtained by Taskin = 48 – 32

In DI section: Marks obtained by Pulkit = 27 – 23
Marks obtained by Qasim = 23 – 27

In VA section: Marks obtained by Rohan = 25 – 35
Marks obtained by Taskin = 35 – 25

Name of Student	QA	LR	DI	VA
Pulkit	12–28	100	23–27	63
Qasim	98	55	27–23	62
Rohan	28–12	32–48	110	25–35
Sameer	72	85	30	65
Taskin	70	48–32	80	35–25
Total	280	320	270	250

14.

Student's Name	Marks Range
Pulkit	198–218
Qasim	238–242
Rohan	179–221
Sameer	252
Taskin	207–233

Rank A must be of Sameer. Rank B must be of Qasim. We cannot determine the ranks of Pulkit, Rohan and Taskin.

15. Minimum possible difference between the two would be if we allocate 28 to Pulkit in QA and 23 in DI. His total would then be: 100 + 63 + 28 + 23 = 214. In such a case, Rohan can reach a total of 48 + 110 + 12 + 35 = 205. The gap between them comes out to be 9. This gap can be reduced to the minimum by reducing Pulkit's score in QA by 4 marks and increasing Rohan's score by 4 marks. Thus, in the even that we use: 100 + 63 + 24 + 23 = 210 for Pulkit and 48 + 110 + 16 + 35 = 209 for Rohan, the difference between Pulkit and Rohan's total scores are reduced to 1. The gap can be further reduced to 0 by taking QA as 23 and 17 for Pulkit and Rohan and then reducing the value of VA for Rohan by 1 to 34. In this case, 100 + 63 + 23 + 23 = 209 (Pulkit) and 110 + 48 + 17 + 34 = 209 (Rohan). In this case, Qasim = 98 + 55 + 27 + 62 = 242; Taskin: 70 + 80 + 32 + 26 = 208. The difference is 242 - 208 = 34. However, we should be able to see that there will be multiple possibilities for getting Pulkit and Rohan's totals equal and the required difference between Qasim and Taskin varies. For Instance: Pulkit:100 + 63 + 20 + 23 = 206; Rohan: 110 + 48 + 20 + 28 = 206 —> Qasim: 98 + 55 + 27 + 62 = 242 and Taskin: 70 + 80 + 32 + 32 = 214. Difference = 28. Hence, we cannot determine the answer.

16. Maximum possible marks scored by Pulkit = 28 + 100 + 27 + 63 = 218

$$\text{Required percentage} = \frac{218}{280+320+270+250} \times 100$$

$$= \frac{218}{1120} \times 100 = 19.46\%$$

Questions 17 to 20:

17. Here we need to find the minimum possible number of farms, so first consider the farm with range of production less than 20 tons. From village A, at least one farm (of area 900 square feet) must be counted.

Now analyze the second range which is between 20 tons and 28 tons. Again we have at least 1 farm from village A and 1 farm from village B.

The next range cannot be analyzed as we cannot be sure about the farms in the 28 tons to 36 tons category, whether the farms did have production less than 30 tons and also had an area less than 1000 square feet. So the required answer is 3.

18. Let's analyze each production range one by one.

Range of Production	0.04 Times of the Farm Area for Village A	0.04 Times of the Farm Area for Village B	Maximum Possible Number of Required Farmers
$p < 20$	5 (36–60)	4 (44–60)	0 + 0 = 0
$20 \le p < 28$	8 (28–44)	7 (30–56)	0 + 0 = 0
$28 \le p < 36$	10 (24–36)	11 (28–44)	9 + 10 = 19
$36 \le p < 44$	6 (18–30)	6 (24–40)	6 + 6 = 12
$44 \le p < 60$	3 (16–24)	4 (20–32)	3 + 4 = 7

Total number of farmers = 0 + 0 + 19 + 12 + 7 = 38.

19. Here we need to find the number of farmers whose farms produce more than 34 tons. So we need to concentrate only on the last three rows of the given table (only for Village B, as stated in the problem). For the range, $28 \le p \le 36$.

For this range, there are at most 10 farms with an area more than 750 square feet and production more than 34 tons.

Similarly for range, $36 \le p \le 44$ there are a maximum of 6 – 1 = 5 farms and for $44 \le p \le 60$ range, there are maximum 4 – 1 = 3 farms with an area greater than 750 square feet.

Hence, the required answer = 10 + 5 + 3 = 18

20. To maximize the average production, we need to maximize the production of farms that falls under a production range. In the < 20 production range, the maximum production can be 19.9999999 ≈ 20. Hence, we would take the limiting value as 20 for the purpose of the calculations.

Required average

$$= \frac{9\times 20 + 15\times 28 + 21\times 36 + 12\times 44 + 7\times 60}{64}$$

$= 36.$

MOCK TEST PAPER 10

Questions 1 to 4:

1. Let's try to decode the information given first.
In additional information it is given that at least one student from each course does not buy the set of books, the percentage of students who bought the set of books can never be 100%
Taking cases – For MBBS course–
If percentage of students in MBBS buying the set of books is less than or equal to 60:
Then the total number of students in MBBS will have to be equal to or more than 1620. This is not possible because then the number of students from remaining 3 courses will be less than or equal to (2700 – 1620) = 1080, but from Table 2, it is clear that it is not possible because then the number of students buying the sets of books would be more than actual number of students available.
If percentage of students in MBBS buying the set of books is either 70 or 80%:
Then the total number of students in MBBS course is not an integral multiple of 10.
If percentage of students in MBBS buying the set of books is equal to 90%:
Then the total number of students in MBBs course = 1080 students
Similarly, for B.Tech course–
Percentage of students in B.Tech buying the set of books cannot be less than or equal to 60, it cannot be 70 either because then the value will not be integral, thus it is = 80%
Similarly, for BA course–
Thus, percentage of students in BA buying set of books is = 70%
Similarly, for B.Com course–
Percentage of students in B.Com buying the set of books is = 60%
Percentage and total number of students in other courses can be found out as :

	Total Number of Students	Percentage of Students Buying Set of Books	Number of Students Buying Set of Books
MBBS	1080	90%	972
B.Tech	810	80%	648
BA	540	70%	378
B.Com	270	60%	162

Therefore, $p + q = n + s = o + r = m + t = 90$
$p + r = n + t = o + s = 80$
$q + r = p + s = 70$
$q + s = 60$
Solving these equations, we get:
$m = 80, q = 40, n = 70, r = 30, o = 60, s = 20, p = 50, t = 10$
Now, Indian Politics books are purchased by only students of course – MBBS, B.Tech and BA =
From Table, the total number of Indian Politics books bought are =
= 90% of MBBS + 80% of B.Tech + 70% of BA
= 972 + 648 + 378 = 1998 books
Answer is option (b)

2. From table above, there are 540 students in BA course
Answer is option (c)

3. From the table above, $m = 80, q = 40, n = 70, r = 30, o = 60, s = 20, p = 50, t = 10$
Thus, m = E1 is the most bought book.
Answer is option (a)

4. From the table above, $m = 80$, $q = 40$, $n = 70$, $r = 30$, $o = 60$, $s = 20$, $p = 50$, $t = 10$. These are the percentage values.
Total number of students who buy E1 $= m + o + p + q$
= 80% of 1080 + 60% of 810 + 50% of 540 + 40% of 270
= 1728
Likewise, we find total number of students who buy P1 $= o + n + q$
= 60% of 1080 + 70% of 810 + 40% of 540
= 1431
Therefore, the required difference = 1728 – 1431 = 297
Answer is option (d)

Questions 5 to 8:

5. The table gives data about the Average weight per marble for each of the boxes. However, the individual weights of marbles of any box is not given, therefore you cannot calculate AWPM hence ESI of the mixture.
Answer is (d)

6. AWPM and corresponding ESI when B2 is mixed with B1, B3, B4 and B5:

B2 and B1: $\frac{16 \times 180 + 48 \times 90}{(16 + 48)} = \frac{7200}{64} = 112.5$,
so ESI = 7.5

B2 and B3: $\frac{48 \times 90 + 32 \times 140}{48 + 32} = \frac{8800}{80} = 110$,
so ESI = 7.5

B2 and B4: $\frac{48\times 90+64\times 130}{48+64}=\frac{12640}{112}=112.85$,

so ESI = 7.5

B2 and B5: $\frac{48\times 90+40\times 170}{48+40}=\frac{11120}{88}=126.36$,

so ESI = 8

Answer is option (d)

7. ASPPM for:
B1, B2 and B3 = 12.17
B2, B3 and B4 = 14.44
B3, B4 and B5 = 16.06
B1, B4 and B5 = 17.27
Only one of the 4 mixtures has ASPPM between 13 and 15, and its ESI would be easily 7.5 as its AWPM would be much more than 100.
Answer is option (b)
8. ASPPM for:
B1, B4 ad B5 = 17.27
B2, B3 and B4 = 14.44
B3, B4 and B5 = 16.06
All give ASPPM between 12 and 18 but none can have ESI as perfect 10 as none of the mixtures mentioned can have AWPM >170
Answer is option (d)

Questions 9 to 12:

9. From A-A-A, Bhavuk now wants to move to any combination amongst- A-A-B or A-A-C (Because question says he'd compromise on rating of only one teacher)
Bhavuk's total score when he is taught by A-A-A combination = 85% of 300 = 255 marks
Case 1 – When the combination becomes A-A-B
His new total score now becomes 80% of 300 = 240 marks
Case 2 – When the combination becomes A-A-C
His new total score becomes 75% of 300 = 225 marks
Clearly, the maximum change occurs when he switches to A-A-C ratings of teachers.
Change = 255 – 225 = 30 marks over 255 marks scored earlier
Percentage change = (30/255) × 100 = 11.76%
Answer is option (c)
10. We are talking about combination B-B-B where Pulkit scores 75% of total marks = 75% of 300 = 225 marks
In order to get minimum possible in one of the 2 sections, we'll have to make marks in other 2 sections as maximum as possible.
Consider Pulkit scored perfect 100 in 2 sections. This would be the case where he'd score the least in the 3rd section. Thus (225 – 2 × 100) = 25 marks
Thus, lowest possible score Pulkit can get in one of the 3 sections = 25 marks
Answer is option (b)
11. From the Bar chart:
A-A-A is manageable
A-A-B is manageable
A-A-C is manageable
B-B-B is manageable
C-B-B is Not manageable- because although the average score is 75%, Pulkit's percentage is 70%.
C-C-A is Not manageable – For the same reason as above
Other 2 are also Not manageable
Therefore, only 4 combinations are manageable
Answer is option (d)
12. Pulkit:(90+80+80+75+70+75+70+65)/8=75.625%
Bhavuk: (85 + 80 + 75 + 75 + 80 + 70 + 65 + 65)/8 = 74.375%
Thus, both are inherently smart
Answer is option (c)

Questions 13 to 16:

13. 2(P + Q + R + S) = (P + Q + R) + (Q + R + S) + (P + S) = 28000
(P + Q + R + S) = 14000
Thus, S = 4800, and P = 1800
And Q – R = 1000
Hence, Q = 4200 and R = 3200

	Number of Faculty Members		
	Non-Experienced	Experienced	Total
Lime	3200	12800	16000
Mindworkzz	4800	7200	12000
Career Lander	4200	9800	14000
ITS	1800	16200	18000

Therefore, number of Non-experienced faculty members in Lime institute = 3200
Answer is (a)
14. 16200 – 4800 = 11400
Answer is option (b)
15. 12000/12800 = 15/16
Answer is option (c)
16. 18000/3 = 6000 faculty members each joined each of the 3 institutes
6000 × 100/12000 = 50%
Answer is option (d)

Questions 17 to 20:

17. If there were a total of 900 permanent employees in 1995, it means that there were 900 employees above 25 years of age. Since there are a total of 315 + 346 = 661 people above 40, we can conclude that there would be exactly 239 people above 25 in the 20 to 40 age group. This means that 329 – 239 = 90 people would be below 25 in that age group. The condition for the maximum number of people in the 40 to 45 category in 2000 would be fulfilled if all these 239 people were aged between 35 to 40 in 1995 and they would have moved to 40 to 45 in 2000. Hence, the required answer is 239.
18. If we look closely at the table, it is evident that any increase in the ≥ 60 age group would occur only because of people shifting from the 40 to 60 age group to the 60+ age group. Also, an increase in the 40 to 60 age group would occur, only because of people shifting from the 20 to 40 age group to the 40 to 60 age group. From 1995 to 2000, there must have been a shift of at least 14 from 20–40 to 40–60. In 2005 this value is 0. In 2010 there must have been a shift of at least 20 and in 2015 this number would be 0. Thus, the minimum shift required is 20 + 14 = 34.
19. There are 329 employees in the age group 20 to 40 in 1995. All these people would go into the age group 40 to 60 in 2015. So, we would expect these 329 employees to be in the 40 to 60 age group in 2015. However, we see that there are only 326 employees in this age group in 2015. If we consider that there are no new employees recruited in this age group during this time period we will get that the minimum number of people leaving the job that must have occurred must have been 3. Likewise, from the 346 people who were in the 40 to 60 age group in 1995, and the 315 people who were in the 60+ age group in 1995, only 340 people are working in the 60+ age group in 2015. Again if we consider no recruitments between 1995 to 2015 in the 60+ age group, we can see that a minimum of 346 + 315 – 340 = 321 must have left the job. Hence, the minimum number of people who must have left the job between 1995 to 2015 must have been 3 + 321 = 324.
20. The minimum number of recruitments would be given by 2 (in 20–40 in 2005) + 48 (in 20–40 in 2010) + 5 (in 20–40 in 2015) + 6 (in 60+ in 2015) = 61.

MOCK TEST PAPER 11

Questions 1 to 6:

1. Fuel consumption between D and K = Distance travelled/Fuel efficiency for this distance
 = 140/14 = 10L
 Fuel consumption between D and M = 420/21 = 20L
 Fuel efficiency between K and M = (distance between K and M)/fuel consumed in this journey
 = (860 – 580)/(20 – 10)
 = 280/10
 = 28 Km/L
 Answer is option (c)
2. We do not know the Fuel efficiency hence the fuel consumption from Debring to Leh, hence we cannot determine the fuel consumed from Delhi to Leh.
 Answer is option (d)
3. At Kurukshetra, it is given that the bike can travel 560 Km more if at the efficiency of 14 Km/L, thus bike must have 40L fuel in the tank left at Kurukshetra.
 Also bike travelled 140 Km from Delhi to Kurukshetra with efficiency of 14 Km/L, thus it consumed 140/14 = 10L fuel to reach Kurukshetra.
 Therefore Bike had 40 + 10 = 50L fuel in it when it started its journey from Delhi.
 Answer is option (a)
4. When Bhavuk reaches Kurukshetra, he analyzes that his fuel efficiency had been 14 Km/L (since the last refill in Delhi) and he is left with 40L in his tank, so he can cover a maximum of 560 Km more with this current efficiency. But Leh is 860 Km away, hence he realizes the need to refuel the tank, however all fuel stations are inactive due to bandh and hence he would not be able to refuel there.
 When he reaches Mandi, he analyzes that his fuel efficiency had been 21 Km/L when considered from Delhi (Fuel last filled at) to Mandi, hence he has consumed 420/21 = 20 L of fuel until now. He realizes that he is left with 30 L of fuel and with current efficiency of 21 Km/L he can actually reach Leh without hassle because he'd need just 580/21 ≈ 28 L of fuel, so he leaves Mandi without refueling.
 When he reaches Debring, he realizes his fuel efficiency had been 23 Km/L when considered from Delhi (Fuel last filled at), he calculates that he has consumed 880/23 ≈ 38 L of fuel so far and is left with 12 L to travel to Leh. He then calculates that at this fuel efficiency he'd need 120/23 ≈ 5 L more, hence he can easily reach Leh without refueling. So he leaves without refueling.

Therefore, Bhavuk did not need to refuel anywhere after Delhi. Yes, if station at Kurukshetra was open, he'd have got a refuel there, but in this question as it states, Kurukshetra was shut down due to bandh.
Therefore answer is option (c)

5. From the table, Range uptil which the fuel could last was only 560 Km from Kurukshetra, however Bhavuk had to travel 860 Km further to Leh. Using data from previous question, yes Bhavuk would have definitely got a refuel done.
Answer is option (a)
6. Fuel efficiency from Delhi to K is 10 and that from K to M is 28 (already calculated in Q1). Fuel efficiency for M to Debring, will be calculated by (total kms from M to D)/(total fuel consumed). The total fuel consumed from M to Debring = Total fuel from Delhi to Debring - Total fuel from Delhi to Mandi = 880/23 - 20 = 18.26. Hence, fuel efficiency from M to Debring = 460/18.26 = 25.19. Simple average = (10+28 + 25.19)/3 = 21.06

Questions 7 to 11:

7. According to the table Hamish's rank is 4th so his weighted total score must have been more than that of the 5th ranked batsman i.e. > 138. Let the runs scored by Hamish in India be 'x' runs, then:

$$150 \times 0.2 + 100 \times 0.4 + x \times 0.2 + 170 \times 0.2 > 138$$

$$30 + 40 + 0.2x + 34 > 138$$

Hence, $x > 170$
Younis's score in India

$$(124 - (140 \times 0.2 + 130 \times 0.4 + 120 \times 0.2)) \div 0.2 = (124 - 28 - 52 - 24) \div 0.2 = 100.$$

Therefore, Hamish must have scored more than anyone else in India. So the required answer is 0.
8. Neel's rank is 8, so his total score should be between 102 and 124.

$$102 < 100 \times 0.2 + 90 \times 0.4 + 110 \times 0.2 + k \times 0.2 < 124$$

$$102 < 78 + k \times 0.2 < 124$$

$$24 < 0.2k < 46$$

$$120 < k < 230$$

But according to the question no player scored more than 190 runs in any country, so the required answer is 190 – 120 = 70.
9. The maximum runs Damian would have scored in South Africa are just less than 160. So at least 5 batsmen – Sachin, Adam, Saurav, Srikant and Hamish scored more than Damian in South Africa.
10. Saurav was in 1st position in the ranking so his total score must be at least 151. If he scored 190 runs in England (maximum possible runs) then his total score would be 160. So the required answer is 160.
11. Saurav is the top ranked batter, so his weighted score has to cross 150. For that to happen, he needs a minimum score of 166 in England.

Questions 12 to 16:

Draw the following table for solving this question:

Team (with number of unknown values)	Penalty Points Got by Cyclists Whose Penalty Points are Exactly Known	Minimum Penalty Points Possible	Maximum Penalty Points Possible	Position
National (1)	155.82	195.97	211.26	
Loreto (0)	198.94	198.94	198.94	5th
Colvin Taluqdar (2)	91.85	172.15	202.73	
St. Francis (1)	141.48	181.63	196.92	
St. Fideles (2)	88.31	168.61	199.19	
St. Anthony (1)	141.23	181.38	196.67	

12. **Since St. Fidelis is sixth, no individual cyclist of St Fideles could break the record as their penalty points have to be greater than 198.94 (Loreto).** We need to similarly look for the other teams in the table.
For National: The total penalties for National (Maximum) can be 198.92 (as 198.94 is for Loreto and Colvin Taluqdars can have a maximum of 198.93) but even if we consider the maximum penalties the penalties Cyclist III of National would still be only 198.92 – 155.82 = 43.10 which still is better than 43.16.
For Loreto: it is very clear that no cyclist of Loreto would have broken the record as all of them are above 43.16 penalty points.
For Colvin Taluqdars: Since the minimum penalties possible for the National team is (155.82 + 40.15) = 195.97 penalty points and Colvin Taluqdars is 4th then they must have greater than 195.97 penalty points. Hence, no Cyclist of Colvin Taluqdars can break the record. (as the maximum possible value for an individual cyclist is 55.44)
St. Francis & St. Anthony: 1 Cyclist each of St. Francis and St. Anthony may or may not break the record.
So at least, 1 Cyclist (National) and at most 3 Cyclists (National, St. Francis and St. Anthony) will break the individual record. Hence, both statements I and II are true. So, answer option is (d).

13. From the above table it is clear that only 2 teams can break the team record (St. Fideles and Colvin Taluqdars) of 178.21.
Colvin Taluqdars: For Colvin Taluqdars the penalty points got by both Cyclists (II &III) should be less than 178.21 – 91.85 = 86.36 i.e., combined timing of II and III can be a maximum of 86.35 penalty points i.e. an average of 43.175. Hence, one among the two cyclists (II and III) of Colvin Taluqdars must break the individual record.
For St. Fidelis: The time taken by II & III Cyclist of St. Fidlis should be less than 178.21 – 88.31 = 89.90 an average of 44.95. So, one of them may or may not break the individual record. Hence, option (a) is correct.
14. (c) In the given condition, the total penalty points of St Anthony's would be 141.23 + 44.30 = 185.53 penalty points.
Every team must have got more than 185.53 penalty points. In such a case, a maximum of 1 Cyclist each of Colvin Taluqdars. St. Fidelis and National could break the individual record.
15. (d) If Cyclist II of St. Francis got 43.16 penalty points, then St. Francis must have got 141 + 43.1 = 184.64 penalty points. As no other Cyclist can break the record, therefore minimum time taken by National will be 155.82 + 43.20 = 199.02. Hence, it will always be in the 6th place as Loreto is fifth with 198.94 penalty points.
Hence, National cannot be third as mentioned by the fourth option.
16. Apart from Loreto, it is possible for each of the other five teams to get the minimum penalty points. Hence, the correct answer is 5.

Questions 17 to 20:

17. For any number in the above table, there are two constraints as defined by statement 2 – With respect to the overall percentile being less than the individual sectional percentiles.
And statement 3 & 4 with respect to the respective percentiles in English and Reasoning as defined for the four batches.
Based on the logic that the overall percentile is lower than the individual sectional percentiles, it can be seen that for Microsoft, 44 students are above 60+ in their overall percentiles, hence, at least that number have to be above 60+ in English for Microsoft. This leaves at most 36 students who can be in the 30+ to 60 bracket. Similarly, for GE, the constraint that works will be that Reasoning < English.
Also, for GE, the minimum number of students who are in the 60+ to 80 percentile in reasoning range would be (36 + 48 + 56) – (38 + 82) = 20. The required difference is 16.
18. Compaq has 52 students in the 0–30 percentile range in English. Hence, we will need to put a minimum of 52 students in the 0–30 percentile category overall. Thus, we can only put 50 students in the 30–60 category (since there are a total of 110 students and 6 + 2 students are in the 60–80 and 80–100 category. Hence, the required difference = 52 – 50 = 2.
19. For the Apple batch the minimum number of students who must be included in the 60+ to 80 percentile range would be 4 (Since there are 160 students who have scored less than 80 percentile in reasoning from this batch and 160 – 60 – 96 = 4).
Besides, the number of students who scored 0 – 30 in the Compaq batch must be at least 52. Hence, the required sum = 4 + 52 = 56.
20. The number of students of GE batch in the 0–60 bracket for reasoning is 120. Also, since there are 164 students in the less than 80 percentile bracket overall and there are 140 students in the less than 80 percentile bracket in English, hence, there must be a maximum of 44 (164 – 120) students in 60+ to 80 in reasoning for the batch and there must be a minimum of 20 students (140 – 120) in the same category. Hence, the required sum = 44 + 20 = 64.

MOCK TEST PAPER 12

Questions 1 to 3:

1. To maximize the production of 2nd highest productive company of a district we need to minimize the production of rest of the companies whose production quantity is unknown.
For district A: If production of 2nd, 3rd, 4th lowest productive companies are 9, 10, 11 metric tons then production of 2nd highest productive company = 100 – (30 + 8 + 9 + 10 + 11) = 32 which is not possible because the production of highest productive company is 30 metric tons. Therefore, the production of the 2nd highest productive company is 29 metric tons. We can do similar calculations for rest of the districts and the resulting data is shown in the table given below.

District	Production of 2nd Highest Productive Company (in metric tons)	Highest Production (in metric tons)
A	30 – 1 = 29	30
B	31	40
C	23	24
D	31	32
E	27	34

District	Production of 2nd Highest Productive Company (in metric tons)	Highest Production (in metric tons)
F	33	34
G	29	30
H	29	30
I	32	45
J	34	35
K	34	40
L	19	35

From the above table we can conclude that there can be only three districts F, J, K for which there are at least two companies whose production is greater than 32 metric tons.

2. For district A maximum possible production of second highest productive company = 30 – 1=29
For district A minimum possible production of second least productive company = 8 + 1 = 9.
For district B minimum possible production of second least productive company = 14 + 1 = 15
For district B maximum possible production of second highest productive company = 100 – (14 + 15 + 40) = 31.
Similarly we can do the same calculation for other companies as well.

District	Production of 2nd Highest Productive Company (in metric tons)	Production of 2nd Lowest Productive Company (in metric tons)	Ratio
A	30 – 1 = 29	8 + 1 = 9	29/9 = 3.22
B	31	15	31/15 = 2.07
C	23	7	23/7 = 3. 29
D	31	21	31/21 = 1.4
E	27	13	27/13 = 2.1
F	33	21	33/21 = 1.6
G	29	9	29/9 = 3.2
H	29	21	29/21 = 1.4
I	32	12	32/12 = 2.7
J	34	10	34/10 = 3.4
K	34	6	34/6 = 5.8
L	19	11	19/11 = 1.77

From the above table it is clear that the required ratio is greater than 3 for five companies. Hence, the correct answer is 5.

3. According to the table given in the question, the number of companies in a given district is either 4 or 5 or 6.
Case 1: When the number of companies in a given district is 4 then less than half i.e. 1 company must produce more than half of the total production i.e. 51 metric tons. No district fulfills this condition.
Case 2: When the number of companies in a given district is 5 then less than half i.e. 2 companies must produce more than half of the total production i.e. 51 metric tons. Districts E, G and J fulfill this condition.
Case 3: When the number of companies in a given district is 6 then less than half i.e. 2 companies must produce more than half of the total production i.e. 51 metric tons. Districts A, C, K, L fulfill this condition. Hence the correct answer is 3 + 4 = 7.

Questions 4 to 8:

4. We know that the difference in cities in between A and B is 8. Hence if A has x cities, B has $x + 8$ or $x - 8$ cities. Also since A – C = 13 and B – C = 5. Hence number of cities C will be having is $x + 13$ or $x - 13$ corresponding to $x + 8$ or $x - 8$ respectively. On similar lines the following two cases may be there:

States	Cities Case 1	Cities Case 2
A	X	X
B	X + 8	X – 8
C	X + 13	X – 13
D	X + 6	X – 6
E	X + 7	X – 7
F	X + 21	X – 21
G	X – 1	X + 1
H	X – 7	X + 7
I	X + 9	X – 9
J	X + 12	X – 12
K	X + 5	X – 5
L	X – 2	X + 2
M	X + 11	X – 11
N	X + 19	X – 19
O	X + 20	X – 20
P	X + 17	X – 17
Q	X + 27	X – 27
R	X + 25	X – 25
S	X + 23	X – 23
T	X + 22	X – 22

In case 1, the number of cities in state H is $x-7$ which must be a natural number. Hence the least possible value of x is 8. Similarly in case 2, state Q has $x-27$ cities and in this case the least possible value of x is 28.

Now states C, J and P are the only states with number of cities in between M and N. Hence number of states that have more or less cities than M and N is 20 – (C, J, P, M, N) = 20 – 5 = 15. Hence (c).

5. As per case 1: $J+K+L+M+N=5x+45$ where $x \geq 8$

   As per case 2: $J+K+L+M+N=5x-45$ where $x \geq 28$

   Clearly in either case the sum cannot be 80.. Hence (b).

6. Since $P \neq (x+17)$, Hence $P=(x-17)$. Hence $x-17 = 15 \Rightarrow x=32$.

   Since $A+C=2x-13 \Rightarrow [(2\times 32)-13]=51$. Hence (a)

7. (i): $A+B+C=3x+21$ or $3x-21$. Since x is a natural number, hence $3x+21 \neq 80$ and $3x-21 \neq 80$. Similarly checking other statements, we find that only option (iii) and (iv) can have 80 cities in total.. Hence (e).

8. In case 1, B has X+8 cities, while R has X + 25. The states of C, EF, I, J, M, N, O, P, S and T have their number of cities between these two numbers. The case 2 also has the same list. Hence, the correct answer is 11.

Questions 9 to 12:

9. The cumulative table can be broken into it's components as follows:

Score	Physics		Chemistry		Mathematics	
	Cumulative Number of Students	Number of Students	Cumulative Number of Students	Number of Students	Cumulative Number of Students	Number of Students
0	100	18	100	25	100	31
10	82	14	75	15	69	19
20	68	16	60	10	50	10
30	52	2	50	15	40	10
40	50	20	35	10	30	10
50	30	18	25	13	20	12
60	12	7	12	5	8	4
70	5	2	7	4	4	3
80	3	1	3	2	1	1
90	2	1	1	1	0	0
100	1	1	0	0	0	0

Consider the marks in Physics. 99 students get less than 100 marks, i.e. exactly one student gets 100. Similarly by calculating the above table can be derived.

50% of the total students imply 50 students. Now, from the table we can see that the first 50 students scored at least 20, 30 and 40 marks in mathematics, chemistry and physics respectively. Hence their overall score is 90 or more. Since the 51st student secured $10+20+30=60$ marks as an overall score. Hence the cutoff is 70. Hence (c) is the correct option

10. The number of students who secured more than 60 marks, i.e. a minimum of 70 marks is 5, 7 and 4 in each of the three subject's physics, chemistry and mathematics respectively. Since 4 minimum students definitely secured more than 60 marks, hence 4 is the answer. Hence (d) is the correct option

11. Now the student who stood first must have got the highest score in all the three subjects as given in the question that when arranged in ascending/ descending order of their scores, it's the same for all the three subjects.

    Hence overall score $= 100+90+80=270$. Hence (d) is the correct option

12. Upon considering the statements ...
    (i) 68 students scored at least 20 marks in the Physics paper and 69 students secured 10 marks in the Mathematics paper. Hence exactly one student scored 10 marks in each of the three exams. Hence (i) is incorrect
    (ii) It is possible and hence not false.
    (iii) The number of students who secured more than 70 marks in each of the three sections is 3, 3 and 1 respectively. Hence only 1 student secured more than 70 marks in each of the three exams. Hence (iii) is false
    (iv) The number of students who secured zero in each of the three exams is 18, 25 and 31 respectively. Since 18 is the minimum, 18 students definitely secured a zero. Hence (iv) is false.

Hence (i), (iii) and (iv) are false. Hence (d) is the correct option.

Questions 13 to 16:

13. From the options the one that satisfies the given conditions is:
Kazakhstan (–19) ⇒ India (+14) and Japan (+5)
Finland (–25) ⇒ Denmark (+16) and Egypt (+9)
Bangladesh (–30) ⇒ Argentina (+19) and Holland (+11)
Clearly option (c) is correct.
14. From the options the one that satisfies the given conditions is:
Japan (–23) ⇒ Holland (+23)
Egypt (–45) ⇒ Finland (+33) and Kazakhstan (+12)
India (–35) ⇒ Bangladesh (+11), Denmark (+8) and Germany (+16)
Clearly option (b) is the correct answer.
15. As we can see from the given data Bangladesh has the highest Doctors deficit. Upon looking further, the following combinations arise in which the deficit of countries Bangladesh, Finland and Kazakhstan can be fulfilled by the surplus of Argentina, Denmark, Egypt, Holland, India, and Japan
Combination (1):
Bangladesh (–30) ⇒ Argentina (+19) and Holland (+11)
Finland (–25) ⇒ Denmark (+16) and Egypt (+9)
Kazakhstan (–19) ⇒ India (+14) and Japan (+5)
Combination (2):
Bangladesh (–30) ⇒ India (+14), Japan (+5) and Holland (+11)
Finland (–25) ⇒ Denmark (+16) and Egypt (+9)
Kazakhstan (–19) ⇒ Argentina (+19)
Combination (3):
Bangladesh (–30) ⇒ Denmark (+16) and India (+14)
Finland (–25) ⇒ Egypt (+9), Holland (+11) and Japan (+5)
Kazakhstan (–19) ⇒ Argentina (+19)
Thus Bangladesh can requisition Doctors from Argentina, Denmark, Holland, India and Japan. Hence (b).
16. As explained in the last question, there are three possible unique combinations in which countries Bangladesh, Finland and Kazakhstan can requisition Engineers. We have already seen that Bangladesh can requisition doctors from 5 different countries. If you look at the previous solution, you can see that Finland can source from 4 different countries (Denmark, Egypt, Holland and Japan. Hence, option (c) is correct.

Questions 17 to 20:

17. It shall be beneficial for the student to draw a diagram illustrating the map of the given condition, i.e. the various cities that connect each other and the traversal time in between each of them. It is left for the student to do this activity.
From the map which the student must have drawn the following table can be inferred. The table given below gives the possible routes the five aircrafts could traverse along with the time taken to traverse the path to start from North Pole (NP) reach the destination of South Pole (SP). Stop over time at each stop over city has obviously not been included.

Route Number	Route	Time in Hours
1	NP-E-H-A-SP	6 + 3 + 4 + 10 = 23
2	NP-E-H-D-G-C-SP	6 + 3 + 4 + 3 + 2 + 8 = 26
3	NP-E-H-B-D-G-C-SP	6 + 3 + 3 + 1 + 3 + 2 + 8 = 26
4	NP-E-H-B-G-C-SP	6 + 3 + 3 + 4 + 2 + 8 = 26
5	NP-F-G-C-SP	8 + 6 + 2 + 8 = 24

After adding the stop over times in each of the stop over cities, we find that the total time (including stop over time) along the five paths is 29, 36, 38, 36 and 30 hours. Clearly, the required answer is 38 – 29 = 9 hours. Hence (a).
18. Reducing the time along the cities B-G reduces the flying time in route 4 to 25 hours. Upon adding the stop over times, we get a total traversal time for the five routes 1 to 5 as 32, 30, 32, 30 and 30 respectively. It can be clearly seen that none of the options are correct. Hence (d).
19. From the given conditions it may be inferred that the stop over time at cities B and D should be 0 each. Similarly to make the traveling time equal, the stop over time at cities A and F should be 7 and 6 hours respectively. Clearly 34 is the correct answer. Hence (c).
20. As shown in the above solutions, when we add the stop over time to each of the given cities, we find that none of the options (a), (b) and (c) satisfy the given conditions. Hence (d).

MOCK TEST PAPER 13

Questions 1 to 4:

1. Let's solve the table first from all the data we have from the question.
Fee paid to celebrities is 25% of the total budget of any campaign, thus we get the following:

According to the question–

1. Digital India:

   Fee to be paid to celebrities for Digital India = 25% of 176 = 44 Lakhs INR

   Fee already paid to celebrities = 26 Lakhs INR

   Fee remaining to pay = 18 Lakhs INR

   From table, only Moni or Kajal + Amir, if added as star campaigners can make a total of 18 Lakhs INR. All other celebrities are not considered.

2. Give It Up India:

   Fee to be paid to celebrities for Give It Up India = 25% of 144 = 36 Lakhs INR

   Fee already paid to celebrities = 26 Lakhs INR

   Fee remaining to pay = 10 Lakhs INR

   From the table, only Anshika when appointed can make up for this amount

3. Startup India:

   Fee to be paid to celebrities for Startup India = 25% of 192 = 48 Lakhs INR

   Fee already paid to celebrities = 24 Lakhs INR

   Fee remaining to pay = 24 Lakhs INR

   From table, only when Anshika and Hansika are appointed, can make up for this sum

4. Swachh Bharat Abhiyaan:

   Fee to be paid to celebrities for Swachh Bharat Abhiyaan = 25% of 288 = 72 Lakhs INR

   Fee already paid to celebrities = 24 Lakhs INR

   Fee remaining to pay = 48 Lakhs INR

   From table, only when Mohli and Imran and Moni/Kajal are appointed, can make up for this sum.

We get the following table:

	Fee Charged Per Campaign (in INR)	Digital India	Give It Up India	Startup India	Swachh Bharat Abhiyaan
Total budget for the campaign (in Lakh INR) Star campaigner		176	144	192	288
Mohli	20	No	Yes	No	Yes
Imran	16	Yes	No	No	Yes
Sairukh	10	Yes	No	No	Yes
Moni	12	*	No	Yes	*
Kajal	12	*	No	Yes	*
Anshika	10	No	Yes	Yes	No
Hansika	14	No	No	Yes	Yes
Amir	6	Yes	Yes	No	No

Clearly, Kajal could have worked in Digital India or Swachh Bharat Abhiyaan. Hence we cannot determine the answer.

Answer is option (d)

2. From the table, Anshika has not worked with Sairukh in any of the given campaigns.

   Answer is option (b)

3. Mohli has worked in Give it Up India and Swachh Bharat Abhiyaan, total budget of which amounts to: 144 + 288 = 432 Lakhs INR

   Moni and Kajal have worked together only in Startup India with budget = 192 Lakhs INR

   Difference = 432 – 192 = 240

   Answer is option (d)

4. We know that every celebrity works in exactly 2 of the 4 campaigns. Therefore, amount these celebrities charge = 2 × (20 + 16 + 10 + 12 + 12 + 10 + 14 + 6) = 2 × (100) = 200 Lakhs INR

   According to question, PM Narendra Modi announced 20% more to be added to it from National treasure

   = 120% of 200 Lakhs INR

   = 240 Lakhs INR

   Amount spent on banners ads = 23% of 240 Lakhs INR

   = 55.2 Lakhs INR

   Answer is option (a)

Questions 5 to 8:

If we look carefully at the second table then we find that C has got his chocolates only in 4 and 6 chocolate packs. Also, the number of chocolates in 4 chocolate packs is twice the number of chocolates that he has in 6 chocolate packs. This gives us the following possibilities of number of chocolates that C has:

	Number of Chocolates C has in 6 Chocolate Packs	Number of Chocolates C has in 4 Chocolate Packs	Total Number of Chocolates C has
Possibility 1	6	12	18
Possibility 2	12	24	36
Possibility 3	18	36	54

However, since we see from the first table that C has a total of 10% of the total number of chocolates. Hence, if we give him 54 chocolates, the total number of chocolates that Charlie must have distributed on that day would have been 540, which is above the limit given in the question. Hence, only possibilities 1 and 2 need to be considered here.

If we consider possibility 1, we can see that the total number of chocolates is 180. In such a case, the number of chocolates given to E, F, G, H, I and J would be 18 too and they would get 6 chocolates each in 6 and 4 chocolate packs. But the number of chocolates someone gets in 4 chocolate packs cannot be 6 (as it has to be a multiple of 4).

Hence, Possibility 1 does not exist.

Considering possibility 2, we get the following scenario:

Solution Table

	Total Number of Chocolates	Number of Chocolates in 4 Chocolate Packs	Number of Chocolates in 6 Chocolate Packs
A	90	12	36
B	108	24	12
C	36	24	12
D	90	36	18
E to J	36	12	12
	360	108	90

The answers can be inferred from the solution table:

5. 108
6. 18/6 = 3
7. Total number of 4 chocolate sets = 108/4 = 27
8. Others (6 people from E–J) have total 36 chocolates. Since, it is given that apart from A and D, no two children had the same number of chocolates, we can only have 1 child as having 0 chocolates. Therefore the maximum number of children who do not have any chocolate = 1

Questions 9 to 12:

9. From the bar-chart, Delhiites is liked by all people surveyed
   Bodyguard is liked by all but one person surveyed
   Dil me is liked by all but 2 persons and so on
   From the information given in question, below table can be deduced:

	Delhiites	Bodyguard	Dil me	Gatekeeper	Junoon	Gharwale	Salam Bombay	Dilwale
Liked by Name of person	10 people	9 people	8 people	6 people	4 people	3 people	2 people	1 person
Bhavye 2	Bhavye 1	Bhavye 0	X	X	X	X	X	X
Dimpy 5	Dimpy 4	Dimpy 3	Dimpy 2	Dimpy 1	Dimpy 0	X	X	X
Pulkit 4	Pulkit 3	Pulkit 2	Pulkit 1	Pulkit 0	X	X	X	X
Bijoy 3	Bijoy 2	Bijoy 1	Bijoy 0	X	X	X	X	X
Charu 1	Charu 0	X	X	X	X	X	X	X
Shanky 8	Shanky 7	Shanky 6	Shanky 5	Shanky 4	Shanky 3	Shanky 2	Shanky 1	Shanky 0
Neha 6	Neha 5	Neha 4	Neha 3	Neha 2	Neha 1	Neha 0	X	X
Guddu 7	Guddu 6	Guddu 5	Guddu 4	Guddu 3	Guddu 2	Guddu 1	Guddu 0	X
Sanju 4	Sanju 3	Sanju 2	Sanju 1	Sanju 0	X	X	X	X
Kanu 3	Kanu 2	Kanu 1	Kanu 0	X	X	X	X	X

Note: "Bhavye 1" means that Bhavye likes this movie (mentioned in that column) and is left with 1 more like from the total number of likes as given in the question. Likewise "Bhavye 0" means Bhavye likes this movie (mentioned in that column) and has no more likes left.

According to this table, 8 people did not like the movie- Salam Bombay
Answer is option (c)

10. From the table above, Dimpy does not like only 3 movies – Gharwale, Salam Bombay and Dilwale
Hence Answer is option (a)

11. From the table above, Pulkit likes Bodyguard, Dil me, Gatekeeper, these movies are not liked Charu
Answer is option (c)

12. From the table above, Kanu dislikes movies – Gatekeeper, Junoon, Gharwale but Neha likes these movies.
Answer is option (b)

Questions 13 to 16:

First we fill the table with the changes in marbles after every round

	Arun	Barun	Charan	Deep	Ela	Faiz
Initial No. of Marbles	160	130	150	180	150	200
No. of Marbles at the end of 1st	140 (–20)	150 (+20)	180 (+30)	160 (–20)	170 (+20)	170 (–30)
No. of Marbles at the end of 2nd	150 (+10)	140 (–10)	190 (+10)	190 (+30)	140 (–30)	160 (–10)
No. of Marbles at the end of 3rd	170 (+20)	130 (–10)	170 (–20)	200 (+10)	–	150 (–10)
No. of Marbles at the end of 4th	180 (+10)	120 (–10)	180 (+10)	190 (–10)	–	170 (+20)
No. of Marbles at the end of 5th						

We can see that during the first round there is an exchange between Charan and Faiz as they both have transacted (+30) and (–30) marbles respectively. Also, further analysis of the first round gives us that Arun and Deep both have a (–20) and Barun and Ela both have a (+20). We can thus deduce from this information that Arun must have dealt with either Barun or Ela and similarly Deep must have dealt with either Ela or Barun.

From the analysis of the second round, it is clear that Deep and Ela must have transacted with each other. Thus we can resolve our doubt about the first round where Deep cannot have transacted with Ela and must have dealt with Barun and at the same time Arun and Ela must have transacted with each other.

In this way we find all the co-relations.

After the 3rd round the No. of Marbles with Ela is missing. We see that Barun and Faiz each has given 10 marbles to two persons and the table is showing only Deep as the recipient of 10 marbles. So Ela must have also received 10 marbles and must have has 150 marbles at the end of the third round.

In the 4th round Faiz has a (+20) and no one else is having a (–20). It automatically means that Faiz has exchanged coins with Ela who must have had –20 and hence ended with 130 at the end of 4th round.

Thus the table at the end of the fourth round would look like:

Players	1	2	3	4	5
Arun	Ela	Faiz	Charan	Barun	Deep
Barun	Deep	Charan	Ela	Arun	Faiz
Charan	Faiz	Barun	Arun	Deep	Ela
Deep	Barun	Ela	Faiz	Charan	Arun
Ela	Arun	Deep	Barun	Faiz	Charan
Faiz	Charan	Arun	Deep	Ela	Barun

So the answers from the above information are as follows:

13. Exact exchanges can be found for all the 5 rounds. Hence the correct option is (d).
14. Faiz exchanges marbles with Barun. Hence the correct option is (c).
15. (a) Charan will get 65 marbles from Ela and have 245 marbles while Deep will get 90 marbles from Arun and have 280 marbles. Thus, the required difference would be 35.
16. Arun transacted with Barun. Hence the correct option is (b).

Questions 17 to 20:

With the help of Table Y, we can make a new Table Z which gives us details of the number of exams in which each of these nine students obtained 100 to 199 marks, 200 to 299 marks, 300 or more marks: **Table Z will look as follows:** (***Note:*** Since A scored 100 + 3 times, 200 + 2 times and 300 + 2 times, he must have scored between 100 to 199 1 time, 200 to 299 zero times and 300+ 2 times)

Student/Marks	100–199	200–299	300+
A	1	0	2
B	0	1	1
C	1	1	2
D	0	1	0
E	2	1	1
F	0	2	0
G	1	0	1
H	2	0	1
I	1	0	0

According to Table Z, E and H scored 100 to 199 marks in two subjects. Therefore they must be from USA and China in any order.

E obtained 200–299 marks in one subject, but no students from China scored 200–299 marks in any subject therefore E is from USA and H is from China.

If we now include this information, we can transform table X to a new **Table X1** (After removing students E and H) This country wise table would look as shown below:

Country/Marks	100 to 199	200 to 299	300+
UK	1	2	2
USA	1	0	1
INDIA	1	2	1
CHINA	0	0	0
FRANCE	1	1	2

From table X1 and table Z it is clear that only G can be from USA and no other student can be from USA.

F can be from UK and India. If F is from India then India needs 1 student who scored 100 to 199 marks in exactly one subject and 1 student who scored 300+ in exactly one subject. But from table Z it is clear that no other student can fulfill this condition, therefore F is not from India and he/she is from UK.

New **table-X2** (After removing students E, H, G and F):

Country/Marks	100 to 199	200 to 299	300+
UK	1	0	2
USA	0	0	0
INDIA	1	2	1
CHINA	0	0	0
FRANCE	1	1	2

From Tables Z and X2 it is clear that A is from UK. C obtained 300+ marks in two subjects therefore he must be from France.

New **Table X3** (After removing students E, H, G, F, A and C):

Country/Marks	100 to 199	200 to 299	300+
UK	0	0	0
USA	0	0	0
INDIA	1	2	1
CHINA	0	0	0
FRANCE	0	0	0

From Table X3 it is clear that rest of the students (B, D, I) were from India.

Country	Students
UK	F, A
USA	E, G
INDIA	B, D, I
CHINA	H
FRANCE	C

17. B. option (c) is correct.
18. India. Option (a) is correct.
19. E. option (c) is correct.
20. 1

MOCK TEST PAPER 14

Questions 1to 5:

1. On 14th May:

   1 dollar = 66 INR = 114 Yen

   ⇨1 INR = 114/66 Yen

   ⇨4000 INR = 4000 × 114/66 = 6909.0909 = 6910 (when rounded off)

   Hence option (b) is correct.

2. Let us convert the value of each currency Bhavuk possesses into equivalent dollar amount and see which currency he has in excess to buy the watch worth $300. Conversion would be done as per the exchange rate on 15th May.

   $ against INR = 19,500/66.5 = $293 → Not sufficient

   $ against £ = 1.45 × 200 = $290 → Not sufficient

   $ against Yen = 34,250/112.5 = $304 (approx.) → Sufficient

   Therefore, Bhavuk can buy this watch by offering Yen to the shopkeeper.

   Hence option (a) is correct.

3. We cannot determine equivalent dollars for Yen on 13th May as the line graph- Yen/Dollar does not have data of that ratio on 13th May.

   Hence option (d) is the correct answer.

4. Devaluing the currency means weakening the currency value against other global currencies. Here it is given that Yen was devalued by 2.22% of its value on 15th May. It stood at 112.5 Yen/dollar. Devaluation was 2.22% that is 2.22% of 112.5 = 2.5 Yen/dollar. Now Yen would stand at 112.5 + 2.5 = 115 Yen/Dollar.

   Therefore, you can buy 56000/115 = $487 (approx) for ¥56000

   Hence option (a) is correct

5. It is given that the base (INR against other currencies) didn't change much on 16th May, hence its

value against dollar remained at 66.5 Rupee/Dollar on 16th May.

On 15th May:

1 dollar = 66.5 INR = 112.5 ¥

⇨1 INR = 112.5/66.5

On 16th May:

1 dollar = 66.5 INR = 115 ¥

⇨1 INR = 115/66.5

We are sure that INR appreciated against Yen, by how much?

⇨2.5/66.5 over 112.5/66.5

⇨2.5/112.5 = 2.22% appreciated

Hence option (a) is the answer

Questions 6 to 10:

In physics paper: Combined score of Pulkit and Rahim in Physics Paper = 405 – (132 + 108 + 90) = 75 and their individual marks cannot be more than 10% of 405 = 40.5. Therefore Pulkit's marks are in the range of 40.5–34.5 and Rahim's marks would be in the range of 34.5–40.5.

In Chemistry paper: Rahim and Tejas obtained 45 marks each, since there are a total of 90 marks to be distributed between them and nobody can get more than 45 marks.

In Biology: Pulkit's and Qasim's marks should be less than or equal to 10% of 360 = 36. But from the table A, Shaan got 30 marks. Therefore Pulkit and Qasim both got less than 30 marks. They can obtain a maximum of 29 marks and a minimum of 19 marks.

In Math: Combined marks of Rahim and Tejas = 58.5

Maximum possible marks of Rahim and Tejas = 30 therefore they can obtain marks in 28.5 to 30 marks.

Student	Physics	Chemistry	Biology	Math
Pulkit	40.5–34.5	150	19–29	79.5
Qasim	132	97.5	29–19	78
Rahim	34.5–40.5	45	165	28.5–30
Shaan	108	112.5	30	84
Tejas	90	45	117	30–28.5

6. Maximum possible marks of Pulkit in Physics = 40.5. Option (d).
7. Maximum marks obtained by Rahim = 40.5 + 45 + 165 + 30 = 280.5

   Required percentage contribution

   $= \frac{280.5}{1515} \times 100 = 18.51\%$. Option (b) is correct
8. The absolute difference of marks obtained by Pulkit and Rahim will be minimum when Pulkit got minimum possible marks and Rahim got maximum possible marks. Minimum possible marks obtained by Pulkit = 34.5 + 150 + 19 + 79.5 = 283

   Maximum possible marks obtained by Rahim = 40.5 + 45 + 165 + 30 = 280.5

   Absolute difference = 283 – 280.5 = 2.5

   In this case (when Pulkit got minimum and Rahim got maximum marks):

   Marks obtained by Qasim = 132 + 97.5 + 29 + 78 = 336.5

   Marks obtained by Tejas = 90 + 45 + 117 + 28.5 = 280.5

   Required difference = 336.5 – 280.5 = 56
9.

Students	Range of scores
Pulkit	283–299
Qasim	326.5–336.5
Rahim	273–280.5
Shaan	334.5
Tejas	280.5–282

From the above table we can conclude that Rahim got the last (5th rank), Tejas got the 4th rank, Pulkit got the 3rd rank and ranks of Qasim and Shaan cannot be determined.

Pulkit got the 3rd rank. Option (c) is correct.

10. If total marks of Qasim is a prime integer then he must score 331 marks therefore he got 2nd rank.

Questions 11 to 15:

11. Consider the below match fixtures in case of no upset in the tournament:

Round-1		Round-2		Round-3		Round-4		Round-5		Round-6	
Seed of Player1	Seed of Player2	Seed of Player1	Seed of Player2	Seed of Player1	Seed of Player2	Seed of Player1	Seed of Player2	Seed of Player1	Seed of Player2	Seed of Player1	Seed of Player2
1	128	1	64	1	32	1	16	1	8	1	4
2	127	2	63	2	31	2	15	2	7	2	3
–	–	–	–	–	–	–	–	3	6		
–	–	–	–	–	–	–	–	4	.5		
–	–	–	–	–	–	–	–	–			
64	65	32	33	16	17	8	9	–			

Round-7	
Seed of Player1	Seed of Player2
1	2

Clearly from above information, we see that the player seeded 8 plays players seeded lower than him till Round-4. In Round-5 player seeded 8 has to play player seeded 1 who is higher seeded than him.
Answer is option (c)

12. In case of no upset, players seeded 17 to 32 won the 1st round and 2nd round that is till the time they played lower seeded players, and were defeated in 3rd round by higher seeded players. Hence 16 players (seeded 17 to 32) won exactly 2 matches.
Answer is option (b)
13. Out of 7 rounds, in the first 3 rounds, player seeded 16 would win all the 3 matches he plays, without any upset. Then in 4th round when seed 16 faces seed 1 and wins – 1st upset happens; then in 5th round seed 16 faces seed 8 and wins – 2nd upset happens; then in 6th round seed 16 faces seed 4 and wins – 3rd upset happens and finally in 7th round seed 16 faces seed 2 and wins – 4th upset happens. Therefore in total 4 upsets happen.
Answer is (c)
14. If no upset happens in previous rounds, then Seed 2 faces Seed 15, but here no information is given on how many upsets had happened earlier in the tournament. In this case consider all possible seeds that can replace Seed 2 in 4th round. Therefore in 2nd round, when Seed 31 faces Seed 34, let's assume that upset happens, so Seed 34 moves ahead. Now in 3rd round, Seed 34 faces seed 2 and again upset happens, so Seed 34 moves ahead in tournament
Now in 4th round Seed 34 will have to face Seed 15. None of the other players mentioned in the other options can face Seed 15 like this in 4th round.
Answer is option (a)
15. From table above, clearly Seed 8 beats Seed 25 in 3rd round.
Answer is option (d)

Questions 16 to 20:

16. From the tables A, G, H and K are the four games of the HI-HI Tournaments. The points awarded to the player are same as that for table 2. Similarly D and J are HA-HA and B, C, I, L and M are HE-HE and E and F are HO-HO. Since the prize money is distributed equally, for each of the semifinalists and each of the first finalists, the total prize money is distributed in 20 + 14 + 9 + 9 + 5 + 5 + 5 + 5 = 72 parts.
Therefore the winner gets 20/72 parts of the money, the runner up gets 14/72 parts of the money, each of the semifinalists get 9/72 parts of the money and the quarter finalists get 5/72 parts of the prize money offered.
The runner up will therefore get 14/72 × [(72000 × 4) + (36000 × 5) + (21600 × 2) + (17700 × 2)] = 106283
Hence (a).
17. In the K game, Scrooge and DD have scored 50 points each and thus they have lost their respective quarter finals. Dexter, Dupey and Scooby have reached to semifinals and finals.
Therefore the possible quarterfinal match must be played in between one of Dexter, Dupey and Scooby against one of Scrooge and DD. Since option (b) satisfies the given conditions.
18. Donald has reached beyond quarter finals in only two games, L and M where he is runner up and both are the HE-HE tournaments. Hence Prize money = 14/72 × 36000 × 2 = 14000. Hence (d).
19. Its best to go through the options to solve the given problem.
Scrooge and Jetson lose in R16 round. Hence (a) is incorrect.
Shaggy loses in quarter final so option (b) is incorrect.
Scrooge and Jetson also loose out before Semifinal, hence (c) is incorrect.
Hence (d) is the correct answer (and can be verified).
20. It can be seen that Dupey has won H, F, B, J, K and C. Bluto has won L, D, I, E, G, M. There are only 13 games in total, so nobody can cross the 6 wins of Dupey and Bluto.
Hence, option (d) is correct.

MOCK TEST PAPER 15

Questions 1 to 4:

1. Maximum loss incurred is due to product G. Hence minimum units of product G should be sold. Hence checking option (c) and (d) shall give the answer. Hence for option (d) ⇒ 6 + 1 – 3 – 2 = 2. Hence option (d) is correct.
2. From the line graph we can see the profit (+) and loss (–) yielded by each of the products, i.e. +3, –1, –5 and 0. Hence to earn profit, maximum units of E and minimum units of G should be sold. Hence profit for each option can be calculated as following (option [a] taken as an example)

$$E = 40, F = 20 \text{ and } G = 10, H = 30$$

$$\text{Profit} = (3 \times 40) - 20 - (5 \times 10) = ₹50$$

Similarly after calculation of other options, we find that [c] is the correct option.

3. For profit: Preparation cost < Tuition cost. It can be seen from the graph that 2 is the correct answer. Hence (d)
4. We can calculate the profit (+)/loss (–) of each of the four products to be –1, +2, +2 and 0 (no profit, no loss). If the number of units sold be e, f, g and h for the respective products. Since company Y suffered a loss of ₹20000 hence we can say that $2f + 2g - e = -20$. Hence $e = 2(f + g) + 20$. We know that $e + f + g + h = 100$ is given. From these equations we may conclude that $3(f + g) + h = 80$. Considering the options, only (a) is correct.

Questions 5 to 8:

5. From the given conditions, Team F's total points must be less than Team E. Since Team E has got 2 points, it had 2 draws and 3 losses and no wins. Team F cannot have any win since it can have a maximum of 1 point, the match in between E and F must have been a draw. Hence Team F got 1 point. Team D could have scored anywhere in between 3 to 7 points. D definitely won against F and had a draw/win against team E.
As can be noticed, total goals for = total goals against. Hence goals for team C are 45 – 43 = 2. Since the number of draws must be an even number, hence the only possibility is that Team D has 4, 2 or 0 draws. Hence also total number of matches won = total number of matches lost. Hence team D should have lost 1 game more than it won. Hence team D definitely lost to team A and C. Hence D cannot have 4 draws.
If we consider that D has 2 draws, i.e. with Team B and E, there is an inconsistency as team C has had 2 draws but as per our hypothesis, there are no countries left to draw against it. Hence the only possibility is that Team D has had 0 draws which automatically means that D beat Team E and F and got 6 points.
The following table gives the details of our analysis thus far:

Position	Country	Won	Draw	Loss	Goals For	Goals Against	Total Points
1	A	5	0	0	17	5	15
2	B	3	1	1	9	6	10
3	C	2	2	1	2	2	8
4	D	2	0	3	2	5	6
5	E	0	2	3	7	11	2
6	F	0	1	4	8	16	1

We can determine each of the three statements. Hence, option (e) is correct.

6. As is clear from the table, all the given statements are false. Hence (d) is correct.
7. As is clear from the table, none of the statements is true. Option (e) is correct.
8. Statement (i): False.
Statement (ii): It can be inferred from the above table that this statement is true.
Statement (iii): It can be inferred from the above table that this statement is false.
Statement (iv): False.
Statement (v): It can be inferred from the above table that this statement is true.
Hence (e) is the correct option.

Questions 9 to 12:

9. From the data the following can be inferred (working out of the inference left for the students)
   (i) D's total points should be greater than 19 (21 or 23) and hence its satisfactory ratings are either 5 or 6
   (ii) C's total points are greater than 19 (21 or 23) satisfactory ratings are either 2 or 3
   (iii) B's total points are greater than or equal to 21 (21 or 24) Good ratings are either 3 or 4
   (iv) From the above B's total points are 24 and the number of Good ratings won by B and F are 4 and 1 respectively

   Clearly (b) is the correct answer
10. If D got 6 satisfactory ratings, C would have to score a minimum of 23 points in order to be ranked 4th. For this C would have to get 3 satisfactory ratings. Option (b) is correct.
11. There are 4 possibilities for A to get to his score of 24 points, B's points get exactly fixed, hence for B there is only one possibility. For C and D there are two possibilities each, while for E there are 6 possible scenarios. Thus, the total number of possible ways in which we can create the table for the first five positions would be got by multiplying these numbers – viz: 4, 2, 2 and 6 = 96 ways. Hence, option (c) is correct.
12. It can be clearly seen that both the options (a) and (c) are true. Hence (d).

Questions 13 to 16:

13. Dogs named 1 through 16 are seated in a row. Dog 1 is seated 6 places to the right of the dog with the tag 1 and is seated 13 places to the left of the dog wearing the tag 3. Hence the dog wearing the tag 1 and 3 are seated on either of the extreme ends of the row. If the positions of the dogs be 1 through 20 (not to confused with their name or tag number) then the following table is obtained:

Name of Dog	Position
1	1 + 6 = 7
13	1 + 2 = 3
19	1 + 16 = 17
16	20 + 0 = 20

Since the positions of the above four dogs is calculated, the positions of the other dogs can also be arrived at. (This activity is left for the students to complete)
The final list is as follows:

Name of Dog	Tag Number	Seating Position
1	6	7
2	12	6
3	5	10
4	16	12
5	10	5
6	14	8
7	20	14
8	7	13
9	19	11
10	13	9
11	15	2
12	1	1
13	11	3
14	2	4
15	4	15
16	3	20
17	18	16
18	9	19
19	8	17
20	17	18

Clearly from the above table, 19 dogs are seated to the left of dog 16 as it is on position 20. Hence (d).

14. As can be seen from the above table, only statements (iv) and (v). Hence [d] is the correct option.
15. The dog with tag 4 is in position 15. Hence the dog to his right is position 16, name 17 and tag 18. Hence (a) is correct.
16. It can be seen and compared from the table above that none of the statements are true. Hence (d)

Questions 17 to 20:

17. Based upon the information given the following table may be drawn which gives us the various possibilities

Possibility	More than Expected		Less than Expected	
	10% more	20% more	10% less	20% less
1	Atron	Ctron	Btron	Dtron
2	Atron	Ctron	Dtron	Btron
3	Atron	Dtron	Btron	Ctron
4	Atron	Dtron	Ctron	Btron
5	Btron	Ctron	Atron	Dtron
6	Btron	Ctron	Dtron	Atron
7	Btron	Dtron	Atron	Ctron
8	Btron	Dtron	Ctron	Atron

On similar lines, the corresponding mean life for each of the above given possibilities is calculated as given below in the table:

Possibility	Atron Expected Mean Life = 60 ns	Btron Expected Mean Life = 90 ns	Ctron Expected Mean Life = 80 ns	Dtron Expected Mean Life = 75 ns	Sum of Mean Life Expected Mean Life = 305 ns
1	66	81	96	60.0	303.0
2	66	72	96	67.5	301.5
3	66	81	64	90.0	301.0
4	66	72	72	90.0	300.0
5	54	99	96	60.0	309.0
6	48	99	96	67.5	310.5
7	54	99	64	90.0	307.0
8	48	99	72	90.0	309.0

Clearly a total mean life of 195 ns of Btron and Ctron corresponds to possibility 5 and 6. Hence (a) is the correct option.

18. Clearly, a sum of mean life of 309 corresponds to possibility 5 and 8 in the table above. As can be seen from the table, none of the given statements hold true. Hence (d) is the correct option.
19. The new mean life of Btron cannot be more than 20% of the old expected life because that violates the rule that the maximum mean life of any sub atomic particle is 100 ns. Hence for maximum difference, the new mean life of every sub atomic particle must be 20% less than that of the old expected mean life. Hence maximum difference =

Old expected mean life – New expected mean life = 310.5 – (0.8 × 305) = 66.5. Hence (c).

20. As seen from the table, only possibility 4 satisfies the given condition. Hence statements i, iii and iv are correct. Hence (c) is correct.

MOCK TEST PAPER 16

Questions 1 to 4:

1. As each team has won/lost different number of matches, the number of matches could be 0, 1, 2, 3, or 4. Also the sum of the number of matches won and lost by any team has to be equal to 4. Also, as the GAIN or LOSS for any team is maximum 40 and the sum of LOSSES and GAINS for A, D and E is more than 40, hence one out of B and C is the team that has either won or lost all the four bets.
Since C has lost more matches than what D has, it implies that C has lost to all the four teams and won none. Hence the LOSS of team C is ₹40. Automatically, B has won against four teams and lost none of the matches and hence its GAIN is ₹37. Again since the GAIN of A is equal to the LOSS of D, hence 1 and 3 teams for each of them. E has won and lost against two teams each (The loss being against A and C). As A lost to B and E, it must have lost 3 matches and won 1, i.e. A lost to D as well. The values of the same are just opposite for D. Also, C had lost to D.
Also total amount of transactions = 55 + 37 + 40 + 55 + 53 = 240. Hence total gains/losses = 240/2 = 120. Since LOSS of D is same as the GAIN of A, hence the sum of money gain/lost by A + D = ₹55. The total amount won by A + B + C + D + E = 55 + 37 + 0 + gain of E. Hence gain of E = 28. Therefore A + C gave 28 to E. Hence A lost 17 to E and C lost 11 to E. Hence the GAIN of C is at least 20 and the amount lost by C to A is at most 21. All this data can be tabulated as given as follows.

	A	B	C	D	E	LOSS
A		*a*	0	*b*	17	35
B	0		0	0	0	0
C	c	*d*		4	11	40
D	0	*f*	0		0	20
E	0	*g*	0	*h*		25
GAIN	20	37	0	35	28	120

From the above, $c = 20$ or 21. But $c = 21$ is not valid because then we know that from the equation $c + d + 4 + 11 = 40 \Rightarrow d = 4$ which is a contradiction as the stakes of no two matches can be the same. Thus $c = 20$ and $d = 5$.
As the total loss of D is equal to the gain of A hence $f = 20$.
Clearly the money involved in the match between B and C is ₹5. Hence (e).

2. As is clear from the discussion, B won the maximum number of matches. Hence (a).
3. As is clear from the discussion, the total loss of A is ₹35. Hence (a).
4. As is clear from the discussion, team E lost to two teams and won against two teams. Hence (e) is the correct option.

Questions 5 to 8:

5. A student can take a maximum of two lab courses since the slots are clashing, i.e, CS002 and SI007. Students have to select five courses with minimum possible credits. All the credits for the classroom courses are either 6 or 8. Thus a student can take any five courses out of $1z$, $2z$, $3z$, $4z$, $5z$, or $6z$ but all the courses of $2z$ and $5z$ have credit 8. Also, z is any of the three days. Thus, minimum possible credits are 3 + 5 + 6 + 6 + 6 + 6 + 8 = 40. Hence (d).
6. The student has already taken courses with the time slot $1z$, $4z$, and $6z$. Also, as it can be seen from the previous answer, he has taken lab courses with time slot ($7a$, $8a$, $9a$). Hence he can take any two out of $2z$, $3z$, and $5z$ courses. From the given options (d) does not satisfy the given conditions. Hence (a).
7. As it can be seen from the given data that all the courses with time slots $2z$ has contact hours of 4 hrs, one out of the three lab courses has a 3 hr contact period. Hence minimum hours that a student should attend is 3 + 4 + (3 × 5) = 22 hrs. Hence (a).
8. From the given courses we can calculate the contact hours and credits. A student has to attend 15 hrs of lecture, 6 hrs of tutorials in the semester. Hence all the given statements are true. Hence (d).

Questions 9 to 14:

We can make the following table for the number of passengers who have a Bachelor's degree:

	Mail Train	Passenger Train	Express Train	Total
Small	100 (#3)	615 (#4)	35 (#3)	750(#1)
Medium	150(#4)	1585(#4)	15(#4)	1750(#1)
Large	1250 (#2)	0(#2)	250(#2)	1500(#1)
Total	1500 (#1)	2200 (#1)	300(#1)	4000(#1)

Deduction 1: Based on the basic information, we can work out that of the 10000 travelers, 4000 travel in mail trains, 5200 in Passenger trains and 800 in Express trains. Also, we can work out that since the small to medium to large ratio is 7:19:14, it means that there must be 1750 travelers in small trains, 4750 in medium trains and 3500 in large trains. From these totals when we subtract the number of people who do not have a bachelor's degree, we get the number of people for each of these categories, who would have a bachelors degree. For instance, there are a total of 10000 people who traveled on that day, and 6000 of them did not have a bachelors degree. So, 4000 would have a bachelors degree.

Likewise, of 4000 people who traveled in mail trains that day, 2500 is given to us in the table for people without a Bachelor's degree. Thus, 4000-2500 = 1500 would be the number of people who traveled in mail trains. For the travelers who have a bachelors degree, the totals for each of mail, passenger and Express trains and small medium and large trains is shown in the solution table with a marking of #1 to indicate the deduction number 1.

Deduction 2: Of the people in large trains, 70% are in Mail trains as given to us in clue 1. This means that there are a total of 2450 people in mail trains (amongst Large trains). Out of this, people without Bachelor's degree is 1200. Hence, people with bachelor's degree would be 2450 – 1200 = 1250. Also, from the other part of the first clue, we can get that there are 0 people with a bachelors degree and traveling in large passenger trains. Hence, in the people with Bachelors degree table that we are making, we will get that there are 1500-1250-250 people in Large express trains.

Deduction 3: The number of people in Small express trains for this table would be 10% of 350 = 35. Also, from Clue 3, we get that the number of small mail train travelers with Bachelor's degree would be 100. Once we fill these numbers, the other missing numbers in the table would be derived from the row and column totals.

The answers to the first three questions can now be read from the table:

9. Option (d) is correct.
10. Option (a) is correct.
11. Option (b) is correct.

For solving the remaining three questions of the set, we need to understand what changes are happening in the respective categories the next time:

Deduction 1: Large passenger trains for Non-Bachelor people = 725 + 500 + 350 = 1575.

Large passenger trains for Bachelor people = 0 + 100 + 35 = 135.

Addition to the number of passengers in Medium mail trains, medium passenger trains, medium express trains, large mail trains and large express trains for non-bachelor people = one fifth of one third of 150 = An addition of 10 each.

Addition to the number of passengers in Medium mail trains, medium passenger trains, medium express trains, large mail trains and large express trains for bachelor people = one fifth of one third of 615 = An addition of 51 each.

Number of people in Jumbo express trains for non-bachelor people = two-thirds of 150=100.

Number of people in Jumbo express trains for bachelor people = two-thirds of 615=410.

These values can be encapsulated in the following tables:

People without a bachelors degree

	Mail Train	Passenger Train	Express Train	Total
Jumbo	0	0	100	100
Medium	810	2135	85	3030
Large	1210	1575	85	2870
Total	2020	3710	270	6000

People with Bachelors' degree

	Mail Train	Passenger Train	Express Train	Total
Jumbo	0	0	410	410
Medium	191	1626	56	1873
Large	1291	135	291	1717
Total	1482	1761	757	4000

Total number of people.

	Mail Train	Passenger Train	Express Train	Total
Jumbo	0	0	510	510
Medium	1001	3761	141	4903
Large	2501	1710	376	4587
Total	3502	5471	1027	10000

The answers can be read off from here:

12. 3761
13. 1626 – 1210 = 415
14. 5471 + 510 = 5981.

Questions 15 to 20 :

From the first paragraph, we can derive the following information:

	Men	Women	Total
Cricket Fans	50	20	70
Football Fans	100	30	130
Total	150	50	200

Total men = 210

Women = x

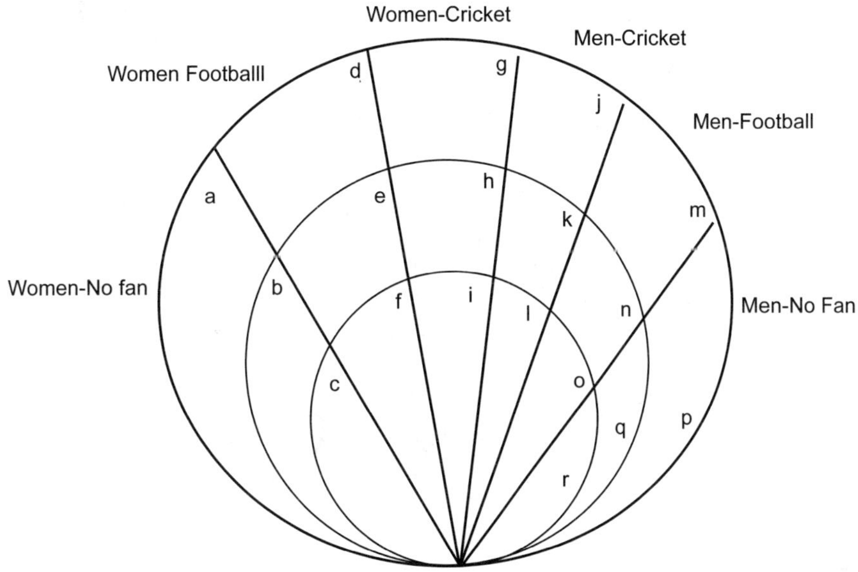

In the above diagram, The inner circle represents the 3 km radius, the middle circle represents the 4 km radius and the outer circle represents the 5 km radius. From clue 6, we know that the number of women is a multiple of 6 and value of region a + d + g = x/6 And that of b + c + e + f + h + i = x/2

From clue 5, we can determine the value of regions f, g, h, and i as 10,0,0 and 20 respectively. Also, since there are only 20 women cricket fans, the value of g = 0. Also, from clue 5 (first part, we have that values of l,o and r as 0 each.

From clue 4, we know that value of b + c = 40% of x/2 Therefore, b+c= x/5.

So x has to be multiple of both 5 and 6. Therefore x is a multiple of 30. So we can test for different values of 30 to find the number of women. We can see that there are at least 50 women in the office (total number of women fans), so possible values of x are 60, 90, 120, 150 and so on. Going through a trial and error of these values, we should be able to eliminate values like 60, 90, 120 and even 180 – as they do not meet the conditions of the problem. The only feasible value is 150 and hence we can fill all the numbers from a to I as follows.

However, before we go there, let us see at least one case of why only 150 fits the situation for the total number of women employees. Suppose, we take the total number of women employees as 120. Then, b + c = 24 (one-fifth); Since, e + f + h + l = 36, e would be 6. Then, we get that d=14 and a = 6 (Since a + d + g = 20 and g = 0). However, clue 7 gives us that the value of a is a two-digit number. Hence, we can reject 120 as a possible value of the number of women employees. Likewise, a value of 180 is rejected because, in such a case e's value comes out as 24 and e + f crosses it's maximum limit of 30. Thus, we conclude, through a trial and error that the only possible value of the number of women = 150.

Deduction 1: e, f, h, I should account for 60% of x/2. Hence, the sum of e, f, h, l should be 45. Since, f = 10, h = 0 and i = 20, e = 15.

Deduction 2: d, e, f, represents the total number of women football fans who live within 5 kms and their sum is equal to 30. Since we know f = 10 and e = 15, we get d = 5. Consequently, we can find out that the value of a = 20 (since a + d = 25). This completes our matrix for the number of women who filled the form in each category. We would need to deduce the number of men from this point.

Deduction 3: Using clue 3, we can work out that since the number of cricket fans living under 4 kms away, is 45 more than the number of football fans living within 4 kms – we get that the value of k = 50 and the value of n = 0. Also, from the second part of clue 4, we get that the value of q = 50 and p = 10.

Our final diagram would look as follows:

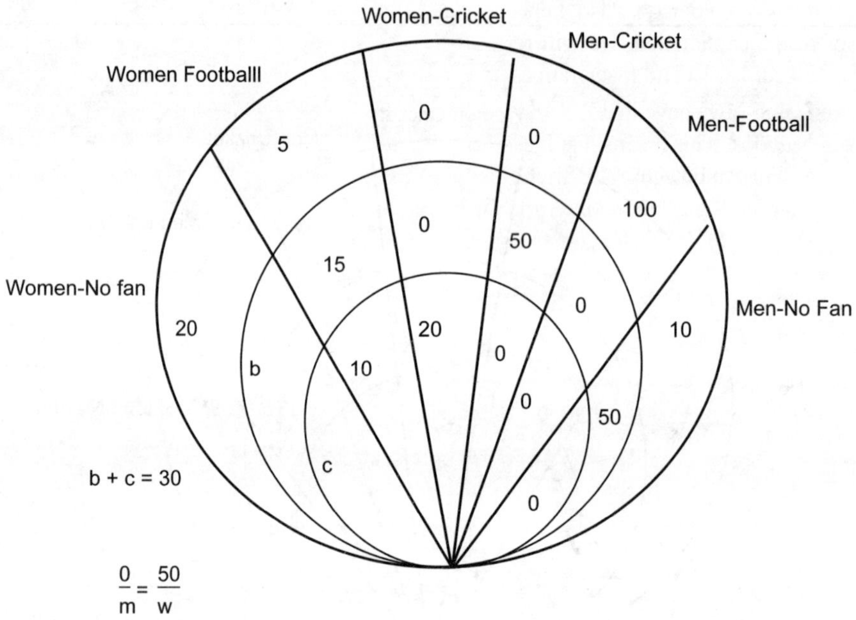

Using the above diagram, we can answer the questions as follows:

15. 150.
16. (c).
We cannot determine the exact values of the number of female employees living within the 3km radius who did not mention their sport. Thus option (c) would be the correct answer.
17. 48.61%
Employees living 4km radius =175
Total number of employees = 360
Percentage of employees living 4km radius = 48.61%
18. 25.
Female football fans living 5km radius=10 + 15 = 25.
19. 0
Male football fans living within 4km radius = 0
20. 50 + 10 = 60.

MOCK TEST PAPER 17

Questions 1 to 5:

The following table represents the spectrum of connections between the seven people. The hash tagged numbers in the brackets are referring to the deduction number – provided in the explanation.

Table 1:

	Facebook	Instagram	LinkedIN
Palak	1 (#2)	1 (#1)	4 (#1)
Qusum	1 (#3)	1 (#3)	4 (#3)
Rashmi		1 (#1)	
Shreya			2 (#1)
Tanya			1 (#1)
Umesh	1 (#1)		
Vivek	1 (#2)	3 (#1)	2 (#1)

Deduction 1: All these numbers are directly given in the paragraph text of the question.

Deduction 2: Since all these connections are amongst themselves, each of them can have a maximum of 6 connections. Hence, Palak and Vivek would have had 1 Facebook friend each.

Deduction 3: From statements 4 and 5 we know that everyone who is a friend of Palak on Facebook follows Qusum on Instagram and every Instagram follower of Qusum is friends with Palak on Facebook and every Facebook friend of Qusum follows Palak on Instagram and every Instagram follower of Palak is a facebook friend of Qusum. This would mean that the number of Instagram and Facebook friends of Qusum are 1 each. Hence, Qusum would have 4 Linkedin connections.

We now move onto trying to identify the specific people who are connected on various platforms with each other. From this point I am renumbering the deductions to present the solution in a cleaner form for you. For this purpose, we are taking the deductions already seen in Table 1, as a given deducing the next set of deductions from this point. We are also using the first letter of the names in order to refer to the person. Also, henceforth for the remainder of the explanation, we will refer to Facebook as FB, Linkedin as LI and Instagram as IG.

Deduction 1: From Clue 2, we have that P, S and U are friends with T on Facebook. This means that P's single FB friend is T. Also, T has minimum 3 FB friends and S has minimum 1 FB friend. Further, an interpretation of clue 4 tells us that T would be Q's IG connect.

Deduction 2: From clue 1, we can mark the LI connections between P, Q, R. Also from clue 3, we can mark R & V as FB connections.

Deduction 3: We can now identify P's IG connection as S – through the following logic: It has to be one of S, U, V. Also, P's IG connection, will also be Q's FB friend- according to clue 5. Now, U or V cannot be Q's FB friend, since both of them have only 1 FB friend who has already been identified. Hence, U or V cannot be P's IG connect and it can only be S. Further, this also means that U and V would be LI connects of Palak. This completes P's complete list.

Further, looking at Q's rows of connections, since we have identified S as Q's FB friend, it means that U,V would also be Q's LI connection. The implication of P's and Q's connections with S, U, V would also come into the table in S, U, V's rows as shown by #3 in table 2.

Deduction 4: Observing the table at this stage tells us that we have identified Vivek's FB and LI connections and hence can fill in his IG connections as S, T, U. This will also have the effect of filling in V as S, T, U's IG connection. At this stage S's 2 LI connects can be deduced as R, U. (since we have identified her 2 FB and 2 IG connects).

Deduction 5: From T's row her LI connect has to be R. Thus, R has T as a LI connect. So R's IG connect would be U. This deduction completes the table.

Table 2:

	Facebook	Instagram	LinkedIn
Palak	1 T (#1)	1 S (#3)	4 Q, R (#2) U,V (#3)
Qusum	1 S (#3)	1 T (#1)	4 P, R (#2) U,V (#3)
Rashmi	V (#2)	1 U (#5)	P, Q (#2) S (#4) T (#5)
Shreya	T (#1) Q (#3)	P (#3), V (#4)	2 R,U (#4)
Tanya	P, S, U	Q (#1) V (#4)	1 R (#5)
Umesh	1 T (#1)	V (#4) R(#5)	P, Q (#3) S (#4)
Vivek	1 R (#2)	3 (S, T, U)	2 P, Q (#3)

1. Option (b)
2. Option (d)
3. Option (a)
4. 3
5. Option (c)

Question 6 to 10

From the information provided to us, We derive the following flowcharts:

If Arun Sharma creates the questions
First review- Pallav, Shaurya
If both accept, then the question is accepted
If both reject, then the question is rejected
If only one of them rejects, then it is reviewed by Anshuman.

If Pallav creates the questions
First review- Shaurya
If he accepts then the question is accepted otherwise it is reviewed by Anshuman

If Shaurya creates the questions
First review- Anshuman
If he accepts then the question is accepted otherwise it is reviewed by Pallav

If Anshuman creates the questions
First review- Pallav
If he accepts then the question is accepted otherwise it is reviewed by Shaurya

Based on the information provided, we can make the following table:

Notes to the table:

1. If only Shaurya & Anshuman or Pallav & Anshuman have reviewed the questions, we can determine that Pallave and Shaurya respectively designed the questions because of the sequence given above
2. From the above flowchart we see that if a question is reviewed by three people then it was definitely created by Arun Sharma. Similarly, we can determine who created the question if only one of them has reviewed that question
3. Thus, we can determine who created Questions 1 through 5 and 7 through 12. The creators of Question 6 and 13 could be either Arun Sharma or Anshuman.
4. The questions rejected or accepted status is given to us for each question in Clue 1. Thus, we can make deductions about acceptance/rejection reaction by the individual reviewers. Some examples are explained here

   Question 1 is only reviewed by Anshuman and is a question that is accepted. Hence, Anshuman must have accepted the question. This also means that Shaurya created the question.

   Question 2 is reviewed by all three people, which means that it was created by Arun Sharma, reviewed first by Pallav and Shaurya – out of which one of them accepted the question the other rejected it – hence the question was sent to Anshuman for a review. Since, the question is finally rejected, Anshuman definitely rejected the question. Question 8 has a similar story, except that Anshuman accepted the question and the question was accepted.

Question 6 is rejected and must have been a question which was made by either Arun Sharma or Anshuman – and both Pallav and Shaurya must have rejected the question.

	Pallav	Shaurya	Anshuman	Accept/ Reject	Created by
Q1			* Accept	Accept	Shaurya
Q2	* Ac/Rj	* Ac/Rj	* Reject	Reject	Arun Sharma
Q3	* Accept		* Reject	Accept	Shaurya
Q4	* Ac/Rj	* Ac/Rj	* Accept	Accept	Arun Sharma
Q5			* Accept	Accept	Shaurya
Q6	* Reject	* Reject		Reject	Arun Sharma/ Anshuman
Q7		* Reject	* Accept	Accept	Pallav
Q8	* Ac/Rj	* Ac/Rj	* Accept	Accept	Arun Sharma
Q9		* Reject	* Reject	Reject	Pallav
Q10	* Accept			Accept	Anshuman
Q11	* Reject		* Reject	Reject	Shaurya
Q12		* Reject	* Reject	Reject	Pallav
Q13	* Ac/Rj	* Accept		Accept	Arun Sharma/ Anshuman

**** means reviewed the question, Ac/Rj means Accept/ Reject***

Using the above table we can answer the questions given to us

6. We can see that Pallav created 3 Questions
7. Anshuman has definitely created only 1 questions
8. Arun Sharma definitely created 3 questions
9. From the above table we can see that Shaurya has rejected 4 questions
10. Shaurya has created a total of 4 questions and Anshuman can create a maximum of 3 Questions. So they both can together create a maximum of 7 questions.

Questions 11 to 15:

From the information provided to us we can form the following table:

Number of students enrolled

	Day 1	Day 2	Total
Fatima	y	20-y	20
Kavita	0	20	20
Jyoti	10	10	20

Number of calls made

	Day 1	Day 2	Total
Fatima	x - 15	x + 15	2x
Kavita	1	2x - 1	2x
Jyoti	x	x	2x

The above two tables are formed from the information we get from the first three clues. Still we have two variables to determine to get to our full solution. Now, the fourth clue becomes an important tool to help us determine those variables.

According to that statement, Fatima's conversion rate was double that of Jyoti on the first day and this figure was 75% of that of Jyoti on the second day.

We get two equations:

$$\frac{y}{x-15} = 2 \times \frac{10}{x} \text{ ---(1)}$$

$$\frac{20-y}{x+15} = 0.75 \times \frac{10}{x} \text{ ---(2)}$$

Solving the above equations we get:

x = 25 and y = 8

Putting the values in the tables we get

Number of students enrolled

	Day 1	Day 2	Total
Fatima	8	12	20
Kavita	0	20	20
Jyoti	10	10	20

Number of calls made

	Day 1	Day 2	Total
Fatima	10	40	50
Kavita	1	49	50
Jyoti	25	25	50

Now we can answer the questions given to us

11. Total number of calls over the two days=3 × 50 = 150
12. Average conversion rate=

$$\frac{\textit{Total Number of Enrollments}}{\textit{Total Calls made}} \times 100 = \frac{60}{150} \times 100 = 40\%$$

13. Conversion rate of each counselor on each day is as follows:

	Day 1	Day 2
Fatima	80	30
Kavita	0	40.81
Jyoti	40	40

From the above table we can see that Fatima had the best conversion rate on day 1.

14. From the table formed for the previous question, we can see that Kavita had the maximum growth.
15. We can see that Fatima enrolled 12 students on the second day.

Questions 16 to 20:

From the above information we can determine the stock prices as follows:
Coal India-₹500
Reliance Ent- ₹500 × 0.6 = 300
Adani Ent- ₹200/Rs 100
Tata Ent- ₹100/Rs 200
Lets test 1 possibility at a time (Adani Ent = ₹200, Tata Ent = ₹100)
Based on clues 2 & 3
We can determine the opening and closing price of each stock on each of the three days
Opening Price:

	Day 1	Day 2	Day 3
Coal India	500	520	546
Reliance Ent	300	315	378
Adani Ent	200	220	242
Tata Steel	100	120	114

Closing Price:

	Day 1	Day 2	Day 3
Coal India	520	546	600.6
Reliance Ent	315	378	415.8
Adani Ent	220	242	266.2
Tata Steel	120	114	125.4

Based on the above, we can find the opening and closing price of each basket on the three days.
Day 1:

Basket	Opening Price	Closing Price
Reliance Basket	800	835
Adani Basket	700	740
Tata Basket	600	640
Mixed Basket	1100	1175
Invesco Basket	600	655

Day 2:

Basket	Opening Price	Closing Price
Reliance Basket	835	924
Adani Basket	740	788
Tata Basket	640	660
Mixed Basket	1175	1280
Invesco Basket	655	734

Day 3:

Basket	Opening Price	Closing Price
Reliance Basket(RB)	924	1016.4
Adani Basket(AB)	788	866.8
Tata Basket(TB)	660	726
Mixed Basket(MB)	1280	1408
Invesco Basket(IB)	734	807.4

We are given the amount received by each person at the end of each day. Using that table we can determine who bought which basket on each day. The below sums are only possible with only a specific combination of baskets as given below

Day	Shaurya	Basket with Shaurya	Pallav	Basket with Pallav	Shubhuti	Basket with Shubuti
1	1575	AB + RB	1830	MB + IB	1830	MB + IB
2	1448	AB + TB	1394	TB + IB	2068	AB + MB
3	2134	TB + MB	2274.8	AB + MB	1883.2	RB + AB

If we check the second possibility that Adani Ent= Rs 100 and Tata Ent = Rs 200, we'll find that the values in the above table will not be satisfied thus rendering this possibility irrelevant.
Using this information we can answer the questions given to us.

16. Answer: 4. In total 4 baskets were traded on the first day.
17. Answer: 340.
    Opening price of Adani Ent on second day = 220
    Opening price of Tata Ent on second day = 120
    Sum = 340
18. Answer: 27.05%
    Cost price of Reliance basket on day 1 = 800
    Selling price of Reliance basket on day 3 = 1016.4
    Percentage growth = 27.05%
19. Answer (c).
    Basket combination for Pallav on third day = Adani Basket + Mixed Basket. Option (c) is correct.
20. Answer (b)
    Basket participation over the three days is given below

	Day 1	Day 2	Day 3	Total
RB	1	0	1	2
AB	1	2	2	5
TB	0	2	1	3
MB	2	1	2	5
IB	2	1	0	3

AB and MB had maximum participation over the three day period. Option (b) is correct.

MOCK TEST PAPER 18

Questions 1 to 3:

The plates are numbered 1, 2, 3 … 9

Therefore, the sum of numbers on all plates = 9 × 10 /2 = 45

If sum of numbers of plates in the 1st casket = X, then Sum of numbers of plates in the 2nd casket = X – 2

Then, sum numbers of plates in the 3rd casket = X – 4

X + X – 2 + X – 4 = 45 or X = 17

Therefore, the three caskets would have plates totaling 17, 15, and 13 respectively. So, each casket should have one plate from each of the following three sets of plates.

1, 2, 3 4, 5, 6, 7, 8, 9

The following combinations are possible if one has to satisfy the requirements.

Casket 1 :	17 = 9 + 6 + 2	9 + 5 + 3	9 + 5 + 3
Casket 2 :	15 = 8 + 4 + 3	8 + 6 + 1	6 + 7 + 2
Casket 3 :	13 = 7 + 5 + 1	7 + 4 + 2	8 + 4 + 1
	Combination 1	Combination 2	Combination 3

But combinations 2 and 3 are not possible because the only way a person can pay ₹7 is if three plates are 4, 2, 1 = 7

But in combination 2 and 3 , this is not possible. Therefore the only combination possible is 1. The lowest possible payment is 3 + 2 + 1 = 6.

1. (c)
2. (c)
   The maximum possible payment is 9 + 8 + 7 = ₹24.
3. (d) A customer can not pay ₹23 as 23 = 9 + 8 + 6 as 9 and 6 are in the same casket. Option (2) is possible as all three plates mentioned are in different casket. A customer can pay ₹19 i.e. 19 = 9 + 3 + 7, as all three plates are in different caskets.

Questions 4 to 8:

The hit sequences are:

Rahul: 12 – 14 – 15 – 16 → Total points = 12 + 14 + 15 + 16 + 15 = 72

Akhil: 14 – 15 – 16 – 18 → Total points = 14 + 15 + 16 + 18 + ? + ? = 97

Tarun 13 – 15. Since Tarun has hit two balls and has G-potted both, his points must be double of the ball numbers he has hit. Only 13 – 15 is a possible combination of 2 balls which give him 28 + 13 + 15 = 56 points.

Samar 18 – 20 – 12 – 14 – 15 → Total points = 18 + 20 + 12 + 14 + 15 + 12 + ? = 106. Hence, his other G-Pocket ball must have been 15.

Ritesh 11 – 15 – 16 – 17 – 18 – 19 – 20 – 12 13 – 14 → 155 points + bonus points on 1 ball. Since his total is 168 he must have G-Potted ball number 13.

Mahim: 11 – 15 – 16 – 17 – 18 – 19 – 20 – 12 – 13 – 14 → 155 points + 19 + ? =188 → The second ball G-potted by Mahim must be 14.

The completed table would look like:

Player's Name	1st Ball Hit	Number of G-Pots Made	G-Pot Ball Number	Total Balls Hit	Total Points
Rahul	12	1	15	4	72
Tarun	13	2	13, 15	2	56
Akhil	14	2	16, 18	4	97
Samar	18	2	12, 15	5	106
Ritesh	11	1	13	10	168
Mahim	11	2	19, 14	10	188

Hence, the answers would be:

4. (d) The pink ball is G-potted exactly twice
5. (d) All the players hit ball number 15 (green)
6. (c) 72 + 56 + 97 + 106 + 168 = 499
7. (a) His second potted ball is a green.
8. (c) 168 – 72 = 96.

Questions 9 to 12:

9. The number of T1 in SS1 is 50. A combination of 50 T1 can be formed by using the following combination of S's:
   (b) S1, S2 and S4
   (c) S1 is used twice
   The number of T2 in SS1 is 45. A combination of 45 T2 can be formed by using the following combinations of S:
   (a) S1, S2 and S4 (b) S1, S3 and S5
   Combination (a) is common for both number of T1 and T2. Hence S1, S2 and S4 are used in SS1
   Similarly, in SS2 we have the following combination: S2 once and S4 twice.
   Hence types of S used are 3. Hence (c).
10. Number of T3 and T4 in SS3 is known. Calculating on similar lines as explained in the last question, we have the following combination of S's: S3 and S4. Hence (b).
11. We know the number of T1 and T5 used in SS4. Again calculating along similar lines, we get that SS4 has the following combination of S's: S1, S3, S4 and S5. Hence number of T2 on SS4 is = 20 + 8 + 15 + 17 = 60
    From the previous results, T2 on SS3 = 23. Hence 83. Hence option (d).
12. As the number of T4's is 63 and the number of T5's is less than 80, the following combinations can be used:
    (a) SS1 and SS3 (b) SS3 and SS4
    (c) SS3 twice and SS2

For combination (a) we have the following combinations of S's: S1, S2 and S5
For combination (b) we have the following combinations of S's: S1, S3, S4, and S5
For combination (c) and (d) we have the following combinations of S's: S2, S3, and S4. Hence option (d) is correct.

Questions 13 to 16:

13. Since P, S and T took leave on Friday; each one of them must have started manufacturing a new unit or product on Saturday. Thus each must have manufactured 2 units on Saturday and thus a total of 6 units of product A. The table given below illustrates this:

	Sun	Mon	Tue	Wed	Thurs	Fri	Sat
P			X			X	A(4) + A(4)
Q	X				X		
R		X		X			

	Sun	Mon	Tue	Wed	Thurs	Fri	Sat
S	X					X	A(4) + A(4)
T			X			X	A(4) + A(4)
U				X			X

On Saturday, 5, 3, and 8 hours were spent on B, C, and D respectively to produce 1, 1 and 2 units of each of the products were completed on Saturday. Thus Q and R must have used their working hours on Friday and Saturday as follows:

	Thurs	Fri	Sat
Q	X	B (5 hrs) + C (3 hrs)	B (5 hrs) + C (3 hrs)
R		A (2 hrs) + D (6 hrs)	D (1 hrs) + D (7 hrs)

When the same rationalisation is applied over every product, workers and the number of hours and units produced on any given day while keeping in mind the days of rest of the workers, the following table is obtained (Deduction of the same left to students)

	Sun	Mon	Tue	Wed	Thurs	Fri	Sat
P	A(4) + D(4)	B(5) + D(3)	X	B(5) + C(3)	B(5) + C(3)	X	A(4) + A(4)
Q	X	C(6) + D(2)	A(3) + D(5)	A(1) + D(7)	X	B(5) + C(3)	B(5) + C(3)
R	A(4) + A(4)	X	A(4) + A(4)	X	A(2) + C(6)	A(2) + D(6)	D(1) + D(7)
S	X	C(1) + D(7)	C(5) + D(3)	B(4) + D(4)	B(1) + D(7)	X	A(4) + A(4)
T	B(5) + C(3)	B(5) + C(3)	X	C(2) + C(6)	A(4) + C(4)	X	A(4) + A(4)
U	A(1) + D(7)	A(3) + D(5)	C(6) + D(2)	X	A(4) + D(4)	B(5) + D(3)	X

It is clear from the above table that the correct answer is A and C. Hence (c).

14. It can be inferred from the above table that C is the correct option. Hence (c).
15. As seen from the table, C and D are the products. Hence (b).
16. It can be counted from the table above that the number of units produced is 8. Hence (d).

Questions 17 to 20:

17. Drawing the following table shall prove useful:

Students	2nd year	3rd year	4th year	Total Score
A	100	*c*	*e*	190 + *c* or 189 + *c*
B	98	96	93	287
C	88	99	94	281
D	92	*d*	97	189 + *d*
E	*a*	87	*f*	176 + *a* or 177 + *a*
F	*b*	91	95	186 + *b*
Total	91 × 6= 546	90 × 6 = 540	93 × 6 = 558	

The missing scores, wherever they were in the question have been replaced with a, b, c, d, e and f and the values of these unknowns has to be found. Clearly $e + 93 + 94 + 97 + f + 95 = 558 \Rightarrow e + f = 179$. Hence the only possible values of e and f are 89 and 90 in no particular order as per the conditions of the question.
Similarly, $100 + 98 + 88 + 92 + a + b = 546 \Rightarrow a + b = 168$. a and b can be any of the combinations (82, 86), (83, 85), (85, 83), (86, 82)
Similarly for c and d the values can be any of \(81, 86), (82, 85), (83, 84), (84, 83), (85, 82), (86, 81)
Now if A and D are ranked the same then $100 + c + e = 189 + d \Rightarrow c + e = d + 89$. But e is either 89 or 90 and hence $c = d$ or $c + 1 = d$. $c = d$ is not possible hence $c = 83$ and $d = 84$. If $e = 90$ and $f = 89$ and hence $(a, b) = (82, 86)$ or $(86, 82)$. Hence (c) is the correct option.

18. From the table above we can see that the maximum possible score of E is 177 + 86 = 263 which is less than the minimum possible score of any of the other five students. Hence E is ranked the lowest. Hence (d).
19. As per the given conditions, the score of E and F must be (82, 86) or (86, 82) respectively. (c, d) is thus (83, 84) or (84, 83). Hence the following possibilities arise:
e = 89 and f = 90, A = 272 or 273, B = 287, C = 281, D = 273 or 272, E = 259 or 263 and F = 272 or 268. Hence two possibilities are there ⇒ A = F = 272 and D = F = 272.
Similarly for e = 90 and f = 89 we have two more set of possibilities (Left for the students to derive) Hence there are four possibilities. Hence (d).
20. If no students are ranked the same then from the previous questions, we can get the following possibilities as the score of students

Possibility	A	B	C	D	E	F
I	272	287	281	273	263	268
II	273	287	281	272	263	268
III	274	287	281	272	262	268

Clearly (c) is the correct option.

MOCK TEST PAPER 19

Questions 1 to 5:

According to the questions condition of Aman, Binay, Charu, Dinesh, Ervin and Fahim's weight carried at the Mumbai airport, being more than or equal to their weights carried at the Delhi airport we get the following relationships that a and b should obey:

$10a \geq 20b, 20a \geq 10b, 25a \geq 15b, 10a \geq 18b, 20a \geq 32b,$
$30a \geq 12b$

Or $a \geq 2b, a \geq 0.5b, a \geq 0.6b, a \geq 1.8b, a \geq 1.6b, a \geq 0.4b$
$a \geq 2b$

Similarly we can conclude: $a \geq 2.5c$ and $0.5d \geq a$

1. According to the question $20b = 8c$ or $b = 0.4c$
Required ratio = $20b/20c = b/c = 0.4$
2. Aman is a light weight passenger in Mumbai and Chennai airports. Binay is a light weight passenger at the Delhi, Chennai, Bangalore airports. Charu is a light weight passenger at the Delhi and Bangalore airports. Dinesh is a light weight passenger at the Mumbai airport. Ervin is a light weight passenger at the Chennai and Bangalore airports. Fahim is a light weight passenger at the Delhi airport. Hence the required number of passengers who are light weight in at least 2 airports is 4.
3. 30d = 30kg → d = 1 kg.
Since, $0.5d \geq a$ or $a \leq 0.5$
Maximum possible weight carried by Aman at the Mumbai airport = 10 × 0.5 = 5 kg
4. D = $20a - 10b$
$a \geq 2b$
Minimum value of D = $40b - 10b = 30b$
Except Ervin rest of the passengers are definitely carrying lesser weight than D at the Delhi airport. Hence the correct answer is 5.
5. $30b = 120$ or $b = 4$

Passenger Name	Maximum Possible Weight (in kg)
Aman	80
Binay	40
Charu	60
Dinesh	72
Ervin	128
Fahim	48

Therefore four passengers definitely carried weight less than 75 kg.

Questions 6 to 8:

6. To minimize the number of EC students we need to minimize the number of EC students who participated in exactly one event or we need to maximize the number of EC students who participated in more than one event.
In Dancing – all the 90 EC students can participate in other events as well as the 30 students who are only in Dancing can all come from CS.
The same logic can be applied to Robotics as well as to Singing and hence there could be 75 EC students from Robotics and 60 students of EC in Singing who can participate in other events as well.
In Bike Riding however, we will need to put a minimum of 30 EC students who would be participating only in Bike riding and 75 EC students who are participating in Bike riding can participate in other events as well.
Now the 90 students who participated in Dancing, can participate in Robotics, Singing as well as Bike riding (and covers up the numbers required in each of those sports who are involved in more than one sport). Also, since 30 EC students did not participate in any other event except bike riding, therefore the minimum number of EC students who participated in Encore = 90 + 30 = 120. Option (b) is correct.
7. To maximize the number of EC students we need to maximize the number of students who participated in exactly one event or we need to minimize the number of students who participated in more than one event.

30 EC students participated only in dancing and 60 students participated in dancing and other events as well.
15 EC students participated only in robotics and 60 students participated in robotics and other events as well.
20 EC students participated only in Singing and 40 students participated in singing and other events as well.
105 students participated only in Bike riding.
Total EC students participated only in one event = 30 + 15 + 20 + 105 = 170.
60 students participated in dancing and other events as well, if we consider 40 out of these 60 students participated in Robotics as well and rest 20 participated in Singing. Similarly 20 students who participated in singing also participated in Robotics as well.
Hence the required number of students = 170 + 20 + 40 + 20 = 250.

8. To minimize the number of CS students we need to minimize the number of students who participated in exactly one event or we need to maximize the number of students who participated in more than one event.
60 students (Dancing): can participate in other events as well.
45 students (Robotics): can participate in other events as well.
40 students (Singing): can participate in other events as well.
15 students (Bike riding): cannot participate in other events.
75 students (Bike riding): can participate in other events as well.
Now the 75 students who participated in bike riding and other events can participate in other events as well – so that would take care of the students from CS in dancing, robotics and singing. Also 15 students of CS who did not participate in any other event except bike riding would need to be added to this.
Therefore the minimum number of CS students participated in Encore = 75 + 15 = 90.

Questions 9 to 12:
We can make the following structure for a tournament with no upsets to analyse the tournament flow:

	Round 1 (32 matches)	Round 2 (16 matches)	Round 3 (8 matches)	Round 4 (4 matches)	Round 5 (2 matches)	Round 6 (1 match)
Match 1	1–64	1–32	1–16	1–8	1–4	1–2
Match 2	2–63	2–31	2–15	2–7	2–3	
Match 3	3–62	3–30	3–14	3–6		
Match 4	4–61	4–29	4–13	4–5		
Match 5	5–60	5–28	5–12			
Match 6	6–59	6–27	6–11			
Match 7	7–58	7–26	7–10			
Match 8	8–57	8–25	8–9			
Match 9	9–56	9–24				
Match 10	10–55	10–23				
Match 11	11–54	11–22				
Match 12	12–53	12–21				

-------------		16–17				
Match 31	31–34					
Match 32	32–33					

9. From the given information we can deduce that the 1st round had 32 matches, 2nd round had 16 matches, 3rd round had 8 matches, 4th round had 4 matches and so on.
If rank-1 team won the tournament then it must have beaten the 64th rank team in the 1st round, the 32nd or 33rd rank team in the second round, the 16th or 17th or 48th and 49th ranked team in the 3rd round. In round 4 it must have beaten one of the following ranked teams: 8, 9, 24, 25, 40, 41, 56 or 57. In round 5 it must have beaten exactly one of the following ranked teams: 4, 5, 28, 29, 12, 13, 20, 21, 44, 45, 36, 37, 60, 61.
Except the above-mentioned teams each team can reach in the final. Hence, option (a) is correct.
Alternately, checking the team rankings from the options we can see that A would have played 4 or 13 only in the round 5 and it would have played team 56 only in round 4. Hence, it is only team 22 from the given options that the rank 1 team could have played in the final.

10. Let each match of the round 1 be an upset except the match played by the 23rd rank team. Then in the

second round the 23rd rank team would meet the 55th ranked team. If except this match, each match of the 2nd round was an upset then in the 3rd round and the next rounds it would meet against a lower ranked team. So, it is possible that there would be 0 upsets created by the team ranked 23, and it could still win the tournament.

11. To maximize the rank of the winner all the upsets must happen in the 1st round. This would make sure that every team has either caused or faced an upset. If every match of the 1st round was an upset, then the 33rd to the 64th ranked team were left in the second round. The highest ranked team that could win the tournament is the 33rd ranked team.
12. If we analyze carefully then we can see that the 16th ranked is the highest ranked team who can win the tournament with four upsets, three caused by it. The 16th ranked team could advance to the 3rd round without any upset. In the 3rd round suppose it played against the 32nd rank team, who beat the 1st rank team in the 2nd round. So the 16th ranked team reaches the 4th round without any upset. From there it could win the tournament by causing three upsets in the 4th round, the semifinal and in the final. You can check that teams below 16, like the 17th ranked team onwards could not win the tournament with only 4 upsets in the tournament.

Questions 13 to 16:

Total score of the class in the five tests are 290, 240, 220, 240 and 260 respectively. This means that the remaining score of the respective tests that students outside the top 3 have scored would be: 87, 84, 66, 84 and 78 respectively.

Also, the scores of the remaining two students (amongst the top 5) would be:

	Abhay	Balwinder	Chetan	David	Faraz
Test 1	90	55	58	0–54	0–54
Test 2	40	0–39	0–39	60	56
Test 3	0–26	75	0–26	27	52
Test 4	54	0–35	0–35	66	36
Test 5	50	62	70	0–49	0–49

Student	Value of C.V.
Abhay	50
Balwinder	55
Chetan	0–39
David	27–54
Faraz	36–52

13. Balwinder had the highest value of C.V.
14. The exact value of C.V. can be calculated only for two students–Abhay and Balwinder.
15.

Student	Value of I.V.
Abhay	90–116
Balwinder	75–110
Chetan	70–96
David	66–93
Faraz	56–92

It is clear from the table that anyone of the five students can have the lowest value of I.V. Hence, the correct answer to this question would be option (d).

16.

Test No.	Maximum Scores of Chetan and Balwinder Together
1	113
2	77
3	101
4	69
5	132
Total	492

Required percentage

$$= \frac{492}{290+240+220+240+260} \times 100$$

$$= \frac{492}{1250} \times 100 = 39.36\%$$

Questions 17 to 20:

17. The following condition would maximise Bio-technology while obeying all the constraints of the problem. In such a case, we can see that Bio Technology can be maximised at $99 + 33 + 33 = 165$

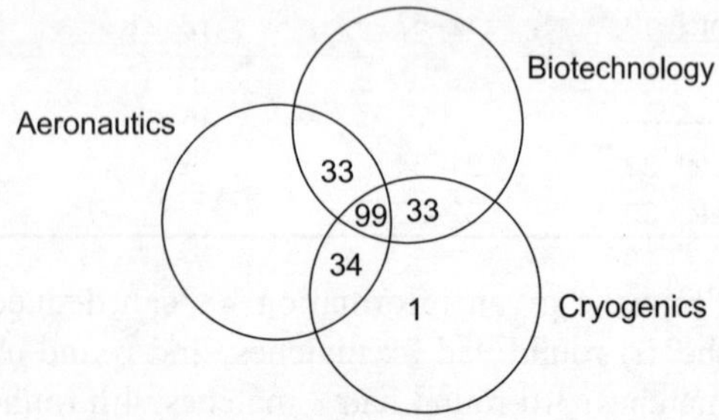

FIGURE 1

18. For minimising Cryogenics, we need to reduce the number in the middle (i.e for all three) to the minimum possible value. This can be done by taking all three as 1 (as we have been given this constraint), only 2 as 2 (as it has to be greater than all three), and the remaining 197 can be distributed as shown in the Figure 2.

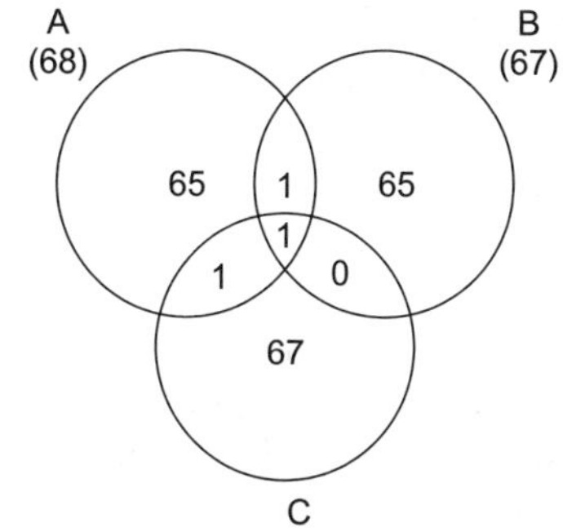

FIGURE 2

This gives us a minimum value of 69 for Cryogenics, while Aeronautics becomes 68 and Biotechnology is 67.

19. The given conditions are satisfied by the following
Figure 3:

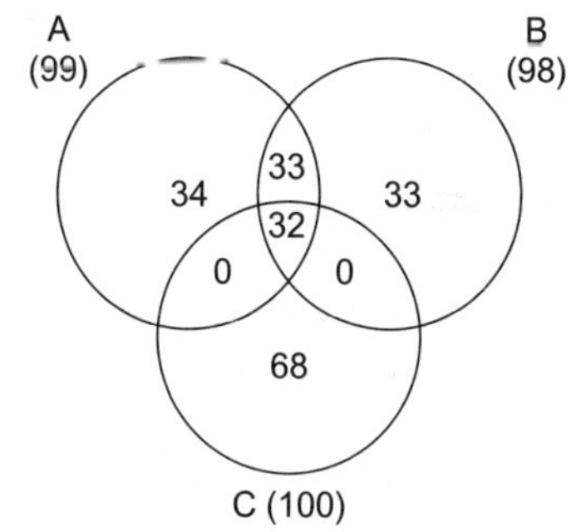

FIGURE 3

Note: If we try to put a value of 33 or more in the central area of the Venn diagram (i.e. for all three), the equilibrium gets disturbed. Hence, the correct answer is 32.

20. In order to maximise only Aeronautics we need to use the following Figure 4.
Hence, Only Aeronautics can be maximised at 99.

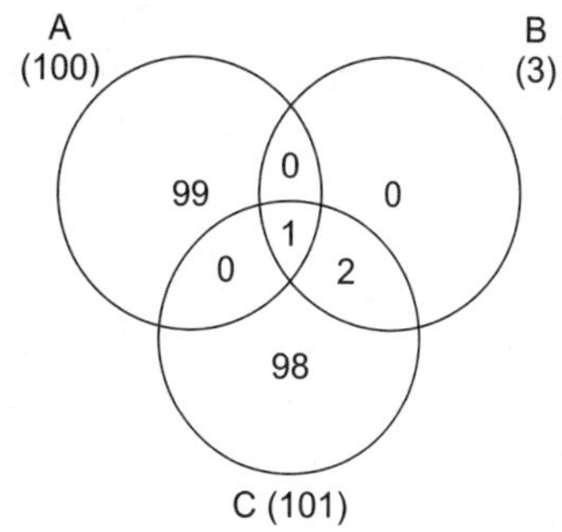

FIGURE 4

MOCK TEST PAPER 20

Questions 1 to 4:

1. Since the total of R7 and R8 is 17 and no two rats secured the same points, hence R7 and R8 must have secured 9 and 8 points (in any order) while R3 and R4 must have secured 10 and 6 points (again in any order). Similarly the ranks and points for others may be derived as seen in the following table (the points and positions of rats may be in any order).

Province		Race 1		Race 2		Race 3	
	Rats	Points	Position	Points	Position	Points	Position
1	R1, R2	5, 2	6, 9	9, 6	2, 5	4, 1	7, 10
2	R3, R4	10, 6	1, 5	5, 3	6, 8	10, 8	1, 3
3	R5, R6	3, 1	8, 10	2, 1	9, 10	7, 3	4, 8
4	R7, R8	9, 8	2, 3	7, 4	4, 7	5, 2	6, 9
5	R9, R10	7, 4	4, 7	10, 8	1, 3	9, 6	2, 5

The rats that came third in race 1 could be either of R7 and R8. Hence (d) is the correct option.

2. To satisfy the given conditions, R1 must have secured 2 points while R5 and R6 must have got 1 and 3 points respectively. Similarly, the positions for others may be deduced as given in the following table:

	Rat	Points	Position
P1	R1	2	9
P1	R2	5	6
P2	R3	6	5
P2	R4	10	1
P3	R5	1	10
P3	R6	3	8
P4	R7	8 or 9	3 or 2
P4	R8	9 or 8	2 or 3
P5	R9	4	7
P5	R10	7	4

We can see from the above table that only (iii) is true. Hence option (d) is correct.

3. As can be seen from the table above, neither the position, nor the points of R7 and R8 can be determined. Hence both the statements (i) and (ii) are true. Hence (c) is the correct option.

4. From the table above, we can see that there are two possible values for each finish position for each rat.
Hence, we cannot make any of conclusions in the first three options. Hence, option (d) is correct.

Questions 5 to 8:

5. As train number AMS008 reaches Lucknow after train number AMS006 and before train number AMS011 as given in the information, the time slot available for the train is at 0915 hrs as landing/arriving slot at 0930 hrs, 0945 hrs and 1000 hrs is already occupied and hence cannot be taken.
Time to traverse from Kanpur to Lucknow via Jaipur is 3 hrs 45 mins as given. As the time taken on a return trip is same, therefore train from Lucknow to Kanpur via Jaipur reaches Kanpur 3 hrs 45 mins after its departure from Lucknow (0800 hrs) and reaches at 1145 hrs. Hence option (b) is the correct alternative.
6. As no train arrives/departs, to/from Lucknow at 0845 hrs other than train number AMS005 and train number AMS002 reaches Agra at 1000 hrs, it means it has left before 1000 hrs. The only slot available for departure from Lucknow before 1000 hrs is at 0815 hrs. So time taken for the journey from Lucknow to Agra is 1 hr 45 mins after its departure from Lucknow at 1100 hrs, i.e. 1245 hrs. Hence (c).
7. As the train between Lucknow and Kanpur takes less than two hours to reach its destination train number AMS023 should reach Lucknow on or before 1300 hrs. All time slots before 1300 hrs are occupied and the slot at 1300 hrs is empty. The train number AMS023 reaches Lucknow at 1300 hrs. Time taken for direct journey in between Lucknow and Kanpur is 1 hr 55 mins. So train number AMS012 leaves Lucknow 1 hr 55 mins before 1125 hrs, i.e. at 0930 hrs. Hence (c).
8. You can observe that trains AMS014 and AMS016 are parallel trains between the same cities. Hence, their time taken would be equal. Now, since train AMS014 reaches Pune at 13:35 hours, it must have left Lucknow before 13:35. Likewise, train AMS016 should reach Lucknow after 8:10 AM. In order to achieve both these outcomes, with the free slots at the Lucknow station between 8:10 and 13:35, we can see that only for a journey timing of 2 hours 35 minutes, do we get a possible solution, where the train AMS016 reaches Lucknow at 10:45 and the train AMS014 leaves Lucknow at 11:00. Hence, option (d) is correct.

Questions 9 to 12:

9. The computers manufactured from the month of Jan and Mar, all computers are sold out before Sept. Computers manufactured in the month of Feb, sold in July = 1077 – (23 + 26 + 45 + 9 + 973) = 1.
On a similar basis, computers manufactured in July sold in the next month = 146 and the computers manufactured in June sold in Sept = 51.
The student is expected to calculate for the other months as well
The unsold computers in Feb are sold at the end of Sept = 1478 – (Summation of the number of computers sold up to Sept) = 0. On the basis of the above information the following table may be drawn:

Month	Unsold Computers
April	1
May	6
June	54
July	72
Aug	139
Sept	510

Hence total computers = 782. Hence (c).
10. From the table, the number of computers sold in Mar = 1421 – 373 = 1098
Total computers sold in April = 1496 + 373 – 459 = 1410. Computers manufactured in the month Mar and sold in Apr = 1410 – 1236 – 41 – 19 = 114
Hence the revenue generated can be calculated to be 718149.5. Hence (e).
11. Computers manufactured in Jan which were not in Jan itself = 1563 – 1231 = 332
and those sold in Feb = (1542 – 1389) = 153. Similarly calculating for May, we get 23 as an answer. Hence (a).
12. Computers manufactured in Feb which were not sold in Feb = 1478 – 1389 = 89. Similarly computers manufactured in Feb and sold in Mar = 1421 – 373 – 875 – 136 = 37. Computers manufactured in Feb that are not sold in Mar = 89 – 37 = 52. Hence (d).

Questions 13 to 16:

13. In the worst case, all the five students will take maximum time to complete their respective questions, i.e. Adam does question 4, Barbie does question 3 and so on and so forth. Hence time taken = 57 + 53 + 53 + 49 + 38 = 250 minutes = 4 hrs 10 min. Hence (a) is the correct option.
14. The best case has to be taken here, i.e. everybody does his question fastest as compared to somebody else doing the same question. Hence 25 + 39 + 29 + 24 + 36 = 153 minutes = 2 hr 33 min. Hence (b).

Question	1	2	3	4	5
Student	Dopey	Estella	Adam	Barbie	Chandler
Time	25	39	29	24	36

15. The most efficient way to assign the questions is: After 24 minutes, Barbie can assist Chandler with question 5 and Dopey joins them after 25 minutes and they will finish the question in approx. 5 min, i.e. 29 min from the start. After 29 min, everybody can work on question 2 which can be completed in under a minute. Hence (c).
16. Under given conditions, the most efficient three students are Adam, Barbie, and Dopey. Upon inspection we find that if we assign them questions 3, 4 and 1 respectively then the time shall come out to be the minimum. Once done with question 3, 4 and 1 they could work on question 2 which would be completed in approx. the 39th minute and then question 5 could be completed in by the 51st minute. Hence (c).

Questions 17 to 20:

17. From Both A and B, we can see that the catches taken by Akash will always be equal to or more than Biplab, while the catches dropped by Biplab are always larger than Akash. Hence, Akash will always win. Option (c) is correct.
18. From A alone, we see that The correct order is B, C, D, A. Likewise we can answer the question using B alone too. Option (e) is correct.
19. From A alone, we can work out that there must have been 20 people paying 30 each initially, and when 5 people left, there were 15 people paying 40 each. There is no other possibility that matches this condition. Hence, option (a) is correct.
20. From Statement A alone, we can see that their ages after 'n' years have to be 10, 30 and 40 respectively – this is the only way in which the given conditions match the constraint given in statement A. Thus, statement A alone gives us a unique solution and hence option (a) is correct.

MOCK TEST PAPER 21

Questions 1 to 4:

1. Decrypting the information in the question, we get the following solution:

Café #	Area it Belongs To
Café – 1	Rohini/Ashok Vihar
Café – 2	Pitampura/Shalimar Bagh
Café – 3	Ashok Vihar
Café – 4	Pitampura
Café – 5	Ashok VIhar/Rohini
Café – 6	Haiderpur
Café – 7	Shalimar Bagh/Pitampura
Café – 8	Rohini

From the table, Haiderpur has only Café 6.
Answer is option (b)

2. From above table, Café 1 belongs to either Rohini or Ashok Vihar. Thus from the given options we get Rohini area as the answer
Answer is option (a)
3. From above table, it is clear that Café 2 can belong to either Pitampura or Shalimar Bagh
Answer is option (c)
4. From above table, it is clear that no area can have more than 2 cafes.
Answer is option (d)

Questions 5 to 8:

5. The total number of votes in round 1 is 164 as the country of Dimply is also allowed to vote. Audi gets 60 votes and Dimply gets 24 votes. Hence total votes obtained by Boxer and Coffee is 164 – (60 + 24) = 80 votes.
Since in round 3, the total number of votes is 147. Hence the 15 countries that are ineligible to vote+, voted for candidate Dimply in round 1, for Coffee in round 2 and were ineligible to vote in round 3. The remaining 24 – 15 – 1 = 8 countries who voted for Dimply in round 1, voted for Boxer in round 2. Since 15 countries who voted for Dimply in round 1, voted for Coffee in round 2 and the number of members who voted for coffee in both the rounds 1 and 2 should be 24 (24 + 15 = 39). As 25% of those who voted for Coffee in round 1 voted for Boxer in round 2, 24 = 75% of those who voted for Coffee in round 1 which is 32. Obviously, number of voted for Boxer in round 1 would be 80 – 32 = 48. In the third round, half of those who voted for Coffee in round 1 voted for Dimply in round 2. Hence total votes for Boxer = 48 + 16 + 8 = 72. Hence total votes in round 3 are 147. So votes for Audi in round 3 = 75.
Hence only statement (ii) is true. Hence (b).
6. From the above discussion it is clear that the answer is 8. Hence (a).
7. From the above discussion it is clear that the answer is 32. Hence (d).
8. Members who voted for Coffee in round 2 = 39 out of which members eligible to vote in round 3 were 39 – 15 – 1 = 23. Also those who voted for candidate

Audi = 15. Hence required percentage = 15/23 × 100 = 65.2%. Hence (d).

Questions 9 to 12:

9. From the basic information we have that if 30% are males, 70% are females and 7% are female engineers. From Statement A we get (25–7) 18% are male engineers which gives us a unique answer to the question asked. Hence, A alone is sufficient. Similarly from Statement B too, we get a unique percentage for the number of male employees who have an engineering background.
10. Both statements together are also insufficient to answer the question because we cannot find for sure whether the match ends in a draw or Mahindra and Mahindra win.
11. Statement A is sufficient while B is not. Hence the answer is Option (a).
12. From Statement A and B as well as the information contained in the question itself, we get that the ranks in increasing order were: A,C,B,E,D. Hence, D gets the highest rank is a unique answer when we use both statements.
Hence, the answer is Option (d).

Questions 13 to 16:

13. From the given conditions, the following table may be derived regarding the industries and the companies associated with it (Deduction of the same left for students).

Name of Industry	Possible Companies
Agriculture	7, 10
Machinery	1, 11
Communication	4, 8, 9
Polyester	2, 6, 12

Also, 3 is either machinery or Polyester based while 5 is either machinery or Agriculture based as derived (left for students)
As it can be seen, only Machinery or Polyester industry could have four companies. Hence (c).

14. As can be seen from the above table, only (iii) and (v) are true and the rest are false. Hence (b) is the correct option.
15. The companies and the industries are:

Name of Industry	Possible Companies
Agriculture	5, 7, 10
Machinery	1, 3, 11
Communication	4, 8, 9
Polyester	2, 6, 12

Hence none of the statements mentioned is true. Hence (d).

16. As seen from the above table, option (a) is correct.

Questions 17 to 20:

17. The question is understood best if done by Venn diagrams. As per the given conditions the following Venn diagram may be drawn:

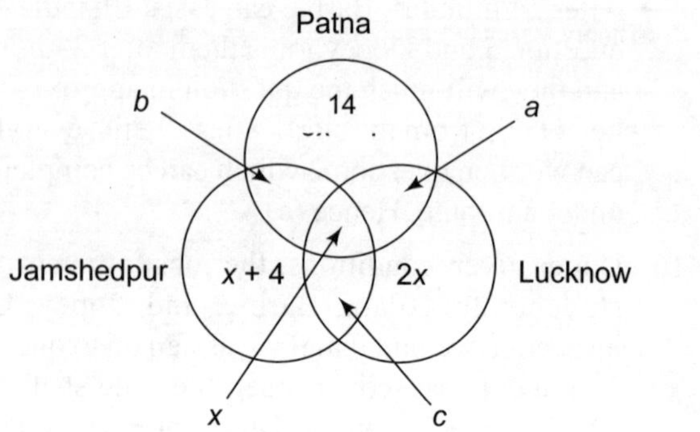

Let the number of teachers teaching in all the three cities be x and the number of teachers teaching in exactly two cities be a, b and c respectively as shown in the above Venn diagram.
As per the given condition $a + x + b = 10$ and $a + b = 4$. Since a, b and c are in the ratio of 1 : 2 : 3 and $a + b = 4$ then obviously $a = 1$ and $b = 3$ or $a = 3$ and $b = 1$. For either case, $c = 2$. Based on this, we can deduce that $x = 6$, $2x = 12$ and $x + 4 = 10$.
Thus total faculty members = 14 + 12 + 10 + 6 + 2 + $(a + b)$ = 44 + 4 = 48.
Hence (d).

18. Statement (i) was inferred by us in the last question. Hence it need not be checked. As per the question, we need to find the exact values of a and b. From statement (ii) $12 + 6 + 2 + a = 21$. Hence $a = 1$ and $b = 3$. Hence statement (ii) can be used.
Similarly from statement (iii), we have $10 + 6 + 2 + b = 21$ and hence $b = 3$ and $a = 1$. Hence statement (iii) can also be used.
Hence (c) is the correct option.
19. All the 6 faculty members teaching at all the three centers have to be withdrawn into two projects. As per the given conditions, if number of teachers withdrawn from Patna is x then those withdrawn from Lucknow and Jamshedpur are $x - 2$ and $x - 4$ respectively. Thus $x + (x - 2) + (x - 4) = 6 \Rightarrow x = 4$
Hence number of teachers working at:
Patna: 24 – 4 = 20
Lucknow: 21 – (4 – 2) = 19
Jamshedpur: 21 – (4 – 4) = 21
Clearly both (a) and (b) are incorrect. Hence (c).
20. From the above question, number of faculty members involved in each of the three centers after withdrawal is known. Hence if 3 new faculty

members are inducted, the numbers shall become equal. Hence (b).

MOCK TEST PAPER 22

Questions 1 to 5:

Theory Marks in Exam of Thermal Physics	Practical Marks in Thermodynamics
1–10	12
11–20	15
21–30	17
31–40	21
41–50	22
51–60	25
61–70	27
71–80	31
81–90	33
91–100	34

1. If theory marks varies from 25 to 76 then practical marks varies from 17 to 31. From table B we can see that for a 17 to 31 marks variation in practical marks in thermodynamics corresponding change in the marks in IQ test is 3 to 9.
2. For grades C to G the practical marks is from 17 to 27. From practical marks from 17 to 27 corresponding theory marks will be from 21–70. Hence, 72 is not a possible score.
3. Theory marks increases → 19 to 63
   Practical marks increases → 15 to 27
   Viva marks increases → 1 to 6

   Percentage increase in viva marks

   $$= \frac{6-1}{1} \times 100 = 500\%$$
4. For grade J, Amit would have got 34 marks in the practical, while Anand would have got 33 marks in the practical. The maximum possible difference in theory marks would be 100 – 81 = 19.
5. G graders score 27 in practical, which occurs in case someone scores 61-70 marks in the theory exam. Also A graders score 12 marks in practical which occurs if the marks in theory exam is between 1-10. The minimum possible difference is 61 – 10 = 51 marks.

Questions 6 to 8:

The logic of this question, is to be based on the fact that the total budget for scientists in each project is 1/8th of the total budget of the project.

Deduction 1: In Project A, the total budget of the project is 352 crores. the total payments to the scientists as their fees would be 1/8th of 352 = 44 crores. Since, we already know that Q and R are working on Project A, it means that the balance budget for scientists' payments in budget A is 18 crores. This can only be fulfilled by using the combinations of S and W or T and W. Using similar logic for what is possible for projects B, C and D, we can come up with the following table. We also realise that: If S works on project A then T must have worked in D and vice versa.

	Fee per project (in Crore ₹)	A	B	C	D
Total Budget (in Crore ₹)		352	288	384	576
P	20	N	Y	N	Y
Q	16	Y	N	N	Y
R	10	Y	N	N	Y
S	12		N	Y	
T	12		N	Y	
U	10	N	Y	Y	N
V	14	N	N	Y	Y
W	6	Y	Y	N	N

6. Required difference = (288 + 576) – (384) = 480
7. (d)
8. (b)

Questions 9 to 12:

According to the statement 4, Sudhir attempted 250 questions and scored 804 marks. He did not attempt 120 questions, because of these 120 questions he lost total 120 × 1 = 120 marks.

If we assume that there are total x incorrect attempts.

$$(250 - x)6 - 2x - 120 = 804$$

$$1500 - 6x - 2x - 120 = 804$$

$$8x = 1500 - 120 - 804 = 576$$

$$x = 72$$

Correct attempts = 250 – 72 = 178.

Total marks obtained in mock test-3 = (34 – 12)6 – 12 × 2 – 36 = 72

From statement-1, total score in mock test-1 = 72 × 2 = 144.

From statement-3, incorrect attempts in test-4 = 72/6 = 12

Because of these 12 incorrect attempts Sudhir lost 24 marks and if the number of correct attempts = c, then according to the question:

$$6c - 24 - (68 - c)1 = 132$$

$$7c - 92 = 132$$

$$c = \frac{92 + 132}{7} = \frac{224}{7} = 32$$

From statement-3: Incorrect attempts in test-1 = 6.
By applying the approach of the previous step we can get: Total attempts in test-1 = 36, Correct attempts in test-1 = 30.
Total problems attempted by Sudhir in Mock test-5 = 250 – (36 + 58 + 34 + 44) = 78.
Incorrect attempts in Mock test-5 = 78 – 60 = 18.

Total marks in test-5 = $60 \times 6 - 18 \times 2 - 12 = 312$
Correct attempts in Mock test-2 = 178 – (30 + 22 + 32 + 60) = 34.
Incorrect attempts in Mock test-2 = 58 – 34 = 24
Total score in test-2 = 144
From the above analysis we can get the following table:

Mock Tests	Total Number of Problems	Attempted Problems	Correct Attempts	Incorrect Attempts	Total Score
1	60	36	30	6	144
2	70	58	34	24	144
3	70	34	22	12	72
4	80	44	32	12	132
5	90	78	60	18	312

9. 144
10. 12
11. 312
12. 3

Questions 13 to 16:

	Rathore	Russell	Bindra
Primary points	23	26	15
Secondary points	21	22	23
Points Scored	79	85	83
Total	123	133	121

13. 133 – 121 = 12 points
14. 26 + 22 = 48
15. 10 + 10 = 20 Bindra
16. Russell

Questions 17 to 20:
5 people out of six, there are 6 ways.
The six groups of 5 students each that can be formed
ABCDE>ABCDF>ABCEF>ABDEF>ACDEF>BCDEF
$5A + 5B + 5C + 5D + 5E + 5F = 5(A + B + C + D + E + F)$
Sum of all 6 correct statements made by the teachers about scores of 5 students must be a multiple of 5.
Total of the numbers given by the 7 teachers

$$232 + 238 + 244 + 245 + 250 + 256 + 235 = 1700$$

232, 238, 244 & 256 are correct values.
One amongst 235, 245, 250 are incorrect.

Case (i): If 250 is incorrect
Total of all six correct statements 1700 – 250 = 1450

$$A + B + C + D + E + F = 1450/5 = 290$$

F = 290 – 256 = 34
E = 290 – 245 = 45
D = 290 – 244 = 46
C = 290 – 238 = 52
B = 290 – 235 = 55
A = 290-232 = 58

Case (ii): If 245 is incorrect
Total of all six correct statements = 1700 – 245 = 1455
A + B + C + D + E + F = 1455/5 = 291
F = 291 – 256 = 35
E = 291 – 250 = 41
D = 291 – 244 = 47
C = 291 – 238 = 53
B = 291 – 235 = 56
A = 291 – 232 = 59

Case (iii): If 235 is incorrect
Total of all 6 correct statements = 1700 – 235 = 1465
A + B + C + D + E + F = 1465/5 = 293
F = 37
E = 43
D = 48
C = 49
B = 55
A = 61

17. A – F = 24
18. 55 or 56
19. 34
20. We are talking about case (iii) here. Sum of 49 + 55 = 104 is a possible value in such a case.

MOCK TEST PAPER 23

Questions 1 to 3:
Deduction 1: The number of horror movies watched in INOX is 7. Therefore, B and C must have watched horror movies in INOX (as they cannot be fit into any other movie category for INOX). From amongst, A, D, E and F we need to find one more person who would have watched a horror movie in INOX.

Deduction 2: From Table-A and Table-B, A watched comedy movies in PVR and Big cinemas.

Deduction 3: D watched a romantic movie in PVR, since there is only one '1' in PVR in both the tables.

Deduction 4: From the given clues, we know that there is one person who has watched horror movies in all the cinemas. From deduction 2 and deduction 3, we conclude that A and D could not have been the ones to have watched horror movies in all the cinemas. Also, F could not have watched a horror movie in all the three cinemas as only one horror movie was watched in Big Cinemas (while F has watched 2 movies in Big Cinemas). Therefore, only E is left for watching one horror movie in INOX. He must also have watched horror movies in PVR and Big Cinemas.

At this point the table starts to look as follows:

Name	PVR	BIG CINEMAS	INOX
A	4-Comedy	4-Comedy	1
B	2	1	2-Horror
C	2	1	4-Horror
D	1-Romance	1	1
E	2-Horror	1-Horror	1-Horror
F	2	2	1

Deduction 5: Exactly two people out of A, D and F watched the same type of movies in all the three multiplexes; the possible person-movie combinations in such a case could be: A-Comedy, D-Romance, F-Dance-based. Exactly 2 out of the given 3 combinations are true. In INOX, they definitely watched these types only, as otherwise the given condition could not be true. So A is definitely one of the persons who watched the same type of movie in all the three multiplexes (as A would then have watched comedy in all three theaters). In Big Cinemas, D did not watch Action, Sci-Fi, comedy or horror movie. D could not have watched a Dance movie in BIG cinemas as in that case even F would not be able to watch dance-based movies in all the three cinemas. Therefore D must have watched one romantic movie in BIG cinemas. Therefore, D is the other person to have watched the same type of movie in all the three multiplexes. The table becomes:

Name	PVR	BIG CINEMAS	INOX
A	4-Comedy	4-Comedy	1-Comedy
B	2	1	2-Horror
C	2	1	4-Horror
D	1-Romance	1-Romance	1-Romance
E	2-Horror	1-Horror	1-Horror
F	2	2	1-Dance

1. 3.

2. F watched one dance-based movie in INOX. He cannot watch dance-based movie in all the three multiplexes as then there will be three students who watched the same type of movie in all the three multiplexes. Hence the required answer for the maximum number of dance-based movies watched by F would be: 1 + 2 = 3.

3. E

Questions 4 to 8:

4. Aroon must have scored at least two 8 pointers (1st ranks) in the first 10 tests. This can be deduced by thinking about his scoring 60 points in the first ten tests to maintain an average of 6 points per test. Since, we have a constraint that a particular score is not repeated for three consecutive times we can try to use the maximum number of sixes first–
   6, 6, _, 6, 6, _, 6, 6, _, _. In the above sequence, the blanks have to be filled in such a way that an average of 6 points is maintained throughout without using any more sixes. This can only be done by using 2 8s and 2 4s. Thus, he must have got the first rank at least twice in the first 10 tests.
   Follow a similar analysis pattern for the remaining tests and you will realise that:
   In tests 11–20, he needs no 1st ranks to get 40 points as there are many combinations without using an 8, that can give 40 points in ten tests. (note; we have to find the minimum number of first ranks and for this we need to use 8's only when and if required!!)
   Similarly, for tests 21 – 30 → No 1st ranks required
   For tests 31 – 40 → No first ranks required,
   For tests 41 – 50 → No first ranks required,
   For tests 51 – 60 → 2 first ranks are necessary.
   Hence, the answer is option (c) (minimum 4 first ranks for Aroon)

5. If we try using twelve 4s (from the options) and three 6s we will get a total of 66 points after 15 tests. In the remaining 5 tests we require a total of 34 points which can be achieved by using four 8's and one 2.

   Note: In case you try to use thirteen 4s and three 6s, then we would need a total of 40 points in 4 tests by using only 8, 2 and 0s. This is not possible to achieve. Hence, 12 is the maximum possible answer.

6. Use an analysis similar to the first question of the set above. This would give you 7 + 7 + 6 + 7 + 2 + 5 (in the respective groups of tests 1–10, 11–20 and so on tlll 51–60) = 34 instances of last rank for Daroon maximum.

7. Twice each in each set of ten tests in the first forty sets. Hence, 8.
8. In the first set of ten tests he requires 20 points overall. Since he uses exactly 2 twos, he must score 16 from the remaining 8 tests. This can be achieved without using a 6 pointer. Hence, he need not have stood second in the first ten tests. Similarly, he need not have stood second in the next ten tests either as the same conditions apply. In the next ten tests he scores 50 points out which he scores 4 points through two two pointers. This means that he needs to score 46 in the remaining 8 tests by using 0, 4, 6 and 8 only. Since 46 is not a multiple of 4 or 8 we need to use at least one 6. Hence, the required answer is 1. [Option (b)].

Questions 9 to 12:

9. Aristotle, being the first to deduce after being told Bach's currency, he must be having Indian currency. Since, Einstein also speaks up at this point, he would also be having Indian currency. Hence, option (b) is correct.
10. Coutin and Dell
11. Aristotle did not know about Bach's Currency. Only Einstein's currency was known to him
12. Aristotle

Questions 13 to 16:

Result of all the matches played in the Honda World Cup Tennis Cup (In the year 2090)

Vs	Fed										
Nad	5-0	**Nad**									
Sam	5-0	4-1	**Sam**								
Mc	4-1	0-5	5-0	**Mc**							
Ldl	0-5	5-0	4-1	1-4	**Ldl**						
Aga	4-1	0-5	5-0	4-1	1-4	**Aga**					
Lee	5-0	5-0	1-4	5-0	1-4	5-0	**Lee**				
Rod	0-5	1-4	4-1	5-0	1-4	5-0	4-1	**Rod**			
Beck	1-4	5-0	0-5	1-4	5-0	1-4	4-1	0-5	**Beck**		
ED	0-5	5-0	1-4	5-0	5-0	0-5	1-4	4-1	0-5	**ED**	
Con	0-5	5-0	1-4	4-1	5-0	0-5	4-1	1-4	1-4	4-1	**Con**
Sti	5-0	4-1	5-0	4-1	4-1	1-4	5-0	4-1	0-5	1-4	5-0

The above table gives the points for each match (The first match shows Nadal vs. Federer where Nadal gets 5 points & Federer gets 0 points.

The points would be

Player	Seeding
Federer (Fed)	26
Nadal (Nad)	5 + 16 = 21
Sampras (Sam)	9 + 19 = 28
McEnroe (Mc)	9 + 11 = 20
Lendl (Ldl)	10 + 13 = 23
Agassi (Aga)	14 + 18 = 32
Leander (Lee)	22 + 7 = 29
Roddick (Rod)	20 + 11 = 31
Becker (Beck)	17 + 14 = 31
Edberg (Ed)	21 + 5 = 26
Connors (Con)	25 + 0 = 25
Stich (Sti)	38

Hence, the answers are:

13. Nadal has only 4 wins in the tournament. Hence, option (b) is correct.
14. Agassi scores 32 points.
15. Stich has the highest points while Agassi has the second highest points. Hence, Agassi-Stich. Option (a) is correct.
16. McEnroe scored only 20 points. Hence, option (b) is correct.

Questions 17 to 20:

17. Since matches lost at home = total matches played – total matches won at home.

Hence the following table may be drawn:

Team	Number of Wins at Home	Number of Losses at Home
Aus	58	27
Ind	69	21
NZ	60	10
SA	75	5
Pak	70	15
SL	69	20

Out of the 80 matches at SA, SA won 75 matches and hence lost 5 matches. NZ defeated SA 11 times while being away from home. Hence at best, NZ won against SA at SA is 5 times. Hence NZ won 6 matches on neutral grounds against SA. Hence (b).

18. As can be seen from the table above, only statements (i) and (iv) stand true. Hence (c).
19. We need to know the maximum number of matches played in between NZ and Pak in either NZ or Pak. NZ won 60 matches at home and lost 10 matches at home against Pak. Hence Pak won 21 – 10 = 11 matches on neutral grounds. Pak had won 70 matches at home which means that Pak lost 15 matches to NZ at home. Similarly NZ won 23 matches against Pak while playing away and hence the number of matches it won on neutral grounds is 23 – 15 = 8. Hence NZ and Pak played at least 11 + 8 = 19 matches on neutral grounds. Hence (d).
20. Total matches played in Aus = 85. Matches won by Aus = 58. Hence Aus lost 27 matches at Aus. SA or Pak with at the most one of Ind, NZ or SL have won all their matches against Aus. Hence at the most 3 teams have won against Aus in Aus. Hence (d).

MOCK TEST PAPER 24

Questions 1 to 5:

Company F has total 7 competitors therefore each of the other company is the competitor of F. Company C has only one competitor therefore it has no competitor other than F. Company D and Company G have six competitors each therefore each of them is a competitor of every other company except C. B and H have three competitors each therefore each of them is a competitor of F, D and G.

E has four competitors. D, G, F are competitors of E and B, C, H cannot be the competitors of E, therefore A must be a competitor of E.

From the above discussion we can conclude that A has four competitors – D, E, F, G.

1. Only option (c) is correct.
2. Required average = (4 + 3 + 1 + 6 + 4 + 7 + 6 + 3)/8 = 34/8 =4 .25
3. The number of competitors of B and H is 3 and 3 respectively. Therefore the number of competitors who sell mobile in the country in which either of B and H sell mobiles can be at most 4.
   Now suppose there is a country in which five companies sell their phones. In such a country five companies A, D, E, F and G can sell their mobile phones. If there is a country where six companies sell their mobile phones then each of the company must have at least five competitors but we have only three such companies (D, F, G). Therefore we cannot have six or more companies selling their phones in a single region. Hence the required answer is 5.
4. According to the analysis we have done above B, E and H are competitors of companies D, F and G. But no two among B, E and H are competitors of each other. If we allot maximum number of countries to C then final distribution will look like this:
   Country 1: B, D, F, G
   Country 2: E, D, F, G, A
   Country 3: H, D, F, G
   Country 4: C, F
   Country 5: C
   Therefore maximum number of countries in which company C sells its mobile phones is 2.
5. From the previous solution it is clear that if P has maximum number of mobile companies then P should have five companies. Hence the required answer is 5.

Questions 6 to 8:

Deduction 1: Since Faraz has scored the highest marks in Gate 2013, hence Faraz cannot be R or S. Hence, Faraz is either P or Q. Similarly Ajay is either Q or P (since he scored the lowest marks in Gate-2012). Therefore, Mohanish and Peter are R & S in any order.

Deduction 2: Total marks obtained by R = 102 + 118 + 56 = 276.

Maximum possible marks obtained by S = 106 + 20 + 150 = 276. Thus, marks of R ≥ Marks of S.

Also, we know from clue 5 that Peter > Mohanish. Therefore, Peter is R and Mohanish is S. The table becomes:

	P = Ajay/Faraz	Q = Faraz/Ajay	Peter	Mohanish
Gate-2012	94		102	106
Gate-2013		124	118	20
Gate-2014	144	50	56	
Total marks	w	x	276	z

Now let's assume Ajay is disguised as Q and his marks in Gate 2012 exam was 'n' then according to statement 2, $50 + n + 124 > 276$

$n > 102$, which is not possible because this violates the third statement, that Ajay scored the lowest marks in Gate 2012. Therefore, our assumption is incorrect and Ajay must be P. The final table would be:

	Ajay	Faraz	Peter	Mohanish
Gate-2012	94	>94	102	106
Gate-2013	>38, but <124	124	118	20
Gate-2014	144	50	56	<150
Total marks	w	x	276	z

6. If Mohanish scored 'k' marks in the Gate-2014 exam then according to the question:
   $106 + 20 + k < 276$. Hence, $k < 150$.
   All the even scores from –50 to +148 are possible in any of the tests, except 140, 146 and 148.
   Therefore, different scores possible for Mohanish = 100 – 3 = 97.
7. Faraz
8. Ajay is disguised as P. Let's assume that Ajay scores q marks in Gate 2013. As Faraz scored the highest in Gate 2013, $q < 124$ and $94 + 144 + q > 102 + 118 + 56$.
   $\therefore 38 < q < 124$
   Ajay's total score is a multiple of 12.
   $\therefore 238 + q$ needs to be a multiple of 12.
   $\therefore q = 12K + 2$, where K is a whole number.
   $38 < 12K + 2 < 124$
   $\therefore 4 \le K \le 10$
   Therefore, 7 different values are possible for w.

Questions 9 to 12:

There are a total of $^6C_2$ = 15 matches played.

Maximum points for all teams together = 45; Minimum points for all teams together = 30.

Deduction 1: We also know that Spain beat England. Since, Spain got a total of 8 points, it could have scored 5 more points in the remaining 4 matches only if it won one game and drew two.

Deduction 2: Also, Brazil's 10 points can only happen if it won 3 matches, drew 1 and lost 1.

Deduction 3: Spain won against England and lost to Argentina. It must have drawn against Brazil and France, while France versus Cameroon must also have been a draw. Also, both of Spain's draws must have been 0-0.

The following would be the final table:

Position	Won	Draw	Loss	Goals For	Goals Against	Total
Argentina	5	0	0	17	5	15
Brazil	3	1	1	9	6	10
Spain	2	2	1	2	2	8
England	2	0	3	2	5	6
France	0	2	3	7	11	2
Cameroon	0	1	4	8	16	1

The answers are quite clear through these deduction and the table:

9. Cameroon vs France
10. England 6 points
11. Brazil vs Spain match is a draw with 0 goals
12. At most 3 goals, since England has two more losses to concede with only 5 goals conceded.

Questions 17 to 20:

The following table would represent the set of possibilities that exist:

	(1)	(2)	(3)	(4)	(5)	Median Index	Differential Index
Sachin	194	60	0-73	124	120	120	134–194
Viru	126	0-59	250	0-66	144	126	191–250
Rahul	112	0–59	0-73	0-66	160	0-73	101–160
Laxman	0–108	170	74	154	0-106	74–108	96–170
Jaffer	0–108	130	124	96	0-106	96-108	34–130

The answers can be read off for the various questions from the above table.

In the 1st match:

Sachin + Viru + Rahul = 432. Total score is 540. Hence, remaining runs = 108.

In the 2nd match, Laxman+ Jaffer + Sachin = 360. Total score is 480. Hence, remaining runs = 120.

In the 3rd match: Viru + Jaffer + Laxman = 448. Total score is 640. Hence, remaining runs = 192.

In the 4th match: Laxman + Sachin + Jaffer = 374. Total score is 440. Hence, remaining runs = 66.

In the 5th match: Rahul + VIru + Sachin = 424. Total score is 530. Hence, remaining runs = 106.

17. Rahul
18. Total 2630. Total of Sachin + Rahul = 1040 → 40% approximately.
19. 2
20. Only Jaffer, Rahul or Laxman

MOCK TEST PAPER 25

Questions 1 to 2:

Team	W	L	T
India	26	30	04
Pakistan	14	36	10
Sri Lanka	24	30	06
South Africa	P	Q	R
Bangladesh	20	32	08
Canada	18	30	12

1. From the table it is clear that, the total number of wins = the total number of losses = 102 + P = 158 + Q

   The total number of matches played = $^6C_2 \times 12$ = 180

   Total matches tied = (40 + R)/2

   Hence at least 20 matches were tied.

   Thus we know that in at least 178 matches of the 180 matches, there were 158 wins/losses and 20 ties in the tournament

   The other 2 matches can have three results:

   (a) No match tied, will mean that R = 0;

   (b) 1 match tied means R = 2;

   (c) 2 matches tied means R = 4.

   In case, R = 0, it means that 20 matches were tied and 160 matches had results. This would mean 102 + P = 158 + Q = 160 → we will get P = 58 and Q = 2 (so that both the W and L columns are equal). In case, R = 2, it means that 21 matches were tied and 159 matches had results. This would mean 102 + P = 158 + Q = 159 → P = 57 and Q = 1 and R = 2. Likewise, when R = 4, P = 56 and Q = 0. Thus, there are three possibilities for W, L and T combinations for South Africa. Option (a) is correct.

2.

	Win	Loss	Tie
South Africa	56-57-58	0-1-2	4-2-0
India	26	30	4
Sri Lanka	24	30	6
Bangladesh	20	32	8
Canada	18	30	12
Pakistan	14	36	10

The third ranked team is Sri Lanka with a total of $24 \times 5 - 30 \times 3 + 6 \times 2 = 42$ points

The second last ranked team is Bangladesh with a total of $20 \times 5 - 32 \times 3 + 8 \times 2 = 20$ points

Thus, the difference between their points is 22 points. Hence, option (e) is correct.

Questions 3 to 5:

The only way to handle this question is through the options. We can see that Vikas's age now should be more than 8. Hence, This gives us 15 as the only viable answer and we start with Vikas = 15.

From the first clue, we get: there was a time when Vikas was 9 times as old as Amit. This means, their age combinations could be 1, 9; 2, 18 etc. But since Vikas is only 15 years old, he cannot have been 9 times Amit in the past. Thus, Amit was 1 when Vikas was 9. Thus, Amit's current age = 15 – 8 = 7. Also, we can work out that at the time Amit and Vikas were 1 and 9 respectively, Vishal was 8 years old. Hence, the answers are:

3. Amit = 7
4. Vishal = 14
5. Vikas = 15

Questions 6 to 9:

6. The only way to score …
   17 token points is: 3 UHL tokens + 1 MHL token
   12 token points is: 2 UHL tokens + 1 MHL token + 1 LHL token
   11 token points is: 1 UHL tokens + 3 MHL token
   7 token points is: 1 UHL tokens +1 MHL token+ 2 LHL tokens
   0 token points is: 4 LHL token
   So on and so forth
   Hence fitting the above values in the given table we get:

City	Number of UHL Tokens	Number of MHL Tokens	Number of LHL Tokens	Token Points
		Stage 1		
A	1	1	2	7
B	2	1	1	12
C	3	1	0	17
D	0	0	4	0
E	1	3	0	11
F	0	3	1	6
G	4	0	0	20
H	1	1	2	7
I	0	2	2	4
J	1	2	1	9

From condition (iii) we know that city E had 11 token points in first stage and is the city with the second highest pollution level with 7 points in the second stage. Hence (b) is the correct answer:

7. Clearly from the above table, the city that ranked 9th in terms of pollution level, i.e. the city with the second lowest token points at the end of the first stage is city I. Hence (d).
8. As mentioned in condition (iii) the city with 20 token points in stage 1 had the highest token points in stage 2 as well, i.e. 12. Clearly city G is the answer. Hence (b)
9. (i) Clearly incorrect as can be verified from the above table.
   (ii) Total UHL tokens = 13, hence total UHL token points = 13 × 5 = 65. Hence correct.
   (iii) MHL tokens = 14 and UHL tokens = 13. Hence incorrect.
   (iv) City D had 0 token points in stage 1. Hence it is obviously the least polluted.
   (v) MHL tokens (first 5 cities) = 6 and LHL tokens (last five cities) = 6. Hence they are equal and hence the statement is incorrect.

   Hence (i), (iii) and (v) are incorrect. Hence (d).

Questions 10 to 13:

10. Statements (iii), (iv) and (v) are conditional statements, some or all of which have been violated in the table given. We need to find the entries in each row that pertain to the specific violations that have to be first identified and then considered for correctness or incorrectness as the case might be. Let the violations of statement (iii) be marked as @, that of statement (iv) be marked as # and of statement (v) be marked as $ in the corresponding table. Then the final tabulated table shall be:

Name of Students	Grade in GD/PI	Marks Obtained In			
		English	Quant	DI	Reasoning
A	@C	@10	40	@20	30
B	B	@40	50	@30	70
C	#$A	60	40	#88	$50
D	B	70	50	60	60
E	$A	50	$80	70	$40
F	B	80	30	90	40
G	B	40	50	80	70
H	@C	@40	60	@50	80
I	$A	@40	30	@60	$50
J	@C	90	85	@40	90

To reduce the number of mistakes, for B there is definitely 1 mistake in his marks of English and DI. Similarly for E, we can either change his grade in his GD/PI or his marks in Quant or reasoning. For minimum changes, we should change his grade. Similarly the other changes should be:
A: Marks in DI (1 change)
C: Grade in GD/PI (from A to B) (1 change)
H: Marks in DI (1 change)
I: Marks in Reasoning and English or Grades in GD/PI and DI (2 changes)
J: Marks in DI (1 change)
Hence a total of 8 changes is required. Hence (d).

11. Now the score of C after correction is Quant = 40, Reasoning = 100 (changed from 50), English = 60 and DI = 80 (changed from 88). Hence his total = 280.
12. A scored the least marks (The inspection has to how we arrived at this is left for the students). A scored 40 in Quant, 30 in Reasoning, 10 in English and 61 in DI. Hence his least possible total is 141. Hence (d).
13. J scored more than 320 marks as his grand total. Hence (a).

Questions 14 to 16:

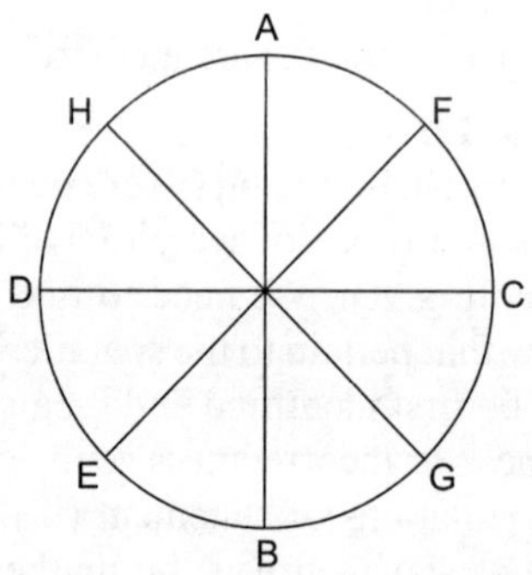

First from A, send 2 planes along with the main plane. The journey consists of 8 parts A-F-C-G-B-E-D-H-A. Let one part of the journey require 1 unit of fuel. Then 3 planes leave A with 4 units of fuel each and reach F with 3 units of fuel left each. One plane gives 1 unit of fuel to the main plane and the other plane and returns back to A. So, at F, the main plane and its' supporting plane both have 4 units of fuel each. Let both planes reach C with 3 units of fuel each. The supporting plane gives 1 unit of fuel to the main plane and returns back. The main plane now has 4 units of fuel and can reach D. At D it would run out of fuel and hence needs refuelling at D. In order to get refueled at D, the main plane needs a support plane from A. But the support plane also needs to go back. So two planes should fly from A anti-clockwise, when the main plane has reached B. One of these two support planes refuels the other at H, and the refueled plane reaches D with 3 units of fuel left. It refuels the main plane with 1 unit of fuel. So at D, there are two planes – the main plane with 1 unit of fuel and the support plane with 2 units of fuel. The support plane can reach A on its' own, but the main pane would need another refuel of 1 unit at H. So, another support plane would need to reach H from A, when the main plane reaches H. The answers can then be read off from this story:

14. Only 2 planes are required to support the main plane in it's journey - since there are only 2 support planes in the air at any point of time. Hence, the correct answer is option (a).
15. Number of flights required is: 2 + 2 + 1 = 5. Option (b) is correct.
16. 2 refuelling planes with one plane flying twice. So a total of 2 planes.

Questions 17 to 20:

17. It can be calculated that there are five slots of 12 seconds each in a minute. In each slot the first second is used by the link to check for the host's job, in the second second th pending job is checked and 10 seconds are taken to complete the job.

For Job 1:

For 1st minute

	1st Second	2nd Second	12th Second	Status
Slot 1	Host	No	User 1	Completed
Slot 2	Host	No	User 2	3 second pending
Slot 3	Host	No	User 3	22 second pending
Slot 4	Host	No	User 4	8 second pending
Slot 5	Host	No	User 5	1 second pending

For 2nd minute

	1st second	2nd second	12th second	Status
Slot 1	No Host job	User 2	User 2	Completed
Slot 2	No Host job	User 3	User 3	12 second pending
Slot 3	Host	No	User 3	2 second pending
Slot 4	Host	No	User 4	Completed
Slot 5	Host	No	User 5	Completed

Students are required to make the table for the 3rd minute of job 1 by themselves to understand the question better.

For job 2:

For 1st Minute

Host	Slot	1st Second	2nd Second	12th Second	Status
User 1	Slot 1	Host	No	User 1	
		9:02:10	9:02:11	9:02:21	10 second pending
User 2	Slot 2	No host job	User 1	User 1	
		9:02:22	9:02:23	9:02:33	Completed

Host	Slot	1st Second	2nd Second	12th Second	Status
User 3	Slot 3	Host	No	User 3	
		9:02:34	9:02:35	9:02:45	21 second pending
User 4	Slot 4	No host job	User 2	User 2	
		9:02:46	9:02:47	9:02:57	3 second pending
User 5	Slot 5	Host	No	User 5	
		9:02:58	9:02:59	9:03:09	5 second pending

For 2nd Minute

Host	Slot	1st Second	2nd Second	12th Second	Status
User 1	Slot 1	No host job	User 2	User 2	
		9:03:10	9:03:11	9:03:21	Completed
User 2	Slot 2	No host job	User 3	User 3	
		9:03:22	9:02:23	9:03:33	11 second pending
User 3	Slot 3	Host	No	User 3	
		9:03:34	9:03:35	9:03:45	1 second pending
User 4	Slot 4	Host	No	User 4	
		9:03:46	9:03:47	9:03:57	1 second pending
User 5	Slot 5	Host	No	User 5	
		9:03:58	9:02:59	9:04:09	Completed

It is left for the students to make the table for the 3rd minute of job 2 by themselves to understand the question better.

From the table, user 3's job gets completed in slot 1 in 3rd minute. Hence (a).

18. From the table, only user 4 did not get access to the link in the first minute of job 2. Hence (c).
19. As seen from the table, no user completes his job in its own slot. Hence (d).
20. Total slots used = 12

    Total time for completion of job 2 = 12 × 12 = 144 seconds

    Actual link – use time = 20 + 13 + 31 + 11 + 15 = 90 seconds

    Time for which the link is idle is therefore = 144 – 90 = 54 seconds.

    Hence (b).

MOCK TEST PAPER 26

Questions 1 to 5:

1. WE ARE ONE with a Caesar cipher of –3 would become TBXXOBXLKB. For doing this, write down the alphabet from A to Z and shift each letter by 3 places to the left. Thus, W becomes T and so on. Also, for the blanks a '–3' cipher means X. Option (e) is correct.
2. For CARTE BLANCHE, we can see that the first letter different in the options is for E. DCUX will be the term used for CART using a ABCDABCD Vegenere cipher. E will get coded using a displacement defined by A – which means we need to do E + 1 = F. Thus, we are only left with options (a) or (d). These are identical and correct till the last letter. The 'E' of BLANCHE is the 13th letter in the word (including the blank). Hence, the Vegenere code to consider will be A and we take a +1 and it becomes F. Option (a) is correct.
3. The added code of ABC & ABCD would become: BDFDBDFD... SECRET would become UIIVGX. Option (e) is correct.
4. Since, the first code would be A + T = U, there would be a +22 change in A to make it V. None of the options starts with V for the encrypted message. Hence, option (e) is correct.
5. The new key would be BDFHE. Option (a) is correct.

Questions 6 to 10:

After the flips the final structure of the table would be:

6	4	3	10	11	15	21	19	18
7	A	2	B	12	C	22	D	17
8	5	1	9	13	14	23	20	16

The answers can be read off the table:

6. 7 numbers have not changed position. These are: 4, 5, 11, 12, 13, 19 and 20. Hence, option (c) is correct.
7. Option (b) is correct.
8. In the third column third row, the number 10 has reduced to 1. This is the highest percentage loss. Option (a) is correct.
9. 9,10,14 and 15 are the 4 numbers exhibiting a numerical value change of 1. Option (c) is correct.
10. 116 has become 131 – an increase of 15. Option (a) is correct.

Questions 11 to 15:

The races were between:

Race 1: A, B, C, D, E
Race 2: B, C, D, E, F
Race 3: C, D, E, F, G
Race 4: D, E, F, G, H
Race 5: E, F, G, H, I

The following deductions can be drawn:

A: must have stood first in the first race since A has scored a total of 5 points and this is the only race he has participated in.

B: B must have stood outside the first three in the first race and first in the second race (this is the only way he could have scored 5 points in 2 races given the point scheme)

C: Since C has scored 8 points overall, he must have got 5 + 3 points. Further since we know that H is the only horse which has scored points in consecutive races, it is clear that C must have scored 3 points in the first race (2nd position) and 5 points in the third race (first position)

D: 2 points without scoring in consecutive races (which is exclusive for H) means that D must have stood third in two races and must have been outside the top three in the remaining 2 races he participates in,

I: Outside the top three in the last race (only race he participates in)

H: 10 points in 2 races, means that H must have won both races 4 and 5.

At this point of our analysis we know the winner of each race.

Race 1: A, Race 2: B, Race 3: C, Race 4: H and Race 5: H

As far as the second position is concerned, we are just aware of the first race (C stood second)

G: 4 points in 3 races, means outside the top three in the fourth race and third once and second once in races 3 and 5 (but not respectively – rather in random order)

F: 6 points can only happen with two 3's and two 0's. Means second position in any two non consecutive races (i.e. Either 2nd and 4th or 2nd and 5th or 3rd and 5th). And two races outside the top three (i.e. Either 3rd and 5th or 3rd and 4th or 2nd and 4th races).

E: 5 points in 5 races, 3 points once and 1 point twice (i.e. one second position and two third positions) Also, these scores must have occurred in the 1st, 3rd and 5th races. (again because of no consecutive scores for anybody except H).

Also, since the second position in the first race goes to C, E must have got the third position in that race.

This gives us the following table:

RACE #	First	Second	Third	Outside the Top Three
1	A	C	E	B, D
2	B			E
3	C			
4	H			G, E
5	H			

Looking at Race 4, D must have scored in it and hence must have got the third position, thus must be out of the top three in Race 3. Also, his other 1 point must have come in Race 2.

RACE #	First	Second	Third	Outside the Top Three
1	A	C	E	B, D
2	B		D	E
3	C			
4	H		D	G, E
5	H			

At this stage we also know that G has one third and one second rank in Races 3 and 5 in some random order, and also E has a third and a second position in the same races in random fashion. This means that the blanks for the third and fifth races would be completely filled by two possibilities as below. We would also then know that F would have finished 2nd in races 2 and 4. Putting these informations in the table, the final table would emerge as follows:

RACE #	First	Second	Third	Outside the Top Three
1-ABCDE	A	C	E	B, D
2-BCDEF	B	F	D	E, C
3-CDEFG	C	G/E	E/G	D, F
4-DEFGH	H	F	D	G, E
5-EFGHI	H	E/G	G/E	I,F

The answers to the questions can be derived from this table.

11. 2nd
12. Could be either 3 : 1 or 1 : 3 we do not know which. Hence, option (d) is correct.
13. Option (d) is correct.
14. Race 4. Hence option (c).
15. If this case occurs, there would be a reduction of 2 points for C and an increase of 2 points for E. The correct answer is option (d).

Questions 16 to 20:

Eahsan has got the maximum number of palaces and number of palaces with Arun is equal to sum of number of palaces with Barun and Charan. As there are 9 palaces, so possible solutions are when Eahsan, Arun, Barun, Charan, and Deep have 3, 2, 1, 1 and 2 or 4, 2, 1, 1 and 1 palaces respectively.

Case I: Barun and Deep have one palace and two palaces respectively.

Let the value of a palace be ₹x. So amount of cash with Barun = x.

So total assets of Barun = $2x$

Total assets of Deep = $x/2 + 2x$.

As Deep has got assets worth 2 crore more than that of Barun,

So $\{x/2 + 2x\} - 2x = 2$ crore, or $x = 4$ crore.

Case II: Barun and Deep have one palace each

Let value of a palace be ₹x. So, amount of cash with Barun = x.

Total assets of Barun= $2x$

$\rightarrow$ Total assets of Deep = $x/2 + x$

As Deep has got assets worth 2 crore more than Barun $\rightarrow \{x/2 + x\}$

$-2x = 2$ crore

Here the value of x is coming as negative.

So this case is not possible.

We can collate the final distribution of assets in the following table:

	Number of Palaces	Cash (in ₹ crore)	Total Assets (in ₹ crore)
Arun	2	1 or 2 or 3	9 or 10 or 11
Barun	1	4	8
Charan	1	1 or 2 or 3	5 or 6 or 7
Deep	2	2	10
Eahsan	3	1 or 2 or 3	13 or 14 or 15

16. (c) Value of 9 palaces is ₹36 crore.
17. (d) Maximum possible assets of Arun is 11 crore. (2 palaces + 3 crore)
18. (d) Maximum possible assets of Eahsan = 15 crore
    Minimum possible assets of Charan = 5 crore
    Ratio = 3 : 1
19. Maximum possible value of assets of all the brothers taken together = 11 + 8 + 7 + 10 + 15 = 51crore. Minimum possible value = 9 + 8 + 5 + 10 + 13 = 45. Thus any value between 45 to 51 crore is possible. Hence (b).
20. Only for Barun and Deep, it is possible to find the exact value of their total assets. Hence (b).

MOCK TEST PAPER 27

Questions 1 to 5:

It would be a good idea to identify the number of blanks row wise and column wise to start solving the question.

In the table, the numbers in brackets with a # indicate the deduction number that helps us fill the value of the blank.

List of final selections in the second auction

List of original selections in the first auction		A	B	C	D	E	F	Total	
	A	3	7	10	1	4	1 (#4)	25 + _	26
	B	0 (#5)	10	8	8	3	3	32 + _	32
	C	2	6	11	0 (#3)	1	1(#6)	20 + _ + _	21
	D	1(#6)	1 (#5)	2	10	1	5	18 + _ + _	20
	E	1 (#7)	11	1	0 (#3)	10	0 (#7)	22 + _ + _ + _	23
	F	1	7	3	1 (#3)	10	8	29 + _	30
	G	4	12	11	5	5	11	48	48
Total		10 + _ + _ + _	53 + _	46	24 + _ + _ + _	34	27 + _ + _ + _	194 + 10 blanks	
		12	54	46	25	34	29		

Logic for filling the table:

Deduction 1: The numbers in the given table add up to 194, while there are 200 players in the auction. This means that out of the 10 blanks in the table, there will be four 0's and six 1's.

Deduction 2: From Clue 1, one can see that the values of C and D, after the first auction would be either 20-19 or 21-20. i.e. either both the blanks in the C row would be 0 each or one blank would be 1 and the other 0. Note: we cannot have C's total players after the first auction as 22, as D's total can reach a maximum of 20 (as D's row has only 2 blanks, which we can put as 1 each – to get D to it's maximum value of 20.) Hence, in D's row the blanks could be both 1's or one blank could be a 1 and the other blank a 0. Also, in D's column, of the three blanks, there has to be exactly one 1, and two 0's. This is because the total of D's column is given to us as 21 less than the total of C's column. Since C's column is fixed at 46- D's column would be exactly 25.

Deduction 3: The blank in the F row would necessarily be equal to 1 – from clue 2. However, when we fill this missing blank in the F row with 1, we see also that it completes the missing 1 from the D column. Thus, the other two blanks of the D column are equal to 0. This also freezes the number of people in the D row as 25. Thus out of the required four zeroes, we have identified two of these.

Deduction 4: After the first auction, E had 34 – 11 = 23 players. At this stage, in the E row, there are two indetermined blanks. This means, that out of these two, one would be filled with a 1 and another with a 0. Thus, one of our remaining two zeroes would be in this row. Also, from clue 3's second part, we can see that the missing number in the A row would be 1, making it 26. Also, the A column would add up to 12 – giving us two 1's and a 0 in the A column.

Deduction 5: We can make out from Clue 4, that the B column's missing number is 0, as it is only then that doubling it would make it 10 more than the B column's number. B's column would also add up to 54, which means that the missing value in the D column would be 1.

Deduction 6: If we try to put a zero in the C row's missing value, then it would mean that the total of C row would be 20. In such a case, from deduction 2, D would need to be 19. For this to happen, we would need a total of five 0's, in the blanks. Hence, this is not possible. Hence, the total of the C row would be 21 (with a 1, in the missing value of the C row. Also, the missing value of the D row's first column would also be 1, making the D row equal to 20.

Deduction 7: From the A column, we already know that there is a total of 12 in it. After the first 6 deductions, we have a total of 11 in the A column. Thus, the value in the blank between the A column, E row would be 1. Hence, the fourth 0 blank would be in the E row's F column. The table is complete with these deductions.

The answers can be read off from this table:

1. 1.
2. 5
3. (a). Team C has gained a total of 25 players – going up from 21 to 46.
4. (d). C with 21 players has the 2nd least number of players, F with 30 players has the third highest number of players.
5. (c). Option (c) represents the correct sequence.

Questions 6 to 10:

We can start to make the table for the situation- by first putting down all the direct information given to us:

	Pragyan	Qusum	Richa	Sherry	Total Marks
Physics	y	x	x	x	27 y > x
Chemistry					26
Data Science			3/4th of Sherry, hence 3 or 6	Multiple of 4 (hence, 4 or 8)	24 (a,b,c,d)
English				10	34 (10, 9, 8, 7)
Total			19		111

From this point, we can go with a series of deductions to reach the answer as follows:

Deduction 1: Total marks in Chemistry = 111-34-24-27=26.

Deduction 2: From Clue 9, since Sherry's marks in Chemistry is 100% more than his marks in DS, it can only mean that he scores 8 marks in Chemistry and 4 in DS. Thus, Richa scores 3 in DS. The other two scores in DS have to be 8 and 9, in some order for Pragyan and Qusum. From clue 4, we can make out that 9 marks should be for Qusum and 8 for Pragyan. Clue 4 also tells us that Qusum's marks in Chemistry and DS are equal. Hence, we can put 9 marks for her in Chemistry.

From Clue 7, we can deduce that Qusum's rank in English is 3rd (as Sherry is ranked 3rd in DS). Hence, Qusum scores 8 marks in English.

Deduction 3: The marks in Physics being x, x, x and y and y being greater than x, can only mean that the value of x = 6 and y = 9. A quick trial and error shows us that no other value fits this constraint and hence we can put x = 6 and y = 9 in the table.

Deduction 4: Pragyan's rank in English is the same as Richa's rank in Chemistry – but we already know that Richa should be 4th in Chemistry. Hence, Pragyan would be 4th in English and would have scored 7 marks in that subject. Consequently Richa scored 9 marks in English and would have scored 1 mark in Chemistry. Also, since Pragyan and Qusum socred the same marks overall, Pragyan's total has to be 32 (we already know this by now). Thus, Pragyan scored 8 marks in Chemistry. The table gets completed with these deductions.

Deduction 5: We can now move onto thinking about the total payment to Anshuman and the tips he must have got. The total payment given to us is 25200 and out of that, he will receive 5000 × 4 = 20000 as his salary. Also, since 2 students have scored more than 30 marks in total, he will get a bonus of 2000 each for the two students – hence a bonus of 4000. This means that he gets a total of 1200 as tips. This means his tips are 500 + 500 + 200. So 3 people tipped Anshuman and Richa must have tipped 200. Amongst Pragyan and Qusum, one of them would have tipped him 500, the other would not have (interpretation of clue 8). Also, Sherry must have given the other 500 tip. We can now work out the answers from our table.

	Pragyan	Qusum	Richa	Sherry	Total Marks
Physics	9	6	6	6	27 y>x
Chemistry	8	9	1	8	26
Data Science	8	9	3	4	24 (a, b, c, d)
English	7	8	9	10	34 (10, 9, 8, 7)
Total	32	32	19 (lowest tip, 200)	28 (tip of 500)	111
	One of Pragyan/ Qusum tipped 500.				

6. Option (b) is correct.
7. Option (c) is correct.
8. Option (a) is correct.
9. Option (a) is correct.
10. 9. There are 9 instances of 8, 9 or 10 marks in the table, which would lead to an award of an A grade.

Questions 11 to 15:

In order to solve this set of questions, we need to identify the data structure. A few things you need to understand here from the given information:

(i) All the cricket players appear for both the tests, while the football players appear for either the Beep Test or the Yoyo test (in the ratio of 2:1).

(ii) From clue B, we realise that:
The number of football players who appear for Yoyo + The number of football players who appear for Beep = The number of cricket players who appear for Beep = The number of cricket players who appear for Yoyo.

(iii) Each player receives a grade of B,G,A or F based on their performance in the tests. At this stage, we can make a tabular structure to get a sense of the variables involved. Some clues used directly to fill the table to this point are:

- Clue F (0 for Football Best Yoyo; 0 for Cricket Fail Yoyo.
- Clue G (ratios of 3:5:2 and 3:7:4 for Yoyo and Beep test give 3n, 5n, 2n and 3m, 7m, 4m respectively as shown in the solution table 1. We can also see that the total cricket players should be 10n)
- Clue C tells us that the number of football players who failed in their respective tests are equal. If we take these as 'x' each, then we also get the value of cricket players who got an A grade in the Beep test as 2x. But we already know that number as 4m. Hence, x = 2m and the total number of football players who fail would be 4m. Also, clue H tells us that the number of cricket players who fail are 1/4th the number of football players who fail. At this stage, we can mark the number of cricket players who fail the beep test as m.
- Hence, the total number of cricket players would be 15m as also 10n. After all these deductions we get the solution table 1 shown here. This also tells us that the total number of football players who took the Beep test were 10m and the Yoyo test were 5m.
- There are 5 values that are not connected to this chain of values at this stage and are shown as a,b,c,d,e in our solution table 1.

SOLUTION TABLE 1:

	Yoyo Test				Totals
Grade→	B	G	A	F	
Cricket	3n	5n	2n	0 (Clue F)	10n
Football	0 (Clue F)	d	e	2m	5m
	Beep Test				
	B	G	A	F	
Cricket	3m	7m	4m	m	10n=15m
Football	a	b	c	2m	10m

From this point, the problem opens up the moment we use clue I. This clue tells us that the value of m + 2m (number of people who fail the beep test) is 60. Hence, we get m = 20 and are able to work out all the marked unknowns in our solution table 1. The following further deductions give us the complete table:

Deduction 1: Calculation for b: From Clue D, we know that of the players who cleared the Beep test, 45.45% got G grades. Since, 60 people have failed the Beep Test, it means that 440 people would have cleared it. 45.45% of 440 is 200. Hence, there were 200 players who got good grades in the Beep test. Out of this, we already know in our table, that the number of cricket players who got a good grade in the Beep test was 140. Hence, the value of b = 60.

Deduction 2: a + c = 100. Also, from Clue E, we have (60 + a)/(80 + c) = 5/7. Hence, a = 40, c = 60.

Deduction 3: d + e = 60. Also from Clue E, we can see that 90/(60 + e) = 9/11. Hence, e = 50 and d = 10. This completes our solution table 2 and we can then read off the answers from it.

Solution Table 2:

Yoyo Test					Totals
Grade→	B	G	A	F	
Cricket	90	150	60	0 (Clue F)	300
Football	0 (Clue F)	10 (#3)	50 (#3)	40	100
	Beep Test				
	B	G	A	F	
Cricket	60	140	80	20	300
Football	40 (#2)	60 (#1)	60 (#2)	40	200

11. Answer: 100. 40 + 40 + 20 = 100.
12. Answer: (d). We do not know how many cricket players are football players too. Hence, Option (d) is correct
13. Answer: 150. The number of cricket players who will get the best grade in at least 1 test, will be maximised if there are no cricket players who got the best grade in both tests. The value would be 90+60=150 in this case.
14. Answer: 190. There will be a total of 60 cricket players who got an average grade in both the tests, there will be 20 cricket players who got an average grade in only the Beep test, while there will be a total of 50 + 60 = 110 football players who got an average grade in either of the tests. The correct answer is 60 + 20 + 110 = 190.
15. Answer: 140. 90 + 50 = 140

Questions 16 to 20:

It is given to us that every conversion buys 1 unit each. That tells us that the total Revenue would be (Number of Conversions) × 150. The Cost of acquisition is given` to us as 20 × (number of Leads) + 60 × (conversions).

When you convert that bar graph into a table, these are the values which emerge.

	A (2019)	B (2019)	C (2019)	A (2020)	B (2020)	C (2020)	A (2021)	B (2021)	C (2021)
Lead	50		65	60	30		90	28	65
Conversions		25	10			15		18	30
	X (2019)	Y (2019)	Z (2019)	X (2020)	Y (2020)	Z (2020)	X (2021)	Y (2021)	Z (2021)
Revenue	1500	3750	1500				3300	2700	
Costs Incurred	1600	2300		4500	2100	2200	3120		3100

For A in 2019, It is given that X had revenues of 1500 that year. Hence, X must have sold 10 products and A's conversion rate would have been 20%.

If the conversions are 10, the total revenue of Company X (as A is the marketing agency for X) would be 10 × 150 = 1500, which is correct as can be seen in the table above. The cost incurred by X would be calculated as 20 × 50 + 60 × 10 = 1000 + 600 = 1600. (which matches the given numbers)

For Y, we know the total Cost incurred is 2300, and the conversions are 25. So 25 × 60 + x × 20 = 2300→ x = 40. Hence the number of leads for B in 2019 would be 40.

Similarly, the cost incurred for Z in 2019 would be 65 × 20 + 10 × 60 = 1900.

We can use this formula to fill the entire table, and after filling in the values, the tables would look like this:

	A (2019)	B (2019)	C (2019)	A (2020)	B (2020)	C (2020)	A (2021)	B (2021)	C (2021)
Lead	50	40	65	60	30	65	90	28	65
Conversions	10	25	10	55	25	15	22	18	30
Lost of Leads	40	15	55	5	5	50	68	10	35
Lead to Conversions	20.00%	62.50%	15.38%	91.67%	83.33%	23.08%	24.44%	64.29%	46.15%

	A (2019)	B (2019)	C (2019)	A (2020)	B (2020)	C (2020)	A (2021)	B (2021)	C (2021)
	X (2019)	Y (2019)	Z (2019)	X (2020)	Y (2020)	Z (2020)	X (2021)	Y (2021)	Z (2021)
Revenue	1500	3750	1500	8250	3750	2250	3300	2700	4500
Costs Incurred	1600	2300	1900	4500	2100	2200	3120	1640	3100
Proft	-100	1450	-400	3750	1650	50	180	1060	1400

16. As can be seen from the table, Company X's overall profit for the 3 years combined would be – 100 + 3750 + 180 = 3830
Company Y's overall proft would be 1450 + 1650 + 1060 = 4160 Company Z's Overall rofit would be – 400 + 50 + 1400 = 1050.
Hence option (b) is correct.
17. As calculated Above, Z has the least overall profit. Option (c) is correct.
18. Lost leads are calculated as Leads-conversions, As can be seen from the table, the highest lost leads are for Company A in 2021. Option (b) is correct.
19. As can be seen from the table, the highest lead to conversion ratio in 2021 is for company B = 64.28%. Option (c) is correct.
20. As can be seen from the table, NPM would be Profit/Revenue. The highest is for Company X in 2020.

	X (2019)	X (2019)	Z (2019)	X (2020)	Y (2020)	Z (2020)	X (2021)	Y (2021)	Z (2021)
Revenue	1500	3750	1500	8250	3750	2250	3300	2700	4500
Cost incure	1600	2300	1900	4500	2100	2200	3120	1640	3100
Proft	-100	1450	-400	3750	1650	50	180	1060	1400
	A (2019)	B (2019)	C (2019)	A (2020)	B (2020)	C (2020)	X (2021)	Y (2021)	Z (2021)
Lead	50	40	65	60	30	65	90	28	65
Conversions	10	25	10	55	25	15		18	30
Lost Leads	40	15	55	5	5	50	68	10	35
Lead to conversions	20.00%	62.50%	15.38%	91.67%	83.33%	23.08%	24.44%	64.29%	46.15%
NPM	-6.67%	38.67%	-26.67%	45.45%	44.00%	2.22%	5.45%	39.26%	31.11%

MOCK TEST PAPER 28

Questions 1 to 5:

We can make a solution table which can be filled first with the direct information from the clues. Note: From clue 6, we know that P is there on all 5 days, and hence we have shown him as part of days 2, 3, 4 and 5 (apart from day 1, which we were given about directly in clue 1). Also, we have put two customers on Day 5, as an interpretation of clue 5.

Day	People	Chit Amounts	Product of chits	Tip Amounts in ₹	Waiter
1	P, S, _	2, 3, 5	30	600	A
2	P, _, _, _	2, 11, 19, 17	7106	142120	B
3	Q, T, P	2, 11, 19	418	8360	D
4	P, _, _	2, 3, 19	114	2280	C
5	P, U	2, 17	34	680	E

From this point in the table, the following deductions will help us get to the complete solution:

Deduction 1: P is the only person present on all 5 days. The chit with the number 2 is the only chit that is present on all 5 days – hence P must have picked the chit with the number 2.

Deduction 2: We can next make out that the chit for U must have been 17, from the last day's chits. Hence, U must also be present on Day 2.

Deduction 3: 2,11 and 19 are commonly available on days 2 and 3 both. Hence, Q,T,P must be present on day 2 also (as they are present on day 3). However, you cannot make out the individual chit values of Q and T between 11 and 19. They will share those chits in some order.

Deduction 4: R must be present on day 1 & R and S must have shared the chits with 3 and 5 – we cannot find who had which chit amongst them.

Day	People	Chit Amounts	Product of chits	Tip Amounts in ₹	Waiter	Chit details
1	P,S,R	2,3,5	30	600	A	P (2);
2	P,Q,T,U	2,11,19,17	7106	142120	B	R/S(3/5) U(17);
3	P,Q,T	2,11,19	418	8360	D	Q/T
4	P,R/ S,Q/T	2,3,19	114	2280	C	(11/19)
5	P,U	2,17	34	680	E	

The answers can be read off this table:

1. Option (a) is correct.
2. Option (b) is correct.
3. According to the question, Q has a chit value of 19, and T has 11. In this case, if R had a chit value of 5, the product would be $2 \times 5 \times 11 \times 17$. So a product of 1870 is possible (though not necessary). If R has a chit of 3, then the total of the chits on day 2 would be $17 + 11 + 3 + 2 = 33$. So, statement 2 can also be true. Again we can see that the third statement can also be true, if R's chit is 3. Hence, option (c) is correct.
4. R has already gone on the first day. So, he must tip A. Also Q has definitely gone on days 2 and 3. Hence, R must definitely tip A, B and D. Hence, option (a) is correct.
5. Option (b) is correct.

Questions 6 to 10:

From Clues A & B, we can determine that the missing ratings in Privee have to be 'F'.

Further if we calculate the value of score with different weightages, we get the following table:

	0.1	0.2	0.3	0.4	0.5
100	10	20	30	40	50
80	8	16	24	32	40
60	6	12	18	24	30
40	4	8	12	16	20
0	0	0	0	0	0

If we look at the above table, then from clue B, we determine that the only score possible for Tamasha in DE & LC is 8, for 38Barracks in FQ & KC is 40 and for MyBarHQ in KC & DQ is 24.

From clue C, we can determine that Local had a rating of B in DQ, McDonalds had a D in KC.

Our final table for the above set would look as follows:

	FQ(0.5)	DE(0.2)	LC(0.1)	KC(0.4)	DQ(0.3)
Tamasha	A	D	B	D	C
McDonalds	B	F	D	D	A
GolaSizzlers	A	C	C	A	D
Local	D	B	A	B	B
Privee	F	A	D	F	A
MyBarHQ	C	B	D	C	B
Harlequin	B	C	C	B	C
38Barracks	B	D	A	A	C

Lets answer the questions:

6. 3
7. To determine this lets calculate the overall ratings for each restaurant:

	FQ(0.5)	DE(0.2)	LC(0.1)	KC(0.4)	DQ(0.3)	Overall
Tamasha	A-50	D-8	B-8	D-16	C-18	100
McDonalds	B-40	F-0	D-4	D-16	A-30	90
Gola Sizzlers	A-50	C-12	C-6	A-40	D-12	120
Local	D-20	B-16	A-10	B-32	B-24	102
Privee	F-0	A-20	D-4	F-0	A-30	54
MyBarHQ	C-30	B-16	D-4	C-24	B-24	98
Harlequin	B-40	C-12	C-6	B-32	C-18	108
38Barracks	B-40	D-8	A-10	A-40	C-18	116

From the above table, we can see that Gola Sizzlers got the maximum rating

8. Privee got the least rating.
9. Maximum difference = Highest rating – Lowest Rating
   $120 - 54 = 66$
10. Tamasha = 100
    Privee = 54
    Sum of ratings = 154

Questions 11 to 14:

We can make a table to reflect the information provided:

First fill in the basic information into the table – (shown with the legend #bi) in the table.

Next, fill out the directly deducible numbers once the basic information is put in. These are marked in the table with cells shown as (#1). Sample logic: Girls in Section 1 would be: Total section 1 students – boys in section 1 = 160 – 64 = 96.

Once, all the deducible information for (#1) is inserted into the table, we get the second set of deductions which are the numbers shown with cells marked as (#2) in the table. For instance, the total number of cricket players in Section 1 = Total number of cricket players – number of cricket players in section 2 and 3 = 379 – 80 – 195 = 104.

	Total Students	Boys	Girls	Football	Cricket
Section 1	160 (#bi)	40%= 64 (#bi)	160-64=96 (#1)	421-285-80=56 (#2)	379-80-195 = 104 (#2)
Section 2	160 (#bi)	50% = 80 (#bi)	160-80=80 (#1)	50%=80 (#bi)	160-80 = 80 (#1)
Section 3	480 (#bi)	336-80-64 = 192 (#2)	464-96-80 = 288 (#2)	59.375% = 285	480-285 = 195 (#1)
	800 (#bi)	42%=336 (#bi)	800-336=464 (#1)	52.625% = 421 (#bi)	800-421 = 379 (#1)

11. Option (a) is correct.
12. 56/160 = 35%. Option (a) is correct.
13. Answer: 42.
    If we have 54 girl cricket players in Section 1, then there will be 42 girl football players in that section. This means that there will be 56 – 42 = 14 boy football players in the section.
14. Answer: 59.83%
    If we have 70 boy football players, we will have 285 – 70 = 215 girl football players. Then, the number of girl cricket players = 288 – 215 = 73 and the number of boy cricket players = 192 – 70 = 122. Required ratio 73/122 = 59.83%

Questions 15 to 20:

We have the following set of data: Table 1:

	LR	VA	QA	Qualified or not
Palak	8/a	9/b	11/16	
Qadir	a/8	b/9	16/11	
Ritika	8/19	4/15	12/c	
Sagar	19/8	15/4	c/12	
Tanya	12/14	7/18	6/14	
Urvashi	14/12	18/7	14/6	
Vivek	14/5	d/e	6/f	Yes
Wriddhi	5/14	e/d	f/6	
Xavier	g/h	8/16	i	Yes
Yash	h/g	16/8	14	

The following series of deductions, helps us identify exact values in the problem:

Deduction 1: Since S,W and X score the same marks in QA, it means that one of this must be true: a) i = 6 = c; b) i = f = 12; c) i = f = c and equal to some number other than 6 or 12.

Also, from the last clue, we know that two of g/h/i are equal to 20 each. Also, the net score of X is 10 less than the composite score of Y. This leads to the following possibilities for X and Y's scores in LR, VA and QA:

Possibility 1: X: 20 + 8 + i, Y:20 + 16 + 14 (not possible, since in this case we get i=12, which means that X would not qualify as he scores less than 70% in two subjects).

Possibility 2: 20 + 16 + i, Y:20 + 8 + 14 (not possible since the value of i turns out negative in this case). Hence, it is not possible for X to score his 20 in LR. Thus, we can conclude the following:

Y=20, 16, 14 (composite score 70); Possible. X would need a sum of 60, in order to be 10 less than Y. Possible with 20 in QA and 8 in VA, 16 in LR

OR Y=20, 8, 14 (composite score 62); Possible. X would need a sum of 52, in order to be 10 less than Y. Possible with 20 in QA and 16 in VA, 8 in LR.

In either case, the missing values for S and W in QA are identified as 20 each and we also know the QA scores of R and V. Also, Yash would definitely qualify, since he scores more than X, and has at max one subject in which he is below 70%.

Deduction 2: Q's score in LR is 2 less than his score in QA. Hence, his score in LR would be either 14 or 9 (depending on whether he scores 16 or 11 in QA). Also, since V has qualified and he has scored only 6 in QA, his score in LR has to be 70% at least. This means that W has a score of 5 in LR.

Deduction 3: Clue (f) tells us that the sectional scores of P, S and X were the same in one or more sections. The possibilities at this stage of S's scores in various sections are: 8, 19, 5, 14. Also we know that he has a score of 20 in QA. X has scores of 8/16, 16/8 and 20 in LR, VA and QA respectively. So we need to think how we can meet this condition. If we try to make a score of 20 for QA equal for all three, we can see that P has either an 11 or 16 in QA and it is not possible to do this. This would mean that their scores are equal to 8 each in LR – as this is the only possibility that can meet this condition.

Deduction 4: From clue H, we can think of the possibilities for W,V and U's consecutive scores.

To do this, we know all possibilities for U's score. We can think about each of these possibilities and try to fit in how many realistic possibilities exist. The following thought structure ensues: U scores 14 in QA and this is the third consecutive score – then W and V should score 12 and 13 in LR/VA or the reverse. Not possible as W and V have scored 5 and 14 in LR.

Likewise, 16,17,18 is not possible (if U scores 18 in VA, there is no 16 or 17 in LR); So also 12, 13, 14 is not possible as well as 10, 11, 12 is not possible (with U as 14 or 12 in LR, as there is no 12/13 or 10/11 in QA for W and V).

Thus, the only possibility for the three consecutive numbers is: W 5 in LR, V 6 in QA and U 7 in VA.

Deduction 5: From Clue G's second part, we get that S would have scored 15 in VA (as giving him 4 in VA would not allow us to meet this clue). This means that R has a composite score of 54, but has not qualified, since she has less than 70% in two subjects. S has a composite score of 51, and he is eligible for selection as far as he is in the top 4.

We can now start looking at the composite scores. In that context, we know that X has qualified with a composite score of 52. V's score has to be below 52 and he has qualified. Also, since S has a composite score of 51, V's best possible score is 50. Hence, if V qualifies (given) S should also qualify. Thus, we know our fourth qualifier is S with 51 points. Thus, we know that P, Q, T, U and W would not have qualified along with R.

Deduction 6: T's possible combinations and their feasibility are: 12, 18, 6 Possible.; 12, 18, 14 (Not Possible, as she would qualify with this combination) ; 14, 18, 6 (Not Possible, as she would score 52); 14, 18, 14 (Not Possible, as she would qualify with this combination). Thus, T has scores of 12, 18, 6 in the three sections and U had scores of 14, 7, 14 for a composite score of 48 and 49 respectively. Consequently, V's VA score would be 16 and his composite score would be 50. W's VA score would be less than 18.

Also, we can see that we cannot determine the exact values of P, Q and W for their composite scores, since some of their values are not determinable.

TABLE 2

	LR	VA	QA	Qualified or not	Composite Score
Palak (P)	8 (#2)	9/b	11/16	No (#5)	Max 47 (#6)
Qadir (Q)	14/9 (#2)	b/9	16/11	No (#5)	Max 47 (#6)
Ritika	19 (#3)	4 (#5)	12 (#1)	No	54
Sagar	8 (#3)	15 (#5)	20 (#1)	Yes (#5)	51
Tanya	12 (#6)	18 (#4)	6 (#6)	No (#5)	48 (#6)
Urvashi	14 (#6)	7 (#4)	14 (#6)	No (#5)	49 (#6)
Vivek	14	16 (#6)	6 (#1)	Yes	50 (#6)
Wriddhi	5	<18	20 (#1)	No (#5)	Max 47 (#6)
Xavier	8/16 (#1). 8 after deduction (#3)	16/8 (#1). 16 after deduction (#3)	20	Yes	52 or 60 (#1). 52 after deduction (#3)
Yash	20	8/16 (#1). 8 after deduction (#3)	14	Yes (#1)	62 or 70 (#1). 62 after deduction (#3)

The answers can be read off from the table:

15. (d). Both 1 and 2 are true. Hence, option (d) is correct.
16. (a). The statement in option (b) is true – as Qadir's score has to be less than 48. If his score is above 48, then the minimum we need for him is 53, in which case he would qualify, which is not possible since we already know that he has not qualified. Statement in option (c) is also definitely true, as also the statement in option (d) is also necessarily true. Only the statement in option (a) is false. Hence, option (a) is the correct answer.
17. In the given condition, Qadir would have scored 16 in QA. Then he would have scored 14 in LR. Since, his maximum possible composite score is 47, it means that he can score at max 3 marks in VA.
18. We know from deduction 6, that Vivek scored 16 marks in VA. Hence, option (c) is correct.
19. We cannot determine the exact composite scores of these three. All we know is that they can reach a maximum of 47. Hence, option (d) is correct.
20. It is possible for the value of b to be greater than 15 (in case, Q has scores of 9 and 11 in LR and QA, his score in VA can go as high as 18). Likewise, the score of Wriddhi could also be greater than 15. Amongst P and Q, there are a maximum of two scores above 15. Amongst R and S, exactly 2, Amongst T& U, exactly 1; Amongst V & W at max 3; Amongst X & Y exactly 3. Hence, the correct answer is 11.

SECTION III

DATA INTERPRETATION FROM THE ARCHIVES

CAT EXAMINATION PAPERS

- CAT Paper 2022
  - Slot-1
  - Slot-2
  - Slot-3
- CAT Paper 2021
  - Slot-1
  - Slot-2
  - Slot-3

SLOT 1

CAT 2022

Directions for Questions 1 to 5

There are 15 girls and some boys among the graduating students in a class. They are planning a get-together, which can be either a 1-day event, or a 2-day event, or a 3-day event. There are 6 singers in the class, 4 of them are boys. There are 10 dancers in the class, 4 of them are girls. No dancer in the class is a singer.

Some students are not interested in attending the get-together. Those students who are interested in attending a 3-day event are also interested in attending a 2-day event; those who are interested in attending a 2-day event are also interested in attending a 1-day event. The following facts are also known:

I. All the girls and 80% of the boys are interested in attending a 1-day event. 60% of the boys are interested in attending a 2-day event.

II. Some of the girls are interested in attending a 1-day event, but not a 2-day event; some of the other girls are interested in attending both.

III. 70% of the boys who are interested in attending a 2-day event are neither singers nor dancers. 60% of the girls who are interested in attending a 2-day event are neither singers nor dancers.

IV. No girl is interested in attending a 3-day event. All male singers and 2 of the dancers are interested in attending a 3-day event.

V. The number of singers interested in attending a 2-day event is one more than the number of dancers interested in attending a 2-day event.

1. How many boys are there in the class?
2. Which of the following can be determined from the given information?
   I. The number of boys who are interested in attending a 1-day event and are neither dancers nor singers.
   II. The number of female dancers who are interested in attending a 1-day event.
   (a) Neither I nor II (b) Both I and II
   (c) Only I (d) Only II
3. What fraction of the class are interested in attending a 2-day event?
   (a) 7/10 (b) 9/13
   (c) 7/13 (d) 2/3
4. What BEST can be concluded about the number of male dancers who are interested in attending a 1-day event?
   (a) 5 or 6 (b) 4 or 6
   (c) 5 (d) 6
5. How many female dancers are interested in attending a 2-day event?
   (a) 0
   (b) 2
   (c) Cannot be determined
   (d) 1

Directions for Questions 6 to 10

Adhara, Bithi, Chhaya, Dhanavi, Esther, and Fathima are the interviewers in a process that awards funding for new initiatives. Every interviewer individually interviews each of the candidates individually and awards a token only if she recommends funding. A token has a face value of 2, 3, 5, 7, 11, or 13. Each interviewer awards tokens of a single face value only. Once all six interviews are over for a candidate, the candidate receives a funding that is ₹1000 times the product of the face values of all the tokens. For example, if a candidate has tokens with face values 2, 5, and 7, then they get a funding of ₹1000 × (2 × 5 × 7) = ₹70,000.

Pragnyaa, Qahira, Rasheeda, Smera, and Tantra were five candidates who received funding. The funds they received, in descending order, were ₹390,000, ₹210,000, ₹165,000, ₹77,000, and ₹66,000.

The following additional facts are known:

I. Fathima awarded tokens to everyone except Qahira, while Adhara awarded tokens to no one except Pragnyaa.

II. Rashida received the highest number of tokens that anyone received, but she did not receive one from Esther.

III. Bithi awarded a token to Smera but not to Qahira, while Dhanavi awarded a token to Qahira but not to Smera.

6. How many tokens did Qahira receive?
7. Who among the following definitely received a token from Bithi but not from Dhanavi?
(a) Qahira (b) Tantra
(c) Pragnyaa (d) Rasheeda
8. How many tokens did Chhaya award?
9. How many tokens did Smera receive?
10. Which of the following could be the amount of funding that Tantra received?
I. ₹ 66,000 II. ₹165,000
(a) Neither (I) nor (II)
(b) Only (I)
(c) Both (I) and (II)
(d) Only (II)

ANSWER KEY

1. 50 2. (d) 3. (c) 4. (a) 5. (a) 6. 2 7. (c)
8. 3 9. 3 10. (c)

SOLUTIONS

Solutions for Questions 1 to 5:
From the first paragraph, we can derive the following information:

	Boys	Girls	Total
Singers	4	2	6
Dancers	6	4	10
Total	10	6	16

Total Girls = 15
Let the total number of Boys be 100B.
From the descriptions in the question we can make out the following data structure for the situation:

	Girls				Boys			
	Singers (Total 2)	Dancers (Total 4)	Neither	Total	Singers (total 4)	Dancers (Total 6)	Neither	
Interested in No event	0	0	0	0	0 (clue 4)			10
Only 1 day event	T	W	G	X	0 (clue 4)	Q	R	
Only 2 day event	P	S	F	Y	0 (clue 4)	M	N	M + N
Only 3 day event	0 (clue 4)	0 (clue 4)	0 (clue 4)	0	4 (clue 4)	2 (clue 4)	A	6 + A

Notes to the values: X + Y = 15 (from clue 1); X > 0 and Y > 0 From clue 2.
L + M + N + 6 + A = 60B (from clue 1, second sentence)

The following deductions will help us fill the table:

Deductions for boys:

Deduction 1: M + 6 = 18B, N + A = 42B (from Clue 3, first sentence). From the basic information of the question, we know that the total of M + 6 cannot be more than 10 (since there are only 10 boy singers or dancers). Thus, we can work out the value of B as 0.5 and we can also work out that the number of boys must be 50. Also, M + 6 = 9 → M = 3; N + A = 21 → Total number of boys interested in 2-day events = 30 (these include boys interested in only 2-day event and boys interested in only 3-day event.)

Deduction 2: Also, Q + R = 10 since there are a total of 80% of the boys who are interested in attending 1-day event i.e. the total number of boys who are interested in attending only a 3-day event + number of boys interested in attending only a 2-day event + number of boys interested in attending only a 1 day event = 40. This also means that the number of boys

not interested in attending any event would be 20% of the boys = 10 boys.
However, we cannot make out the individual values of Q and R, since, we do not know whether the 6th dancer is actually a part of these 40 people or is outside them.

Deduction about the girls:

Deduction 3: Girl singers interested in attending only a 2-day event (P) will have to be 2, by an interpretation of clue 5. This is the only way to make the condition 'The number of singers interested in attending a 2-day event is one more than the number of dancers interested in attending a 2-day event' true. Hence, we will have to put T and S as 0 each. The value of W will become 4.

Deduction 4: The value of F has to be 3 (from clue 3's second statement), consequently Y becomes 5 (sum of P, S, F) and X would become 10. So, G = 6.

	GIRLS				BOYS			
	Singers (2)	Dancers (4)	Neither	Total	Singers (4)	Dancers (6)	Neither	
Interested in No event	0	0	0	0	0	1 or 0	9 or 10	10
Only 1 day event	0 (#3)	4 (#3)	6	10	0	Q (0 or 1)	R (10 or 9)	
Only 2 day event	2 (#3)	0 (#3)	3	5	0	3 (#1)	N	L + M + N
Only 3 day event	0 (clue 4)	0 (clue 4)	0 (clue 4)	0	4 (clue 4)	2 (clue 4)	A	6 + A

We can read off the answers from the table.

1. There are 50 boys in all.
2. Only II can be determined. Option (d) is correct.
3. 35 out of 65 = 7/13. Option (c) is correct.
4. 2 + 3 + 0/1 = 5 or 6. Option (a) is correct.
5. 0. Option (a) is correct.

Solutions for Questions 6 to 10:
According to the information given to us, we can find out the tokens for different amounts as:

₹390,000 = 2 × 3 × 5 × 13 (number of tokens 4)
₹210,000 = 2 × 3 × 5 × 7 (number of tokens 4)
₹165,000 = 3 × 5 × 11 (number of tokens 3)
₹77,000 = 7 × 11 (number of tokens 2)
₹66,000 = 2 × 3 × 11 (number of tokens 3)

Token Value	Quantity
2	3
3	4
5	3
7	2
11	3
13	1
Total tokens given	6

Using the information above and the ones given to us in form of clues and also using the deductions explained below, we can formulate the table as given below.

Deduction 1: Apart from the directly given information in the clues, we can also deduce from clue 2, that Rashida must have received 4 tokens and these must be from Bithi, Chayya and Dhanavi apart from Fathima.

Deduction 2: Adhara has handed out only 1 token and since it is given to us that every interviewer gives only 1 kind of token, it follows that Adhara would have given out the tokens of value 13. Also, since Fathima has handed out 4 tokens, the value of the tokens handed out by her have to be necessarily 3 each.

Deduction 3: At this stage we know that Pragnyaa has received a token from Adhara as well as from Fathima. Hence, she has received the 13 and 3 tokens. Funding of 390000 is the only possible value which is feasible for her. Also, funding for Qahira has to be necessarily 77000 (since she has received a token neither from Fathima nor from Adhara, meaning she has not received either the token of value 3 or of value 13. 7 × 11 is the only combination that is feasible for her,

Deduction 4: Rashida has received 4 tokens and must have received a funding of 210000, with token values of 2, 3, 5 and 7. This is so, because the only other combination of maximum number of 4 tokens is for funding of 390000, which is already fixed for Pragnyaa in our value chain.

Deduction 5: From the deduction about 210000, we can make out that the tokens for Bithi, Chhaya and Dhanavi are between 2, 5, 7. This means that Esther must have a token of 11. Consequently, from Qahira's funding of 77000, we can make out that Dhanavi. Must have handed out the value 7 tokens.

Deduction 6: Pragnyaa must have received tokens from Bithi and Chhaya, who would have shared the 2 and 5 value tokens in random order.

Deduction 7: At this point, we also know that Smera receives a token from Bithi and Bithi has also given tokens to Rashida (deduction 1) and Pragnyaa (deduction 6). Hence, Bithi would not give a token to Tantra. Also, since Smera and Tantra have to share funding of 66000 and 165000 in some order. Hence, they would have got tokens from 3 interviewers each.

	Pragnyaa	Qahira	Rashida	Smera	Tantra	No of Tokens	Value of Token
Adhara	Y	N	N	N	N	1	13 (#2)
Bithi	Y (#6)	N	Y (#1)	Y	N (#7)	3	2/5 (#6)
Chayya	Y (#6)	N (#5)	Y (#1)	N (#7)	Y (#7)	3	5/2 (#6)
Dhanavi	N (#5)	Y	Y (#1)	N	N (#5)	2	7 (#5)
Esther	N	Y (#5)	N	Y (#5)	Y (#5)	3	11 (#5)
Fathima	Y	N	Y	Y	Y	4	3 (#2)
Amount Received	390000 (#3)	77000 (#3)	210000 (#4)	66000/165000	165000/66000		

Using the above table, we can answer the given questions:

6. Ans: 2
7. Ans: C
8. Ans: 3
9. Ans: 3
10. Ans: C

SLOT 2

CAT 2022

Directions for Questions 1 to 5

A few salesmen are employed to sell a product called TRICCEK among households in various housing complexes. On each day, a salesman is assigned to visit one housing complex. Once a salesman enters a housing complex, he can meet any number of households in the time available. However, if a household makes a complaint against the salesman, then he must leave the housing complex immediately and cannot meet any other household on that day. A household may buy any number of TRICCEK items or may not buy any item. The salesman needs to record the total number of TRICCEK items sold as well as the number of households met in each day. The success rate of a salesman for a day is defined as the ratio of the number of items sold to the number of households met on that day. Some details about the performances of three salesmen - Tohri, Hokli and Lahur, on two particular days are given below.

I. Over the two days, all three of them met the same total number of households, and each of them sold a total of 100 items.
II. On both days, Lahur met the same number of households and sold the same number of items.
III. Hokli could not sell any item on the second day because the first household he met on that day complained against him.
IV. Tohri met 30 more households on the second day than on the first day.
V. Tohri's success rate was twice that of Lahur's on the first day, and it was 75% of Lahur's on the second day.

1. What was the total number of households met by Tohri, Hokli and Lahur on the first day?
2. How many TRICCEK items were sold by Tohri on the first day?
3. How many households did Lahur meet on the second day?
   (a) 20 or less (b) between 21 and 29
   (c) between 30 and 35 (d) more than 35
4. How many households did Tohri meet on the first day?
   (a) more than 40 (b) 10 or less
   (c) between 11 and 20 (d) between 21 and 40
5. Which of the following statements is FALSE?
   (a) Among the three, Tohri had the highest success rate on the first day.
   (b) Tohri had a higher success rate on the first day compared to the second day.
   (c) Among the three, Lahur had the lowest success rate on the first day.
   (d) Among the three, Tohri had the highest success rate on the second day.

Directions for Questions 6 to 10

The two plots below show data for four companies code-named A, B, C, and D over three years - 2019, 2020, and 2021.

The first plot shows the revenues and costs incurred by the companies during these years. For example, in 2021, company C earned ₹100 crores in revenue and spent ₹30 crores. The profit of a company is defined as its revenue minus its costs.

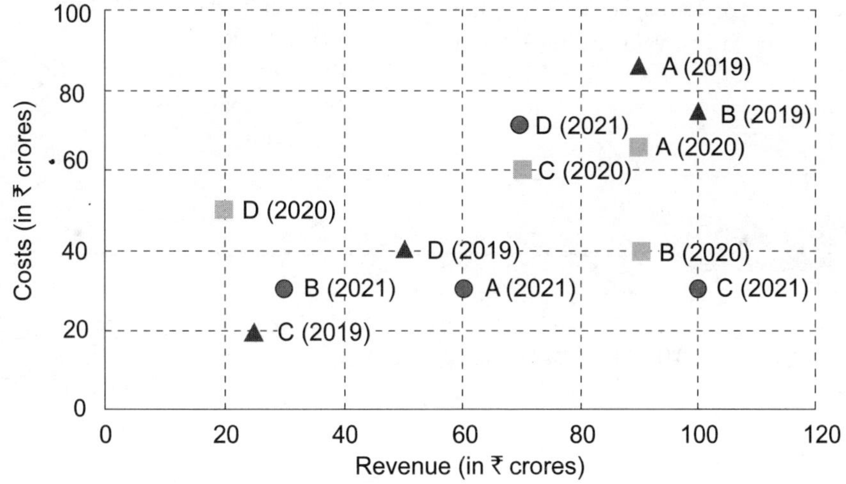

The second plot shows the number of employees employed by the company (employee strength) at the start of each of these three years, as well as the number of new employees hired each year (new hires). For example, Company B had 250 employees at the start of 2021, and 30 new employees joined the company during the year.

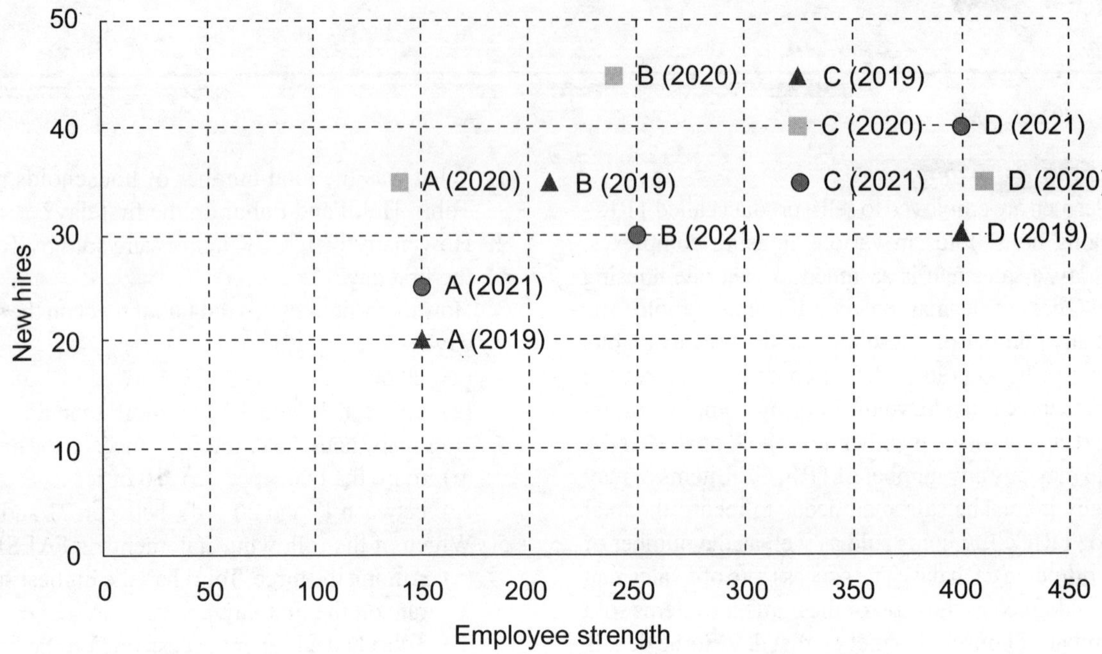

6. Considering all three years, which company had the highest annual profit?
   (a) Company C
   (b) Company B
   (c) Company A
   (d) Company D
7. Which of the four companies experienced the highest annual loss in any of the years?
   (a) Company D
   (b) Company C
   (c) Company A
   (d) Company B
8. The ratio of a company's annual profit to its annual costs is a measure of its performance. Which of the four companies had the lowest value of this ratio in 2019?
   (a) Company A
   (b) Company B
   (c) Company C
   (d) Company D
9. The total number of employees lost in 2019 and 2020 was the least for:
   (a) Company A
   (b) Company C
   (c) Company B
   (d) Company D
10. Profit per employee is the ratio of a company's profit to its employee strength. For this purpose, the employee strength in a year is the average of the employee strength at the beginning of that year and the beginning of the next year. In 2020, which of the four companies had the highest profit per employee?
   (a) Company B
   (b) Company A
   (c) Company D
   (d) Company C

ANSWER KEY

1. 84	2. 40	3. (b)	4. (b)	5. (d)	6. (a)	7. (a)
8. (a)	9. (b)	10. (a)				

SOLUTIONS

Solutions for Questions 1 to 5:

From the information given to us, we can deduce the following:

Triccek Sold

	Day 1	Day 2	Total
Tohri	a	100 – a	100
Hokli	100	0	100
Lahur	50	50	100

Households Visited

	Day 1	Day 2	Total
Tohri	x – 15	x + 15	2x
Hokli	2x – 1	1	2x
Lahur	x	x	2x

For day 1:

Success rate of Tohri = 2 × Success rate of Lahur →

$$\frac{a}{(x-15)} = 2 \times \frac{50}{x} \quad \text{———— (1)}$$

& For day 2 Success rate of Tohri= 0.75 × Success rate of Lahur:

$$\frac{(100-a)}{(x+15)} = 0.75 \times \frac{50}{x} \quad \text{———— (2)}$$

We have 2 variable, 2 equations. On solving the 2 equations we get, $a = 40$ and $x = 25$.

Our final tables would look as follows:

Triccek Sold

	Day 1	Day 2	Total
Tohri	40	60	100
Hokli	100	0	100
Lahur	50	50	100

Households Visited

	Day 1	Day 2	Total
Tohri	10	40	50
Hokli	49	1	50
Lahur	x	x	50

Using the above tables we can answer the questions given to us.

1. Total households visited = 10 + 49 + 25 = 84.
2. Tohri sold 40 items on the first day.
3. He met 25 households on the second day. Hence, option (b) is correct.
4. He met 10 households on the first day. Hence, option (b) is correct.
5. The statements in options (a), (b) and (c) can all be seen to be true. The statement in option (d) is false, as we can see that Tohri's success rate on the second day was not the highest amongst the three – as Lahur had a higher success rate on the second day than Tohri. Hence, option (d) is correct.

Solutions for Questions 6 to 10:

The data given in the charts can be noted in a tabular form as follows:

2019

		Revenue	Cost	Profit/ Loss	Employee Strength	New Hires
A	2019	90	85	5	150	20
	2020	90	65	25	140	35
	2021	60	30	30	150	25
B	2019	100	75	25	210	35
	2020	90	40	50	240	45
	2021	30	30	0	250	30
C	2019	25	20	5	325	45
	2020	70	60	10	325	40
	2021	100	30	70	325	35
D	2019	50	40	10	400	30
	2020	20	50	–30	410	35
	2021	70	70	0	400	40

Using this table we can answer the questions given to us.

6. Total profit of company A = 5 + 25 + 30 = 60
   Total profit of company B = 25 + 50 + 0 = 75
   Total profit of company C = 5 + 10 + 70 = 85
   Total profit of company D = 10 – 30 + 0 = -20
   Highest total profit was achieved by Company C. Hence, Option (a) is the correct Answer.
7. Company D was the only company to experience a loss in 2020. Hence, Option (a) is the correct answer.
8. Performance Ratio = Annual Profit/Annual Cost
   Ratio for Company A = 5/85 = 0.0588
   Ratio for Company B = 25/75 = 0.333
   Ratio for Company C = 5/20 = 0.25
   Ratio for Company D = 10/40 = 0.25

We can see that Company A had the lowest ratio in the year 2019. Hence, Option (a) is the correct answer.

9. Company A had 150 employees at the start of 2019 and it hired 20 new people. So in 2020 the total should have been 170 at the start of the year but it is only 140. This happened because 30 employees left in 2019. This figure for 2020 for company A is 25. Similarly, we can find the figures for the remaining companies

	Employees who left in 2019	Employees who left in 2020	Total
Company A	30	25	55
Company B	5	35	40
Company C	45	40	85
Company D	20	45	65

From the above table it is clear that Option (b) is the correct answer.

10. Year 2020

Profit per Employee for Company A = 25/145
Profit per Employee for Company B = 50/245
Profit per Employee for Company C = 10/325
Since company D made a loss in 2020, we need not calculate this value for D.
From the above calculations it is clear that Company B had the highest profit per employee.
Hence, Option (a) is the correct answer.

SLOT 3

CAT 2022

Directions for Questions 1 to 5

There are only four neighbourhoods in a city - Levmisto, Tyhrmisto, Pesmisto and Kitmisto. During the onset of a pandemic, the number of new cases of a disease in each of these neighbourhoods was recorded over a period of five days. On each day, the number of new cases recorded in any of the neighbourhoods was either 0, 1, 2 or 3.

The following facts are also known:

I. There was at least one new case in every neighbourhood on Day 1.

II. On each of the five days, there were more new cases in Kitmisto than in Pesmisto.

III. The number of new cases in the city in a day kept increasing during the five-day period. The number of new cases on Day 3 was exactly one more than that on Day 2.

IV. The maximum number of new cases in a day in Pesmisto was 2, and this happened only once during the five-day period.

V. Kitmisto is the only place to have 3 new cases on Day 2.

VI. The total numbers of new cases in Levmisto, Tyhrmisto, Pesmisto and Kitmisto over the five-day period were 12, 12, 5 and 14 respectively.

1. What BEST can be concluded about the total number of new cases in the city on Day 2?
   (a) Either 6 or 7
   (b) Exactly 8
   (c) Exactly 7
   (d) Either 7 or 8
2. What BEST can be concluded about the number of new cases in Levmisto on Day 3?
   (a) Exactly 3
   (b) Either 2 or 3
   (c) Exactly 2
   (d) Either 0 or 1
3. On which day(s) did Pesmisto not have any new case?
   (a) Only Day 3
   (b) Only Day 2
   (c) Both Day 2 and Day 4
   (d) Both Day 2 and Day 3
4. Which of the two statements below is/are necessarily false?
   Statement A: There were 2 new cases in Tyhrmisto on Day 3.
   Statement B: There were no new cases in Pesmisto on Day 2.
   (a) Statement B only
   (b) Both Statement A and Statement B
   (c) Statement A only
   (d) Neither Statement A nor Statement B
5. On how many days did Levmisto and Tyhrmisto have the same number of new cases?
   (a) 4 (b) 5
   (c) 3 (d) 2

Directions for Questions 6 to 10

In the following, a year corresponds to 1st of January of that year.

A study to determine the mortality rate for a disease began in 1980. The study chose 1000 males and 1000 females and followed them for forty years or until they died, whichever came first. The 1000 males chosen in 1980 consisted of 250 each of ages 10 to less than 20, 20 to less than 30, 30 to less than 40, and 40 to less than 50. The 1000 females chosen in 1980 also consisted of 250 each of ages 10 to less than 20, 20 to less than 30, 30 to less than 40, and 40 to less than 50.

The four figures below depict the age profile of those among the 2000 individuals who were still alive in 1990, 2000, 2010, and 2020. The dark grey bars in each figure represent the number of males in each age group at that point in time; while the light grey bars represent the number of females in each age group at that point in time. The numbers next to the bars give the exact numbers being represented by the bars. For example, we know that 230 males among those tracked and who were alive in 1990 were aged between 20 and 30.

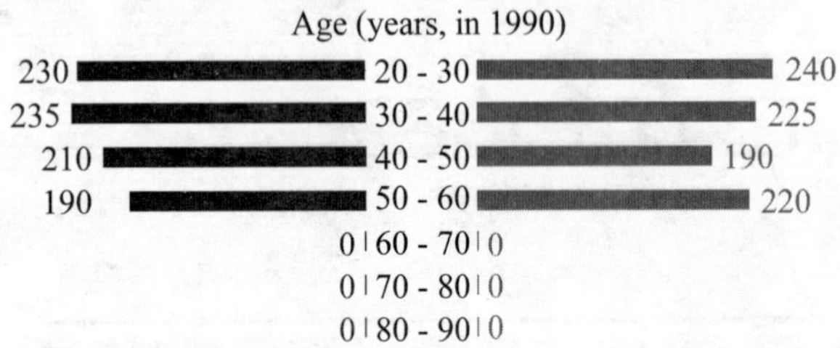

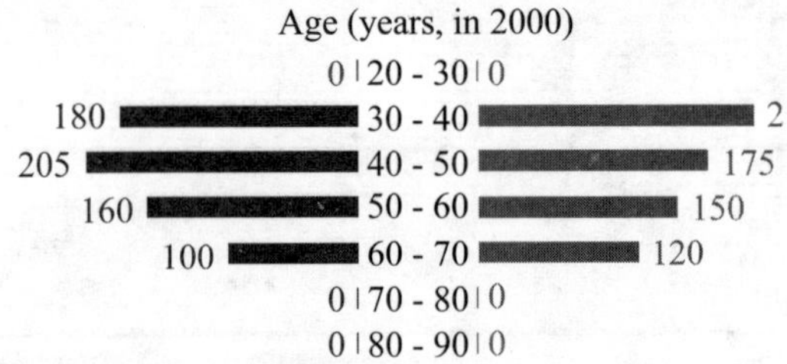

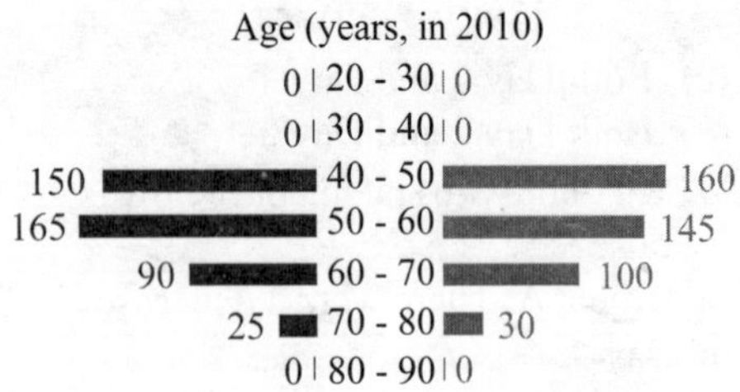

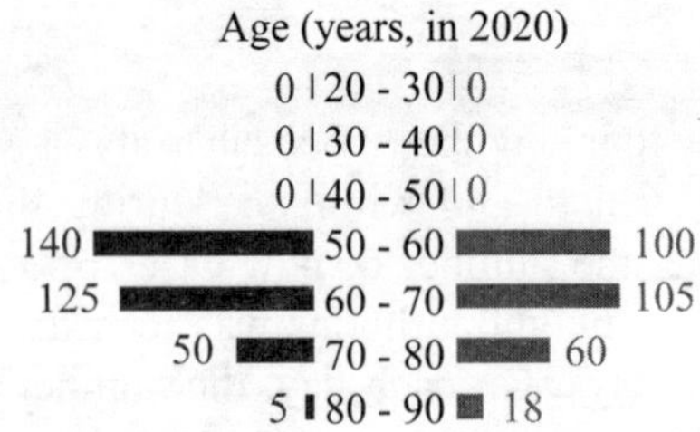

6. In 2000, what was the ratio of the number of dead males to dead females among those being tracked?
   (a) 109 : 107 (b) 129 : 131
   (c) 71 : 69 (d) 41 : 43
7. How many people who were being tracked and who were between 30 and 40 years of age in 1980 survived until 2010?
   (a) 90 (b) 190
   (c) 110 (d) 310
8. How many individuals who were being tracked and who were less than 30 years of age in 1980 survived until 2020?
   (a) 470 (b) 580
   (c) 240 (d) 230
9. How many of the males who were being tracked and who were between 20 and 30 years of age in 1980 died in the period 2000 to 2010?
10. How many of the females who were being tracked and who were between 20 and 30 years of age in 1980 died between the ages of 50 and 60?

ANSWER KEY

1. (b) 2. (a) 3. (a) 4. (b) 5. (b) 6. (c) 7. (b)
8. (a) 9. 40 10. 30

SOLUTIONS

Solutions for Questions 1 to 5:

From the information given to us, we can deduce the following table:

	Levmisto	Tyhrmisto	Pesmisto	Kitmisto	Total
Day 1	> = 1	> = 1	> = 1	> = 2	> = 5
Day 2	not (3)	not (3)	not (3)	3	x
Day 3					x + 1
Day 4					Y (more than x + 1)
Day 5	= < 3	= < 3	= < 2	= < 3	= < 11
Total	12	12	5	14	43

From this point the following deductions will lead us to the answers:

Deduction 1: The total of Kitmisto of 14, which can only be achieved if we use four 3's and one 2. Likewise, for Pesmisto, the total of 5 (with one instance of 2) can only be achieved if we use one 2, three 1's and one 0.

Deduction 2: The minimum number of cases on day 1 is 5, the maximum number of cases on day 5 is 11 (since Pesmisto cannot have a 3, even if we put 3's in all the other neighbourhoods, the total can at max be 11.

Deduction 3: From this point, let us try to think about what value/s can fit into the total cases for day 1. If there are 7 cases on day 1, the minimum total of the 5 days would be 7 + 8 + 9 + 10 + 11 = 45 (hence, 7 is not possible on day 1 and neither is anything more than that). Next, if we try to fit in 6 in the day 1 total, with an increasing trend, if we try 6 + 7 + 8 + 9 + 11 = 41 (2 short); 6 + 8 + 9 + 10 + 11 = 44 (1 more than 43). Hence, we can rule out 6 as day 1's total. This leaves us with 5 as day 1's total and the number of cases in the four neighbourhoods has to be 1, 1, 1, 2 (2 in Kitmitso).

Deduction 4: 5 + 6 + 7 + 8 + 9 gives us a total of 35. We need to increase it to 43. The only way to do it is 5 + 8 + 9 + 10 + 11 (by increasing each of the 2nd to 5th day by 2 each).

Deduction 5: Pesmisto will need to have it's 2 on day 5. Thus, Pesmisto cannot have a 2 on day 2. So, on day 2, the total of 8 – can only be made using 2 + 2 + 1 + 3. Levmisto and Tyhrmisto can only have 3's on day 3 – 4 – 5 to get to their respective totals of 12. Likewise, since the 2 of Kitmisto has been used on day 1, the remaining days for Kitmisto would be 3 each. The table completes as shown:

	Levmisto	Tyhrmisto	Pesmisto	Kitmisto	Total
Day 1	1	1	1	2	5
Day 2	2	2	1	3	8
Day 3	3	3	0	3	9
Day 4	3	3	1	3	10
Day 5	3	3	2	3	11
Total	12	12	5	14	43
	3, 3, 3, 2, 1	3, 3, 3, 2, 1	2, 1, 1, 1, 0	3, 3, 3, 3, 2	

We can use the table to answer the questions given to us.

1. We can see that the number of new cases on day 2 are exactly 8. Option (b) is correct.
2. Exactly 3. Option (a) is correct.
3. Day 3. Option (a) is correct.
4. Both the statements are necessarily false. Option (b) is correct.
5. On all five days their cases were equal. Option (b) is correct.

Solutions for Questions 6 to 10:

6. From the graph for 2000, we see that
   Total males who were alive = 180 + 205 + 160 + 100 = 645
   Total females who were alive = 210 + 175 + 150 + 120 = 655
   Therefore, the ratio for dead males to dead females = 355/345 = 71/69
   Hence Option (c) is the correct answer.
7. People who were under the bracket of 30–40 years in 1980, would be under the bracket of 60–70 years in 2010. We can see that in 2010, the number of men alive is 90, while the number of women alive is 100. So, 90 + 100 = 190 people were alive. Hence, Option (b) is the correct answer.
8. There were a total of 250 + 250 + 250 + 250 = 1000 individuals between 10 to 30 in 1980. In 2020 these people will be in the age group of 50–70. There are a total of 140 + 125 + 100 + 105 = 470 individuals who would have survived till 2020. Hence, Option (a) is the correct answer.
9. Males who were between 20 to 30 in 1980, would be 40 to 50 in 2000. We can see that in 2000, 205 males in that age group are alive. In 2010, these people would have moved to the age group of 50 to 60 and we can see that in males in 50–60 in 2010, there are a total of 165 people alive. This means that a total of 205 – 165 = 40 males from that age group died in the period 2000 to 2010. Hence, the correct answer is 40.
10. Females who were aged between 20–30 years in 1980 would have come in the category of 50–60 years in the year 2010. So, a total of 30 females died in that age group. Hence, the answer is 30.

SLOT 1

CAT 2021

Directions for Questions 1 to 4

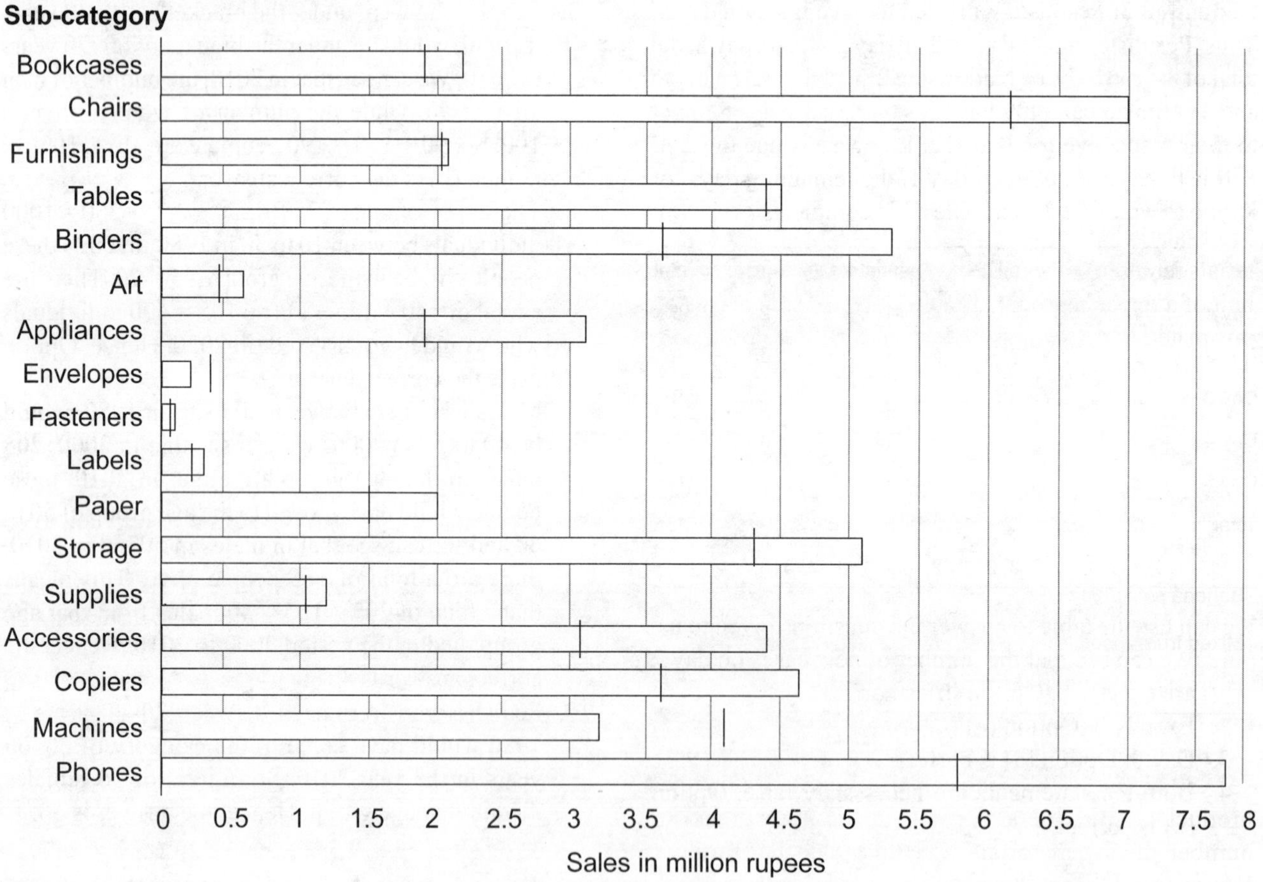

The horizontal bars in the above diagram represent 2020 aggregate sales (in ₹ million) of a company for the different subcategories of its products. The top four product subcategories (Bookcases, Chairs, Furnishings, Tables) belong to furniture product category; the bottom four product subcategories (Accessories, Copiers, Machines, Phones) belong to the technology product category while all other product subcategories belong to the office supply product category. For each of the product subcategories, there is a vertical line indicating the sales of the corresponding subcategory in 2019.

1. The total sales (in ₹ million) in 2019 from products in office supplies category is closest to
   (a) 16.5
   (b) 12.5
   (c) 18.0
   (d) 13.5
2. The percentage increase in sales in Furniture category from 2019 to 2020 is closest to
   (a) 1%
   (b) 8%
   (c) 20%
   (d) 25%

3. How many subcategories had sales of ₹4 million or more in 2019 and registered an increase in sales in excess of 25% in 2020?
4. The improvement index for a category is the maximum percentage increase in sales from 2019 to 2020 among any of its subcategories. The correct order of categories in increasing order of this improvement index is
   (a) office supply, technology, furniture
   (b) technology, furniture, office supply
   (c) office supply, furniture, technology
   (d) furniture, technology, office supply

Directions for Questions 5 to 10

Ganga, Kaveri, and Narmada are three women who buy four raw materials (Mango, Apple, Banana and Milk) and sell five finished products (Mango smoothie, Apple smoothie, Banana smoothie, Mixed fruit smoothie and Fruit salad). Table-1 gives information about the raw materials required to produce the five finished products. One unit of a finished product requires one unit of each of the raw materials mentioned in the second column of the table.

TABLE-1

Finished product	Raw materials required
Mango smoothie	Mango, Milk
Apple smoothie	Apple, Milk
Banana smoothie	Banana, Milk
Mixed fruit smoothie	Mango, Apple, Banana, Milk
Fruit salad	Mango, Apple, Banana

One unit of milk, mango, apple, and banana cost ₹5, ₹3, ₹2, and ₹1 respectively. Each unit of a finished product is sold for a profit equal to two times the number of raw materials used to make that product. For example, apple smoothie is made with two raw materials (apple and milk) and will be sold for a profit of ₹4 per unit. Leftover raw materials are sold during the last business hour of the day for a loss of ₹1 per unit.

The amount, in rupees, received from sales (revenue) for each woman in each of the four business hours of the day is given in Table-2.

TABLE-2

Business Hour	Ganga	Kaveri	Narmada
Hour 1	23	19	31
Hour 2	21	22	21
Hour 3	29	30	23
Hour 4 (last hour)	30	27	22

The following additional facts are known.

I. No one except possibly Ganga sold any Mango smoothie.
II. Each woman sold either zero or one unit of any single finished product in any hour.
III. Each woman had exactly one unit each of two different raw materials as leftovers.
IV. No one had any banana leftover.

5. What BEST can be concluded about the number of units of fruit salad sold in the first hour?
   (a) Either 0 or 1 or 2.
   (b) Exactly 1.
   (c) Exactly 2.
   (d) Either 1 or 2.
6. Which of the following is NECESSARILY true?
   (a) Narmada sold one unit of leftover milk.
   (b) Kaveri sold one unit of leftover mangoes.
   (c) Ganga did not sell any leftover apples.
   (d) Ganga did not sell any leftover mangoes.
7. What BEST can be concluded about the total number of units of milk the three women had in the beginning?
   (a) Either 18 or 19 or 20 units.
   (b) Either 17 or 18 or 19 units.
   (c) Either 19 or 20 units.
   (d) Either 18 or 19 units.
8. If it is known that three leftover units of mangoes were sold during the last business hour of the day, how many apple smoothies were sold during the day?

ANSWER KEY

1. (d) 2. (b) 3. 1 4. (d) 5. (d) 6. (c) 7. (a)
8. 6

SOLUTIONS

Solutions for Questions 1 to 4:

1. Sales of 2019 is represented by the vertical line in the graph. The addition of 3.6 (binders); 0.4 (Art); 1.9 (Appliances); 0.3 (Envelopes); 0.15 (Fasteners); 0.3 (Labels); 1.5 (Paper); 4.3 (Storage) and 1.1 (Supplies) gets us a value of 13.5 approximately. Option (d) is correct.
2. Sales in 2019 in Furniture Category = 14.5
   Sales in 2020 in Furniture Category = 15.7
   Percentage increase = 8% (approximately). Option (b) is correct.
3. A total of 5 categories had sales of more than 4 Million in 2019. Out of these 5 only 1 (phones) registered a growth in excess of 25%. Hence, the answer is 1
4. The Furniture Category showed the least growth (Approximately 8% as calculated for the second question of this set). Meanwhile, the Office Supply category has grown from 13.5 to approximately 18, which is a growth of about 33.33% and is the maximum growth from 2019 to 2020 for any of the three categories. We can confirm that Technology product category grows by more than 8% but less than 33% Hence the correct answer is Option (d).

Solutions for Questions 5 to 8:

Cost of mango, apple , Banana and milk is given as ₹3, 2, 1 and 5 respectively.

From the information given to us, we can calculate the CP & SP of the goods sold by the three people. The logic given to us to do so, is that the profit value is twice the number of raw materials used to make the product. For instance, Mango Smoothie (MS), Banana Smoothie (BS) and Apple Smoothie (AS) are all made from two raw materials. Hence, the profit amount on those products would be ₹4 each. Mixed fruit smoothie is made out of 4 raw materials and hence the profit for it would be ₹8 and for fruit salad it would be ₹6. The cost price, profit and selling price for each of the five products can be tabulated as shown.

	Cost Price	Profit	Selling Price
Mango Smoothie (MS)	8	4	12
Apple Smoothie (AS)	7	4	11
Banana Smoothie (BS)	6	4	10
Mixed Fruit Smoothie (MFS)	11	8	19
Fruit Salad (FS)	6	6	12

Once we have these values tabulated, we can think of the hourly sales revenue for each woman – and come up with the table shown for the first 3 hours. To do so, we use the information that each finished product had a sale of zero or one unit in any hour for each woman (Clue 2). Also, we use the information that Mango Smoothie can be sold only by Ganga – and not Kaveri or Narmada (Clue 1).

TABLE OF PRODUCTS (INCLUDING POSSIBLE COMBINATIONS) FOR FIRST 3 HOURS

	Ganga	Kaveri	Narmada
Hour 1	AS + (FS/MS)	MFS	MFS + FS
Hour 2	AS + BS	FS + BS	AS + BS
Hour 3	BS + MFS	AS + MFS	FS + AS
Final Hour	30	27	22

There will be a set of 9 deductions to arrive at the table. I will now explain the hour 1 deductions for you.

Deductions for Hour 1: Ganga earns ₹23. This is only possible through a combination sale of 12 + 11. The 11 rupee product is only AS. The 12 rupee product for Ganga could be a FS/MS. The 19 rupees earned by Kaveri in hour 1 can only be through a sale of a MFS. Narmada's 31 can only be created using a 19 + 12 structure. Also, since she cannot sell MS, her 12 rupee revenue would be received by selling a FS. Hence, Narmada would have sold 1 unit of MFS and 1 unit of FS in the first hour.

I would encourage you to make similar deductions for the other two hours to complete the table.

For the analysis of the fourth hour, we need to see the possibility of earning the revenues mentioned by including a combination of two raw materials sold as left overs at 1 rupee below their cost price. Also we know from clue 4 that there was no banana leftover.

Hence, we can have Mango + apple, Mango + Milk, Apple + Milk as leftovers. The amount received from these combinations is ₹3, 6 and 5 respectively. We would need to see which combination of leftover sale is possible for each woman to justify the revenue she earns in the fourth hour and also, what are the products sold by her. The following deductions lead to the table shown:

Deduction1: Since Narmada earned 22 rupees in the last hour, this is only possible if she earned 19 (1 unit of MFS sale) + 3 (by selling leftover 1 unit mango + 1 unit apple). Note that it is not possible for Narmada to sell Mango + Milk or Apple + Milk as leftovers, as those combinations would not justify the ₹22 she earns in that hour.

Deduction 2: Since Ganga earned 30 rupees in the last hour, this is only possible if she earned 24 (1 unit of MS + 1 unit FS sale) + 6 (by selling leftover 1 unit mango + 1 unit milk). Note that it is not possible for her to sell Mango + Apple or Apple + Milk as leftovers, as those combinations would not justify the ₹30 she earns in that hour.

Deduction 3: Since Kaveri earned 27 rupees in the last hour, this is possible if she earned 22 (Product sale of BS + FS) + 5 (by selling leftover 1 unit Milk + 1 unit apple) OR if she earned 21 (Product sale of AS + BS) + 6 (by selling leftover 1 unit Milk + 1 unit mango). Note that it is not possible for Kaveri to sell Mango + Apple as leftover, as we cannot create a structure of 24 (product sale) + 3 (leftover sale) for her. These deductions can be tabulated as shown in the table for the 4th hour.

TABLE FOR THE 4th HOUR:

Last Hour	₹3 (Mango + Apple)	₹6 (Mango + Milk)	₹5 (Apple + Milk)
Ganga (₹30)	Not possible	MS + FS	Not Possible
Kaveri (₹27)	Not Possible	AS + BS	BS + FS
Narmada (₹22)	MFS	Not possible	Not possible

From the above tables, we can answer the questions.

5. In the first hour, Ganga might have sold 1 unit FS plus Narmada definitely sold 1 unit of FS. Hence, the number of units of FS in hour 1 is 1 or 2. Option (d) is correct.
6. Option (c) necessarily true.
7. 1 unit of milk is required for any product except fruit salad. There are 16 definite instances of product sales other than FS in the 4 hours (To count this we have assumed Ganga sold a FS in the first hour and Kaveri sold a FS in the 4th hour). Also, each of Ganga and Kaveri definitely sold 1 unit of milk in the last hour as leftover. Thus, the minimum count of milk they should have had at the start is 18. Besides, it is possible that Ganga in the first hour sold a MS instead of a FS. Likewise, it is also possible that Kaveri in the 4th hour sold AS + BS instead of BS + FS. Hence, the number of units of milk can be either 18 or 19 or 20. Option (a) is correct.
8. If 3 units of mangoes were sold as leftovers in the last hour, it means that Kaveri must have sold a combination of AS + BS in the 4th hour. The total number of AS sold in the 4 hours would be 1 + 2 + 2 + 1 (hour wise) = 6. Hence, the correct answer is 6.

SLOT 2

CAT 2021

Directions for Questions 1 to 6

Ravi works in an online food-delivery company. After each delivery, customers rate Ravi on each of four parameters – Behaviour, Packaging, Hygiene, and Timeliness, on a scale from 1 to 9. If the total of the four rating points is 25 or more, then Ravi gets a bonus of ₹20 for that delivery. Additionally, a customer may or may not give Ravi a tip. If the customer gives a tip, it is either ₹30 or ₹50.

One day, Ravi made four deliveries - one to each of Atal, Bihari, Chirag and Deepak, and received a total of ₹120 in bonus and tips. He did not get both a bonus and a tip from the same customer.

The following additional facts are also known.

I. In Timeliness, Ravi received a total of 21 points, and three of the customers gave him the same rating points in this parameter. Atal gave higher rating points than Bihari and Chirag in this parameter.

II. Ravi received distinct rating points in Packaging from the four customers adding up to 29 points. Similarly, Ravi received distinct rating points in Hygiene from the four customers adding up to 26 points.

III. Chirag gave the same rating points for Packaging and Hygiene.

IV. Among the four customers, Bihari gave the highest rating points in Packaging, and Chirag gave the highest rating points in Hygiene.

V. Everyone rated Ravi between 5 and 7 in Behaviour. Unique maximum and minimum ratings in this parameter were given by Atal and Deepak respectively.

VI. If the customers are ranked based on ratings given by them in individual parameters, then Atal's rank based on Packaging is the same as that based on Hygiene. This is also true for Deepak.

1. What was the minimum rating that Ravi received from any customer in any parameter?

2. The COMPLETE list of customers who gave the maximum total rating points to Ravi is
   (a) Bihari
   (b) Bihari and Chirag
   (c) Atal
   (d) Atal and Bihari

3. What rating did Atal give on Timeliness?

4. What BEST can be concluded about the tip amount given by Deepak?
   (a) Either ₹30 or ₹50
   (b) Either ₹0 or ₹30 or ₹50
   (c) ₹50
   (d) ₹30

5. In which parameter did Atal give the maximum rating points to Ravi?
   (a) Behavior
   (b) Hygiene
   (c) Packaging
   (d) Timeliness

6. What rating did Deepak give on Packaging?
   (a) 5
   (b) 7
   (c) 8
   (d) 6

Directions for Questions 7 to 10

The different bars in the diagram below provide information about different orders in various categories (Art, Binders, ….) that were booked in the first two weeks of September of a store for one client. The pattern of a bar denotes the ship mode (First Class / Second Class / Standard Class). The left end point of a bar indicates the booking day of the order, while the right end point indicates the dispatch day of the order. The difference between the dispatch day and the booking day (measured in terms of the number of days) is called the processing time of the order. For the same category, an order is considered for booking only after the previous order of the same category is dispatched. No two consecutive orders of the same category had identical ship mode during this period.

For example, there were only two orders in the furnishing category during this period. The first one was shipped in the Second Class. It was booked on Sep 1 and dispatched on Sep 5. The second order was shipped in the Standard class. It was booked on Sep 5 (although the order might have been placed before that) and dispatched on Sep 12. So the processing times were 4 and 7 days respectively for these orders.

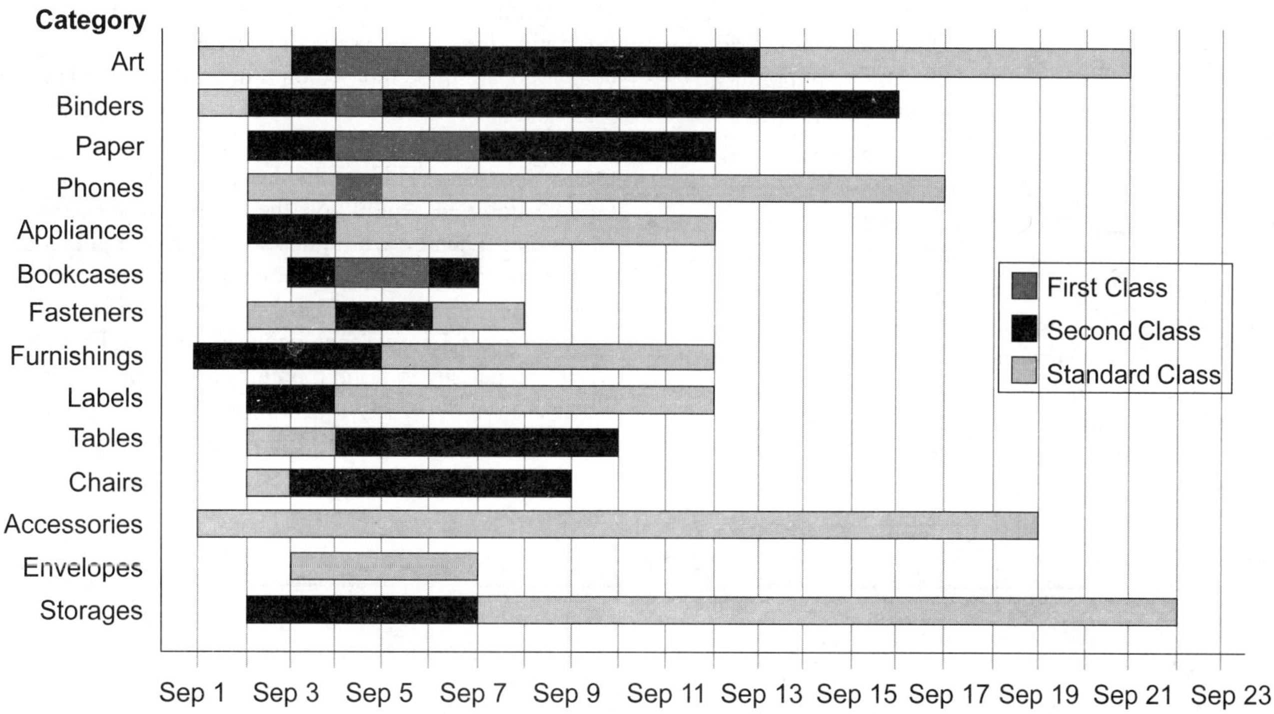

7. How many days between Sep 1 and Sep 14 (both inclusive) had no booking from this client considering all the above categories?
8. What was the average processing time of all orders in the categories which had only one type of ship mode?
9. The sequence of categories – Art, Binders, Paper and Phones – in decreasing order of average processing time of their orders in this period is:
   (a) Art, Binders, Paper, Phones
   (b) Paper, Binders, Art, Phones
   (c) Phones, Binders, Art, Paper
   (d) Phones, Art, Binders, Paper
10. Approximately what percentage of orders had a processing time of one day during the period Sep 1 to Sep 22 (both dates inclusive)?
   (a) 16%
   (b) 20%
   (c) 25%
   (d) 22%

ANSWER KEY

1. 5	2. (b)	3. 6	4. (a)	5. (a)	6. (b)	7. 6
8. 11	9. (d)	10. (b)				

SOLUTIONS

Solutions for Questions 1 to 6:

From the information given to us we can determine the following directly:

Deduction 1: From Clue 5, we can make out that Atal would have given 7 points on Behaviour, while Deepak would have given 5 points on that parameter. Also, since these are unique maximum and minimum respectively, it follows that Bihari and Chirag would give 6 points each on Behaviour.

Deduction 2: The only way to make up 29 points with 4 distinct numbers is 9, 8, 7, 5. Hence, Bihari would have given Ravi 9 points on packaging (since he gives the highest points on that parameter).

Deduction 3: From clues 3 and 4, we can make out that Chirag's value of points would be the same for packaging and hygiene. Hence, he cannot give 9 points on Hygiene. Also, since he has given the highest points on hygiene and the total of hygiene is 26, with 4 distinct numbers, it follows that the only way to make a total of 26 for hygiene is 8 + 7 + 6 + 5. Hence, the number of points given by Chirag on Hygiene and Packaging would be 8 each.

Deduction 4: From clue 1, we can make out that each of Bihari, Chirag and Deepak would have given the same points to Ravi on Timeliness (say x). Also, Atal gives more points than the other three (say y). We have $3x + y = 21$, which gives us that the alternatives possible for the timeliness points are 9, 4, 4, 4 or 6, 5, 5, 5 for A, B, C, D respectively. We will need to work out subsequently which of the two sets of values have to be filled for x and y. Apart from that, we have to only fill up the remaining values for Packaging and hygiene.

Deduction 5: Clue 6 helps us do that with a multiple possibility thought outcome. It is given to us that 'If the customers are ranked based on ratings given by them in individual parameters, then Atal's rank based on Packaging is the same as that based on Hygiene. This is also true for Deepak.' This means that if Atal gives 7 points on packaging, he would give the third highest points in packaging. Then he would necessarily give 6 points on hygiene. In that case, Deepak would give 5 points each on each of these parameters. The opposite can also be true – viz: Atal gives 5 points each on Packaging and Hygiene, while Deepak gives 7 and 6 points each respectively. In either case, it definitely follows that Bihari would have given 7 points on Hygiene.

Table after Deduction 5:

	Behavior	Packaging	Hygiene	Timeliness	Total
Atal	7 (#1)	7/5 (#5)	6/5 (#5)	y (#4)	
Bihari	6 (#1)	9 (#2)	7 (#5)	x (#4)	
Chirag	6 (#1)	8 (#3)	8 (#3)	x (#4)	
Deepak	5 (#1)	5/7 (#5)	5/6 (#5)	x (#4)	
Total	24	29	26	21 (#4)	
		Distinct (9, 8, 7, 5) (#2)	Distinct (8, 7, 6, 5) (#3)	(9, 4, 4, 4) / (6, 5, 5, 5) (#4)	

Thus, at this stage we are standing at a 4-possibility situation (2 possibilities for the timeliness values and 2 possibilities for the packaging hygiene values distributed amongst Atal and Deepak. To proceed further, it is important to be able to use the fact that he has earned a total of bonus plus tips of 120. With a combination of 50/30 for tips and 20 for bonus, it is not possible to create a total earning of 120 for him if he gets bonus on 3 deliveries (Since he does not receive a bonus plus a tip from any single customer, and 20 + 20 + 20 + 50 can maximum reach a total earning of 110). If you try the 4 possibilities one by one, in three of the four it emerges that the sum of points given by an individual customer is 25 or more – and he would get a bonus 3 times, which is not possible. For instance, if we use 9, 4, 4, 4 for timeliness and 7, 6 for Atal and 5, 5, for Deepak, we can see that Atal (29) Bihari (26) and Chirag (26) are all crossing 25 points which is not possible. The only possibility that would give us an answer is shown in the final solution table and the answers can be read off from here.

	Behavior	Packaging	Hygiene	Timeliness	Total	Tip/Bonus
Atal	7	5	5	6	23	30/50
Bihari	6	9	7	5	27	20
Chirag	6	8	8	5	27	20
Deepak	5	7	6	5	23	50/30
Total	24	29	26	21		120

1. The lowest rating in the table is 5
2. Both Bihari and Chirag have given the maximum total rating points of 27. Hence, option (b) is correct.
3. 6
4. Option (a) is correct.
5. Option (a) is correct.

6. Option (b) is correct.

Solutions for Questions 7 to 10:

7. From the chart, it is evident that there was no booking from Sept 8 to Sept 12 and Sept 14. So a total of 6 Days.
8. Only 2 categories had only 1 shipping mode. They were Accessories and Envelopes.
   Processing time for Accessories = 18 Days
   Processing time for Envelopes = 4 days
   Average processing time = 11 days
9. Phones have an average processing time of 16/3 = 5.33 (total processing time for all orders/no of orders) = 5.33. Art has an average processing time of 20/5 = 4. For paper, it is 10/3 = 3.33 and for Binders it is 15/4 = 3.75. The correct decreasing order would be Phones, Art, Binders, Paper. Option (d) is correct.
10. Total number of orders during the given period: 35
    Orders with processing time of 1 day: 7
    Percentage of orders = 20%
    Hence, option (b) is the correct answer.

SLOT 3

CAT 2021

Directions for Questions 1 to 4

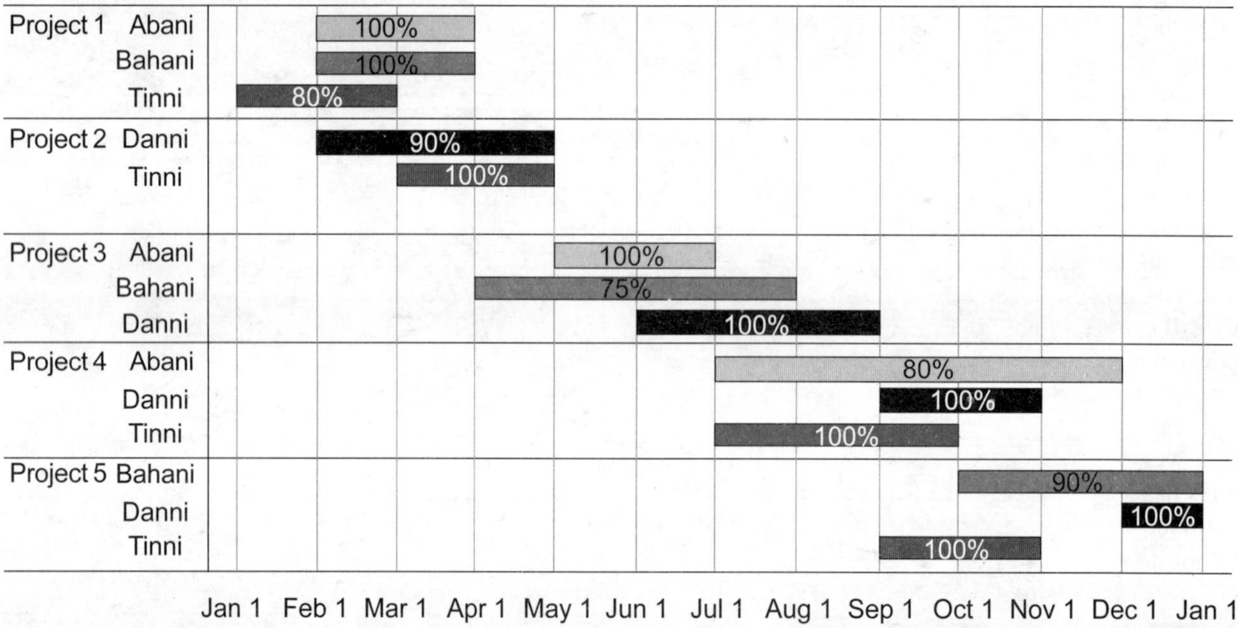

The figure above shows the schedule of four employees – Abani, Bahni, Danni and Tinni – whom Dhoni supervised in 2020. Altogether, there were five projects which started and concluded in 2020 in which they were all involved. For each of these projects and for each employee, the starting day was at the beginning of a month and the concluding day was the end of a month; and these days are indicated by the left and right end points of the corresponding horizontal bars. The number within each bar indicates the percentage of assigned work completed by the employee for that project, as assessed by Dhoni.

For each employee, their total project-month (in 2020) is the sum of the number of months they worked across the five projects, while their annual completion index is the weighted average of the completion percentage assigned from the different projects, with the weights being the corresponding number of months they worked in these projects. For each project, the total employee-month is the sum of the number of months four employees worked in this project, while its completion index is the weighted average of the completion percentage assigned for the employees who worked in this project, with the weights being the corresponding number of months they worked in this project.

1. Which of the following statements is/are true?
   I: The total project-month was the same for the four employees.
   II: The total employee-month was the same for the five projects.
   (a) Neither I nor II (b) Only II
   (c) Both I and II (d) Only I
2. Which employees did not work in multiple projects for any of the months in 2020?
   (a) Only Abani and Bahni
   (b) All four of them
   (c) Only Tinni
   (d) Only Abani, Bahni and Danni
3. The project duration, measured in terms of the number of months, is the time during which at least one employee worked in the project. Which of the following pairs of the projects had the same duration?

(a) Project 3, Project 5
(b) Project 1, Project 5
(c) Project 4, Project 5
(d) Project 3, Project 4

4. The list of employees in decreasing order of annual completion index is:
(a) Danni, Tinni, Bahni, Abani
(b) Bahni, Abani, Tinni, Danni
(c) Danni, Tinni, Abani, Bahni
(d) Tinni, Danni, Abani, Bahni

Directions for Questions 5 to 8

Each of the bottles mentioned in this question contains 50 ml of liquid. The liquid in any bottle can be 100% pure content (P) or can have certain amount of impurity (I). Visually it is not possible to distinguish between P and I. There is a testing device which detects impurity, as long as the percentage of impurity in the content tested is 10% or more.

For example, suppose bottle 1 contains only P, and bottle 2 contains 80% P and 20% I. If content from bottle 1 is tested, it will be found out that it contains only P. If content of bottle 2 is tested, the test will reveal that it contains some amount of I. If 10 ml of content from bottle 1 is mixed with 20 ml content from bottle 2, the test will show that the mixture has impurity, and hence we can conclude that at least one of the two bottles has I. However, if 10 ml of content from bottle 1 is mixed with 5 ml of content from bottle 2. the test will not detect any impurity in the resultant mixture.

5. 5 ml of content from bottle A is mixed with 5 ml of content from bottle B. The resultant mixture, when tested, detects the presence of I. If it is known that bottle A contains only P, what BEST can be concluded about the volume of I in bottle B?
(a) 10 ml or more
(b) Less than 1 ml
(c) 10 ml
(d) 1 ml

6. There are four bottles. Each bottle is known to contain only P or only I. They will be considered to be "collectively ready for despatch" if all of them contain only P. In minimum how many tests, is it possible to ascertain whether these four bottles are "collectively ready for despatch"?

7. There are four bottles. It is known that three of these bottles contain only P, while the remaining one contains 80% P and 20% I. What is the minimum number of tests required to definitely identify the bottle containing some amount of I?

8. There are four bottles. It is known that either one or two of these bottles contain(s) only P, while the remaining ones contain 85% P and 15% I. What is the minimum number of tests required to ascertain the exact number of bottles containing only P?
(a) 1 (b) 4
(c) 3 (d) 2

ANSWER KEY

1. (d) 2. (d) 3. (d) 4. (c) 5. (a) 6. 1 7. 2
8. (a)

SOLUTIONS

Solutions for Questions 1 to 4:

1. Project months for Abani = 2 +2 + 5 = 9 Months
Project months for Bahni = 2 + 4 + 3 = 9 Months
Project months for Tinni = 2 + 2 + 3+2 = 9 Months
Project months for Danni =3 + 3 + 2 + 1 = 9 Months
Statement 1 is true.
Employee month for Project 1= 6 Months
Employee month for Project 2= 5 Months
Statement 2 is False.
Hence, Option (d) is the correct answer.
2. From the given chart we can see that, Abani, Bahni and Danni did not work on multiple projects during a given month. Hence, Option (d) is the correct answer.
3. Duration of Project 1: 3 Months (Jan to March)
Duration of Project 2: 3 Months (Feb to April)
Duration of Project 3: 5 Months (April to August)
Duration of Project 4: 5 Months (July to November)
Duration of Project 5: 4 Months (September to December)
Projects 1 & 2 and 3 & 4 have the same project duration. From the given options, Opiton (d) contains our answer pair.
4. Annual completion Index for
Abani: $(2 \times 100 + 2 \times 100 + 5 \times 80)/9 = 800/9$
Bahni: $(2 \times 100 + 4 \times 75 + 3 \times 90)/9 = 770/9$

Tinni: (2 × 80 + 2 × 100 + 3 × 100 + 2 × 100)/9 = 860/9

Danni: (3 × 90 + 3 × 100 + 2 × 100 + 1 × 100)/9 = 870/9

Decreasing Order: Danni, Tinni, Abani, Bahni

Option (c) is the correct answer.

Solutions for Questions 5 to 8:

5. Bottle B would have at least 20% I, since only then a 1:1 mixture of A and B would show some impurity. Since all the bottles mentioned in the question have 50 ml of liquid, it follows that B will have 10 ml or more of I. Option (a) is correct.
6. If we take a 1:1:1:1 mixture from the 4 bottles and test this mixture, the test result would come out P, only if all 4 bottles are only P. In the event that even if one of the 4 bottles contains I, the test would show the presence of I and would not be considered ready for dispatch. Think of this as: If 3 of the bottles are P and 1 bottle is I, and you were to test a 1:1:1:1 mixture from the four bottles, the resultant mixture would have 25% I and 75% P. The test would be able to find that the bottles are not collectively ready for dispatch. Hence, the correct answer is 1.
7. Let the bottles be A, B, C, D. Test any two bottles first, Say A,B. Two things can happen:
   (a) **If both the bottles A and B are P,** then the test will not detect I. This means that the 20% I is in one of the remaining bottles (C or D). Test any one of the remaining two bottles alone. If you test C and it shows I, you have detected C as the bottle with I. If you test C and it shows no I, it means that D has I and C is pure. In either case, we know the bottle with I in 2 tests.
   (b) **If one of the bottles A and B has 20% I,** then the test will detect I. This means that the 20% I is in one of A or B. Test any one of these two bottles alone. If you test A and it shows I, you have detected A as the bottle with I. If you test A and it shows no I, it means that B has I and A is pure. In either case, we know the bottle with I in 2 tests.

   Thus, the minimum number of tests required to find the bottle with 20% I is 2.
8. The number of bottles with only P can be identified in exactly 1 test and this can be thought of as follows. There are two cases here: **Case 1:** 2 bottles with only P and 2 bottles with 0.85 P and 0.15 I. **Case 2:** 1 bottle with only P and 3 bottles with 0.85 P and 0.15 I. To find how many bottles have only P, pour all the contents from all the bottles (50 ml each) into a larger container. In case 1, the 200 ml mixture will have 15 ml of I, and the test will not detect any I. In the second case, the 200 ml mixture will have 22.5 ml of I and the test will detect I. Thus, if the test detects I, we can conclude that there is only 1 bottle with only P. If the test does not detect I, we can conclude that there are 2 bottles with only P. Hence, the correct answer is option (a)